The Information Age

Economy, Society and Culture

Volume I

The Rise of the Network Society

For Emma Kiselyova-Castells,
without whose love, work, and support
this book would not exist

The Rise of the Network Society

Manuel Castells

BLACKWELL
Publishers

First published 1996
Reprinted 1997 (three times),
1998 (three times), 1999

Blackwell Publishers Inc
350 Main Street
Massachusetts 02148, USA

Blackwell Publishers Ltd
108 Cowley Road
Oxford OX4 1JF, UK

Library of Congress Cataloging in Publication Data
Castells, Manuel.
The rise of the network society / Manuel Castells.
p.   cm. — (Informational age : 1)
Includes bibliographical references and index.
ISBN 1-55786-616-3 — ISBN 1-55786-617-1 (pbk)
1. Information technology — Economic aspects. 2. Information technology —
Social aspects. 3. Information society. 4. Information networks. 5. Technology and
civilization. I. Title. II. Series: Castells, Manuel. Information age : 1
HC79.I55C373   1996   95-45082
303.48'33 — dc20   CIP

British Library Cataloguing in Publication Data
A CIP catalogue record for this book is available from the British Library

Printed and bound in Great Britain
by T. J. International Limited, Padstow, Cornwall

This book is printed on acid-free paper

Contents

Contents

4 The transformation of work and employment: networkers, jobless, and flextimers

Figures

Tables

Acknowledgements

This book has been twelve years in the making, as my research and writing were trying to catch up with an object of study expanding faster than my working capacity. That I have been able to reach some form of completion, however tentative, is due to the cooperation, help, and support of a number of persons and institutions.

My first and deepest expression of gratitude goes to Emma Kiselyova, whose collaboration was essential in obtaining information for several chapters, in helping with the elaboration of the book, in securing access to languages that I do not know, and in commenting, assessing, and advising on the entire manuscript.

I also want to thank the organizers of four exceptional forums where the main ideas of the book were discussed in depth, and duly rectified, in 1994–5, in the final stage of its elaboration: the special session on this book at the 1994 Meeting of the American Anthropological Association, organized by Ida Susser; the Department of Sociology Colloquium at Berkeley, organized by Loic Wacquant; the international seminar on new world trends organized in Brasilia around Fernando Henrique Cardoso, as he was assuming the Presidency of Brazil; and the series of seminars on the book at Tokyo's Hitotsubashi University, organized by Shujiro Yazawa.

Several colleagues in several countries read carefully the draft of the book, in full or specific chapters, and spent considerable time commenting on it, leading to substantial and extensive revisions of the text. The mistakes that remain in the book are entirely mine. Many positive contributions are theirs. I want to acknowledge the collegial efforts of Stephen S. Cohen, Martin Carnoy, Alain Touraine, Anthony Giddens, Daniel Bell, Jesus Leal, Shujiro Yazawa, Peter Hall, Chu-joe Hsia, You-tien Hsing, François Bar, Michael Borrus, Harley Shaiken, Claude Fischer, Nicole Woolsey-Biggart, Bennett Harrison, Anne Marie Guillemard, Richard Nelson, Loic Wacquant, Ida Susser,

Fernando Calderon, Roberto Laserna, Alejandro Foxley, John Urry, Guy Benveniste, Katherine Burlen, Vicente Navarro, Dieter Ernst, Padmanabha Gopinath, Franz Lehner, Julia Trilling, Robert Benson, David Lyon and Melvin Kranzberg.

Throughout the last twelve years a number of institutions have constituted the basis for this work. First of all is my intellectual home, the University of California at Berkeley, and more specifically the academic units where I work: the Department of City and Regional Planning, the Department of Sociology, the Center for Western European Studies, the Institute of Urban and Regional Development, and the Berkeley Roundtable on the International Economy. They have all helped me, and my research, with their material and institutional support, and in providing the appropriate environment to think, imagine, dare, investigate, discuss and write. A key part of this environment, and therefore of my understanding of the world, is the intelligence and openness of graduate students with whom I have been fortunate to interact. Some of them have also been most helpful research assistants, whose contribution to this book must be recognized: You-tien Hsing, Roberto Laserna, Yuko Aoyama, Chris Benner, and Sandra Moog. I also wish to acknowledge the valuable research assistance from Kekuei Hasegawa at Hitotsubashi University.

Other institutions in various countries have also provided support to conduct the research presented in this book. By naming them, I extend my gratitude to their directors and to the many colleagues in these institutions who have taught me about what I have written in this book. These are: Instituto de Sociología de Nuevas Tecnologías, Universidad Autónoma de Madrid; International Institute of Labour Studies, International Labour Office, Geneva; Soviet (later Russian) Sociological Association; Institute of Economics and Industrial Engineering, Siberian Branch of the USSR (later Russian) Academy of Sciences; Universidad Mayor de San Simon, Cochabamba, Bolivia; Instituto de Investigaciónes Sociales, Universidad Nacional Autónoma de Mexico; Center for Urban Studies, University of Hong Kong; Center for Advanced Studies, National University of Singapore; Institute of Technology and International Economy, The State Council, Beijing; National Taiwan University, Taipei; Korean Research Institute for Human Settlement, Seoul; and Faculty of Social Studies, Hitotsubashi University, Tokyo.

I reserve a special thought for John Davey, Blackwell's editorial director, whose intellectual interaction and helpful criticism over more than twenty years have been precious to the development of my writing, helping me out of frequent dead ends by constantly reminding me that books are about communicating ideas, not about printing words.

Last but not least, I want to thank my surgeon, Dr Lawrence Werboff, and my physician, Dr James Davis, both from the University of California at San Francisco's Mount Zion Hospital, whose care and professionalism gave me the time and energy to finish this book, and maybe others.

March 1996 Berkeley, California

Prologue: The Net and the Self

"Do you think me a learned, well-read man?"
"Certainly," replied Zi-gong, "Aren't you?"
"Not at all," said Confucius. "I have simply grasped one thread which
*links up the rest."**

Toward the end of the second millennium of the Christian Era several
events of historical significance have transformed the social landscape
of human life. A technological revolution, centered around information technologies, is reshaping, at accelerated pace, the material basis
of society. Economies throughout the world have become globally
interdependent, introducing a new form of relationship between
economy, state, and society, in a system of variable geometry. The
collapse of Soviet statism, and the subsequent demise of the international communist movement, has undermined for the time being
the historical challenge to capitalism, rescued the political left (and
Marxian theory) from the fatal attraction of Marxism–Leninism,
brought the Cold War to an end, reduced the risk of nuclear holocaust, and fundamentally altered global geopolitics. Capitalism itself
has undergone a process of profound restructuring, characterized by
greater flexibility in management; decentralization and networking
of firms both internally and in their relationships to other firms;
considerable empowering of capital *vis-à-vis* labor, with the concomitant decline of influence of the labor movement; increasing
individualization and diversification of working relationships; massive
incorporation of women into the paid labor force, usually under

* Recounted in Sima Qian (145–ca. 89BC), "Confucius," in Hu Shi, *The
Development of Logical Methods in Ancient China*, Shanghai: Oriental Book
Company, 1922; quoted in Qian 1985: 125.

discriminatory conditions; intervention of the state to deregulate markets selectively, and to undo the welfare state, with different intensity and orientations depending upon the nature of political forces and institutions in each society; stepped-up global economic competition, in a context of increasing geographic and cultural differentiation of settings for capital accumulation and management. As a consequence of this general overhauling of the capitalist system, still under way, we have witnessed the global integration of financial markets, the rise of the Asian Pacific as the new dominant, global manufacturing center, the arduous economic unification of Europe, the emergence of a North American regional economy, the diversification, then disintegration, of the former Third World, the gradual transformation of Russia and the ex-Soviet area of influence in market economies, the incorporation of valuable segments of economies throughout the world into an interdependent system working as a unit in real time. Because of these trends, there has also been an accentuation of uneven development, this time not only between North and South, but between the dynamic segments and territories of societies everywhere, and those others that risk becoming irrelevant from the perspective of the system's logic. Indeed, we observe the parallel unleashing of formidable productive forces of the informational revolution, and the consolidation of black holes of human misery in the global economy, be it in Burkina Faso, South Bronx, Kamagasaki, Chiapas, or La Courneuve.

Simultaneously, criminal activities and mafia-like organizations around the world have also become global and informational, providing the means for stimulation of mental hyperactivity and forbidden desire, along with any form of illicit trade demanded by our societies, from sophisticated weaponry to human flesh. Besides, a new communication system, increasingly speaking a universal, digital language is both integrating globally the production and distribution of words, sounds and images of our culture, and customizing them to the tastes of identities and moods of individuals. Interactive computer networks are growing exponentially, creating new forms and channels of communication, shaping life and being shaped by life at the same time.

Social changes are as dramatic as technological and economic processes of transformation. For all the difficulty in the process of transformation of women's condition, patriarchalism has come under attack, and has been shaken in a number of societies. Thus, gender relationships have become, in much of the world, a contested domain, rather than a sphere of cultural reproduction. It follows a fundamental redefinition of relationships between women, men and children, and thus, of family, sexuality, and personality.

Environmental consciousness has permeated down to the institutions of society, and its values have won political appeal, at the price of being belied and manipulated in the daily practice of corporations and bureaucracies. Political systems are engulfed in a structural crisis of legitimacy, periodically wrecked by scandals, essentially dependent on media coverage and personalized leadership, and increasingly isolated from the citizenry. Social movements tend to be fragmented, localistic, single-issue oriented, and ephemeral, either retrenched in their inner worlds, or flaring up for just an instant around a media symbol. In such a world of uncontrolled, confusing change, people tend to regroup around primary identities: religious, ethnic, territorial, national. Religious fundamentalism, Christian, Islamic, Jewish, Hindu, and even Buddhist (in what seems to be a contradiction in terms), is probably the most formidable force of personal security and collective mobilization in these troubled years. In a world of global flows of wealth, power, and images, the search for identity, collective or individual, ascribed or constructed, becomes the fundamental source of social meaning. This is not a new trend, since identity, and particularly religious and ethnic identity, have been at the roots of meaning since the dawn of human society. Yet identity is becoming the main, and sometimes the only, source of meaning in a historical period characterized by widespread destructuring of organizations, delegitimation of institutions, fading away of major social movements, and ephemeral cultural expressions. People increasingly organize their meaning not around what they do but on the basis of what they are, or believe they are. Meanwhile, on the other hand, global networks of instrumental exchanges selectively switch on and off individuals, groups, regions, and even countries, according to their relevance in fulfilling the goals processed in the network, in a relentless flow of strategic decisions. It follows a fundamental split between abstract, universal instrumentalism, and historically rooted, particularistic identities. **Our societies are increasingly structured around a bipolar opposition between the Net and the Self.**

In this condition of structural schizophrenia between function and meaning, patterns of social communication become increasingly under stress. And when communication breaks down, when it does not exist any longer, even in the form of conflictual communication (as would be the case in social struggles or political opposition), social groups and individuals become alienated from each other, and see the other as a stranger, eventually as a threat. In this process, social fragmentation spreads, as identities become more specific and increasingly difficult to share. The informational society, in its global manifestation, is also the world of Aum Shinrikyo, of American Militia,

of Islamic/Christian theocratic ambitions, and of Hutu/Tutsi reciprocal genocide.

Bewildered by the scale and scope of historical change, culture and
thinking in our time often embrace a new millenarism. Prophets of
technology preach the new age, extrapolating to social trends and
organization the barely understood logic of computers and DNA.
Postmodern culture, and theory, indulge in celebrating the end of
history, and, to some extent, the end of Reason, giving up on our
capacity to understand and make sense, even of nonsense. The
implicit assumption is the acceptance of full individualization of
behaviour, and of society's powerlessness over its destiny.

The project informing this book swims against streams of destruction, and takes exception to various forms of intellectual nihilism,
social skepticism, and political cynicism. I believe in rationality, and
in the possibility of calling upon reason, without worshipping its
goddess. I believe in the chances of meaningful social action, and
transformative politics, without necessarily drifting towards the deadly
rapids of absolute utopias. I believe in the liberating power of identity, without accepting the necessity of either its individualization or
its capture by fundamentalism. And I propose the hypothesis that all
major trends of change constituting our new, confusing world are
related, and that we can make sense of their interrelationship. And,
yes, I believe, in spite of a long tradition of sometimes tragic intellectual errors, that observing, analyzing, and theorizing is a way of
helping to build a different, better world. Not by providing the
answers, that will be specific to each society and found by social actors
themselves, but by raising some relevant questions. This book would
like to be a modest contribution to a necessarily collective, analytical
effort, already underway from many horizons, aimed at understanding our new world on the basis of available evidence and
exploratory theory.

To walk preliminary steps in this direction, we must take technology
seriously, using it as the point of departure of this inquiry; we ought
to locate this process of revolutionary technological change in the
social context in which it takes place and by which it is being shaped;
and we should keep in mind that the search for identity is as powerful
as techno–economic change in charting the new history. Then, after
saying the words, we will depart for our intellectual journey, following
an itinerary that will take us to numerous domains, and will cross
through several cultures and institutional contexts, since the understanding of a global transformation requires a perspective as global as
possible, within the obvious limits of this author's experience and
knowledge.

Technology, Society, and Historical Change

The information technology revolution, because of its pervasiveness throughout the whole realm of human activity, will be my entry point in analyzing the complexity of new economy, society, and culture in the making. This methodological choice does not imply that new social forms and processes emerge as consequences of technological change. Of course technology does not determine society.[1] Neither does society script the course of technological change, since many factors, including individual inventiveness and entrepreneurialism, intervene in the process of scientific discovery, technological innovation, and social applications, so that the final outcome depends on a complex pattern of interaction.[2] Indeed, the dilemma of technological determinism is probably a false problem,[3] since technology *is* society, and society cannot be understood or represented without its technological tools.[4] Thus, when in the 1970s a new technological paradigm, organized around information technology, came to be constituted, mainly in the United States (see chapter 1), it was a specific segment of American society, in interaction with the global economy and with world geopolitics, that materialized into a new way of producing, communicating, managing, and living. That the constitution of this paradigm took place in the United States, and to some extent in California, and in the 1970s, probably had considerable consequences for the forms and evolution of new information technologies. For instance, in spite of the decisive role of military funding and markets in fostering early stages of the electronics industry during the 1940s–1960s, the technological blossoming that took place in the early 1970s can be somehow related to the culture of freedom, individual innovation, and entrepreneurialism that grew out from the 1960s culture of American campuses. Not so much in terms of its politics, since Silicon Valley was, and is, a solid bastion of the conservative vote, and most innovators were meta-political, but in regard to social values of breaking away from established patterns of behavior, both in society at large and in the business world. The emphasis on personalized devices, on interactivity, on networking, and the relentless

[1]   See the interesting debate on the matter in Smith and Marx 1994.
[2]   Technology does not determine society: it embodies it. But neither does society determine technological innovation: it uses it. This dialectical interaction between society and technology is present in the works of the best historians, such as Fernand Braudel.
[3]   Classic historian of technology Melvin Kranzberg has forcefully argued against the false dilemma of technological determinism. See, for instance, Kranzberg's (1992) acceptance speech of the Award to Honorary Membership in NASTS.
[4]   Bijker et al. (1987).

pursuit of new technological breakthroughs, even when it apparently did not make much business sense, was clearly in discontinuity with the somewhat cautious tradition of the corporate world. The information technology revolution half-consciously[5] diffused through the material culture of our societies the libertarian spirit that flourished in the 1960s movements. Yet, as soon as new information technologies diffused, and were appropriated by different countries, various cultures, diverse organizations, and miscellaneous goals, they exploded in all kinds of applications and uses that fed back into technological innovation, accelerating the speed, broadening the scope of technological change, and diversifying its sources.[6] An illustration will help us to understand the importance of unintended social consequences of technology.[7]

As is known, the Internet originated in a daring scheme imagined in the 1960s by the technological warriors of US Defense Department Advanced Research Projects Agency (the mythical DARPA) to prevent a Soviet takeover or destruction of American communications in case of nuclear war. To some extent, it was the electronic equivalent of the Maoist tactics of dispersal of guerrilla forces around a vast territory to counter an enemy's might with versatility and knowledge of terrain. The outcome was a network architecture that, as its inventors wanted, cannot be controlled from any center, and is made up of thousands of autonomous computer networks that have innumerable ways to

[5]   There is still to be written a fascinating social history of the values and personal views of some of the key innovators of the 1970s Silicon Valley revolution in computer technologies. But a few indications seem to point to the fact that they were intentionally trying to undo the centralizing technologies of the corporate world, both out of conviction and as their market niche. As evidence, I recall the famous Apple Computer 1984 advertising spot to launch Macintosh, in explicit opposition to Big Brother IBM of Orwellian mythology. As for the countercultural character of many of these innovators, I shall also refer to the life story of the genius developer of the personal computer, Steve Wozniak: after quitting Apple, bored by its transformation into another multinational corporation, he spent a fortune for a few years subsidizing rock groups that he liked, before creating another company to develop technologies of his taste. At one point, after having created the personal computer, Wozniak realized that he had no formal education in computer sciences, so he enrolled at UC Berkeley. But in order to avoid embarrassing publicity he used another name.
[6]   For selected evidence concerning the variation of information technology diffusion patterns in different social and institutional contexts see, among other works: Guile (1985); Landau and Rosenberg (1986); Wang (1994); Watanuki (1990); Bianchi et al. (1988); Freeman et al. (1991); Bertazzoni et al (1984); Agence de L'Informatique (1986); Castells et al. (1986).
[7]   For an informed and cautious discussion of relationships between society and technology, see Fischer (1985).

link up, going around electronic barriers. Ultimately ARPANET, the network set up by the US Defense Department, became the foundation of a global, horizontal communication network of thousands of computer networks (admittedly for a computer literate elite of about 20 million users in the mid-1990s, but growing exponentially), that has been appropriated for all kinds of purposes, quite removed from the concerns of an extinct Cold War, by individuals and groups around the world. Indeed, it was via the Internet that Subcomandante Marcos, the leader of Chiapas' *zapatistas*, communicated with the world, and with the media, from the depth of Lacandon forest, during his escape in February 1995.

Yet, if society does not determine technology, it can, mainly through the state, suffocate its development. Or alternatively, again mainly by state intervention, it can embark on an accelerated process of technological modernization able to change the fate of economies, military power, and social well-being in a few years. Indeed, the ability or inability of societies to master technology, and particularly technologies that are strategically decisive in each historical period, largely shapes their destiny, to the point where we could say that while technology *per se* does not determine historical evolution and social change, technology (or the lack of it) embodies the capacity of societies to transform themselves, as well as the uses to which societies, always in a conflictive process, decide to put their technological potential.[8]

Thus, around 1400, when the European Renaissance was planting the intellectual seeds of technological change that would dominate the world three centuries later, China was the most advanced technological civilization in the world, according to Mokyr.[9] Key inventions had developed in China centuries earlier, even a millennium and a half earlier, as in the case of blast furnaces that allowed the casting of iron in China by 200BC. Also, Su Sung introduced the water clock in AD1086, surpassing the accuracy of measurement of European mechanical clocks of the same date. The iron plow was introduced in the sixth century, and adapted to wet-field rice cultivation two centuries later. In textiles, the spinning wheel appeared at the same time as in the West, by the thirteenth century, but advanced much faster in China because there was an old-established tradition of sophisticated weaving equipment: draw looms to weave silk were used in Han times.

[8]   See the analyses presented in Castells (1988b); also Webster (1991).
[9]   My discussion on China's interrupted technological development relies mainly, on the one hand, on an extraordinary chapter by Joel Mokyr (1990: 209–38); on the other hand, on a most insightful, although controversial book, Qian (1985).

The adoption of water power was parallel to Europe: by the eight century the Chinese were using hydraulic trip hammers, and in 1280 there was wide diffusion of the vertical water wheel. Ocean travel was easier for the Chinese at an earlier date than for European vessels: they invented the compass around AD960, and their junks were the most advanced ships in the world by the end of the fourteenth century, enabling long sea trips. In military matters, the Chinese, besides inventing powder, developed a chemical industry that was able to provide powerful explosives, and the crossbow and the trebuchet were used by Chinese armies centuries ahead of Europe. In medicine, techniques such as acupuncture were yielding extraordinary results that only recently have been universally acknowledged. And of course, the first information processing revolution was Chinese: paper and printing were Chinese inventions. Paper was introduced in China 1,000 years earlier than in the West, and printing probably began in the late seventh century. As Jones writes: "China came within a hair's breadth of industrializing in the fourteenth century."[10] That it did not, changed the history of the world. When in 1842 the Opium Wars led to Britain's colonial impositions, China realized, too late, that isolation could not protect the Middle Kingdom from the evil consequences of technological inferiority. It took more than one century thereafter for China to start recovering from such a catastrophic deviation from its historical trajectory.

Explanations for such a stunning historical course are both numerous and controversial. There is no place in this Prologue to enter the complexity of the debate. But, on the basis of research and analysis by historians such as Needham,[11] Qian,[12] Jones,[13] and Mokyr,[14] it is possible to suggest an interpretation that may help to understand, in general terms, the interaction between society, history, and technology. Indeed, most hypotheses concerning cultural differences (even those without implicitly racist undertones), fail to explain, as Mokyr points out, the difference not between China and Europe but between China in 1300 and China in 1800. Why did a culture and a kingdom that had been the technological leader of the world for thousands of years suddenly become technologically stagnant precisely at the moment when Europe embarked on the age of discoveries, and then on the industrial revolution?

Needham has proposed that Chinese culture was more prone than

---

[10]   Jones (1981: 160), cited by Mokyr (1990: 219).
[11]   Needham (1954–88, 1969, 1981).
[12]   Qian (1985).
[13]   Jones (1988).
[14]   Mokyr (1990).

Western values to a harmonious relationship between man and nature, something that could be jeopardized by fast technological innovation. Furthermore, he objects to the Western criteria used to measure technological development. However, this cultural emphasis on a holistic approach to development had not impeded technological innovation for millennia, nor stopped ecological deterioration as a result of irrigation works in Southern China, when the conservation of nature was subordinated to agricultural production in order to feed a growing population. In fact, Wen-yuan Qian, in his powerful book, takes exception to Needham's somewhat excessive enthusiasm for the feats of Chinese traditional technology, notwithstanding his shared admiration for Needham's monumental life-long work. Qian calls for a closer analytical linkage between the development of Chinese science and the characteristics of Chinese civilization dominated by the dynamics of state. Mokyr also considers the state to be the crucial factor in explaining Chinese technological retardation in modern times. The explanation may be proposed in three steps: technological innovation was, for centuries, fundamentally in the hands of the state; after 1400 the Chinese state, under the Ming and Qing dynasties, lost interest in technological innovation; and, partly because of their dedication to serve the state, cultural and social elites were focused on arts, humanities, and self-promotion *vis-à-vis* the imperial bureaucracy. Thus, what does seem to be crucial is the role of the state, and the changing orientation of state policy. Why would a state that had been the greatest hydraulic engineer in history, and had established an agricultural extension system to improve agricultural productivity since the Han period, suddenly become inhibited from technological innovation, even forbidding geographical exploration, and abandoning the construction of large ships by 1430? The obvious answer is that it was not the same state; not only because they were of different dynasties, but because the bureaucratic class became more deeply entrenched in the administration due to a longer than usual period of uncontested domination.

According to Mokyr, it appears that the determining factor for technological conservatism was the rulers' fears of the potentially disruptive impacts of technological change on social stability. Numerous forces opposed the diffusion of technology in China, as in other societies, particularly the urban guilds. Bureaucrats content with the status quo were concerned by the possibility of triggering social conflicts that could coalesce with other sources of latent opposition in a society that had been kept under control for several centuries. Even the two enlightened Manchu despots of the eighteenth century, K'ang Chi and Ch'ien Lung, focused their efforts on pacification and order, rather than on unleashing new development. Conversely, exploration and contacts with foreigners, beyond controlled trade and acquisition of weapons, were deemed at best unnecessary, at worst threatening, because of the uncertainty they would imply. A bureaucratic state without external incentive and with internal disincentives to engage in technological modernization opted for the most prudent neutrality, as a result stalling the technological trajectory that China had been following for centuries, if not millennia, precisely under state guidance. The discussion of the factors underlying the dynamics of the Chinese state under the Ming and Qing dynasties is clearly beyond the scope of this book. What matters for our research purpose are two teachings from this fundamental experience of interrupted technological development: on the one hand, the state can be, and has been in history, in China and elsewhere, a leading force of technological innovation; on the other hand, precisely because of this, when the state reverses its interest in technological development, or becomes unable to perform it under new conditions, a statist model of innovation leads to stagnation, because of the sterilization of society's autonomous innovative energy to create and apply technology. That the Chinese state could, centuries later, build anew an advanced technological basis, in nuclear technology, missiles, satellite launching, and electronics,[15] demonstrates again the emptiness of a predominantly cultural interpretation of technological development and backwardness: the same culture may induce very different technological trajectories depending on the pattern of relationships between state and society. However, the exclusive dependence on the state has a price, and the price for China was that of retardation, famine, epidemics, colonial domination, and civil war, until at least the middle of the twentieth century.

A rather similar, contemporary story can be told, and will be told in this book (in volume III), of the inability of Soviet statism to master the information technology revolution, thus stalling its productive capacity and undermining its military might. Yet we should not jump to the ideological conclusion that all state intervention is counterproductive to technological development, indulging in ahistorical reverence for unfettered, individual entrepreneurialism. Japan is of course the counter-example, both to Chinese historical experience and to the inability of the Soviet state to adapt to the American-initiated revolution in information technology.

Historically, Japan went, even deeper than China, through a period of historical isolation under the Tokugawa Shogunate (established in

[15]   Wang (1993).

1603), between 1636 and 1853, precisely during the critical period of formation of an industrial system in the western hemisphere. Thus, while at the turn of the seventeenth century Japanese merchants were trading throughout East and Southeast Asia, using modern vessels of up to 700 tons, the construction of ships above 50 tons was prohibited in 1635, and all Japanese ports, except Nagasaki, were closed to foreigners, while trade was restricted to China, Korea, and Holland.[16] Technological isolation was not total during these two centuries, and endogenous innovation did allow Japan to proceed with incremental change at a faster pace than China.[17] Yet, because Japan's technological level was lower than China's, by the mid-nineteenth century the *kurobune* (black ships) of Commodore Perry could impose trade and diplomatic relations on a country substantially lagging behind Western technology. However, as soon as the 1868 *Ishin Meiji* (Meiji Restoration) created the political conditions for a decisive state-led modernization,[18] Japan progressed in advanced technology by leaps and bounds in a very short time span.[19] Just as one significant illustration, because of its current strategic importance, let us briefly recall the extraordinary development of electrical engineering and communication applications in Japan in the last quarter of the nineteenth century.[20] Indeed, the first independent department of electrical engineering in the world was established in 1873 in the newly founded Imperial College of Engineering in Tokyo, under the leadership of its Dean, Henry Dyer, a Scottish mechanical engineer. Between 1887 and 1892, a leading academic in electrical engineering, British professor William Ayrton, was invited to teach at the College, being instrumental in disseminating knowledge to the new generation of Japanese engineers, so that by the end of the century the Telegraph Bureau was able to replace foreigners in all its technical departments. Technology

[16] Chida and Davies (1990).
[17] Ito (1993).
[18] Several distinguished Japanese scholars, and I tend to concur with them, consider that the best Western account of the Meiji Restoration, and of the social roots of Japanese modernization, is Norman (1940). It has been translated into Japanese and is widely read in Japanese universities. A brilliant historian, educated at Cambridge and Harvard, before joining the Canadian diplomatic corps Norman was denounced as a communist by Karl Wittfogel to the McCarthy Senate Committee in the 1950s, and then submitted to constant pressure from Western intelligence agencies. Appointed Canadian Ambassador to Egypt he committed suicide in Cairo in 1957. On the contribution of this truly exceptional scholar to the understanding of the Japanese state, see Dower (1975); for a different perspective, see Beasley (1990).
[19] Matsumoto and Sinclair (1994); Kamatani (1988).
[20] Uchida (1991).

transfer from the West was sought after through a variety of mechanisms. In 1873, the Machine Shop of the Telegraph Bureau sent a Japanese clockmaker, Tanaka Seisuke, to the International Machines exhibition in Vienna to obtain information on the machines. About ten years later, all the Bureau's machines were made in Japan. Based on this technology, Tanaka Daikichi founded in 1882 an electrical factory, Shibaura Works, that, after its acquisition by Mitsui, went on to become Toshiba. Engineers were sent to Europe and to America. And Western Electric was permitted to produce and sell in Japan in 1899, in a joint venture with Japanese industrialists: the name of the company was NEC. On such a technological basis Japan went full speed into the electrical and communications age before 1914: by 1914 total power production had reached·1,555,000 kw/hour, and 3,000 telephone offices were relaying a billion messages a year. It is indeed symbolic that Commodore Perry's gift to the Shogun in 1857 was a set of American telegraphs, until then never seen in Japan: the first telegraph line was laid in 1869, and ten years later Japan was connected to the whole world through a transcontinental information network, via Siberia, operated by the Great Northern Telegraph Co., jointly managed by Western and Japanese engineers and transmitting in both English and Japanese.

The story of how Japan became a major world player in information technology industries in the last quarter of the twentieth century, under the strategic guidance of the state, is now general public knowledge, so it will be assumed in our discussion.[21] What is relevant for the ideas presented here is that it happened at the same time as an industrial and scientific superpower, the Soviet Union, failed this fundamental technological transition. It is obvious, as the preceding reminders show, that Japanese technological development since the 1960s did not happen in an historical vacuum, but was rooted in a decades-old tradition of engineering excellence. Yet what matters for the purpose of this analysis is to emphasize what dramatically different results state intervention (and lack of intervention) had in the cases of China and the Soviet Union, as compared to Japan in both the Meiji period and the post-second World War period. The characteristics of the Japanese state at the roots of both processes of modernization and development are well known, both for *Ishin Meiji*[22] and for the contemporary developmental state,[23] and

---

[21]   Ito (1994); Japan Informatization Processing Center (1994); for a western perspective, see Forester (1993).
[22]   See Norman (1940) and Dower (1975); see also Allen (1981a).
[23]   Johnson (1995).

their presentation would take us excessively away from the focus of these preliminary reflections. What must be retained for the understanding of the relationship between technology and society is that the role of the state, by either stalling, unleashing, or leading technological innovation, is a decisive factor in the overall process, as it expresses and organizes the social and cultural forces that dominate in a given space and time. To a large extent, technology expresses the ability of a society to propel itself into technological mastery through the institutions of society, including the state. The historical process through which such development of productive forces takes place earmarks the characteristics of technology and its interweaving in social relationships.

This is not different in the case of the current technological revolution. It originated and diffused, not by accident, in a historical period of the global restructuring of capitalism, for which it was an essential tool. Thus, the new society emerging from such a process of change is both capitalist and informational, while presenting considerable historical variation in different countries, according to their history, culture, institutions, and to their specific relationship to global capitalism and information technology.

Informationalism, Industrialism, Capitalism, Statism: Modes of Development and Modes of Production

The information technology revolution has been instrumental in allowing the implementation of a fundamental process of restructuring of the capitalist system from the 1980s onwards. In the process, this technological revolution was itself shaped, in its development and manifestations, by the logic and interests of advanced capitalism, without being reducible to the expression of such interests. The alternative system of social organization present in our historical period, statism, also tried to redefine the means of accomplishing its structural goals while preserving the essence of these goals: that is the meaning of restructuring (or *perestroyka*, in Russian). Yet Soviet statism failed in its attempt, to the point of collapsing the whole system, to a large extent because of the incapacity of statism to assimilate and use the principles of informationalism embodied in new information technologies, as I shall argue in this book (volume III) on the basis of empirical analysis. Chinese statism seemed to succeed by shifting from statism to state-led capitalism and integration in global economic networks, actually becoming closer to the developmental state model of East Asian capitalism than to the "Socialism with Chinese characteristics" of official ideology,[24] as I shall also try to discuss in volume III. Nonetheless, it is highly likely that the process of structural transformation in China will undergo major political conflicts and institutional change in the coming years. The collapse of statism (with rare exceptions, for example, Vietnam, North Korea, Cuba, which are, however, in the process of linking up with global capitalism) has established a close relationship between the new, global capitalist system shaped by its relatively successful *perestroyka*, and the emergence of informationalism, as the new material, technological basis of economic activity and social organization. Yet both processes (capitalist restructuring, the rise of informationalism) are distinct, and their interaction can only be understood if we separate them analytically. At this point in my introductory presentation of the book's *idées fortes*, it seems necessary to propose some theoretical distinctions and definitions concerning capitalism, statism, industrialism, and informationalism.

It is a well-established tradition in theories of postindustrialism and informationalism, starting with classic works by Alain Touraine[25] and Daniel Bell,[26] to place the distinction between pre-industrialism, industrialism, and informationalism (or postindustrialism) on a different axis than the one opposing capitalism and statism (or collectivism, in Bell's terms). While societies can be characterized along the two axes (so that we have industrial statism, industrial capitalism, and so on), it is essential for the understanding of social dynamics to maintain the analytical distance and empirical interrelation between modes of production (capitalism, statism) and modes of development (industrialism, informationalism). To root these distinctions in a theoretical basis, that will inform the specific analyses presented in this book, it is unavoidable to take the reader, for a few paragraphs, into the somewhat arcane domains of sociological theory.

This book studies the emergence of a new social structure, manifested under various forms, depending on the diversity of cultures and institutions throughout the planet. This new social structure is associated with the emergence of a new mode of development, informationalism, historically shaped by the restructuring of the capitalist mode of production towards the end of the twentieth century.

The theoretical perspective underlying this approach postulates that societies are organized around human processes structured by historically determined relationships of *production, experience,* and

---

[24]   Nolan and Furen (1990); Hsing (1996).
[25]   Touraine (1969).
[26]   Bell (1973). All quotes are from the 1976 edition, which includes a new, substantial "Foreword 1976."

power. *Production* is the action of humankind on matter (nature) to appropriate it and transform it for its benefit by obtaining a product, consuming (unevenly) part of it, and accumulating surplus for investment, according to a variety of socially determined goals. *Experience* is the action of human subjects on themselves, determined by the interaction between their biological and cultural identities, and in relationship to their social and natural environment. It is constructed around the endless search for fulfillment of human needs and desires. *Power* is that relationship between human subjects which, on the basis of production and experience, imposes the will of some subjects upon others by the potential or actual use of violence, physical or symbolic. Institutions of society are built to enforce power relationships existing in each historical period, including the controls, limits, and social contracts achieved in the power struggles.

Production is organized in class relationships that define the process by which some human subjects, on the basis of their position in the production process, decide the sharing and uses of the product in relationship to consumption and investment. Experience is structured around gender/sexual relationships, historically organized around the family, and characterized hitherto by the domination of men over women. Family relationships and sexuality structure personality and frame symbolic interaction.

Power is founded upon the state and its institutionalized monopoly of violence, although what Foucault labels the microphysics of power, embodied in institutions and organizations, diffuses throughout the entire society, from work places to hospitals, enclosing subjects in a tight framework of formal duties and informal aggressions.

Symbolic communication between humans, and the relationship between humans and nature, on the basis of production (with its complement, consumption), experience, and power, crystallize over history in specific territories, thus generating *cultures and collective identities*.

Production is a socially complex process, because each one of its elements is internally differentiated. Thus, humankind as collective producer includes both labor and the organizers of production, and labor is highly differentiated and stratified according to the role of each worker in the production process. Matter includes nature, human-modified nature, human-produced nature, and human nature itself, the labors of history forcing us to move away from the classic distinction between humankind and nature, since millennia of human action have incorporated the natural environment into society, making us, materially and symbolically, an inseparable part of this environment. The relationship between labor and matter in the process of work involves the use of means of production to act upon matter on the basis of energy, knowledge, and information. Technology is the specific form of this relationship.

The product of the production process is socially used under two forms: consumption and surplus. Social structures interact with production processes by determining the rules for the appropriation, distribution, and uses of the surplus. These rules constitute modes of production, and these modes define social relationships of production, determining the existence of social classes that become constituted as such classes through their historical practice. The structural principle under which surplus is appropriated and controlled characterizes a mode of production. In the twentieth century we have lived, essentially, with two predominant modes of production: capitalism and statism. Under capitalism, the separation between producers and their means of production, the commodification of labor, and the private ownership of means of production on the basis of the control of capital (commodified surplus), determined the basic principle of appropriation and distribution of surplus by capitalists, although who is (are) the capitalist class(es) is a matter of social inquiry in each historical context, rather than an abstract category. Under statism, the control of surplus is external to the economic sphere: it lies in the hands of the power-holders in the state: let us call them *apparatchiki* or *ling-dao*. Capitalism is oriented toward profit-maximizing, that is, toward increasing the amount of surplus appropriated by capital on the basis of the private control over the means of production and circulation. Statism is (was?) oriented toward power-maximizing, that is, toward increasing the military and ideological capacity of the political apparatus for imposing its goals on a greater number of subjects and at deeper levels of their consciousness.

The social relationships of production, and thus the mode of production, determine the appropriation and uses of surplus. A separate yet fundamental question is the level of such surplus, determined by the productivity of a particular process of production, that is by the ratio of the value of each unit of output to the value of each unit of input. Productivity levels are themselves dependent on the relationship between labor and matter, as a function of the use of the means of production by the application of energy and knowledge. This process is characterized by technical relationships of production, defining modes of development. Thus, modes of development are the technological arrangements through which labor works on matter to generate the product, ultimately determining the level and quality of surplus. Each mode of development is defined by the element that is fundamental in fostering productivity in the production process. Thus, in the agrarian mode of development, the source of increasing surplus results from quantitative increases of labor and natural resources (particularly land) in the production process, as well as from the natural endowment of these resources. In the industrial mode of development, the main source of productivity lies in the introduction of new energy sources, and in the ability to decentralize the use of energy throughout the production and circulation processes. In the new, informational mode of development the source of productivity lies in the technology of knowledge generation, information processing, and symbol communication. To be sure, knowledge and information are critical elements in all modes of development, since the process of production is always based on some level of knowledge and in the processing of information.[27] However, what is specific to the informational mode of development is the action of knowledge upon knowledge itself as the main source of productivity (see chapter 2). Information processing is focused on improving the technology of information processing as a source of productivity, in a virtuous circle of interaction between the knowledge sources of technology and the application of technology to improve knowledge generation and information processing: this is why, rejoining popular fashion, I call this new mode of development informational, constituted by the emergence of a new technological paradigm based on information technology (see chapter 1).

Each mode of development has also a structurally determined performance principle around which technological processes are organized: industrialism is oriented toward economic growth, that is toward maximizing output; informationalism is oriented towards technological development, that is toward the accumulation of knowledge and towards higher levels of complexity in information processing. While higher levels of knowledge may normally result in higher levels of output per unit of input, it is the pursuit of knowledge

[27] For the sake of clarity in this book, I find it necessary to provide a definition of knowledge and information, even if such an intellectually satisfying gesture introduces a dose of the arbitrary in the discourse, as social scientists who have struggled with the issue know well. I have no compelling reason to improve on Daniel Bell's (1973: 175) own definition of *knowledge:* "Knowledge: a set of organized statements of facts or ideas, presenting a reasoned judgment or an experimental result, which is transmitted to others through some communication medium in some systematic form. Thus, I distinguish knowledge from news and entertainment." As for *information,* some established authors in the field, such as Machlup, simply define information as the communication of knowledge (see Machlup 1962: 15). However, this is because Machlup's definition of knowledge seems to be excessively broad, as Bell argues. Thus, I would rejoin the operational definition of information proposed by Porat in his classic work (1977:2): "Information is data that have been organized and communicated."

and information that characterizes the technological production function under informationalism.

Although technology and technical relationships of production are organized in paradigms originating in the dominant spheres of society (for example, the production process, the military industrial complex) they diffuse throughout the whole set of social relationships and social structures, so penetrating and modifying power and experience.[28] Thus, modes of development shape the entire realm of social behavior, of course including symbolic communication. Because informationalism is based on the technology of knowledge and information, there is a specially close linkage between culture and productive forces, between spirit and matter, in the informational mode of development. It follows that we should expect the emergence of historically new forms of social interaction, social control, and social change.

Informationalism and capitalist *perestroyka*

Shifting from theoretical categories to historical change, what truly matters for social processes and forms making the living flesh of societies is the actual interaction between modes of production and modes of development, enacted and fought for by social actors, in unpredictable ways, within the constraining framework of past history and current conditions of technological and economic development. Thus, the world, and societies, would have been very different if Gorbachev had succeeded in his own *perestroyka*, a target that was politically difficult, but not out of reach. Or if the Asian Pacific had not been able to blend its traditional business networking form of economic organization with the tools provided by information technology. Yet the most decisive historical factor accelerating, channeling and shaping the information technology paradigm, and inducing its associated social forms, was/is the process of capitalist restructuring undertaken since the 1980s, so that the new techno-economic system can be adequately characterized as *informational capitalism*.

The Keynesian model of capitalist growth that brought unprece-

[28] When technological innovation does not diffuse in society, because of institutional obstacles to such diffusion, what follows is technological retardation because of the absence of necessary social/cultural feedback into the institutions of innovation and into the innovators themselves. This is the fundamental lesson that can be drawn from such important experiences as Qing's China, or the Soviet Union. For the Soviet Union, see vol. III. For China, see Qian (1985) and Mokyr (1990).

dented economic prosperity and social stability to most market economies for almost three decades after the Second World War, hit the wall of its built-in limitations in the early 1970s, and its crisis was manifested in the form of rampant inflation.[29] When the oil price increases of 1974 and 1979 threatened to spiral inflation out of control, governments and firms engaged in a process of restructuring in a pragmatic process of trial and error that is still underway in the mid-1990s with a more decisive effort at deregulation, privatization, and the dismantling of the social contract between capital and labor that underlay the stability of the previous growth model. In a nutshell, a series of reforms, both at the level of institutions and in the management of firms, aimed at four main goals: deepening the capitalist logic of profit-seeking in capital–labor relationships; enhancing the productivity of labor and capital; globalizing production, circulation, and markets, seizing the opportunity of the most advantageous conditions for profit-making everywhere; and marshaling the state's support for productivity gains and competitiveness of national economies, often to the detriment of social protection and public interest regulations. Technological innovation and organizational change, focusing on flexibility and adaptability, were absolutely critical in ensuring the speed and efficiency of restructuring. It can be argued that without new information technology global capitalism would have been a much-limited reality, flexible management would have been reduced to labor trimming, and the new round of spending in both capital goods and new consumer products would not have been sufficient to compensate for the reduction in public spending. Thus, informationalism is linked to the expansion and rejuvenation of capitalism, as industrialism was linked to its constitution as a mode of production. To be sure, the process of restructuring had very different manifestations in areas and societies around the world, as I shall briefly survey in chapter 2: it was diverted from its fundamental logic by the military Keynesianism of the Reagan Administration, actually creating even greater difficulties for the American economy at the end of the euphoria of artificial stimulation; it was somewhat limited in Western Europe because of society's resistance to the dismantling of the welfare state and to one-sided labor market flexibility, with the

[29] I presented years ago my interpretation of the causes of the 1970s worldwide economic crisis, as well as a tentative prognosis of avenues for capitalist restructuring. Notwithstanding the excessively rigid theoretical framework I juxtaposed to the empirical analysis, I think that the main points I made in that book (written in 1977–8), including the prediction of Reagonomics under that name, are still useful to understand the qualitative changes operated in capitalism during the last two decades (see Castells 1980).

result of raising unemployment in the European Union; it was absorbed in Japan without dramatic changes by emphasizing productivity and competitiveness on the basis of technology and cooperation rather than by increasing exploitation, until international pressures forced Japan to offshore production and to broadening the role of an unprotected, secondary labor market; and it plunged into a major recession, in the 1980s, the economies of Africa (except South Africa and Botswana) and Latin America (with the exception of Chile and Colombia), when International Monetary Fund policies cut money supply, reduced wages and imports, to homogenize conditions of global capital accumulation around the world. Restructuring proceeded on the basis of the political defeat of organized labor in major capitalist countries, and the acceptance of a common economic discipline by countries of the OECD area. Such discipline, although enforced when necessary by the Bundesbank, the Federal Reserve Board, and International Monetary Fund, was in fact inscribed in the integration of global financial markets that took place in the early 1980s using new information technologies. Under conditions of global financial integration, autonomous, national monetary policies became literally unfeasible, thus equalizing basic economic parameters of restructuring processes throughout the planet.

While capitalism's restructuring and the diffusion of informationalism were inseparable processes on a global scale, societies did act/react differently to such processes, according to the specificity of their history, culture, and institutions. Thus, to some extent it would be improper to refer to an Informational Society, which would imply the homogeneity of social forms everywhere under the new system. This is obviously an untenable proposition, empirically and theoretically. Yet we could speak of an Informational Society in the same way that sociologists have been referring to the existence of an Industrial Society, characterized by common fundamental features in their socio-technical systems, for instance in Raymond Aron's formulation.[30] But with two important qualifications: on the one hand, informational societies, as they exist currently, are capitalist (unlike industrial societies, some of which were statist); on the other hand, we must stress the cultural and institutional diversity of informational societies. Thus, Japanese uniqueness[31] or Spain's difference[32] are not going to fade away in a process of cultural indifferentiation, marching anew towards universal modernization, this time measured

[30]   Aron (1963).
[31]   On Japanese uniqueness in a sociological perspective, see Shoji (1990).
[32]   On the social roots of Spanish differences, and similarities, vis-à-vis other countries, see Zaldivar and Castells (1992).

by rates of computer diffusion. Neither are China or Brazil going to be melted in the global pot of informational capitalism by continuing their current high-speed developmental path. But Japan, Spain, China, Brazil, as well as the United States, are and will be more so in the future, informational societies, in the sense that the core processes of knowledge generation, economic productivity, polit-ical/military power and media communication are already deeply transformed by the informational paradigm, and are connected to global networks of wealth, power, and symbols working under such a logic. Thus, all societies are affected by capitalism and information-alism, and many societies (certainly all major societies) are already informational,[33] although of different kinds, in different settings, and with specific cultural/institutional expressions. A theory of the infor-mational society, as distinct from a global/informational economy,

[33] I should like to draw an analytical distinction between the notions of "infor-mation society" and "informational society," with similar implications for information/informational economy. The term information society emphasizes the role of information in society. But I argue that information, in its broadest sense, e.g. as communication of knowledge, has been critical in all societies, including medieval Europe which was culturally structured, and to some extent unified, around scholasticism, that is, by and large an intellectual framework (see Southern 1995). In contrast, the term informational indicates the attribute of a specific form of social organization in which information generation, processing, and transmission become the fundamental sources of productivity and power, because of new technological conditions emerging in this historical period. My terminology tries to establish a parallel with the distinction between industry and industrial. An industrial society (a usual notion in the sociological tradition) is not just a society where there is industry, but a society where the social and tech-nological forms of industrial organization permeate all spheres of activity, starting with the dominant activities, located in the economic system and in military tech-nology, and reaching the objects and habits of everyday life. My use of the terms informational society and informational economy attempts a more precise char-acterization of current transformations, beyond the commonsense observation that information and knowledge are important to our societies. However, the actual content of "informational society" has to be determined by observation and analysis. This is precisely the object of this book. For instance, one of the key features of informational society is the networking logic of its basic structure, which explains the use of the concept of "network society," as defined and spec-ified in the conclusion of this volume. However, other components of "informational society," such as social movements or the state, exhibit features that go beyond the networking logic, although they are substantially influenced by such logic, as characteristic of the new social structure. Thus, "the network society" does not exhaust all the meaning of the "informational society". Finally, why, after all these precisions, have I kept *The Information Age* as the overall title of the book, without including medieval Europe in my inquiry? Titles are commu-nicating devices. They should be user-friendly, clear enough for the reader to guess what is the real topic of the book, and worded in a fashion that does not

will always have to be attentive to historical/cultural specificity as much as to structural similarities related to a largely shared techno-economic paradigm. As for the actual content of this common social structure that could be considered to be the essence of the new informational society, I'm afraid I am unable to summarize it in one paragraph: indeed, the structure and processes that characterize informational societies are the subject matter covered in this book.

The Self in the Informational Society

New information technologies are integrating the world in global networks of instrumentality. Computer-mediated communication begets a vast array of virtual communities. Yet the distinctive social and political trend of the 1990s is the construction of social action and politics around primary identities, either ascribed, rooted in history and geography, or newly built in an anxious search for meaning and spirituality. The first historical steps of informational societies seem to characterize them by the preeminence of identity as their organizing principle. I understand by identity the process by which a social actor recognizes itself and constructs meaning primarily on the basis of a given cultural attribute or set of attributes, to the exclusion of a broader reference to other social structures. Affirmation of identity does not necessarily mean incapacity to relate to other identities (for example, women still relate to men), or to embrace the whole society under such identity (for example, religious fundamentalism aspires to convert everybody). But social relationships are defined vis-à-vis the others on the basis of those cultural attributes that specify identity. For instance, Yoshino, in his study on *nihonjiron* (ideas of Japanese uniqueness), pointedly defines cultural nationalism as "the aim to regenerate the national community by creating, preserving or strengthening a people's cultural identity when it is felt to be lacking, or threatened. The cultural nationalist regards the nation as the product of its unique history and culture and as a collective solidarity endowed with unique attributes."[34] Calhoun, although rejecting the historical newness of the phenomenon, has also emphasized the decisive role

---

depart excessively from the semantic frame of reference. Thus, in a world built around information technologies, information society, informatization, information superhighway, and the like (all terminologies originated in Japan in the mid-1960s – *Johoka Shakai*, in Japanese – and were transmitted to the West in 1978 by Simon Nora and Alain Minc, indulging in exoticism), a title such as *The Information Age* points straightforwardly to the questions to be raised, without prejudging the answers.

[34]   Yoshino (1992: 1).

of identity in defining politics in contemporary American society, particularly in the women's movement, in the gay movement, in the civil rights movement, movements "that sought not only various instrumental goals but the affirmation of excluded identities as publicly good and politically salient."[35] Alain Touraine goes further, arguing that "in a post-industrial society, in which cultural services have replaced material goods at the core of production, *it is the defense of the subject, in its personality and in its culture, against the logic of apparatuses and markets, that replaces the idea of class struggle.*"[36] Then the key issue becomes, as stated by Calderon and Laserna, in a world characterized by simultaneous globalization and fragmentation, "how to combine new technologies and collective memory, universal science and communitarian cultures, passion and reason?"[37] How, indeed! And why do we observe the opposite trend throughout the world, namely, the increasing distance between globalization and identity, between the Net and the Self?

Raymond Barglow, in his illuminating essay on this matter, from a socio-psychoanalytical perspective, points at the paradox that while information systems and networking augment human powers of organization and integration, they simultaneously subvert the traditional Western concept of a separate, independent subject: "The historical shift from mechanical to information technologies helps to subvert the notions of sovereignty and self-sufficiency that have provided an ideological anchoring for individual identity since Greek philosophers elaborated the concept more than two millennia ago. In short, technology is helping to dismantle the very vision of the world that in the past it fostered."[38] Then he goes on to present a fascinating comparison between classic dreams reported in Freud's writing and his own patients' dreams in the high tech environment of 1990s' San Francisco: "Image of a head . . . and behind it is suspended a computer keyboard . . . I'm this programmed head!"[39] This feeling of absolute solitude is new in comparison to classic Freudian representation: "the dreamers . . . express a sense of solitude experienced as existential and inescapable, built into the structure of the world . . . Totally isolated, the self seems irretrievably lost to itself."[40] Thus, the search for new connectedness around shared, reconstructed identity.

[35]   Calhoun (1994: 4).
[36]   Touraine (1994: 168; my translation, his italics).
[37]   Calderon and Laserna (1994: 90; my translation).
[38]   Barglow (1994: 6).
[39]   Ibid.: 53.
[40]   Ibid.: 185.

However insightful, this hypothesis may be only part of the explanation. On the one hand, it would imply a crisis of the self limited to a Western individualist conception, shaken by uncontrollable connectedness. Yet the search for new identity and new spirituality is on also in the East, in spite of a stronger sense of collective identity and the traditional, cultural subordination of individual to the family. The resonance of Aum Shinrikyo in Japan in 1995, particularly among the young, highly educated generations, could be considered a symptom of the crisis of established patterns of identity, coupled with the desperate need to build a new, collective self, significantly mixing spirituality, advanced technology (chemicals, biology, laser), global business connections, and the culture of millenarist doom.[41]

On the other hand, elements of an interpretative framework to explain the rising power of identity must also be found at a broader level, in relationship to macroprocesses of institutional change, to a large extent connected to the emergence of a new global system. Thus, widespread currents of racism and xenophobia in Western Europe may be related, as Alain Touraine[42] and Michel Wieviorka[43] have suggested, to an identity crisis on becoming an abstraction (European), at the same time that European societies, while seeing their national identity blurred, discovered within themselves the lasting existence of ethnic minorities in European societies (a demographic fact since at least the 1960s). Or again, in Russia and the ex-Soviet Union, the strong development of nationalism in the post-communist period can be related, as I shall argue in volume III, to the cultural emptiness created by 70 years of imposition of an exclusionary ideological identity, coupled with the return to primary, historical identity (Russian, Georgian), as the only source of meaning after the crumbling of the historically fragile *sovetskii narod* (Soviet people).

The emergence of religious fundamentalism seems also to be linked both to a global trend and to an institutional crisis. We know from history that ideas and beliefs of all brands are always in stock waiting to catch fire under the right circumstances.[44] It is significant that fundamentalism, be it Islamic or Christian, has spread, and will spread, throughout the world at the historical moment when global networks of wealth and power connect nodal points and valued

[41]   For the new forms of revolt linked to identity in explicit opposition to globalization, see the exploratory analysis undertaken in Castells, Yazawa, and Kiselyova, (1996b).

[42]   Touraine (1991).

[43]   Wieviorka (1993).

[44]   See, for instance Kepel (1993); Colas (1992).

individuals throughout the planet, while disconnecting, and excluding, large segments of societies, regions, and even entire countries. Why did Algeria, one of most modernized Muslim societies, suddenly turn to fundamentalist saviors, who became terrorists (as did their anti-colonialist predecessors) when they were denied their electoral victory in democratic elections? Why did the traditionalist teachings of Pope John Paul II find an undisputable echo among the impoverished masses of the Third World, so that the Vatican could afford to ignore the protests of a minority of feminists in a few advanced countries where precisely the progress of reproductive rights contributes to diminishing the number of souls to be saved? There seems to be a logic of excluding the excluders, of redefining the criteria for value and meaning in a world where there is shrinking room for the computer illiterate, for consumptionless groups, and for under-communicated territories. When the Net switches off the Self, the Self, individual or collective, constructs its meaning without global, instrumental reference: the process of disconnection becomes reciprocal, after the refusal by the excluded of the one-sided logic of structural domination and social exclusion.

Such is the terrain to be explored, not just declared. The few ideas advanced here on the paradoxical manifestation of the self in the informational society are only intended to chart the course of my inquiry for the reader's information, not to draw conclusions beforehand.

A Word on Method

This is not a book about books. While relying on evidence of various sorts, and on analyses and accounts from multiple sources, it does not intend to discuss existing theories of postindustrialism or the information society. There are available several, thorough, balanced presentations of these theories,[45] as well as various critiques,[46] including my own.[47] Similarly, I shall not contribute, except when

[45]   A useful overview of sociological theories on postindustrialism and informationalism is Lyon (1988). For the intellectual and terminological origins of notions of "information society," see Ito (1991a) and Nora and Minc (1978). See also Beniger (1986); Katz (1988); Salvaggio (1989); Williams (1988).

[46]   For critical perspectives on postindustrialism, see, among others, Lyon (1988); Touraine (1992); Shoji (1990); Woodward (1980); Roszak (1986). For a cultural critique of our society's emphasis on information technology, see Postman (1992).

[47]   For my own critique on postindustrialism, see Castells (1994, 1995, 1996).

necessary for the sake of the argument, to the cottage industry created in the 1980s around postmodern theory,[48] being for my part fully satisfied with the excellent criticism elaborated by David Harvey on the social and ideological foundations of "post-modernity,"[49] as well as with the sociological dissection of postmodern theories performed by Scott Lash.[50] I certainly owe many thoughts to many authors, and particularly to the forebears of informationalism, Alain Touraine and Daniel Bell, as well as to the one Marxist theorist who sensed the new, relevant issues just before his death in 1979, Nicos Poulantzas.[51] And I duly acknowledge borrowed concepts when I use them as tools in my specific analyses. Yet I have tried to construct a discourse as autonomous and nonredundant as possible, integrating materials and observations from various sources, without submitting the reader to the painful revisiting of the bibliographic jungle where I have lived (fortunately, among other activities) for the past 12 years.

In a similar vein, while using a significant amount of statistical sources and empirical studies, I have tried to minimize the processing of data, to simplify an already excessively cumbersome book. Therefore, I tend to use data sources that find broad, accepted consensus among social scientists (for example, OECD, United Nations, World Bank, governments' official statistics, authoritative research monographs, generally reliable academic or business sources), except when such sources seem to be erroneous (such as Soviet GNP statistics or the World Bank's report on adjustment policies in Africa). I am aware of limitations in lending credibility to information that may not always be accurate, yet the reader will realize that there are numerous precautions taken in this text, so as to form conclusions usually on the basis of convergent trends from several sources, according to a methodology of triangulation with a well-established, successful tradition among historians, policemen, and investigative reporters. Furthermore, the data, observations, and references presented in this book do not really aim at demonstrating but at suggesting hypotheses while constraining the ideas within a corpus of observation, admittedly selected with my research questions in mind but certainly not organized around preconceived answers. The methodology followed in this book, whose specific implications will be discussed in each chapter, is at the service of the overarching purpose of its intellectual endeavor: to propose some elements of an

[48] See Lyon (1993); also Seidman and Wagner (1992).
[49] Harvey (1990).
[50] Lash (1990).
[51] Poulantzas (1978: esp. 160–9).

exploratory, cross-cultural theory of economy and society in the information age, *as it specifically refers to the emergence of a new social structure*. The broad scope of my analysis is required by the pervasiveness of the object of such analysis (informationalism) throughout social domains and cultural expressions. But I certainly do not intend to address the whole range of themes and issues in contemporary societies, since writing encyclopedias is not my trade.

The book is divided into three parts that the publisher has wisely transformed into three volumes, to appear within the span of approximately one year. They are analytically interrelated, but they have been organized to make their reading independent. The only exception to this rule concerns the General Conclusion, in volume III, that is the overall conclusion of the book, and presents a synthetic interpretation of its findings and ideas.

The division into three volumes, while making the book publishable and readable, raises some problems in communicating my overall theory. Indeed, some critical topics that cut across all the themes treated in this book are presented in the second volume. Such is the case, particularly, of the analysis of women and patriarchalism, and of power relationships and the state. I warn the reader that I do not share a traditional view of society as made up of superimposed levels, with technology and economy in the basement, power on the mezzanine, and culture in the penthouse. Yet, for the sake of clarity, I am forced to a systematic, somewhat linear presentation of topics that, while relating to each other, cannot fully integrate all the elements until they have been discussed in some depth throughout the intellectual journey on which the reader is invited by this book. The first volume, in the reader's hands, deals primarily with the logic of what I call the Net, while the second (*The Power of Identity*) analyzes the formation of the Self, and the interaction between the Net and the Self in the crisis of two central institutions of society: the patriarchal family and the national state. The third volume (*End of Millennium*) attempts an interpretation of current historical transformations as a result of the dynamics of processes studied in the two first volumes. It is only at the end of the third volume that a general integration between theory and observation,. linking up the analyses concerning the various domains, will be proposed, although each volume concludes with an effort at synthesizing the main findings and ideas presented in the volume. While volume III is more directly concerned with specific processes of historical change in various contexts, throughout the whole book I have tried my best to accomplish two goals: to ground analysis in observation, without reducing theorization to commentary; to diversify culturally my sources of observation *and of ideas*, as much as possible. This approach stems from my conviction that we have entered a truly multicultural, interdependent world, that can only be understood, and changed, from a plural perspective that brings together cultural identity, global networking, and multidimensional politics.

— 1 —

The Information Technology Revolution

Which Revolution?

"Gradualism," wrote paleontologist Stephen J. Gould, "the idea that all change must be smooth, slow, and steady, was never read from the rocks. It represented a common cultural bias, in part a response of nineteenth century liberalism to a world in revolution. But it continues to color our supposedly objective reading of life's history. . . . . The history of life, as I read it, is a series of stable states, punctuated at rare intervals by major events that occur with great rapidity and help to establish the next stable era."[1] My starting point, and I am not alone in this assumption,[2] is that, at the end of the twentieth century, we are living through one of these rare intervals in history. An interval characterized by the transformation of our "material culture"[3] by the works of a new technological paradigm organized around information technologies.

By technology I understand, in straight line with Harvey Brooks and Daniel Bell, "the use of scientific knowledge to specify ways of doing

[1]   Gould (1980: 226).
[2]   Melvin Kranzberg, one of the leading historians of technology, wrote "The Information Age has indeed revolutionized the technical elements of industrial society" (1985: 42). As for its societal effects: "While it might be evolutionary, in the sense that all changes and benefits will not appear overnight, it will be revolutionary in its effects upon our society" (ibid. 52). Along the same lines of argument, see also, for instance, Perez (1983); Forester (1985); Dizard (1982); Nora and Minc (1978); Stourdze (1987); Negroponte (1995); Ministry of Posts and Telecommunications (Japan) (1995); Bishop and Waldholz (1990); Darbon and Robin (1987); Salomon (1992); Dosi et al. (1988b); Petrella (1993).
[3]   On the definition of technology as "material culture" which I consider to be the appropriate sociological perspective, see the discussion in Fischer (1992: 1–32, esp): "Technology here is similar to the idea of material culture.'

things in a *reproducible* manner."[4] Among information technologies, I include, like everybody else, the *converging set* of technologies in microelectronics, computing (machines and software), telecommunications/broadcasting, and optoelectronics.[5] In addition, unlike some analysts, I also include in the realm of information technologies genetic engineering and its expanding set of developments and applications.[6] This is, first, because genetic engineering is focused on the decoding, manipulation, and eventual reprogramming of information codes of the living matter. But also because, in the 1990s, biology, electronics, and informatics seem to be converging and interacting in their applications, in their materials, and, more fundamentally, in their conceptual approach, a topic that deserves further mention below in this chapter.[7] Around this nucleus of information technologies, in the broad sense as defined, a constellation of major technological breakthroughs has been taking place in the last two decades of the twentieth century in advanced materials, in energy sources, in medical applications, in manufacturing techniques (current or potential, such as nanotechnology), and in transportation technology, among others.[8] Furthermore, the current process of technological transformation expands exponentially because of its ability to create an interface between technological fields through common digital language in which information is generated, stored, retrieved, processed, and transmitted. We live in a world that, in the expression of Nicholas Negroponte, has become digital.[9]

The prophetic hype and ideological manipulation characterizing most discourses on the information technology revolution should not mislead us into underestimating its truly fundamental significance. It is, as this book will try to show, at least as major a historical event as was the eighteenth-century Industrial Revolution, inducing a pattern of discontinuity in the material basis of economy, society, and culture. The historical record of technological revolutions, as compiled by Melvin Kranzberg and Carroll Pursell,[10] shows that they are all

[4]   Brooks (1971: 13) from unpublished text, quoted with emphasis added by Bell (1976: 29).
[5]   Saxby (1990); Mulgan (1991).
[6]   Marx (1989); Hall (1987).
[7]   For a stimulating, informed, although deliberately controversial, account of the convergence between the biological revolution and the broader Information Technology Revolution, see Kelly (1995).
[8]   Forester (1988); Herman (1990); Lyon and Gorner (1995); Lincoln and Essin (1993); Edquist and Jacobsson (1989); Drexler and Peterson (1991); Lovins and Lovins (1995); Dondero (1995).
[9]   Negroponte (1995).
[10]   Kranzberg and Pursell (1967).

characterized by their *pervasiveness*, that is by their penetration of all domains of human activity, not as an exogenous source of impact, but as the fabric in which such activity is woven. In other words, *they are process-oriented*, besides inducing new products. On the other hand, unlike any other revolution, *the core* of the transformation we are experiencing in the current revolution refers to *technologies of information processing and communication*.[11] Information technology is to this revolution what new sources of energy were to the successive Industrial Revolutions, from the steam engine to electricity, to fossil fuels, and even to nuclear power, since the generation and distribution of energy was the key element underlying the industrial socie However, this statement on the preeminent role of information technology is often confused with the characterization of the current revolution as essentially dependent on new knowledge and information. This is true of the current process of technological change, but so it is of preceding technological revolutions, as is shown by leading historians of technology, such as Melvin Kranzberg and Joel Mokyr.[12] The first Industrial Revolution, although not science-based, relied on

---

[11]   The full understanding of the current technological revolution would require the discussion of the specificity of new information technologies *vis-à-vis* their historical ancestors of equally revolutionary character, such as the discovery of printing in China probably in the late seventh century, and in Europe in the fifteenth century, a classical theme of communications literature. Without being able to address the issue within the limits of this book focused on the sociological dimension of technological change, let me suggest a few topics to the reader's attention. Electronic-based information technologies (including electronic printing) feature incomparable memory storage capacity and speed of combination and transmission of bits. Electronic text allows for substantially greater flexibility of feedbacks, interaction, and reconfiguration of text, as any word-processing writer will acknowledge, thus altering the process of communication itself. On-line communication, combined with flexibility of text, allows for ubiquitous, asynchronous space/time programming. As for the social effects of information technologies, I propose the hypothesis that the depth of their impact is a function of the pervasiveness of information throughout the social structure. Thus, while printing did substantially affect European societies in the Modern Age, as well as Medieval China to a lesser extent, its effects were somewhat limited because of widespread illiteracy in the population and because of the low intensity of information in the productive structure. Thus, the industrial society, by educating citizens and by gradually organizing the economy around knowledge and information, prepared the ground for the empowering of the human mind when new information technologies became available. See, for a historical comment on this earlier information technology revolution, Boureau et al. (1989). For some elements of the debate on technological specificity of electronic communication, including McLuhan's perspective, see chapter 5.
[12]   M. Kranzberg, "Prerequisites for industrialization," in Kranzberg and Pursell (1967: I. ch. 13); Mokyr (1990).

the extensive use of information, applying and developing preexisting knowledge. And the second Industrial Revolution, after 1850, was characterized by the decisive role of science in fostering innovation. Indeed, R&D laboratories appeared for the first time in the German chemical industry in the last decades of the nineteenth century.[13]

What characterizes the current technological revolution is not the centrality of knowledge and information, but the application of such knowledge and information to knowledge generation and information processing/communication devices, in a cumulative feedback loop between innovation and the uses of innovation.[14] An illustration may clarify this analysis. The uses of new telecommunications technologies in the last two decades have gone through three distinct stages: automation of tasks, experimentation of uses, reconfiguration of applications.[15] In the first two stages, technological innovation progressed through learning *by using*, in Rosenberg's terminology.[16] In the third stage, the users learned technology *by doing*, and ended up reconfiguring the networks, and finding new applications. The feedback loop between introducing new technology, using it, and developing it into new realms becomes much faster under the new technological paradigm. As a result, diffusion of technology endlessly amplifies the power of technology, as it becomes appropriated and redefined by its users. New information technologies are not simply tools to be applied, but processes to be developed. Users and doers may become the same. Thus users can take control of technology, as in the case of Internet (see chapter 5). It follows a close relationship between the social processes of creating and manipulating symbols (the culture of society) and the capacity to produce and distribute goods and services (the productive forces). For the first time in history, the human mind is a direct productive force, not just a decisive element of the production system.

Thus, computers, communication systems, and genetic decoding and programming are all amplifiers and extensions of the human mind. What we think, and how we think, become expressed in goods, services, material and intellectual output, be it food, shelter, transportation and communications systems, computers, missiles, health, education, or images. The growing integration between minds and machines, including the DNA machine, is canceling what Bruce Mazlish calls the "fourth discontinuity"[17] (the one between humans

---

[13]   Ashton (1948); Landes (1969); Mokyr (1990: 112); Clow and Clow (1952).
[14]   Hall and Preston (1988); Saxby (1990); Dizard (1982); Forester (1985).
[15]   Bar (1990).
[16]   Rosenberg (1982); Bar (1992).

and machines), fundamentally altering the way we are born, we live, we learn, we work, we produce, we consume, we dream, we fight, or we die. Of course, cultural/institutional contexts and purposeful social action decisively interact with the new technological system, but this system has its own, embedded logic, characterized by the capacity to translate all inputs into a common information system, and to process such information at increasing speed, with increasing power, at decreasing cost, in a potentially ubiquitous retrieval and distribution network.

There is an additional feature characterizing the information technology revolution in comparison with its historical predecessors. Mokyr[18] has shown that technological revolutions took place only in a few societies, and diffused in a relatively limited geographic area, often living in isolated space and time *vis-à-vis* other regions of the planet. Thus, while Europeans borrowed some of the discoveries that took place in China, for many centuries China and Japan adopted European technology only on a very limited basis, mainly restricted to military applications. The contact between civilizations at different technological levels often took the form of the destruction of the least developed, or of those who had predominantly applied their knowledge to non-military technology, as in the case of American civilizations annihilated by Spanish conquerors, sometimes through accidental biological warfare.[19] The Industrial Revolution did extend to most of the globe from its original West European shores during the next two centuries. But its expansion was highly selective, and its pace rather slow by current standards of technological diffusion. Indeed, even in Britain by the mid-nineteenth century, sectors that accounted for the majority of the labor force, and at least half the gross national product, were not affected by new industrial technologies.[20] Furthermore, its planetary reach in the following decades more often than not took the form of colonial domination, be it in India under the British Empire; in Latin America under commercial/industrial dependency on Britain and the United States; in the dismembering of Africa under the Berlin Treaty; or in the opening to foreign trade of Japan and China by the guns of Western ships. In contrast, new information technologies have spread throughout the globe with lightning speed in less than two decades, between the mid-1970s and the mid-1990s, displaying a logic that I propose as characteristic of this technological revolution: the immediate

[17] Mazlish (1993).
[18] Mokyr (1990: 293, 209 ff).
[19] See, for instance, Thomas (1993).
[20] Mokyr (1990: 83).

application to its own development of technologies it generates, connecting the world through information technology.[21] To be sure, there are large areas of the world, and considerable segments of the population, switched off from the new technological system: this is precisely one of the central arguments of this book. Furthermore, the speed of technological diffusion is selective, both socially and functionally. Differential timing in access to the power of technology for people, countries, and regions is a critical source of inequality in our society. The switched-off areas are culturally and spatially discontinuous: they are in the American inner cities or in the French *banlieues*, as much as in the shanty towns of Africa or in the deprived rural areas of China or India. Yet dominant functions, social groups, and territories across the globe are connected by the mid-1990s in a new technological system that, as such, started to take shape only in the 1970s.

How did this fundamental transformation happen in what amounts to an historical instant? Why is it diffusing throughout the globe at such an accelerated, if uneven, pace? Why is it a "revolution"? Since our experience of the new is shaped by our recent past, I think the answers to these basic questions could be helped by a brief reminder of the historical record of the Industrial Revolution, still present in our institutions, and therefore in our mind-set.

Lessons from the Industrial Revolution

Historians have shown that there were at least two Industrial Revolutions: the first started in the last third of the eighteenth century, characterized by new technologies such as the steam engine, the spinning jenny, the Cort's process in metallurgy, and, more broadly, by the replacement of hand-tools by machines; the second one, about 100 years later, featured the development of electricity, the internal combustion engine, science-based chemicals, efficient steel casting, and the beginning of communication technologies, with the diffusion of the telegraph and the invention of the telephone. Between the two there are fundamental continuities, as well as some critical differences, the main one being the decisive importance of scientific knowledge in sustaining and guiding technological development after 1850.[22] It is precisely because of their differences that

---

[21]   Pool (1990); Mulgan (1991).

[22]   Singer et al. (1958); Mokyr (1985). However, as Mokyr himself points out, an interface between science and technology was also present in the first Industrial Revolution in Britain. Thus, Watt's decisive improvement of the steam engine

features common to both may offer precious insights in understanding the logic of technological revolutions.

First of all, in both cases, we witness what Mokyr describes as a period of "accelerating and unprecedented technological change"[23] by historical standards. A set of macro-inventions prepared the ground for the blossoming of micro-inventions in the realms of agriculture, industry, and communications. Fundamental historical discontinuity, in an irreversible form, was introduced into the material basis of the human species, in a path-dependent process whose inner, sequential logic has been researched by Paul David and theorized by Brian Arthur.[24] They were indeed "revolutions," in the sense that a sudden, unexpected surge of technological applications transformed the processes of production and distribution, created a flurry of new products, and shifted decisively the location of wealth and power in a planet that became suddenly under the reach of those countries and elites able to master the new technological system. The dark side of this technological adventure is that it was inextricably tied to imperialist ambitions and inter-imperialist conflicts.

Yet this is precisely a confirmation of the revolutionary character of new industrial technologies. The historical ascent of the so-called West, in fact limited to Britain and a handful of nations in Western Europe as well as to their North American, and Australian offspring, is fundamentally linked to the technological superiority achieved during the two Industrial Revolutions.[25] Nothing in the cultural, scientific, political or military history of the world prior to the Industrial Revolution would explain such undisputable "Western" (Anglo-Saxon/German, with a French touch) supremacy between the 1750s and the 1940s. China was a far superior culture for most of pre-Renaissance history; the Muslim civilization (taking the liberty of using such a term) dominated much of the Mediterranean and exerted a significant influence in Africa and Asia throughout the Modern age; Asia and Africa remained by and large organized around autonomous cultural and political centers; Russia ruled in splendid

---

designed by Newcomen took place in interaction with his friend and protector Joseph Black, professor of chemistry at the University of Glasgow, where Watts was appointed in 1757 as "Mathematical Instrument Maker to the University," and where he conducted his own experiments on a model of the Newcomen engine (see Dickinson 1958). Indeed, Ubbelohde (1958: 673) reports that "Watt's development of a condenser for the steam, separated from the cylinder in which the piston moved, was closely linked up with and inspired by the scientific researches of Joseph Black (1728–99) the professor of chemistry at Glasgow University.'

[23]   Mokyr (1990: 82).

[24]   David (1975); David and Bunn (1988); Arthur (1989).

[25]   Rosenberg and Birdzell (1986).

isolation a vast expanse across East Europe and Asia; and the Spanish Empire, the laggard European culture of the Industrial Revolution, was the major world power for more than two centuries after 1492. Technology, expressing specific social conditions, introduced a new historical path in the second half of the eighteenth century.

This path originated in Britain, although its intellectual roots can be traced back all over Europe and to the Renaissance's spirit of discovery.[26] Indeed, some historians insist that the necessary scientific knowledge underlying the first Industrial Revolution was available 100 years earlier, ready to be used under mature social conditions; or, as others argue, waiting for the technical ingenuity of self-trained inventors, such as Newcomen, Watts, Crompton or Arkwright, able to translate available knowledge, combined with craft experience, into decisive new industrial technologies.[27] However, the second Industrial Revolution, more dependent on new scientific knowledge, shifted its center of gravity towards Germany and the United States, where the main developments in chemicals, electricity, and telephony took place.[28] Historians have painstakingly dissected the social conditions of the shifting geography of technical innovation, often focusing on the characteristics of education and science systems, or on the institutionalization of property rights. However, the contextual explanation for the uneven trajectory of technological innovation seems to be excessively broad and open to alternative interpretations. Hall and Preston, in their analysis of the changing geography of technological innovation between 1846 and 2003, show the importance of *local* seedbeds of innovation, of which Berlin, New York, and Boston are crowned as the "high technology industrial centers of the world" between 1880 and 1914, while "London in that period was a pale shadow of Berlin."[29] The reason lies in the territorial basis for the interaction of systems of technological discovery and applications, namely in the synergistic properties of what is known in the literature as "milieux of innovation."[30]

---

[26]   Singer et al. (1957).
[27]   Rostow (1975); see Jewkes et al. (1969) for the argument, and Singer et al. (1958) for the historical evidence.
[28]   Mokyr (1990).
[29]   Hall and Preston (1988: 123).
[30]   The origin of the concept of "milieu of innovation" can be traced back to Aydalot (1985). It was also implicitly present in the work by Anderson (1985); and in the elaboration by Arthur (1985). Around the same dates Peter Hall and I in Berkeley, Roberto Camagni in Milan, and Denis Maillat in Lausanne, together for a brief period with the late Philippe Aydalot, started to develop empirical analyses of milieux of innovation, a theme that, rightly so, has become a cottage research industry in the 1990s.

Indeed, technological breakthroughs came in clusters, interacting with each other in a process of increasing returns. Whichever conditions determined such clustering, the key lesson to be retained is that *technological innovation is not an isolated instance.*[31] It reflects a given state of knowledge, a particular institutional and industrial environment, a certain availability of skills to define a technical problem and to solve it, an economic mentality to make such application cost-efficient, and a network of producers and users who can communicate their experiences cumulatively, learning by using and by doing: elites learn by doing, thereby modifying the applications of technology, while most people learn by using, thus remaining within the constraints of the packaging of technology. The interactivity of systems of technological innovation and their dependence on certain "milieux" of exchange of ideas, problems, and solutions are critical features that can be generalized from the experience of past revolutions to the current one.[32]

The positive effects of new industrial technologies on economic growth, living standards, and the human mastery of a hostile Nature (reflected in the dramatic lengthening of life expectancy, which did not improve steadily before the eighteenth century) over the long run are undisputable in the historical record. However, they did not come early, in spite of the diffusion of the steam engine and new machinery. Mokyr reminds us that "per capita consumption and living standards increased little initially [at the end of the eighteenth century] but production technologies changed dramatically in many industries and sectors, preparing the way for sustained Schumpeterian growth in the second half of the 19th century when technological progress spread to previously unaffected industries."[33] This is a critical assessment that forces us to evaluate the actual effects of major technological changes in light of a time lag highly dependent on the specific conditions of each society. The historical record seems to indicate however that, in general terms, the closer the relationship between the sites of innovation, production, and use of new technologies, the faster the transformation of societies, and the greater the positive feedback from social conditions on the general conditions for further innovation. Thus, in Spain, the Industrial Revolution diffused rapidly in Catalonia, as early as the late eighteenth century,

[31]   The specific discussion of the historical conditions for the clustering of technological innovations cannot be undertaken within the limits of this chapter. Useful reflections on the matter can be found in Mokyr (1990); and in Gille (1978). See also Mokyr (1990: 298).

[32]   Rosenberg (1976, 1982); Dosi (1988).

[33]   Mokyr (1990: 83).

but followed a much slower pace in the rest of Spain, particularly in Madrid and in the South; only the Basque Country and Asturias had joined the process of industrialization by the end of the nineteenth century.[34] The boundaries of industrial innovation were to a large extent coterminous with areas that were prohibited to trade with the Spanish American colonies for about two centuries: while Andalusian and Castilian elites, as well as the Crown, could live from their American rents, Catalans had to provide for themselves through their trade and ingenuity, while being submitted to the pressure of a centralist state. Partly as a result of this historical trajectory, Catalonia and the Basque Country were the only fully industrialized regions until the 1950s and the main seedbeds of entrepreneurialism and innovation, in sharp contrast with trends in the rest of Spain. Thus, specific social conditions foster technological innovation that itself feeds into the path of economic development and further innovation. Yet the reproduction of such conditions is cultural and institutional, as much as economic and technological. The transformation of social and institutional environments may alter the pace and geography of technological development (for example, Japan after the Meiji Restoration, or Russia for a brief period under Stolypin), although past history does bear considerable inertia.

A last and essential lesson from the Industrial Revolutions, that I consider relevant to this analysis, is controversial: although they both brought a whole array of new technologies that actually formed and transformed an industrial system in successive stages, at their core there was fundamental innovation in the generation and distribution of energy. R.J. Forbes, a classic historian of technology, affirms that "the invention of the steam engine is the central fact in the industrial revolution", followed by the introduction of new prime movers and by the mobile prime mover, under which "the power of the steam-engine could be created where needed and to the extent desired."[35] And although Mokyr insists on the multifaceted character of the Industrial Revolution, he also thinks that "the protestations of some economic historians notwithstanding, the steam engine is still widely regarded as the quintessential invention of the Industrial Revolution."[36] Electricity was the central force of the second revolution, in spite of other extraordinary developments in chemicals, steel, the internal combustion engine, telegraphy and telephony. This is because only through electrical generation and distribution were all the other fields able to develop their applications and be connected

---

[34] Fontana (1988); Nadal and Carreras (1990).
[35] Forbes (1958: 150).
[36] Mokyr (1990: 84).

to each other. A case in point is the electric telegraph which, first used experimentally in the 1790s and widely in existence since 1837, could only grow into a communication network, connecting the world on a large scale, when it could rely on the diffusion of electricity. The widespread use of electricity from the 1870s onwards changed transportation, telegraphy, lighting, and, not least, factory work by diffusing power in the form of the electrical engine. Indeed, while factories have been associated with the first Industrial Revolution, for almost a century they were not concomitant with the use of the steam engine that was widely used in craft shops, while many large factories continued to use improved water-power sources (and thus were known for a long time as mills). It was the electrical engine that both made possible and induced large-scale organization of work in the industrial factory.[37] As R.J. Forbes wrote (in 1958):

> During the last 250 years five great new prime movers have produced what is often called the Machine Age. The eighteenth century brought the steam-engine; the nineteenth century the water-turbine, the internal combustion engine and the steam-turbine; and the twentieth the gas-turbine. Historians have often coined catch-phrases to denote movements or currents in history. Such is "The Industrial Revolution," the title for a development often described as starting in the early eighteenth century and extending through much of the nineteenth. It was a slow movement, but wrought changes so profound in their combination of material progress and social dislocation that collectively they may well be described as revolutionary if we consider these extreme dates.[38]

Thus, by acting on the process at the core of all processes – that is, the necessary power to produce, distribute, and communicate – the two Industrial Revolutions diffused throughout the entire economic system and permeated the whole social fabric. Cheap, accessible, mobile energy sources extended and augmented the power of the

[37]   Hall and Preston (1988); Canby (1962); Jarvis (1958). One of the first detailed specifications for an electric telegraph is contained in a letter signed C.M. and published in *Scots Magazine* in 1753. One of the first practical experiments with an electrical system was proposed by the Catalan Francisco de Salva in 1795. There are unconfirmed reports that a single-wire telegraph, using Salva's scheme, was actually constructed between Madrid and Aranjuez (26 miles) in 1798. However, it was only in the 1830s (William Cooke in England, Samuel Morse in America) that the electric telegraph was established, and in 1851 the first submarine cable laid out between Dover and Calais (Garratt 1958); see also Mokyr (1990); Sharlin (1967).

[38]   Forbes (1958: 148).

human body, creating the material basis for the historical continuation of a similar movement towards the expansion of the human
mind.

The Historical Sequence of the Information Technology Revolution

The brief, yet intense history of the Information Technology
Revolution has been told so many times in recent years as to render
it unnecessary to provide the reader with another full account.[39]
Besides, given the acceleration of its pace, any such an account would
be instantly obsolete, so that between this writing and your reading
(let's say 18 months), microchips will have doubled in performance
at a given price, according to the generally acknowledged "Moore's
law."[40] Nevertheless, I find it analytically useful to recall the main axes
of technological transformation in information generation/
processing/transmission, and to place them in the sequence that
drifted towards the formation of a new socio-technical paradigm.[41]
This brief summary will allow me, later on, to skip references to technological features when discussing their specific interaction with
economy, culture, and society throughout the intellectual itinerary of
this book, except when new elements of information are required.

[39] A good history of the origins of the Information Technology Revolution,
naturally superseded by developments since the 1980s, is Braun and Macdonald
(1982). The most systematic effort at summarizing the developments of the
Information Technology Revolution has been conducted by Tom Forester in a
series of books (1980, 1985, 1987, 1989, 1993). For good accounts of the origins
of genetic engineering, see Russell (1988) and Elkington (1985).
[40] An accepted "law" in the electronics industry, originated by Gordon Moore,
Chairman of Intel, the legendary Silicon Valley start-up company, today the
world's largest and one of the most profitable firms in microelectronics.
[41] The information reported in this chapter is widely available in newspapers
and magazines. I extracted much of it from my reading of *Business Week, The
Economist, Wired, Scientific American,* the *New York Times, El Pais* and the *San
Francisco Chronicle,* which constitute my daily/weekly information staple. It also
comes from occasional chats on technology matters with colleagues and friends
around Berkeley and Stanford, knowledgeable about electronics and biology and
acquainted with industry sources. I do not consider it necessary to provide
detailed references to data of such general character, except when a given figure
or quote could be hard to find.

Micro-engineering macro changes: electronics and information

Although the scientific and industrial predecessors of electronics-based information technologies can be found decades before the 1940s[42] (not the least being the invention of the telephone by Bell in 1876, of the radio by Marconi in 1898, and of the vacuum tube by De Forest in 1906), it was during the Second World War, and in its aftermath, that major technological breakthroughs in electronics took place: the first programmable computer, and the transistor, source of microelectronics, the true core of the Information Technology Revolution in the twentieth century.[43] Yet I contend that only in the 1970s did new information technologies diffuse widely, accelerating their synergistic development and converging into a new paradigm. Let us retrace the stages of innovation in the three main technological fields that, although closely interrelated, constituted the history of electronics-based technologies: microelectronics, computers, and telecommunications.

The transistor, invented in 1947 at Bell Laboratories in Murray Hill, New Jersey, by three physicists, Bardeen, Brattain, and Shockley (recipients of the Nobel Prize for this discovery), made possible the processing of electric impulses at a fast pace in a binary mode of interruption and amplification, thus enabling the coding of logic and of communication with and between machines: we call these processing devices semiconductors, and people commonly call them chips (actually now made of millions of transistors). The first step in the transistor's diffusion was taken with the invention by Shockley of the junction transistor in 1951. Yet its fabrication and widespread use required new manufacturing technologies and the use of an appropriate material. The shift to silicon, literally building the new revolution on sand, was first accomplished by Texas Instruments (in Dallas) in 1954 (a move facilitated by the hiring in 1953 of Gordon Teal, another leading scientist from Bell Labs). The invention of the planar process in 1959 by Fairchild Semiconductors (in Silicon Valley) opened up the possibility of the integration of miniaturized components with precision manufacturing.

[42] See Hall and Preston (1988); Mazlish(1993).
[43] I think that, as with the Industrial Revolutions, there will be several Information Technology Revolutions, of which the one constituted in the 1970s is only the first. Probably the second, in the early twenty-first century, will give a more important role to the biological revolution, in close interaction with new computer technologies.

Yet the decisive step in microelectronics had taken place in 1957: the integrated circuit was co-invented by Jack Kilby, a Texas Instrument engineer (who patented it), and Bob Noyce, one of the founders of Fairchild. But it was Noyce who first manufactured ICs by using the planar process. It triggered a technological explosion: in only three years, between 1959 and 1962, prices of semiconductors fell by 85%, and in the next ten years production increased by 20 times, 50% of which went to military uses.[44] As a point of historical comparison, it took 70 years (1780–1850) for the price of cotton cloth to drop by 85% in Britain during the Industrial Revolution.[45] Then, the movement accelerated during the 1960s: as manufacturing technology improved and better chip design was helped by computers using faster and more powerful microelectronic devices, the average price of an integrated circuit fell from $50 in 1962 to $1 in 1971.

The giant leap forward in the diffusion of microelectronics in all machines came in 1971 with the invention by an Intel engineer, Ted Hoff (also in Silicon Valley), of the microprocessor, that is the computer on a chip. Thus, information processing power could be installed everywhere. The race was on for ever-greater integration capacity of circuits on a single chip, the technology of design and manufacturing constantly exceeding the limits of integration previously thought to be physically impossible without abandoning the use of silicon material. In the mid-1990s, technical evaluations still give 10 to 20 years of good life for silicon-based circuits, although research in alternative materials has been stepped up. The level of integration has progressed by leaps and bounds in the last two decades. While technical details have no place in this book, it is analytically relevant to indicate the speed and extent of technological change.

As is known, the power of chips can be evaluated by a combination of three characteristics: their integration capacity, indicated by the smallest line width in the chip measured in microns (1 micron = 1 millionth of an inch); their memory capacity, measured in bits: thousands (k), and millions (megabits); and the speed of the microprocessor measured in megahertz. Thus, the first 1971 processor was laid in lines of about 6.5 microns; in 1980, it reached 4 microns; in 1987, 1 micron; in 1995, Intel's Pentium chip featured a size in the 0.35 micron range; and at the time of writing projections were for reaching 0.25 micron in 1999. Thus, where in 1971 2,300 transistors were packed on a chip the size of a thumbtack, in 1993 there were 35 million transistors. Memory capacity, as indicated by DRAM (dynamic random access memory) capacity was in 1971, 1,024

[44] Braun and Macdonald (1982).
[45] Mokyr (1990: 111).

bits; in 1980, 64,000; in 1987, 1,024,000; in 1993, 16,384,000; and projected in 1999, 256,000,000. As for the speed, current 64-bit microprocessors are 550 times faster than the first Intel chip in 1972; and MPUs are doubling every 18 months. Projections to 2002 forecast an acceleration of microelectronics technology in integration (0.18 micron chips), in DRAM capacity (1,024 megabits), and microprocessor speed (500+ megahertz as compared to 150 in 1993). Combined with dramatic developments in parallel processing using multiple microprocessors (including, in the future, linking multiple microprocessors on a single chip), it appears that the power of microelectronics is still being unleashed, thus relentlessly increasing computing capacity. Furthermore, greater miniaturization, further specialization, and the decreasing price of increasingly powerful chips made it possible to place them in every machine in our everyday life, from dishwashers and microwave ovens to automobiles, whose electronics, in the 1990s standard models, was more valuable than their steel.

Computers were also conceived from the mother of all technologies that was the Second World War, but they were only born in 1946 in Philadelphia, if we except the war-related tools of the 1943 British Colossus applied to deciphering enemy codes, and the German Z-3 reportedly produced in 1941 to help aircraft calculations.[46] Yet most Allied effort in electronics was concentrated in research programs at MIT, and the actual experimentation of the calculators' power, under US Army sponsorship, took place at the University of Pennsylvania, where Mauchly and Eckert produced in 1946 the first general purpose computer, the ENIAC (Electronic Numerical Integrator and Calculator). Historians will recall that the first electronic computer weighed 30 tons, was built on metal modules nine feet tall, had 70,000 resistors and 18,000 vacuum tubes, and occupied the area of a gymnasium. When it was turned on, its electricity consumption was so high that Philadelphia's lighting twinkled.[47]

Yet the first commercial version of this primitive machine, UNIVAC–1, produced in 1951 by the same team, then under the Remington Rand brand name, was extremely successful in processing the 1950 US Census. IBM, also supported by military contracts and relying partly on MIT research, overcame its early reservations about the computer age, and entered the race in 1953 with its 701 vacuum tube machine. In 1958, when Sperry Rand introduced a second-generation computer mainframe machine, IBM immediately

---

[46]   Hall and Preston (1988).
[47]   See the description by Forester (1987).

followed up with its 7090 model. But it was only in 1964 that IBM, with its 360/370 mainframe computer, came to dominate the computer industry, populated by new (Control Data, Digital), and old (Sperry, Honeywell, Burroughs, NCR) business machines companies. Most of these firms were ailing or had vanished by the 1990s: this is how fast Schumpeterian "creative destruction" has proceeded in the electronics industry. In that ancient age, that is 30 years ago from the time of writing, the industry organized itself in a well-defined hierarchy of mainframes, minicomputers (in fact, rather bulky machines), and terminals, with some specialty informatics left to the esoteric world of supercomputers (a cross-fertilization of weather forecasting and war games), in which the extraordinary ingenuity of Seymour Cray, in spite of his lack of technological vision, reigned for some time.

Microelectronics changed all this, inducing a "revolution within the revolution." The advent of the microprocessor in 1971, with the capacity to put a computer on a chip, turned the electronics world, and indeed the world itself, upside down. In 1975, Ed Roberts, an engineer who had created a small calculator company, MITS, in Albuquerque, New Mexico, built a computing box with the improbable name of Altair, after a character in the *Star Trek* TV series, that was the object of admiration of the inventor's young daughter. The machine was a primitive object, but it was built as a small-scale computer around a microprocessor. It was the basis for the design of Apple I, then of Apple II, the first commercially successful microcomputer, realized in the garage of their parents' home by two young school drop-outs, Steve Wozniak and Steve Jobs, in Menlo Park, Silicon Valley, in a truly extraordinary saga that has by now become the founding legend of the Information Age. Launched in 1976, with three partners and $91,000 capital, Apple Computers had by 1982 reached $583 million in sales, ushering in the age of diffusion of computer power. IBM reacted quickly: in 1981 it introduced its own version of the microcomputer, with a brilliant name: the Personal Computer (PC), that became in fact the generic name for microcomputers. But because it was not based on IBM's proprietary technology, but on technology developed for IBM by other sources, it became vulnerable to cloning, which was soon practiced on a massive scale, particularly in Asia. Yet while this fact eventually doomed IBM's business dominance in PCs, it also spread the use of IBM clones throughout the world, diffusing a common standard, in spite of the superiority of Apple machines. Apple's Macintosh, launched in 1984, was the first step towards user-friendly computing, with the introduction of icon-based, user interface technology, originally developed by Xerox's Palo Alto Research Center.

A fundamental condition for the diffusion of microcomputers was fulfilled with the development of new software adapted to their operation.[48] PC software also emerged in the mid-1970s out of the enthusiasm generated by Altair: two young Harvard drop-outs, Bill Gates and Paul Allen, adapted BASIC for operating the Altair machine in 1976. Having realized its potential, they went on to found Microsoft (first in Albuquerque, two years later moving to Seattle, home of Bill Gates' parents), today's software giant, that parlayed dominance in operating system software into dominance in software for the exponentially growing microcomputer market as a whole.

In the last 15 years, increasing chip power has resulted in a dramatic enhancement of microcomputing power, thus shrinking the function of larger computers. By the early 1990s, single-chip microcomputers had the processing power of IBM only five years earlier. Networked microprocessor-based systems, composed of smaller desktop machines (clients), served by more powerful, more dedicated machines (servers), may eventually supplant more specialized information-processing computers, such as traditional mainframes and supercomputers. Indeed, to advances in microelectronics and software we have to add major leaps forward in networking capabilities. Since the mid-1980s, microcomputers cannot be conceived of in isolation: they perform in networks, with increasing mobility, on the basis of portable computers. This extraordinary versatility, and the capacity to add memory and processing capacity by sharing computing power in an electronic network, decisively shifted the computer age in the 1990s from centralized data storage and processing to networked, interactive computer power-sharing. Not only the whole technological system changed, but its social and organizational interactions as well. Thus, the average cost of processing information fell from around $75 per million operations in 1960 to less than one-hundredth of a cent in 1990.

This networking capability only became possible, naturally, because of major developments both in telecommunication and computer networking technologies during the 1970s. But, at the same time, such changes were only made possible by new microelectronic devices and stepped-up computing capacity, in a striking illustration of the synergistic relationships in the Information Technology Revolution.

Telecommunications have been revolutionized also by the combination of "node" technologies (electronic switches and routers) and new linkages (transmission technologies). The first industrially produced electronic switch, the ESS-1, was introduced by Bell Labs in 1969. By the mid-1970s, progress in integrated circuit technologies had made possible the digital switch, increasing speed, power, and

[48]   Egan (1995).

flexibility, while saving space, energy, and labor, *vis-à-vis* analog devices. Although ATT, parent of the discoverer Bell Labs, was initially reluctant about its introduction, because of the need to amortize the investment already made in analog equipment, when in 1977 Canada's Northern Telecom captured a share of the US market through its lead in digital switching, the Bell companies joined the race and triggered a similar movement around the world.

Major advances in optoelectronics (fiber optics and laser transmission) and digital packet transmission technology dramatically broadened the capacity of transmission lines. The Integrated Broadband Networks (IBN) envisioned in the 1990s could surpass substantially the revolutionary 1970s proposals for an Integrated Services Digital Network (ISDN): while the carrying capacity of ISDN on copper wire was estimated at 144,000 bits, the 1990s IBN on optic fibers, if and when they can be realized, though at a high price, could carry a quadrillion bits. To measure the pace of change, let us recall that in 1956 the first transatlantic cable phone carried 50 compressed voice circuits; in 1995, optical fibers could carry 85,000 such circuits. This optoelectronics-based transmission capacity, together with advanced switching and routing architectures, such as the Asynchronous Transmission Mode (ATM) and Transmission Control Protocol/Interconnection Protocol (TCP/IP), are the basis of the so-called 1990s Information Superhighway, whose characteristics are discussed in chapter 5.

Different forms of utilization of the radio spectrum (traditional broadcasting, direct satellite broadcasting, microwaves, digital cellular telephony), as well as coaxial cable and fiber optics, offer a diversity and versatility of transmission technologies, that are being adapted to a whole range of uses, and make possible ubiquitous communication between mobile users. Thus, cellular telephony diffused with force all over the world in the 1990s, literally dotting Asia with unsophisticated pagers and Latin America with status-symbol cellular phones, relying on the promise (from Motorola for example) of an upcoming universal-coverage, personal communication device before 2000. Each leap and bound in a specific technological field amplifies the effects of related information technologies. Thus, mobile telephony, relying on computing power to route the messages, provides at the same time the basis for ubiquitous computing and for real-time, untethered, interactive electronic communication.

The 1970s technological divide

This technological system in which we are fully immersed in the 1990s came together in the 1970s. Because of the significance of specific historical contexts for technological trajectories, and for the particular form of interaction between technology and society, it is important to recall a few dates associated with essential discoveries in information technologies. All of them have something essential in common: while mainly based on previously existing knowledge, and developed in prolongation of key technologies, they represented a qualitative leap forward in the massive diffusion of technology in commercial and civilian applications because of their accessibility and their decreasing cost with increasing quality. Thus, the microprocessor, the key device in spreading microelectronics, was invented in 1971 and began to diffuse by the mid-1970s. The microcomputer was invented in 1975 and the first successful commercial product, Apple II, was introduced in April 1977, around the same date that Microsoft started to produce operating systems for microcomputers. The Xerox Alto, the matrix of many software technologies for 1990s personal computers, was developed at PARC labs in Palo Alto in 1973. The first industrial electronic switch appeared in 1969, and digital switching was developed in the mid-1970s and commercially diffused in 1977. Optic fiber was first industrially produced by Corning Glass in the early 1970s. Also by the mid-1970s, Sony started to produce VCR machines commercially, on the basis of 1960s discoveries in America and England that never reached mass production. And last, but not least, it was in 1969 that the US Defense Department's Advanced Research Projects Agency (ARPA) set up a new, revolutionary electronic communication network, that would grow during the 1970s to become the current Internet. It was greatly helped by the invention by Cerf and Kahn in 1974 of TCP/IP, the interconnection network protocol that ushered in "gateway" technology, allowing different types of networks to be connected.[49] I think we can say, without exaggeration, that the Information Technology Revolution, as a revolution, was born in the 1970s, particularly if we include in it the parallel emergence and diffusion of genetic engineering around the same dates and places, a development that deserves, to say the least, a few lines of attention.

Technologies of life

Although biotechnology can be traced all the way back to a 6000BC Babylonian tablet on brewing, and the revolution in microbiology to the scientific discovery of the basic structure of life, DNA's double helix, by Francis Crick and James Watson at Cambridge University in

[49]   Hart et al. (1992).

1953, it was only in the early 1970s that gene splicing and recombinant DNA, the technological foundation of genetic engineering, made possible the application of cumulative knowledge. Stanford's Stanley Cohen and University of California at San Francisco's Herbert Boyer are generally credited with the discovery of gene cloning procedures in 1973, although their work was based on research by Stanford's Nobel Prize winner Paul Berg. In 1975 researchers at Harvard isolated the first mammalian gene, out of rabbit hemoglobin; and in 1977 the first human gene was cloned.

What followed was a rush to start up commercial firms, most of them spin-offs from major universities and hospital research centers, clusters of such firms emerging in Northern California, New England, and Maryland. Journalists, investors, and social activists alike were struck by the awesome possibilities opened up by the potential ability to engineer life, including human life. Genentech in South San Francisco, Cetus in Berkeley, and Biogen in Cambridge, Massachusetts, were among the first companies, organized around Nobel Prize winners, to use new genetic technologies for medical applications. Agro-business followed soon; and micro-organisms, some of them genetically altered, were given an increasing number of assignments, not least to clean up pollution, often generated by the same companies and agencies that were selling the superbugs. Yet scientific difficulties, technical problems, and major legal obstacles derived from justified ethical and safety concerns slowed down the much-vaunted biotechnological revolution during the 1980s. A considerable amount of venture capital investment was lost and some of the most innovative companies, including Genentech, were absorbed by pharmaceutical giants (Hoffman-La Roche, Merck) who, better than anybody else, understood that they could not replicate the costly arrogance that established computer firms had displayed towards innovative start-ups: to buy small, innovative firms, along with their scientists' services, became a major insurance policy for pharmaceutical and chemical multinationals, to both internalize the commercial benefits of the biological revolution and to control its pace. A slowing down of this pace followed, at least in the diffusion of its applications.

However, in the late 1980s and in the 1990s a major science push, and a new generation of daring scientist entrepreneurs, revitalized biotechnology, with a decisive focus on genetic engineering, the truly revolutionary technology in the field. Genetic cloning entered a new stage when, in 1988, Harvard formally patented a genetically engineered mouse, thus taking the copyright of life away from God and Nature. In the next seven years, an additional seven mice were also patented as newly created forms of life, identified as the property of their engineers. In August 1989 researchers from the University of Michigan and Toronto discovered the gene responsible for cystic fibrosis, opening the way for genetic therapy.

In the wake of expectations generated by this discovery, the US Government decided in 1990 to sponsor and fund a $3 billion, 15-year collaborative program, coordinated by James Watson, bringing together some of the most advanced microbiology research teams to map the human genome, that is to identify and locate the 60,000 to 80,000 genes that compose the alphabet of the human species.[50] Through this and other efforts, a continuous stream of human genes related to various diseases are being identified, so that by the mid-1990s about 7% of human genes have been located, with a proper understanding of their function. This of course creates the possibility of acting on such genes, and on those identified in the future, making humankind able not only to control some diseases, but to identify biological predispositions and to intervene in such predispositions, potentially altering genetic fate. Lyon and Gorner conclude their balanced survey of developments in human genetic engineering, with a prediction and an admonition:

> We could in a few generations do away with certain mental illnesses, perhaps, or diabetes, or high blood pressure, or almost any affliction we selected. The important thing to keep in mind is that the quality of decision making dictates whether the choices to be made are going to be wise and just . . . The rather inglorious way that the scientific and administrative elite are handling the earliest fruits of gene therapy is ominous . . . We humans have evolved intellectually to the point that, relatively soon, we will be able to understand the composition, function, and dynamics of the genome in much of its intimidating complexity. Emotionally however, we are still apes, with all the behavioral baggage that the issue brings. Perhaps the ultimate form of gene therapy would be for our species to rise above its baser heritage and learn to apply its new knowledge wisely and benignly.[51]

Yet, while scientists, regulators, and ethicists debate the humanistic implications of genetic engineering, researchers-turned-business-entrepreneurs are taking the short path, setting up mechanisms for

---

[50] On the development of biotechnology and genetic engineering, see, for instance, Teitelman (1989); Hall (1987); US Congress, Office of Technology Assessment (1991); Bishop and Waldholz (1990).
[51] Lyon and Gorner (1995: 567).

legal and financial control of the human genome. The most daring attempt in this sense was the project initiated in 1990 in Rockville, Maryland, by two scientists, J. Craig Venter, then with the National Institute of Health, and William Haseltine, then at Harvard. Using supercomputer power, they sequenced in only five years parts of about 85% of all human genes, creating a gigantic genetic data base.[52] The problem is that they do not know, and will not know for a long time, which gene's piece is what or where it is located: their data base comprises hundreds of thousands of gene fragments with unknown functions. What is then the interest? On the one hand, focused research on specific genes may (and does in fact) use to its advantage the data contained in such sequences. But, more importantly and the main reason for the whole project, Craig and Haseltine have been busy patenting all their data, so that, literally, they may own one day the legal rights to a large portion of the knowledge to manipulate the human genome. The threat posed by such a development was serious enough that, while on the one hand they have attracted tens of millions of dollars from investors, on the other hand, a major pharmaceutical company, Merck, gave in 1994 substantial funding to Washington University to proceed with the same blind sequencing and to make the data public, so that there would be no private control of bits and pieces of knowledge which could block development of products based on a future, systematic understanding of the human genome.

The lesson for the sociologist of such business battles is not just another instance of human greed. It signals an accelerating tempo in the spread and deepening of the genetic revolution. Because of its specificity, both scientific and social, the diffusion of genetic engineering proceeded at a slower pace of development in the 1970s–1990s period than the one we observed in electronics. But in the 1990s, more open markets and greater education and research capabilities throughout the world have accelerated the biotechnological revolution. All indications point towards the explosion of its applications at the turn of the millennium, thus triggering a most fundamental debate at the now blurred frontier between nature and society.

Social context and the dynamics of technological change

Why were discoveries of new information technologies clustered in the 1970s, and mostly in the United States? And what are the conse-

---

[52] See *Business Week* (1995e).

quences of such timed/placed clustering for their future development and for their interaction with societies? It would be tempting to relate directly the formation of this technological paradigm to the characteristics of its social context; particularly if we remember that in the mid-1970s the United States and the capitalist world were shaken by a major economic crisis, epitomized (but not caused) by the oil shock of 1973–4: a crisis that prompted the dramatic restructuring of the capitalist system on a global scale, actually inducing a new model of accumulation in historical discontinuity with post-Second World War capitalism, as I proposed in the Prologue of this book. Was the new technological paradigm a response by the capitalist system to overcome its internal contradictions? Or, alternatively, was it a way to ensure military superiority over the Soviet foe, responding to its technological challenge in the space race and nuclear weaponry? Neither explanation seems to be convincing. While there is a historical coincidence between the clustering of new technologies and the economic crisis of the 1970s, their timing was too close, the "technological fix" would have been too quick, and too mechanical, when we know from the lessons of the Industrial Revolution and other historical processes of technological change that economic, industrial, and technological paths, while related, are slow-moving and imperfectly fitting in their interaction. As for the military argument, the Sputnik shock of 1957–60 was answered in kind by the massive technological build up of the 1960s, not the 1970s; and the new major American military technology push was launched in 1983 around the "Star Wars" program, actually using and furthering technologies developed in the preceding, prodigious decade. In fact, it seems that the emergence of a new technological system in the 1970s must be traced to the autonomous dynamics of technological discovery and diffusion, including synergistic effects between various key technologies. Thus, the microprocessor made possible the microcomputer; advances in telecommunications, as mentioned above, enabled microcomputers to function in networks, thus increasing their power and flexibility. Applications of these technologies to electronics manufacturing enhanced the potential for new design and fabrication technologies in semiconductor production. New software was stimulated by the fast-growing microcomputer market that, in turn, exploded on the basis of new applications and user-friendly technologies churned out from software writers' minds. And so on.

The strong, military-induced technological push of the 1960s prepared American technology for the leap forward. But Ted Hoff's invention of the microprocessor while trying to fulfill an order for a Japanese hand calculator company in 1971 came out of knowledge and ingenuity accumulated at Intel, in close interaction with the milieu of innovation created since the 1950s in Silicon Valley. In other words, the first Information Technology Revolution clustered in America, and to some extent in California, in the 1970s, building on developments of the two preceding decades, and under the influence of various institutional, economic, and cultural factors. But it did not come out of any preestablished necessity: it was technologically induced rather than socially determined. However, once it came into existence as a system, on the basis of the clustering I have described, its development and applications, and ultimately its content, were decisively shaped by the historical context where it expanded. Indeed, by the 1980s capitalism (specifically: major corporations and governments of the club of G-7 countries) did undertake a substantial process of economic and organizational restructuring, in which new information technology played a fundamental role and was decisively shaped by the role it played. For instance, the business-led movement towards deregulation and liberalization in the 1980s was decisive in the reorganization and growth of telecommunications, most notably after the 1984 divestiture of ATT. In turn, the availability of new telecommunication networks and information systems prepared the ground for the global integration of financial markets and the segmented articulation of production and trade throughout the world, as I shall examine in the next chapter.

Thus, to some extent, the availability of new technologies constituted as a system in the 1970s was a fundamental basis for the process of socio-economic restructuring in the 1980s. And the uses of such technologies in the 1980s largely conditioned their uses and trajectories in the 1990s. The rise of the network society, which I shall attempt to analyze in the following chapters of this volume, cannot be understood without the interaction between these two relatively autonomous trends: development of new information technologies, and the old society's attempt to retool itself by using the power of technology to serve the technology of power. However, the historical outcome of such a half-conscious strategy is largely undetermined, since the interaction of technology and society depends on stochastic relationships between an excessive number of quasi-independent variables. Without necessarily surrendering to historical relativism, it can be said that the Information Technology Revolution was culturally, historically, and spatially contingent on a very specific set of circumstances whose characteristics earmarked its future evolution.

Models, Actors, and Sites of the Information Technology Revolution

If the first Industrial Revolution was British, the first Information Technology Revolution was American, with a Californian inclination. In both cases scientists and industrialists from other countries did play an important role, both in the discovery and in the diffusion of new technologies. France and Germany were key sources of talent and applications in the Industrial Revolution. Scientific discoveries originated in England, France, Germany, and Italy were at the roots of new technologies in electronics and biology. The ingenuity of Japanese companies has been critical in the improvement of manufacturing processes in electronics and in the penetration of information technologies into everyday life around the world through a flurry of innovative products, from VCRs and faxes to video games and pagers.[53] Indeed, in the 1980s Japanese companies came to dominate semiconductor production in the world market, although by the mid-1990s American companies by and large had retaken the competitive lead. The whole industry evolved towards interpenetration, strategic alliances, and networking between firms of different countries, as I shall analyze in chapter 3. This made differentiation by national origin somewhat less relevant. Yet not only were US innovators, firms, and institutions at the origins of the revolution in the 1970s, but they have continued to play a leading role in its expansion, which is likely to be sustained into the twenty-first century; although we shall undoubtedly witness an increasing presence of Japanese, Chinese, Korean, and Indian firms, as well as significant European contributions in biotechnology and telecommunications.

To understand the social roots of the Information Technology Revolution in America, beyond the myths surrounding it, I shall recall briefly the process of formation of its most notorious seedbed of innovation: Silicon Valley. As I already mentioned, it was in Silicon Valley that the integrated circuit, the microprocessor, the microcomputer, among other key technologies, were developed, and that the heart of electronics innovation has beat for four decades, sustained by about a quarter of a million information technology workers.[54] Besides, the San Francisco Bay Area at large (including other centers of innovation such as Berkeley, Emeryville, Marin County, and San Francisco itself) was also at the origins of genetic engineering and is, in the

[53]   Forester (1993).
[54]   On the history of formation of Silicon Valley, two useful, easy-reading books are Rogers and Larsen (1984) and Malone (1985).

1990s, one of the world's leading centers of advanced software, genetic engineering, and multimedia computing design.

Silicon Valley (Santa Clara County, 30 miles south of San Francisco, between Stanford and San Jose) was formed as a milieu of innovation by the convergence on one site of new technological knowledge; a large pool of skilled engineers and scientists from major universities in the area; generous funding from an assured market with the Defense Department; and, in the early stages, the institutional leadership of Stanford University. Indeed, the unlikely location of the electronics industry in a charming, semi-rural area of Northern California can be traced back to the establishment in 1951 of Stanford Industrial Park by Stanford University's visionary Dean of Engineering and Provost, Frederick Terman. He had personally supported two of his graduate students, William Hewlett and David Packard, in creating an electronics company in 1938. The Second World War was a bonanza for Hewlett-Packard and other start-up electronics companies. Thus, naturally, they were the first tenants of a new, privileged location where only firms that Stanford judged innovative could benefit from a notional rent. As the Park was soon filled, new electronics firms started to locate down freeway 101 towards San Jose.

The decisive move was the hiring by Stanford in 1956 of William Shockley, the inventor of the transistor. And this was a fortuitous development, although it reflects on the historical inability of established electronics firms to seize revolutionary microelectronics technology. Shockley had solicited the support of large companies on the East Coast, such as RCA and Raytheon, to develop his discovery into industrial production. When he was turned down he accepted Stanford's offer, mainly because his mother lived in Palo Alto, and he decided to create there his own company, Shockley Transistors, with the backing of Beckman Instruments. He recruited eight brilliant young engineers, mainly from Bell Labs, attracted by the possibility of working with Shockley; one of them, although not precisely from Bell Labs, was Bob Noyce. They were soon disappointed. While learning the fundamentals of cutting-edge microelectronics from Shockley, they were turned off by his authoritarianism and stubbornness that led the firm into dead-ends. Particularly they wanted, against his decision, to work on silicon as the most promising route to the larger integration of transistors. Thus, after only one year they left Shockley (whose firm collapsed), and created (with the help of Fairchild Cameras) Fairchild Semiconductors, where the invention of the planar process and of the integrated circuit took place in the next two years. As soon as they discovered the technological and business potential of their knowledge, each one of these brilliant engineers left

Fairchild to start his own firm. And their new recruits did the same after some time, so that one-half of the 85 largest American semiconductors firms, including today's leading producers such as Intel, Advanced Micro Devices, National Semiconductors, Signetics, and so on, can be traced back to this spin-off from Fairchild.

It was this technology transfer from Shockley to Fairchild, then to a network of spin-off companies, that constituted the initial source of innovation on which Silicon Valley, and the microelectronics revolution, were built. Indeed, by the mid-1950s Stanford and Berkeley were not yet leading centers in electronics: MIT was, and this was reflected in the original location of the electronics industry in New England. However, as soon as knowledge was available in Silicon Valley, the dynamism of its industrial structure and the continuous creation of start-up firms anchored Silicon Valley as the world's microelectronics center by the early 1970s. Anna Saxenian compared the development of electronics complexes in the two areas (Boston's Route 128 and Silicon Valley) and concluded that the decisive role was played by the social and industrial organization of companies in fostering or stymying innovation.[55] Thus, while large, established companies in the East were too rigid (and too arrogant) to constantly retool themselves towards new technological frontiers, Silicon Valley kept churning out new firms, and practicing cross-fertilization and knowledge diffusion by job-hopping and spin-offs. Late-evening conversations at the Walker's Wagon Wheel Bar and Grill in Mountain View did more for the diffusion of technological innovation than most seminars in Stanford.

A similar process took place in the development of the microcomputer, which introduced a historical divide in the uses of information technology.[56] By the mid-1970s Silicon Valley had attracted tens of thousands of bright young minds from around the world, coming to the excitement of the new technological Mecca in a search for the talisman of invention and money. They gathered in loose clubs, to exchange ideas and information on the latest developments. One of such gatherings was the Home Brew Computer Club, whose young visionaries (including Bill Gates, Steve Jobs, and Steve Wozniak) would go on to create in the following years up to 22 companies, including Microsoft, Apple, Comenco, and North Star. It was the club's reading, in *Popular Electronics*, of an article reporting Ed Roberts' Altair machine which inspired Wozniak to design a microcomputer, Apple I, in his Menlo Park garage in the summer of 1976. Steve Jobs saw the potential, and together they founded Apple, with

[55] Saxenian (1994).
[56] Levy (1984); Egan (1995).

a $91,000 loan from an Intel executive, Mike Markkula, who came in as a partner. At about the same time Bill Gates founded Microsoft to provide the operating system for microcomputers, although he located his company in 1978 in Seattle to take advantage of the social contacts of his family.

A rather similar story could be told about the development of genetic engineering, with leading scientists at Stanford, UC San Francisco and Berkeley bridging into companies, first located in the Bay Area. They would also go through frequent processes of spin-off while keeping close ties with their alma maters.[57] Very similar processes took place in Boston/Cambridge around Harvard–MIT, in the Research Triangle around Duke University and the University of North Carolina, and, more importantly, in Maryland around major hospitals, national health research institutes, and Johns Hopkins University.

The fundamental learning from these colorful stories is two-fold: the development of the information technology revolution contributed to the formation of the milieux of innovation where discoveries and applications would interact, and be tested, in a recurrent process of trial and error, of learning by doing; these milieus required (and still do in the 1990s, in spite of on-line networking) spatial concentration of research centers, higher education institutions, advanced technology companies, a network of ancillary suppliers of goods and services, and business networks of venture capital to finance start-ups. Once a milieu is consolidated, as Silicon Valley was in the 1970s, it tends to generate its own dynamics, and to attract knowledge, investment and talent from around the world. Indeed, in the 1990s Silicon Valley is witnessing a proliferation of Japanese, Taiwanese, Korean, Indian, and European companies for whom an active presence in the Valley is the most productive linkage to the sources of new technology and valuable business information. Furthermore, because of its positioning in the networks of technological innovation, the San Francisco Bay Area has been able to jump on any new development. For instance, the coming of multimedia in the mid-1990s created a network of technological and business linkages between computer design capabilities from Silicon Valley companies and image-producing studios in Hollywood, immediately labeled the "Siliwood" industry. And in a run-down corner of San Francisco, artists, graphic designers, and software writers came together in the so-called "Multimedia Gulch" that threatens to flood our living rooms with images coming from their fevered minds.

[57] Blakely et al. (1988); Hall et al. (1988).

Can this social, cultural, and spatial pattern of innovation be extrapolated throughout the world? To answer this question, in 1988 my colleague Peter Hall and I undertook a several years' tour of the world that brought us to visit and analyze some of the main scientific/technological centers of this planet, from California to Japan, New England to Old England, Paris-Sud to Hsinchu-Taiwan, Sophia-Antipolis to Akademgorodok, Szelenograd to Daeduck, Munich to Seoul. Our conclusions[58] confirm the critical role played by milieus of innovation in the development of the Information Technology Revolution: clusters of scientific/technical knowledge, institutions, firms, and skilled labor are the furnaces of innovation in the Information Age. Yet they do not need to reproduce the cultural, spatial, institutional and industrial pattern of Silicon Valley, or for that matter, of other American centers of technological innovation, such as Southern California, Boston, Seattle, or Austin.

Our most striking discovery is that the largest, old metropolitan areas of the industrialized world are the main centers of innovation and production in information technology outside the United States. In Europe, Paris-Sud constitutes the largest concentration of high-technology production and research; and London's M4 corridor is still Britain's preeminent electronics site, in historical continuity with ordnance factories working for the Crown since the nineteenth century. The displacement of Berlin by Munich was obviously related to the German defeat in the Second World War, with Siemens deliberately moving from Berlin to Bavaria in anticipation of American occupation of that area. Tokyo-Yokohama continues to be the technological core of the Japanese information technology industry, in spite of the decentralization of branch plants operated under the Technopolis Program. Moscow-Szelenograd and St Petersburg were and are the centers of Soviet and Russian technological knowledge and production, after the failure of Khrushchev's Siberian dream. Hsinchu is in fact a satellite of Taipei; Daeduck never played a significant role vis-à-vis Seoul-Inchon, in spite of being in the home province of dictator Park; and Beijing and Shanghai are, and will be, the core of Chinese technological development. And so are Mexico City in Mexico, Sao Paulo-Campinas in Brazil, and Buenos Aires in Argentina. In this sense, the technological fading of old American metropolises (New York-New Jersey, in spite of its prominent role up to the 1960s; Chicago; Detroit; Philadelphia) is the exception at the international level, linked to American exceptionalism of frontier spirit, and to its endless escapism from the contradictions of built

[58] Castells and Hall (1994).

cities and constituted societies. On the other hand, it would be intriguing to explore the relationship between this American exceptionalism and the indisputable American preeminence in a technological revolution characterized by the need to break mental molds to spur creativity.

Yet the metropolitan character of most sites of the Information Technology Revolution around the world seems to indicate that the critical ingredient in its development is not the newness of the institutional and cultural setting, but its ability to generate synergy on the basis of knowledge and information, directly related to industrial production and commercial applications. The cultural and business strength of the metropolis (old or new – after all, the San Francisco Bay Area is a metropolis of about 6 million people) makes it the privileged environment of this new technological revolution, actually demystifying the notion of placelessness of innovation in the information age.

Similarly, the entrepreneurial model of the Information Technology Revolution seems to be overshadowed by ideology. Not only are the Japanese, European, and Chinese models of technological innovation quite different from the American experience, but even this leading experience is often misunderstood. The role of the state is generally acknowledged as decisive in Japan, where large corporations were guided and supported by MITI for a long time, well into the 1980s, through a series of bold technological programs, some of which failed (for example, the Fifth Generation Computer), but most of which helped to transform Japan into a technological superpower in just about 20 years, as Michael Borrus has documented.[59] No start-up innovative firms and little role for universities can be found in the Japanese experience. Strategic planning by MITI and the constant interface between the *keiretsu* and government are key elements in explaining the Japanese prowess that overwhelmed Europe and overtook the US in several segments of information technology industries. A similar story can be told about South Korea and Taiwan, although in the latter case multinationals played a greater role. India's and China's strong technological bases are directly related to their military–industrial complex, under state funding and guidance.

But so was also the case for much of the British and French electronics industries, centered on telecommunications and defense, until the 1980s.[60] In the last quarter of the twentieth century, the

[59]   Borrus (1988).
[60]   Hall et al. (1987).

European Union has proceeded with a series of technological programs to keep up with international competition, systematically supporting "national champions", even at a loss, without much result. Indeed, the only way for European information technology companies to survive technologically has been to use their considerable resources (a substantial share of which comes from government funds) to make alliances with Japanese and American companies, which are increasingly their main source of know-how in advanced information technology.[61]

Even in the US it is a well-known fact that military contracts and Defense Department technological initiatives played decisive roles in the formative stage of the Information Technology Revolution, that is, between the 1940s and the 1960s. Even the major source of electronics discovery, Bell Laboratories, in fact played the role of a national laboratory: its parent company (ATT) enjoyed a government-enforced monopoly of telecommunications; a significant part of its research funds came from the US Government; and ATT was in fact forced by the Government from 1956, in return for its monopoly on public telecommunications, to diffuse technological discoveries in the public domain.[62] MIT, Harvard, Stanford, Berkeley, UCLA, Chicago, Johns Hopkins, and national weapons laboratories such as Livermore, Los Alamos, Sandia, and Lincoln, worked with and for Defense Department agencies on programs that led to fundamental breakthroughs, from the 1940s computers to optoelectronics and artificial intelligence technologies of the 1980s "Star Wars" programs. DARPA, the extraordinarily innovative Defense Department Research Agency, played in the US a role not too different from that of MITI in Japan's technological development, including the design and initial funding of the Internet.[63] Indeed, in the 1980s, when the ultra-*laissez-faire* Reagan Administration felt the pinch of Japanese competition, the Defense Department funded SEMATECH, a consortium of American electronics companies to support costly R&D programs in electronics manufacturing, for reasons of national security. And the federal government also helped the cooperative effort by major firms to cooperate in microelectronics by creating MCC, with both SEMATECH and MCC locating in Austin, Texas.[64] Also, during the decisive 1950s and 1960s, military contracts and the space program were essential markets for the electronics industry, both for the giant defense contractors of Southern California and for the

[61]   Freeman et al. (1991); Castells et al. (1991).
[62]   Bar (1990).
[63]   Tirman (1984); Broad (1985); Stowsky (1992).
[64]   Borrus (1988); Gibson and Rogers (1994).

start-up innovators of Silicon Valley and New England.[65] They could not have survived without the generous funding and protected markets of a US Government anxious to recover technological superiority over the Soviet Union, a strategy that eventually paid off. Genetic engineering spun off from major research universities, hospitals, and health research institutes, largely funded and sponsored by government money.[66] Thus, the state, not the innovative entrepreneur in his garage, both in America and throughout the world, was the initiator of the Information Technology Revolution.[67]

However, without these innovative entrepreneurs, such as those at the origin of Silicon Valley or of Taiwan's PC clones, the Information Technology Revolution would have had very different characteristics, and it is unlikely that it would have evolved toward the kind of decentralized, flexible technological devices that are diffusing through all realms of human activity. Indeed, since the early 1970s, technological innovation has been essentially market driven:[68] and innovators, while still often employed by major companies, particularly in Japan and Europe, continue to establish their own businesses in America and, increasingly, around the world. This gives rise to an acceleration of technological innovation and a faster diffusion of such innovation, as ingenious minds, driven by passion and greed, constantly scan the industry for market niches in products and processes. **It is indeed by this interface between macro-research programs and large markets developed by the state, on the one hand, and decentralized innovation stimulated by a culture of technological creativity and role models of fast personal success, on the other hand, that new information technologies came to blossom.** In so doing, they clustered around networks of firms, organizations, and institutions to form a new socio-technical paradigm.

The Information Technology Paradigm

As Christopher Freeman writes:

A techno-economic paradigm is a cluster of interrelated technical, organizational, and managerial innovations whose advantages are to be found not only in a new range of products and systems, but most of all in the dynamics of the relative cost

---

[65]   Roberts (1991).
[66]   Kenney (1986).
[67]   See the analyses gathered in Castells (1988b).
[68]   Banegas (1993).

structure of all possible inputs to production. *In each new paradigm a particular input or set of inputs may be described as the "key factor" in that paradigm characterized by falling relative costs and universal availability.* The contemporary change of paradigm may be seen as a shift from a technology based primarily on cheap inputs of energy to one *predominantly based on cheap inputs of information derived from advances in microelectronic and telecommunications technology.*[69]

The notion of the technological paradigm, elaborated by Carlota Perez, Christopher Freeman, and Giovanni Dosi, adapting the classic analysis of scientific revolutions by Kuhn, helps to organize the essence of current technological transformation as it interacts with economy and society.[70] Rather than refining the definition to include social processes beyond the economy, I think it would be useful, as a guide to our upcoming journey along the paths of social transformation, to pinpoint those features that constitute the heart of the information technology paradigm. Taken together, they are the material foundation of the informational society.

The first characteristic of the new paradigm is that information is its raw material: *these are technologies to act on information,* not just information to act on technology, as was the case in previous technological revolutions.

The second feature refers to the *pervasiveness of effects of new technologies.* Because information is an integral part of all human activity, all processes of our individual and collective existence are directly shaped (although certainly not determined) by the new technological medium.

The third characteristic refers to the *networking logic* of any system or set of relationships using these new information technologies. The morphology of the network seems to be well adapted to increasing complexity of interaction and to unpredictable patterns of development arising from the creative power of such interaction.[71] This

---

[69] C. Freeman, "Preface to Part II," in Dosi et al. (1988b: 10).

[70] Perez (1983); Dosi et al. (1988b); Kuhn (1962).

[71] Kelly (1995: 25–7) elaborates on the properties of networking logic in a few telling paragraphs:

The Atom is the past. The symbol of science for the next century is the dynamical Net . . . Whereas the Atom represents clean simplicity, the Net channels the messy power of complexity . . . The only organization capable of nonprejudiced growth, or unguided learning is a network. All other topologies limit what can happen. A network swarm is all edges and therefore open ended any way you come at it. Indeed, the network is the least structured organization that can be said to have any structure at all . . . In

topological configuration, the network, can now be materially implemented, in all kinds of processes and organizations, by newly available information technologies. Without them, the networking logic would be too cumbersome to implement. Yet this networking logic is needed to structure the unstructured while preserving flexibility, since the unstructured is the driving force of innovation in human activity.

Fourthly, related to networking but a clearly distinct feature, the information technology paradigm is based on *flexibility*. Not only processes are reversible, but organizations and institutions can be modified, and even fundamentally altered, by rearranging their components. What is distinctive to the configuration of the new technological paradigm is its ability to reconfigure, a decisive feature in a society characterized by constant change and organizational fluidity. Turning the rules upside down without destroying the organization has become a possibility, because the material basis of the organization can be reprogrammed and retooled. However, we must stop short of a value judgment attached to this technological feature. This is because flexibility could be a liberating force, but also a repressive tendency if the rewriters of rules are always the powers that be. As Mulgan wrote: "Networks are created not just to communicate, but also to gain position, to outcommunicate.'[72] It is thus essential to keep a distance between assessing the emergence of new social forms and processes, as induced and allowed by new technologies, and extrapolating the potential consequences of such developments for society and people: only specific analyses and empirical observation will be able to determine the outcome of interaction between new technologies and emerging social forms. Yet it is essential as well to identify the logic embedded in the new technological paradigm.

Then, a fifth characteristic of this technological revolution is the growing *convergence of specific technologies into a highly integrated system,* within which old, separate technological trajectories become literally indistinguishable. Thus, microelectronics, telecommunications, optoelectronics, and computers are all now integrated into informa-

---

fact a plurality of truly divergent components can only remain coherent in a network. No other arrangement – chain, pyramid, tree, circle, hub – can contain true diversity working as a whole.

Although physicists and mathematicians may take exception to some of these statements, Kelly's basic message is an interesting one: the convergence between the evolutionary topology of living matter, the open-ended nature of an increasingly complex society, and the interactive logic of new information technologies.
[72]   Mulgan (1991: 21).

tion systems. There still exists, and will exist for some time, some business distinction between chip makers and software writers, for instance. But even such differentiation is blurred by the growing integration of business firms in strategic alliances and cooperative projects, as well as by the inscription of software programs into chip hardware. Furthermore, in terms of technological system one element cannot be imagined without the other: microcomputers are largely determined by chip power, and both the design and the parallel processing of microprocessors depend on computer architecture. Telecommunications is now but one form of processing information; transmission and linkage technologies are at the same time increasingly diversified and integrated into the same network, operated by computers.[73]

Technological convergence increasingly extends to growing interdependence between the biological and microelectronics revolutions, both materially and methodologically. Thus, decisive advances in biological research, such as the identification of human genes or segments of human DNA, can only proceed because of massive computing power.[74] On the other hand, the use of biological materials in microelectronics, although still very far from a generalized application, was already at the experimentation stage in 1995. Leonard Adleman, a computer scientist at the University of Southern California, used synthetic DNA molecules, and with the help of a chemical reaction made them work according to the DNA combining logic as the material basis for computing.[75] Although research has still a long way to go toward the material integration of biology and electronics, the logic of biology (the ability to self-generate unprogrammed, coherent sequences) is increasingly being introduced in electronic machines.[76] The cutting edge of robotics is the field of learning robots, using neural network theory. Thus, at the European Union Joint Research Centre's neural network laboratory in Ispra, Italy, computer scientist Jose Millan has for years been patiently teaching a couple of robots to learn by themselves, with the hope that, in the near future, they will find a good job working in applications such as surveillance and material handling in nuclear installations.[77] The ongoing convergence between different

[73] Williams (1991).
[74] *Business Week* (1995e); Bishop and Waldholz (1990).
[75] Allen (1995).
[76] See, for an analysis of trends, Kelly (1995); for a historical perspective on the convergence between mind and machines, see Mazlish (1994); for a theoretical reflection, see Levy (1994).
[77] Millan (1996); and Kaiser et al. (1995).

technological fields in the information paradigm results from their shared logic of information generation, a logic that is most apparent in the working of DNA and in natural evolution and that is increasingly replicated in the most advanced information systems, as chips, computers, and software reach new frontiers of speed, storage capacity, and flexible treatment of information from multiple sources. While the reproduction of the human brain, with its billions of circuits and unsurpassable recombining capacity, is strictly science fiction, the boundaries of information power of today's computers are being transgressed month by month.[78]

From the observation of such extraordinary changes in our machines and knowledge of life, and with the help provided by these machines and this knowledge, a deeper technological transformation is taking place: that of categories under which we think all processes. Historian of technology Bruce Mazlish proposes the idea of the necessary

> recognition that human biological evolution, now best under-stood in cultural terms, forces upon humankind – us – the consciousness that tools and machines are inseparable from evolving human nature. It also requires us to realize that the development of machines, culminating in the computer, makes inescapable the awareness that the same theories that are useful in explaining the workings of mechanical contrivances are also useful in understanding the human animal – and vice versa, for the understanding of the human brain sheds light in the nature of artificial intelligence.[79]

From a different perspective, based on fashionable discourses of the 1980s on "chaos theory", in the 1990s a network of scientists and researchers converged towards a shared epistemological approach, identified by the code word "complexity". Organized around seminars held at the Santa Fe Institute in New Mexico (originally a club of high-level physicists from Los Alamos Laboratory, soon joined by a select network of Nobel Prize winners and their friends), this intellectual circle aims at communicating scientific thought (including social sciences) under a new paradigm. They focus on understanding the emergence of self-organizing structures that create complexity out of simplicity and superior order out of chaos, through several orders of interactivity between the basic elements at the origin of the process.[80] Although this project is often dismissed by mainstream

---

[78] See the excellent prospective analysis by Gelernter (1991).
[79] Mazlish (1993: 233).

science as a nonverifiable proposition, it is one example of the effort being made from different quarters towards finding a common ground for intellectual cross-fertilization of science and technology in the Information Age. Yet this approach seems to forbid any integrating, systemic framework. Complexity thinking should be considered as a method for understanding diversity, rather than a unified meta-theory. Its epistemological value could come from acknowledging the serendipitous nature of Nature and of society. Not that there are no rules, but that rules are created, and changed, in a relentless process of deliberate actions and unique interactions.

The information technology paradigm does not evolve towards its closure as a system, but towards its openness as a multi-edged network. It is powerful and imposing in its materiality, but adaptive and open-ended in its historical development. Comprehensiveness, complexity, and networking are its decisive qualities.

Thus, the social dimension of the Information Technology Revolution seems bound to follow the law on the relationship between technology and society proposed some time ago by Melvin Kranzberg: **"Kranzberg's First Law reads as follows: Technology is neither good nor bad, nor is it neutral."**[81] It is indeed a force, probably more than ever under the current technological paradigm that penetrates the core of life and mind.[82] But its actual deployment in the realm of conscious social action, and the complex matrix of interaction between the technological forces unleashed by our species, and the species itself, are matters of inquiry rather than of fate. I shall now proceed with such an inquiry.

[80]   The diffusion of chaos theory to a broad audience was largely due to the best-seller by Gleick (1987); see also Hall (1991). For a clearly written, intriguing history of the "complexity" school, see Waldrop (1992).

[81]   Kranzberg (1985: 50).

[82]   For an informative, casual discussion of recent developments at the crossroads of science and the human mind, see Baumgartner and Payr (1995). For a more forceful, if controversial, interpretation by one of the founders of the genetic revolution, see Crick (1994).

━━ 2 ━━

The Informational Economy and the Process of Globalization

Introduction

A new economy has emerged in the last two decades on a worldwide scale. I call it informational and global to identify its fundamental distinctive features and to emphasize their intertwining. It is *informational* because the productivity and competitiveness of units or agents in this economy (be it firms, regions, or nations) fundamentally depend upon their capacity to generate, process, and apply efficiently knowledge-based information. It is *global* because the core activities of production, consumption, and circulation, as well as their components (capital, labor, raw materials, management, information, technology, markets) are organized on a global scale, either directly or through a network of linkages between economic agents. It is informational *and* global because, under the new historical conditions, productivity is generated through and competition is played out in a global network of interaction. And it has emerged in the last quarter of the twentieth century because the Information Technology Revolution provides the indispensable, material basis for such a new economy. It is the historical linkage between the knowledge-information base of the economy, its global reach, and the Information Technology Revolution that gives birth to a new, distinctive economic system, whose structure and dynamics I shall explore in this chapter.

To be sure, information and knowledge have always been critical components of economic growth, and the evolution of technology has indeed largely determined the productive capacity of society and standards of living, as well as social forms of economic organization.[1] Yet,

---

[1] Rosenberg and Birdzell (1986); Mokyr (1990).

as argued in chapter 1, we are witnessing a point of historical discontinuity. The emergence of a new technological paradigm organized around new, more powerful, and more flexible information technologies makes it possible for information itself to become the product of the production process. To be more precise: the products of new information technology industries are information-processing devices or information processing itself.[2] New information technologies, by transforming the processes of information processing, act upon all domains of human activity, and make it possible to establish endless connections between different domains, as well as between elements and agents of such activities. A networked, deeply interdependent economy emerges that becomes increasingly able to apply its progress in technology, knowledge, and management to technology, knowledge, and management themselves. Such a virtuous circle should lead to greater productivity and efficiency, given the right conditions of equally dramatic organizational and institutional changes.[3] In this chapter I shall try to assess the historical specificity of a new informational, global economy, outline its main features, and explore the structure and dynamics of a worldwide economic system emerging as a transitional form toward the informational mode of development that is likely to characterize the coming decades.

Productivity, Competitiveness, and the Informational Economy

The productivity enigma

Productivity drives economic progress. It is by increasing the yields of output per unit of input over time that humankind eventually mastered the forces of Nature and, in the process, shaped itself as Culture. No wonder that the debate over the sources of productivity is the cornerstone of classical political economy, from the Physiocrats to Marx, via Ricardo, and remains at the forefront of that dwindling stream of economic theory still concerned with the real economy.[4] Indeed, the specific ways of increasing productivity define the structure and dynamics of a given economic system. If there is a new, informational economy, we should be able to pinpoint the historically

[2]   Monk (1989); Freeman (1982).
[3]   Machlup (1980, 1982, 1984); Dosi et al. (1988a).
[4]   Nelson (1994); Boyer (ed.) (1986); Arthur (1989); Krugman (1990); Nelson and Winter (1982); Dosi et al. (1988a).

novel sources of productivity that make such an economy a distinctive
one. But as soon as we raise this fundamental question we sense the
complexity and uncertainty of the answer. Few economic matters are
more questioned and more questionable than the sources of productivity and productivity growth.[5]

Academic discussions on productivity in advanced economies ritu-
ally start with the reference to the pioneering work by Robert Solow
in 1956–7 and to the aggregate production function he proposed
within a strict neoclassical framework to explain the sources and
evolution of productivity growth in the American economy. On the
basis of his calculations he contended that gross output per man
doubled in the American private nonfarm sector between 1909 and
1949, "with 87½% of the increase attributable to technical change and
the remaining 12½% to increased use of capital."[6] Parallel work by
Kendrick converged toward similar results.[7] However, although Solow
interpreted his findings as reflecting the influence of technical
change on productivity, statistically speaking what he showed was that
increasing output per hour of work was not the result of adding more
labor, and only slightly of adding capital, but came from some other
source, expressed as a statistical residual in his production function
equation. Most econometric research on productivity growth in the
two decades after Solow's pathbreaking work concentrated on
explaining the "residual," by finding ad hoc factors that would
account for the variation in the evolution of productivity, such as
energy supply, government regulation, education of the labor force,
and so on, without succeeding very much in clarifying this enigmatic
"residual."[8] Economists, sociologists, and economic historians,
supporting Solow's intuition, did not hesitate to interpret the
"residual" as being equivalent to technological change. In the most
refined elaborations, "science and technology" were understood in
the broad sense, namely as knowledge and information, so that the
technology of management was considered to be as important as the
management of technology.[9] One of the most insightful, systematic
research efforts on productivity, that by Richard Nelson,[10] starts from

[5]   Nelson (1981).
[6]   Solow (1957: 32); see also Solow (1956).
[7]   Kendrick (1961).
[8]   See, for the USA, Denison (1974, 1979); Kendrick (1973); Jorgerson and
      Griliches (1967); Mansfield (1969); Baumol et al. (1989). For France, Carre
      et al. (1984); Sautter (1978); Dubois (1985). For international comparison,
      see Denison (1967) and Maddison (1984).
[9]   Bell (1976); Nelson (1981); Rosenberg (1982); Stonier (1983); Freeman
      (1982).
[10] Nelson (1980, 1981, 1988, 1994) and Nelson and Winter (1982).

the widespread assumption of the central role of technological change in productivity growth, thus recasting the question about the sources of productivity to shift the emphasis toward the origins of such change. In other words, the economics of technology would be the explanatory framework for the analysis of the sources of growth. However, this analytical intellectual perspective may in fact complicate the matter even further. This is because a stream of research, particularly by the University of Sussex's Science and Policy Research Unit economists,[11] has demonstrated the fundamental role of institutional environment and historical trajectories in fostering and guiding technological change, thus ultimately inducing productivity growth. Therefore, to argue that productivity creates economic growth, and that productivity is a function of technological change, is tantamount to stating that the characteristics of society are the crucial factors underlying economic growth, by their impact on technological innovation.

This Schumpeterian approach to economic growth[12] raises an even more fundamental question concerning the structure and dynamics of the informational economy. Namely, what is historically new about our economy? What is its specificity *vis-à-vis* other economic systems, and particularly *vis-à-vis* the industrial economy?

Is knowledge-based productivity specific to the informational economy?

Economic historians have shown the fundamental role played by technology in economic growth, via productivity increase, throughout history and especially in the industrial era.[13] The hypothesis of the critical role of technology as a source of productivity in advanced economies seems also able to comprehend much of the past experience of economic growth, cutting across different intellectual traditions in economic theory.

Furthermore, the analysis by Solow, repeatedly used as the starting point of the argument in favor of the emergence of a post-industrial economy by Bell and others, *is based on data for the 1909–49 period of the American economy, namely the heyday of the American industrial economy.* Indeed, in 1950 the proportion of manufacturing employment in the US was almost at its peak (the highest point was reached in 1960), so that by the most usual indicator of "industrialism" Solow's calculations

---

[11]   Dosi et al. (1988a).
[12]   Schumpeter (1939).
[13]   Basalla (1988); Mokyr (1990); David (1975); Rosenberg (1976); Arthur (1986).

were referring to the process of expansion of the industrial economy. What is the analytical meaning of this observation? If the explanation of productivity growth introduced by the aggregate production function school is not substantially different from the results of historical analysis of the relationship between technology and economic growth over longer periods, at least for the industrial economy, does this mean that there is nothing new about the "informational" economy? Are we simply observing the mature stage of the industrial economic system whose steady accumulation of productive capacity frees labor from direct material production for the benefit of information-processing activities, as it was suggested in the pioneering work by Marc Porat?[14]

Table 2.1 Productivity rate: growth rates of output per worker; average annual percentage change by period

Country	1870–1913	1913–29	1929–50	1950–60	1960–9
Canada	1.7	0.7	2.0	2.1	2.2
France[a]	1.4	2.0	0.3	5.4	5.0
Germany[b]	1.6	-0.2	1.2	6.0	4.6
Italy[a]	0.8	1.5	1.0	4.5	6.4
Japan[c]	–	–	–	6.7	9.5
United Kingdom	1.0	0.4	1.1	1.9	2.5
United States[d]	1.9	1.5	1.7	2.1	2.6

[a] Initial year for period 1950–60 is 1954.
[b] Initial year for 1870–1913 is 1871.
[c] Initial year for 1950–1960 is 1953.
[d] Initial year for period 1870–1913 is 1871.
Historical Statistics of the United States: Colonial Times to 1970, Part 1, Series F10–16.

To answer this question, let us look at the long-term evolution of productivity growth in advanced market economies (see tables 2.1 for the so-called G-7 countries and 2.2 for the OECD countries). For the purpose of my analysis, what is relevant is the change of trends between four periods: 1870–1950, 1950–73, 1973–9, and 1979–93. Because we use two different statistical sources we cannot compare levels of productivity growth rates between the periods before and after 1969, but we can reason on the evolution of growth rates within and between periods for each source. Overall, there was a moderate rate of growth of productivity for the 1870–1950 period (never surpassing 2% for any country or subperiod, except for Canada), a high rate of growth during the 1950–73 period (always over 2%,

[14]   Porat (1977).

except for the UK) with Japan leading the charge; and a low growth rate in 1973–93 (very low for the US and Canada), always below 2% in total factor productivity, except Italy in the 1970s. Even if we account for the specificity of some countries, what appears clearly is that *we observe a downward trend of productivity growth starting roughly around the same time that the Information Technology Revolution took shape in the early 1970s.* Highest growth rates of productivity took place during the 1950–73 period when industrial technological innovations that came together as a system during the Second World War were woven into a dynamic model of economic growth. But by the early 1970s, the productivity potential of these technologies seemed to be exhausted, and new information technologies did not appear to reverse the productivity slowdown for the next two decades.[15] Indeed, in the United States, the famous "residual", after accounting for about 1.5 points of annual productivity growth during the 1960s, made no contribution at all in 1972–92.[16] In a comparative perspective, calculations by the reliable Centre d'Etudes Prospectives et d'Informations Internationales[17] show a general reduction of total factor productivity growth for the main market economies during the 1970s and 1980s. Even for Japan, the role of capital in productivity growth was more important than that of multifactor productivity for the 1973–90 period. This decline was particularly marked in all countries for service activities, where new information-processing devices could be thought to have increased productivity, if the relationship between technology and productivity were simple and direct. Evidently, it is not.

Thus, over the long term,[18] there was a steady, moderate productivity growth, with some downturns, in the period of formation of the

---

[15]   Maddison (1984); Krugman (1994a).

[16]   See Council of Economic Advisers (1995).

[17]   Centre d'Etudes Prospectives et d'Informations Internationales (CEPII), 1992. I have relied on key information in the 1992 report on the world economy prepared by CEPII, on the basis of the MIMOSA model of the world economy elaborated by the researchers of this leading economic research center linked to the French Prime Minister's office. Although the data base has been produced by this research center, and thus does not coincide entirely in its periodization and estimates with various international sources (OECD, US Government statistics, etc.), it is a reliable model that allows me to compare very different economic trends in the whole world, and for the same periods, without changing the data base, thus furthering consistency and comparability. However, I have also felt the necessity of relying on additional sources from standard statistical publications, which I have cited where necessary. For a presentation of the characteristics of this model, see CEPII–OFCE (1990).

[18]   Kindleberger (1964); Maddison (1984); Freeman (ed.) (1986); Dosi et al. (1988a).

Table 2.2 Productivity in the business sector: percentage changes at annual rates

	Total factor productivity[a]			Labor productivity[b]			Capital productivity		
	1960c–73	1973–79	1979–93d	1960c–73	1973–79	1979–93d	1960c–73	1973–79	1979–93d
United States	1.6	-0.4	0.4	2.2	0	0.8	0.2	-1.3	-0.5
Japan	5.6	1.3	1.4	8.3	2.9	2.5	-2.6	-3.4	-1.9
Germany[e]	2.6	1.8	1.0	4.5	3.1	1.7	-1.4	-1.0	-0.6
France	3.7	1.6	1.2	5.3	2.9	2.2	0.6	-1.0	-0.7
Italy	4.4	2.0	1.0	6.3	2.9	1.8	0.4	0.3	-0.7
United Kingdom	2.6	0.6	1.4	3.9	1.5	2.0	-0.3	-1.5	0.2
Canada	1.9	0.6	-0.3	2.9	1.5	1.0	0.1	-1.1	-2.8
Total of above countries[f]	2.9	0.6	0.8	4.3	1.4	1.5	-0.5	-1.5	-0.8
Australia	2.3	1.0	0.5	3.4	2.3	1.2	0.2	-1.5	-0.7
Austria	3.3	1.2	0.7	5.8	3.2	1.7	-2.0	-3.1	-1.5
Belgium	3.8	1.4	1.4	5.2	2.7	2.3	0.6	-1.9	-0.7
Denmark	2.3	0.9	1.3	3.9	2.4	2.3	-1.4	-2.6	-0.8
Finland	4.0	1.9	2.1	5.0	3.2	3.2	1.4	-1.6	-0.8
Greece	3.1	0.9	-0.2	9.1	3.4	0.7	-8.8	-4.2	-2.1
Ireland	3.6	3.0	3.3	4.8	4.1	4.1	-0.9	-1.2	0.2
Netherlands	3.5	1.8	0.8	4.8	2.8	1.3	0.8	0	-0.2
New Zealand	0.7	-2.1	0.4	1.6	-1.4	1.6	-0.7	-3.2	-1.4
Norway[g]	2.3	1.4	0	3.8	2.5	1.3	0	-0.3	-1.9
Portugal	5.4	-0.2	1.6	7.4	0.5	2.4	-0.7	-2.5	-0.8
Spain	3.2	0.9	1.6	6.0	3.2	2.9	-3.6	-5.0	-1.5
Sweden	2.0	0	0.8	3.7	1.4	1.7	-2.2	-3.2	-1.4
Switzerland	2.0	-0.4	0.4	3.2	0.8	1.0	-1.4	-3.5	-1.3
Total of above smaller countries[f]	3.0	0.9	1.1	5.0	2.5	2.0	-1.5	-2.8	-1.1

Total of above North American countries[f]	1.6	-0.4	0.4	2.3	0.1	0.9	0.2	-1.3	-0.7
Total of above European countries[f]	3.3	1.4	1.2	5.1	2.6	2.0	-0.7	-1.4	-0.7
Total of above OECD countries[f]	2.9	0.6	0.9	4.4	1.6	1.6	-0.7	-1.7	-0.9

[a] TFP growth is equal to a weighted average of the growth in labor and capital productivity. The sample-period averages for capital and labor shares are used as weights.

[b] Output per employed person.

[c] Or earliest year available, i.e. 1961 for Australia, Greece and Ireland; 1962 for Japan, the United Kingdom and New Zealand; 1964 for Spain; 1965 for France and Sweden; 1966 for Canada and Norway and 1970 for Belgium and the Netherlands

[d] Or latest available year, i.e. 1991 for Norway and Switzerland; 1992 for Italy, Australia, Austria, Belgium, Ireland, New Zealand, Portugal and Sweden and 1994 for the United States, Western Germany and Denmark.

[e] Western Germany

[f] Aggregates were calculated on the basis of 1992 GDP for the business sector expressed in 1992 purchasing power parities.

[g] Mainland business sector (i.e. excluding shipping as well as crude petroleum and gas extraction).

Source: OECD Economic Outlook, June 1995.

industrial economy between the late nineteenth century and the Second World War; a substantial acceleration of productivity growth in the mature period of industrialism (1950–73); and a slowing down of productivity growth rates in the 1973–93 period, in spite of a substantial increase in technology inputs and acceleration in the pace of technological change. Thus, on the one hand, we should expand the argument on the central role of technology in economic growth to past historical periods, at least for the Western economies in the industrial era. On the other hand, the pace of productivity growth in the last two decades does not seem to covariate with the timing of technological change. This could indicate the absence of substantial differences between the "industrial" and the "informational" regimes of economic growth, at least with reference to their differential impact on productivity growth, thus forcing us to reconsider the theoretical relevance of the distinction altogether. However, before surrendering to the enigma of vanishing productivity growth in the midst of one of the fastest and most comprehensive technological revolutions in history, I shall advance a number of hypotheses that could help to unveil the mystery.

First, economic historians argue that a considerable time lag between technological innovation and economic productivity is characteristic of past technological revolutions. For instance, Paul David, analyzing the diffusion of the electrical engine, showed that while it was introduced in the 1880s, its real impact on productivity had to wait until the 1920s.[19] For new technological discoveries to be able to diffuse throughout the whole economy, thus enhancing productivity growth at an observable rate, the culture and institutions of society, business firms, and the factors intervening in the production process need to undergo substantial change. This general statement is particularly appropriate in the case of a technological revolution centered around knowledge and information, embodied in symbol-processing operations that are necessarily linked to the culture of society, and to the education/skills of its people. If we date the emergence of the new technological paradigm to the mid-1970s, and its consolidation to the 1990s, it appears that society as a whole, business firms, institutions, organizations, and people, hardly had time to process technological change and decide on its uses. As a result, the new techno-economic system did not yet characterize entire national economies in the 1970s and 1980s, and could not be reflected in such synthetic, aggregate measure as the productivity growth rate for the whole economy.

However, this wise, historical perspective requires social specificity.

---

[19]   David (1989).

Namely, why and how *these* new technologies had to wait to deliver their promise in enhancing productivity? Which are the conditions for such enhancement? How do they differ depending on the characteristics of technology? How different is the rate of diffusion of technology, and thus its impact on productivity, in various industries? Do such differences make overall productivity dependent on the industrial mix of each country? Accordingly, can the process of economic maturation of new technologies be accelerated or restrained in different countries, or by different policies? In other words, the time lag between technology and productivity cannot be reduced to a black box. It has to be specified. So let us have a closer look at the differential evolution of productivity by countries and industries over the last two decades, restricting our observation to leading market economies, so as not to lose the thread of the argument in excessive empirical detail (see tables 2.3 and 2.4).

A fundamental observation concerns the fact that the slowdown of productivity has taken place mainly in service industries. And since these industries account for the majority of employment and GNP, its weight is statistically reflected in overall productivity growth rate. This simple remark raises two fundamental problems. The first one refers to the difficulty of measuring productivity in many service industries,[20] particularly in those that account for the bulk of employment in services: education, health services, government. There are endless paradoxes, and instances of economic nonsense, in many of the indexes used to measure productivity in these services. But even when considering only the business sector, measurement problems are substantial. For instance, in the US in the 1990s the banking industry, according to Bureau of Labor Statistics, increased its productivity by about 2% a year. But this calculation seems an underestimate, because growth in real output in banking and other financial services is assumed equal to the increase in hours worked in the industry, and therefore labor productivity is eliminated by assumption.[21] Until we develop a more accurate economic analysis of services, with its corresponding statistical apparatus, measuring productivity in many services is subject to considerable margins of error.

Secondly, under the term services are dumped together miscellaneous activities with little in common except being other than agriculture, extractive industries, utilities, construction, and manufacturing. The "services" category is a residual, negative notion,

---

[20]   See the interesting effort at measuring services productivity by McKinsey Global Institute (1992). However, they focused on just five services industries which were relatively easy to measure.
[21]   Council of Economic Advisers (1995: 110).

Table 2.3 Evolution of the productivity of business sectors (% average annual growth rate)

Country	1973/60[a]	1979/73	1989/79[b]	1985/79	1989/85[b]
Total factor productivity					
United States	2.2	0.4	0.9	0.6	1.4
Japan	3.2	1.5	1.6	1.5	1.6
W. Germany	3.2	2.2	1.2	0.9	1.7
France	3.3	2.0	2.1	2.1	2.0
UK[c]	2.2	0.5	1.8	1.6	2.2
Productivity of capital					
United States	0.6	-1.1	-0.5	-1.0	0.7
Japan	-6.0	-4.1	-2.6	-2.3	-3.0
W. Germany	-1.5	-1.3	-1.1	-1.8	0.0
France	-1.9	-2.5	-0.9	-1.8	0.4
UK[c]	-0.8	-1.7	0.3	-0.7	1.9
Productivity of labor (output per person/hour)					
United States	2.9	1.1	1.5	1.3	1.8
Japan	6.9	3.7	3.2	3.0	3.4
W. Germany	5.6	4.1	2.4	2.3	2.5
France	5.6	3.9	3.3	3.7	2.7
UK[c]	3.5	1.5	2.5	2.6	2.4

[a] The period starts in 1970 in Japan, 1971 in France, and 1966 in the UK.
[b] The period ends in 1988 in the United States.
[c] For the UK the work factor is measured in number of workers and not in hours worked.
Source: CEPII–OFCE, data base of the MIMOSA model.

Table 2.4 Evolution of productivity in sectors not open to free trade
(% average annual growth rate)

Country	1973/60[a]	1979/73	1989/79[b]	1985/79	1989/85[b]
Total factor productivity					
United States	1.9	0.6	-0.1	-0.1	0.0
Japan	0.1	0.3	-0.2	-0.1	-0.4
W. Germany	1.4	0.9	0.7	0.0	1.6
France	2.4	0.6	1.6	1.6	1.7
UK[c]	1.3	-0.3	1.2	0.5	2.3
Productivity of capital					
United States	0.4	-0.6	-1.2	-1.4	-0.7
Japan	-7.9	-4.5	-5.3	-4.3	-6.7
W. Germany	-2.4	-2.2	-1.6	-2.7	0.1
France	-1.7	-3.2	-0.6	-1.6	0.9
UK[c]	-1.1	-2.6	-0.1	-0.9	1.1
Productivity per person/hour					
United States	2.5	1.1	0.4	0.4	0.3
Japan	4.0	2.6	2.1	1.8	2.6
W. Germany	4.3	3.2	2.4	2.1	2.8
France	4.7	2.7	2.8	3.3	2.1
UK[c]	2.2	0.5	1.5	1.0	2.3

[a] The period starts in 1970 in Japan, 1971 in France, and 1966 in the UK.
[b] The period ends in 1988 in the United States.
[c] For the UK the work factor is measured in number of workers and not in hours worked.
Source: CEDII–OFCE, data base of the MIMOSA model.

inducing analytical confusion, as I shall argue in some detail below (chapter 4). Thus, when we analyze specific service industries we observe a great disparity in the evolution of their productivity in the last two decades. One of the leading experts in this area, Quinn, observes that "initial analyses [in the mid-1980s] indicate that measured added value in the services sector is at least as high as in manufacturing.'[22] Some service industries in the US, such as telecommunications, air transportation, and railroads, displayed substantial increases in productivity, between 4.5% and 6.8% per year for the period 1970–83. On a comparative basis, the evolution of labor productivity in services as a whole shows wide disparity between countries, increasing much faster in France and Germany than in the US and the UK, with Japan in between.[23] This indicates that the evolution of productivity in services is to a large extent dependent on the actual structure of services in each country (for example, much lower weight of retail employment in France and Germany vis-à-vis the USA and Japan in the 1970s and 1980s).

By and large, the observation of stagnant productivity in services as a whole is counterintuitive to observers and business managers, who have been witnessing staggering changes in technology and procedures in office work for more than a decade.[24] Indeed, detailed analysis of accounting methods for economic productivity reveals considerable sources of measurement error. One of the most important distortions in US calculating procedures refers to the difficulty of measuring software and R&D investment, a major item of investment goods in the new economy, yet categorized as "intermediate goods and services," and not showing up in final demand, thus lowering the actual rate of growth of both output and productivity. An even more important source of distortion is the difficulty in measuring prices for many services in an economy that has become so diversified and has submitted to rapid change in the goods and services produced.[25] In sum, it may well be that a significant proportion of the mysterious productivity slowdown results from a growing inadequacy of economic statistics to capture movements of the new informational economy, *precisely because of the broad scope of its transformation under the impact of information technology and related organizational change.*

If that is the case, manufacturing productivity, relatively easier to measure for all its problems, should offer a different picture. And this is indeed what we observe. Using the CEPII data base, for the US and

---

22   Quinn (1987: 122–7).
23   CEPII (1992: 61).
24   *Business Week* (1995f: 86–96).
25   Council of Economic Advisers (1995: 110).

Japan multifactor productivity in manufacturing in 1979–89 increased by an annual average of 3% and 4.1% respectively, dramatically upgrading the performance of 1973–9, *and increasing productivity at a faster pace than during the 1960s.* The UK displayed a similar trend, although at a slightly slower pace than productivity increases in the 1960s. On the other hand, Germany and France continued their slowdown in manufacturing productivity growth, with annual increases of 1.5% and 2.4% respectively in 1979–89, way below their past performance. Thus, instead of a catch-up effect on productivity in European countries *vis-à-vis* higher US productivity, we observe the opposite, maybe an indication of their technological lagging *vis-à-vis* the US and Japan. The better-than-usually-thought performance of manufacturing productivity growth in the US in the 1980s is also documented by the US Department of Labor, although the periods selected and methods used offer a lower estimate than CEPII's data base. According to its calculations, output per hour in the manufacturing sector went from 3.3% annual increase in 1963–72, to 2.6% in 1972–8, and again 2.6% in 1978–87, hardly a spectacular drop. Productivity increases in manufacturing are much more significant in the United States and Japan in the sectors that include electronics manufacturing. According to the CEPII data base, in these sectors productivity increased by 1% per year in 1973–9, but it exploded by 11% per year in 1979–87, accounting for the largest share of total increase in manufacturing productivity.[26] While Japan displays similar trends, France and Germany experienced a decline of productivity in the electronics industry, again probably as a reflection of the accumulated technological gap in information technologies *vis-à-vis* America and Japan.

So maybe after all, productivity is not really vanishing but is increasing through partly hidden avenues, in expanding circles. Technology, and the management of technology involving organizational change, could be diffusing from information technology manufacturing, telecommunications, and financial services (the original sites of technological revolution) into manufacturing at large, then into business services, to reach gradually miscellaneous service activities, where there are lower incentives for the diffusion of

---

[26]   Source: CEPII (1992); see tables 2.3 and 2.4 in this chapter, and CEPII (1992: 58–9). Data on manufacturing productivity do not coincide with those of US Bureau of Labor Statistics because of different periodization and calculation procedures. However, trends in both sources coincide in not showing a slowdown in manufacturing productivity growth during the 1980s: according to BLS data there was a stabilization of growth rates; according to CEPII data, there was an increase in growth rates.

technology and greater resistance to organizational change. This interpretation seems to be plausible in light of the evolution of productivity in the US in the early 1990s. According to some sources, in 1993 and 1994 factory productivity grew by an annual 5.4% (while real factory wages declined by 2.7%), with electronics again leading the trend.[27] Moreover, together with the diffusion of technology and new methods of management in services, this increase in manufacturing productivity pushed productivity for the whole economy between 1991 and 1994 to a level of growth of about 2% per year, more than doubling the performance of the past decade.[28] So the productivity dividend of technological revolution *could be* on its way to pay off. Yet the picture is still confusing, as data at the time of writing are insufficient to establish a trend.[29] It seems that commentary on the data may ground our understanding of the informational economy, but cannot tell the real story until we introduce some analytical tools to broaden the scope of analysis beyond the boundaries of uncertain productivity statistics.

Informationalism and capitalism, productivity and profitability

Yes, in the long term productivity is the source of the wealth of nations. And technology, including organizational and managerial technology, is the major productivity-inducing factor. But, from the perspective of economic agents, productivity is not a goal in itself. Neither is investing in technology for the sake of technological innovation. This is why Richard Nelson, in a recent paper on the matter, considers that the new agenda for formal growth theorizing should be built around the relationships between technical change, firm capabilities, and national institutions.[30] Firms and nations (or political entities of different levels, such as regions or the European Union) are the actual agents of economic growth. They do not seek technology for the sake of technology or productivity enhancement for the betterment of humankind. They behave in a given historical context, within the rules of an economic system (informational

[27]   Cooper (ed.) (1994: 62), using data from US Department of Labor.
[28]   Council of Economic Advisers (1995: 108).
[29]   Upward trends in productivity growth rates by the mid-1990s in the US should still be taken with a grain of salt. As the Council of Economic Advisers' Report to the President (1995) wrote: "While the evidence in favor of a slight improvement in the productivity growth trend is encouraging, it is not yet decisive. The experience of the next few years will be quite telling for this issue." Indeed.
[30]   Nelson (1994: 41).

capitalism, as I proposed above), which will ultimately reward or penalize their conduct. Thus, *firms will be motivated not by productivity, but by profitability*, for which productivity and technology may be important means, but certainly not the only ones. And *political institutions*, being shaped by a broader set of values and interests, *will be oriented, in the economic realm, towards maximizing the competitiveness of their constituent economies*. **Profitability and competitiveness are the actual determinants of technological innovation and productivity growth.** It is in their concrete, historical dynamics that we may find the clues for understanding productivity's vagaries.

The 1970s were at the same time the likely birth date of the Information Technology Revolution and a watershed in the evolution of capitalism, as I argued above. Firms in all countries reacted to actual or feared decline in profitability by adopting new strategies.[31] Some of them, such as technological innovation and organizational decentralization, while essential in their potential impact, had a relatively long-term horizon. But firms looked for shorter-term results that could show up in their bookkeeping and, for American firms, in their quarterly reports. To increase profits, for a given financial environment and with prices set by the market, there are four main ways: to reduce production costs (starting with labor costs); to increase productivity; to broaden the market; and to accelerate capital turnover.

With different emphases, depending on firms and countries, all were used during the last decade. In all of them, new information technologies were essential tools. But I propose the hypothesis that one strategy was implemented earlier and with more immediate results: the broadening of markets and the fight for market share. This is because to increase productivity without a prior expansion of demand, or the potential for it, is too risky from the investor's point of view. This is why the American electronics industry desperately needed military markets in its infant years until investments in technological innovation could pay off in a broad range of markets. And this is why Japanese firms, and after them Korean firms, used a protected market and clever targeting of industries and segments of industries at the global level as ways to build up economies of scale in order to reach economies of scope. The real crisis of the 1970s was not the oil prices shock. It was the inability of the public sector to keep expanding its markets, and thus income-generating employment, without either increasing taxes on capital or fueling inflation through additional money supply and public

[31]   Boyer (ed.) (1986); Boyer (1988a); Boyer and Ralle (1986a); Aglietta (1976).

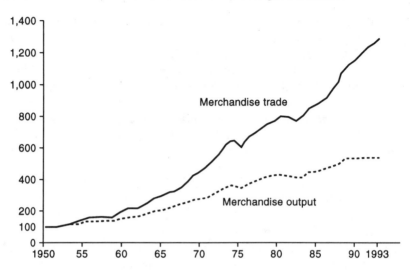

Figure 2.1 Long-term trends of world merchandise trade and
output, 1950–93 (indices and percentages)
Source: GATT (1994).

indebtedness.[32] While some short-term answers to the profitability
crisis focused on labor trimming and wage attrition, the real challenge for individual firms and for capitalism as a whole was to find
new markets able to absorb a growing productive capacity of goods
and services.[33] This is at the root of the substantial expansion of
trade relative to output, and, later, that of foreign direct investment
in the last two decades (see figure 2.1 and table 2.5). They became
the engines of economic growth throughout the world.[34] It is true
that world trade grew at a lower rate in these years than during the
1960s (because of a lower rate of economic growth overall), but the
critical figure is the relationship between the expansion of trade and
GDP growth: in 1970–80, while world's GDP grew at an annual 3.4%,
exports of merchandise trade grew at 4% per year. In 1980–92, the

[32]   The critique by the monetarist school on sources of inflation in the American
economy seems to be plausible. See Milton Friedman (1968). However, it omitted
the fact that expansionary monetary policies were also responsible for unprecedented, stable economic growth in the 1950s and 1960s. On this point, see my
own analysis (Castells 1980).
[33]   The old underconsumption theory, at the heart of Marxian economics, but
also of Keynesian policies, still has relevance when placed in the new context of
global capitalism. On this issue, see Castells and Tyson (1988).
[34]   I refer the reader to the excellent overview of global economic transformations by Chesnais (1994).

Table 2.5   Worldwide foreign direct investment and selected economic indicators, 1991, and growth rates for 1981–5, 1986–90

Indicator	Value at current prices, 1991 (US$ bn)	Annual growth %[a]	
		1981–5	1986–90
All countries[b]			
Foreign direct investment outflows	180	4	24
Foreign direct investment stock	1,800	7	16
Sales of transnational corporations	5,500[c]	2[d]	15
Gross domestic product at market prices	21,500	2	9
Gross domestic investment	4,900	0.5	10
Exports of goods and non-factor services	4,000	-0.2	12
Royalties and fees receipts	34	0.1	19
Developed countries			
Foreign direct investment outflows	177	3	24
Gross domestic product at market prices	17,200	3	10
Gross domestic investment	3,800	2	11
Exports of goods and non-factor services	3,000	2	12
Royalty and fees receipts	33	0.2	19
Developing economies			
Foreign direct investment inflows	39	-4	17
Gross domestic product at market prices	3,400	0.2	8
Gross domestic investment	800	-3	9
Exports of goods and non-factor services	930	-3	13
Royalties and fees payments	2	-1	23

[a] Growth rates were calculated at an annual compounded rate, derived from a semi-logarithmic regression equation.
[b] Data on developed and developing economies do not equal those for all countries because of the inclusion of Central and Eastern Europe in the item on "countries."
[c] For 1990.
[d] For 1982–5.
*Sources:*UNCTAD, Programme on Transnational Corporations, based on International Monetary Fund (IMF) balance-of-payments tape, retrieved in February 1993; and unpublished data provided by the World Bank, International Economics Department.

Table 2.6 Growth in the value of world exports by major product group, 1985–93
(Billion dollars and percentage)

	Value US$ bn 1993	Average annual change (%)			
		1985–90	1991	1992	1993
World merchandise exports[a]	3,640	12.3	1.5	6.3	-0.4
Agricultural products	438	10.1	1.1	6.8	-2.1
Mining products	433	2.5	-5.0	-1.8	-2.7
Manufactures	2,668	15.5	3.0	7.9	0.1
World exports of commercial services	1,020	—	5.5	12.5	0.5

[a] Including unspecified products
Note: The statistics for commercial services and for merchandise trade are not directly comparable because (i) the country coverage of available data on commercial services trade is less comprehensive than that for merchandise trade, and (ii) the data on commercial services are subject to other sources of (primarily downward) bias.
Source: GATT (1994).

corresponding figures were 3% and 4.9%. Table 2.6 shows the substantial acceleration of world trade, when measured in value, in the second half of the 1980s: an average annual growth of 12.3%. And although in 1993 world trade experienced a downturn, in 1993–5 it continued to grow at rates over 4%.[35] For nine major manufacturing sectors considered in the CEPII model of the world economy,[36] the proportion of internationally traded manufactured goods in total world production was in 1973 15.3%, in 1980 19.7%, in 1988 22.2%, and in the year 2000 should reach 24.8%. As for foreign direct investment, scanning the globe in search of better production conditions and market penetration, according to UNCTAD's World Investment Report, it increased at an annual rate of 4% in 1981–5, and at a staggering 24% per year in 1986–90. The stock of foreign direct investment reached $2 trillion in 1992. Over 170,000 affiliates of 37,000 parent firms generated about $5.5 trillion in worldwide sales in 1990. This figure can be put into perspective compared to $4 trillion of total world exports and nonfactor services in 1992.[37]

To open up new markets, linking in a global network valuable

[35]   World Bank (1995); GATT (1994).
[36]   CEPII (1992: MIMOSA model).
[37]   UNCTAD (1993: 13 ff).

market segments of each country, capital required extreme mobility, and firms needed dramatically enhanced communication capabilities. Deregulation of markets and new information technologies, in close interaction, provided such conditions. The earliest and most direct beneficiaries of such restructuring were the very actors of techno-economic transformation: high-technology firms and financial corporations. The global integration of financial markets since the early 1980s, made possible by new information technologies, had a dramatic impact on the growing disassociation of capital flows from national economies. Thus, Chesnais measures the movement of internationalization of capital by calculating the percentage over GDP of crossborder operations in shares and obligations:[38] in 1980, this percentage was not over 10% in any major country; in 1992, it varied between 72.2% of GDP (Japan) and 122.2% (France), with the US standing at 109.3%.

By extending its global reach, integrating markets, and maximizing comparative advantages of location, capital, capitalists, and capitalist firms have, as a whole, substantially increased their profitability in the last decade, and particularly in the 1990s, restoring for the time being the preconditions for investment on which a capitalist economy depends.[39]

This recapitalization of capitalism may explain to some extent the uneven progress of productivity. Throughout the 1980s there was massive technological investment in the communications/information infrastructure that made possible the twin movements of deregulation of markets and globalization of capital. Firms and industries that were directly affected by such dramatic transformation (such as microelectronics, microcomputers, telecommunications, financial institutions) experienced a surge in productivity as well as in profitability.[40] Around this hard core of new, dynamic, global capitalist firms and ancillary networks, successive layers of firms and industries were

---

[38]   Chesnais (1994: 209).

[39]   For the US, a good measure of profitability, for non-financial corporations, is the after-tax profit per unit of output (the higher the ratio, the higher the profit, of course). The ratio stood at 0.024 in 1959; went down to 0.020 in 1970 and 0.017 in 1974; bounced back to 0.040 in 1978, to decline again to 0.027 in 1980. Then, since 1983 (0.048) it kept an upward trend that accelerated substantially during the 1990s: 1991, 0.061; 1992, 0.067; 1993, 0.073; third quarter 1994, 0.080. See Council of Economic Advisers (1995: 291, Table B-14).

[40]   Source: CEPII (1992). Profitability was high since the 1980s in electronics, telecommunications, and finance as a whole. However, cut-throat competition, and risky financial deals, did cause a number of setbacks and bankruptcies. Indeed, without the US government bail-out of a number of savings & loan associations, a major financial crash could have been a very serious possibility.

either integrated in the new technological system or phased out. Thus, the slow movement of productivity in national economies taken as a whole may hide contradictory trends of explosive productivity growth in leading industries, decline of obsolete firms, and persistence of low-productivity service activities. Furthermore, the more this dynamic sector constituted around highly profitable firms becomes globalized across boundaries, the less it is meaningful to calculate productivity of "national economies," or of industries defined within national boundaries. Although the largest proportion of GDP, and of employment, of most countries continues to depend on activities aimed at the domestic economy, rather than at the global market, it is indeed what happens to competition in these global markets, in manufacturing as in finance, telecommunications or entertainment, that determines the share of wealth appropriated by firms and, ultimately, by people in each country.[41] This is why, together with the search for profitability as the driving motivation of the firm, the informational economy is also shaped by the vested interest of political institutions in fostering the competitiveness of those economies they are supposed to represent.

As for *competitiveness*, it is an elusive, indeed controversial, notion that has become a rallying flag for governments and a battleground for real-life economists opposing academic model-makers.[42] Competitiveness is an attribute of economic collectives, such as countries or regions, rather than of firms, for which the traditional, and rather complex, notion of "competitive position" seems to be

---

[41]   The decisive role played by global competition in the economic prosperity of the nation is widely accepted all over the world, except in the United States, where, in some economists' circles, and in sectors of the public opinion, there is still the conviction that because exports only account for about 10% of GNP in the early 1990s, the country's economic health depends essentially on the domestic market (see Krugman 1994a). Although the size and productivity of the American economy does make it much more autonomous than any other country in the world, the idea of quasi-self reliance is a dangerous illusion that is in fact not shared by either business or government elites. For arguments and data concerning the critical role of global competition for the American economy, as for all economies in the world, see Cohen and Zysman (1987); Castells and Tyson (1989); Reich (1991); Thurow (1992); Carnoy et al. (1993b).

[42]   The debate over productivity versus competitiveness as keys to renewed economic growth has raged in American academic and political circles in the 1990s. Paul Krugman, one of the most brilliant academic economists in America, can be credited with triggering a necessary debate by his vigorous critique of the notion of competitiveness, unfortunately tainted and obscured by manners inappropriate to a scholar. For a sample of the debate, see Krugman (1994b). For a reply, Cohen (1994).

more adequate. One reasonable definition, by Stephen Cohen et al. states:

> Competitiveness has different meanings for the firm and for the national economy. A nation's competitiveness is the degree to which it can, under free and fair market conditions, produce goods and services that meet the test of international markets while simultaneously expanding the real incomes of its citizens. Competitiveness at the national level is based on superior productivity performance by the economy and the economy's ability to shift output to high productivity activities which in turn can generate high levels of real wages.[43]

Naturally, since "free and fair market conditions" belong to the unreal world, political agencies acting in the international economy seek to interpret such a principle in a way that maximizes the competitive advantage of firms under their jurisdiction. The emphasis here is on the *relative position of national economies* vis-à-vis *other countries*, as a major legitimizing force for governments.[44]

The strategic importance of competitiveness, both for economic policies and political ideologies, comes from two factors. On the one hand, the growing interdependence of economies, and particularly of capital markets and currencies, makes increasingly difficult the existence of genuine national economic policies. Practically all countries have to steer their economies both in cooperation and in competition with others, while the tempos of their societies and polities is unlikely to be synchronized with their economic moves. Therefore, to compete is to strengthen relative position in order to acquire greater bargaining power in the necessary negotiation process in which all political units must adjust their strategies in an interdependent system.

On the other hand, competitiveness has come to the foreground of business, governments, media, political scientists, and, lately, of economists as well, as a result of the challenge mounted by nationalist policies in the Asian Pacific to previously unchallenged domination by American companies in the international arena. That Japan first, then the Asian tigers, and finally maybe giant China could enter *en force* global competition, and win substantial market share while protecting their own markets for a long time, came as a rude awakening to American business and government.[45] It prompted a

---

[43]   Cohen et al. (1985: 1).
[44]   Tyson and Zysman (1983).
[45]   Cohen (1993).

confused mobilization that soon found similar echoes in Europe, this time against both American and Japanese competition. New technologies and the new industries associated with them were seen, rightly, as the main tool for global competition and a good indication of competitiveness. Therefore, programs of technological innovation and of managerial restructuring were induced or supported by governments, first in Asian Pacific countries, then in Europe, finally, somehow, in the US, under the label of competitiveness policies.[46] Their differential diffusion, their variable accuracy, and their mixed record of success have induced distinct technological trajectories, with equally diverse outcomes on productivity, in spite of a largely shared technological stock.

Ultimately, the process of globalization feeds back into productivity growth, since firms must improve their performance when faced with stronger competition from around the world, or when they vie to win market shares internationally. Thus a 1993 McKinsey Global Institute Study on manufacturing productivity in the US, Japan, and Germany found a high correlation between an index of globalization, measuring exposure to international competition, and the relative productivity performance of nine industries analyzed in the three countries.[47] Thus, the linkage path between information technology, organizational change, and productivity growth goes, to a large extent, through global competition.

This is how firms' search for profitability and nations' mobilization towards competitiveness induced variable arrangements in the new historical equation between technology and productivity. In the process, they created, and shaped, a new, global economy that may be the most characteristic and important feature of informational capitalism.

The repoliticization of informational capitalism

There is an additional, critical element in the economy, old and new: the state. By integrating countries in a global economy, the specific political interests of the state in each nation become directly linked with the fate of economic competition for firms that are either national or located in the country's territory.[48] In key instances of development, governments use economic competition by their countries' firms as an instrument of fulfillment of their national

[46]   Tyson (1992); Borrus and Zysman (1992).
[47]   McKinsey Global Institute (1993).
[48]   Carnoy et al. (1993b).

interest, as G.C. Allen and Chalmers Johnson have argued for Japan, and Amsdem for Taiwan and South Korea, as I have tried to suggest for the four "Asian tigers with a dragon head," or as Peter Evans has proposed in general terms, on the basis of his comparative analysis of Brazil, India, and South Korea.[49] The new form of state intervention in the economy links up, in an explicit strategy, competitiveness, productivity, and technology. The new developmental state supports technological development in their countries' industries and in their productive infrastructure as a way of fostering productivity and helping "its" firms to compete in the world market. Simultaneously, some governments have restrained as much as possible the penetration of their markets by foreign competition, thus creating competitive advantage for specific industries in their period of nurturing. In the analysis by Johnson, Tyson, and Zysman, politics and productivity become intertwined as key instruments for competitiveness.[50]

On the other hand, since the mid-1980s states all over the world have also engaged in deregulating markets and privatizing public companies, particularly in strategic, profitable sectors, such as energy, telecommunications, media, and finance.[51] In many cases, particularly in Latin America, it can be argued that liberalization and privatization have opened up investment opportunities, increased productivity in privatized companies, induced technological modernization and, ultimately, spurred economic growth overall, as was shown by the cases of Chile in the 1980s and of Brazil, Argentina, and Peru in the 1990s.[52] However, deregulation *per se* or privatization *per se* are not developmental mechanisms. Under the conditions of a globalized capitalist economy they are often prerequisites for economic growth. But countries that are left exclusively to the impulses of market forces, in a world where established power relationships of governments and multinational corporations bend and shape market trends, become extremely vulnerable to volatile financial flows and technological dependency.[53] After the immediate benefits of liberalization (for example, massive inflows of fresh capital searching for new opportunities in emergent markets) dissolve in the real economy of the country, economic shock therapy tends to substitute for

---

[49] Allen (1981a); Johnson (1982, 1995); Amsdem (1979, 1989); Castells (1992); Evans (1995).
[50] Tyson (1992); Johnson et al. (eds) (1989).
[51] Haggard and Kaufman (eds) (1992).
[52] Calderon and dos Santos (1995); Frankel et al. (1990), Gereffi and Wyman (eds) (1990); Massad and Eyzaguirre (1990); *Economist* (1995c).
[53] Stallings (1993).

consumption euphoria, as Spain realized after the 1992 feasts, and Mexico and Argentina discovered in 1994–5.

Thus, surprising as it may be to emphasize the economic role of states in the age of deregulation, *it is precisely because of the interdependence and openness of international economy that states must become engaged in fostering development strategies on behalf of their economic constituencies.* Traditional economic policies managed within the boundaries of regulated national economies are increasingly ineffective, as key factors, such as monetary policy, interest rates, or technological innovation, are highly dependent on global movements. In the new, global economy, if states want to increase the wealth and power of their nations, they must enter the arena of international competition, steering their policies towards enhancing collective competitiveness of firms under their jurisdiction, as well as the quality of production factors in their territories. Deregulation and privatization may be elements of states' developmental strategy, but their impact on economic growth will depend on the actual content of these measures and on their linkage to strategies of positive intervention, such as technological and educational policies to enhance the country's endowment in informational production factors.[54] Notwithstanding the persistence of the economic ideology of out-of-this-world, unfettered markets, successful experiences of economic growth in the last two decades have often been associated with active development strategies by the state *within the context of a market economy*, particularly in the Asian Pacific, and to a lesser extent in the European Union (see volume III). The counterexample is obviously the undermining of America's competitiveness, the massive indebtedness of the United States, and the deterioration of living standards for most Americans, by the unfair, shortsighted, and ideological *laissez-faire* policies of the 1980s, as Stephen Cohen and Lester Thurow have documented.[55]

The informational, global economy is indeed a highly politicized economy. Stepped-up market competition played on a global scale takes place under conditions of managed trade. Rapid technological change combines entrepreneurial innovation with deliberate government strategies in supporting research and targeting technology. Countries that fall victims to their own ideology see their technological and economic positions rapidly deteriorate relative to others. Thus, the new economy, based upon socio-economic restructuring and technological revolution will be shaped, to some extent, according to political processes played out in and by the state.

---

[54] Sagasti and Araoz (eds) (1988); Castells and Laserna (1989).
[55] Cohen (1993); Thurow (1992).

The historical specificity of informationalism

A complex picture emerges regarding the process of historical development of the new informational economy. This complexity explains why highly aggregated statistical data cannot reflect directly the extent and pace of economic transformation under the impact of technological change. The informational economy is a distinctive socio-economic system in relationship to the industrial economy, but not because they differ in the sources of their productivity growth. In both cases, knowledge and information processing are critical elements in economic growth, as can be illustrated by the history of the science-based chemical industry[56] or by the managerial revolution that created Fordism.[57] **What is distinctive is the eventual realization of the productivity potential contained in the mature industrial economy because of the shift toward a technological paradigm based on information technologies.** The new technological paradigm changed first the scope and dynamics of the industrial economy, creating a global economy and fostering a new wave of competition between existing economic agents as well as between them and a legion of newcomers. This new competition, played out by firms but conditioned by the state, led to substantial technological changes in processes and products that made some firms, some sectors, and some areas more productive. Yet, at the same time, creative destruction did occur in large segments of the economy, also affecting disproportionately firms, sectors, regions, and countries. The net result in the first stage of the informational revolution was thus a mixed blessing for economic progress. Furthermore, the generalization of knowledge-based production and management to the whole realm of economic processes on a global scale requires fundamental social, cultural, and institutional transformations that, if the historical record of other technological revolutions is considered, will take some time. This is why the economy is informational, not just information-based, because the cultural-institutional attributes of the whole social system must be included in the diffusion and implementation of the new technological paradigm, as the industrial economy was not merely based on the use of new sources of energy for manufacturing but on the emergence of an industrial culture, characterized by a new social and technical division of labor.

Thus, while the informational/global economy is distinct from the industrial economy, it does not oppose its logic. It subsumes it

---

[56] Hohenberg (1967).
[57] Coriat (1990).

through technological deepening, embodying knowledge and information in all processes of material production and distribution on the basis of a gigantic leap forward in the reach and scope of the circulation sphere. In other words: the industrial economy had to become informational and global or collapse. A case in point is the dramatic breakdown of the hyperindustrial society, the Soviet Union, because of its structural inability to shift into the informational paradigm and to pursue its growth in relative isolation from the international economy (see volume III). An additional argument to support this interpretation refers to the process of increasingly divergent development paths in the Third World, in fact ending the very notion of "a Third World,"[58] on the basis of the differential ability of countries and economic agents to link up with informational processes and to compete in the global economy.[59] Thus, the shift from industrialism to informationalism is not the historical equivalent of the transition from agricultural to industrial economies, and cannot be equated to the emergence of the service economy. There are informational agriculture, informational manufacturing, and informational service activities that produce and distribute on the basis of information and knowledge embodied in the work process by the increasing power of information technologies. What has changed is not the kind of activities humankind is engaged on, but its technological ability to use as a direct productive force what distinguishes our species as a biological oddity: its superior capacity to process symbols.

The Global Economy: Genesis, Structure, and Dynamics

The informational economy is global. A global economy is a historically new reality, distinct from a world economy. A world economy, that is an economy in which capital accumulation proceeds throughout the world, has existed in the West at least since the sixteenth century, as Fernand Braudel and Immanuel Wallerstein have taught us.[60] **A global economy is something different: it is an economy with the capacity to work as a unit in real time on a planetary scale.** While the capitalist mode of production is characterized by its relentless expansion, always trying to overcome limits of time and

---

[58]   Harris (1987).
[59]   Castells and Tyson (1988); Kincaid and Portes (eds) (1994); Katz (ed.) (1987); Fajnzylber (1990).
[60]   Braudel (1967); Wallerstein (1974).

space, it is only in the late twentieth century that the world economy was able to become truly global on the basis of the new infrastructure provided by information and communication technologies. This globality concerns the core processes and elements of the economic system.

Capital is managed around the clock in globally integrated financial markets working in real time for the first time in history:[61] billion dollars-worth of transactions take place in seconds in the electronic circuits throughout the globe. Table 2.7 provides a measure of the phenomenal growth and dimension of transborder financial flows for major market economies: their share of GDP increased by a factor of about 10 in 1980–92. New technologies allow capital to be shuttled back and forth between economies in very short time, so that capital, and therefore savings and investment, are interconnected worldwide, from banks to pension funds, stock exchange markets, and currency exchange. Since currencies are interdependent, so are economies everywhere. Although major corporate centers provide the human resources and facilities necessary to manage an increasingly complex financial network,[62] it is in the information networks connecting such centers that the actual operations of capital take place. Capital flows become at the same time global and increasingly autonomous *vis-à-vis* the actual performance of economies.[63]

Labor markets are not truly global, except for a small but growing segment of professionals and scientists (see chapter 4), but labor is a global resource at least in three ways:[64] firms may choose to locate in a variety of places worldwide to find the labor supply they need, be it in terms of skills, costs, or social control; firms everywhere may also solicit highly skilled labor from everywhere, and they will obtain it provided they offer the right remuneration and working conditions; and labor will enter any market on its own initiative, coming from anywhere, when human beings are pushed from their homes by poverty and war or pulled towards a new life by hope for their children. Immigrant labor from all over the planet may flow to wherever jobs are, but its mobility is increasingly restricted by xenophobic movements leading to much stricter immigration controls. Indeed, citizens and politicians of affluent societies seem to be determined to keep barbarians of impoverished areas off their world, protected behind the walls of immigration authorities.[65]

---

[61] Chesnais (1994: 206–48); Shirref (1994); Heavey (1994); *Economist* (1995b); Khoury and Ghosh (1987).
[62] Sassen (1991).
[63] Lee et al. (1994); Chesnais (1994: 206–48).
[64] Sengenberger and Campbell (eds) (1994).

Table 2.7 Transborder financial flows, 1980–92 (% of GDP)[a]

Country	1980	1981	1982	1983	1984	1985	1986	1987	1988	1989	1990	1991	1992
United States	9.3	9.4	11.8	15.9	20.8	36.4	71.7	86.1	85.3	104.3	92.1	98.8	109.3
Japan	n.a.	n.a.	n.a.	n.a.	25.0	62.8	163.7	147.3	128.5	156.7	120.7	92.9	72.2
Germany	7.5	7.8	12.5	16.0	20.7	33.9	45.6	55.2	60.7	67.3	61.1	59.2	90.8
France	n.a.	n.a.	8.4	13.8	14.0	21.4	28.0	37.3	34.6	51.6	53.6	78.9	122.2
Italy	1.1	1.4	1.0	1.4	1.9	4.0	6.9	8.1	10.3	17.6	26.6	60.4	118.4
UK	n.a.	n.a.	n.a.	n.a.	n.a.	366.1	648.9	830.1	642.6	766.6	689.0	1,016.6	n.a.
Canada	9.6	8.0	7.4	10.5	15.8	26.7	40.5	58.9	39.1	54.5	64.1	81.4	111.2

[a] Estimated purchases and scales of stocks between residents and non-residents.

n.a. = not available.

Source: Bank for International Settlements, *62nd Annual Report*, 15 June 1992.

Science, technology, and information are also organized in global flows, albeit in an asymmetrical structure. Proprietary technological information plays a major role in creating competitive advantage, and R&D centers are heavily concentrated in certain areas and in some companies and institutions.[66] However, the characteristics of new productive knowledge favor its diffusion. Innovation centers cannot live in secrecy without drying up their innovative capacity. Communication of knowledge in a global network of interaction is at the same time the condition to keep up with fast advancement of knowledge and the obstacle to its proprietary control.[67] In addition, the capacity to innovate is fundamentally stored in human brains, which makes possible the diffusion of innovation by the movement of scientists, engineers, and managers between organizations and production systems.

In spite of the persistence of protectionism and restrictions to free trade, markets for goods and services are becoming increasingly globalized.[68] This does not mean that all firms sell worldwide. But it does mean that the strategic aim of firms, large and small, is to sell wherever they can throughout the world, either directly or via their linkage with networks that operate in the world market. And there are indeed, to a large extent thanks to new communication and transportation technologies, channels and opportunities to sell everywhere. This statement must be qualified, however, by the fact that domestic markets account for the largest share of GDP in most countries, and that in developing countries, informal economies, mainly aimed at local markets, constitute the bulk of urban employment. Also, some major economies, for instance Japan, have important segments (for example, public works, retail trade) sheltered from worldwide competition by government protection and by cultural/institutional insulation.[69] And public services and government institutions throughout the world, accounting for between one-third and over a half of jobs in each country, are, and will be, by and large removed from international competition. Yet, the *dominant segments and firms, the strategic cores* of all economies are deeply connected to the world market, and their fate is a function of their performance in such a market. The dynamism of domestic markets depends ultimately on the capacity of domestic firms and networks of firms to compete

---

[65]   Baldwin-Evans and Schain (eds) (1995); Portes and Rumbault (1990); Soysal (1994).

[66]   Sagasti and Alberto (1988); Soete (1991); Johnston and Sasson (1986).

[67]   Castells and Hall (1994); Arthur (1985); Hall and Preston (1988); Soete (1991).

[68]   Andrieu et al. (eds) (1992); Daniels (1993); Chesnais (1994: 181–206).

[69]   Tyson (1992).

globally.[70] Here again, the globalization of markets has only been made possible in the late twentieth century by dramatic changes in transportation and communication technologies, for information, people, goods, and services.

However, the most important transformation underlying the emergence of a global economy concerns the management of production and distribution, and of the production process itself.[71] The dominant segments of most economic sectors (either for goods or for services) are organized worldwide in their actual operating procedures, forming what Robert Reich has labeled "the global web." The production process incorporates components produced in many different locations by different firms, and assembled for specific purposes and specific markets in a new form of production and commercialization: high-volume, flexible, customized production. Such a web does not correspond only to the vision of a global corporation obtaining its supplies from different units around the world. The new production system relies on a combination of strategic alliances and ad hoc cooperation projects between corporations, decentralized units of each major corporation, and networks of small and medium enterprises connecting among themselves and/or with large corporations or networks of corporations. These transborder production networks operate under two main configurations: in Gereffi's terminology, producer-driven commodity chains (in industries such as automobiles, computers, aircraft, electrical machinery), and buyer-driven commodity chains (in industries such as garment, footwear, toys, housewares). What is fundamental in this web-like industrial structure it that it is territorially spread throughout the world, and its geometry keeps changing, as a whole and for each individual unit. In such a structure, the most important element for a successful managerial strategy is to position a firm (or a given industrial project) in the web in such a way as to gain competitive advantage for its relative position. Thus, the structure tends to reproduce itself and to keep expanding as competition goes on, so deepening the global character of the economy. For the firm to operate in such a variable geometry of production and distribution a very flexible form of management is required, a form that is dependent on the flexibility of the firm itself and on the access to communication and production technologies suited to such flexibility (see chapter 3). For instance, to be able to assemble parts produced from very distant sources, it is necessary to have, on the one hand, a microelectronics-based

[70] Chesnais (1994); UNCTAD (1993); Reich (1991); Stallings (1993); Porter (1990).
[71] BRIE (1992); Dicken (1992); Reich (1991); Gereffi (1993); Imai (1990b).

precision quality in the fabrication process, so that the parts are compatible to the smallest detail of specification;[72] on the other hand, a computer-based flexibility enabling the factory to program production runs according to the volume and customized characteristics required by each order.[73] In addition, the management of inventories will depend on the existence of an adequate network of trained suppliers, whose performance was enhanced in the last decade by new technological capability to adjust demand and supply on-line.[74]

The limits to globalization

After reviewing the operation of current economic processes, it appears that the new, informational economy works on a global scale. Yet the notion of globalization has come under spirited attack, particularly from Stephen Cohen.[75] Some of the criticism is based on a commonsense, often forgotten observation: the international economy is not global *yet*. Markets, even for strategic industries and major firms, are still far away from being fully integrated; capital flows are restricted by currency and banking regulations (although the offshoring of financial centers and the prevalence of computer transactions tend to increasingly circumvent such regulations);[76] the mobility of labor is undermined by immigration controls and people's xenophobia; and multinational corporations still keep most of their assets and their strategic command centers in their historically defined "home" nations.[77] However, this is a very important objection only when dealing with economic policy issues, a concern that is marginal for the intellectual purpose of this book. If the argument is simply that the trends toward globalization are not yet fully realized, it would be only a matter of time down the historical sequence to observe in all clarity the profile of the new, global economy.

But there is something else in the critical appraisal of the notion of globalization: in its simplistic version[78] the globalization thesis ignores the persistence of the nation state and the crucial role of government in influencing the structure and dynamics of the new economy (see, in particular, the forceful critique by Stephen Cohen and the group of BRIE researchers on the matter;[79] as well as the argument by Martin

---

[72] Henderson (1989).
[73] Coriat (1990).
[74] Gereffi and Wyman (eds) (1990); Tetsuro and Steven (eds) (1994).
[75] Cohen (1990).
[76] Bertrand and Noyelle (1988).
[77] Carnoy et al. (1993).
[78] Ohmae (1990).
[79] Cohen (1990); BRIE (1992); Sandholtz et al. (1992).

Carnoy concerning the role of the nation state[80]). Evidence shows that government regulation and policies affect the international boundaries and structure of the global economy.[81] There is not, and there will not be in the foreseeable future, a *fully integrated*, open world market for labor, technology, goods, and services, as long as nation states (or associations of nation states, such as the European Union) exist, and as long as governments are there to foster the interests of their citizens and of firms in the territories under their jurisdiction, in the global competition. Furthermore, corporate nationality is not irrelevant to corporate behavior, as is shown by the stream of research produced by the United Nations Center on Transnational Corporations. This is quite obvious to observers from developing countries, but it is also the conclusion reached by Martin Carnoy after reviewing the literature on this question concerning multinationals in advanced economies. Japanese multinationals have been supported fully by the Japanese Government, and they have kept their main financial and technological assets at home. European multinationals have been the object of systematic support by their own governments, as well as by the European Union, both in technology and in market protection. German multinationals (such as Volkswagen) have disinvested in West European countries to undertake financially risky investments in East Germany to fulfill the national ideal of German unification.[82] American multinationals (for example, IBM) have followed the instructions of their Government, sometimes reluctantly, when it came to withholding technology or restraining trade with countries at odds with US foreign policy. Accordingly, the US Government has supported technology projects for American corporations or intervened in business transactions in the name of national security interests. Indeed, some analysts have stressed the need to protect the American microelectronics industry from Japanese unfair competition to prevent Japan from controlling strategic military inputs.[83] The US Defense Department is confronting, in some areas, the kind of military technological dependency that countries around the world, including West European nations, had been experiencing for decades *vis-à-vis* key technology held by American corporations.

Furthermore, it is rightly claimed that market penetration is not reciprocal. While the American and, to a lesser extent, European

---

[80]   Carnoy et al. (1993).
[81]   Johnson et al. (1989); Evans (1995).
[82]   UNCTAD (1993); Carnoy et al. (1993); Okimoto (1984); Johnson et al. (1989); Abbeglen and Stalk (1985); Van Tulder and Junne (1988); Dunning (ed.) (1985); Cohen (1990).
[83]   Reich (1991); Borrus (1988).

economies are relatively open markets (for trade and for foreign direct investment), the Japanese economy, as well as the Chinese, Korean, Taiwanese, Indian, or Russian economies, remain highly protected. For instance, in 1989–91 Japanese direct investment in the US amounted to 46% of total Japanese direct investment abroad, and in the European Union, to 23%. However, both US and European direct investment in Japan amounted to only about 1% of their total direct investment abroad.[84] Because the mentioned Asian economies represented over one-fifth of world markets in the early 1990s this "exception" to the formation of a world market is significant.[85]

Nevertheless, the overall, dominant trend points toward the increasing interpenetration of markets, particularly after the reasonably successful Uruguay Round of GATT, the birth of the World Trade Organization, the slow but steady progress in European unification, the signing of the North American Free Trade Agreement, the intensification of economic exchanges within Asia, the gradual incorporation of Eastern Europe and Russia into the global economy, and the growing role played by trade and foreign investment in economic growth everywhere. Furthermore, the quasi-total integration of capital markets makes all economies globally interdependent. Yet, because of the persistence of nations and national governments, and because of the role of governments in using economic competition as a tool of political strategy, boundaries and cleavages between major economic regions are likely to remain for a long period, establishing a regional differentiation of the global economy.

The regional differentiation of the global economy

The global economy is internally diversified into three major regions and their areas of influence: North America (including Canada and Mexico, after NAFTA); the European Union (particularly after some revised version of the Maastricht Treaty trickles down into policy-making); and the Asian Pacific region, centered around Japan, but with the increasing weight of South Korea, Indonesia, Taiwan, Singapore, Overseas Chinese, and, most of all, China itself, in the region's economic potential. Barbara Stallings has proposed an insightful analysis of simultaneous concentration and regionalization of the global economy, arguing that

> present data show that trade and investment are increasing *both*
> within the so-called triad area (the United States, Japan, and

[84]   Stallings (1993).
[85]   CEPII (1992).

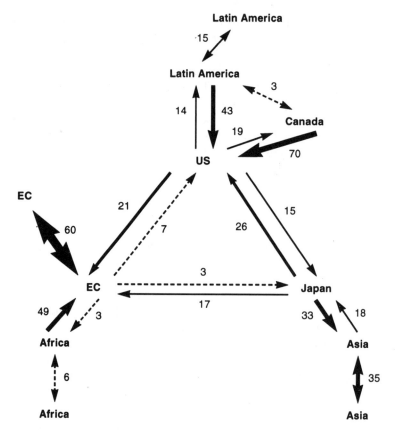

Figure 2.2   Structure of world trade, 1991
Figures are percentages of total trade (exports plus imports). Weight
of lines between trading partners indicates intensity of exchanges.
Source: International Monetary Fund, *Direction of Trade Statistics
Yearbook, 1992*, Washington, DC: IMF, 1992; elaborated by Stallings
(1993).

Europe) *and* within the three blocs. Other areas are being
marginalized in the process. . . . [The concept is] nonhegemonic
interdependence. The different types of capitalism that exist in
the three regions have given rise to differential economic performance. The result is conflict *and* cooperation, divergence *and*
convergence.[86]

From a different perspective, Lester Thurow reaches a similar con-

---

[86]   Stallings (1993: 21).

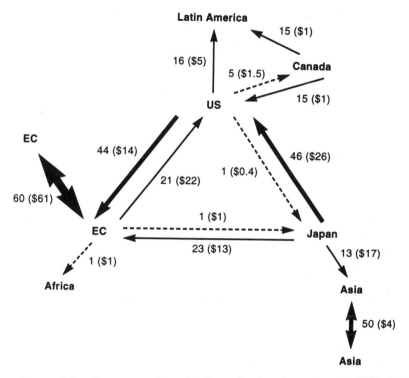

Figure 2.3   Structure of world direct foreign investment, 1989–91
(average)
Figures are percentages of total direct investment; those in
parentheses are absolute values in US$ bn. Weight of lines between
trading partners indicates intensity of exchanges.
Sources: For US: *Survey of Current Business*, August 1992; for Japan:
Ministry of Finance, unpublished data; for Europe: UNTNC: *World
Investment Report, 1992, Survey of Current Business* (inflow to US), and
IMF, *Balance of Payments Yearbook, 1992*. Other figures are estimates.
Data elaborated by Stallings (1993).

clusion, although he emphasizes the process of growing competition
between the three regions, and the undermining of American hegemony first by Japan and, in the future, by the European Union.[87]
Around this triangle of wealth, power, and technology, the rest of the
world becomes organized in a hierarchical and asymmetrically interdependent web, as different countries and regions compete to attract
capital, human skills, and technology to their shores. Stallings

---

[87]   Thurow (1992).

illustrates the argument by mapping flows of trade and foreign investment between the three centers, and between each one of them and their areas of influence, as shown in figures 2.2 and 2.3.

The notion of a regionalized, global economy is not a contradiction in terms. There is indeed a global economy because economic agents do operate in a global network of interaction that transcends national and geographic boundaries. But such an economy is not politically undifferentiated, and national governments play a major role in influencing economic processes. Yet the economic accounting unit is the global economy, because it is at such a global scale that strategic production and trade activities take place, as well as capital accumulation, knowledge generation, and information management. The political differentiation of this global system defines economic processes and shapes the strategies of competing agents. In this sense, **I consider internal regionalization to be a systemic attribute of the informational/global economy.** This is because states are the expression of societies, not of economies. **What becomes crucial, in the informational economy, is the complex interaction between historically rooted political institutions and increasingly globalized economic agents.**

The segmentation of the global economy

An additional qualification is essential in defining the contours of the global economy: *it is not a planetary economy.* In other words, the global economy does not embrace all economic processes in the planet, it does not include all territories, and it does not include all people in its workings, although it does affect directly or indirectly the livelihood of the entire humankind. While its effects reach out to the whole planet, **its actual operation and structure concern only segments of economic structures, countries, and regions, in proportions that vary according to the particular position of a country or region in the international division of labor.**[88] Furthermore, such a position can be transformed over time, placing countries, regions, and populations constantly on the move, which is tantamount to structurally induced instability. Thus, the new, global economic system is at the same time highly dynamic, highly exclusionary, and highly unstable in its boundaries. While dominant segments of all national economies are linked into the global web, segments of countries, regions, economic sectors, and local societies are disconnected from the processes of accumulation and consumption that characterize the informational/global

[88] Sengenberger and Campbell (eds); UNCTAD (1993); Portes et al. (eds) (1989); Carnoy et al. (1993); Sassen (1988); Mingione (1991).

economy. I do not pretend that these "marginal" sectors are not socially connected to the rest of the system, since there is no such thing as a social vacuum. But their social and economic logic is based upon mechanisms clearly distinct from those of the informational economy.[89] Thus, while the informational economy shapes the entire planet, and in this sense it is indeed global, most people in the planet do not work for or buy from the informational/global economy. Yet all economic and social processes do relate to the structurally dominant logic of such an economy. How and why such a connection is operated, and who and what is connected and disconnected over time is a fundamental feature of our societies that requires specific, careful analysis (see "The Rise of the Fourth World" in volume III).

The sources of competitiveness in the global economy

The structure of the global economy is produced by the dynamics of competition between economic agents and between the locales (countries, regions, economic areas) where they are situated. Such competition is played out on the basis of factors that are specific to the new, informational economy, in a global system articulated by a network based on information technologies. Four main processes determine the form and outcome of competition.

The first is *technological capacity*. Under such a notion should be included the science base of the production and management process, the R&D strength, the human resources necessary for technological innovation, the adequate utilization of new technologies, and the level of their diffusion into the whole network of economic interaction. In other words, technological capacity is not simply what results from adding up various elements, but is an attribute of a system: what I called the science–technology–industry–society system (the STIS system).[90] It refers to the appropriate articulation of science, technology, management, and production in a system of complementaries, each level being provided, by the educational system, with the necessary human resources in skills and quantity. The excellence of a given element in a given economic unit, for instance a strong science base or a long manufacturing tradition in a country, is not enough to ensure the successful adoption of a new technological paradigm based on information technologies. It is the articulation of different elements that becomes critical. This is why technological capacity can hardly be the attribute of individual firms (even giant

[89]   I elaborated on the new processes of dualism in a comparative perspective in Castells (1990).
[90]   Castells et al. (1986).

global firms such as IBM). It is related to production complexes that tend to have a territorial basis, although they connect to each other once they have established themselves in a given territory, and they diffuse and interact globally via telecommunication/transportation networks.[91] The operational expression of this production form in advanced technological systems is what BRIE researchers call the "supply base":

> By the supply base of an economy we mean the parts, components, subsystems, materials, and equipment technologies available for new product and process development, as well as the structure of relations among the firms that supply and use these elements.[92]

However, a technologically advanced "supply base" needs to be anchored in a fully fledged STIS system that acts as the provider of the components of the supply base and as the recipient of feedback effects resulting from technological learning in the production process.

Available evidence shows that competitiveness of industrial sectors in OECD countries is largely determined by the technological level of each sector. Similarly, the ability of countries to compete in the international economy is directly related to their technological potential.[93]

The second major factor influencing competitiveness is *access to a large, integrated, affluent market*, such as the European Union, the United States/North American Trade Zone or, to a lesser extent, Japan. The best competitive position is the one that enables firms to operate unchallenged within one of these large markets, and still have the possibility of access to the others with as few restrictions as possible.[94] Thus, the larger and deeper the integration of a given economic area, the greater the chances of spurring productivity and profitability for firms locating in that zone.[95] Therefore, the dynamics of trade and foreign investment between countries and macro-regions affect decisively the performance of individual firms or networks of firms.

The third factor that explains competitive performance in the global market is *the differential between production costs at the production site and prices at the market of destination* – a calculation that is more appropriate than the simplistic formula that focuses only on labor costs, since other cost factors may be as important (for example, land

[91]   Castells and Hall (1994).
[92]   Borrus and Zysman (1992: 25).
[93]   Dosi et al. (1988a); Dosi and Soete (1983); OECD (1992); Soete (1991); Castells and Tyson (1988); Tyson (1992).
[94]   Lafay and Herzog (1989).
[95]   Cecchini (1988); Spence and Hazard (1988).

costs, taxes, environmental regulations, and so on).[96] However, this factor can only affect competitiveness if the two preceding factors are integrated positively in the firm's commercial strategy. That is, the potential profit involved in lower production costs can only be realized if there is access to a large, rich market. Also, cost-price differentials are no substitute for technological capacity. Given the level of technological diffusion worldwide, a competitive strategy based on low cost still needs to operate within the information technology paradigm. The winning formula is the addition of technological/managerial excellence and production costs lower than those of competitors, lower costs and technological excellence being understood in terms relative to the characteristics of each product.[97] This observation is critical because it precludes in fact the possibility for developing countries to compete on the basis of low costs if they are not able, at the same time, to adapt their production system to the requirements of the information age.

Finally, competitiveness in the new global economy, as stated above, seems to be highly dependent on *the political capacity of national and supranational institutions to steer the growth strategy of those countries or areas under their jurisdiction,* including the creation of competitive advantages in the world market for those firms considered to serve the interests of the populations in their territories by generating jobs and income. Governments' actions are not limited to managing trade: they also may provide the necessary support for technological development and human resources training, the fundamental basis for the informational economy to work. Furthermore, government markets (for example, defense, telecommunications), and government subsidies and soft loans (for R&D, training, exports) have been critical in positioning firms in the global competition.[98] Thus, the active intervention by Japanese and South Korean governments has been decisive in fostering the competitiveness of their firms. European self-sufficiency in the critical commercial aviation industry could never have been achieved without decisive help from French, German, British, and Spanish governments to launch and sell the Airbus. The ideology of positive non-intervention practiced by the Reagan and

---

[96]   Cohen et al. (1985); Krugman (ed.) (1986). For an analysis of sources of competitiveness in the new global economy on the basis of experiences in the Asian Pacific, see my monograph, and the economic analyses on which I relied, most of them from Asian scholars, on the sources of economic development of Hong Kong and Singapore: Castells et al. (1990).

[97]   Katz (ed.) (1987); Dahlman et al. (1987).

[98]   Freeman (ed.) (1990); Johnson (1982); Deyo (ed.) (1987); Tyson and Zysman (1983); Castells (1989a); Evans (1995); Reich (1991); Amsdem (1989); Johnson et al. (eds) (1988); Cohen (1993).

Thatcher administrations in the midst of world turmoil wrecked the manufacturing and trade bases of both the American and British economies in the 1980s. On the other hand, the mixed record of the European Union's interventionist policies in sectors as diverse as electronics, automobiles, and agriculture shows that there are limits to governments' capacity to reverse technological or economic decline (for example, French farmers' productivity; European microelectronics manufacturing). However, such governmental efforts made it possible to help European competitiveness in some critical market segments (consumer electronics, telecommunications, aerospace, pharmaceuticals, nuclear energy, and so on), while buying time for restructuring in other sectors (automobiles, steel).

The above-mentioned factors jointly determine the dynamics and forms of competition between firms, regions, and countries in the new global economy, thus ushering in a new international division of labor.

The Newest International Division of Labor

The global economy emerging from informational-based production and competition is characterized by its *interdependence*, its *asymmetry*, its *regionalization*, the *increasing diversification within each region*, its *selective inclusiveness*, its *exclusionary segmentation*, and, as a result of all these features, an extraordinarily *variable geometry* that tends to dissolve historical, economic geography.

I shall try to assess this newest pattern of international division of labor in the late twentieth century[99] by focusing sequentially on each one of these characteristics. To support the argument I shall use, unless indicated otherwise, the same data source, to avoid problems of statistical comparability between countries and periods of time. Thus, when referring to broad areas of the global economy, data are cited from the model of the world economy 1990–2000 elaborated in 992 by Centre d'Etudes Prospectives et d'Information Internationales (CEPII), a research institution linked to the French Prime Minister's Office, working in cooperation with technical staff of the French Government's Commissariat du Plan.[100] Naturally, data for 2000 are projections from the model. Sources for other global data are the World Bank's Development Reports.

[99] I use the term "newest international division of labor" to differentiate my analysis from the somewhat simplistic perspective introduced in the 1970s by "new international division of labor" theorists, as represented, for instance, by the powerful book by Froebel et al. (1980).
[100] CEPII (1992).

Changing patterns of international division of labor in the informational/global economy: triad power, the rise of the Pacific, and the end of the Third World

As mentioned above, the global economy is still far from being a single, undifferentiated system. Yet the interdependence of its processes and agents has advanced at a fast pace in a short period of time. For the nine major manufacturing industrial sectors considered in CEPII's MIMOSA model, the proportion of internationally traded manufactured goods in total world production for the same manufacturing sectors in 1973 was 15.3%, in 1980 19.7%, in 1988 22.2%, and in the year 2000 should reach 28.5%. If we consider the growth of foreign investment for the same sectors, the proportion of manufacturing production under foreign control for the whole world was 13.2% in 1973, 14.7% in 1980, 16.5% in 1988, and should reach 24.8% in 2000, that is almost doubling in the last quarter of the century. Interdependence is particularly strong between Western Europe and the United States. In the year 2000 Western European companies are projected to control 14% of American manufacturing production, and American companies 16% of Western European production. As stated above, Japan is also deeply embedded in the trade and investment networks in both Western Europe and North America,[101] but in this case the level of penetration is not reciprocal, since Japan is, for the time being, less open to imports and almost closed to direct foreign investment (less than 1% of total investment).

International trade is concentrated in the exchanges between Western Europe, the United States, and the Asian Pacific, with a clear advantage for the latter region. Thus, as an illustration of the intertwining of trade flows, in 1992 the European Union exported goods and services worth $95 billion to the US and imported from America $111 billion; it exported $96 billion to the Asian Pacific, and imported $153 billion. As for the US, it exported goods and services worth $128 billion to the Pacific Rim and imported from that region a staggering $215 billion.[102] If we add financial interdependence, technology transfer, and alliances, interlockings, and joint ventures between firms, it is obvious that the core of the global economy is a tightly interdependent network between USA, Japan, and Western Europe that is becoming increasingly so, constituting what Ohmae labeled years ago "Triad Power."[103] Around this core, as argued by

[101] Glickman and Woodward (1987); Humbert (ed.) (1990).
[102] Sources: for Europe, German Ministry of Economy; for US, US Department of Commerce.
[103] Ohmae (1985).

Barbara Stallings,[104] all the other areas of the world organize their economies in a multiple dependency relationship. However, patterns are changing. Japan has substantially increased its investments in Asia in recent years, as well as opening its markets to a greater extent to Asian exports, although the bulk of Japanese imports from Asia still originate from Japanese companies offshore.[105] Japan is also investing heavily in Latin America, particularly in Mexico. And South American exports in the mid-1990s are more oriented toward the European Union and the Asian Pacific than toward the United States.

The global economy is deeply asymmetric. But not in the simplistic form of a center, semi-periphery, and a periphery, or following an outright opposition between North and South; because there are several "centers" and several "peripheries," and because both North and South are so internally diversified as to make little analytical sense in using these categories.[106] Still, a group of countries that corresponds, approximately, to the membership of the Organization for Economic Cooperation and Development (OECD), concentrates an overwhelming proportion of technological capacity, capital, markets, and industrial production. If we add to the OECD the four newly industrialized countries of Asia, in 1988 the three major economic regions represented 72.8% of world's manufacturing production, and in 2000 their share should still amount to 69.5%, while the population of these three regions in 2000 would only be 15.7% of world population. The concentration of resources is even greater at the core of the system, in the G-7 countries, particularly in terms of technology, skills, and informational infrastrcture, key determinants of competitiveness. Thus, in 1990 the G-7 countries accounted for 90.5% of high-technology manufacturing in the world, and were holding 80.4% of global computing power.[107] The differential in human resources is critical: while the world average of scientific and technical manpower in 1985 was 23,442 per million population, the actual figure for developing countries was 8,263; for developed countries, 70,452; and for North America, 126,200, that is more than 15 times the level of developing countries. As for R&D expenditures, while North America accounted for 42.8% of the world's total in 1990, Latin America and Africa *together* represented less than 1% of the same total.[108]

104 Stallings (1993).
105 Doherty (ed.) (1995); Cohen and Borrus (1995b).
106 Coutrot and Husson (1993); Harris (1987).
107 US National Science Board (1991).
108 UNESCO (1990).

Thus, the new competitive paradigm, based on technological capacity,[109] while inducing interdependency in the new global economy, has also reinforced dependency in an asymmetrical relationship that, by and large, has reinforced patterns of domination created by previous forms of dependency throughout history.

However, this apparent historical continuity must be corrected by observing processes of diversification taking place both in the so-called "North" and in the so-called "South" under the impact of the factors of competitiveness I presented above. First of all, a dramatic realignment in the distribution of capital, technology, and manufacturing capacity has taken place among the three dominant regions in the last third of the century, to the benefit of the Asian Pacific Region (see figure 2.4). Adding the newly industrialized Asian countries to Japan to form the "developed Asia" region, such a region is poised to become the largest industrial region of the world, with 26.9% of world manufacturing in the year 2000, against 24.6% for Western Europe, and just 18% for North America. And this is without counting China, whose rapid growth and technological modernization will make it a major economic power before long. Furthermore, the importance of manufacturing in developed Asia, extrapolating on the basis of current tendencies, would be particularly significant in electronics, the critical sector for the informational economy, and may also take the lead in automobile manufacturing.[110]

In addition, if we include in the picture the growing linkages between Japan and the "four tigers" with China and the South East Asian region, what seems to be emerging at the turn of century is a powerful, semi-integrated Asian Pacific economy that has become a major center of capital accumulation in the world.[111] The Asian Pacific economy is internally differentiated among at least five distinct networks of economic power: the Japanese corporations; the Korean corporations; American multinational corporations, particularly in electronics and finance, established in the area for many years; the powerful networks of ethnic Chinese capital, connecting Hong Kong, Taipei, Singapore, and "overseas" Chinese business groups (often operating through Hong Kong), all of them with direct linkages to China, forming what observers are calling "the China Circle"; the

---

[109]   Foray and Freeman (eds) (1992).
[110]   CEPII (1992); Guerrieri (1991); Mortimore (1992); Bergsten and Noland (eds) (1993).
[111]   Urata, in Bergsten and Noland (1993); Soesastro and Pangestu (eds) (1990); Ernst (1994b); *Business Week* (1994c); Bergsten and Noland (1993); Ernst and O'Connor (1992); Ernst, in Doherty (ed.) (1995).

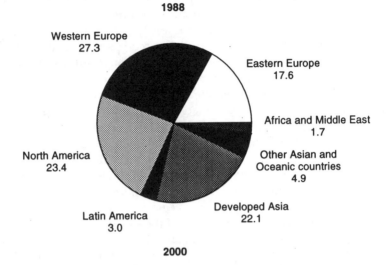

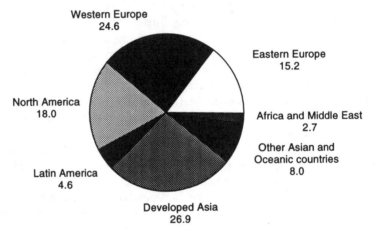

Figure 2.4   Share by region of the world's manufacturing
production: 2000 projections (%)
Source: CEPII calculations from the Industrie 2000 model and the
CHELEM and PIM data bases.

Chinese Government and Chinese provincial and local governments, with their diversified financial and industrial interests.[112]

Indeed, the rapid incorporation of China's new market economy into the global system is the economic miracle of the last decade. China's GDP grew at an average rate of 9.4% in 1980–91, and at a rate of 12.8% in 1992, and 13.4% in 1993.[113] During the same period, China's exports increased over 11% per year on average. Foreign direct investment in China grew from under $1billion in 1983 to $26 billion in 1993, making China the second-largest investment host country in the world after the US. Of this investment 70% came from Hong Kong and Taiwan, giving substance to the notion of the "China circle." You-tien Hsing has analyzed the social and political linkages created between Taiwanese and Hong Kong investors and local and provincial officials in Southern China: this is the true face of new Chinese capitalism.[114]

The economic power accumulated in the Asian Pacific region, even without counting Japan, is staggering. In 1993, East Asian governments had foreign currency reserves of $250 billion, three times those of Japan. In addition, private corporations outside Japan were holding another $600 billion in cash reserves. Savings were expected to increase by $550 billion per year during the 1990s, so that by the year 2000 the gross domestic product of East Asia (including China) could reach $2 trillion, and surpass Japan.[115] According to another calculation, taking together China, Hong Kong, and Taiwan (which would correspond to the stricter definition of the "China circle"), in 1993 the three economies together were approaching two-thirds of Japanese GDP.[116] An indirect and substantial impact of China's entry into the Asian economy has been the reaction by South East Asian countries, particularly Indonesia and Thailand, to stimulate their growth and to open up their economies to offer alternatives to foreign investment.[117] Vietnam and the Philippines are following this example.[118]

Thus, if we consider together the lasting technological and economic power of Japan, the sustained process of economic growth and international integration of China, the explosion of investment by Japanese, ethnic Chinese, and Korean firms in the East and South

[112]   Sung (1994); Naughton (1994); Hsing (1994).
[113]   Jia (1994).
[114]   Hsing (1996).
[115]   *Business Week* (1993).
[116]   Estimates by Jia (1994: 3).
[117]   Tan Kong Yam (1994).
[118]   *Economist* (1995d).

East Asia region, the meaning of the "North" in the new global economy is definitively blurred. The emergence of Asian Pacific fast-growth capitalism is, with the end of the Soviet Empire and the process of European unification, one of the most important structural changes taking place in the world at the turn of the century. Although I shall analyze the historical roots and social consequences of this process in some detail (see "Towards the Pacific Era?" in volume III), it is important to trace back the possibility of such a phenomenon to the structural trends that, in my hypothesis, constitute the source of competitiveness in the new global economy. Among them, the ability of these countries to use new information technologies, both in processes and in products, to reverse the established pattern of the international division of labor, mainly on the base of endogenous processes, since American multinationals played a minor role in the process, with the exception of Malaysia and Singapore. The openness of the global economy, enabling access to major markets, and the role of governments, steering their countries' competitiveness in the global, capitalist economy; altogether, the recentering of capital accumulation and high technology manufacturing around the Asian Pacific is a process of historical proportions whose shockwaves in the rest of the world, and particularly in Western Europe and North America, were only starting to be felt in the early 1990s.[119]

This process of extreme diversification of development trajectories is also visible at the other end of the global economy, the so-called "South," to the point that Nigel Harris was proven to be correct when announcing "the end of the Third World."[120] To be sure, there is widespread poverty and human suffering throughout the planet, and it will unfortunately continue to be so in the foreseeable future.[121] Indeed, there is a growing polarization of income at the world level, as shown in the calculations of the CEPII model on the evolution of GDP per capita by world areas in 1960–2000. Yet, there is also increasing differentiation of economic growth, technological capacity, and social conditions between areas of the world, between countries, within countries, and even within regions. Thus, South Asia, and particularly some areas of India, in the 1990s started upon a process of fast economic growth and integration into the global economy, improving over the moderate performance of the previous decade: in

[119]   For an overview of the process, see Appelbaum and Henderson (eds) (1992); and Fouquin et al. (1992); Martin (1987); Wade (1990); Amsdem (1992).
[120]   Harris (1987).
[121]   Rodgers (ed.) (1995); Nayyar (1994); Baghwati and Srinivasan (1993); ILO-ARTEP (1993); Lachaud (1994); Lustig (1995); Tchernina (1993); Islam (1995).

the 1980s, South Asia's GDP per capita increased at an average annual rate of 3.2% (5.5% in GDP growth), contrasting to the meager 0.6% per capita growth during the 1970s. After the economic crisis of 1990, India went into a new policy of internationalization and liberalization of its economy that induced an economic boom around areas such as Ahmedabad, Bombay, Bangalore (a new node in the world's electronics industry), and New Delhi. However, economic quasi-stagnation continues in most rural areas, as well as in some major metropolitan centers such as Calcutta. Furthermore, social inequality and a new brand of unrestrained capitalism keep the majority of the Indian population, including in the most dynamic urban centers, in miserable living conditions. Sub-Saharan Africa is projected to continue to stagnate at a subhuman level. Latin America as a whole has hardly recovered from the social costs inflicted by the "lost decade" of the 1980s, in spite of its dynamic integration into the global economy in the mid-1990s. Most of the ex-Soviet Empire countries for the remaining years of the century will still be catching up with their standards of living in the 1960s. And even Asia as a whole, while experiencing substantial growth (about 6% per year on average during the 1980s, most likely to be improved in the 1990s), will still remain at an abysmal distance from living standards of developed regions, with the obvious exceptions of Japan and the four Asian tigers.

Nevertheless, there is a substantial process of development under way for millions of people in some areas, particularly in China, home of one-fifth of the world's population, but also in most of Asia (over two-thirds of humankind), and in major Latin American countries. By development I mean, for the sake of this analysis, the simultaneous process of improvement in living standards, structural change in the productive system, and growing competitiveness in the global economy. While theorizing on postindustrialism we are experiencing, toward the end of the twentieth century, one of the largest waves of industrialization in history, if we use a simple indicator such as the absolute number of manufacturing workers, at its peak in 1990 (see figure 2.5) and growing: in the Pearl River Delta alone at least 6 million new manufacturing jobs were created in the last decade. On the other hand, some rural regions of China, India, and Latin America, entire countries around the world, and large segments of the population everywhere are becoming irrelevant (*from the perspective of dominant economic interests*) in the new pattern of international division of labor, and thus they are being socially excluded.[122] To enter

---

[122]   Rodgers et al. (eds) (1995).

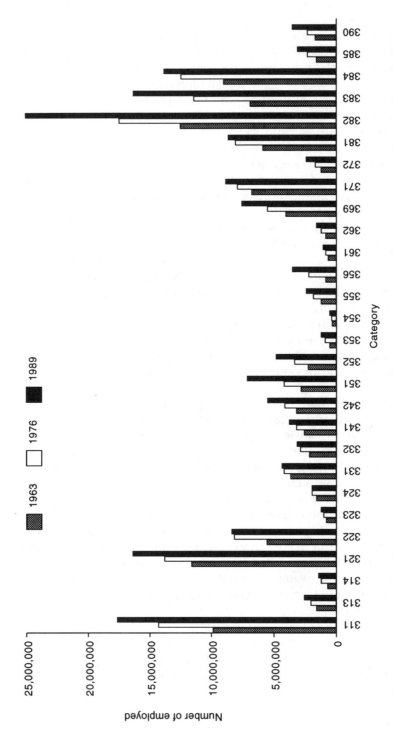

Figure 2.5 Evolution of world manufacturing employment, by three-digit ISIC categories, 1963, 1976, and 1989
Source: UNIDO; elaborated by Wieczorek (1995).

the complexity of this process of development, I shall examine sequentially the contradictory trends experienced by Latin America in the last two decades, and the structural logic that threatens to exclude most of Africa from the global economy.

Sources of growth and stagnation in the international division of labor: the changing fortunes of Latin America

Latin America, whose economic stagnation in the 1980s has been repeatedly contrasted to the East Asian development saga,[123] is a much more diversified and dynamic reality than the image presented by the dogmatic version of dependency theory.[124] Indeed, until the mid-1970s Latin America's major countries' growth rates were not far away from those of East Asia (see table 2.8). It was the "lost decade" of the 1980s, as a consequence of the debt crisis and of deterioration in terms of trade, that set back Latin America.[125] Even countries with high export performances such as Brazil had to use their earnings to cover their financial obligations, being forced to cut imports and public spending at a critical moment when international competition and technological revolution required the modernization of the productive structure.

Taking the long-term view, it is possible to say that Latin America has struggled in the half-century after the Second World War to make the transition along three distinct, albeit overlapping, models of development.[126] The first model was based on exports of raw materials and agricultural products, within the traditional pattern of unequal exchange, trading primary commodities for manufactured goods and know-how from most advanced regions in the world. The second

---

[123]   Gereffi (1989); Evans (1987).

[124]   Dependency theory has played a decisive role in the study of development by transforming and diversifying a theoretical paradigm dominated until the 1960s by modernization theory, based on an ethnocentric approach, often irrelevant to historical reality in developing countries. Fernando Henrique Cardoso and Enzo Faletto (1969) were the intellectual source of the most productive, sensitive approach to the analysis of the relationship between dependency and development. However, at about the same time, a dogmatic brand of dependency theory spread all over the world, and particularly in Latin America, oversimplifying issues and reducing the complexity of development process to the sheer dynamics of foreign domination. The best-known author of what I consider to be the dogmatic dependency school is Andre Gunder Frank (1967), a most honorable scholar, yet carried away by his ideological commitment. For an intelligent, up-to-date discussion on dependency theory, see Lidia Goldenstein (1994).

[125]   Sainz and Calcagno (1992); Frischtak (1989).

[126]   Bradford (ed.) (1992); Fajnzylber (1988); Kuwayama (1992); Castells and Laserna (1989).

Table 2.8 Latin America: gross domestic product, by type of expenditure, at constant 1980 prices

	1950–65	1965–74	Annual growth rates[a] 1974–80	1980–5	1985–90	1950–90
Gross domestic product	5.3	6.2	5.1	0.3	1.8	4.8
Private consumption	4.7	6.5	5.5	-0.4	1.8	4.7
General government consumption	4.7	7.0	5.2	1.9	1.7	4.9
Gross domestic investment	5.0	8.9	4.7	-8.7	-0.2	4.7
Exports	6.3	3.7	4.7	5.5	5.8	4.5
Imports	3.1	8.7	5.7	-9.5	6.0	4.3

[a] Calculated by regression.
Source: ECLAC, on the basis of official data.

model was based on import-substitution industrialization, along the policies designed and implemented by United Nations–CEPAL economists (most notably Raul Prebisch and Anibal Pinto), counting on the expansion of protected domestic markets. The third was based on an outward development strategy, using comparative cost advantages to win market shares in the global economy, trying to imitate the successful path of Asia's newly industrialized countries. I argue, for the sake of simplicity, that the first model deteriorated in the 1960s, the second was exhausted by the end of the 1970s, and the third failed by and large in the 1980s (with the exception of Chile, to be considered), leaving the 1990s as a critical period of restructuring in the relationship of Latin America to the new, global economy. I also propose the idea that such failures were determined by the combined effect of transformations taking place in the informational/global economy and of the institutional inability of most Latin American countries to adapt to such transformations.[127] Reactions to structural decline in the 1990s, with different timing for different countries, led to a growing diversification between Latin American economies, as each society looked for a specific form of incorporation into the increasingly intrusive global economy. Because this analysis is critical to understanding the differential dynamics of new global economy, I shall go in some detail into Latin America's changing pattern of dependency and development in the last three decades.

The first model of development, the most traditional form of commercial dependency, was exhausted from the 1960s onwards as a result of the structural transformation of world trade and production. For the world as a whole, the part of non-energy primary commodities in total trade in 1970 was only 16%, while for Latin America it was over 48%. Indeed, up to the 1980s, for all Latin American countries, with the major exception of Brazil, primary commodities represented more than 50% of their exports. This dependency on primary exports put Latin America at a disadvantage in the world economy because of three main reasons: the constant deterioration in terms of trade of primary products relative to manufactured goods; the increasing productivity in agricultural production in the most developed economies, leading to lower prices and decreasing demand in world markets; technological change that induced gradual substitution of synthetic products and advanced materials for traditional raw materials, also reducing their consumption via the recycling of used metals.

The weakness of economies that were dependent on low-priced

---

[127]   Fajnzylber (1983); Touraine (1987); Stallings and Kaufman (eds) (1989); Calderon and Dos Santos (1989, 1995).

primary commodity exports was a key argument for a government-supported, import-substitution industrialization strategy in protected domestic markets. Indeed, traditional sources of revenue were dwindling, and competition in the open economy was considered to be hopeless against the technological and financial power of firms in dominant countries. Although these policies were initiated in the 1930s and 1940s, as a response to the 1930s crisis, they expanded considerably in the 1960s with a substantial flow of foreign direct investment, mainly from the US, aimed at domestic markets. In addition to import-substitution industrialization, in the case of three major countries (Brazil, Mexico, and Argentina), exports also grew substantially in the 1960s and 1970s, particularly in primary resource-intensive sectors. These policies were quite successful in Latin America up to the mid-1970s, albeit at a price of generating high (but not hyper) inflation: GDP for the whole region grew at an average annual rate of 5.3% in 1950–65, and at 6.2% in 1965–74. Average annual growth of manufacturing exports in 1970–80 was a robust 11.9%, lower than but not too far from the 15.95% of the four Asian tigers in the same period.[128] The exhaustion of the import-substitution industrialization model came as a consequence of various factors, against the background of the technological and economic restructuring that took place in the world economy from the mid-seventies onwards. It will be easier to recall this process in historical sequence.

The decline of the primary commodity export model, with the exception of oil exporting countries, depleted government reserves on which the economy depended for its imports. The two oil shocks (1974, 1979) forced a realignment in the external sector. Eroded by rampant inflation, domestic demand started to fall, shrinking the basis for import substitution as an accumulation strategy. The resulting social tensions brought an end by the late 1960s to most of the social alliances that had been at the root of Latin American populist states, and opened the way for a variety of military regimes that introduced, more often than not, widespread corruption and inefficiency, besides political repression and social inequity. Yet the economic difficulties experienced by the import-substitution model could have been coped with, in due time, except for the intervention of external factors directly linked to the dynamics of the new global economy. After all, the Asian Pacific countries, including Japan, Taiwan, and South Korea, went in the 1950s and 1960s through a prolonged period of import-substitution policies in highly protected

---

[128]   World Bank (1994).

markets, until their industries were ready for the gradual assault on the world economy. What decisively twisted the development process in Latin America were the massive, irresponsible indebtedness of the late 1970s and the monetary policies designed to deal with the debt crisis in the 1980s.

Much has been written on the origins and processes that led to the debt crisis, in Latin America and in other areas of the world, and much of this writing is straightforwardly ideological, both by dogmatic leftist critics,[129] and by orthodox neoclassical economists.[130] Yet the story is relatively simple.[131] In a nutshell, there was a surplus of petrodollars to be recycled in the global financial markets at the very moment when advanced economies were in the worst recession since the 1930s and low interest rates were yielding negative returns in real terms. Private international banks, particularly in the US, saw the opportunity to lend to Latin American governments, particularly to those who were oil-rich and therefore potentially solvent. But they were not particularly picky: any government wanting a major loan could obtain it, the banks counting on the possibility of applying political pressures on the Latin governments if they were to default, as eventually happened.

Governments used loans in a variety of ways, often unproductive, sometimes extravagant: Argentina's military dictators used the money to buy military hardware to try to take the Malvinas from Britain, helping on the way Thatcher's political career; Mexico's Lopez Portillo and many of the Mexican state companies indulged in greater than usual corruption, succeeding in creating the largest debt in Mexican history precisely during the years of the boom in oil prices, production and exports; Venezuela sank much of the money in unprofitable public corporations, particularly in steel and petrochemicals, ruining the country for the benefit of technocrats running such corporations; Banzer's Bolivia used public money to expand public expenditure with little productive impact, and to support export-oriented private investment in the lowlands, setting the stage for the growing of coca and the illegal processing of cocaine; perhaps only Brazil tried to invest at least some of the loans in rebuilding the country's industrial and communications infrastructure, yet in the

---

[129]   Payer (1974).
[130]   Feldstein et al. (1987).
[131]   The interpretation of the debt crisis presented here is, naturally, my responsibility alone. However, I have relied on analyses and information from several sources, among which: Stallings (1992); French-Davis (ed.) (1983); Arancibia (1988); Schatan (1987); Griffith-Jones (1988); Calderon and Dos Santos (1995); Sunkel (ed.) (1993).

midst of wasteful management practices by a confused military regime. Thus, the convergence of interests between irresponsible lending by private financial firms, mainly from the United States, and the misuse of loans by Latin American governments created a financial time bomb that exploded in 1982 when Mexico renounced the payment of its debt.

The stage was set for the second act of the drama: enter the international lending institutions, spearheaded by the International Monetary Fund (IMF).[132] With their economies in financial bankruptcy, major Latin American countries were confronted with a choice: either sever their damaged ties with the global economy; or else accept a profound restructuring of their economies, strictly following the policies designed for each country by the IMF on behalf of the creditors' club. Few governments dared to resist.[133] And those who tried, did so from such a weak position, relying on unrealistic demagoguery without real political support, that they rapidly sank into disgrace, Peru's Alan Garcia being the clearest example of such a doomed strategy. Thus, with the acquiescence of entrapped governments, IMF-inspired economists went to work on the restructuring of Latin America during the 1980s. While the principles of neoclassical, free-trade orthodoxy were proclaimed relentlessly (ignoring the diversity of economic theories and experiences, and thus the impudence of *any* orthodoxy), two measures became the centerpiece of all new policies, and one simple goal presided over the overall strategy. The two measures were: (a) control of inflation, particularly by sharply reducing government spending, imposing fiscal austerity, tightening credit and money supply, and lowering real wages; and (b) privatization of as much as possible of the public sector, particularly its most profitable companies, offering them up to foreign capital bidding. The fundamental goal pursued through these measures was

[132]   Stallings (1992); Siddell (1987); Gwin and Feinberg (1989); Haggard and Kaufman (eds) (1992).

[133]   Brazil showed the world in 1993 that international debt payments can be negotiated directly with the creditor banks without the intervention of the International Monetary Fund. The then Finance Minister Fernando Henrique Cardoso reached an agreement in New York with Brazil's main creditors without involving IMF in the negotiations, thus avoiding losing his freedom in economic policy. I do not think that this freedom to maneuver, and to design a policy having in mind the specific conditions of the country, is unrelated to the spectacular success of Cardoso's *Plan Real* in controlling inflation in 1994. To be sure, not all countries have the weight of Brazil to help them escape IMF's diktat. However, the astonishing case of Russia's submissiveness to IMF's policies (in exchange for meager aid), in spite of its power as a nation, shows that a government's self-confidence is a major factor in managing processes in the new global economy.

to homogenize the macroeconomic features of Latin America, aligning them with those of the open, global economy. Thus, investment could come in from, and go out to, anywhere in the world, free trade could proceed, and production could be transferred to whatever location in the region. In the process, interest on the outstanding debt could be paid by increasingly competitive economies. Although the immediate goal of these policies was to avoid massive default on international loans, thus avoiding a major crisis for international banking, the ultimate design of the debt-induced restructuring of Latin America was to incorporate the continent into the new, global economy, or at least the most productive, potentially dynamic segments of the economy of each country. Thus, the sequence went from irresponsible lending to irresponsible spending, then to a monetarist diktat by IMF and the creditors' club, which entrusted a capable, well-intentioned alliance of democrats and technocrats to take their countries into the high seas of the global economy.

In fact, in spite of all the hype on Latin America at the moment of writing, it did not exactly work out the way it was supposed to do. The strategic aim of the restructuring program was to make Latin American economies competitive in the new world economy, which implied their ability to compete in manufacturing exports. Yet the precondition for such competitiveness was the technological modernization of Latin America's productive base.[134] Without such technological capacity, the exports of the region could increase on the basis of cost-cutting strategies at the low end of manufacturing goods, but could never rise to competitive exports of high-value manufactured goods. Yet the modernization of technological infrastructure (from telecommunications to R&D, and the training of human resources) required massive public and private investment at the very moment when austerity policies and cuts in spending left Latin American governments and companies without resources.[135] Furthermore, companies and affluent individuals looked to their own survival, placing their savings in the international financial networks, so that in the 1980s the net transfer of private capital out of Latin America was larger than the region's total debt.[136] As for the evolution of trade, following Paolo Guerrieri's careful statistical analysis of Brazil, Mexico, and Argentina,[137] during the 1970s and until the debt crisis of the early 1980s exports grew faster than the world average,

---

[134]   Bradford (ed.) (1994); Fajnzylber (1990); Katz (1994); Katz (ed.) (1987); Castells and Laserna (1989).
[135]   Massad (1991).
[136]   Sainz and Calcagno (1992).
[137]   Guerrieri (1994).

Table 2.9 Shares of Latin American NIEs in world exports, 1970–90[a]

	1970	1976	1979	1982	1984	1986	1988	1990
Total trade	1.99	1.94	2.10	2.89	3.51	2.69	2.41	2.13
Agricultural products	5.84	5.62	5.21	4.91	5.63	5.02	4.18	5.23
Fuels	0.04	0.56	1.70	5.70	6.34	4.15	3.98	3.94
Other raw materials	4.50	7.57	6.38	9.18	8.65	5.01	5.17	9.80
Food industries	6.63	6.87	7.14	7.00	8.89	8.03	7.98	5.62
Traditional products	1.02	1.40	1.53	1.34	2.09	1.93	1.52	1.18
Primary resource-intensive products	0.61	0.57	0.75	1.99	3.28	2.94	3.52	2.58
Scale-intensive products	0.60	0.76	1.12	1.43	2.06	1.76	2.12	1.84
Specialized supplier products	0.32	0.58	0.83	0.90	1.32	1.41	1.00	0.92
Science-based products	0.43	0.56	0.65	0.80	1.40	1.94	1.17	0.97
Others	10.32	10.31	7.59	6.66	7.61	1.87	0.46	0.67

[a]The ratio of Latin American NIEs' exports to world exports in each product group; percentage shares in values.
Source: SIE-World Trade data base; elaborated by Guerrieri (1994).

and the share of world exports for the three countries increased by 76%. In contrast, during the 1980s the whole region suffered industrial stagnation, and world export share of the three countries declined by 39%. At the root of the decreasing competitiveness of Latin American economies lies, according to Guerrieri, in line with a number of Latin American economists, the inability of countries and firms to transform their technological basis in a context where manufacturing exports had become critical for economic growth. Thus, on the one hand, for the three countries the share of manufactures in exports increased from 25.6% of total exports in early 1970s to about 55% in late 1980s. But the picture becomes troublesome when analyzing differential growth of manufacturing exports by sectors. Following Guerrieri's typology, and observing his data for Mexico, Brazil, and Argentina (see table 2.9), growth of manufacturing exports was concentrated in primary resource-intensive products and food industries (in the case of Brazil, also in scale-intensive products, such as automobiles). On the other hand, science-based products (for example, electronics, specialty chemicals) and specialized-supplier products (such as mechanical engineering), sectors with higher value added and with the highest rate of growth in world trade, not only had a modest role in total exports, but decreased substantially their competitiveness in the second half of the 1980s. The policies of the 1980s reversed in fact the reduction in technological dependency attained by Latin America in the 1970s.[138] Decreasing technological capacity affected negatively the whole productive structure, undermining productivity and competitiveness in strategic sectors, because of the interdependent nature of technological linkages in the informational economy. According to Guerrieri:

> In the case of Latin American newly industrialized economies, these technological linkages among firms and sectors either were absent or performed very poorly, especially during the past decade [1980s]. This weak technological interdependence has greatly contributed to the substantial deterioration of the long-term competitive position of the three Latin American economies.[139]

The net result of the 1980s restructuring policies for Latin America was economic retardation and a painful social crisis.[140] Sharply

---

[138]   Guerrieri (1994); Katz (1994).
[139]   Guerrieri (1994: 198).
[140]   Sainz and Calcagno (1992); CEPAL (1990b); for an example of the increase of poverty in dynamic Latin American metropolitan areas, see the analysis of Sao Paulo in SEADE Foundation (1995). Sources for growth data are World Bank's Development Reports.

Table 2.10 Shares of major Latin American countries in world exports, 1970–90

	Mexcio			Brazil			Argentina			Chile		
	1970 -3	1970 -82	1987 -90	1970 -3	1979 -82	1987 -90	1970 -3	1979 -82	1987 -90	1970 -3	1979 -82	1987 -90
Total trade	0.455	0.943	0.815	1.023	1.143	1.135	0.573	0.475	0.330	0.300	0.238	0.255
Agricultural products	1.260	1.143	1.345	1.850	1.223	1.770	2.290	2.815	1.495	0.108	0.318	0.668
Fuels	0.018	3.603	4.173	0.050	0.043	0.000	0.000	0.000	0.033	0.005	0.000	0.000
Other raw materials	1.193	1.523	1.753	3.600	6.073	5.385	0.078	0.080	0.080	1.698	1.730	2.823
Food industries	0.853	0.338	0.538	3.408	4.973	4.190	3.178	2.158	2.030	0.123	0.340	0.498
Traditional products	0.430	0.223	0.350	0.673	0.938	0.838	0.228	0.288	0.190	0.023	0.063	0.078
Primary resource-intensive products	0.503	0.450	0.725	0.160	0.805	1.925	0.043	0.313	0.285	2.500	1.483	1.553
Scale-intensive products	0.288	0.255	0.650	0.225	0.855	1.115	0.168	0.198	0.195	0.033	0.048	0.043
Specialized supplier products	0.058	0.138	0.298	0.205	0.663	0.583	0.133	0.148	0.088	0.003	0.013	0.008
Science-based products	0.208	0.113	0.535	0.140	0.523	0.503	0.130	0.093	0.073	0.005	0.015	0.005
Others	0.858	1.193	0.175	8.590	5.658	0.350	0.085	0.033	0.013	0.003	0.030	0.295

Source: SIE-World Trade data base; elaborated by Guerrieri (1994).

contrasting with past experience in this century, characterized by steady economic growth, in 1980–91 Latin America's per capita GDP experienced a negative average annual rate of growth (–0.3%). To be sure, with the major exception of Brazil, inflation came gradually under control: the dead do not move. And the economies of major countries, when measured on a per capita basis, were almost dead during the 1980s decade (although Brazil, consistent with its character, still went up and down): per capita GDP in 1990 in major countries was below or barely at the level of 1982, with the exception of Colombia and Chile. These exceptions must be taken into consideration. Colombia performed very well during the 1980s, both in terms of growth and in controlling inflation. The explanation, notwithstanding protests from Colombia's official economists, is very simple: precisely during the 1980s it became a key center of capital accumulation and trade management for one of the most flourishing industries in the world, cocaine production and distribution.[141] I shall analyze in detail this new form of incorporation into the global economy (see volume III).

As for Chile, the quintessential model of free-trade ideologists (initially advised in the 1970s by the so-called "Chicago boys" and supported by the International Monetary Fund under the Pinochet dictatorship), it is indeed a successful case of transition to a new strategy of export-driven growth.[142] Yet it is often misunderstood because, seen from the perspective of the 1990s, Chilean development mixed sequentially two very different models of growth:[143] the first one, under General Pinochet's dictatorship (1974–89), went through a crisis in 1980–2, and met serious difficulties by the late 1980s. The second model, under conditions of political democracy in the 1990s, may represent the chance for sustained economic growth in the new global economy. The two Chilean models are in fact representative of divergent paths for the future of Latin America. Thus, because of the confusion created in international circles by making Chile the show case of Latin American economic development while mixing substantially different economic policies, I find it necessary to recall some of the features of this unique experience.

Chile's economic performance during the 1980s has been overstated by self-serving discourses of the International Monetary Fund and other free marketeers. Check the data: Chile's average annual growth rate of GNP per capita in 1980–9 was 1.0%. For the whole period of the dictatorship, between 1974 and 1989, Chilean GDP grew

---

[141]   Handinghaus (1989); Garcia Sayan (ed.) (1989); Arrieta et al. (1991).
[142]   Fontaine (1988); CEPAL (1986, 1994); Sainz and Calcagno (1992).
[143]   Foxley (1995). For data on Chile, see MIDEPLAN (1994).

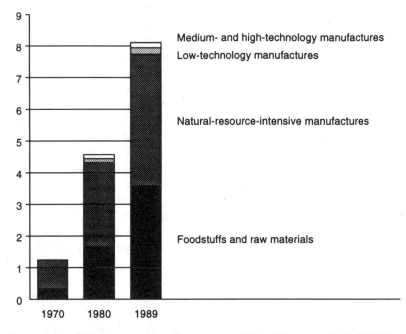

Figure 2.6   Chile: evolution of exports, 1970, 1980, and 1989 (US$ bn)
The classification is based on the Standard International Trade
Classification (SITC) at the three-digit level in line with the criteria
used by ECLAC in *El comercio de manufacturas de América Latina:
Evolución y estructura 1962–1989* (LC/R.1056, Santiago, Chile,
September 1991) and in *Interindustry Trade: A comparison between
Latin America and some industrial countries* (LC/R.1101, Santiago,
Chile, November 1991).
Source: Estimates on the basis of primary data from the Latin American
and Caribbean External Trade Data Bank (BADECEL); Statistics and
Projections Division, ECLAC.

at an average annual rate of 3%, certainly improving on Latin
America's dismal performance in the 1980s, but hardly comparable
to East Asian growth rates. Annual inflation in the 1980s was, on
average, over 20%, comparing favorably with neighbors sick from
hyperinflation, but still disturbing for international standards. As for
exports, while they grew at a high rate (10.4% per year) in the 1970s,
their growth was halved (to 5.2% annual average) in 1980–91.
Furthermore, table 2.10, calculated by Guerrieri from his world data
base, provides surprising information: Chile's share of world exports
in 1987–90, after one and a half decades of growth, was lower than its
share during the Allende government in 1970–3. The first reason for
such a fact is very obvious: total world trade grew faster than Chile's.

The second reason is less apparent and more important: it concerns the structure of Chilean trade. As shown in table 2.10, while Chilean exports performed very well in agricultural products and food industries, they remained stagnant in high value-added science-based products and specialized-supplier products. Exports were concentrated in two categories: foodstuffs and raw materials (copper, wood products, produce, wine, and so on); and natural-resource-intensive manufactures (such as fishmeal, canned seafood, paper pulp, farmed fish) (see figure 2.6). The share of manufactured goods in exports was very small: indeed, Chile, unlike the Asian Pacific countries that it likes to imitate, suffered a severe deindustrialization process, particularly during the 1970s: in 1982 per capita manufacturing GDP had fallen to 69% of the 1972 level, and risen to 93% in 1990. GNP per capita in 1990 was still under $2,000. As for the benefits of economic growth for the Chilean people, the percentage of GDP that went into wages decreased from 42.7% in 1970 to 33% in 1985, so that between 1982 and 1989 real wages declined slightly, and the purchasing power of minimum wages fell substantially. As a result, in 1987, 44.7% of the population was living under the poverty level, with 17% being in conditions of extreme misery.[144] Yet with all these caveats, Chile did better than the rest of Latin America during the "lost decade" of the 1980s. Why so? The critical element in spurring economic growth was the surge in exports: they went from 12% of GDP in 1974 to 32% in 1989. The conditions for this performance were linked to five main factors:

(a) until the end of the 1980s, a ruthless authoritarian government allowed for very low labor costs and, most importantly, for a natural-resource economy, for an absolute lack of environmental controls that made Chilean products highly competitive in sectors where the compliance with environmental regulations is a major obstacle to quick profits[145] (for example, Chilean fishmeal processing was made easy by allowing firms to gobble up entire fish banks off the coast and send them to the mixer without any further procedure);

(b) the existence of a very strong Chilean agro-business bourgeoisie, with the capital and entrepreneurial skills to take on the world market on the basis of their learning of technology. A good example of this strategy is the development of Chilean fish farming, a booming exports sector, on the basis of imitating Norwegian technology;

[144]   Sainz and Calcagno (1992); Foxley (1995).
[145]   Collado (1995); Quiroga Martinez (ed.) (1994).

(c) major support by international lending institutions, and particularly by the International Monetary Fund, committed to make Chile a show case for trade-driven development in the new open, world economy;

(d) substantial foreign direct investment (almost $1 billion per year in 1983–90), encouraged by Chile's credibility with the international institutions;

(e) and also, ironically, the persistence of a strong revenue-generating public sector under Pinochet allowed the Chilean Government to keep receiving the necessary revenue to proceed with its infrastructural development projects, in spite of the restriction of imports linked to tight monetary policy. CODELCO, the monopoly of copper production in Chile nationalized under Allende, was not privatized under Pinochet and kept feeding the Chilean Government and through it, Chilean business. In ardent free-marketeer Chile, public-sector investment as a percentage of GDP grew from 4.7% in 1982 to 8% in 1987.[146])

However, by the late 1980s the "neo-liberal" Chilean model was reaching its limits. On the one hand, widespread poverty and stagnation of average real wages restricted the domestic market to a growing, but relatively small affluent middle class. On the other hand, the outward orientation of the economy required enhancement of technological capacity, including information and commercial networking in external markets, to ensure the transition into higher value-added markets. Besides, the growing opposition of a traditionally democratic Chilean society to dictator Pinochet was inducing political instability, creating potential risks for essential foreign investment. In the last period of the Pinochet regime, economic growth was reduced to 3%, the investment rate fell below 18% of GDP, and inflation hit an annual rate of 30% at the end of 1989.

The new, democratically elected government that took over in Chile in March 1990 aimed at consolidating growth in an open economy, while engaging in income redistribution and fostering social programs to improve living conditions, ensure social stability, and broaden domestic markets. The four years of President Aylwin's administration were rather successful on most fronts. GDP growth increased at an average annual rate of 7% in 1990–3, again driven by exports that increased their share of GDP from 32% to 35%. But the key difference from previous policies was that real wages increased 4% per year, the minimum wage rose by 24%, income redistribution substantially improved, and the percentage of the population under

---

[146]   Sainz and Calcagno (1992: 22, n. 6).

the poverty level decreased to 32.7% of the total, while the government engaged in a large-scale housing program. Inflation was reduced at about 12% per year by 1993. Two policies were critical in this overhauling of the shaky Chilean miracle: on the one hand, a social pact between government, business, and labor unions that gave the government room, and time, to maneuver; on the other hand fiscal reform that substantially increased tax revenues, providing the resources for increased social expenditure and the beginning of modernization of the technological infrastructure. Unfortunately, environmental policies, while rewritten into politically correct language in official statements, continued to be bent for the sake of the profitability of a natural-resources-based export economy. Chile still faces a structural problem, related to its weak technological basis, that would need improvement to shift into higher value-added exports, particularly if Chile joins NAFTA. Yet it may be able to make its full transition to the new model of competition in an open economy thanks to its attractiveness to foreign investment. Indeed, competent economic management, the recovery of democratic stability, and its entrepreneurial class have made Chile a favorite destination of foreign investment. The headstart of Chile in the new model of development during the 1990s could be rewarded by its incorporation into the global economic networks just on time to offset the effects of the exhaustion of its model of exports based on extensive, and somewhat destructive, exploitation of natural resources.

There is a key lesson to be drawn from the Chilean experience. After the crumbling of the import-substitution model, under the pressures of the global economy enacted by international private banks and the IMF, Latin American economies could only survive in a new form of incorporation to the global economy in which the export capacity of the economy and the ability to attract foreign investment are the critical factors. Chile, in its two-stage sequence, showed the feasibility, but also the social and environmental costs, of such strategy.

On the other hand, Mexico was the country that took the boldest step in the direction of the new outward-oriented model, fully integrating itself into the North American economy.[147] As a result, even before the signing of NAFTA, Mexico received over $28 billion in 1990–1, and an additional $35 billion foreign investment in 1992, accounting for over a half of total foreign investment in Latin America. An expanding manufacturing base, beyond the *maquiladoras* enclaves, is transforming Mexico into an industrial platform to sell in

[147]   Martinez and Farber (1994); Skezely (1993); Pozas (1993); Rogozinski (1993); Randall (ed.) (1992); Cook, Middlebrook, and Molinar (eds) (1994).

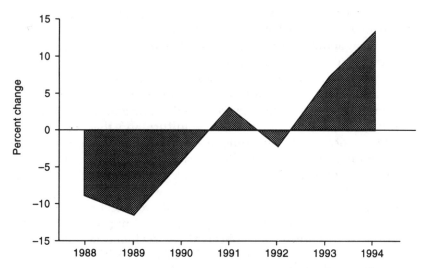

Figure 2.7   Peru: percentage change in total GDP, 1988–94
Source: Banco Central de Reserva.

the integrated North American market industrial goods produced in Mexico at lower costs, and with similar productivity levels, than in the United States.[148] Exports from Mexico accounted in 1992 for almost a quarter of its GDP. However, Mexico's trade deficit, its extreme dependence on global capital flows, and the sensitivity of financial flows to the political context of the country, plunged Mexico into a devastating financial crisis in 1994, a crisis that brought down the dollar after the US came to the rescue of a Mexican economy that is now inextricably linked with that of its powerful neighbor.[149]

Latin America, with all the singularities of such a diverse continent, was in the 1990s in the process of being integrated into the new global economy, albeit, again, in a subordinate position. Discounting Chile and Mexico, exports for the whole region, representing about 15% of GDP in 1980, accounted for 20.6% of GDP in 1992. Foreign invest-ment has poured into some countries, particularly Mexico, Chile, Brazil, and Argentina since the early 1990s.[150] Even Peru, which was literally in a process of economic disintegration during the 1980s, spectacularly reversed its decline in 1993–5 (see figure 2.7), under the impact of massive foreign direct investment flows and fast expanding trade, once President Fujimori established some sort of political stability and imposed the "Fujishock" to regain the good

[148]   Shaiken (1990).
[149]   *Business Week* (1995b).
[150]   Bradford (ed.) (1994).

reputation with IMF that the country had lost under Alan Garcia.[151] That about 60% of the Peruvian population remains below the poverty level does not undermine the importance of the fact that a country that in 1992 was 30% below its GDP per capita level of a decade earlier, became in 1994 the country with the highest rate of growth in the world (12%).

However, since massive foreign investment, both in stocks and in real estate assets, is an essential part of new economic dynamism in Argentina, Peru, Bolivia, Mexico, and to some extent Brazil, we may be observing an artificial increase of the wealth of these economies, by labeling as investment what is basically a transfer in ownership of existing assets, particularly in privatized state companies in strategic sectors. Thus, some of the region's new prosperity could be a financial mirage, subject to reversible capital flows relentlessly scanning the planet for short-term profitability, as well as for positioning in strategic sectors (such as telecommunications). The competitiveness of export-oriented economies, including Brazil, is hampered by the technological gap which Latin America still suffers, Furthermore, the social and environmental devastation of IMF-inspired policies of the 1980s[152] has not been reversed by a new model of economic growth that gives priority to fiscal austerity and external competitiveness over any other criteria. Therefore, widespread poverty shrinks potential domestic markets, forcing economies to survive in the global competition by cutting costs on labor, social welfare, and environmental protection.

Yet overall, after the painful restructuring of the 1980s, Latin America in the 1990s has been incorporated into the new global economy, with dynamic segments in all countries being immersed in the international competition for selling goods and attracting capital. The price of this incorporation has been very high:[153] a substantial proportion of the Latin American population has been excluded from such dynamic sectors, both as producers and consumers. In some cases people, cities and regions are reconnected through the local informal economy and the outward-oriented criminal economy (see "The criminal global economy" in volume III). This is why the

---

[151]   Chion (1995).
[152]   Nelson (ed.) (1990, 1992); see the literature review on poverty in Latin America in the 1980s and 1990s, in Faria (1995); for processes of environmental destruction linked to the new pattern of growth advocated by IMF, see Vaquero (ed.) (1994).
[153]   For a collective reflection by distinguished Latin American intellectuals on the new historical course of development, see the three volumes of the symposium held in Mexico in 1991: Coloquio de Invierno (1992).

future of Latin America, and its actual form of incorporation into the informational/global economy, will depend on the relative weight of two opposed models of development: one closer to Pinochet's Chile, based on absolute exploitation of population and devastation of the environment, to support cut-throat competition in external markets; or a different one, closer to that of democratic Chile in the 1990s, linking up external competitiveness, social well-being, and expansion of the internal market, on the basis of redistribution of wealth and stepped-up technological/managerial modernization. Indeed, it is this latter model that mirrors the reality of East Asian development experiences that are often proposed as role models to Latin America.

Two processes of economic restructuring, under way in the mid-1990s, will decide the fate of Latin America through the early twenty-first century. The first is the successful integration of Mexico, but also of Chile, and later on, of other economies, in NAFTA. For all the painful consequences that such integration implies for both American workers and Mexican peasants, mobility of capital, labor, and technology within such a large, dynamic, integrated economic area will foster investment, bypass some of the wasteful closets of government corruption, open up new markets, and stimulate technological diffusion. Furthermore, one-sided dependency will be more difficult to operate under the complexity created by the new regional economy. The feasibility of NAFTA will, however, depend on the capacity of Mexico to democratize the state and to redistribute wealth among the population at large.

The second process is the project of economic restructuring and social reform undertaken by President Cardoso in Brazil in 1995. Brazil is the economic and technological powerhouse of Latin America, and the tenth largest economy in the world. But it is also one of the most unequal countries on the planet, and a giant weakened by the illiteracy and lack of education of a substantial proportion of its population.[154] With labor aristocracy and populist politicians blocking the reforms, and business elites entrenched in a tradition of claiming government subsidies and illegally exporting profits, the chances of success are uncertain. However, if by the beginning of the twenty-first century Brazil has proceeded with the technological overhauling of its productive structure, with some improvement in income distribution and with a large-scale program of public investment in education and health it could become a substantial component of the global economy and carry along the development path much of Latin America. Yet neither in Brazil or Mexico will

[154] SEADE (1995); *Economist* (1995c).

a successful incorporation in the new, informational economy guarantee the integration of their people, many of whom could become, as my co-author Fernando Henrique Cardoso, in his former incarnation, wrote in 1992, "not even considered worth the trouble of exploitation; they will become inconsequential, of no interest to the developing globalized economy."[155]

The dynamics of exclusion from the new global economy: Africa's fate?

The dynamics of social exclusion of a significant proportion of the population as a result of new forms of inclusion of countries in the global economy operates on a larger scale in the case of Africa.[156] Because of the importance of the matter, both in human terms and for understanding the uneven logic of the new economy, I shall analyze this process in some detail in another volume, in what I consider to be one of the most relevant chapters in this book (see "The rise of the Fourth World" in volume III). Yet it is necessary to include an overview of Africa's recent economic evolution for any understanding of the new global economy. It is precisely the feature of this new economy: that it affects the whole planet either by inclusion or exclusion in the processes of production, circulation, and consumption, that have become at the same time globalized and informationalized.

Thus, the exhaustion of the model of primary-commodity production, due to the deterioration in the terms of trade, led most African countries, and particularly the countries of Sub-Saharan Africa, to virtual economic bankruptcy in the 1970s.[157] In 1970 the proportion of primary commodities in total exports was over 52% for Sub-Saharan Africa and over 70% for Northern Africa. Worldwide restructuring, based on manufacturing trade and foreign direct investment, during the 1970s made increasingly difficult the continuation of the traditional trade model on which most African economies operated. African governments, as in the case of Latin America, tried a conversion to industrialization and commercially oriented agriculture, and to do so, they borrowed heavily from the lending-happy international banks.[158] But the conditions of competitiveness in the new informational, global economy were too far away

[155]   Cardoso (1993: 156).
[156]   CEPII (1992); Lachaud (1994); Sandbrook (1985); Illiffe (1987); Ungar (1985); Jamal (1995).
[157]   Leys (1987, 1994); Ghai and Rodwan (eds) (1983).
[158]   Brown (1992).

from what could be accomplished in the short term by rather primitive economies that were by and large still committed to the trade channels of the old and new (USSR) colonial powers. When the oil shock of 1979 and the rise in interest rates provoked their financial bankruptcy, most African economies came under the direct control of policies of international financial institutions that imposed liberalization measures supposedly aimed at generating trade and investment. The fragile African economies did not resist the shock. Even the jewel of the former French colonial crown, the Ivory Coast, sank into economic disintegration:[159] after having grown at a hefty 6.6% per year in the 1970s, it turned into negative growth (annual average rate of –0.5%) in 1980–91; in fact, on a per capita basis, its GDP regressed at a rate of –4.6% per year during the 1980s. The competitive position of African countries in international trade was not brilliant in the 1960s, but deteriorated dramatically after the intervention of international financial institutions in African economic policies (see appendix to this chapter): the share of Sub-Saharan Africa in world trade of manufactured goods in 1970 was just 1.2%, but it went down to 0.5% in 1980, and to 0.4% in 1989.[160] Furthermore, the primary commodities trade also collapsed: from 7.2% of world trade of primary goods in 1970, it went down to 5.5% in 1980, and to 3.7% in 1989. Furthermore, the damage done to the agricultural production of Africa was even greater than the data show. While liberalization policies were not able to attract investment or improve competitiveness, what they did was to destroy large sectors of agricultural production for local markets, and in some cases, subsistence agriculture.[161] As a result, African countries were left without defense against the impact of bad harvests. When drought struck in Central and Eastern Africa, widespread famine followed (the Sahel, Ethiopia, Sudan), aggravated by civil wars and banditry induced by the heritage of surrogate military confrontation between the superpowers (Ethiopia, Somalia, Angola, Mozambique). Because states, as intermediaries between their countries and the meager resources transferred from abroad, were the main source of income, control of the state became a matter of survival.[162] And because tribal and ethnic networks were the safest bet for people's support, the fight to control the state (often equated to control of the military) was organized around ethnic cleavages, reviving centuries-old hatred and prejudice:

[159]   Glewwe and de Tray (1988).
[160]   CEPII (1992).
[161]   Durufle (1988); African Development Bank (1990).
[162]   Bayart (1992); Rothchild and Chazan (eds) (1988); Wilson (1991); Davidson (1992); Leys (1994).

genocidal tendencies and widespread banditry are rooted in the political economy of Africa's disconnection from the new, global economy.

North African economies, because of their proximity to Europe geographically, demographically, and economically, did not suffer as much as the rest of Africa during the restructuring process. They found new forms of insertion in the European economy through the export of workers (remittances from emigrants is one of the most important items in their balance of payments),[163] and the beginning of a strategy of exporting low-priced manufactured goods, particularly Morocco (4.2% annual growth of manufacturing production in the 1980s). Still, the Soviet-style industrialization process of Algeria collapsed because of the limits of the domestic market, Egypt saw its 1970s strong growth halved during the 1980s, and Tunisia (the modernized example of the region in the eyes of international institutions) grew at a meager 1.1% per capita annual GDP in 1980–91. In the 1990s, widespread poverty and mechanisms of social exclusion were prevailing in much of the Maghreb and the Machreq.[164]

Overall, the systematic logic of the new global economy does not have much of a role for the majority of the African population in the newest international division of labor. Most primary commodities are useless or low priced, markets are too narrow, investment too risky, labor not skilled enough, communication and telecommunication infrastructure clearly inadequate, politics too unpredictable, and government bureaucracies inefficiently corrupt (since no official international criticism has been heard about other bureaucracies equally corrupt but still efficient, for example, in South Korea until the presidency of Kim Young Sam). Under such conditions, the only real concern of the "North" (particularly of Western Europe) was the fear of being invaded by millions of uprooted peasants and workers unable to survive in their own countries. This is why international aid was channeled to African countries in the hope of still taking advantage of some valuable natural resources and with the purpose of preventing massive famines that could trigger large-scale migrations. Yet what can be said of the experience of the transition of Africa into the new global economy is that *structural irrelevance* (from the systems point of view) is a more threatening condition than dependency. Such structural irrelevance was revealed when policies of adjustment were imposed on Africa during the 1980s, in the wake of the debt crisis, applying abstract formulae to specific historical conditions: under the dominance of free market conditions, internationally and

---

[163]   Choucri (1986).
[164]   Bedoui (1995).

domestically, most of Africa ceased to exist as an economically viable entity in the informational/global economy.

This is why the most hopeful prospects for future development in Africa come from the potential role that could be played by the new, democratic, black-majority South Africa, with strong economic and technological linkages to the global economy. The stability and prosperity of South Africa, and its willingness and capacity to lead its neighbors as *primus inter pares*, offers the best chance to avoid the human holocaust that threatens Africa, and through Africa, the sense of humanity in all of us.

The last frontier of the global economy: the segmented incorporation of Russia and the ex-Soviet republics

The restructuring of the international economy has been further complicated by the disintegration of the Soviet Empire, and by the eventual incorporation of the broken pieces of former command economies into the global market economy. The collapse of communism and of the Soviet Union are major historical events that I consider to be directly related to the structural difficulties of the statist mode of production in making the transition to the informational mode of development (see volume III). But whatever the origins of such a phenomenon, the integration of resulting economic ruins into the global economy is the last frontier for the expansion of capitalism. These economies can hardly survive without linkages to the world system of circulation of capital, commodities, and technology. Indeed, their transition to the market economies, operated with the support (but not much help) from advanced capitalist countries and international financial institutions, means primarily the implementation of macroeconomic policies enabling foreign capital and foreign trade to operate in the ex-command economies. The sheer size of these economies, their educated population, their strong scientific basis, and their immense reserves of energy and natural resources will substantially impact the world's economic system. In the long term, a critical contribution of this area to the global economy could be to add a dynamic market of 400 million consumers, thus providing outlets for the excess capacity being accumulated in the high-technology productive structures of the West, particularly in Western Europe. However, such a long-term view would require a process of economic growth to make these consumers solvent enough to pay for their consumption, on a scale large enough to make the market significant. Yet, since the late 1980s, ex-command economies are posting negative growth rates, and the estimate is that, in the best though unlikely scenarios, they could only recover their modest standards of living of 1980 by the year 2000.[165] In fact, it appears that for Russia and the ex-Soviet republics economic deterioration could continue well into the twenty-first century.[166] Thus, the process of incorporation of the ex-Soviet Empire into the global economy is highly complex, and requires careful consideration. While not being able fully to address the issue within the limits of this chapter, I shall briefly sketch what seem to be the main trends developing in the 1990s.[167]

Eastern European countries are being annexed, by bits and pieces, into the European Union area of influence, particularly through German investment and trade (see "The unification of Europe" in volume III). The Baltic states are developing a close relationship to Scandinavian countries, and their small size and high level of education could make them potential subcontracting sites for Western European high-technology industries, in addition to their current role as import–export platforms for Russian trade. As for the other ex-Soviet republics, and particularly for Ukraine, their form of incorporation in the global economy will largely follow the path of the new, capitalist Russia.

Western fears and hopes about the immediate economic impact of post-Soviet Russia never materialized. The 25 million Russians who, according to a report for the Commission of the European Union, were supposed to invade Europe after the collapse of their economy and the granting of freedom to travel abroad, stayed home. Emigration was by and large limited to Jewish people (but much less than anticipated), and to hundreds of thousands, not millions (through 1995), mainly scientists and skilled professionals. Total direct foreign investment in 1990–4 posted a modest total of US$5 billion or $3 billion, depending upon estimates. This figure may be

---

[165] CEPII (1992).

[166] Khanin (1994).

[167] This section is mainly based on my ongoing field-work research on the crisis of the Soviet Union and the process of social transformation in Russia, from 1989 to the present. Specifically, more recent information comes from field-work and interviews conducted, jointly with Emma Kiselyova, in June and July 1995 in Khabarovsk, Sakhalin, Novosibirsk, and Moscow. Key ideas and information were obtained from interviews and conversations with several leading economists of the Russian Academy of Sciences, including Valery Kuleshov, Gregory Khanin, Galina Kovalyova, and Valery Kryukov from the Novosibirsk's Institute of Economics and Industrial Engineering, and Alexander Granberg, director of SOPS Institute in Moscow. Naturally, the responsibility for the analysis presented here is exclusively mine, since I have interpreted in my own terms the substance of our conversations. For a different view on Russian economic transition, seen from an informed, orthodox economic perspective, see Aslund (1995).

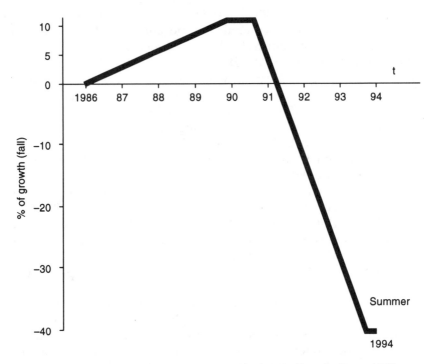

Figure 2.8   Changes in industrial production in Russia from 1986 to
second half 1994 (approximate scale)
Base level for comparison: early 1970s.
Source: Kuleshov (1994).

compared to the $26 billion of foreign investment in China just in
1993, or to $63 billion of foreign investment in Mexico in 1990–2.
Foreign trade shrank in 1991–3 (exports were in 1993 at 86% of their
1991 level, and imports went down to 61% of the 1991 level),
although both exports and imports increased in 1994 (increase of
9.1% in exports, and 5.1% in imports over 1993 by November 1994),
and were on their way to similar increases in 1995 at the time of writing. Yet the one fulfilled prediction was that of fast
internationalization of the Russian economy: in November 1994,
exports represented about 25% of Russian GDP and imports about
17%, thus making the proportion of the external sector over GDP
about twice as high as in the US.[168]

---

[168]   Source: data from various Russian sources, compiled and cited by Kur'yerov
(1994, 1995a, 1995b). See also Economist Intelligence Unit (1995).

The reason for such an apparent paradox (fast internationalization of the economy in spite of declining exports and imports and meager foreign investment) is sadly simple: the collapse of the Russian economy, with stunning negative rates in GDP growth (see figure 2.8).[169] Thus, GDP fell by 29% in 1992/1991, and by 12% in 1993/92. Material production fell by 63% between 1989 and 1993. Total investment in the economy fell by 15% in 1991, by 40% in 1992, and by 16% in 1993. Fall in investment was much greater in manufacturing, so that by 1994 it was estimated that 60% of industrial machinery was used up since, according to a survey, in 1993 only a quarter of company managers were ready to invest in new equipment. In agriculture, investment fell by a factor of 7 between 1991 and 1993. The overall rate of accumulation in the economy (*dolya nakopleniya osnovnykh fondov*) decreased by 33.8% in 1989, by 32% in 1992, and by 25.8% in 1993.[170] In spite of official optimism in 1995, independent academic economists reported the continuation of the decline in production in agriculture and the construction industry.[171] Additional manufacturing decline was considered likely because of lack of markets, obsolescence of equipment, and the high level of indebtedness of most enterprises.[172] By the mid-1990s the military-industrial sector, the heart of Soviet industry, was essentially wrecked; science and technology institutions were in shambles; production of oil and gas in some important areas, particularly in Tyumen, was disorganized and still declining; and transportation and telecommunications infrastructures were in desperate need of equipment and repairs.[173] As for the country's financial situation, Russian foreign debt in 1993 represented 64% of Russian GDP and 262% of annual exports. It was projected to reach US$130 billion by the end of 1995.[174]

Thus, it is because the Russian economy as a whole is in a process of disintegration and decline that its external sector becomes a relatively bright spot. The small segments of the economy that link up with global processes and markets are the most dynamic and those which feed the wealth being accumulated in an equally small segment of the

---

[169] Kuleshov (1994). Figure 2.8 is elaborated by Kuleshov on a different statistical basis than that of Kur'yerov data cited in the text. However, both sources, and both authors, converge in assessing a steep decline of Russian production since during the first half of the 1990s.

[170] Kur'yerov (1994).

[171] Professor Valery Kuleshov, interview, Novosibirsk, July 1995.

[172] Professor Gregory Khanin, interview, Novosibirsk, July 1995.

[173] Castells and Natalushko (1993); Natalushko, personal communication, Moscow, July 1995; Schweitzer (1995); Kryukov (1994).

[174] Kur'yerov (1994).

Table 2.11 Foreign trade of Russia (including trade with CIS countries), 1995

	Volume[b]	Value (US$ m)	% of level in same period of 1994[a]
Exports of principal goods, January–June 1995			
Crude oil (million tons)	58.9	6,259	99
Oil products (million tons)	19.4	1,939	92
Natural gas (billion m³)	98.4	6,625	105
Coal	12.4	404	121
Coke	527	27.6	73
Iron ores & concentrates	6,965	129	118
Cast iron	1,307	162	73
Ferro-alloys	197	191	76
Copper	187	457	147
Aluminium unprocessed	986	1,430	88
Nickel	60.7	515	137
Round timber (thousand m³)	6,841	457	101
Saw-timber (thousand m³)	1,839	284	73
Plywood (thousand m³)	287	82.5	88
Cellulose	631	439	154
Newsprint	488	242	161
Ammonia	1,880	230	97
Methanol	491	160	86
Nitrogen fertilizers	3,714	420	111
Potash fertilizers	2,379	165	149
Rubber synthetic	191	219	122
Fish frozen	588	486	88
Machinery, equipment	—	1,756	82
Imports of principal goods January–May 1995			
Grain	—	151	55
Sugar, incl. raw sugar	1,027	422	109
Meat frozen	321	455	127
Chicken frozen	262	224	147
Butter	126	223	135
Sunflower oil	111	107	336
Citrus fruits	281	155	84
Coffee	10.8	53.4	92
Tea	—	133	123
Medicines	—	386	86
Clothing, knitted and textile	—	269	62
Leather shoes (million pairs)	12.1	88.1	64
Non-ferrous metals	—	234	85
Pipes	455	243	85
Machinery and equipment	—	6,111	137

[a] Comparison refers to volume except when no data are available; otherwise, to value.
[b] Volume is in thousands of tons unless otherwise stated.
Source: Kur'yerov (1995b).

population, formed by *nomenklatura* leaders turned capitalists, mafia-related businesses, new daring entrepreneurs, and a growing group of young professionals with the skills to operate the connection between Russia and the global economy.

Thus, after years of decline, exports are on the rise, but they are increasingly concentrated in the fuel and energy sector (accounting for about 50% of total exports), natural resources, and raw materials[175] (see table 2.11). Share of machinery and equipment in exports, already at a low 6.7% of total in 1993, fell even further, to 5.2% in 1994. As a result, Russia has become increasingly dependent on Siberia and the Far East: almost two-thirds of its exports originate in this area. As for the structure of imports, it also displays the trends of a deteriorating economy increasingly oriented towards its survival: in 1994 the share of machinery imports went down from 33% to 30%, while the share of food imports (in spite of a good harvest) increased from 23% to 33%. Imports of poultry from America, including the famous "Bush's legs,"[176] accounted for a substantial proportion of food imports.

The other major linkage developing between the global economy and the Russian economy is portfolio investment by foreign capital. Indeed, foreign capital is considered to account for about 80% of transactions on the Russian stock exchange. The main reason for such interest is that Russian companies' shares were hugely undervalued during the phase of accelerated privatization accomplished by the Russian Government in 1992–5.[177] According to some sources, through 1994 about $11 billion have been committed (though not invested as yet) in shares of companies in sectors such as oil and gas, electronics and telecommunications, leisure and hotels, transportation equipment and shipping, and real estate. These investments not only may pay off in the future, when and if a giant Russian market economy starts working, but they have already revalued the acquired assets by three to ten times.[178] A case in point is Gazprom, the giant gas consortium, managing 40% of the world's natural gas reserves, privatized, but still under control of Russian state holdings. In 1994,

---

[175]   Kovalyova (1995); Kur'yerov (1995a and b); Castells, Granberg and Kiselyova (1996a, in progress).

[176] In the early 1990s, as an expression of American support, President Bush stepped up subsidized exports of frozen food and poultry to Russia. Thus, in many Russian homes, the only meat seen for months were chicken drumsticks, quickly named by people "Bush's legs," in fact a sign of appreciation, with a little ironic twist. In 1995, the Russian government argued that some of their poultry imports presented a health risk.

[177]   Denisova (1995); Stevenson (1994).

[178]   *Economist* (1994b); Denisova (1995).

the stock market valued its reserves at three-tenths of $1 per barrel of oil equivalent, compared with $10.30 for British Gas:[179] whoever bought its shares is sure to make a hefty profit in not such a long time. Thus, most of this portfolio investment aims more at financial speculation than at reconstructing the Russian economy. Russian interests, and particularly company managers and government *apparatchiki* who presided over the privatization process, kept the most valuable property under their control, yet devalued stocks of privatized companies in order to offer substantial profits to foreign partners in exchange for instant cash, most often kept in bank accounts abroad.

Foreign direct investment in production is proceeding with extraordinary precautions in the situation of legal uncertainty, bureaucratic arbitrariness, and safety concerns that characterize Russia's wild capitalism. Even in the potentially profitable oil and gas sector, prudence is the rule. Our own research on investment by American and Japanese companies in the most promising offshore oil and gas drilling in Sakhalin[180] shows that, while substantial investment could come from these companies (about $25 billion in 20 years), firm commitments await the final passage of special legislation that would guarantee entire freedom of movement for capital and management of production to foreign companies. In contrast, huge gas reserves in Western Siberia appear to be less attractive to foreign direct investment because of the need to rely on Russian controls for production and transportation of gas. In other words: foreign capital approaches to Russia aim at taking advantage of energy and natural resources, as well as of good financial deals, while being as little involved as possible in the Russian economy and setting up its own operating infrastructure. On the other hand, Russian government and Russian business strategy seems to be to attract foreign capital to prepackaged deals, without relinquishing control except when there is no alternative (for example, lack of technology and equipment for offshore drilling).

Yet understanding the dynamics of Russian transition to the market economy, including its connection to the global economy, lies in what is fundamentally at stake in this transition: primitive accumulation of capital on a gigantic scale. Or, in less analytical terms, the pillage of Russia's wealth, as the old class of *apparatchiki* strives to become fully fledged partners of global capitalism, sometimes by using unruly methods. Indeed, a non-negligible fraction of new business elites are sometimes connected to various criminal economy networks,

[179]   Stevenson (1994).
[180]   Castells, Granberg, and Kiselyova (1996a, in progress).

probably the most internationalized sector of the Russian economy. Iurii Sukhotin, using several sources, estimated that in 1992 criminal business income in Russia accounted for about 14.5% of Russian GDP. Since then, the proportion has probably increased.[181] While the process of primitive accumulation goes on, and as long as the struggle continues between different groups and persons to appropriate individually what was state property through a largely biased privatization process blessed by the world's financial institutions, nothing can be settled, investment can hardly proceed, and the real economy continues to decline. Indeed, survival mechanisms and petty commodity trade are the staple of daily life for most Russian people. The quasi-informal kiosk economy as the basis for trade, and cultivation at dachas for self-subsistence are the real pillars of Russia's transition to the market economy.[182] Limited linkages to the international economy, overwhelmingly concentrated in Moscow and St Petersburg and connected to a few nodes from Nizhni-Novgorod to Khabarovsk, through Yekaterinburg, Tomsk, and Novosibirsk, constitute the dynamic pole of the new economy, making a few hundred millionaires (in dollars) and a few thousand billionaires (in rubles) as the living proof of success on the wildest capitalist frontier.

In the mean time, living standards for the large majority of the population continue to decline, and, together with a catastrophic environmental heritage, have prompted the spectacular rise of mortality rates in Russia, reversing for the first time a worldwide historical trend towards increasing life expectancy.[183] There is a growing polarization between small segments of Russia that are being fully globalized and the majority of people who are being drawn into an increasingly primitive, local economy, often submitted to racketeering and violence. Such a tendency may trigger unpredictable social responses and help the political chances of a populist, ultra-nationalist movement. In 1995, a celebrated joke in Russian intellectual circles attributed *perestroyka* to a genial design by Andropov to relegitimize communism among the Russian people after a few years of experiencing capitalism. I doubt memories are so

---

[181]   Handelman (1995); Voshchanov (1995); *Commersant Weekly* (1995); Sukhotin (1994).

[182]   Kuleshov (1994).

[183]   Male life expectancy in Russia in 1990 was 64 years, compared with 72 years for American men. But it dropped further to 57 years in 1994, putting Russia at a lower level than Egypt or Bolivia. Infant mortality rate increased by 15% per year in 1992–4. In 1994, the death rate in Russia reached 15.6 per 1,000 people, an increase of about 30% since 1992 (death rate in the US was 9 per 1,000). See Specter (1995).

short in Russia. However, I do not think either that the social segmentation and social exclusion implicit in the logic of the new global economy can proceed further in Russia without being challenged.

In April 1992 the Advisory Committee to the Russian Government on the Social Problems of the Transition, which I chaired, delivered a confidential report to the Acting Prime Minister and Deputy Prime Ministers,[184] in which we wrote:

> A market economy does not operate outside of an institutional context. The key task for the Reform Movement in Russia today is to build the institutional context in order to create the conditions necessary for a market economy. Without such structures the market economy cannot develop beyond petty speculation and one shot looting. That is to say, a functioning, or productive market economy is fundamentally different from the simple task of transferring assets from the state and the old nomenklatura to their successors. . . . This social, political, and institutional infrastructure includes many elements, such as: laws, rules, codes, and procedures for resolving conflicts, for determining responsibility, for defining property, for defining and bounding property rights. [It is also necessary] to generate quickly a widespread conviction that those rules are indeed the rules governing economic life, and not just pieces of paper. For that to happen, a functioning public administration is needed. The market is not a substitute for the state: it is a complement. Without it the market cannot work.

The report was praised by the then Russian leaders, yet was not very influential in policy-making. A few months later, our duly warned interlocutors, Gaidar and Burbulis, were evicted from the government. A year later, tanks were necessary to promulgate a new constitution. Two years later, Zhirinovsky and the communists scored

---

[184] In January 1992, the Prime Minister's Office of the first democratic government of post-Soviet Russia asked me to organize an international advisory committee of leading social scientists to help the Russian Government to manage social problems during the transition period. I accepted the task, and a Committee comprising Fernando Henrique Cardoso, Martin Carnoy, Stephen S. Cohen, Alain Touraine, and me went to work on the matter. During 1992 we/I had several meetings with Russian leaders in Moscow (including a closed-door, two full days meeting of the whole committee with Gaidar, Burbulis, Shokhin, and their staff in March 1992). We wrote a report, and several working notes, all confidential, although I decided that the short paragraph quoted in this book does not compromise international security. For press reports on the activities of this Committee, which faded away by the end of 1992 after Gaidar's resignation, see *Izvestia*, 1 April 1992: 2, and 9 July 1992: 1.

major wins in parliamentary elections. Three years later, in 1995, the communists won in the parliamentary elections. In 1994, an in-depth assessment of the Russian economy published in *EKO*, the prestigious economics journal of the Siberian Academy of Sciences, concluded that

> there is an obvious and evidently final failure of government's economic policy, with its one-sided accent on financial stabiliz-ation, with disregard of interests of material production, with an excessively simplified, and politicized approach to problems of market development, and with its primitive understanding of role and functions of the state in the market economy.[185]

Yet the apparent inattention to obvious warnings can be easily explained in terms of social interests served by this economic policy. The segmented incorporation of Russia to the global economy, a fundamental matter for the future structure and dynamics of this economy, is taking place not according to the a-historical logic of markets, but to historically determined processes that, as in the origins of capitalism in other latitudes, were motivated by greed and imposed by force.

The Architecture and Geometry of the Informational/Global Economy

I can now sum up the structure and dynamics of the new global economy emerging from the historical interaction between the rise of informationalism and capitalist restructuring.

The structure of this economy is characterized by the combination of an enduring architecture and a variable geometry. The architecture of the global economy features an asymmetrically interdependent world, organized around three major economic regions and increas-ingly polarized along an axis of opposition between productive, information-rich, affluent areas, and impoverished areas, economi-cally devalued and socially excluded. Between the three dominant regions, Europe, North America, and the Asian Pacific, the latter appears to be the most dynamic yet the most vulnerable because of its dependence upon the openness of the markets of the other regions. However, the intertwining of economic processes between the three regions makes them practically inseparable in their fate. Around each region an economic hinterland has been created, with some countries

---

[185] Kur'yerov (1994: 7, translation by E. Kiselyova). For an alternative view on the Russian economic record, with which I disagree, see the informed book by Aslund (1995).

being gradually incorporated into the global economy, usually through the dominant regions that are their geographic neighbors: North America for Latin America; the European Union for Eastern Europe, Russia, and the South Mediterranean; Japan and the Asian Pacific for the rest of Asia, as well as for Australia and New Zealand, and maybe for the Russian Pacific, Eastern Siberia and Kazakhstan; Africa, while still dependent on ex-colonial economic networks, seems to be increasingly marginalized in the global economy; the Middle East is, by and large, integrated into the global networks of finance and energy supply, although highly dependent on the avatars of the world's geopolitics.

To be sure, there is nothing automatic in the emergence of such a world economic order: Russia is likely to emerge as a power on its own and could link up with Japan, providing much-needed energy and natural resources, once Japanese nationalism is ready to settle the Kuriles dispute; Kazakhstan has strong connections with American oil companies, and with South Korean *chaebol*; MERCOSUR[186] exports more to Europe than to North America, and Chilean markets are increasingly in the Asian Pacific; China is linking up with the ethnic Chinese networks in the Pacific rather than with Japan, most likely constituting in the future a formidable, economic subregion with more capital and labor than the Japanese-centered area; South Korea is not, by any means, an appendage of Japan, and is becoming a major world player in high-technology industries. The "South" is increasingly differentiated internally, and some of its fragments are being incorporated into the "North" over time; for example, Indonesia is being drawn into the dynamic waters of the Asian Pacific economy, both through Japanese and through ethnic Chinese investments. Even Africa is not necessarily sentenced to poverty: as mentioned above, the new democratic, black-majority-ruled South Africa could be the industrial, financial, and technological magnet of the Southern African subcontinent, maybe linking up with Angola, Namibia, Mozambique, Botswana, and Zimbabwe to form a viable subregional entity. Yet, in spite of all the complexity of this pattern, there is a basic architecture, inherited from history, that frames the development of the global economy.

However, this is not the whole story. Within this visible architecture there are dynamic processes of competition and change that infuse a variable geometry into the global system of economic processes.

---

[186] MERCOSUR is the trade association between Brazil, Argentina, Uruguay, and Paraguay, that represents the embryo of a future South American Common Market. In 1995, the largest share of MERCOSUR exports went to the European Union.

Indeed, the evolution that I have recalled somewhat schematically in the preceding pages shows the emergence of a new pattern of international division of labor, characteristic of the global economy. What I call the newest international division of labor is constructed around four different positions in the informational/global economy: the producers of high value, based on informational labor; the producers of high volume, based on lower-cost labor; the producers of raw materials, based on natural endowments; and the redundant producers, reduced to devalued labor. The differential location of such different types of labor also determines the affluence of markets, since income generation will depend upon the capacity to create value incorporated in each segment of the global economy. The critical matter is that these different positions do not coincide with countries. *They are organized in networks and flows, using the technological infrastructure of the informational economy.* They feature geographic concentrations in some areas of the planet, so that the global economy is not geographically undifferentiated. Yet the newest international division of labor does not take place between countries but between economic agents placed in the four positions I have indicated along a global structure of networks and flows. In this sense, all countries are penetrated by the four positions indicated because all networks are global in their reality or in their target. Even marginalized economies have a small segment of their directional functions connected to the high-value producers network, at least to ensure the transfer of whatever capital or information is still accumulated in the country. And certainly, the most powerful economies have marginal segments of their population placed in a position of devalued labor, be it in New York,[187] in Osaka,[188] in London,[189] or in Madrid.[190]

Because the position in the international division of labor does not depend, fundamentally, on the characteristics of the country but on the characteristics of its labor (including embodied knowledge) and of its insertion into the global economy, changes may occur, and indeed do, in a short time span. Actions by governments and by entrepreneurial sectors of societies are critical in this matter. The newest international division of labor is organized on the basis of labor and technology, but is enacted and modified by governments and entrepreneurs. The relentlessly variable geometry that results from such processes of innovation and competition struggles with the historically produced architecture of the world economic order, inducing the creative chaos that characterizes the new economy.

[187] Mollenkopf and Castells (eds) (1991).
[188] Sugihara et al. (1988).
[189] Lee and Townsend (1993).
[190] Leal (1993).

Appendix: Some methodological comments on adjustment policies in Africa and their evaluation

In 1993, the World Bank's Development Vice-Presidency conducted a study aimed at responding to criticisms of its adjustment policies in Africa. Indeed the record, in the words of the World's Bank Development Vice-President and Chief Economist "raised troubling questions about the extent and efficacy of the policy reform efforts" (World Bank 1994a xi). The study, published in 1994, intended to provide evidence on the economic benefits of adjustment policies recommended by the Bank. It received wide publicity in the media, as well as in development forums, as proof of the rightful attitude of international institutions in advocating macroeconomic adjustment policies in spite of the social and political costs of such policies. Because of the relevance of this matter, and of this report, to the debate on development and underdevelopment in the new global economy, I believe it can be helpful to challenge the empirical evidence presented in it, at the price of going into some petty details concerning the use of statistics in justifying failed policies. Within the limits of this note, I shall simply point to faulty procedures, inviting the reader to judge by checking the report. To simplify the matter, I am not introducing different data sources, but taking at face value (a nonobvious approach) data as presented.

In a nutshell, the procedure followed by the authors of the report was to classify 26 Sub-Saharan countries according to their good or bad behavior on macroeconomic policies into three groups: large improvement in macroeconomic policies, small improvement, and deterioration. The terminology of course suggests that economic improvement, measured by rates of variation in GDP per capita, would follow broadly within the same groupings. Then for each country and group of countries their percentage of average annual GDP growth is compared for two periods: 1981–6 (before adjustment policies) and 1987–91 (after adjustment policies). Although countries as a whole did not improve much (0.5 percentage points of difference between periods), the difference in percentage points by group shows that "good policy countries" fared somewhat better than "small improving policy countries" (median of 1.8 points difference versus 1.5), and much better than the "deteriorating policy countries" (median of –2.6) (see World Bank 1994a: 138, table 5.1).

I argue that the conclusion that "There are rewards to adjustment, as countries that have come further in implementing good policies –

particularly good macroeconomic policies – have enjoyed a resurgence of growth" (Vice-President's foreword, p. xi) is inaccurate and misleading as stated, and overall is based on a statistical artifact. It is inaccurate as stated because two out of the six "good policy countries," according to World Bank criteria, actually decreased their rate of growth between periods: Burkina Faso by 1.7 points, and The Gambia by 0.8 of a point. It is misleading because the highest performing country of all 26, Mozambique, which improved its growth rate by 7.6 points, is ranked deep down in the "bad policy countries" group of the report. It is also misleading because the three highest performers, Nigeria, Ghana, and Tanzania, improved their rate to a large extent because they were coming from substantially negative rates of growth in the preceding period (–4.6%, –2.4%, –1.7%), which was also the case for Mozambique. And it is a statistical artifact because the calculations by group (median and mean) are biased by groupings in widely different sizes for each group (six good policy countries, nine medium policy countries, and eleven bad policy countries).

It works like this: if you have 26 countries in a generally bad situation, and you group together eleven as "deteriorating" and six under "good policy," it will be more difficult for the eleven-member pool than for the six-member pool to show a good mean value, simply because more "low values" will go into the eleven member-pool by simple statistical probability.

Let us change the procedure, and group the countries by their actual performance in improving the growth rate. Let us now take the top one-third of the distribution, that is eight countries (cutting, by the natural break point of the curve, between 2.2 and 1.6). What kind of countries do we find in such a group of "economic performers"? Using World Bank categories: three "good policy countries" (Nigeria, Ghana, and Tanzania), three "small improvement" countries, and two "deterioration" countries (Mozambique and Sierra Leone, both among the top six). This is hardly the basis for a significant correlation, let alone for drawing conclusions about development policies. Indeed, if we rank 26 countries in two scales, one of improvement in GDP per capita, and another of obedience to adjustment policies, the two rankings differ considerably.

The report does calculate a linear regression between policy and GDP growth, which is shown to be significant, but only after controlling the equation to eliminate the effect of the growth rate before adjustment, since its authors acknowledge that countries which were doing particularly poorly are more likely to experience an improvement (p. 140), thus voiding of meaning such a calculation. If we eliminate from the "good six" group, countries that were doing badly in the first period (Nigeria, Ghana, and Tanzania), the whole group disappears since, as stated, the growth rate of two others in fact decreased, so that the only star, at the end, would be Zimbabwe, displaying a staggering performance from 0.3% growth to 1.0% growth.

In the final analysis, it is difficult to understand why the authors of the report go through all this pain to prove their point, gearing up to the ultimate policy goal of improving export performance as the development tool in the global economy, only to find in their regression analysis that "the terms-of-trade effect is not significant and generally has the wrong sign (improved terms of trade slows growth)" (p. 140). Never mind, the authors have an answer: "This result reflects the peculiarities of the short time period under study and should not be taken to contradict the well-established positive relation in the long run between growth and the terms of trade" (p. 140). But "the peculiarities of the short time period under study" do not deter the authors from taking less negative trends of growth as proof of goodness of adjustment policies. This is how decisions are taken, and legitimized *ex post*, in the wonderland of international financial institutions.

═ 3 ═

The Network Enterprise:
The Culture, Institutions, and
Organizations of the Informational
Economy

Introduction

The informational economy, as with all historically distinctive forms of production, is characterized by its specific culture and institutions. Yet culture, in this analytical framework, should not be considered as a set of values and beliefs linked to a particular society. What characterizes the development of the informational, global economy is precisely its emergence in very different cultural/national contexts: in North America, in Western Europe, in Japan, in the "China circle," in Russia, in Latin America, as well as its planetary reach, affecting all countries, and leading to a multi-cultural framework of reference. Indeed, the attempts to propose a theory of "cultural economics" to account for new development processes on the basis of philosophies and mentalities (such as Confucianism), particularly in the Asian Pacific,[1] have not resisted the scrutiny of empirical research.[2] But the diversity of cultural contexts where the informational economy emerges and evolves does not preclude the existence of a common matrix of organizational forms in the processes of production, consumption, and distribution. Without such organizational arrangements, neither technological change, state policies, nor firms' strategies would be able to come together in a new economic system. I contend, along with a growing number of scholars, that cultures manifest themselves fundamentally through their embeddedness in institutions and organizations.[3] By organizations I understand specific

---

[1]   Berger (1987); Berger and Hsiao (eds) (1988).
[2]   Hamilton and Biggart (1988); Biggart (1991); Clegg (1990); Whitley (1993); Janelli (1993).
[3]   Granovetter (1985); Clegg (1992); Evans (1995).

systems of means oriented to the performance of specific goals. By
institutions I understand organizations invested with the necessary
authority to perform some specific tasks on behalf of society as a
whole. The culture that matters for the constitution and development
of a given economic system is the one that materializes in organizational logics, using Nicole Biggart's concept: "By organizational logics
I mean a legitimating principle that is elaborated in an array of derivative social practices. In other words, organizational logics are the
ideational bases for institutionalized authority relations."[4]

My thesis is that the rise of the informational economy is characterized by the development of a new organizational logic which is
related to the current process of technological change, but not dependent upon it. It is the convergence and interaction between a new
technological paradigm and a new organizational logic that constitutes the historical foundation of the informational economy.
However, this organizational logic manifests itself under different
forms in various cultural and institutional contexts. Thus, in this
chapter I shall try to account at the same time for the commonality of
organizational arrangements in the informational economy, and for
their contextual variety. In addition, I shall examine the genesis of this
new organizational form and the conditions of its interaction with
the new technological paradigm.

Organizational Trajectories in the Restructuring of Capitalism and in the Transition from Industrialism to Informationalism

The economic restructuring of the 1980s induced a number of reorganizing strategies in business firms.[5] Some analysts, particularly Piore
and Sabel, argue that the economic crisis of the 1970s resulted from
the exhaustion of the mass-production system, constituting a "second
industrial divide" in the history of capitalism.[6] For others, such as
Harrison and Storper,[7] the diffusion of new organizational forms,
some of which had already been practiced in some countries or firms
for many years, was the response to the crisis of profitability in the
process of capital accumulation. Others, like Coriat[8] suggest a

---

[4] Biggart (1992: 49).
[5] Harrison (1994); Sengenberger and Campbell (eds) (1992); Williamson (1985).
[6] Piore and Sabel (1984).
[7] Harrison (1994).
[8] Coriat (1990).

long-term evolution from "Fordism" to "post-Fordism," as an expression of a "grand transition," the historical transformation of the relationships between, on the one hand, production and productivity, and on the other hand, consumption and competition. But in spite of the diversity of approaches there is coincidence in four fundamental points of the analysis:

(a) whichever the causes and the genesis of the organizational transformation, there was from the mid-1970s onwards a major divide (industrial or otherwise) in the organization of production and markets in the global economy;
(b) organizational changes interacted with the diffusion of information technology but by and large were independent, and in general preceded the diffusion of information technologies in business firms;
(c) the fundamental goal of organizational changes, in various forms, was to cope with the uncertainty caused by the fast pace of change in the economic, institutional, and technological environment of the firm by enhancing flexibility in production, management, and marketing;
(d) many organizational changes were aimed at redefining labor processes and employment practices, introducing the model of "lean production" with the objective of saving labor, by the automation of jobs, elimination of tasks, and suppression of managerial layers.

However, these sweeping interpretations of major organizational changes in the last two decades display an excessive tendency to merge in one single evolutionary trend various processes of change that are in fact different, albeit interrelated. In a parallel analysis to the notion of technological trajectories,[9] I propose to consider the development of different organizational trajectories, namely specific arrangements of systems of means oriented toward increasing productivity and competitiveness in the new technological paradigm and in the new global economy. In most cases, these trajectories evolved from industrial organizational forms, such as the vertically integrated corporation and the independent small business firm, that had become unable to perform their tasks under the new structural conditions of production and markets, a trend that became fully apparent in the crisis of the 1970s. In other cultural contexts, new organizational forms emerged from preexisting ones that had been pushed aside by the classical model of industrial·organization, to find

[9] Dosi (1988).

new life in the requirements of the new economy and in the possibilities offered by new technologies. Several organizational trends evolved from the process of capitalist restructuring and industrial transition. They must be considered separately before proposing their potential convergence in a new kind of organizational paradigm.

From mass production to flexible production

The first, and broader, trend of organizational evolution that has been identified, particularly in the pioneering work by Piore and Sabel, is the **transition from mass production to flexible production, or from "Fordism" to "post-Fordism"** in Coriat's formulation. The mass-production model was based on productivity gains obtained by economies of scale in an assembly-line-based, mechanized process of production of a standardized product, under the conditions of control of a large market by a *specific organizational form: the large corporation structured on the principles of vertical integration, and institutionalized social and technical division of labor.* These principles were embedded in the management methods known as "Taylorism" and "scientific organization of work," methods adopted as guidelines by both Henry Ford and Lenin.

When demand became unpredictable in quantity and quality, when markets were diversified worldwide and thereby difficult to control, and when the pace of technological change made obsolete single-purpose production equipment, the mass-production system became too rigid and too costly for the characteristics of the new economy. A tentative answer to overcome such rigidity was the flexible production system. It has been practiced and theorized in two different forms: first, as flexible specialization, in the formulation of Piore and Sabel, on the basis of the experience of the Northern Italian industrial districts, when "production accommodates to ceaseless change without pretending to control it"[10] in a pattern of industrial craft, or customized production. Similar practices have been observed by researchers in firms performing advanced services, such as banking.[11]

Yet industrial management practice in recent years has introduced another form of flexibility: dynamic flexibility in the formulation of Coriat, or high-volume flexible production in the formula proposed by Cohen and Zysman, also shown by Baran to characterize the transformation of the insurance industry.[12] High-volume flexible

---

[10]   Piore and Sabel (1984: 17).
[11]   Hirschhorn (1985); Bettinger (1991); Daniels (1993).
[12]   Coriat (1990: 165); Cohen and Zysman (1987); Baran (1985).

production systems, usually linked to a situation of growing demand for a given product, combine high-volume production, permitting economies of scale, and customized, reprogrammable production systems, capturing economies of scope. New technologies allow for the transformation of assembly lines characteristic of the large corporation into easy-to-program production units that can be sensitive to variations in the market (product flexibility) and in the changes of technological inputs (process flexibility).

Small business and the crisis of the large corporation: myth and reality

A second, distinct trend emphasized by analysts in recent years, is *the crisis of the large corporation, and the resilience of small and medium firms as agents of innovation and sources of job creation.*[13] For some observers, the crisis of the corporation is the necessary consequence of the crisis of standardized mass production, while the revival of customized, craft production and flexible specialization is better enacted by small businesses.[14] Bennett Harrison has written a devastating empirical critique of this thesis.[15] According to his analysis, based on data from the United States, Western Europe, and Japan, large corporations have continued to concentrate a growing proportion of capital and markets in all major economies; their share of employment has not changed in the last decade, except in the UK; small and medium firms remain by and large under the financial, commercial, and technological control of large corporations; he also contends that small businesses are less technologically advanced, and less able to innovate technologically in process and in product than larger firms. Furthermore, on the basis of the work of a number of Italian researchers (Bianchi and Belussi, particularly) he shows how the archetype of flexible specialization, the Italian firms in the industrial districts of Emilia Romagna during the early 1990s, went through a series of mergers, and either came under the control of large corporations or became large corporations themselves (for example, Benetton), or else were unable to keep up with the pace of competition if they remained small and fragmented, as in the Prato district.

Some of these statements are controversial. The work by other researchers points to somewhat different conclusions.[16] For instance,

---

[13]   Weiss (1988); Sengenberger et al. (eds) (1990); Clegg (1990).
[14]   Piore and Sabel (1984); Lorenz (1988); Birch (1987).
[15]   Harrison (1994).
[16]   Weiss (1988, 1992).

the study by Schiatarella on Italian small firms suggests that small businesses have outperformed large firms in job creation, profit margins, investment per capita, technological change, productivity, and value added. Friedman's study on Japanese industrial structure even pretends that it is precisely this dense network of small and medium subcontracting enterprises which lies at the root of Japanese competitiveness. Also the calculations by Michael Teitz and collaborators, years ago, on California's small businesses pointed at the enduring vitality and critical economic role of small businesses.[17]

In fact, we must separate the argument concerning the shift of economic power and technological capability from the large corporation to small firms (a trend that, as Harrison argues, does not seem to be supported by empirical evidence) from the argument referring to the decline of the large, vertically integrated corporation as an organizational model. Indeed, Piore and Sabel foresaw the possibility of survival of the corporate model through what they called "multinational Keynesianism," that is the expansion and conquest of world markets by corporate conglomerates, counting on growing demand from a rapidly industrializing world. But to do so, corporations did have to change their organizational structures. Some of the changes implied the growing use of subcontracting to small and medium businesses, whose vitality and flexibility allowed gains in productivity and efficiency for large corporations, as well as for the economy as a whole.[18]

Thus, at the same time, it is true that small and medium businesses appear to be forms of organization well adapted to the flexible production system of the informational economy, and it is also true that their renewed dynamism comes under the control of large corporations that remain at the center of the structure of economic power in the new global economy. We are not witnessing the demise of powerful, large corporations, but we are indeed observing the crisis of the traditional corporate model of organization based on vertical integration, and hierarchical, functional management: the "staff and line" system of strict technical and social division of labor within the firm.

[17]   Schiatarella (1984); Friedman (1988); Teitz et al. (1981).
[18]   Gereffi (1993).

"Toyotism": management–worker cooperation, multifunctional labor, total quality control, and reduction of uncertainty

A third development concerns *new methods of management*, most of them originating in Japanese firms,[19] although in some cases they were experimenting within other contexts, for example in Volvo's Kalmar complex in Sweden.[20] The substantial success in productivity and competitiveness obtained by Japanese automobile firms has been attributed to a large extent to this managerial revolution, so that in the business literature "Toyotism" is opposed to "Fordism" as the new winning formula adapted to the global economy and to the flexible production system.[21] The original Japanese model has been widely imitated by other companies, as well as transplanted by Japanese firms to their foreign locations, often leading to a substantial improvement in the performance of these firms *vis-à-vis* the traditional industrial system.[22] Some elements of this model are well known:[23] the *kan-ban* (or "just in time") system of supplies, by which inventories are eliminated or reduced substantially through delivery from the suppliers to the production site at the exact required time and with the characteristics specified for the production line; "total quality control" of products in the production process, aiming at near-zero defects and best use of resources; workers' involvement in the production process, by using team work, decentralized initiative, greater autonomy of decision on the shop floor, rewards for team performance, and a flat management hierarchy with few status symbols in the daily life of the firm.

Culture may have been important in generating "Toyotism" (particularly the consensus-building, cooperative model of team work) but it is certainly not a determinant for its implementation. The model works equally well in Japanese firms in Europe, and in the United States, and several of its elements have been successfully adopted by American (GM-Saturn) or German (Volkswagen) factories. Indeed, the model was perfected by Toyota engineers over a period of 20 years, after its first, limited introduction in 1948. To be able to generalize the method to the whole factory system, Japanese engineers studied the control procedures used in American supermarkets to assess stock on their shelves, so it could be argued that "just in time"

---

[19] Nonaka (1990); Coriat (1990); Durlabhji and Marks (eds) (1993).
[20] Sandkull (1992).
[21] Cusumano (1985); McMillan (1984).
[22] Wilkinson et al. (1992).
[23] Coriat (1990); Aoki (1988); Dohse et al. (1985).

is to some extent an American mass-production method, adapted to flexible management by using the specificity of Japanese firms, particularly the cooperative relationship between management and workers.

The stability and complementarity of relationships between the core firm and the suppliers' network are extremely important for the implementation of this model: Toyota maintains in Japan a three-tier network of suppliers embracing thousands of firms of different sizes.[24] Most of the markets for most of the firms are captive markets for Toyota, and the same can be said of other major firms. How different is this from the structure of divisions and departments in a vertically integrated corporation? Most of the key suppliers are in fact controlled or influenced by financial, commercial or technological undertakings, belonging either to the parent firm or to the overarching *keiretsu*. Under such conditions, are we not observing a system of planned production under the premise of relative market control by the large corporation? Thus, what is important in this model is the vertical disintegration of production along a network of firms, a process that substitutes for the vertical integration of departments within the same corporate structure. The network allows for greater differentiation of the labor and capital components of the production unit, and probably builds in greater incentives and stepped-up responsibility, without necessarily altering the pattern of concentration of industrial power and technological innovation.

The performance of the model relies also on the absence of major disruptions in the overall process of production and distribution. Or, to put it in other words, it is based on the assumption of the "five zeros": zero defect in the parts; zero mischief in the machines; zero inventory; zero delay; zero paperwork. Such performances can only be predicated on the basis of an absence of work stoppages and total control over labor, on entirely reliable suppliers, and on adequately predicted markets. **"Toyotism" is a management system designed to reduce uncertainty rather than to encourage adaptability.** The flexibility is in the process, not in the product. Thus, some analysts have suggested that it could be considered as an extension of "Fordism,"[25] keeping the same principles of mass production, yet organizing the production process on the basis of human initiative and feedback capacity to eliminate waste (of time, work, and resources) while maintaining the characteristics of output close to the business plan. Is this

---

[24]   Friedman (1988); Weiss (1992).
[25]   Tetsuro and Steven (eds) (1994).

really a management system well fitted to a global economy in constant swirl? Or, as Stephen Cohen likes to say, "Is it too late for 'just in time'?".

In fact, the truly distinctive character of Toyotism, as distinct from Fordism, does not concern relationships between firms, but between management and workers. As Coriat argued, in the international seminar convened in Tokyo to debate the question "Is Japanese Management Post-Fordism?," in fact, "it is neither pre- nor post-Fordist, but an original and new way of managing the labor process: the central and distinctive feature of the Japanese path was to de-specialize the professional workers and, instead of scattering them, to turn them into multi-functional specialists."[26] A distinguished Japanese economist, Aoki, also emphasizes labor organization as the key to the success of Japanese firms:

> The main difference between the American firm and the Japanese firm may be summarized as follows: the American firm emphasizes efficiency attained through fine specialization and sharp job demarcation, whereas the Japanese firm emphasizes the capability of the workers' group to cope with local emergencies autonomously, which is developed through learning by doing and sharing knowledge on the shopfloor.[27]

Indeed, some of the most important organizational mechanisms underlying productivity growth in Japanese firms seem to have been overlooked by Western experts of management. Thus, Ikujiro Nonaka,[28] on the basis of his studies of major Japanese companies, has proposed a simple, elegant model to account for the generation of knowledge in the firm. What he labels "the knowledge-creating company" is based on the organizational interaction between "explicit knowledge" and "tacit knowledge" at the source of innovation. He argues that much of the knowledge accumulated in the firm is made out of experience, and cannot be communicated by workers under excessively formalized management procedures. And yet the sources of innovation multiply when organizations are able to establish bridges to transfer tacit into explicit knowledge, explicit into tacit knowledge, tacit into tacit, and explicit into explicit. By so doing, not only is worker experience communicated and amplified to increase the formal body of knowledge in the company, but also knowledge generated in the outside world can be incorporated into the tacit

---

[26]   Coriat (1994: 182).
[27]   Aoki (1988: 16).
[28]   Nonaka (1991); Nonaka and Takeuchi (1994).

habits of workers, enabling them to work out their own uses and to improve on the standard procedures. In an economic system where innovation is critical, the organizational ability to increase its sources from all forms of knowledge becomes the foundation of the innovative firm. This organizational process, however, requires the full participation of workers in the innovation process, so that they do not keep their tacit knowledge solely for their own benefit. It also requires stability of the labor force in the company, because only then does it become rational for the individual to transfer his/her knowledge to the company, and for the company to diffuse explicit knowledge among its workers. Thus, this apparently simple mechanism, the dramatic effects of which in enhancing productivity and quality are shown in a number of case studies, in fact engages a profound transformation of management–labor relationships. Although information technology does not play a prominent role in Nonaka's "explicit analysis," in our personal conversations we shared the thought that on-line communication and computerized storage capacity have become powerful tools in developing the complexity of organizational links between tacit and explicit knowledge. Yet this form of innovation preceded the development of information technologies, and was, in fact, for the last two decades "tacit knowledge" of Japanese management, removed from the observation of foreign managerial experts, but truly decisive in improving performance of the Japanese firms.

Interfirm networking

Let us now turn to consider two other forms of organizational flexibility in the international experience, characterized by interfirm linkages. These are *the multidirectional network model enacted by small and medium businesses* and *the licensing–subcontracting model of production under an umbrella corporation.* I shall briefly describe these two distinct organizational models that have played a considerable role in the economic growth of several countries in the last two decades.

Small and medium enterprises, as I wrote, in concurrence with Bennett Harrison's argument, are often under the control of subcontracting arrangements or financial/technological domination from large corporations. Yet they also frequently take the initiative in establishing networking relationships with several large firms and/or with other small and medium enterprises, finding market niches and cooperative ventures. Besides the classical example of the Italian industrial districts, a good case in point is represented by Hong Kong's manufacturing firms. As I argued in my book on Hong Kong, on the basis of work by Victor Sit and other researchers of the Hong Kong scene,[29] its export success was based, for a long period between the late 1950s and the early 1980s, on domestic small businesses networks competing in the world economy. Over 85% of Hong Kong manufacturing exports up to the early 1980s originated from Chinese family-based firms, of which 41% were small enterprises employing fewer than 50 workers. In most cases they did not subcontract to larger firms, but exported through the network of Hong Kong's import–export firms – also small, also Chinese, and also family-based – that numbered 14,000 in the late 1970s. Networks of production and distribution formed, disappeared, and reformed on the basis of the variations in the world market, through the signals transmitted by flexible intermediaries often using a network of "commercial spies" in the main world markets. Very often the same person would be entrepreneur or salaried worker at different points in time, according to the circumstances of the business cycle and his own family needs.

Taiwan's exports during the 1960s came also mainly from a similar small and medium enterprise system, although in this case the traditional Japanese trading companies were the main intermediaries.[30] Granted, as Hong Kong prospered, many of the small enterprises merged, refinanced, and grew bigger, sometimes linking up with large department stores or manufacturers in Europe and America, to become their surrogate producers. Yet the, by then, medium-large businesses subcontracted much of their own production to firms (small, medium, and large) across the Chinese border in the Pearl River Delta. By the mid-1990s, somewhere between six and ten million workers, depending upon the estimates used, were involved in Guandong province in these subcontracting production networks.

Taiwanese companies took an even more complex circuit. In order to produce in China, taking advantage of low labor costs, social control, and China's export quotas, they set up intermediary firms in Hong Kong. These firms linked up with local governments in Guandong and Fujian provinces, setting up manufacturing subsidiaries in China.[31] These subsidiaries put out work to small shops and homes in the surrounding villages. The flexibility of such a system allowed it to capture cost advantages in different locations, to diffuse technology throughout the system, to benefit from various supports from various governments, and to use several countries as export platforms.

In a very different context, Ybarra found a similar networking

[29]   Castells et al. (1990); Sit et al. (1979); Sit and Wong (1988).
[30]   Gold (1986).
[31]   Hsing (1996).

production pattern among small and medium footwear, textile, and toy-making enterprises in the Valencia region of Spain.[32] There are numerous examples of such horizontal networks of enterprises in other countries and industries, as reported in the specialized literature.[33]

A different kind of production network is the one exemplified by the so-called "Benetton Model," the object of much commentary in the business world, as well as of some limited but revealing research, particularly that by Fiorenza Belussi and by Bennett Harrison.[34] The Italian knitwear firm, a multinational enterprise grown from a small family business in the Veneto region, operates on the basis of licensing commercial franchises, reaching about 5,000 stores in the whole world, for the exclusive distribution of its products under the strictest control of the core firm. On-line feedback is received by the center from all distribution points, triggering resupply of stock, as well as defining market trends in shapes and colors. The network model is also effective at the production level by putting out work to small firms and homes in Italy and other Mediterranean countries, such as Turkey. This type of network organization is an intermediate form of arrangement between vertical disintegration through the subcontracting arrangements of a large firm and the horizontal networks of small businesses. It is a horizontal network, but based on a set of core-periphery relationships, both on the supply and on the demand side of the process.

Similar forms of horizontal business networks integrated vertically by financial control have been shown to characterize direct sales operations in America, as researched by Nicole Biggart, and to inform the decentralized structure of many business consulting firms in France, organized under an umbrella of quality control.[35]

Corporate strategic alliances

A sixth organizational pattern emerging in recent years refers to *the intertwining of large corporations* in what has come to be known as strategic alliances.[36] Such alliances are very different from the traditional forms of cartels and other oligopolistic agreements, because they concern specific times, markets, products, and processes, and they do not exclude competition in all the areas (the majority)

---

[32] Ybarra (1989).
[33] Powell (1990).
[34] Belussi (1992); Harrison (1994).
[35] Biggart (1990b); Leo and Philippe (1989).
[36] Imai (1980); Gerlach (1992); Ernst (1995); Cohen and Borrus (1995b).

not covered by the agreements.[37] They have been particularly relevant in high-technology industries, as the cost of R&D has skyrocketed and access to privileged information has become increasingly difficult in an industry where innovation is the main competitive weapon.[38] Access to markets and capital resources is often exchanged for technology and manufacturing skills; in other cases joint efforts by two or more companies are undertaken to develop a new product or refine a new technology, often under the sponsorship of governments or public agencies. In Europe, the European Union has even forced companies from different countries to cooperate as a condition of receiving subsidies, as was the case with Philips, Thomson-SGS, and Siemens in the microelectronics JESSI program. Small and medium firms receive European Union and EUREKA program support for R&D on the basis of establishing joint ventures between firms of more than one country.[39] The structure of high-technology industries in the world is an increasingly complex web of alliances, agreements, and joint ventures in which most large corporations are interlinked. Such linkages do not preclude stepped-up competition. Rather, strategic alliances are decisive instruments in this competition, with today's partners becoming tomorrow's foes, while collaboration in a given market is in sharp contrast to the ferocious struggle for market share in another region of the world.[40] Furthermore, because large corporations are the tip of the pyramid of a vast network of subcontracting arrangements, their patterns of alliance and competition involve also their subcontractors. Often, practices such as securing supplies from subcontracting firms or barring access to a network are competitive weapons used by firms. Reciprocally, subcontractors use whatever margin of freedom they have to diversify their clients and hedge their bets, while absorbing technology and information for their own use. This is why proprietary information and technological copyright are so critical in the new global economy.

In sum, the large corporation in such an economy is not, and will no longer be, self-contained and self-sufficient. The arrogance of the IBMs, the Philips, or the Mitsuis of the world has become a matter of cultural history.[41] Their actual operations are conducted with other firms: not only with the hundreds or thousands of subcontracting and ancillary enterprises, but with the dozens of relatively equal partners

---

[37] Dunning (1993).
[38] Van Tulder and Junne (1988); Ernst and O'Connor (1992); Ernst (1995).
[39] Baranano (1994).
[40] Mowery (ed.) (1988).
[41] Bennett (1990).

with whom they cooperate and compete at the same time in this new brave economic world where friends and foes are the same.

The horizontal corporation and global business networks

The corporation itself has changed its organizational model, to adapt to the conditions of unpredictability ushered in by rapid economic and technological change.[42] *The main shift can be characterized as the shift from vertical bureaucracies to the horizontal corporation.* The horizontal corporation seems to be characterized by seven main trends: organization around process, not task; a flat hierarchy; team management; measuring performance by customer satisfaction; rewards based on team performance; maximization of contacts with suppliers and customers; information, training, and retraining of employees at all levels.[43] This transformation of the corporate model, particularly visible in the 1990s in some leading American companies (such as ATT), follows the realization of the limits of the "lean production" model attempted in the 1980s. This "lean model" (justifiably called by its critics "lean and mean") was fundamentally predicated on labor savings, by using a combination of automation, computerized worker control, "putting out" work, and retrenchment of production. In its most extreme manifestation, it created what has been labelled the "hollow corporation," that is a business specialized in intermediation between financing, production, and market sales, on the basis of an established trade mark or industrial image. A direct expression of capitalist restructuring to overcome the crisis of profitability of the 1970s, the "lean production" model reduced costs but also perpetuated obsolete organizational structures rooted in the logic of the mass-production model under the conditions of oligopolistic market control. To maneuver in the new global economy, characterized by an endless flurry of new competitors using new technologies and cost-cutting capabilities, the large corporations had to become primarily more effective rather than more thrifty. The networking strategies added flexibility to the system, but they did not solve the problem of adaptability for the corporation. To be able to internalize the benefits of network flexibility the corporation had to become a network itself and dynamize each element of its internal structure: this is in essence the meaning and the purpose of the "horizontal corporation" model, often extended in the decentralization of its units and in the growing autonomy given to each of these units, even allowing them

---

[42] Drucker (1988).
[43] *Business Week* (1993); *Business Week* (1995).

to compete against each other, albeit within a common overall strategy.[44]

Ken'ichi Imai is probably the organizational analyst who has gone the furthest in proposing and documenting the thesis of the transformation of corporations into networks.[45] On the basis of his studies of Japanese and American multinational corporations, he argues that the process of internationalization of business activity has proceeded along three different strategies for firms. The first, and most traditional, refers to a multidomestic market strategy for companies investing abroad from their national platform. The second targets the global market, and organizes different company functions in different locations, which are integrated within an articulated, global strategy. The third strategy, characteristic of the most advanced economic and technological stage, is based on cross-border networks. Under this strategy, on the one hand, companies relate to a variety of domestic markets; on the other hand, there is an exchange of information between these various markets. Rather than controlling markets from the outside, companies try to integrate their market shares and market information across borders. Thus, in the old strategy, foreign direct investment aimed at taking control. Under the most recent strategy, investment is geared toward the construction of a set of relationships between companies in different institutional environments. Global competition is greatly helped by "on the spot information" from each market, so that designing strategy in a top-down approach will invite failure in a constantly changing environment and with highly diverse market dynamics. Information coming from specific time and space is the crucial factor. Information technology allows simultaneously for the decentralized retrieval of such information and for its integration into a flexible system of strategy-making. This cross-border structure allows small and medium businesses to link up with major corporations, forming networks that are able to innovate and adapt relentlessly. Thus, *the actual operating unit becomes the business project, enacted by a network*, rather than individual companies or formal groupings of companies. Business projects are implemented in fields of activity, which can be product lines, organizational tasks, or territorial areas. Appropriate information is critical to companies' performance. And the most important information, under new economic conditions, is that processed between companies, on the basis of experience received from each field. Information circulates through networks: networks between companies, networks within

---

[44] Goodman, Sproull, and Associates (1990).
[45] Imai (1990a).

companies, personal networks, and computer networks. New information technologies are decisive in allowing such a flexible, adaptive model to actually work. For Imai, this cross-border network model, closer to the experience of Japanese corporations than to that of American companies, which are generally sticking to the old model of a unified global strategy, is at the root of competitiveness of Japanese firms.

Provided the large corporation can reform itself, transforming its organization into an articulated network of multifunctional decision-making centers, it could actually be a superior form of management in the new economy. The reason for this is that the most important management problem in a highly decentralized, extremely flexible structure is the correction of what organizational theorist Guy Benveniste calls "articulation errors." I agree with his definition: "Articulation errors are the partial or total lack of fit between what is wanted and what is available."[46] With the increasing interconnectedness and extreme decentralization of processes in the global economy, articulation errors become more difficult to avoid, and their micro- and macroeconomic impacts have greater intensity. The flexible production model, in its different forms, maximizes the response of economic agents and units to a fast-changing environment. But it also increases the difficulty of controlling and correcting articulation errors. The large corporations, with adequate levels of information and resources, could handle such errors better than fragmented, decentralized networks, provided they use adaptability on top of flexibility. This implies the capacity of the corporation to restructure itself, not simply by eliminating redundancy, but by allocating reprogramming capabilities to all its sensors while reintegrating the overarching logic of the corporate system into a decision-making center, working on-line with the networked units in real time. Many of the debates and experiments concerning the transformation of large-scale organizations, be they private or public, business-oriented or mission-oriented, are attempts to combine flexibility and coordination capabilities, to ensure both innovation and continuity in a fast-changing environment. The "horizontal corporation" is a dynamic and strategically planned network of self-programmed, self-directed units based on decentralization, participation, and coordination.

[46]   Benveniste (1994: 74).

The crisis of the vertical corporation model and the rise of business networks

These different trends in the organizational transformation of the informational economy are relatively independent of each other. The formation of subcontracting networks centered in large enterprises is a different phenomenon from the formation of horizontal networks of small and medium businesses. The web-like structure of strategic alliances between large corporations is different from the shift toward the horizontal corporation. Workers' involvement in the production process is not necessarily reduced to the Japanese model based also on *kan-ban* and total quality control. These various trends interact with each other, influence each other, but they all are different dimensions of a fundamental process: the process of disintegration of the organizational model of vertical, rational bureaucracies, characteristic of the large corporation under the conditions of standardized mass production and oligopolistic markets.[47] The historic timing of these various trends is also different, and the time sequence of their diffusion is extremely important to the understanding of their social and economic meaning. For instance, *kan-ban* originated in Japan in 1948, and was designed by Ono Taiichi, a former labor union staff member, who became a Toyota manager.[48] "Toyotism" was gradually adopted by the Japanese automobile firms at a historical moment (the 1960s) when they still did not represent a competitive threat to the rest of the world.[49] "Toyotism" was able to develop by taking advantage of two specific mechanisms historically available to Toyota: its control over labor and its total control over a huge network of suppliers that were external to the firm but internal to the *keiretsu*. When in the 1990s Toyota had to offshore some of its production, it was not always possible to reproduce the *kan-ban* model (it was not in the symbolic NUMMI plant of Toyota-GM in Fremont, California). Thus "Toyotism" is a transitional model between standardized, mass production and a more efficient work organization characterized by the introduction of craft practices, as well as by workers' and suppliers' involvement, in an assembly-line based, industrial model.

Thus, what emerges from the observation of major organizational changes in the last two decades of the century is not a new, "one best way" of production, but the crisis of an old, powerful but excessively rigid model associated with the large, vertical corporation, and with

---

[47]   Vaill (1990).

[48]   Cusumano (1985).

[49]   McMillan (1984).

oligopolistic control over markets. A variety of models and organizational arrangements emerged from this crisis, prospering or failing according to their adaptability to various institutional contexts and competitive structures. As Piore and Sabel conclude in their book:

> Whether our economy is based on mass production or on flexible specialization are open questions. The answers will depend in part on the capacity of nations and social classes to envision the future that they want.[50]

Yet recent historical experience has already provided some of the answers concerning the new organizational forms of the informational economy. Under different organizational arrangements, and through diverse cultural expressions, they are all based in networks. **Networks are the fundamental stuff of which new organizations are and will be made.** And they are able to form and expand all over the main streets and back alleys of the global economy because of their reliance on the information power provided by the new technological paradigm.

Information Technology and the Network Enterprise

The new organizational trajectories I have described were not the mechanical consequence of technological change. Some of them preceded the rise of new information technologies. For instance, as mentioned, the *kan-ban* system was first introduced in Toyota in 1948, and its implementation did not require on-line electronic linkages. Instructions and information were written on standardized cards posted at different working points, and exchanged between suppliers and factory operators.[51] Most of the workers' involvement methods experimented with by Japanese, Swedish, and American companies, required a change of mentality rather than a change in machinery.[52] The most important obstacle in adapting the vertical corporation to the flexibility requirements of the global economy was the rigidity of traditional corporate cultures. Furthermore, at the moment of its massive diffusion, in the 1980s, information technology was supposed to be the magic tool to reform and change the industrial corporation.[53] But its introduction in the absence of fundamental organizational change in fact aggravated the problems of bureau-

---

[50]   Piore and Sabel (1984: 308).
[51]   McMillan (1984); Cusumano (1985).
[52]   Dodgson (ed.) (1989).
[53]   Kotter and Heskett (1992); Harrington (1991).

cratization and rigidity. Computerized controls are even more para-lyzing than traditional face-to-face chains of command in which there was still place for some form of implicit bargaining.[54] In the 1980s in America, more often than not, new technology was viewed as a labor-saving device and as an opportunity to take control of labor, not as an instrument of organizational change.[55]

Thus, organizational change happened, independently from tech-nological change, as a response to the need to cope with a constantly changing operational environment.[56] Yet, once it started to take place, the feasibility or organizational change was extraordinarily enhanced by new information technologies. As Boyett and Conn write:

> The ability of large American companies to reconfigure them-selves to look and act like small businesses can, at least in part, be attributed to the development of new technology that makes whole layers of managers and their staffs unnecessary.[57]

The ability of small and medium businesses to link up in networks among themselves and with large corporations also became depen-dent on the availability of new technologies, once the networks' horizon (if not their daily operations) became global.[58] True, Chinese business had been based on networks of trust and cooperation for centuries. But when in the 1980s they stretched out across the Pacific, from Tachung to Fukien, from Hong Kong to Guandong, from Jakarta to Bangkok, from Hsinchu to Mountain View, from Singapore to Shanghai, from Hong Kong to Vancouver, and, above all, from Taipei and Hong Kong to Guangzhou and Shanghai, only reliance on new communication and information technologies allowed them to work on an ongoing basis, once the family, regional, and personal codes established the basis for the rules of the game to be followed up in their computers.

The complexity of the web of strategic alliances, of subcontracting agreements, and of decentralized decision-making for large firms would have been simply impossible to manage without the develop-ment of computer networks;[59] more specifically, without powerful microprocessors installed in desktop computers linked up via digitally switched telecommunication networks. This is a case in which organ-izational change induced to some extent the technological trajectory.

[54]   Hirschhorn (1985); Mowshowitz (1986).
[55]   Shaiken (1985).
[56]   Cohendet and Llerena (1989).
[57]   Boyett and Conn (1991: 23).
[58]   Shapira (1990); Hsing (1996).
[59]   Whightman (1987).

If the large, vertical corporations had been able to continue to operate successfully in the new economy, the crisis of IBM, Digital, Fujitsu, and of the mainframe computer industry in general might not have happened. It was because of the networking needs of new organizations, large and small, that personal computers and computer networking underwent an explosive diffusion. And because of the massive need for the flexible, interactive manipulation of computers, software became the most dynamic segment of the industry and the information-producing activity that is likely to shape processes of production and management in the future. On the other hand, it was because of the availability of these technologies (due to the stubbornness of innovators in Silicon Valley resisting the "1984" model of informatics) that networking became the key for organizational flexibility and business performance.[60]

Bar and Borrus have shown, in a stream of important research papers, that information networking technology jumped by a quantum leap in the early 1990s, due to the convergence of three trends: digitization of the telecommunications network, development of broadband transmission, and a dramatic increase in the performance of computers connected by the network, performance that was in turn determined by technological breakthrough in microelectronics and software. Then, computer interactive systems that had been limited until then to Local Area Networks, became operational in Wide Area Networks, and the computer paradigm shifted from the mere linkage between computers to "cooperative computing," regardless of the location of the interacting partners. Qualitative advances in information technology, not available until the 1990s, allowed the emergence of fully interactive, computer-based, flexible processes of management, production, and distribution, involving simultaneous cooperation between different firms and units of such firms.[61]

On the other hand, Dieter Ernst has shown that the convergence between organizational requirements and technological change has established networking as the fundamental form of competition in the new, global economy. Barriers to entry in the most advanced industries, such as electronics or automobiles, have skyrocketed, making it extremely difficult for new competitors to enter the market by themselves, and even hampering large corporations' ability to open up new product lines or to innovate their own processes in accordance with the pace of technological change.[62] Thus, co-

---

[60]   Fulk and Steinfield (eds) (1990); *Business Week* (1996).
[61]   Bar and Borrus (1993).
[62]   Ernst (1994b).

operation and networking offer the only possibility to share costs, and risks, as well as to keep up with constantly renewed information. Yet networks also act as gatekeepers. Inside the networks, new possibilities are relentlessly created. Outside the networks, survival is increasingly difficult. Under the conditions of fast technological change, networks, not firms, have become the actual operating unit. In other words, through the interaction between organizational crisis and change and new information technologies a new organizational form has emerged as characteristic of the informational/global economy: the **network enterprise**.

To define more precisely the network enterprise, I need to recall my definition of organization: a system of means structured around the purpose of achieving specific goals. I would add a second analytical distinction, adapted (in a personal version) from Alain Touraine's theory.[63] In a dynamic, evolutionary perspective there is a fundamental difference between two types of organizations: organizations for which the reproduction of their system of means becomes their main organizational goal; and organizations in which goals, and the change of goals, shape and endlessly reshape the structure of means. I call the first type of organizations bureaucracies; the second type, enterprises.

On the basis of these conceptual distinctions, I propose what I believe to be a potentially useful (non-nominalist) definition of the network enterprise: **that specific form of enterprise whose system of means is constituted by the intersection of segments of autonomous systems of goals.** Thus, the components of the network are both autonomous and dependent *vis-à-vis* the network, and may be a part of other networks, and therefore of other systems of means aimed at other goals. The performance of a given network will then depend on two fundamental attributes of the network: its *connectedness*, that is its structural ability to facilitate noise-free communication between its components; its *consistency*, that is the extent to which there is sharing of interests between the network's goals and the goals of its components.

Why is the network enterprise the organizational form of the informational/global economy? One easy answer would be predicated on an empiricist approach: it is what has emerged in the formative period of the new economy, and it is what seems to be performing. But it is intellectually more satisfying to understand that this performance seems to be in accordance with the characteristics of the informational economy: the successful organizations are those able to generate knowledge and process information efficiently; to

---

[63] Touraine (1959).

adapt to the variable geometry of the global economy; to be flexible enough to change its means as rapidly as goals change, under the impact of fast cultural, technological, and institutional change; and to innovate, as innovation becomes the key competitive weapon. These characteristics are indeed features of the new economic system we have analyzed in the preceding chapter. In this sense, **the network enterprise makes material the culture of the informational/global economy: it transforms signals into commodities by processing knowledge.**

Culture, Institutions, and Economic Organization: East Asian Business Networks

Forms of economic organization do not develop in a social vacuum: they are rooted in cultures and institutions. Each society tends to generate its own organizational arrangements. The more a society is historically distinct, the more it evolves in isolation from other societies, and the more its organizational forms are specific. However, when technology broadens the scope of economic activity, and when business systems interact on a global scale, organizational forms diffuse, borrow from each other, and create a mixture that responds to largely common patterns of production and competition, while adapting to the specific social environments in which they operate.[64] This is tantamount to saying that the "market logic" is so deeply mediated by organizations, culture, and institutions that economic agents daring to follow an abstract market logic, as dictated by neoclassical economics orthodoxy, would be at a loss.[65] Most firms do not follow such logic. Some governments do, out of ideology, and they end up losing control over their economies (for example, the Reagan Administration in the US in the 1980s, or the Spanish Socialist Government in the early 1990s). In other words: market mechanisms change over history and work through a variety of organizational forms. The critical question is then: Which are the sources of market specificity? And such a question can only be answered by comparative studies of economic organization.

A major stream of research in comparative organizational theory has shown the fundamental differences in firms' organization and behavior in contexts very different from the traditional Anglo-Saxon pattern embedded in property rights, individualism, and separation

---

[64]   Hamilton (1991).
[65]   Abolaffia and Biggart (1991).

between state and enterprises.[66] The focus of much of this research has been on the East Asian economies, an obvious choice because of the astounding performance of such economies in the last quarter of the twentieth century. The findings of organizational research on East Asian economies are extremely important for a general theory of economic organization, for two reasons.

First, it can be shown that patterns of business organization in East Asian societies are produced by the interplay of culture, history, and institutions, with the latter being the fundamental factor in the formation of specific business systems. Furthermore, as expected in the institutionalist theory of economics, such patterns present common trends, linked to cultural similarity, as well as very distinct features that can be traced to major differences in institutions, as a result of specific historical processes.

Secondly, the fundamental common trend of East Asian business systems is that they are based on networks, albeit on different forms of networks. The building block of such systems is not the firm or the individual entrepreneur, but networks or business groups of different kinds, in a pattern that, with all its variations, tends to fit with the organizational form that I have characterized as the network enterprise. If this is the case, and if the informational/global economy is better suited to the network form of business organization, then East Asian societies, and their organizational forms of economic activity, would have a distinctive comparative advantage in global competition, because such an organizational model is embedded in their culture and institutions. Their historical specificity would tend to converge with the sociotechnical logic of the informational paradigm. The historical record supports such a hypothesis: East Asian economies and firms have adapted more rapidly than any other area of the world to the new technologies and to the new forms of global competition, actually altering the balance of world trade and capital accumulation in favor of the Asian Pacific in only 30 years (see chapter 2). But I must introduce a word of caution: historical coincidence does not mean structural causality. Aren't we repeating the same ethnocentric mistake of the neoclassical paradigm, arguing for "one best way" of universal value, this time from another cultural source? To discuss this issue we need to consider, simultaneously, the historical specificity of cultures, the historical trajectories of institutions, the structural requisites of the informational paradigm, and the forms of competition in the global economy. It is in the interplay of these different social domains that we can find some tentative answers on "the spirit of informationalism."

---

[66] Clegg and Redding (eds) (1990).

A typology of East Asian business networks

Let us first set forth the record on the formation, structure, and dynamics of East Asian business networks. Fortunately, this is a subject that has received sufficient attention in social research,[67] and in which I can rely on the systematic efforts of comparative analysis and theorization by the leading social scientists in this field, Nicole Woolsey Biggart and Gary Hamilton,[68] in addition to my own research work in the Asian Pacific between 1983 and 1995.

The organized network of independent firms is the prevailing form of economic activity in the market economies of East Asia. There are three distinctive, basic types of networks, each one of them characterizing Japanese, Korean, and Chinese businesses.[69]

Japan

In Japan, business groups are organized around networks of firms that mutually own each other (*kabushiki mochiai*), and whose main companies are run by managers. There are two sub-types of these networks:[70]

(a) horizontal networks based on intermarket linkages among large firms (*kigyo shudan*). These networks reach out across a variety of economic sectors. Some of them are the heirs of the *zaibatsu*, the giant conglomerates that led Japanese industrialization and trade before the Second World War, prior to their formal (and ineffective) dissolution during the American occupation. The three largest old networks, are Mitsui, Mitsubishi, and Sumitomo. After the war three new networks were formed around major banks: Fuyo, Dao-Ichi Kangin, and Sanwa. Each one of the networks has its own sources of financing, and competes in all main sectors of activity;

(b) vertical networks (*keiretsu*), built around a *kaisha*, or large specialized industrial corporation, comprising hundreds, and even thousands, of suppliers and their related subsidiaries. Main *keiretsu* are those centered around Toyota, Nissan, Hitachi, Matsushita, Toshiba, Tokai Bank, and Industrial Bank of Japan.

These stable business groups practically control the core of the Japanese economy, organizing a dense network of mutual obligations, financial interdependency, market agreements, personnel transfer,

[67] Whitley (1993).
[68] Biggart (1991); Hamilton and Biggart (1988); Biggart and Hamilton (1992); Hamilton (1991).
[69] Hamilton et al. (1990).
[70] Gerlach (1992); Imai and Yonekura (1991); Whitley (1993).

and information sharing. A critical component of the system is the General Trading Company (*sogo shosha*) for each network, which acts as a general intermediary between suppliers and consumers, and adjusts inputs and outputs.[71] It is the system integrator. Such a business organization works as a flexible unit in the competitive market, allocating resources to each member of the network as it sees fit. This also makes it extremely difficult for any external firm to penetrate markets. This specific economic organization explains to a large extent the problems that foreign firms meet in penetrating the Japanese market, since all operations must be established anew, and suppliers refuse to serve other customers unless their parent *kaisha* agrees with the deal.[72]

Labor practices and work organization reflect this hierarchical network structure.[73] At the core, large companies offer their workers lifetime employment, reward systems based on seniority, and co-operation with firm-based unions. Team work and autonomy of task performance is the rule, counting on workers' commitment to the prosperity of their company. Management is involved at the shop-floor level, and they share facilities and working conditions with manual workers. Consensus-building is sought through a number of procedures, from the organization of work to symbolic action such as the singing of a corporate anthem to start the day.[74]

On the other hand, the more that firms are in the periphery of the network, the more labor is considered expendable and exchangeable, most of it being accounted for by temporary workers and part-time employees (see chapter 4). Women and poorly-educated youth are the bulk of such peripheral labor.[75] Thus, networked business groups lead both to flexible cooperation and to highly segmented labor markets that induce a dual social structure, mainly organized along gender lines. Only the relative stability of the patriarchal Japanese family integrates both ends of the social structure, downplaying the trends towards a polarized society – but only for as long as Japanese women can be kept in subservience, both at home and at work.[76]

Korea

The Korean networks (*chaebol*), although historically inspired by the Japanese *zaibatsu*, are far more hierarchical than their Japanese

---

[71]   Yoshino and Lifson (1986).
[72]   Abegglen and Stalk (1985).
[73]   Koike (1988); Clark (1979); Durlabhji and Marks (eds) (1993).
[74]   Kuwahara (1989).
[75]   Jacoby (1979); Shinotsuka (1994).
[76]   Chizuko (1987); Chizuko (1988); Seki (1988).

counterparts.[77] Their main distinctive trend is that all firms in the network are controlled by a central holding company owned by an individual and his family.[78] In addition, the central holding company is backed by government banks and by government-controlled trading companies. The founding family keeps tight control by appointing members of the family, regional acquaintances, and close friends to top managerial posts throughout the *chaebol*.[79] Small and medium businesses play a minor role, unlike in the Japanese *keiretsu*. Most of the firms of the *chaebol* are relatively sizable, and they work under the coordinated initiative of the top, centralized management of the *chaebol*, often reproducing the military style that their government backers brought to it, particularly after 1961. *Chaebol* are multisectoral, and their managers are transferred from one sector of activity to another, thus ensuring unity of strategy, and cross-fertilization of experience. The four largest Korean *chaebol* (Hyundai, Samsung, Lucky Gold Star, and Daewoo) figure today among the world's largest economic conglomerates, and together accounted in 1985 for 45% of all South Korean gross domestic product. *Chaebol* are largely self-sufficient entities, only dependent on government. Most contractual relations are internal to the *chaebol*, and subcontracting plays a minor role. Markets are shaped by the state, and developed by competition between *chaebol*.[80] Mutual obligation networks external to the *chaebol* are rare. Internal *chaebol* relations are a matter of discipline down the network, rather than of cooperation and reciprocity.

Labor policies and practices also fit this authoritarian pattern. There is, as in Japan, a sharp segmentation of labor markets between core workers and temporary workers, depending on the centrality of the firm in the *chaebol*.[81] Women play a much reduced role, since patriarchalism is even more intense in Korea than in Japan,[82] and men are reluctant to let women work outside the household. But core workers do not receive the same kind of commitment to long-term employment and working conditions from their firms.[83] Neither are they expected to commit themselves by taking the initiative. They are mainly supposed to fulfill the orders they receive. Unions were state-controlled and were kept subservient for a long period. When in the 1980s democracy made substantial gains in Korea, the unions'

[77]   Steers et al. (1989).
[78]   Biggart (1990a).
[79]   Yoo and Lee (1987).
[80]   Kim (1989).
[81]   Wilkinson (1988).
[82]   Gelb and Lief Palley (eds) (1994).
[83]   Park (1992).

growing independence was met with confrontational tactics from *chaebol* leaders, leading to a highly conflictual pattern of industrial relations,[84] a trend that belies the racist ideology about Asian labor's supposedly obedient attitude, sometimes mistakenly attributed to Confucianism.

However, while distrust of workers is the rule, trust is a fundamental feature between different levels of management in the Korean networks, to the point that such trust is mainly embedded in kinship relationships: in 1978, 13.5% of the directors of the largest 100 *chaebol* were part of the owner's family, and they were in control of 21% of top management positions.[85] Additional managerial positions are generally held by persons trusted by the owner's family on the basis of direct knowledge, enforced by mechanism of social control (local social networks, family networks, school networks). However, the interests of the *chaebol* are paramount, even in relationship to the family. If there is a contradiction between the two, government makes sure that *chaebol*'s interests, not individuals' or families' concerns, prevail.[86]

China

The Chinese business organization is based on family firms (*jiazuqiye*), and cross-sectoral, business networks (*jituanqiye*), often controlled by one family. Although most of the detailed research available concerns the formation and development of business networks in Taiwan,[87] empirical evidence, as well as my personal knowledge, allow for an extrapolation of such a pattern to Hong Kong and to overseas Chinese communities in South-East Asia.[88] Interestingly enough, similar networks seem to be at work in the fast process of market-driven indus-trialization in South China, if we extend the networks' reach to include among them the officials of local government.[89]

The key component of Chinese business organization is the family.[90] Firms are family property, and the dominant value concerns the family, not the firm. When the firm prospers, so does the family. Thus, after enough wealth has been accumulated, it is divided among family members who invest in other businesses, most often unrelated to the activity of the original firm. Sometimes, the pattern of creation

---

[84] Koo and Kim (1992).
[85] Shin and Chin (1989).
[86] Amsdem (1989); Evans (1995).
[87] Hamilton and Kao (1990).
[88] Sit and Wong (1988); Yoshihara (1988).
[89] Hsing (1994); Hamilton (1991).
[90] Greenhalgh (1988).

of new businesses, as the family increases its wealth, is intragenerational. But if this does not happen in the life of the founder of the firm, it will after his death. This is because, unlike in Japan and Korea, the family system is based on patrilineage and equal inheritance among the sons, and thus each son will receive his share of the family assets, to start a business of his own. Wong, for instance, considers that successful Chinese businesses go through four phases in three generations: emergent, centralized, segmented, and disintegrative, after which the cycle starts all over again.[91] In spite of frequent intrafamily rivalries, personal trust is still the basis for business deals, beyond and aside from legal–contractual rules. Thus, families prosper by creating new firms in any sector of activity deemed profitable. Family-based firms are linked by subcontracting arrangements, exchange of investment, sharing of stock. Firms are specialized in their trade, families are diversified in their investments. Connections between firms are highly personalized, fluid, and changeable, unlike the long-term commitment patterns of Japanese networks. Sources of finance tend to be informal (family savings, loans from trusted friends, revolving credit associations, or other forms of informal lending, such as Taiwan's "curb market").[92]

In such a structure, management is highly centralized and authoritarian. Middle management, not being part of the family, is considered only as a transmission belt; and workers' loyalty is not expected, since the workers' ideal is to start their own businesses, and thus they are suspect as future competitors. Commitments are short-term, which undermines long-range planning strategies. On the other hand, the extreme decentralization and flexibility of such a system allows for fast adjustments to new products, to new processes, and to new markets. Through alliances between families, and their corresponding networks, capital turnover is accelerated, and allocation of resources is optimized.

The weak point in these small-scale Chinese business networks is their inability to undertake major strategic transformations, requiring for instance R&D investment, knowledge of world markets, large-scale technological modernization, or offshoring of production. I shall argue below, unlike some observers of Chinese business, that the state, particularly in Taiwan but also in other contexts, such as Hong Kong and certainly in China, has provided this critical strategic backing for Chinese networks to prosper in the informational/global economy beyond their profitable, but limited, local horizon. The ideology of entrepreneurial familism, rooted in an ancestral distrust of the state

[91]   Wong (1985).
[92]   Hamilton and Biggart (1988).

in Southern China, cannot be taken at face value, even it if shapes, to a large extent, the behavior of Chinese businessmen.

Entrepreneurial familism was only part of the success story of Chinese business networks, albeit the substantial one. Another element was the Chinese version of the developmental state, in Taiwan, Hong Kong, or China. Under different forms, the state, after so many historic failures, had the intelligence finally to find the formula to support Chinese entrepreneurialism, based on familistic, trustworthy, information relationships, without suffocating its autonomy, once it became clear that the lasting glory of Chinese civilization was in fact dependent upon the relentless vitality of selfishly bustling families. It is probably not by accident that the convergence between families and the state occurred in the Chinese culture at the dawn of the informational/global age, when power and wealth depend more on network flexibility than on bureaucratic might.

Culture, organizations, and institutions: Asian business networks and the developmental state

Thus, East Asian economic organization, without question the most successful in world competition in the last third of the twentieth century, is based on business networks, both formal and informal. But there are considerable differences between the three cultural areas where these networks have arisen. As Nicole Biggart and Gary Hamilton put it, within the network Japanese firms enact a communitarian logic, Korean firms a patrimonial logic, and Taiwanese firms a patrilineal logic.[93]

Both the similarities and differences of East Asian business networks can be traced back to the cultural and institutional characteristics of these societies.

The three cultures intermixed over centuries, and were deeply permeated by philosophical/religious values of Confucianism and Buddhism, in their various national patterns.[94] Their relative isolation from other areas of the world until the nineteenth century reinforced their specificity. The basic social unit was the family, not the individual. Loyalty is due to the family, and contractual obligations to other individuals are subordinated to familistic "natural law." Education is of central value, both for social ascension and for personal enhancement. Trust and reputation, within a given network

---

[93] Hamilton and Biggart (1988).
[94] Whitley (1993).

of obligation, are the most valued qualities, and the most severely sanctioned rule in case of failure.[95]

Although the shaping of organizational forms by cultural attributes is sometimes too indeterminate an argument, because of its lack of specificity, it would seem that the commonality of network forms in East Asia can be related to these common cultural trends. If the unit of economic transaction is not the individual, property rights take second place to family rights. And if the hierarchy of obligations is structured along mutual trust, stable networks have to be established on the basis of such trust, while agents external to these networks will not be treated equally in the market place.

But if culture fosters the commonality of network business patterns, institutions seem to account for their substantial differences while, at the same time, reinforcing their networking logic. The fundamental difference between the three cultures concerns the role of the state, both historically and in the process of industrialization. In all cases, the state preempted civil society: merchant and industrial elites came under the guidance, alternatively benevolent and repressive, of the state. But in each case, the state was historically different and played a different role. At this point in the argument, I must set a distinction between the role of state in history and the performance of the contemporary, developmental state.[96]

In recent history, the substantial difference was between the Japanese state[97] and the Chinese state.[98] The Japanese state not only molded Japan, but also Korea and Taiwan under its colonial domination.[99] Since the Meiji period it was an agent of authoritarian modernization, but working through, and with, clan-based business groups (the *zaibatsu*), some of which (Mitsui, for instance) can be traced back to merchant houses linked to powerful feudal lords.[100] The Japanese imperial state set up a modern, insulated technocracy that sharpened its skills in the preparation of the Japanese war machine (the immediate ancestor of MITI was the Ministry of Munitions, core of the Japanese military industry).[101] It is only when we introduce this particular institutional setting that we understand the precise workings of culture on organizations. For instance, Hamilton and Biggart show the institutional background of

95   Baker (1979); Willmott (ed.) (1972).
96   Biggart (1991); Wade (1990); Whitley (1993).
97   Beasley (1990); Johnson (1995).
98   Feuerwerker (1984).
99   Amsdem (1979, 1985, 1989, 1992).
100   Norman (1940).
101   Johnson (1982).

the cultural explanation usually provided for Japanese consensus-building in the work process through the notion of *Wa* or harmony. *Wa* searches for the integration of the world order, through the subordination of the individual to the group practices. But Biggart and Hamilton refuse to accept the direct determination of Japanese management practices as the cultural expression of *Wa*. They argue that such organizational arrangements result from an industrial system, fostered and enforced by the state, that finds support for its implementation in the elements of traditional culture, the building materials with which institutions work to produce organizations. As they write, citing Sayle, "the Japanese government does not stand apart from or over the community: it is rather the place where *Wa* deals are negotiated."[102] Thus, business groups in Japan, as was historically the case in the areas of Japanese influence, tend to be organized vertically, around a core corporation with direct access to the state.

The Chinese state had a very different relationship to business, and particularly to business in Southern China, the fundamental source of Chinese entrepreneurialism. Both in the last decades of the imperial state and in the brief period of the Kuomintang state in China, business was at the same time abused and solicited, seen as a source of income rather than as an engine of wealth. This led, on the one hand, to the harmful practices of excessive taxation and lack of support for industrialization; on the other hand, to favoritism for some business groups, thus breaking the rules of competition. Reactions to this state of affairs led Chinese business to stay away from the state as much as possible, building on a secular fear imposed on southern entrepreneurial Chinese by their northern conquerors. Such a distance from the state emphasized the role of family, as well as of local and regional connections, in setting up business transactions, a trend that Hamilton shows can be dated back to the Qin dynasty.[103]

Without a reliable state enforcing property rights, you do not need to be Confucian in order to place your trust in kin rather than in a legal contract on paper. Significantly enough, it was the active involvement of the state in the West in enforcing property rights, as North has shown,[104] and not the lack of state intervention, that became the critical factor in organizing economic activity along market transactions between free individual agents. When the state did not act to create the market, as in China, families did it on their own, bypassing

[102]   Hamilton and Biggart (1988: 72).
[103]   Hamilton (1984, 1985).
[104]   North (1981).

the state and embedding market mechanisms in socially constructed networks.

But the dynamic configuration of East Asian business networks, able to take on the global economy, came in the second half of the twentieth century, under the decisive impulse of what Chalmers Johnson labeled the developmental state.[105] To extend this fundamental concept, which originated in Johnson's study of the role of MITI in the Japanese economy, to the broader experience of East Asian industrialization, I used in my own work a somewhat modified definition of the developmental state.[106] A state is developmental when it establishes as its principle of legitimacy its ability to promote and sustain development, understanding by development the combination of steady high rates of economic growth and structural change in the economic system, both domestically and in its relationship to the international economy. This definition is misleading, however, unless we specify the meaning of legitimacy in a given historical context. Most political theorists remain prisoners of an ethnocentric conception of legitimacy, related to the democratic state. But not all states have attempted to ground their legitimacy on the consensus of the civil society. The legitimacy principle may be exercised on behalf of the society-as-it-is (in the case of the democratic state), or on behalf of a societal project carried on by the state, as self-proclaimed interpreter of the "historical needs" of the society (the state as social "vanguard," in the Leninist tradition). When such a societal project involves a fundamental transformation of the social order, I refer to it as a revolutionary state, based on revolutionary legitimacy, regardless of the degree of internalization of such legitimacy by its subjects, for example the Communist Party state. When the societal project carried forward by the state respects the broader parameters of social order (although not necessarily of a specific social structure, for example an agrarian society), I consider it to be a developmental state. The historical expression of this societal project in East Asia took the form of the affirmation of national identity, and national culture, building or rebuilding the nation as a force in the world, in this case by means of economic competitiveness and socioeconomic improvement. Ultimately, for the developmental state economic development is not a goal, but a means: the means of implementing a nationalist project, superseding a situation of material destruction and political defeat after a major war, or, in the

---

[105] Johnson (1982, 1995).
[106] Castells (1992). Chalmers Johnson, in his latest book (1995) converged on my redefinition of the developmental state, accepting it as a further refinement of his theory, which it is.

case of Hong Kong and Singapore, after the severance of their ties
with their economic and cultural environment (communist China,
independent Malaysia). Along with a number of researchers,[107] I have
empirically argued in several writings that at the roots of the rise of
Asian Pacific economies lies the nationalist project of the developmental state. This is now generally acknowledged in the case of Japan,
Korea, and Singapore. There is some debate on the matter in the case
of Taiwan, although it does seem to fit the model.[108] And I raised a few
eyebrows when I extended the analysis to Hong Kong, albeit with due
specifications.[109]

I cannot go into the empirical detail of this debate in the framework of this text. It would take the analysis of Asian business too far
away from the focus of this chapter, namely the emergence of the
network enterprise as the prevailing organizational form in the information economy. But it is possible and useful for the sake of the
argument to show the correspondence between the characteristics of
state intervention in each East Asian context and the variety
of network forms of business organization.

In Japan, government guides economic development by advising
business on product lines, export markets, technology, and work organization.[110] It backs its guidance with powerful financial and fiscal
measures, as well as with selective support for strategic R&D programs.
At the core of government industrial policy was (is) the activity of the
Ministry of International Trade and Industry, MITI, that periodically
elaborates "visions" for Japan's development trajectory, and sets up
the industrial policy measures that are necessary to implement the
desirable course along this trajectory. The crucial mechanism in
ensuring that private business broadly follows government's policies
relies on financing. Japanese corporations are highly dependent on
bank loans. Credit is channeled to the banks of each major business
network by the Central Bank of Japan, under instructions from the
Finance Ministry, in coordination with MITI. Indeed, while MITI took
responsibility for strategic planning, real power in the Japanese
government always lay in the Finance Ministry. Furthermore,
much of the lending funds comes from postal savings, a massive
supply of available finance controlled by the Ministry of Posts and

[107] Deyo (ed.) (1987); Wade (1990); Johnson (1982, 1985, 1987, 1995); Gold
(1986); Amsdem (1989, 1992); Appelbaum and Henderson (eds) (1992); Evans
(1995).
[108] Amsdem (1985); Gold (1986).
[109] Castells et al. (1990).
[110] Johnson (1982, 1995); Johnson et al. (eds) (1989); Gerlach (1992).

Telecommunications. MITI targeted specific industries for their competitive potential, and provided a number of incentives, such as tax breaks, subsidies, market and technology information, and support for R&D and personnel training. Until the 1980s, MITI also enforced protectionist measures, insulating specific industries from world competition during their nurturing period. Such long-standing practices have created a protectionist inertia that survives to some extent after the formal abolition of restrictions on free trade.

Government's economic intervention in Japan is organized around the autonomy of the state *vis-à-vis* business, and to a large extent *vis-à-vis* the political party system, although the conservative Liberal Democratic Party ruled uncontested until 1993. Recruitment of the top-level bureaucracy on the basis of merit, most often from Tokyo University graduates and particularly from the Law School, and always from elite universities (Kyoto, Hitotsubashi, Keio, and so on), ensures a tight social network of highly professional, well-trained, and largely apolitical technocrats, who constitute the actual ruling elite of contemporary Japan. Furthermore, only about 1% of these high-level bureaucrats reach the top of the hierarchy. The others in the later stage of their career take well-paid jobs either in para-public sector institutions, in corporate business, or in mainstream political parties, thus ensuring the diffusion of the values of the bureaucratic elite among the political and economic agents who are in charge of implementing government's strategic vision of Japan's national interests.

This form of state intervention, based on consensus, strategic planning, and advice, largely determines the organization of Japanese business in networks, and the particular structure of such networks. Without a centralized planning mechanism to allocate resources, Japan's industrial policy can only be effective if business itself is tightly organized in hierarchical networks that can carry out the guidelines issued by MITI. Such coordinating mechanisms have very concrete expressions. One of them is the *shacho-kai*, or monthly meetings, that bring together the presidents of the core companies of a major intermarket network. These meetings are occasions to build social cohesion in the networks, in addition to carrying out the directives that are signaled by government's formal or informal communications. The actual structure of the network also reflects the type of government intervention: financial dependency on government-approved loans gives a strategic role to the main bank (or banks) of the network; international trade restrictions and incentives are channeled through the general trading company of each network which works as a system integrator, both between the members of the network and between the network and MITI. Thus, for a firm to break the discipline of government's industrial policy is tantamount to excluding itself from the network, being cut off from access to financing, technology, and import-export licensing. Japan's strategic planning, and the centralized network structure of Japanese business are but two faces of the same model of economic organization.

The connection between government policy and business organization is even more evident in the case of the Republic of Korea.[111] Yet it is important to notice that the developmental state in Korea was not characteristic of Korea during the 1950s. After the war, Syngman Rhee's dictatorship was a corrupt regime, playing simply the role of a vassal government of the United States. It was the nationalistic project of the Park Chung Hee regime, after the 1961 military coup, that set up the bases for a state-led process of industrialization and competition in the world economy, enacted by Korean business on behalf of the interests of the nation and under the strict guidance of the state. The Park government aimed at creating the equivalent of the Japanese *zaibatsu*, on the basis of existing large Korean companies. But because the resulting networks were forced into existence by the state they were even more centralized and authoritarian than their Japanese predecessors. To achieve its design, the Korean government closed the domestic market to international competition and practiced an import-substitution policy. As soon as Korean firms started to operate, it targeted the enhancement of their competitiveness, and favored an export-oriented strategy along a trajectory of increasingly capital- and technology-intensive industries, with specific goals outlined in five-year economic plans established by the Economic Planning Board, the brain and engine of Korea's economic miracle. In the vision of the Korean military, to be competitive Korean firms had to be concentrated in large conglomerates. They were forced to do so by government's control of the banking system, and of the export-import licenses. Both credit and licences were selectively given to firms on condition of joining a *chaebol*, since government's privileges were accorded to the central firm (owned by a family) in the *chaebol*. Business was also explicitly requested to finance government's political activities, as well as to pay in cash for any special favors obtained from top-level bureaucrats, generally military officers. To enforce strict business discipline, the Park government did not relinquish control over the banking system. Thus, unlike in Japan, Korean *chaebol* were not financially independent until the 1980s. Labor policies were also shaped by military-induced authoritarianism, with

[111] Amsdem (1989); Evans (1995); Jacobs (1985); Lim (1982); Jones and Sakong (1980).

the unions being directly under government control to make sure that they would be purged of any communist influence. These labor policies led to the ferocious repression of any independent labor organization, thus destroying the possibility of consensus-building in the work process of Korean industry.[112] The military state origin of *chaebol* was certainly more influential in shaping the authoritarian and patrilineal character of Korean business networks than the Confucian tradition of rural Korea.[113]

The interaction between state and business is far more complex in the case of Chinese family firms, rooted in centuries-old distrust of government interference. And yet government planning and policy have been a decisive factor in Taiwan's economic development.[114] Not only does Taiwan have the largest public enterprise sector of the capitalist Asian Pacific (amounting to about 25% of GDP up to the late 1970s), but government guidance was formalized in successive four-year economic plans. As in Korea, control of banks and of export–import licenses were the main instruments for the implementation of government's economic policy, also based on the combination of an import-substitution policy and export-oriented industrialization. Yet, unlike in Korea, Chinese firms did not depend primarily on bank credits but, as mentioned above, relied on family savings, credit cooperatives, and informal capital markets, largely autonomous from the government. Thus, small and medium-size enterprises thrived on their own, and established the horizontal, family-based networks I have described. The intelligence of the KMT state, having learned from its historical mistakes in 1930s Shanghai, was to build on the foundations of these dynamic networks of small enterprises, many of them in the rural fringes of the metropolitan areas, sharing farming and craft industrial production. However, it is doubtful that these small enterprises would have been able to compete on the world market without critical, strategic support from the state. Such support took three main forms: (a) subsidized health and education, public infrastructure, and income redistribution, on the basis of a radical agrarian reform; (b) attraction of foreign capital, via tax incentives, and the establishment of the first export-processing zones in the world, thus ensuring linkages, subcontracting and enhancement of quality standards for Taiwanese firms and workers that came into contact with foreign companies; (c) decisive government support for R&D, technology transfer, and diffusion. This latter point was particularly critical to enable Taiwanese firms to climb up

---

[112]   Kim (ed.) (1987).
[113]   Janelli (1993).
[114]   Amsdem (1979, 1985); Gold (1986); Kuo (1983); Chen (1979).

the ladder of the technological division of labor. For instance, the process of diffusion of advanced electronics technology, at the origin of the expansion of the most dynamic sector of Taiwan's industry in the 1980s, PC clone manufacturing, was directly organized by the government in the 1960s.[115] The government acquired the license for chip design technology from RCA, together with the training of Chinese engineers by the American company. Relying on these engineers, the government created a public research center, ETRI, that kept up to date with developments in the world's electronic technology, emphasizing its commercial applications. Under government directives, ETRI organized enterprise seminars to diffuse, at no cost, the technology it was generating among Taiwanese small firms. Furthermore, ETRI engineers were encouraged to leave the Institute after a few years, and were provided with government funding and technology support to start up their own businesses. Thus, although in more traditional industries government support in Taiwan was more indirect than in South Korea or Japan, what is characteristic is that productive interaction was found between government and business networks: networks continued to be family-based and relatively small in the size of their firms (although there are also major industrial groups in Taiwan, for example Tatung); but government policies assumed the coordinating and strategic planning functions when it was necessary for such networks to broaden and upgrade the scope of their activities in products, processes, and markets.

The story is more complex in the case of Hong Kong, but the outcome is not too dissimilar.[116] The basis of the export-oriented industrial structure of Hong Kong was made from small and medium businesses that originated mainly from family savings, starting with 21 industrialists' families who emigrated from Shanghai after the communist revolution. But the colonial government aimed at making Hong Kong into a showcase for the successful implementation of British benevolent colonialism, and in the process also tried to make the Territory self-sufficient in its finances in order to put off pressures for decolonization from the Labour Party back home. To do so behind the ideological screen of "positive nonintervention" (eagerly consumed by the Milton Friedmans of the world) the Hong Kong "cadets," career civil servants from the British Colonial Service, introduced an active developmental policy, half by design, half by accident. [117] They strictly controlled the distribution of textile and garment export

[115] Castells et al. (1990); Wong (1988); Chen (1979); Lin et al. (1980).
[116] Castells (1989c); Castells and Hall (1994).
[117] Miners (1986); Mushkat (1982); Lethbridge (1978).

quotas among firms, allocating them on the basis of their knowledge
of competitive capabilities. They built a network of government institutions (Productivity Center, Trade Council, and so on) to diffuse
information about markets, technology, management, and other critical matters throughout the networks of small enterprises, thus
accomplishing the coordinating and strategic functions without
which such networks would never have been able to tap into the
markets of the US and of Commonwealth countries. They built the
largest public housing program in the world in terms of the proportion of the population housed in its premises (later it became second
to Singapore, after Singapore had imitated the formula). Not only
were there thousands of factories in high-rise buildings (called
"flatted factories") paying low rents as an integral part of the public
housing program, but the subsidy of the program substantially
lowered labor costs, and the safety net it provided made it possible for
workers to venture into starting their own businesses without excessive risk (seven starts on average before succeeding). In Taiwan, the
rural dwelling and the family plot of land, resulting from the persistence of farming in the industrial areas, was the safety mechanism that
allows for movements back and forth between self-employment and
salaried employment.[118] In Hong Kong, the functional equivalent was
the public housing program. In both cases, networks of small businesses could emerge, disappear, and re-emerge under a different
form because there was a safety net provided by family solidarity and
a peculiar colonial version of the welfare state.[119]

A similar form of linkage between supportive government and
family-based business networks seems to be emerging in the process
of export-oriented industrialization in Southern China in the
1990s.[120] On the one hand, Hong Kong and Taiwanese manufacturers
tapped into the regional networks of their villages of origin in
Guandong and Fukien provinces to create subsidiaries and to establish subcontractors, in order to offshore the low end of their
manufacturing production (for example, in shoes, plastics, or
consumer electronics). On the other hand, such production networks
can only exist on the basis of the support of provincial and local
governments, which provide the necessary infrastructure, enforce
labor discipline, and act as intermediaries between management,
labor, and export firms. As Hsing writes in concluding her pioneering

---

[118]   Chin (1988).
[119]   Schiffer (1983).
[120]   Hsing (1994, 1996); Hamilton (1991).

effort of research on Taiwanese manufacturing investment in Southern China:

> The new pattern of foreign direct investment in the rapidly industrializing regions of China is characterized by the dominant role played by small and medium-sized investors and their collaboration with low-level local authorities in new production sites. The institutional basis that maintains and enhances the flexibility of their operations is a network form of production and marketing organizations, as well as the increasing autonomy of the local governments. Of equal importance, the cultural affinity of overseas investors and their local agents, including local officials and local workers, facilitates a much smoother and faster process of establishing transnational production networks.[121]

Thus, the form of Chinese business networks is also a function of the indirect, subtle, yet real and effective form of state intervention in the process of economic development in various contexts. However, a process of historical transformation may be under way, as Chinese business networks have grown extraordinarily in wealth, influence, and global reach. Interestingly enough, they continue to be family-based, and their interlocking seems to reproduce the early forms of networking between small entrepreneurs. But they are certainly powerful enough to bypass directives from government in Taiwan, in Hong Kong, and for that matter, in other South-East Asian countries, with the exception of the strong Singaporean state. Chinese business networks, while keeping in essence their organizational structure and cultural dynamics, appear to have reached a qualitatively larger size, one that allows them finally to be set free from the state.[122] But such a perception might be an illusion linked to a period of historical transition; because what is looming on the horizon is the gradual linkage between powerful Chinese business networks and the multilayered structure of the mainland Chinese state. Indeed, the most profitable investments of Chinese businesses are already taking place in China. When and if such linkage takes place, the autonomy of Chinese business networks will be tested, as will be the ability of a developmental state constructed by a Communist Party to evolve into a form of government able to steer without subduing the flexible, family-based, network enterprises. If such convergence takes place, the world's economic landscape will be transformed.

Thus, the observation of East Asian business networks shows the

---

[121]   Hsing (1996: 307).
[122]   Mackie (1992b, 1992b).

cultural and institutional sources of such organizational forms, both
in their common features and in their significant differences. Let us
now return to the general analytical implications of this conclusion.
Are such networking forms of economic organization able to develop
in other cultural/institutional contexts? How does contextual variation influence their morphology and performance? What is common
to the new rules of the game in the informational/global economy,
and what is specific to particular social systems (for example, East
Asian business systems, the "Anglo-Saxon model," the "French
Model," the "Northern Italian model," and so on)? And the most
important question of all: How will the organizational forms of the
late industrial economy, such as the large multi-unit corporation,
interact with the emerging network enterprise in its various
manifestations?

Multinational Enterprises, Transnational Corporations, and International Networks

The analysis of East Asian business networks shows the insti-
tutional/cultural production of organizational forms. But it also
shows the limits of the market-driven theory of business organizations,
ethnocentrically rooted in the Anglo-Saxon experience. Thus,
Williamson's influential interpretation[123] of the emergence of the
large corporation as the best way to reduce uncertainty and minimize
transaction costs by internalizing transactions within the corporation,
simply does not hold when confronted with the empirical evidence of
the spectacular process of capitalist development in the Asian Pacific,
based on networks external to the corporation.[124]

Similarly, the process of economic globalization based on network
formation seems also to contradict the classical analysis by Chandler[125]
that attributes the rise of the large multi-unit corporation to the
growing size of the market, and to the availability of communications
technology that enables the large firm to take hold on such a broad
market, thus reaping economies of scale and scope, and internalizing
them within the firm. Chandler extended his historical analysis of the
expansion of the large firm in the US market to the rise of the multinational enterprise as a response to the globalization of the economy,
this time by using enhanced information technologies.[126] In most of

[123]   Williamson (1985).
[124]   Hamilton and Biggart (1988).
[125]   Chandler (1977).
[126]   Chandler (1986).

the literature of the last 20 years it seems as if the multinational enterprise, with its divisional, centralized structure, was the organizational expression of the new, global economy.[127] The only debate on the matter was between those who argued for the persistence of the national roots of the multinational enterprise,[128] and those who considered the new forms of enterprise as truly transnational corporations, having superseded in their vision, interests, and commitments any particular country, regardless of their historical origin.[129] Yet empirical analyses of the structure and practice of large corporations with a global scope appear to show that both visions are outdated and should be replaced by the emergence of international networks of firms, and of subunits of firms, as the basic organizational form of the informational/global economy. Dieter Ernst has summarized a substantial amount of available evidence concerning the formation of interfirm networks in the global economy, and considers that most economic activity in leading industries is organized around five different types of networks (electronics and automobiles being the most advanced industries in the diffusion of this organizational pattern). These five types of networks are:

- *Supplier networks* which are defined to include subcontracting, OEM (Original Equipment Manufacturing) and ODM (Original Design Manufacturing) arrangements between a client (the "focal company") and its suppliers of intermediate production inputs.
- *Producer networks* which are defined to include all co-production arrangements that enable competing producers to pool their production capacities, financial, and human resources in order to broaden their product portfolios and geographic coverage.
- *Customer networks* which are defined as the forward linkages of manufacturing companies with distributors, marketing channels, value-added resellers and end users, either in the major export markets or in domestic markets.
- *Standard coalitions* which are initiated by potential global standard setters with the explicit purpose of locking-in as many firms as possible into their proprietary product or interface standards.
- *Technology cooperation networks* which facilitate the acquisition of product design and production technology, enable joint production and process development, and permit generic scientific knowledge and R&D to be shared.[130]

127   De Anne (1990); Dunning (1992); Enderwick (ed.) (1989).
128   Ghoshal and Westney (1993).
129   Ohmae (1990).
130   Ernst (1994b: 5–6).

However, the formation of these networks does not imply the demise of the multinational enterprise. Ernst, concurring with a number of observers on this matter,[131] considers that networks are either centered on a major multinational enterprise or are formed on the basis of alliances and cooperation between such enterprises. Cooperative networks of small and medium enterprises do exist (for example, in Italy and in East Asia), but they play a minor role in the global economy, at least in the key industries. Oligopolistic concentration seems to have been maintained or increased in most sectors of major industries, not only in spite of but because of the networked form of organization. This is because entry into the strategic networks requires either considerable resources (financial, technological, market share) or an alliance with a major player in the network.

Multinational enterprises seem to be still highly dependent on their national basis. The idea of transnational corporations being "citizens of the world economy" does not seem to hold. Yet the networks formed by multinational corporations do transcend national boundaries, identities, and interests.[132] My hypothesis is that, as the process of globalization progresses, organizational forms evolve from *multinational enterprises* to *international networks*, actually bypassing the so-called "transnationals" that belong more to the world of mythical representation (or self-serving image-making by management consultants) than to the institutionally bounded realities of the world economy.

Furthermore, as mentioned above, multinational enterprises are not only engaged in networking, but are increasingly organized themselves in decentralized networks. Ghoshal and Bartlett, after summarizing evidence on the transformation of multinational corporations, define the contemporary multinational as "an inter-organizational network," or, more precisely, as "a network that is embedded within an external network."[133] This approach is critical to our understanding because, so the argument goes, the characteristics of the institutional environments where the various components of the corporation are located actually shape the structure and dynamics of the corporation's internal network. Thus, multinational corporations are indeed the power-holders of wealth and technology in the global economy, since most networks are structured around such corporations. But at the same time, they are internally differentiated in decentralized networks, and externally dependent on their

---

[131]   Harrison (1994).
[132]   Imai (1990a).
[133]   Ghoshal and Bartlett (1993: 81).

membership in a complex, changing structure of interlocked networks, cross-border networks in Imai's formulation.[134] Besides, each one of the components of such networks, internal and external, is embedded in specific cultural/institutional environments (nations, regions, locales) that affect the network in varying degrees. Overall, the networks are asymmetrical, but each single element of the network can hardly survive by itself or impose its diktat. The logic of the network is more powerful than the powers in the network. The management of uncertainty becomes critical in a situation of asymmetrical interdependency.

Why are networks central in the new economic competition? Ernst argues that two factors are foremost sources in this process of organizational transformation: globalization of markets and inputs; dramatic technological change that makes equipment constantly obsolete and forces firms to be relentlessly updated with information on processes and products. In such a context, cooperation is not only a way of sharing costs and resources, but also an insurance policy against a bad technological decision: the consequences of such a decision would also be suffered by the competitors, since networks are ubiquitous and intertwined.

Interestingly enough, Ernst's explanation for the emergence of the international network enterprise echoes the argument of market theorists, that I have tried to personalize in Chandler, for the classics, and in Williamson, for the new wave of neoclassical economists. Market characteristics and technology are suggested to be the key variables. However, in Ernst's analysis, the organizational effects are exactly the opposite of those expected by the traditional economic theory: whilst market size was supposed to induce the formation of the vertical, multi-unit corporation, the globalization of competition dissolves the large corporation in a web of multidirectional networks, that become the actual operating unit. The increase of transaction costs, because of added technological complexity, does not result in the internalization of transactions within the corporation but in the externalization of transactions and sharing of costs throughout the network, obviously increasing uncertainty, but also making possible the spreading and sharing of uncertainty. Thus, either the mainstream explanation of business organization, based on neoclassical market theory, is wrong, or else available evidence on the emergence of business networks is faulty. I am inclined to think the former.

Thus, the network enterprise, a predominant form of business

[134]   Imai (1990a).

organization in East Asia, seems to be flourishing in various institutional/cultural contexts, in Europe,[135] as in the United States,[136] while the large, multi-unit corporation, hierarchically organized around vertical lines of command seems to be ill-adapted to the informational/global economy. Globalization and informationalization seem to be structurally related to networking and flexibility. Does this trend mean that we are shifting to an Asian model of development that would replace the Anglo-Saxon model of the classical corporation? I do not think so, in spite of the diffusion of work and management practices across countries. Cultures and institutions continue to shape the organizational requirements of the new economy, in an interaction between the logic of production, the changing technological basis, and the institutional features of the social environment. A survey of business cultures in Europe shows the variation within Europe of organizational patterns, particularly *vis-à-vis* the relationships between governments and firms.[137] The architecture and composition of business networks being formed around the world are influenced by the national characteristics of societies where such networks are embedded. For instance, the content and strategies of electronic firms in Europe are highly contingent on the policies of the European Union, regarding the reduction of technological dependency on Japan and the US. But, on the other hand, the alliance of Siemens with IBM and Toshiba in microelectronics is dictated by technological imperatives. The formation of high-technology networks around defense programs in the US is an institutional characteristic of the American industry, and one that tends to exclude foreign partnership. The gradual incorporation of Northern Italian industrial districts by major Italian firms was favored by agreements between government, large firms, and labor unions concerning the convenience of stabilizing and consolidating the productive base formed during the 1970s, with the support of regional governments that were dominated by left-wing parties. In other words, the network enterprise is increasingly international (not transnational), and its conduct will result from the managed interaction between the global strategy of the network and the nationally/regionally rooted interests of its components. Since most multinational firms participate in a variety of networks depending on products, processes, and countries, the new economy cannot be characterized as being centered any longer on multinational corporations, even if they continue to exercise

---

[135] Danton de Rouffignac (1991).
[136] Bower (1987); Harrison (1994).
[137] Randlesome et al. (1990).

jointly oligopolistic control over most markets. This is because corporations have transformed themselves into a web of multiple networks embedded in a multiplicity of institutional environments. Power still exists, but it is randomly exercised. Markets still trade, but purely economic calculations are hampered by their dependency on unsolvable equations overdetermined by too many variables. The market's hand that institutional economists tried to make visible has returned to invisibility. But this time, its structural logic is not only governed by supply and demand but also influenced by hidden strategies and untold discoveries played out in the global information networks.

The Spirit of Informationalism

Max Weber's classic essay on *The Protestant Ethic and the Spirit of Capitalism,* originally published in 1904–5[138] still remains the methodological cornerstone of any theoretical attempt at grasping the essence of cultural/institutional transformations that in history usher in a new paradigm of economic organization. His substantive analysis of the roots of capitalist development has certainly been challenged by historians, who have pointed at alternative historical configurations that sustained capitalism as effectively as the Anglo-Saxon culture did, albeit in different institutional forms. Furthermore, the focus of this chapter is not so much on capitalism, which is alive and well in spite of its social contradictions, as on informationalism, a new mode of development that alters, but does not replace, the dominant mode of production. Yet the theoretical principles proposed by Max Weber almost a century ago still provide a useful guideline to make sense of the series of analyses and observations I have presented in this chapter, bringing them together to highlight the new cultural/institutional configuration underlying the organizational forms of economic life. In homage to one of sociology's founding fathers, I shall call this configuration "the spirit of informationalism."
Where to start? How to proceed? Let us read Weber again:

The spirit of capitalism. What is to be understood by it? . . . If any object can be found to which this term can be applied with any understandable meaning, it can only be an historical individual, i.e. a complex of elements associated in historical reality which we unite into a conceptual whole from the standpoint of their cultural significance. Such an historical concept, however, since it refers in its content to a phenomenon significant for its unique

[138] Weber (1958).

individuality . . . must be gradually put together out of the individual parts which are taken from historical reality to make it up. Thus the final and definitive concept cannot stand at the beginning of the investigation, but must come at the end.[139]

We are at the end, at least of this chapter. Which are the elements of historical reality we have uncovered as being associated in the new organizational paradigm? And how can we unite them in a conceptual whole of historical significance?

They are, first of all, *business networks*, under different forms, in different contexts, and from different cultural expressions. Family-based networks in Chinese societies and Northern Italy; entrepreneurial networks emerging from technological seedbeds in the milieux of innovation, as in Silicon Valley; hierarchical, communal networks of the Japanese *keiretsu* type; organizational networks of decentralized corporate units from former vertically integrated corporations forced to adapt to the realities of the time; and cross-border networks resulting from strategic alliances between firms.

There are also *technological tools*: new telecommunication networks; new, powerful desktop computers; new, adaptive, self-evolving software; new, mobile communication devices that extend on-line linkages to any space at any time; new workers and managers, connected to each other around tasks and performance, able to speak the same language, the digital language.

There is *global competition*, forcing constant redefinitions of products, processes, markets, and economic inputs, including capital and information.

And there is, as always, *the state*: developmental in the take-off stage of the new economy, as in East Asia; agent of incorporation when economic institutions have to be rebuilt, as in the process of European unification; coordinating when territorially based networks need the nurturing support of local or regional governments to generate synergistic effects that will set up milieux of innovation; and mission-oriented messenger when it steers a national economy, or the world economic order, into a new historical course, scripted in the technology but not fulfilled in the business practice, as in the US Government's design to built the twenty-first century's information superhighway, notwithstanding the budget deficit. All these elements come together to give rise to the network enterprise.

The *emergence and consolidation of the network enterprise*, in all its different manifestations, may well be the answer to the "productivity

---

[139] Weber (1958: 47).

enigma" that cast such a long shadow on my analysis of the informational economy in the preceding chapter. Because, as Bar and Borrus argue in their study on the future of networking:

> One reason Information Technology investments have not translated into higher productivity is that they have primarily served to automate existing tasks. They often automate inefficient ways of doing things. Realizing the potential of Information Technology requires substantial re-organization. The ability to re-organize tasks as they become automated rests largely on the availability of a coherent infrastructure, i.e. a flexible network able to interconnect the various computer-based business activities.

They go on to establish a historical parallel with the impact of decentralization of small electrical generators to the shop floor of industrial factories, to conclude;

> These decentralized computers are only now [1993] being interconnected, so as to allow and support re-organization. Where this has been effectively accomplished, there are corresponding gains in productivity.[140]

Yet, while all these elements are ingredients of the new developmental paradigm, they still lack the cultural glue that brings them together. Because, as Max Weber wrote:

> The capitalism of today, which has come to dominate economic life, educates and selects the economic subjects which it needs through a process of economic survival of the fittest. But here one can easily see the limits of the concept of selection as a means of historical explanation. In order that a manner of life so well adapted to the peculiarities of capitalism could be selected at all, i.e. should come to dominate others, it had to originate somewhere, and not in isolated individuals alone, but as a way of life common to a whole group of men. This origin is what really needs explanation . . . In the country of Benjamin Franklin's birth . . . the spirit of capitalism was present before the capitalistic order.

And he adds:

> The fact to be explained historically is that in the most highly capitalistic centre of that time, in Florence of the fourteenth and fifteenth centuries, the money and capital market of all the great

---

[140]   Bar and Borrus (1993: 6).

political Powers, this attitude [Benjamin Franklin's defense of profit-searching] was considered ethically unjustifiable, or at best to be tolerated. But in the backwoods small bourgeois circumstances of Pennsylvania in the eighteenth century, where business threatened for simple lack of money to fall back into barter, where there was hardly a sign of large enterprise, where only the earliest beginnings of banking were to be found, the same thing was considered the essence of moral conduct, even commanded in the name of duty. To speak here of a reflection of material conditions in the ideal superstructure would be patent nonsense. What was the background of ideas which could account for the sort of activity apparently directed toward profit alone as a calling toward which the individual feels himself to have an ethical obligation? For it was this idea which gave the way of life of the new entrepreneur its ethical foundation and justification.[141]

What is the ethical foundation of informationalism? And does it need an ethical foundation at all? I should remind the patient reader that in the historical period of the rise of informationalism, capitalism, albeit in new, profoundly modified forms *vis-à-vis* the time of Weber's writing, is still operating as the dominant economic form. Thus, the corporate ethos of accumulation, the renewed appeal of consumerism, are driving cultural forms in the organizations of informationalism. Additionally, the state and the affirmation of national/cultural collective identity have been shown to muster decisive force in the arena of global competition. Families, in their complexity, continue to thrive and reproduce by the means of economic competition, accumulation, and heritage. But while all these elements seem to account, together, for the cultural sustainment of renewed capitalist competition, they do not seem to be specific enough to distinguish the new agent of such capitalist competition: the network enterprise.

For the first time in history, the basic unit of economic organization is not a subject, be it individual (such as the entrepreneur, or the entrepreneurial family) or collective (such as the capitalist class, the corporation, the state). As I have tried to show, **the unit is the network**, made up of a variety of subjects and organizations, relentlessly modified as networks adapt to supportive environments and market structures. What glues together these networks? Are there purely instrumental, accidental alliances? It may be so for particular networks, but the networking form of organization must have a

---

[141]   Weber (1958: 55 and 75).

cultural dimension of its own. Otherwise, economic activity would be
performed in a social/cultural vacuum, a statement that can be
sustained by some ultrarationalist economists, but that is fully belied
by the historical record. What is, then, this *"ethical foundation of the
network enterprise"* this *"spirit of informationalism?"*

It is certainly not a new culture, in the traditional sense of a system
of values, because the multiplicity of subjects in the network and the
diversity of networks reject such unifying "network culture." Neither
is it a set of institutions, because we have observed the diverse development of the network enterprise in a variety of institutional
environments, to the point of being shaped by such environments
into a broad range of forms. But there is indeed a common cultural
code in the diverse workings of the network enterprise. It is made of
many cultures, many values, many projects, that cross through the
minds and inform the strategies of the various participants in the
networks, changing at the same pace as the network's members, and
following the organizational and cultural transformation of the units
of the network. It is a culture, indeed, but a culture of the ephemeral,
a culture of each strategic decision, a patchwork of experiences and
interests, rather than a charter of rights and obligations. It is a *multifaceted, virtual culture,* as in the visual experiences created by
computers in cyberspace by rearranging reality. It is not a fantasy, it
is a material force because it informs, and enforces, powerful
economic decisions at every moment in the life of the network. But it
does not stay long: it goes into the computer's memory as raw material
of past successes and failures. The network enterprise learns to live
within this virtual culture. Any attempt at crystallizing the position in
the network as a cultural code in a particular time and space sentences
the network to obsolescence, since it becomes too rigid for the variable geometry required by informationalism. The "spirit of
informationalism" is the culture of "creative destruction" accelerated
to the speed of the optoelectronic circuits that process its signals.
Schumpeter meets Weber in the cyberspace of the network
enterprise.

As for the potential social consequences of this new economic
history, the voice of the master resonates with force 100 years later:

> The modern economic order . . . is now bound to the technical
> and economic conditions of machine production which today
> determine the lives of all individuals who are born into this
> mechanism, not only those directly concerned with economic
> acquisition, with irresistible force . . . The care for external goods
> should only lie on the shoulders of the "saint like a light cloak,
> which can be thrown aside at any moment." But fate decreed that

the cloak should become an iron cage . . . Today the spirit of religious asceticism . . . has escaped from the cage. But victorious capitalism, since it rests on mechanical foundations, needs its support no longer . . . No one knows who will live in this cage in the future, or whether at the end of this tremendous development, entirely new prophets will arise, or there will be a great rebirth of old ideas, or, if neither, mechanized petrification, embellished with a sort of convulsive self-importance. For of the last stage of this cultural development, it might well be truly said: "Specialists without spirit, sensualists without heart; this nullity imagines that it has attained a level of civilization never before achieved."[142]

---

[142] Weber (1958: 180–2).

— 4 —

The Transformation of Work and Employment: Networkers, Jobless, and Flextimers

The process of work is at the core of social structure. The technological and managerial transformation of labor, and of production relationships, in and around the emerging network enterprise is the main lever by which the informational paradigm and the process of globalization affect society at large. In this chapter I shall analyze this transformation on the basis of available evidence, while attempting to make sense of contradictory trends observed in the changes of work and employment patterns over the last decades. I shall first address the classic question of secular transformation of employment structure that underlies theories of postindustrialism, by analyzing its evolution in the main capitalist countries between 1920 and 2005. Next, to reach beyond the borders of OECD countries, I shall consider the arguments on the emergence of a global labor force. I shall then turn to analyze the specific impact of new information technologies on the process of work itself, and on the level of employment, trying to assess the widespread fear of a jobless society. Finally, I shall treat the potential impacts of the transformation of work and employment on the social structure, by focusing on processes of social polarization that have been associated with the emergence of the informational paradigm. In fact, I shall suggest an alternative hypothesis that, while acknowledging these trends, will place them in the broader framework of a more fundamental transformation: the individualization of work and the fragmentation of societies.[1] All along such an

I want to acknowledge the significant input to this chapter from Martin Carnoy and Harley Shaiken. I have also relied extensively on data and material provided by the International Institute of Labour Studies, International Labour Office. For this, I am particularly grateful to Padmanabha Gopinath and to Gerry Rodgers.
[1]   To understand the transformation of work in the informational paradigm it is necessary to root this analysis in a comparative and historical perspective. For this, I have relied on what I consider to be the best available source of ideas and

intellectual itinerary, I shall use data and research findings from a flurry of monographs, simulation models, and standard statistics that have treated these questions with minute attention over many years in many countries. Yet the purpose of my inquiry, as for this book in general, is analytical: it aims at raising new questions rather than answering old concerns.

The Historical Evolution of Employment and Occupational Structure in Advanced Capitalist Countries: The G-7, 1920–2005

In any process of historical transition one of the most direct expressions of systemic change is the transformation of employment and occupational structure. Indeed, theories of postindustrialism and informationalism use as the strongest empirical evidence for the change in historical course the coming into being of a new social structure, characterized by the shift from goods to services, by the rise of managerial and professional occupations, by the demise of agricultural and manufacturing jobs, and by the growing information content of work in the most advanced economies. Implicit in much of these formulations is a sort of natural law of economies and societies, that should follow a single path along a trajectory of modernity in which American society has led the way.

I take a different approach. I contend that while there is a common trend in the unfolding of the employment structure characteristic of informational societies, there is also a historical variation of employment patterns according to specific institutions, culture, and political environments. In order to assess both the commonality and the variation of employment structures in the informational paradigm I have examined the evolution of employment structure between 1920 and 1990 for the major capitalist countries that constitute the core of the global economy, the so-called G-7 countries. All of them are in an advanced stage of transition to the informational society, thus can be used to observe the emergence of new employment patterns. They also represent very distinct cultures and institutional systems, allowing us to examine historical variety. In conducting this analysis I am not implying that all other societies, at different levels of development,

---

research on the matter: Pahl (ed.) (1988). The central thesis of this chapter on the transition toward individualization of work, inducing potentially fragmented societies, is also related, although from a very different analytical perspective, to an important book that builds on Polanyi's theory, and relies on empirical analysis of Italian social structure: Mingione (1991).

will conform to one or another of the historical trajectories represented by these countries. As I have argued in the general
introduction to this book, the new, informational paradigm interacts
with history, institutions, levels of development, and position in the
global system of interaction along the lines of different networks. The
analysis presented in the following pages has a more precise purpose:
to unveil the interaction between technology, economy, and institutions in the patterning of employment and occupation, in the process
of transition between agricultural, industrial, and informational
modes of development.

By differentiating the internal composition of service employment,
and by analyzing the differential evolution of the employment and
occupational structure in each one of the seven countries (United
States, Japan, Germany, France, Italy, the United Kingdom and
Canada) between *circa* 1920 and *circa* 1990, the analysis presented
here introduces an empirically grounded discussion on the
cultural/institutional diversity of the informational society. To
proceed in such a direction, I shall introduce the analytical issues
researched in this section, define the concepts, and describe briefly
the methodology I have used in this study. [2]

Postindustrialism, the service economy, and the informational society

The classical theory of postindustrialism combined three statements
and predictions that ought to be analytically differentiated:[3]

(1) The source of productivity and growth lies in the generation of
   knowledge, extended to all realms of economic activity through
   information processing.
(2) Economic activity would shift from goods production to services
   delivery. The demise of agricultural employment would be
   followed by the irreversible decline of manufacturing jobs, to the
   benefit of service jobs which would ultimately form the overwhelming proportion of employment. The more advanced an
   economy, the more its employment and its production would be
   focused on services.
(3) The new economy would increase the importance of occupations

[2]   The analysis of the evolution of employment structure of G-7 countries was
conducted with considerable help from Dr Yuko Aoyama, formerly my research
assistant at Berkeley, particularly for the construction of the international,
comparative data base on which this analysis is grounded.
[3]   Bell (1976); Dordick and Wang (1993).

with a high information and knowledge content in their activity. Managerial, professional, and technical occupations would grow faster than any other occupational position and would constitute the core of the new social structure.

Although various interpretations would extend the theory of postindustrialism in different versions to the realm of social classes, politics, and culture, the preceding three interrelated statements anchor the theory at the level of the social structure, the level where, in Bell's thinking, the theory belongs.

Each one of these major assertions deserves qualification. In addition, the historical linkage between the three processes has still to be submitted to empirical verification.

First, as we argued in chapter 2, knowledge and information seem indeed to be major sources of productivity and growth in advanced societies. However, as we also mentioned above, it is important to notice that theories of postindustrialism based their original assertion on research by Solow and by Kendrick, both referring to the first half of the twentieth century in America, at the height of the industrial era. This is to say that the knowledge base of productivity growth has been a feature of the industrial economy, when manufacturing employment was at its peak in the most advanced countries. Thus, although the late twentieth-century economies are clearly different from the pre-World War II economies, the feature that distinguishes these two types of economies does not seem to be rooted primarily in the source of their productivity growth. **The appropriate distinction is not between an industrial and a postindustrial economy, but between two forms of knowledge-based industrial, agricultural, and services production.** As I have argued in the opening chapters of this book, what is most distinctive, in historical terms, between the economic structures of the first half and of the second half of the twentieth century is the revolution in information technologies, and its diffusion in all spheres of social and economic activity, including its contribution in providing the infrastructure for the formation of a global economy. Therefore, I propose to shift the analytical emphasis from *postindustrialism* (a relevant question of social forecasting still without an answer at the moment of its formulation) to *informationalism*. In this perspective, societies will be informational, not because they fit into a particular model of social structure, but because they organize their production system around the principles of maximizing knowledge-based productivity through the development and diffusion of information technologies, and by fulfilling the prerequisites for their utilization (primarily human resources and communications infrastructure).

The second criterion of postindustrialist theory by which to consider a society as postindustrial concerns the shift to service activities and the demise of manufacturing. It is an obvious fact that most employment in advanced economies is in services, and that the service sector accounts for the largest contribution to GNP. Yet it does not follow that manufacturing industries are disappearing or that the structure and dynamics of manufacturing activity are indifferent to the health of a service economy. Cohen and Zysman,[4] among others, have forcefully argued that many services depend on their direct linkage to manufacturing, and that manufacturing activity (distinct from manufacturing employment) is critical to the productivity and competitiveness of the economy. For the United States, Cohen and Zysman estimate that 24% of GNP comes from the value added by manufacturing firms, and another 25% of GNP comes from the contribution of services directly linked to manufacturing. Thus, they argue that the postindustrial economy is a "myth," and that we are in fact in a different kind of industrial economy.

Furthermore, the notion of "services" is often considered to be ambiguous at best, misleading at worst.[5] In employment statistics, it has been used as a residual notion that embraces all that is not agriculture, mining, construction, utilities, or manufacturing. Thus, the category of services includes activities of all kinds, historically originated from various social structures and productive systems. The only common feature for these service activities is what they are not. Attempts at defining services by some intrinsic characteristics, such as their "intangibility," opposed to the "materiality" of goods, have been definitely voided of meaning by the evolution of the informational economy. Computer software, video production, microelectronics design, biotechnology-based agriculture, and so on, and many other critical processes characteristic of advanced economies, merge inextricably their information content with the material support of the product, making it impossible to distinguish the boundaries between "goods" and "services." To understand the new type of economy and social structure, we must start by characterizing different types of "services," in order to establish clear distinctions between them. In understanding the informational economy, each one of the specific categories of services becomes as important a distinction as was the old borderline between manufacturing and services in the preceding type of industrial economy. As economies become more complex, we must diversify the concepts through which we categorize economic

[4]   Cohen and Zysman (1987).
[5]   Gershuny and Miles (1983); Castells (1976); Daniels (1993); Cohen and Zysman (1987); De Bandt (ed.) (1985); Stanback (1979).

activities, and ultimately abandon Colin Clark's old paradigm based on the primary/secondary/tertiary sectors distinction. Such a distinction has become an epistemological obstacle to the understanding of our societies.

The third major prediction of the original theory of postindustrialism refers to the expansion of information-rich occupations, such as managerial, professional, and technical positions, as the core of the new occupational structure. This prediction also requires qualification. A number of analysts have argued that this trend is not the only characteristic of the new occupational structure. Simultaneous to this trend there is also the growth of low-end, unskilled, service occupations. These low-skilled jobs, despite their slower growth rate, may represent a substantial proportion of the postindustrial social structure in terms of their absolute numbers. In other words, advanced, informational societies could also be characterized by an increasingly polarized social structure, where the top and the bottom increase their share at the expense of the middle.[6] In addition, there is a widespread challenge in the literature to the notion that knowledge, science, and expertise are the critical components in most of the managerial/professional occupations. A harder, closer look must be taken at the actual content of such general statistical classifications before we jump to characterizing our future as the republic of the learned elite.

Yet the most important argument against a simplistic version of postindustrialism is the critique of the assumption according to which the three features we have examined coalesce in the historical evolution, and that such an evolution leads to a single model of the informational society. This analytical construct is in fact similar to the formulation of the concept of capitalism by classical political economists (from Adam Smith to Marx) exclusively based on the experience of English industrialization, only to find continuous "exceptions" to the pattern throughout the diversity of economic and social experience in the world. Only if we start from the analytical separation between the structural logic of the production system of the informational society and its social structure can we observe empirically if a specific techno-economic paradigm induces a specific social structure and to what extent. And only if we open up the cultural and institutional scope of our observation can we separate what belongs to the structure of the informational society (as expressing a new mode of development) from what is specific to the historical trajectory

---

[6]   Kuttner (1983); Rumberger and Levin (1984); Bluestone and Harrison (1988); Leal et al. (1993); Sayer and Walker (1992).

of a given country. To make some tentative steps in such a direction, I have compiled and made somewhat comparable basic statistics for the seven largest market economies in the world, the so-called G-7 countries. Thus I can compare, with reasonable approximation, the evolution of their employment and occupational structure over the last 70 years. I have also considered some employment projections for Japan and the United States through the early twenty-first century. The empirical core of this analysis consists in an attempt at differentiating between various service activities. To do so, I have followed the well-known typology of services employment constructed by Singelmann almost 20 years ago.[7] Singelmann's conceptualization is not without flaws, but has a fundamental merit: it is well adapted to the usual statistical categories, as shown in Singelmann's own doctoral dissertation that analyzed the change of employment structure in various countries between 1920 and 1970. Since the main purpose of this book is analytical I decided to build on Singelmann's work, to compare the 1970–90 period with his findings for the 1920–79 period. Thus, I constructed a similar typology of sectoral employment, and processed the statistics of the G-7 countries along roughly comparable categories, extending Singelmann's analysis to the critical period of development of informational societies, from the 1970s onwards. Because I cannot ensure the absolute equivalence of my decisions in classifying activities with those taken earlier by Singelmann, I present our data separately for the two periods: they must not be read as a statistical series, but as two distinct statistical trends made roughly equivalent in terms of the analytical categories used to compile the data. I did find considerable methodological difficulties in establishing equivalent categories among different countries. The appendix to this chapter provides details on the procedures followed in building this data base. In analyzing these data I have used the simplest statistical procedures, always trying to show the actual trends in the social structure, rather than using analytical methods that would be unnecessarily sophisticated for the current level of elaboration of the data base. I have opted for using descriptive statistics that would simply suggest lines of new theoretical understanding.

By adopting Singelmann's categories of service activities I have embraced a structuralist view of employment, dividing it up according to the place of the activity in the chain of linkages that starts from the production process. Thus, distributive services refer both to communication and transportation activities, as well as to commercial distribution networks (wholesale and retail). Producer services refer

---

[7]   Singelmann (1978).

more directly to those services that appear to be critical inputs in the economy, although they also include auxiliary services to business that may not be necessarily highly skilled. Social services include a whole realm of government activities, as well as collective consumption-related jobs. Personal services are those related to individual consumption, from entertainment to eating and drinking places. Although these distinctions are admittedly broad, they do allow us to think differentially about the evolution of the employment structure across countries, at least with greater analytical depth than the usual statistical accounts. I have also tried to establish a difference between the services/goods dichotomy and the classification of employment between information-processing and goods-handling activities, since each one of these distinctions belongs to a different approach in the analysis of social structure. To do so, I built two elementary indexes of service-delivery employment/goods-producing employment, and of information-processing employment/goods-handling employment, and calculated these indexes for the countries and periods under consideration. Finally, I also calculated a simplified typology of occupations across countries, building the various countries' categories around those used by American and Japanese statistics. Although I have serious concerns about the definitions of such occupational categories which mix, in fact, occupational positions and types of activities, using standard statistics that are widely available gives us the opportunity of looking at the evolution of occupational structures in roughly comparative terms. The purpose of this exercise is to recast the sociological analysis of informational societies by assessing in a comparative framework the differences in the evolution of their employment structure as a fundamental indicator for both their commonality and their diversity.

The transformation of employment structure, 1920–70 and 1970–90

The analysis of the evolution of employment structure in the G-7 countries must start from the distinction between two periods that, by sheer luck, match our two different data bases: *circa* 1920–70 and *circa* 1970–90. *The major analytical distinction between the two periods stems from the fact that during the first period the societies under consideration became postagricultural, while in the second period they did become postindustrial.* I understand obviously by such terms the massive decline of agricultural employment in the first case and the rapid decline of manufacturing employment in the second period. Indeed, *all G-7 countries maintained or increased (in some cases substantially) the percentage of their employment in transformative activities and in manufacturing between*

1920 and 1970. Thus, if we exclude construction and utilities in order to have a sharper view of the manufacturing labor force, England and Wales decreased only slightly the level of their manufacturing labor force from 36.8% in 1921 to 34.9% in 1971; the United States increased manufacturing employment from 24.5% in 1930 to 25.9% in 1970; Canada from 17.0% in 1921 to 22.0% in 1971; Japan saw a dramatic increase in manufacturing from 16.6% in 1920 to 26.0% in 1970; Germany (although with a different national territory) increased its manufacturing labor force from 33.0% to 40.2%; France, from 26.4% to 28.1%; and Italy, from 19.9% to 27.4%. Thus, as Singelmann argues, the shift in the structure of employment in this half century (1920–70) was from agriculture to services and construction, not out of manufacturing.

The story is a very different one in the 1970–90 period, when the process of economic restructuring and technological transformation that took place during these two decades led to a reduction of manufacturing employment in all countries (See tables 4.1 to 4.14 in Appendix A). However, while this trend was general, the shrinkage of manufacturing employment was uneven, clearly indicating the fundamental variety of social structures according to differences in economic policies and in firms' strategies. Thus, while the United Kingdom, the United States, and Italy experienced rapid deindustrialization (reducing the share of their manufacturing employment in 1970–90 from 38.7% to 22.5%; from 25.9% to 17.5%; from 27.3% to 21.8%, respectively), Japan and Germany reduced their share of manufacturing labor force moderately: from 26.0% to 23.6% in the case of Japan, and from 38.6% to a still rather high level of 32.2% in 1987 in the case of Germany. Canada and France occupy an intermediate position, reducing manufacturing employment from 19.7% (in 1971) to 14.9%, and from 27.7% to 21.3%, respectively.

In fact, England and Wales had already become a postagricultural society in 1921, with only 7.1% of their labor force in agriculture. The United States, Germany, and Canada still had a sizable agricultural population (from a quarter to a third of total employment), and Japan, Italy, and France were, by and large, societies dominated by agricultural and commercial occupations. From this differential starting point in the historical period under study, trends converged toward an employment structure characterized by simultaneous growth of manufacturing and services at the expense of agriculture. Such a convergence is explained by very rapid processes of industrialization in Germany, Japan, Italy, and France, that distributed the surplus of agricultural population between manufacturing and services.

Thus, if we calculate the employment ratio of services to industry (our indicator of the "service economy") it shows only a moderate increase for most countries between 1920 and 1970. Only the United States (change from 1.1 to 2.0) and Canada (1.3 to 2.0) witnessed a significant increase of the relative proportion of service employment during the period that I call postagricultural. In this sense, it is true that the United States was the standard-bearer of the employment structure characteristic of the service economy. Thus, when the trend toward service employment accelerated and generalized in the post-industrial period, the United States and Canada increased even more their service predominance, with indexes of 3.0 and 3.3 respectively. All other countries followed the same tendency, but at different speeds, thus reaching different levels of deindustrialization. While the United Kingdom, France, and Italy seem to be on the same path, North America, Japan, and Germany clearly stand out as strong industrial economies, with lower rates of increase of service employment, and lower service to industry employment ratios: 1.8 and 1.4 respectively in 1987–90. This is a fundamental observation that deserves careful discussion below. Yet, as a trend, in the 1990s the majority of the population in all G-7 countries is employed in services.

Is employment also concentrating on information processing? Our ratio of information-processing to goods-handling employment provides some interesting clues for the analysis. First, we must put aside Japan for further consideration.

For all other countries there has been a trend toward a higher percentage of information-processing employment. Although Italy and Germany had no or only slow increase in 1920–70, their share of information employment grew considerably in the last two decades. The United States holds the highest information employment ratio among the seven countries, but the United Kingdom, Canada, and France are almost at the same level. Thus, the trend toward information processing is clearly not a distinctive feature of the United States: the American employment structure is more clearly set apart from the others as a "service economy" than as an "information economy." Germany and Italy have a significantly lower rate of information employment, but they have doubled it in the last two decades, thus displaying the same trend.

The data on Japan are most interesting. They show only a moderate increase of information employment in 50 years (from 0.3 to 0.4), and an even slower increase in the last 20 years, from 0.4 to 0.5. Thus, what is probably the society to put the strongest emphasis on information technologies, and in which high technology plays a most significant role in productivity and competitiveness, also appears to have the lowest level of information-processing employment, and the lowest rate of progression of such employment. The expansion of information employment and the development of an "information society" (*johoka shakai*, in the Japanese concept) seem to be different, although interrelated, processes. It is indeed interesting, and problematic for some interpretations of postindustrialism, that Japan and Germany, the two most competitive economies among major economies in the 1970s and 1980s, are those with the strongest manufacturing employment, the lowest service to industry employment ratio, the lowest information to goods employment ratio, and, for Japan (which has experienced the fastest productivity growth), the lowest rate of increase in information employment throughout the century. I suggest the idea that information processing is most productive when it is embedded in material production or in the handling of goods, instead of being disjointed in a stepped-up technical division of labor. After all, most of automation refers precisely to the integration of information processing in goods handling.

This hypothesis may also help to interpret another important observation: none of the seven countries had a ratio of information employment over 1 in 1990, and only the United States was approaching that threshold. Thus, if information is a critical component in the functioning of the economy and in the organization of society, it does not follow that most jobs are or will be in information processing. The march toward information employment is proceeding at a significantly slower pace, and reaching much lower levels, than the trend toward service employment. Thus, to understand the actual profile of the transformation of employment in advanced societies we must now turn to the differential evolution of each type of services in the G-7 countries.

To do so, I shall first comment on the evolution of each category of services in each country; then I shall compare the relative importance of each type of service *vis-à-vis* each other in each country; finally, I shall consider the trends of evolution of employment in those services that have been identified in the literature as characteristic of "postindustrial" societies. In proceeding with this analysis I must remind the reader that the further we go into the fine-grain analysis of specific categories of employment, the less solid the data base becomes. The inability to obtain reliable data for some categories, countries, and periods will make it difficult to be systematic in our analysis across the board. Yet the observation of the tables presented here still suggests that there are some features that merit closer analysis and further elaboration on country-specific data bases.

Let us start with *producer services*. They are considered in the literature to be the strategic services of the new economy, the providers of information and support for the increase in the productivity and efficiency of firms. Thus, their expansion should go hand in hand with the increasing sophistication and productivity of the economy. Indeed, we observe throughout the two periods (1920–1970, 1970–1990) a significant expansion of employment in these activities in all countries. For instance, in the United Kingdom employment in producer services shot up from 5% in 1970 to 12% in 1990; in the United States, for the same period, from 8.2% to 14%; in France, it doubled, from 5% to 10%. It is significant that Japan increased dramatically its producer services employment between 1921 (0.8%) and 1970 (5.1%), most of this increase taking place during the 1960s, the moment when the Japanese economy internationalized its scope. On the other hand, focusing on 1970–90 on a different data base, the increase of Japanese employment in producer services between 1971 and 1990 (from 4.8% to 9.6%), while substantial, still leaves Japan in the lower tier of employment in producer services among the advanced economies. This could suggest that a significant proportion of producer services are internalized in Japan in manufacturing companies, which could appear to be a more efficient formula, if we consider the competitiveness and productivity of the Japanese economy.

This hypothesis receives additional support from the observation of data concerning Germany. While increasing significantly the share of employment in producer services from 4.5% in 1970 to 7.3% in 1987, Germany still displays the lowest level of producer services employment of the G-7 countries. This could imply a great degree of internalization of service activities in German firms. If these data were confirmed, we must emphasize that the two most dynamic economies (Japan and Germany) have also the lowest rate of employment in producer services, while it is obvious that their firms do use such services in great amount, yet probably with a different organizational structure that links up more closely producer services to the production process.

While it is evident that producer services are strategically crucial in an advanced economy, they still do not represent a substantial proportion of employment in most advanced countries, in spite of their rapid rate of growth in several of them. With the unknown position of Italy, the proportion of employment varies between 7.3% and 14% in the other countries, of course putting them well ahead of agriculture, but far behind in manufacturing. The battalions of professionals and managers have indeed swelled the ranks of employment in advanced economies, but not always, and not predominantly, in the visible spots of the management of capital and the control of information. It seems that the expansion of producer services is linked to the processes of vertical disintegration and outsourcing that characterize the informational corporation.

Social services form the second employment category which, according to the postindustrial literature, should characterize the new society. And indeed it does. With, again, the exception of Japan, employment in social services represents between one-fifth and one-quarter of total employment in the G-7 countries. But the interesting observation here is that the major increase in social services took place during the roaring sixties, actually linking their expansion with the impact of social movements rather than with the advent of post-industrialism. Indeed, the United States, Canada, and France had very moderate rates of growth of employment in social services in the 1970–90 period, while in Germany, Japan, and Britain it grew at a robust rate.

Overall, it would seem that the expansion of the welfare state has been a secular trend since the beginning of the century, with moments of acceleration in periods that vary for each society, and a tendency to slow down in the 1980s. Japan is the exception because it appears to be catching up. It maintained a very low level of employment in social services until 1970, probably linked to a greater decentralization of social support both by the firm and the family. Then, when Japan became a major industrial power, and when more traditional forms of support could not be maintained, Japan engaged in forms of social redistribution similar to the other advanced economies, providing services and creating jobs in the social services sector. Overall, we can say that although the expansion of social services employment at a very high level is a feature of all advanced societies, the pace of such expansion seems to be directly dependent on the relationship between the state and society, rather than on the stage of development of the economy. Indeed, the expansion of social services employment (except in Japan) is more characteristic of the 1950–70 period than of the 1970–90 period, at the dawn of the informational society.

Distributive services combine transportation and communication, relational activities of all advanced economies, with wholesale and retail trade, the supposedly typical service activities of less industrialized societies. Is employment declining in these low-productivity, labor-intensive activities, as the economy progresses toward the automation of work, and toward the modernization of commercial shops? In fact, employment in distributive services remains at a very high level in advanced societies, also oscillating between one-fifth and one-quarter of total employment, with the exception of Germany, which stood at 17.7% in 1987. This level of employment is substantially higher than that of 1920, and has only declined slightly in the last 20 years in the United States (from 22.4% to 20.6%). Thus employment in distributive services is roughly double that in producer services, considered typical of advanced economies. Japan, Canada, and France have increased the share of such employment in the 1970–90 period. About half of employment in distributive services in the G-7 countries corresponds to retail services, although it is often impossible to differentiate the data between wholesale and retail trade. Overall, retail employment has not significantly declined over a 70-year period. In the United States, for instance, it grew from 1.8% in 1940 to 12.8% in 1970, later declining slightly from 12.9% in 1970 to 11.7% in 1991. Japan has increased retail employment from 8.9% in 1960 to 11.2% in 1990, and Germany, while having a lower level of employment in such activity (8.6% in 1987) has actually increased it over its 1970 figure. Thus, there is a large sector of employment still engaged in distribution, as the movements of the employment structure are in fact very slow in the so-called service activities.

Personal services are viewed, at the same time, as the remnants of a proto-industrial structure, and as the expression (at least for some of them) of the social dualism that, according to observers, characterizes the informational society. Here also, the observation of the long-term evolution in the seven countries invites the introduction of a word of caution. They continue to represent a sizable proportion of employment in 1990: with the exception of Germany (6.3% in 1987), they vary in the range between 9.7% and 14.1%, that is roughly equivalent to the quintessential postindustrialist producer services. Overall, they have increased their share since 1970. Focusing on the famous/ infamous "eating and drinking places" jobs, a favorite theme of the literature critical of postindustrialism, we do find a significant expansion of such jobs in the last two decades, particularly in the United Kingdom and in Canada, although the data often mix restaurants and bars with hotel employment which could also be considered as characteristic of the "leisure society." In the United States, eating and drinking places employment stood at 4.9% of total employment in 1991 (up from 3.2% in 1970), which is about twice the size of agricultural employment, but still less than we are asked to believe by the essays elaborating on the notion of the "hamburger society." The main remark to be made on employment in personal services is that it is not fading away in the advanced economies, thus providing ground for the argument that the changes in the social/economic structure concern more the type of services and the type of jobs than the activities themselves.

Let us try now to evaluate some of the traditional theses on postindustrialism in the light of the evolution of employment structure since 1970, more or less at the moment when Touraine, Bell, Richta, and other early theorists of the new, information society were publishing their analyses. In terms of activity, producer services and social services were considered to be typical of postindustrial economies, both as sources of productivity and as responses to social demands and changing values. If we aggregate employment in producer services and social services, we do observe a substantial increase in what could be labeled the "postindustrial services category" in all countries between 1970 and 1990: from 22.8% to 39.2% in the United Kingdom; from 30.2% to 39.5% in the United States; from 28.6% to 33.8% in Canada; from 15.1% to 24.0% in Japan, from 20.2% to 31.7% in Germany; from 21.1% to 29.5% in France (Italian data in our data base do not allow any serious evaluation of this trend). Thus, the trend is there, but it is uneven since it starts from a very different base in 1970: the Anglo-Saxon countries had already developed a strong basis in advanced services employment, while Japan, Germany, and France kept much higher employment in manufacturing, as well as in agriculture. Thus, we observe two different paths in the expansion of "postindustrial" services' employment: one, the Anglo-Saxon model, that shifts from manufacturing to advanced services, maintaining employment in the traditional services; the other, the Japanese/German model, that both expands advanced services and preserves a manufacturing basis, while internalizing some of the service activities in the industrial sector. France is in-between, although leaning toward the Anglo-Saxon model.

In sum, the evolution of employment during what we called the "postindustrial" period (1970–90) shows, at the same time, a general pattern of shifting away from manufacturing jobs, and two different paths regarding manufacturing activity: the first amounts to a rapid phasing away of manufacturing, coupled with a strong expansion of employment in producer services (in rate) and in social services (in size), while other service activities are still kept as sources of employment. A second, different path more closely links manufacturing and producer services, more cautiously increases social services employment, and maintains distributive services. The variation within this second path is between Japan, with a greater agricultural and retail trade population, and Germany with a significantly higher manufacturing employment.

In the process of transformation of the employment structure there is no disappearance of any major service category with the exception of domestic service as compared to 1920. What happens is an increasing diversity of activities, and the emergence of a set of linkages between different activities that makes the employment categories obsolete. There is indeed a postmanufacturing employment structure emerging in the last quarter of the twentieth century. But there is a great deal of variation in the emerging structures of various countries, and it does not seem that great productivity, social stability, and international competitiveness are directly associated with the highest degree of service-related or information-processing jobs. On the contrary, those societies in the G-7 group that have been at the forefront of economic progress and social stability in recent years (Japan and Germany) seem to have developed a more efficient linkage system between manufacturing, producer services, social services, and distributive services than Anglo-Saxon societies, with France and Italy being at the crossroads between the two paths. In all of these societies, informationalization seems to be more decisive than information processing.

Thus, when societies massively destroy manufacturing jobs in a short period of time, instead of gradually phasing the industrial transformation, it is not necessarily because they are more advanced, but because they follow specific policies and strategies that are based in their cultural, social, and political backdrop. And the options taken to conduct the transformation of the national economy and of the labor force have profound consequences for the evolution of the occupational structure that provides the foundations for the new class system of the informational society.

The new occupational structure

A major statement of theories on postindustrialism is that people, besides being engaged in different activities, also hold new positions in the occupational structure. By and large, it was predicted that as we move into what we call the informational society we would observe an increasing importance of managerial, professional, and technical positions, a decreasing proportion of workers in the craft and operator positions, and a swelling in the numbers of clerical and sales workers. In addition, the "left-wing" version of postindustrialism points at the growing importance of semiskilled (often unskilled) service occupations as a counterpart to the growth of professional jobs.

To examine the accuracy of such predictions in the evolution of G-7 countries over the last 40 years is not an easy task, both because the statistical categories do not always correspond exactly across countries and because dates for the various available statistics do not always coincide. Thus, in spite of our methodological efforts to clean up the data, our analysis on this point remains rather tentative, and should be taken only as a first empirical approach to suggest lines of analysis on the evolution of the social structure.

First, let us start with the *diversity of the occupational profiles across societies.* Table 4.15 in Appendix A brings together the distribution of the labor force in the main occupational categories for each country at the time of the latest available statistical information when we conducted this study (1992–3). The first and most important conclusion of our observation is that there are very strong differences between the occupational structures of societies equally entitled to be considered as informational. Thus, if we take the category that groups managers, professionals, and technicians, the epitome of the informational occupations, it was indeed very strong in the United States and in Canada, amounting to almost one-third of the labor force in the early 1990s. But in early 1990s Japan it was only 14.9%. And in France and Germany in 1989 it was only at about one-quarter of all labor. On the other hand, while crafts and operators have substantially dwindled down in North America, they still represented 31.8% of the labor force of Japan, and they were over 27% in both France and Germany, Similarly, sales workers are not a major category in France (3.8%) but they are still important in the United States (11.9%) and truly significant in Japan (15.1%). Japan had a very low proportion of managers (only 3.8%) in 1990, compared to 12.8% in the United States, which could be an indicator of a much more hierarchical structure. France's distinctive feature is the strong component of technicians in the higher professional groups (12.4% of all labor force), in contrast to Germany's 8.7%. On the other hand, Germany has many more jobs than France in the "professionals" category: 13.9% against 6.0%.

Another factor of diversity is the variation in the proportion of semi-skilled service workers: it is significant in the United States, Canada, and Germany, much lower in Japan and France, precisely the countries that, together with Italy, have preserved somewhat more sizable traditional agricultural and commercial activities.

Overall, **Japan and the United States represent the opposite ends of the comparison, and their contrast emphasizes the need to recast the theory of postindustrialism and informationalism.** The data on the United States fit well with the predominant model in the literature, very simply because the "model" was but a theorization of the evolution of the US employment structure. Meanwhile, Japan appears to combine an increase in the professional occupations with the persistence of a strong craft labor force, linked to the industrial era, and with the durability of the agricultural labor force and of sales workers that witness the continuity, under new forms, of the occupations characteristic of the pre-industrial era. The US model progresses into informationalism by substituting new occupations for the old ones. The Japanese model does equally progress into informationalism but following a different route: by increasing some of the required new occupations while redefining the content of occupations of a previous era, yet phasing out those positions that become an obstacle to increase productivity (particularly in agriculture). In between these two "models," Germany and France combine elements of both: they are closer to the United States in terms of the professional/managerial occupations, but closer to Japan in the slower decline of craft/operators jobs.

The second major observation refers, in spite of the diversity we have shown, to the existence of a **common trend toward the increase of the relative weight of the most clearly informational occupation (managers, professionals, and technicians)**, as well as of the overall "white-collar" occupations (including sales and clerical workers). Having first established my call for diversity I also want to give empirical credit to the notion that there is indeed a tendency toward a greater informational content in the occupational structure of advanced societies, in spite of their diverse cultural/political system, and in spite also of the different historical moments of their processes of industrialization.

To observe such a common trend, we must concentrate on the growth of each occupation in each country over time. Let us compare for instance (see tables 4.16 to 4.21 in Appendix A) the evolution of four critical groups of occupations: craft/operators; technicians, professionals, and managers; sales and clerical workers; farm workers and managers. Calculating the rates of change in share of each occupation and group of occupations, we observe some general trends and some critical differences. The share of the managerial/professional/technical occupations showed strong growth in all countries except France. Crafts and operators declined substantially in the United States, the United Kingdom and Canada, and moderately in Germany, France and Japan. Sales and clericals increased moderately their share in the United Kingdom and France and strongly in the four other countries. Farm workers and managers declined substantially in all countries. And semiskilled service and transportation workers presented clearly different trends: they increased their share strongly in the United States and in the United Kingdom; they increased moderately in France; they declined or stabilized in Japan and Germany.

Of all countries considered, Japan was the one that most dramatically upgraded its occupational structure, increasing its share of managers by 46.2% in a 20-year period, and the share of its professional/technical labor force by 91.4%. The United Kingdom also increased the share of its managers by 96.3%, although the increase of its professional/technical workers was much more moderate (5.2%). Thus, we observe a great diversity of rates of change in the share of its occupational group in the overall employment structure. There is diversity in rates because there is some degree of convergence toward a relatively similar occupational structure. At the same time, the differences in management style and in the importance of manufacturing in each country also introduce some variation in the process of change.

Overall, the tendency toward a predominantly white-collar labor force skewed toward its higher tier seems to be the general trend (in the United States in 1991, 57.3% of the labor force was white collar), with the exceptions of Japan and Germany, whose white-collar labor force still does not exceed 50% of total employment. However, even in Japan and Germany, the rates of growth of the informational occupations have been the highest among the various occupational positions; thus, as a trend Japan will count increasingly on a substantial professional labor force, although still holding onto a broader craft and commercial basis than in other societies.

Thirdly, **the widespread argument concerning the increasing polarization of the occupational structure of informational society does not seem to fit with this data set**, if by polarization we mean the simultaneous expansion in equivalent terms of the top and of the bottom of the occupational scale. If such were the case the managerial–professional–technical labor force and the semiskilled service and transport workers would be expanding at similar rates and in similar numbers. Such is clearly not the case. In the United States, semiskilled service workers have indeed increased their share in the occupational structure but at a lower rate than the managerial/professional labor force, and they only represented 13.7% of the labor force in 1991. By contrast, managers, at the top of the scale, have increased their share between 1950 and 1991 at a rate much higher than that of the semiskilled service workers, increasing their number to 12.8% of the labor force in 1991, almost at the same level as that of semiskilled service workers. Even if we add semiskilled transportation workers, we still reach a mere 17.9% of the labor force in 1991, in sharp contrast with the 29.7% of the top managerial–professional–technical category. Of course, many jobs among clerical and sales workers, as well as among operators, are also semiskilled, so that we cannot truly assess the evolution of the occupational structure in terms of skills. Additionally, we know from other sources that *there has been a polarization of income distribution in the United States and in other countries in the last two decades.*[8] However, here I am objecting to the popular image of the informational economy as providing an increasing number of low-level service jobs at a disproportionately higher rate than the rate of increase in the share of the professional/technical component of the labor force. According to this data base, this is simply not the case. In the United

[8] Esping-Andersen (1993); Mishel and Bernstein (1994).

Kingdom there was however a substantial increase in such semiskilled service jobs between 1961 and 1981, but, even there, the share of the higher occupational level increased faster. In Canada, semi-skilled service workers also increased their share substantially to reach 13.7% in 1992 but managerial–professional–technical jobs progressed even more, almost doubling their representation to account for 30.6% of the labor force in 1992. A similar pattern can be found in Germany: low-end service jobs remained relatively stable and well below the progression in rate and in size of the upper occupational tier. France, while increasing substantially such service jobs during the 1980s, still counted them only as 7.2% of the labor force in 1989. As for Japan, semiskilled service jobs experienced a slow growth, from 5.4% in 1955 to a modest 8.6% in 1990.

Thus, while there are certainly signs of social and economic polarization in advanced societies, they do not take the form of divergent paths in the occupational structure, but of different positions of similar occupations across sectors and between firms. Sectoral, territorial, firm-specific, and gender/ethnic/age characteristics are clearer sources of social polarization than occupational differentiation per se.

Informational societies are certainly unequal societies, but inequalities stem less from their relatively upgraded occupational structure than from the exclusions and discriminations that take place in and around the labor force.

Finally, a view of the transformation of the labor force in advanced societies must also consider the *evolution of its employment status*. Again, the data challenge predominant views of postindustrialism, exclusively based on the American experience. Thus, the hypothesis on the fading away of self-employment in mature, informational economies is somewhat supported by the US experience, where the percentage of self-employment in the total labor force declined from 17.6% in 1950 to 8.8% in 1991 *although it has been almost at a standstill for the last 20 years*. But other countries present different patterns. Germany declined at a slow, steady pace, from 13.8% in 1955 to 9.5% in 1975, then to 8.9% in 1989. France has maintained its share of self-employment in the labor force between 1977 and 1987 (12.8% and 12.7% respectively). Italy, while being the fifth largest market economy in the world, still retained 24.8% of its labor force in self-employment in 1989. Japan, while experiencing a decline in self-employment from 19.2% in 1970 to 14.1% in 1990, still has a significant level of such autonomous employment, to which we must add 8.3% of family workers, which places almost one-quarter of the Japanese labor force outside salaried work. As for Canada and the United Kingdom, they have reversed the supposed secular pattern of corporatization of employment in the last 20 years, as Canada increased the proportion of self-employed in its population from 8.4% in 1970 to 9.7% in 1992, and the United Kingdom increased the share of self-employment and family workers in the labor force from 7.6% in 1969 to 13.0% in 1989: a trend that has continued in the 1990s, as I shall show later in this chapter (pp. 266–7).

Granted, the majority of the labor force in the advanced economies is under salaried conditions. But the diversity of the levels, the unevenness of the process, and the reversal of the trend in some cases calls for a differential view of the patterns of evolution of the occupational structure. We could even formulate the hypothesis that as networking and flexibility become characteristic of the new industrial organization, and as new technologies make it possible for small business to find market niches, we witness a resurgence of self-employment and mixed employment status. Thus, the occupational profile of the informational societies, as they emerge historically, will be far more diverse than that imagined by the quasi-naturalistic vision of postindustrial theories biased by an American ethnocentrism that did not fully represent even the American experience.

The maturing of the informational society: employment projections to the twenty-first century

The informational society, in its historically diverse manifestations, is only taking shape in the twilight of the twentieth century. Thus, an analytical clue for its future direction and mature profile could be provided by employment and occupational projections that forecast the social structure of advanced societies into the early years of the coming century. Such projections are always subject to a number of economic, technological, and institutional assumptions that are hardly established on solid ground. Thus, the status of the data that I shall be using in this section is even more tentative than the analysis of the employment trends up to 1990. Yet, by using reliable sources, such as the US Bureau of Labor Statistics, the Japanese Ministry of Labor, and government data compiled by OECD, and by keeping in mind the approximative nature of the exercise, we may be able to generate some hypotheses on the future path of informational employment.

My analysis of employment projections will be mainly focusing on the United States and Japan, because I want to keep within limits the empirical complexity of the study in order to be able to focus on the main argument of my analysis.[9] Thus, by pinpointing the United

[9] For employment projections concerning other OECD countries, see OECD (1994a: 71–100).

States and Japan, which appear to be two different models of the informational society, I can better assess the hypotheses on the convergence and/or divergence of the informational society's employment and occupational structure.

For the United States, the US Bureau of Labor Statistics (BLS) published in 1991–93 a series of studies, updated in 1994,[10] that together offer a meaningful overview of the evolution of employment and occupational structure between 1990–2 and 2005. To simplify the analysis, I shall refer to the "moderative alternative projection" of the three scenarios considered by the Bureau.

The American economy is projected to create over 26 million jobs between 1992 and 2005. That is a total increase of 22%, slightly higher than the increase in the previous 13-year period, 1979–92. The most apparent features in the projections are the continuation of the trend toward the decline of agricultural and manufacturing jobs, which in 1990–2005 would decline, respectively, at an average annual rate of -0.4 and -0.2. However, manufacturing output would continue to grow at a slightly higher rate than the economy as a whole, at 2.3% per year. Thus the differential growth rate between employment and output in manufacturing and in services shows a substantial gap in labor productivity in favor of manufacturing, in spite of the introduction of new technologies in information-processing activities. Higher than average manufacturing productivity continues to be the key to sustained economic growth able to provide jobs for all other sectors in the economy.

An interesting observation comes from the fact that although employment in agriculture would decline, to a low 2.5% of total employment, agriculture-related *occupations* are expected to grow: this is because, while farmers are expected to decrease by 231,000, an increase of 311,000 jobs for gardeners and groundskeepers is expected: the surpassing of farming jobs by urban-oriented agricultural service jobs underlines how far informational societies have come in their post-agricultural status.

Although only 1 million of the projected 26.4 million new jobs are expected to be created in the goods-producing industries, decline in manufacturing employment is expected to slow down, and some occupational categories in manufacturing, such as precision production, craft, and repair, are actually expected to increase. Yet the bulk of new job growth in the United States is expected to take place in "service activities." About half of such growth is expected to be contributed by the so-called "services division," whose main components are *health*

---

[10]   See Kutscher (1991); Carey and Franklin (1991); Silvestri and Lukasiewicz (1991); Braddock (1992); Bureau of Labor Statistics (1994).

services and *business services.* Business services, which were the fastest-growing service sector in 1975–90, will continue to be at the top of the expansion through 2005, although with a slower growth rate of about 2.5% per year. One should be aware, though, that not all business services are knowledge intensive: an important component of them are computer data-processing jobs, but *in the 1975–90 period the fastest growing activity was personnel supply services, linked to the increase of temporary work and of contracting out services by firms.* Other fast-growing services in the coming years are expected to be legal services (particularly para-legal), engineering and architectural services, and educational services (*private schools*). In the BLS categories, finance, insurance, and real estate (FIRE) are not included in business services. Thus, to the strong growth in business services we must add the moderate but steady growth projected for this FIRE category, expected to be at about 1.3% per year, to reach 6.1% of total employment by 2005. When comparing these data with my analysis of "producer services" in the preceding sections, both business services and FIRE should be taken into consideration.

Health services will be among the fastest growing activities, at a rate twice as fast as its own increase for the 1975–90 period. By 2005, health services are projected to count for 11.5 million jobs, that is 8.7% of all nonfarm wage and salary employment. To put this figure into perspective, the comparable number for all manufacturing employment in 2005 is projected to be 14% of the labor force. Home healthcare services, particularly for the elderly, would be the fastest growing activity.

Retail trade, growing at a healthy 1.6% average annual rate, and starting from a high level in absolute numbers of jobs, represents the third major source of potential new growth, with 5.1 million new jobs. Within this sector, eating and drinking places would account for 42% of total jobs in retail in 2005.

State and local government jobs would also add to employment in sizable numbers, rising from 15.2 million in 1990 to 18.3 million by 2005. More than half of this increase is expected to take place in education.

Thus, overall, the projected employment structure for the United States closely fits the original blueprint for the informational society:

- agricultural jobs are being phased out;
- manufacturing employment will continue to decline, although at a lower pace, being reduced to a hard core of craft and engineering workforce. Most of the employment impact of manufacturing production will be transferred to services for manufacturing;

- producer services, as well as health and education, lead employment growth in terms of rate, also becoming increasingly important in terms of absolute numbers;
- retail jobs and service jobs continue to swell the ranks of low-skilled activities of the new economy.

If we now turn to examine the projected occupational structure, at first sight the hypothesis of informationalism seems to be confirmed: the fastest-growing rates among occupational groups are those of professionals (32.3% for the period) and technicians (36.9%). But "service occupations," mostly semiskilled, are also growing fast (29.2%) and they would still represent 16.9% of the occupational structure in 2005. Altogether, managers, professionals, and technicians would increase their share of total occupational employment from 24.5% in 1990 to 28.9% in 2005. Sales and clerical workers, taken as a group, would remain stable at about 28.8% of total employment. Craft workers would actually increase their share, confirming the tendency to stabilize a hard core of manual workers around craft skills.

Let us examine more closely this argument: is the future informational society characterized by an increasing polarization of occupational structure? In the case of the United States, the Bureau of Labor Statistics included in its projections an analysis of the educational level required for the 30 occupations that were expected to grow most rapidly and for the 30 occupations that were expected to decline fastest between 1990 and 2005. The analysis considered both the rate of growth or decline of the occupations and their variation in absolute numbers. The conclusion of the authors of the study is that "in general, a majority of the [growing] occupations require education or training beyond high school. In fact, more than 2 out of 3 of the 30 fastest growing occupations, and nearly half of the 30 with the largest number of jobs added had a majority of workers with education or training beyond high school in 1990."[11] The largest job declines, on the other hand, are expected in manufacturing industries, and in some clerical jobs that will be swept away by office automation, generally in the lower tier of skills. Yet at the aggregate level of new jobs being created in the 1992–2005 period Silvestri foresees only modest changes in the distribution of the educational level of the labor force.[12] The proportion of workers who are college graduates is projected to increase by 1.4 percentage points, and the proportion of those with some college education would increase slightly. Conversely, the proportion of high school graduates

[11] Silvestri and Lukasiewicz (1991: 82).
[12] Silvestri (1993).

decreases by 1 percentage point and the proportion of the lowest educated decreases slightly. Thus, some trends point at an upgrading of the occupational structure, in line with the predictions of post-industrial theory. However, on the other hand the fact that high-skill occupations tend to grow faster does not mean that society at large necessarily avoids polarization and dualism, because of the relative weight of unskilled jobs when they are counted in absolute numbers. BLS projections for 1992–2005 show that the shares of employment for professionals and for service workers are expected to increase approximately by the same amount, about 1.8 and 1.5 percentage points respectively. Since these two groups account together for about half of total job growth, in absolute numbers they do tend to concentrate jobs at both ends of the occupational ladder: 6.2 million new professional workers, and 6.5 million new service workers, whose earnings in 1992 were about 40% below the average for all occupational groups. As Silvestri writes, "part of the reason [for lower earnings of service workers] is that almost a third of these employees had less than a high school education and twice as many worked part-time than the average for all workers."[13] Trying to provide a synthetic vision of projected changes in the occupational structure, I calculated a simplified stratification model on the basis of the detailed data provided by another study by Silvestri concerning distribution of employment by occupation, education, and earnings, for 1992 (actual data) and 2005 (projection).[14] Using median weekly earnings as a most direct indicator of social stratification, I constructed four social groups: upper class (managers and professionals); middle class (technicians and craft workers); lower middle class (sales, clerical, and operators); and lower class (service occupations and agricultural workers). Recalculating under these categories Silvestri's data, I found for the upper class an increase in its share of employment from 23.7% in 1992 to 25.3% in 2005 (+1.6); a slight decline for the middle class, from 14.7% to 14.3% (-0.3); a decline for the lower middle class, from 42.7% to 40.0% (-2.7); and an increase for the lower class, from 18.9% to 20% (+1.1). Two facts deserve comment: on the one hand, there is at the same time relative upgrading of the stratification system and a moderate trend towards occupational polarization. This is because there are simultaneous increases at both the top and the bottom of the social ladder, although the increase at the top is of greater magnitude.

Let us now turn to examine the projections on the Japanese employment and occupational structure. We have two projections, both from

[13]   Ibid.: 85.
[14]   Ibid.: table 9.

the Ministry of Labor. One of them, published in 1991, projects (on the basis of the 1980–85 data) to 1989, 1995, and 2000. The other, published in 1987, projects to 1990, 1995, 2000, and 2005. Both project the employment structure by industry and the occupational structure. I have chosen to elaborate on the basis of the 1987 projection because, while being equally reliable, it is more detailed in its breakdown by industries and reaches out to 2005.[15]

The most significant feature of these projections is the slow decline of manufacturing employment in Japan in spite of the acceleration of the transformation of Japan into an informational society. In the 1987 statistical projection, manufacturing employment stood at 25.9% in 1985 and was projected to remain at 23.9% of total employment in 2005. As a reminder, in the US projection, manufacturing employment was expected to decline from 17.5% in 1990 to 14% in 2005, a much sharper decline from a substantially lower base. Japan achieves this relative stability of manufacturing jobs by compensating declines in the traditional sectors with actual increases in the newest sectors. Thus, while employment in textiles would decline from 1.6% in 1985 to 1.1% in 2005, in the same period employment in electrical machinery would increase from 4.1% to 4.9%. Metalworkers will decline substantially, but jobs in the food processing industry will jump from 2.4% to 3.5%.

Overall, the most spectacular increase in employment in Japan is projected to be in business services (from 3.3% in 1985 to 8.1% in 2005), thus showing the increasing role of information-intensive activities in the Japanese economy. However, the employment share of activities in financial, insurance and real estate is projected to remain stable for the 20-year period of the projection. Coupled with the preceding observation, this seems to imply that these rapidly growing business services are, mainly, services to manufacturing and to other services, that is services which input knowledge and information into production. Health services are projected to grow slightly, and education employment is expected to remain at the same share as in 1985.

On the other hand, agricultural employment is expected to decline sharply, from 9.1% in 1985 to 3.9% in 2005, as if Japan had finally assumed its transition to the postagricultural (not postindustrial) age.

In general terms, with the exception of business services and agriculture, the Japanese employment structure is projected to remain remarkably stable, verifying again this gradual transition to the informational paradigm, reworking the content of existing jobs into the new paradigm without necessarily phasing out such jobs.

[15] Ministry of Labor (1991).

As for the occupational structure, the most substantial change projected would be the increase in the share of professional and technical occupations, which would grow from 10.5% in 1985 to a staggering 17% in 2005. On the other hand, managerial occupations, while growing significantly in their share, will grow at a slower rate, and they still would represent less than 6% of total employment in 2005. This would confirm the tendency toward the reproduction of the lean hierarchical structure of Japanese organizations with power concentrated in the hands of a few managers. The data also seem to indicate the increase in the professionalization of middle-level workers and the specialization of tasks in information processing and knowledge generation. Crafts and operators are expected to decline, but will still represent over one-quarter of the labor force in 2005, about 3 percentage points ahead of the corresponding occupational categories for the United States at the same date. Clerical workers are also expected to increase at a moderate rate, while farming occupations would be reduced by about two-thirds in relationship to their 1985 level.

Thus, the projections of the employment structure in the United States and Japan seem to continue the trends observed for the 1970–90 period. These are clearly two different employment and occupational structures corresponding to two societies which can be equally labeled informational in terms of their sociotechnical paradigm of production, yet with clearly distinct performances in productivity growth, economic competitiveness, and social cohesion. While the United States appears to be emphasizing its tendency to move away from manufacturing jobs, and to concentrate in both producer and social services, Japan is maintaining a more balanced structure, with a strong manufacturing sector and a wide cushion of retail service activities. Japanese emphasis in business services is significantly less concentrated in finance and real estate, and the expansion of employment in social services is also more limited. The projections on the occupational structure confirm different styles of management, with Japanese organizations establishing cooperative structures at the shop-floor and office level while at the same time continuing to concentrate decision-making into a leaner managerial rank. Overall, the general hypothesis of diverse paths to the informational paradigm within a common pattern of employment structure seems to be confirmed by the limited test offered by the projections presented here.

Summing up: the evolution of employment structure and its implications for a comparative analysis of the informational society

The historical evolution of employment structure, at the roots of social structure, has been dominated by the secular trend toward the increasing productivity of human labor. As technological and organizational innovations have allowed men and women to put out more and better product with less effort and resources, work and workers have shifted from direct production to indirect production, from cultivation, extraction, and fabrication to consumption services and management work, and from a narrow range of economic activities to an increasingly diverse occupational universe.

But the tale of human creativity and economic progress throughout history has been often told in simplistic terms, thus obscuring the understanding not only of our past but of our future. The usual version of this process of historical transition as a shift from agriculture, to industry, then to services, as an explanatory framework for the current transformation of our societies, presents three fundamental flaws:

(1) It assumes homogeneity between the transition from agriculture to industry and that from industry to services, overlooking the ambiguity and internal diversity of the activities included under the label of "services."
(2) It does not pay enough attention to the truly revolutionary nature of new information technologies, which, by allowing a direct, on-line linkage between different types of activity in the same process of production, management, and distribution, establish a close, structural connection between spheres of work and employment artificially separated by obsolete statistical categories.
(3) It forgets the cultural, historical, and institutional diversity of advanced societies, as well as the fact that they are interdependent in a global economy. Thus, the shift to the sociotechnical paradigm of informational production takes place along different lines, determined by the trajectory of each society and by the interaction between these various trajectories. It follows a diversity of employment/occupational structures within the common paradigm of the informational society.

Our empirical observation of the evolution of employment in the G-7 countries shows some fundamental common features that seem indeed to be characteristic of informational societies:

• the phasing out of agricultural employment;

- the steady decline of traditional manufacturing employment;
- the rise of both producer services and social services, with the emphasis on business services in the first category, and health services in the second group;
- the increasing diversification of service activities as sources of jobs;
- the rapid rise of managerial, professional, and technical jobs;
- the formation of a "white-collar" proletariat, made up of clerical and sales workers;
- the relative stability of a substantial share of employment in retail trade;
- the simultaneous increase of the upper and lower levels of the occupational structure;
- the relative upgrading of the occupational structure over time, with an increasing share of those occupations that require higher skills and advanced education proportionally higher than the increase of the lower-level categories.

It does not follow that societies at large are upgraded in their skills, education, or income status, nor in their stratification system. The impact of a somewhat upgraded employment structure into the social structure will depend on the ability of the institutions to incorporate the labor demand into the labor force and to reward workers proportionally to their skills.

On the other hand, the analysis of the differential evolution of the G-7 countries clearly shows some variation in their employment and occupational structures. At the risk of oversimplifying, we can propose the hypothesis of two different informational models:

(1) The "Service Economy Model," represented by the United States, the United Kingdom, and Canada. It is characterized by a rapid phasing out of manufacturing employment after 1970, as the pace towards informationalism accelerated. Having already eliminated almost all agricultural employment, this model emphasizes an entirely new employment structure where the differentiation among various service activities becomes the key element to analyze social structure. This model emphasizes capital management services over producer services, and keeps expanding the social service sector because of a dramatic rise in healthcare jobs and, to a lesser extent, in education employment. It is also characterized by the expansion of the managerial category that includes a considerable number of middle managers.

(2) The "Industrial Production Model," clearly represented by Japan and to a considerable extent by Germany, which, while reducing also the share of their manufacturing employment, continues to keep it at a relatively high level (around one-quarter of the labor

force) in a much more gradual movement that allows for the restructuring of manufacturing activities into the new sociotechnical paradigm. Indeed, this model reduces manufacturing jobs while reinforcing manufacturing activity. Partly as a reflection of this orientation, producer services are much more important than financial services, and they seem to be more directly linked to manufacturing firms. This is not to say that financial activities are not important in Japan and Germany: after all, eight of the world's ten largest banks are Japanese. Yet, while financial services are indeed important and have increased their share in both countries, the bulk of service growth is in services to companies, and in social services. However, Japan is also specific in showing a significantly lower level of employment in social services than other informational societies. This is probably linked to the structure of the Japanese family and to the internalization of some social services into the structure of the firms: a cultural and institutional analysis of the variegations of employment structure seems to be a necessity to account for the diversity of informational societies.

In between, France seems to be leaning toward the service economy model, but maintaining a relatively strong manufacturing basis and emphasizing both producer and social services. The close linkage between the French and the German economies in the European Union is probably creating a division of labor between management and manufacturing activities that could ultimately benefit the German component of the emerging European economy. Italy characterizes itself as keeping almost one-quarter of employment in self-employed status, maybe introducing a third model that would emphasize a different organizational arrangement, based on networks of small and medium businesses adapted to the changing conditions of the global economy, thus laying the ground for an interesting transition from proto-industrialism to proto-informationalism.

The different expressions of such models in each one of the G-7 countries are dependent upon their position in the global economy. In other words, for a country to be focused on the "service economy" model means that other countries are exercising their role as industrial production economies. The implicit assumption of postindustrial theory that the advanced countries would be service economies and the less advanced countries would specialize in agriculture and manufacturing has been rejected by historical experience. Throughout the world, many economies are quasi-subsistence economies, while agricultural and industrial activities that thrive outside of the informational core do so on the basis of their close connection to the global economy, dominated by the G-7 countries. Thus, the employment structure of the United States and of Japan reflect their different forms of articulation to the global economy, and not just their degree of advancement in the informational scale. The fact that there is a lower proportion of manufacturing jobs or a higher proportion of managers in the United States is partly due to the offshoring of manufacturing jobs by US firms, and to the concentration of management and information-processing activities in the United States at the expense of production activities generated in other countries by US consumption of these countries' products.

Furthermore, different modes of articulation to the global economy are not only due to different institutional environments and economic trajectories, but to different government policies and firms' strategies. Thus, the observed trends can be reversed. If policies and strategies can modify the service and industrial mix of a given economy it means that the variations of the informational paradigm are as important as its basic structure. It is a socially open, politically managed paradigm, whose main common feature is technological.

As economies rapidly evolve towards their integration and inter-penetration, the resulting employment structure will largely reflect the position of each country and region in the interdependent, global structure of production, distribution, and management. Thus, the artificial separation of social structures by institutional boundaries of different nations (the United States, Japan, Germany, and so on) limits the interest of analyzing the occupational structure of the infor-mational society in a given country in isolation from what happens in another country whose economy is so closely interrelated. If Japanese manufacturers produce many of the cars consumed by the American market and many of the chips consumed in Europe, we are not just witnessing the demise of American or British manufacturing, but the impact on the employment structure of each country of the division of labor among different types of informational societies.

The implications of such an observation for the theory of infor-mationalism are far-reaching: the unit of analysis to comprehend the new society will necessarily have to change. The focus of the theory must shift to a comparative paradigm able to explain at the same time the sharing of technology, the interdependence of the economy, and the variations of history in the determination of an employment structure spread across national boundaries.

Is There a Global Labor Force?

If there is a global economy, it should be a global labor market and a global labor force.[16] Yet, as with many of such obvious statements, taken in its literal sense it is empirically wrong and analytically misleading. While capital flows freely in the electronic circuits of global financial networks, labor is still highly constrained, and will be for the foreseeable future, by institutions, culture, borders, police, and xenophobia. Only about 1.5% of the global labor force (about 80 million workers) worked outside their country in 1993, and half of them were concentrated in Sub-Saharan Africa and the Middle-East.[17] In the European Union, in spite of free movement of their citizens in the member countries, only 2% of its nationals worked in another Union country in 1993, a proportion unchanged for ten years.[18] Notwithstanding the public perception in the North concerning the invasion of immigrants from the South and East, in major West European countries in the late 1980s, the impact of immigration on labor was at a lower level than in 1975. Thus, the percentage of foreign labor in the total labor force in Britain was 6.5% in 1975, and 4.5% in 1985–7; in France, it went down from 8.5% to 6.9%; in Germany from 8% to 7.9%; in Sweden from 6% to 4.9%; and in Switzerland from 24% to 18.2%.[19] In the early 1990s, because of social disruption in Eastern Europe (mainly in Yugoslavia), political asylum increased the number of immigrants, particularly in Germany. Yet overall, in the European Union it is estimated that total foreign population of non-European citizens amounts to about 13 million, of which about one-quarter would be undocumented.[20] For the whole of Western Europe, the proportion of foreigners in the total population in 1990 was 4.5% (see table 4.22 in Appendix A), and France and the UK had a lower proportion in 1990 than in 1982. Furthermore, the proportion of foreigners in the total population, for the five largest countries of the European Union in 1994, only surpassed 5% in Germany (to reach almost 7%); it was actually lower than in 1986 in France; and it was only slightly over the 1986 level in the UK.[21] As for the United States, where a significant new wave of immigration did indeed occur during the 1980s and 1990s, it was always an immigrant society, and current trends are in

---

[16]   Johnston (1991).
[17]   Campbell (1994).
[18]   *Newsweek* (1993).
[19]   Sources collected and elaborated by Soysal (1994: 23); see also Stalker (1994).
[20]   Soysal (1994: 22).
[21]   *Economist* (1994).

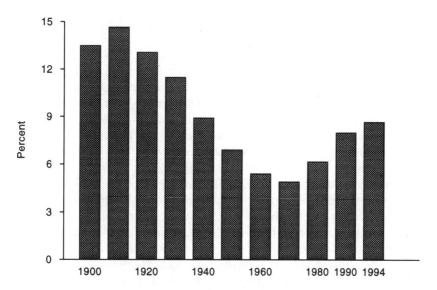

Figure 4.1 Percentage of United States population that is foreign-born
Source: US Census Bureau.

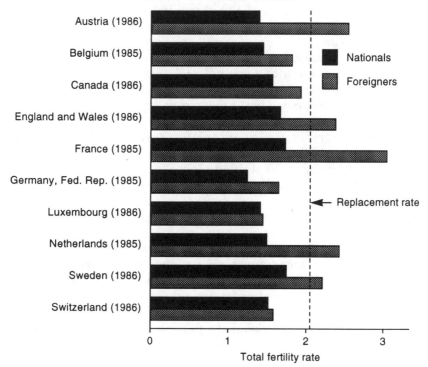

Figure 4.2 Total fertility rates for nationals and foreigners, selected OECD countries
Sources: SOPEMI/OECD; elaborated by Stalker (1994).

the line of historical continuity (see figure 4.1).[22] What has changed, in both contexts, is the ethnic composition of immigration, with a decreasing proportion of immigrants of European stock in America, and with a higher proportion of Muslim immigrants in European countries. What is also happening is that because of differential birth rates between the native population and the residents and citizens of immigrant origin, affluent societies are becoming more ethnically diverse (figure 4.2). The visibility of immigrant workers, and their descendants, has increased because of their concentration in the largest metropolitan areas and in a few regions.[23] As a result of both features, in the 1990s ethnicity and cultural diversity have become a major social problem in Europe, are a new issue in Japan, and continue to be, as they always were, at the top of the American agenda. Yet this is a different argument than saying that the labor market has become global. There is indeed a global market for a tiny fraction of the labor force, concerning the highest-skilled professionals in innovative R&D, cutting-edge engineering, financial management, advanced business services, and entertainment, who shift and commute between nodes of the global networks that control the planet.[24] Yet while this integration of the best talent in the global networks is critical for the commanding heights of the informational economy, the overwhelming proportion of labor, in developed as well as in developing countries, remains largely nation-bound. Indeed, for two-thirds of workers in the world, employment still means agricultural employment, rooted in the fields, usually in their region.[25] Thus, in the strictest sense, with the exception of the highest level of knowledge generators/symbol manipulators (what I call below the *networkers, commanders,* and *innovators*), there is not, and will not be in the foreseeable future, a unified global labor market, in spite of emigration flows to OECD countries, to the Arabian peninsula, and to the booming metropolitan centers in the Asian Pacific. More important for movements of people are massive displacements of population because of war and hunger.

However, there is a historical tendency toward increasing interdependence of the labor force on a global scale, through three mechanisms: global employment in the multinational corporations and their associated cross-border networks; impacts of international trade on employment and labor conditions, both in the North and in the South; and effects of global competition and of the new mode of

---

[22]   Bouvier and Grant (1994); Stalker (1994); Borjas et al. (1991).
[23]   Machimura (1994); Stalker (1994).
[24]   Johnston (1991).
[25]   ILO (1994).

flexible management on each country's labor force. In each case, information technology is the indispensable medium for the linkages between different segments of the labor force across national boundaries.

As stated in chapter 2, foreign direct investment has become the driving force of globalization, more significant than trade as a conductor of transborder interdependence.[26] The worldwide stock of FDI tripled from an estimated value of US$500 billion in 1980 to over US$1,500 billion in 1990. While in the early 1970s and early 1980s foreign direct investment grew at the same pace as other economic indicators, from the mid-1980s it accelerated, with annual growth rates for FDI outflows of 33% during 1986–90. The most significant agents of the new pattern of foreign direct investment are multi-national corporations and their associated networks: together they organize the core labor force in the global economy. The number of multinational firms increased from 7,000 in 1970 to 37,000 in 1993, with 150,000 affiliates around the world. Although they employ directly "only" 70 million workers, these workers produce one-third of the world's total private output. Global value of their sales in 1992 was US$5,500 billion, a figure 25% greater than the total value of world trade. Labor force located in different countries depends on the division of labor between distinct functions and strategies of such multinational networks. Thus, most of the labor force does not circulate in the network, but becomes dependent on the function, evolution and behavior of other segments in the network. It results in a process of hierarchical, segmented interdependence of the labor force, under the impulse of relentless movements by firms in the circuits of their global network (see figure 4.3).

The second major mechanism of global labor interdependence concerns the impacts of trade on employment, both in the North and in the South.[27] On the one hand, the combination of North-bound exports, foreign direct investment, and growth of domestic markets in the South has triggered a gigantic wave of industrialization in some developing countries.[28] Simply accounting for the direct impact of trade, Wood[29] estimates that between 1960 and 1990 20 million manu-facturing jobs have been created in the South. In Guandong province's Pearl River Delta alone, between 5 and 6 million workers have been hired in factories in semirural areas in the last ten years. (Kwok and So (eds) 1995). But while there is agreement on the signif-

[26]   Bailey et al. (eds) (1993); Tyson et al. (eds) (1988); UNCTAD (1993, 1994).
[27]   Rothstein (1993); Mishel and Bernstein (1993).
[28]   Patel (1992); Singh (1994); ILO (1993, 1994).
[29]   Wood (1994).

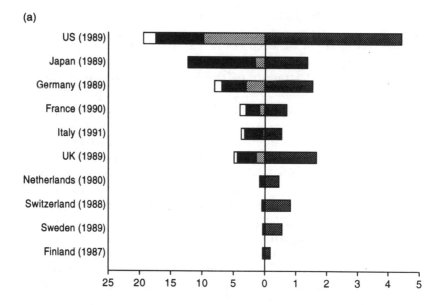

(a)

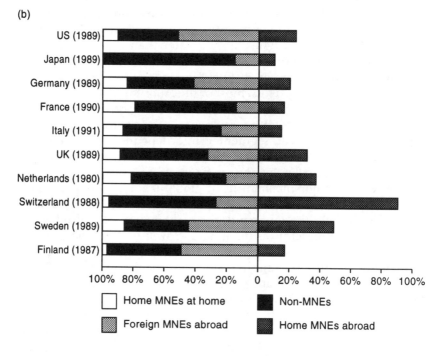

(b)

Figure 4.3 Paid employment in manufacturing firms in selected industrialized countries by ownership, latest available year
(a) Million employees
(b) Share of domestic paid employment
Source: Bailey et al. (1993).

icance of the new process of industrialization triggered in Asia and
Latin America by the new outward orientation of developing
economies, an intense debate has raged on the actual impact of trade
on employment and labor conditions in OECD countries. The White
Paper of the Commission of European Communities (1994) considered global competition to be a significant factor in the rise of
unemployment in Europe. In sharp contrast, the 1994 employment
study of the OECD Secretariat rejects this relationship, arguing that
imports from industrializing countries account only for 1.5% of total
demand in the OECD area. Some noted economists, such as Paul
Krugman and Robert Lawrence,[30] have proposed empirical analyses
according to which the impact of trade on employment and wages in
the United States is very small. Yet their analysis has been submitted
to serious criticism, both methodological and substantive, by Cohen,
Sachs and Shatz, and Mishel and Bernstein, among others.[31] Indeed,
the complexity of the new global economy is not easily captured by
traditional trade and employment statistics. UNCTAD and ILO estimate that intrafirm trade represents the equivalent of about 32% of
world trade. Such exchanges do not take place through the market,
but are internalized (through ownership) or quasi-internalized
(through networks).[32] It is this kind of trade that affects most directly
the labor force in OECD countries. Subcontracting of services by
companies around the globe, using telecommunications linkages,
further integrates the labor force without displacing it or trading its
output. But even using standard trade statistics, it seems that the
impact of trade on the labor force has been underestimated by some
economic analyses. Perhaps a balanced view of this matter is the
empirical study by Adrian Wood on the impact of trade on employment and inequality between 1960 and 1990.[33] According to his
calculations (that revise, on the basis of a sound methodological
critique, usual estimates), skilled workers in the North greatly benefited from global trade on two grounds: first, they took advantage of
higher economic growth brought about by increased trade; second,
the new international division of labor gave their firms, and themselves, a comparative advantage in higher value-added products and
processes. On the other hand, unskilled workers in the North considerably suffered because of the competition with producers in
lower-cost areas. Wood estimates that overall demand for unskilled
labor was reduced by 20%. When government and firms could not

[30]   Krugman and Lawrence (1994); Krugman (1994).
[31]   See, for instance, Cohen (1994); Mishel and Bernstein (1994).
[32]   UNCTAD (1993); Bailey et al. (eds) (1993); Campbell (1994).
[33]   Wood (1994).

change the conditions of labor contracts, as in the European Union, unskilled labor became too costly with reference to commodities traded with newly industrializing countries. It followed unemployment of unskilled labor that was, in comparative standards, too expensive for its low skills. Because skilled workers, on the contrary, were still in demand, wage inequality surged in the OECD area.

Yet the new international division of labor theory that underlies the analyses on the differential impact of trade and globalization on the labor force relies on an assumption that has been questioned by empirical observation of production processes in newly industrializing areas, namely the persistence of a productivity gap between workers and factories in the South and the North. The pioneering research by Harley Shaiken on American automobile and computer plants and on Japanese consumer electronic plants in Northern Mexico shows that the productivity of Mexican workers and factories is comparable to that of American plants.[34] Mexican production lines are not at a lower technological level than those in the United States either in process (CAM manufacturing) or products (engines, computers), yet they operate at a fraction of the cost north of the Rio Grande. In another typical example of new labor interdependence, Bombay and Bangalore have become major subcontractors of software for companies around the globe, using the work of thousands of highly skilled Indian engineers and computer scientists who receive about 20% of the wage paid in the United States for similar jobs.[35] Similar trends were taking place in finance and business services in Singapore, Hong Kong and Taipei.[36] In sum, the more the process of economic globalization deepens, the more the interpenetration of networks of production and management expands across borders, and the closer become the links between the conditions of the labor force in different countries, placed at different levels of wages and social protection, but decreasingly distinct in terms of skills and technology.

Thus, a wide range of opportunities opens up for companies in advanced capitalist countries, concerning their strategies toward labor, both skilled and unskilled. They can either:

(a) downsize the firm, keeping the indispensable highly skilled labor force in the North, and importing inputs from low-cost areas; or,
(b) subcontract part of the work to their transnational establishments and to the auxiliary networks whose production can be internalized in the network enterprise system; or,

[34] Shaiken (1990).
[35] Balaji (1994).

(c) use temporary labor, part-time workers, or informal firms as suppliers in the home country; or,

(d) automate or relocate tasks and functions for which the standard labor market prices are considered too high *vis-à-vis* alternative formulae; or,

(e) obtain from their labor force, including the core labor force, acquiescence to more stringent conditions of work and pay as a condition for the continuation of their jobs, thus reversing social contracts established under circumstances more favorable for labor.

In the real world, this range of possibilities translates into the actual use of all of them, depending upon firms, countries, and periods of time. Thus, although global competition may not affect directly the majority of the labor force in OECD countries, its indirect effects entirely transform the condition of labor and labor institutions everywhere.[37] Furthermore, the alignment of labor conditions across countries does not take place only because of competition from low-cost areas: it also forces Europe, America, and Japan to converge. The pressures toward greater flexibility of the labor market and toward the reversal of the welfare state in Western Europe come less from the pressures derived from East Asia than from the comparison with the United States.[38] It will become increasingly difficult for Japanese firms to continue life employment practices for the privileged 30% of its labor force if they have to compete in an open economy with American companies practicing flexible employment.[39] Lean production, downsizing, restructuring, consolidation, and flexible management practices are induced and made possible by the intertwined impact of economic globalization and diffusion of information technologies. The indirect effects of such tendencies on the conditions of labor in all countries are far more important than the measurable impact of international trade or cross-border direct employment.

Thus, while there is not a unified global labor market, and therefore not a global labor force, there is indeed global interdependence of the labor force in the informational economy. Such interdependence is characterized by the hierarchical segmentation of labor not between countries but across borders.

The new model of global production and management is

---

[36]   Fouquin et al. (1991); Tan and Kapur (eds) (1986); Kwok and So (eds) (1995).

[37]   Rothstein (1994); Sengenberger and Campbell (1994).

[38]   Navarro (1994).

[39]   Joussaud (1994); NIKKEIREN (1993).

tantamount to the simultaneous integration of work process and disintegration of the workforce. This model is not the inevitable consequence of the informational paradigm but the result of an economic and political choice made by governments and companies selecting the "low road" in the process of transition to the new, informational economy, mainly using productivity increases for short-term profitability. These policies contrast sharply, in fact, with the possibilities of work enhancement and sustained, high productivity opened up by the transformation of the work process under the informational paradigm.

The Work Process in the Informational Paradigm

The maturation of the information technology revolution in the 1990s has transformed the work process, introducing new forms of social and technical division of labor. It took the 1980s for micro-electronics-based machinery to fully penetrate manufacturing, and it is only in the 1990s that networked computers have widely diffused throughout the information-processing activities at the core of the so-called services sector. By the mid-1990s the new informational paradigm, associated with the emergence of the network enterprise, is well in place and set for its unfolding.[40]

There is an old and honorable tradition of sociological and organizational research on the relationship between technology and work.[41] Thus, we know that technology per se is not the cause of the work arrangements to be found in the workplace. Management decisions, systems of industrial relations, cultural and institutional environments, and government policies are such fundamental sources of labor practices and production organization that the impact of technology can only be understood in complex interaction within a social system comprising all these elements. Furthermore, the process of capitalist restructuring decisively marked the forms and outcomes of introducing information technologies into the work process.[42] The means and ways of such a restructuring were also diverse depending upon countries' technological capability, political culture, and labor traditions. Thus, the new informational paradigm of work and labor is not a neat model but a messy quilt, woven from the historical inter-

---

[40]   For a documented view of developments in the diffusion of information technology in the workplace up to 1995 see *Business Week* (1994a, 1995a).
[41]   For a review of relevant literature, see Child (1986); see also Appelbaum and Schettkat (eds) (1990); Buitelaar (ed.) (1988); Noble (1984).
[42]   Shaiken (1985); Castano (1994a).

action between technological change, industrial relations policy, and conflictive social action. To find patterns of regularity behind this confusing scene, we must have the patience to abstract successive layers of social causation, to first deconstruct, then reconstruct the emerging pattern of work, workers, and labor organization that characterize the new, informational society.

Let us start with information technology. Mechanization first, automation later, have been transforming human labor for decades, always triggering similar debates around issues of workers' displacement, deskilling versus reskilling, productivity versus alienation, management control versus labor autonomy.[43] To follow a French "*filière*" of analysis over the last half-century, George Friedmann criticized "*le travail en miettes*" (piecemeal work) of the Taylorist factory; Pierre Naville denounced the alienation of workers under mechanization; Alain Touraine, on the basis of his pioneering sociological study in the late 1940s on the technological transformation of Renault factories, proposed his typology of work processes as A/B/C (craft, assembly line, and innovation work); Serge Mallet announced the birth of "a new working class" focused on the capacity to manage and operate advanced technology; and Benjamin Coriat analyzed the emergence of a post-Fordist model in the labor process, on the basis of linking up flexibility and integration in a new model of relationships between production and consumption. At the end of this intellectual itinerary, impressive on many grounds, one fundamental idea emerges: automation, which received its full meaning only with the deployment of information technology, increases dramatically the importance of human brain input into the work process.[44] While automated machinery, and later computers, have indeed been used for transforming workers into second-order robots, as Braverman argued,[45] this is not the corollary of technology, but of a social organization of labor that stalled (and still does) the full utilization of the productive capacity generated by the new technologies. As Harley Shaiken, Maryellen Kelley, Larry Hirschhorn, Shoshana Zuboff, and others have shown in their empirical work, the broader and deeper the diffusion of advanced information technology in factories and offices, the greater the need for an autonomous, educated worker able and willing to program and decide entire sequences of work.[46]

[43]   Hirschhorn (1984).
[44]   Friedmann (1956); Friedmann and Naville (eds) (1961); Touraine (1955); Mallet (1963); Coriat (1990).
[45]   Braverman (1973).
[46]   Shaiken (1985, 1993); Kelley (1986, 1990); Hirschhorn (1984); Zuboff (1988); Japan Institute of Labour (1985). For a discussion on the literature, see Adler (1992); for a comparative approach, see Ozaki et al. (1992).

Notwithstanding the formidable obstacles of authoritarian management and exploitative capitalism, information technologies call for
greater freedom for better-informed workers to deliver the full
promise of its productivity potential. The networker is the necessary
agent of the network enterprise made possible by new information
technologies.

In the 1990s several factors accelerated the transformation of the
work process: computer technology, and its applications, progressing
by quantum leaps, became increasingly cheaper and better, thus
being affordable and manageable on a large scale; global competition
triggered a technology/management race between companies all
over the world; organizations evolved and adopted new shapes that
were generally based on flexibility and networking; managers, and
their consultants, finally understood the potential of new technology
and how to use it, although more often than not they constrained such
potential within the limits of the old set of organizational goals (such
as a short-term increase of profits calculated on a quarterly basis).

The massive diffusion of information technologies has caused
rather similar effects in factories, offices, and service organizations.[47]
These effects are not, as was forecasted, the shift towards indirect work
at the expense of direct work which would become automated. On
the contrary: the role of direct work has increased because information technology has empowered the direct worker at the shop floor
level (be it in the process of testing chips or underwriting insurance
policies). What *tends* to disappear through integral automation are
the routine, repetitive tasks, that can be precoded and programmed
for their execution by machines. It is the Taylorist assembly line that
becomes a historic relic (although it is still the harsh reality for
millions of workers in the industrializing world). It should not be
surprising that information technologies do precisely that: replace
work that can be encoded in a programmable sequence and enhance
work that requires analysis, decision, and reprogramming capabilities
in real time at a level that only the human brain can master. Every
other activity, given the extraordinary rate of progress in information
technology and its constant lowering in price per information unit, is
potentially susceptible of automation, and thus the labor engaged in
it is expendable (although workers as such are not, depending upon
their social organization and political capacity).

The informational work process is determined by the characteristics of the informational production process. Keeping in mind the
analyses presented in previous chapters on the informational/global

---

[47]   Quinn (1988); Bushnell (1994).

economy, and on the network enterprise as its organizational form, such process can be summarized as follows:

(1) Value added is mainly generated by innovation, both of process and products. New designs of chips, new software-writing largely condition the fate of the electronics industry. The invention of new financial products (for example, the creation of the "derivatives market" on the stock exchanges during the late 1980s) are at the roots of the boom (however risky) of financial services, and of the prosperity (or collapse) of financial firms, and of their clients.

(2) Innovation is itself dependent upon two conditions: research potential and specification capability. That is, new knowledge has to be discovered, then applied to specific purposes in a given organizational/institutional context. Custom design is critical for microelectronics in the 1990s; instant reaction to macroeconomic changes is fundamental in managing the volatile financial products created in the global market.

(3) Execution tasks are more efficient when they are able to adapt higher-level instructions to their specific application, and when they can generate feedback effects into the system. An optimum combination of worker/machine in the execution tasks is set to automate all standard procedures, and to reserve human potential for adaptation and feedback effects.

(4) Most production activity takes place in organizations. Since the two main features of the predominant organizational form (the network enterprise) are internal adaptability and external flexibility, the two key features for the work process will be: the ability to generate flexible strategic decision-making; and the capacity to achieve organizational integration between all elements of the production process.

(5) Information technology becomes the critical ingredient of the process of work as described because:
   • it largely determines innovation capability;
   • it makes possible the correction of errors and generation of feedback effects at the level of execution;
   • it provides the infrastructure for flexibility and adaptability throughout the management of the production process.

This specific production process introduces a *new division of labor* that characterizes the emerging informational paradigm. The new division of labor can be better understood by presenting a typology constructed around three dimensions. **The first dimension refers to the actual tasks performed in a given work process. The second dimension concerns the relationship between a given organization and its environment, including other organizations. The third**

dimension considers the relationship between managers and employees in a given organization or network. I call the first dimension value-making, the second dimension relation-making, and the third dimension decision-making.

In terms of *value-making*, in a production process organized around information technology (be it goods production or service delivery), the following fundamental tasks, and their corresponding workers, can be distinguished:

- strategic decision-making and planning by the *commanders*;
- innovation in products and process by the *researchers*;
- adaptation, packaging, and targeting of innovation by the *designers*;
- management of the relationships between the decision, innovation, design, and execution, taking into consideration the means available to the organization to achieve the stated goals, by the *integrators*;
- execution of tasks under their own initiative and understanding by the *operators*;
- execution of ancillary, preprogrammed tasks that have not been, or cannot be, automated, by what I dare to call the "*operated*" (or human robots).

This typology must be combined with another referring to the need and capacity of each task (and its performer) to link up with other workers in real time, be it within the same organization or in the overall system of the network enterprise. According to this relational capacity we may distinguish between three fundamental positions:

- the *networkers*, who set up connections on their initiative (for example, joint engineering with other departments of companies), and navigate the routes of the network enterprise;
- the *networked*, workers who are on-line but without deciding when, how, why, or with whom;
- the *switched-off* workers, tied to their own specific tasks, defined by non-interactive, one-way instructions.

Finally, in terms of the capacity to input the *decision-making process* we can differentiate between:

- the *deciders*, who make the decision in the last resort;
- the *participants*, who are involved in decision-making;
- the *executants*, who merely implement decisions.

The three typologies do not coincide, and the difference in the relational dimension or in the decision-making process can occur, and indeed does in practice, at all levels of the value-making structure.

This construction is not an ideal type of organization, or some futuristic scenario. It is a synthetic representation of what seems to be emerging as the main task-performing positions in the informational work process, according to empirical studies on the transformation of work and organizations under the impact of information technologies.[48] Yet my argument is certainly not that all or most work processes and workers in our society are reducible to these typologies. Archaic forms of sociotechnical organization do survive, and will for a long, long time remain in many countries, in the same way as preindustrial, handicraft forms of production were combined with mechanization of industrial production for an extended historical period. But it is critical to distinguish the complex and diverse forms of work and workers in our observation from the emerging patterns of production and management that, because they are rooted in a dynamic sociotechnical system, will tend to become dominant through the dynamics of competition and demonstration effects. My hypothesis is that the work organization sketched in this analytical scheme represents the emerging informational work paradigm. I shall illustrate this emerging paradigm by referring briefly to some case studies on the impacts of computer-aided manufacturing and office automation on work, in order to make somewhat concrete the analytical construction I have proposed.

Thus, Harley Shaiken studied in 1994 the practice of so-called "high performance work organization" in two up-to-date American automobile factories: the GM-Saturn Complex on the outskirts of Nashville, Tennessee, and the Chrysler Jefferson North Plant on the east side of Detroit.[49] Both are cases of successful, highly productive organizations that have integrated the most advanced computer-based machinery in their operation, and have simultaneously transformed the organization of work and management. While acknowledging differences between the two plants, Shaiken points at the critical factors accounting for high performance in both of them, on the basis of new technological tools. The first is the high level of skills of an experienced industrial labor force, whose knowledge of production and products was critical to modifying a complex process when necessary. In order to develop these skills, at the heart of the new work system there is regular work training, on special courses outside the plant and on the job. Saturn workers spent 5% of their

---

[48]   See, among others, Mowery and Henderson (eds) (1989); Wood (ed.) (1989); Hyman and Streeck (eds) (1988); ILO (1988); Carnoy (1989); Wall et al. (1987); Rees (1992); Hartmann (ed.) (1987); Buitelaar (ed.) (1988); Dean et al. (1992).
[49]   Shaiken, personal communication, 1994, 1995; Shaiken (1995).

annual working time in training sessions, most of them in the Work Development Center, a facility adjacent to the plant.

The second factor fostering high performance was increased worker autonomy, as compared to other factories, allowing for shop-floor cooperation, quality circles, and feedback from workers in real time during the production process. Both plants organize production in work teams, with a flat occupational classification system. Saturn eliminated the position of first line supervisor, and Chrysler was moving in the same direction. Workers are able to work with consider-able freedom, and are encouraged to increase formal interaction in the performance of their tasks.

Workers' involvement in the upgraded process is dependent on two conditions that were met in both factories: job security and labor union participation in negotiating and implementing the reorgani-zation of work. The building of the new Chrysler plant in Detroit was preceded by a "Modern Operating Agreement," emphasizing managerial flexibility and workers' input. Of course, this is not an ideal world, exempt from social conflicts. Shaiken observed the exis-tence of tensions, and potential sources of labor disputes, between labor and management, as well as between the local union (increas-ingly behaving as a factory union, in the case of Saturn), and the United Auto Workers leadership. Yet the nature of the informational work process calls for cooperation, team work, workers' autonomy and responsibility, without which new technologies cannot be used up to their potential. The networked character of informational produc-tion permeates the whole firm, and requires constant interaction and processing of information between workers, between workers and management, and between humans and machines.

As for office automation, it has gone through three different phases, largely determined by available technology.[50] In the first phase, characteristic of the 1960s and 1970s, mainframe computers were used for batch processing of data; centralized computing by specialists in data-processing centers formed the basis of a system characterized by the rigidity and hierarchical control of information flows; data entry operations required substantial efforts since the goal of the system was the accumulation of large amounts of information in a central memory; work was standardized, routinized, and, in essence, deskilled for the majority of clerical workers, in a process analyzed, and denounced, by Braverman in his classic study. The following stages of automation, however, were substantially different. The second phase, in the early 1980s, was characterized by the

---

[50] Zuboff (1988); Dy (ed.) (1990).

emphasis on the use of microcomputers by the employees in charge of the actual work process; although they were supported by centralized data bases, they interacted directly in the process of generating information, although often requiring the support of computer experts. By the mid-1980s, the combination of advances in telecommunications, and the development of microcomputers, led to the formation of networks of workstations and literally revolutionized office work, although the organizational changes required for the full use of new technology delayed the widespread diffusion of the new model of automation until the 1990s. In this third phase of automation, office systems are integrated and networked, with multiple microcomputers interacting among themselves and with mainframes, forming an interactive web that is capable of processing information, communicating, and making decisions in real time.[51] Interactive information systems, not just computers, are the basis of the automated office, and of the so-called "alternative officing" or "virtual offices," networking tasks performed in distant locations. There might be a fourth phase of office automation brewing up in the technological cauldrons of the last years of the century: the mobile office, performed by individual workers provided with portable, powerful information processing/transmitting devices.[52] If it does develop, as seems likely, it will enhance the organizational logic I have described under the concept of the network enterprise, and it will deepen the process of transformation of work and workers along the lines proposed in this chapter.

The effects of these technological changes on office work are not yet fully identified, because empirical studies, and their interpretation, are running behind the fast process of technological change. However, during the 1980s, a number of doctoral students at Berkeley, whose work I followed and supervised, were able to produce a number of detailed monographs documenting the trends of change that seem to be confirmed by the evolution in the 1990s.[53] Particularly revealing was the doctoral dissertation by Barbara Baran on the impact of office automation on the work process in some large insurance companies in the United States.[54] Her work, as well as other sources, showed a tendency for firms to automate the lower end of clerical jobs, those routine tasks that, because they can be reduced to

[51] Strassman (1985).
[52] Thach and Woodman (1994).
[53] Particularly, I relied on work performed in their doctoral dissertations at Berkeley by Barbara Baran (1989), Carol Parsons (1987), Penny Gurstein (1990), Lisa Bornstein (1993), and Lionel Nicol (1985).
[54] Baran (1989).

a number of standard steps, can be easily programmed. Also, data entry was decentralized, gathering the information and entering it into the system as close as possible to the source. For instance, sales accounting is now linked to scanning and storage at the cashier's point-of-sale machine. ATMs (automated teller machines) constantly update bank accounts. Insurance claims are directly stored in memory with regard to all elements that do not call for a business judgement; and so on. The net result of these trends is the possibility of eliminating most of the mechanical, routine clerical work. On the other hand, higher-level operations are concentrated in the hands of skilled clerical workers and professionals, who make decisions on the basis of the information they have stored in their computer files. So, while at the bottom of the process there is increasing routinization (and thus automation), at the middle level there is reintegration of several tasks into an informed decision-making operation, generally processed, evaluated, and performed by a team made up of clerical workers with increasing autonomy in making decisions. In a more advanced stage of this process of reintegration of tasks, middle managers' supervision also disappears, and controls and safety procedures are standardized in the computer. The critical linkage then becomes the one between professionals, evaluating and making decisions on important matters, and informed clerks making decisions on day-to-day operations on the basis of their computer files and their networking capabilities. Thus the third phase of office automation, instead of simply rationalizing the task (as was the case in batch-processing automation) rationalizes the process, because the technology allows the integration of information from many different sources and its redistribution, once processed, to different, decentralized units of execution. So, instead of automating discrete tasks (such as typing, calculating), the new system rationalizes an entire procedure (for example, new business insurance, claims processing, underwriting), and then integrates various procedures by product lines or segmented markets. Workers are then functionally reintegrated instead of being organizationally distributed.

A similar trend has been observed by Hirschhorn in his analyses of American banks, and by Castano in her study of Spanish banking.[55] While routine operations have been increasingly automated (ATMs, telephone information services, electronic banking), the remaining bank clerks are increasingly working as sales persons, to sell financial services to customers, and as controllers of the repayment of the money they sell. In the United States the federal government plans to

[55]   Hirschhorn (1985); Castano (1991).

automate tax and social security payments by the end of the century, thus extending a similar change of the work process to the public sector agencies.

However, the emergence of the informational paradigm in the work process does not tell the whole story of labor and workers in our societies. The social context, and particularly the relationship between capital and labor according to specific decisions by the management of firms, drastically affects the actual shape of the work process and the consequences of the change for workers. This was particularly true during the 1980s when the acceleration of technological change went hand in hand with the process of capitalist restructuring, as I have argued above. Thus, the classic study by Watanabe [56] on the impact of introduction of robots in the automobile industry in Japan, the United States, France, and Italy, showed substantially different impacts of a similar technology in the same industry: in the United States and Italy, workers were displaced, because the main goal of introducing new technology was to reduce labor costs; in France, job loss was lower than in the two other countries, because of government policies to cushion the social impacts of modernization; and in Japan, where companies were committed to life-tenured employment, employment actually increased, and productivity shot up, as a result of retraining and higher team-work effort which increased the competitiveness of firms and took market share away from their American counterparts.

Studies conducted on the interaction between technological change and capitalist restructuring during the 1980s also showed that more often than not technologies were introduced, first of all, to save labor, to subdue unions, and to trim costs, rather than to improve quality or to enhance productivity by means other than downsizing. Thus, another of my former students, Carol Parsons, studied in her Berkeley doctoral dissertation the social-technological restructuring of metalworking and apparel industries in America.[57] In the metalworking sector, among the firms surveyed by Parsons, the most-often cited purpose for the introduction of technology was the reduction of direct labor. Furthermore, instead of retooling their factories, firms often closed plants that were unionized and opened new ones, generally without a union, even if firms did not change region for their new location. As a result of the restructuring process, employment fell substantially in all metalworking industries, with the exception of office equipment. In addition, production workers saw their relative

[56] Watanabe (1986).
[57] Parsons (1987).

numbers reduced *vis-à-vis* managers and professionals. Within production workers there was a polarization between craft workers and unskilled laborers, with assembly line workers being substantially squeezed by automation. A similar development was observed by Parsons in the apparel industry in relation to the introduction of microelectronics-based technology. Direct production workforce was rapidly being phased out, and the industry was becoming a dispatching center connecting the demand of the American market with manufacturing suppliers all over the world. The net result was a bipolar labor force composed of highly skilled designers and telecommunicating sales managers on the one hand, and low-skill, low-paid manufacturing workers, located either offshore or in American, often illegal, domestic sweatshops. This is a strikingly similar model to the one I have described in the preceding chapter for Benetton, the worldwide knitwear networked firm, considered to be the epitome of flexible production.

Eileen Appelbaum[58] found similar trends in the insurance industry, whose dramatic technological changes I have described above on the basis of Barbara Baran's work. Indeed, the story concerning technological innovation, organizational change, and work reintegration in the insurance industry must be completed with the observation of massive layoffs and underpayment of skilled work in the same industry. Appelbaum links the process of rapid technological change in the insurance industry to the impact of deregulation and global competition in the financial markets. As a result, it became critical to ensure the mobility of capital and the versatility of labor. Labor was both trimmed and reskilled. Unskilled data-entry jobs, where ethnic minority women were concentrated, were projected to be all but eliminated by automation by the end of the century. On the other hand, the remaining clerical positions were reskilled, by integrating tasks into multiskilled, multifunctional jobs susceptible of greater flexibility and adaptation to the changing needs of an increasingly diversified industry. Professional jobs were also polarized between less-skilled tasks, taken on by upgraded clerical workers, and highly specialized tasks that generally required college education. These occupational changes were specified by gender, class, and race: while machines mainly replaced ethnic-minority, less-educated women at the bottom of the scale, educated, mainly white women went into replacing white men in the lower professional positions, yet for a lower pay and reduced career prospects *vis-à-vis* those which men used to have. Multiskilling of jobs and individualization of responsibility were often accompanied by ideologically tailored new titles (for example, "assis-

---

[58]   Appelbaum (1984).

tant manager" instead of "secretary"), thus enhancing the potential for commitment of clerical workers without correspondingly increasing their professional rewards.

Thus, new information technology is redefining work processes, and workers, and therefore employment and occupational structure. While a substantial number of jobs are being upgraded in skills, and sometimes in wages and working conditions in the most dynamic sectors, a large number of jobs are being phased out by automation in both manufacturing and services. These are generally jobs that are not skilled enough to escape to automation but are expensive enough to be worth the investment in technology to replace them. Increasing educational qualifications, either general or specialized, required in the reskilled positions of the occupational structure further segregate the labor force on the basis of education, itself a highly segregated system because it roughly corresponds institutionally to a segregated residential structure. Downgraded labor, particularly in the entry positions for a new generation of workers made up of women, ethnic minorities, immigrants, and youth, is concentrated in low-skill, low-paid activities, as well as in temporary work and/or miscellaneous services. The resulting bifurcation of work patterns and polarization of labor is not the necessary result of technological progress or of inexorable evolutionary trends (for example, the rise of the "postindustrial society" or of the "service economy"). It is socially determined and managerially designed in the process of the capitalist restructuring taking place at the shop-floor level, within the framework and with the help of the process of technological change at the roots of the informational paradigm. Under such conditions, work, employment, and occupations are transformed, and the very notion of work and working time may be changed for ever.

The Effects of Information Technology on Employment: Toward a Jobless Society?

The diffusion of information technology in factories, offices, and services has reignited a centuries-old fear by workers of being displaced by machines, thus becoming irrelevant for the productivist logic that still dominates our social organization. While the information age version of the Luddite movement that terrorized English industrialists in 1811 has not appeared yet, increasing unemployment in Western Europe in the 1980s and 1990s has prompted questions about the potential disruption of labor markets, and therefore of the whole social structure, by the massive impact of labor-saving technologies.

The debate on this question has raged over the last decade, and is far from generating a clear-cut answer.[59] On the one hand, it is argued that historical experience shows the secular transfer from one kind of activity to another as technological progress replaces labor with more efficient tools of production.[60] Thus, in Britain, between 1780 and 1988 the agricultural labor force was reduced by half in absolute numbers, and fell off from 50% to 2.2% of the total labor force; yet productivity per capita increased by a factor of 68, and the increase in productivity allowed for the investment of capital and labor in manufacturing, then in services, so as to employ an increasing population. The extraordinary rate of technological change in the American economy during the twentieth century also massively displaced labor from agriculture, but the number of total jobs created by the US economy climbed from about 27 million in 1900 to 124.5 million in 1994. In this view, most traditional manufacturing jobs will know the same fate as agricultural jobs, but new jobs are being created, and will be created, in high-technology manufacturing and, more significantly, in "services."[61] As evidence of the continuity of this technical trend, it is easy to point to the experience of the most technologically advanced industrial economies, Japan and the United States: they are precisely the ones which have created most jobs during the 1980s and 1990s.[62] According to the 1994 White Paper of the European Commission on *Growth, Competitiveness, and Employment*, between 1970 and 1992, the US economy grew in real terms by 70%, and employment by 49%. Japan's economy grew by 173%, and its employment by 25%. While the European Community's economy grew by 81%, but with an employment increase of only 9% (Commission of the European Union 1994: 141). And what the Commission does not say is that almost all of this new employment was created by the public sector: private employment creation in the European Community remained at a standstill during the 1980s. In the 1990s, the gap in employment creation between Europe, on the one hand, and the US, Japan, and South East Asia, on the other hand, has increased (see figure 4.4). Furthermore, between 1993 and 1996, when most of Europe experienced high unemployment, the United States economy, while stepping up technological diffusion in offices and factories, created over eight million new jobs. And the skills profile of

[59]   For a balanced and thorough analysis of unemployment trends in the last two decades, see Freeman and Soete (1994).
[60]   Lawrence (1984); Commission of the European Communities (1994); Cyert and Mowery (eds) (1987); OECD (1994b); Jones (1982); Hinrichs et al. (eds) (1991); Bosch et al. (1994).
[61]   OECD (1994b).
[62]   OECD *Employment Outlook*, several years.

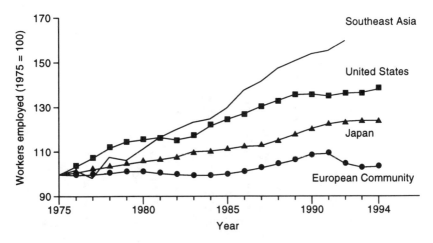

Figure 4.4   Index of employment growth, by region, 1975–94
Sources: ILO, OECD.

the new jobs was, on average, of a higher level than that of the average
skills of the overall labor force. Indeed, what characterizes the new
labor market of the last two decades is the massive incorporation of
women in paid work: the rate of participation of women in the labor
force for ages 15–64 increased from 1970 to 1990, from 48.9% to
69.1% in the US; from 55.4% to 61.8% in Japan, from 48.1% to 61.3%
in Germany; from 50.8% to 65.3% in the UK; from 47.5% to 59% in
France; from 33.5% to 43.3% in Italy; and from 29.2% to 42.8% in
Spain (source: OECD, *Main Economic Indicators*, 1995). Yet the
pressure of this substantial increase in labor supply did not create high
unemployment in the US and Japan as it did in Western Europe.
    In a broader context, while the number of manufacturing jobs is
declining in OECD countries, it is rapidly growing in developing
countries, more than offsetting the losses at world level (see figures
4.5(a) and 4.5(b), and figure 2.5 in chapter 2). All evidence points to
the fact that high unemployment is mainly a European problem,
caused by mistaken macroeconomic policies and by an institutional
environment that discourages private job creation. Thus, in a long-
term perspective, between 1960 and 1995, employment has increased
at 1.8% per annum in North America, 1.7% in Oceania, 1.2% in
Japan, 0.6% in the EFTA countries, but only 0.3% in the European
Union.[63] In 1993–4, within the area of the European Union, countries
with the highest diffusion of electronic technologies (Austria,

[63]   OECD (1994b: 13).

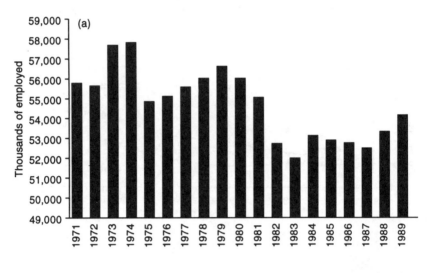

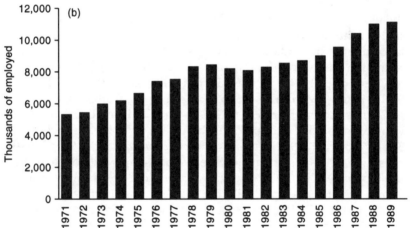

Figure 4.5   Annual progression of employment in manufacturing
(ISIC 3) , 1971–89
(a) In nine industrialized countries
(b) In twelve developing countries
Source: International Labour Office: STAT data base; elaborated by
Wieczorek (1995).

Sweden, Germany) were also those with the lowest unemployment rate, while Spain, a technological laggard, displayed by far the highest rate of unemployment. Yet no rule can be established in the opposite direction: low-tech Portugal had relatively low unemployment, while high-tech Finland had the second largest unemployment rate. As table 4.23 (in Appendix A) indicates, institutional variation seems to account for levels of unemployment, while effects of technological levels do not follow a consistent pattern. If any pattern did emerge from international data it would be in the opposite direction of Luddite predictions: higher technological level is generally associated with lower unemployment rate.

Yet the prophets of massive unemployment, led by the honorable Club of Rome, argue that such calculations are based on a different historical experience that underestimates the radically new impacts of technologies, whose effects are universal and pervasive because they relate to information processing. Thus, so the argument goes, if manufacturing jobs go the way farmers did, there will be not enough service jobs to replace them because service jobs themselves are being rapidly automated and phased out, and the movement is just accelerating in the 1990s.[64] The obvious consequence of this analysis is that our societies will have to choose between massive unemployment, with its corollary, the sharp division of society between the employed and the unemployed/occasional workers, or else a redefinition of work and employment, opening the way to a full restructuring of social organization and cultural values.

Given the importance of the matter, international institutions, governments, and researchers have made extraordinary efforts to assess the impact of new technologies. Dozens of technically sophisticated studies have been conducted in the last 15 years, particularly during the 1980s, when there was still hope that the data could provide the answer. The reading of such studies reveals the difficulty of the search. It is obvious that introducing robots in an assembly line

---

[64] King (1991); Rifkin (1995); Aznar (1993); Aronowitz and Di Fazio (1994). The most salient characteristic of all these writings announcing a jobless society is that they do not provide any consistent, rigorous evidence of their claims, relying on isolated press clippings, random examples of firms in some countries and sectors, and "commonsense" arguments on the "obvious" impact of computers on jobs. There is no serious analysis to explain, for instance, the high rate of job creation in the United States and Japan, as compared to Western Europe; and hardly any reference to the explosion of employment growth, particularly in manufacturing, in East and South-East Asia. Since most of these writers relate themselves to the "political left," their credibility must be challenged before their unfounded theses lead labor and the political left to a new dead end, in the best tradition of ideological self-destructiveness.

reduces human working time for a given level of output. But it does not follow that this reduces employment for the firm or even for the industry. If the superior quality and productivity achieved by introducing electronic machinery increases competitiveness, both the firm and the industry would need to increase employment to supply the broader demand resulting from a larger market share. Thus, the question is raised at the level of the nation: the new growth strategy would imply increased competitiveness at the cost of reducing employment in some sectors, while using the surplus thus generated to invest and create jobs in other sectors, such as business services or environmental technology industries. In the last resort, the net employment results will depend on inter-nation competition. Trade theorists would then argue that there is no zero-sum game, since an expansion of global trade will benefit most of its partners by increasing overall demand. According to this line of argument, there would be a potential reduction of employment as a consequence of the diffusion of new information technologies only if:

- expansion in demand does not offset the increase in labor productivity; *and*
- there is no institutional reaction to such a mismatch by reducing working time, not jobs.

This second condition is particularly important. After all, the history of industrialization has shown a long-term increase in unemployment, production, productivity, real wages, profits, and demand, while significantly reducing working time, on the basis of progress in technology and management.[65] Why should it not be the case in the current stage of techno-economic transformation? Why would information technologies be more destructive for overall employment than mechanization or automation were during the earlier decades of the twentieth century? Let us check the empirical record.

Facing a plethora of studies on different countries and industries in the 1980s, the International Labour Office commissioned some literature reviews that would indicate the state of the knowledge on the relationship between microelectronics and employment in various contexts. Among such reviews two stand out as well documented and analytical: those by Raphael Kaplinsky[66] and by John Bessant.[67] Kaplinsky emphasized the need to distinguish the findings at eight different levels: process level, plant level, firm level, industry

[65]   OECD (1994c).
[66]   Kaplinsky (1986).
[67]   Bessant (1989).

level, region level, sector level, national level, and meta level (meaning the discussion of differential effects related to alternative sociotechnical paradigms). After reviewing the evidence for each one of these levels, he concluded:

> Insofar as the individual studies offer any clear statement on the issue, it would appear that the quantitative macro and micro studies are drawn to fundamentally different conclusions. Process and plant level investigations generally seem to point to a significant displacement of labour. On the other hand, national level simulations more often reach the conclusion that there is no significant employment problem on hand.[68]

Bessant dismisses as excessive what he calls the "repeated scares about automation and employment" that have been stated since the 1950s. Then, after closer examination of the study findings, he writes that "it became increasingly clear that the pattern of employment effects associated with microelectronics would vary widely." According to evidence reviewed by Bessant, on the one hand, microelectronics displaces some jobs in some industries. But, on the other hand, it will also contribute to create jobs, and it will also modify the characteristics of such jobs. The overall equation must take into consideration several elements at the same time:

> new employment generated by new product industries based on microelectronics; new employment in advanced technologies generated in existing industries; employment displaced by process changes in existing industries; employment displaced in industries whose products are being replaced by those based on microelectronics, such as telecommunications equipment; employment lost through a lack of overall competitiveness caused by non-adoption of microelectronics. All things considered, across the whole spectrum the pattern is one of both losses and gains, with overall relatively small change in employment.[69]

Looking at studies of specific countries during the 1980s, the findings are somewhat contradictory although, overall, the same pattern of indetermination seems to emerge. In Japan, a 1985 study of the Japan Institute of Labour, concerning employment and work effects of new electronic technologies in industries as diverse as automobiles, newspaper, electrical machinery, and software, concluded that "in any of

---

[68] Kaplinsky (1986: 153).
[69] Bessant (1989: 27, 28, 30).

the cases, the introduction of new technologies neither aimed at reducing the size of the work force in practice nor reduced it subsequently."[70]

In Germany, a major research effort, the so-called Meta Study, was commissioned by the Minister of Research and Technology during the 1980s to conduct both econometric and case-study research on the impacts of technological change on employment. Although the diversity of studies included in the research program does not allow a firm conclusion , the synthesis by its authors concluded that it is "the context" that counts for the variation in observed effects. In any case, technological innovation was understood to be an accelerating factor of existing trends in the labor market, rather than its cause. The study forecast that in the short term unskilled jobs would be displaced, although enhanced productivity would probably result in greater job creation in the long term.[71]

In the United States, Flynn analyzed 200 case studies of the employ-ment impacts of process innovations between 1940 and 1982. He concluded that, while process innovations in manufacturing elimin-ated high-skill jobs and helped to create low-skill jobs, the opposite was true for information-processing in offices, where technological innovation suppressed low-skill jobs and created high-skill ones. Thus, according to Flynn, the effects of process innovation were variable, depending upon specific situations of industries and firms. At the industry level, again in the US, the analysis by Levy et al. of five indus-tries showed different effects of technological innovation: in iron mining, coal mining, and aluminium, technological change increased output and resulted in higher employment levels; in steel and auto-mobiles, on the other hand, growth of demand did not match reduction of labor per unit of output and job losses resulted. Also in the United States, the analysis by Miller in the 1980s of the available evidence on the impact of industrial robotics concluded that most of the displaced workers would be reabsorbed in the labor force.[72]

In the UK, the study by Daniel on the employment impacts of tech-nology in factories and offices concluded there would be a negligible effect. Another study by the London Policy Studies Institute on a sample of 1,200 firms in France, Germany, and the UK estimated that, on average, for the three countries considered, the impact of micro-electronics amounted to a job loss equivalent to, respectively, 0.5%, 0.6%, and 0.8% of annual decrease of employment in manufacturing.[73]

[70] Japan Institute of Labour (1985: 27).
[71] Schettkat and Wagner (eds) (1990).
[72] Miller (1989: 80); Flynn (1985); Levy et al. (1984); OTA (1984, 1986).

In the synthesis of studies directed by Watanabe on the impacts of robotization in the automobile industry in Japan, the United States, France, and Italy, the total job loss was estimated at between 2% and 3.5%, but with the additional caveat of the differential effects I mentioned above, namely the increase in employment in Japanese factories because of their use of microelectronics to retrain workers and enhance competitiveness.[74] In the case of Brazil, Silva found no effect of technology on employment in the automobile industry, although employment varied considerably depending on the levels of output.[75]

In the study I directed on the impacts of new technologies on the Spanish economy in the early 1980s we found no statistical relationship between employment variation and technological level in the manufacturing and service sectors. Furthermore, a study within the same research program conducted by Cecilia Castano on the automobile and banking industry in Spain found a trend towards a positive association between the introduction of information technology and employment. An econometric study by Saez on the evolution of employment in Spain, by sector in the 1980s, found also a positive statistical relationship between technological modernization and employment gains, due to increased productivity and competitiveness.[76]

Studies commissioned by the International Labour Office on the UK, on the OECD as a whole, and on South Korea seem also to point to the lack of systematic links between information technology and employment.[77] The other variables in the equation (such as the countries' industrial mix, institutional contexts, place in the international division of labor, competitiveness, management policies, and so on) overwhelm, by and large, the specific impact of technology.

Yet the argument has often been advanced that observed trends during the 1980s did not fully represent the extent of the employment impact of information technologies because their diffusion into the whole economy and society was still to come.[78] Which forces us to

---

[73]   Daniel (1987); Northcott (1986).
[74]   Watanabe (ed.) (1987).
[75]   Cited in Watanabe (1987).
[76]   Castells et al. (1986); Castano (1994b); Saez et al. (1991).
[77]   Swann (1986); Ebel and Ulrich (1987); Pyo (1986).
[78]   See, for instance, the apocalyptic prophecies of Adam Schaff (1992). It is surprising, to say the least, to see the credit given in the media to books such as Rifkin (1995), announcing "the end of work," published in a country, the United States, where between 1993 and 1996 over 8 million new jobs were created. A different matter is the quality of and pay for these jobs (although their skills profile was higher than that of overall employment structure). Work and employ-

venture onto the shaky ground of projections dealing with two uncertain variables (new information technologies and employment) and their even more uncertain relationship. Nevertheless, there have been a number of fairly sophisticated simulation models that have shed some light on the issues under discussion. One of them is the model built by Blazejczak, Eber, and Horn to evaluate the macroeconomics impacts of investment in R&D in the West German economy between 1987 and 2000. They built three scenarios. Only under the most favorable circumstances does technological change increase employment by enhancing competitiveness. Indeed, they conclude that employment losses are imminent unless compensatory demand effects occur, and this demand cannot be generated only by a better performance in international trade. Yet according to the projections in their model, "at the aggregate level demand effects do in fact compensate a relevant part of the predicted employment decrease."[79] Thus, it is likely that technological innovation will negatively affect employment in Germany, but at a rather moderate level. Here again, other elements such as macroeconomic policies, competitiveness, and industrial relations seem to be much more important as factors determining the evolution of employment.

In the United States, the most widely cited simulation study was that performed in 1984 by Leontieff and Duchin to evaluate the impact of computers on employment for the period 1963–2000 using a dynamic input–output matrix of the US economy.[80] Focusing on their intermediate scenario, they found that 20 million fewer workers would be required in relationship to the number of workers that would have to be employed to achieve the same output while keeping constant the level of technology. This figure, according to their calculations, represents a drop of 11.7% in required labor. However, the impact is strongly differentiated among industries and occupations. Services, and particularly office activities, were predicted to suffer greater job losses than manufacturing as a result of massive diffusion of office

---

ment are indeed being transformed, as this book tries to argue. But the number of paid jobs in the world, notwithstanding the Western European malaise, linked to institutional factors, is at its highest peak in history and going up. And rates of participation of labor force in the adult population are increasing everywhere, because of the unprecedented incorporation of women into the labor market. To ignore these elementary data is to ignore our society.

[79] One of the most systematic efforts at forecasting the economic and employment effects of new technologies was the "Meta Study" conducted in Germany in the late 1980s. Main findings are presented in Matzner and Wagner (eds) (1990). See especially the chapter "Sectoral and Macroeconomic Impacts of Research and Development on Employment," in Blazejczak et al. (1990: 231).

[80] Leontieff and Duchin (1985).

automation. Clerical workers and managers would see their prospects of employment significantly reduced while those for professionals would increase substantially, and craftsmen and operatives would maintain their relative position in the labor force. The methodology of the Leontieff–Duchin study has, however, been strongly criticized, because it relies on a number of assumptions that, on the basis of limited case studies, maximize the potential impact of computer automation while limiting technological change to computers. Furthermore, as argued by Lawrence, the fundamental flaw in this, and other models, is that they assumed a fixed level of final demand and output.[81] *This is precisely what past experience of technological innovation seems to reject as the most likely hypothesis.*[82] If the economy does not grow, it is obvious that labor-saving technologies will reduce the amount of working time required (even on this hypothesis by a somewhat limited amount – 11.7%). But in the past, rapid technological change has generally been associated with an expansionary trend that, by increasing demand and output, has generated the need for more working time in absolute terms, even if it represents less working time per unit of output. However, the key point in the new historical period is that in an internationally integrated economic system, expansion of demand and output will depend on the competitiveness of each economic unit and on their location in a given institutional setting (also called a nation). Since quality and production costs, the determinants of competitiveness, will largely depend on product and process innovation, it is likely that faster technological change for a given firm, industry, or national economy would result in a higher, not a lower, employment level. This is in line with the findings of Young and Lawson's study on the effect of technology on employment and output in US between 1972 and 1984.[83] In 44 of the 79 industries they examined, the labor-saving effects of new technologies were more than compensated for by higher final demand, so that, overall, employment expanded. At the level of national economies, studies on the newly industrialized countries of the Asian Pacific have also shown a dramatic increase in employment, particularly in manufacturing, following the technological upgrading of industries that enhanced their international competitiveness.[84]

In a more analytical vein, reflecting on the empirical findings in different European countries, the intellectual leader of the

[81]   See Cyert and Mowery (eds) (1987); Lawrence (1984).
[82]   See Landau and Rosenberg (eds) (1986); OECD (1994b); Lawrence (1984).
[83]   Young and Lawson (1984).
[84]   Rodgers (ed.) (1994).

"regulation school," Robert Boyer, summarizes his argument on the matter in several key points:[85]

(1) All other variables being constant, technological change (measured by R&D density) improves productivity and obviously reduces the level of employment for any given demand.
(2) However, productivity gains can be used to reduce relative prices, thus stimulating demand for a given product. If price elasticities are greater than one, a decline in price parallel to a rise in production will in fact enhance employment.
(3) If prices are constant, productivity increases could be converted into real wage or profit increases. Consumption and/or investment will then be higher with stepped-up technological change. If price elasticities are high, employment losses will be compensated by extra demand from both old and new sectors.
(4) Yet the critical matter is the right mix between process innovation and product innovation. If process innovation progresses faster, a decline in employment will occur, all other factors being equal. If product innovation leads the pace, then newly induced demand could result in higher employment.

The problem with such elegant economic analyses is always in the assumptions: all other factors are never equal . . . Boyer himself acknowledges this fact, and then examines the empirical fit of his model, observing, again, a wide range of variation between different industries and countries. While Boyer and Mistral found a negative relationship between productivity and employment for the OECD as a whole in the 1980–86 period, a comparative analysis by Boyer on OECD countries identified three different patterns of employment in areas with similar levels of R&D density.[86]

(1) In Japan an efficient model of mass production and consumption was able to sustain productivity growth and employment growth, on the basis of enhanced competitiveness.
(2) In the United States, there was an impressive rate of job creation, but by concentrating on generating large numbers of low-wage, low-productivity jobs in traditional service activities.
(3) In Western Europe, most economies entered a vicious circle: to cope with increased international competition, firms introduced labor-saving technologies, thus increasing output but leveling off the capacity to generate jobs, particularly in manufacturing. Technological innovation does *not* increase employment. Given

---

[85]   Boyer (1990).
[86]   Boyer and Mistral (1988); Boyer (1988b).

the European characteristics of what Boyer calls "the mode of regulation" (for example, government economic policies and business strategies on labor and technology), innovation is likely to destroy employment in the European context. Yet innovation is increasingly required by competition.

The employment study conducted by the OECD Secretariat in 1994, after examining historical and current evidence on the relationship between technology and employment, concluded that:

> Detailed information, mainly from the manufacturing sector provides evidence that technology is creating jobs. Since 1970 employment in high technology manufacturing has expanded, in sharp contrast to stagnation of medium and low technology sectors and job losses in low-skill manufacturing – at around 1% per year. Countries that have adapted best to new technologies and have shifted production and exports to rapidly growing high tech markets have tended to create more jobs. . . Japan realized a 4% increase in manufacturing employment in the 1970s and 1980s compared with a 1.5% increase in the US. Over the same period the European Community, where exports were increasingly specialized in relatively low-wage, low-tech industries, experienced a 20% drop in manufacturing employment.[87]

In sum, it seems, as a general trend, **that there is no systematic structural relationship between the diffusion of information technologies and the evolution of employment levels in the economy as a whole.** Jobs are being displaced and new jobs are being created, but the quantitative relationship between the losses and the gains varies among firms, industries, sectors, regions, and countries, depending upon competitiveness, firms' strategies, government policies, institutional environments, and relative position in the global economy. The specific outcome of the interaction between information technology and employment is largely dependent upon macroeconomic factors, economic strategies, and sociopolitical contexts. Overall, the employment projections for OECD countries in the early twenty-first century forecast a significant increase in jobs for the US and moderate growth for Japan and the European Community (12 countries): for the 1992–2005 period the projected net increase of jobs would be 24 million (a total increase of 19% over the period) in the US; for Japan, 4 million (an increase of 6%); and for the European Union about 10 million (an increase of between 6% and 7%).[88] However,

[87]   OECD (1994b: 32).
[88]   OECD (194b). For a broader discussion of these data and the policy issues related to the future of work and employment, see Stevens and Michalski (1994).

these projections are highly sensitive to variations in the assumptions on which they are based (such as migration and labor participation rates). This is precisely my argument. The evolution of the level of employment is not a given, which would result from the combination of stable demographic data and a projected rate of diffusion of information technology. It will largely depend on socially determined decisions on the uses of technology, on immigration policy, on the evolution of the family, on the institutional distribution of working time in the lifecycle, and on the new system of industrial relations.

Thus, information technology per se does not cause unemployment, even if it obviously reduces working time per unit of output. But, under the informational paradigm, the kind of jobs change, in quantity, in quality, and in the nature of the work being performed. Thus, a new production system requires a new labor force; those individuals and groups unable to acquire informational skills could be excluded from work or downgraded as workers. Also, because the informational economy is a global economy, widespread unemployment concentrated in some segments of the population (for example, French youth) and in some regions (such as Asturias) could indeed become a threat in the OECD area if global competition is unrestricted, and if the "mode of regulation" of capital–labor relationships is not transformed.

The hardening of capitalist logic since the 1980s has fostered social polarization in spite of occupational upgrading. This tendency is not irreversible: it can be rectified by deliberate policies aimed at rebalancing the social structure. But left to themselves, the forces of unfettered competition in the informational paradigm will push employment and social structure towards dualization. Finally, the flexibility of labor processes and labor markets induced by the network enterprise, and allowed by information technologies, affects profoundly the social relationships of production inherited from industrialism, introducing a new model of flexible work, and a new type of worker: the flex-timer.

Work and the Informational Divide: Flextimers

Linda's new working life is not without its drawbacks. Chief among them is a constant cloud of anxiety about finding the next job. In some ways Linda feels isolated and vulnerable. Fearful of the stigma of having been laid off, for example, she doesn't want her last name to appear in this article.

But the freedom of being her own boss makes up for the insecurity.

Linda gets to build her schedule around her son's. She gets to pick her own assignments. And she gets to be a pioneer of the new work force. (*Newsweek*, June 14 1993: 17)

A new specter haunts Europe (not so much America and Japan): the emergence of a jobless society under the impact of information technologies in factories, offices, and services. Yet, as is usually the case with specters in the electronic age, in a close-up it appears to be more a matter of special effects than a terrifying reality. The lessons of history, current empirical evidence, employment projections in OECD countries, and economic theory do not support these fears in the long term, notwithstanding painful adjustments in the process of transition to the informational paradigm. Institutions and social organizations of work seem to play a greater role than technology in inducing job creation or destruction. However, if technology per se does not create or destroy employment, it does profoundly transform the nature of work and the organization of production. The restructuring of firms and organizations, allowed by information technology and stimulated by global competition, is ushering in a fundamental transformation of work: *the individualization of labor in the labor process.* We are witnessing the reversal of the historical trend of salarization of work and socialization of production that was the dominant feature of the industrial era. The new social and economic organization based on information technologies aims at decentralizing management, individualizing work, and customizing markets, thereby segmenting work and fragmenting societies. New information technologies allow at the same time for the decentralization of work tasks and for their coordination in an interactive network of communication in real time, be it between continents or between floors of the same building. The emergence of lean production methods goes hand in hand with widespread business practices of subcontracting, outsourcing, offshoring, consulting, downsizing, and customizing.

Competition-induced, technology-driven trends towards flexibility underlie the current transformation of working arrangements. The fastest growing categories of work are temporary labor and part-time work. In some countries, such as Italy and the UK, self-employment is becoming again a substantial component of the labor force. Thus, in the UK, the seed-bed of the industrial revolution that spearheaded the historical process of salarization and standardization of labor, the 1993 Labour Force Survey indicated that 38% of people in employment were not employed on a permanent, full-time basis: the bulk of such group is formed by part-timers (85% of whom were women), who accounted for 23.9% of the employed population.[89] Both the OECD and the ILO report that part-time work increased during the 1980s in practically all industrialized countries, rising by about 30% in the decade to reach 50 million workers, of which 40% were in North America.[90] Between 1979 and 1990, part-time work increased from 16.4% to 21.8% of total employment in the UK; from 8.2% to 12% in France; from 11.4% to 13.2% in Germany; from 15.4% to 17.6% in Japan; and from 16.4% to 16.9% in the US.[91]

As shown in table 4.24 (in Appendix A), self-employment as a percentage of total employment largely varies in industrialized countries, in a range that goes between 9.4% (Canada) and 29.1% (Italy) in 1990; temporary work is on the rise in France and Germany, countries with lower part-time work (see figure 4.6). But temporary work is declining in the UK (a country with a high proportion of part-time workers) and in Italy (a country with a high proportion of self-employed). This observation might suggest that the broader category of "flexible work" takes different forms (self-employment, part-time, temporary work) depending on countries' fiscal and labor regulations. Thus, if we add in France in 1990 the self-employed (15.0%), the part-timers (12.0%), and temporary workers (at least 9.2%), we obtain a percentage of non-standard employment close to the British figure (36.2%) – even accounting for some overlapping between these categories. Indeed, in the 1983–88 period, while the full-time employment variation in France was -1.6%, part-time increased by 36.6%. Similar data for Japan, Germany, Italy, and the United Kingdom are shown in table 4.24.

As for the United States, in 1990 self-employment accounted for 10.8% of the workforce, part-time for 16.9%, and "contract" or temporary work for about 2%, adding up to 27.9% of the labor force, although, again, categories overlap to some extent. According to a different estimate, the contingent workforce with no benefits, no job security, and no career amounted in the US in 1992 to about 25% of the labor force, up from 20% in 1982. The projections were for this type of labor to increase to 35% of the US labor force in the year 2000.[92] Outsourcing, facilitated by on-line transactions, concerns not just manufacturing but increasingly services. In a 1994 survey of 392 of America's fastest growing firms, 68% of them were subcontracting

[89]   "Non-standard working under review," *Industrial Relations & Review Report*, no. 565, August 1994: 5–14.
[90]   Robinson (1993).
[91]   OECD (1994b); see also Bosch et al. (eds) (1994): esp. 11–20.
[92]   Jost (1993).

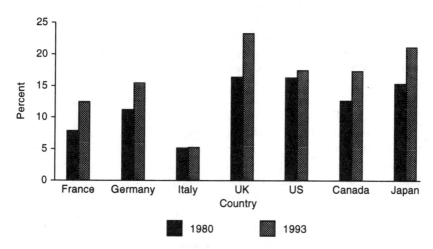

Figure 4.6 OECD countries: part-time employment, 1980–93 (% of total employment)
Source: OECD, *Employment Outlook*, 1994; elaborated by Freeman and Soete (1994).

payroll services, 48% tax compliance services, 46% claim benefits administration, and the like.[93]

The mobility of labor concerns both unskilled and skilled workers. While a core labor force is still the norm in most firms, subcontracting and consulting is a fast-growing form of obtaining professional work. Not only the firm benefits from flexibility. Many professionals add to their main job (full- or part-time) consulting venues which help both their income and their bargaining power. The logic of this highly dynamic work system interacts with the labor institutions of each country: the greater the constraints to such flexibility, and the greater the bargaining power of the labor unions, the lesser will be the impact on wages and benefits, and the greater will be the difficulty for newcomers to enter the core labor force, thus limiting job creation.

While the social costs of flexibility can be high, a growing stream of research emphasizes the transformative value of new work arrangements for social life, and particularly for improved family relationships, and greater egalitarian patterns between genders.[94] A British researcher, P. Hewitt,[95] reports on the growing diversity of

[93] Marshall (1994)
[94] Bielenski (ed.) (1994); for social problems associated with part-time work, see Warme et al. (eds) (1992).
[95] Hewitt (1993). This interesting study is pointedly cited by Freeman and Soete (1994).

working formulae and schedules, and the potential offered by work-sharing between those currently full-time employed and those barely employed *within the same household*. Overall, **the traditional form of work, based on full-time employment, clear-cut occupational assignments, and a career pattern over the lifecycle is being slowly but surely eroded away.**

Japan is different, although not as much as observers usually think. Any analytical framework aimed at explaining new historical trends in the organization of work, and their impact on employment structure, must be able to account for "Japanese exceptionalism:" it is too important an exception to be left aside as an oddity for comparative theory. Therefore, let us consider the matter in some detail.

In May 1995, in spite of economic quasi-stagnation after the prolonged recession that started in 1991, the Japanese unemployment rate, while reaching a record high level for the last two decades, was still at a low 3.2%. Indeed, the main concern of Japanese labor planners is the potential shortage of Japanese workers in the future, given the aging of the demographic structure and Japanese reluctance about foreign immigration.[96] Furthermore, the *Chuki Koyo* system, that provides assurance of long-term employment for the core labor force of large companies, while coming under pressure, did not seem in danger of being dismantled *in the short term*. Thus, it would seem that Japanese exceptionalism belies the general trend towards flexibility of the labor market and the individualization of work that characterizes the other informational, capitalist societies.[97] In fact, I would argue that while Japan has indeed created a highly original system of industrial relations and employment procedures, flexibility has been a structural trend of such a system for the last two decades, and it is increasing along with the transformation of the technological basis and occupational structure.[98]

The Japanese employment structure is characterized by extraordinary internal diversity, as well as by a complex pattern of fluid situations that resist generalization and standardization. The very definition of the *Chuki Koyo* system needs precision.[99] For most workers under such a system it means simply that they can work until retirement in the same company, under normal circumstances, as a matter of custom, not of right. This employment practice is in fact limited to large companies (those with over 1,000 employees), and in most cases concerns only the male, core labor force. In addition to

[96]   NIKKEIREN (1993).
[97]   Kumazawa and Yamada (1989).
[98]   Kuwahara (1989).
[99]   Inoki and Higuchi (eds) (1995).

their regular workers, companies also employ at least three different kinds of workers: part-time workers, temporary workers, and workers sent to the company by another company, or by a recruiting agent ("dispatched workers"). None of these categories has job security, retirement benefits, or is entitled to receive the customary annual bonuses to reward productivity and commitment to the company. In addition, very often workers, particularly older men, are reallocated to other jobs in other companies within the same corporate group (*Shukko*). This includes the practice of separating married men from their families (*Tanshin-Funin*) because of difficulties in finding housing and, most of all, because of the family's reluctance to relocate children to a different school in the middle of their education. *Tanshin-Funin* is said to concern about 30% of managerial employees.[100] Nomura estimates that long-term job security in the same company applies only to about one-third of Japanese employees, including public sector employees.[101] Joussaud provides a similar estimate.[102] Besides, the incidence of job tenure varies widely, even for men, depending on age, level of qualification, and size of the company. Table 4.25 (in Appendix A) provides an illustration of the profile of *Chuki Koyo* in 1991–2.

The critical point in this labor market structure concerns the definition of part-time. According to the government's labor status definitions, 'part-time' workers are those considered as such by the company.[103] In fact, they work almost full-time (6 hours a day, compared to the schedule of 7.5 hours of regular workers), although the number of working days in a month is slightly less than for regular workers. Yet they receive, on average, about 60% of a regular worker's salary, and about 15% of the annual bonus. More importantly, they have no job security, so they are fired and hired according to the company's convenience. Part-timers and temporary workers provide the required labor flexibility. Their role has substantially increased since the 1970s, when the oil shock induced major economic restructuring in Japan. In the 1975–90 period, the number of part-time workers increased by 42.6% for male workers and by 253% for female workers.

Indeed, women account for two-thirds of part-timers. Women are the skilled, adaptable workers that provide flexibility to Japanese labor management practices. This is in fact an old practice in Japanese industrialization. In 1872, the Meiji Government recruited women to work in the nascent textile industry. A pioneer was Wada Ei, daughter of a samurai from Matsuhiro, who went to work in the Tomioka

---

[100]   Collective Author (1994).
[101]   Nomura (1994).
[102]   Joussaud (1994).
[103]   Shinotsuka (1994); Collective Author (1994).

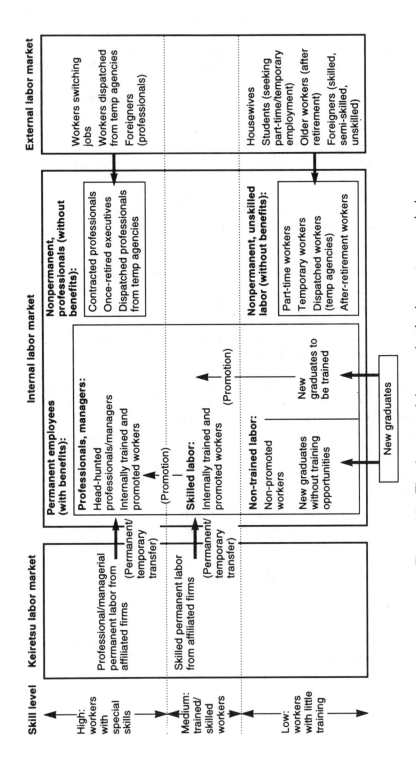

Figure 4.7 The Japanese labor market in the postwar period

Source: Elaborated by Yuko Aoyama, based on information from Japan's Economic Planning Agency, *Gaikokujin rodosha to shakai no shinro*, 1989: p. 99: figure 4.1

Silk-reeling Mill, learned the technology, and helped to train women in other mills. In 1899, women accounted for 70% of workers in spinning mills, and outnumbered male workers in the iron mills. However, at times of crisis women would be fired, while men would be kept as long as possible, emphasizing their role as the last-resort bread-winners of the family. In the last three decades, this historical pattern of gender-based division of labor has hardly changed, although a 1986 Equal Opportunity Law corrected some of the most blatant legal discriminations. Women's participation in the labor force in 1990 features a rate of 61.8% (as compared to 90.2% for men), lower than in the US, but similar to that of Western Europe. Yet their working status varies widely with age and marriage. Thus, 70% of the women who are hired in conditions roughly comparable with men (*sogoshoku*) are under 29 years of age; while 85% of part-timers are married. Women massively enter the labor force in their early twenties, stop working after marriage to raise their children, and return later to the labor force as part-timers. This structure of the occupational lifecycle is reinforced by the Japanese tax code, which makes it more advantageous for women to contribute in a relatively small proportion to the family income than to add a second salary. The stability of the Japanese patriarchal family, with a low rate of divorce and separation and strong intergenerational solidarity,[104] keeps men and women together in the same household, avoiding the polarization of social structure as the result of this obvious pattern of labor market dualism. Uneducated youth and elderly workers of small and medium companies are the other groups accounting for this segment of unstable employees, whose boundaries are difficult to establish because of the fluidity of labor status in Japanese networks of firms.[105] Figure 4.7 attempts to represent schematically the complexity of the Japanese labor market structure.

Thus, it seems that Japan has been practicing for some time the dual labor market logic that is spreading in Western economies. By so doing, it has combined the benefits of the commitment of a core labor force with the flexibility of a peripheral labor market. The former has been essential because it has guaranteed social peace through cooperation between management and company unions; and because it has increased productivity by accumulating knowledge in the firm, and quickly assimilating new technologies. The latter has allowed for quick reaction to changes in labor demand, as well as to competitive pressures from offshored manufacturing in the 1980s. In the 1990s, figures for foreign immigration and day laborers started to

[104]   Gelb and Lief Palley (1995).
[105]   Takenori and Higuchi (1995).

rise, introducing additional choice and flexibility in the lower-skilled segments of the workforce. Altogether, Japanese firms seemed to be able to cope with competitive pressures by retraining their core labor force and adding technology, while multiplying their flexible labor, both in Japan and in their globalized production networks. However, since this labor practice relies essentially on the occupational subservience of highly educated Japanese women, which will not last for ever, I propose the hypothesis that it is just a matter of time until the hidden flexibility of the Japanese labor market diffuses to the core labor force, calling into question what has been the most stable and productive labor relations system of the late industrial era.[106]

Thus, overall, there is indeed a fundamental transformation of work, workers, and working organizations in our societies, but it cannot be apprehended in the traditional categories of obsolete debates over the "end of work" or the "deskilling of labor." The prevailing model for labor in the new, information-based economy is that of a *core labor force*, formed by information-based managers and by those whom Reich calls "symbolic analysts," and a *disposable labor force* that can be automated and/or hired/fired/offshored, depending upon market demand and labor costs. Furthermore, the networked form of business organization allows outsourcing and subcontracting as forms of externalizing labor in a flexible adaptation to market conditions. Analysts have rightly distinguished between various forms of flexibility in wages, geographical mobility, occupational status, contractual security, and task performance, among others.[107] Often all these forms are lumped together in a self-serving strategy to present as inevitable what is in fact a business or policy decision. Yet it is true that current technological trends foster all forms of flexibility, so that in the absence of specific agreements on stabilizing one or various dimensions of work, the system will evolve into multifaceted, generalized flexibility for workers and working conditions. This transformation has shaken our institutions, inducing a crisis in the relationship between work and society.

Information Technology and the Restructuring of Capital–Labor Relationships: Social Dualism or Fragmented Societies?

The diffusion of information technology in the economy does not directly induce unemployment and may create more jobs in the long

---

[106]   Kuwahara (1989); Whitaker (1990).
[107]   Freeman and Soete (1994).

run. The transformation of management and work upgrades the occupational structure to a greater extent in that it increases the number of low-skill jobs. Increasing global trade and investment do not seem to be, by themselves, major causal factors in eliminating jobs and degrading work conditions in the North, while they contribute to create millions of jobs in newly industrializing countries. And yet the process of historical transition toward an informational society and a global economy is characterized by the widespread deterioration of living and working conditions for labor.[108] This deterioration takes different forms in different contexts: the rise of structural unemployment in Europe; declining real wages, increasing inequality, and job instability in the United States; underemployment and stepped-up segmentation of the labor force in Japan; informalization and downgrading of newly incorporated urban labor in industrializing countries; and increasing marginalization of the agricultural labor force in stagnant, underdeveloped economies. As argued above, these trends do not stem from the structural logic of the informational paradigm, but are the result of the current restructuring of capital–labor relationships, helped by the powerful tools provided by new information technologies, and facilitated by a new organizational form, the network enterprise. Furthermore, although the potential of information technologies could have provided for higher productivity, higher living standards, and higher employment simultaneously, once certain technological choices are in place, technological trajectories are "locked in,"[109] and the informational society could become at the same time (without the technological or historical necessity to be so) a dual society.

Alternative views prevailing in the OECD, IMF, and government circles in major Western countries have suggested that observed trends of rising unemployment, underemployment, income inequality, poverty, and social polarization are by and large the result of a skills mismatch, worsened by the lack of flexibility in the labor markets.[110] According to such views, while the occupational/employment structure is upgraded in terms of the educational content of the skills required for the informational jobs, the labor force is not up to the new tasks, either because of the low quality of the educational system or because of the inadequacy of this system

---

[108]   Harrison (1994); ILO (1994).

[109]   Arthur (1989).

[110]   This is the view usually expressed by Alan Greenspan, chairman of the US Federal Reserve Board, and by the International Monetary Fund and other international expert circles. For an economic discourse articulating this thesis, see Krugman (1994); and Krugman and Lawrence (1994).

to provide the new skills needed in the emerging occupational structure.[111]

In their report to the ILO's research institute, Carnoy and Fluitman have submitted this broadly accepted view to a devastating critique. After extensively reviewing the literature and evidence on the relationship between skills, employment, and wages in the OECD countries, they conclude that

> Despite the apparent consensus around the supply-side, skill mismatch argument, the supporting evidence for it is extremely thin, especially in terms of improved education and more and better training solving either the problem of open unemployment (Europe) or the problem of wage distribution (US). It is much more convincing, we argue, that better education and more training could, in the longer run, contribute to higher productivity and economic growth rates.[112]

In the same sense, David Howell has shown for the US that while there has been an increasing demand for higher skills, this is not the cause of the substantial decline in average wages for American workers between 1973 to 1990 (a fall from a weekly wage of $327 to $265 in 1990, measured in 1982 dollars). Neither is the skill mix the source of increasing income inequality. In his study with Wolff, Howell shows that while the share of low-skilled workers in the US is decreasing across industries, the share of low-wage workers has increased in these same industries. Several studies also suggest that higher skills are in demand, although not in shortage, but higher skills do not necessarily translate into higher wages.[113] Thus, in the US, while decline in real wages was more pronounced for the lowest-educated, salaries for the college-educated also stagnated between 1987 and 1993.[114]

The direct consequence of economic restructuring in the United States is that in the 1980s and 1990s family income has plummeted (see figure 4.8). Wages and living conditions continued to decline in the 1990s in spite of a strong economic recovery in 1993.[115] A study by the US Census Bureau in 1994[116] showed that, in spite of significant

---

[111]   Cappelli and Rogovsky (1994).

[112]   Carnoy and Fluitman (1994).

[113]   Howell (1994); Howell and Wolff (1991); Mishel and Teixeira (1991).

[114]   Center for Budget and Policy Priorities, Washington, D.C., cited by *New York Times*, October 7 1994: 9; see also Murphy and Welch (1993); Bernstein and Adler (1994).

[115]   Mishel and Bernstein (1994).

[116]   Cited by *New York Times*, October 7 1994. See also Newman (1993).

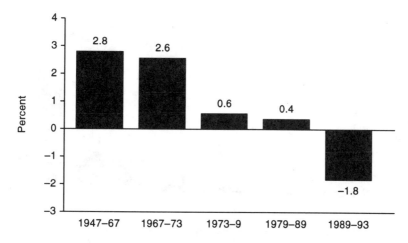

Figure 4.8   United States: annual growth of median family income,
1947–93
Data for 1989 and 1993 were revised using 1990 census weights.
Source: US Bureau of Census (1994); elaborated by Mishel and Bernstein
(1994).

economic growth for the economy as a whole (3%), and an average
increase of 1.8% in the per capita income, median household income
in 1993 declined by 1% in comparison with 1992. From 1989 to 1993
the typical American household lost 7% in annual income. The
percentage of Americans under the poverty line also increased in
1993 to 15.1% (up from 13.1% in 1989), and income inequality
continued to increase to record levels: in 1993, the top fifth of
American households earned 48.2% of total income, while the
bottom fifth earned 3.6%, accentuating the pattern of income
inequality established in the 1980s. According to Thurow (1995: 78),
the median wage for men working full-time began to fall in 1973, and
fell in 20 years from $34,048 to $30,407. In the same period, 1973–93,
the earnings of the top 20% grew steadily and real per capita GDP rose
29%. At the same time, women's wages sustained the family income,
but by the late 1980s they too started to fall in real terms, thus
inducing a decline in household income. By the early 1990s the top
1% of the population owned 40% of all assets, double what it had been
in the mid-1970s, and at the level of the late 1920s, before progressive
taxation. For an illustration of the staggering progression of income
inequality in the US, see figure 4.9. Furthermore, half a century after
Gunnar Myrdal pointed at the "American Dilemma," Martin Carnoy
in a powerful recent book has documented that racial discrimination

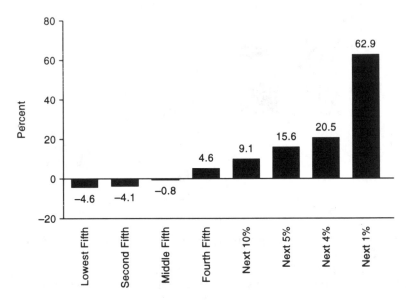

Figure 4.9   United States: income growth, among the top one-fifth
and by fifths, 1980–9
Source: US Congressional Budget Office (1991); compiled by Mishel and
Bernstein (1994).

continues to increase social inequality, contributing to marginalizing
a large proportion of America's ethnic minorities.[117]

While America is an extreme case of income inequality and
declining real wages among the industrialized nations, its evolution is
significant because it does represent the flexible labor market model
at which most European nations, and certainly European firms, are
aiming.[118] And the social consequences of such a trend are similar in
Europe. Thus, in Greater London between 1979 and 1991 real disposable income of households in the lowest decile of income
distribution declined by 14%, and the ratio of real income of the
richest decile over the poorest one almost doubled in the decade,
from 5.6 to 10.2.[119]

The new vulnerability of labor under conditions of unrestrained
flexibility does not concern only the unskilled labor force. The core
labor force, while better paid and more stable, is submitted to mobility
by shortening the working-life period in which professionals are

[117]   Carnoy (1994).
[118]   Sayer and Walker (1992).
[119]   Lee and Townsend (1993: 18–20).

recruited to the core of the enterprise. In American business, the bottom line in the 1990s is the 50/50 rule: those who are over 50 years old and earn over $50,000 have their jobs first in line for any potential downsizing.[120]

The logic of this highly dynamic labor market model interacts with the specificity of labor institutions in each country. Thus, a study of German labor relationships shows that reduction of labor as a result of the introduction of computerized machinery in the 1980s was inversely related to the level of workers' protection provided by the unions in the industry. On the other hand, firms with high levels of protection were also those with the highest change in innovation. This study shows that there is not necessarily a conflict between upgrading the technological basis of the firm and keeping most of the workers, generally retraining them. These firms were also those with the highest level of unionization.[121] The study by Harley Shaiken on Japanese automobile companies in the United States, and on the Saturn automobile plant in Tennessee, reaches similar conclusions, showing the effectiveness of workers' input and unions' participation in the successful introduction of technological innovations, while limiting labor losses.[122]

This institutional variation is what explains the difference we have shown between the United States and the European Union. Social restructuring takes the form of pressuring wages and labor conditions in the US. In the European Union, where labor institutions defend better their historically conquered positions, the net result is increasing unemployment, because of limited entry to young workers and because of the early exit from the labor force for the oldest, or for those trapped in noncompetitive sectors and firms.[123]

As for industrializing countries, they have been featuring for at least three decades a model of articulation between the formal and informal urban labor markets that is tantamount to the flexible forms diffused in the mature economies by the new technological/organizational paradigm.[124]

Why and how has this restructuring of the capital–labor relationship taken place at the dawn of the information age? It resulted from historical circumstances, technological opportunities, and economic imperatives. To reverse the profit squeeze without triggering inflation, national economies and private firms have acted on labor

[120]   Byrne (1994).
[121]   Warnken and Ronning (1990).
[122]   Shaiken (1993, 1995).
[123]   Bosch (1995).
[124]   Portes et al. (1989); Gereffi (1993)

costs since the early 1980s, either by increasing productivity without employment creation (Europe) or by lowering the cost of a plethora of new jobs (US). Labor unions, the main obstacle to one-sided restructuring strategy, were weakened by their inadaptability to representing new kinds of workers (women, youth, immigrants), to acting in new work places (private sector offices, high-technology industries), and to functioning in the new forms of organization (the network enterprise on a global scale).[125] When necessary, politically induced offensive strategies helped the historical/structural trends working against the unions (for example, Reagan on air traffic controllers, Thatcher on the coal miners). But even socialist governments in France and Spain went on changing the conditions of the labor market, thus weakening the unions, when the pressures of competition made it difficult to depart sharply from the new management rules of the global economy.

What made possible this historical redefinition of the relationship between capital and labor was the use of powerful information technologies and of organizational forms facilitated by the new technological medium. The ability to assemble and disperse labor on specific projects and tasks anywhere, any time, created the possibility for the coming into being of the virtual enterprise as a functional entity. From then on, it was a matter of overcoming institutional resistance to the development of such logic, and/or of obtaining concessions from labor and unions under the potential threat of virtualization. The extraordinary increase in flexibility and adaptability permitted by new technologies opposed the rigidity of labor to the mobility of capital. It followed a relentless pressure to make the labor contribution as flexible as it could be. Productivity and profitability were enhanced, yet labor lost institutional protection and became increasingly dependent on individual bargaining conditions in a constantly changing labor market.

Society became divided, as it was for most of human history, between winners and losers of the endless process of individualized, unequal bargaining. But this time there were few rules about how to win and how to lose. Skills were not enough, since the process of technological change accelerated its pace, constantly superseding the definition of appropriate skills. Membership of corporations, or even countries, ceased to have its privileges, because stepped-up global competition kept redesigning the variable geometry of work and markets. Never was labor more central to the process of value-making.

---

[125]   For assessments of the decline of traditional unionism under new economic/technological conditions, see Carnoy et al. (1993a); see also Gourevitch (ed.) (1984); Adler and Suarez (1993).

But never were the workers (regardless of their skills) more vulnerable to the organization, since they had become lean individuals, farmed out in a flexible network whose whereabouts were unknown to the network itself.

Thus, on the surface, societies were/are becoming dualized, with a substantial top and a substantial bottom growing at both ends of the occupational structure, so shrinking the middle, at a pace and in a proportion that depend on each country's position in the international division of labor and on its political climate. But down in the deep of the nascent social structure, a more fundamental process has been triggered by informational work: the disaggregation of labor, ushering in the network society.

Appendix A: Statistical tables for chapter 4

Table 4.1 United States: percentage distribution of employment by industrial sector and intermediate industry group

Industry	(a) 1920–70						(b) 1970–91				
	1920	1930	1940	1950	1960	1970	1970	1980	1985	1990	1991
I Extractive	28.9	25.4	21.3	14.4	8.1	4.5	4.6	4.5	4.0	3.5	3.5
Agriculture	26.3	22.9	19.2	12.7	7.0	3.7	3.7	3.6	3.1	2.8	2.9
Mining	2.6	2.5	2.1	1.7	1.1	0.8	0.8	1.0	0.9	0.6	0.6
II Transformative	32.9	31.6	29.8	33.9	35.9	33.1	33.0	29.6	27.2	25.6	24.7
Constructive	<	6.5	4.7	6.2	6.2	5.8	6.0	6.2	6.5	6.5	6.1
Utilities	<	0.6	1.2	1.4	1.4	1.4	1.1	1.2	1.2	1.1	1.1
Manufacturing	<	24.5	23.9	26.2	28.3	25.9	25.9	22.2	19.5	18.0	17.5
Food	<	2.3	2.7	2.7	3.1	2.0	1.9	1.9	1.7	1.6	1.5
Textiles	<	4.2	2.0	2.2	3.3	3.0	1.3	0.8	0.7	0.6	0.6
Metal	<	7.7	2.9	3.6	3.9	3.3	3.1	2.7	2.0	1.8	1.7
Machinery	<	^	2.4	3.7	7.5	8.3	5.1	5.2	4.5	3.8	3.7
Chemical	<	1.3	1.5	1.7	1.8	1.6	1.5	1.6	1.3	1.3	1.3
Misc. mfg.	<	9.0	11.8	12.3	8.7	7.7	12.9	10.0	9.4	8.9	8.6
III Distributive services	18.7	19.6	20.4	22.4	21.9	22.3	22.4	21.0	20.9	20.6	20.6
Transportation	7.6	6.0	4.9	5.3	4.4	3.9	3.9	3.7	3.5	3.5	3.6
Communication	<	1.0	0.9	1.2	1.3	1.5	1.5	1.5	1.5	1.3	1.4
Wholesale	11.1	12.6	2.7	3.5	3.6	4.1	4.0	3.9	4.1	3.9	4.0
Retail	<	^	11.8	12.3	12.5	12.8	12.9	11.9	11.9	11.8	11.7
IV Producer services	2.8	3.2	4.6	4.8	6.6	8.5	8.2	10.5	12.7	14.0	14.0
Banking	<	1.3	1.1	1.1	1.6	2.6	2.2	2.6	2.9	2.9	2.8
Insurance	<	1.1	1.2	1.4	1.7	1.8	1.8	1.9	1.9	2.1	2.1
Real Estate	<	0.6	1.1	1.0	1.0	1.0	1.0	1.6	1.7	1.8	1.8
Engineering	<	—	1.3	0.2	0.3	0.4	0.4	0.6	0.7	0.7	0.7

Accounting	^	—	^	0.2	0.3	0.4	0.4	0.5	0.5	0.5	0.6
Misc. business serv.	^	0.1	^	0.6	1.2	1.8	1.8	2.6	4.0	4.9	5.0
Legal services	^	—	^	0.4	0.5	0.5	0.5	0.8	0.9	1.0	1.1
V Social services	8.7	9.2	10.0	12.4	16.3	21.9	22.0	23.7	23.6	24.9	25.5
Medical, health serv.	^	—	2.3	1.1	1.4	2.2	2.4	2.3	3.6	4.3	4.5
Hospital	^	—	^	1.8	2.7	3.7	3.7	5.3	4.0	4.0	4.1
Education	^	—	3.5	3.8	5.4	8.6	8.5	8.3	7.8	7.9	8.0
Welfare, relig. serv.	^	—	0.9	0.7	1.0	1.2	1.2	1.6	2.2	2.6	2.7
Nonprofit org.	^	—	^	0.3	0.4	0.4	0.4	0.5	0.4	0.4	0.4
Postal service	^	0.6	0.7	0.8	0.9	1.0	1.0	0.7	0.7	0.7	0.7
Government	^	2.2	2.6	3.7	4.3	4.6	4.5	4.7	4.7	4.8	4.8
Misc. social services	^	6.3	—	0.1	0.2	0.3	0.3	0.4	0.2	0.2	0.2
VI Personal services	8.2	11.2	14.0	12.1	11.3	10.	10.0	10.5	11.7	11.5	11.7
Domestic serv.	^	6.5	5.3	3.2	3.1	1.7	1.7	1.3	1.2	0.9	0.9
Hotel	^	2.9	1.3	1.0	1.0	1.0	1.0	1.1	1.4	1.5	1.6
Eating, drinking places	^	^	2.5	3.0	2.9	3.3	3.2	4.4	4.9	4.8	4.9
Repair services	^	—	1.5	1.7	1.4	1.3	1.4	1.3	1.5	1.4	1.4
Laundry	^	—	1.0	1.2	1.0	0.8	0.8	0.4	0.4	0.5	0.4
Barber, beauty shops	^	0.9	—	—	0.8	0.9	0.9	0.7	0.8	0.7	0.4
Entertainment	^	0.9	0.9	1.0	0.8	0.8	0.8	1.0	1.2	1.3	0.7
Misc. personal serv.	^	—	1.6	1.2	0.4	0.3	0.3	0.3	0.4	0.4	0.4
Total	100	100	100	100	100	100	100	100	100	100	100

^ signifies that the figure is included in the above category.

The numbers may not add up due to rounding.

Sources: (a) Singelmann (1978); (b) 1970: Population Census; 1980–1991: *Current Population Survey*, Bureau of Labor Statistics; Labor statistics: *Employment and Earnings*, various issues.

Table 4.2 Japan: percentage distribution of employment by industrial sector and intermediate industry group

Industry	(a) 1920–70						(b) 1970–90			
	1920	1930	1940	1950	1960	1970	1970	1980	1985	1990
I Extractive	56.4	50.9	46.3	50.3	34.1	19.6	19.8	11.2	9.5	7.2
Agriculture	54.9	49.9	44.0	48.6	32.9	19.4	19.4	11.0	9.3	7.1
Mining	1.5	1.0	2.2	1.7	1.2	0.3	0.4	0.2	0.2	0.1
II Transformative	19.6	19.8	24.9	21.0	28.5	34.2	34.1	33.7	33.4	33.7
Construction	2.7	3.3	3.0	4.3	6.2	7.6	7.6	9.7	9.1	9.6
Utilities	0.3	0.4	0.4	0.6	0.6	0.6	0.6	0.6	0.6	0.6
Manufacturing	16.6	16.1	21.6	16.1	21.7	26.0	26.0	23.4	23.7	23.6
Food	2.0	1.8	1.4	2.2	2.1	2.1	2.1	2.1	2.2	2.3
Textiles	5.0	4.8	3.9	3.1	3.2	2.7	2.7	1.7	1.5	1.2
Metal	1.0	0.8	1.4	1.6	2.9	1.5	4.0	3.6	3.2	3.2
Machinery	0.4	0.7	2.9	1.6	3.1	4.9	5.0	4.6	5.9	5.9
Chemical	0.4	0.6	1.1	1.2	1.2	1.3	1.3	1.1	1.0	1.1
Misc. mfg.	7.8	7.4	10.9	6.4	9.2	13.5	10.9	10.3	10.0	10.0
III Distributive services	12.4	15.6	15.2	14.6	18.6	22.5	22.4	25.1	24.8	24.3
Transportation	3.5	3.2	3.4	3.5	4.0	5.1	5.1	5.1	5.0	5.0
Communication	0.4	0.7	0.9	1.0	1.1	1.2	1.1	1.2	1.1	1.0
Wholesale	8.5	11.6	10.9	2.3	4.7	6.1	6.1	6.9	7.2	7.1
Retail	^	^	^	7.8	8.9	10.2	10.2	11.9	11.5	11.2
IV Producer services	0.8	0.9	1.2	1.5	2.9	5.1	4.8	7.5	8.6	9.6
Banking	0.4	0.5	0.6	0.7	1.2	1.4	1.4	2.8	3.0	1.9
Insurance	0.1	0.2	0.3	0.2	0.5	0.7	0.7	^	^	1.3
Real Estate	—	—	0.1	0.0	0.2	0.5	0.5	0.8	0.8	1.1
Engineering	0.0	—	0.3	0.3	1.0	0.5	0.5	—	—	0.8

	(1)	(2)	(3)	(4)	(5)	(6)	(7)	(8)	(9)	(10)
Accounting	—	—	<	<	<	0.2	0.2	—	—	0.3
Misc. business services	0.2	0.2	<	<	<	1.7	1.4	3.9	4.8	4.0
Legal services	0.1	0.0	0.0	0.2	0.1	0.1	0.1	—	—	0.1
V Social services	4.9	5.5	6.0	7.2	8.3	10.1	10.3	12.9	13.5	14.3
Medical, health serv.	0.4	0.3	0.4	1.1	0.3	0.2	0.4	2.9	3.4	1.5
Hospital	0.3	0.5	0.7	<	1.3	1.8	1.8	<	<	2.2
Education	0.9	1.3	1.5	2.2	2.4	2.7	2.9	3.6	3.7	4.5
Welfare, relig. serv.	0.6	0.6	0.6	0.3	0.6	0.7	0.7	1.3	1.3	1.4
Nonprofit org.	0.1	—	0.7	0.2	0.2	0.5	1.0	1.1	1.1	1.1
Postal service	2.2	2.5	1.9	3.3	3.1	3.3	—	—	—	—
Government	<	<	<	<	<	<	3.4	3.6	3.6	3.4
Misc. social services	0.3	0.3	0.3	0.1	0.6	0.9	0.0	0.5	0.4	0.4
VI Personal services	5.7	7.3	6.3	5.3	7.6	8.5	8.5	9.6	10.1	10.2
Domestic serv.	2.5	2.7	2.2	0.8	0.7	0.3	0.3	0.1	0.1	0.1
Hotel	0.5	0.5	0.5	0.5	0.8	0.9	0.9	1.0	1.1	1.1
Eating, drinking places	1.4	2.4	1.8	1.1	2.2	3.1	3.0	4.1	4.3	4.1
Repair services	0.0	0.1	—	0.9	0.7	0.9	0.9	1.1	0.9	1.0
Laundry	0.1	0.2	0.2	0.2	0.4	0.5	0.5	1.6	1.7	0.6
Barber, beauty shops	0.5	0.7	0.6	0.6	1.1	1.1	1.1	<	<	1.1
Entertainment	0.4	0.3	0.8	0.5	0.7	0.7	0.8	0.9	1.0	1.3
Misc. personal serv.	0.2	0.3	0.3	0.7	1.0	1.0	1.0	0.9	0.9	0.9
Unclassifiable	—	—	—	—	—	—	—	—	—	0.6
Total	100	100	100	100	100	100	100	100	100	100

^ signifies that the figure is included in the category immediately above.
The numbers may not add up due to rounding.
Source: (a) Singelmann (1978); (b) Population Census, Bureau of Statistics.

286

Table 4.3 Germany: percentage distribution of employment by industrial sector and intermediate industry group

Industry	(a) 1925–70					(b) 1970–87	
	1925	1933	1950	1961	1970	1970	1987
I Extractive	33.5	31.5	16.1	9.0	5.1	8.7	4.1
Agriculture	30.9	29.1	12.9	6.8	3.8	7.5	3.2
Mining	2.6	2.4	3.2	2.2	1.3	1.2	0.9
II Transformative	38.9	36.3	47.3	51.3	49.0	47.1	40.3
Construction	5.3	6.1	9.3	8.5	8.0	7.7	7.1
Utilities	0.6	0.6	0.8	1.2	0.8	0.8	1.0
Manufacturing	33.0	31.6	37.1	41.6	40.2	38.6	32.2
Food	4.3	5.1	4.6	3.1	3.8	3.6	2.9
Textiles	3.7	3.5	3.5	5.1	2.2	2.4	1.1
Metal	3.7	4.5	2.3	3.7	3.7	4.7	4.3
Machinery	2.9	3.4	3.0	5.0	4.8	9.5	4.9
Chemical	1.1	1.1	1.7	2.4	2.7	2.4	2.7
Misc. mfg.	17.3	14.0	22.0	22.3	23.0	16.0	16.2
III Distributive services	11.9	12.8	15.7	16.4	16.4	17.9	17.7
Transportation	4.0	4.2	5.1	4.5	3.9	5.4	5.9
Communication	—	—	—	0.5	—	^	^
Wholesale	7.9	8.6	10.6	3.9	4.4	4.2	3.2
Retail	^	^	^	7.5	8.6	8.2	8.6
IV Producer services	2.1	2.7	2.5	4.2	5.1	4.5	7.3
Banking	0.7	0.6	0.7	1.2	1.7	1.7	2.4
Insurance	0.4	0.6	0.8	0.7	1.0	0.9	1.0
Real estate	0.0	0.6	0.1	0.3	0.4	0.3	0.4
Engineering	0.1	0.1	0.2	0.4	0.6	0.6	0.7

	(1)	(2)	(3)	(4)	(5)	(6)	(7)
Accounting	0.5	0.3	0.3	1.0	0.7	—	—
Misc. business serv.	<	<	<	<	<	0.9	2.8
Legal services	0.3	0.6	0.5	0.6	0.8	—	—
V Social services	6.0	6.8	11.1	12.5	17.4	15.7	24.3
Medical, health serv.	0.4	1.3	2.4	2.5	3.2	3.1	5.4
Hospital	0.6	<	<	<	<	—	—
Education	1.1	1.2	1.5	2.1	3.0	3.0	4.9
Welfare, relig. serv.	0.5	0.8	1.0	0.9	0.4	0.9	1.5
Nonprofit org.	—	—	—	—	0.4	0.4	0.2
Postal service	1.1	1.1	1.5	1.7	1.8	—	—
Government	2.1	2.2	4.1	5.3	8.6	7.7	9.5
Misc. social services	0.1	0.2	0.6	—	—	0.5	2.8
VI Personal services	7.7	7.8	6.9	6.4	7.4	6.1	6.3
Domestic serv.	4.4	4.0	3.2	1.5	0.5	0.4	0.2
Hotel	2.1	2.4	2.2	2.6	2.9	2.8	2.7
Eating, drinking places	<	<	<	<	<	<	<
Repair services	—	—	—	—	1.1	1.0	1.1
Laundry	0.2	—	—	0.6	0.5	0.5	0.2
Barber, beauty shops	0.4	0.7	0.8	0.9	0.9	0.9	1.0
Entertainment	0.4	0.5	0.1	—	0.4	0.4	0.9
Misc. personal serv.	0.1	0.2	0.6	0.8	0.4	0.1	0.1
Total	100	100	100	100	100	100	100

< signifies that the figure is included in the category immediately above.
The numbers may not add up due to rounding.
Sources: (a) Singelmann (1978); (b) Statistisches Bundesamt, Volkszählung.

288

Table 4.4 France: percentage distribution of employment by industrial sector and intermediate industry group

Industry	(a) 1921–68						(b) 1968–89					
	1921	1931	1946	1954	1962	1968	1968	1970	1975	1980	1985	1989p
I Extractive	43.6	38.3	40.2	30.9	23.0	17.0	15.6	13.5	10.3	8.7	7.6	6.4
Agriculture	42.4	36.6	38.8	28.6	20.6	15.9	14.8	12.9	9.9	8.4	7.4	6.3
Mining	1.2	1.7	1.4	2.3	2.4	1.1	0.2	0.6	0.4	0.3	0.2	0.1
II Transformative	29.7	32.8	29.6	35.2	37.7	39.3	39.4	38.0	37.3	34.8	30.9	29.5
Construction	3.0	4.2	5.1	7.4	8.7	10.3	9.5	9.5	8.9	8.5	7.1	7.2
Utilities	0.2	0.0	0.6	0.7	0.8	0.8	0.8	0.8	0.8	0.9	1.0	1.0
Manufacturing	26.4	28.5	23.8	27.2	28.0	26.0	27.0	27.7	27.6	25.5	22.9	21.3
Food	2.3	2.6	2.2	3.2	3.1	3.0	3.0	3.0	2.9	2.9	2.9	2.8
Textiles	9.4	4.4	2.5	6.0	4.9	2.3	3.8	3.6	3.1	2.5	2.1	1.7
Metal	0.6	2.1	7.3	0.9	1.1	1.5	5.0	5.1	5.0	4.3	3.6	3.5
Machinery	—	—	<	0.9	1.2	1.3	4.9	5.3	5.6	5.2	4.8	4.5
Chemical	0.9	1.1	1.1	1.3	1.4	1.5	1.8	1.9	1.9	1.8	1.7	1.6
Misc. mfg.	13.2	18.3	10.7	14.9	16.3	18.5	8.4	8.8	9.1	8.7	7.7	7.3
III Distributive services	14.4	13.6	15.1	14.2	16.4	15.5	18.8	18.7	19.2	19.9	20.2	20.5
Transportation	5.6	5.1	6.1	4.2	4.3	4.3	4.2	4.1	4.1	4.1	4.2	4.3
Communication	0.7	<	<	1.3	1.7	0.1	1.8	1.8	2.0	2.1	2.3	2.2
Wholesale	8.1	8.5	9.1	2.3	3.2	3.6	3.7	3.8	4.0	4.4	4.4	4.5
Retail	<	<	<	6.5	7.3	7.5	9.1	9.0	9.2	9.3	9.3	9.5
IV Producer services	1.6	2.1	1.9	2.6	3.2	5.5	5.0	5.5	6.5	7.8	8.5	10.0
Banking	0.6	0.9	1.2	0.8	1.1	2.0	1.3	1.4	1.8	2.0	2.8	2.0
Insurance	0.2	0.3	0.4	0.5	0.7	0.8	0.5	0.5	0.6	0.7	0.7	0.8
Real estate	0.0	0.0	0.0	0.4	0.2	0.4	0.1	0.2	0.3	0.3	0.3	0.3
Engineering	0.5	0.7	—	0.9	1.1	0.3	—	—	—	—	—	—
Accounting	<	<	—	<	<	1.6	—	—	—	—	—	—

	1	2	3	4	5	6	7	8	9	10	11	12
Misc. business serv.	^	^	^	^	^	^	3.1	3.4	3.8	4.9	5.3	6.9
Legal services	0.3	0.3	0.3	^	^	0.4	—	—	—	—	—	—
V Social services	5.3	6.1	6.8	9.4	12.3	14.5	15.1	15.6	16.4	17.1	19.8	19.5
Medical, health serv.	0.9	1.1	1.2	2.2	2.9	1.0	—	—	—	—	—	—
Hospital	^	^	^	^	^	2.2	—	—	—	—	—	—
Education	1.3	1.4	1.5	2.4	3.5	4.4	—	—	—	—	—	—
Welfare, relig. serv.	0.5	0.5	0.7	0.6	1.1	1.1	—	—	—	—	—	—
Nonprofit org.	—	—	—	—	1.0	0.7	—	—	—	—	—	—
Postal services	2.3	2.8	3.2	4.0	3.4	1.8	—	—	—	—	—	—
Government	^	^	^	^	^	3.3	—	—	—	—	—	—
Misc. social services	0.2	0.2	0.1	0.2	0.4	0.0	—	—	—	—	—	—
VI Personal services	5.6	7.2	6.4	7.4	7.4	7.9	8.2	8.7	10.2	11.6	13.1	14.1
Domestic serv.	3.7	3.8	1.3	3.1	3.0	2.7	—	—	—	—	—	—
Hotel	1.5	2.8	1.4	1.5	1.6	0.9	2.7	2.7	2.7	2.8	3.1	3.5
Eating, drinking places	^	^	^	1.4	1.2	1.8	^	^	^	^	^	^
Repair services	—	—	—	—	0.3	1.1	—	—	—	—	—	—
Laundry	—	—	0.2	1.0	1.2	0.5	—	—	—	—	—	—
Barber, beauty shops	0.3	0.2	^	^	^	0.7	—	—	—	—	—	—
Entertainment	0.1	0.5	0.3	0.4	0.2	0.2	—	—	—	—	—	—
Misc. personal serv.	0.0	—	0.5	—	0.0	0.0	5.6	6.0	7.4	8.8	10.0	10.6
Total	100	100	100	100	100	100	100	100	100	100	100	100

^ signifies the figure is included in the category immediately above.

The numbers may not add up due to rounding.

1989 figures are preliminary. Communication includes postal services.

Miscellaneous services includes all non-profit services in 1968–89.

Sources: (a) Singelmann (1978); (b) INSEE, Annuaire statistique de la France.

Table 4.5 Italy: percentage distribution of employment by industrial sector and intermediate industry group.

Industry	(a) 1921–61				(b) 1961–90			
	1921	1931	1951	1961	1961	1971	1981	1990
I Extractive	57.1	48.1	42.9	29.8	29.8	17.2	11.7	9.5
Agriculture	56.7	47.7	42.5	29.1	29.1	17.2	11.4	9.5
Mining	0.4	0.4	0.4	0.7	0.7	—	0.3	—
II Transformative	24.3	29.0	31.8	40.0	39.9	44.3	40.5	29.7
Constructive	4.1	6.0	7.6	12.0	12.0	10.8	9.4	7.0
Utilities	0.3	0.6	0.5	0.6	0.6	0.9	0.9	0.8
Manufacturing	19.9	22.4	23.7	27.4	27.3	32.7	30.2	21.8
Food	1.2	1.5	2.4	2.4	—	—	1.8	1.6
Textiles	3.2	4.2	3.7	3.4	—	—	6.3	5.0
Metal	1.8	4.4	1.2	1.5	—	—	7.0	4.7
Machinery	1.5	^	1.4	1.8	—	—	4.8	3.3
Chemical	0.4	1.0	1.1	1.4	—	—	1.4	1.3
Misc. mfg.	11.8	11.3	13.9	16.9	—	—	8.8	5.9
III Distributive services	8.6	10.1	10.6	13.0	15.3	18.7	16.2	25.8
Transportation	3.9	4.2	3.4	4.1	4.9	5.3	4.9	5.2
Communication	0.4	0.5	0.6	0.8	^	^	1.5	1.3
Wholesale	4.3	5.4	1.2	1.4	10.3	13.4	3.6	17.3
Retail	^	^	5.4	6.7	^	^	6.1	^
IV Producer services	1.2	1.8	1.9	2.0	—	—	4.6	—
Banking	0.2	0.5	0.8	0.9	1.1	1.5	1.7	1.8
Insurance	^	0.1	0.1	0.2	^	^	0.5	^
Real estate	^	^	^	0.0	—	—	0.0	—
Engineering	0.8	^	^	0.3	—	—	1.4	—
Accounting	^	1.0	0.7	^	—	—	0.4	—

Misc. business serv.	^	^	^	0.2			—	0.1
Legal services	0.2	0.2	0.3	0.4			—	0.4
V Social services	4.1	5.1	7.9	9.3			—	19.1
Medical, health serv.	0.6	0.8	1.1	0.7			—	1.7
Hospital	^	^	^	0.9			—	2.6
Education	1.0	1.1	2.0	2.7			—	7.4
Welfare, relig. serv.	0.6	0.7	1.2	0.2			—	0.2
Nonprofit org.	—	0.1	0.1	—			—	0.3
Postal service	1.3	2.1	3.4	4.8			—	—
Government	^	^	^	^	6.9	6.5	15.5	6.5
Misc. social services	0.6	0.3	0.1	—			—	0.4
VI Personal services	4.6	5.6	4.7	5.9			—	7.9
Domestic serv.	2.4	3.2	2.2	2.2			—	1.2
Hotel	0.2	0.6	1.4	0.7			4.1	0.9
Eating, drinking places	0.8	0.7	^	1.4			^	2.0
Repair services	—	—	—	—			—	2.0
Laundry	0.3	0.2	0.1	0.2			—	0.3
Barber, beauty shops	0.4	0.7	0.6	0.9			—	1.0
Entertainment	0.0	0.1	0.3	0.3			—	0.5
Misc. personal serv.	0.5	0.1	0.1	0.2			—	0.1
All other services					7.0	11.8	15.6	15.6
Total	100	100	100	100	100	100	100	100

^ signifies that the figure is included in the category immediately above.

The numbers may not add up due to rounding.

1990 figures may not be comparable to figures from earlier years due to the difference in sources.

Sources: (a) Singelmann (1978); (b) 1961–81: Istituto Centrale di statistica, *Censimento generale della popolazione;* 1990: Istituto nazionale di statistica, *Annuario Statistico Italiano,* 1991.

Table 4.6 United Kingdom: percentage distribution of employment by industrial sector and intermediate industry group

Industry	(a) England and Wales 1921–71					(b) UK (employees) 1970–90					(c) Great Britain (employees) 1970–92						(d) Great Britain (employed) 1971–81	
	1921	1931	1951	1961	1971	1970	1975	1980	1985	1990	1970	1971	1980	1981	1990	1992	1971	1981
I Extractive	14.2	11.8	8.9	6.6	4.3	3.6	3.3	4.7	4.4	3.3	3.6	3.4	4.3	4.9	3.2	1.8	4.3	3.9
Agriculture	7.1	6.1	5.0	3.5	2.6	1.7	1.8	1.6	1.6	1.3	1.7	1.6	1.6	1.6	1.2	1.2	2.7	2.3
Mining	7.1	5.7	3.9	3.1	1.7	1.9	1.6	3.2	2.8	2.0	1.9	1.9	3.2	3.3	2.0	0.5	1.6	1.6
II Transformative	42.2	39.3	45.4	46.0	43.8	46.7	40.3	35.7	29.8	27.3	46.6	45.9	35.7	33.7	27.3	26.3	42.8	35.6
Construction	4.4	5.2	6.5	6.9	7.1	6.3	5.8	5.5	4.8	4.8	6.2	6.0	5.4	5.2	4.8	4.0	7.0	7.0
Utilities	1.0	1.3	1.7	1.7	1.6	1.7	1.6	—	—	—	1.7	1.7	—	—	—	1.2	1.5	1.5
Manufacturing	36.8	32.9	37.2	37.4	34.9	38.7	33.0	30.2	25.0	22.5	38.8	38.2	30.3	28.5	22.5	21.1	34.2	27.1
Food	3.3	3.4	3.0	3.0	3.0	3.9	3.2	3.2	2.8	2.4	3.8	3.8	3.1	3.1	2.9	2.9	3.1	3.0
Textiles	5.9	5.9	4.5	3.4	2.4	3.1	2.1	1.5	1.1	0.9	3.0	2.8	1.5	1.5	0.9	0.8	2.5	1.3
Metal	2.8	2.1	2.7	2.7	2.3	5.4	4.6	6.8	3.6	3.1	5.5	5.3	6.9	6.2	3.2	2.7	4.8	4.1
Machinery	1.6	1.4	3.0	3.2	4.8	9.2	7.7	7.9	6.8	6.1	9.3	9.1	8.0	7.6	6.2	5.8	8.3	7.1
Chemical	1.1	1.1	2.1	2.3	2.0	2.3	2.1	—	1.6	1.4	2.4	2.4	—	—	1.5	1.4	2.2	1.7
Misc. mfg.	22.1	19.0	21.9	22.8	20.4	14.8	13.1	10.8	9.2	8.6	14.8	14.8	10.8	10.2	8.5	8.0	13.4	10.0
III Distributive services	19.3	21.6	19.2	19.7	17.9	18.7	18.9	19.9	20.4	20.6	18.8	18.7	20.2	20.4	20.4	20.7	19.3	20.3
Transportation	7.3	7.0	6.4	5.7	4.8	4.9	4.7	6.5	4.2	4.1	4.9	5.0	6.5	6.6	4.2	4.3	4.8	4.6
Communication	—	—	—	—	—	2.0	2.0	<	2.0	1.9	2.0	2.1	<	<	1.9	1.9	1.8	1.9
Wholesale	12.0	14.6	12.8	14.0	3.4	2.3	3.7	4.0	4.5	4.5	2.3	2.4	4.1	4.2	4.3	4.5	2.1	3.9
Retail	<	<	<	<	9.6	9.5	8.4	9.5	9.7	10.1	9.5	9.3	9.5	9.6	10.1	10.0	10.7	9.8
IV Producer services	2.6	3.1	3.2	4.5	5.6	5.0	5.7	7.5	9.7	12.0	5.1	5.2	7.5	8.0	12.1	12.3	5.6	7.9
Banking	0.8	0.8	0.9	1.2	1.6	1.6	1.9	2.0	2.4	2.8	1.6	1.7	2.0	2.2	2.8	2.8	1.6	2.1
Insurance	0.7	0.9	0.9	1.1	1.2	1.3	1.2	0.9	1.1	1.2	1.3	1.3	1.0	1.0	1.2	1.2	1.2	1.1
Real estate	—	0.3	0.3	0.3	0.4	0.3	0.4	—	0.6	0.6	0.3	0.3	—	—	0.6	0.7	0.4	0.4

	1	2	3	4	5	6	7	8	9	10	11	12	13	14	15	16	17	18
Engineering	0.2	0.2	0.2	—	0.4	0.4	0.4	—	—	—	0.4	0.4	—	—	—	—	0.5	—
Accounting	0.0	0.3	0.3	0.4	0.4	1.0	1.4	—	—	—	1.1	1.1	—	—	—	—	0.4	—
Misc. business serv.	0.4	0.2	0.1	1.1	1.0	1.2	1.2	4.5	5.6	7.4	1.2	1.2	4.5	4.8	7.5	5.9	1.1	4.3
Legal services	0.4	0.4	0.4	0.4	0.5	0.5	0.5	—	—	—	0.5	0.5	—	—	—	—	0.5	—
V Social services	8.9	9.7	12.1	14.1	19.4	17.7	22.1	24.2	26.8	27.2	17.7	18.3	23.9	24.9	27.2	28.9	18.9	22.8
Medical, health serv.	1.0	1.1	2.9	3.4	0.8	4.5	5.5	6.8	7.8	8.1	4.4	4.6	6.8	7.1	8.1	8.7	1.0	6.3
Hospital	<	<	<	<	3.1	<	<	<	<	<	<	<	<	<	<	<	3.2	—
Education	2.1	2.2	2.4	3.9	5.8	6.4	8.5	7.6	8.1	8.3	6.4	6.7	7.5	7.8	8.2	8.7	6.2	6.7
Welfare, relig. serv.	0.6	0.6	0.6	0.7	1.0	0.1	0.1	2.5	3.5	3.9	0.1	0.1	2.4	2.6	3.2	3.4	1.1	—
Nonprofit org.	0.1	0.1	—	0.0	0.2	—	—	—	—	—	—	—	—	—	—	—	0.1	—
Postal service	1.1	1.2	1.6	1.6	1.8	—	—	—	—	—	—	—	—	—	—	—	—	—
Government	3.8	4.3	4.2	4.0	6.0	6.2	7.3	7.3	7.4	6.8	6.2	6.4	7.2	7.0	7.4	7.4	6.8	7.2
Misc. social services	0.2	0.2	0.4	0.6	0.6	0.6	0.6	—	—	—	0.5	0.5	—	0.6	0.6	0.7	0.4	2.6
VI Personal services	12.9	14.5	11.3	9.0	9.0	8.1	9.7	8.1	9.0	9.7	8.1	8.1	7.9	8.1	9.8	9.7	8.4	8.9
Domestic serv.	7.5	8.2	2.4	1.6	1.0	1.2	1.1	4.3	4.9	5.6	1.2	0.4	4.3	4.4	1.2	1.3	1.0	0.4
Hotel	2.4	2.2	4.2	2.7	1.6	1.3	2.5	<	<	<	1.3	1.2	<	<	4.4	4.0	1.0	4.1
Eating, drinking places	0.8	1.3	<	<	1.0	1.3	1.9	0.9	1.0	1.0	1.9	1.3	0.9	0.9	1.0	1.1	1.9	<
Repair services	—	—	1.4	1.8	2.1	1.8	1.9	—	—	—	1.8	1.9	—	—	—	—	2.1	1.5
Laundry	0.8	0.9	0.8	0.7	0.4	0.5	0.4	—	—	—	0.5	0.5	—	—	—	—	0.4	—
Barber, beauty shops	0.3	0.5	0.4	0.7	1.1	0.4	0.4	—	—	—	0.4	0.4	—	—	—	—	0.6	—
Entertainment	0.7	0.9	1.1	1.0	1.1	1.1	1.3	1.9	2.3	2.3	1.1	1.1	1.9	2.0	2.3	2.3	1.1	1.9
Misc. personal serv.	0.5	0.3	1.0	1.0	1.3	1.3	2.1	1.0	0.9	0.9	1.3	1.4	0.8	0.8	0.9	0.9	0.2	1.1
Unclassifiable	—	—	—	0.5	0.8	0.2	0.0	0.0	0.0	—	0.2	0.3	—	—	0.0	0.3	0.7	0.6
Total	100	100	100	100	100	100	100	100	100	100	100	100	100	100	100	100	100	100

^ signifies that the figure is included in the category immediately above.
The numbers may not add up due to rounding.
The data for Great Britain are of the employed, while the data for United Kingdom are of employees in employment.
Postal service is included in Communication.
From 1980 UK figures, utilities is included under Mining. Chemical is included in Metal in 1980.
Sources: (a) Singelmann (1978); (b)–(d) 1970–92: Annual Abstract of Statistics, and Employment Gazette; 1971–81: Office of Population Censuses and Surveys, Census Reports.

Table 4.7 Canada: percentage distribution of employment by industrial sector and intermediate industry group.

Industry	(a) 1921–71						(b) 1971–92		
	1921	1931	1941	1951	1961	1971	1971	1981	1992
I Extractive	36.9	34.4	31.7	21.6	14.7	9.1	8.3	7.1	5.7
Agriculture	35.2	32.5	29.5	19.7	12.8	7.4	6.6	5.3	4.4
Mining	1.6	1.9	2.2	1.9	1.9	1.7	1.6	1.8	1.3
II Transformative	26.1	24.7	28.2	33.7	31.1	30.0	27.1	26.8	22.3
Construction	9.0	6.8	5.3	6.9	7.0	6.9	6.3	6.5	6.3
Utilities	—	1.5	0.6	1.2	1.1	1.1	1.0	1.1	1.2
Manufacturing	17.0	16.4	22.3	25.6	23.0	22.0	19.7	19.2	14.9
Food	1.2	2.2	3.4	3.1	3.7	3.2	2.9	2.7	—
Textiles	2.7	2.6	3.7	1.6	1.3	0.9	1.0	0.7	—
Metal	2.9	1.9	2.3	3.9	3.2	1.5	3.0	3.4	—
Machinery	<	0.7	0.9	<	0.8	1.0	2.3	2.2	—
Chemical	0.2	0.4	0.8	1.3	1.4	1.0	1.2	1.1	—
Misc. mfg.	10.0	8.6	11.2	15.7	12.6	14.4	9.3	9.0	14.9
III Distributive services	19.2	18.4	17.7	21.8	23.9	23.0	20.8	22.9	24.0
Transportation	8.5	7.2	5.8	6.8	6.6	5.4	5.0	4.8	4.1
Communication	—	0.9	0.7	1.1	2.1	2.1	1.9	2.1	2.1
Wholesale	10.7	1.6	2.4	3.8	4.7	4.5	4.1	4.8	4.5
Retail	<	8.7	8.8	10.1	10.5	11.0	9.8	11.1	13.2
IV Producer services	3.7	3.3	2.7	3.9	5.3	7.3	6.6	9.7	11.3
Banking	1.2	1.2	0.9	1.3	1.8	2.4	2.2	2.7	3.7
Insurance	<	1.0	0.9	1.1	1.9	2.2	2.0	0.9	<
Real estate	<	0.2	0.3	0.4	<	<	<	1.7	2.2
Engineering	2.3	—	—	0.2	0.4	0.7	0.6	0.9	+
Accounting	<	0.1	0.1	0.2	0.3	0.4	0.4	0.5	—

Misc. business serv.	<	0.4	0.2	0.4	0.5	1.1	1.0	2.3	5.4
Legal services	0.2	0.4	0.3	0.3	0.4	0.5	0.4	0.6	—
V Social services	7.5	8.9	9.4	11.3	15.4	21.1	22.0	24.0	22.6
Medical, health serv.	1.1	1.8	2.2	3.1	0.9	1.0	1.8	2.0	9.1
Hospital	<	<	<	<	3.7	4.7	4.1	4.0	<
Education	2.0	2.7	2.7	2.9	4.4	7.3	6.0	6.6	7.0
Welfare, relig. serv.	0.9	1.0	0.7	1.1	1.3	1.4	1.3	1.9	—
Nonprofit org.	—	—	—	—	—	0.2	0.2	0.2	—
Postal service	3.0	0.5	0.5	0.6	5.1	5.4	—	—	—
Government	<	2.6	2.8	3.4	<	<	7.4	7.6	6.5
Misc. social services	0.5	0.3	0.5	0.2	—	—	1.1	1.6	—
VI Personal services	6.7	10.2	10.2	7.8	9.5	9.6	7.5	9.5	13.5
Domestic serv.	—	4.2	4.5	1.6	1.6	0.7	0.6	0.4	—
Hotel	—	2.8	1.6	1.5	3.9	1.7	1.5	5.7	6.5
Eating, drinking places	—	<	1.3	1.6	<	2.6	2.2	—	<
Repair services	—	0.5	1.1	1.1	1.1	0.9	1.0	1.1	—
Laundry	—	0.5	0.5	0.7	0.6	0.5	0.5	0.3	—
Barber, beauty shops	—	0.6	0.6	0.5	0.7	0.7	0.6	0.5	—
Entertainment	—	0.4	0.4	0.5	0.6	1.0	0.9	1.2	—
Misc. personal serv.	—	1.2	0.2	0.3	1.0	1.5	0.3	0.3	7.0
Unclassifiable	—	—	—	—	—	—	7.3	—	0.7
Total	100	100	100	100	100	100	100	100	100

^ signifies that the figure is included in the category immediately above.

The numbers may not add up due to rounding.

1992 figures may not be comparable to the earlier years due to the difference in sources.

Sources: (a) Singelmann (1978); (b) 1971–81: Population Census; 1992: *Statistics Canada* (The Labour Force) May.

Table 4.8 United States: employment statistics by industry

(a) 1920–70

	1920	1930	1940	1950	1960	1970
Industry	48.0%	43.3%	37.9%	39.2%	38.2%	33.6%
Services	52.0%	56.7%	62.1%	60.8%	61.8%	66.4%
Goods handling	73.3%	69.0%	67.4%	69.3%	65.8%	61.1%
Information handling	26.7%	31.0%	32.5%	30.6%	34.0%	38.9%
Services: industry	1.1	1.3	1.6	1.6	1.6	2.0
Information: goods	0.4	0.5	0.5	0.4	0.5	0.6

(b) 1970–91

	1970	1980	1985	1990	1991
Industry	34.0%	30.5%	27.7%	25.8%	24.9%
Services	66.0%	69.5%	72.3%	74.2%	75.1%
Goods handling	61.2%	57.3%	54.7%	52.6%	51.7%
Information handling	39.0%	42.7%	45.3%	47.4%	48.3%
Services: industry	1.9	2.3	2.6	2.9	3.0
Information: goods	0.6	0.7	0.8	0.9	0.9

Industry = mining, construction, manufacturing.
Services = remaining categories.
Goods handling = mining, construction, manufacturing, transportation, wholesale/retail trade.
Information handling = communications; finance, insurance, and real estate (FIRE); services; government.
Services: industry = ratio between services and industry employment.
Information: goods = ratio between information handling and goods handling employment.
Source: See table 4.1.

Table 4.9 Japan: employment statistics by industry

	(a) 1920–70							(b) 1970–91				
	1920	1930	1940	1950	1960	1970	1970	1980	1985	1990
Industry	46.3%	40.7%	47.8%	43.1%	43.4%	42.1%	42.1%	37.4%	36.3%	35.8%
Services	53.7%	59.3%	52.2%	56.9%	56.6%	57.9%	57.9%	62.6%	63.7%	64.2%
Goods handling	76.8%	75.8%	77.3%	72.9%	73.8%	73.2%	73.0%	69.6%	67.9%	65.9%
Information handling	23.2%	24.0%	22.5%	27.1%	26.4%	27.0%	26.9%	30.4%	31.9%	33.4%
Services: industry	1.2	1.5	1.1	1.3	1.3	1.4	1.4	1.7	1.8	1.8
Information: goods	0.3	0.3	0.3	0.4	0.4	0.4	0.4	0.4	0.5	0.5

Industry = mining, construction, manufacturing.
Services = remaining categories.
Goods handling = mining, construction, manufacturing, transportation, wholesale/retail trade.
Information handling = communications; finance, insurance, and real estate (FIRE); services, government.
Services: industry = ratio between services and industry employment.
Information: goods = ratio between information handling and goods handling employment.
Source: See table 4.2.

Table 4.10 Germany: employment statistics by industry

| | (a) 1925–70 | | | | | (b) 1970–87 | |
	1925	1933	1950	1961	1970	1970	1987
Industry	59.1%	56.6%	57.3%	56.2%	51.2%	51.4%	41.5%
Services	40.9%	43.4%	42.7%	43.8%	48.8%	48.6%	58.5%
Goods handling	78.8%	77.1%	78.1%	76.5%	71.4%	71.6%	60.8%
Information handling	21.2%	22.9%	21.9%	23.5%	29.1%	28.4%	39.2%
Services: industry	0.7	0.8	0.7	0.8	1.0	0.9	1.4
Information: goods	0.3	0.3	0.3	0.3	0.4	0.4	0.6

Industry = mining, construction, manufacturing.
Services = remaining categories.
Goods handling = mining, construction, manufacturing, transportation, wholesale/retail trade.
Information handling = communications; finance, insurance, and real estate (FIRE); services; government.
Services: industry = ratio between services and industry employment.
Information: goods = ratio between information handling and goods handling employment.
Source: See table 4.3.

Table 4.11 France: employment statistics by industry

| | (a) 1921–68 | | | | | | (b) 1968–89 | | | | | |
	1921	1931	1946	1954	1962	1968	1968	1970	1975	1980	1985	1989
Industry	53.1%	54.3%	49.7%	51.8%	49.5%	47.3%	43.8%	43.4%	41.0%	37.4%	32.5%	30.6%
Services	46.9%	45.7%	50.3%	48.2%	50.5%	52.7%	56.2%	56.6%	59.0%	62.6%	67.5%	69.4%
Goods handling	79.8%	80.2%	77.8%	73.1%	71.2%	67.7%	67.8%	66.8%	64.1%	60.8%	56.3%	54.9%
Information handling	20.2%	19.8%	22.4%	27.0%	29.0%	32.3%	32.2%	33.2%	35.9%	39.2%	43.7%	45.1%
Services: industry	0.9	0.8	1.0	0.9	1.0	1.1	1.3	1.3	1.4	1.7	2.1	2.3
Information: goods	0.3	0.2	0.3	0.4	0.4	0.5	0.5	0.5	0.6	0.6	0.8	0.8

Industry = mining, construction, manufacturing.
Services = remaining categories.
Goods handling = mining, construction, manufacturing, transportation, wholesale/retail trade, hotels/lodging places.
Information handling = communications; finance, insurance, and real estate (FIRE); services; government.
Services: industry = ratio between services and industry employment.
Information: goods = ratio between information handling and goods handling employment.
Source: See table 4.4.

Table 4.12 Italy: employment statistics by industry

	(a) 1921–61				(b) 1961–90			
	1921	1931	1951	1961	1961	1971	1981	1990
Industry	56.5%	55.4%	55.3%	56.6%	56.4%	52.5%	45.0%	31.9%
Services	43.5%	44.6%	44.7%	43.4%	43.6%	47.5%	55.0%	68.1%
Goods handling	76.6%	76.2%	76.1%	75.6%	78.8%	76.1%	63.6%	62.2%
Information handling	23.4%	23.8%	23.9%	24.4%	21.2%	23.9%	36.4%	37.8%
Services: industry	0.8	0.8	0.8	0.8	0.8	0.9	1.2	2.1
Information: goods	0.3	0.3	0.3	0.3	0.3	0.3	0.6	0.6

Industry = mining, construction, manufacturing.
Services = remaining categories.
Goods handling = mining, construction, manufacturing, transportation, wholesale/retail trade, hotels/lodging places.
Information handling = communications; finance, insurance, and real estate (FIRE); services; government.
Services: industry = ratio between services and industry employment.
Information: goods = ratio between information handling and goods handling employment.
1990 figures may not be comparable to figures from earlier years due to the difference in sources.
Source: See table 4.5.

Table 4.13 United Kingdom: employment statistics by industry

	(a) England and Wales, 1921–71					(b) UK, 1970–90				
	1921	1931	1951	1961	1971	1970	1975	1980	1985	1990
Industry	53.0%	47.9%	51.8%	50.9%	46.7%	49.4%	42.6%	39.4%	33.1%	29.6%
Services	47.0%	52.1%	48.2%	49.1%	53.3%	50.6%	57.4%	60.6%	66.9%	70.4%
Goods handling	76.3%	73.3%	76.4%	74.2%	66.6%	67.6%	61.0%	64.0%	56.7%	54.2%
Information handling	23.7%	26.7%	23.6%	25.8%	33.3%	32.2%	39.0%	36.0%	43.3%	45.8%
Services: industry	0.9	1.1	0.9	1.0	1.1	1.0	1.3	1.5	2.0	2.4
Information: goods	0.3	0.4	0.3	0.3	0.5	0.5	0.6	0.6	0.8	0.8

Industry = mining, construction, manufacturing.

Services = remaining categories.

Goods handling = mining, construction, manufacturing, transportation, wholesale/retail trade, hotels/lodging places.

Information handling = communications; finance, insurance, and real estate (FIRE); services; government.

Services: industry = ratio between services and industry employment.

Information: goods = ratio between information handling and goods handling employment.

Source: See table 4.6

Table 4.14 Canada: employment statistics by industry

	(a) 1921–71						(b) 1971–92		
	1921	1931	1941	1951	1961	1971	1971	1981	1992
Industry	42.7%	37.2%	42.3%	42.8%	36.6%	33.0%	29.8%	29.0%	23.5%
Services	57.3%	62.8%	57.7%	57.2%	63.4%	67.0%	70.2%	71.0%	76.5%
Goods handling	72.3%	69.6%	69.6%	71.9%	67.4%	58.6%	52.8%	58.1%	54.3%
Information handling	27.6%	30.4%	30.4%	28.1%	32.6%	41.4%	47.2%	41.9%	45.7%
Services: industry	1.3	1.7	1.4	1.3	1.7	2.0	2.4	2.4	3.3
Information: goods	0.4	0.4	0.4	0.4	0.5	0.7	0.9	0.7	0.8

Industry = mining, construction, manufacturing.
Services = remaining categories.
Goods handling = mining, construction, manufacturing, transportation, wholesale/retail trade, hotels/lodging places.
Information handling = communications; finance, insurance, and real estate (FIRE); services; government.
Services: industry = ratio between services and industry employment.
Information: goods = ratio between information handling and goods handling employment.
· 1992 figures may not be comparable to figures from previous years due to the difference in sources.
Source: See table 4.7.

Table 4.15 Occupational structure of selected countries (%)

Categories	USA 1991	Canada 1992	UK 1990	France 1989	Germany 1987	Japan 1990
Managers	12.8	13.0	11.0	7.5	4.1	3.8
Professionals	13.7	17.6	21.8	6.0	13.9	11.1
Technicians	3.2	^	^	12.4	8.7	^
Subtotal	29.7	30.6	32.8	25.9	26.7	14.9
Sales	11.9	9.9	6.6	3.8	7.8	15.1
Clerical	15.7	16.0	17.3	24.2	13.7	18.6
Subtotal	27.6	25.9	23.9	28.0	21.5	33.7
Crafts & operators	21.8	21.1	22.4	28.1	27.9	31.8
Semiskilled service workers	13.7	13.7	12.8	7.2	12.3	8.6
Semiskilled transport workers	4.2	3.5	5.6	4.2	5.5	3.7
Subtotal	17.9	17.2	18.4	11.4	17.3	12.3
Farm workers & managers	3.0	5.1	1.6	6.6	3.1	7.2
Unclassified	—	—	1.0	—	3.0	—
Total	100	100	100	100	100	100

1 The figures may not add up due to rounding.
2 the ^ signifies that figure is included in the category immediately above.
Source: Author's elaboration; see Appendix B.

Table 4.16 United States: percentage distribution of employment by occupation, 1960–91 (%)

Occupational category	1960	1970	1980	1985	1990	1990
Managerial	11.1	10.5	11.2	11.4	12.6	12.8
Professional	11.8	14.2	16.1	12.7	13.4	13.7
Technicians	^	^	^	3.0	3.3	3.2
Sales	7.3	6.2	6.3	11.8	12.0	11.9
Clerical	14.8	17.4	18.6	16.2	15.8	15.7
Crafts and operators	30.2	32.2	28.1	23.9	22.5	21.8
Semiskilled service workers	13.0	12.4	13.3	13.5	13.4	13.7
Semiskilled transport workers	4.9	3.2	3.6	4.2	4.1	4.2
Farm workers and managers	7.0	4.0	2.8	3.2	2.9	3.0
Total	100.	100.	100.	100.	100.	100.

^signifies that figure is included in the category immediately above.

Figures are seasonally adjusted annual data except the 1960 data, which are those of December.

Source: *Labor Statistics: Employment and Earnings*, various issues.

Table 4.17 Japan: percentage distribution of employment by occupation, 1955–90 (%)

Occupational category	1955	1960	1965	1970	1975	1980	1985	1990
Managerial	2.2	2.1	2.8	2.6	4.0	4.0	3.6	3.8
Professional	4.6	5.0	5.0	5.8	7.0	7.9	9.3	11.1
Technicians	^	^	^	^	^	^	^	^
Sales	13.3	13.4	13.0	13.0	14.2	14.4	14.9	15.1
Clerical	9.0	11.2	13.4	14.8	15.7	16.7	17.7	18.6
Crafts and operators	27.0	29.5	31.4	34.2	33.3	33.1	33.2	31.8
Semiskilled service workers	5.4	6.7	7.5	7.6	8.8	9.1	8.7	8.6
Semiskilled transport workers	1.7	2.3	3.7	4.6	4.5	4.5	3.9	3.7
Farm workers and managers	36.7	29.8	23.1	17.3	12.5	10.3	8.7	7.2
Total	100	100	100	100	100	100	100	100

^ signifies that figure is included in the category immediately above.
Sweepers and garbage collectors are included in Semiskilled service category between 1970 and 1980. From 1985, they are included in Crafts & Operators category.
Source: Statistical Yearbook of Japan, 1991.

Table 4.18   Germany: percentage distribution of employment by occupation, 1976–89 (%)

Occupational category	1976	1980	1985	1989
Managerial	3.8	3.2	3.9	4.1
Professional	11.0	11.1	12.6	13.9
Technicians	7.0	7.2	7.8	8.7
Sales	7.6	7.6	7.5	7.8
Clerical	13.1	14.2	12.5	13.7
Crafts & Operators	31.8	32.0	28.3	27.9
Semiskilled service workers	12.5	12.5	15.8	12.3
Semiskilled transport workers	6.3	6.1	5.5	5.5
Farm workers and managers	5.8	4.8	3.9	3.1
Not classifiable	1.1	1.2	2.1	3.0
Total	100	100	100	100

^ signifies that figure is included in the category immediately above.
Source: 1976–89: *Statistisches Bundesamt, Statistisches Jahrbuch*, various issues.

Table 4.19   France: percentage distribution of employment by occupation, 1982–9 (%)

Occupational category	1982	1989
Managerial	7.1	7.5
Professional	4.8	6.0
Technicians	12.3	12.4
Sales	3.3	3.8
Clerical	22.8	24.2
Crafts and operators	30.9	28.1
Semiskilled service workers	6.2	7.2
Semiskilled transport workers	4.6	4.2
Farm workers and managers	8.0	6.6
Not classifiable		
Total	100	100

^ signifies that figure is included in the category immediately above.
Source: 1982: *Enquête sur l'emploi de mars 1982*; 1989: *Enquête sur l'emploi de mars 1989*.

Table 4.20   Great Britain: percentage distribution of employment by occupation, 1961–90 (%)

Occupational category	1961	1971	1981	1990
Managerial	2.7	3.7	5.3	11.0
Professional	8.7	8.6	11.8	21.8
Technicians	^	2.4	2.0	^
Sales	9.7	8.9	8.8	6.6
Clerical	13.3	14.1	14.8	17.3
Crafts and operators	43.1	34.2	27.9	22.4
Semiskilled service workers	11.9	12.7	14.0	12.8
Semiskilled transport workers	6.5	10.0	9.1	5.6
Farm workers and managers	4.0	2.9	2.4	1.6
Not classifiable		2.6	3.8	1.0
Total	100	100	100	100

^ signifies that figure is included in the category immediately above.
Source: Census, 1961, 1971, 1981; 1990: (Spring) *Labour Force Survey 1991*.

Table 4.21   Canada: percentage distribution of employment by occupation, 1950–92 (%)

Occupational category	1950	1970	1980	1985	1992
Managerial	8.4	10.0	7.7	11.4	13.0
Professional	7.0	13.6	15.6	17.1	17.6
Technicians	1.5	^	^	^	^
Sales	6.9	7.1	10.8	9.6	9.9
Clerical	10.6	14.8	17.5	17.3	16.0
Crafts and operators	28.2	29.6	26.0	22.3	21.1
Semiskilled service workers	8.8	12.3	13.1	13.7	13.7
Semiskilled transport workers	6.9	5.3	4.1	3.8	3.5
Farm workers and managers	21.7	7.4	5.3	4.7	5.1
Total	100	100	100	100	100

^ signifies that figure is included in the category immediately above.
1950 figures were taken on March 4 1950; 1980 and 1985 figures are those of January. 1992 figures are those of July.
Source: Statistics Canada, *The Labour Force*, various issues.

Table 4.22 Foreign resident population in Western Europe, 1950–90 (in thousands and as % of total population)

Country	1950		1970		1982[a]		1990	
	No.	%	No.	%	No.	%	No.	%
Austria	323	4.7	212	2.8	303	4.0	512	6.6
Belgium	368	4.3	696	7.2	886	9.0	905	9.1
Denmark	—	—	—	—	102	2.0	161	3.1
Finland	11	0.3	6	0.1	12	0.3	35	0.9
France	1765	4.1	2621	5.3	3680	6.8	3608	6.4
Germany, Fed. Rep.	568	1.1	2977	4.9	4667	7.6	5242	8.2
Greece	31	0.4	93	1.1	60	0.7	70	0.9
Ireland	—	—	—	—	69	2.0	90	2.5
Italy	47	0.1	—	—	312	0.5	781	1.4
Liechtenstein	3	19.6	7	36.0	9	36.1	—	—
Luxembourg	29	9.9	63	18.4	96	26.4	109	28.0
Netherlands	104	1.1	255	2.0	547	3.9	692	4.6
Norway	16	0.5	—	—	91	2.2	143	3.4
Portugal	21	0.3	—	—	64	0.6	108	1.0
Spain	93	0.3	291	0.9	418	1.1	415	1.1
Sweden	124	1.8	411	1.8	406	4.9	484	5.6
Switzerland	285	6.1	1080	17.2	926	14.7	1100	16.3
United Kingdom	—	—	—	—	2137	3.9	1875	3.3
Total[b]	5100	1.3	10200	2.2	15000	3.1	16600	4.5

[a] 1982 is a reference year, rather than 1980 since the data are better for 1982.
[b] Includes interpolated figures for the missing (—) data.
Source: Fassman and Münz (1992).

Table 4.23 Unemployment in various countries, 1933–93 (as % of the labour force)

Country	1933	1959–67 average	1982–92 average	1992	1993
Belgium	10.6	2.4	11.3	10.3	12.1
Denmark	14.5	1.4	9.1	11.1	12.1
France	4.5[a]	0.7	9.5	10.4	11.7
Germany	14.8	1.2[b]	7.4	7.7	8.9
Ireland	n.a.	4.6	15.5	17.2	17.6
Italy	5.9	6.2	10.9	10.7	10.2
Netherlands	9.7	0.9	9.8	6.8	8.3
Spain	n.a.	2.3	19.0	18.4	22.7
UK	13.9	1.8	9.7	10.1	10.3
Austria	16.3	1.7	3.5	3.7	4.2
Finland	6.2	1.7	4.8	13.1	18.2
Norway	9.7	2.1	3.2	5.9	6.0
Sweden	7.3	1.3	2.3	5.3	8.2
Switzerland	3.5	0.2	0.7	2.5	4.5
USA	24.7	5.3	7.1	7.4	6.9
Canada	19.3	4.9	9.6	11.3	11.2
Japan	n.a.	1.5	2.5	2.2	2.5
Australia	17.4	2.2	7.8	10.7	10.9

[a] 1936
[b] The Federal Republic for the period 1959–92.
n.a. = not available.
Sources: Freeman and Soete (1994); OECD *Employment Outlook*, 1993.

Table 4.24 Indicators for self-employment and part-time employment, 1990 (%)

	Share of self-employment in total employment		Share of part-time in total employment
	Total economy	Non-agricultural sector	
Canada	9.4	7.5	15.1
France	15.0	9.1	12.0
Germany	11.0	8.0	13.4
Italy	29.1	22.2	5.7
Japan	23.6	11.6	17.6
United Kingdom	14.1	12.4	21.7
United States	10.8	7.7	17.0

Source: OECD *Jobs Study* (1994: 77, table 6.8).

Table 4.25 Percentage of standard workers included in the *Chuki Koyo* system of Japanese firms, according to size of the firm, age of workers and level of education

A. Size of the firm, education of workers and *Chuki Koyo* membership (% calculated on the total of workers in each cell)

	Number of employees		
	>1,000	100–999	10–99
Elementary/new junior high	8.4	4.9	3.9
Old junior high/new high	24.3	11.7	4.8
Professional high/2-year college	14.1	7.2	2.8
University	53.2	35.0	15.7

B. Percentage of workers in firms with over 1,000 employees included in *Chuki Koyo* system, according to their age and education

Education	Age (years)							
	20–24	25–29	30–34	35–39	40–44	45–49	50–54	55–59
Elementary/new junior high	13.1	13.1	27.9	32.5	25.6	17.1	8.4	6.2
Old junior high/new senior high	53.4	50.3	42.9	52.6	41.4	39.1	24.3	14.3
Professional high, 2-year college	50.8	34.1	31.3	37.2	30.9	15.8	14.1	8.6
University	88.9	59.5	57.1	49.9	58.9	53.4	53.2	31.7

Source: Nomura (1994).

Appendix B: Methodological Note and Statistical References for the Analysis of Employment and Occupational Structure of G-7 Countries, 1920–2005

Three sets of statistics have been compiled to illustrate the development of the service and information sectors. Data have been collected for seven countries (Canada, France, Germany, Italy, Japan, the United Kingdom and the United States) beginning from the 1920s up to the most recently available date. The following describes each set of statistics compiled for this exercise.

1 Percentage distribution of employment by industrial sector and intermediate industry group

Employment statistics by industry have been compiled for seven countries. Industries are classified into 6 industrial sectors and 37 intermediate industry groups, according to the classification developed and used by Singelmann (1978). The six industrial sectors are:

I	Extractive
II	Transformative
III	Distributive services
IV	Producer services
V	Social services
VI	Personal services

Within each sector, two to eight intermediate industry groups are included, as shown in table A4.1. Employment statistics with detailed industrial breakdown, from national census or statistical abstracts, have been aggregated and reclassified into these categories.

*This appendix was written by Manuel Castells and Yuko Aoyama.

Classification of industrial sectors and intermediate industry groups

I Extractive	V Social services
Agriculture	Medical, health services
Mining	Hospital
II Transformative	Education
Construction	Welfare, religious services
Utilities	Nonprofit organizations
Manufacturing	Postal service
Food	Government
Textiles	Miscellaneous social
Metal	services
Machinery	VI Personal services
Chemicals	Domestic services
Miscellaneous manufac-	Hotel
turing	Eating, drinking places
III Distributive services	Repair services
Transportation	Laundry
Communication	Barber, beauty shops
Wholesale	Entertainment
Retail	Miscellaneous personal
IV Producer services	services
Banking	
Insurance	
Real estate	
Engineering	
Accounting	
Miscellaneous business	
services	
Legal services	

Source: Singelmann (1978)

Instead of reconstructing the data base from the 1920s, we chose to build upon Singelmann's work by extending his data base beyond 1970. We put the best possible effort into making our classification of industries identical to that used by Singelmann, so that the data base would be comparable in time series.

For the purpose of clarification, table A4.2 shows the industrial breakdown we used in updating the employment distribution by industry. The table lists all detailed industrial categories included in each intermediate industrial group for the seven countries. Any major variations from other countries concerning the classification is noted in each statistical table produced. For all countries, figures that represent annual averages of the number of employed persons (including self-employed, nonsalaried employees) by industry have been used for this analysis.

Note that the sectoral categories (categories I through VI) do not take into account detailed industries which may be included in another sector. For instance, when a country's statistics include eating and drinking places in retail services, but cannot be disaggregated due to the lack of detailed breakdown, the percentage for distributive services (III) becomes overestimated and personal services (VI) becomes underestimated. As a result, proportions for certain industrial sectors may be inflated or deflated.

Also, priority was given to comparability across countries rather than to strict breakdown of detailed industry by our classification. This was done to avoid assigning industries to different categories in each country, which would have disturbed the comparability of the shares of employment in the large categories (I through VI). This was due to the fact that data from some countries combined various sectors and we were unable to disaggregate them. For instance, many countries regarded paper, printing and publishing as one sector, and we have allocated it to miscellaneous manufacturing, although it was theoretically favorable to consider publishing as business services. As a result, we have allocated publishing statistics from all countries under miscellaneous manufacturing, even those countries which provide disaggregated data on publishing, in order to maintain cross-national comparability.

For the same reasons, the following industries are allotted to the following detailed categories.

- products that are made from textile or fabrics, including apparel, shoes and clothing are classified as "miscellaneous manufacturing";
- transport equipment (including automobile, shipbuilding and aerospace industry products) are classified under "miscellaneous manufacturing";
- scientific equipment, including optical, photography, and precision instruments are classified under "miscellaneous manufacturing";
- printing and publishing is classified under "miscellaneous manufacturing";
- depending on the breakdown available in each country, broadcasting (radio and TV) is classified under either "communication" or "entertainment";
- miscellaneous professional and related services may be classified in any miscellaneous services, depending on the country. After

Classification of industries by countries

	Canada	France	Germany	Italy	Japan	United Kingdom	United States
Agriculture	Agriculture, forestry, fishing, trapping	Agriculture, forestry, fisheries	Agriculture, forestry, fisheries, gardening	Agriculture, forestry, fisheries	Agriculture, forestry, fisheries	Agriculture, forestry, fishing	Agriculture, forestry, fisheries
Mining	Mining, quarries oil wells	Solid mineral extraction/coking	Coal mining, ore mining, petroleum/gas extraction	Extraction of combustible solids, liquids	Mining	Coal extraction, solid fuels, electricity/gas	Metal, coal mining, crude petroleum and natural gas extraction
Construction	Construction	Building/civil engineering/agricole	Construction	Construction	Construction	Construction	Construction
Food	Food/beverage, tobacco	Food, meat/milk	Food, beverage, tobacco	Food, beverage, tobacco	Food, beverage, tobacco, feed	Food, drink, tobacco	Food/kindred prods, tobacco manufactures
Textiles	Textiles, knitting mills	Textiles, clothing	Textiles	Textiles	Textiles	Textiles	Textile mill prods
Metal	Primary metal, metal fabricating	Ferrous metals, steel, construction materials, foundry	Foundry, metal, steel	Nonferrous metal, fabricated metal, foundry	Nonferrous metal, fabricated metal, iron/steel	Metal, nonmetallic mineral prods	Primary metal, fabricated metal
Machinery	Machinery, electrical products	Machinery, electric/electronic prods, household appliances	Machinery, electrical, office equipment	Machinery, electrical/electronics machinery	Machinery, electrical/ electronic products	Mechanical engineering, data-processing equip., electrical/ electronic engineering	Machinery, electrical machinery
Chemical	Chemical petroleum/coal products	Basic chemical/ artificial fibers, pharmaceutical	Chemical/fibers	Chemical	Basic chemical, petroleum/coal prods	Chemical/man-made fibers	Chemical/allied prods, petroleum/coal prods
Miscellaneous manufacturing	Rubber/plastic, leather, clothing, wood, furniture/fixtures, paper, printing/publishing, transp. equipment, nonmetallic mineral products, misc. manufacturing	Automobiles, ship/aerospace/ military equip., apparel, misc. mfg, wood, plastic, glass, paper/printing/ publishing, shoe/leather prods	Stone/clay, rubber, transport equip., aircraft/shipbldg, wood, plastic, glass, paper, printing/publishing, leather, music instr., clothing	Leather, transport equip., clothing/footwear, paper/printing/ publishing, rubber/plastic, misc. mfg	Apparel/other fabric prods, transp. equip., precision instr., misc. mfg, lumber/wood/furni- ture, plastic, rubber, pulp/paper, printing/publishing leather/fur, ceramic/stone/ clay prods	Motor vehicle/parts, other transp. equip., instrument engineering, footwear/clothing, timber/wood furniture/paper/ printing/publishing, rubber/plastics, other mfg	Transportation equip., apparel, prof. photographic equipment/watches, toys/sporting goods, lumber/wood, furniture/fixtures, stone/clay/glass, paper, publishing, printing, rubber/ plastic, leather, misc. mfg

Utilities	Electric power, gas, water utilities	Electricity production/distrib., gas/water distrib.	Electricity, gas, water supply	Electricity, gas, water	Electricity distr., water/gas/heat supply	Gas/electricity/water	Utilities/sanitary serv.
Transportation	Transportation, storage	Transport	Railways, water transport	Railways, air transport	Railways, road passenger/freight, water/air, other rel. serv., auto parking	Railways, other inland transport, sea, air transport, supporting serv.	Railroads, bus/urban transit, taxicab trucking, water/air transp., warehousing
Communication	Communications	Telecommunications/postal services	Communications, postal services	Communications	Communication	Communications/postal services	Communications, broadcasting
Wholesale	Wholesale trade	Food wholesale, non-food wholesale	Wholesale	Wholesale	Wholesale, warehousing	Wholesale	Wholesale trade
Retail	Retail trade	Food retail, non-food retail, auto repair/sales	Retail	Retail	Retail	Retail	Retail trade
Banking	Banks, credit agencies, security brokers/dealers	Financial organizations	Financial institutions	Financial institutions, securities	Financing/insurance	Banking/finance	Banking, S&L, credit agencies, security brokerage
Insurance	Insurance carriers/agencies/real estate	Insurance	Insurance	Insurance	Insurance	Insurance, except social security	Insurance
Real estate	n.a.	Real estate rental/finance	Real estate, rental	Real estate	Real estate	Owning/dealing real estate	Real estate, real estate insurance law offices
Engineering	Engineering/scientific services	n.a.	Technical consulting	Technical services	Civil engineering, architecture	n.a.	Engineering/archictectural/survey
Accounting	Accountants	n.a.	n.a.	Accounting	Accounting	Accounting	Accounting/auditing
Misc. business services	Services to business management	Services to enterprises	Legal/accounting/other business services	Other business services, renting	Goods rental/leasing, info. serv./research/advertising, professional serv.	Business services, renting of movables	Advertising, commercial R&D, personnel supply serv., bus. mgmt consulting, computer serv., detective serv., bus. serv.
Legal services	Office of lawyers/notaries	n.a.	n.a.	Legal	Legal services	Legal	Legal serv.

	Canada	France	Germany	Italy	Japan	United Kingdom	United States
Medical, health services	Office of physicians/surgeons, paramedical, dentists, etc.	n.a.	Health/veterinary	Health services, veterinary	Medical/health serv., public health serv.	Medical/other health serv., sanitary serv.	Health serv. except hospitals
Hospital	Hospitals	n.a.	n.a.	Hospitals	Hospitals	Hospitals	Hospitals
Education	Education and related services	n.a.	Education, science/research institutions	Education, research, museums, botanical/zoological gardens	Education, science research institutions	Education, research and development	Schools, libraries, vocational schools, educational serv.
Welfare, religious services	Welfare, religious organizations	n.a.	Social serv./employment offices	Religious organizations	Welfare/social insurance, religion	Other serv. incl. social welfare	Religious organizations
Nonprofit organizations	Labor organizations, trade associations	n.a.	Nonprofit organizations	Economic org., professional associations	Co-ops, pol./bus./cultural organizations	n.a.	Membership organizations
Postal service	n.a.	n.a.	n.a.	Postal services	n.a.	n.a.	Postal serv.
Government	Public administration defense	n.a.	Public administration	Public administration, armed forces, international organizations	National gov't serv., local gov't serv., foreign gov'ts/int'l org.	Public administration and defense	Public administration, defense, justice, public order
Misc.social services	Miscellaneous services	n.a.	Trash removal, residential institutions	Other social services	Waste treatment, other services	Other professional/scientific services	Misc. prof. and related serv.
Domestic services	Private households	n.a.	Private households	Domestic services	Domestic services	n.a.	Private households
Hotel	Hotels/motels lodging houses/residential clubs, camping grounds	Hotels/cafés/restaurants	Hotels/restaurants	Hotels (with or without restaurants)	Hotels/lodging places	Hotels/catering (restaurants, cafés clubs/canteens)	Hotels/motels, lodging places
Eating drinking places	Restaurants/caterers/taverns	n.a.	n.a.	Restaurants, camping	Eating/drinking places	Restaurants/cafés/snack bars	Eating/drinking pl.

Repair services	Repair of shoe, auto, jewelry, electrical appliance	n.a.	Auto/bicycle repair	Repair	Repair services	Repair of consumer goods/vehicles	Auto, electrical, misc. repair
Laundry	Laundries/cleaners/pressor, self-service laundries	n.a.	Laundry/cleaning	Laundry	Laundry	Laundry/dry cleaning	Laundry/cleaning
Barber, beauty shops	Barber/beauty shops	n.a.	Barber/body care businesses	Barber/beauty shops	Barber/beauty shops	Hairdressing/manicure	Beauty shops, barber shops
Entertainment	Amusement/recreational services	n.a.	Culture/sports/entertainment	Entertainment, cinema, broadcasting, sports	Motion pictures, recreation, broadcasting, amusement	Recreation/cultural services	Entertainment, theaters/movies, bowling alleys/billiard/pool places
Misc. personal services	Funeral services misc. personal services	All for-profit personal services	Other personal services	Cemetery administration	Misc. personal services	Personal services	Funeral service/crematories

carefully analyzing the data and finding some further disaggregated data, "other professional services" was classified as "business
services" for Japan. For the United States, it is classified as "miscellaneous social services."

In addition, the following specificities should be noted for the countries studied.

Canada

The 1971 figures are based on the census data for persons 15 years
and over who worked in 1970. The 1981 figures are based on the 20%
sample data from the 1981 census on the labor force 15 years and over.
Due to the unavailability of the breakdown of the labor force in
detailed industry from the results of the 1991 census as of November
1992, we have used the latest statistics available (May 1992) from
Statistics Canada, published in the monthly report, *The Labour Force.*
The figures are derived from the sample of about 62,000 representative households across the country (excluding the Yukon and
Northwest Territories). The survey has been designed to represent all
persons in the population 15 years of age and over residing in the
provinces of Canada, with the exception of the following: persons
living on Indian reserves; full-time members of the armed forces; and
people living in institutions (that is, inmates of penal institutions and
patients in hospitals or nursing homes who have resided in the institution for more than six months). The 1992 figures reflect the labor
force in May 1992, and have been based on the 1980 Standard
Industrial Classification since 1984 (Statistics Canada, 1992).

France

Figures are based on the employed population on December 31 of
every year, published in the annual statistical abstract. 1989 figures are
preliminary. Problems have been encountered due to the general lack
of detailed breakdown of statistics on the service sector employment.
Whenever a detailed breakdown of service industries is unavailable,
the category "not-for-profit services" is classified as miscellaneous
social services, and "for-profit services" is classified as miscellaneous
personal services. However, the data from the annual statistical
abstract was used instead of the census data since the most recent
results currently available to us from the census are those of 1982.

Germany

In this analysis we used the former Federal Republic of Germany prior
to unification as a unit of analysis. The figures are based on the census

data on the employed for 1970 and 1987. No census was conducted in Germany between these years.

Italy

Figures are based on the census data on labor force in 1971 and 1981; 1990 figures may not be directly comparable to the data in earlier years due to the difference in sources. Since the 1991 census figures are not available at the time of this writing, the 1990 figures have been used as a rough indicator of recent trends.

Japan

Figures are based on the census data from October 1970, 1980 and 1990 on employed persons 15 years of age and over. The 1970 and 1980 figures are that of 20% sample tabulation, and the 1990 figures are that of 1% sample tabulation.

United Kingdom

Figures for England and Wales are used for the years between 1921 and 1971. From 1971 onwards, figures for employees in employment for the entire United Kingdom in June every year are used. These figures are chosen in preference to the census data on employed persons due to the unavailability of 1991 census results at the time of this writing, and the 1971 and 1981 figures available to us do not include the entire United Kingdom. In addition, careful comparisons of the census data on the employed and the Department of Employment data on employees in employment for Great Britain revealed that differences are minor in terms of employment distribution.[126] Thus we have decided that the employees-in-employment figures would serve as a rough estimate of the trends in the United Kingdom between 1970 and 1990. These figures exclude private domestic servants and a small number of employees of agricultural machinery contractors but included seasonal and temporary workers. Family workers are included in the figures for Great Britain but not for Northern Ireland. The figures on the employees in employment also excludes the self-employed. The figures are from censuses of employment conducted in Great Britain by the Department of Employment and for the United Kingdom include information from similar censuses conducted in Northern Ireland by the Department of Manpower Services.

[126]   There is a tendency, however, for share of agricultural employment to be estimated lower than that of the entire employed population, as shown in table 4.16.

United States

The detailed breakdown of employment from the current population survey for 1970 was not published in the *Employment and Earnings* issues. Thus we have substituted the 1970 data with that of the census, since the intercensal statistics provided by the current population survey are, in general, designed to be comparable with the decennial statistics (see p. VII of 1970 census, volume 2: 7B, Subject Reports: Industrial Characteristics). The US figures are based on all civilians who, during the survey week, did any work at all as paid employees, in their own business, profession, or on their own farm, or who worked 15 hours or more as unpaid workers in an enterprise operated by a member of a family; and all those who were not working but who had jobs or businesses from which they were temporarily absent because of illness, bad weather, vacation, labor–management disputes, or personal reasons, whether they were paid for the time off or were working in other jobs. Members of the armed forces stationed in the United States are also included in the employed total. Each employed person is counted only once. Those who held more than one job are counted in the job at which they worked the greatest number of hours during the survey week. Included in the total are employed citizens of foreign countries who are temporarily in the United States but not living on the premises of an embassy. Excluded are persons whose only activity consisted of work around the house (painting, repairing, or own-home housework) or volunteer work for religious, charitable, and similar organizations (Department of Labor Statistics 1992). Due to the reclassification of the SIC codes for the 1980 census, figures before and after that date may not be strictly comparable.

Employment statistics by industry

Hall proposes two ways of dividing employment sectors: industry versus services, and goods handling versus information handling (Hall 1988). "Industry" includes all mining, construction and manufacturing sectors, and "services"' includes all remaining categories. "Goods handling" sector includes mining, construction, manufacturing, transportation, wholesale/retail trade, and "Information handling" sector includes communications, finance, insurance and real estate (FIRE), all remaining services and government.

In our analysis, employment statistics with Singelmann's classification has been aggregated and reorganized to fit into Hall's classification.[127] Further, the ratio between services and industry

[127] In order to comply with the standard classification of services, eating and drinking places are included in retail trade.

employment, as well as the ratio between information handling and goods handling employment have been derived from the data used in tables 4.10 through 4.17.

Employment by occupations

Standard occupational classifications of most countries habitually confuse sectoral activities with skill levels, and thus are unfavorable for our use. However, after careful consideration based on the available data from the countries, it became clear that a reconfiguration of occupational classifications would be a major project by itself. Since our primary purpose in this appendix excludes such analysis, we decided to use the existing classification as a rough indicator for the occupational breakdown of these countries. As a result, the following rough breakdown of occupations has been determined:

- managerial;
- professional;
- technicians;
- sales;
- clerical;
- crafts and operators;
- semiskilled service workers;
- semiskilled transport workers;
- farm workers and managers.

For most countries, it was impossible to separate professional and technician categories. Also, in some countries, craft workers and operators are mixed, thus we have collapsed these categories into one in order to avoid misleading conclusions from the data. The same applies to the collapse of farm workers and farm managers into one category. "Crafts and operators" also includes laborers, handlers and miners. Those categorized as service workers have been included in semiskilled service workers.

The specificity for each country is described as follows:

Canada

Figures are based on the occupational classification of the employed. Professional and technician categories also include those whose professions are in natural science, social science, teaching, medicine/health and artistic/recreational. Crafts and operators category also included mining/quarrying, machining, processing, construction trades, materials handling, and other crafts/equipment operating. Farm workers and managers also includes agriculture, fishing/hunting/trapping and forestry/logging.

France

Figures are based on the occupational classification of the population aged 15 years and over, excluding unemployed, retired, students, and others who have never worked, according to employment surveys, the results of which are included in the statistical abstract. Managerial category also includes high-level public officials and high-level administrative/commercial workers in business enterprises. Professional category includes professors/scientific occupations, information/art and engineers/technical workers. Technicians includes intermediate professions, workers in religion, and social/health mid-level workers. Clerical category includes civil servants and administrative workers. Crafts and operators category includes qualified and unqualified workers in industries.

Germany

Figures are based on the occupational classification of the employed persons, according to the statistical abstract. Managerial category includes accountants, public officials and entrepreneurs. Professional category includes engineers, scientists, artists, and health service workers. Crafts and operators includes most industrial workers. Technicians includes social workers. Farm workers and managers category includes workers in forestry and fisheries.

Japan

Figures are based on the occupational classification of employed persons, according to Labour Force Survey, the results of which are included in the statistical abstract. Farm workers and managers includes workers in forestry and fisheries. Semiskilled service workers category also includes protective service workers. Semiskilled transport workers includes communications occupations.

United Kingdom

Figures are based on the 10% sample of Great Britain, derived from the censuses. Professional category includes judges, economists, environmental health officers, etc. Technicians includes estimators, welfare occupations, medical technicians, draughtsmen, foremen, tracers, supervisors of tracers, and technician engineers. Crafts and operators includes most industrial workers. Semiskilled transport workers includes warehousemen/storekeepers/packers/bottlers.

Semiskilled service workers includes sport/recreation workers and protective services. The 1990 figures are based on the Labour Force Survey (1990 and 1991) conducted by the Office of Censuses and Surveys. The 1990 figures are not directly comparable to previous years due to the different survey methodology and categories employed. However, since the 1991 census data are not available at the time of this writing, these 1990 figures provide a rough estimate of current employment structure in Great Britain.

United States

Figures are based on the annual averages of employed persons according to the household survey, conducted as part of the Current Population Survey by the Bureau of the Census for the Department of Labor. Managerial category includes executive and administrative occupations. Clerical category includes administrative support. Semiskilled service worker category includes private household and protective services. Crafts and operators category includes precision production, repair, machine operators/assemblers/inspectors, handlers, equipment cleaners, helpers and laborers. Semiskilled transport workers includes material-moving occupations. Farm workers and managers includes forestry and fishing.

Distribution of employment status

The status of the employed persons are broadly categorized as employees, self-employed and family workers. When figures for family workers are not available, they may be included within the self-employed categories. Self-employed generally include employers, unless otherwise noted.

The following lists the specificity for each country.

Canada

Those employers who are paid workers (rather than the self-employed) are included in the employees category.

France

Figures are based on civilian employment, indicated in OECD Labour Force Statistics.

Germany

Figures are based on the annual statistical abstract.

Italy

Figures are based on civilian employment, indicated in OECD Labour Force Statistics.

Japan

Figures are based on the Labour Force Survey on employed persons, included in the annual statistical abstract.

United Kingdom

Figures are based on civilian employment, indicated in OECD Labour Force Statistics.

United States

Figures are based on the annual averages of employed civilians in agriculture and nonagricultural industries.

Statistical references

Canada

Statistics Canada. *1971 Census of Canada*, vol. 3: *Economic Characteristics*, 1973.

——*1981 Census of Canada: Population, Labor Force – Industry by demographic and educational characteristics, Canada, provinces, urban, rural, nonfarm and rural farm*, January 1984.

——*The Labour Force*, various issues.

——*Labour Force: Annual Averages, 1975–1983*, January 1984

France

Institut national de la statistique et des études économiques (INSEE). *Annuaire statistique de la France 1979: résultats de 1978*, Ministère de l'économie, des finances et du budget, Paris: INSEE, 1979.

——*Recensement général de la population de 1982: résultats définitifs*, par Pierre-Alain Audirac, no. 483 des Collections de l'INSEE, série D, no. 103, Ministère de l'économie, des finances et du budget, Paris: INSEE, 1985

——*Enquêtes sur l'emploi de 1982 et 1983: résultats redressés*, no. 120, February 1985.

——*Enquêtes sur l'emploi de mars 1989: résultats détaillés*, no. 28–29, October 1989.

——*Annuaire statistique de la France 1990: résultats de 1989*, vol. 95, nouvelle série no. 37, Ministère de l'économie, des finances et du budget, Paris: INSEE, 1990.

Germany

Statistisches Bundesamt. *Statistisches Jahrbuch 1977: für die Bundesrepublik Deutschland*, Metzler-Poeschel Verlag Stuttgart, 1977
——*Statistisches Jahrbuch 1991: für die Bundesrepublik Deutschland*, Metzler-Poeschel Verlag Stuttgart, 1991.
——*Bevölkerung und Kultur:Volkszählung vom 27. Mai 1970*, Heft 17, Erwerbstätige in wirtschaftlicher Gliederung nach Wochenarbeitszeit und weiterer Tätigkeit, Fachserie A, Stuttgart and Mainz: Verlag W. Kohlhammer.
——*Volkszählung vom 25 Mai 1987*, Bevölkerung und Erwerbstätigkeit, Stuttgart: Metzler-Poeschel, 1989.

Italy

Istituto Centrale di Statistica. *10° Censimento Generale della Popolazione, 15 Ottobre 1961, Vol. IX:* Dati Generali Riassuntivi, Rome, 1969.
——*11° Censimento Generale della Popolazione, 24 Ottobre,1971*, vol. VI: *Professioni e Attività Economiche*, Tomo 1: *Attività Economiche*, Rome, 1975.
——*12° Censimento Generale della Popolazione, 25 Ottobre, 1981*, vol. II: *Dati sulle caratteristiche strutturali della popolazione e delle abitazioni*, Tomo 3: *Italia*, Rome, 1985.
Istituto Nazionale di Statistica (ISTAT). *Annuario Statistico Italiano*, edizione 1991.

Japan

Statistics Bureau, Management and Coordination Agency (1977) *Japan Statistical Yearbook*, Tokyo.
——(1983) *Japan Statistical Yearbook*, Tokyo.
——(1991) *Japan Statistical Yearbook*, Tokyo.
Bureau of Statistics, Office of the Prime Minister. *Summary of the Results of 1970 Population Census of Japan*, Tokyo: Bureau of Statistics, 1975
——*1980 Population Census of Japan*, Tokyo: Bureau of Statistics, 1980.
——*1990 Population Census of Japan*, Prompt report (results of 1% sample tabulation), Tokyo: Bureau of Statistics, 1990.

United Kingdom

Office of Population Censuses and Surveys, General Registrar Office. *Census 1971: Great Britain, Economic Activity*, Part IV (10% Sample), London: HMSO, 1974.
——*Census 1981: Economic Activity, Great Britain*, London: HMSO, 1984.

——*Labour Force Survey 1990 and 1991: A survey conducted by OPCS and the Department of Economic Development in Northern Ireland on behalf of the Employment Department and the European Community*, Series LFS no. 9, London: HMSO, 1992.

Central Statistical Office. *Annual Abstract of Statistics: 1977*, London: HMSO, 1977.

——*Annual Abstract of Statistics: 1985*, London: HMSO, 1985.

——*Annual Abstract of Statistics: 1992,* no. 128, London: HMSO, 1992.

Department of Employment. *Employment Gazette* vol. 100, no. 8 (August 1992).

United States

United States Department of Labor. *Handbook of Labor Statistics*, Bulletin 2175, Bureau of Labor Statistics, December.

——*Labor Force Statistics: Derived from the current population survey, 1948–87*, Bureau of Labor Statistics, August 1988.

——*Handbook of Labor Statistics*, Bulletin 2340, Bureau of Labor Statistics, March, 1990.

——*Employment and Earnings*, various issues.

Other

Eurostat. *Labour Force Sample Survey*, Luxembourg: Eurostat, various issues.

——*Labour Force Survey*, Theme 3, Series C, *Population and Social Statistics, Accounts, Surveys and Statistics*, Luxembourg: Eurostat, various issues.

Hall, Peter (1988) "Regions in the Transition to the Information Economy," in G. Sternlieb and J.W. Hughes (eds), *America's New Market Geography: Nation, region and metropolis*, Rutgers, N.J.: State University of New Jersey, Center for Urban Policy Research, New Brunswick, pp. 137–59.

Mori, K. (1989) *Hai-teku shakai to rōdō: naniga okite iruka*, Iwanami Shinsho no. 70, Tokyo: Iwanami Shoten.

Organization for Economic Cooperation and Development (OECD) (1991) *OECD Labour Force Statistics: 1969–1989*, Paris: OECD.

——(1992a) *OECD Economic Outlook: Historical Statistics: 1960–90*, Paris: OECD.

——(1992b) *OECD Economic Outlook*, no. 51, June.

— 5 —

The Culture of Real Virtuality: The Integration of Electronic Communication, the End of the Mass Audience, and the Rise of Interactive Networks

Introduction

Around 700BC a major invention took place in Greece: the alphabet. This conceptual technology, it has been argued by leading classics scholars such as Havelock, was the foundation for the development of Western philosophy and science as we know it today. It made it possible to bridge the gap from spoken tongue to language, thus separating the spoken from the speaker, and making possible conceptual discourse. This historical turning point was prepared for by about 3,000 years of evolution in oral tradition and nonalphabetic communication, until Greek society reached what Havelock calls a new state of mind, "the alphabetic mind," that prompted the qualitative transformation of human communication.[1] Widespread literacy did not occur until many centuries later, after the invention and diffusion of the printing press and the manufacturing of paper. Yet it was the alphabet that, in the West, provided the mental infrastructure for cumulative, knowledge-based communication.

However, the new alphabetic order, while allowing rational discourse, separated written communication from the audiovisual system of symbols and perceptions, so critical for the full-fledged expression of the human mind. By implicitly and explicitly establishing a social hierarchy between literate culture and audiovisual expression, the price paid for the foundation of human practice in the written discourse was to relegate the world of sounds and images

---

[1] Havelock (1982: esp. 6–7).

to the backstage of the arts, dealing with the private domain of emotions and with the public world of liturgy. Of course, audiovisual culture took an historical revenge in the twentieth century, first with film and radio, then with television, overwhelming the influence of written communication in the hearts and souls of most people. Indeed, this tension between noble, alphabetic communication and sensorial, nonreflective communication underlies the intellectuals' frustration against the influence of television that still dominates the social critique of mass media.[2]

A technological transformation of similar historic dimensions is taking place 2,700 years later, namely the integration of various modes of communication into an interactive network. Or, in other words, the formation of a Super-Text and a Meta-Language that, for the first time in history, integrates into the same system the written, oral, and audio-visual modalities of human communication. The human spirit reunites its dimensions in a new interaction between the two sides of the brain, machines, and social contexts. For all the science fiction ideology and commercial hype surrounding the emergence of the so-called Information Superhighway, we can hardly underestimate its significance.[3] The potential integration of text, images, and sounds in the same system, interacting from multiple points, in chosen time (real or delayed) along a global network, in conditions of open and affordable access, does fundamentally change the character of communication. And communication decisively shapes culture, because as Postman writes "we do not see . . . reality . . . as 'it' is, but as our languages are. And our languages are our media. Our media are our metaphors. Our metaphors create the content of our culture."[4] Because culture is mediated and enacted through communication, cultures themselves, that is our historically produced systems of beliefs and codes, become fundamentally transformed, and will be more so over time, by the new technological system. At the moment of this writing, such a new system is not fully in place, and its development will occur at uneven pace and with uneven geography in the coming years. Yet it is a certainty that it will develop and embrace at least the dominant activities and the core segments of the population in the whole planet. Furthermore, it already exists in bits and pieces, in the new media system, in the rapidly changing telecommunications

[2]   For a critical presentation of these ideas, see Postman (1985).
[3]   For a documented exposition of the data on the Information Superhighway, as of end of 1994, see Sullivan-Trainor (1994). For an overview of social and economic trends in news media and computer-mediated communication at the international level, see the informed, special supplement of the Spanish newspaper *El Pais/World Media*, "*Habla el Futuro*," March 9 1995.
[4]   Postman (1985: 15).

systems, in the networks of interaction already formed around Internet, in the imagination of people, in the policies of governments, and on the drawing boards of corporate offices. The emergence of a new electronic communication system characterized by its global reach, its integration of all communication media, and its potential interactivity is changing and will change forever our culture. However, the issue arises of the actual conditions, characteristics, and effects of such change. Given the still embryonic development of an otherwise clearly identified trend, how can we assess its potential impact without falling into the excesses of futurology from which this book tries to depart sharply? On the other hand, without analyzing the transformation of cultures under the new electronic communication system, the overall analysis of the information society would be fundamentally flawed. Fortunately, while there is technological discontinuity, there is in history a great deal of social continuity that allows analysis of tendencies on the basis of the observation of trends that have prepared the formation of the new system over the last two decades. Indeed, one of the major components of the new communication system, the mass media of communication, structured around television, have been studied in minute detail.[5] Their evolution towards globalization and decentralization was foreseen in the early 1960s by McLuhan, the great visionary who revolutionized thinking in communications in spite of his unrestrained use of hyperbole.[6] In this chapter I shall first retrace the formation of the mass media, and their interplay with culture and social behavior. Then I shall assess their transformation during the 1980s, with the emergence of decentralized and diversified "new media" that prepared the formation of a multimedia system in the 1990s. I shall later turn my attention to a different system of communication, organized around computer networking, with the emergence of Internet and the surprising, spontaneous development of new kinds of virtual communities. While this is a relatively new phenomenon, we have enough empirical observations, both from France and from the United States, to formulate some hypotheses on reasonable grounds. Finally, I shall try to bring together what we know about the two systems to speculate on the social dimension of their coming merger, and the impact of such a merger on the processes of communication and cultural expression. I argue that through the powerful influence of the new communication system, mediated by social interests, government policies, and business strategies, a new culture is emerging: the *culture of real*

[5]   See the evolution of media research synthesized in Williams et al. (1988).
[6]   For a retrospective of McLuhan's theories, see his posthumous book: McLuhan and Powers (1989).

virtuality, whose content, dynamics, and significance will be presented and analyzed in the following pages.

From the Gutenberg Galaxy to the McLuhan Galaxy: the Rise of Mass Media Culture

The diffusion of television in the three decades following World War II (in different times and with variable intensity depending on countries) created a new Galaxy of communication, if I may use the McLuhanian terminology.[7] Not that other media disappeared, but they were restructured and reorganized in a system whose heart was made of vacuum tubes and whose appealing face was a television screen.[8] Radio lost its centrality but won in pervasiveness and flexibility, adapting modes and themes to the rhythm of people's everyday lives. Films transformed themselves to fit television audiences, with the exceptions of government subsidized art and of special-effects shows on large screens. Newspapers and magazines specialized in deepening their content or targeting their audience, while being attentive to providing strategic information to the dominant TV medium.[9] As for books, they remained books, although the unconscious desire behind many books was to become a TV script; the best sellers' lists soon became filled with titles referring to TV characters or to TV-popularized themes.

Why television became such a prevailing communication mode is still the object of raging debate among scholars and media critics.[10] W. Russell Neuman's hypothesis, which I would rephrase as being the consequence of the basic instinct of a lazy audience, seems to be a plausible explanation in regard to available evidence. In his own words: "The key finding from the realm of research on educational and advertising effects that must be dealt with candidly if we are to understand the nature of low-salience learning in regard to politics and culture is simply that people are attracted to the path of least resistance."[11] He grounds his interpretation in the broader psychological theories by Herbert Simon and Anthony Downs, emphasizing the psychological costs of obtaining and processing information. I would be inclined to place the roots of such logic not in human nature, but in the conditions of home life after long days of strenuous

---

[7]   McLuhan (1964).
[8]   Ball-Rokeach and Cantor (eds) (1986).
[9]   Postman (1985).
[10]   Ferguson (ed.) (1986); Withey and Abeles (eds) (1980).
[11]   Neuman (1991: 103).

work, and in the lack of alternatives for personal/cultural involvement.[12] Yet social conditions in our societies being as they are, the minimum-effort syndrome that seems to be associated with TV-mediated communication could explain the rapidity and pervasiveness of its dominance as a communication medium as soon as it appeared on the historical scene. For instance, according to media studies, [13] only a small proportion of people choose in advance the program they will view. In general, the first decision is to watch television, then programs are scanned until the most attractive is selected or, more often, the least boring.

The TV-dominated system could be easily characterized as mass media.[14] A similar message was simultaneously emitted from a few centralized senders to an audience of millions of receivers. Thus, the content and format of messages were tailored to the lowest common denominator. In the case of private TV, predominant in the original TV country, the US, it was the lowest common denominator of the audience as evaluated by marketing experts. For most of the world, dominated by government television until at least the 1980s, the standard was the lowest common denominator in the minds of bureaucrats in control of broadcasting, although increasingly audience ratings played a role. In both cases, the audience was seen as largely homogeneous, or susceptible to being made homogeneous.[15] The notion of mass culture, arising from mass society, was a direct expression of the media system resulting from the control of new electronic communication technology by governments and corporate oligopolies.[16]

What was fundamentally new in television? The novelty was not so much its centralizing power and its potential as a propaganda instrument. After all, Hitler showed how radio could be a formidable instrument of resonance for one-way single-purpose messages. What TV represented, first of all, was the end of the Gutenberg Galaxy, that is of a system of communication essentially dominated by the typographic mind and the phonetic alphabet order.[17] For all his critics (generally turned off by the obscurity of his mosaic language) Marshall McLuhan struck a universal chord when, in all simplicity, he declared that the "medium is the message":

[12] Mattelart and Stourdze (1982); Trejo Delarbre (1992).
[13] Neuman (1991).
[14] Blumler and Katz (eds) (1974).
[15] Botein and Rice (eds) (1980).
[16] Neuman (1991).
[17] McLuhan (1962).

The mode of TV image has nothing in common with film or photo, except that it offers also a nonverbal gestalt or posture of forms. With TV, the viewer is the screen. He is bombarded with light impulses that James Joyce called "The Charge of the Light Brigade". . . . The TV image is not a still shot. It is not a photo in any sense, but a ceaselessly forming contour of things limned by the scanning-finger. The resulting plastic contour appears by light through, not light on, and the image so formed has the quality of sculptures and icon, rather than a picture. The TV image offers some three million dots per second to the receiver. From these he accepts only a few dozen each instant, from which to make an image.[18]

Because of the low definition of TV, McLuhan argued, viewers have to fill in the gaps in the image, thus becoming more emotionally involved in the viewing (what he, paradoxically, characterized as a "cool medium"). Such involvement does not contradict the hypothesis of the least effort, because TV appeals to the associative/lyrical mind, not involving the psychological effort of information retrieving and analyzing to which Herbert Simon's theory refers. This is why Neil Postman, a leading media scholar, considers that television represents an historical rupture with the typographic mind. While print favors systematic exposition, TV is best suited to casual conversation. To make the distinction sharply, in his own words:

Typography has the strongest possible bias towards exposition: a sophisticated ability to think conceptually, deductively and sequentially; a high valuation of reason and order; an abhorrence of contradiction; a large capacity for detachment and objectivity; and a tolerance for delayed response.[19]

While for television, "entertainment is the supra-ideology of all discourse on television. No matter what is depicted or from what point of view, the overarching presumption is that it is there for our amusement and pleasure."[20] Beyond the discrepancies in the social/political implications of this analysis, from McLuhan's belief about the universal communitarian potential of television to the Luddite attitudes of Jerry Mander[21] and some of the critics of mass culture,[22] the diagnoses converge toward two fundamental points: a few years after

18   McLuhan (1964: 313).
19   Postman (1985: 87).
20   Ibid.
21   Mander (1978).
22   Mankiewicz and Swerdlow (eds) (1979).

its development television became the cultural epicenter of our societies;[23] and the television modality of communication is a fundamentally new medium, characterized by its seductiveness, its sensorial simulation of reality, and its easy communicability along the lines of least psychological effort.

Led by television, there has been in the last three decades a communication explosion throughout the world.[24] In the most TV-oriented country, the United States, in the late 1980s TV presented 3,600 images per minute per channel. According to the Nielsen Report the average American home had the TV set on for about seven hours a day, and actual viewing was estimated at 4.5 daily hours per adult. To this had to be added radio, which offered 100 words per minute and was listened to an average of two hours a day, mainly in the car. An average daily newspaper offered 150,000 words, and it was estimated to take between 18 and 49 minutes of daily reading time, while magazines were browsed over for about 6 to 30 minutes, and book reading, including schoolwork-related books, took about 18 minutes per day.[25] Media exposure is cumulative. According to some studies, US homes with cable TV watch more network TV than homes without cable. All in all, the average adult American uses 6.43 hours a day in media attention.[26] This figure can be contrasted (although in rigor it is not comparable) to other data that give the number of 14 minutes per day and per person for interpersonal interaction in the household.[27] In Japan in 1992, the weekly average of television watching time per household was 8 hours and 17 minutes per day, up by 25 minutes from 1980.[28] Other countries seem to be less intensive consumers of media: for example, in the late 1980s French adults watched TV only about three hours a day.[29] Still, the predominant pattern of behavior around the world seems to be that in urban societies media consumption is the second largest category of activity behind work, and certainly the predominant activity at home.[30] This observation must however be qualified to truly understand the role of media in our culture: media watching/listening is by no means an exclusive activity. It is generally mixed with the performance of home tasks, with shared meals, with social interaction. It is the almost constant background presence, the

---

[23] See Williams (1974); and Martin and Chaudhary (eds) (1983).
[24] Williams (1982).
[25] Data from various sources, reported by Neuman (1991).
[26] Data reported by Sabbah (1985); Neuman (1991).
[27] Sabbah (1985).
[28] Dentsu Institute for Human Studies/DataFlow International (1994: 67).
[29] Neuman (1991); for Japan, see Sato et al. (1995).
[30] Sorlin (1994).

fabric of our lives. We live with the media and by the media. McLuhan used the expression of technological media as staples or natural resources.[31] Rather, the media, particularly radio and television, have become the audiovisual environment with which we interact endlessly and automatically. Very often television, above all, is a presence in the home. A precious feature in a society where increasing numbers of people live alone: in the 1990s, 25% of American households were formed by one single person. Although the situation is not so extreme in other societies, the trend towards decreasing size of households is similar in Europe.

This pervasive, powerful presence of such subliminally provoking messages of sounds and images could be assumed to produce dramatic impacts on social behavior. Yet most available research points to the opposite conclusion. After reviewing the literature, W. Russell Neumann concludes that

> the accumulated findings from five decades of systematic social science research reveal that mass media audience, youthful or otherwise, is not helpless, and the media are not all-powerful. The evolving theory of modest and conditional media effects helps to put in perspective the historical cycle of moral panic over new media.[32]

Furthermore, the barrage of advertising messages received through the media seems to have limited effect. According to Draper,[33] although in the US the average person is exposed to 1,600 advertising messages per day, people respond (and not necessarily positively) to only about 12 of them. Indeed, McGuire,[34] after reviewing accumulated evidence on the effects of media advertising, concluded that there is no substantial evidence of specific impacts by media advertising on actual behavior, an ironic conclusion for an industry that spent at that time US$50 billion a year. Why, then, do companies keep insisting on advertising? For one thing, companies pass on the cost of advertising to consumers: according to *The Economist* in 1993, "free TV" in the US cost every American household $30 per month. Yet a substantive answer to such an important question requires that we first analyze the mechanisms through which television and other media influence behavior.

---

[31] McLuhan (1964: 21).
[32] Neuman (1991: 87).
[33] Roger Draper, "The Faithless Shepard," *New York Review of Books,* June 26, reported by Neuman (1991).
[34] McGuire (1986).

The key issue is that while mass media are a one-way communication system, the actual process of communication is not, but depends on the interaction between the sender and the receiver in the interpretation of the message. Umberto Eco provided an insightful perspective to interpret media effects in his 1977 seminal paper titled "Does the Audience have Bad Effects on Television?" As Eco wrote:

> There exist, depending on sociocultural circumstances, a variety of codes, or rather of rules of competence and interpretation. The message has a signifying form that can be filled with different meanings . . . So the suspicion grew that the sender organized the televisual image on the basis of his own codes, which coincided with those of the dominant ideology, while the addressees filled it with "aberrant" meanings according to their particular cultural codes.[35]

The consequence of this analysis is that

> One thing we do know is that there doesn't exist a Mass Culture in the sense imagined by the apocalyptic critics of mass communications because this model competes with others (constituted by historical vestiges, class culture, aspects of high culture transmitted through education etc.).[36]

While historians and empirical researchers of the media would find this statement pure common sense, in fact, taking it seriously, as I do, it decisively undermines a fundamental aspect of critical social theory from Marcuse to Habermas. It is one of the ironies of intellectual history that it is precisely those thinkers who advocate social change who often view people as passive receptacles of ideological manipulation, in fact precluding the notions of social movements and social change except under the mode of exceptional, singular events generated outside the social system. If people have some level of autonomy in organizing and deciding their behavior, the messages sent through the media should interact with their receivers, and thus the notion of mass media refers to a technological system, not to a form of culture, the mass culture. Indeed, some experiments in psychology found that even if TV presents 3,600 images per minute per channel, the brain responds consciously to only one sensory stimulus among each million stimuli being sent.[37]

Yet to emphasize the autonomy of human mind and of individual cultural systems in filling in the actual meaning of the messages

[35] Eco (1977: 90).
[36] Ibid.: 98.
[37] Neuman (1991: 91).

received does not imply that the media are neutral institutions, or that their effects are negligible. What empirical studies show is that the media are not independent variables in inducing behavior. Their messages, explicit or subliminal, are worked out, processed by individuals placed in specific social contexts, thus modifying what was the intended effect of the message. But the media, and particularly audiovisual media in our culture, are indeed the basic material of communication processes. We live in a media environment, and most of our symbolic stimuli come from the media. Furthermore, as Cecilia Tichi has shown in her wonderful book *The Electronic Hearth*,[38] the diffusion of television took place in a television environment, that is a culture in which objects and symbols are referred to television, from the shapes of home furniture to acting styles and themes of conversation. The real power of television, as Eco and Postman have also argued, is that it sets the stage for all processes that intend to be communicated to society at large, from politics to business, including sports and art. Television frames the language of societal communication. If advertisers keep spending billions in spite of reasonable doubts about the actual direct impact of advertising on their sales, it may be because an absence of television usually means conceding name recognition in the mass market to those competitors who do advertise. While the effects of television on political choices is highly diverse, politics and politicians that are not on television in advanced societies simply do not stand a chance of obtaining people's support, since people's minds are informed fundamentally by the media, with television being foremost among such media.[39] The social impact of television works in the binary mode: to be or not to be. Once a message is on television, it can be changed, transformed, or even subverted. But in a society organized around mass media, the existence of messages that are outside the media is restricted to interpersonal networks, thus disappearing from the collective mind. However, the price to be paid for a message to be on television is not just money or power. It is to accept being mixed in a multisemantic text whose syntax is extremely lax. Thus, information and entertainment, education and propaganda, relaxation and hypnosis are all blurred in the language of television. Because the context of the viewing is controllable and familiar to the receiver, all messages are absorbed into the reassuring mode of the home or quasi-home situations (for instance, sports bars as one of the few real extended families left . . .).

This normalization of messages, where atrocious images of real war

---

[38]   Tichi (1991).
[39]   Lichtenberg (ed.) (1990).

can almost be absorbed as part of action movies, does have a fundamental impact: the leveling of all content into each person's frame of images. Thus, because they are the symbolic fabric of our life, the media tend to work on consciousness and behavior as real experience works on dreams, providing the raw material out of which our brain works. It is as if the world of visual dreams (the information/entertainment provided by television) would give back to our consciousness the power to select, recombine, and interpret the images and sounds that we have generated through our collective practices or by our individual preferences. It is a system of feedbacks between distorting mirrors: the media are the expression of our culture, and our culture works primarily through the materials provided by the media. In this fundamental sense, the mass media system fulfilled most of the features suggested by McLuhan in the early 1960s: it was the McLuhan Galaxy.[40] Yet the fact that the audience is not a passive object but an interactive subject opened the way to its differentiation, and to the subsequent transformation of the media from mass communication to segmentation, customization and individualization, from the moment technology, corporations, and institutions allowed such moves.

The New Media and the Diversification of Mass Audience

During the 1980s new technologies transformed the world of media.[41] Newspapers were written, edited and printed at distance, allowing for simultaneous editions of the same newspaper tailored to several major areas (for example, *Le Figaro* in several French cities; *The New York Times* in parallel East Coast/West Coast editions; *International Herald Tribune*, printed daily in several locations in three continents, and so on). Walkman devices made personally selected music a portable audio environment, allowing people, particularly teenagers, to build

[40] I label the mass media electronic communication system the McLuhan Galaxy in homage to the revolutionary thinker who visualized its existence as a distinctive mode of cognitive expression. It should be emphasized, however, that we are entering a new communication system, clearly distinct from the one McLuhan envisaged, as this chapter tries to argue.

[41] This section relies partly on the information and ideas on new developments in the media worldwide provided by Manuel Campo Vidal, leading television journalist in Spain and Latin America, vice-president of Antena-3 Television: see Campo Vidal (1996). For projections on these trends elaborated in the academic world during the 1980s, see also Rogers (1986). For a visionary analysis of media diversification in a historical perspective, I recall De Sola Pool (1983).

walls of sounds against the outside world. Radio became increasingly specialized, with thematic and subthematic stations (such as 24-hour easy-listening music or exclusive dedication to a singer or pop group for several months until the new hit comes in). Radio's hosted talk-shows filled the time of commuters and flexible workers. VCRs exploded all over the world and became in many developing countries a major alternative to boring, official television broadcasting.[42] Although the multiplicity of potential uses of VCRs were not fully exploited, because of lack of consumers' technological skills, and because of rapid commercialization of its use by video rental stores, their diffusion provided a great deal of flexibility to the use of visual media. Films survived in the form of video-cassettes. Music video, accounting for over 25% of total video production, became a new cultural form that shaped the images of a whole generation of youth, and actually changed the music industry. The ability to record TV programs and watch them at selected times changed the habits of TV audiences and reinforced their selective viewing, counteracting the pattern of least resistance that I discussed above. On the basis of VCRs, any future diversification of television offerings was amplified in its effects by the second-step choice of the recording audience, further segmenting it.

People started to tape their own events, from vacation to family celebrations, thus producing their own images beyond the photo album. For all the limits of this self-production of images, it actually modified the one-way flow of images and reintegrated life experience and the screen. In many countries, from Andalusia to Southern India, local community video technology allowed for the blossoming of rudimentary local broadcasting that mixed diffusion of video films with local events and announcements, often on the fringes of communications regulations.

But the decisive move was the multiplication of television channels, leading to their increasing diversification.[43] Development of cable television technologies, to be fostered in the 1990s by fiber optics and digitization, and of direct satellite broadcasting dramatically expanded the spectrum of transmission and put pressure on the authorities to deregulate communications in general and television in particular. It followed an explosion of cable television programming in the United States and of satellite television in Europe, Asia, and Latin America. Soon, new networks were formed that came to challenge the established ones, and in Europe governments lost

[42]   Alvarado (ed.) (1988).
[43]   Doyle (1992); Dentsu Institute for Human Studies/DataFlow International (1994).

control of much of television. In the US the number of independent TV stations grew during the 1980s from 62 to 330. Cable systems in major metropolitan areas feature up to 60 channels, mixing network TV, independent stations, cable networks, most of them specialized, and pay TV. In the countries of the European Union, the number of TV networks increased from 40 in 1980 to 150 by the mid-1990s, one-third of them being satellite broadcasted. In Japan, the NHK public network has two terrestrial networks and two specialized satellite services; in addition there are five commercial networks. From 1980 to the mid-1990s, the number of satellite-TV stations grew from 0 to 300.

According to UNESCO, in 1992 there were over 1 billion TV sets in the world (35% of which were in Europe, 32% in Asia, 20% in North America, 8% in Latin America, 4% in the Middle East, and 1% in Africa). Ownership of TV sets was expected to grow at 5% per year up to the year 2000, with Asia leading the charge. The impact of such a proliferation of television offerings on the audience was deep in all contexts. In the US, while the three major networks controlled 90% of prime-time audience in 1980, their share went down to 65% in 1990, and the trend has accelerated since: it stands at slightly over 60% in 1995. CNN established itself as the major global news producer worldwide, to the point that in emergency situations in countries around the world politicians and journalists alike turn on CNN full time. In 1995 the embryo of a similar global channel in Spanish, *Telenoticias*, was launched by a consortium of Spanish, Hispanic American, and Latin American television companies. Direct satellite television is making a major penetration in the Asian market, broadcasting from Hong Kong to the whole Asian Pacific. Hubbard Communications and Hughes Corporation launched in 1994 two competing direct satellite broadcasting systems that sell 'à la carte' almost any program from anywhere to anywhere in the US, the Asian Pacific, and Latin America. Chinese communities in the US can watch daily Hong Kong news while Chinese in China may have access to American soap operas (*Falcon Crest* recorded 450 million viewers in China). Thus, as Françoise Sabbah wrote in 1985 in one of the best and earliest assessments of new trends in the media:

> In sum, the new media determine a segmented, differentiated audience that, although massive in terms of numbers, is no longer a mass audience in terms of simultaneity and uniformity of the message it receives. The new media are no longer mass media in the traditional sense of sending a limited number of messages to a homogeneous mass audience. Because of the multiplicity of messages and sources, the audience itself

becomes more selective. The targeted audience tends to choose its messages, so deepening its segmentation, enhancing the individual relationship between sender and receiver.[44]

Youichi Ito, analyzing the evolution of media uses in Japan, has also concluded that there is evolution from a mass society to a "segmented society" (*Bunshu Shakai*), as a result of new communication technologies that focus on diversified, specialized information, so that the audience becomes increasingly segmented by ideologies, values, tastes, and lifestyles.[45]

Thus, because of the diversity of media and the possibility of targeting the audience, we can say that in the new media system, **the message is the medium**. That is, the characteristics of the message will shape the characteristics of the medium. For instance, if feeding the musical environment of teenagers is the message (a very explicit one), MTV will be tailored to the rites and language of this audience, not only in the content but in the whole organization of the station and in the technology and design of image production/broadcasting. Or, again, to produce a 24-hour world news service requires a different setting, programming, and broadcasting, such as weather report shows of global and continental scope. This is indeed the present and future of television: decentralization, diversification, and customization. Within the broader parameters of the McLuhanian language, the message of the medium (still operating as such) is shaping different media for different messages.

Yet diversification of messages and media expressions do not imply loss of control by major corporations and governments over television. Indeed, it is the opposite trend that has been observed during the last decade.[46] Investment has poured into the communications field, as mega-groups have been formed and strategic alliances have been established to carve out market shares in a market in complete transformation. In the 1980–95 period, the three major US TV networks have changed ownership, two of them twice: the merger of Disney and ABC in 1995 was a turning point in integrating TV into the emerging multimedia business. TF1, the leading French channel was privatized. Berlusconi took control of all private TV stations in Italy, organizing them in three private networks. Private television flourished in Spain, with the development of three private networks, including Antena-3, and made significant inroads in the UK and in Germany, always under the control of powerful financial groups, both

[44]   Sabbah (1985: 219).
[45]   Ito (1991b).
[46]   See, for instance, data cited in *The Economist* (1994a); also Doyle (1992); Trejo Delarbre (ed.) (1988); Campo Vidal (1996).

national and international. Russian television became diversified, including private, independent television channels. Latin American television experienced a process of concentration around a few major players. The Asian Pacific became the most hotly contested terrain for new television mavericks, such as Murdoch's Star channel, as well as for "old Television hands" such as the new, global BBC, pitted in competition against CNN. In Japan, the government's NHK was joined in competition by private networks: Fuji TV, NTV, TBS, TV Asahi, and TV Tokyo, as well as by cable and direct satellite broadcasting operations. In 1993–95, about US$80 billion were spent in television programming worldwide, and spending was rising by 10% a year. Between 1994 and 1997 some 70 new communications satellites are expected to be launched, most of them destined for TV broadcasting.

The net result of such business competition and concentration is that while the audience has been segmented and diversified, television has become more commercialized than ever, and increasingly oligopolistic at the global level. The actual content of most programming is not substantially different from one network to the other, if we consider the underlying semantic formulae of most popular programs as a whole. Yet the fact that not everybody watches the same thing at the same time, and that each culture and social group has a specific relationship to the media system, does make a fundamental difference *vis-à-vis* the old system of standardized mass media. In addition, the widespread practice of "surfing" (simultaneously watching several programs) introduces the creation by the audience of their own visual mosaics. While the media have become indeed globally interconnected, and programs and messages circulate in the global network, **we are not living in a global village, but in customized cottages globally produced and locally distributed.**

However, the diversification of the media, because of the conditions of their corporate and institutional control, did not transform the unidirectional logic of their message, nor truly allowed the audience's feedback except in the most primitive form of market reaction. While the audience received more and more diverse raw material from which to construct each person's own image of the universe, the McLuhan Galaxy was a world of one-way communication, not of interaction. It was, and still is, the extension of mass production, industrial logic into the realm of signs, and it fell short, McLuhan's genius notwithstanding, of expressing the culture of the information age. This is because information processing goes far beyond one-way communication. Television needed the computer to be free from the screen. But their coupling, with major potential consequences over society at large, came after a long detour taken by computers in order to be able to talk to television only after learning to talk to each other. Only then could the audience speak up.

Computer-Mediated Communication, Institutional Control, Social Networks, and Virtual Communities

History will recall that the two first large-scale experiments of what Ithiel de Sola Pool labeled "technologies of freedom" were induced by the state: the French MINITEL, as a device to steer France into the information society; the American ARPANET, predecessor of Internet, as a military strategy to enable communication networks to survive a nuclear attack. They were very different, both being deeply rooted in the culture and institutions of their respective societies. Leo Scheer has highlighted their contrasting logic in a synthetic view of each system's features:

> Both announced the information superhighways, but their differences are full of lessons. First of all, Internet links up computers while Minitel links, via Transpac, server centers that can be questioned by terminals with low capacity of memory. Internet is an American initiative of worldwide scope, initiated, with military support, by computer companies, financed by the American government, to create a world club of computer users and data banks. Minitel is a French system that, until now [1994] could never go beyond its national boundaries because of [foreign] regulatory constraints. It is the product of the boldest imagination from high level State technocrats in their effort to remedy the weakness of French electronic industries. On the side of Internet: the random topology of local networks of computer fanatics. On the side of Minitel: the orderly arrangement of the telephone book. Internet: an anarchic tariff system of uncontrollable services. Minitel: a kiosk system that allows for homogeneous tariffs and a transparent sharing of revenues. On the one hand, the uprooting and the phantasm of generalized connections beyond boundaries and cultures; on the other hand, the electronic version of communal roots.[47]

The comparative analysis of the development of these two systems, in relationship to their social and institutional environments, helps to shed some light on the characteristics of the emerging, interactive communication system.[48]

---

[47] Scheer (1994: 97–8), my translation.
[48] Case (1994).

The Minitel story: *l'état et l'amour*

Teletel, the network feeding Minitel terminals, is a videotex system designed in 1978 by the French Telephone Company and introduced to the market in 1984, after years of localized experiments. The earliest and largest of such systems in the world, in spite of its primitive technology, almost unchanged for 15 years, it won a wide acceptance among French households and grew to phenomenal proportions. By the mid-1990s, it was offering 23,000 services, and billing FFr7 billion to 6.5 million Minitel terminals in service, being used in one out of four French households and by one-third of the adult population.[49]

This success is particularly striking when contrasted to the general failure of videotex systems such as Prestel in Britain and Germany, and Japan's Captain, and to the limited receptivity to Minitel or other videotex networks in the United States.[50] Such success came in spite of very limited video and transmission technology: thus, until the early 1990s it transmitted at 1,200 baud speed, to be compared with typical computer information services in the US operating at 9,600 bauds.[51] Behind the success of Minitel lie two fundamental reasons: the first was the commitment of the French government to the experiment as an element of the challenge presented by the Nora-Minc report on the "informatization of society" prepared in 1978 at the request of the Prime Minister.[52] The second was the simplicity of its use, and the straightforwardness of its kiosk billing system that made it accessible and trustworthy to the average citizen.[53] Still, people needed an extra incentive to use it and this is the most revealing part of the Minitel story.[54]

The government's commitment, through French Telecom, was spectacularly shown in the launching of the program: each household was given the option of the delivery of a free Minitel terminal in place of the usual telephone book. Furthermore, the telephone company subsidized the system until it broke even for the first time in 1995. It was a way of stimulating telecommunications usage, creating a captive market for the troubled French electronics industry and, above all, inducing familiarity with the new medium for both companies and people.[55] However, the most intelligent strategy from French Telecom

---

[49] Thery (1994); Myers (1981); Lehman (1994).
[50] McGowan and Compaine (1989).
[51] Thery (1994); Preston (1994); Rosenbaum (1992).
[52] Nora and Minc (1978).
[53] McGowan (1988).
[54] Mehta (1993).

was to open the system wide to private providers of services, and first of all to French newspapers, which quickly became the defenders and popularizers of Minitel.[56]

But there was a second, major reason for the widespread use of Minitel: the appropriation of the medium by the French people for their personal expression. The first services provided by Minitel were the same that were available via traditional telephone communication: telephone directory, weather reports, transportation information and reservations, advance purchase of tickets for entertainment and cultural events, and so on. As the system and people became more sophisticated, and thousands of providers of services came on line, advertising, tele-shopping, tele-banking, and various business services were offered through Minitel. Yet the social impact of Minitel was limited in the early stages of its development.[57] In terms of volume, the telephone directory accounted for over 40% of total calls; in terms of value, in 1988 36% of Minitel revenues came from 2% of its users, which were businesses.[58] The system caught fire with the introduction of chat-lines or *messageries*, most of which quickly specialized in sex offerings or in sex-related conversations (*les messageries roses*), that by 1990 accounted for more than half of the calls.[59] Some of these services were commercial porno-electronic conversations, equivalent to the phone sex so pervasive in other societies. The main difference was the accessibility of such services over the videotex network, and their massive advertising in public places. But most of the erotic uses of Minitel were initiated by people themselves over the general-purpose chat-lines. Yet there was not a generalized sex bazaar, but a democratized sexual fantasy. More often than not (source: author's participant observation), the on-line exchanges were based on impersonation of ages, genders and physical characteristics, so that Minitel became the vehicle of sexual and personal dreams rather than the substitute for pick-up bars. This infatuation with the intimate use of Minitel was critical to ensure its rapid diffusion among the French people, in spite of the solemn protests of prudish puritans. By the early 1990s, the erotic uses of Minitel dwindled down, as the fashion faded away, and the rudimentary character of the technology limited its sex appeal: chat-lines

[55] For a comprehensive analysis of the policy that led to the development of Minitel, see Cats-Baril and Jelassi (1994).
[56] Preston (1994).
[57] Mehta (1993).
[58] Honigsbaum (1988).
[59] Maital (1991); Rheingold (1993).

came to account for less than 10% of the traffic.[60] Once the system was fully settled, the fastest growing services in the 1990s were developed by businesses for their internal use, with the highest growth being that of high value-added services, such as legal services, accounting for over 30% of the traffic.[61] Yet the hooking-up of a substantial proportion of the French people to the system needed the detour through their personal psyche, and the partial fulfillment of their communication needs, at least for a while.

When in the 1990s Minitel emphasized its role as service provider, it also made evident its built-in limitations as a means of communication.[62] Technologically, it was relying on ages-old video and transmission technology whose overhaul would end its basic appeal as a free electronic device. Furthermore, it was not based on personal computing but, by and large, on dumb terminals, thus substantially limiting autonomous capacity for information processing. Institutionally, its architecture, organized around a hierarchy of server networks, with little capacity for horizontal communication, was too inflexible for a society as culturally sophisticated as France, once new realms of communication were available beyond Minitel. The obvious solution adopted by the French system was to offer the option, at a price, of linking up with Internet worldwide. In so doing, Minitel became internally split between a bureaucratic information service, a networked system of business services, and the tributary gateway to the vast communication system of the Internet constellation.

The Internet constellation

The Internet network is the backbone of global computer-mediated communication (CMC) in the 1990s, since it gradually links up most networks. In the mid-1990s it connected 44,000 computer networks and about 3.2 million host computers worldwide with an estimated 25 million users, and it was expanding rapidly (see figure 5.1). According to a survey of the United States conducted in August 1995 by Nielsen Media Research, 24 million people were Internet users, and 36 million had access to it. However, a different survey, conducted by the Emerging Technologies Research Group in November–December 1995 evaluated the number of Americans that used Internet regularly at only 9.5 million, of whom two-thirds signed on only once a week.

---

[60] Wilson (1991).
[61] Ibid.
[62] Dalloz and Portnoff (1994).

346

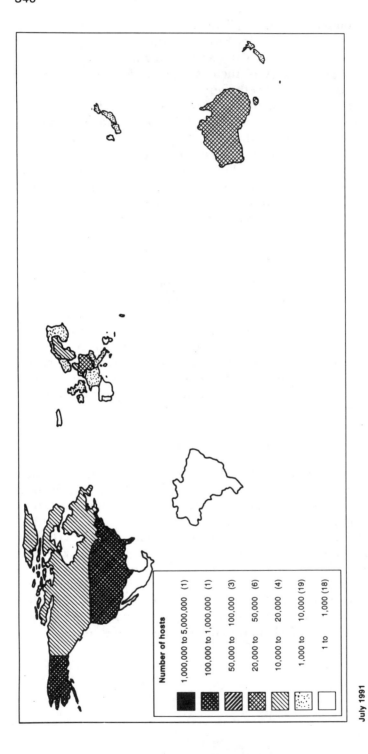

Figure 5.1 The diffusion of the Internet
Source: Batty and Barr (1994).

July 1991

Number of hosts

1,000,000 to 5,000,000 (1)

100,000 to 1,000,000 (1)

50,000 to 100,000 (3)

20,000 to 50,000 (6)

10,000 to 20,000 (4)

1,000 to 10,000 (19)

1 to 1,000 (18)

Number of hosts

■	1,000,000 to 5,000,000 (1)
▨	100,000 to 1,000,000 (1)
▩	50,000 to 100,000 (3)
▨	20,000 to 50,000 (6)
▨	10,000 to 20,000 (4)
⠿	1,000 to 10,000 (19)
□	1 to 1,000 (18)

July 1992

Figure 5.1 – cont.

348

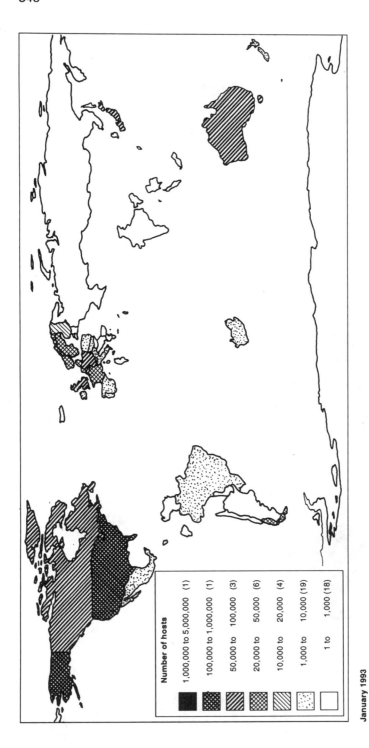

Figure 5.1 – cont.

Number of hosts

1,000,000 to 5,000,000 (1)

100,000 to 1,000,000 (1)

50,000 to 100,000 (3)

20,000 to 50,000 (6)

10,000 to 20,000 (4)

1,000 to 10,000 (19)

1 to 1,000 (18)

349

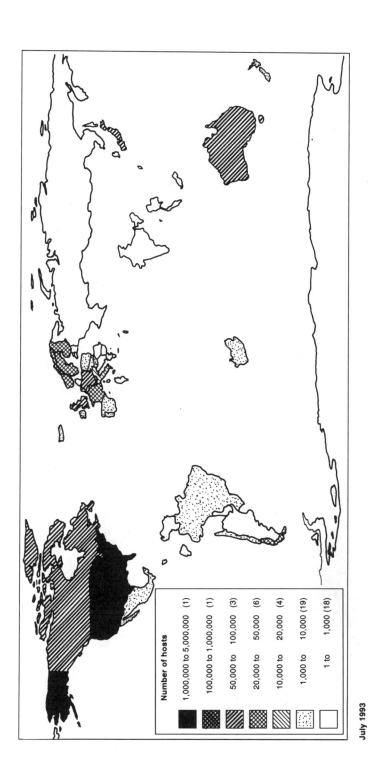

Figure 5.1 – cont.

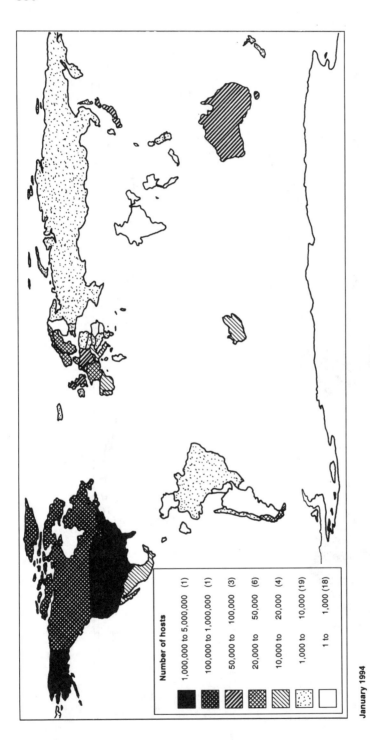

Number of hosts

■	1,000,000 to 5,000,000 (1)
▨	100,000 to 1,000,000 (1)
▨	50,000 to 100,000 (3)
▨	20,000 to 50,000 (6)
▨	10,000 to 20,000 (4)
░	1,000 to 10,000 (19)
□	1 to 1,000 (18)

January 1994

Figure 5.1 – cont.

Yet the projections were for the number of users to double in a year.[63] Overall, while there is wide disagreement about how many users are currently connected to Internet, there is a convergence of opinion that it has the potential to explode into hundreds of millions of users by early in the twenty-first century. Experts consider that, technically, Internet could one day link up 600 million computer networks. This is to be compared with its size in earlier stages of development: in 1973, there were 25 computers in the network; through the 1970s, it could only support 256 computers; in the early 1980s, after substantial enhancement, it was still limited to about 25 networks with only a few hundred primary computers and a few thousand users.[64] The history of Internet's development and of the convergence of other communication networks into the Net provides essential material to understanding the technical, organizational and cultural characteristics of this Net, thus opening the way for assessing its social impacts.[65]

It is indeed a unique blending of military strategy, big science cooperation, and countercultural innovation.[66] At the origins of Internet is the work of one of the most innovative research institutions in the world: the US Defense Department's Advanced Research Projects Agency (DARPA). When in the late 1950s the launching of the first Sputnik alarmed the American high-tech military establishment, DARPA undertook a number of bold initiatives, some of which changed the history of technology and ushered in the information age on a grand scale. One of these strategies, developing an idea conceived by Paul Baran at Rand Corporation, was to design a communications system invulnerable to nuclear attack. Based on packet-switching communication technology, the system made the network independent of command and control centers, so that message units would find their own routes along the network, being reassembled in coherent meaning at any point in the network.

When, later on, digital technology allowed the packaging of all kind of messages, including sound, images, and data, a network was formed that was able to communicate all kinds of symbols without using

[63] McLeod (1996).
[64] Sullivan-Trainor (1994); *Business Week* (1994a); Hafner and Markoff (1991); *El Pais/World Media* (1995); McLeod (1996).
[65] For documented and intelligent analyses of the origins, development, and characteristics of Internet and other CMC networks, see Hart et al. (1992); Rheingold (1993). For an empirical study of the growth of Internet, see Batty and Barr (1994). For a discussion of Internet's prospects, see a study by the Rand Corporation available only on-line at the time of this writing: Rand Corporation (1995).
[66] Hafner and Markoff (1991).

control centers. The universality of digital language and the pure networking logic of the communication system created the technological conditions for horizontal, global communication. Furthermore, the architecture of this network technology is such that it is very difficult to censor or control it. The only way to control the network is not to be into it, and this is a high price to pay for any institution or organization once the network becomes pervasive and channels all kinds of information around the world.

The first such network, named ARPANET after its powerful sponsor, went on-line in 1969. It was opened to research centers cooperating with the US Defense Department, but scientists started to use it for all kinds of communication purposes. At one point it became difficult to separate military-oriented research from scientific communication and from personal chatting. Thus, scientists of all disciplines were given access to the network, and in 1983 there was a split between ARPANET, dedicated to scientific purposes, and MILNET, directly oriented to military applications. The National Science Foundation also became involved in the 1980s in creating another scientific network, CSNET, and – in cooperation with IBM – still another network for non-science scholars, BITNET. Yet all networks used ARPANET as their communication system. The network of networks that formed during the 1980s was called ARPA-INTERNET, then INTERNET, still supported by the Defense Department and operated by the National Science Foundation.

For the network to be able to sustain the fantastic growth in the volume of communication, transmission technology had to be enhanced. In the 1970s, ARPANET was using 56,000 bits-per-second links, In 1987, the network lines transmitted 1.5 million bits per second. By 1992, the NSFNET, backbone network behind Internet, operated at transmission speeds of 45 million bits per second: enough capacity to send 5,000 pages per second. In 1995, gigabit transmission technology was in the prototype stage, with capacity equivalent to transmitting the US Library of Congress in one minute.

However, transmission capacity was not enough to establish a worldwide communication web. Computers had to be able to talk to each other. The obstacle was overcome with the creation of UNIX, an operating system enabling access from computer to computer. The system was invented by Bell Laboratories in 1969, but became widely used only after 1983, when Berkeley researchers (again funded by ARPA) adapted to UNIX the TCP/IP protocol that made it possible for computers not only to communicate but to encode and decode data packages traveling at high speed in the Internet network. Since the new version of Unix was financed with public funds, the software was made available just for the cost of distribution. Networking was born on a large scale as local area networks and regional networks connected to each other, and started to spread anywhere where there were telephone lines and computers were equipped with modems, an inexpensive piece of equipment.

Behind the development of Internet there was the scientific, institutional, and personal networks cutting across the Defense Department, National Science Foundation, major research universities, and specialized technological think-tanks, such as MIT's Lincoln Laboratory, SRI (formerly Stanford Research Institute), Palo Alto Research Corporation (funded by Xerox), ATT's Bell Laboratories, Rand Corporation, BBN (Bolt, Beranek & Newman), the research company where the TCP/IP protocol was invented, and so on. Key technological players in the 1950s–1970s period, such as J.C.R. Licklider, Douglas Engelbart, Robert Taylor, Ivan Sutherland, Lawrence Roberts, Robert Kahn, Alan Kay, Robert Thomas, and the rest, moved back and forth between these institutions, creating a networked milieu of innovation whose dynamics and goals became largely autonomous from the specific purposes of military strategy or supercomputing link-ups. They were technological crusaders, convinced that they were changing the world, as eventually they did.

But this is only one side of the story; because in parallel to the efforts by the Pentagon and Big Science to establish a universal computer network with public access, within "acceptable use" norms, a sprawling computer counterculture emerged in the United States, often mentally associated with the aftershocks of the 1960s movements, in their most libertarian/utopian version. An important element of the system, the modem, was one of the technological breakthroughs emerging from the pioneers of this counterculture, originally labeled "the hackers" before the term took on its malignant connotation. The modem was invented by two Chicago students, Ward Christensen and Randy Suess, in 1978, when they were trying to find a system to transfer microcomputer programs to each other through the telephone to avoid traveling in the Chicago winter between their distant locations. In 1979 they diffused the XModem protocol that allowed computers to transfer files directly without going through a host system. And they diffused the technology at no cost, because their purpose was to spread communication capabilities as much as possible. Computer networks that were excluded from ARPANET (reserved to elite science universities in its early stages) found their way to start communicating with each other on their own. In 1979, three students at Duke University and University of North Carolina, not included in ARPANET, created a modified version of the Unix protocol that made it possible to link up computers over the regular telephone line. They used it to start a forum of on-line computer discussion, Usenet, that quickly became one of the first large-scale electronic conversation systems. The inventors of Usenet News also diffused freely their software in a leaflet circulated at the Unix users conference.

Ironically, this countercultural approach to technology had a similar effect to the military-inspired strategy of horizontal networking: it made available technological means to whoever had the technical knowledge and a computing tool, the PC, which soon would start a spectacular progression of increasing power and decreasing price at the same time. The advent of personal computing and the communicability of networks spurred the development of Bulletin Board Systems (BBS), first in the United States, then world-wide: the electronic protests to the Tian An Men events in China in 1989 via computer networks operated by Chinese students abroad were one of the most notorious manifestations of the potential of the new communication devices. Bulletin Board Systems did not need sophisticated computer networks, just PCs, modems, and the telephone line. Thus, they became the electronic notice-boards of all kinds of interests and affinities, creating what Howard Rheingold names "virtual communities."[67]

Thousands and thousands of such micro-networks exist today around the world, covering the whole spectrum of human communication, from politics and religion to sex and research. By the mid-1990s, the majority of them were also connected to Internet, but they were keeping their own identity and enforcing their own rules of behavior. One of the most important rules was (and is) the rejection of the intrusion into BBS of undeclared commercial interests. While it is considered legitimate to create commercial BBS or business-oriented networks, it is not legitimate to invade cyberspaces created for other purposes. The sanction against intruders is devastating: thousands of hostile messages "flame" the bad electronic citizen. When the fault is particularly serious, huge files are dumped onto the guilty system, bringing it to a halt, and usually provoking the expulsion of the culprit from the network of its host computer. This electronics grass-roots culture marked for ever the evolution and use of the net. While its most heroic tones and its countercultural ideology fade away with the generalization of the medium on a global scale, the technological features and social codes that developed from the original free use of the network have framed its utilization.

In the 1990s, business has realized the extraordinary potential of

---

[67]   Rheingold (1993).

Internet, as the National Science Foundation decided to privatize some of the major operations of the network to the usual large corporation consortiums (ATT, MCI-IBM, and so on). The commercialization of Internet grew at a fast rate: while in 1991 there were about 9,000 commercial domains (or sub-networks) by the end of 1994 they had increased to 21,700.[68] Several commercial computer services networks were created, providing services on the basis of an organized grid, with adjusted pricing. Yet the capacity of the network is such that the majority of the communication process was, and still is, largely spontaneous, unorganized, and diversified in purpose and membership. In fact, commercial and government interests coincide in favoring the expanding use of the network: the greater the diversity of messages and participants, the higher the critical mass in the network, and the higher the value. The peaceful coexistence of various interests and cultures in the net took the form of the World Wide Web (WWW), a flexible network of networks within the Internet where institutions, businesses, associations, and individuals create their own "sites," on the basis of which everybody with access can produce her/his/its "home page," made of a variable collage of text and images. Helped by software technology first developed in Mosaic (a Web browser software program invented in 1992 by students in Illinois, at the National Center for Supercomputing Applications, the Web allowed for groupings of interests and projects in the net, overcoming the time-costly chaotic browsing of pre-WWW Internet. On the basis of these groupings, individuals and organizations were able to interact meaningfully on what has become, literally, a World Wide Web of individualized, interactive communication.[69] The price to pay for such diverse and widespread participation is to let spontaneous, informal communication flourish at the same time. The commercialization of cyberspace will be closer to the historical experience of merchant streets that sprout out from vibrant urban culture, than to the shopping centers spread in the dullness of anonymous suburbs.

The two sources of the Net, the military/science establishment and the personal computing counterculture, did have a common ground: the university world. The first ARPANET node was set up in 1969 at UCLA, and six other nodes were added in 1970–1 at UC Santa Barbara, SRI, University of Utah, BBN, MIT, and Harvard. From there, they spread primarily over the academic community, with the exception of the internal networks of large electronic corporations. This university origin of the Net has been, and is, decisive for the development and diffusion of electronic communication throughout

---

[68]   *Business Week* (1994).
[69]   Markoff (1995).

the world. The large-scale initiation to CMC in the United States took place among graduate students and faculties of universities in the early 1990s. And a similar process took place only a few years later in the rest of the world. In Spain, in the mid-1990s the largest contingent of "internetters" came from the computer networks built around Universidad Complutense de Madrid and Universitat Politécnica de Catalunya. The story seems to be the same around the world. This university-based process of diffusion is significant because it has the highest potential for spreading both the know-how and the habits of CMC. Indeed, against the assumption of social isolation suggested by the image of the ivory tower, universities are major agents of diffusion of social innovation because generation after generation of young people go through them, becoming aware of and accustomed to new ways of thinking, managing, acting, and communicating. As CMC becomes pervasive in the university system on an international scale during the 1990s, the graduates that will take over companies and institutions in the early twenty-first century will bring with them the message of the new medium into the mainstream of society.

The process of the formation and diffusion of Internet, and related CMC networks, in the last quarter of the century shaped for ever the structure of the new medium, in the architecture of the network, in the culture of the networkers, and in the actual patterns of communication. The architecture of the network is, and will remain, technologically open, enabling widespread public access and seriously limiting governmental or commercial restrictions to such access, although social inequality will powerfully manifest itself in the electronic domain, as I shall analyze below. This openness is the consequence, on the one hand, of the original design conceived partly for the above-mentioned military strategic reasons; partly because the scientists managing military research programs wanted to set up such a new system, both to show technological prowess and as a utopian endeavor. On the other hand, the openness of the system also results from the constant process of innovation and free accessibility enacted by early computer hackers and the network hobbyists who still populate the net by the thousands.

This constant, multisided effort to improve the communicability of the network is a remarkable example of how the technological productivity of cooperation through the net ended up enhancing the net itself. Furthermore, the open architecture of the network makes it very difficult to ensure its secrecy against sophisticated intruders. In January 1995 Tsutomu Shimomura, a computer security expert at the San Diego Supercomputer Center, revealed that his security-proof files had been accessed and downloaded onto computers in Rochester University, and that other protected files in several locations have been submitted to similar attacks, providing strong evidence that Internet's network security screens were useless against advanced software invasion. Shimomura took revenge on this professional offense. He went to work to track the hacker and, using strictly electronic means, a few weeks later led the FBI to the housing complex where they made the arrest of Kevin Mitnick, a legendary outlaw of the network frontier. Yet this well-publicized event underscored the difficulty of protecting information in the network. The issue came down to the choice between closing down Internet as it was or finding other communication networks for commercial interests that require protected transmission of information. Given that it would be almost impossible to shut down Internet in its current format (precisely because of the genius of DARPA's researchers), my hypothesis is that, slowly but surely, commercial uses requiring credit card and bank account numbers will develop separate networks, while Internet will expand as an electronic global agora, with its inevitable small dose of psychological deviance.

The culture of first-generation users, with its utopian, communal, and libertarian undercurrents, shaped the Net in two opposite directions. On the one hand, it tended to restrict access to a minority of computer hobbyists, the only people able and willing to spend time and energy living in cyberspace. From this era there remains a pioneering spirit that looks with distrust at the commercialization of the network, and watches with apprehension how the realization of the dream of generalized communication for the people brings with it the limits and misery of humankind as it is. But as the heroics of early computer tribes recedes under the relentless flow of "newbies," what remains from the countercultural origins of the network is the informality and self-directedness of communication, the idea that many contribute to many, and yet each one has her own voice and expects an individualized answer. The multipersonalization of CMC does express to some extent the same tension that arose in the 1960s between the "me culture" and the communal dreams of each individual.[70] In fact, there are more bridges than communication experts usually acknowledge between the countercultural origins of CMC and the mainstream Internetters of the 1990s, as is shown by the business acceptance of *Wired* magazine, created as a countercultural outfit, but to become the hottest expression of Internet culture and how-to advice in the mid-1990s.

Thus, in spite of all efforts to regulate, privatize, and commercialize Internet and its tributary systems, CMC networks, inside and outside Internet, are characterized by their pervasiveness, their multifaceted

[70] Gitlin (1987); Rand Corporation (1995).

decentralization, and their flexibility. They sprawl as colonies of micro-organisms, to follow Rheingold's biological image. They will certainly reflect commercial interests, as they will extend the controlling logic of major public and private organizations into the whole realm of communication. But unlike the mass media of the McLuhan Galaxy, they have technologically and culturally embedded properties of interactivity and individualization. However, do these potentialities translate into new patterns of communication? Which are the cultural attributes emerging from the process of electronic interaction? Let us turn to an examination of the meager empirical record on this matter.

The interactive society

Computer-mediated communication is too recent and has been too narrowly experienced at the time of this writing (1995) to have been the object of rigorous, reliable research. Most of the often-cited evidence is anecdotal, and some of the most accurate sources come in fact from journalists' reports. Furthermore, changes in technology are so fast and the diffusion of CMC is so rapid that most of the available research from the 1980s is hardly applicable to social trends in the 1990s, precisely the historic moment when the new communication culture is taking shape. Yet it is methodologically useful to discuss the social implications of new communication processes within the constraints of reported evidence, in spite of a pattern of somewhat contradictory findings. I shall rely on a nonexhaustive review of social sciences literature on CMC to suggest some tentative lines of interpretation of the relationship between communication and society under the conditions of computer-based interactive technology.[71] First of all, CMC is not a general medium of communication and will not be so in the foreseeable future. While its use expands at phenomenal rates it will exclude for a long time the large majority of humankind, unlike television and other mass media. To be sure, in 1994 more than one-third of American households were equipped with personal computers, and spending on PCs toppled purchases of television sets for the first time. Western Europe also experienced a computer shopping spree by the mid-1990s but rates of household penetration were held at a lower level (less than 20% if we exclude videotex terminals). Japan lags considerably in home computer

[71] I have used extensively an excellent literature review on computer-mediated communication prepared by UC Berkeley graduate student Rod Benson (1994). For some empirical evidence on Japan, based on the analysis of a 1993 survey, see Sato et al. (1995). For an intellectual reflection on the culture of Internet see the insightful book by Turkle (1995).

equipment and computer use outside the work place.[72] And the rest of the world (excluding Singapore), in spite of high rates of growth of computer penetration (with the exception of Africa), was clearly in a different communication age, notwithstanding beepers and pagers relentlessly buzzing all along the Asian Pacific. This will change over time, undoubtedly, but the rate of diffusion of interactive CMC will hardly match that of television for a long historical period.[73]

A different matter, which I shall analyze in the next section, is that of the use of interactive communication in the operation of multimedia systems, which will probably be made available, in extremely simplified versions, to a large proportion of the population in many countries. But CMC as such will remain the domain of an educated segment of the population of the most advanced countries, numbered in tens of millions but still counting as an elite on a global scale. Even the number of Internet users, as cited above, has been challenged by knowledgeable experts on grounds that connection to Internet does not mean actual use of it, even less than the multiplier of ten persons to one link that has been generally used in the estimates.[74] And even among those who use it, only a minority is really active in the medium. A survey of American users of BBSs, published in 1993, indicated that only 18% of them were active on a weekly basis; that the average number of calls was 50 per week and per BBS; that 38% of transactions were uploads of the system; and that 66% of board content was in fact devoted to computer-related matters.[75] As expected, surveys of PC owners show that they are above-average affluent, full-time employed, and single, and less likely to be retired.[76] The large majority of PC users, as well as users of bulletin board systems, are men. As for Internet users, a survey conducted on a national sample in the United States found that 67% of those with Internet access were male, over half of them aged 18–34. Their median household income was between $50,000 and $75,000, and the most frequently mentioned occupations were education, sales, and engineering.[77] A different survey, also for the United States in 1995, again found that 65% of

---

[72]   See *Business Week* (1994a); *Business Week* (1994e, f, g); *El Pais/World Media* (1995). For data on the diffusion of electronic communication in Japan, see Soumu-cho Toukei-kyoku (Bureau of Statistics, Management and Coordination Agency) (1995); Ministry of Posts and Telecommunications (1994a); Japan Information Processing Center (1994).

[73]   Hamelink (1990).

[74]   Revised estimates by John S. Quarterman, University of Texas at Austin, reported by *New York Times*, August 10 1994.

[75]   Rafaeli and LaRose (1993).

[76]   Schweitzer (1995); Sato et al. (1995).

[77]   Lohr (1995).

users were male and affluent (average household income $62,000), although older than indicated by other surveys (average age 36).[78] Thus, CMC starts as the medium of communication for the most educated and affluent segment of the population of the most educated and affluent countries, and more often than not in the largest and most sophisticated metropolitan areas.

Clearly, in the near future use of CMC will expand, particularly via the educational system, and will reach substantial proportions of the population *in the industrialized world*: it will not be exclusively an elite phenomenon, although it will be much less pervasive than the mass media. Yet the fact that it will expand through successive waves, starting from a cultural elite, means that it will shape habits of communication through the usages of its first-wave practitioners. Increasingly CMC will be critical in shaping future culture, and increasingly the elites who have shaped its format will be structurally advantaged in the emerging society. Thus, while CMC is truly revolutionizing the process of communication, and through it culture at large, it is a revolution developing in concentric waves, starting from the higher levels of education and wealth, and probably unable to reach large segments of the uneducated masses and poor countries.

On the other hand, within the segment of regular users of CMC, it appears that the medium favors uninhibited communication and stimulates participation from lower-status workers in company-based networks.[79] Along the same line of argument, women, and other oppressed groups of society, seem to be more likely to express themselves openly through the protection of the electronic medium, although we must keep in mind that, as a whole, women are a minority of users up to this point.[80] It works as though the symbolism of power embedded in face-to-face communication has not yet found its language in the new CMC. Because of the historical newness of the medium and the relative improvement of the relative status of power for traditionally subordinated groups, such as women, CMC could offer a chance to reverse traditional power games in the communication process.

Shifting the analysis from the *users* to the *uses*, it must be emphasized that *the overwhelming proportion of CMC activity takes place at work or in work-related situations*. I have discussed above in chapters 3 and 4 the critical importance of the computer medium for the new form of networked organization and for the specific labor conditions of the networkers. In the context of the present analysis on cultural impacts,

---

[78] McLeod (1996).
[79] Sproull and Kiesler (1991); Rand Corporation (1995).

what should be considered is the symbolic isomorphism in the processes of work, home services, and entertainment in the new structure of communication. Is the relationship to the computer specific enough to connect work, home and entertainment into the same system of symbol processing? Or, on the contrary, does the context determine the perception and uses of the medium? We do not have reliable research on the matter at this point, but some preliminary observations by Penny Gurstein in her doctoral dissertation[81] seem to indicate that while people using computers at home enjoy their self-reliance in the management of time and space, they resent the lack of distinct separation between work and leisure, family and business, personality and function. Let us say, as a hypothesis to be kept in the back of our mind, that the convergence of experience in the same medium blurs somewhat the institutional separation of domains of activity, and confuses codes of behavior.

Beyond the performance of professional tasks, the uses of CMC already reach the whole realm of social activity. While tele-banking has never been a favorite of average people (until they are pushed into it against their will, as will happen), and tele-shopping is dependent on the coming blossoming of virtual reality multimedia, personal communication is exploding in e-mail, the most usual CMC activity outside work.[82] In fact, its widespread use does not substitute for inter-personal communication but for telephone communication, since answering machines and voice-phone services have created a communication barrier that makes e-mail the best alternative for direct communication at a chosen time. Computer sex is another major use of CMC, and is expanding quickly. While there is a fast-growing business market in computerized sexual stimulation, increasingly associated with virtual reality technology,[83] most computer sex takes place on conversation lines, either on specialized BBSs or as a spontaneous derivation of personal interaction. The interactive power of new networks make this activity more dynamic in 1990s California than it was in 1980s French Minitel.[84] Increasingly afraid of contagion and of personal aggression, people search for alternatives to express their sexuality, and in our culture of symbolic overstimulation CMC certainly offers avenues to sexual fantasy, particularly as long as the interaction is not visual and identities can be concealed.

[80]   Hiltz and Turoff (1993); Sato et al. (1995).
[81]   Gurstein (1990).
[82]   Lanham (1993).; Rand Corporation (1995).
[83]   Specter (1994).
[84]   Armstrong (1994).

Politics is also a growing area of utilization of CMC.[85] On the one hand, e-mail is being used for mass diffusion of targeted political propaganda with the possibility of interaction. Christian fundamentalist groups, the American militia in the US, and the Zapatistas in Mexico are pioneering this political technology.[86] On the other hand, local democracy is being enhanced through experiments in electronic citizen participation, such as the PEN program organized by the City of Santa Monica, California,[87] through which citizens debate public issues and make their feelings known to the city government: a raging debate on homelessness (with electronic participation by the homeless themselves!) was one of the most highly publicized results of this experiment in the early 1990s.

Beyond casual social interaction and instrumental uses of CMC, observers have detected the phenomenon of the formation of virtual communities. By this, in line with Rheingold's argument,[88] is generally understood a self-defined electronic network of interactive communication organized around a shared interest or purpose, although sometimes communication becomes the goal in itself. Such communities may be relatively formalized, as in the case of hosted conferences or bulletin boards systems, or be spontaneously formed by social networks which keep logging into the network to send and retrieve messages in a chosen time pattern (either delayed or in real time).Tens of thousands of such "communities" existed throughout the world in the mid-1990s, most of them based in the US but increasingly reaching out on a global scale. It is still unclear how much sociability is taking place in such electronic networks, and what are the cultural effects of such a new form of sociability. Yet one feature can be highlighted: such networks are ephemeral from the point of view of the participants. While a given conference or BBS can go on for a long time, around a nucleus of dedicated computer users, most of the contributions to the interaction are sporadic, with most people moving in and out of networks as their interests change or their expectations remain unfulfilled. I would advance the hypothesis that two very different populations "live" in such virtual communities: a tiny minority of electronic villagers "homesteading in the electronic frontier,"[89] and a transient crowd for whom their casual incursions into various networks is tantamount to exploring several existences under the mode of the ephemeral.[90]

---

[85]   Abramson et al. (1988); Epstein (1995).
[86]   Castells, Yazawa and Kiselyova (1996).
[87]   Varley (1991); Ganley (1991).
[88]   Rheingold (1993).
[89]   Ibid.

How specific is the language of CMC as a new medium? To some analysts, CMC, and particularly e-mail, represents the revenge of the written medium, the return to the typographic mind, and the recuperation of the constructed, rational discourse. For others, on the contrary, the informality, spontaneity, and anonymity of the medium stimulates what they call a new form of "orality," expressed by an electronic text.[91] If we can consider such behavior as informal, unconstructed writing in real-time interaction, in the mode of a synchronist chat (a writing telephone . . .), maybe we can foresee the emergence of a new medium, mixing forms of communication that were previously separated in different domains of the human mind.

Overall, when assessing the social and cultural impacts of CMC we must keep in mind the accumulated sociological research on the social uses of technology. More to the point, the masterful work by Claude Fischer on the social history of the telephone in America to 1940 shows the high social elasticity of any given technology.[92] Thus, the Northern California communities he studied adopted the telephone to enhance their existing social networks of communication, and to reinforce their deep-rooted social habits. Telephone was adapted, not just adopted. People shape technology to fit it to their own needs, as I have argued above in relationship to the personal and contextual reception of television messages by the audience, and as is clearly shown by the mass adoption of Minitel by French people to fulfill their sexual fantasy needs. The many-to-many electronic communication mode represented by CMC has been used in different ways and for different purposes, as many as in the range of social and contextual variation among its users. What is common to CMC is that, according to the few existing studies on the matter, it does not substitute for other means of communication nor does it create new networks: it reinforces the preexisting social patterns. It adds to telephone and transportation communication, it expands the reach of social networks, and makes it possible for them to interact more actively and in chosen time patterns. Because access to CMC is culturally, educationally, and economically restrictive, and will be so for a long time, the most important cultural impact of CMC could be potentially the reinforcement of the culturally dominant social networks, as well as the increase of their cosmopolitanism and globalization. This is not because CMC per se is more cosmopolitan: as Fischer showed, early telephone networks favored local over

---

[90]   Turkle (1995).
[91]   John December, "Characteristics of Oral Culture in Discourse on the Net," 1993 unpublished paper, cited and summarized by Benson (1994).
[92]   Fischer (1992).

long-distance communication. In some of the virtual communities, for instance in the San Francisco Bay Area's SFNET, the majority of their "regulars" are local residents, and some of them periodically celebrate face-to-face parties, in order to nurture their electronic intimacy.[93] Yet for electronic networks at large, they tend to reinforce the cosmopolitanism of the new professional and managerial classes living symbolically in a global frame of reference, unlike most of the population in any country. Thus, CMC may be a powerful medium to reinforce the social cohesion of the cosmopolitan elite, providing material support to the meaning of a global culture, from the chic of an e-mail address to the rapid circulation of fashionable messages.

In contrast, for the majority of the population in all countries, beyond the work place, the experience and uses of CMC will be increasingly intertwined with the new world of communication associated with the emergence of multimedia.

The Grand Fusion: Multimedia as Symbolic Environment

In the second half of the 1990s a new electronic communication system started to be formed out of the merger of globalized, customized mass media and computer-mediated communication. As I mentioned above, the new system is characterized by the integration of different media and by its interactive potential. Multimedia, as the new system was hastily labeled, extend the realm of electronic communication into the whole domain of life, from home to work, from schools to hospitals, from entertainment to travel. By the mid-1990s governments and companies around the world were in a frantic race to position themselves in setting up the new system, considered to be a tool of power, potential source of huge profits, and symbol of hypermodernity. In the US Vice-president Albert Gore launched the National Information Infrastructure program, to renew America's leadership in the twenty-first century.[94] In Japan, the Telecommunications Council proposed the necessary "Reforms toward the Intellectually Creative Society of the Twenty-first Century," and the Ministry of Posts and Telecommunications obliged with a strategy to create a multimedia system in Japan, to overcome the lagging of the nation *vis-à-vis* the United States.[95] The French Prime Minister

[93]   Rheingold (1993).
[94]   Sullivan-Trainor (1994).
[95]   Telecommunications Council (1994).

commissioned a report in 1994 on *"autoroutes de l'information,"* which concluded that it was to the potential advantage of France in the field, building on the society's experience with Minitel and on French advanced technology, to foster the next stage of multimedia, putting emphasis on providing a media content less dependent on Hollywood.[96] European technology programs, particularly Esprit and Eureka, stepped up efforts to develop a European standard of high-definition television, as well as telecommunication protocols that could integrate different communication systems across the borders.[97] In February 1995 the G-7 club held a special meeting in Brussels to jointly address the issues involved in the transition to the "Information Society." And in early 1995, Brazil's new president, distinguished sociologist Fernando Henrique Cardoso, decided, as one of the key measures of his new administration, to overhaul Brazil's communication system, to link up with the emerging global super-highway.

Yet business, not governments, was shaping the new multimedia system.[98] Indeed, the scale of investment in infrastructure prevented any government from acting by itself: for the United States alone, the estimates for the launch phase of the so-called Information Super-highway were $US400 billion. Companies from all over the world were positioning themselves to enter a market that could become, in the early twenty-first century, the equivalent of what the automobile–oil–rubber–highway industrial complex was in the first half of the twentieth century. Furthermore, because the actual tech-nological shape of the system is uncertain, whoever controls its first stages could decisively influence its future evolution, thus acquiring structural competitive advantage. Because of technological conver-gence between computers, telecommunications, and mass media in all its modalities, global/regional consortia were formed, and dissolved, on a gigantic scale.[99] Telephone companies, cable TV oper-ators, and TV satellite broadcasting were both competing and merging to hedge the risks of the new market. Computer companies were hurrying to provide "the box," this magic device that would embody the potential to hook up the electronic home to a new galaxy of communication, while providing people with a navigating and self-programming capability in a "user-friendly" mode, hopefully by just

[96]   Thery (1994).
[97]   Banegas (ed.) (1993).
[98]   See, among a myriad of business sources on the matter, Bunker (1994); Herther (1994); Dalloz and Portnoff (1994); Bird (1994).
[99]   *The Economist* (1994a).
[100] *Business Week* (1994h).

speaking to "it."[100] Software companies, from Microsoft to Japanese video-games creators such as Nintendo and Saga, were generating the new interactive know-how that would unleash the fantasy of immersion in the virtual reality of the electronic environment.[101] Television networks, music companies, and movie studios were cranking up their production to feed an entire world supposedly hungry for info-entertainment and audiovisual product lines.[102]

The business control over the first stages of development of multimedia systems will have lasting consequences on the characteristics of the new electronic culture. For all the ideology of the potential of new communication technologies in education, health, and cultural enhancement, the prevailing strategy aims at developing a giant electronic entertainment system, considered the safest investment from a business perspective. Indeed, in the pioneer country, the United States, entertainment in all its forms was in the mid-1990s the fastest growing industry, with over $350 billion of consumer spending per year, and about 5 million workers, with employment increasing at 12% per year.[103] In Japan, a 1992 national market survey on the distribution of multimedia software by product category found that entertainment accounted for 85.7% of the value, while education represented only 0.8%.[104] Thus, while governments and futurologists speak of wiring classrooms, doing surgery at a distance, and tele-consulting the *Encyclopedia Britannica*, most of the actual construction of the new system focuses on "video-on-demand," tele-gambling, and virtual reality theme parks. In the analytical vein of this book, I am not opposing the noble goals of new technologies to their mediocre materialization. I am simply indicating that their actual use in the early stages of the new system will considerably shape the uses, perceptions, and ultimately the social consequences of multimedia.

However, the process of formation of the new system is likely to be slower, and more contradictory, than anticipated. In 1994, there were a number of experiments with multimedia interactive systems in a number of areas: in Kansai Science City in Japan; a coordinated program in eight European telecommunication networks, to test the Asymmetrical Digital Subscriber Loop (ASDL);[105] and in several areas of the United States, from Orlando to Vermont, from Brooklyn to

---

[101]   Poirier (1993); *Business Week* (1994d); Elmer-Dewwit (1993).
[102]   *New Media Markets* (1993).
[103]   *Business Week* (1994f).
[104]   Dentsu Institute for Human Studies (1994: 117).
[105]   Ministry of Posts and Telecommunications (1994b); *New Media Markets* (1994).

Denver.[106] The results did not match the expectations. Major technological problems were still unsolved, particularly the ability of the
software system to make possible interaction on a very large scale, for
thousands of homes and hundreds of communication sources. While
"video-on-demand" companies advertise unlimited possibilities, the
technological ability to handle requests still does not go too far
beyond the range of choice provided by existing cable and satellite-
based systems or on-line servers of the Minitel type. While adequate
technology will undoubtedly be developed, the investment necessary
to speed it up depends on the existence of a mass market which
cannot materialize until efficient technology becomes available. Here
again, the issue is not if a multimedia system will develop (it will) but
when and how, and under what conditions in different countries,
because the cultural meaning of the system will be deeply modified
by the timing and shape of the technological trajectory.

Furthermore, the expectations of unlimited demand for entertainment seem to be overstated and heavily influenced by the ideology of
the "leisure society." While entertainment spending appears to be
recession-resilient, payment for the full range of possibilities
proposed on-line clearly exceeds the expected evolution of households' income in the near future. Time is also a scarce resource. There
are indications that in the United States leisure time decreased by
37% between 1973 and 1994. In addition, media viewing time
declined in the second half of the 1980s: between 1985 and 1990 total
time spent reading and watching TV and movies declined by 45 hours
per year; hours spent watching TV declined by 4%; and hours
watching network TV declined by 20%.[107] Although decreasing media
exposure seems to be linked more to an overworked society (dual-job
families) than to lack of interest, multimedia business is betting on
another interpretation: lack of sufficiently attractive content. Indeed,
most experts of the media industry consider that the real bottleneck
for the expansion of multimedia is that content does not follow the
technological transformation of the system: the message is lagging the
medium.[108] A dramatic expansion of broadcasting capacity, coupled
with interactive choice, will fall short of its potential if there is no real
choice in terms of the content: the on-line availability of 50 distinct-
but-similar sex/violence movies does not justify the dramatic
broadening of transmission capacity. This is why the acquisition of
Hollywood studios, movie companies, and TV documentary archives

---

[106] Wexler (1994); Lizzio (1994); Sellers (1993); Kaplan (1992); Booker (1994);
Business Week (1994e).
[107] Martin (1994).
[108] Bunker (1994); Cuneo (1994); *The Economist* (1994a); *Business Week* (1994f).

is a must for any global multimedia consortium. Entrepreneurial creators, such as Steven Spielberg, seem to have understood that, **in the new system, because of the potential diversity of contents, the message is the message**: it is the ability to differentiate a product that yields the greatest competitive potential. Thus, any conglomerate with enough financial resources could have access to multimedia technology and, in an increasingly deregulated context, could access almost any market. But whoever controls Bogart's films or the capacity to generate the new electronic Marilyn or the next Jurassic Park episode will be in the position to supply the much-needed commodity to whichever communication support.

However, it is not sure that what people want, even if given the time and resources, is more entertainment with an increasingly sophisticated format, from sadistic video-games to endless sports events. Although there is scant evidence on the matter, some indications point to a more complex demand pattern. One of the most complete surveys on multimedia demand, carried out by Charles Piller on a national sample of 600 adults in 1994 in the United States,[109] revealed a much deeper interest in using multimedia for information access, community affairs, political involvement, and education, than in adding television and movies to their choice. Only 28% of consumers considered video-on-demand as highly desirable, and the lack of interest in entertainment was equally strong among Internet users. On the other hand, political uses were highly valued: 57% would like to participate in electronic town-hall meetings; 46% wanted to use e-mail to send messages to their representatives; and about 50% valued the possibility of voting electronically. Additional services in high demand were: educational/instructional courses; interactive reports on local schools; access to reference materials; access to information about government services. Respondents were ready to back up their opinions with their pocket: 34% were ready to pay an additional $10 a month for distant learning, while only 19% were ready to pay that amount for additional entertainment choice. Also, experiments conducted by multimedia companies for video-on-demand in local markets have shown that people are not ready for a substantial increase in their entertainment dose. Thus, the 18-month experiment conducted by US West/ATT video in Littleton, Colorado, in 1993–4, showed that households had indeed switched from standard video viewing to customized video offerings, but they did not increase the number of films they were viewing: it stayed at 2.5 movies per month, priced at $3 per movie.[110]

[109]   Piller (1994).
[110]   Tobenkin (1993); Martin (1994).

Coupled with the large-scale success of French Minitel, offering services rather than entertainment, and the fast diffusion of personal communication in Internet, observation tends to suggest that mass-produced, diversified entertainment on demand may not be the obvious choice for multimedia users, although it is clear that this is the strategic choice of business firms shaping the field. It may result in an increasing tension between infotainment products, guided by the ideology of what people are, as imagined in marketing think-tanks, and the need for personal communication and information enhancement that asserts itself with great determination in CMC networks. It may well also be that this tension is diluted through the social stratification of different multimedia expressions, a critical theme to which I shall return.

Because of the newness of multimedia, it is difficult to assess their implications for the culture of society, beyond acknowledging that fundamental changes are indeed under way. Nevertheless, scattered empirical evidence and informed commentary on the different components of new communications system provide a basis to ground some hypotheses on the emerging social and cultural trends. Thus, a "scanning report" by the European Foundation for the Improvement of Living and Working Conditions on the development of the "electronic home" emphasizes two critical features of the new life style: its "home centredness," and its individualism.[111] On the one hand, the increasing electronic equipment in European homes has increased their comfort and stepped up their self-sufficiency, enabling them to link up with the whole world from the safety of the home. Together with the increase in the size of housing units and the decrease in size of the household, more space per person is available, making home a cozier place. Indeed, time spent at home went up in the early 1990s. On the other hand, the new electronic home and portable communication devices increase the chances of individual members of the family to organize their own time and space. For instance, microwave ovens, allowing for individual consumption of precooked food, has reduced the incidence of collective family dinners. Individual TV dinner sets represent a growing market. VCRs and walkman devices, together with the decrease in the price of TV sets, radio, and CD players, allow a large segment of the population to be individually hooked into selected audiovisual worlds. Family care is also helped/transformed by electronics: children are monitored from a distance through remote control; studies show the increased use of TV as a baby-sitter while parents do their house work; elderly persons

[111]   Moran (1993).

living alone are provided with alarm systems for emergency situations. Yet some social features seem to endure beyond the technological revolution: the sharing of home tasks between genders (or, rather, lack of it) is unaffected by the electronic means; VCR use and the handling of remote control devices reflect the authority structure in the family; and the use of electronic devices is differentiated along gender and age lines, with men more often using computers, women handling electrical home maintenance and telematic services, and children obsessed with video-games.

New electronic media do not depart from traditional cultures: they absorb them. A case in point is the Japanese invention of *karaoke*, rapidly diffusing all over Asia in the 1990s, and most likely spreading to the rest of the world in the near future. In 1991, *karaoke* dissemination in Japan reached 100% of recreational hotels and inns, and about 90% of bars and clubs, to which should be added an explosion of specialized *karaoke* rooms, from under 2,000 in 1989 to over 107,000 in 1992. In 1992, about 52% of Japanese participated in *karaoke*, including 79% of all teenage women.[112] At first sight, *karaoke* extends and amplifies the traditional habit of singing together in bars, something as popular in Japan as it was (and is) in Spain or the UK, thus escaping the world of electronic communication. Yet what in fact it does is to integrate this habit into a preprogrammed machine, whose musical rhythms and repertoire have to be followed by the singer, reciting the words that appear on the screen. Indeed, competition with friends to reach a higher score depends on the reward given by the machine to whoever best follows its pace. The *karaoke* machine is not a musical instrument: the singer is swallowed by the machine to supplement its sounds and images. While in the *karaoke* room we become part of a musical hypertext, we physically enter the multimedia system, and we separate our singing from that of our friends waiting their turn to substitute a linear sequence of performance for the disorderly chorus of traditional pub singing.

Overall, in Europe as in America or in Asia, multimedia appear to be supporting, even in their early stage, a social/cultural pattern characterized by the following features. First, *widespread social and cultural differentation*, leading to the segmentation of the users/viewers/readers/listeners. Not only are the messages segmented by markets following senders' strategies, but they are also increasingly diversified by users of the media, acccording to their interests, taking advantage of interactive capacities. As some experts put it, in the new system,

---

[112]   Dentsu Institute for Human Studies (1994: 140–3).

"prime time is my time. "[113] The formation of virtual communities is but one of the expressions of such differentiation.

Secondly, *increasing social stratification among the users.* Not only will choice of multimedia be restrained to those with time and money to access, and to countries and regions with enough market potential, but cultural/educational differences will be decisive in using interaction to the advantage of each user. The information about what to look for and the knowledge about how to use the message will be essential to truly experience a system different from standard customized mass media. **Thus, the multimedia world will be populated by two essentially distinct populations: the** *interacting and the interacted,* meaning those who are able to select their multidirectional circuits of communication, and those who are provided with a restricted number of prepackaged choices. And who is what will be largely determined by class, race, gender, and country. The unifying cultural power of mass television (from which only a tiny cultural elite had escaped in the past) is now replaced by a socially stratified differentiation, leading to the coexistence of a customized mass media culture and an interactive electronic communication network of self-selected communes.

Thirdly, the communication of all kinds of messages in the same system, even if the system is interactive and selective (in fact, precisely because of this), induces an *integration of all messages in a common cognitive pattern.* Accessing audiovisual news, education, and shows on the same medium, even from different sources, takes one step further the blurring of contents that was already taking place in mass television. From the perspective of the medium, different communication modes tend to borrow codes from each other: interactive educational programs look like video-games; newscasts are constructed as audio-visual shows; trial cases are broadcast as soap operas; pop music is composed for MTV; sports games are choreographed for their distant viewers, so that their messages becomes less and less distinguishable from action movies; and the like. From the perspective of the user (both as receiver and sender, in an interactive system), the choice of various messages under the same communication mode, with easy switching from one to the other, reduces the mental distance between various sources of cognitive and sensorial involvement. The issue at stake is not that the medium is the message: messages are messages. And because they keep their distinctiveness as messages, while being mixed in their symbolic communication process, they blur their codes in this process, creating a multifaceted semantic context made of a random mixture of various meanings.

[113] Negroponte (1995).

Finally, perhaps *the most important feature of multimedia is that they capture within their domain most cultural expressions, in all their diversity.* Their advent is tantamount to ending the separation, and even the distinction, between audiovisual media and printed media, popular culture and learned culture, entertainment and information, education and persuasion. Every cultural expression, from the worst to the best, from the most elitist to the most popular, comes together in this digital universe that links up in a giant, a historical supertext, past, present, and future manifestations of the communicative mind. By so doing, they construct a new symbolic environment. They make virtuality our reality.

The Culture of Real Virtuality

Cultures are made up of communication processes. And all forms of communication, as Roland Barthes and Jean Baudrillard taught us many years ago, are based on the production and consumption of signs.[114] Thus there is no separation between "reality" and symbolic representation. In all societies humankind has existed in and acted through a symbolic environment. Therefore, what is historically specific to the new communication system, organized around the electronic integration of all communication modes from the typographic to the multisensorial, is not its inducement of virtual reality but the construction of real virtuality. I shall explain, with the help of the dictionary, according to which : "*virtual*: being so in practice though not strictly or in name," and "*real*: actually existing."[115] Thus reality, as experienced, has always been virtual because it is always perceived through symbols that frame practice with some meaning that escapes their strict semantic definition. It is precisely this ability of all forms of language to encode ambiguity and to open up a diversity of interpretations that makes cultural expressions distinct from formal/logical/mathematical reasoning. It is through the polysemic character of our discourses that the complexity and even contradictory quality of messages of the human brain manifest themselves. This range of cultural variation of the meaning of messages is what enables us to interact with each other in a multiplicity of dimensions, some explicit, some implicit. Thus, when critics of electronic media argue that the new symbolic environment does not represent "reality," they

[114] Barthes (1978); Baudrillard (1972).
[115] *Oxford Dictionary of Current English* (1992).

implicitly refer to an absurdly primitive notion of "uncoded" real experience that never existed. All realities are communicated through symbols. And in human, interactive communication, regardless of the medium, all symbols are somewhat displaced in relationship to their assigned semantic meaning. In a sense, all reality is virtually perceived.

What is then a communication system that, in contrast to earlier historical experience, generates *real virtuality*? **It is a system in which reality itself (that is, people's material/symbolic existence) is entirely captured, fully immersed in a virtual image setting, in the world of make believe, in which appearances are not just on the screen through which experience is communicated, but they become the experience**. All messages of all kinds become enclosed in the medium, because the medium has become so comprehensive, so diversified, so malleable, that it absorbs in the same multimedia text the whole of human experience, past, present, and future, as in that unique point of the Universe that Jorge Luis Borges called "Aleph." Let me give an example.

In the 1992 American presidential campaign, then Vice-president Dan Quayle, wanted to make a stand in defense of traditional family values. Armed with his moral convictions he initiated an unusual debate with Murphy Brown. Murphy Brown, played by a fine actress, Candice Bergen, was the main character of a popular television soap opera who (re)presented the values and problems of a new kind of woman: the single, working professional woman with her own criteria about life. Around the weeks of the presidential campaign, Murphy Brown (not Candice Bergen) decided to have a child out of wedlock. Vice-president Quayle hurried to condemn her behavior as improper, prompting national outrage, particularly among working women. Murphy Brown (not just Candice Bergen) retaliated: in her next episode, she appeared watching the television interview in which Vice-president Quayle was criticizing her, and she spoke up, sharply criticizing politicians' interference with women's life, and defending her right to a new morality. Eventually *Murphy Brown* increased its share of the audience and Dan Quayle's outdated conservatism contributed to the electoral defeat of President Bush, both events being real and, to some extent, socially relevant. Yet a new text of the real and the imaginary had been composed throughout the dialogue. The unsolicited presence of Murphy Brown's imaginary world in the real life presidential campaign induced the transformation of Quayle (or rather, of his "real" television image) into a character of Murphy Brown's imaginary life: a supertext had been made, blending in the same discourse passionately argued messages emitted from both levels of experience. In this case, virtuality (that is Murphy Brown being in practice what many women were, without being so in the name of any woman) had become real, in the sense that it actually interacted, with some significant impact, with the process of election to the most powerful political office on earth. Granted, the example is extreme and unusual, but I believe it illustrates my analysis, helping to reduce the obscurity of its abstraction. Hoping that such is the case, let me be more precise.

What characterizes the new system of communication, based in the digitized, networked integration of multiple communication modes, is its inclusiveness and comprehensiveness of all cultural expressions. Because of its existence, all kinds of messages in the new type of society work in a binary mode: presence/absence in the multimedia communication system. Only presence in this integrated system permits communicability and socialization of the message. All other messages are reduced to individual imagination or to increasingly marginalized face-to-face subcultures. From society's perspective, *electronically-based communication (typographic, audiovisual, or computer-mediated) is communication.* Yet it does not follow that there is homogenization of cultural expressions and full domination of codes by a few central senders. It is precisely because of the diversification, multimodality, and versatility of the new communication system that it is able to embrace and integrate all forms of expression, as well as the diversity of interests, values, and imaginations, including the expression of social conflicts. But the price to pay for inclusion in the system is to adapt to its logic, to its language, to its points of entry, to its encoding and decoding. This is why it is so critical for different kinds of social effects that there should be the development of a multinodal, horizontal network of communication, of Internet type, instead of a centrally dispatched multimedia system, as in the video-on-demand configuration. The setting of barriers to entry into this communication system, and the creation of passwords for the circulation and diffusion of messages throughout the system, are critical cultural battles for the new society, the outcome of which predetermines the fate of symbolically mediated conflicts to be fought in this new historical environment. Who are the *interacting* and who are the *interacted* in the new system, to use the terminology whose meaning I suggested above, largely frames the system of domination and the processes of liberation in the informational society.

The inclusion of most cultural expressions within the integrated communication system based in digitized electronic production, distribution, and exchange of signals, has major consequences for social forms and processes. On the one hand, it weakens considerably the symbolic power of traditional senders external to the system, transmitting through historically encoded social habits: religion, morality, authority, traditional values, political ideology. Not that they disappear, but they are weakened unless they recode themselves in the new system, where their power becomes multiplied by the electronic materialization of spiritually transmitted habits: electronic preachers and interactive fundamentalist networks are a more efficient, more penetrating form of indoctrination in our societies than face-to-face transmission of distant, charismatic authority. But by having to concede the earthly coexistence of transcendental messages, on-demand pornography, soap operas, and chat-lines within the same system, superior spiritual powers still conquer souls but lose their suprahuman status. The final step of secularization of society follows, even if it sometimes takes the paradoxical form of conspicuous consumption of religion, under all kinds of generic and brand names. Societies are finally and truly disenchanted because all wonders are on-line and can be combined into self-constructed image worlds.

On the other hand, the new communication system radically transforms space and time, the fundamental dimensions of human life. Localities become disembodied from their cultural, historical, geographic meaning, and reintegrated into functional networks, or into image collages, inducing a space of flows that substitutes for the space of places. Time is erased in the new communication system when past, present, and future can be programmed to interact with each other in the same message. The *space of flows* and *timeless time* are the material foundations of a new culture, that transcends and includes the diversity of historically transmitted systems of representation: the culture of real virtuality where make-believe is belief in the making.

— 6 —

The Space of Flows

Introduction

Space and time are the fundamental, material dimensions of human life. Physicists have unveiled the complexity of such notions, beyond their fallacious intuitive simplicity. School children know that space and time are related. And superstring theory, the latest fashion in physics, advances the hypothesis of a hyperspace that articulates ten dimensions, including time.[1] There is of course no place for such a discussion in my analysis, strictly concerned with the *social meaning of space and time.* But my reference to such complexity goes beyond rhetorical pedantry. It invites us to consider social forms of time and space that are not reducible to what have been our perceptions to date, based upon socio-technical structures superseded by current historical experience.

Since space and time are intertwined in nature and in society, so they will be in my analysis, although for the sake of clarity I shall focus sequentially first on space, in this chapter, and then on time in the next one. The ordering in the sequence is not random: unlike most classical social theories, that assume the domination of space by time, I propose the hypothesis that space organizes time in the network society.This statement will hopefully make more sense at the end of the intellectual journey I propose to the reader in these two chapters.

Both space and time are being transformed under the combined effect of the information technology paradigm, and of social forms and processes induced by the current process of historical change, as presented in this book. However, the actual profile of such transformation sharply departs from common-sense extrapolations of technological determinism. For instance, it appears to be obvious

[1]   Kaku (1994).

that advanced telecommunications would make location of offices ubiquitous, thus enabling corporate headquarters to quit expensive, congested, and unpleasant central business districts for custom-made sites in beautiful spots around the world. Yet Mitchell Moss' empirical analysis on the impact of telecommunications on Manhattan's business in the 1980s found that these new, advanced telecommunications facilities were among the factors responsible for slowing down corporate relocation away from New York, for reasons that I shall expose below. Or, to use another example on a different social domain, home-based electronic communication was supposed to induce the decline of dense urban forms, and to diminish spatially localized social interaction. Yet the first mass diffused system of computer mediated communication, the French Minitel, described in the previous chapter, originated in the 1980s in an intense urban environment, whose vitality and face-to-face interaction was hardly undermined by the new medium. Indeed, French students used Minitel to successfully stage *street* demonstrations against the government. In the early 1990s tele-commuting, that is working at home on-line, was practiced by a very small fraction of the labor force, in the United States (between 1% and 2% on a given day), Europe, or Japan, if we except the old, customary practice of professionals to keep working at home or to organize their activity in flexible time and space when they have the leisure to do so.[2] While working at home part-time seems to be emerging as a mode of professional activity in the future, it develops out of the rise of the network enterprise and of the flexible work process, as analyzed in preceding chapters, not as the direct consequence of available technology. The theoretical and practical consequences of such precisions are critical. It is this complexity of the interaction between technology, society, and space that I shall address in the following pages.

To proceed in this direction, I shall examine the empirical record on the transformation of location patterns of core economic activities under the new technological system, both for advanced services and for manufacturing. Afterwards, I shall try to assess the scarce evidence on the interaction between the rise of the electronic home and the evolution of the city, and I shall elaborate on the recent evolution of urban forms in various contexts. I shall then synthesize the observed

[2]   For an excellent overview of the interaction between telecommunications and spatial processes, see Graham and Marvin (1996). For evidence on the impact of telecommunications on business districts, see Moss (1987, 1991, 1992:147–58). For summary of evidence on teleworking and telecommuting in advanced societies, see Qvortup (1992); and Korte et al. (1988).

tendencies under a new spatial logic that I label *space of flows*. I shall oppose to such logic the historically rooted spatial organization of our common experience: *the space of places*. And I shall refer to the reflection of such dialectical opposition between the space of flows and the space of places in current debates in architecture and urban design. The purpose of this intellectual itinerary is to draw the profile of this new spatial process, the space of flows, that is becoming the dominant spatial manifestation of power and function in our societies. In spite of all my efforts to anchor the new spatial logic in the empirical record, I am afraid it is unavoidable, towards the end of the chapter, to confront the reader with some fundamentals of a social theory of space, as a way to approach the current transformation of the material basis of our experience. Yet my ability to communicate a rather abstract theorization of new spatial forms and processes will hopefully be enhanced by a brief survey of available evidence on recent spatial patterning of dominant economic functions and social practices.[3]

Advanced Services, Information Flows, and the Global City

The informational/global economy is organized around command and control centers able to coordinate, innovate, and manage the intertwined activities of networks of firms.[4] Advanced services, including finance, insurance, real estate, consulting, legal services, advertising, design, marketing, public relations, security, information gathering, and management of information systems, but also R&D and scientific innovation, are at the core of all economic processes, be it in manufacturing, agriculture, energy, or services of different kinds.[5] They all can be reduced to knowledge generation and

[3] To a large extent, the empirical basis and the analytical foundations of this chapter rely on the research work I did in the 1980s, summarized and elaborated in my book *The Informational City: Information Technology, Economic Restructuring, and the Urban–Regional Process* (Castells 1989). Although this chapter contains updated, additional information on various countries, as well as further theoretical elaboration, I still refer the reader to the cited book for more detailed analysis and empirical support of the analysis presented here. Accordingly, *I shall not repeat here again the empirical sources that have been used and cited in the above-mentioned book.* This note should be considered as a generic reference to the sources and material contained in *The Informational City*. For an up-to-date discussion on these matters, see also Graham and Marvin (1996).
[4] For an excellent overview of current transformations of spatial forms and processes at the global level, see Hall (1995: 3–32).
[5] Daniels (1993).

information flows.[6] Thus, advanced telecommunications systems could make possible their scattered location around the globe. Yet more than a decade of studies on the matter have established a different spatial pattern, characterized by the simultaneous dispersion and concentration of advanced services.[7] On the one hand, advanced services have substantially increased their share in employment and GNP in most countries, and they display the highest growth in employment and the highest investment rates in the leading metropolitan areas of the world.[8] They are pervasive, and they are located throughout the geography of the planet, excepting the "black holes" of marginality. On the other hand, there has been a spatial concentration of the upper tier of such activities in a few nodal centers of a few countries.[9] Such concentration follows a hierarchy between tiers of urban centers, with the higher-level functions, in terms of both power and skill, being concentrated in some major metropolitan areas.[10] Saskia Sassen's classic study on the global city has shown the joint dominance of New York, Tokyo, and London in international finance, and in most consulting and business services of international scope.[11] These three centers together cover the spectrum of time zones for the purpose of financial trading, and work largely as a unit in the same system of endless transactions. But other centers are important, and even more preeminent in some specific segments of trade, for example Chicago and Singapore in futures' contracts (in fact, first practiced in Chicago in 1972). Hong Kong, Osaka, Frankfurt, Zurich, Paris, Los Angeles, San Francisco, Amsterdam, and Milan are also major centers both in finance and in international business services.[12] And a number of "regional centers" are rapidly joining the network, as "emergent markets" develop all over the world: Madrid, São Paulo, Buenos Aires, Mexico, Taipei, Moscow, Budapest, among others.

As the global economy expands and incorporates new markets it also organizes the production of advanced services required to manage the new units joining the system, and the conditions of their ever-changing linkages.[13] A case in point that illustrates such process is Madrid, relatively a backwater of the global economy until 1986. In

[6]   Norman (1993).
[7]   Graham (1994).
[8]   Enderwick (ed.) (1989).
[9]   Daniels (1993).
[10]   Thrift (1986); Thrift and Leyshon (1992).
[11]   Sassen (1991).
[12]   Daniels (1993).
[13]   Borja et al. (eds) (1991).

that year Spain joined the European Community, opening up fully to foreign capital investment in the stock exchange markets, in banking operations, and in acquisition of companies equity, as well as in real estate. As shown in our study[14], in the 1986–90 period foreign direct investment in Madrid and in Madrid's stock exchange fueled a period of rapid regional economic growth, together with a boom in real estate and a fast expansion of employment in business services. Acquisitions of stocks in Madrid by foreign investors between 1982 and 1988 jumped from 4,494 million pesetas (pts) to 623,445 million pts. Foreign direct investment in Madrid went up from 8,000 million pts in 1985 to almost 400,000 million pts in 1988. Accordingly, office construction in downtown Madrid, and high-level residential real estate, went in the late 1980s through the same kind of frenzy experienced in New York and London. The city was deeply transformed both through the saturation of valuable space in the core city, and through a process of massive suburbanization that, until then, had been a somewhat limited phenomenon in Madrid.

Along the same line of argument, the study by Cappelin on services networking in European cities shows the increasing interdependence and complementarity between medium-sized urban centers in the European Union.[15] He concluded that

> The relative importance of the city–region relationships seems to decrease with respect to the importance of the relationships which interlink various cities of different regions and countries ... New activities concentrate in particular poles and that implies an increase of disparities between the urban poles and their respective hinterlands.[16]

Thus, the global city phenomenon cannot be reduced to a few urban cores at the top of the hierarchy. It is a process that connects advanced services, producer centers, and markets in a global network, with different intensity and at a different scale depending upon the relative importance of the activities located in each area *vis-à-vis* the global network. Inside each country, the networking architecture reproduces itself into regional and local centers, so that the whole system becomes interconnected at the global level. Territories surrounding these nodes play an increasingly subordinate function, sometimes becoming irrelevant or even dysfunctional) for example, Mexico City's *colonias populares* (originally squatter settlements) that account for about two-thirds of the megapolitan population, without

[14] For a summary of the research report, see Castells (1991).
[15] Cappelin (1991).
[16] Ibid.: 237.

playing any distinctive role in the functioning of Mexico City as an international business center).[17] Furthermore, globalization stimulates regionalization. In his studies on European regions in the 1990s, Philip Cooke has shown, on the basis of available evidence, that the growing internationalization of economic activities throughout Europe has made regions more dependent on these activities. Accordingly, regions, under the impulse of their governments and business elites, have restructured themselves to compete in the global economy, and they have established networks of cooperation between regional institutions and between region-based companies. Thus, regions and localities do not disappear, but become integrated in international networks that link up their most dynamic sectors.[18]

An approximation to the evolving architecture of information flows in the global economy has been obtained by Michelson and Wheeler on the basis of data analysis of traffic for one of the leading business couriers, Federal Express Corporation.[19] They studied the 1990s movement of overnight letters, packages, and boxes between US metropolitan areas, as well as between the US major sending centers and international destinations. The results of their analysis, illustrated in figures 6.1 and 6.2 show two basic trends: (a) dominance of some nodes, particularly New York, followed by Los Angeles, increasing over time; (b) selected national and international circuits of connection. As they conclude:

> All indicators point to a strengthening of the hierarchical structure of command-and-control functions and the resulting exchange of information . . . The locational concentration of information results from high levels of uncertainty, driven in turn by technological change, market demassification, deregulation and market globalization. . . . (However) as the current epoch unfolds, the importance of flexibility as a basic coping mechanism, and of agglomeration economies as the preeminent locational force will persist. The importance of the city as a center of gravity for economic transactions thus will not vanish. But with the impending regulation of international markets . . . with less uncertainty about the rules of the economic game and the players involved, the concentration of the information industry will slow and certain aspects of production and distribution will filter into lower levels of an internationalized urban hierarchy.[20]

[17]   Davis (1994).
[18]   Cooke (1994); Cooke and Morgan (1993).
[19]   Michelson and Wheeler (1994).
[20]   Ibid.: 102–3.

Origin		Destination
New York	4,523	Los Angeles
Los Angeles	4,391	New York
New York	2,768	Washington
Washington	2,249	New York
Los Angeles	2,182	San Francisco
New York	2,161	Boston
New York	2,077	Philadelphia
Boston	1,947	New York
New York	1,691	Miami
Philadelphia	1,684	New York
Atlanta	1,654	New York
San Francisco	1,632	New York
New York	1,628	Atlanta
Dallas	1,609	Los Angeles
Chicago	1,555	Los Angeles

Figure 6.1   Largest absolute growth in information flows, 1982 and 1990
Source: Federal Express data; elaborated by Michelson and Wheeler (1994).

Indeed, the hierarchy in the network is by no means assured or stable: it is subject to fierce inter-city competition, as well as to the venture of highly risky investments in both finance and real estate. Thus, P.W.Daniels, in one of the most comprehensive studies on the matter, explains the partial failure of the major redevelopment project of Canary Wharf in London's Docklands because of the overextended strategy of its developer, the notorious Canadian firm Olympia & York, unable to absorb the office development glut of the early 1990s, in the wake of retrenchment of financial services employment in both London and New York. He concludes that:

The expansion of services into the international market place has therefore introduced a greater degree of flexibility, and ultimately competition, into the global urban system than was

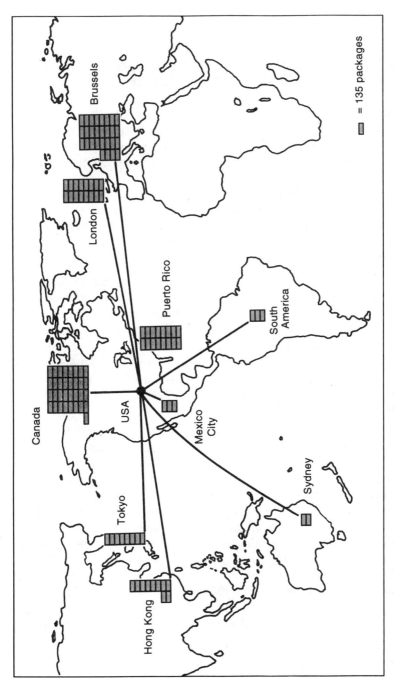

Figure 6.2 Exports of information from the United States to major world regions and centers
Source: Federal Express data, 1990; elaborated by Michelson and Wheeler (1994).

the case in the past. As the experience with Canary Wharf has shown, it also made the outcome of large-scale planning and redevelopment within cities a hostage to external international factors over which they can have limited control.[21]

Thus, in the early 1990s, while business-led explosive urban growth was experienced in cities such as Bangkok, Taipei, Shanghai, Mexico D.F., or Bogota, on the other hand, Madrid, along with New York, London, and Paris, went into a slump that triggered a sharp downturn in real estate prices and halted new construction. This urban roller coaster at different periods, across areas of the world, illustrates both the dependence and vulnerability of any locale, including major cities, to changing global flows.

But why must these advanced service systems still be dependent on agglomeration in a few large metropolitan nodes? Here again, Saskia Sassen, capping years of field work research by herself and other researchers in different contexts, offers convincing answers. She argues that:

> The combination of spatial dispersal and global integration has created a new strategic role for major cities. Beyond their long history as centers for international trade and banking, these cities now function in four new ways: first, as highly concentrated command points in the organization of the world economy; second, as key locations for finance and for specialized service firms . . . ; third, as sites of production, including the production of innovation in these leading industries; and fourth, as markets for the products and innovations produced.[22]

These cities, or rather, their business districts, are information-based, value production complexes, where corporate headquarters and advanced financial firms can find both the suppliers and the highly skilled, specialized labor they require. They constitute indeed networks of production and management, whose flexibility needs *not* to internalize workers and suppliers, but to be able to access them when it fits, and in the time and quantities that are required in each particular instance. Flexibility and adaptability are better served by this combination between agglomeration of core networks, and global networking of these cores and of their dispersed, ancillary networks, via telecommunications and air transportation. Other factors seem also to contribute to strengthen concentration of high-level activities in a few nodes: once they are constituted, heavy

[21] Daniels (1993: 166).
[22] Sassen (1991: 3–4).

investment in valuable real estate by corporations explains their reluctance to move because such a move would devalue their fixed assets; also, face-to-face contacts for critical decisions are still necessary in the age of widespread eavesdropping, since, as Saskia Sassen reports a manager confessed to her during an interview, sometimes business deals are, of necessity, marginally illegal.[23] And, finally, major metropolitan centers still offer the greatest opportunities for the personal enhancement, social status, and individual self-gratification of the much-needed upper-level professionals, from good schools for their children to symbolic membership at the heights of conspicuous consumption, including art and entertainment.[24]

Nevertheless, advanced services, and even more so services at large, do indeed disperse and decentralize to the periphery of metropolitan areas, to smaller metropolitan areas, to less-developed regions, and to some less-developed countries.[25] New regional centers of service processing activities have emerged in the United States (for example, Atlanta, Georgia, or Omaha, Nebraska), in Europe (for example, Barcelona, Nice, Stuttgart, Bristol), or in Asia (for example, Bombay, Bangkok, Shanghai). The peripheries of major metropolitan areas are bustling with new office development, be it Walnut Creek in San Francisco or Reading near London. And in some cases, new major service centers have sprung up on the edge of the historic city, Paris' La Défense being the most notorious and successful example. Yet, in almost all instances, decentralization of office work affects "back offices," that is the mass processing of transactions that execute strategies decided and designed in the corporate centers of high finance and advanced services.[26] These are precisely the activities that employ the bulk of semi-skilled office workers, most of them suburbanite women, many of them replaceable or recyclable, as technology evolves and the economic roller coaster goes on.

What is significant about this spatial system of advanced service activities is neither their concentration nor decentralization, since both processes are indeed taking place at the same time throughout countries and continents. Nor is it the hierarchy of their geography, since this is in fact tributary to the variable geometry of money and

[23] Personal notes, reported by Sassen over a glass of Argentinian wine, Harvard Inn, April 22 1994.

[24] For an approximation to the differentiation of social worlds in global cities, using New York as an illustration, see the various essays collected in Mollenkopf and Castells (eds) (1991); and Mollenkopf (ed.) (1989); also Zukin (1992).

[25] For evidence on spatial decentralization of services, see Castells (1989: ch.3); Daniels 1993: ch. 5); and Marshall et al. (1988).

[26] See Castells (1989b: ch.3); and Dunford and Kafkalas (eds) (1992).

information flows. After all, who could predict in the early 1980s that Taipei, Madrid or Buenos Aires could emerge as important international financial and business centers? I believe that the megalopolis Hong Kong–Shenzhen–Guangzhou–Zhuhai–Macau will be one of the major financial and business capitals in the early twenty-first century, thus inducing a major realignment in the global geography of advanced services.[27] But for the sake of the spatial analysis I am proposing here, it is secondary if I miss my prediction. Because, while the actual location of high-level centers in each period is critical for the distribution of wealth and power in the world, from the perspective of the spatial logic of the new system what matters is the versatility of its networks. The global city is not a place, but a process. A process by which centers of production and consumption of advanced services, and their ancillary local societies, are connected in a global network, while simultaneously downplaying the linkages with their hinterlands, on the basis of information flows.

The New Industrial Space

The advent of high-technology manufacturing, namely microelectronics-based, computer-aided manufacturing, ushered in a new logic of industrial location. Electronic firms, the producers of new information technology devices, were also the first to practice the locational strategy both allowed and required by the information-based production process. During the 1980s, a number of empirical studies conducted by faculty and graduate students at the University of California Berkeley's Institute of Urban and Regional Development provided a solid grasp on the profile of "the new industrial space."[28] It is characterized by the technological and organizational ability to separate the production process in different locations while reintegrating its unity through telecommunications linkages, and microelectronics-based precision and flexibility in the fabrication of components. Furthermore, geographic specificity of each phase of the production process is made advisable by the singularity of the labor force required at each stage, and by the different social and environmental features involved in the living conditions of highly distinct segments of this labor force. This is because high-technology manufacturing presents an occupational composition very different

[27]   See Kwok and So (1992); Henderson (1991); Kwok and So (eds) (1995).
[28]   For an analytical summary of the evidence gathered by these studies on new patterns of manufacturing location see Castells (1988a). See also Scott (1988); Henderson (1989).

from traditional manufacturing: it is organized in a bipolar structure around two predominant groups of roughly similar size; a highly skilled, science- and technology-based labor force, on the one hand; a mass of unskilled workers engaged in routine assembly and auxiliary operations, on the other hand. While automation has increasingly enabled companies to eliminate the lower tier of workers, the staggering increase in the volume of production still employs, and will for some time, a considerable number of unskilled and semi-skilled workers whose location in the same areas as scientists and engineers is neither economically feasible nor socially suitable, in the prevailing social context. In between, skilled operators also represent a distinctive group that can be separated from the high levels of high-technology production. Because of the light weight of the final product, and because of easy communication linkages developed by companies throughout the globe, electronics firms, particularly American, developed from the origins of the industry (as early as Fairchild's plant location in Hong Kong in 1962) a locational pattern characterized by the international spatial division of labor.[29] Roughly speaking, both for microelectronics and computers, four different types of location were sought for each one of the four distinctive operations in the production process:

a) R&D, innovation, and prototype fabrication were concentrated in highly innovative industrial centers in core areas, generally with good quality of life before their development process degraded the environment to some extent;

b) skilled fabrication in branch plants, generally in newly industrializing areas in the home country, which in the case of the US generally meant in medium-sized towns in the Western states;

c) semi-skilled, large-scale assembly and testing work that from the very beginning was located offshore in a substantial proportion, particularly in South East Asia, with Singapore and Malaysia pioneering the movement of attracting factories of American electronics corporations;

d) customization of devices and aftersales maintenance and technical support, which was organized in regional centers throughout the globe, generally in the area of major electronics markets, originally in America and Western Europe, although in the 1990s the Asian markets rose to equal status.

European companies, used to cozy locations on their protected home turfs, were pushed to decentralize their production systems in

---

[29] Cooper (ed.) (1994).

a similar global chain, as markets opened up, and they started to feel the pinch of competition from Asian-based operations, and from American and Japanese technological advantage.[30] Japanese companies tried to resist for a long time to quit "fortress Japan," both for reasons of nationalism (at the request of their government) and because of their close dependence on "just in time" networks of suppliers. However, unbearable congestion and skyrocketing prices of operation in the Tokyo–Yokohama area forced first regional decentralization (helped by MITI's Technopolis program) in less-developed areas of Japan, particularly in Kyushu;[31] and then, from the late 1980s, Japanese companies proceeded to follow the locational pattern initiated by their American competitors two decades earlier: offshore production facilities in South East Asia, searching for lower labor costs and looser environmental constraints, and dissemination of factories throughout the main markets in America, Europe, and Asia as a preemption to overcome future protectionism.[32] Thus, the end of Japanese exceptionalism confirmed the accuracy of the locational model that, together with a number of colleagues, we proposed to understand the new spatial logic of high technology industry. Figure 6.3 displays schematically the spatial logic of this model, elaborated on the basis of empirical evidence gathered by a number of researchers in different contexts.[33]

A key element in this location pattern is the decisive importance of technological innovation production complexes for the whole system. This is what Peter Hall and I, as well as the pioneer in this field of research, Philippe Aydalot, called "milieux of innovation."[34] By milieu of innovation I understand a specific set of relationships of production and management, based on a social organization that by and

---

[30]   Chesnais (1994).

[31]   Castells and Hall (1994).

[32]   Aoyama (1995).

[33]   Castells (1989b: ch.2).

[34]   The concept of milieu of innovation, as applied to technological/industrial development emerged in the early 1980s in a series of exchanges, in Berkeley, between Peter Hall, the late Philippe Aydalot, and myself. We were also influenced by some economic writings on the matter, around the same time, by B. Arthur, and by A.E. Anderson. Peter Hall and I, in separate papers, attempted formulations of the concept in 1984 and subsequent years; and in Europe the research network originally organized by Philippe Aydalot, the Groupe de Recherche sur les Milieux Innovateurs (GREMI), undertook systematic research on the matter, published in 1986 and subsequent years. Among GREMI researchers, Roberto Camagni provided, in my personal opinion, the most precise analysis on this topic.

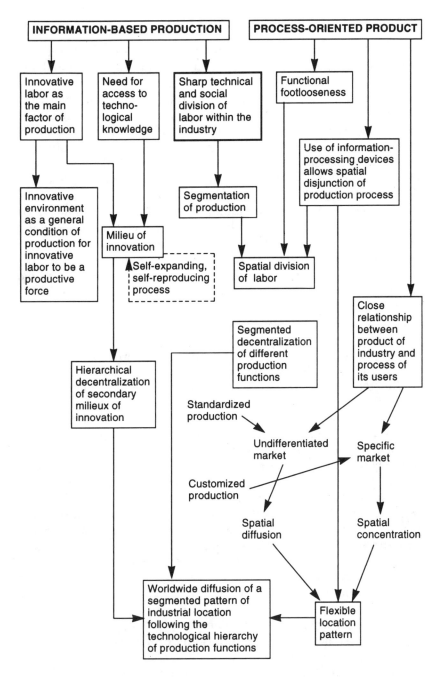

Figure 6.3 System of relationships between the characteristics of information technology manufacturing and the industry's spatial pattern
Source: Elaborated by Castells (1989a).

large shares a work culture and instrumental goals aimed at generating new knowledge, new processes, and new products. Although the
concept of milieu does not necessarily include a spatial dimension, I
argue that in the case of information technology industries, at least in
this century, spatial proximity is a necessary material condition for the
existence of such milieux, because of the nature of the interaction in
the innovation process. What defines the specificity of a milieu of
innovation is its capacity to generate synergy, that is the added value
resulting not from the cumulative effect of the elements present in
the milieu but from their interaction. Milieux of innovation are the
fundamental sources of innovation and of generation of value added
in the process of industrial production in the information age. Peter
Hall and I studied for several years the formation, structure, and
dynamics of the main technological milieux of innovation around the
world, both actual and supposed. The results of our inquiry added
some elements to the understanding of the locational pattern of information technology industry.[35]

First of all, high-technology-led industrial milieux of innovation,
which we called "technopoles," come in a variety of urban formats.
Most notably, it is clear that in most countries, with the important
exceptions of the United States and, to some extent Germany, the
leading technopoles are in fact contained in the leading metropolitan
areas: Tokyo, Paris-Sud, London–M4 Corridor, Milan, Seoul–Inchon,
Moscow–Zelenograd, and at a considerable distance Nice–Sophia
Antipolis, Taipei–Hsinchu, Singapore, Shanghai, São Paulo,
Barcelona, and so on. The partial exception of Germany (after all,
Munich is a major metropolitan area) relates directly to political
history: the destruction of Berlin, the preeminent European science-
based industrial center, and the relocation of Siemens from Berlin to
Munich in the last months of the Third Reich, under the anticipated
protection of American occupation forces and with the subsequent
support of the Bavarian CSU party. Thus, against the excessive
imagery of upstart technopoles there is indeed continuity in the
spatial history of technology and industrialization in the information
age: major metropolitan centers around the world continue to cumu-
late innovation-inducing factors and to generate synergy, in
manufacturing as in advanced services.

However, some of the most important innovation centers of information-technology manufacturing are indeed new, particularly in the
world's technological leader, the United States. Silicon Valley,
Boston's Route 128 (rejuvenating an old, traditional manufacturing

[35]   Castells and Hall (1994).

structure), the Southern California Technopole, North Carolina's Research Triangle, Seattle, and Austin, among others, were by and large linked to the latest wave of information-technology-based industrialization. We have shown that their development resulted from the clustering of specific varieties of the usual factors of production: capital, labor, and raw material, brought together by some kind of institutional entrepreneur, and constituted by a particular form of social organization. Their raw material was made up of new knowledge, related to strategically important fields of application, produced by major centers of innovation, such as Stanford University, CalTech, or MIT schools of engineering research teams, and the networks built around them. Their labor, distinct from the knowledge factor, required the concentration of a large number of highly skilled scientists and engineers, from a variety of locally based schools, including those above mentioned but also others, such as Berkeley, San Jose State, or Santa Clara, in the case of Silicon Valley. Their capital was also specific, willing to take the high risks of investing in pioneering high tech: either because of the military imperative on performance (defense-related spending); or else because of the high stakes of venture capital betting on the extra rewards of risk-taking investments. The articulation of these production factors was generally the fact, at the onset of the process, of an institutional actor, such as Stanford University launching the Stanford Industrial Park that induced Silicon Valley; or the Air Force commanders who, relying on Los Angeles boosterism, won for Southern California the defense contracts that would make the new Western metropolis the largest high-technology defense complex in the world. Finally, social networks, of different kinds, powerfully contributed to the consolidation of the milieu of innovation, and to its dynamism, ensuring the communication of ideas, the circulation of labor, and the cross-fertilization of technological innovation and business entrepreneurialism.

What our research on the new milieux of innovation, in the US or elsewhere, shows is that while there is indeed spatial continuity in metropolitan dominance, it can also be reversed given the right conditions. And that the right conditions concern the capacity to spatially concentrate the proper ingredients for inducing synergy. If such is the case, as our evidence seems to support, then we do have a new industrial space marked by fundamental discontinuity: milieux of innovation, new and old, constitute themselves on the basis of their internal structure and dynamics, later attracting firms, capital and labor to the seedbed of innovation they constituted. Once established, milieux of innovation both compete and cooperate between different regions, creating a network of interaction that brings them together in a common industrial structure beyond their geographical discontinuity. Research by Camagni and the research teams organized around the GREMI network[36] shows the growing interdependence of these milieux of innovation all over the globe, while at the same time emphasizing how decisive for their fate is the capacity of each milieu to enhance its synergy. Finally, milieux of innovation command global networks of production and distribution that extend their reach all over the planet. This is why some researchers, such as Amin and Robins, argue that the new industrial system is neither global nor local but "a new articulation of global and local dynamics."[37]

However, to have a clear vision of the new industrial space consti-tuted in the information age we must add some precision. This is because too often the emphasis of the analysis has been placed on the hierarchical spatial division of labor between different functions located in different territories. This is important, but not essential in the new spatial logic. Territorial hierarchies can be blurred, and even reversed, as the industry expands throughout the world, and as competition enhances or depresses entire agglomerations, including milieux of innovation themselves. Also, secondary milieux of innova-tion are constituted, sometimes as decentralized systems spun off from primary centers, but they often find their niches in competition with their original matrices, examples to the point being Seattle *vis-à-vis* Silicon Valley and Boston in software, or Austin, Texas, *vis-à-vis* New York or Minneapolis in computers. Furthermore, in the 1990s, the development of electronics industry in Asia, mainly under the impulse of American–Japanese competition, has complicated extra-ordinarily the geography of the industry in its mature stage, as shown in the analyses by Cohen and Borrus and by Dieter Ernst.[38] On the one hand, there has been substantial upgrading of the technological potential of American multinationals' subsidiaries, particularly in Singapore, Malaysia, and Taiwan, and this upgrading has trickled down to their local subsidiaries. On the other hand, Japanese elec-tronics firms, as mentioned above, have massively decentralized their production in Asia, both to export globally and to supply their onshore parent plants. In both cases, a substantial supply base has been built in Asia, thus rendering obsolete the old spatial division of labor in which South East and East Asian subsidiaries occupied the bottom level of the hierarchy.

Furthermore, on the basis of the review of available evidence up to 1994, including his own company surveys, Richard Gordon con-

[36]   Camagni (1991).
[37]   Amin and Robins (1991).
[38]   Cohen and Borrus (1995a); Ernst (1994c).

vincingly argues for the emergence of a new spatial division of labor, one characterized by its variable geometry, and its back and forth linkages between firms located in different territorial complexes, including the leading milieux of innovation. His detailed analysis of developments in 1990s' Silicon Valley shows the importance of extraregional relationships for the most technologically sophisticated and transaction-intensive interactions of regional high technology firms. Thus he argues that

> in this new global context, localized agglomeration, far from constituting an alternative to spatial dispersion, becomes the principal basis for participation in a global network of regional economies . . . Regions and networks in fact constitute interdependent poles within the new spatial mosaic of global innovation. Globalization in this context involves not the leavening impact of universal processes but, on the contrary, the calculated synthesis of cultural diversity in the form of differentiated regional innovation logics and capabilities.[39]

The new industrial space does not represent the demise of old, established metropolitan areas and the rising sun of new, high-tech regions. Nor can it be apprehended under the simplistic opposition between automation at the center and low-cost manufacturing at the periphery. It is organized in a hierarchy of innovation and fabrication articulated in global networks. But the direction and architecture of these networks are submitted to the endless changing movements of cooperation and competition between firms and between locales, sometimes historically cumulative, sometimes reversing the established pattern through deliberate institutional entrepreneurialism. What does remain as the characteristic logic of the new industrial location is its geographical discontinuity, paradoxically made up of territorial production complexes. The new industrial space is organized around flows of information that bring together and separate at the same time – depending upon cycles or firms, – their territorial components. And as the logic of information technology manufacturing trickles down from the producers of information technology devices to the users of such devices in the whole realm of manufacturing, so the new spatial logic expands, creating a multiplicity of global industrial networks whose intersections and exclusions transform the very notion of industrial location from factory sites to manufacturing flows.

[39] Gordon (1994: 46).

Everyday Life in the Electronic Cottage: the End of Cities?

The development of electronic communication and information systems allows for an increasing disassociation between spatial proximity and the performance of everyday life's functions: work, shopping, entertainment, healthcare, education, public services, governance, and the like. Accordingly, futurologists often predict the demise of the city, or at least of cities as we have known them until now, once they are voided of their functional necessity. Processes of spatial transformation are of course much more complicated, as history shows. Therefore, it is worthwhile to consider the scant empirical record on the matter.[40]

A dramatic increase of teleworking is the most usual assumption about the impact of information technology on cities, and the last hope for metropolitan transportation planners before surrendering to the inevitability of the mega-gridlock. Yet, in 1988, a leading European researcher on telecommuting could write, without the shadow of a joke, that "There are more people doing research on telework than there are actual teleworkers."[41] In fact, as pointed by Qvortup, the whole debate is biased by the lack of precision in defining telework, leading to considerable uncertainty when measuring the phenomenon.[42] After reviewing available evidence, he adequately distinguishes between three categories; (a) "Substitutors, those who substitute work done at home for work done in a traditional work setting." These are telecommuters in the strict sense; (b) self-employed, working on-line from their homes; (c) supplementers, "bringing supplementary work home from their conventional office." Furthermore, in some cases this "supplementary work" takes most of the working time; for example, according to Kraut,[43] in the case of university professors. By most reliable accounts the first category, telecommuters *stricto sensu* employed regularly to work on-line at home, is very small overall, and is not expected to grow substantially in the foreseeable future.[44] In the United States the highest estimates evaluated in 1991 about 5.5 million home-based telecommuters, but of this total only 16% telecommuted 35 hours or more per week, 25% telecommuted less than one day a week, with two days a week being

---

[40]   For sources on topics covered in this section, see Graham and Marvin (1996).
[41]   Steinle (1988:8).
[42]   Qvortup (1992:8).
[43]   Kraut (1989).
[44]   Rijn and Williams (eds) (1988); Nilles (1988); Huws et al. (1990).

the most common pattern. Thus, the percentage of workers who on any given day are telecommuting ranges, depending on estimates, between 1% and 2% of total labor force, with major metropolitan areas in California displaying the highest percentages.[45] On the other hand, what seems to be emerging is telecommuting from telecenters, that is networked computer facilities scattered in the suburbs of metropolitan areas for workers to work on-line with their companies.[46] If these trends are confirmed, homes would not become workplaces, but work activity could spread considerably throughout the metropolitan area, increasing urban decentralization. Increase of home work may also result as a form of electronic outworking by temporary workers, paid by the piece of information processing under an individualized subcontracting arrangement.[47] Interestingly enough, in the United States, a 1991 national survey showed that fewer than a half of home telecommuters used computers: the rest worked with a telephone, pen, and paper.[48] Examples of such activities are social workers and welfare fraud investigators in Los Angeles County.[49] What is certainly significant, and on the rise, is the development of self-employment, and of "supplementers," either full-time or part-time, as part of the broader trend toward the disaggregation of labor and the formation of virtual business networks, as indicated in previous chapters. This does not imply the end of the office, but the diversification of working sites for a large fraction of the population, and particularly for its most dynamic, professional segment. Increasingly mobile tele-computing equipment will enhance this trend toward the office-on-the-run, in the most literal sense.[50]

How do these tendencies affect cities? Scattered data seem to indicate that transportation problems will get worse, not better, because increasing activity and time compression allowed by new networking organization translate into higher concentration of markets in certain areas, and into greater physical mobility for a labor force that was previously confined to its working sites during working hours.[51] Work-related commuting time is kept at a steady level in the US metropolitan areas, not because of improved technology, but because of a more decentralized location pattern of jobs and residences that

[45] Mokhtarian (1991a, 1991b); Handy and Mokhtarian (1995).
[46] Mokhtarian (1991b).
[47] See Lozano (1989); Gurstein (1990).
[48] "Telecommuting Data form Link Resources Corporation", cited by Mokhtarian (1991b).
[49] Mokhtarian (1992:12).
[50] "The New Face of Business," in *Business Week* (1994a: 99ff).
[51] I have relied on a balanced evaluation of impacts by Vessali (1995).

allows easier, suburb-to-suburb traffic flows. In those cities, particularly in Europe, where a radioconcentric pattern still dominates daily commuting (such as Paris, Madrid, or Milan), commuting time is sharply up, particularly for stubborn automobile addicts.[52] As for the new, sprawling metropolises of Asia, their coming into the information age is parallel to their discovery of the most awesome traffic jams in history, from Bangkok to Shanghai.

Teleshopping is also slow to live up to its promise. While it is increasing in most countries, in fact it is mainly substituting for traditional mail catalog orders, rather than for actual presence in shopping malls and merchant streets. As with other on-line activities of everyday life, it supplements rather than replaces commercial areas.[53] A similar story can be told of most on-line consumer services. For instance, telebanking[54] is spreading fast, mainly under the impulse of banks interested in eliminating branch offices and replacing them by on-line customer services and automated teller machines. However, the consolidated bank branches continue as service centers, to sell financial products to their customers through a personalized relationship. Even on-line, cultural features of localities may be important as locational factors for information-oriented transactions. Thus, First Direct, the telephone banking branch of Midland Bank in Britain, located in Leeds because its research "showed West Yorkshire's plain accent, with its flat vowel sounds but clear diction and apparent classlessness, to be the most easily understood and acceptable throughout the UK – a vital element of any telephone-based business."[55] Thus, it is the system of branch office sellers, automated tellers, customer service-by-telephone, and on-line transactions that constitutes the new banking industry.

Health services offer an even more interesting case of the emerging dialectics between concentration and centralization of people-oriented services. On the one hand, expert systems, on-line communications, and high-resolution video transmission allow for the distant interconnection of medical care. For instance, in a practice that has become usual, if not yet routine, in 1995, highly skilled surgeons supervise by videoconference surgery performed at the other end of the country or of the world, literally guiding the less-expert hand of another surgeon into a human body. Regular health checks are also conducted via computer and telephone on the basis of patients' computerized, updated information. Neighborhood

---

[52] Cervero (1989, 1991); Bendixon (1991).
[53] Miles (1988); Schoonmaker (1993); Menotti (1995).
[54] Silverstone (1991); Castano (1991).
[55] Fazy (1995).

healthcare centers are backed by information systems to improve the
quality and efficiency of their primary-level attention. Yet, on
the other hand, in most countries major medical complexes emerge
in specific locales, generally in large metropolitan areas. Usually
organized around a big hospital, often connected to medical and
nursing schools, they include in their physical proximity private
clinics headed by the most prominent hospital doctors, radiology
centers, test laboratories, specialized pharmacists, and, not in-
frequently, gift shops and mortuaries, to cater to the whole range of
possibilities. Indeed, such medical complexes are a major economic
and cultural force in the areas and cities where they are located, and
tend to expand in their surrounding vicinity over time. When forced
to relocate, the whole complex moves together.[56]

Schools and universities are paradoxically the institutions least
affected by the virtual logic embedded in information technology, in
spite of the foreseeable quasi-universal use of computers in the classrooms of advanced countries. But they will hardly vanish into the
virtual space. In the case of elementary and secondary schools, this is
because they are as much childcare centers and/or children's warehouses as they are learning institutions. In the case of universities, this
is because the quality of education is still and will be for a long time,
associated with the intensity of face-to-face interaction. Thus, the
large-scale experiences of "distant universities," regardless of their
quality (bad in Spain, good in Britain), seem to show that they are
second-option forms of education which could play a significant role
in a future, enhanced system of adult education, but which could
hardly replace current higher education institutions.

On the other hand, computer-mediated communication is
diffusing around the world, although with an extremely uneven geography, as mentioned above in chapter 5. Thus, some segments of
societies across the globe, invariably concentrated in the upper
professional strata, interact with each other, reinforcing the social
dimension of the space of flows.[57]

There is no point in exhausting the list of empirical illustrations of
the actual impacts of information technology on the spatial dimension of everyday life. What emerges from different observations is a
similar picture of simultaneous spatial dispersion and concentration
via information technologies. People increasingly work and manage
services from their home, as the 1993 survey of the European
Foundation for the Improvement of Living Conditions shows.[58] Thus,

[56]   Lincoln et al. (1993); Moran (1990); Miller and Swensson (1995).
[57]   Batty and Barr (1994); Graham and Marvin (1996).
[58]   Moran (1993).

"home centeredness" is an important trend of the new society. Yet it does not mean the end of the city. Because workplaces, schools, medical complexes, consumer services outlets, recreational areas, commercial streets, shopping centers, sports stadiums, and parks still exist and will exist, and people will shuttle between all these places with increasing mobility precisely because of the newly acquired looseness of working arrangements and social networking: as time becomes more flexible, places become more singular, as people circulate among them in an increasingly mobile pattern.

However, the interaction between new information technology and current processes of social change does have a substantial impact on cities and space. On the one hand, the urban form is considerably transformed in its layout. But this transformation does not follow a single, universal pattern: it shows considerable variation depending upon the characteristics of historic, territorial, and institutional contexts. On the other hand, the emphasis on interactivity between places breaks up spatial patterns of behavior into a fluid network of exchanges that underlies the emergence of a new kind of space, the space of flows. On both counts, I must tighten the analysis and raise it to a more theoretical level.

The Transformation of Urban Form: the Informational City

The information age is ushering in a new urban form, the informational city. Yet, as the industrial city was not a worldwide replica of Manchester, the emerging informational city will not copy Silicon Valley, let alone Los Angeles. On the other hand, as in the industrial era, in spite of the extraordinary diversity of cultural and physical contexts there are some fundamental common features in the transcultural development of the informational city. I shall argue that, because of the nature of the new society, based upon knowledge, organized around networks, and partly made up of flows, the informational city is not a form but a process, a process characterized by the structural domination of the space of flows. Before developing this idea, I think it is first necessary to introduce the diversity of emerging urban forms in the new historical period, to counter a primitive technological vision that sees the world through the simplified lenses of endless freeways and fiber optic networks.

America's last suburban frontier

The image of a homogeneous, endless suburban/exurban sprawl as the city of the future is belied even by its unwilling model, Los Angeles, whose contradictory complexity is revealed by Mike Davis' marvelous *City of Quartz*.[59] Yet it does evoke a powerful trend in the relentless waves of suburban development in the American metropolis, West and South as well as North and East, toward the end of the millennium. Joel Garreau has captured the similarities of this spatial model across America in his journalistic account of the rise of *Edge City*, as the core of the new urbanization process. He empirically defines Edge City by the combination of five criteria:

> Edge City is any place that: a) Has five million square feet or more of leasable office space – the work place of the Information Age. . . b) Has 600,000 square feet or more of leasable retail space . . . c) Has more jobs than bedrooms. d) Is perceived by the population as one place . . . e) Was nothing like 'city' as recently as thirty years ago.

He reports the mushrooming of such places around Boston, New Jersey, Detroit, Atlanta, Phoenix, Texas, Southern California, San Francisco Bay Area, and Washington, D.C. They are both working areas and service centers around which mile after mile of increasingly dense, single-family dwelling residential units, organize the "home centeredness" of private life. He remarks that these exurban constellations are

> tied together not by locomotives and subways, but by freeways, jetways, and rooftop satellite dishes thirty feet across. Their characteristic monument is not a horse-mounted hero, but the atria reaching for the sun and shielding trees perpetually in leaf at the core of corporate headquarters, fitness centers, and shopping plazas. These new urban areas are marked not by the penthouses of the old urban rich or the tenements of the old urban poor. Instead, their landmark structure is the celebrated single-family detached dwelling, the suburban home with grass all around that made America the best housed civilization the world has ever known.[60]

Naturally, where Garreau sees the relentless frontier spirit of American culture, always creating new forms of life and space, James Howard Kunstler sees the regrettable domination of the "geography

---

[59]   Davis (1990).
[60]   Garreau (1991).

of nowhere,"[61] thus reigniting a decades-long debate between partisans and detractors of America's sharp spatial departure from its European ancestry. Yet, for the purpose of my analysis, I will retain just two major points of this debate.

First, the development of these loosely interrelated exurban constellations emphasizes the functional interdependence of different units and processes in a given urban system over very long distances, minimizing the role of territorial contiguity, and maximizing the communication networks in all their dimensions. Flows of exchange are at the core of the American Edge City.[62]

Second, this spatial form is indeed very specific to the American experience. Because, as Garreau acknowledges, it is embedded in a classic pattern of American history, always pushing for the endless search for a promised land in new settlements. While the extraordinary dynamism that this represents did indeed build one of the most vital nations in history, it did so at the price of creating, over time, staggering social and environmental problems. Each wave of social and physical escapism (for example, the abandonment of inner cities, leaving the lower social classes and ethnic minorities trapped in their ruins) deepened the crisis of American cities,[63] and made more difficult the management of an overextended infrastructure and of an overstressed society. Unless the development of private "jails-for-rent" in Western Texas is considered a welcome process to complement the social and physical disinvestment in American inner cities, the "fuite en avant" of American culture and space seems to have reached the limits of refusing to face unpleasant realities. Thus, the profile of America's Informational City is not fully represented by the "Edge City" phenomenon, but by the relationship between fast exurban development, inner-city decay, and obsolescence of the suburban built environment.[64]

European cities have entered the information age along a different line of spatial restructuring linked to their historical heritage, although finding new issues, not always dissimilar to those emerging in the American context.

---

[61] Kunstler (1993).
[62] See the collection of papers gathered in Caves (1994).
[63] Goldsmith and Blakely (1992).
[64] Fainstein et al. (eds) (1992); Gottdiener (1985).

The fading charm of European cities

A number of trends constitute together the new urban dynamics of major European metropolitan areas in the 1990s.[65]

The business center is, as in America, the economic engine of the city, networked in the global economy. The business center is made up of an infrastructure of telecommunications, communications, advanced services, and office space, based upon technology-generating centers and educational institutions. It thrives upon information processing and control functions. It is usually complemented by tourism and travel facilities. It is a node of the inter-metropolitan network.[66] Thus, the business center does not exist by itself but by its connection to other equivalent locales organized in a network that forms the actual unit of management, innovation, and work.[67]

The new managerial–technocratic–political elite does create exclusive spaces, as segregated and removed from the city at large as the bourgeois quarters of the industrial society, but, because the professional class is larger, on a much larger scale. In most European cities (Paris, Rome, Madrid, Amsterdam), unlike in America – if we except New York, the most un-American of US cities – the truly exclusive residential areas tend to appropriate urban culture and history, by locating in rehabilitated or well-preserved areas of the central city. By so doing, they emphasize the fact that when domination is clearly established and enforced (unlike in nouveau-riche America) the elite does not need to go into suburban exile to escape the populace. This trend is however limited in the case of the UK where the nostalgia for the life of the gentry in the countryside translates into up-scale residence in selected suburbs of metropolitan areas, sometimes urbanizing charming historic villages in the vicinity of a major city.

The suburban world of European cities is a socially diversified space, that is segmented in different peripheries around the central city. There are the traditional working-class suburbs, often organized around large, public housing estates, lately in home ownership. There are the new towns, French, British, or Swedish, inhabited by a younger population of the middle classes, whose age made it difficult for them to penetrate the housing market of the central city. And there are also the peripheral ghettos of older public housing estates, exemplified by Paris' La Courneuve, where new immigrant populations and poor

---

[65] For developments on European cities, see Hall (1995); Martinotti (1993); Borja et al. (eds) (1991); Siino (1994); Deben et al. (eds) (1993).
[66] Dunford and Kafkalas (eds) (1992); Robson (1992).
[67] Tarr and Dupuy (eds) (1988).

working families experience exclusion from their "right to the city." Suburbs are also the locus of manufacturing production in European cities, both for traditional manufacturing and for new, high-technology industries that locate in the newest and environmentally most desirable peripheries of metropolitan areas, close enough to the communication centers but removed from old industrial districts.

Central cities are still shaped by their history. Thus, traditional working-class neighborhoods, increasingly populated by service workers, constitute a distinctive space, a space that, because it is the most vulnerable, becomes the battleground between the redevelopment efforts of business and the upper middle class, and the invasion attempts of countercultures (Amsterdam, Copenhagen, Berlin) trying to reappropriate the use value of the city. Thus, they often become defensive spaces for workers who only have their home to fight for, being at the same time meaningful popular neighborhoods and likely bastions of xenophobia and localism.

The new professional middle class in Europe is torn between the attraction to the peaceful comfort of boring suburbs and the excitement of a hectic, and often too expensive, urban life. The trade-offs between the differential spatial patterns of work of dual-job families often determine the location of their household.

The central city, in Europe as well, is also the focus for the ghettos of immigrants. However, unlike American ghettos, most of these areas are not so economically deprived, because immigrant residents are generally workers, with strong family ties, thus counting on a very strong support structure that makes European ghettos family-oriented communities, unlikely to be taken over by street crime. England again seems exceptional in this regard, with some ethnic-minority neighborhoods in London (for example, Tower Hamlets, or Hackney) being closer to the American experience than to Paris' La Goutte d'Or. Paradoxically, it is in the core administrative and entertainment districts of European cities, be it Frankfurt or Barcelona, where urban marginality makes itself present. Its pervasive occupation of the busiest streets and public transportation nodal points is a survival strategy destined to be present, so that they can receive public attention or private business, be it welfare assistance, a drug transaction, a prostitution deal, or the customary police attention.

Major European metropolitan centres present some variation around the urban structure I have outlined, depending upon their differential role in the European network of cities. The lower their position in the new informational network, the greater the difficulty of their transition from the industrial stage, and the more traditional will be their urban structure, with old established neighborhoods and commercial quarters playing the determinant role in the dynamics of the city. On the other hand, the higher their position in the competitive structure of the new European economy, the greater the role of their advanced services in the business district, and the more intense will be the restructuring of urban space.

The critical factor in the new urban processes, in Europe as elsewhere, is the fact that urban space is increasingly differentiated in social terms, while being functionally interrelated beyond physical contiguity. It follows the separation between symbolic meaning, location of functions, and the social appropriation of space in the metropolitan area. This is the trend underlying the most important transformation of urban forms worldwide, with particular force in the newly industrializing areas: the rise of megacities.

Third millennium urbanization: megacities

The new global economy and the emerging informational society have indeed a new spatial form, which develops in a variety of social and geographical contexts: megacities.[68] Megacities are, certainly, very large agglomerations of human beings, all of them (13 in the United Nations classification) with over 10 million people in 1992 (see table 6.1 and figure 6.4), and four of them projected to be well over 20 million in 2010. But size is not their defining quality. They are the nodes of the global economy, concentrating the directional, productive, and managerial upper functions all over the planet; the control of the media; the real politics of power; and the symbolic capacity to create and diffuse messages. They have names, most of them alien to the still dominant European/North American cultural matrix: Tokyo, São Paulo, New York, Ciudad de Mexico, Shanghai, Bombay, Los Angeles, Buenos Aires, Seoul, Beijing, Rio de Janeiro, Calcutta, Osaka. In addition, Moscow, Jakarta, Cairo, New Delhi, London, Paris, Lagos, Dacca, Karachi, Tianjin, and possibly others, are in fact members of the club.[69] Not all of them (for example Dacca or Lagos) are dominant centers of the global economy, but they do connect to this global system huge segments of the human population. They also function as magnets for their hinterlands, that is the whole country or regional area where they are located. Megacities cannot be seen only in terms of their size, but as a function of their gravitational power toward major regions of the world. Thus, Hong

[68]   The notion of megacities has been popularized by several urban experts on the international arena, most notably by Janice Perlman, founder and director of the New York-based "Megacities Project." For a journalistic account of her vision, see *Time* (1993), which also offers basic data on the topic.

[69]   See Borja and Castells (1996).

Table 6.1   World's largest urban agglomerations, 1992

Rank	Agglomeration	Country	Population (millions)
1	Tokyo	Japan	25,772
2	São Paulo	Brazil	19,235
3	New York	United States of America	16,158
4	Mexico City	Mexico	15,276
5	Shanghai	China	14,053
6	Bombay	India	13,322
7	Los Angeles	United States of America	11,853
8	Buenos Aires	Argentina	11,753
9	Seoul	Republic of Korea	11,589
10	Beijing	China	11,433
11	Rio de Janeiro	Brazil	11,257
12	Calcutta	India	11,106
13	Isaka	Japan	10,535

Source: United Nations (1992).

Kong is not just its six million people, and Guangzhou is not just its six and a half million people: what is emerging is a megacity of 40 to 50 million people, connecting Hong Kong, Shenzhen, Guangzhou, Zhuhai, Macau, and small towns in the Pearl River Delta, as I shall develop below. Megacities articulate the global economy, link up the informational networks, and concentrate the world's power. But they are also the depositories of all these segments of the population who fight to survive, as well as of those groups who want to make visible their dereliction, so that they will not die ignored in areas bypassed by communication networks. Megacities concentrate the best and the worst, from the innovators and the powers that be to their structurally irrelevant people, ready to sell their irrelevance or to make "the others" pay for it. Yet what is most significant about megacities is that they are connected externally to global networks and to segments of their own countries, while internally disconnecting local populations that are either functionally unnecessary or socially disruptive. I argue that this is true of New York as well as of Mexico or Jakarta. **It is this distinctive feature of being globally connected and locally disconnected, physically and socially, that makes megacities a new urban form.** A form that is characterized by the functional linkages it establishes across vast expanses of territory, yet with a great deal of discontinuity in land use patterns. Megacities' functional and social hierarchies are spatially blurred and mixed, organized in retrenched encampments, and unevenly patched by unexpected pockets of

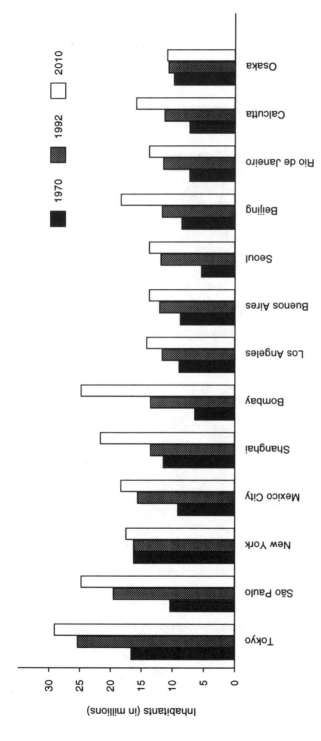

Figure 6.4 The world's largest urban agglomerations (> 10 million inhabitants in 1992)
Source: United Nations (1992).

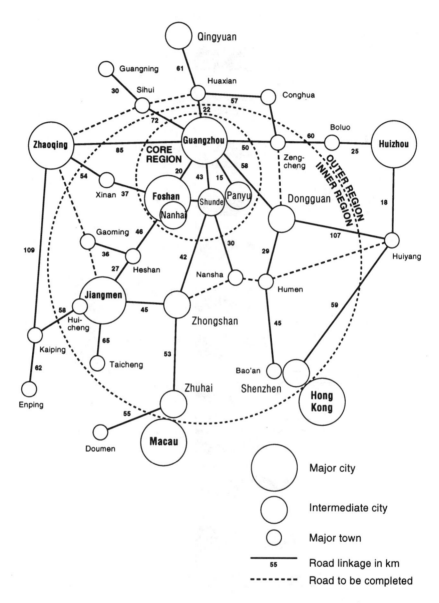

Figure 6.5 Diagrammatic representation of major nodes and links in
the urban region of the Pearl River Delta
Source: Elaborated by Woo (1994).

un-desirable uses. Megacities are discontinuous constellations of spatial fragments, functional pieces, and social segments.[70]

To illustrate my analysis I shall refer to a megacity in the making that is not even yet on the map but that, in my opinion, will be one of the preeminent industrial, business, and cultural centers of the twenty-first century, without indulging in futurology: the Hong Kong–Shenzhen–Canton–Pearl River Delta–Macau–Zhuhai metropolitan regional system.[71] Let us look at the mega-urban future from this vantage point (see figure 6.5). In 1995, this spatial system, still without a name, extended itself over 50,000 km², with a total population of between 40 and 50 million, depending on where boundaries are defined. Its units, scattered in a predominantly rural landscape, were functionally connected on a daily basis, and communicated through a multimodal transportation system that included railways, freeways, country roads, hovercrafts, boats, and planes. New super-highways were under construction, and the railway was being fully electrified and double-tracked. An optic fiber telecommunications system was in process of connecting the whole area internally and with the world, mainly via earth stations and cellular telephony. Five new airports were under construction in Hong Kong, Macau, Shenzhen, Zhuhai, and Guangzhou, with a projected passenger traffic capacity of 150 million per year. New container ports were also being built in North Lantau (Hong Kong), Yiantian (Shenzhen), Gaolan (Zhuhai), Huangpo (Guangzhou) and Macau, adding up to the world's largest port capacity in a given location. At the heart of such staggering metropolitan development are three interlinked phenomena:

1. The economic transformation of China, and its link-up to the global economy, with Hong Kong being one of the nodal points in such connection. Thus, in 1981–91, Guandong province's GDP grew at 12.8% per year in real terms. Hong Kong-based investors accounted at the end of 1993 for US$40 billion invested in China, representing two-thirds of total foreign direct investment. At the same time, China was also the largest foreign investor in Hong Kong, with about US$25 billion a year (compared with Japan's US$12.7 billion). The management of these capital flows was

[70] Mollenkopf and Castells (eds) (1991).
[71] My analysis on the emerging Southern China Metropolis is based, on the one hand, on my personal knowledge of the area, particularly of Hong Kong and Shenzhen, where I conducted research in the 1980s; on the other hand, particularly for developments in the 1990s, on a number of sources of which the most relevant are the following: Sit (1991); Hsing (1995); Lo (1994); Leung (1993); Ling (1995); Kwok and So (eds) (1995).

dependent upon the business transactions operated in, and inbetween, the various units of this metropolitan system. Thus, Guanghzou was the actual connecting point between Hong Kong business and the governments and enterprises not only of Guandong province, but of inland China.

2.   The restructuring of Hong Kong's economic basis in the 1990s led to a dramatic shrinkage of Hong Kong's traditional manufacturing basis, to be replaced by employment in advanced services. Thus, manufacturing workers in Hong Kong decreased from 837,000 in 1988 to 484,000 in 1993, while employees in trading and business sectors increased, in the same period, from 947,000 to 1.3 million. Hong Kong developed its functions as a global business center.

3.   However, Hong Kong's manufacturing exports capacity did not fade away: it simply modified its industrial organization and its spatial location. In about ten years, between the mid-1980s and the mid-1990s, Hong Kong's industrialists induced one of the largest-scale processes of industrialization in human history in the small towns of the Pearl River Delta. By the end of 1994, Hong Kong investors, often using family and village connections, had established in the Pearl River Delta 10,000 joint ventures and 20,000 processing factories, in which were working about 6 million workers, depending upon various estimates. Much of this population, housed in company dormitories in semi-rural locations, came from surrounding provinces beyond the borders of Guandong. This gigantic industrial system was being managed on a daily basis from a multilayered managerial structure, based in Hong Kong, regularly traveling to Guangzhou, with production runs being supervised by local managers throughout the rural area. Materials, technology, and managers were being sent from Hong Kong and Shenzhen, and manufactured goods were generally exported from Hong Kong (actually surpassing the value of Hong Kong-made exports), although the building of new container ports in Yiantian and Gaolan aimed at diversifying export sites.

This accelerated process of export-oriented industrialization and business linkages between China and the global economy led to an unprecedented urban explosion. Shenzhen Special Economic Zone, on the Hong Kong border, grew from zero to 1.5 million inhabitants between 1982 and 1995. Local governments in the whole area, full of cash from overseas Chinese investors, embarked on the construction of major infrastructural projects, the most amazing of which, still in the planning stage at the time of this writing, was the decision by

Zhuhai's local government to build a 60 km bridge over the South China Sea to link by road Zhuhai and Hong Kong.

The Southern China Metropolis, still in the making but a sure reality, is a new spatial form. It is not the traditional Megalopolis identified by Gottman in the 1960s on the north-eastern seaboard of the United States. Unlike this classical case, the Hong Kong–Guandong metropolitan region is not made up of the physical conurbation of successive urban/suburban units with relative functional autonomy in each one of them. It is rapidly becoming an interdependent unit, economically, functionally, and socially, and it will be even more so after Hong Kong becomes formally part of China in 1997, with Macau joining the flag in 1999. But there is considerable spatial discontinuity within the area, with rural settlements, agricultural land, and undeveloped areas separating urban centers, and industrial factories being scattered all over the region. The internal linkages of the area and the indispensable connection of the whole system to the global economy via multiple communication links are the real backbone of this new spatial unit. Flows define the spatial form and processes. Within each city, within each area, processes of segregation and segmentation take place, in a pattern of endless variation. But such segmented diversity is dependent upon a functional unity marked by gigantic, technology-intensive infrastructures, which seem to know as their only limit the amount of fresh water that the region can still retrieve from the East River area. The Southern China Metropolis, only vaguely perceived in most of the world at this time, is likely to become the most representative urban face of the twenty-first century.

Current trends point in the direction of another Asian megacity on an even greater scale when, in the early twenty-first century, the corridor Tokyo–Yokohama–Nagoya (already a functional unit) links up with Osaka–Kobe–Kyoto, creating the largest metropolitan agglomeration in human history, not only in terms of population, but in economic and technological power.

Thus, in spite of all their social, urban and environmental problems, megacities will continue to grow, both in their size and in their attractiveness for the location of high-level functions and for people's choice. The ecological dream of small, quasi-rural communes will be pushed away to countercultural marginality by the historical tide of megacity development. This is because megacities are:

a) centers of economic, technological, and social dynamism, in their countries and on a global scale. They are the actual development engines. Their countries' economic fate, be it the United States

or China, depends on megacities' performance, in spite of the small-town ideology still pervasive in both countries;
b) they are centers of cultural and political innovation;
c) they are the connecting points to the global networks of every kind. Internet cannot bypass megacities: it depends on the telecommunications and on the "telecommunicators" located in those centers.

To be sure, some factors will slow down their pace of growth, depending on the accuracy and effectiveness of policies designed to limit megacities' growth. Family planning is working, in spite of the Vatican, so we can expect a continuation of the decline in the birthrate already taking place. Policies of regional development may be able to diversify the concentration of jobs and population to other areas. And I foresee large-scale epidemics, and disintegration of social control that will make megacities less attractive. However, overall, megacities will grow in size and dominance, because they keep feeding themselves on population, wealth, power, and innovators, from their extended hinterland. Furthermore, they are the nodal points connecting to the global networks. Thus, in a fundamental sense, the future of humankind, and of each megacity's country, is being played out in the evolution and management of these areas. Megacities are the nodal points, and the power centers of the new spatial form/process of the information age: the space of flows.

Having laid out the empirical landscape of new territorial phenomena, we now have to come to grips with the understanding of such a new spatial reality. This requires an unavoidable excursus through the uncertain trails of the theory of space.

The Social Theory of Space and the Theory of the Space of Flows

Space is the expression of society. Since our societies are undergoing structural transformation, it is a reasonable hypothesis to suggest that new spatial forms and processes are currently emerging. The purpose of the analysis presented here is to identify the new logic underlying such forms and processes.

The task is not an easy one, because the apparently simple acknowledgement of a meaningful relationship between society and space hides a fundamental complexity. This is because space is not a reflection of society, it is its expression. In other words: space is not a photocopy of society, it is society. Spatial forms and processes are formed by the dynamics of the overall social structure. This includes contradictory trends derived from conflicts and strategies between social actors playing out their opposing interests and values. Furthermore, social processes influence space by acting on the built environment inherited from previous socio-spatial structures. Indeed, **space is crystallized time**. To approach in the simplest possible terms such a complexity, let us proceed step by step.

What is space? In physics, it cannot be defined outside the dynamics of matter. In social theory it cannot be defined without reference to social practices. This area of theorizing being one of my old trades, I still approach the issue under the assumption that "space is a material product, in relationship to other material products – including people – who engage in [historically] determined social relationships that provide space with a form, a function, and a social meaning."[72] In a convergent and clearer formulation, David Harvey, in his recent book *The Condition of Postmodernity*, states that

> from a materialist perspective, we can argue that objective conceptions of time and space are necessarily created through material practices and processes which serve to reproduce social life . . . It is a fundamental axiom of my enquiry that time and space cannot be understood independently of social action.[73]

Thus, we have to define, at a general level, what space is, from the point of view of social practices; then, we must identify the historical specificity of social practices, for example those in the informational society that underlie the emergence and consolidation of new spatial forms and processes.

From the point of view of social theory, **space is the material support of time-sharing social practices**. I immediately add that any material support bears always a symbolic meaning. By time-sharing social practices I refer to the fact that space brings together those practices that are simultaneous in time. It is the material articulation of this simultaneity that gives sense to space *vis-à-vis* society. Traditionally, this notion was assimilated to contiguity. Yet it is fundamental that we separate the basic concept of material support of simultaneous practices from the notion of contiguity, in order to account for the possible existence of material supports of simultaneity that do not rely on physical contiguity, since this is precisely the case of the dominant social practices of the information age.

I have argued in the preceding chapters that our society is

---

[72] Castells (1972: 152) (my own translation).
[73] Harvey (1990: 204).

constructed around flows: flows of capital, flows of information, flows of technology, flows of organizational interaction, flows of images, sounds, and symbols. Flows are not just one element of the social organization: they are the expression of processes *dominating* our economic, political, and symbolic life. If such is the case, the material support of the dominant processes in our societies will be the ensemble of elements supporting such flows, and making materially possible their articulation in simultaneous time. Thus, I propose the idea that there is a new spatial form characteristic of social practices that dominate and shape the network society: the space of flows. **The space of flows is the material organization of time-sharing social practices that work through flows.** By flows I understand purposeful, repetitive, programmable sequences of exchange and interaction between physically disjointed positions held by social actors in the economic, political, and symbolic structures of society. Dominant social practices are those which are embedded in dominant social structures. By dominant structures I understand those arrangements of organizations and institutions whose internal logic plays a strategic role in shaping social practices and social consciousness for society at large.

The abstraction of the concept of the space of flows can be better understood by specifying its content. The space of flows, as the material form of support of dominant processes and functions in the informational society, can be described (rather than defined) by the combination of at least three layers of material supports that, together, constitute the space of flows. **The first layer, the first material support of the space of flows, is actually constituted by a circuit of electronic impulses** (microelectronics, telecommunications, computer processing, broadcasting systems, and high-speed transportation – also based on information technologies) that, together, form the material basis for the processes we have observed as being strategically crucial in the network of society. This is indeed a material support of simultaneous practices. Thus, it is a spatial form, just as it could be "the city" or "the region" in the organization of the merchant society or of the industrial society. The spatial articulation of dominant functions does take place in our societies in the network of interactions made possible by information technology devices. In this network, no place exists by itself, since the positions are defined by flows. Thus, the network of communication is the fundamental spatial configuration: places do not disappear, but their logic and their meaning become absorbed in the network. The technological infrastructure that builds up the network defines the new space, very much like railways defined "economic regions" and "national markets" in the industrial economy; or the boundary-specific, institutional rules of citizenry (and their technologically advanced armies) defined "cities" in the merchant origins of capitalism and democracy. This technological infrastructure is itself the expression of the network of flows whose architecture and content is determined by the powers that be in our world.

The second layer of the space of flows is constituted by its nodes and hubs. The space of flows is not placeless, although its structural logic is. It is based on an electronic network, but this network links up specific places, with well-defined social, cultural, physical, and functional characteristics. Some places are exchangers, communication hubs playing a role of coordination for the smooth interaction of all the elements integrated into the network. Other places are the nodes of the network, that is the location of strategically important functions that build a series of locality-based activities and organizations around a key function in the network. Location in the node links up the locality with the whole network. Both nodes and hubs are hierarchically organized according to their relative weight in the network. But such hierarchy may change depending upon the evolution of activities processed through the network. Indeed, in some instances, some places may be switched off the network, their disconnection resulting in instant decline, and thus in economic, social and physical deterioration. The characteristics of nodes are dependent upon the type of functions performed by a given network.

Some examples of networks, and their corresponding nodes, will help to communicate the concept. The easiest type of network to visualize as representative of the space of flows is the network constituted by decision-making systems of the global economy, particularly those relative to the financial system. This refers to the analysis of the global city as a process rather than a place, as presented in this chapter. The analysis of the "global city" as the production site of the informational, global economy has shown the critical role of these global cities in our societies, and the dependence of local societies and economies upon the directional functions located in such cities. But beyond the main global cities, other continental, national, and regional economies have their own nodes that connect to the global network. Each one of these nodes requires an adequate technological infrastructure, a system of ancillary firms providing the support services, a specialized labor market, and the system of services required by the professional labor force.

As I showed above, what is true for top managerial functions and financial markets is also applicable to high-technology manufacturing (both to industries producing high technology and to those using high technology, that is all advanced manufacturing). The spatial division of labor that characterizes high-technology manufacturing

translates into the worldwide connection between the milieux of innovation, the skilled manufacturing sites, the assembly lines, and the
market-oriented factories, with a series of intra-firm linkages between
the different operations in different locations along the production
lines; and another series of inter-firm linkages among similar functions of production located in specific sites that become production
complexes. Directional nodes, production sites and communication
hubs are defined along the network and articulated in a common
logic by communication technologies and programmable, micro-
electronic-based, flexible integrated manufacturing.

The functions to be fulfilled by each network define the characteristics of places that become their privileged nodes. In some cases, the
most unlikely sites become central nodes because of historical
specificity that ended up centering a given network around a particular locality. For instance, it was unlikely that Rochester, Minnesota,
or the Parisian suburb of Villejuif would become central nodes of a
world network of advanced medical treatment and health research,
in close interaction with each other. But the location of the Mayo
Clinic at Rochester and of one of the main centers for cancer treatment of the French Health Administration at Villejuif, in both cases
for accidental, historical reasons, have articulated a complex of knowledge generation and advanced medical treatment around these two
odd locales. Once established they attracted researchers, doctors, and
patients from around the world: they became a node in the world's
medical network.

Each network defines its sites according to the functions and
hierarchy of each site, and to the characteristics of the product or
service to be processed in the network. Thus, one of the most powerful
networks in our society, narcotics production and distribution
(including its money-laundering component), has constructed a
specific geography that has redefined the meaning, structure, and
culture of societies, regions, and cities connected in the network.[74]
Thus, in cocaine production and trade, the coca production sites of
Chapare or Alto Beni in Bolivia or Alto Huallanga in Peru are
connected to the refineries and management centers in Colombia,
which were subsidiary, until 1995, to the Medellin or Cali headquarters, themselves connected to financial centers such as Miami,
Panama, the Cayman Islands, and Luxembourg, and to transportation centers, such as the Tamaulipas or Tijuana drug traffic networks
in Mexico, then finally to distribution points in the main metropolitan
areas of America and Western Europe. None of these localities can
exist by itself in such network. The Medellin and Cali cartels, and their

[74] Arrieta et al. (1991); Laserna (1995).

close American and Italian allies, would soon be out of business without the raw materials produced in Bolivia or Peru, without the chemicals (precursors) provided by Swiss and German laboratories, without the semi-legal financial networks of free-banking paradises, and without the distribution networks starting in Miami, Los Angeles, New York, Amsterdam or La Coruña.

Therefore, while the analysis of global cities provides the most direct illustration of the place-based orientation of the space of flows in nodes and hubs, this logic is not limited by any means to capital flows. The main dominant processes in our society are articulated in networks that link up different places and assign to each one of them a role and a weight in a hierarchy of wealth generation, information processing, and power making that ultimately conditions the fate of each locale.

The third important layer of the space of flows refers to the spatial organization of the dominant, managerial elites (rather than classes) that exercise the directional functions around which such space is articulated. The theory of the space of flows starts from the implicit assumption that societies are asymmetrically organized around the dominant interests specific to each social structure. The space of flows is not the only spatial logic of our societies. It is, however, the dominant spatial logic because it is the spatial logic of the dominant interests/functions in our society. But such domination is not purely structural. It is enacted, indeed conceived, decided, and implemented by social actors. Thus, the technocratic–financial–managerial elite that occupies the leading positions in our societies will also have specific spatial requirements regarding the material/spatial support of their interests and practices. The spatial manifestation of the informational elite constitutes another fundamental dimension of the space of flows. What is this spatial manifestation?

The fundamental form of domination in our society is based on the organizational capacity of the dominant elite that goes hand in hand with its capacity to disorganize those groups in society which, while constituting a numerical majority, see their interests partially (if ever) represented only within the framework of the fulfillment of the dominant interests. Articulation of the elites, segmentation and disorganization of the masses seem to be the twin mechanisms of social domination in our societies.[75] Space plays a fundamental role in this mechanism. In short: elites are cosmopolitan, people are local. The space of power and wealth is projected throughout the world, while people's life and experience is rooted in places, in their culture,

---

[75] See Zukin (1992).

in their history. Thus, the more a social organization is based upon ahistorical flows, superseding the logic of any specific place, the more the logic of global power escapes the socio-political control of historically specific local/national societies.

On the other hand, the elites do not want and cannot become flows themselves, if they are to preserve their social cohesion, develop the set of rules and the cultural codes by which they can understand each other and dominate the others, thus establishing the "in" and "out" boundaries of their cultural/political community. The more a society is democratic in its institutions, the more the elites have to become clearly distinct from the populace, so avoiding the excessive penetration of political representatives into the inner world of strategic decision-making. However, my analysis does not share the hypothesis about the improbable existence of a "power elite" *à la* Wright Mills. On the contrary, the real social domination stems from the fact that cultural codes are embedded in the social structure in such a way that the possession of these codes opens the access to the power structure without the elite needing to conspire to bar access to its networks.

The spatial manifestation of such logic of domination takes two main forms in the space of flows. On the one hand, the elites form their own society, and constitute symbolically secluded communities, retrenched behind the very material barrier of real estate pricing. They define their community as a spatially bound, interpersonally networked subculture. I propose the hypothesis that the space of flows is made up of personal micro-networks that project their interests in functional macro-networks throughout the global set of interactions in the space of flows. This is a well-known phenomenon in the financial networks: major strategic decisions are taken over business luncheons in exclusive restaurants, or in country house week-ends over golf playing, as in the good old times. But such decisions will be executed in instant decision-making processes over telecommunicated computers which can trigger their own decisions to react to market trends. Thus, the nodes of the space of flows include residential and leisure-oriented spaces which, along with the location of headquarters and their ancillary services, tend to cluster dominant functions in carefully segregated spaces, with easy access to cosmopolitan complexes of arts, culture, and entertainment. Segregation happens both by location in different places and by security control of certain spaces open only to the elite. From the pinnacles of power and their cultural centers, a series of symbolic socio-spatial hierarchies are organized, so that lower levels of management can mirror the symbols of power and appropriate such symbols by constructing second-order spatial communities that will also tend to isolate themselves from the rest of society, in a succession of hierarchical segregation processes that, together, are tantamount to socio-spatial fragmentation.

A second major trend of cultural distinctiveness of the elites in the informational society is to create a lifestyle and to design spatial forms aimed at unifying the symbolic environment of the elite around the world, thus superseding the historical specificity of each locale. Thus, there is the construction of a (relatively) secluded space across the world along the connecting lines of the space of flows: international hotels whose decoration, from the design of the room to the color of the towels, is similar all over the world to create a sense of familiarity with the inner world, while inducing abstraction from the surrounding world; airports' VIP lounges, designed to maintain the distance *vis-à-vis* society in the highways of the space of flows; mobile, personal, on-line access to telecommunications networks, so that the traveler is never lost; and a system of travel arrangements, secretarial services, and reciprocal hosting that maintains a close circle of the corporate elite together through the worshipping of similar rites in all countries. Furthermore, there is an increasingly homogeneous lifestyle among the information elite that transcends the cultural borders of all societies: the regular use of SPA installations (even when traveling), and the practice of jogging; the mandatory diet of grilled salmon and green salad, with *udon* and *sashimi* providing a Japanese functional equivalent; the "pale chamois" wall color intended to create the cozy atmosphere of the inner space; the ubiquitous laptop computer; the combination of business suits and sportswear; the unisex dressing style, and so on. All these are symbols of an international culture whose identity is not linked to any specific society but to membership in the managerial circles of the informational economy across a global cultural spectrum.

The call for cultural connectedness of the space of flows between its different nodes is also reflected in the tendency toward the architectural uniformity of the new directional centers in various societies. Paradoxically, the attempt by postmodern architecture to break the molds and patterns of architectural discipline has resulted in an over-imposed postmodern monumentality which became the generalized rule of new corporate headquarters from New York to Kaoshiung during the 1980s. Thus, the space of flows includes the symbolic connection of homogeneous architecture in the places that constitute the nodes of each network across the world, so that architecture escapes from the history and culture of each society and becomes captured into the new imaginary, wonderland world of unlimited possibilities that underlies the logic transmitted by multimedia: the culture of electronic surfing, as if we could reinvent all forms in any place, on the sole condition of leaping into the cultural indefinition of the flows of power. The enclosure of architecture into a historical abstraction is the formal frontier of the space of flows.

The Architecture of the End of History

Nomada, sigo siendo un nomada.   Ricardo Bofill[76]

If the space of flows is truly the dominant spatial form of the network society, architecture and design are likely to be redefined in their form, function, process, and value in the coming years. Indeed, I would argue that all over history, architecture has been the "failed act" of society, the mediated expression of the deeper tendencies of society, of those that could not be openly declared but yet were strong enough to be cast in stone, in concrete, in steel, in glass, and in the visual perception of the human beings who were to dwell, deal, or worship in such forms.

Panofsky on the Gothic cathedrals, Tafuri on the American skyscrapers, Venturi on the surprisingly kitsch American city, Lynch on city images, Harvey on postmodernism as the expression of time/space compression by capitalism, are some of the best illustrations of an intellectual tradition that has used the forms of the built environment as one of the most signifying codes to read the basic structures of society's dominant values.[77] To be sure, there is no simple, direct interpretation of the formal expression of social values. But as research by scholars and analysts has revealed, and as works by architects have demonstrated, there has always been a strong, semiconscious connection between what society (in its diversity) was saying and what architects wanted to say.[78]

Not any more. My hypothesis is that the coming of the space of flows is blurring the meaningful relationship between architecture and society. Because the spatial manifestation of the dominant interests takes place around the world, and across cultures, the uprooting of experience, history, and specific culture as the background of meaning is leading to the generalization of ahistorical, acultural architecture.

[76]   Opening statement of Ricardo Bofill's architectural autobiography, *Espacio y Vida* (Bofill 1990).
[77]   Panofsky (1957); Tafuri (1971); Venturi et al. (1977); Lynch (1960); Harvey (1990).
[78]   See Burlen (1972).

Figure 6.6   Downtown Kaoshiung (photograph: Professor Hsia
Chu-joe)

Some tendencies of "postmodern architecture," as represented for instance by the works of Philip Johnson or Charles Moore, under the pretext of breaking down the tyranny of codes, such as modernism, attempt to cut off all ties with specific social environments. So did modernism in its time, but as the expression of a historically rooted culture that asserted the belief in progress, technology and rationality. In contrast, postmodern architecture declares the end of all systems of meaning. It creates a mixture of elements that searches formal harmony out of transhistorical, stylistic provocation. Irony becomes the preferred mode of expression. Yet, in fact what most postmodernism does is to express, in almost direct terms, the new dominant ideology: the end of history and the supersession of places in the space of flows.[79] Because only if we are at the end of history can we now mix up everything we knew before (see figure 6.6: Downtown Kaoshiung). Because we do not belong any longer to any place, to any culture, the extreme version of postmodernism imposes its codified code-breaking logic anywhere something is built. The liberation from cultural codes hides in fact the escape from historically rooted

[79]   I find my own understanding of postmodernism and postmodern architecture very close to David Harvey's analysis. But I shall not take responsibility for using his work in support of my position.

Figure 6.7   The entrance hall of Barcelona airport.
Source: Original drawing by Ricardo Bofill; reproduced by kind
permission of Ricardo Bofill.

societies. In this perspective, postmodernism could be considered the architecture of the space of flows.[80]

The more that societies try to recover their identity beyond the global logic of uncontrolled power of flows, the more they need an architecture that exposes their own reality, without faking beauty from a transhistorical spatial repertoire. But at the same time, over-significant architecture, trying to give a very definite message or to express directly the codes of a given culture, is too primitive a form to be able to penetrate our saturated visual imaginary. The meaning of its messages will be lost in the culture of "surfing" that characterizes our symbolic behavior. This is why, paradoxically, the architecture that seems most charged with meaning in societies shaped by the logic of the space of flows is what I call "the architecture of nudity." That is, the architecture whose forms are so neutral, so pure, so diaphanous, that they do not pretend to say anything. And by not saying anything they confront the experience with the solitude of the space of flows. Its message is the silence.

For the sake of communication, I shall use two examples drawn from Spanish architecture, an architectural milieu that is widely

---

[80]   For a balanced, intelligent discussion of the social meaning of postmodern architecture, see Kolb (1990); for a broader discussion of the interaction between globalization/informationalization processes and architecture, see Saunders, (ed.) (1996).

recognized as being currently at the forefront of design. Both concern, not by accident, the design of major communication nodes, where the space of flows materializes ephemerally. The Spanish festivities of 1992 provided the occasion for the construction of major functional buildings designed by some of the best architects. Thus, the new Barcelona airport, designed by Bofill, simply combines beautiful marble floor, dark glass facade, and transparent glass separating panels in an immense, open space (see figure 6.7). No cover up of the fear and anxiety that people experience in an airport. No carpeting, no cozy rooms, no indirect lighting. In the middle of the cold beauty of this airport passengers have to face their terrible truth: they are alone, in the middle of the space of flows, they may lose their connection, they are suspended in the emptiness of transition. They are, literally, in the hands of Iberia Airlines. And there is no escape.

Let us take another example: the new Madrid AVE (high speed train) station, designed by Rafael Moneo. It is simply a wonderful old station, exquisitely rehabilitated, and made into an indoor palm-tree park, full of birds that sing and fly in the enclosed space of the station. In a nearby structure, adjacent to such a beautiful, monumental space, there is the real station with the high-speed train. Thus, people go to the pseudo-station, to visit it, to walk through its different levels and paths, as they go to a park or a museum. The too-obvious message is that we are in a park, not in a station; that in the old station, trees grew, and birds nested, operating a metamorphosis. Thus, the high-speed train becomes the oddity in this space. And this is in fact the question everybody in the world asks: what is a high-speed train doing there, just to go from Madrid to Seville, with no connection whatsoever with the European high-speed network, at a cost of US$4 billion? The broken mirror of a segment of the space of flows becomes exposed, and the use value of the station recovered, in a simple, elegant design that does not say much but makes everything evident.

Some prominent architects, such as Rem Koolhas, the designer of the Lille Grand Palais Convention Center, theorize the need to adapt architecture to the process of de-localization, and to the relevance of communication nodes in people's experience: Koolhas actually sees his project as an expression of the "space of flows." Or, in another instance of a growing self-awareness of architects about the structural transformation of space, the American Institute of Architects' award-winning design of D.E. Shaw & Company's offices by Steven Holl in New York's West 45th Street

> offers – in Herbert Muschamp's words – a poetic interpretation of . . . the space of flows. . . . Mr Holl's design takes the Shaw offices to a place as novel as the information technology that

Figure 6.8   The waiting room at D.E. Shaw & Company: no ficus
trees, no sectional sofas, no corporate art on the walls
Source: Muschamp (1992).

paid to build them. When we walk in the door of D.E. Shaw [see
figure 6.8] we know we are not in 1960s Manhattan or Colonial
New England. For that matter, we have left even much of present
day New York far below on the ground. Standing inside the Holl
atrium we have got our head in the clouds and our feet firmly
planted on solid air.[81]

Granted we may be forcing Bofill, Moneo, and even Holl into discourses that are not theirs.[82] But the simple fact that their

[81]   Muschamp (1992).
[82]   For Bofill's own interpretation of the Barcelona airport (whose formal
antecedent, I believe, is in his design of Paris' Marché St Honoré), see his book
(Bofill 1990). However, in a long personal conversation, after reading the draft
of my analysis, he did not disagree with my interpretation of the project of an
"architecture of nudity," although he conceived it rather as an innovative attempt
to bring together high-tech and classic design. We both agreed that the new architectural monuments of our epoch are likely to be built as "communication
exchangers" (airports, train stations, intermodal transfer areas, telecommunication infrastructures, harbors, and computerized trading centers).

architecture would allow me, or Herbert Muschamp, to relate forms to symbols, to functions, to social situations, means that their strict, retained architecture (in rather formally different styles) is in fact full of meaning. Indeed, architecture and design, because their forms either resist or interpret the abstract materiality of the dominant space of flows, could become essential devices of cultural innovation and intellectual autonomy in the informational society through two main avenues. Either the new architecture builds the palaces of the new masters, thus exposing their deformity hidden behind the abstraction of the space of flows; or it roots itself into places, thus into culture, and into people.[83] In both cases, under different forms, architecture and design may be digging the trenches of resistance for the preservation of meaning in the generation of knowledge. Or, what is the same, for the reconciliation of culture and technology.

Space of Flows and Space of Places

The space of flows does not permeate down to the whole realm of human experience in the network society. Indeed, the overwhelming majority of people, in advanced and traditional societies alike, live in places, and so they perceive their space as place-based. **A place is a locale whose form, function and meaning are self-contained within the boundaries of physical contiguity.** A place, to illustrate my argument, is the Parisian *quartier* of Belleville.

Belleville was, as for so many immigrants throughout its history, my entry point to Paris, in 1962. As a 20-year-old political exile, without much to lose except my revolutionary ideals, I was given shelter by a Spanish construction worker, an anarchist union leader, who introduced me to the tradition of the place. Nine years later, this time as a sociologist, I was still walking Belleville, working with immigrant workers' committees, and studying social movements against urban renewal: the struggles of what I labeled "*La Cité du Peuple*," reported in my first book.[84] Thirty years after our first encounter, both Belleville and I have changed. But Belleville is still a place, while I am afraid I look more like a flow. The new immigrants (Asians, Yugoslavs) have joined a long-established stream of Tunisian Jews, Maghrebian Muslims, and Southern Europeans, themselves the successors of the intra-urban exiles pushed into Belleville in the nineteenth century by

[83] For a useful debate on the matter, see Lillyman et al. (eds) (1994).
[84] Castells (1972: 496ff).

Figure 6.9 An Urban Place: Rambla de les Flors, Barcelona, 1996,
Photograph by Olga Torres.

the Hausmannian design of building a bourgeois Paris. Belleville itself
has been hit by several waves of urban renewal, intensified in the
1970s.[85] Its traditional physical landscape of a poor but harmonious
historic *faubourg* has been messed up with plastic postmodernism,
cheap modernism, and sanitized gardens on top of a still somewhat
dilapidated housing stock. And yet, Belleville in 1995 is a clearly identifiable place, both from the outside and from the inside. Ethnic
communities that often degenerate in hostility toward each other
coexist peacefully in Belleville, although keeping track of their own
turf, and certainly not without tensions. New middle-class households,
generally young, have joined the neighborhood because of its urban
vitality, and powerfully contribute to its survival, while self-controlling
the impacts of gentrification. Cultures and histories, in a truly plural
urbanity, interact in the space, giving meaning to it, linking up with
the "city of collective memory," *à la* Christine Boyer.[86] The landscape
pattern swallows and digests substantial physical modifications, by
integrating them in its mixed uses and active street life. Yet Belleville

[85] For an updated social and spatial, illustrated history of Belleville, see the
delightful book: Morier (ed.) (1994); on urban renewal in Paris in the 1970s, see
Godard et al. (1973).
[86] Boyer (1994).

is by no means the idealized version of the lost community, which probably never existed, as Oscar Lewis demonstrated in his revisit of Tepoztlan. Places are not necessarily communities, although they may contribute to community-building. But the life of their inhabitants is marked by their characteristics, so they are indeed good and bad places depending on the value judgement of what a good life is. In Belleville, its dwellers, without loving each other, and while certainly not being loved by the police, have constructed throughout history a meaningful, interacting space, with a diversity of uses and a wide range of functions and expressions. They actively interact with their daily physical environment. In between home and the world, there is a place called Belleville.

Not all places are socially interactive and spatially rich. It is precisely because their physical/symbolic qualities make them different that they are places. Thus Allan Jacobs, in his great book about "great streets".[87] examines the difference in urban quality between Barcelona and Irvine (the epitome of suburban Southern California) on the basis of the number and frequency of intersections in the street pattern: his findings go even beyond what any informed urbanist could imagine (see figures 6.10 and 6.11). So Irvine is indeed a place, although a special kind of place, where the space of experience shrinks inward toward the home, as flows take over increasing shares of time and space.

The relationships between the space of flows and the space of places, between simultaneous globalization and localization are not predetermined in their outcome. For instance, Tokyo has undergone a substantial process of urban restructuring during the 1980s, to live up to its role as "a global city," a process fully documented by Machimura. The city government, sensitive to the deep-seated Japanese fear about the loss of identity, added to its business-oriented restructuring policy an image-making policy of singing the virtues of old Edo, Pre-Meiji Tokyo. A historical museum (*Edo-Tokyo Hakubutsakan*) was opened in 1993, a public relations magazine was published, exhibitions regularly organized. As Machimura writes:

> Although these views seem to go in totally different directions, both of them seek for redefinition of the Westernized image of the city in more domestic ways. Now, "Japanization" of the Westernized city provides an important context for the discourse about "global city" Tokyo after modernism.[88]

[87] Jacobs (1994).
[88] Machimura (1995:16). See his book on the social and political forces underlying the restructuring of Tokyo: Machimura (1994).

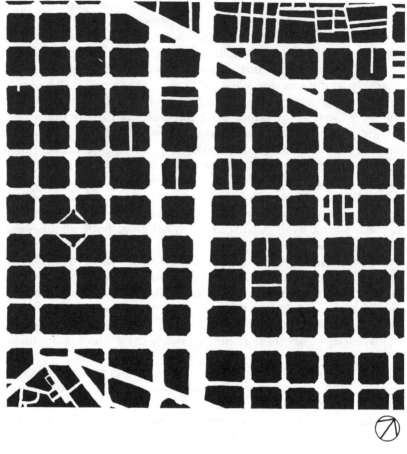

Figure 6.10   Barcelona: Paseo de Gracia
Source: Jacobs (1993).

Yet Tokyo citizens were not complaining just about the loss of historical essence, but about the reduction of their everyday life's space to
the instrumental logic of the global city. A project symbolized this
logic: the celebration of a World City Fair in 1997, a good occasion to
build another, major business complex on reclaimed land in Tokyo
Harbor. Large construction companies happily obliged, and work was

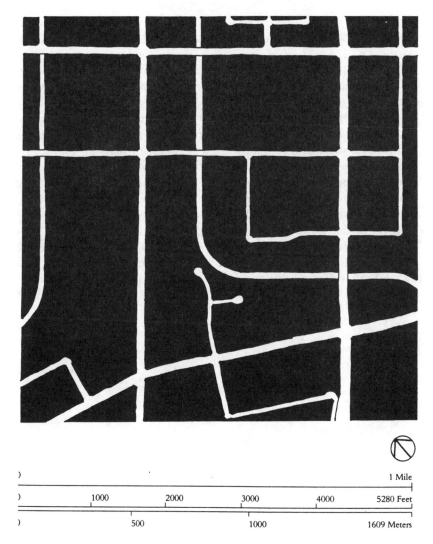

Figure 6.11   Irvine, California: business complex
Source: Jacobs (1993).

well under way in 1995. Suddenly, in the 1995 municipal election, an independent candidate, Aoshima, a television comedian without backing from political parties or financial circles, campaigned on a one-issue program: to cancel the World City Fair. He won the election by a large margin, and became Governor of Tokyo. A few weeks later, he kept his campaign promise and canceled the World City Fair, to the disbelief of the corporate elite. The local logic of civil society was catching up with, and contradicting, the global logic of international business.

Thus, people do still live in places. But because function and power in our societies are organized in the space of flows, the structural domination of its logic essentially alters the meaning and dynamic of places. Experience, by being related to places, becomes abstracted from power, and meaning is increasingly separated from knowledge. It follows a structural schizophrenia between two spatial logics that threatens to break down communication channels in society. The dominant tendency is toward a horizon of networked, ahistorical space of flows, aiming at imposing its logic over scattered, segmented places, increasingly unrelated to each other, less and less able to share cultural codes. Unless cultural *and physical* bridges are deliberately built between these two forms of space, we may be heading toward life in parallel universes whose times cannot meet because they are warped into different dimensions of a social hyperspace.

—— 7 ——

The Edge of Forever:
Timeless Time

Introduction

We are embodied time, and so are our societies, made out of history. Yet the simplicity of this statement hides the complexity of the concept of time, one of the most controversial categories in the natural and social sciences alike, whose centrality is underlined by current debates in social theory.[1] Indeed, the transformation of time under the information technology paradigm, as shaped by social practices, is one of the foundations of the new society we have entered, inextricably linked to the emergence of the space of flows. Furthermore, according to the illuminating essay by Barbara Adam on time and social theory, recent research in physics and biology seems to converge with social sciences in adopting a contextual notion of human time.[2] All time, in nature as in society, seems to be specific to a given context: time is local. Focusing on the emerging social structure, I argue, in the tradition of Harold Innis, that "the fashionable mind is the time-denying mind,"[3] and that this new "time regime" is linked to the development of communication technologies. Thus, in

[1]   The analysis of time plays a central role in the thought of Anthony Giddens, one of the leading sociological theorists of our intellectual generation. See, particularly, Giddens (1981, 1984). An extremely stimulating theorization of the relationship between time, space, and society is the work by Lash and Urry (1994); see also Young (1988). For a more traditional, empirical approach to social analysis of time, see Kirsch et al.(eds) (1988). For recent debates, see Friedland and Boden (eds) (1994). Of course, for sociologists, the classic references on social time continue to be Durkheim (1912) and Sorokin and Merton (1937). See also, the pioneering work by Innis (1950, 1951, 1952) on regimes of time and space as defining historical epochs.
[2]   Adam (1990: 81, 87-90).
[3]   Innis (1951: 89ff); see also Innis (1950).

order to appreciate the transformation of human time under the new social socio-technical context it may be helpful to introduce briefly a historical perspective on the changing relationship between time and society.

Time, History, and Society

In a classic book, Whitrow has shown how conceptions of time have varied considerably throughout history, from the determination of human fate under the Babylonian horoscopes, to the Newtonian revolution of absolute time as an organizing principle of nature.[4] And Nigel Thrift has reminded us of the fact that time in medieval societies was a loose notion, with some major events (religious celebrations, market fairs, the coming of the seasons) becoming time markers around which most of the daily life went by without precise timing.[5] To illustrate the wide contextual variation of such an apparently simple fact of life, let us recall in a few paragraphs the transformation of the notion of time in Russian culture in two critical historical periods: the reforms of Peter the Great, and the rise and fall of the Soviet Union.[6]

Traditional, popular Russian culture viewed time as eternal, without beginning or end. Writing in the 1920s, Andrey Platonov emphasized this deep-seated notion of Russia as a timeless society. Yet Russia was periodically shaken by statist modernization efforts to organize life around time. The first deliberate attempt at timing life came from Peter the Great. Upon his return from a long trip abroad to educate himself about ways and means in more advanced countries, he decided to bring Russia, literally, to a new departure, by shifting to the Western European (Julian) calendar, and starting the new year in January instead of September, as had been the case until then. On

[4] Whitrow (1988). For a good example of cultural/historical variation of time and time measures, see the fascinating book by Zerubavel (1985).
[5] Thrift (1990).
[6] The plural source for this analysis of the evolution of time in the Russian culture is the set of unpublished presentations and discussions at the Conference on Time and Money in the Russian Culture, organized by the University of California at Berkeley's Center for Slavic and Eastern European Studies, and the Stanford University's Center for Russian and East European Studies, held at Berkeley on March 17 1995 (personal notes and summary of the proceedings by Emma G. Kiselyova). Among the various significant contributions to this conference, I have used Zhivov (1995). Additionally, for the time implications of Peter the Great's reforms, see Waliszewski (1990); Kara-Murza and Polyakov (1994); Anisimov (1993).

December 19 and 20 1699, he issued two decrees that would start the eighteenth century in Russia a few days later. He prescribed detailed instructions about celebrating the new year, including the adoption of the Christmas tree, and adding a new holiday to entice the traditionalists. While some people marveled at the Czar's power to alter the course of the sun, many were concerned about offending God: was not September 1 the day of the Creation in 5508BC? And was it not supposed to be so because the daring act of Creation had to take place in warm weather, an occurrence extremely unlikely in the Russian January? Peter the Great argued personally with his critics, in his customary pedagogic mode, indulging in teaching them about global time geography. His stubbornness was rooted in his reformist motivation to homogenize Russia with Europe, and to emphasize time-measured obligations of people towards the state. Although these decrees focused strictly on calendar changes, Peter the Great's reforms, in broader terms, introduced a distinction between the time of religious duty and secular time to be given to the state. Measuring and taxing people's time, and giving his own personal example of an intense, timed work schedule, Peter the Great inaugurated a centuries-old tradition of associating service to the country, submission to the state, and the timing of life.

In the early stage of the Soviet Union, Lenin shared with Henry Ford the admiration for Taylorism and the "scientific organization of work," based on measuring working time to the smallest movement in the assembly line. But time compression under communism came with a decisive ideological twist.[7] While under Fordism the speeding up of work was associated with money, by increasing pay, under Stalinism not only was money evil, in line with the Russian tradition, but time should be accelerated by ideological motivation. Thus, Stakhanovism meant working more per unit of time as a service to the country, and five-year plans were fulfilled in four years as a proof of the ability of the new society to revolutionize time. In May 1929, at the Fifth Congress of the Soviets of the Union which marked the triumph of Stalin, an even more extreme acceleration of time was attempted: the uninterrupted *(nepreryvka)* work week. Although increase in production was the explicit goal of the reform, the destruction of the weekly rhythm of religious observance was an even greater motivation, in the tradition of the French Revolution. So, in November 1931, a resting day was introduced every sixth day, but the traditional seven-

---

[7]   For analysis of time in the Soviet Union, see Hanson (1991); Castillo (1994); on developments related to "uninterrupted workweek" under Stalin, see Zerubavel (1985: 35–43).

day cycle was still denied. Protests arising from families separated by differences in schedules between their members brought the seven-day week back in 1940, particularly after it was realized that cities were on the six-day pattern, but most of the countryside was still observing the traditional week, introducing a dangerous cultural cleavage between peasants and industrial workers. Indeed, while forced collectivization of agriculture aimed at eliminating the communal notion of slow-paced time, rooted in nature, family, and history, the social and cultural resistance to such brutal imposition was widespread, showing the depth of the time foundation of social life. Yet, while compressing time at the workplace, the time horizon of communism was always in the long term and to some extent eternal, as expressed in Lenin's embodied immortality, and in Stalin's attempt to make an idol of himself during life. Accordingly, in the 1990s, the collapse of communism shifted Russians, and particularly the new professional classes, from the long-term horizon of historical time to the short term of monetized time characteristic of capitalism, thus ending the centuries-old statist separation between time and money. By so doing Russia joined the West at the very moment advanced capitalism was revolutionizing its own time frame.

Contemporary societies are still by and large dominated by the notion of clock time, a mechanical/categorical discovery that E.P. Thompson,[8] among others, considers to be critical to the constitution of industrial capitalism. Modernity can be conceived, in material terms, as the dominance of clock time over space and society, a theme that has been developed by Giddens, Lash and Urry, and Harvey. Time as repetition of daily routine, as Giddens proposes,[9] or as "the mastery of nature, as all sorts of phenomena, practices and places become subjected to the disembedding, centralizing and universalizing march of time," in the words of Lash and Urry,[10] is at the core of both industrial capitalism and statism. Industrial machinism brought the chronometer to the assembly lines of Fordist and Leninist factories almost at the same moment.[11] Long-distance travel in the West became organized by the late nineteenth century around Greenwich Mean Time, as the materialization of the hegemony of the British Empire. While, half a century later, the constitution of the Soviet Union was marked by the organization of an immense territory around Moscow time, with time zones arbitrarily decided by the bureaucrats' convenience without proportion to geographical

---

[8]   Thompson (1967).
[9]   Giddens (1984).
[10] Lash and Urry (1994: 229).

distance. Significantly the first act of defiance of the Baltic Republics during Gorbachev's *perestroyka* was to vote for the adoption of Finland's time zone as the official time in their territories.

This linear, irreversible, measurable, predictable time is being shattered in the network society, in a movement of extraordinary historical significance. But we are not just witnessing a relativization of time according to social contexts or alternatively the return to time reversibility as if reality could become entirely captured in cyclical myths. The transformation is more profound: it is the mixing of tenses to create a forever universe, not self-expanding but self-maintaining, not cyclical but random, not recursive but incursive: timeless time, using technology to escape the contexts of its existence, and to appropriate selectively any value each context could offer to the ever-present. I argue that this is happening now not only because capitalism strives to free itself from all constraints, since this has been the capitalist system's tendency all along, without being able fully to materialize it.[12] Neither is it sufficient to refer to the cultural and social revolts against clock time, since they have characterized the history of the last century without actually reversing its domination, indeed furthering its logic by including clock time distribution of life in the social contract.[13] Capital's freedom from time and culture's escape from the clock are decisively facilitated by new information technologies, and embedded in the structure of the network society.

Having said the words, I shall proceed with the specification of their meaning, so that by the end of this chapter sociological analysis has a chance to replace metaphorical statements. To do so without annoying repetition I shall rely on the empirical observations presented in other chapters of this book on the transformation of various domains of social structure, while adding illustrations or analyses when necessary to complete our understanding. Thus, I shall sequentially explore the effects on time of transformations occurring in the economic, political, cultural, and social spheres, and end with an attempt at reintegrating time and space in their new, contradictory relationship. In this exploration of ongoing transformation of time in very different social spheres, I shall be somewhat schematic in my statements, since it is materially impossible to develop fully in a few pages the analysis of domains as complex and diverse as global finance, working time, the life-cycle, death, war-making, and the media. However, by dealing with so many and different matters I try to extract, beyond such diversity, the shared logic of new temporality

---

[11] Castillo (1994).
[12] As Harvey (1990) shows.
[13] Hinrichs et al. (eds) (1991); see also Rifkin (1987).

manifesting itself in the whole range of human experience. Thus, the purpose of this chapter is not to summarize the transformation of social life in all its dimensions, but, rather, to show the consistency of patterns in the emergence of a new concept of temporality, that I call *timeless time*.

Another word of caution must be added. The transformation of time as surveyed in this chapter does not concern all processes, social groupings, and territories in our societies, although it does affect the entire planet. What I call *timeless time* is only the emerging, *dominant* form of social time in the network society, as the space of flows does not negate the existence of places. It is precisely my argument that social domination is exercised through the selective inclusion and exclusion of functions and people in different temporal and spatial frames. I shall return to this theme at the end of the chapter after having explored the profile of time in its new, dominant form.

Time as the Source of Value: the Global Casino

David Harvey adequately represents current transformations in capitalism under the formula of "time-space compression."[14] Nowhere is this logic more evident than in the circulation of capital at the global level. As we analyzed in chapter 2, during the 1980s the convergence of global deregulation of finance and the availability of new information technologies and new management techniques transformed the nature of capital markets. For the first time in history, a unified global capital market, *working in real time,* has emerged.[15] The explanation, and the real issue, of the phenomenal volume of transborder financial flows, as shown in chapter 2, lies in the *speed* of the transactions.[16] The same capital is shuttled back and forth between economies in a matter of hours, minutes, and some times seconds.[17] Favored by deregulation, disintermediation, and the opening of domestic financial markets, powerful computer programs and skillful financial analysts/computer wizards sitting at the global nodes of a selective telecommunications network play games, literally, with billions of dollars.[18] The main card room in this electronic casino is the currency market, which has exploded in the last decade, taking advantage of floating exchange rates. In 1995, US$1.2 trillion were exchanged

[14]   See Harvey (1990: 284–5).
[15]   Chesnais (1994); O'Brien (1992).
[16]   Reynolds (1992), Javetski and Glasgall (1994).
[17]   Shirref (1994); Breeden (1993).
[18]   *Time* (1994); Jones (1993). For a revealing "financial fiction" allegory, enjoy the reading of Kimsey (1994).

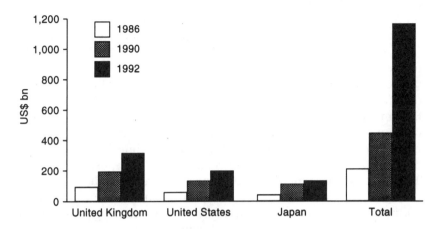

Figure 7.1   Average daily transactions on stock exchanges, 1986–92
(US$bn)
Source: Chesnais and Serfati (1994), quoted in Chesnais (1994); based on
triennial reports of the Bank for International Settlement.

every day in the currency market (see figure 7.1).[19] These global
gamblers are not obscure speculators, but major investment banks,
pension funds, multinational corporations (of course including
manufacturing corporations), and mutual funds organized precisely
for the sake of financial manipulation.[20] François Chesnais identified
about 50 major players in the global financial markets.[21] Yet, as argued
above, once turbulences are generated in the market, flows take over,
as central banks have repeatedly learned to their heavy cost. Time is
critical to the profit-making of the whole system. It is the speed of the
transaction, sometimes automatically preprogrammed in
the computer to make quasi-instantaneous decisions, that generates the gain – or the loss. But it is also the time circularity of the
process, a relentless sequence of buying and selling which characterizes the system. The architecture of global finance is indeed
constructed around time zones, with London, New York, and Tokyo
anchoring the three shifts of capital, and a number of financial
maverick centers working on the slight discrepancies between market
values at their opening and closing times.[22] Furthermore, a significant
and growing number of financial transactions are based on making

[19]   *Economist* (1995b).
[20]   Heavey (1994).
[21]   Chesnais (1994).
[22]   Lee and Schmidt-Marwede (1993).

value out of the capture of future time in present transactions, as in the futures, options, and other derivative capital markets.[23] Together these new financial products dramatically increase the mass of nominal capital *vis-à-vis* bank deposits and assets, so that it can be said properly that time creates money, as everybody bets on and with future money anticipated in computer projections.[24] The very process of marketing future development affects these developments, so that the time frame of capital is constantly dissolved into its present manipulation after being given a fictitious value for the purpose of monetizing it. Thus capital not only compresses time: it absorbs it, and lives out of (that is, generates rent) its digested seconds and years.

The material consequences of this apparently abstract disgression on time and capital are increasingly felt in economies and daily lives around the world: recurrent monetary crises, ushering in an era of structural economic instability and actually jeopardizing European integration; the inability of capital investment to anticipate the future, thus undermining incentives for productive investment; the wrecking of companies, and of their jobs, regardless of performance because of sudden, unforeseen changes in the financial environment in which they operate; the increasing gap between profits in the production of goods and services and rents generated in the sphere of circulation, thus shifting an increasing share of world savings to financial gambling; the growing risks for pension funds and private insurance liabilities, thus introducing a question mark into the hard-bought security of working people around the world; the dependence of entire economies, and particularly those of developing countries, on movements of capital largely determined by subjective perception and speculative turbulence; the destruction in the collective experience of societies of the deferred-gratification pattern of behavior, in favour of the "quick buck" common ideology, emphasizing individual gambling with life and the economy; and the fundamental damage to the social perception of the correspondence between production and reward, work and meaning, ethics and wealth. Puritanism seems to have been buried in Singapore in 1995 along with the venerable Barings Bank.[25] And Confucianism will last in the new economy only as long as "blood is thicker than water,"[26] that is while family ties still provide social cohesion beyond pure speculation in the brave new world of gambling finance. The annihilation and manipulation of

---

[23] Lee et al. (1994); *Asian Money, Asian Issuers & Capital Markets Supplement* (1993-4); Fager (1994).
[24] Chesnais (1994).
[25] *Economist* (1995a).
[26] Hsing (1994).

time by electronically managed global capital markets are at the source of new forms of devastating economic crises, looming into the twenty-first century.

Flextime and the Network Enterprise

The supersession of time is also at the core of new organizational forms of economic activity that I have identified as the *network enterprise*. Flexible forms of management, relentless utilization of fixed capital, intensified performance by labor, strategic alliances, and inter-organizational linkages, all come down to shortening time per operation and to speeding up turnover of resources. Indeed, the "just in time" inventory management procedure has been the symbol of lean production, even if, as I mentioned above, it belongs to a pre-electronic age of manufacturing technology. Yet, in the informational economy, this time compression does not primarily rely on extracting more time from labor or more labor from time under the clock imperative. Because the value-making potential of labor and organizations is highly dependent on the autonomy of informed labor to make decisions in real time, traditional disciplinary management of labor does not fit the new production system.[27] Instead, skilled labor is required to manage its own time in a flexible manner, sometimes adding more work time, at other times adjusting to flexible schedules, in some instances reducing working hours, and thus pay. This new time-oriented management of labor could be called, as John Urry suggests, "just-in-time labor."

For the networked firm, the time frame of its adaptability to market demand and technology changes is also at the roots of its competitiveness. Thus, the showcase of networking production, the Italian knitwear multinational firm Benetton, was overtaken in 1995 by its American competitor Gap mainly because of its inability to follow Gap's speed in introducing new models according to evolving consumer taste: every two months, as compared to twice a year for Benetton.[28] Another example: in the software industry in the mid-1990s firms started to give away their products for free, over the line, in order to attract customers at a faster pace.[29] The rationale behind this final dematerialization of software products is that profits are to be made in the long term, mainly out of customized relationships with users over development and improvements of a given program. But

---

[27] See the discussion of the matter in Freeman (ed.) (1994).
[28] *Business Week* (1995d).
[29] *Business Week* (1995c).

Table 7.1 Annual hours worked per person, 1870–1979

	1870	1880	1890	1900	1913	1929	1938	1950	1960	1970	1979
Canada	2,964	2,871	2,789	2,707	2,605	2,399	2,240	1,967	1,877	1,805	1,730
France	2,945	2,852	2,770	2,688	2,588	2,297	1,848	1,989	1,983	1,888	1,727
Germany	2,941	2,848	2,765	2,684	2,584	2,284	2,316	2,316	2,083	1,907	1,719
Italy	2,886	2,795	2,714	2,634	2,536	2,228	1,927	1,997	2,059	1,768	1,556
Japan	2,945	2,852	2,770	2,688	2,588	2,364	2,391	2,272	2,432	2,252	2,129
United Kingdom	2,984	2,890	2,807	2,725	2,624	2,286	2,267	1,958	1,913	1,735	1,617
United States	2,964	2,871	2,789	2,707	2,605	2,342	2,062	1,867	1,794	1,707	1,607

For Italy, 1978 figure is used for 1979.
Source: Maddison (1982); Bosch et. al. (eds) (1994: 8, table 1).

Table 7.2 Potential lifelong working hours, 1950–85

	1950	1960	1979	1980	1985
France	113,729	107,849	101,871	92,708	77,748
West Germany	114,170	104,076	93,051	87,367	85,015
East Germany	108,252	n.a.	97,046	93,698	93,372
Hungary	97,940	96,695	92,918	85,946	78,642
Italy	n.a.	n.a.	n.a.	n.a.	82,584
Japan	109,694	109,647	100,068	95,418	93,976
United Kingdom	n.a.	n.a.	n.a.	n.a.	82,677
USA	n.a.	n.a.	n.a.	n.a.	93,688
USSR	n.a.	n.a.	n.a.	n.a.	77,148

n.a. = not available
Source: Schuldt (1990: 43).

the initial adoption of such a program depends on the advantage of solutions offered by a product over other products in the market, thus putting a premium on the quick availability of new breakthroughs, as soon as they are generated by a firm or an individual. The flexible management system of networked production relies on flexible temporality, on the ability to accelerate or slow down product and profit cycles, on the time-sharing of equipment and personnel, and on the control of time lags of available technology *vis-à-vis* the competition. Time is managed as a resource, not under the linear, chronological manner of mass production, but as a differential factor in reference to the temporality of other firms, networks, processes or products. Only the networked form of organization and increasingly powerful and mobile information-processing machines are able to ensure the flexible management of time as the new frontier of high-performance firms.[30] Under such conditions time is not only compressed: it is processed.

The Shrinking and Twisting of Life Working Time

Work is, and will be for the foreseeable future, the nucleus of people's life. More specifically in modern societies, *paid working time* structures social time. Working time in industrialized countries has experienced a secular decline in the last 100 years, measured in annual working hours *per person,* as shown in the study by Maddison[31] (see table 7.1). I should remind the reader that this reduction in working time hides in fact a substantial increase in total labor, as a result of the increase in the number of jobs since, as I showed in chapter 4, aggregate employment is less a function of technology than of the expansion of investment and demand, depending on social and institutional organization. Calculations on the potential lifelong working hours per person also show a significant reduction in the last four decades, although with important variations in the number of hours between countries[32] (see table 7.2).

The number of working hours and their distribution in the lifecycle and in the annual, monthly, and weekly cycles of people's lives, are a central feature of how they feel, enjoy, and suffer. Their differential evolution in various countries and historical periods reflects

---

[30]   Benveniste (1994).

[31]   Maddison (1982).

[32]   K. Schuldt, *Soziale und ökonomische Gestaltung der Elemente der Lebensarbeitszeit der Werktätigen,* Dissertation, Berlin (GDR), 1990; cited in Bosch et al. (eds) (1994:15).

Table 7.3 Duration and reduction of working time, 1970–87

	Agreed working hours	Reduction of agreed hours (%)		Actual working hours per employee		Change (%)	Working hours per person, working age 55–64 years		Change (%)	Working hours per person
		1970–80	1980–7	1980	1987	1980–7	1980	1987	1980–7	
Sweden	1,796 (9)	-8.2(3)	0(8)	1,438 (1)	1,482 (1)	+3.1 (10)	1,133 (7)	1,188 (6)	+4.9 (8)	770 (6)
Norway	1,714 (2)	-6.2(4)	-6.6(3)	1,563 (2)	1,537 (2)	-1.7 (7)	1,131 (6)	1,210 (7)	+7.0 (9)	788 (7)
Denmark	1,733 (4)	-2.6(6)	-6.0(4)	1,720 (4)	1,596 (4)	-7.2 (2)	1,246 (8)	1,211 (8)	-2.8 (4)	812 (8)
Finland	1,720 (3)	0 (8)	-7.5(1)	1,818 (8)	1,782 (10)	-2.0 (6)	1,299 (9)	1,305 (10)	+0.5 (6)	890 (10)
Germany	1,712 (1)	-5.9(5)	-4.7(6)	1,736 (7)	1,672 (6)	-3.7 (4)	1,090 (3)	1,020 (4)	-6.4 (2)	712 (4)
Netherlands	1,744 (5)	-9.1(2)	-7.0(2)	1,720 (4)	1,645 (5)	-4.5 (3)	881 (1)	864 (1)	-1.9 (5)	603 (2)
Belgium	1,759 (6)	-9.2(1)	-5.0(5)	1,590 (3)	1,550 (3)	-3.0 (5)	925 (2)	875 (2)	-5.4 (3)	601 (1)
France	1,767 (7)	0 (8)	-4.6(7)	1,850 (9)	1,696 (7)	-3.3 (1)	1,122 (5)	1,001 (3)	-10.8 (1)	672 (5)
United Kingdom	1,782 (8)	-2.1(7)	-4.6(7)	—	1,730 (8)	—	—	1,183 (5)	—	765 (5)
USA	1,916 (10)	0 (8)	0 (8)	1,735 (6)	1,770 (9)	+2.0 (9)	1,106 (4)	1,231 (9)	+11.3 (10)	832 (9)
Japan	2,121 (11)	-5.9 (5)	0 (8)	2,113 (10)	2,085 (11)	-1.3 (8)	1,446 (10)	1,469 (11)	+1.6 (7)	1,020 (11)

The table is based on Eurostat figures. It is assumed that hours of part-timers are 25% lower than those of full-time employees and that hours outside industry are 2.5% longer than in industry.
Figures in brackets are rankings.
Source: Pettersson (1989).

economic organization, the state of technology, the intensity of social struggles, and the outcomes of social contracts and institutional reforms.[33] French workers were the first in Europe to conquer the 40-hour week and the right to paid vacation, after bitter social struggles and the election to government of the Popular Front in 1936. The UK, the USA, and Japan have been the bastions of business-imposed Stakhanovism, with workers having half or one-third less vacation time than workers in Germany, France, or Spain, with no apparent effect on productivity (actually, in terms of productivity growth in the last 30 years, if we except Japan, vacation time seems to correlate positively with growth in labor productivity). Yet overall, for more than one century, between 1870 and 1980, we could observe two related trends in industrialized economies toward decreasing labor time per person and per worker, and toward increasing homogenization and regulation of working time as part of the social contract underlying the welfare state. However, recently these trends have been modified toward an increasingly complex and variable pattern[34] (see table 7.3). The key phenomenon seems to be the increasing diversification of working time and working schedules, reflecting the trend toward the disaggregation of labor in the work process, as analyzed in chapter 4. Thus the 1994 ILO study on the evolution of working time in 14 industrialized countries synthesizes its observations as follows:

> In the long term, the reduction of working time obviously is the dominant trend. Also, in the last 20 years working hours were reduced in most countries, but by very different combinations of increasing part time work, reducing agreed and actual weekly and yearly working hours and lifetime hours. However, in analyzing this main trend one easily overlooks some manifest tendencies towards an extension of hours at least in some countries and for some groups of workers within different countries. *These tendencies may indicate the increasing differentiation of the duration of working hours between and within countries after a long period of standardization and harmonization of working hours.*[35]

What are the sources of such diversity? On the one hand, institutional differences in the regulation of labor markets, with the US, Japan, and the European Union displaying clear-cut contrasting logics. On the other hand, within countries, longer working hours are concentrated in two groups: high-level professionals and unskilled service workers. The former, because of their value-making contribu-

---

[33] Hinrichs et al. (eds) (1991).
[34] Bosch et al. (eds) (1994).
[35] Ibid.:19 (my added emphasis).

tion, the latter because of their weak bargaining power, often associated with immigrant status or informal work arrangements. As for shorter working time and atypical schedules, they are linked to part-time and temporary work, and concern mainly women and low-educated youth. The massive entry of women into the labor force is, to some extent, associated with the diversification of work status and working schedules. As a result, as shown above in chapter 4, between one-quarter and one-third of the employed population of major industrialized countries (including self-employment) does not follow the classic pattern of a full-time job with a regular working schedule. The number of workers in variable job assignments is rapidly increasing everywhere. In addition, a considerable proportion of full-time workers (probably a majority of the professional labor force) are heading toward flexible time schedules, generally increasing their work load. The technological ability to reintegrate in a network of stored information contributions from various workers at various times induces the constant variation of the actual time of work performance, undermining the structuring capacity of working time over everyday life. Thus, in his insightful analysis on the transformation of work and firms in France, Frederic de Conninck focuses on the fact that "the enterprise is affected by plural and divergent temporalities," "the economy is dominated more and more by the search for flexibility, or organized around short run time," with the result that "today, the individual is overwhelmed by the various temporalities he has to confront;" thus, while work remains integrated, society tends toward its *éclatement,* out of the unmanageable development of contradictory temporalities within the same structure.[36]

Therefore, the real issue in our societies is not so much that technology allows us to work less for the same unit of output: it does so, but the impact of this technological fact on actual working time and schedules is undetermined. What is at stake, and what appears to be the prevailing trend in most advanced sectors of most advanced societies, is the general diversification of working time, depending on firms, networks, jobs, occupations, and characteristics of the workers. Such diversity ends up, in fact, being measured in terms of each worker's and each job's differential capacity to manage time. Without anticipating my analysis on the evolution of the family (in volume II), it seems that the heterogeneity of working schedules in a society with similar participation by the genders in the labor force, imposes a dramatic readjustment of household arrangements. Not necessarily for the worse, since in fact added work-time flexibility could provide

[36] De Conninck (1995); quotes are, in sequential order, from pp.200, 193, and 193 (my translation).

the basis for time-sharing in the household. Yet new household partnerships would have to be built on the ruins of patriarchal family rules.[37] Since flex-time and part-time have penetrated the contractual structures of working time on the basis of women's work, largely to accommodate women's needs to combine their child-rearing endeavors and their working lives, the extension of this logic to men and to other domains of social life other than child-rearing could actually introduce (it is in fact already introducing in many instances)[38] a new articulation of life time and work time at different ages and under different conditions, for both men and women. Thus, under such new arrangements, working time may lose its traditional centrality throughout the lifecycle.

A convergent trend pointing in the same direction comes from the dramatic shortening of actual working *years* in major industrialized countries, precisely at the moment of a substantial increase in life expectancy. This is, on the one hand, because the age of entry into the labor force, both for men and women, is increasingly higher, as a greater proportion of the population attends universities: a trend that results from cultural expectations, the tightening of labor markets, and employers' increasing requirement for higher education credentials in the labor force.[39] On the other hand, Anne Marie Guillemard has conducted comparative studies that show the dramatic decline of actual employment for the labor force over 50 years, and specially over 55 years.[40] As figure 7.2 shows, the rate of activity of men between 55 and 65 has declined precipitously in the last 20 years in major industrialized economies, and in 1991 was down to 65% in the US, 64% in the UK, 54% in Germany, and 43% in France. For these countries, be it by early retirement, disability, permanent unemployment, attrition, or discouragement, between one-third and over one-half of the male labor force *permanently* quits the labor market in their early fifties. Guillemard puts forward a solid argument in the sense that this tendency is not temporary but rooted in shortsighted government and business policies, and in the belief of the inability of the aged worker to adapt to the current speed of technological and organizational innovation.[41] Under such circumstances, the actual working lifetime could be shortened to about 30 years (from 24 to 54), out of a real lifetime span of about 75–80 years. Then, not only working time

[37] Martin Carnoy and I have jointly elaborated on this theme in Carnoy and Castells (1996).
[38] Hewitt (1993).
[39] Carnoy and Levin (1985).
[40] Guillemard (1993).
[41] Guillemard and Rein (1993).

444

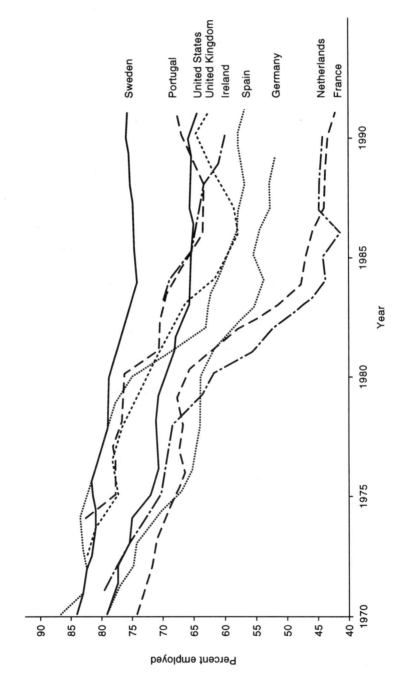

Figure 7.2 Labor force participation rate (%) for men 55–64 years old in nine countries, 1970–91
Source: Guillemard (1993).

loses its centrality *vis-à-vis* life in general, but the accounting system on which pensions and healthcare are calculated collapses, not because there are too many elderly persons, but because the proportion between contributing workers and nonworking recipients becomes unbearable, unless productivity increases are dramatic and society accepts a massive intergenerational redistribution.[42]

Thus, the real challenge of the new relationship between work and technology does not concern mass unemployment, as I tried to discuss in chapter 4, but the overall shortening of life working time for a substantial proportion of the population. Unless the basis of calculation for social benefits is modified through a new social contract, the shrinkage of valuable working time and the accelerated obsolescence of labor will bring to an end the institutions of social solidarity, ushering in the age wars.

The Blurring of Lifecycle: Toward Social Arrhythmia?

It seems that all living beings, including us, are biological clocks.[43] Biological rhythms, be it individual, related to the species, or even cosmic, are essential in human life. People and societies ignore them at their peril.[44] For millennia human rhythmicity was constructed in close relationship to the rhythms of nature, generally with little bargaining power against hostile natural forces, so that it seemed reasonable to go with the flow, and to model the lifecycle in accordance with a society where most babies would die as infants, where women's reproductive power had to be used early, where youth was ephemeral (Ronsard), where growing elderly was such a privilege that it brought with it the respect due to a unique source of experience and wisdom, and where plagues would periodically wipe out a sizable share of the population.[45] In the developed world, the industrial revolution, the constitution of medical science, the triumph of Reason, and the affirmation of social rights has altered this pattern in the last two centuries, prolonging life, overcoming illness, regulating births, alleviating death, calling into question the biological determination of roles in society, and constructing the lifecycle around social categories, among which education, working time, career patterns, and the right to retirement became paramount. However, although the principle of a sequential life shifted from being bio-social to becoming

---

[42] Lenoir (1994).
[43] Berger (1984), cited by Adam (1990).
[44] Schor (1991).
[45] McNeill (1977).

socio-biological, there was (indeed, there still is) a lifecycle pattern to which advanced societies tend to conform, and toward which developing countries try to evolve. Now, organizational, technological, and cultural developments characteristic of the new, emerging society, are decisively undermining this orderly lifecycle without replacing it with an alternative sequence. **I propose the hypothesis that the network society is characterized by the breaking down of rhythmicity, either biological or social, associated with the notion of a lifecycle.**

I have already examined one of the reasons for this new trend, namely the variable chronology of working time. But an even more important development is the increasing ability to control, within obvious limits, the reproduction of our species, and the average duration of the life of its individuals (see chapter 1). Although the upper limit of longevity has a biological boundary, the prolongation of the average duration of life to the late seventies (early eighties for women), and the increasing share of the population reaching well beyond the average, into the eighties age group, has considerable consequences for our societies and for the ways we conceive of ourselves. While old age was once considered a homogeneous last stage of life, in fact dominated by "social death," as demonstrated in the French study that Anne Marie Guillemard conducted many years ago with my collaboration,[46] it is now a highly diverse universe, made up of early retirees, average retirees, able elders, and elders with various degrees and forms of disability. So, suddenly, the "third age" is extended toward younger and older groups, and substantially redefines the lifecycle in three ways: it denies the exit from the labor market as the defining criterion, since for a substantial proportion of the population about one-third of their life may occur after this event; it differentiates the elderly fundamentally in terms of their level of disability, not always correlating with age, thus assimilating to some extent their disabled condition to other disabled groups of a younger age, thus inducing new social category; and it compels the distinction between several age groups, whose actual differentiation will greatly depend on their social, cultural, and relational capital accumulated throughout their lives.[47] Depending on each one of these variables, the social attributes of these distinct old ages will differ considerably, thus breaking down the relationship between social condition and biological stage at the roots of the lifecycle.

Simultaneously, this relationship is being called into question at the other end: reproduction is coming under increasing control around the world. In advanced societies the norm is birth control, although

---

[46]   Guillemard (1972); Castells and Guillemard (1971).
[47]   Guillemard (1988).

social marginality and religious beliefs constitute areas of resistance to planned motherhood. In close interaction with the cultural and professional emancipation of women, the development of reproductive rights has altered the demographic structure and biological rhythms of our societies in just two decades (see table 7.4). Overall, the most industrialized countries have entered an era of low birth rates (below the reproduction rate for the native population), of delayed time for marriage and reproduction, and of variable stages for women to have children throughout their lifecycle, as they strive to combine education, work, personal life, and children in an increasingly individualized pattern of decision-making (see table 7.5). Together with the transformation of the family and the increasing diversification of lifestyles (see volume II) we observe a substantial modification of the time and forms for mothering and fathering in the lifecycle, where the new rule is, increasingly, that there are few rules. Furthermore, new reproductive technologies and new cultural models make it possible, to a considerable extent, to disassociate age and biological condition from reproduction and from parenthood. In strictly technical terms it is possible today to differentiate the legal parent(s) of a child; whose is the sperm; whose is the egg; where and how the fertilization is performed, in real or delayed time, even after the death of the father; and whose is the womb which gives birth to the child. *All combinations are possible and are socially decided.* Our society has already reached the technological capacity to separate social reproduction and biological reproduction of the species. I am obviously referring to exceptions to the rule, but to tens of thousands of exceptions throughout the world. Some of them are showcases of the possibility for aged women (in their late fifties or early sixties) actually to give birth. Others are soap opera happenings about a dead lover whose frozen sperm is fought by irate heirs. Most are secluded events often whispered over dinner in high-tech California or in gossipy Madrid. Since these developments are related to very simple reproductive technologies which do not involve genetic engineering, it is plausible to imagine a much greater range for the possible manipulation of reproductive ages and reproduction conditions when human genetic engineering ends up finding a legal and ethical accommodation in society, as all technologies do in the long term.

Since I am not speculating on future projections but elaborating on well-known facts of our everyday life, I believe it is legitimate to think about the on-going consequences of these developments for human life, and particularly for the lifecycle. It is very simple: they lead to the final blurring of the biological foundation of the lifecycle concept. Sixty-year-old parents of infants; children of different marriages enjoying brothers and sisters 30 years older with no intermediate age

Table 7.4(a) Principal demographic characteristics by main regions of the world, 1970–95[a]

	Total fertility rate			Life expectancy at birth			Infant mortality rate		
	1970–5	1980–5	1990–5	1970–5	1980–5	1990–5	1970–5	1980–5	1990–5
World	4.4	3.5	3.3	57	60	65	93	78	62
More-developed regions	2.2	2.0	1.9	71	73	75	22	16	12
Less-developed regions	5.4	4.1	3.6	54	57	62	104	88	69
Africa	6.5	6.3	6.0	46	49	53	142	112	95
Asia	5.1	3.5	3.2	56	59	65	97	83	62
Europe	2.2	1.9	1.7	71	73	75	24	15	10
Americas	3.6	3.1	—	64	67	68	64	49	—
Latin	—	—	3.1	—	—	—	—	—	47
Northern	—	—	2.0	—	—	—	—	—	8
Oceania	3.2	2.7	2.5	66	68	73	39	31	22
USSR	2.4	2.4	2.3	70	71	70	26	25	21

[a] Data for 1990–5 all projections.

Sources: United Nations, World Population Prospects. Estimates and Projections as Assessed in 1984; United Nations, World Population at the Turn of the Century, 1989, p. 9, table 3; United Nations Population Fund, The State of World Population: Choices and Responsibilities, 1994.

Table 7.4(b) Total fertility rates of some industrialized countries, 1901–85

	Denmark	Finland	France	Germany[a]	Italy	Netherlands	Portugal	Sweden	Switzerland	United Kingdom	United States
1901–05	4.04	4.22	2.78	4.74	—	4.48	—	3.91	3.82	3.40	—
1906–10	3.83	4.15	2.59	4.25	—	4.15	—	3.76	3.56	3.14	—
1911–15	3.44	3.68	2.26	3.19	—	3.79	—	3.31	3.02	2.84	—
1916–20	3.15	3.49	1.66	2.13	—	3.58	—	2.94	2.46	2.40	3.22
1921–25	2.85	3.33	2.43	2.49	—	3.47	—	2.58	2.43	2.39	3.08
1926–30	2.41	2.88	2.29	2.05	—	3.08	—	2.08	2.10	2.01	2.65
1931–35	2.15	2.41	2.18	1.86	3.06	2.73	3.88	1.77	1.91	1.79	2.21
1936–40	2.17	2.38	2.07	2.43	3.00	2.58	3.45	1.82	1.80	1.80	2.14
1941–45	2.64	2.60	2.11	2.05	2.56	2.85	3.43	2.35	2.38	2.00	2.45
1946–50	2.75	2.86	2.99	2.05	2.78	3.48	3.29	2.45	2.52	2.38	2.97
1951–55	2.55	2.99	2.73	2.09	2.30	3.05	3.05	2.23	2.30	2.19	3.27
1956–60	2.54	2.78	2.70	2.34	2.32	3.11	3.02	2.24	2.40	2.52	3.53
1961–65	2.59	2.58	2.83	2.50	2.56	3.15	3.10	2.33	2.61	2.83	3.16
1966–70	2.20	2.06	2.60	2.33	2.50	2.74	2.91	2.12	2.29	2.56	2.41
1971–75	1.96	1.62	2.26	1.62	2.31	1.99	2.64	1.89	1.82	2.06	1.84
1976–80	1.65	1.67	1.88	1.41	1.88	1.59	2.32	1.66	1.51	1.76	1.69
1981–85	1.38	1.74	1.82	1.32	1.53	1.47	1.97	1.61	1.50	1.75	1.66

Note: [a] German figures include both FRG and GDR.

Sources: J. Bourgeois-Pichat, "Comparative fertility trends in Europe," in Causes and Consequences of Non-Replacement Fertility (Hoover Institution, 1985); United Nations, World Population at the Turn of the Century, 1989, p. 90, table 21.

Table 7.5 First live births per 1,000 women, USA, by age-group of mother (30–49 years) and by race, 1960 and 1990

| | Age group | | | |
	30–34 years	35–39 years	40–44 years	45–49 years
Total				
1960	8.6	3.2	0.8	0.0
1990	21.2	6.7	1.0	0.0
White				
1960	8.9	3.3	0.8	0.0
1990	21.6	6.8	1.0	0.0
All other				
1960	6.9	2.9	0.7	0.1
1990	19.1	6.3	1.1	0.1
Black				
1964	5.4	2.2	0.6	0.0
1990	12.9	4.0	0.7	0.0

Note the dramatic increase in the first live birth rate between 1960 and 1990: an increase of 146.5% for the 30–34 year age group, and of 109% for the 35–39 year age group.
Sources: US Bureau of Census, *Historical Statistics of the United States: Colonial Times to 1970*, vol. 1, p. 50, Series B 11–19, 1975; US Dept of Health and Human Services. *Vital Statistics of the United States: 1990*, vol. 1, section 1, table 1.9, 1994.

groups; men and women deciding to procreate, with or without coupling, at whichever age; grandmothers giving birth to the baby originated in her daughter's egg (also cases in real life); posthumous babies; and an increasing gap between social institutions and reproductive practices (children out of wedlock represent about 25% of all births in Sweden, and about 50% of African Americans). It is essential that we do not include a value judgement in this observation. What for traditionalists amounts to challenging the divine wrath, for cultural revolutionaries is the triumph of individual desire, and indeed the ultimate affirmation of women's rights to their bodies and their lives. Yet what is essential is that we are not on the fringes of society, even if these are still embryos of a new relationship between our social and biological condition. These are growing social trends, whose technological and cultural diffusion seems unstoppable, except under conditions of a new theocracy. And their direct implication is another form of the annihilation of time, of human biological time, of the time rhythm by which our species has been regulated since its origins. Regardless of our opinion, we may have to live without the clock that told our parents when they were supposed to procreate us, and that told us when, how, and if, to pass our life on to our children. A secular biological rhythm has been replaced by a moment of existential decision.

Death Denied

The belief in the probability of death with dignity is our, and society's attempt to deal with the reality of what is all too frequently a series of destructive events that involve by their very nature the disintegration of the dying person's humanity. I have not often seen much dignity in the process by which we die. The quest to achieve true dignity fails when our bodies fail . . . The greatest dignity to be found in death is the dignity of the life that preceded it. Sherwin B. Nuland[48]

Time in society and life is measured by death. Death is and has been the central theme of cultures throughout history, either revered as God's will or defied as the ultimate human challenge.[49] It has been exorcised in the rites destined to calm the living, accepted with the resignation of the serene, tamed in the carnivals of the simple, fought with the desperation of the romantics, but never denied.[50] It is a distinctive feature of our new culture, the attempt to exile death from our lives. Although the matrix of this attempt lies in the rationalist belief in all mighty progress, it is the extraordinary breakthroughs of medical technology and biological research in the last two decades that provide a material basis for the oldest aspiration of humankind: to live as if death did not exist, in spite of its being our only certainty. By so doing, the ultimate subversion of the lifecycle is accomplished, and life becomes this flat landscape punctuated by chosen moments of high and low experiences, in the endless boutique of customized feelings. So when death does happen it is simply an additional blip on the screen of distracted spectators. If it is true that, as Ionesco said, "each of us is the first one to die,"[51] social mechanisms make sure that we are also the last, namely that the dead are truly alone, and do not take away the vital energy of the living. Yet this old, and healthy, aspiration to survival, documented by Philippe Aries as being present in Western culture since the Middle Ages,[52] takes a new turn under the biological revolution. Because we are so close to unveiling the secrets

[48] Nuland (1994: xvii, 242).
[49] Morin, (1970).
[50] Thomas (1988, 1985).
[51] Quoted by Thomas (1988: 17).
[52] Aries (1977, 1983).

of life, two major trends have diffused from the medical sciences towards the rest of the society: obsessive prevention, and the fight to the end.

According to the first trend, every biological study, every medical exploration relating human health to the environment becomes quickly translated into hygienic advice or mandatory prescription (for example, the anti-smoking crusade in the US, the same country where submachine guns can be purchased by mail) which increasingly transforms society into a symbolically sanitized environment, with the full cooperation of the media. Indeed, newscasters have found in the health crusade an endless source of public attention, more so since the results of studies are periodically refuted and replaced by new specific instructions. A whole "healthy living" industry is directly related to this crusade, from hygienized food to fashionable sportswear and to mainly irrelevant vitamin pills. This perverted use of medical research is particularly pathetic when contrasted to the indifference of health insurance companies and mainstream business towards primary care and occupational safety.[53] Thus, an increasing proportion of people in advanced societies, and the professional classes throughout the world, spend considerable time, money, and psychological energy all through their lives pursuing health fashions in ways and with outcomes only slightly different from traditional shaman rites. For instance, while recent studies show that weight is largely linked to genetically programmed metabolism, and that people oscillate in a 10–15% range around their age and size average regardless of their efforts,[54] diet is a social obsession, either real or manipulated. True, personal aesthetics and the relationship to the body is also linked to the culture of individualism and narcissism, but the hygienist view of our societies adds a decisive instrumental twist to it (indeed, it is often linked with rejecting the objectification of woman's body). It aims at delaying and fighting death and aging every minute of life, with the support of medical science, the health industry, and media information.

Yet the real offensive against death is the good-faith, all-out medical struggle to push back the ineluctable as much as humanly possible. Sherwin B. Nuland, a surgeon and historian of medicine, writes in his soul-shaking book *How We Die:*

> Every medical specialist must admit that he has at times convinced patients to undergo diagnostic or therapeutic measures at a point in illness so far beyond reason that The

---

[53]   Navarro (1994).
[54]   Kolata (1995).

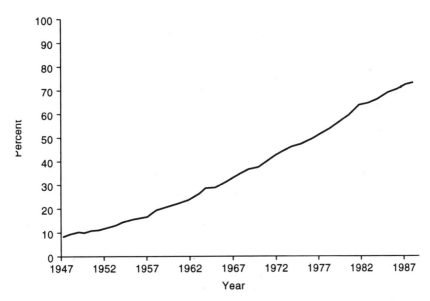

Figure 7.3 Ratio of hospitalized deaths to total deaths (%), by year, 1947–87

Source: Koichiri Kuroda, "Medicalization of Death: Changes in Site of Death in Japan after World War Two," Hyogo: Kobe College, Department of Intercultural Studies, 1990, unpublished research paper.

Riddle might better have remained unsolved. Too often near the end, were the doctor able to see deeply within himself, he might recognize that his decisions and advice are motivated by his inability to give up The Riddle and admit defeat as long as there is any chance of solving it. Though he be kind and considerate of the patient he treats, he allows himself to push his kindness aside because the seduction of The Riddle is so strong and the failure to solve it renders him so weak.[55]

This medical impulse to repulse death has nothing to do with capitalism. In fact, some insurance companies would rather welcome euthanasia, and would like to send patients home as soon as possible, a cynical view daily fought against by doctors. Without this relentless will to reject the inevitable, valuable lessons would be lost, and our collective ability to survive and overcome suffering would be hampered. Yet the societal impact of such efforts, along with less-noble enterprises of using terminal patients as experimental subjects, is tantamount to the denial of death until its very last act. So strong is

[55] Nuland (1994: 249).

the temporal and spatial confinement of death that the overwhelming majority of deaths (80% in the US, and a growing proportion in all countries: see figure 7.3 for Japan, a society with a strong family culture) take place in the hospital, very often in special intensive care units, with the bodies already removed from their social and emotional environments. In spite of some limited movements in defense of humane hospices for terminal patients, and even more limited tendencies towards bringing the dying back home, our last episode is increasingly sanitized, and our loved ones do not have the courage to object: it is too messy, too dirty, too painful, too inhuman, too degrading in fact. Life is interrupted at the threshold of the last possible smile, and death becomes visible only for a brief, ceremonial moment, after specialized image-makers perform their soothing *mise-en-scène*. Afterwards, mourning is becoming out of fashion in our societies, both as a reaction against traditional social hypocrisy, and as a down-to-earth philosophy of survival. Yet psychoanalysts and anthropologists have shown the social functions and individual benefits of mourning, both in its ritual and in its feeling.[56] But forfeiting mourning is the price to pay for accessing eternity in our lifetime through the denial of death.

The dominant trend in our societies, as an expression of our technological ambition, and in line with our celebration of the ephemeral, is to erase death from life, or to make it meaningless by its repeated representation in the media, always as the other's death, so that our own is met with the surprise of the unexpected. By separating death from life, and by creating the technological system to make this belief last long enough, we construct eternity in our life span. Thus, eternal we become except for that brief moment when embraced by the light.

Instant Wars

Death, war, and time are secular historical associates. It is one of the most striking characteristics of the emerging technological paradigm that this association is essentially altered, at least for the decisive warfare of dominant powers. Indeed, the advent of nuclear technology, and the possibility of planetary holocaust had the paradoxical effect of canceling large-scale, global warfare between major powers, superseding a condition that marked the first half of the twentieth century as the most destructive, lethal period in history.[57] However,

[56] Thomas (1975).
[57] Van Creveld (1989); Tilly (1995).

geopolitical interests and societal confrontations continue to fuel international, inter-ethnic, and ideological hostility to the limit of aiming at physical destruction:[58] the roots of war, we must acknowledge, are in human nature, at least as historically experienced.[59] Yet in the last two decades, democratic, technologically advanced societies, in North America, Western Europe, Japan, and Oceania, have come to reject warfare and to oppose extraordinary resistance to governments' calling their citizens to the ultimate sacrifice. The Algerian war in France, the Vietnam war in the United States, and the Afghanistan war in Russia[60] were turning points in the capacity of states to commit their societies to destruction for not so compelling

[58] For some useful information, of questionable conceptualization, see US House of Representatives, Committee on Armed Services, Readiness Subcommittee (1990). See also Gurr (1993); Harff (1986).

[59] I have to confess that my understanding of war, and of the social context of warfare, is influenced by what is probably the oldest military treatise on strategy: Sun Tzu's *On the Art of War* (c.505–496BC). If the reader suspects that I indulge in exoticism, I invite her or him to its reading, on the condition of having the patience to extract the logic embedded in the analysis from its historical context. Read a sample of it:

> The art of war is of vital importance to the State. It is a matter of life and death, a road either to safety or ruin. Hence it is a subject of inquiry which can on no account be neglected. The art of war, then, is governed by five constant factors, to be taken into account in one's deliberations, when seeking to determine the conditions obtaining in the field. These are (1) The Moral Law (2) Heaven (3) Earth (4) The Commander (5) Method and Discipline. The Moral Law causes the people to be in complete accord with their ruler, so that they will follow him regardless of their lives. Heaven signifies night and day, cold and heat, times and seasons. Earth comprises distances, great and small; danger and security; open ground and narrow passes; the chances of life and death. The Commander stands for the virtues of wisdom, sincerity, benevolence, courage, and strictness. By Method and Discipline are to be understood the marshalling of the army in its proper subdivisions, the gradations of rank among the officers, the maintenance of roads by which supplies may reach the army, and *the control of military expenditure.* (pp.1–3; my emphasis)

[60] Public opinion in Russia is probably, with Japan and Germany, one of the most pacifist in the world, since in the twentieth century Russian people have suffered more from war than anyone else in the world. This pacifism could not express itself in the open until the 1980s for obvious reasons, but widespread discontent with the war in Afghanistan was an important factor in inducing Gorbachev's *perestroyka.* Furthermore, although the war in Chechnya in 1994 seemed to belie this statement, in fact it provoked the disaffection of a large proportion of the population *vis-à-vis* Yeltsin's policies, and precipitated the split between the Russian President and many of the democrats who had supported him in the past. On the basis of my personal knowledge of Russia and of some

reasons. Since warfare, and the credible threat of resorting to it, is still at the core of state power, since the end of the Vietnam war strategists have been busy finding ways still to make war. Only under this condition can economic, technological, and demographic power be translated into domination over other states, the oldest game in humankind. Three conclusions were rapidly reached in advanced, democratic countries, regarding the conditions necessary to make war somewhat acceptable to society:[61]

1 It should not involve common citizens, thus being enacted by a professional army, so that the mandatory draft should be reserved for truly exceptional circumstances, perceived as unlikely.
2 It should be short, even instantaneous, so that the consequences would not linger on, draining human and economic resources, and raising questions about the justification for military action.
3. It should be clean, surgical, with destruction, even of the enemy, kept within reasonable limits and as hidden as possible from public view, with the consequence of linking closely information-handling, image-making, and war-making.

Dramatic breakthroughs in military technology in the last two decades provided the tools to implement this socio-military strategy. Well-trained, well-equipped, full-time, professional armed forces do not require the involvement of the population at large in the war effort, except for viewing and cheering from their living rooms a particularly exciting show, punctuated with deep patriotic feelings.[62] Professional management of news reporting, in an intelligent form that understands the needs of the media while monitoring them, can bring the war live to people's homes with limited, sanitized

survey data, I would propose the admittedly optimistic hypothesis that Russia's military lobby will face in the future as serious a popular opposition to war-making as Western countries do, thus inducing a shift to technological emphasis in warfare.
[61] See the reassessment of American military strategy, in fact initiated in the late 1970s, in an important report from a blue-ribbon Commission for the US Defense Department: Ikle and Wohlsletter (1988). See my elaboration on the impact of technology on military strategy, in Castells and Skinner (1988).
[62] Most Western European countries still had no strictly professional armed forces in the mid-1990s. Yet, although a time-limited draft (less than a year in general) was still practiced, actual military operations were in the hands of a core of professional soldiers with appropriate technological training and ready to fight. Indeed, given widespread opposition to risk life for the sake of the country, the more an army relies on the draft the less these troops are likely to be engaged in combat. The overall trend points clearly to a purely symbolic military service for the large majority of the population in advanced, democratic societies.

perception of killing and suffering, a theme that Baudrillard has elaborated thoroughly.[63] Most importantly, communications and electronic weapons technology allow for devastating strikes against the enemy in extremely brief time spans. The Gulf War was of course the general rehearsal for a new type of war, and its 100 hours' denouement, against a large, and well-equipped Iraqi army, was a demonstration of the decisiveness of new military powers when an important issue is at stake (the West's oil supply in that case).[64] Of course, this analysis, and the Gulf War itself, would require some lengthy qualifications. The US and its allies did send half a million soldiers for several months to launch a ground attack, although many experts suspect that this was in fact due to internal politics in the Defense Department, not yet ready to concede to the Air Force that wars can be won from the air and the sea. This was indeed the case, since land forces did not in practice meet much resistance after the punishment inflicted on the Iraqis at a distance. True, the allies did not press their drive into Baghdad, yet this decision was not because of serious military obstacles, but because of their political calculation in keeping Iraq as a military power in the area, to check Iran and Syria. The lack of support from a major state (Russia or China) made the Iraqis particularly vulnerable, so that other major wars are not potentially so easy for the Western powers' coalition. Technologically equivalent powers would have greater difficulty going after each other. However, given the mutual cancellation of nuclear exchange between major military powers, their potential wars, and the wars between their surrogate states, are likely to depend on rapid exchanges that set the real state of technological imbalance between the warring forces.Massive destruction, or a quick demonstration of its possibility, in minimum time seems to be the accepted strategy to fight advanced wars in the information age.

However, this military strategy can only be pursued by dominant technological powers, and it contrasts sharply with numerous, endless internal and international violent conflicts that have plagued the world since 1945.[65] This temporal difference in war-making is one of the most striking manifestations of the difference in temporality that characterizes our segmented global system, a theme on which I shall elaborate below.

In dominant societies, this new age of warfare has considerable impact on time, and on the notion of time, as experienced in history. Extraordinarily intense moments of military decision-making will

[63]   Baudrillard (1991).
[64]   See, for instance, Morrocco (1991).
[65]   Tilly (1995); Carver (1980); Holsti (1991).

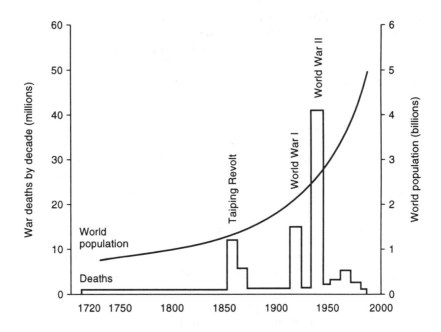

Figure 7.4   War deaths relative to world population, by decade,
1729–2000
Source: Kaye et al. (1985).

emerge as shaping instants over long periods of peace or restrained tension. For instance, according to a historical quantitative study on armed conflicts, conducted for the Canadian Defense Ministry, the duration of conflicts in the first half of the 1980s was reduced, on average, by more than half in comparison to the 1970s, and by more than two-thirds with reference to the 1960s.[66] Relying on the same source, figure 7.4 displays the decrease in the scale of death as the result of war *in recent years,* particularly when compared to the size of world population. However, observation of the same figure shows the extent to which war has been historically a way of life, with particular intensity in the first half of the twentieth century. Other sources indicate that per capita deaths from war in Western Europe, North America, Japan, and Latin America were much lower in 1945–89 than in 1815–1913.[67] Under the new warfare temporality, induced by the convergence of technology and the pressure from civil societies in

[66]   Kaye et al. (1985).
[67]   Tilly (1995), citing Derriennic (1990).

advanced countries, it seems likely that war will recede to the background of these dominant societies, to flare up from time to time in
a sudden reminder of human nature.

In several societies, this disappearance of war from the lifecycle of
most people has already decisively impacted culture and behavior. In
industrialized, democratic countries, if we except a minority of the
population for a short period of time in France, in Portugal, and in
the United States, the generations born after the Second World War
are the first in history not to have experienced war in their lifetime,
with the exception of the lucky Swedes and Swiss. This is a fundamental discontinuity in the human experience. Indeed, this
essentially affects masculinity and the culture of manhood, for
instance. Up to these generations, in the life of all men it was assumed
that at one point something terrible would happen: they would be
sent to be killed, to be killers, to live with death and the destruction
of bodies, to experience dehumanization on a large scale, and yet be
proud of it, or else be banned from the esteem of their society and,
frequently, of their families. It is impossible to understand the
women's extraordinary patience in the traditional, patriarchal family
without a reference to this moment of truth, to this male's atrocious
fate, to which mothers, wives, and daughters did pay their respect, a
recurrent theme in the literature of all countries.[68] Anyone who has
grown up, as in my case, in the first generation without war in their
life, knows how decisive the experience of war was for our fathers, how
much childhood and the life of the family was filled with the wounds
and the reconstructed memories of those years, sometimes only
months, but still shaping men's personality for ever, and with it, the
personality of their families throughout the lifecycle. This acceleration of time by cohabitation with death, regularly experienced by
generation over generation for most of human history, is now over in
some societies.[69] And this truly ushers in a new age in our experience.

However, we must be strongly reminded that instant, surgical,
secluded, technology-driven wars are the privilege of technologically
dominant nations. All around the world, half-ignored, cruel wars
linger on for years and years, often fought with primitive means,

---

[68] This theme has been elaborated by French feminist writer Annie Leclerc.
Although I discovered this idea through our personal conversations, it is also
present in some of her essays; see especially Leclerc (1975).

[69] In his cultural study of post-War World II Japanese youth, Inoue Syun found
that the "non-war" generation differed sharply from its fathers by thinking of life
apart from death. He writes: "We might very loosely label the war-time generation
as death-acceptors and the non-war generation as death-defiers" (Syun 1975). For
a broader analysis on the matter, see Freud (1947).

although global diffusion of high-tech weaponry is also catching up in this market. In the 1989–92 period alone the United Nations counted 82 armed conflicts in the world, of which 79 were internal to a nation.[70] The Indian guerrillas of Guatemala, the endless revolutionary struggles in Colombia and Peru, the Christian rebellion of Southern Sudan, the liberation struggles of Kurdish people, the Muslim rebellion of Mindanao, the mixing of drug traffic and national struggles in Myanmar and Thailand, the tribal/ideological wars in Angola, the warlords' confrontations in Somalia or Liberia, the ethnic civil wars of Rwanda and Burundi, the Sahara resistance to Morocco, the civil war in Algeria, the civil war in Afghanistan, the civil war in Sri Lanka, the civil war in Bosnia, the decades-old Arab–Israeli wars and struggles, the wars in the Caucasus, and so many other armed confrontations and wars that last for years and decades, clearly demonstrate that slow-motion, debilitating wars are still, and will be for the foreseeable future, the hideous sign of our destructive capacity.[71] It is precisely the asymmetry of various countries in their relationship to power, wealth, and technology that determines different temporalities, and particularly the time of their warfare. Furthermore, the same country may shift from slow-motion wars to instant wars depending on its relationship to the global system and to the interests of dominant powers. Thus, Iran and Iraq fought for seven years an atrocious war, carefully fed by Western countries supporting both sides of the carnage (US and France helping Iraq, Israel helping Iran, Spain selling chemical weapons to both), so that their reciprocal destruction would undermine the capacity of either of them to jeopardize the oil supply. When Iraq, with a well-equipped, combat-hardened army, went on to affirm its leadership in the region (indeed, counting on the acquiescence of Western powers), it found itself confronted by instant war technology, in a demonstration of force that was intended as a warning of future world disorder. Or elsewhere, the lingering, atrocious war in Bosnia, the shame of the European Union, was transformed in a few days, and a peace process was imposed at Dayton, Ohio, in August 1995, once the NATO countries settled their differences, and shifted the technological mode to a few days of selective, devastating strikes that crippled the Bosnian Serbs' fighting capacity. When and if a conflict becomes included in the high-priority plans of world powers, it shifts to a different tempo.

To be sure, even for dominant societies, the end of war does not mean the end of violence and of violent confrontation with political

[70] *Economist* (1993).
[71] Tillema (1991).

apparatuses of various kinds. The transformation of war ushers in new forms of violent conflict, terrorism being foremost among them. Potential nuclear, chemical, and bacteriological terrorism, in addition to indiscriminate massacres and hostage-taking, with the media as the focus of the action, are likely to become the expressions of warfare in advanced societies. Yet even these violent acts, susceptible to affecting everybody's psyche, are experienced as discontinuous instants in the course of peaceful normality. This is in striking contrast to the pervasiveness of state-induced violence in much of the planet.[72]

Instant wars, and their technologically induced temporality, are an attribute of informational societies, but, as with other dimensions of the new temporality, they characterize the forms of domination of the new system, to the exclusion of countries and events that are not central to the emerging, dominant logic.

Virtual Time

The culture of real virtuality associated with an electronically integrated multimedia system, as argued in chapter 5, contributes to the transformation of time in our society in two different forms: simultaneity and timelessness.

On the one hand, instant information throughout the globe, mixed with live reporting from across the neighborhood, provides unprecedented temporal immediacy to social events and cultural expressions.[73] To follow minute by minute in real time the collapse of the Soviet state in August 1991, with simultaneous translation of Russian political debates, introduced a new era of communication, when the making of history can be directly witnessed, provided it is deemed interesting enough by the controllers of information. Also, computer-mediated communication makes possible real-time dialogue, bringing people together around their interests, in interactive, multilateral chat writing. Time-delayed answers can be easily overcome, as new communication technologies provide a sense of immediacy that conquers time barriers, as much as the telephone did but with greater flexibility, with the communicating parties able to lapse for a few seconds, or minutes, to bring in other information, to expand the realm of communication, without the pressure of the telephone, ill-adapted to long silences.

---

[72] Tilly (1995).
[73] Wark (1994); Campo Vidal (1996).

On the other hand, the mixing of times in the media, within the same channel of communication and at the choice of the viewer/interactor, creates a temporal collage, where not only genres are mixed, but their timing becomes synchronous in a flat horizon, with no beginning, no end, no sequence. The timelessness of multi-media's hypertext is a decisive feature of our culture, shaping the minds and memories of children educated in the new cultural context. History is first organized according to the availability of visual material, then submitted to the computerized possibility of selecting seconds of frames to be pieced together, or split apart, according to specific discourses. School education, media entertainment, special news reports or advertising organize temporality as it fits, so that the overall effect is a nonsequential time of cultural products available from the whole realm of the human experience. If encyclopedias have organized human knowledge by alphabetical order, electronic media provide access to information, expression, and perception according to the impulses of the consumer or to the decisions of the producer. By so doing, the whole ordering of meaningful events loses its internal, chronological rhythm, and becomes arranged in time sequences depending upon the social context of their utilization. Thus, **it is a culture at the same time of the eternal and of the ephemeral.** It is eternal because it reaches back and forth to the whole sequence of cultural expressions. It is ephemeral because each arrangement, each specific sequencing, depends on the context and purpose under which any given cultural construct is solicited. We are not in a culture of circularity, but in a universe of undifferentiated temporality of cultural expressions.

I have discussed the relationship between the ideology of the end of history, the material conditions created under the logic of the space of flows, and the emergence of postmodern architecture, where all cultural codes can be mixed without sequencing or ordering, since we are in a world of finite cultural expressions. Eternal/ephemeral time also fits in this particular cultural mode, as it transcends any partic-ular sequencing. David Harvey, along similar lines of argument, has brilliantly shown the interaction between postmodern culture, be it in architecture, cinema, art, or philosophy, and what he calls the "post-modern condition" induced by space-time compression. Although I believe that he gives to capitalist logic more responsibility than it deserves for current processes of cultural transformation, his analysis unveils the social sources of the sudden convergence of cultural expressions towards the negation of meaning and the affir-mation of irony as the supreme value.[74] Time is compressed and

[74]   Harvey (1990: 284ff).

ultimately denied in culture, as a primitive replica of the fast turnover in production, consumption, ideology, and politics on which our society is based. A speed only made possible because of new communication technologies.

Yet culture does not simply reproduce in all its manifestations the logic of the economic system. The historical correspondence between the political economy of signs and the signs of political economy is not a sufficient argument to characterize the emergence of timeless time in postmodernism. I think we must add something else: the specificity of new cultural expressions, their ideological and technological freedom to scan the planet and the whole history of humankind, and to integrate, and mix, in the supertext any sign from anywhere, from the rap culture of American ghettoes, mimicked a few months later in the pop groups of Taipei or Tokyo, to Buddhist spiritualism transformed in electronic music. The eternal/ephemeral time of the new culture does fit with the logic of flexible capitalism and with the dynamics of the network society, but it adds its own, powerful layer, installing individual dreams and collective representations in a no-time mental landscape.

Perhaps New Age music, so characteristic of the taste of today's professionals throughout the world, is representative of the timeless dimension of the emerging culture, bringing together reconstructed Buddhist meditation, electronic sound-making, and sophisticated Californian composition. The electric harp of Hillary Staggs, modulating the range of elementary notes in an endless variation of a simple melody, or the long pauses and sudden volume alterations of Ray Lynch's painful serenity, combine within the same musical text a feeling of distance and repetition with the sudden surge of restrained sentiment, as blips of life in the ocean of eternity, a feeling often underscored by background sound of ocean waves or of the desert's wind in many New Age compositions. Assuming, as I do, that New Age is the classic music of our epoch, and observing its influence in so many different contexts but always among the same social groups, it can be suggested that the manipulation of time is the recurrent theme of new cultural expressions. A manipulation obsessed with the binary reference to instantaneity and eternity: me and the universe, the self and the net. Such reconciliation, actually fusing the biological individual into the cosmological whole, can only be achieved under the condition of the merger of all times, from the creation of ourselves to the end of the universe. Timelessness is the recurrent theme of our age's cultural expressions, be it in the sudden flashes of video clips or in the eternal echoes of electronic spiritualism.

Time, Space, and Society: the Edge of Forever

So, in the end, what is time, this elusive notion that bewildered St Augustine, misled Newton, inspired Einstein, obsessed Heidegger? And how is it being transformed in our society?

For the sake of my exploration, I find it helpful to call upon Leibniz, for whom time is the order of succession of "things," so that without "things" there would be no time.[75] Current knowledge on the concept of time in physics, biology, history, and sociology does not seem to be contradicted by such clear, synthetic conceptualization. Furthermore, we may better understand the on-going transformation of temporality by reference to the Leibnizian notion of time. I propose the idea that **timeless time,** as I label the dominant temporality of our society, **occurs when the characteristics of a given context, namely, the informational paradigm and the network society, induce systemic perturbation in the sequential order of phenomena performed in that context.** This perturbation may take the form of compressing the occurrence of phenomena, aiming at instantaneity, or else by introducing random discontinuity in the sequence. Elimination of sequencing creates undifferentiated time, which is tantamount to eternity.

The specific analyses presented in this chapter provide illustrations of the substantive issues involved under such abstract characterization. Split-second capital transactions, flex-time enterprises, variable life working time, the blurring of the lifecycle, the search for eternity through the denial of death, instant wars, and the culture of virtual time, all are fundamental phenomena, characteristic of the network society, that systemically mix tenses in their occurrence.

However, this characterization does not refer to all time in human experience. In fact, in our world, most people and most spaces live in a different temporality. I mentioned the dramatic contrast between

---

[75] Although the analysis of space and time is embedded in the whole philosophical vision of Leibniz, one of the most clear formulations of his thinking is the following paragraph, extracted from his correspondence with Clark (1715–16):

> I have more than once stated that I held *space* to be something purely relative, like *time; space being an order of co-existences as time is an order of successions.* For space denotes in terms of possibility an order of things which exist at the same time, in so far as they exist together, and is not concerned with their particular ways of existing: and when we see several things together we perceive this order of things among themselves . . . The same is true of time . . . *Instants apart from things are nothing, and they only consist in the successive order of things.*   (Quoted from Parkinson (ed.) 1973: 211–12, my added emphasis)

instant wars and the elimination of war in the life horizon of most people in the dominant countries, on the one hand, and the endless, daily war-making in places scattered all over the planet, on the other hand. A similar argument may be extended to each instance associated with the new temporality. Infant mortality rates in Uruguay and in the former USSR are more than twice the average of those in the US, but so are the rates for infant mortality in Washington, D.C. (see table 7.6). Although death and illness are being pushed back throughout the world, yet in 1990 people from the least-developed countries were expected to live 25 years less than those in the most advanced areas. Flex-time, networked production, and self-management of time in Northern Italy or Silicon Valley have very little meaning for the millions of workers brought into the clock-run assembly lines of China and South-East Asia. Flexible schedules still mean for the vast majority of the world's urban population their survival in unpredictable work patterns of the informal economy, where the notion of unemployment is strange to a system where you work or you die. For instance, mobile telephony adds time/space flexibility to personal and professional connections, but in the streets of Lima, in 1995, it spurred a new form of informal business, nicknamed *cholular*,[76] in which street communication vendors wandered around carrying cellular phones, offering rental calls to people walking by: maximum flexibility in endless working days of unpredictable future. Or, again, virtual culture is still associated for a large segment of people with passive TV viewing at the end of exhausting days, with the mind captured in images of soap operas about Texas millionaires, strangely equally familiar to youngsters in Marrakech and to housewives in Barcelona where, naturally proud of their identity, they watch it in Catalan.

Timeless time belongs to the space of flows, while time discipline, biological time, and socially determined sequencing characterize places around the world, materially structuring and destructuring our segmented societies. Space shapes time in our society, thus reversing a historical trend: flows induce timeless time, places are time-bounded.[77] The idea of progress, at the roots of our culture and society for the last two centuries, was based on the movement of

---

[76] "Cholo" is the common language name received by the people of the coast in Peru. "Cholular" plays with the linguistic integration between cellular telephony and Lima's identity.

[77] This conceptualization has some similarity with the construction of space-time regimes proposed by Innis (1950, 1951). I do not claim, however, an intellectual lineage with his theory, since I believe he would probably have disagreed with my overall analysis of time.

Table 7.6 Comparisons of infant mortality rates, selected countries, 1990–5 estimates

	Deaths per 1,000 live births
United States Total	9
White	8
Other	16
Black	18
Counties and cities	
Norfolk City, VA	20
Portsmouth City, VA	19
Suffolk City, VA	25
New York City, NY	12
Bronx	13
Orleans, LA	17
Los Angeles Co., CA	8
Wayne Co. (Detroit), MI	16
Washington, DC	21
Africa	95
Algeria	61
Egypt	57
Kenya	66
Morocco	68
Nigeria	96
South Africa	53
Tanzania	102
Zaire	93
Asia	62
Europe	10
Latin America	47
Northern America	8
Oceania	22
USSR (former)	21
Other countries	
Bulgaria	14
Canada	7
Chile	17
China	27
Costa Rica	14
France	7
Germany	7
Hong Kong	6
Jamaica	14
Japan	5
Korea	21
Malaysia	14
Poland	15
Singapore	8
Thailand	26
Ukraine	14
Uruguay	20
United Kingdom	7

Sources: United Nations Population Fund, *The State of World Population*, 1994; US Dept of Health and Human Services, *Vital Statistics of the United States: 1990*, vol. II section 2, table 2-1, 1994.

history, indeed on the predetermined sequence of history under the lead of reason and with the impulse of productive forces, escaping the constraints of spatially bounded societies and cultures. The mastery of time, the control of rhythmicity colonized territories and transformed space in the vast movement of industrialization and urbanization accomplished by the twin historical processes of formation of capitalism and statism. *Becoming* structured *being*, time conformed space.

The dominant trend in our society displays the historical revenge of space, structuring temporality in different, even contradictory logics according to spatial dynamics. The space of flows, as analyzed in the preceding chapter, dissolves time by disordering the sequence of events and making them simultaneous, thus installing society in eternal ephemerality. The multiple space of places, scattered, fragmented, and disconnected, displays diverse temporalities, from the most primitive domination of natural rhythms to the strictest tyranny of clock time. Selected functions and individuals transcend time,[78] while downgraded activities and subordinate people endure life as time goes by. While the emerging logic of the new social structure aims at the relentless supersession of time as an ordered sequence of events, most of society, in a globally interdependent system, remains on the edge of the new universe. Timelessness sails in an ocean surrounded by time-bound shores, from where still can be heard the laments of time-chained creatures.

Furthermore, the logic of timelessness is not displayed without resistance in society. As places and localities aim at regaining control over the social interests embedded in the space of flows, so time-conscious social actors try to bring under control the ahistorical domination of timelessness. Precisely because our society reaches the understanding of material interactions for the whole environment, science and technology provide us with the potential to foresee a new kind of temporality, also placed within the framework of eternity, but taking into account historical sequences. This is what Lash and Urry call "glacial time," a notion in which "the relation between humans and nature is very long-term and evolutionary. It moves back out of immediate human history and forwards into a wholly unspecifiable

---

[78] It would seem counterintuitive to argue that the professional elite in our societies is time-transcendent. Are not they (we) constantly running against the clock? My argument is that this behavioral pattern is precisely the consequence of aiming at the relentless supersession of time and of the rhythmicity of the life-cycle (aging, career advancement), induced by our culture/organization, and apparently facilitated by new technological means. What can be more time stressful than the daily battle against time?

future."[79] In fact, the opposition between the management of glacial time and the search for timelessness anchors in contradictory positions in the social structure the environmentalist movement and the powers that be in our society, as I shall elaborate further in volume II. What must be retained from the discussion at this point is the conflictive differentiation of time, understood as the impact of opposed social interests on the sequencing of phenomena. Such differentiation concerns, on the one hand, the contrasting logic between timelessness, structured by the space of flows, and multiple, subordinate temporalities, associated with the space of places. On the other hand, the contradictory dynamics of society opposes the search for human eternity, through the annihilation of time in life, to the realization of cosmological eternity, through the respect of glacial time. Between subdued temporalities and evolutionary nature the network society rises on the edge of forever.

[79]   Lash and Urry (1994: 243).

Conclusion:
The Network Society

Our exploration of emergent social structures across domains of human activity and experience leads to an overarching conclusion: as a historical trend, dominant functions and processes in the information age are increasingly organized around networks. Networks constitute the new social morphology of our societies, and the diffusion of networking logic substantially modifies the operation and outcomes in processes of production, experience, power, and culture. While the networking form of social organization has existed in other times and spaces, the new information technology paradigm provides the material basis for its pervasive expansion throughout the entire social structure. Furthermore, I would argue that this networking logic induces a social determination of a higher level than that of the specific social interests expressed through the networks: the power of flows takes precedence over the flows of power. Presence or absence in the network and the dynamics of each network *vis-à-vis* others are critical sources of domination and change in our society: a society that, therefore, we may properly call the network society, characterized by the preeminence of social morphology over social action.

To clarify this statement, I shall try to link up the main lines of analysis presented in this volume with the broader theoretical perspective outlined in the Prologue. It should, however, be kept in mind that I cannot address the full range of theoretical questions introduced at the onset of this inquiry until after examining (in volumes II and III) fundamental issues such as gender relationships, the construction of identity, social movements, the transformation of political process, and the crisis of the state in the information age. It is only after treating these matters, and observing their actual expression in the macro-processes reshaping societies in this end of millennium, that I shall try to propose some exploratory hypotheses to interpret the new society in the making. Nevertheless, enough information and ideas have been submitted to the reader's attention in this volume to be able to reach some provisional conclusions concerning the new structure of dominant functions and processes, a necessary starting point to understand the overall dynamics of society.

I shall first define the concept of network, since it plays such a central role in my characterization of society in the information age.[1] A network is a set of interconnected nodes. A node is the point at which a curve intersects itself. What a node is, concretely speaking, depends on the kind of concrete networks of which we speak. They are stock exchange markets, and their ancillary advanced services centers, in the network of global financial flows. They are national councils of ministers and European Commissioners in the political network that governs the European Union. They are coca fields and poppy fields, clandestine laboratories, secret landing strips, street gangs, and money-laundering financial institutions, in the network of drug traffic that penetrates economies, societies, and states throughout the world. They are television systems, entertainment studios, computer graphics milieux, news teams, and mobile devices generating, transmitting, and receiving signals, in the global network of the new media at the roots of cultural expression and public opinion in the information age. The topology defined by networks determines that the distance (or intensity and frequence of interaction) between two points (or social positions) is shorter (or more frequent, or more intense) if both points are nodes in a network than if they do not belong to the same network. On the other hand, within a given network flows have no distance, or the same distance, between nodes. Thus, distance (physical, social, economic, political, cultural) for a given point or position varies between zero (for any node in the same network) and infinite (for any point external to the network). The inclusion/exclusion in networks, and the architecture of relationships between networks, enacted by light-speed operating information technologies, configurate dominant processes and functions in our societies.

Networks are open structures, able to expand without limits, integrating new nodes as long as they are able to communicate within the network, namely as long as they share the same communication codes (for example, values or performance goals). A network-based social structure is a highly dynamic, open system, susceptible to innovating without threatening its balance. Networks are appropriate instru-

[1]   I am indebted for my conceptualization of networks to my on-going intellectual dialogue with François Bar.

ments for a capitalist economy based on innovation, globalization, and decentralized concentration; for work, workers, and firms based on flexibility, and adaptability; for a culture of endless deconstruction and reconstruction; for a polity geared towards the instant processing of new values and public moods; and for a social organization aiming at the supersession of space and the annihilation of time. Yet the network morphology is also a source of dramatic reorganization of power relationships. Switches connecting the networks (for example, financial flows taking control of media empires that influence political processes) are the privileged instruments of power. Thus, the switchers are the power holders. Since networks are multiple, the interoperating codes and switches between networks become the fundamental sources in shaping, guiding, and misguiding societies. The convergence of social evolution and information technologies has created a new material basis for the performance of activities throughout the social structure. This material basis, built in networks, earmarks dominant social processes, thus shaping social structure itself.

So observations and analyses presented in this volume seem to indicate that the new economy is organized around global networks of capital, management, and information, whose access to technological know-how is at the roots of productivity and competitiveness. Business firms and, increasingly, organizations and institutions are organized in networks of variable geometry whose intertwining supersedes the traditional distinction between corporations and small business, cutting across sectors, and spreading along different geographic clusters of economic units. Accordingly, the work process is increasingly individualized, labor is disaggregated in its performance, and reintegrated in its outcome through a multiplicity of interconnected tasks in different sites, ushering in a new division of labor based on the attributes/capacities of each worker rather than on the organization of the task.

However, this evolution towards networking forms of management and production does not imply the demise of capitalism. The network society, in its various institutional expressions, is, for the time being, a capitalist society. Furthermore, for the first time in history, the capitalist mode of production shapes social relationships over the entire planet. But this brand of capitalism is profoundly different from its historical predecessors. It has two fundamental distinctive features: it is global, and it is structured to a large extent, around a network of financial flows. Capital works globally as a unit in real time; and it is realized, invested, and accumulated mainly in the sphere of circulation, that is as finance capital. While finance capital has generally been among the dominant fractions of capital, we are witnessing the emergence of something different: capital accumulation proceeds, and its value-making is generated, increasingly, in the global financial markets enacted by information networks in the timeless space of financial flows. From these networks, capital is invested, globally, in all sectors of activity: information industries, media business, advanced services, agricultural production, health, education, technology, old and new manufacturing, transportation, trade, tourism, culture, environmental management, real estate, war-making and peace-selling, religion, entertainment, and sports. Some activities are more profitable than others, as they go through cycles, market upswings and downturns, and segmented global competition. Yet whatever is extracted as profit (from producers, consumers, technology, nature, and institutions) is reverted to the meta-network of financial flows, where all capital is equalized in the commodified democracy of profit-making. In this electronically operated global casino specific capitals boom or bust, settling the fate of corporations, household savings, national currencies, and regional economies. The net result sums to zero: the losers pay for the winners. But who are the winners and the losers changes by the year, the month, the day, the second, and permeates down to the world of firms, jobs, salaries, taxes, and public services. To the world of what is sometimes called "the real economy," and of what I would be tempted to call the "unreal economy," since in the age of networked capitalism the fundamental reality, where money is made and lost, invested or saved, is in the financial sphere. All other activities (except those of the dwindling public sector) are primarily the basis to generate the necessary surplus to invest in global flows, or the result of investment originated in these financial networks.

Financial capital needs, however, to rely for its operation and competition on knowledge and information generated and enhanced by information technology. This is the concrete meaning of the articulation between the capitalist mode of production and the informational mode of development. Thus, capital that would remain purely speculative is submitted to excessive risk, and ultimately washed out by simple statistical probability in the random movements of the financial markets. It is in the interaction between investment in profitable firms and using accumulated profits to make them fructify in the global financial networks that the process of accumulation lies. So it depends on productivity, on competitiveness, and on adequate information on investment and long-term planning in every sector. High-technology firms depend on financial resources to go on with their endless drive toward innovation, productivity, and competitiveness. Financial capital, acting directly through financial institutions or indirectly through the dynamics of stock exchange markets, conditions the fate of high-technology industries. On the other hand, technology and information are decisive tools in generating profits and in appropriating market shares. Thus, financial capital and high-technology, industrial capital are increasingly interdependent, even if their modes of operation are specific to each industry. Hilferding and Schumpeter were both right, but their historical coupling had to wait until it was dreamed of in Palo Alto and consummated in Ginza.

Thus, capital is either global or becomes global to enter the accumulation process in the electronically networked economy. Firms, as I have tried to show in chapter 3, are increasingly organized in networks, both internally and in their relationship. So capital flows, and their induced production/management/distribution activities are spread in interconnected networks of variable geometry. Under these new technological, organizational, and economic conditions, who are the capitalists? They are certainly not the legal owners of the means of production, who range from your/my pension fund to a passer-by in a Singapore ATM suddenly deciding to buy stock in Buenos Aires' emergent market. But this has been to some extent true since the 1930s, as shown by Berle and Means' classic study on control and ownership in United States corporations. Yet neither are the corporate managers, as suggested in their study, and, thereafter, by other analysts. For managers control specific corporations, and specific segments of the global economy, but do not control, and do not even know about, the actual, systemic movements of capital in the networks of financial flows, of knowledge in the information networks, of strategies in the multifaceted set of network enterprises. Some actors at the top of this global capitalist system are indeed managers, as in the case of Japanese corporations. Others could still be identified under the traditional category of bourgeoisie, as in the overseas Chinese business networks, who are culturally bonded, often family or personally related, share values and, sometimes, political connections. In the United States, a mixture of historical layers provides to the capitalist characters a colorful array of traditional bankers, nouveau riche speculators, self-made geniuses-turned-entrepreneurs, global tycoons, and multinational managers. In other cases, public corporations (as in French banking or electronics firms) are the capitalist actors. In Russia, survivors of communist *nomenklatura* compete with wild young capitalists in recycling state property in the constitution of the newest capitalist province. And all over the world, money-laundering from miscellaneous criminal businesses flows toward this mother of all accumulations that is the global financial network.

So all these are capitalists, presiding over all sorts of economies, and people's lives. But a capitalist class? There is not, sociologically and economically, such a thing as a global capitalist class. But there is an integrated, global capital network, whose movements and variable logic ultimately determine economies and influence societies. Thus, above a diversity of human-flesh capitalists and capitalist groups there is a faceless collective capitalist, made up of financial flows operated by electronic networks. This is not simply the expression of the abstract logic of the market, because it does not truly follow the law of supply and demand: it responds to the turbulences, and unpredictable movements, of noncalculable anticipations, induced by psychology and society, as much as by economic processes. This network of networks of capital both unifies and commands specific centers of capitalist accumulation, structuring the behavior of capitalists around their submission to the global network. They play their competing, or converging, strategies by and through the circuits of this global network, and so they are ultimately dependent upon the nonhuman capitalist logic of an electronically operated, random processing of information. It is indeed capitalism in its pure expression of the endless search for money by money through the production of commodities by commodities. But money has become almost entirely independent from production, including production of services, by escaping into the networks of higher-order electronic interactions barely understood by its managers. While capitalism still rules, capitalists are randomly incarnated, and the capitalist classes are restricted to specific areas of the world where they prosper as appendixes to a mighty whirlwind which manifests its will by spread points and futures options ratings in the global flashes of computer screens.

What happens to labor, and to the social relationships of production, in this brave new world of informational, global capitalism? Workers do not disappear in the space of flows, and, down to earth, work is plentiful. Indeed, belying apocalyptic prophecies of simplistic analyses, there are more jobs and a higher proportion of working-age people employed than at any time in history. This is mainly because of the massive incorporation of women in paid work in all industrialized societies, an incorporation that has generally been absorbed, and to a large extent induced, by the labor market without major disruptions. So the diffusion of information technologies, while certainly displacing workers and eliminating some jobs, has not resulted, and it does not seem that it will result in the foreseeable future, in mass unemployment. This in spite of the rise of unemployment in European economies, a trend that is related to social institutions rather than to the new production system. But, if work, workers, and working classes exist, and even expand, around the world, the social relationships between capital and labor are profoundly transformed.

At its core, capital is global. As a rule, labor is local. Informationalism, in its historical reality, leads to the concentration and globalization of capital, precisely by using the decentralizing power of networks. Labor is disaggregated in its performance, fragmented in its organization, diversified in its existence, divided in its collective action. Networks converge toward a meta-network of capital that integrates capitalist interests at the global level and across sectors and realms of activity: not without conflict, but under the same overarching logic. Labor loses its collective identity, becomes increasingly individualized in its capacities, in its working conditions, and in its interests and projects. Who are the owners, who the producers, who the managers, and who the servants, becomes increasingly blurred in a production system of variable geometry, of teamwork, of networking, outsourcing, and subcontracting. Can we say that the producers of value are the computer nerds who invent new financial instruments to be dispossessed from their work by corporate brokers? Who is contributing to value creation in the electronics industry: the Silicon Valley chip designer, or the young woman on the assembly line of a South-East Asian factory? Certainly both, albeit in quite substantially different proportions. Thus, are they jointly the new working class? Why not include in it the Bombay computer consultant subcontracted to program this particular design? Or the flying manager who commutes or telecommutes between California and Singapore customizing chip production and electronics consumption? There is unity of the work process throughout the complex, global networks of interaction. But there is at the same time differentiation of work, segmentation of workers, and disaggregation of labor on a global scale. So while capitalist relationships of production still persist (indeed, in many economies the dominant logic is more strictly capitalist than ever before), capital and labor increasingly tend to exist in different spaces and times: the space of flows and the space of places, instant time of computerized networks versus clock time of everyday life. Thus, they live by each other, but do not relate to each other, as the life of global capital depends less and less on specific labor, and more and more on accumulated, generic labor, operated by a small brains trust inhabiting the virtual palaces of global networks. Beyond this fundamental dichotomy a great deal of social diversity still exists, made up of investors' bids, workers' efforts, human ingenuity, human suffering, hirings and layoffs, promotions and demotions, conflicts and negotiations, competition and alliances: working life goes on. Yet, at a deeper level of the new social reality, social relationships of production have been disconnected in their actual existence. Capital tends to escape in its hyperspace of pure circulation, while labor dissolves its collective entity into an infinite variation of individual existences. Under the conditions of the network society, capital is globally coordinated, labor is individualized. The struggle between diverse capitalists and miscellaneous working classes is subsumed into the more fundamental opposition between the bare logic of capital flows and the cultural values of human experience.

Processes of social transformation summarized under the ideal type of the network society go beyond the sphere of social and technical relationships of production: they deeply affect culture and power as well. Cultural expressions are abstracted from history and geography, and become predominantly mediated by electronic communication networks that interact with the audience and by the audience in a diversity of codes and values, ultimately subsumed in a digitized, audiovisual hypertext. Because information and communication circulate primarily through the diversified, yet comprehensive media system, politics becomes increasingly played out in the space of media. Leadership is personalized, and image-making is power-making. Not that all politics can be reduced to media effects, or that values and interests are indifferent to political outcomes. But whoever the political actors and whatever their orientations, they exist in the power game through and by the media, in the whole variety of an increasingly diverse media system, that includes computer-mediated communication networks. The fact that politics has to be framed in the language of electronically based media has profound consequences on the characteristics, organization, and goals of political processes, political actors, and political institutions. Ultimately, the powers that are in the media networks take second place to the power of flows embodied in the structure and language of these networks.

At a deeper level, the material foundations of society, space and time are being transformed, organized around the space of flows and timeless time. Beyond the metaphorical value of these expressions, supported by a number of analyses and illustrations in preceding chapters, a major hypothesis is put forward: dominant functions are organized in networks pertaining to a space of flows that links them up around the world, while fragmenting subordinate functions, and people, in the multiple space of places, made of locales increasingly segregated and disconnected from each other. Timeless time appears to be the result of the negation of time, past and future, in the networks of the space of flows. Meanwhile clock time, measured and valued differentially for each process according to its position in the network, continues to characterize subordinate functions and specific locales. The end of history, enacted in the circularity of computerized financial flows or in the instantaneity of surgical wars, overpowers the biological time of poverty or the mechanical time of industrial work. The social construction of new dominant forms of space and time develops a meta-network that switches off nonessential functions, subordinate social groups, and devalued territories. By so doing, infinite social distance is created between this meta-network and most individuals, activities, and locales around the world. Not that people, locales, or activities disappear. But their structural meaning does, subsumed in the unseen logic of the meta-network where value is produced, cultural codes are created, and power is decided. The new social order, the network society, increasingly appears to most people as a meta-social disorder. Namely, as an automated, random sequence of events, derived from the uncontrollable logic of markets, technology, geopolitical order, or biological determination.

In a broader historical perspective, the network society represents a qualitative change in the human experience. If we refer to an old sociological tradition according to which social action at the most fundamental level can be understood as the changing pattern of relationships between Nature and Culture, we are indeed in a new era.

The first model of relationship between these two fundamental poles of human existence was characterized for millennia by the domination of Nature over Culture. The codes of social organization almost directly expressed the struggle for survival under the uncontrolled harshness of Nature, as anthropology taught us by tracing the codes of social life back to the roots of our biological entity.

The second pattern of the relationship established at the origins of the Modern Age, and associated with the Industrial Revolution and with the triumph of Reason, saw the domination of Nature by Culture, making society out of the process of work by which Humankind found both its liberation from natural forces and its submission to its own abysses of oppression and exploitation.

We are just entering a new stage in which Culture refers to Culture, having superseded Nature to the point that Nature is artificially revived ("preserved") as a cultural form: this is in fact the meaning of the environmental movement, to reconstruct Nature as an ideal cultural form. Because of the convergence of historical evolution and technological change we have entered a purely cultural pattern of social interaction and social organization. This is why information is the key ingredient of our social organization and why flows of messages and images between networks constitute the basic thread of our social structure. This is not to say that history has ended in a happy reconciliation of Humankind with itself. It is in fact quite the opposite: history is just beginning, if by history we understand the moment when, after millennia of a prehistoric battle with Nature, first to survive, then to conquer it, our species has reached the level of knowledge and social organization that will allow us to live in a predominantly social world. It is the beginning of a new existence, and indeed the beginning of a new age, the information age, marked by the autonomy of culture *vis-à-vis* the material bases of our existence. But this is not necessarily an exhilarating moment. Because, alone at last in our human world, we shall have to look at ourselves in the mirror of historical reality. And we may not like the vision.

To be continued.

Summary of the Contents of Volumes II and III

Throughout this volume reference has been made to the themes to be presented in the subsequent volumes of this work (to be published by Blackwell Publishers in 1997). An outline of their contents is given below.

Volume II: *The Power of Identity*

Introduction: Our lives, our world

1 Communal Heavens: Identity and meaning in the network society

2 The end of patriarchalism: the transformation of gender, family, sexuality, and personality

3 Social movements and social change in a world of flows

4 The powerless state

5 Informational politics and the crisis of democracy

Conclusion: The subjects of social change in the network society

Bibliography

Abegglen, J.C. and Stalk, G. (1985) *Kaisha: The Japanese Corporation*, New York: Basic Books.

Abolaffia, Michael Y. and Biggart, Nicole W. (1991) "Competition and markets: an institutional perspective." In Amitai Etzioni and Paul R. Lawrence (eds), *Socio-economics: Towards a New Synthesis*, Armonk, NY: M.E. Sharpe, pp. 211–31.

Adam, Barbara (1990) *Time and Social Theory*, Cambridge: Polity Press.

Adler, Glenn and Suarez, Doris (1993) *Union Voices: Labor's Responses to Crisis*, Albany, NY: State University of New York Press.

Adler, Paul S. (1992) *Technology and the Future of Work*, New York: Oxford University Press.

African Development Bank (1990) *The Social Dimensions of Adjustment in Africa: A Policy Agenda*, Washington D.C.: World Bank.

Agence de l'Informatique (1986) *L'Etat d'informatisation de la France*, Paris: Economica.

Aglietta, Michel (1976) *Régulation et crise du capitalisme: l'expérience des Etats-Unis*, Paris: Calmann-Levy.

Allen, G.C. (1981a) *The Japanese Economy*, New York: St Martin's Press.

—— (1981b) *A Short Economic History of Modern Japan*, London: Macmillan.

Allen, Jane E. (1995) "New computers may use DNA instead of chips." *San Francisco Chronicle*, May 13: B2.

Alvarado, Manuel (ed.) (1988) *Video World-wide*, London and Paris: John Libbey.

Amin, Ash and Robins, Kevin (1991) "These are not Marshallian times." In Roberto Camagni (ed.) *Innovation Networks: Spatial Perspectives*, London: Belhaven Press, pp. 105–20.

Amsdem, Alice (1979) "Taiwan's economic history: a case of étatisme and a challenge to dependency theory," *Modern China*, 5(3): 341–80.

—— (1985) "The state and Taiwan's economic development." In Peter B.

Evans, Dietrich Rueschemeyer and Theda Skocpol (eds), *Bringing the State Back in*, Cambridge: Cambridge University Press.

—— (1989) *Asia's Next Giant: South Korea and Late Industrialization*, New York: Oxford University Press.

—— (1992) "A theory of government intervention in late industrialization." In Louis Putterman and Dietrich Rueschemeyer (eds), *State and Market in Development: Synergy or Rivalry?*, Boulder, CO: Lynne Rienner.

Anderson, A.E. (1985) *Creativity and Regional Development*, Laxenburg: International Institute for Applied Systems Analysis, Working Paper 85/14.

Andrieu, Michel, Michalski, Wolfgang and Stevens, Barrie (eds) (1992) *Long-term Prospects for the World Economy*, Paris: OECD.

Anisimov, Evgenii (1993) *The Reforms of Peter the Great: Progress Through Coercion in Russia*, Armonk, NY: M.E. Sharpe.

Aoki, Masahiko (1988) *Information, incentives, and bargaining in the Japanese economy*, Cambridge: Cambridge University Press.

Aoyama, Yuko (1995 in progress) "Locational strategies of Japanese multi-national corporations in electronics," University of California, PhD dissertation in city and regional planning.

Appelbaum, Eileen (1984) *Technology and the Redesign of Work in the Insurance Industry*, Research Report, Stanford, CA: Stanford University Institute of Research on Educational Finance and Governance.

—— and Schettkat, Ronald (eds) (1990) *Labor Markets, Adjustments to Structural Change and Technological Progress*, New York: Praeger.

Appelbaum, Richard P. and Henderson, Jeffrey (eds) (1992) *States and Development in the Asian Pacific Rim*, London: Sage.

Arancibia, Sergio (1988) *Dependencia y deuda externa*, Lima: Taller Popular.

Aries, Philippe (1977) *L'homme devant la mort*, Paris: Seuil.

—— (1983) *Images de l'homme devant la mort*, Paris: Seuil.

Armstrong, David (1994) "Computer sex: log on; talk dirty; get off." *San Francisco Examiner*, April 10.

Aron, Raymond (1963) *Dix-huit leçons sur la société industrielle*, Paris: Idées-Gallimard.

Aronowitz, Stanley and Di Fazio, Williams (1994) *The Jobless Future*, Minneapolis: University of Minnesota.

Arrieta, Carlos G. et al. (1991) *Narcotrafico en Colombia. Dimensiones politicas, economicas, juridicas e internacionales*, Bogota: Tercer Mundo Editores.

Arthur, Brian (1985) *Industry Location and the Economics of Agglomeration: Why a Silicon Valley?*, Stanford, CA: Stanford University Center for Economic Policy Research, Working Paper.

—— (1986) *Industry Location Patterns and the Importance of History*, Stanford, CA: Stanford University Food Research Institute, Research Paper.

—— (1989) "Competing technologies, increasing returns, and lock-in by historical events." *Economic Journal*, 99 (March): 116–31.

Ashton, Thomas S. (1948) *The Industrial Revolution, 1760–1830*, Oxford: Oxford University Press.

Asian Money, Asian Issuers & Capital Markets Supplement (1993/1994) "Derivatives: making more room to manoeuvre," Dec.–Jan.: 30–2.

Aslund, Anders (1995) *How Russia Became a Market Economy*, Washington D.C.: Brookings Institution.

Aydalot, Philippe (1985) "L'aptitude des milieux locaux a promouvoir innovation technologique," communication au symposium *Nouvelles technologies et regions en crise*, Association de science régionale de langue française, Brussels, April 22–23.

Aznar, Guy (1993) *Travailler moins pour travailler tous*, Paris: Syros.

Baghwati, J. and Srinivasan, T.M. (1993) *Indian Economic Reforms*, New Delhi: Ministry of Finance.

Bailey, Paul, Parisotto, Aurelio and Renshaw, Geoffrey (eds) (1993) *Multinationals and Employment: The Global Economy of the 1990s*, Geneva: International Labour Organization.

Baker, Hugh (1979) *Chinese Family and Kinship*, New York: Columbia University Press.

Balaji, R. (1994) "The formation and structure of the high technology industrial complex in Bangalore, India," Berkeley, CA: University of California, PhD dissertation in City and Regional Planning (in progress).

Baldwin-Evans, Martin and Schain, Martin (eds) (1995) *The Politics of Immigration in Western Europe*, London: Frank Cass.

Ball-Rokeach, Sandra J. and Cantor, Muriel (eds) (1986) *Media, Audience and Social Structure*, Beverly Hills, CA: Sage.

Banegas, Jesus (ed.) (1993) *La industria de la información. Situación actual y perspectivas*, Madrid: Fundesco.

Bar, François (1990) *Configuring the Telecommunications Infrastructure for the Computer Age: The Economics of Network Control*, Berkeley, CA: University of California, PhD dissertation.

—— (1992) "Network flexibility: a new challenge for telecom policy." *Communications and Strategies*, special issue, June: 111–22.

—— and Borrus, M. (1993) *The Future of Networking*, Berkeley, CA: University of California, BRIE Working Paper.

—— and —— with Coriat, Benjamin (1991) *Information Networks and Competitive Advantage: Issues for Government Policy and Corporate Strategy Development*, Brussels: Commission of European Communities, DGIII-BRIE-OECD Research Program.

Baran, Barbara (1985) "Office automation and women's work: the technological transformation of the insurance industry." In Manuel Castells (ed.), *High Technology, Space, and Society*, Beverly Hills, CA: Sage, pp. 143–71.

—— (1989) *Technological Innovation and Deregulation: The Transformation of the Labor Process in the Insurance Industry*, Berkeley, CA: University of California, PhD dissertation in City and Regional Planning.

Baranano, Ana M. (1994) "La empresa española en los programas europeos de cooperación tecnológica," Madrid: Universidad Autonoma de Madrid, unpublished doctoral thesis in Business Economics.

Barglow, Raymond (1994) *The Crisis of the Self in the Age of Information: Computers, Dolphins, and Dreams*, London: Routledge.

Barthes, Roland (1978) *Leçon inaugurale de la chaire de sémiologie littéraire du Collège de France, prononcée le 7 Janvier 1977*, Paris: Seuil.

Bassalla, George (1988) *The Evolution of Technology*, Cambridge: Cambridge University Press.

Batty, Michael and Barr, Bob (1994) "The electronic frontier: exploring and mapping cyberspace," *Futures*, 26(7): 699–712.

Baudrillard, Jean (1972) *Pour une critique de l'économie politique du signe*, Paris: Gallimard.

—— (1991) *La Guerre du Golfe n'a pas eu lieu*, Paris: Fayard.

Baumgartner, Peter and Payr, Sabine (eds) (1995) *Speaking Minds: Interviews with Twenty Eminent Cognitive Scientists*, Princeton, NJ: Princeton University Press.

Baumol, W.J., Blackman S.A.B. and Wolf, E.N. (1989) *Productivity and American Leadership: The Long View*, Cambridge, MA: MIT Press.

Bayart, Jean-François (1992) *The State in Africa: The Politics of the Belly*, London: Longman.

Beasley, W.G. (1990) *The Rise of Modern Japan*, London: Weidenfeld & Nicolson.

Bedi, Hari (1991) *Understanding the Asian Manager*, Sydney: Allen & Unwin.

Bedoui, Mongi (1995) *Bibliographie sur l'exclusion dans les pays arabes du Mahgreb et du Machreq*, Geneva: International Institute of Labour Studies, Discussion paper 80/1995.

Bell, Daniel (1976) *The Coming of Post-industrial Society: A Venture in Social Forecasting*, New York: Basic Books. (First published 1973.)

Belussi, Fiorenza (1992) "La flessibilita si fa gerarchia: la Benetton." In F. Belussi (ed.), *Nuovi Modelli d'Impresa, Gerarchie Organizzative e Imprese Rete*, Milan: Franco Angeli.

Bendixon, Terence (1991) "El transporte urbano." In Jordi Borja et al., pp 427–53. *Las grandes ciudades en la decada de los noventa*, Madrid: Editorial Sistema.

Beniger, James R. (1986) *The Control Revolution: Technological and Economic Origins of the Information Society*, Cambridge, MA: Harvard University Press.

Bennett, A. (1990) *The Death of Organization Man*, New York: William Morrow.

Benson, Rod (1994) "Telecommunications and society: a review on the research literature on computer-mediated communication," Berkeley, CA: University of California, Berkeley Roundtable on the International Economy, Compuscript.

Benveniste, Guy (1994) *Twenty-first Century Organization: Analyzing Current Trends, Imagining the Future*, San Francisco, CA: Jossey Bass.

Berger, J. (1984) *And Our Faces, My Heart, Brief as Photos*, London: Writers & Readers.

Berger, Peter (1987) *The Capitalist Revolution*, London: Wildwood.

Berger, Peter and Hsiao, M. (eds) (1988) *In Search of an East Asian Development Model*, New Brunswick, NJ: Transaction Books.

Bergsten, C. Fred and Noland, Marcus (eds) (1993) *Pacific Dynamism and the*

International Economic System, Washington D.C.: Institute for International Economics.

Bernstein, Michael A. and Adler, David E. (1994) *Understanding American Economic Decline*, New York: Cambridge University Press.

Bertazzoni, F. et al. (1984) *Odissea Informatica. Alle soglie della nuova era: intinerario nelle societa informatiche*, Milan: Istituto A. Gemelli per I Problemi della Comunicazione, Gruppo Editoriale Jackson.

Bertrand, O. and Noyelle, T.J. (1988) *Corporate and Human Resources: Technological Change in Banks and Insurance Companies in Five OECD Countries*, Paris, OECD.

Bessant, John (1989) *Microelectronics and · Change at Work*, Geneva: International Labour Organization.

Bettinger, Cass (1991) *High Performance in the 1990s: Leading the Strategic and Cultural Revolution in Banking*, Homewood, IL: Business One Irwin.

Bianchi, Patrizio, Carnoy, Martin and Castells, Manuel (1988) *Economic Modernization and Technology Policy in the People's Republic of China*, Stanford, CA: Stanford University Center for Education Research, Research Monograph.

Bielenski, Harald (ed.) (1994) *New Forms of Work and Activity: Survey of Experience at Establishment Level in Eight European Countries*, Dublin: European Foundation for the Improvement of Living and Working Conditions.

Biggart, Nicole Woolsey (1990a) *Charismatic Capitalism*, Chicago, IL: University of Chicago Press.

—— (1990b) "Institutionalized patrimonialism in Korean business." *Comparative Social Research*, 12: 113–33.

—— (1991) "Explaining Asian economic organization: toward a Weberian institutional perspective." *Theory and Society*, 20: 199–232.

—— (1992) "Institutional logic and economic explanation." In Jane Marceau (ed.), *Reworking the World: Organizations, Technologies, and Cultures in Comparative Perspective*, Berlin: Walter de Gruyter, pp. 29–54.

—— and Hamilton, G.G. (1992) "On the limits of a firm-based theory to explain business networks: the western bias of neoclassical economics." In Nitin Nohria and Robert G. Ecckles (eds), *Networks and Organizations: Structure, Form, and Action*, Boston, MA: Harvard Business School Press.

Bijker, Wiebe E., Hughes, Thomas P. and Pinch, Trevor (eds) (1987) *The Social Construction of Technological Systems: New Directions in the Sociology and History of Technology*, Cambridge, MA: MIT Press.

Birch, David L. (1987) *Job Generation in America*, New York: Free Press.

Bird, Jane (1994) "Dial M for multimedia." *Management Today*, July: 50–3.

Bishop, Jerry E. and Waldholz, Michael (1990) *Genome*, New York: Simon & Schuster.

Blakely, Edward, Scotchmer, S. and Levine, J. (1988) *The Locational and Economic Patterns of California's Biotech Industry*, Berkeley, CA: University of California Institute of Urban and Regional Development, Biotech Industry Research Group Report.

Blazejczak, Jurgen, Eber, Georg and Horn, Gustav A. (1990) "Sectoral and

macroeconomic impacts of research and development on employment."
In Egon Matzner and Michael Wagner (eds), *The Employment Impact of New Technology: The Case of West Germany*, Aldershot, Hants: Avebury, pp. 221–33.

Bluestone, Barry and Harrison, Bennett (1988) *The Great American Job Machine: The Proliferation of Low-wage Employment in the U.S. Economy*, New York: Basic Books.

Blumler, Jay G. and Katz, Elihu (eds) (1974) *The Uses of Mass Communications*, Newport Beach, CA: Sage.

Bofill, Ricardo (1990) *Espacio y Vida*, Barcelona: Tusquets Editores.

Booker, Ellis (1994) "Interactive TV comes to public broadcasting." *Computerworld*, 28(3): 59.

Borja, Jordi and Castells, Manuel (1996) *The Local and the Global: Cities in the Information Age*, report commissioned by the United Nations Habitat Center for Habitat II – United Nations Conference *The City Summit*, Istanbul, 1996; to be published by Earthscan, London.

Borja, Jordi et al. (eds) (1991) *Las grandes ciudades en la decada de los noventa*, Madrid: Editorial Sistema.

Borjas, George F., Freeman, Richard B. and Katz, Lawrence F. (1991) *On the Labour Market Effects of Immigration and Trade*, Cambridge, MA: National Bureau of Economic Research.

Bornstein, Lisa (1993) "Flexible production in the unstable state: the Brazilian information technology industry." Unpublished PhD dissertation, University of California, Berkeley, Department of City and Regional Planning.

Borrus, Michael G. (1988) *Competing for Control: America's Stake in Microelectronics*, Cambridge, MA: Ballinger.

—— and Zysman, John (1992) "Industrial competitiveness and American national security." In W. Sandholtz et al., *The Highest Stakes: The Economic Foundations of the Next Security System*, New York: Oxford University Press.

Bosch, Gerhard (1995) *Flexibility and Work Organization: Report of Expert Working Group*, Brussels: European Commission, Directorate General for Employment, Industrial Relations, and Social Affairs.

——, Dawkins, Peter and Michon, François (eds) (1994) *Times Are Changing: Working Time in 14 Industrialised Countries*, Geneva: International Labour Organization.

Botein, Michael and Rice, David M. (eds) (1980) *Network Television and the Public Interest*, Lexington, MA: Lexington Books.

Boureau, Allain et al. (1989) *The Culture of Print: Power and the Uses of Print in Early Modern Europe*, ed. Roder Chartier, Princeton, NJ: Princeton University Press.

Bouvier, Leon F. and Grant, Lindsay (1994) *How Many Americans? Population, Immigration, and the Environment*, San Francisco, CA: Sierra Club Books.

Bower, J.L. (1987) *When Markets Quake*, Boston, MA: Harvard Business School Press.

Boyer, Christine (1994) *The City of Collective Memory*, Cambridge, MA: MIT Press.

Boyer, Robert (1988a) "Is a new socio-technical system emerging?" Paper prepared for a conference on *Structural Change and Labour Market Policy*, Var, Gard, 6–9 June.

—— (1988b) "Technical change and the theory of regulation." In G. Dosi, et al., *Technical Change and Economic Theory*, London: Pinter, pp. 67–94.

—— (1990) "Assessing the impact of R&D on employment: puzzle or consensus?" In E. Matzner and M. Wagner (eds), *The Employment Impact of New Technology: The Case of West Germany*, Aldershot, Hants: Avebury, pp. 234–54.

—— (ed.) (1986) *Capitalismes fin de siècle*, Paris: Presses Universitaires de France.

Boyer, R. and Mistral, J. (1988) "Le bout du tunnel? Stratégies conservatrices et nouveau régime d'accumulation," paper delivered at the International Conference on the Theory of Regulation, Barcelona, June 16–18.

—— and Ralle, P. (1986a) "Croissances nationales et contrainte extérieure avant et après 1973." *Economie et société*, no. P29.

—— and —— (1986b) "L'Insertion internationale conditionne-t-elle les formes nationales d'emploi? Convergences ou différentiations des pays européens." *Economie et société*, no. P29

Boyett, Joseph H. and Conn, Henry P. (1991) *Workplace 2000: The Revolution Reshaping American Business*, New York: Dutton.

Braddock, D.J. (1992) "Scientific and technical employment, 1900–2005." *Monthly Labor Review*, February: 28–41.

Bradford, Colin I. (ed.) (1992) *Strategic Options for Latin America in the 1990s*, Paris: OECD Development Center.

—— (1994) *The New Paradigm of Systemic Competitiveness: Toward More Integrated Policies in Latin America*, Paris: OECD Development Center.

Braudel, Fernand (1967) *Civilisation matérielle et capitalisme. XVe–XVIIe siècle*, Paris: Armand Colin.

Braun, Ernest and Macdonald, Stuart (1982) *Revolution in Miniature: The History and Impact of Semiconductor Electronics Re-explored*, 2nd edn, Cambridge: Cambridge University Press.

Braverman, Harry (1973) *Labor and Monopoly Capital*, New York: Monthly Review Press.

Breeden, Richard C. (1993) "The globalization of law and business in the 1990s." *Wake Forest Law Review*, 28(3): 509–17.

BRIE (1992) *Globalization and Production*, Berkeley, CA: University of California, BRIE Working Paper 45.

Broad, William J. (1985) *Star Warriors*, New York: Simon & Schuster.

Brooks, Harvey (1971) "Technology and the ecological crisis," lecture given at Amherst, May 9.

Brown, Richard P.C. (1992) *Public Debt and Private Wealth: Debt, Capital Flight and the IMF in Sudan*, London: Macmillan.

Brusco, S. (1982) "The Emilian model: productive decentralization and social integration." *Cambridge Journal of Economics* 6(2): 167–84.

Buitelaar, Wout (ed.) (1988) *Technology and Work: Labour Studies in England, Germany and the Netherlands*, Aldershot, Hants: Avebury.

Bunker, Ted (1994) "The multimedia infotainment I-way: telephone, cable, and media companies are pursuing video-on-demand, interactive education, multimedia politicking, and more." *LAN Magazine*, 9(10): S24.

Bureau of Labor Statistics (1994) *Occupational Projections and Training Data*, Statistical and Research Supplement to the 1994–5 *Occupational Outlook Handbook*, Bulletin 2451, May.

Burlen, Katherine (1972) "La réalisation spatiale du désir et l'image spatialisée du besoin." *Espaces et sociétés*, n.5: 145–59.

Bushnell, P. Timothy (1994) *The Transformation of the American Manufacturing Paradigm*, New York: Garland.

Business Week (1993) "The horizontal corporation." October 28.

—— (1993b) "Asia's wealth: special report." November 29.

—— (1994a) "The information technology revolution: how digital technology is changing the way we work and live." Special Issue.

—— (1994b) "The new face of business." In Special issue on "The Information Revolution," pp. 99ff.

—— (1994c) "China: birth of a new economy." January 31: 42–8.

—— (1994d) "Sega: it's blasting beyond games and racing to build a high-tech entertainment empire." February 21: cover story.

—— (1994e) "Interactive TV: not ready for prime time." March 14: 30.

—— (1994f) "The entertainment economy." March 14: 58–73.

—— (1994g) "How the Internet will change the way you do business." November 14.

—— (1994h) "Home computers: sales explode as new uses turn PCs into all-purpose information appliances." November 28: 89ff.

—— (1995a) "The networked corporation." Special issue.

—— (1995b) "Mexico: can it cope?" January 16.

—— (1995c) "Software industry." February 27: 78–86.

—— (1995d) "Benetton's new age." April 14.

—— (1995e) "The gene kings." May 8: 72ff.

—— (1995f) "The networked corporation." June 26: 85ff.

—— (1996) "Sun's rise." January 22.

Byrne, John H. (1994) "The pain of downsizing." *Business Week*, May 9.

Calderon, Fernando and Dos Santos, Mario (directors) (1989) *Hacia un nuevo orden estatal? Democratizacion, modernizacion y actores socio-politicos*, 4 vols, Buenos Aires: CLACSO.

—— and —— Mario R. (1995) *Sociedades sin atajos. Cultura politica y restructuracion económica en America Latina*, Buenos Aires: Paidos.

—— and Laserna, Roberto (1994) *Paradojas de la modernidad. Sociedad y cambios en Bolivia*, La Paz: Fundacion Milenio.

Calhoun, Craig (ed.) (1994) *Social Theory and the Politics of Identity*, Oxford: Blackwell.

Camagni, Roberto (1991) "Local milieu, uncertainty and innovation networks: towards a new dynamic theory of economic space." In Roberto Camagni (ed.), *Innovation Networks: Spatial Perspectives*, London: Belhaven Press, pp. 121–44.

Campbell, Duncan (1994) "Foreign investment, labor immobility and the quality of employment." *International Labour Review*, 2: 185–203.

Campo Vidal, Manuel (1996) "La transición audiovisual." Madrid: Antena-3 TV (unpublished).

Campos Alvarez, Tostado (1993) *El Fondo Monetario y la dueda externa mexicana*, Mexico: Plaza y Valdes Editores.

Canby, E.T. (1962) *A History of Electricity*, Englewood Cliffs, NJ: Prentice-Hall.

Cappelin, Riccardo (1991) "International networks of cities." In Roberto Camagni (ed.), *Innovation Networks: Spatial Perspectives*, London: Belhaven Press.

Cappelli, Peter and Rogovsky, Nicolai (1994) "New work systems and skill requirements." *International Labour Review*, 133(2): 205–20.

Cardoso, Fernando H. (1993) "New North/South relations in the present context: a new dependency?" In Martin Carnoy et al., *The New Global Economy in the Information Age*, University Park, PA: Penn State University Press, pp. 149–59.

—— and Faletto, Enzo (1969) *Desarrollo y dependencia en America Latina*, Mexico D.F.: Siglo XXI Editores; English trans. in expanded edition, Berkeley, CA: University of California Press, 1979.

Carey, M. and Franklin, J.C. (1991) "Outlook: 1990–2005 industry output and job growth continues slow into next century." *Monthly Labor Review*, Nov.: 45–60.

Carnoy, Martin (1989) *The New Information Technology: International Diffusion and Its Impact on Employment and Skills. A Review of the Literature*, Washington D.C.: World Bank, PHREE.

—— (1994) *Faded Dreams: The Politics and Economics of Race in America*, New York: Cambridge University Press.

—— and Castells, Manuel (1996) "Sustainable flexibility: work, family, and society in the information age," Berkeley: University of California, Center for Western European Studies.

—— and Fluitman, Fred (1994) "Training and the reduction of unemployment in industrialized countries," Geneva: International Labour Organization, unpublished report.

—— and Levin, Henry (1985) *Schooling and Work in the Democratic State*, Stanford, CA: Stanford University Press.

——, Pollack, Seth and Wong, Pia L. (1993a) *Labor Institutions and Technological Change: A Framework for Analysis and Review of the Literature*, Stanford, CA: Stanford University International Development Education Center, report prepared for the International Labour Organization, Geneva.

—— et al. (1993b) *The New Global Economy in the Information Age*, University Park, PA: Penn State University Press.

Carre, Jean-Jacques, Dubois, Paul and Malinvaud, Edmond (1984) *Abrégé de la croissance française: un essai d'analyse économique causale de l'après guerre*, Paris: Editions du Seuil.

Carver, M. (1980) *War since 1945*, London: Weidenfeld & Nicolson.

Case, Donald O. (1994) "The social shaping of videotex: how information services for the public have evolved." *Journal of the American Society for Information Science*, 45(7): 483–9.

Castano, Cecilia (1991) *La Informatizacion de la banca en Espana*, Madrid: Ministerio de Economia/Universidad Autónoma de Madrid.

—— (1994a) *Nuevas Tecnologias, Trabajo y Empleo en Espana*, Madrid: Alianza Editorial.

—— (1994b) *Tecnologia, empleo y trabajo en Espana*, Madrid: Alianza Editorial.

Castells, Manuel (1972) *La Question urbaine*, Paris: François Maspero.

—— (1976) "The service economy and the postindustrial society: a sociological critique." *International Journal of Health Services*, 6(4): 595–607.

—— (1980) *The Economic Crisis and American Society*, Princeton, NJ: Princeton University Press, and Oxford: Blackwell.

—— (1988a) "The new industrial space: information technology manufacturing and spatial structure in the United States." In G. Sternlieb and J. Hughes (eds), *America's New Market Geography: Nation, Region and Metropolis*, New Brunswick, NJ: Rutgers University.

—— (director) (1988b) *The State and Technology Policy: A Comparative Analysis of U.S. Strategic Defense Initiative, Informatics Policy in Brazil, and Electronics Policy in China*, Berkeley, CA: University of California, Berkeley Roundtable on the International Economy (BRIE), Research Monograph.

—— (1989a), "High technology and the new international division of labor." *Labour Studies*, October.

—— (1989b) *The Informational City: Information Technology, Economic Restructuring, and the Urban–Regional Process*, Oxford: Blackwell.

—— (1989c), "Notes of field work in the industrial areas of Taiwan," unpublished.

—— (1990) "Die zweigeteilte Stadt. Arm und Reich in den Stadten Lateinamerikas, der USA and Europas." In Tilo Schabert (ed.), *Die Weldt der Stadt*, Munich: Piper, pp. 199–216.

—— (1991) "Estrategias de desarrollo metropolitano en las grandes ciudades españolas: la articulación entre crecimiento economico y calidad de vida." In Jordi Borja et al. (eds), *Las grandes ciudades en la decada de los noventa*, Madrid: Editorial Sistema, pp. 17–64.

—— (1992), "Four Asian tigers with a dragon head: a comparative analysis of the state, economy, and society in the Asian Pacific Rim." In Richard Appelbaum and Jeffrey Henderson (eds), *States and Development in the Asian Pacific Rim*, Newbury Park, CA: Sage, pp. 33–70.

—— (1994) "Paths towards the informational society: employment structure in G-7 countries, 1920–1990." *International Labour Review*, 133(1): 5–33 (with Yuko Aoyama).

—— (1996) "The net and the self: working notes for a critical theory of informational society." *Critique of Anthropology*, 16(1): 9–38.

—— (ed.) (1985) *High Technology, Space and Society*, Beverly Hills, CA: Sage.

—— and Guillemard, Anne Marie (1971) "Analyse sociologique des pratiques sociales en situation de retraite." *Sociologie du travail*, 3: 282–307.

—— and Hall, Peter (1994) *Technopoles of the World: The Makings of 21st Century Industrial Complexes*, London: Routledge.

—— and Laserna, Roberto (1989) "The new dependency: technology and social change in Latin America." *Sociological Forum*, Fall.

—— and Natalushko, Svetlana (1993) "La modernizacion tecnologica de las empresas de electrónica y telecomunicaciónes en Rusia: un estudio de Szelenograd," Madrid: Universidad Autónoma de Madrid, Programa de Estudios Rusos, unpublished research monograph.

—— and Skinner, Rebecca (1988) "State and technological policy in the U.S.: the SDI program." In Manuel Castells (director) *The State and Technological Policy: A Comparative Analysis*, Berkeley, CA: University of California, BRIE Research Monograph.

—— and Tyson, Laura d'Andrea (1988) "High technology choices ahead: restructuring interdependence." In John W. Sewell and Stuart Tucker (eds), *Growth, Exports, and Jobs in a Changing World Economy*, New Brunswick, NJ: Transaction Books.

—— and —— (1989) "High technology and the changing international division of production: Implications for the U.S. economy." In Randall B. Purcell (ed.), *The Newly Industrializing Countries in the World Economy: Challenges for U.S. Policy*, Boulder, CO: Lynne Rienner, pp. 13–50.

—— et al. (1986) *Nuevas tecnologias, economia y sociedad en España*, 2 vols, Madrid: Alianza Editorial.

——, Goh, Lee and Kwok, R.W.Y. (1990) *The* Shek Kip Mei *Syndrome: Economic Development and Public Housing in Hong Kong and Singapore*, London: Pion.

—— (director), Gamella, Manuel, De la Puerta, Enrique, Ayala, Luis and Matias, Carmen (1991) *La industria de las tecnologias de informacion (1985–90). España en el contexto mundial*, Madrid: Fundesco.

——, Granberg, Alexander and Kiselyova, Emma (1996a – in progress) *The Development of Siberia and the Russian Far East and its Implications for the Pacific Economy*, Berkeley, CA: University of California Pacific Rim Research Program and Institute of Urban and Regional Development, Research Monograph.

——, Yazawa, Shujiro and Kiselyova, Emma (1996b), "Insurgents against the global order: a comparative analysis of Chiapas Zapatistas, American militia movement, and Aum Shinrikyo." *Berkeley Journal of Sociology*, forthcoming.

Castillo, Gregory (1994) "Henry Ford, Lenin, and the scientific organization of work in capitalist and soviet industrialization," Berkeley, CA: University of California Department of City and Regional Planning, Seminar paper for CP 275, unpublished.

Cats-Baril, William L. and Jelassi, Tawfik (1994) "The French videotex system Minitel: a successful implementation of a national information technology infrastructure." *MIS Quarterly*, 18(1): 1–20.

Caves, Roger W. (1994) *Exploring Urban America*, Thousand Oaks, CA: Sage.

Cecchini, Paolo (1988) *The European Challenge, 1992: The Benefits of a Single Market*, Aldershot, Hants: Gower.

Centre d'Etudes Prospectives et d'Informations Internationales (CEPII) (1992) *L'Economie mondiale 1990–2000: l'impératif de la croissance*, Paris: Economica.

—— and OFCE (1990) Mimosa: une modelisation de l'économie mondiale, *Observations et diagnostics économiques*, 30 January.

CEPAL (Comision Economica para America Latina, Naciones Unidas) (1986) *El desarrollo fruticola y forestal en Chile y sus derivaciones sociales*, Santiago, Chile: Informe CEPAL.

—— (1990a) *La apertura financiera de Chile y el comportamiento de los bancos transnacionales*, Santiago, Chile: Informe CEPAL.

—— (1990b) *Transformacion productiva con equidad*, Santiago de Chile: Naciones Unidas, CEPAL.

—— (1994) *El crecimiento economico y su difusion social: el caso de Chile de 1987 a 1992*, Santiago de Chile: CEPAL, Division de Estadisticas y Proyecciones.

Cervero, Robert (1989) *America's Suburban Centers: The Land Use–Transportation Link*, Boston, MA: Unwin Hyman.

—— (1991) "Changing live-work spatial relationships: implications for metropolitan structure and mobility." In John Brotchie et al. (eds), *Cities in the 21st Century: New Technologies and Spatial Systems*, Melbourne: Longman & Cheshire, pp. 330–47.

Chandler, Alfred D. (1977) *The Visible Hand: The Managerial Revolution in American Business*, Cambridge, MA: Harvard University Press.

—— (1986) "The evolution of modern global competition." In M.E. Porter (ed.), *Competition in Global Industries*, Boston, MA: Harvard Business School Press, pp. 405–48.

Chen, Edward K.Y. (1979) *Hypergrowth in Asian Economies: A Comparative Analysis of Hong Kong, Japan, Korea, Singapore and Taiwan*, London: Macmillan.

Chesnais, François (1994) *La Mondialisation du capital*, Paris: Syros.

Chida, Tomohei and Davies, Peter N. (1990) *The Japanese Shipping and Shipbuilding Industries: A History of Their Modern Growth*, London: Athlone Press.

Child, John (1986) "Technology and work: An outline of theory and research in the western social sciences." In Peter Grootings (ed.), *Technology and Work: East–West Comparison*, London: Croom Helm, pp. 7–66.

Chin, Pei-Hsiung (1988) *Housing Policy and Economic Development in Taiwan*, Berkeley, CA: University of California, IURD.

Chion, Miriam (1995) "Recent process of globalization in Peru," Berkeley, CA: University of California Department of City and Regional Planning, unpublished research paper for CP229.

Chizuko, Ueno (1987) "The position of Japanese women reconsidered." *Current Anthropology*, 28(4): 75–84.

—— (1988) "The Japanese women's movement: the counter-values to industrialism." In Grakan McCormack and Yoshio Sugimoto (eds), *Modernization and Beyond: The Japanese Trajectory*, Cambridge: Cambridge University Press, pp. 167–85.

Choucri, Nazli (1986) "The hidden economy: a new view of remittances in the Arab World." *World Development Report*, 14: 702–9.

Chung, K.H., Lee H.C. and Okumura, A. (1988) "The managerial practices of Korean, American, and Japanese firms." *Journal of East and West Studies*, 17: 45–74.

Clark, R. (1979) *The Japanese Company*, New Haven, CT: Yale University Press.

Clegg, Stewart (1990) *Modern Organizations: Organization Studies in the Postmodern World*, London: Sage.

——— (1992) "French bread, Italian fashions, and Asian enterprises: modern passions and postmodern prognoses." In Jane Marceau (ed.), *Reworking the World*, Berlin: Walter de Gruyter, pp. 55–94.

——— and Redding, S. Gordon (eds) (1990) *Capitalism in Contrasting Cultures*, Berlin: Walter de Gruyter.

Clow Archibald and Clow, Nan L. (1952) *The Chemical Revolution*, London: Batchworth Press.

Coclough, Christopher and Manor, James (eds) (1991) *States or Markets? Neoliberalism and the Development Policy Debate*, Oxford: Clarendon Press.

Cohen Stephen (1990) "Corporate nationality can matter a lot," testimony before the US Congress Joint Economic Committee, September.

——— (1993) "Geo-economics: lessons from America's mistakes." In Martin Carnoy et al., *The New Global Economy in the Information Age*, University Park, PA: Penn State University Press, pp. 97–147.

——— (1994) "Competitiveness: a reply to Krugman." *Foreign Affairs*, 73: 3.

——— and Borrus, Michael (1995a) *Networks of American and Japanese Electronics Companies in Asia*, Berkeley, CA: University of California, BRIE Research Paper.

——— and ——— (1995b) *Networks of Companies in Asia*, Berkeley, CA: University of California, BRIE Research Paper.

——— and Guerrieri, Paolo (1995) "The variable geometry of Asian trade." In Eileen M. Doherty (ed.), *Japanese Investment in Asia*, proceedings of a conference organized with Berkeley Roundtable on the International Economy, San Francisco: Asia Foundation, pp. 189–208.

——— and Zysman, John (1987) *Manufacturing Matters: The Myth of Postindustrial Economy*, New York: Basic Books.

——— et al., (1985) *Global Competition: The New Reality*, vol. III of John Young (chair), *Competitiveness. The Report of the President's Commission on Industrial Competitiveness*, Washington D.C.: Government Printing Office, p. 1.

Cohendet, P. and Llerena, P. (1989) *Flexibilité, information et décision*, Paris: Economica.

Colas, Dominique (1992) *La Glaive et le fléau. Genéalogie du fanatisme et de la société civile*. Paris: Grasset.

Collado, Cecilia (1995) "Unsustainable development: environmental policy and regional development in Chile," Berkeley, University of California: Department of City and Regional Planning, PhD dissertation, in progress.

Collective Author (1994) *The State of Working Women: 1994 Edition*, Tokyo: 21 Seiki Zoidan (in Japanese).

Coloquio de Invierno (1992) *Los grandes cambios de nuestro tiempo: la situación internacional, America Latina y Mexico*, 3 vols, Mexico DF: Universidad Nacional Autónoma de Mexico/Fondo de Cultura Economica.

Comision Economica para America Latina, Naciones Unidas, *see* CEPAL.

Commersant Weekly (1995) "Survey on commercial crime in Russia." June 13.

Commission of the European Union (1994) *Growth, Competitiveness, Employment: The Challenges and Ways Forward into the 21st Century, White Paper*, Luxembourg: Office of the European Communities.

Conference on Time and Money in the Russian Culture (1995), organized by the University of California at Berkeley's Center for Slavic and Eastern European Studies, and the Stanford University's Center for Russian and Eastern European Studies, held at Berkeley on March 17 1995, unpublished presentations and discussions (personal notes and summary of the proceedings by Emma G. Kiselyova).

Cooke, Philip (1994) "The cooperative advantage of regions," paper prepared for Harold Innis Centenary Celebration Conference *Regions, Institutions and Technology*, University of Toronto, September 23–25.

—— and Morgan, K. (1993) "The network paradigm: new departures in corporate and regional development." *Society and Space*, 11: 543–64.

Cooper, Charles (ed.) (1994) *Technology and Innovation in the International Economy*, Aldershot, Hants.: Edward Elgar and United Nations University Press.

Cooper, James C. (1995) "The new golden age of productivity." *Business Week*, September 26: 62.

Coriat, Benjamin (1990) *L'Atelier et le robot*, Paris: Christian Bourgois Editeur.

—— (1994) "Neither pre- nor post-fordism: an original and new way of managing the labour process." In K. Tetsuro and R. Steven (eds), *Is Japanese Management Post-Fordism?*, Tokyo: Mado-sha, p. 182.

Council of Economic Advisers (1995) *Economic Report to the President of the United States. Transmitted to the Congress, February 1995*, Washington D.C.: Government Printing Office, pp. 95–127.

Coutrot, T. and Husson, M. (1993) *Les Destins du tiers monde*, Paris: Nathan.

Crick, Francis (1994) *The Astonishing Hypothesis: The Scientific Search for the Soul*, New York: Charles Scribner's Sons.

Cuneo, Alice (1994) "Getting wired in the Gulch: creative and coding merge in San Francisco's multimedia community." *Advertising Age*, 65(50).

Cusumano, M. (1985) *The Japanese Automobile Industry: Technology and Management at Nissan and Toyota*, Cambridge, MA: Harvard University Press.

Cyert, Richard M. and Mowery, David C. (eds) (1987) *Technology and Employment: Innovation and Growth in the U.S. Economy*, Washington D.C.: National Academy Press.

Dahlman, C., Ross-Larsen, B. and Westphal, L.E. (1987) "Managing technological development: lessons from newly industrialising countries." *World Development*, 15(6).

Dalloz, Xavier and Portnoff, Andre-Yves (1994) "Les promesses de l'unimedia." *Futuribles*, n. 191: 11–36.

Daniel, W. (1987) *Workplace Survey of Industrial Relations*, London: Policy Studies Institute.

Daniels, P.W. (1993) *Service Industries in the World Economy*, Oxford: Blackwell.

Danton de Rouffignac, Peter (1991) *Europe's New Business Culture*, London: Pitman.

Darbon, Pierre and Robin, Jacques (eds) (1987) *Le Jaillissement des biotechnologies*, Paris: Fayard-Fondation Diderot.

David, Paul (1989) *Computer and Dynamo: The Modern Productivity Paradox in Historical Perspective*, Stanford, CA: Stanford University Center for Economic Policy Research, Working Paper No. 172.

David, P.A. (1975) *Technical Choice Innovation and Economic Growth: Essays on American and British Experience in the Nineteenth Century*, London: Cambridge University Press.

—— and Bunn, J.A. (1988) "The economics of gateways' technologies and network evolution: lessons from the electricity supply industry." *Information Economics and Policy*, 3 (April): 165–202.

Davidson, Basil (1992) *The Black Man's Burden: Africa and the Curse of the Nation-state*, London: James Currey.

Davis, Diane (1994) *Urban Leviathan: Mexico in the 20th Century*, Philadelphia, PA: Temple University Press.

Davis, Mike (1990) *City of Quartz*, London: Verso.

Dean, James W., Yoon, Se Joon and Susman, Gerald I. (1992) "Advanced manufacturing technology and organization structure: empowerment or subordination?" *Organization Science*, 3(2): 203–29.

De Anne, Julius (1990) *Global Companies and Public Policy: The Growing Challenge of Foreign Direct Investment*, New York: Council of Foreign Relations Press.

De Bandt, J (ed.) (1985) *Les Services dans les sociétés industrielles avancées*, Paris: Economica.

Deben, Leon et al. (eds) (1993) *Understanding Amsterdam: Essays on Economic Vitality, City Life, and Urban Form*, Amsterdam: Het Spinhuis.

De Conninck, Frederic (1995) *Société éclatée. Travail intégré*, Paris: Presses Universitaires de France.

Denison, Edward F. (1967) *Why Growth Rates differ: Postwar Experience in Nine Western Countries*, Washington D.C.: Brookings Institution.

—— (1974) *Accounting for United States Economic Growth, 1929–69*, Washington D.C.: Brookings Institution.

—— (1979) *Accounting for Slower Economic Growth: The United States in the 1970s*, Washington D.C.: Brookings Institution.

Denisova, L.I. (1995) "Fondovyi rynok i inostrannye investitsii [Stock exchange market and foreign investment]." *EKO*, no. 4: 65–73.

Dentsu Institute for Human Studies/DataFlow International (1994) *Media in Japan*, Tokyo: DataFlow International.

Derriennic, J.P. (1990) "Tentative de polémologie nécrométrique," Quebec: Université Laval, unpublished paper.

Deyo, Frederick (ed.) (1987) *The Political Economy of New Asian Industrialism*, Ithaca, NY: Cornell University Press.

Dicken, Peter (1992) *Global Shift: The Internationalization of Economic Activity*, New York: Guilford Press.

Dickens, William T., Tyson, Laura D'Andrea and Zysman, John, (eds) (1988) *The Dynamics of Trade and Employment*, Cambridge, MA: Ballinger Press.

Dickinson, H.W. (1958) "The steam engine to 1830." In C. Singer (ed.), *A History of Technology*, vol. 4: *The Industrial Revolution, 1750–1850*, Oxford: Oxford University Press, pp. 168–97.

Dizard, Wilson P. (1982) *The Coming Information Age*, New York: Longman.

Dodgson, M. (ed.) (1989) *Technology Strategy and the Firm: Management and Public Policy*, Harlow, Essex: Longman.

Doherty, Eileen M. (ed.) (1995) *Japanese Investment in Asia: International Production Strategies in a Rapidly Changing World*, proceedings of a conference organized with Berkeley Roundtable on the International Economy, San Francisco: Asia Foundation.

Dohse, K., Jurgens, V. and Malsch, T. (1985) "From Fordism to Toyotism? The social organization of the labour process in the Japanese automobile industry." *Politics and Society*, 14(2): 115–46.

Dondero, George (1995) "Information, communication, and vehicle technology," Berkeley, CA: University of California Department of City and Regional Planning, Spring, unpublished seminar paper for CP-298I.

Dordick, Herbert S. and Wang, Georgette (1993) *The Information Society: A Retrospective View*, Newbury Park, CA: Sage.

Dosi, Giovanni (1988) "The nature of the innovative process." In G. Dosi et al., *Technical Change and Economic Theory*, London: Pinter, 221–39.

—— and Soete, Luc (1983), "Technology, competitiveness, and international trade." *Econometrica*, 3.

—— Pavitt, K and Soete, L. (1988a) *The Economics of Technical Change and International Trade*, Brighton, Sussex: Wheatsheaf.

——, Freeman, Christopher, Nelson, Richard, Silverberg, Gerald and Soete Luc (eds) (1988b) *Technical Change and Economic Theory*, London: Pinter.

Dower, John W. (ed.) (1975) *Origins of the Modern Japanese State: Selected Writings of E.H. Norman*, New York: Pantheon Books.

Doyle, Marc (1992) *The Future of Television: A Global Overview of Programming, Advertising, Technology and Growth*, Lincolnwood, IL: NTC Business Books.

Drexler, K. Eric and Peterson, Chris (1991) *Unbounding the Future: The Nanotechnology Revolution*, New York: Quill/William Morrow.

Drucker, Peter F. (1988) "The coming of the new organization." *Harvard Business Review*, 88: 45–53.

Dubois, Pierre (1985) "Rupture de croissance et progrès technique." *Economie et statistique*, 181.

Dunford, M. and Kafkalas, G. (eds) (1992) *Cities and Regions in the New Europe: The Global–Local interplay and Spatial Development Strategies*, London: Belhaven Press.

Dunning, John (ed.) (1985) *Multinational Enterprises, Economic Structure, and International Competitiveness*, New York: John Wiley.

—— (1992) *Multinational Enterprises and the Global Economy*, Reading, MA: Addison-Wesley.

—— (1993) *Multinational Enterprises and the Global Economy*, Reading, MA: Addison Wesley.

Durlabhji, Subhash and Marks, Norton (eds) (1993) *Japanese Business: Cultural Perspectives*, Albany, NY: State University of New York Press.

Durufle, G. (1988) *L'Ajustement structurel en Afrique (Sénégal, Côte d'Ivoire, Madagascar*, Paris: Karthala.

Dy, Josefina (ed.) (1990) *Advanced Technology in Commerce, Offices, and Health Service*, Aldershot, Hants: Avebury.

Ebel, K. and Ulrich, E. (1987) *Social and Labour Effects of CAD/CAM*, Geneva: International Labour Organization.

Eco, Umberto (1977) "Dalla periferia dell'impero," cited in the English translation as Eco, Umberto, "Does the audience have bad effects on television?" In Umberto Eco, *Apocalypse Postponed*, Bloomington: Indiana University Press, 1994, pp. 87–102.

Economist, (1993) 7 July 27.

—— (1994a) "Feeling for the future: survey of television." February 12: special report.

—— (1994b) "Sale of the century." May 14: 67–9.

—— (1995a) "The bank that disappeared." February 27.

—— (1995b) "Currencies in a spin." March 11: 69–70.

—— (1995c) "A survey of Brazil: half-empty or half-full?" April 29.

—— (1995d) "A survey of Vietnam: the road to capitalism." July 8.

Economist Intelligence Unit (1995) "Country report: Russian Federation, 2nd quarter."

Edquist, Charles and Jacobsson, Stefan (1989) *Flexible Automation: The Global Diffusion of New Technologies in the Engineering Industry*, Oxford: Blackwell.

Egan, Ted (1995) "The development and location patterns of software industry in the U.S.," Berkeley, CA: University of California, PhD dissertation in City and Regional Planning (in progress).

Elkington, John (1985) *The Gene Factory: Inside the Business and Science of Biotechnology*, New York: Carroll & Graf.

Elmer-Dewwit, Philip (1993) "The amazing video game boom." *Time*, September 27: 67–72.

El Pais/World Media (1995) "Habla el futuro." March 9: supplement.

Enderwick, Peter (ed.) (1989) *Multinational Service Firms*, London: Routledge.

Epstein, Edward (1995) "Presidential contender's campaign online." *San Francisco Chronicle*, November 27.

Ernst, Dieter (1994a) *Carriers of Regionalization? The East Asian Production Networks of Japanese Electronics Firms*, Berkeley, CA: University of California, BRIE Working Paper 73.

—— (1994b) *Inter-Firms Networks and Market Structure: Driving Forces, Barriers and Patterns of Control*, Berkeley, CA: University of California, BRIE Research Paper.

—— (1994c) *Networks in Electronics*, Berkeley, CA: University of California, BRIE Research Monograph.

—— (1995) "International production networks in Asian electronics: how do they differ and what are their impacts?" Unpublished paper presented at the Berkeley Roundtable on the International Economy/Asia Foundation

Conference on Competing Production Networks in Asia, San Francisco, 27–28 April.

—— and O'Connor, David (1992) *Competing in the Electronics Industry: The Experience of Newly Industrializing Economies*, Paris: OECD, Development Centre Studies.

Esping-Andersen, G (ed.) (1993) *Changing Classes*, London: Sage.

Evans, Peter (1987) "Class, state and dependence in East Asia: lessons for Latin Americanists." In Frederic Deyo (ed.), *The Political Economy of East Asian Industrialism*, Ithaca, NY: Cornell University Press.

—— (1995) *Embedded Autonomy: States and Industrial Transformation*, Princeton, NJ: Princeton University Press.

Fager, Gregory (1994) "Financial flows to the major emerging markets in Asia." *Business Economics*, 29(2): 21–7.

Fainstein, Susan S., Gordon, Ian and Harloe, Michael (eds.) (1992) *Divided Cities*, Oxford: Blackwell.

Fajnzylber, Fernando (1983) *La industrializacion truncada de America Latina*, Mexico: Nueva Imagen.

—— (1988) "Competitividad internacional, evolución y lecciónes." *Revista de la CEPAL*, no. 36.

—— (1990) *Unavoidable Industrial Restructuring in Latin America*, Durham, NC: Duke University Press.

Faria, Vilmar E. (1995) "Social exclusion and Latin American analyses of poverty and deprivation." In Gerry Rodgers, Charles Gore and Jose B. Figueredo (eds), *Social Exclusion: Rhetoric, Reality, Responses*, Geneva: International Institute of Labor Studies and United Nations Development Programme.

Fassmann H. and Münz, R. (1992) Patterns and trends of international migration in Western Europe. *Population and Development Review*, 18(3).

Fazy, Ian Hamilton (1995) "The superhighway pioneers." *The Financial Times*, June 20.

Feldstein, Martin et al. (1987) *Restructuring Growth in the Debt-laden Third World*, New York: Trilateral Commission.

Ferguson, Marjorie (ed.) (1986) *New Communications Technologies and the Public Interest: Comparative Perspectives on Policies and Research*, Newbury Park, CA: Sage.

Feuerwerker, Albert (1984) "The state and economy in late imperial China." *Theory and Society*, 13: 297–326.

Fischer, Claude (1985) "Studying technology and social life." In Manuel Castells (ed.), *High Technology, Space, and Society*, Beverly Hills, CA: Sage (*Urban Affairs Annual Reviews*, 28: 284–301).

—— (1992) *America Calling: A Social History of the Telephone to 1940*, Berkeley, CA: University of California Press.

Flynn, P.M. (1985) *The Impact of Technological Change on Jobs and Workers*, paper prepared for the US Department of Labor, Employment Training Administration.

Fontaine, Arturo (1988) *Los economistas y el Presidente Pinochet*, Santiago de Chile: Zig-Zag.

Fontana, Josep (1988) *La fin de l'Antic Regim i l'industrialitzacio, 1787–1868,* vol. V of Pierre Vilar (director), *Historia de Catalunya,* Barcelona: Edicions 62.

Foray, Dominique and Freeman, Christopher (eds) (1992) *Technologie et richesse des nations,* Paris: Economica.

Forbes, R.J. (1958) "Power to 1850." In C. Singer (ed.), *A History of Technology,* vol. 4: *The Industrial Revolution, 1750–1850,* Oxford: Oxford University Press.

Forester, Tom (1987) *High-tech Society,* Oxford: Blackwell.

—— (1993) *Silicon Samurai: How Japan Conquered the World Information Technology Industry,* Oxford: Blackwell.

—— (ed.) (1980) *The Microelectronics Revolution,* Oxford: Blackwell.

—— (ed.) (1985) *The Information Technology Revolution,* Oxford: Blackwell.

—— (ed.) (1988) *The Materials Revolution,* Oxford: Blackwell Business.

—— (ed.) (1989) *Computers in the Human Context,* Oxford: Blackwell.

Fouquin, Michel, Dourille-Feer, Evelyne and Oliveira-Martins, Joaquim, (1992) *Pacifique: le recentrage asiatique,* Paris: Economica.

Foxley, Alejandro (1995) *Los objetivos economicos y sociales en la transicion a la democracia,* Santiago: Universidad de Chile.

Frank, Andre Gunder (1967) *Capitalism and Underdevelopment in Latin America,* New York: Monthly Review Press.

Frankel, Robert et al. (1990) "Growth and structural reform in Latin America." *Cuadernos CEDES* (Buenos Aires).

Freeman, Christopher (1982) *The Economics of Industrial Innovation,* London: Pinter.

—— (ed.) (1986) *Design, Innovation, and Long Cycles in Economic Development,* London: Pinter.

—— (ed.) (1990) *The Economics of Innovation,* Aldershot, Hants.: Edward Elgar.

—— and Soete, Luc (1994) *Work for All or Mass Unemployment?* London: Pinter.

——, Sharp, Margaret and Walker, William (eds) (1991) *Technology and the Future of Europe,* London: Pinter.

Freeman, Richard (ed.) (1994) *Working Under Different Rules,* Cambridge, MA: Harvard University Press.

French-Davis, Ricardo (ed.) (1983) *Relaciones financieras externas: su efecto en la economia latinoamericana,* Mexico: Fondo de Cultura Economica – CIEPLAN.

Freud, Sigmund (1947) "Thoughts for the times on war and death." In his *On War, Sex, and Neurosis,* New York: Arts and Science Press, pp. 243–76.

Friedland, Roger and Boden, Deirdre (eds) (1994) *Nowhere: Space, Time, and Modernity,* Berkeley, CA: University of California Press.

Friedman, D. (1988) *The Misunderstood Miracle* Ithaca, NY: Cornell University Press.

Friedman, Milton (1968) *Dollars and Deficits: Living with America's economic problems,* Englewood Cliffs, N.J.: Prentice-Hall.

Friedmann, Georges (1956) *Le Travail en miettes,* Paris: Gallimard.

—— and Naville, Pierre (eds) (1961) *Traité de sociologie du travail*, Paris: Armand Colin.

—— (1957) *Countries in the World Economy: Challenges for US Policy*, Boulder, CO: Lynne Reinner, pp. 159–86.

Frischtak, Claudio (1989) "Structural change and trade in Brazil and in the newly industrializing Latin American economies." In Randall B. Purcell (ed.), *The Newly Industrializing*.

Froebel, Friedrich, Henricks, Jurgen and Kreye, Otto (1980) *The New International Division of Labor*, Cambridge: Cambridge University Press.

Fulk, J. and Steinfield, C. (eds) (1990) *Organizations and Communication Technology*, Newbury, CA: Sage.

Ganley, Gladys D. (1991) "Power to the people via electronic media." *Washington Quarterly*, Spring: 5–22.

Garcia-Sayan, Diego (ed.) (1989) *Coca, cocaina y narcotrafico. Laberinto en los Andes*, Lima: Comision Andina de Juristas.

Garratt, G.R.M. (1958) "Telegraphy." In C. Singer (ed.), *A History of Technology*, vol. 4: *The Industrial Revolution, 1750–1850*, Oxford: Oxford University Press, pp. 644–62.

Garreau, Joel (1991) *Edge City: Life on the New Frontier*, New York: Doubleday.

GATT (General Agreement on Tariffs and Trade) (1994) *International Trade*, Geneva: GATT, Trends and Statistics.

Gelb, Joyce and Lief Palley, Marian (eds) (1994) *Women of Japan and Korea: Continuity and Change*, Philadelphia, PA: Temple University Press.

Gelernter, David (1991) *Mirror Worlds*, New York: Oxford University Press.

Gereffi, Gary (1989) "Rethinking development theory: insights from East Asia and Latin America." *Sociological Forum*, 4: 505–35.

—— (1993) *Global Production Systems and Third World Development*, Madison: University of Wisconsin Global Studies Research Program, Working Paper Series, August.

—— and Wyman, Donald (eds) (1990) *Manufacturing Miracles: Paths of Industrialization in Latin America and East Asia*, Princeton, NJ: Princeton University Press.

Gerlach, Michael L. (1992) *Alliance Capitalism: The Social Organization of Japanese Business*, Berkeley, CA: University of California Press.

Gershuny, J.I. and Miles, I.D. (1983) *The New Service Economy: The Transformation of Employment in Industrial Societies*, London: Pinter.

Ghai, Dharam and Rodwan, Samir (eds) (1983) *Agrarian Policies and Rural Poverty in Africa*, Geneva: International Labour Organization.

Ghoshal, Sumantra and Bartlett, Christopher (1993) "The multinational corporation as an inter-organizational network." In Sumantra Ghoshal and D. Eleanor Westney (eds), *Organization Theory and Multinational Corporations*, New York: St Martin's Press, pp. 77–104.

—— and Westney, E. Eleanor (eds) (1993) *Organization Theory and Multinational Corporations*, New York: St Martin's Press.

Gibson, David G. and Rogers, Everett (1994) *R&D: Collaboration on Trial. The Microelectronics Computer Technology Corporation*, Boston, MA: Harvard Business School Press.

Giddens, A. (1981) *A Contemporary Critique of Historical Materialism*, Berkeley, CA: University of California Press.

—— (1984) *The Constitution of Society: Outline of a Theory of Structuration*, Cambridge: Polity Press.

Gill, Bertrand (1978) *Histoire des techniques: technique et civilisations, technique et sciences*, Paris: Gallimard.

Gitlin, Todd (1987) *The Sixties: Years of Hope, Days of Rage*, Toronto and New York: Bantam Books.

Gleick, James (1987) *Chaos*, New York: Viking Penguin.

Glewwe, Paul and de Tray, Dennis (1988) *The Poor During Adjustment: A Case Study of Côte d'Ivoire*, Washington D.C.: World Bank.

Glickman, Norman J. and Woodward, Douglas P. (1987) *Regional Patterns of Manufacturing Investment in the United States*, Special Project Report for the US Department of Commerce, Austin, TX: University of Texas, Lyndon B. Johnson School of Public Affairs.

Godard, Francis et al. (1973) *La Renovation urbaine à Paris*, Paris: Mouton.

Gold, Thomas (1986) *State and Society in the Taiwan Miracle*, Armonk, NY: M.E. Sharpe.

Goldenstein, Lidia (1994) *Repensando a Dependencia*, Rio de Janeiro: Paz e Terra.

Goldsmith, William W. and Blakely, Edward J. (1992) *Separate Societies: Poverty and Inequality in U.S. cities*, Philadelphia, PA: Temple University Press.

Goodman, P.S., Sproull, L.S. and Associates (1990) *Technology and Organization*, San Francisco, CA: Jossey-Bass.

Gordon, Richard (1994) *Internationalization, Multinationalization, Globalization: Contradictory World Economies and New Spatial Divisions of Labor*, Santa Cruz, CA: University of California Center for the Study of Global Transformations, Working Paper 94.

Gorgen, Armelle and Mathieu, Rene (1992) "Developing partnerships: new organizational practices in manufacturer–supplier relationships in the French automobile and aerospace industry." In Jane Marceau (ed.) *Reworking the World: Organizations, Technologies, and Cultures in Comparative Perspective*, Berlin: Walter de Gruyter, pp. 171–80.

Gottdiener, Marc (1985) *The Social Production of Urban Space*, Austin TX: University of Texas Press.

Gould, Stephen J. (1980) *The Panda's Thumb: More Reflections on Natural History*, New York: W.W. Norton.

Gourevitch, Peter A. (ed.) (1984) *Unions and Economic Crisis: Britain, West Germany and Sweden*, Boston, MA: Allen & Unwin.

Graham, Stephen (1994) "Networking cities: telematics in urban policy – a critical review." *International Journal of Urban and Regional Research*, 18(3): 416–31.

—— and Marvin, Simon (1996) *Telecommunications and the City: Electronic Spaces, Urban Places*, London: Routledge.

Granovetter, M. (1985) "Economic action and social structure: the problem of embeddedness." *American Journal of Sociology*, 49: 323–34.

Greenhalgh, S. (1988) "Families and networks in Taiwan's economic development." In E.A. Winckler and S. Greenhalgh (eds), *Contending Approaches to the Political Economy of Taiwan*, Armonk, NY: M.E. Sharpe.

Griffith-Jones, Stephany (ed.) (1988) *Managing Third World Debt*, New York: St Martin's Press.

Guerrieri, Paolo (1991) *Technology and International Trade Performance in the Most Advanced Countries*, Berkeley, CA: University of California BRIE Working Paper 49.

—— (1993) "Patterns of technological capability and international trade performance: an empirical analysis." In M. Kreinin (ed.), *The Political Economy of International Commercial Policy: Issues for the 1990s*, London: Taylor & Francis.

—— (1994) "International competitiveness, trade integration and technological interdependence." In Colin I. Bradford (ed.), *The New Paradigm of Systemic Competitiveness: Toward More Integrated Policies in Latin America*, Paris: OECD Development Centre, pp. 171–206.

Guile, Bruce R. (ed.) (1985) *Information Technologies and Social Transformation*, Washington D.C.: National Academy of Engineering, National Academy Press.

—— and Brooks, Harvey (eds) (1987) *Technology and Global Industry: Companies and Nations in the World Economy*, Washington D.C.: National Academy of Engineering.

Guillemard, Anne Marie (1972) *La Retraite: une mort sociale*, Paris: Mouton.

—— (1988) *Le Déclin du social*, Paris: Presses Universitaires de France.

—— (1993) "Travailleurs vieillissants et marché du travail en Europe." *Travail et emploi*, Sept.: 60–79.

—— and Rein, Martin (1993) "Comparative patterns of retirement: recent trends in developed societies." *Annual Review of Sociology*, 19: 469–503.

Gurr, T.R. (1993) *Minorities at Risk: A Global View of Ethnopolitical Conflicts*, Washington D.C.: US Institute of Peace Press.

Gurstein, Penny (1990) "Working at home in the live-in office: computers, space, and the social life of household," Berkeley, CA: University of California, unpublished PhD dissertation.

Gwin, Catherine and Feinberg, Richard (eds) (1989) *Pulling Together: The IMF in a Multipolar World*, New Brunswick, NJ: Transaction Books.

Hafner, Katie and Markoff, John (1991) *Cyberpunk: Outlaws and Hackers in the Computer Frontier*, New York: Touchstone.

Haggard, Stephan and Kaufman, Robert R. (eds) (1992) *The Politics of Economic Adjustment: International Constraints, Distributive Conflicts, and the State*, Princeton, NJ: Princeton University Press.

Hall, Nina (ed.) (1991) *Exploring Chaos: A Guide to the New Science of Disorder*, New York: W.W. Norton.

Hall, Peter (1995) "Towards a general urban theory." In John Brotchie et al. (eds), *Cities in Competition: Productive and Sustainable Cities for the 21st Century*, Sydney: Longman Australia, pp. 3–32.

—— and Preston, Pascal (1988) *The Carrier Wave: New Information Technology and the Geography of Innovation, 1846–2003*, London: Unwin Hyman.

—— et al. (1987) *Western Sunrise: The Genesis and Growth of Britain's Major High Technology Corridor*, London: Allen & Unwin.

——, Bornstein, Lisa, Grier, Reed and Webber, Melvin (1988) *Biotechnology: The Next Industrial Frontier*, Berkeley, CA: University of California Institute of Urban and Regional Development, Biotech Industry Research Group Report.

Hall, Stephen S. (1987) *Invisible Frontiers: The Race to Synthesize a Human Gene*, New York: Atlantic Monthly Press.

Hamelink, Cees (1990) "Information imbalance: core and periphery." In C. Downing et al., *Questioning the Media*, Newbury Park: Sage, pp. 217–28.

Hamilton, Gary G. (1991) *Business Networks and Economic Development in East and Southeast Asia*, Hong Kong: University of Hong Kong, Centre of Asian Studies.

—— and Biggart, N.W. (1988) "Market, culture, and authority: a comparative analysis of management and organization in the Far East." In C. Winship and S. Rosen (eds), *Organization and Institutions: Sociological Approaches to the Analysis of Social Structure*, Chicago, IL: University of Chicago Press, American Journal of Sociology Supplement, pp. S52–S95.

——, Zeile, W. and Kim, W.J. (1990) "The networks structures of East Asian economies." In Stewart R. Clegg and S. Gordon Redding (eds), *Capitalism in Contrasting Cultures*, Berlin: Walter de Gruyter.

Hamilton, Gary G. (1984) "Patriarchalism in Imperial China and Western Europe." *Theory and Society*, 13: 293–426.

—— (1985) "Why no capitalism in China? Negative questions in historical comparative research." *Journal of Asian Perspectives*, 2: 2.

—— and Kao, C.S. (1990) "The institutional foundation of Chinese business: the family firm in Taiwan." *Comparative Social Research*, 12: 95–112.

Handelman, Stephen (1995) *Comrade Criminal: Russia's New Mafiya*, New Haven, CT: Yale University Press.

Handinghaus, Nicolas H. (1989) "Droga y crecimiento economico: el narcotrafico en las cuentas nacionales." *Nueva Sociedad* (Bogota), no. 102.

Handy, Susan and Mokhtarian, Patricia L. (1995) "Planning for telecommuting." *Journal of the American Planning Association*, 61(1): 99–111.

Hanks, Roma S. and Sussman, Marvin B. (eds) (1990) *Corporations, Businesses and Families*, New York: Haworth Press.

Hanson, Stephen E. (1991) "Time and Soviet industrialization," Berkeley, CA: University of California, unpublished PhD dissertation.

Harff, B. (1986) "Genocide as state terrorism." In Michael Stohl and George A. Lopez, *Government Violence and Repression*, Westport, CT: Greenwood Press.

Harrington, Jon (1991) *Organizational Structure and Information Technology*, New York: Prentice-Hall.

Harris, Nigel (1987) *The End of the Third World*, Harmondsworth, Middx.: Penguin.

Harrison, Bennett (1994) *Lean and Mean: The Changing Landscape of Corporate Power in the Age of Flexibility*, New York: Basic Books.

Hart, Jeffrey A., Reed, Robert R. and Bar, François (1992) *The Building of Internet*, Berkeley, CA: University of California, BRIE Working Paper.

Hartmann, Heidi (ed.) (1987) *Computer Chips and Paper Clips: Technology and Women's Employment*, Washington D.C.: National Academy Press.

Harvey, David (1990) *The Condition of Postmodernity*, Oxford: Blackwell.

Havelock, Eric A. (1982) *The Literate Revolution in Greece and its Cultural Consequences*, Princeton, NJ: Princeton University Press.

Heavey, Laurie (1994) "Global integration." *Pension World*, 30(7): 24–7.

Henderson, Jeffrey (1989) *The Globalisation of High Technology Production: Society, Space and Semiconductors in the Restructuring of the Modern World*, London: Routledge.

—— (1990) *The American Semiconductors Industry and the New International Division of Labor*, London: Routledge.

—— (1991) "Urbanization in the Hong Kong–South China region: an introduction to dynamics and dilemmas." *International Journal of Urban and Regional Research* 15(2): 169–79.

Herman, Robin (1990) *Fusion: The Search for Endless Energy*, Cambridge: Cambridge University Press.

Herther, Nancy K. (1994) "Multimedia and the 'information superhighway'." *Online*, 18(5): 24.

Hewitt, P. (1993) *About Time: The Revolution in Work and Family Life*, London: IPPR/Rivers Oram Press.

Hiltz, Starr Roxanne and Turoff, Murray (1993) *The Network Nation: Human Communication via Computer*, Cambridge, MA: MIT Press.

Hinrichs, Karl, Roche, William and Sirianni, Carmen (eds) (1991) *The Political Economy of Working Hours in Industrial Nations*, Philadelphia, PA: Temple University Press.

Hirschhorn, Larry (1984) *Beyond Mechanization: Work and Technology in a Postindustrial Age*, Cambridge, MA: MIT Press.

—— (1985) "Information technology and the new services game." In Manuel Castells (ed.), *High Technology, Space and Society*, Beverly Hills, CA: Sage, pp. 172–90.

Ho, H.C.Y. (1979) *The Fiscal System of Hong Kong*, London: Croom Helm.

Hohenberg, Paul (1967) *Chemicals in Western Europe, 1850-1914*, Chicago, IL: Rand-McNally.

Holsti, K.J. (1991) *Peace and War: Armed Conflicts and International Order, 1648–1989*, Cambridge: Cambridge University Press.

Honigsbaum, Mark (1988) "Minitel loses fads image, moves toward money." *MIS Week*, 9(36): 22.

Howell, David (1994) "The skills myth." *American Prospect*, 18 (Summer): 81–90.

—— and Wolff, Edward (1991) "Trends in the growth and distribution of skills in the U.S. workplace, 1960–85." *Industrial and Labor Relations Review*, 44(3): 486–502.

Hsing, You-tien (1994) "Blood thicker than water: networks of local Chinese officials and Taiwanese investors in Southern China." Paper delivered at the conference sponsored by the University of California Institute on

Global Conflict and Cooperation, *The Economies of the China Circle*, Hong Kong, September 1–3.

—— (1995) *Migrant Workers, Foreign Capital, and Diversification of Labor Markets in Southern China*, Vancouver: University of British Columbia, Asian Urban Research Networks, Working Paper Series.

—— (1996) *Making Capitalism in China: The Taiwan Connection*, New York: Oxford University Press.

Humbert, M. (ed.) (1993) *The Impact of Globalisation on Europe's Firms and Industries*, London: Pinter.

Huws, U., Korte, W.B. and Robinson, S. (1990) *Telework: Towards the Elusive Office*, Chichester, Sussex: John Wiley.

Hyman, Richard and Streeck, Wolfgang (eds) (1988) *New Technology and Industrial Relations*, Oxford: Blackwell.

Ikle, Fred C. and Wohlsletter, Albert (co-chairmen) (1988) *Discriminate Deterrence: Report of the Commission on Integrated Long-term Strategy to the Secretary of Defense*, Washington D.C.: US Government Printing Office.

Illife, John (1987) *The African Poor*, Cambridge: Cambridge University Press.

ILO-ARTEP (1993) *India: Employment, Poverty, and Economic Policies*, New Delhi: ILO-ARTEP.

Imai, Ken'ichi (1980) *Japan's Industrial Organization and its Vertical Structure*, Kunitachi: Hitotsubashi University, Institute of Business Research, Discussion paper no. 101.

—— (1990a) *Joho netto waku shakai no tenbo* [The information network society], Tokyo: Chikuma Shobo.

—— (1990b) *Jouhon Network Shakai no Tenkai* [The development of information network society], Tokyo: Tikuma Shobou.

—— and Yonekura, Seiichiro (1991) "Network and network-in strategy," paper presented at the international conference between Bocconi University and Hitotsubashi University, Milan, September 20.

Innis, Harold A. (1950) *Empire and Communications*, Oxford: Oxford University Press.

—— (1951) *The Bias of Communication*, Toronto: University of Toronto Press.

—— (1952) *Changing Concepts of Time*, Toronto: University of Toronto Press.

Inoki, Takenori and Higuchi, Yoshio (eds) (1995) *Nihon no Koyou system to lodo shijo* [Japanese employment system and labor market], Tokyo: Nihon Keizai Shinbunsha.

International Labor Organization (ILO) (1993 and 1994) *World Labor Report*, Geneva: International Labor Organization.

—— (1988) *Technological Change, Work Organization and Pay: Lessons from Asia*, Geneva: ILO Labor-Management Relations Series, no. 68.

Islam, Rizwanul (1995) "Rural institutions and poverty in Asia." In Gerry Rodgers and Rolph van der Hoeven, (eds), *The Poverty Agenda: Trends and Policy Options*, Geneva: International Institute of Labour Studies, pp. 33–58.

Ito, Youichi (1991a) "Birth of *Joho Shakai* and *Johoka* concepts in Japan and their diffusion outside Japan." *Keio Communication Review*, no. 13: 3–12.

—— (1991b) "*Johoka* as a driving force of social change." *Keio Communication Review*, no. 12: 33–58.

—— (1993) "How Japan modernised earlier and faster than other non-western countries: an information sociology approach." *Journal of Development Communication*, 4(2).

—— (1994) "Japan." In Georgette Wang (ed.), *Treading Different Paths: Informatization in Asian Nations*, Norwood, NJ: Ablex, pp. 68–97.

Jackson, John H. (1989) *The World Trading System*, Cambridge, MA: MIT Press.

Jacobs, Allan (1993) *Great Streets*, Cambridge, MA: MIT Press.

Jacobs, N. (1985) *The Korean Road to Modernization and Development*, Urbana, IL: University of Illinois Press.

Jacoby, S. (1979) "The origins of internal labor markets in Japan." *Industrial Relations*, 18: 184–96.

Jamal, Vali (1995) "Changing poverty and employment patterns under crisis in Africa." In Gerry Rodgers and Rolph van der Hoeven (eds), *The Poverty Agenda: Trends and Policy Options*, Geneva: International Institute of Labour Studies, pp. 59–88.

James, William E., Naya, Seiji and Meier, Gerald M. (1989) *Asian Development: Economic Success and Policy Lessons*, Madison, WIS: University of Wisconsin Press.

Janelli, Roger with Yim, Downhee (1993) *Making Capitalism: The Social and Cultural Construction of a South Korean Conglomerate*, Stanford, CA: Stanford University Press.

Japan Informatization Processing Center (1994) *Informatization White Paper*, Tokyo: JIPDEC.

Japan Institute of Labour (1985) *Technological Innovation and Industrial Relations*, Tokyo: JIL.

Jarvis, C.M. (1958) "The distribution and utilization of electricity." In Charles Singer et al., *A History of Technology*, vol.5: *The Late Nineteenth Century*, Oxford: Clarendon Press, pp. 177–207.

Javetski, Bill and Glasgall, William (1994) "Borderless finance: fuel for growth." *Business Week*, Nov. 18: 40–50.

Jewkes, J., Sawers, D. and Stillerman, R. (1969) *The sources of invention*, New York: W.W. Norton.

Jia, Qingguo (1994) "Threat or opportunity? Implications of the growth of the China Circle for the distribution of economic and political power in the Asia-Pacific region." Beijing: Beijing University, Department of International Politics, unpublished discussion paper.

Johnson, Chalmers (1982) *MITI and the Japanese Miracle*, Stanford, CA: Stanford University Press.

—— (1985) "The institutional foundations of Japanese industrial policy." *California Management Review*, 27(4).

—— (1987) "Political institutions and economic performance: the government–business relationship in Japan, South Korea, and Taiwan." In Frederick Deyo (ed.), *The Political Economy of New Asian Industrialism*, Ithaca, NY: Cornell University Press, pp. 136–64.

—— (1995) *Japan: Who Governs? The Rise of the Developmental State*, New York: W.W. Norton.

——, Tyson, L. and Zysman, J. (eds) (1989) *Politics and Productivity: How Japan's Development Strategy Works*, New York: Harper Business.

Johnston, Ann and Sasson, Albert (1986) *New Technologies and Development*, Paris UNESCO.

Johnston, William B. (1991) "Global labor force 2000: the new world labor market." *Harvard Business Review*, March–April.

Jones, Barry (1982) *Sleepers, Wake! Technology and the Future of Work*, Melbourne: Oxford University Press (references are to the 1990 rev. edn).

Jones, David (1993) "Banks move to cut currency dealing costs." *Financial Technology International Bulletin*, 10(6): 1–3.

Jones, Eric L. (1981) *The European Miracle*, Cambridge: Cambridge University Press.

—— (1988) *Growth Recurring: Economic Change in World History*, Oxford: Clarendon Press.

Jones, L.P. and Sakong, I. (1980) *Government Business and Entrepreneurship in Economic Development: The Korean Case*, Cambridge, MA: Council on East Asian Studies.

Jorgerson, Dale W. and Griliches, Z. (1967) "The explanation of productivity growth." *Review of Economic Studies*, 34 (July): 249–83.

Jost, Kennet (1993) "Downward mobility." *CQ Researcher*, 3(27): 627–47.

Joussaud, Jacques (1994) "Diversité des statuts des travailleurs et flexibilité des entreprises au Japon." *Japan in Extenso*, no.31: 49–53.

Kaiser, M., Klingspor, V., Millan, J. de R., Accami, M., Wallner, F. and Dillman, R. (1995) "Using machine learning techniques in real-world mobile robots." *IEEE Expert*, 10(2).

Kaku, Michio (1994) *Hyperspace: A Scientific Odyssey Through Parallel Universes, Time Warps, and the 10th Dimension*, New York: Oxford University Press.

Kamatani, Chikatoshi (1988) *Gijutsu Taikoku Hyakunen no Kei: Nippon no Kindaika to Kokuritsu Kenkyu Kikan* [The road to techno-nationalism: Japanese modernization and national research institutes from the Meiji era], Tokyo: Heibonsha.

Kaplan, Rachel (1992) "Video on demand." *American Demographics*, 14(6): 38–43.

Kaplinsky, Raphael (1986) *Microelectronics and Work Revisited: A Review*, report prepared for the International Labor Organization, Brighton: University of Sussex Institute of Development Studies.

Kara-Murza, A.A. and Polyakov, L.V. (1994) *Reformator. Opyt analiticheskoy antologii*, Moscow: Institut Filosofii Rossiiskoi Akademii Nauk, Flora.

Katz, Jorge (1994) "Industrial organization, international competitiveness and public policy." In Colin I. Bradford (ed.), *The New Paradigm of Systemic Competitiveness: Toward More Integrated Policies in Latin America*, Paris: OECD Development Center.

Katz, Jorge (ed.) (1987) *Technology Generation in Latin American Manufacturing Industries*, London: Macmillan.

Katz, Raul L. (1988) *The Information Society: An International Perspective*, New York: Praeger.

Kaye, G.D., Grant, D.A. and Emond, E.J. (1985) *Major Armed Conflicts: A Compendium of Interstate and Intrastate Conflict, 1720 to 1985*, Ottawa: Operational Research and Analysis Establishment, Report to National Defense, Canada.

Kelley, Maryellen (1986) "Programmable automation and the skill question: a re-interpretation of the cross-national evidence." *Human Systems Management*, 6.

—— (1990) "New process technology, job design and work organization: a contingency model." *American Sociological Review*, 55 (April): 191–208.

Kelly, Kevin (1995) *Out of Control: The Rise of Neo-biological Civilization*, Menlo Park, CA: Addison-Wesley.

Kendrick, John W. (1961) *Productivity Trends in the United States*, National Bureau of Economic Research, Princeton, NJ: Princeton University Press.

—— (1973) *Postwar Productivity Trends in the United States, 1948–69*, National Bureau of Economic Research New York: Columbia University Press.

—— (1984) *International Comparisons of Productivity and Causes of the Slowdown*, Cambridge, MA: Ballinger.

—— and Grossman, E. (1980) *Productivity in the United States: Trends and Cycles*, Baltimore, MD: Johns Hopkins University Press.

Kenney, Martin (1986) *Biotechnology: The University–Industrial Complex*, New Haven, CT: Yale University Press.

Kepel, G. (ed.) (1993) *Les Politiques de Dieu*, Paris: Seuil.

Khanin, Gregory I. (1994) "Nachalo Krakha [Beginning of collapse]." *EKO*, no. 7.

Khoury, Sarkis and Ghosh, Alo (1987) *Recent Developments in International Banking and Finance*, Lexington, MA: D.C. Heath.

Kim, E.M. (1989) "From domination to symbiosis: state and chaebol in Korea." *Pacific Focus*, 2: 105–21.

Kim, Kyong-Dong (ed.) (1987) *Dependency Issues in Korean Development*, Seoul: Seoul National University Press.

Kimsey, Stephen (1994) "The virtual flight of the cyber-trader." *Euromoney*, June: 45–6.

Kincaid, A. Douglas and Portes, Alejandro (eds) (1994) *Comparative National Development: Society and Economy in the New Global Order*, Chapel Hill, NC: University of North Carolina Press.

Kindleberger, Charles (1964) *Economic Growth in France and Britain, 1851–1950*, Cambridge, MA: Harvard University Press.

King, Alexander (1991) *The First Global Revolution: A Report by the Council of the Club of Rome*, New York: Pantheon Books.

Kirsch, Guy, Nijkamp, Peter and Zimmermann, Klaus (eds) (1988) *The Formulation of Time Preferences in a Multidisciplinary Perspective*, Aldershot, Hants: Gower.

Koike, Kazuo (1988) *Understanding Industrial Relations in Modern Japan*, London: Macmillan.

Kolata, Gina (1995) "Metabolism found to adjust for a body's natural weight." *New York Times*, March 9: A 1/A 11.

Kolb, David (1990) *Postmodern Sophistications: Philosophy, Architecture and Tradition*, Chicago, IL: University of Chicago Press.

Koo, H. and Kim, E.M. (1992) "The developmental state and capital accumulation in South Korea." In Richard P. Appelbaum and Jeffrey Henderson (eds), *States and Development in the Asian Pacific Rim*, London: Sage, pp. 121–49.

Korte, W.B., Robinson, S. and Steinle, W.K. (eds) (1988) *Telework: Present Situation and Future Development of a New Form of Work Organization*, Amsterdam: North-Holland.

Kotter, John P. and Heskett, James L. (1992) *Corporate Culture and Performance*, New York: Free Press.

Kovalyova, Galina (1995) *Sibir' na mirovom rynke: Tekyshchyi obzor vneshney torgovli* [Siberia in the world market: current survey of foreign trade], Novosibirsk: Institute of Economics and Industrial Engineering, Russian Academy of Sciences, Siberian Branch, Research Report.

Kranzberg, M. (1985) "The information age: evolution or revolution?" In Bruce R. Guile (ed.), *Information Technologies and Social Transformation*, Washington D.C.: National Academy of Engineering.

—— (1992) "The scientific and technological age." *Bulletin of Science and Technology Society*, 12: 63–5.

—— and Pursell, Carroll W. Jr (eds) (1967) *Technology in Western Civilization*, 2 vols, New York: Oxford University Press.

Kraut, R.E. (1989) "Tele-commuting: the trade-offs of home-work." *Journal of Communications*, 39: 19–47.

Krugman, Paul (1990) *The Age of Diminished Expectations*, Cambridge, MA: MIT Press.

—— (1994a) *Peddling Prosperity: Economic Sense and Nonsense in the Age of Diminished Expectations*, New York: W.W. Norton.

—— (1994b) "Competitiveness: a dangerous obsession." *Foreign Affairs*, 73(2): 28–44.

—— (ed.) (1986) *Strategic Trade Policy and the New International Economics*, Cambridge, MA: MIT Press.

—— and Lawrence, Robert Z. (1994) "Trade, jobs and wages." *Scientific American*, April: 44–9.

Krykov, Valery (1994) "Polnye kanistry i pystyye karmany [Full jerricans and empty pockets]." *EKO*, 1: 53–62.

Kuhn, Thomas (1962) *The Structure of Scientific Revolutions*, Chicago, IL: University of Chicago Press.

Kuleshov, Valery I. (1994) "Perekhodnaya economika: proidennye etapy, nametivshiyesya tendentsii [Transition economy: past stages, emerging trends]." *EKO*, 12: 54–63.

Kumazawa, M. and Yamada, J. (1989) "Jobs and skills under the lifelong Nenko employment practice." In Stephen Wood (ed.), *The Transformation of Work?: Skill, Flexibility and the Labour Process*, London: Unwin Hyman.

Kunstler, James Howard (1993) *The Geography of Nowhere: The Rise and Decline of America's Man Made Landscape*, New York: Simon & Schuster.

Kuo, Shirley W.Y. (1983) *The Taiwan Economy in Transition*, Boulder,CO: Westview Press.

Kur'yerov, V.G. (1994) "Ekonomika Rossii: Obshchiye Tendentsii [Russian economy: general trends]." *EKO*, no. 5: 2–7.

—— (1995a) "Vneshneekonomicheskiye svyazi [Foreign economic relations]." *EKO*, no. 3: 77–98.

—— (1995b) "Vneshneekonomicheskiye svyazi [Foreign economic relations]." *EKO*, no. 9: 51–75.

Kutscher, R.E. (1991) "Outlook 1990–2005. New BLS projections: findings and implications." *Monthly Labor Review*, November: 3–12.

Kuttner, Robert (1983) "The declining middle." *Atlantic Monthly*, July: 60–72.

Kuwahara, Yasuo (1989) *Japanese Industrial Relations System: A New Interpretation*, Tokyo: Japan Institute of Labour.

Kuwayama, M. (1992) "America Latina y la internacionalizacion de la economia mundial." *Revista de la CEPAL*, no. 46.

Kwok, R. Yin-Wang and So, Alvin (1992) *Hong Kong–Guandong Interaction: Joint Enterprise of Market Capitalism and State Socialism*, Manoa: University of Hawaii, Research paper.

Kwok and So (eds) (1995) *The Hong Kong–Guandong Link: Partnership in Flux*, Armouk, NY: M.E. Sharpe.

Lachaud, Jean-Pierre (1994) *The Labour Market in Africa*, Geneva: International Institute of Labour Studies, Research Series.

Lafay, Gerard and Herzog, Colette (1989) *Commerce international: la fin des avantages acquis*, Paris: Economica/Centre d'Etudes Prospectives et d'Informations Internationales.

Landau, Ralph and Rosenberg, Nathan (eds) (1986) *The Positive Sum Strategy: Harnessing Technology for Economic Growth*, Washington D.C.: National Academy Press.

Landes, David (1969) *The Unbound Prometheus: Technical Change and Industrial Development in Western Europe from 1750 to the Present*, London: Cambridge University Press.

Lanham, Richard A. (1993) *The Electronic Ward*, Chicago, IL: University of Chicago Press.

Laserna, Roberto (1995) "Regional development and coca production in Cochabamba, Bolivia," Berkeley, CA: University of California, unpublished PhD dissertation in City and Regional Planning.

—— (1996) "El circuito coca-cocaine y sus implicaciones," La Paz: ILDIS.

Lash, Scott (1990) *Sociology of Postmodernism*, London: Routledge.

—— and Urry, John (1994) *Economies of Signs and Space*, London: Sage.

Lawrence, Robert Z. (1984) "The employment effects of information technologies: an optimistic view," paper delivered at the OECD *Conference on the Social Challenge of Information Technologies*, Berlin, November: 28–30.

Leal, Jesus (1993) *La desigualdad social en España*, 10 vols, Madrid: Universidad

Autonóma de Madrid, Instituto de Sociologia de Nuevas Tecnologias, Research Monograph.

Leclerc, Annie (1975) *Parole de femme*, Paris: Grasset.

Lee, Peter and Townsend, Peter (1993) *Trends in Deprivation in the London Labour Market: A Study of Low-Incomes and Unemployment in London between 1985 and 1992*, Geneva: International Institute of Labour Studies, Discussion paper 59/1993.

Lee, Peter, King, Paul, Shirref, David and Dyer, Geof (1994) "All change." *Euromoney*, June: 89–101.

Lee, Roger and Schmidt-Marwede, Ulrich (1993) "Interurban competition? Financial centres and the geography of financial production." *International Journal of Urban and Regional Research*, 17(4): 492–515.

Lehman, Yves (1994) "Videotex: a Japanese lesson." *Telecommunications*, 28(7): 53–4.

Lenoir, Daniel (1994) *L'Europe sociale*, Paris: La Découverte.

Leo, P.Y. and Philippe, J. (1989) "Réseaux et services aux entreprises. Marchés locaux et développement global," papers of Seminar 32, 1989-II, CEP, pp. 79–103.

Leontieff, Wassily and Duchin, Faye (1985) *The Future Impact of Automation on Workers*, New York: Oxford University Press.

Lethbridge, Henry J. (1978) *Hong Kong: Stability and Change*, Hong Kong: Oxford University Press.

Leung, Chi Kin (1993) "Personal contacts, subcontracting linkages, and development in the Hong Kong–Zhujiang Delta Region." *Annals of the Association of American Geographers*, 83(2): 272–302.

Levy, Pierre (1994) *L'Intelligence collective: pour une anthropologie du cyberspace*, Paris: La Découverte.

Levy, R.A., Bowes, M. and Jondrow, J.M. (1984) "Technical advance and other sources of employment change in basic industry." In E.L. Collins and L.D. Tanner (eds), *American Jobs and the Changing Industrial Base*, Cambridge, MA: Ballinger, pp. 77–95.

Levy, Stephen (1984) *Hackers: Heroes of the Computer Revolution*, Garden City, NY: Doubleday.

Leys, Colin (1987) "The state and the crisis of simple commodity production in Africa." *Institute of Development Studies Bulletin*, 8(3): 45–8.

—— (1994) "Confronting the African tragedy." *New Left Review*, no. 204: 33–47.

Lichtenberg, Judith (ed.) (1990) *Democracy and Mass Media*, New York: Cambridge University Press.

Lillyman, William, Moriarty, Marilyn F. and Neuman, David J. (eds) (1994) *Critical Architecture and Contemporary Culture*, New York: Oxford University Press.

Lim, Hyun-Chin (1982) *Dependent Development in Korea (1963–79)*, Seoul: Seoul National University Press.

Lin, T.B., Mok, V. and Ho, Y.P. (1980) *Manufactured Exports and Employment in Hong Kong*, Hong Kong: Chinese University Press.

Lincoln, Edward J. (1990) *Japan's Unequal Trade*, Washington, DC: Brookings Institution.

Lincoln, Thomas L. and Essin, Daniel J. (1993) "The electronic medical record: a challenge for computer science to develop clinically and socially relevant computer systems to coordinate information for patient care and analysis." *Information Society*, 9:157–88.

——, —— and Ware, Willis H. (1993) "The electronic medical record." *Information Society*, 9(2): 157–88.

Ling, K.K. (1995) "A case for regional planning: the Greater Pearl River Delta: a Hong Kong perspective," unpublished Research Seminar Paper, CP 229, Berkeley, CA: University of California Department of City and Regional Planning.

Lizzio, James R. (1994) "Real-time RAID storage: the enabling technology for video on demand." *Telephony*, 226(21): 24–32.

Lo, C.P. (1994) "Economic reforms and socialist city structure: a case study of Guangzhou, China." *Urban Geography*, 15(2) 128–49.

Lohr, Steve (1995) "Who uses Internet?" *New York Times*, September 22.

Lorenz, E. (1988) "Neither friends nor strangers: informal networks of subcontracting in French industry." In D. Gambetta, (ed.), *Trust: Making and Breaking Cooperative Relations*, Oxford: Blackwell, pp. 194–210.

Lovins, Amory B. and Lovins, L. Hunter (1995) "Reinventing the wheels." *Atlantic Monthly*, January: 75–86.

Lozano, Beverly (1989) *The Invisible Work Force: Transforming American Business with Outside and Home-based Workers*, New York: Free Press.

Lustig, Nora (1995) "Coping with austerity: poverty and inequality in Latin America." In Gerry Rodgers and Rolph van der Hoeven (eds), *The Poverty Agenda: Trends and Policy Options*, Geneva: International Institute of Labour Studies, pp. 89–126.

Lynch, Kevin (1960) *The Image of the City*, Cambridge, MA: MIT Press.

Lyon, David (1988) *The Information Society: Issues and Illusions*, Cambridge: Polity Press.

—— (1995) *Postmodernity*, Oxford: Blackwell.

Lyon, Jeff and Gorner, Peter (1995) *Altered Fates: Gene Therapy and the Retooling of Human Life*, New York: W.W. Norton.

Machimura, T. (1994) *Sekai Toshi Tokyo no Kozo* [The structural transformation of a global city Tokyo], Tokyo: Tokyo University Press.

—— (1995) *Symbolic Use of Globalization in Urban Politics in Tokyo*, Kunitachi: Hitotsubashi University Faculty of Social Sciences, Research Paper.

Machlup, Fritz (1962) *The Production and Distribution of Knowledge in the United States*, Princeton, NJ: Princeton University Press.

—— (1980) *Knowledge: Its Creation, Distribution, and Economic Significance*, vol. I: *Knowledge and Knowledge Production*, Princeton, NJ: Princeton University Press.

—— (1982) *Knowledge: Its Creation, Distribution and Economic Significance*, vol. II: *The Branches of Learning*, Princeton, NJ: Princeton University Press.

—— (1984) *Knowledge: Its Creation, Distribution and Economic Significance*, vol.

III, *The Economics of Information and Human Capital*, Princeton, NJ: Princeton University Press.

Mackie, J.A.C. (1992a) "Changing patterns of Chinese big business in Southeast Asia." In Ruth McVey (ed.), *Southeast Asian Capitalists*, Ithaca, N.Y.: Cornell University, Southeast Asian Program.

—— (1992b) "Overseas Chinese entrepreneurship." *Asian Pacific Economic Literature*, 6(1): 41–64.

Maddison, A. (1982) *Phases of Capitalised Development*, New York: Oxford University Press.

Maddison, Angus (1984) "Comparative analysis of the productivity situation in the advanced capitalist countries." In John W. Kendrick (ed.), *International Comparisons of Productivity and Causes of the Slowdown*, Cambridge, MA: Ballinger.

Maital, Shlomo (1991) "Why the French do it better." *Across the Board*, 28(11): 7–10.

Malinvaud, Edmond et al. (1974) *Fresque historique du système productif français*, Paris: Collections de l'INSEE, Séries E, 27 (October).

Mallet, Serge (1963) *La Nouvelle Classe ouvrière*, Paris: Seuil.

Malone, M.S. (1985) *The Big Score: The Billion-dollar Story of Silicon Valley*, Garden City, NY: Doubleday.

Mander, Jerry (1978) *Four Arguments for the Elimination of Television*, New York: William Morrow.

Mankiewicz, Frank and Swerdlow, Joel (eds) (1979) *Remote Control: Television and the Manipulation of American Life*, New York: Ballantine.

Mansfield, Edwin (1982) *Technology Transfer, Productivity, and Economic Policy*, Englewood Cliffs, NJ: Prentice-Hall.

Marceau, Jane (ed.) (1992) *Reworking the World: Organisations, Technologies, and Cultures in Comparative Perspective*, Berlin: Walter De Gruyter.

Markoff, John (1995) "If the medium is the message, the message is the Web." *New York Times*, 20 November: A1, C5.

Marshall, Alfred (1919) *Industry and Trade*, London: Macmillan.

Marshall, Jonathan (1994) "Contracting out catching on: firms find it's more efficient to farm out jobs." *San Francisco Chronicle*, August 22: D2–D3.

Marshall, J.N. et al. (1988) *Services and Uneven Development*, Oxford: Oxford University Press.

Martin, L. John and Chaudhary, Anja Grover (eds) (1983) *Comparative Mass Media Systems*, New York: Longman.

Martin, Linda G. (1987) *The ASEAN Success Story: Social, Economic, and Political Dimensions*, Honolulu: University of Hawaii Press.

Martin, Patricia (1994) "The consumer market for interactive services: observing past trends and current demographics." *Telephony*, 226(18): 126–30.

Martinez, Gabriel and Farber, Guillermo (1994) *Desregulacion economica 1989–93*, Mexico DF: Fondo de Cultura Economica.

Martinotti, Guido (1993) *Metropoli. La Nuova morfologia sociale della citta*, Bologna: Il Mulino.

Marx, Jean L. (ed.) (1989) *A Revolution in Biotechnology*, Cambridge:

Cambridge University Press for the International Council of Scientific Unions.

Massad, Carlos (1991) "El financiamiento del desarrollo industrial en un continente empobrecido." In *Industrializacion y desarrollo tecnologico*, Santiago, Chile: Joint ECLAC/UNIDO Industry and Technology Division, Informe no.11, August.

—— and Eyzaguirre, N. (1990) *Ahorro y formacion de capital. Experiencias latinoamericanas: Argentina, Brasil, Chile, El Salvador y Mexico*, Buenos Aires: CEPAL/PNUD, Grupo Editor Latinoamericano.

Matsumoto, Miwao and Sinclair, Bruce (1994) "How did Japan adapt itself to scientific and technological revolution at the turn of the 20th Century?" *Japan Journal for Science, Technology, and Society*, 3: 133–55.

Mattelart, Armand and Stourdze, Yves (1982) *Technologie, culture et communication*, Paris: La Documentation française.

Matzner, Egon and Wagner, Michael (eds) (1990) *The Employment Impact of New Technology: The Case of West Germany*, Aldershot, Hants.: Avebury.

Mazlish, Bruce (1993) *The Fourth Discontinuity: The Co-evolution of Humans and Machines*, New Haven, CT: Yale University Press.

McGowan, James (1988) "Lessons learned from the Minitel phenomenon." *Network World*, 5(49): 27.

—— and Compaine, Benjamin (1989) "Is Minitel a good model for the North American market?" *Network World*, 6(36).

McGuire, William J. (1986) "The myth of massive media impact: savagings and salvagings." In George Comstock (ed.), *Public Communication and Behavior*, Orlando, FLA: Academic Press, pp. 173–257.

McKinsey Global Institute (1992) *Service Sector Productivity*, Washington D.C.: McKinsey Global Institute.

—— (1993) *Manufacturing Productivity*, Washington D.C.: McKinsey Global Institute.

McLeod, Roger (1996) "Internet users abandoning TV, survey finds." *San Francisco Chronicle*, 12 January: 1, 17.

McLuhan, Marshall (1962) *The Gutenberg Galaxy: The Making of Typographic Man*, Toronto: University of Toronto Press.

—— (1964) *Understanding Media: The Extensions of Man*, New York: Macmillan.

—— and Powers, Bruce R. (1989) *The Global Village: Transformations in World Life and Media in the 21st Century*, New York: Oxford University Press.

McMillan, C. (1984) *The Japanese Industrial System*, Berlin: De Gruyter.

McNeill, William H. (1977) *Plagues and People*, New York: Doubleday.

Mehta, Suketu (1993) "The French connection." *LAN Magazine*, 8(5).

Menotti, Val (1995) "The transformation of retail social space: an analysis of virtual shopping's impact on retail centers." Unpublished research paper for seminar CP298I, University of California, Berkeley, Department of City and Regional Planning.

Michelson, Ronald L. and Wheeler, James O. (1994) "The flow of information in a global economy: the role of the American urban system in 1990." *Annals of the Association of American Geographers*, 84 (1): 87–107.

MIDEPLAN (1994) *Integracion al Desarrollo: Balance de la Politica Social 1990–93, Santiago de Chile: Ministerio de Desarrollo y Planificacion.*

Miles, Ian (1988) *Home Informatics: Information Technology and the Transformation of Everyday Life,* London: Pinter.

Millan, Jose del Rocio (1996) "Rapid, safe, and incremental learning of navigation strategies." *IEEE Transactions on Systems, Man, and Cybernetics,* 26(6).

Miller, Steven, M. (1989) *Impacts of Industrial Robotics: Potential Effects of Labor and Costs within the Metalworking Industries,* Madison, WIS: University of Wisconsin Press.

Miller, Richard L. and Swensson, Earl S. (1995) *New Directions in Hospital and Health Care Facility Design,* New York: McGraw-Hill.

Miners, N. (1986) *The Government and Politics of Hong Kong,* Hong Kong: Oxford University Press.

Mingione, Enzo (1991) *Fragmented Societies,* Oxford, Blackwell.

Ministry of Labor [Japan] (1991) *Statistical Yearbook,* Tokyo: Government of Japan.

Ministry of Posts and Telecommunications [Japan] (1994a) *1994 White Paper: Communications in Japan,* Tokyo: Ministry of Posts and Telecommunications.

—— (1994b) *Communications in Japan 1994,* Part 3: *Multimedia: Opening up a New World of Info-communication,* Tokyo: Ministry of Posts and Telecommunications.

—— (1995) *Tsushin Hakusho Heisei 7 nenban* [White Paper on Communication in Japan], Tokyo: Yusei shou.

Mishel, Lawrence and Bernstein, Jared (1993) *The State of Working America,* New York: M.E. Sharpe.

—— and —— (1994) *The State of Working America 1994–95,* Washington D.C.: Economic Policy Institute.

—— and Teixeira, Ruy A. (1991) *The Myth of the Coming Labor Shortage: Jobs, Skills, and Incomes of America's Workforce 2000,* Washington, D.C.: Economic Policy Institute Report.

Mokhtarian, Patricia L. (1991a) "Defining telecommuting." *Transportation Research Record,* 1305: 273–81.

—— (1991b) "Telecommuting and travel: state of the practice, state of the art." *Transportation,* 18: 319–42.

—— (1992) "Telecommuting in the United States: letting our fingers do the commuting." *Telecommuting Review: the Gordon Report,* 9(5): 12.

Mokyr, Joel (1990) *The Lever of Riches: Technological Creativity and Economic Progress,* New York: Oxford University Press.

—— (ed.) (1985) *The Economics of the Industrial Revolution,* Totowa, NJ: Rowman & Allanheld.

Mollenkopf, John (ed.) (1989) *Power, Culture, and Place: Essays on New York City,* New York: Russell Sage Foundation.

—— and Castells, Manuel (eds) (1991) *Dual City: Restructuring New York,* New York: Russell Sage Foundation.

Monk, Peter (1989) *Technological Change in the Information Economy,* London: Pinter.

Moran, R. (1990) "Health environment and healthy environment." In R. Moran, R. Anderson and P. Paoli, *Building for People in Hospitals, Workers, and Consumers*, Dublin: European Foundation for the Improvement of Living and Working Conditions.

—— (1993) *The Electronic Home: Social and Spatial Aspects. A Scoping Report*, Dublin: European Foundation for the Improvement of Living and Working Conditions.

Morier, Françoise (ed.) (1994) *Belleville, Belleville. Visages d'un planète*, Paris: Editions Creaphis.

Morin, Edgar (1970) *L'homme et la mort*, Paris: Seuil.

Morrocco, John D. (1991) "Gulf War boosts prospects for high-technology weapons." *Aviation Week & Space Technology*, 134(11): 45–7.

Mortimore, Michael (1992) "A new international industrial order." *CEPAL Review*, no. 48: 39–59.

Moss, Mitchell (1987) "Telecommunications, world cities, and urban policy." *Urban Studies*, 24: 534–46.

—— (1991) "The new fibers of economic development." *Portfolio*, 4: 11–18.

—— (1992) "Telecommunications and urban economic development." In OECD, *Cities and New Technologies*, Paris: OECD, pp. 147–58.

Mowery, David (ed.) (1988) *International Collaborative Ventures in U.S. Manufacturing*, Cambridge, MA: Ballinger.

—— and Henderson, Bruce E. (eds) (1989) *The Challenge of New Technology to Labor–Management Relations*, Washington D.C.: Dept of Labor, Bureau of Labor Management Relations.

Mowshowitz, Abbe (1986) "Social dimensions of office automation." In *Advances in Computers*, vol. 25, New York: Academic Press.

Mulgan, G.J. (1991) *Communication and Control: Networks and the New Economies of Communication*, New York: Guilford Press.

Murphy, Kevin M. and Welch, Finis (1993) "Inequality and relative wages." *American Economic Review*, May.

Muschamp, Herbert (1992) "A design that taps into the 'Informational City'." *Sunday New York Times*, August 9, Architecture View Section: 32.

Mushkat, Miron (1982) *The Making of the Hong Kong Administrative Class*, Hong Kong: University of Hong Kong Centre of Asian Studies.

Myers, Edith (1981) "In France it's Teletel." *Datamation*, 27(10): 78–88.

Nadal, Jordi and Carreras, Albert (eds) (1990) *Pautas regionales de la industrializacion española. Siglos XIX y XX*, Barcelona: Ariel.

National Science Board (1991) *Science and Engineering Indicators, 1991*, 10th edn (NSB 91–1), Washington, D.C.: US Government Printing Office.

Naughton, Barry (1994) "Increasing economic interaction in the China Circle in the context of East Asian Growth," paper delivered at the Conference sponsored by the University of California Institute on Global Conflict and Cooperation, *The Economics of the China Circle*, Hong Kong, September 1–3.

Navarro, Vicente (1994a) *The Politics of Health Policy*, Oxford: Blackwell.

—— (1994b) "La economia y el Estado de bienestar," unpublished paper presented at the 10th Meeting on the Future of the Welfare State, Madrid.

Nayyar, Deepak (1994) *Macroeconomic Adjustment, Liberalization and Growth: The Indian Experience*, Geneva: International Institute of Labour Studies, Discussion paper 73/1994.

Needham, Joseph (1954–88) *Science and Civilization in China*, Cambridge: Cambridge University Press.

—— (1969) *The Grand Titration*, Toronto: Toronto University Press.

—— (1981) *Science in Traditional China*, Cambridge, MA: Harvard University Press.

Negroponte, Nicholas (1995) *Being Digital*, New York: Alfred A. Knopf.

Nelson, Joan M. (ed.) (1990) *Economic Crisis and Policy Choice: The Politics of Adjustment in the Third World*, Princeton, NJ: Princeton University Press.

Nelson, Richard (1980) "Production sets, technological knowledge, and R&D: fragile and overworked constructs for analysis of productivity growth?" *American Economic Review*, 70(2): 62–7.

—— (1981) "Research on productivity growth and productivity differences: dead ends and new departures." *Journal of Economic Literature*, 19(3): 1029–64.

—— (1984) *High Technology Policies: A Five Nations Comparison*, Washington D.C.: American Enterprise Institute.

—— (1988) "Institutions supporting technical change in the United States." In G. Dosi et al. *Technical Change and Economic Theory*, London: Pinter, pp. 312–29.

—— (1994) "An agenda for formal growth theory," New York: Columbia University Department of Economics, unpublished paper (communicated by the author).

—— and Winter, S.G. (1982) *An Evolutionary Theory of Economic Change*, Cambridge, MA: Harvard University Press.

Neuman, W. Russell (1991) *The Future of Mass Audience*, New York: Cambridge University Press.

New Media Markets (1993) "Video on demand will provide Hollywood studios with much-needed boost." 11(10): 13–15.

—— (1994) "Video-on-demand trials planned across Europe." 12(1): 8.

Newman, Katherine S. (1993) *Declining Fortunes: The Withering of the American Dream*, New York: Basic Books.

Newsweek (1993) "Jobs." Special issue, June 14.

Nicol, Lionel (1985) Communications technology: economic and social impacts. In Manuel Castells (ed.), *High Technology, Space and Society*, Beverly Hills, CA: Sage.

NIKKEIREN [Japan Federation of Employers Associations] (1993) *The Current Labor Economy in Japan*, Tokyo: NIKKEIREN, Information Report.

Nilles, J.M. (1988) "Traffic reduction by telecommuting: a status review and selected bibliography." *Transportation Research A*, 22A(4): 301–17.

Noble, David F. (1984) *Forces of Production: A Social History of Industrial Automation*, New York: Alfred A. Knopf.

Nolan, Peter and Furen, Dong (eds) (1990) *The Chinese Economy and its Future: Achievements and Problems of Post-Mao Reform*, Cambridge: Polity Press.

Nomura, Masami (1994) *Syushin Koyo*, Tokyo: Iwanami Shoten.

Nonaka, Ikujiro (1990) *Chisiki souzou no keiei* [Knowledge creation: epistemology of the Japanese firms], Tokyo: Nikkei shinbunsha.

—— (1991) "The knowledge-creating company." *Harvard Business Review,* Nov.–Dec.: 96–104.

—— and Takeuchi, Hirotaka (1994) *The Knowledge-creating Company: How Japanese Companies Created the Dynamics of Innovation,* New York: Oxford University Press.

"Non-standard working under review." (1994) *Industrial Relations & Review Report,* no. 565: 5–14.

Nora, Simon and Minc, Alain (1978) *L'Informatisation de la société.* Paris: La Documentation française.

Norman, Alfred Lorn (1993) *Informational Society: An Economic Theory of Discovery, Invention and Innovation,* Boston/Dordrecht/London: Kluwer Academic Publishers.

Norman, E. Herbert (1940) *Japan's Emergence as a Modern State: Political and Economic Problems of the Meiji Period,* New York: Institute of Pacific Relations.

North, Douglas (1981) *Structure and Change in Economic History,* New York: W.W. Norton.

Northcott, J. (1986) *Microelectronics in Industry,* London: Policy Studies Institute.

Nuland, Sherwin B. (1994) *How We Die: Reflections on Life's Final Chapter,* New York: Alfred A. Knopf.

O'Brien, Richard (1992) *Global Financial Integration: The End of Geography,* London: Pinter.

OECD (Organization for Economic Cooperation and Development) *Cities and New Technologies,* Paris: OECD.

—— (1994a) *Employment Outlook,* July, Paris: OECD.

—— (1994b) *Employment/Unemployment Study: Policy Report,* Paris: OECD, document for Council at ministerial level, May.

—— (1994c) *The OECD Jobs Study,* Paris: OECD.

—— (1995) *Economic Outlook,* June, Paris: OECD.

Office of Technology Assessment (OTA) (US Congress) (1984) *Computerized Manufacturing Automation: Employment, Education, and the Workplace,* Washington D.C.: US Government Printing Office.

—— (1986) *Technology and Structural Unemployment,* Washington D.C.: US Government Printing Office.

Ohmae, Kenichi (1985) *Triad Power: The Coming Shape of Global Competition,* New York: Free Press.

—— (1990) *The Borderless World: Power and Strategy in the Interlinked Economy,* New York: Harper.

Okimoto, Daniel (1984), "Political context." In Daniel Okimoto, Takuo Sugano and Franklin B. Weinstein (eds), *Competitive Edge,* Stanford, CA: Stanford University Press.

Ozaki, Muneto et al. (1992) *Technological Change and Labour Relations,* Geneva: International Labour Organization.

Pahl, Ray (ed.) (1988) *On Work: Historical, Comparative, and Theoretical Approaches,* Oxford: Blackwell.

Panofsky, Erwin (1957) *Gothic Architecture and Scholasticism*, New York: Meridian Books.

Park, Young-bum (1992) *Wage-fixing Institutions in the Republic of Korea*, Geneva: International Institute of Labour Studies, Discussion paper 51/1992.

Parkinson, G.H.R. (ed.) (1973) *Leibniz: Philosophical Writings*, London: J.M. Dent.

Parsons, Carol A. (1987) *Flexible Production Technology and Industrial Restructuring: Case Studies of the Metalworking, Semiconductor, and Apparel Industries*, PhD dissertation, Berkeley, University of California.

Patel, S.J. (1992) "In tribute to the Golden Age of the South's development." *World Development*, 20(5): 767–77.

Payer, Cheryl (1974) *The Debt Trap*, New York: Monthly Review Press.

Perez, Carlotta (1983) "Structural change and the assimilation of new technologies in the economic and social systems." *Futures*, 15: 357–75.

Petrella, Ricardo (1993) *Un techno-monde en construction. Synthèse des résultats et des recommendations FAST 1989–1992/93*, Brussels: European Commission: FAST Programme.

Petterson, L.O. (1989) "Arbetstider i tolv Lander." *Statens offentliga utrednigar*, 53: cited in Bosch et al. (eds) (1994).

Piller, Charles (1994) "Dreamnet." *Macworld* 11(10): 96–9.

Piore, Michael J. and Sabel, Charles F. (1984) *The Second Industrial Divide: Possibilities for Prosperity*, New York: Basic Books.

Poirier, Mark (1993) "The multimedia trail blazers." *Catalog Age*, 10(7): 49.

Pool, Ithiel de Sola (1983) *Technologies of Freedom: On Free Speech in the Electronic Age*, Cambridge, MA: Belknap Press of Harvard University Press.

—— (1990) *Technologies Without Boundaries*, ed. Eli M. Noam, Cambridge, MA: Harvard University Press.

Porat, Marc (1977) *The Information Economy: Definition and Measurement*, Washington D.C.: US Department of Commerce, Office of Telecommunications, publication 77–12 (1).

Porter, Michael (1990) *The Competitive Advantage of Nations*, New York: Free Press.

Portes, Alejandro and Rumbault, Ruben (1990) *Immigrant America: A Portrait*, Berkeley, CA: University of California Press.

——, Castells, Manuel and Benton, Lauren (eds) (1989) *The Informal Economy: Studies on Advanced and Less Developed Countries*, Baltimore; MD: Johns Hopkins University Press.

Postman, Neil (1985) *Amusing Ourselves to Death: Public Discourse in the Age of Show Business*, New York: Penguin Books.

—— (1992) *Technopoly*, New York: Pantheon.

Poulantzas, Nicos (1978) *L'Etat, le pouvoir, le socialisme*, Paris: Presses Universitaires de France.

Powell, Walter W. (1990) "Neither market nor hierarchy: network forms of organization." In Barry M. Straw and Larry L. Cummings (eds), *Research in Organizational Behavior*, Greenwich, CT: JAI Press, pp. 295–336.

Pozas, Maria de los Angeles (1993) *Industrial Restructuring in Mexico*, San Diego: University of California Center for US–Mexican Studies.

Preston, Holly H. (1994) "Minitel reigns in Paris with key French connection." *Computer Reseller News*, no. 594: 49–50.

Pyo, H. (1986) *The Impact of Microelectronics and Indigenous Technological Capacity in the Republic of Korea*, Geneva: International Labour Organization.

Qian, Wen-yuan (1985) *The Great Inertia: Scientific Stagnation in Traditional China*, London: Croom Helm.

Qingguo Jia (1994) "Threat or opportunity? Implications of the growth of the China Circle for the distribution of economic and political power in the Asia Pacific Region," paper delivered at the conference sponsored by the University of California Institute on Global Conflict and Cooperation, *The Economics of the China Circle*, Hong Kong, September 1–3.

Quinn, James Brian (1987) "The impacts of technology in the services sector." In Bruce R. Guile and Harvey Brooks (eds), *Technology and Global Industry: Companies and Nations in the World Economy*, Washington D.C.: National Academy of Engineering: National Academy Press, pp. 119–159.

—— (1988) "Technology in services: past myths and future challenges." In Bruce R. Guile and James B. Quinn (eds), *Technology in Services*, Washington D.C.: National Academy Press, pp. 16–46.

Quiroga Martinez, Layen (ed.) (1994) *El tigre sin selva: consecuencias ambientales de la transformacion economica de Chile, 1974–1993*, Santiago de Chile: Instituto de Ecologia Politica.

Qvortup, Lars (1992) "Telework: visions, definitions, realities, barriers." In OECD *Cities and New Technologies*, Paris: OECD, pp. 77–108.

Rafaeli, Sheifaz and LaRose, Robert J. (1993) "Electronic bulletin boards and public goods explanations of collaborative mass media." *Communications Research*, 20(2): 277–97.

Ramamurthy, K. (1994) "Moderating influences of organizational attitude and compatibility on implementation success from computer-integrated manufacturing technology." *International Journal of Production Research*, 32(10):2251–73

Rand Corporation (1995) *Universal Access to E-Mail: Feasibility and Social Implications*, World Wide Web, ttp://www.rand.org/publications/MR/MR650/

Randall, Stephen J. (ed.) (1992) *North America Without Borders?*, Calgary: University of Calgary Press.

Randlesome, Collin, Brierly, William, Bruton, Kevin, Gordon, Colin and King, Peter (1990) *Business Cultures in Europe*, Oxford: Heinemann.

Redding, S. Gordon (1990) *The Spirit of Chinese Capitalism*, Berlin: Walter de Gruyter.

Rees, Teresa (1992) *Skill Shortages, Women, and the New Information Technologies*, Report of the Task Force of Human Resources, Education, Training, and Youth, Brussels: Commission of the European Communities, January.

Reich, Robert (1991) *The Work of Nations*, New York: Random House.

Reynolds, Larry (1992) "Fast money: global markets change the investment game." *Management Review*, 81(2): 60–1.

Rheingold, Howard (1993) *The Virtual Community*, Reading, MA: Addison-Wesley.

Rice, Ronald E. "Issues and concepts on research on computer-mediated communication systems." *Communication Yearbook*, 12: 436–76.

Rifkin, Jeremy (1987) *Time Wars: The Primary Conflict in Human History*, New York: Henry Holt.

—— (1995) *The End of Work*, New York: Putnam.

Rijn, F.V. and Williams, R. (eds) (1988) *Concerning Home Telematics*, Amsterdam: North-Holland.

Roberts, Edward B. (1991) *Entrepreneurs in High Technology: MIT and Beyond*, New York: Oxford University Press.

Robinson, Olive (1993) "Employment in services: perspectives on part-time employment growth in North America." *Service Industries Journal*, 13(3): 1–18.

Robson, B. (1992) "Competing and collaborating through urban networks." *Town and Country Planning*, Sept: 236–8.

Rodgers, Gerry (ed.) (1994) *Workers, Institutions, and Economic Growth in Asia*, Geneva: International Institute of Labour Studies.

—— (ed.) (1995) *The Poverty Agenda and the ILO: Issues for Research and Action. A Contribution to the World Summit for Social Development*, Geneva: International Institute of Labour Studies.

——, Gore, Charles and Figueiredo, Jose B. (eds) (1995) *Social Exclusion: Rhetoric, Reality, Responses*, Geneva: International Institute of Labour Studies.

Rogers, Everett M. (1986) *Communication Technology: The New Media in Society*, New York: Free Press.

—— and Larsen, Judith K. (1984) *Silicon Valley Fever: Growth of High Technology Culture*, New York: Basic Books.

Rogozinski, Jacques (1993) *La privatizacion de las empresas estatales*, Mexico DF: Fondo de Cultura Economica.

Rosenbaum, Andrew (1992) "France's Minitel has finally grown up." *Electronics*, 65(6).

Rosenberg, Nathan (1976) *Perspectives on Technology*, Cambridge: Cambridge University Press.

—— (1982) *Inside the Black Box: Technology and Economics*, Cambridge: Cambridge University Press.

—— and Birdzell, L.E. (1986) *How the West Grew Rich: The Economic Transformation of the Industrial World*, New York: Basic Books.

Rostow, W.W. (1975) *How It All Began*, New York: McGraw Hill.

Roszak, Theodore (1986) *The Cult of Information*, New York: Pantheon.

Rothchild, Donald and Chazan, Naomi (eds) (1988) *The Precarious Balance: State and Society in Africa*, Boulder, CO: Westview Press.

Rothstein, Richard (1993) *Workforce Globalization: A Policy Response*, Washington D.C.: Economic Policy Institute, Report prepared for the Women's Bureau of the US Department of Labor.

—— (1994) "The global hiring hall: why we need worldwide labor standards."
   American Prospect, no. 17: 54–61.
Rumberger, R.W. and Levin, H.M. (1984) *Forecasting the Impact of New
   Technologies on the Future Job Market*, Stanford, CA: Stanford University
   School of Education, Research Report.
Russell, Alan M. (1988) *The Biotechnology Revolution: An International
   Perspective*, Brighton, Sussex: Wheatsheaf Books.
Sabbah, Françoise (1985) "The new media." In Manuel Castells (ed.), *High
   Technology, Space, and Society*, Beverly Hills, CA: Sage.
Sabel, C. and Zeitlin, J. (1985) "Historical alternatives to mass production:
   politics, markets, and technology in 19th century industrialization." *Past
   and Present*, 108 (August): 133–76.
Saez, Felipe et al. (1991) *Tecnologia y empleo en España: situación y perspectivas*,
   Madrid: Universidad Autónoma de Madrid–Instituto de Sociologia de
   Nuevas Tecnologias y Ministerio de Economia–Instituto de Estudios de
   Prospectiva.
Sagasti, Francisco and Araoz, Alberto (eds) (1988) *La planificacion cientifica y
   tecnologica en los paises en desarrollo. La experiencia del proyecto STPI*, Mexico:
   Fondo de Cultura Economica.
—— et al. (1988) *Conocimiento y desarrollo: ensayos sobre ciencia y tecnologia*,
   Lima: GRADE.
Sainz, Pedro and Calcagno, Alfredo (1992) "In search of another form of
   development." *CEPAL Review*, 48 (December): 7–38.
Salomon, Jean-Jacques (1992) *Le Destin technologique*, Paris: Editions Balland.
Salvaggio, Jerry L. (ed.) (1989) *The Information Society: Economic, Social, and
   Structural Issues*, Hillsdale, NJ: Lawrence Erlbaum Associates.
Sandbrook, Richard (1985) *The Politics of Africa's Economic Stagnation*,
   Cambridge: Cambridge University Press.
Sandholtz, Wayne et al. (1992) *The Highest Stakes: The Economic Foundations of
   the Next Security System*, New York: Oxford University Press (a BRIE Project).
Sandkull, Bengdt (1992) "Reorganizing labour: the Volvo experience." In
   Jane Marceau (ed.), *Reworking the World: Organisations, Technologies, and
   Cultures in Comparative Perspective*, Berlin: Walter de Gruyter, pp. 399–409.
Sassen, Saskia (1988) *The Mobility of Labor and Capital*, Cambridge: Cambridge
   University Press.
—— (1991) *The Global City: New York, London, Tokyo*, Princeton, NJ: Princeton
   University Press.
Sato, Takeshi et al. (1995) *Johoza to taisyu bunka* [Informationalization and
   mass culture], Kunitachi: Hitotsubashi University Department of Social
   Psychology, Research Report.
Saunders, William (ed.) (1996) *Architectural Practices in the 1990s*, Princeton,
   NJ: Princeton University Press.
Sautter, Christian (1978) "L'efficacité et la rentabilité de l'économie
   française de 1954 à 1976." *Economie et statistique*, 68.
Saxby, Stephen (1990) *The Age of Information*, London: Macmillan.
Saxenian, Anna L. (1994) *Regional Advantage: Culture and Competition in Silicon
   Valley and Route 128*, Cambridge, MA: Harvard University Press.

Sayer, Andrew and Walker, Richard (1992) *The New Social Economy: Reworking the Division of Labor*, Oxford: Blackwell.

Schaff, Adam (1992) *El Socialismo del Futuro*, no. 4: special issue on the future of labor.

Schatan, Jacobo (1987) *World Debt: Who is to Pay?*, London: Zed Books.

Scheer, Leo (1994) *La Démocratie virtuelle*, Paris: Flammarion.

Schettkat, R. and Wagner, M. (eds) (1990) *Technological Change and Employment Innovation in the German Economy*, Berlin: Walter De Gruyter.

Schiatarella, R. (1984) *Mercato di Lavoro e struttura produttiva*, Milan: Franco Angeli.

Schiffer, Jonathan (1983) *Anatomy of a Laissez-faire Government: The Hong Kong Growth Model Reconsidered*, Hong Kong: University of Hong Kong Centre for Asian Studies.

Schoonmaker, Sara (1993) "Trading on-line: information flows in advanced capitalism." *Information Society*, 9(1): 39–49.

Schor, Juliet (1991) *The Overworked American*, New York: Basic Books.

Schuldt, K. (1990) *Soziale und ökonomische Gestaltung der Elemente der Lebensarbeitzeit der Werktätigen*, Dissertation, Berlin; cited in Bosch et al. (eds) (1994).

Schumpeter, J.A. (1939) *Business Cycles: A Theoretical, Historical, and Statistical Analysis of the Capitalist Process*, New York: McGraw-Hill.

Schweitzer, John C. (1995) "Personal computers and media use." *Journalism Quarterly*, 68(4): 689–97.

Schwitzer, Glenn E. (1995) "Can research and development recover in Russia?" *Business World of Russia Weekly*, May 15–20: 10–12; reprinted from *Journal of Technology and Society*, 17(2).

Scott, Allen (1988) *New Industrial Spaces*, London: Pion.

SEADE Foundation (1995) *Survey of Living Conditions in the Metropolitan Area of São Paulo*, Geneva: International Institute of Labour Studies, Research Series.

Seidman, Steven and Wagner, David G. (eds) (1992) *Postmodernism and Social Theory*, Oxford: Blackwell.

Seki, Kiyohide (1988) *Summary of the National Opinion Survey of Family in Japan*, Tokyo: Nihon University Research Center, Research Paper.

Sellers, Patricia (1993) "The best way to reach buyers." *Fortune*, 128(13): 14–17.

Sengenberger, Werner and Campbell, Duncan (eds) (1992) *Is the Single Firm Vanishing? Inter-enterprise Networks, Labour, and Labour Institutions*, Geneva: International Institute of Labour Studies.

—— and —— (eds) (1994) *International Labour Standards and Economic Interdependence*, Geneva: International Institute of Labour Studies.

——, Loveman, Gary and Piore, Michael (eds) (1990) *The Re-emergence of Small Enterprises: Industrial Restructuring in Industrialized Countries*, Geneva: International Institute for Labour Studies.

Shaiken, Harley (1985) *Work Transformed: Automation and Labor in the Computer Age*, New York: Holt, Rinehart & Winston.

—— (1990) *Mexico in the Global Economy: High Technology and Work*

Organization in Export Industries, La Jolla, CA: University of California at San Diego, Center for US–Mexican Studies.

—— (1993) "Beyond lean production." *Stanford Law & Policy Review*, 5(1): 41–52.

—— (1995) "Experienced workers and high performance work organization: a case study of two automobile assembly plants," unpublished paper presented at the Industrial Relations Research Association Annual Meetings, Washington D.C., January 6.

Shapira, Phillip (1990) *Modernizing Manufacturing*, Washington D.C.: Economic Policy Institute.

Sharlin, Harold I. (1967) "Electrical generation and transmission." In Melvin Kranzberg and Carroll W. Pursell Jr (eds), *Technology in Western Civilization*, 2 vols, New York: Oxford University Press, vol. 2, pp. 578–91.

Shin, E.H. and Chin S.W. (1989) "Social affinity among top managerial executives of large corporations in Korea." *Sociological Forum*, 4: 3–26.

Shinotsuka, Eiko (1994) "Women workers in Japan: past, present, and future." In Joyce Gelb and Marian Lief Palley (eds), *Women of Japan and Korea: Continuity and Change*, Philadelphia, PA: Temple University Press, pp. 95–119.

Shirref, David (1994) "The metamorphosis of finance." *Euromoney*, June: 36–42.

Shoji, Kokichi (1990) *Le Nipponisme comme méthode sociologique. Originalité, particularité, universalité*, Tokyo: Tokyo University Department of Sociology, Discussion paper.

Shujiro Urata (1993) "Changing patterns of direct investment and its implications for trade and development." In C. Fred Bergsten and Marcus Noland (eds), *Pacific Dynamism and the International Economic System*, Washington, D.C.: Institute for International Economics, pp. 273–99.

Siddell, Scott (1987) *The IMF and Third World Political Instability*, London: Macmillan.

Siino, Corinne (1994) "La ville et le chomage." *Revue d'économie régionale et urbaine*, no. 3: 324–52.

Silverstone, R. (1991) *Beneath the bottom line: households and information and communication technologies in the age of the consumer*, London: Brunel University Center for Research on Innovation, Culture, and Technology.

Silvestri, George T. (1993) "The American work force, 1992–2005: occupational employment, wide variations in growth." *Monthly Labor Review*, November: 58–86.

—— and Lukasiewicz, J. (1991) "Outlook 1990–2005: occupational employment projections." *Monthly Labor Review*, November:

Singleman, Joachim (1978) *The Transformation of Industry: From Agriculture to Service Employment*, Beverly Hills, CA: Sage.

Singer, Charles et al. (1957) *A History of Technology*, vol. 3: *From the Renaissance to the Industrial Revolution*, Oxford: Clarendon Press.

——, Holmyard, E.J., Hall, A.R. and Williams, Trevor I. (eds) (1958) *A History of Technology*, vol. 4: *The Industrial Revolution, c.1750 to c.1850*, Oxford: Clarendon Press.

Singh, Ajit (1994) "Global economic changes, skills, and international competitiveness." *International Labour Review*, 133(2): 107–83.

Sit, Victor Fueng-Shuen (1991) "Transnational capital flows and urbanization in the Pearl River Delta, China." *Southeast Asian Journal of Social Science*, 19(1–2): 154–79.

—— and Wong, S.L. (1988) *Changes in the Industrial Structure and the Role of Small and Medium Industries in Asian Countries: The Case of Hong Kong*, Hong Kong: University of Hong Kong Centre of Asian Studies.

Sit, Victor F.S., Wong, Sin Lun and Kiang, Tsiu-Sing (1979) *Small-scale Industry in a Laissez-faire Economy: A Hong Kong Case Study*, Hong Kong: University of Hong Kong, Centre of Asian Studies.

Skezely, Gabriel (1993) "Mexico's international strategy: looking east and north." In Barbara Stallings and Gabriel Skezely (eds), *Japan, the United States, and Latin America*, Baltimore, MD: Johns Hopkins University Press.

Smith, Merrit Roe and Marx, Leo (eds) (1994) *Does Technology Drive History? The Dilemma of Technological Determinism*, Cambridge, MA: MIT Press.

Soesastro, Hadi and Pangetsu, Mari (eds) (1990) *Technological Challenge in the Asia–Pacific Economy*, Sydney: Allen & Unwin.

Soete, Luc (1987) "The impact of technological innovation on international trade patterns: the evidence reconsidered." *Research Policy*, 16.

—— (1991) "Technology and economy in a changing world," background paper prepared for the OECD International Policy Conference on *Technology and the Global Economy*, Montreal, February.

Solow, Robert M. (1956) "A contribution to the theory of economic growth." *Quarterly Journal of Economics*, 70 (Feb.): 65–94.

—— (1957) "Technical change and the aggregate production function." *Revue of Economics and Statistics*, 39 (Aug.): 214–31.

Sorlin, Pierre (1994) *Mass Media*, London: Routledge.

Sorokin, P.A. and Merton, R.K. (1937) "Social time: a methodological and functional analysis." *American Journal of Sociology*, 42: 615–29.

Soumu-cho Toukei-kyoku (Bureau of Statistics, Management and Coordination Agency, Japan) (1995) *Nihon no Toukei*, Tokyo.

Southern, R.W. (1995) *Scholastic Humanism and the Unification of Europe*, vol. 1: *Foundations*, Oxford: Blackwell Publishers.

Soysal, Yasemin Nuhoglu (1994) *Limits of citizenship: Migrants and Postnational Membership in Europe*, Chicago, IL: University of Chicago Press.

Specter, Michael (1994) "Russians' newest space adventure: cyberspace." *New York Times*, March 9: C1–C2.

—— (1995) "Plunging life expectancy puzzles Russia." *New York Times*, August 2: 1.

Spence, Michael and Hazard, Heather A. (eds) (1988) *International Competitiveness*, Cambridge, MA: Ballinger.

Sproull, Lee and Kiesler, Sara (1991) *Connections: New Ways of Working in the Networked Organization*, Cambridge, MA: MIT Press.

Stalker, Peter (1994) *The Work of Strangers: A Survey of International Labour Migration*, Geneva: International Labour Organization.

Stallings, Barbara (1992) "International influence on economic policy: debt, stabilization and structural reform." In Stephen Haggard and Robert R. Kaufman (eds), *The Politics of Adjustment*, Princeton, NJ: Princeton University Press, pp. 41–88.

—— (1993) *The New International Context of Development*, Madison, WIS: University of Wisconsin, Working Paper Series on the New International Context of Development, no. 1.

—— and Kaufman, Robert (eds) (1989) *Debt and Democracy in Latin America*, Boulder, CO: Westview Press.

Stanback, T.M. (1979) *Understanding the Service Economy: Employment, Productivity, Location*, Baltimore, MD: Johns Hopkins University Press.

Steers, R.M., Shin, Y.K. and Ungson, G.R. (1989) *The Chaebol*, New York: Harper & Row.

Steinle, W.J. (1988) "Telework: opening remarks and opening debate." In W.B. Korte, S. Robinson and W.K. Steinle (eds), *Telework: Present Situation and Future Development of a New Form of Work Organization*, Amsterdam: North-Holland.

Stevens, Barrie and Michalski, Wolfgang (1994) *Long-term Prospects for Work and Social Cohesion in OECD Countries: An Overview of the Issues*, Paris: Report to the OECD Forum for the Future.

Stevenson, Richard W. (1994) "Foreign capitalists brush risks aside to invest in Russia." *New York Times*, October 11: cl, p. 4.

Stonier, Tom (1983) *The Wealth of Information*, London: Methuen.

Stourdze, Yves (1987) *Pour une poignée d'électrons*, Paris: Fayard.

Stowsky, Jay (1992) "From spin-off to spin-on: redefining the military's role in American technology development." In Wayne Sandholtz, Michael Borrus and John Zysman et al., *The Highest Stakes: The Economic Foundations of the Next Security System*, New York: Oxford University Press.

Strassman, Paul A. (1985) *Information Payoff: The Transformation of Work in the Electronic Age*, New York: Free Press.

Sugihara, Kaoru et al. (1988) *Taisho, Osaka, and the Slum: Another Modern History of Japan*, Tokyo: Shinhyoron.

Sukhotin, Iurii (1994) "Stabilization of the economy and social contrasts." *Problems of Economic Transition*, November: 44–61.

Sullivan-Trainor, Michael (1994) *Detour: The Truth about the Information SuperHighway*, San Mateo, CA: IDG Books.

Sun Tzu (*c.* 505–496BC) *On the Art of War*, trans. from Chinese with critical notes by Lionel Giles, Singapore: Graham Brash, 1988 (first published in English in 1910).

Sung, Yun-Wing (1994) "Hong Kong and the economic integration of the China Circle." Paper delivered at the conference sponsored by the University of California Institute on Global Conflict and Cooperation, *The Economies of the China Circle*, Hong Kong, September 1–3.

Sunkel, Osvaldo (ed.) (1993) *Development from Within: Toward a Neostructuralist Approach for Latin America*, Boulder, CO: Lynne Reiner.

Swann, J. (1986) *The Employment Effects of Microelectronics in the UK Service Sector*, Geneva: International Labour Organization.

Syun, Inoue (1975) The loss of meaning in death. *Japan Interpreter*, 9(3): 336.

Tafuri, Manfredo (1971) *L'urbanistica del riformismo*, Milan: Franco Angeli.

Takenori, Inoki and Higuchi, Yoshio (eds) (1995) *Nihon no Koyou system to lodo shijo* [Japanese employment system and labour market], Tokyo: Nihon Keizai Shinbunsha.

Tan, Augustine H.H. and Kapur, Basant (eds) (1986) *Pacific Growth and Financial Interdependence*, Sydney: Allen & Unwin.

Tan Kong Yam (1994) "China and ASEAN: competitive industrialization through foreign direct investment," paper delivered at the conference sponsored by the University of California Institute on Global Conflict and Cooperation, *The Economics of the China Circle*, Hong Kong, September 1–3.

Tarr, J. and Dupuy, G. (eds) (1988) *Technology and the Rise of the Networked City in Europe and North America*, Philadelphia, PA: Temple University Press.

Tchernina, Natalia (1993) *Employment, Deprivation, and Poverty: The Ways in which Poverty is Emerging in the Course of Economic Reform in Russia*, Geneva: International Institute of Labour Studies, Discussion Paper no. 60/1993.

Teitelman, Robert (1989) *Gene Dreams: Wall Street, Academia, and the Rise of Biotechnology*, New York: Basic Books.

Teitz, Michael B., Glasmeier, Amy and Shapira, Philip (1981) *Small Business and Employment Growth in California*, Berkeley, CA: Institute of Urban and Regional Development, Working Paper no. 348.

Telecommunications Council (Japan) (1994) *Reforms Toward the Intellectually Creative Society of the 21st Century: Program for the Establishment of High-performance Info-communications Infrastructure*, Report–response to Inquiry no. 5, 1993, Tokyo: May 31 (unofficial translation, July 1994).

Tetsuro, Kato and Steven, Rob (eds) (1994) *Is Japanese Management Post-Fordism?*, Tokyo: Mado-sha.

Thach, Liz and Woodman, Richard W. (1994) "Organizational change and information technology: managing on the edge of cyberspace." *Organizational Dynamics*, 1: 30–46.

Thery, Gérard (1994) *Les autoroutes de l'information. Rapport au Premier Ministre*, Paris: La Documentation française.

Thomas, Hugh (1993) *The Conquest of Mexico*, London: Hutchinson.

Thomas, Louis-Vincent (1975) *Anthropologie de la mort*, Paris: Payot.

—— (1985) *Rites de mort pour la paix des vivants*, Paris: Fayard.

—— (1988) *La Mort*, Paris: Presses Universitaires de France.

Thompson, E.P. (1967) "Time, work-discipline, and industrial capitalism." *Past and Present*, 36: 57–97.

Thrift, Nigel J. (1986) *The "Fixers": The Urban Geography of International Financial Capital*, Lampeter: University of Wales Department of Geography.

—— (1990) "The making of capitalism in time consciousness." In J. Hassard (ed.), *The Sociology of Time*, London: Macmillan, pp. 105–29.

—— and Leyshon, A. (1992) "In the wake of money: the City of London and the accumulation of value." In L. Budd and S. Whimster (eds), *Global Finance and Urban Living: A Study of Metropolitan Change*, London: Routledge, pp. 282–311.

Thurow, Lester (1992) *Head to Head: The Coming Economic Battle among Japan, Europe, and America*, New York: William Morrow.

—— (1995) "How much inequality can a democracy take?" *New York Times Magazine*, special issue: *The Rich*, November 19: 78.

Tichi, Cecilia (1991) *Electronic Hearth: Creating an American Television Culture*, New York: Oxford University Press.

Tillema, H.K. (1991) *International Armed Conflict Since 1945: A Bibliographic Handbook of Wars and Military Intervention*, Boulder, CO: Westview Press.

Tilly, Charles (1995) "State-incited violence, 1900–1999." *Political Power and Social Theory*, 9: 161–79.

Time (1993) Special issue on Megacities, January 11.

—— (1994) "Risky business in Wall Street: high-tech supernerds are playing dangerous games with money." Special report, April 11: 24–35.

Tirman, John (ed.) (1984) *The Militarization of High Technology*, Cambridge, MA: Ballinger.

Tobenkin, David (1993) "Customers respond to video on demand." *Broadcasting & Cable*, 123(48): 16.

Touraine, Alain (1955) *L'Evolution du travail ouvrier aux usines Renault*, Paris: Centre National de la Recherche Scientifique.

—— (1959) "Entreprise et bureaucratie." *Sociologie du travail*, no. 1: 58–71.

—— (1969) *La Société post-industrielle*, Paris: Denoel.

—— (1987) *La Parole et le sang. Politique et société en Amerique Latine*, Paris: Odile Jacob.

—— (1991) "Existe-t-il encore une société française?" *Contemporary French Civilization*, 15: 329–52.

—— (1992) *Critique de la modernité*, Paris: Fayard.

—— (1994) *Qu'est-ce que la démocratie?*, Paris: Fayard.

Trejo Delarbre, Raul (1992) *La Sociedad Ausente. Comunicacion, democracia y modernidad*, Mexico: Cal y Arena.

—— (ed.) (1988) *Las Redes de Televisa*, Mexico: Como/Rotativo.

Turkle, Sherry (1995) *Life on the Screen: Identity in the Age of the Internet*, New York: Simon & Schuster.

Tyson, Laura D'Andrea (1992) *Who's Bashing Whom? Trade Conflict in High-technology Industries*, Washington D.C.: Institute of International Economics.

—— and Zysman, John (1983) *American Industry in International Competition*, Ithaca, N.Y.: Cornell University Press.

——, Dickens, William T. and Zysman, John (eds) (1988) *The Dynamics of Trade and Employment*, Cambridge, MA: Ballinger.

Ubbelhode, A.R.J.P. (1958) "The beginnings of the change from craft mystery to science as a basis for technology." In C. Singer et al., *A History of Technology*, vol. 4: *The Industrial Revolution, 1750–1850*, Oxford: Clarendon Press.

Uchida, Hoshimi (1991) "The transfer of electrical technologies from the U.S. and Europe to Japan, 1869–1914." In David J. Jeremy (ed.), *International Technology Transfer: Europe, Japan, and the USA, 1700–1914*, Aldershot, Hants: Edward Elgar, pp. 219–41.

Ungar, Sanford J. (1985) *Africa: The People and Politics of an Emerging Continent,* New York: Simon & Schuster.

United Nations Center on Transnational Corporations (1991) *Transnational Banks and the External Indebtedness of Developing Countries,* New York: United Nations, UNCTC Current Studies, Series A, No.22.

United Nations Conference on Trade and Development (UNCTAD), Programme on Transnational Corporations (1993) *World Investment Report 1993: Transnational Corporations and Integrated International Production,* New York: United Nations.

—— (1994) *Transnational Corporations and Employment,* report by the UNCTAD Secretariat to the Commission on Transnational Corporations, 2–11 May.

US Congress, Office of Technology Assessment (1991) *Biotechnology in a Global Economy,* Washington D.C.: US Government Printing Office.

US House of Representatives, Committee on Armed Services, Readiness Subcommittee (1990) *U.S. Low-intensity Conflicts, 1899–1990,* a study by the Congressional Research Service, Library of Congress, Washington D.C.: US Government Printing Office.

US National Science Board (1991) *Science and Engineering Indicators: 1991,* 10th edn, Washington D.C.: US Government Printing Office.

Vaill, P.B. (1990) *Managing as a Performing Art: New Ideas for a World of Chaotic Change,* San Francisco, CA: Jossey-Bass.

Van Creveld, Martin (1989) *Technology and War from 2000 BC to the Present,* New York: Free Press.

Van Tulder, Rob and Junne, Gerd (1988) *European Multinationals in Core Technologies,* New York: John Wiley.

Vaquero, Carlos (ed.) (1994) *Desarrollo, probreza y medio ambiente. FMI, Banco Mundial, GATT al final del siglo,* Madrid: Talasa Ediciones.

Varley, Pamela (1991) "Electronic democracy." *Technology Review,* Nov/Dec: 43–51.

Velloso, Joao Paulo dos Reis (1994) "Innovation and society: the modern bases for development with equity." In Colin I. Bradford (ed.), *The New Paradigm of Systemic Competitiveness: Toward More Integrated Policies in Latin America,* Paris: OECD Development Center, pp. 97–118.

Venturi, Robert et al. (1977) *Learning from Las Vegas: The Forgotten Symbolism of Architectural Form,* Cambridge, MA: MIT Press.

Vessali, Kaveh V. (1995) "Transportation, urban form, and information technology," Berkeley, CA: University of California, unpublished seminar paper for CP 298 I.

Voshchanov, Pavel (1995) "Mafia godfathers become fathers of the nation." *Business World of Russia Weekly,* May 25–30: 13–14.

Wade, Richard (1990) *Governing the Market: Economic Theory and the Role of Government in East Asian Industrialization,* Princeton, NJ: Princeton University Press.

Waldrop, M. Mitchell (1992) *Complexity: The Emerging Science at the Edge of Order and Chaos,* New York: Simon & Schuster.

Waliszewski, Kasimierz (1900) *Peter the Great,* New York: D. Appleton and Co.

Wall, Toby D. et al. (eds) (1987) *The Human Side of Advanced Manufacturing Technology*, Chichester, Sussex: John Wiley.

Wallerstein, Immanuel (1974) *The Modern World System*, New York: Academic Press.

Wang, Georgette (ed.) (1994) *Treading Different Paths: Informatization in Asian Nations*, Norwood, NJ: Ablex.

Wang, Yeu-fain (1993) *China's Science and Technology Policy, 1949–1989*, Brookfield, VT: Avebury.

Wark, McKenzie (1994) *Virtual Geography: Living with Global Media Events*, Bloomington, IND: Indiana University Press.

Warme, Barbara et al. (eds) (1992) *Working Part-time: Risks and Opportunities*, New York: Praeger.

Warnken, Jurgen and Ronning, Gerd, "Technological change and employment structures." In R. Schettkat and M. Wagner (eds), *Technological Change and Employment Innovation in the German Economy*, Berlin: Walter De Gruyter, pp. 214–53.

Watanabe, Susumu (1986) "Labour-saving versus work-amplifying effects of microelectronics." *International Labour Review*, 125(3): 243–59.

—— (ed.) (1987) *Microelectronics, Automation, and Employment in the Automobile Industry*, Chichester, Sussex: John Wiley.

Watanuki, Joji (1990) *The Development of Information Technology and its Impact on Japanese Society*, Tokyo: Sophia University Institute of International Relations, Research Paper.

Weber, Marx (1958) *The Protestant Ethic and the Spirit of Capitalism*, trans. Talcott Parsons, New York: Charles Scribner's Sons. First published 1904–5.

Webster, Andrew (1991) *Science, Technology, and Society: New Directions*, London: Macmillan.

Weiss, Linda (1988) *Creating Capitalism: The State and Small Business since 1945*, Oxford: Blackwell.

—— (1992) "The politics of industrial organization: a comparative view." In Jane Marceau (ed.), *Reworking the World: Organizations, Technologies, and Cultures in Comparative Perspective*, Berlin: Walter De Gruyter, pp. 95–124.

Wexler, Joanie (1994) "ATT preps service for video on demand." *Network World*, 11(25): 6.

Whightman, D.W. (1987) "Competitive advantage through information technology." *Journal of General Management*, 12(4).

Whitaker, D.H. (1990) "The end of Japanese-style employment." *Work, Employment & Society*, 4(3): 321–47.

Whitley, Richard (1993) *Business Systems in East Asia: Firms, Markets, and Societies*, London: Sage.

Whitrow, G.J. (1988) *Time in History: The Evolution of our General Awareness of Time and Temporal Perspective*, Oxford: Oxford University Press.

Wieczorek, Jaroslaw (1995) *Sectoral Trends in World Employment*, Working Paper 82, Geneva: International Labour Organization, Industrial Activities Branch.

Wieviorka, Michel (1993) *La Démocratie a l'épreuve. Nationalisme, populisme, ethnicité*, Paris: La Découverte.

Wilkinson, B. (1988) "A comparative analysis." In *Technological Change, Work, Organization and Pay: Lessons from Asia*, Geneva: International Labour Organization.

Wilkinson, Barry, Morris, Jonathan and Nich, Oliver (1992) "Japanizing the world: the case of Toyota." In Jane Marceau (ed.), *Reworking the World: Organizations, Technologies, and Cultures in Comparative Perspective*, Berlin: Walter de Gruyter, pp. 133–50.

Williams, Frederick (1982) *The Communications Revolution*, Beverly Hills, CA: Sage.

—— (1991) *The New Telecommunications: Infrastructure for the Information Age*, New York: Free Press.

—— (ed.) (1988) *Measuring the Information Society*, Beverly Hills, CA: Sage.

——, Rice, Ronald E. and Rogers, Everett M. (1988) *Research Methods and the New Media*, New York: Free Press.

Williams, Raymond (1974) *Television: Technology and Cultural Form*, New York: Schocken Books.

Williamson, Oliver E. (1975) *Markets and Hierarchies: Analysis and Anti-trust Implications*, New York: Free Press.

—— (1985) *The Economic Institutions of Capitalism*, New York: Free Press.

Willmott, W.E. (ed.) (1972) *Economic Organization in Chinese Society*, Stanford, CA: Stanford University Press.

Wilson, Carol (1991) "The myths and magic of Minitel." *Telephony*, 221(23): 52.

Wilson, Ernest J. (1991) "Strategies of state control of the economy: nationalization and indigenization in Africa." *Comparative Politics*, July: 411.

Withey, Stephen B. and Abeles, Ronald P. (eds) (1980) *Television and Social Behavior*, Hillsdale, NJ: Lawrence Erlbaum.

Wong, Siulun (1988) *Emigrant Entrepreneurs: Shanghai Industrialists in Hong Kong*, Hong Kong: Oxford University Press.

Wong, S.L. (1985) "The Chinese family firm: a model." *British Journal of Sociology*, 36: 58–72.

Woo, Edward S.W. (1994) Urban development. In Y.M. Yeung and David K.Y. Chu, *Guandong: Survey of a Province Undergoing Rapid Change*, Hong Kong: Chinese University Press.

Wood, Adrian (1994) *North–South Trade, Employment and Inequality*, Oxford: Clarendon Press.

Wood, Stephen (ed.) (1989) *The Transformation of Work*, London: Unwin Hyman.

Woodward, Kathleen (ed.) (1980) *The Myths of Information: Technology and Postindustrial Culture*, London: Routledge & Kegan Paul.

World Bank (1994a) *Adjustment in Africa: Reforms, Results and the Road Ahead*, New York: Oxford University Press.

—— (1994b) *World Development Report: Infrastructure for Development. World Development Indicators*, Washington D.C.: World Bank.

—— (1995) *World Development Report, 1995*, Washington, D.C.: World Bank.

Ybarra, Josep-Antoni (1989) "Informationalization in the Valencian economy: a model for underdevelopment." In A. Portes, M. Castells and L. Benton *The Informal Economy*, Baltimore, MD: Johns Hopkins University Press.

Yoo, S. and Lee, S.M. (1987) "Management style and practice in Korean chaebols." *California Management Review*, 29: 95–110.

Yoshihara, K. (1988) *The Rise of Ersatz Capitalism in South East Asia*, Oxford: Oxford University Press.

Yoshino, Kosaku (1992) *Cultural Nationalism in Contemporary Japan*, London: Routledge.

Yoshino, M.Y. and Lifson, T.B. (1986) *The Invisible Link: Japan's Sogo Shosha and the Organization of Trade*, Cambridge, MA: MIT Press.

Young, K. and Lawson, C. (1984) "What fuels U.S. job growth? Changes in technology and demand on employment growth," paper prepared for the Panel on Technology and Employment of the National Academy of Sciences, Washington D.C.

Young, Michael (1988) *The Metronomic Society*, Cambridge, Mass.: Harvard University Press.

Youngson, A.J. (1982) *Hong Kong: Economic Growth and Policy*, Hong Kong: Oxford University Press.

Zaldivar, Carlos Alonso and Castells, Manuel (1992) *España, fin de siglo*, Madrid: Alianza Editorial.

Zerubavel, Eviatar (1985) *The Seven Day Circle: The History and Meaning of the Week*, New York: Free Press.

Zhivov, Victor M. (1995) "Time and money in Imperial Russia." Unpublished paper delivered at the conference on *Time and Money in the Russian Culture*, University of California at Berkeley, Center for Slavic and Eastern European Studies, March 17.

Zuboff, Shoshana (1988) *In the Age of the Smart Machine*, New York: Basic Books.

Zukin, Sharon (1992) *Landscapes of Power*, Berkeley, CA: University of California Press.

Index

The Information Age

Economy, Society and Culture

Volume II

The Power of Identity

Para Irene Castells Oliván,
historiadora de utopías

The Power of Identity

Manuel Castells

First published 1997

Reprinted 1997 (twice), 1998, 1999

Blackwell Publishers Inc
350 Main Street
Massachusetts 02148, USA

Blackwell Publishers Ltd
108 Cowley Road
Oxford OX4 1JF, UK

Library of Congress Cataloging in Publication Data
Castells, Manuel.
The power of identity / Manuel Castells
p. cm. — (Information age : v.2)
Includes bibliographical references and index.
ISBN 1–55786–873–5 — ISBN 1–55786–874–3 (pbk)
1. Information society. 2. Social movements. 3. Information technology—
Social aspects. 4. Information technology—Political aspects. 5. Identity.
I. Title. II. Series: Castells, Manuel. Information age : 2
HM221.C366 1997 96–36317
303.48'33—dc20 CIP

British Library Cataloguing in Publication Data
A CIP catalogue record for this book is available from the British Library

Printed and bound in Great Britain
by T. J. International Limited, Padstow, Cornwall

This book is printed on acid-free paper

Contents

Figures

Tables

Charts

Acknowledgments

The ideas and analyses presented in this volume have grown out of 25 years of study which I have conducted on social movements and political processes in various areas of the world, although they are now re-elaborated and integrated in a broader theory of the Information Age, as presented in the three volumes of this book. A number of academic institutions were essential environments for the development of my work in this specific area of inquiry. Foremost among them was the Centre d'Étude des Mouvements Sociaux, École des Hautes Etudes en Sciences Sociales, Paris, founded and directed by Alain Touraine, where I was a researcher between 1965 and 1979. Other research institutions that helped my work on social movements and politics were: Centro Interdisciplinario de Desarrollo Urbano, Universidad Catolica de Chile; Instituto de Investigaciones Sociales, Universidad Nacional Autonoma de Mexico; Center for Urban Studies, University of Hong Kong; Instituto de Sociologia de Nuevas Tecnologias, Universidad Autonoma de Madrid; Faculty of Social Sciences, Hitotsubashi University, Tokyo. The final elaboration and writing of the material presented here took place in the 1990s in what has been, since 1979, my intellectual home, the University of California at Berkeley. Many of the ideas were discussed and refined in my graduate seminar on "Sociology of the Information Society." For this, I thank my students, a constant source of inspiration for and criticism of my work. This volume has benefited from exceptional research assistance by Sandra Moog, a sociology graduate student at Berkeley, and a future outstanding scholar. Additional valuable research assistance was provided by Lan-chih Po, a doctoral student in city and regional planning, also at Berkeley. As with the other volumes of this book, Emma Kiselyova considerably helped my research by facilitating access to languages that I do not know, as well as by assessing and commenting on various sections of the volume.

Several colleagues read drafts of the whole volume, or of specific chapters, and commented extensively, helping me to correct some mistakes and to tighten up the analysis, although I obviously take full responsibility for the final interpretation. My gratitude goes to: Ira Katznelson, Ida Susser, Alain Touraine, Anthony Giddens, Martin Carnoy, Stephen Cohen, Alejandra Moreno Toscano, Roberto Laserna, Fernando Calderon, Rula Sadik, You-tien Hsing, Shujiro Yazawa, Chu-joe Hsia, Nancy Whittier, Barbara Epstein, David Hooson, Irene Castells, Eva Serra, Tim Duane, and Elsie Harper-Anderson. I wish to express my special thanks to John Davey, Blackwell's editorial director, who provided his expert insight, as well as careful suggestions on substance in several key sections of the volume.

This is to say that, as with the other volumes of this book, the process of thinking and writing is largely a collective endeavour, albeit ultimately assumed in the solitude of authorship.

November 1996   Berkeley, California

The author and publishers gratefully acknowledge permission from the following to reproduce copyright material:

Professor Ines Alberdi: for figures 4.2 and 4.5.

The Economist: for figures 5.1 and 5.2, both copyright © The Economist, London 1996.

The University of Texas Press and the authors: for table 6.2 from 'Political Corruption and Presidential Elections, 1929–1992' in *The Journal of Politics*, volume 57:4.

The Southern Poverty Law Center, Alabama: for figure 2.1 obtained from their Klanwatch Milita Task Force Programs.

The University of Chicago Press: for figures 4.10 and 4.14 from E. O. Laumann et al., *The Social Organization of Sexuality: Sexual Practices in the United States* (1994), copyright © 1994 by Edward O. Laumann, Robert T. Michael, CSG Enterprises, Inc., and Stuart Michaels. All rights reserved.

Westview Press, Inc.: for figure 4.1 from *The New Role of Women: Family Formation in Modern Societies* by Hans-Peter Blossfeld et al. (1995), copyright © 1995 by Westview Press.

Our World, our Lives

Lift up your faces, you have a piercing need
For this bright morning dawning for you.
History, despite its wrenching pain,
Cannot be unlived, and if faced
With courage, need not be lived again.

Lift up your eyes upon
This day breaking for you.
Give birth again
To the dream.
                    Maya Angelou, "On the Pulse of Morning"[1]

Our world, and our lives, are being shaped by the conflicting trends of globalization and identity. The information technology revolution, and the restructuring of capitalism, have induced a new form of society, the network society. It is characterized by the globalization of strategically decisive economic activities. By the networking form of organization. By the flexibility and instability of work, and the individualization of labor. By a culture of real virtuality constructed by a pervasive, interconnected, and diversified media system. And by the transformation of material foundations of life, space and time, through the constitution of a space of flows and of timeless time, as expressions of dominant activities and controlling elites. This new form of social organization, in its pervasive globality, is diffusing throughout the world, as industrial capitalism and its twin enemy, industrial statism, did in the twentieth century, shaking institutions, transforming cultures, creating wealth and inducing poverty, spurring greed, innovation, and hope, while simultaneously

---

[1] Poem on the inauguration of the US President, January 22, 1993.

imposing hardship and instilling despair. It is indeed, brave or not, a new world.

But this is not the whole story. Along with the technological revolution, the transformation of capitalism, and the demise of statism, we have experienced, in the last quarter of the century, the widespread surge of powerful expressions of collective identity that challenge globalization and cosmopolitanism on behalf of cultural singularity and people's control over their lives and environment. These expressions are multiple, highly diversified, following the contours of each culture, and of historical sources of formation of each identity. They include proactive movements, aiming at transforming human relationships at their most fundamental level, such as feminism and environmentalism. But they also include a whole array of reactive movements that build trenches of resistance on behalf of God, nation, ethnicity, family, locality, that is, the fundamental categories of millennial existence now threatened under the combined, contradictory assault of techno-economic forces and transformative social movements. Caught between these opposing trends, the nation-state is called into question, drawing into its crisis the very notion of political democracy, predicated upon the historical construction of a sovereign, representative nation-state. More often than not, new, powerful technological media, such as worldwide, interactive telecommunication networks, are used by various contenders, amplifying and sharpening their struggle, as, for instance, when the Internet becomes an instrument of international environmentalists, Mexican *Zapatistas*, or American militia, responding in kind to computerized globalization of financial markets and information processing.

This is the world explored in this volume, focusing primarily on social movements and politics, as they result from the interplay between technology-induced globalization, the power of identity (gender, religious, national, ethnic, territorial, socio-biological), and the institutions of the state. Inviting the reader to this intellectual journey through the landscapes of contemporary social struggles and political conflicts, I will start with a few remarks that may help the voyage.

This is not a book about books. Thus, I will not discuss existing theories on each topic, or cite every possible source on the issues presented here. Indeed, it would be pretentious to attempt setting, even superficially, the scholarly record on the whole realm of themes covered in this book. The sources and authors that I do use for each topic are materials that I consider relevant to construct the hypotheses I am proposing on each theme, as well as on the meaning of these analyses for a broader theory of social change in the network society. Readers interested in bibliography, and in critical evaluations of such a bibliography, should consult the many available good textbooks on each matter.

The method I have followed aims at communicating theory by analyzing practice, in successive waves of observation of social movements in various cultural and institutional contexts. Thus, empirical analysis is mainly used as a communication device, and as a method of disciplining my theoretical discourse, of making it difficult, if not impossible, to say something that observed collective action rejects in practice. However, I have tried to provide a few empirical elements, within the space constraints of this volume, to make my interpretation plausible, and to allow the reader to judge for her/himself.

There is in this book a deliberate obsession with multiculturalism, with scanning the planet, in its diverse social and political manifestations. This approach stems from my view that the process of techno-economic globalization shaping our world is being challenged, and will eventually be transformed, from a multiplicity of sources, according to different cultures, histories, and geographies. Thus, moving thematically between the United States, Western Europe, Russia, Mexico, Bolivia, the Islamic world, China or Japan, as I do in this volume, has the specific purpose of using the same analytical framework to understand very different social processes that are, none the less, interrelated in their meaning. I would also like, within the obvious limits of my knowledge and experience, to break the ethnocentric approach still dominating much social science at the very moment when our societies have become globally interconnected and culturally intertwined.

One word about theory. The sociological theory informing this book is diluted for your convenience in the presentation of themes in each chapter. It is also blended with empirical analysis as far as it could be done. Only when it is unavoidable will I submit the reader to a brief theoretical excursus, since for me social theory is a tool to understand the world, not an end for intellectual self-enjoyment. I shall try, in the conclusion to this volume, to tighten up the analysis in a more formal, systematic manner, bringing together the various threads woven in each chapter. However, since the book focuses on social movements, and since there is a great deal of disagreement on the meaning of the concept, I advance my definition of social movements as being: purposive collective actions whose outcome, in victory as in defeat, transforms the values and institutions of society. Since there is no sense of history other than the history we sense, *from an analytical perspective* there are no "good" and "bad," progressive and regressive social movements. They are all symptoms of who we are, and avenues of our transformation, since transformation may equally lead to a whole range of heavens, hells, or heavenly hells. This is not an incidental remark, since processes of social change in our world often take forms of fanaticism and violence that we do not usually associate with positive social change. And yet, this is our world, this is us, in our contradictory plurality, and this is what we have to understand, if necessarily to face it, and to overcome it. As for the meaning of *this* and *us*, please dare to read on.

— 1 —

Communal Heavens: Identity and Meaning in the Network Society

The capital is established near Zhong Mountain;
The palaces and thresholds are brilliant and shining;
The forests and gardens are fragrant and flourishing;
Epidendrums and cassia complement each other in beauty.
The forbidden palace is magnificent;
Buildings and pavilions a hundred stories high.
Halls and gates are beautiful and lustrous;
Bells and chimes sound musically.
The towers reach up to the sky;
Upon altars sacrificial animals are burned.
Cleansed and purified,
We fast and bathe.
We are respectful and devout in worship,
Dignified and serene in prayer.
Supplicating with fervor,
Each seeks happiness and joy.
The uncivilized and border people offer tribute,
And all the barbarians are submissive.
No matter how vast the territory,
All will be eventually under our rule.

Hong Xiuquan

Such were the words of the "Imperially Written Tale of a Thousand Words," composed by Hong Xiuquan, the guide and prophet of the Taiping Rebellion, after establishing his heavenly kingdom in Nanjing in 1853.[1] The insurgency of Taiping Tao (Way of Great

---

[1] Cited by Spence (1996: 190–1).

Peace) aimed at creating a communal, neo-Christian fundamentalist kingdom in China. The kingdom was organized, for more than a decade, in conformity with the revelation of the Bible that, by his own account, Hong Xiuquan received from his elder brother, Jesus Christ, after being initiated into Christianity by evangelical missionaries. Between 1845 and 1864, Hong's prayers, teachings, and armies shook up China, and the world, as they interfered with the growing foreign control of the Middle Kingdom. The Taiping Kingdom perished, as it lived, in blood and fire, taking the lives of 20 million Chinese. It longed to establish an earthly paradise by fighting the demons that had taken over China, so that "all people may live together in perpetual joy, until at last they are raised to Heaven to greet their Father."[2] It was a time of crisis for state bureaucracies and moral traditions, of globalization of trade, of profitable drug traffic, of rapid industrialization spreading in the world, of religious missions, of impoverished peasants, of the shaking of families and communities, of local bandits and international armies, of the diffusion of printing and mass illiteracy, a time of uncertainty and hopelessness, of identity crisis. It was another time. Or was it?

The Construction of Identity

Identity is people's source of meaning and experience. As Calhoun writes:

> We know of no people without names, no languages or cultures in which some manner of distinctions between self and other, we and they, are not made . . . Self-knowledge – always a construction no matter how much it feels like a discovery – is never altogether separable from claims to be known in specific ways by others.[3]

By identity, as it refers to social actors, I understand the process of construction of meaning on the basis of a cultural attribute, or related set of cultural attributes, that is/are given priority over other sources of meaning. For a given individual, or for a collective actor, there may be a plurality of identities. Yet, such a plurality is a source of stress and contradiction in both self-representation and social action. This is because identity must be distinguished from what, traditionally, sociologists have called roles, and role-sets. Roles (for example, to be a worker, a mother, a neighbor, a socialist militant, a union member,

---

[2]   Spence (1996: 172).
[3]   Calhoun (1994: 9–10).

a basketball player, a churchgoer, and a smoker, at the same time) are defined by norms structured by the institutions and organizations of society. Their relative weight in influencing people's behavior depend upon negotiations and arrangements between individuals and these institutions and organizations. Identities are sources of meaning for the actors themselves, and by themselves, constructed through a process of individuation.[4] Although, as I will argue below, identities can also be originated from dominant institutions, they become identities only when and if social actors internalize them, and construct their meaning around this internalization. To be sure, some self-definitions can also coincide with social roles, for instance when to be a father is the most important self-definition from the point of view of the actor. Yet, identities are stronger sources of meaning than roles, because of the process of self-construction and individuation that they involve. In simple terms, identities organize the meaning while roles organize the functions. I define *meaning* as the symbolic identification by a social actor of the purpose of her/his action. I also propose the idea that, *in the network society*, for reasons that I will develop below, for most social actors, meaning is organized around a primary identity (that is an identity that frames the others), that is self-sustaining across time and space. While this approach is close to Erikson's formulation of identity, my focus here will be primarily on collective, rather than on individual, identity. However, individualism (different from individual identity) may also be a form of "collective identity," as analyzed in Lasch's "culture of narcissism."[5]

It is easy to agree on the fact that, from a sociological perspective, all identities are constructed. The real issue is how, from what, by whom, and for what. The construction of identities uses building materials from history, from geography, from biology, from productive and reproductive institutions, from collective memory and from personal fantasies, from power apparatuses and religious revelations. But individuals, social groups, and societies process all these materials, and rearrange their meaning, according to social determinations and cultural projects that are rooted in their social structure, and in their space/time framework. I propose, as a hypothesis, that, in general terms, who constructs collective identity, and for what, largely determines the symbolic content of this identity, and its meaning for those identifying with it or placing themselves outside of it. Since the social construction of identity always takes place in a context marked by power relationships, I propose a distinction between three forms and origins of identity building:

---

[4] Giddens (1991).
[5] Lasch (1980).

- *Legitimizing identity*: introduced by the dominant institutions of society to extend and rationalize their domination *vis à vis* social actors, a theme that is at the heart of Sennett's theory of authority and domination,[6] but also fits with various theories of nationalism.[7]
- *Resistance identity*: generated by those actors that are in positions/conditions devalued and/or stigmatized by the logic of domination, thus building trenches of resistance and survival on the basis of principles different from, or opposed to, those permeating the institutions of society, as Calhoun proposes when explaining the emergence of identity politics.[8]
- *Project identity*: when social actors, on the basis of whichever cultural materials are available to them, build a new identity that redefines their position in society and, by so doing, seek the transformation of overall social structure. This is the case, for instance, when feminism moves out from the trenches of resistance of women's identity and women's rights, to challenge patriarchalism, thus the patriarchal family, thus the entire structure of production, reproduction, sexuality, and personality on which societies have been historically based.

Naturally, identities that start as resistance may induce projects, and may also, along the course of history, become dominant in the institutions of society, thus becoming legitimizing identities to rationalize their domination. Indeed, the dynamics of identities along this sequence shows that, from the point of view of social theory, no identity can be an essence, and no identity has, *per se*, progressive or regressive value outside its historical context. A different, and very important matter, is the benefits of each identity for the people who belong.

In my view, each type of identity-building process leads to a different outcome in constituting society. *Legitimizing identity generates a civil society*; that is, a set of organizations and institutions, as well as a series of structured and organized social actors, which reproduce, albeit sometimes in a conflictive manner, the identity that rationalizes the sources of structural domination. This statement may come as a surprise to some readers, since civil society generally suggests a positive connotation of democratic social change. However, this is in fact the original conception of civil society, as formulated by Gramsci, the intellectual father of this ambiguous concept. Indeed, in Gramsci's conception, civil society is formed by a series of "apparatuses," such as the Church(es), unions, parties, cooperatives, civic associations and

---

[6]   Sennett (1986).
[7]   Anderson (1983); Gellner (1983).
[8]   Calhoun (1994: 17).

so on, which, on the one hand, prolong the dynamics of the state, but, on the other hand, are deeply rooted among people.[9] It is precisely this double character of civil society that makes it a privileged terrain of political change by making it possible to seize the state without launching a direct, violent assault. The conquest of the state by the forces of change (let's say the forces of socialism, in Gramsci's ideology), present in the civil society, is made possible exactly because of the continuity between civil society's institutions and the power apparatuses of the state, organized around a similar identity (citizenship, democracy, the politicization of social change, the confinement of power to the state and its ramifications, and the like). Where Gramsci, and de Tocqueville, see democracy and civility, Foucault or Sennett, and before them Horkheimer or Marcuse, see internalized domination and legitimation of an over-imposed, undifferentiated, normalizing identity.

The second type of identity-building, *identity for resistance*, leads to the formation of *communes*, or *communities*, in Etzioni's formulation.[10] This may be the most important type of identity-building in our society. It constructs forms of collective resistance against otherwise unbearable oppression, usually on the basis of identities that were, apparently, clearly defined by history, geography, or biology, making it easier to essentialize the boundaries of resistance. For instance, ethnically based nationalism, as Scheff proposes, often "arises out of a sense of alienation, on the one hand, and resentment against unfair exclusion, whether political, economic or social."[11] Religious fundamentalism, territorial communities, nationalist self-affirmation, or even the pride of self-denigration, inverting the terms of oppressive discourse (as in the "queer culture" of some tendencies in the gay movement), are all expressions of what I name *the exclusion of the excluders by the excluded.* That is, the building of defensive identity in the terms of dominant institutions/ideologies, reversing the value judgment while reinforcing the boundary. In such a case, the issue arises of the reciprocal communicability between these excluded/exclusionary identities. The answer to this question, that can only be empirical and historical, determines whether societies remain as societies or else fragment into a constellation of tribes, some times euphemistically renamed communities.

The third process of constructing identity, that is *project identity*, produces *subjects*, as defined by Alain Touraine:

[9] Buci-Glucksman (1978).
[10] Etzioni (1993).
[11] Scheff (1994: 281).

> I name subject the desire of being an individual, of creating a personal history, of giving meaning to the whole realm of experiences of individual life . . . The transformation of individuals into subjects results from the necessary combination of two affirmations: that of individuals against communities, and that of individuals against the market.[12]

Subjects are not individuals, even if they are made by and in individuals. They are the collective social actor through which individuals reach holistic meaning in their experience.[13] In this case, the building of identity is a project of a different life, perhaps on the basis of an oppressed identity, but expanding toward the transformation of society as the prolongation of this project of identity, as in the above-mentioned example of a post-patriarchal society, liberating women, men, and children, through the realization of women's identity. Or, in a very different perspective, the final reconciliation of all human beings as believers, brothers and sisters, under the guidance of God's law, be it Allah or Jesus, as a result of the religious conversion of godless, anti-family, materialist societies, otherwise unable to fufill human needs and God's design.

How, and by whom, different types of identities are constructed, and with what outcomes, cannot be addressed in general, abstract terms: it is a matter of social context. Identity politics, as Zaretsky writes, "must be situated historically."[14]

Thus, our discussion must refer to a specific context, the rise of the network society. The dynamics of identity in this context can be better understood by contrasting it with Giddens' characterization of identity in "late modernity," a historical period which, I believe, is an era reaching its end – by which I do not mean to suggest that we are in some way reaching the "end of history" as posited in some postmodern vagaries. In a powerful theorization whose main lines I share, Giddens states that "self-identity is not a distinctive trait possessed by the individual. It is the self as reflexively understood by the person in terms of her/his biography." Indeed, "to be a human being is to know . . . both what one is doing and why one is doing it . . . In the context of post-traditional order, the self becomes a reflexive project."[15]

How does "late modernity" impact this reflexive project? In Giddens' terms,

---

[12]   Touraine (1995: 29–30); my translation.
[13]   Touraine (1992).
[14]   Zaretsky (1994: 198).
[15]   Giddens (1991: 53, 35, 32).

one of the distinctive features of modernity is an increasing inter-connection between the two extremes of extensionality and intentionality: globalising influences on the one hand and personal dispositions on the other . . . The more tradition loses its hold, and the more daily life is reconstituted in terms of the dialectical interplay of the local and the global, the more indi-viduals are forced to negotiate lifestyle choices among a diversity of options . . . Reflexively organized life-planning . . . becomes a central feature of the structuring of self-identity."[16]

While agreeing with Giddens' theoretical characterization of identity-building in the period of "late modernity," I argue, on the basis of analyses presented in volume I of this book, that the rise of the network society calls into question the processes of construction of identity during that period, thus inducing new forms of social change. This is because the network society is based on the systemic disjunction between the local and the global for most individuals and social groups. And, I will add, by the separation in different time–space frames between power and experience (volume I, chap-ters 6 and 7). Therefore, reflexive life-planning becomes impossible, except for the elite inhabiting the timeless space of flows of global net-works and their ancillary locales. And the building of intimacy on the basis of trust requires a redefinition of identity fully autonomous *vis à vis* the networking logic of dominant institutions and organizations.

Under such new conditions, civil societies shrink and disarticulate because there is no longer continuity between the logic of power-making in the global network and the logic of association and representation in specific societies and cultures. The search for meaning takes place then in the reconstruction of defensive identi-ties around communal principles. Most of social action becomes organized in the opposition between unidentified flows and secluded identities. As for the emergence of project identities, it still happens, or may happen, depending on societies. But, I propose the hypothesis that the constitution of subjects, at the heart of the process of social change, takes a different route to the one we knew during modernity, and late modernity: namely, *subjects, if and when constructed, are not built any longer on the basis of civil societies, that are in the process of disintegra-tion, but as prolongation of communal resistance.* While in modernity (early or late) project identity was constituted from civil society (as in the case of socialism on the basis of the labor movement), in the network society, project identity, if it develops at all, grows from communal resistance. This is the actual meaning of the new primacy of identity politics in the network society. The analysis of processes,

[16] Giddens (1991: 1, 5).

conditions, and outcomes of the transformation of communal resistance into transformative subjects is the precise realm for a theory of social change in the information age.

Having reached a tentative formulation of my hypotheses, it would be against the methodological principles of this book to go any further down the path of abstract theorizing that could quickly divert into bibliographical commentary. I shall try to suggest the precise implications of my analysis by focusing on a number of key processes in the construction of collective identity selected by their particular relevance to the process of social change in the network society. I will start with *religious fundamentalism*, both in its Islamic and Christian versions, although this does not imply that other religions (for example, Hinduism, Buddhism, Judaism) are less important or less prone to fundamentalism. I shall continue with *nationalism*, considering, after some overview of the issue, two very different, but significant processes: the role of nationalism in the disintegration of the Soviet Union, and in post-Soviet republics; and the formation, and re-emergence of Catalan nationalism. I will then turn to *ethnic identity*, focusing on contemporary African-American identity. And I will end by considering, briefly, *territorial identity*, on the basis of my observation of urban movements and local communities around the world. In conclusion, I shall try a succinct synthesis of major lines of inquiry that will emerge from examining various contemporary processes of the (re)construction of identity on the basis of communal resistance.

God's Heavens: Religious Fundamentalism and Cultural Identity

It is an attribute of society, and I would dare to say of human nature if such an entity were to exist, to find solace and refuge in religion. The fear of death, the pain of life, need God, and faith in God, whichever of God's manifestations, for people just to go on. Indeed, outside us God would become homeless.

Religious fundamentalism is something else. And I contend that this "something else" is a most important source of constructing identity in the network society for reasons that will become clearer, I hope, in the following pages. As for its actual content, experiences, opinions, history, and theories are so diverse as to defy synthesis. Fortunately, the American Academy of Arts and Sciences undertook, in the late 1980s, a major comparative project aimed at observing fundamentalisms in various social and institutional contexts.[17] Thus,

---

[17]   Marty and Appleby (1991).

we know that "fundamentalists are always reactive, reactionary,"[18] and that:

> fundamentalists are selective. They may well consider that they are adopting the whole of the pure past, but their energies go into employing those features which will best reinforce their identity, keep their movement together, build defenses around its boundaries, and keep others at a distance . . . Fundamentalists fight under God – in the case of theistic religion – or under the signs of some transcendent reference.[19]

To be more precise, I believe, to be consistent with the collection of essays gathered in the "Fundamentalism Observed" Project, in defining *fundamentalism*, in my own understanding, as *the construction of collective identity under the identification of individual behavior and society's institutions to the norms derived from God's law, interpreted by a definite authority that intermediates between God and humanity.* Thus, as Marty writes, "It is impossible for fundamentalists to argue or settle anything with people who do not share their commitment to an authority, whether it be an inerrant Bible, an infallible Pope, the *Shari'a* codes in Islam, or the implications of *halacha* in Judaism."[20]

Religious fundamentalism has, of course, existed throughout the whole of human history, but it appears to be surprisingly strong and influential as a source of identity in this end of millennium. Why so? My analyses of Islamic fundamentalism, and of Christian fundamentalism, in this section, will try to propose some clues to understand one of the most defining trends in the making of our historical epoch.[21]

Umma versus *Jahiliya*: Islamic fundamentalism

The only way to accede to modernity is by our own path, that which has been traced for us by our religion, our history and our civilization.

Rached Gannouchi[22]

The 1970s, the birthdate of the information technology revolution in Silicon Valley, and the starting point of global capitalist restructuring, had a different meaning for the Muslim world: it marked the

---

[18]   Marty (1988: 20).
[19]   Marty and Appleby (1991: ix–x).
[20]   Marty (1988: 22).
[21]   See also Misztal and Shupe (1992a).
[22]   Rached Gannouchi, interview with *Jeune Afrique*, July 1990. Gannouchi is a leading intellectual in the Tunisian Islamist movement.

beginning of the fourteenth century of the *Hegira*, a period of Islamic revival, purification, and strengthening, as at the onset of each new century. Indeed, in the next two decades an authentic cultural/religious revolution spread throughout Muslim lands, sometimes victorious, as in Iran, sometimes subdued, as in Egypt, sometimes triggering civil war, as in Algeria, sometimes formally acknowledged in the institutions of the state, as in the Sudan or Bangladesh, most times establishing an uneasy coexistence with a formally Islamic nation-state, fully integrated in global capitalism, as in Saudi Arabia, Indonesia, or Morocco. Overall, the cultural identity and political fate of almost a billion people were being fought for in the mosques and in the wards of Muslim cities, crowded by accelerated urbanization, and disintegrated by failed modernization. Islamic fundamentalism, as a reconstructed identity, and as a political project, is at the center of a most decisive process, largely conditioning the world's future.[23]

But, what is Islamic fundamentalism? Islam, in Arabic, means state of submission, and a Muslim is one who has submitted to Allah. Thus, according to the definition of fundamentalism I presented above, it would appear that all Islam is fundamentalist: societies, and their state institutions, must be organized around uncontested religious principles. However, a number of distinguished scholars[24] argue that, while the primacy of religious principles as formulated in the Qur'ān is common to all of Islam, Islamic societies and institutions are also based on multivocal interpretation. Furthermore, in most traditional Islamic societies, the pre-eminence of religious principles over political authority was purely formal. Indeed, the *shari'a* (divine law, formed by the Qur'ān and the *Hadiths*) relates in classic Arabic language to the verb *shara'a*, to walk toward a source. Thus, for most Muslims, *shari'a* is not an invariable, rigid command, but a guide to walk toward God, with the adaptations required by each historical and social context.[25] In contrast to this openness of Islam, Islamic fundamentalism implies the fusion of *shari'a* with *fiqh*, or interpretation and application by jurists and authorities, under the absolute domination of *shari'a*. Naturally, the actual meaning depends on the process of interpretation, and on who interprets. Thus, there is a wide range of variation between conservative fundamentalism, such as the one represented by the House of Saud, and radical fundamentalism, as elaborated in the writings of al-Mawdudi or Sayyid Qtub in the 1950s

---

[23]   Hiro (1989); Balta (1991); Sisk (1992); Choueri (1993); Juergensmayer (1993); Dekmejian (1995).
[24]   See, for example, Bassam Tibi (1988, 1992a); Aziz Al-Azmeh (1993); Farhad Khosrokhavar (1995), among others.
[25]   Garaudy (1990).

and 1960s.[26] There are also considerable differences between the Shia tradition, the one inspiring Khomeini, and the Sunni tradition which constitutes the faith for about 85 percent of Muslims, including revolutionary movements such as Algeria's *Front Islamique de Salvation* (FIS), or Egypt's *Takfir wal-Hijrah*. Yet, in the vision of writers who constitute Islamist thought in this century, such as Egypt's Hassan al Banna and Sayyid Qtub, India's Ali al-Nadawi, or Pakistan's Sayyid Abul al-Mawdudi, the history of Islam is reconstructed to show the perennial submission of state to religion.[27] For a Muslim, the fundamental attachment is not to the *watan* (homeland), but to the *umma*, or community of believers, all made equal in their submission to Allah. This universal confraternity supersedes the institutions of the nation-state, which is seen as a source of division among believers.[28] For the *umma* to live, and expand, until embracing the whole of humanity, it has to accomplish a godly task: to undertake, anew, the fight against *Jahiliya* (the state of ignorance of God, or of lack of observance of God's teachings), in which societies have fallen again. To regenerate humanity, Islamization must proceed first in the Muslim societies that have secularized and departed from the strict obedience of God's law, then in the entire world. This process must start with a spiritual rebirth based on *al-sirat al-mustaqin* (straight path), modeled after the community organized by the Prophet Muhammad in Medina. Yet, to overcome impious forces, it may be necessary to proceed through *jihad* (struggle on behalf of Islam) against the infidels, which may include, in extreme cases, the resort to holy war. In the Shia tradition, martyrdom, re-enacting Imam Ali's sacrifice in 681, is indeed at the heart of religious purity. But the whole of Islam shares the praise for the necessary sacrifices implied by the call of God (*al-da'wah*). As stated by Hassan al Banna, the founder and leader of Muslim Brotherhood, assassinated in 1949: "The Qur'ān is our constitution, the Prophet is our Guide; death for the glory of Allah is our greatest ambition."[29] The ultimate goal of all human actions must be the establishment of God's law over the whole of humankind, thus ending the current opposition between *Dar al-Islam* (the Muslim world), and *Dar al-Harb* (the non-Muslim world).

In this cultural/religious/political framework, Islamic identity is constructed on the basis of a double deconstruction, by the social actors, and by the institutions of society.

Social actors must deconstruct themselves as subjects, be it as indi-

---

[26]   Carre (1984); Choueri (1993).
[27]   Hiro (1989); Al-Azmeh (1993); Choueri (1993); Dekmejian (1995).
[28]   Oumlil (1992).
[29]   Cited by Hiro (1989: 63).

viduals, as members of an ethnic group, or as citizens of a nation. In addition, women must submit to their guardian men, as they are encouraged to fulfill themselves primarily in the framework of the family: "Men are the protectors and maintainers of women, because God has given the one more (strength) than the other, and because they support them from their means."[30] As Bassam Tibi writes, "Habermas' principle of subjectivity is a heresy for Islamic fundamentalists."[31] Only in the *umma* can the individual be fully himself/herself, as part of the confraternity of believers, a basic equalizing mechanism that provides mutual support, solidarity, and shared meaning. On the other hand, the nation-state itself must negate its identity: *al-dawla islamiiyya* (Islamic state), based on the *Shari'a*, takes precedence over the nation-state (*al-dawla qawmiyya*). This proposition is particularly effective in the Middle East, a region where, according to Tibi, "the nation-state is alien and is virtually imposed on its parts . . . The political culture of secular nationalism is not only a novelty in the Middle East, but also remains on the surface of involved societies."[32]

However, and this is essential, Islamic fundamentalism is not a traditionalist movement. For all the efforts of exegesis to root Islamic identity in history and the holy texts, Islamists proceeded, for the sake of social resistance and political insurgency, with a reconstruction of cultural identity that is in fact hypermodern.[33] As Al-Azmeh writes: "The politicization of the sacred, the sacralization of politics, and the transformation of Islamic pseudo-legal institutes into 'social devotions', are all means of realizing the politics of the authentic ego, a politics of identity, and therefore the means for the very formation, indeed the invention, of this identity."[34]

But, if Islamism (although rooted in the writings of nineteenth-century Islamic reformers and revivalists, such as al-Afghani) is essentially a contemporary identity, why now? Why has it exploded in the past two decades, after being repeatedly subdued by nationalism in the post-colonial period, as exemplified by the repression of the Muslim Brothers in Egypt and Syria (including the execution of Qtub in 1966), the rise of Sukarno in Indonesia or of the *Front de Liberation Nationale* in Algeria?[35]

---

[30] Qur'ān, surah IV, v. 34 (trans. Abdullah Yusuf Ali, 1988). See Hiro (1989: 202); Delcroix (1995); Gerami (1996).
[31] Tibi (1992b: 8).
[32] Tibi (1992b: 5).
[33] Gole (1995).
[34] Al-Azmeh (1993: 31).
[35] Piscatori (1986); Moen and Gustafson (1992); Tibi (1992a); Burgat and Dowell (1993); Juergensmayer (1993); Dekmejian (1995).

For Tibi, "the rise of Islamic fundamentalism in the Middle East is inter-related with the exposure of this part of the world of Islam, which perceives itself as a collective entity, to the processes of globalization, to nationalism and the nation-state as globalized principles of organization."[36]

Indeed, the explosion of Islamic movements seems to be related to both the disruption of traditional societies (including the undermining of the power of traditional clergy), and to the failure of the nation-state, created by nationalist movements, to accomplish modernization, develop the economy, and/or to distribute the benefits of economic growth among the population at large. Thus, Islamic identity is (re)constructed by fundamentalists in opposition to capitalism, to socialism, and to nationalism, Arab or otherwise, which are, in their view, all failing ideologies of the post-colonial order.

A case in point is, of course, Iran.[37] The Shah's White Revolution, launched in 1963, was a most ambitious attempt to modernize the economy and society, with the support of the United States, and with the deliberate project of linking up with new global capitalism in the making. So doing, it undermined basic structures of traditional society, from agriculture to the calendar. Indeed, a major conflict between the Shah and the *ulemas* concerned control over time, when, on April 24, 1976, the Shah changed the Islamic calendar to the pre-Islamic Achemenian dynasty calendar. When Khomeini landed in Tehran on February 1, 1979, to lead the revolution, he returned as representative of Imam Nacoste, Lord of Time (*wali al-zaman*) to assert the pre-eminence of religious principles. The Islamic revolution opposed simultaneously the institution of monarchy (Khomeini: "Islam is fundamentally opposed to the whole notion of monarchy");[38] the nation-state (article 10 of the new Iranian Constitution: "All Muslims form a single nation"); and modernization as an expression of Westernization (article 43 of the Iranian Constitution asserts the "prohibition of extravagance and wastefulness in all matters related to the economy, including consumption, investment, production, distribution, and services"). The power of the *ulemas*, the main targets of the Shah's institutional reforms, became enshrined as the intermediary between the *shari'a* and society. The radicalization of the Islamic regime, after Iraq's attack in 1980 and the atrocious war that followed, led to the purification of society, and the setting up of special religious judges to repress impious acts, such as "adultery, homosexuality, gambling, hypocrisy, sympathy for atheists and

[36]   Tibi (1992b: 7).
[37]   Hiro (1989); Bakhash (1990); Esposito (1990); Khosrokhavar (1995).
[38]   Hiro (1989: 161).

hypocrites, and treason."[39] There followed thousands of imprison-
ments, flagellations, and executions, on different grounds. The cycle
of terror, particularly aimed at leftist critics and Marxist guerrillas,
closed the circle of fundamentalist logic in Iran.

What are the social bases of fundamentalism? In Iran, where other
revolutionary forces participated in the long, hard-fought mobilizations to topple the Pahlavis' bloody dictatorship, the leaders were
the clerics, and mosques were the sites of revolutionary committees
that organized popular insurgency. As for the social actors, the
strength of the movement was in Tehran and other large cities, particularly among the students, intellectuals, bazaar merchants and
artisans. When the movement came onto the streets, it was joined by
the masses of recent rural immigrants that populated Tehran's
sprawling shanty towns in the 1970s, after the modernization of agriculture expelled them from their villages.

Islamists in Algeria and Tunisia seem to present a similar social
profile, according to some scattered data: support for FIS originated
in a heterogeneous group of educated intellectuals, university
teachers, and low-level civil servants, joined by small merchants and
artisans. However, these movements, taking place in the 1980s, also
had their social roots in rural exodus. Thus, a survey in Tunisia found
that 48 percent of fathers of militants were illiterate, as they migrated
to the cities in the 1970s, from impoverished rural areas. The militants themselves were young: in Tunisia, the average age of 72
militants sentenced in a major trial in 1987 was 32 years.[40] In Egypt,
Islamism is predominant among university students (most student
unions have been under Islamic fundamentalist leadership since the
mid-1980s), and receives support from government employees, particularly teachers, with a growing influence in the police and the
army.[41]

The social roots of radical fundamentalism appear to derive from
the combination of successful state-led modernization in the 1950s
and 1960s and the failure of economic modernization in most Muslim
countries during the 1970s and 1980s, as their economies could not
adapt to the new conditions of global competition and technological
revolution in the latter period. Thus, a young, urban population, with
a high level of education as a result of the first wave of modernization,
was frustrated in its expectations, as the economy faltered and new
forms of cultural dependency settled in. It was joined in its discontent
by impoverished masses expelled from rural areas to cities by the

[39]   Official documents reported in the press, quoted by Hiro (1989: 190)
[40]   Data reported by Burgat and Dowell (1993).
[41]   Hiro (1989); Dekmejian (1995).

unbalanced modernization of agriculture. This social mixture was made explosive by the crisis of the nation-state, whose employees, including military personnel, suffered declining living standards, and lost faith in the nationalist project. The crisis of legitimacy of the nation-state was the result of its widespread corruption, inefficiency, dependency upon foreign powers, and, in the Middle East, repeated military humiliation by Israel, followed by accommodation with the Zionist enemy. The construction of contemporary Islamic identity proceeds as a reaction against unreachable modernization (be it capitalist or socialist), the evil consequences of globalization, and the collapse of the post-colonial nationalist project. This is why the differential development of fundamentalism in the Muslim world seems to be linked to variations in the capacity of the nation-state to integrate in its project both the urban masses, through economic welfare, and the Muslim clergy, through official sanction of their religious power under the aegis of the state, as had been the case in the Ummayyad caliphate or the Ottoman Empire.[42] Thus, while Saudi Arabia is formally an Islamic monarchy, the *ulemas* are on the payroll of the House of Saud, which succeeded in being, at the same time, guardian of the holy sites and guardian of Western oil. Indonesia and Malaysia seem to be able to integrate Islamist pressures within their authoritarian nation-states by ensuring fast economic growth, thus providing some promising prospects to their subjects, although Indonesian cities are accumulating social tensions. On the other hand, the nationalist projects of Egypt, Algeria, and Tunisia, some of the most Westernized Muslim countries, collapsed by and large in the 1980s, thus ushering in social tensions that were predominantly captured by Islamists under moderate (Muslim Brotherhood), radical (*Jama'ah al-Islamiyya*), or democratic-radical versions (Algeria's FIS).[43] In the 1990s, the challenge by Hamas to the proto-Palestinian state constituted around the leadership of Yasser Arafat, in cooperation with Israel, may constitute one of the most dramatic schisms between Arab nationalism (of which the Palestinian movement is the epitome) and radical Islamic fundamentalism.

When Islamist electoral victories, such as in Algeria in December 1991, were voided by military repression, widespread violence and civil war ensued.[44] Even in the most Westernized Muslim country, Turkey, Kemal Atatürk's secular, nationalist heritage came under historical challenge when, in the elections of 1995, Islamists became the country's first political force, relying on the vote of radicalized

[42]   Balta (1991).
[43]   Sisk (1992).
[44]   Nair (1996).

intellectuals and the urban poor, and formed the government in 1996.

Political Islamism, and Islamic fundamentalist identity, seem to be expanding in the 1990s in a variety of social and institutional contexts, always related to the dynamics of social exclusion and/or the crisis of the nation-state. Thus, social segregation, discrimination, and unemployment among French youth of Maghrebian origin, among young Turks born in Germany, among Pakistanis in Britain, or among African-Americans, induces the emergence of a new Islamic identity among disaffected youth, in a dramatic transference of radical Islamism to the socially excluded areas of advanced capitalist societies.[45] On the other hand, the collapse of the Soviet state triggered the emergence of Islamic movements in the Caucasus and Central Asia, and even the formation of an Islamic Revival Party in Russia, threatening to realize the fears of a spread of Islamic revolutions in Afghanistan and Iran into the former Soviet republics.[46]

Through a variety of political processes, depending upon the dynamics of each nation-state, and the form of global articulation of each economy, an Islamic fundamentalist project has emerged in all Muslim societies, and among Muslim minorities in non-Muslim societies. A new identity is being constructed, not by returning to tradition, but by working on traditional materials in the formation of a new godly, communal world, where deprived masses and disaffected intellectuals may reconstruct meaning in a global alternative to the exclusionary global order.[47] Furthermore, as Khosrokhavar writes:

> When the project of constituting individuals fully participating in modernity reveals its absurdity in the actual experience of everyday life, violence becomes the only form of self-affirmation of the new subject ... The neo-community becomes then a necro-community. The exclusion from modernity takes a religious meaning: thus, self-immolation becomes the way to fight against exclusion.[48]

Through the negation of exclusion, even in the extreme form of self-sacrifice, a new Islamic identity emerges in the historical process of building the *umma*, the communal heaven for the true believers.

---

[45] Luecke (1993); Kepel (1995).
[46] Mikulsky (1992).
[47] Tibi (1992a, b); Gole (1995).
[48] Khosrokhavar (1995: 249–50); my translation.

God Save Me! American Christian fundamentalism

We have come into an electronic dark age, in which the new pagan hordes, with all the power of technology at their command, are on the verge of obliterating the last strongholds of civilized humanity. A vision of death lies before us. As we leave the shores of Christian western man behind, only a dark and turbulent sea of despair stretches endlessly ahead . . . unless we fight!

Francis Schaeffer, *Time for Anger*[49]

Christian fundamentalism is a perennial feature of American history, from the ideas of post-revolutionary federalists, like Timothy Dwight and Jedidiah Morse, to the pre-millennial eschatology of Pat Robertson, through the 1900 revivalists, such as Dwight L. Moody, and the 1970s reconstructionists inspired by Rousas J. Rushdoony.[50] A society relentlessly at the frontier of social change and individual mobility is bound to doubt periodically the benefits of modernity and secularization, yearning for the security of traditional values and institutions rooted in God's eternal truth. Indeed, the very term "fundamentalism," widely used around the world, originated in America, in reference to a series of ten volumes entitled *The Fundamentals*, privately published by two businessmen brothers between 1910 and 1915, to collect holy texts edited by conservative evangelical theologians at the turn of the century. While fundamentalist influence has varied in different historical periods, it has never faded away. In the 1980s and 1990s it certainly surged. While the disintegration of Jerry Falwell's Moral Majority in 1989 led some observers to announce the decline of fundamentalism (parallel to the end of the Communist Satan whose opposition was a major source of legitimacy and funding for fundamentalists), it quickly became obvious that it was the crisis of an organization, and of a political ploy, rather than that of fundamentalist identity.[51] In the 1990s, in the wake of Clinton's presidential victory in 1992, fundamentalism came to the forefront of the political scene, this time in the form of the Christian Coalition, led by Pat Robertson and Ralph Reed, claiming 1.5 million organized members, and marshalling considerable political influence

---

[49] Schaeffer (1982: 122). Francis Schaeffer is one of the leading inspirations of contemporary American Christian fundamentalism. His *Christian Manifesto*, published in 1981, shortly after his death, was the most influential pamphlet in the 1980s' anti-abortion movement in America.
[50] Marsden (1980); Ammerman (1987); Misztal and Shupe (1992b); Wilcox (1992).
[51] Lawton (1989); Moen (1992); Wilcox (1992).

among the Republican electorate. Furthermore, the ideas and world vision of fundamentalists seem to find considerable echo in *fin-de-siècle* America. For instance, according to a Gallup poll on a national sample in 1979, one in three adults declared they had had an experience of religious conversion; almost half of them believed that the Bible was inerrant; and more than 80 percent thought that Jesus Christ was divine.[52] To be sure, America has always been, and still is, a very religious society, much more so, for instance, than Western Europe or Japan. But, this religious sentiment seems to take increasingly a revivalist tone, drifting toward a powerful fundamentalist current. According to Simpson:

> fundamentalism, in its original sense is a set of Christian beliefs and experiences that include (1) subscription to the verbal, plenary inspiration of the Bible and its inerrancy; (2) individual salvation through and acceptance of Christ as a personal Saviour (being born-again) on account of Christ's efficacious, substitutionary atonement for sin in his death and resurrection; (3) the expectation of Christ's premillennial return to earth from heaven; (4) the endorsement of such Protestant orthodox Christian doctrines as the Virgin birth and the trinity.[53]

Yet, Christian fundamentalism is such a wide, diversified trend that it defies a simple definition cutting across the cleavages between pentecostal and charismatic evangelicals, pre-millennial or post-millennial, pietists and activists. Fortunately, we can rely on an excellent, well-documented, scholarly synthesis of American fundamentalist writings and doctrines by Michael Lienesch, on the basis of which, and with the support of other sources that confirm, in general terms, his record and arguments, I will attempt to reconstruct the main traits of Christian fundamentalist identity.[54]

As Lienesch writes, "at the center of Christian conservative thinking, shaping its sense of the self, lies the concept of Conversion, the act of faith and forgiveness through which sinners are brought from sin into a state of everlasting salvation."[55] Through this personal experience of being born again, the whole personality is reconstructed, and becomes "the starting place for constructing a sense not only of autonomy and identity, but also of social order and political purpose."[56] The linkage between personality and society goes through

[52]   Lienesch (1993: 1).
[53]   Simpson (1992: 26).
[54]   Zeskind (1986); Jelen (1989, 1991); Barron and Shupe (1992); Lienesch (1993); Riesebrodt (1993); Hicks (1994).
[55]   Lienesch (1993: 23).
[56]   Lienesch (1993: 23).

the reconstruction of the family, the central institution of society, that used to be the refuge against a harsh, hostile world, and is now crumbling in our society. This "fortress of Christian life" has to be reconstructed by asserting patriarchalism, that is the sanctity of marriage (excluding divorce and adultery) and, above all, the authority of men over women (as established in biblical literality: Genesis 1; Ephesians 5, 22–23), and the strict obedience of children, if necessary enforced by spanking. Indeed, children are born in sin: "it is of great benefit to the parent when he realizes that it is natural for his child to have desire for evil."[57] Thus, it is essential for the family to educate children in God's fear and in respect for parental authority, and to count on the full support of a Christian education in school. As an obvious consequence of this vision, public schools become the battleground between good and evil, between the Christian family and the institutions of secularism.

A bounty of earthly rewards awaits the Christian who dares to stand up for these principles, and chooses God's plans over his/her own, imperfect, life planning. To start with, a great sex life in marriage. Best-selling authors Tim and Beverly La Haye propose their sex manual as "fully biblical and highly practical,"[58] and show, with the support of illustrations, all the joys of sexuality that, once sanctified and channeled toward procreation, are in strict accordance with Christianity. Under such conditions, men can be men again: instead of current "Christianettes," men should look and act like men, another Christian tradition: "Jesus was not sissified."[59] Indeed, the channeling of male aggressive sexuality in a fulfilling marriage is essential for society, both for the control of violence, and because it is the source of the "Protestant work ethic," and thus of economic productivity. In this view, sexual sublimation is the foundation of civilization. As for women, they are biologically determined to be mothers, and to be the emotional complement of rational men (as per Phyllis Schlafly). Their submission will help them to achieve a sense of self-esteem. It is through sacrifice that women assert their identity as independent from men. Thus, as Beverly La Haye writes "Don't be afraid to give, and give, and give."[60] The result will be the salvation of the family, "this little commonwealth, the foundation on which all of society stands."[61]

With salvation guaranteed, as long as a Christian strictly observes the Bible, and with a stable patriarchal family as a solid footing for life,

[57] Beverly La Haye, quoted in Lienesch (1993: 78).
[58] Quoted in Lienesch (1993: 56).
[59] Edwin L. Cole, quoted in Lienesch (1993: 63).
[60] Beverly La Haye, quoted in Lienesch (1993: 77).
[61] Lienesch (1993: 77).

business will also be good, provided that government does not interfere with the economy, leaves alone the undeserving poor, and brings
taxes within reasonable limits (at about 10 percent of income).
Indeed, Christian fundamentalists do not seem to be bothered by the
contradiction between being moral theocratists and economic libertarians.[62] Furthermore, God will help the good Christian in his
business life: after all he has to provide for the family. A living proof
is offered, by his own account, by the very leader of the Christian
Coalition, Pat Robertson, a noted tele-evangelist. After his conversion,
armed with his newborn self-assurance, he went to his business: "God
has sent me here to buy your television station," and he offered a sum,
based on "God's figure": "The Lord spoke: 'Don't go over two and a
half million.'"[63] Overall, it turned out to be an excellent deal, for
which Pat Robertson weekly thanked God in his "700 Club" television
show.

Yet, the Christian way cannot be fulfilled individually because institutions of society, and particularly government, the media, and the
public school system, are controlled by humanists of various origins,
associated, in different fundamentalist versions, with communists,
bankers, heretics, and Jews. The most insidious and dangerous
enemies are feminists and homosexuals because they are the ones
undermining the family, the main source of social stability, Christian
life, and personal fulfillment. (Phyllis Schlafly referred to "the disease
called women's liberation.")[64] The fight against abortion symbolizes
all the struggles to preserve family, life, and Christianity, bridging over
to other Christian faiths. This is why the pro-life movement is the most
militant and influential expression of Christian fundamentalism in
America.

The struggle must be intensified, and the necessary political
compromises with institutional politics must be achieved, because
time is becoming short. The "end of times" is approaching, and we
must repent, and clean up our society, to be ready for Jesus Christ's
Second Coming, which will open a new era, a new millennium of
unprecedented peace and prosperity. Yet, there is a dangerous
passage because we will have to go through the atrocious Battle of
Armageddon, originating in the Middle East, then expanding to the
whole world. Israel, and the New Israel (America), will finally prevail
over their enemies, but at a terrible cost, and only counting on the
capacity of our society to regenerate. This is why the transformation
of society (through grassroots Christian politics), and the regener-

---

[62]   Hicks (1994).
[63]   Reported by Pat Robertson and quoted in Lienesch (1993: 40).
[64]   Quoted by Lienesch (1993: 71).

ation of the self (through a pious, family life), are both necessary and complementary.

Who are the contemporary American fundamentalists? Clyde Wilcox provides some interesting data on the demographic characteristics of evangelicals, as compared to the whole population, in 1988.[65] Taking into account the characteristics of the doctrinal evangelicals, it would seem that they are less educated, poorer, more influential among housewives, more often residents of the South, significantly more religious, and 100 percent of them consider the Bible to be inerrant (as compared to 27 percent for the population at large). According to other sources,[66] the recent expansion of Christian fundamentalism is particularly strong in the suburbs of the new South, South West, and Southern California, among low-middle class and service workers, recently migrated to the new suburbs of fast-expanding metropolitan areas. This prompts Lienesch to hypothesize that they may represent "the first modernized generation of traditional people of recent immigration maintaining rural values in a secular urban society."[67] However, it appears that values, beliefs, and political stands are more important than demographic, occupational, or residential characteristics in spurring Christian fundamentalism. After reviewing a substantial body of available evidence on the matter, Wilcox concludes that "the data demonstrate that the best predictors of support for the Christian Right are religious identities, doctrines, behaviors, affiliations, and political beliefs."[68] Fundamentalism does not appear to be a rationalization of class interests, or territorial positioning. Rather, it acts on the political process in the defense of moral, Christian values.[69] It is, as most fundamentalisms in history, a reactive movement, aiming at constructing social and personal identity on the basis of images of the past and projecting them into a utopian future, to overcome unbearable present times.

But a reaction to what? What is unbearable? Two seem to be the most immediate sources of Christian fundamentalism: the threat of globalization, and the crisis of patriarchalism.

As Misztal and Shupe write, "the dynamics of globalization have promoted the dynamics of fundamentalism in a dialectical fashion."[70] Lechner elaborates further the reasons for this dialectic:

---

[65]   Wilcox (1992).
[66]   Cited by Lienesch (1993).
[67]   Lienesch (1993: 10).
[68]   Wilcox (1992: 223).
[69]   Jelen (1991).
[70]   Misztal and Shupe (1992a: 8).

In the process of globalization societies have become institutionalized as global facts. As organizations, they operate in
secular terms; in their relations, they follow secular rules; hardly
any religious tradition attributes transcendent significance to
worldly societies in their present form . . . By the standards of
most religious traditions, institutionalized societalism amounts
to idolatry. But this means that life within society also has become
a challenge for traditional religion . . . Precisely because global
order is an institutionalized normative order it is plausible that
there emerges some search for an "ultimate" foundation, for
some transcendent reality beyond this world in relation to which
the latter could be more clearly defined.[71]

Furthermore, while the communist threat provided ground for
identification between the interests of the US government,
Christianity, and America as the chosen nation, the collapse of the
Soviet Union, and the emergence of a new global order, creates a
threatening uncertainty over the control of America's destiny. A
recurrent theme of Christian fundamentalism in the US in the 1990s
is opposition to the control of the country by a "world government,"
superseding the US federal government (which it believes complicit
in this development), enacted by the United Nations, the International Monetary Fund, and the World Trade Organization, among
other international bodies. In some eschatological writings, this new
"world government" is assimilated to the Anti-Christ, and its symbols,
including the microchip, are the Mark of the Beast that announces
the "end of times." The construction of Christian fundamentalist
identity seems to be an attempt to reassert control over life, and
over the country, in direct response to uncontrollable processes of
globalization that are increasingly sensed in the economy and in the
media.
     Yet, probably the most important source of Christian funda-
mentalism in the 1980s and 1990s is the reaction against the challenge
to patriarchalism, issued from the 1960s revolts, and expressed in
women's, lesbian, and gay movements.[72] Furthermore, the battle is
not just ideological. American patriarchal family is indeed in crisis,
according to all indicators of divorce, separation, violence in the
family, children born out of wedlock, delayed marriages, shrinking
motherhood, single lifestyles, gay and lesbian couples, and widespread rejection of patriarchal authority (see chapter 4). There is an
obvious reaction by men to defend their privileges, which is better
suited to divine legitimacy, after their diminishing role as sole bread-

[71] Lechner (1991: 276–7).
[72] Lamberts-Bendroth (1993).

winners undermined the material and ideological bases of patriarchalism. But there is something else, shared by men, women, and children. A deep-seated fear of the unknown, particularly scary when the unknown concerns the everyday basis of personal life. Unable to live under secular patriarchalism, but terrified of solitude and uncertainty in a wildly competitive, individualistic society, where family, as a myth and a reality, represented the only safe haven, many men, women, and children, pray God to return them to the state of innocence where they could be content with benevolent patriarchalism under God's rules. And by praying together they become able to live together again. This is why American Christian fundamentalism is deeply marked by the characteristics of American culture, by its familistic individualism, by its pragmatism, and by the personalized relationship to God, and to God's design, as a methodology for solving personal problems in an increasingly unpredictable and uncontrollable life. As if the fundamental prayer were to receive from God's mercy the restoration of the lost American Way of Life in exchange for the sinner's commitment to repentance and Christian testimony.

Nations and Nationalisms in the Age of Globalization: Imagined Communities or Communal Images?

Only when all of us – all of us – recover our memory, will we be able, we and them, to stop being nationalists.

Rubert de Ventos, *Nacionalismos*[73]

The age of globalization is also the age of nationalist resurgence, expressed both in the challenge to established nation-states and in the widespread (re)construction of identity on the basis of nationality, always affirmed against the alien. This historical trend has surprised some observers, after nationalism had been declared deceased from a triple death: the globalization of economy and the internationalization of political institutions; the universalism of a largely shared culture, diffused by electronic media, education, literacy, urbanization, and modernization; and the scholarly assault on the very concept of nations, declared to be "imagined communities"[74] in the mild version of anti-nationalist theory, or even "arbitrary historical inventions," in Gellner's forceful formulation,[75] arising from

---

[73]   Rubert de Ventos (1994: 241); my translation.
[74]   Anderson (1983).
[75]   Gellner (1983: 56).

elite-dominated nationalist movements in their way to build the modern nation-state. Indeed, for Gellner, "nationalisms are simply those tribalisms, or for that matter any other kind of groups, which through luck, effort or circumstance succeed in becoming an effective force under modern circumstances."[76] Success means, both for Gellner and for Hobsbawm,[77] the construction of a modern, sovereign nation-state. Thus, in this view, nationalist movements, as rationalizers of interests of a certain elite, invent a national identity that, if successful, is enshrined by the nation-state, and then diffused by propaganda among its subjects, to the point that "nationals" will then become ready to die for their nation. Hobsbawm does accept the historical evidence of nationalism that emerged from the bottom up (from sharing linguistic, territorial, ethnic, religious, and historical political attributes), but he labels it "proto-nationalism," since only when the nation-state is constituted, do nations and nationalism come into existence, either as an expression of this nation-state or as a challenge to it on behalf of a future state. The explosion of nationalisms in this late millennium, in close relationship to the weakening of existing nation-states, does not fit well into this theoretical model that assimilates nations and nationalism to the emergence and consolidation of the modern nation-state after the French Revolution, which operated in much of the world as its founding mold. Never mind. For Hobsbawm, this apparent resurgence is in fact the historical product of unsolved national problems, created in the territorial restructuring of Europe between 1918 and 1921.[78] However, as David Hooson writes, in his introduction to the global survey he edited, *Geography and National Identity*:

> the last half of the twentieth century will go down in history as a new age of rampant and proliferating nationalisms of a more durable nature than the dreadful but now banished tyrannies which have also characterized our century ... The urge to express one's identity, and to have it recognized tangibly by others, is increasingly contagious and has to be recognized as an elemental force even in the shrunken, apparently homogenizing, high-tech world of the end of the twentieth century.[79]

And, as Eley and Suny write, in the introduction to their most insightful reader, *Becoming National*:

[76] Gellner (1983: 87).
[77] Hobsbawm (1992).
[78] Hobsbawm (1992: 173–202).
[79] Hooson (1994b: 2–3).

Does the stress on subjectivity and consciousness rule out any "objective" basis for the existence of nationality? Clearly, such a radically subjectivist view would be absurd. Most successful nationalisms presume some prior community of territory, language, or culture, which provide the raw material for the intellectual project of nationality. Yet, those prior communities should not be "naturalized", as if they had always existed in some essential way, or have simply prefigured a history yet to come . . . Culture is more often not what people share, but what they choose to fight over.[80]

In my view, the incongruence between some social theory and contemporary practice comes from the fact that nationalism, and nations, have a life of their own, independent from statehood, albeit embedded in cultural constructs and political projects. However attractive the influential notion of "imagined communities" may be, it is either obvious or empirically inadequate. Obvious for a social scientist if it is to say that all feelings of belonging, all worshipping of icons, is culturally constructed. Nations would not be an exception to this. The opposition between "real" and "imagined" communities is of little analytical use beyond the laudable effort at demystifying ideologies of essentialist nationalism à la Michelet. But if the meaning of the statement is, as it is explicit in Gellner's theory, that nations are pure ideological artefacts, constructed through arbitrary manipulation of historical myths by intellectuals for the interests of social and economic elites, then the historical record seems to belie such an excessive deconstructionism.[81] To be sure, ethnicity, religion, language, territory, *per se*, do not suffice to build nations, and induce nationalism. Shared experience does: both the United States and Japan are countries of strong national identity, and most of their nationals do feel, and express, strong patriotic feelings. Yet, Japan is one of the most ethnically homogeneous nations on earth, and the United States one of the most ethnically heterogeneous. But in both cases there is a shared history and a shared project, and their historical narratives build on an experience, socially, ethnically, territorially, and genderly diversified, but common to the people of each country on many grounds. Other nations, and nationalisms did not reach modern nation-statehood (for example, Scotland, Catalonia, Quebec, Kurdistan, Palestine), and yet they display, and some have displayed

---

[80]   Eley and Suny (1996: 9).
[81]   Moser (1985); Smith (1986); Johnston et al. (1988); Touraine (1988); Perez-Argote (1989); Chatterjee (1993); Blas Guerrero (1994); Hooson (1994b); Rubert de Ventos (1994); Eley and Suny (1996).

for several centuries, a strong cultural/territorial identity that expresses itself as a national character.

Thus, four major analytical points must be emphasized when discussing contemporary nationalism with regard to social theories of nationalism. First, contemporary nationalism may or may not be oriented toward the construction of a sovereign nation-state, and thus nations are, historically and analytically, entities independent from the state.[82] Secondly, nations, and nation-states, are not historically limited to the modern nation-state as constituted in Europe in the two hundred years following the French Revolution. Current political experience seems to reject the idea that nationalism is exclusively linked to the period of formation of the modern nation-state, with its climax in the nineteenth century, replicated in the decolonization process of the mid-twentieth century by the import of the Western nation-state into the Third World.[83] To assert so, as it has become fashionable, is simply Euro-centrism, as argued by Chatterjee.[84] As Panarin writes:

> The misunderstanding of the century was the confusion of self-determination of people with the self-determination of nation. The mechanical transference of certain West European principles to the soil of non-European cultures often spawns monsters. One of these monsters was the concept of national sovereignty transplanted to non-European soil . . . The syncretism of the concept of nation in the political lexicon of Europe prevents Europeans from making extremely important differentiations touching on the "sovereignty of people", "national sovereignty", and "rights of an ethnos."[85]

Indeed, Panarin's analysis is vindicated by the development of nationalist movements in many areas of the world, following a wide variety of cultural orientations and political projects, toward the end of the twentieth century.

Thirdly, nationalism is not necessarily an elite phenomenon, and, in fact, nationalism nowadays is more often than not a reaction against the global elites. To be sure, as in all social movements, the leadership tends to be more educated and literate (or computer literate in our time) than the popular masses that mobilize around nationalist goals, but this does not reduce the appeal and significance of nationalism to the manipulation of the masses by elites for the self-interest of these elites. As Smith writes, with obvious regret:

[82]   Keating (1995).
[83]   Badie (1992).
[84]   Chatterjee (1993).
[85]   Panarin (1994/1996: 37).

Through a community of history and destiny, memories may be kept alive and actions retain their glory. For only in the chain of generations of those who share an historic and quasi-familial bond, can individuals hope to achieve a sense of immortality in eras of purely terrestrial horizons. In this sense, the formation of nations and the rise of ethnic nationalisms appears more like the institutionalization of "surrogate religion" than a political ideology, and therefore far more durable and potent than we care to admit.[86]

Fourthly, because contemporary nationalism is more reactive than proactive, it tends to be more cultural than political, and thus more oriented toward the defense of an already institutionalized culture than toward the construction or defense of a state. When new political institutions are created, or recreated, they are defensive trenches of identity, rather than launching platforms of political sovereignty. This is why I think that a more appropriate point of theoretical departure for understanding contemporary nationalism is Kosaku Yoshino's analysis of cultural nationalism in Japan:

> Cultural nationalism aims to regenerate the national community by creating, preserving, or strengthening a people's cultural identity when it is felt to be lacking or threatened. The cultural nationalist regards the nation as a product of its unique history and culture, and as a collective solidarity endowed with unique attributes. In short, cultural nationalism is concerned with the distinctiveness of the cultural community as the essence of a nation.[87]

Thus, nationalism is constructed by social action and reaction, both by elites and by the masses, as Hobsbawm argues, countering Gellner's emphasis on "high culture" as the exclusive origin of nationalism. But, against Hobsbawm's or Anderson's views, nationalism as a source of identity cannot be reduced to a particular historical period and to the exclusive workings of the modern nation-state. To reduce nations and nationalisms to the process of construction of the nation-state makes it impossible to explain the simultaneous rise of postmodern nationalism and decline of the modern state.

Rubert de Ventos, in an updated, refined version of Deutsch's classical perspective,[88] has suggested a more complex theory that sees the emergence of national identity through the historical interaction of four series of factors: *primary factors*, such as ethnicity, territory,

---

[86]   Smith (1989/1996: 125).
[87]   Yoshino (1992: 1).
[88]   Deutsch (1953); Rubert de Ventos (1994).

language, religion, and the like; *generative factors*, such as the development of communications and technology, the formation of cities, the emergence of modern armies and centralized monarchies; *induced factors*, such as the codification of language in official grammars, the growth of bureaucracies, and the establishment of a national education system; and *reactive factors*, that is the defense of oppressed identities and subdued interests by a dominant social group or institutional apparatus, triggering the search for alternative identities in the collective memory of people.[89] Which factors play which role in the formation of each nationalism, and of each nation, depends on historical contexts, on the materials available to collective memory, and on the interaction between conflicting power strategies. Thus, nationalism is indeed culturally, and politically, constructed, but what really matters, both theoretically and practically, is, as for all identities, how, from what, by whom, and for what it is constructed.

In this *fin de siècle*, the explosion of nationalisms, some of them deconstructing multinational states, others constructing plurinational entities, is not associated with the formation of classical, sovereign, modern states. Rather, nationalism appears to be a major force behind the constitution of quasi-states; that is, political entities of shared sovereignty, either in stepped-up federalism (as in the Canadian (re)constitution in process, or in the "nation of nationalities," proclaimed in the Spanish Constitution of 1978, and widely expanded in its practice in the 1990s); or in international multilateralism (as in the European Union, or in the renegotiation of the Commonwealth of Independent States of ex-Soviet republics). Centralized nation-states resisting this trend of nationalist movements in search of quasi-statehood as a new historical reality (for example, Indonesia, Nigeria, Sri Lanka, even India) may well fall victim to this fatal error of assimilating the nation to the state, as a state as strong as Pakistan realized after the secession of Bangladesh.

In order to explore the complexity of the (re)construction of national identity in our new historical context, I will briefly elaborate on two cases that represent the two poles of the dialectic I am proposing as characteristic of this period: the deconstruction of a centralized, multinational state, the former Soviet Union, and the subsequent formation of what I consider to be quasi-nation-states; and the national quasi-state emerging in Catalonia through the double movement of federalism in Spain and of confederalism in the European Union. After illustrating the analysis with these two case studies, I shall offer some hints on the new historical avenues of nationalism as a renewed source of collective identity.

[89] Rubert de Ventos (1994: 139–200).

Nations against the state: the breakup of the Soviet Union and the Commonwealth of Impossible States (*Sojuz Nevozmoznykh Gosudarstv*)

The Russian people of the cities and villages, half-savage beasts, stupid, almost frightening, will die to make room for a new human race.
Maxim Gorki, "On the Russian peasantry"[90]

The revolt of constituent nations against the Soviet state was a major factor, albeit not the only one, in the surprising collapse of the Soviet Union, as argued by Helene Carrere d'Encausse and Ronald Grigor Suny,[91] among other scholars. I shall analyze (in volume III) the complex intertwining of economic, technological, political, and national identity elements that, *together*, explain one of the most extraordinary developments in history, as the Russian Revolutions both opened and closed the political span of the twentieth century. Yet, while discussing the formation of national identity, and its new contours in the 1990s, it is essential to refer to the Soviet experience, and its aftermath, because it is a privileged terrain for observing the interplay between nations and the state, two entities that, in my view, are historically and analytically distinct. Indeed, the nationalist revolt against the Soviet Union was particularly significant because it was one of the few modern states explicitly built as a pluri-national state, with nationalities affirmed both for individuals (every Soviet citizen had an ascribed nationality written in his/her passport), and in the territorial administration of the Soviet Union. The Soviet state was organized in a complex system of 15 federal republics, to which were added autonomous republics within the federal republics, territories (*krai*), and autonomous native districts (*okrag*), each republic comprising also several provinces (*oblasti*). Each federal republic, as well as autonomous republics within the federal republics, was based on a territorial nationality principle. This institutional construction was not a simple fiction. Certainly, autonomous nationalist expressions in contradiction to the will of the Soviet Communist party were ruthlessly repressed, particularly during the Stalinist period, and millions of Ukrainians, Estonians, Latvians, Lithuanians, Volga Germans, Crimean Tatars, Chechens, Mesketyans, Ingushi, Balkars, Karachai, and Kalmyks were deported to Siberia and Central Asia to prevent their cooperation with German invaders, or with other potential enemies, or simply to clear land for strategic projects of the state. But so were millions of Russians, for a variety of reasons, often randomly

---

[90] 1922, in *SSR vnutrennie protivorechiia*, Tchalidze Publications, 1987: 128, as cited by Carrere d'Encausse (1993: 173).
[91] Carrere d'Encausse (1993); Suny (1993).

assigned. Yet, the reality of nationality-based administrations went beyond token appointments of national elites to leading positions in the republics' administration.[92] Policies of nativization *(korenizatsiya)* were supported by Lenin and Stalin until the 1930s, and renewed in the 1960s. They encouraged native languages and customs, implemented "affirmative action" programs, favoring recruitment and promotion of non-Russian nationalities in the state and party apparatuses of the republics, as well as in educational institutions, and fostered the development of national cultural elites, naturally on the condition of their subservience to Soviet power. As Suny writes:

> Lost in the powerful nationalist rhetoric is any sense of the degree to which the long and difficult years of Communist party rule actually continued the "making of nations" of the pre-revolutionary period . . . It thereby increased ethnic solidarity and national consciousness in the non-Russian republics, even as it frustrated full articulation of a national agenda by requiring conformity to an imposed political order.[93]

The reasons for this apparent openness to national self-determination (enshrined in the Soviet Constitution in the right of republics to secede from the Union) lie deep in the history and strategy of the Soviet state.[94] Soviet pluri-national federalism was the result of a compromise following intense political and ideological debates during the revolutionary period. Originally, the Bolshevik position, in line with classical Marxist thought, denied the relevance of nationality as a significant criterion to build the new state: proletarian internationalism was intended to supersede "artificial," or "secondary," national differences between the working classes, manipulated into inter-ethnic bloody confrontations by imperialist interests, as shown by World War I. But in January 1918, the urgency of finding military alliances in the civil war, and in the resistance against foreign invasion, convinced Lenin of the need for support from nationalist forces outside Russia, particularly in Ukraine, after observing the vitality of national consciousness. The Third All-Russian Congress of Soviets adopted the "Declaration of the Rights of Working and Exploited People," transforming the ruins of the Russian Empire into "the fraternal union of Soviet Republics of Russia freely meeting on an internal basis." To this "internal federalization" of Russia, the Bolsheviks added, in April, the call for "external

---

[92]   Slezkine (1994).
[93]   Suny (1993: 101, 130).
[94]   Pipes (1954); Conquest (1967); Carrere d'Encausse (1987); Suny (1993); Slezkine (1994).

federalization" of other nations, explicitly naming the people of Poland, Ukraine, Crimea, Transcaucasia, Turkestan, Kirghiz, "and others."[95] The critical debate concerned the principle under which national identity would be recognized in the new federal state. The Bundists, and other socialist tendencies, wanted national cultures recognized throughout the whole structure of the state, without distinguishing them territorially, since the goal of the revolution was precisely to transcend ancestral bondings of ethnicity and territory on behalf of new, class-based, socialist universalism. To this view, Lenin and Stalin opposed the principle of territoriality as the basis for nationhood. The result was the multilayered national structure of the Soviet state: national identity was recognized in the institutions of governance. However, in application of the principle of democratic centralism, this diversity of territorial subjects would be under the control of the dominant apparatuses of the Soviet Communist party, and of the Soviet state. Thus, the Soviet Union was constructed around a double identity: on the one hand, ethnic/national identities (including Russian); on the other hand, Soviet identity as the foundation of the new society: *sovetskii narod* (the Soviet people) would be the new cultural identity to be achieved in the historical horizon of Communist construction.

There were also strategic reasons in this conversion of proletarian internationalists into territorial nationalists. A. M. Salmin has proposed an interesting model for interpreting the Leninist–Stalinist strategy underlying Soviet federalism.[96] The Soviet Union was a centralized, but flexible institutional system whose structure should remain open and adaptive to receive new countries as members of the Union, as the cause of communism would advance throughout the world. Five concentric circles were designed as both security areas and waves of expansion of the Soviet state as vanguard of the revolution. The first was Russia, and its satellite republics, organized in the RSFSR. Paradoxically Russia, and the Russian Federation, was the only republic with no autonomous Communist party, no President of the republican Supreme Soviet, and with the least developed republican institutions: it was the exclusive domain of the Soviet Communist party. To make safer this bastion, Russia did not have land borders with the potentially aggressive capitalist world. Thus, around Russia, Soviet republics were organized, in the outlying borders of the Soviet Union, so that they would eventually protect, at the same time, Soviet power and their national independence. This is why some ethnically based areas, such as Azerbaijan, became Soviet republics

[95] Singh (1982: 61).
[96] Salmin (1992).

because they were bordering the outside world, while others, equally distinctive in its ethnic composition, like Chechn'ya, were kept in the Russian Federation because they were geographically closer to the core. The third ring of Soviet geopolitics was constituted by people's democracies under Soviet military power: this was originally the case for Khoresm, Bukhara, Mongolia, and Tannu-Tura, and became the precedent for the incorporation of Eastern Europe after World War II. The fourth circle would be formed by distant socialist countries, such as, years later, Cuba, North Korea, or Vietnam. China was never considered to be a part of this category because of deep distrust of future Chinese power. Finally, allied progressive governments and revolutionary movements around the world constituted the fifth circle, and their potential would depend on keeping a balance between their internationalism (meaning their pro-Soviet stand) and their national representativeness. It was this constant tension between the class-based universalism of communist utopia and geopolitical interests based on the ethnic/national concerns of potential allies that determined the schizophrenia of Soviet policy toward the national question.

The result of these contradictions throughout the tormented history of the Soviet Union was an incoherent patchwork of people, nationalities, and state institutions.[97] The more than one hundred nationalities and ethnic groups of the Soviet Union were dispatched all along its immense geography, following geopolitical strategies, collective punishments and rewards, and individual caprices. Thus, Armenian-populated Nagorno-Karabaj was included by Stalin in Azerbaijan to please Turkey by putting its ancestral enemies under Azeri control (Azeris are a Turkic people); Volga Germans ended up in Kazakhstan, in whose northern territory they are now the driving economic force, supported by German subsidies to keep them off Germany; Cossack settlements proliferated in Siberia and in the Far East; Ossetians were split between Russia (North) and Georgia (South), while Ingushis were distributed between Chechn'ya, North Ossetia, and Georgia; Crimea, taken by Russia from Tatars in 1783, and from where the Tatars were deported by Stalin during World War II, was transferred by Khrushchev (himself a Ukrainian) to Ukraine in 1954 to commemorate 300 years of Russian–Ukrainian friendship, reportedly after a night of heavy drinking. Furthermore, Russians were sent all over the territory of the Soviet Union, most often as skilled workers or willing pioneers, sometimes as rulers, sometimes as exiles. Thus, when the Soviet Union disintegrated, the principle of territorial nationality trapped inside the newly independent republics

[97] Kozlov (1988); Suny (1993); Slezkine (1994).

tens of millions of suddenly "foreign nationals." The problem seems to be particularly acute for the 25 million Russians living outside the new Russian frontiers.

One of the greatest paradoxes of Soviet federalism is that Russia was probably the most discriminated of nationalities. The Russian Federation had much less political autonomy from the central Soviet state than any other republic. Analysis by regional economists showed that, in general terms, there was a net transfer of wealth, resources, and skills from Russia to the other republics (Siberia, which is the most ethnically Russian area of the Russian Federation, was the funda-mental source of exports, and thus of hard currency for the Soviet Union).[98] As for national identity, it was Russian history, religion, and traditional identity that became the main target of Soviet cultural repression, as documented in the 1980s by Russian writers and intellectuals, such as Likhachev, Belov, Astafiev, Rasputin, Solukhin, or Zalygin.[99] After all, the new Soviet identity had to be built on the ruins of the historical Russian identity, with some tactical exceptions during World War II, when Stalin needed to mobilize everything against the Germans, including Alexander Nevsky's memory. Thus, while there was indeed a policy of russification of culture throughout the Soviet Union (indeed, contradictory to the parallel trend of *korenizatsiya*), and ethnic Russians kept control of party, army, and KGB (but Stalin was Georgian, and Khrushchev was Ukrainian), Russian identity as a national identity was repressed to a much greater extent than other nationalities, some of which were in fact symboli-cally revived for the sake of pluri-national federalism.

This paradoxical constitution of the Soviet state expressed itself in the revolt against the Soviet Union, using the breathing space provided by Gorbachev's *glasnost*. The Baltic republics, forcefully annexed in 1940 in defiance of international law, were the first to claim their right to self-determination. But they were closely followed by a strong Russian nationalist movement that was in fact the most potent mobilizing force against the Soviet state. It was the merger of the struggle for democracy, and the recovery of Russian national identity under Yeltsin's leadership in 1989–91, that created the con-ditions for the demise of Soviet communism and the breakup of the Soviet Union.[100] Indeed, the first democratic election of the head of state in Russian history, with the election of Yeltsin on June 12, 1991, marked the beginning of the new Russia and, with it, the end of the Soviet Union. It was Russia's traditional flag that led the resistance to

[98]   Granberg and Spehl (1989); Granberg (1993).
[99]   Carrere d'Encausse (1993: ch. 9).
[100] Castells (1992b); Carrere d'Encausse (1993).

the Communist coup in August 1991. And it was Yeltsin's strategy of dismantling the Soviet state, by concentrating power and resources in the republican institutions, that led to the agreement with other republics, first of all with Ukraine and Belarus, in December 1991, to end the Soviet Union, and to transform the ex-Soviet republics into sovereign states, loosely confederated in the Commonwealth of Independent States (*Sojuz Nezavisimykh Gosudarstv*). The assault on the Soviet state was not conducted only by nationalist movements: it linked up with democrats' demands, and with the interests of political elites in a number of republics, carving their own turf among the ruins of a crumbling empire. But it took a nationalist form, and received popular support on behalf of the nation. The interesting matter is that nationalism was much less active in the most ethnically distinctive republics (for example, in Central Asia) than in the Baltic states, and in Russia.[101]

The first years of existence of this new conglomerate of independent states revealed the fragility of their construction, as well as the durability of historically rooted nationalities, across the borders inherited from the disintegration of the Soviet Union.[102] Russia's most intractable problem became the war in Chechn'ya. The Baltic republics practiced discrimination against their Russian population, inducing new inter-ethnic strife. Ukraine saw the peaceful revolt of the Russian majority in Crimea against Ukrainian rule, and continued to experience the tension between strong nationalist sentiment in western Ukraine, and pan-Slavic feelings in eastern Ukraine. Moldova was torn between its historical Romanian identity and the Russian character of its eastern population that tried to create the Republic of Dniester. Georgia exploded in a bloody confrontation between its multiple nationalities (Georgians, Abkhazians, Armenians, Ossetians, Adzharis, Meshketians, Russians). Azerbaijan continued to fight intermittently with Armenia over Nagorno-Karabaj, and induced pogroms against Armenians in Baku. And the Muslim republics of Central Asia were torn between their historic links with Russia and the perspective of joining the Islamic fundamentalist whirlwind spinning from Iran and Afghanistan. As a result, Tajikistan suffered a full-scale civil war, and other republics Islamized their institutions and education to integrate radical Islamism before it was too late. Thus, the historical record seems to show that artificial, half-hearted, acknowledgment of the national question by Marxism–Leninism not only did not solve historical conflicts, but actually made them more virulent.[103]

[101]   Carrere d'Encausse (1993); Starovoytova (1994).
[102]   Hooson (1994b); Lyday (1994); Stebelsky (1994); Khazanov (1995).
[103]   Twinning (1993); Panarin (1994); Khazanov (1995).

Reflecting on this extraordinary episode, and on its aftermath in the 1990s, several key issues of theoretical relevance deserve commentary.

First of all, one of the most powerful states in the history of humankind was not able, after 74 years, to create a new national identity. *Sovetskii narod* was not a myth, in spite of what Carrere d'Encausse says.[104] It did have some reality in the minds and lives of the generations born in the Soviet Union, in the reality of people making families with people from other nationalities, and living and working throughout the whole Soviet territory. Resistance against the Nazi juggernaut rallied people around the Soviet flag. After the Stalinist terror subsided, in the late 1950s, and when material conditions improved, in the 1960s, a certain pride in being part of a superpower nation did develop. And, in spite of widespread cynicism and withdrawal, the ideology of equality and human solidarity took root in the Soviet citizenry, so that, overall, a new Soviet identity started to emerge. However, it was so fragile, and so dependent on the lack of information about the real situation of the country and of the world, that it did not resist the shocks of economic stagnation and the learning of the truth. In the 1980s, Russians who dared to proclaim themselves as "Soviet citizens" were derided as *Sovoks* by their compatriots. While *sovetskii narod* was not necessarily a failing identity project, it disintegrated before it could settle in the minds and lives of the people of the Soviet Union. Thus, the Soviet experience belies the theory according to which the state can construct national identity by itself. The most powerful state, using the most comprehensive ideological apparatus in history for more than seven decades, failed in recombining historical materials and projected myths into the making of a new identity. Communities may be imagined, but not necessarily believed.

Secondly, the formal acknowledgment of national identities in the territorial administration of the Soviet state, as well as policies of "nativization," did not succeed in integrating these nationalities into the Soviet system, with one significant exception: the Muslim republics of Central Asia, precisely those that were most distinctive from the dominant Slavic culture. These republics were so dependent on central power for their daily survival that only in the last moments of the disintegration of the Soviet Union did their elites dare to lead the drive for independence. In the rest of the Soviet Union, national identities could not find themselves expressed in the artificially constructed institutions of Soviet federalism. A case in point is Georgia, a multi-ethnic puzzle constructed on the basis of a historic kingdom. Georgians represent about 70 percent of the 5.5 million

[104]   Carrere d'Encausse (1993: 234).

population. They generally belong to the Georgian Orthodox
Church. But they had to coexist with Ossetians, primarily Russian
Orthodox, whose population is split between North Ossetia
Autonomous Republic (in Russia) and South Ossetia Autonomous
Oblast (in Georgia). In the north-western corner of Georgia, the
Abkhaz, a Sunni Muslim Turkic people, number only about 80,000,
but they constituted 17 percent of the Abkhaz Autonomous Soviet
Socialist Republic, created inside Georgia as a counterpoint to
Georgian nationalism. It did succeed: in the 1990s, the Abkhaz, with
support from Russia, fought to obtain quasi-independence in their
territory, in spite of being a minority of the population. Georgia's
second autonomous republic, Adzharia, is also Sunni Muslim, but
from ethnic Georgians, thus supporting Georgia, while seeking their
autonomy. Muslim Ingushis are in conflict with Ossetians in the
border areas between Georgia, Ossetia, and Chechn'ya-Ingushetia. In
addition, Meshketian Turks, deported by Stalin, are returning to
Georgia, and Turkey has expressed its willingness to protect them,
inducing distrust in Georgia's Armenian population. The net result
of this territorially entangled history was that, in 1990–91, when
Gamsakhurdia led a radical Georgian nationalist movement, and
proclaimed independence without considering the interests of
Georgia's national minorities, and without respecting civil liberties,
he triggered a civil war (in which he died), both between his
forces and Georgian democrats, and between Georgian forces,
Abkhazians, and Ossetians. The intervention of Russia, and the paci-
fying role of Shevernadze, elected president in 1991 as a last resort to
save the country, brought an unstable peace to the region, only to see
neighboring Chechn'ya explode in an atrocious, protracted, debilitating guerrilla war. Thus, the failure of integrating national identities
into the Soviet Union did not come from their recognition, but from
the fact that their artificial institutionalization, following a bureaucratic and geopolitical logic, did not pay attention to the actual history
and cultural/religious identity of each national community, and their
geographical specificity. This is what authorizes Suny to speak of "the
revenge of the past,"[105] or David Hooson to write:

> The question of identity is clearly the most insistent to have
> surfaced after the long freeze [in the former Soviet Union]. But
> it is not enough to treat it as a purely ethnic or cultural question.
> What is involved here is a re-search for the real regions of
> cultures, economies *and* environment which mean something
> (or in some cases everything) to the peoples who inhabit them.

[105]   Suny (1993).

The process of crystallization of these regions, beyond the bald and flawed "Republic" boundaries of today, promises to be long and painful but inevitable and ultimately right.[106]

Thirdly, the ideological emptiness created by the failure of Marxism–Leninism to actually indoctrinate the masses was replaced, in the 1980s, when people were able to express themselves, by the only source of identity that was kept in the collective memory: *national identity*. This is why most anti-Soviet mobilizations, including democratic movements, were carried under the respective national flag. It is true, as it has been argued, and as I have argued, that political elites, in Russia, and in the federal republics, utilized nationalism as the ultimate weapon against failing communist ideology, to undermine the Soviet state, and seize power in the institutions of each republic.[107] However, the elites used this strategy because it was effective, because nationalist ideology resonated more in people's minds than abstract appeals to democracy, or to the virtues of the market, often assimilated to speculation in people's personal experience. Thus, the resurgence of nationalism cannot be explained by political manipulation: rather, its use by the elites is a proof of the resilience and vitality of national identity as a mobilizing principle. When, after 74 years of endless repetition of official socialist ideology, people discovered that the king was naked, the reconstruction of their identity could only take place around basic institutions of their collective memory: family, community, the rural past, sometimes religion, and, above all, the nation. But the nation was not meant as the equivalent of statehood and officialdom, but as personal self-identification in this now confusing world: I am Ukrainian, I am Russian, I am Armenian, became the rallying cry, the perennial foundation from which to reconstruct life in collectivity. This is why the Soviet experience is a testimony to the perdurability of nations beyond, and despite, the state.

Perhaps the greatest paradox of all is that when, at the end of this historical *parcours*, new nation-states emerged to assert their suppressed identities, *it is unlikely that they could really function as fully sovereign states*. This is, first of all, because of the intertwining of a mosaic of nationalities and historical identities within the current boundaries of independent states.[108] The most obvious issue refers to the 25 million Russians living under a different flag. But the Russian Federation (although currently populated by 82 percent of ethnic

---

[106]   Hooson (1994a: 140).
[107]   Castells (1992b); Hobsbawm (1994).
[108]   Twinning (1993); Hooson (1994b).

Russians) is also made up of 60 different ethnic/national groups, some of which are sitting on top of a wealth of natural and mineral resources, as in Sakha-Yakutia, or Tatarstan. As for the other republics, besides the illustrative case of Georgia, Kazakhs are only a minority in Kazakhstan; Tajikistan has 62 percent of Tajiks, and 24 percent Uzbeks; Kyrgyz make up only 52 percent of Kyrgyztan's population; Uzbekistan has 72 percent of Uzbeks, and a wide diversity of different nationalities; 14 percent of Moldova's residents are Ukrainian, and 13 percent Russian. Ukrainians account for only 73 percent of Ukraine's population. Latvians are 52 percent of Latvia, and Estonians 62 percent of Estonia. Thus, any strict definition of national interests around the institutionally dominant nationality would lead to intractable conflicts in the whole Eurasian continent, as Shevernadze conceded, explaining his willingness to cooperate with Russia, after his initial hostility. Furthermore, the interpenetration of the economies, and the sharing of infrastructure, from the electrical grid to pipelines and water supply, makes extremely costly the disentanglement of the territories of the former Soviet Union, and puts a decisive premium on cooperation. More so in a process of multilateral integration in the global economy that requires inter-regional linkages to operate efficiently. Naturally, the deep-seated fears of a new form of Russian imperialism will loom large in the future evolution of these new states. This is why there will be no reconstruction of the Soviet Union, regardless of who is in power in Russia. Yet, the full recognition of national identity cannot be expressed in the full independence of the new states, *precisely because of the strength of identities that cut across state borders.* This is why I propose, as the most likely, and indeed promising future, the notion of the Commonwealth of Inseparable States (*Sojuz Nerazdelimykh Gosudarstv*); that is, of a web of institutions flexible and dynamic enough to articulate the autonomy of national identity and the sharing of political instrumentality in the context of the global economy. Otherwise, the affirmation of sheer state power over a fragmented map of historical identities will be a caricature of nineteenth-century European nationalism: it will lead in fact to a Commonwealth of Impossible States (*Sojuz Nevozmoznykh Gosudarstv*).

Nations without a state: *Catalunya*

The State must be fundamentally differentiated from the Nation because the State is a political organization, an independent power externally, a supreme power internally, with material forces in manpower and money to maintain its independence and authority. We cannot identify the one with the other, as it was usual, even by Catalan patriots themselves who were speaking or writing of a Catalan nation in the sense of an inde-pendent Catalan state . . . Catalunya continued to be Catalunya after centuries of having lost its self-government. Thus, we have reached a clear, distinct idea of nationality, the concept of a primary, fundamental social unit, destined to be in the world society, in Humanity, what man is for the civil society.

Enric Prat de la Riba, *La nacionalitat catalana*[109]

If the analysis of the Soviet Union shows the possibility of states, however powerful, failing to produce nations, the experience of Catalonia (or *Catalunya*, in Catalan) allows us to reflect on the con-ditions under which nations exist, and (re)construct themselves over history, without a nation-state, and without searching to establish one.[110] Indeed, as stated by the current president, and national leader of *Catalunya* in the last quarter of the twentieth century, Jordi Pujol: "*Catalunya* is a nation without a state. We belong to the Spanish state, but we do not have secessionist ambitions. This must be clearly affirmed . . . The case of *Catalunya* is peculiar: we have our own language, and culture, we are a nation without a state."[111] To clarify this statement, and to elaborate on its broader, analytical impli-cations, a brief historical reminder is necessary. Since not every reader is familiar with Catalonian history, I shall put forward, succinctly, the historical elements that authorize one to speak of the continuity of *Catalunya* as a materially lived, distinctive, national reality, of which the persistence of its language, and its contemporary widespread use against all odds, is a powerful indicator.[112]

Catalunya's official birthday as a nation is generally dated to 988, when Count Borrell finally severed links with the remnants of the Carolingian Empire that, around 800, had taken the lands and in-habitants of this southern frontier of the empire under its protection to counteract the threat from Arab invaders to Occitania. By the end of the ninth century, Count Guifrè el Pelòs, who had fought success-fully against Arab domination, received from the French king the counties of Barcelona, Urgell, Cerdanya-Conflent, and Girona. His heirs became counts in their own right, without needing to be appointed by the French kings, assuring the hegemony of the Casal

---

[109] Originally published 1906; this edition 1978: 49–50.
[110] Keating (1995).
[111] 1986; quoted in Pi (1996: 254).
[112] For historical sources, see the compendium of Catalan history in Vilar (1987–90); and the special issue of *L'Avenc: Revista d'Historia* (1996). See also Vicens Vives and Llorens (1958); Vicens Vives (1959); Vilar (1964); Jutglar (1966); Sole-Tura (1967); McDonogh (1986); Rovira i Virgili (1988); Azevedo (1991); Garcia-Ramon and Nogue-Font (1994); Keating (1995); Salrach (1996).

de Barcelona over the borderlands that would be called *Catalunya* in the twelfth century. Thus, while most of Christian Spain was engaged in the "Reconquest" against the Arabs for eight centuries, building in the process the kingdom of Castile and Leon, *Catalunya*, after a period of Arab domination in the eighth and ninth centuries, evolved from its Carolingian origins to become, between the early thirteenth and mid-fifteenth centuries, a Mediterranean empire. It extended to Mallorca (1229), Valencia (1238), Sicily (1282), part of Greece, with Athens (1303), Sardinia (1323), and Naples (1442), including, as well, French territories beyond the Pyrénées, particularly Roussillon and Cerdagne. Although *Catalunya* had a significant rural hinterland, it was primarily a commercial empire, governed by the alliance of nobility and urban merchant elites, along lines similar to those of the merchant republics of northern Italy. Concerned with the military power of Castile, the prudent Catalans accepted the merger proposed by the small, but conveniently located, kingdom of Aragon in 1137. It was only in the late fifteenth century, after the voluntary merger with proto-imperial Castile, through the marriage of Fernando, king of *Catalunya*, Valencia and Aragon, with Isabel, queen of Castile, in application of the Compromiso de Caspe (1412), that *Catalunya* ceased to be a sovereign political entity. The marriage of the two nations was supposed to respect language, customs, and institutions, as well as sharing wealth. Yet, the power and wealth of the Spanish Crown and of its landowning nobility, as well as the influence of the fundamentalist Church built around the Counter-Reformation, steered the historical course in a different direction, subjugating non-Castilian peoples, in Europe, and in the Iberian peninsula, as well as in America. *Catalunya*, as the rest of Europe, was excluded from commerce with the American colonies, a major source of wealth in the Spanish kingdom. It reacted by developing its own consumer goods industry and by trading in its regional environment, triggering a process of incipient industrialization and capital accumulation from the second half of the sixteenth century. In the meantime Castile, after crushing, in 1520–23, the free Castilian cities (*Comunidades*) where an artisan class and a proto-bourgeoisie were emerging, went on to build a *rentier* economy to finance a warrior-theocratic state with proceeds from its American colonies and from heavy taxation on its subjects. The clash of culture and institutions accelerated in the seventeenth century when Philip IV, in need of additional fiscal revenues, tightened up centralism, leading to the insurrection of both Portugal and *Catalunya* (where the Revolt of the Reapers took place) in 1640. Portugal, with the support of England, regained its independence. *Catalunya* was defeated, and most of its freedoms were taken away. Again, between 1705 and 1714, *Catalunya* fought for its autonomy, supporting the cause of the Austrians against Philip V, from the Bourbon dynasty, in the Spanish War of Succession. It is a mark of the Catalan character that its defeat, and the entry of Philip V's armies into Barcelona on September 11, 1714, is now celebrated as *Catalunya*'s national day. *Catalunya* lost all its political institutions of self-government, established since the Middle Ages: the municipal government based on democratic councils, the parliament, the Catalan sovereign government (*Generalitat*). The new institutions, established by the *Decreto de nueva planta*, issued by Philip V, concentrated authority in the hands of the military commander, or General Captain of Catalunya. It followed a long period of outright institutional and cultural repression from central powers, that, as documented by historians, deliberately aimed at the gradual elimination of the Catalan language, which was first banned in the administration, then in commercial transactions, and, finally, in the schools, reducing its practice to the domains of family and Church.[113] Again, Catalans reacted by closing themselves off from state matters, and going back to work, reportedly just two days after the occupation of Barcelona, in a concerted attitude. Thus, *Catalunya* industrialized by the end of the eighteenth century, and was, for more than a century, the only truly industrial area of Spain.

The economic strength of the Catalan bourgeoisie, and the relatively high educational and cultural level of the society at large, contrasted throughout the nineteenth century with its political marginality. Then, when trade policies from Madrid began to threaten the still fragile Catalan industry, which required protectionism, a strong Catalan nationalist movement developed from the late nineteenth century, inspired by articulate ideologues, such as pragmatic nationalist Enric Prat de la Riba, or the federalists Valenti Almirall and Francesc Pi i Margall, sung by national poets, such as Joan Maragall, chronicled by historians, such as Rovira i Virgili, and supported by the work of philologists, such as Pompeu Fabra, who codified the modern Catalan language in the twentieth century. Yet, the Madrid political class never really accepted the alliance with Catalan nationalists, not even with the Lliga Regionalista, a clearly conservative party, probably the first modern political party in Spain, created in 1901 as a reaction to the control of elections by local bosses (*caciques*) on behalf of the central government. On the other hand, the growth of a powerful working-class movement, mainly anarcho-syndicalist, in *Catalunya* in the first third of the twentieth century, pushed Catalan nationalists, by and large dominated by their conservative wing until the 1920s, to rely on Madrid's

[113]   Ferrer i Girones (1985).

protection against workers' demands, and threats of social revolution.[114] However, when in 1931 the Republic was proclaimed in Spain, the left-wing republicans *(Esquerra republicana de Catalunya)* were able to establish a bridge between the Catalan working class, the petty bourgeoisie, and the nationalist ideals, and they became the dominant force in Catalan nationalism. Under the leadership of Lluis Companys, a labor lawyer elected president of the restored *Generalitat, Esquerra* made a Spain-wide alliance with the Spanish Republicans, the Socialists, the Communists, and the labor unions (Anarchists, and Socialists). In 1932, under popular pressure expressed in a referendum, the Spanish government approved a Statute of Autonomy that re-stated liberties, self-government, and cultural/linguistic autonomy to *Catalunya.* Indeed, the satisfaction of nationalist demands from *Catalunya* and the Basque Country by the Spanish Republic was one of the most powerful triggers of the military insurrection that provoked the 1936–9 Civil War. Consequently, after the Civil War, the systematic repression of Catalan institutions, language, culture, identity, and political leaders (starting with the execution of Companys in 1940, after being delivered to Franco by the Gestapo) became a distinctive mark of Franco's dictatorship. It included the deliberate elimination of Catalan-speaking teachers from schools, so as to make impossible the teaching of Catalan. In a corresponding movement, nationalism became a rallying cry for the anti-Franco forces in *Catalunya,* as it was in the Basque Country, to the point that all democratic political forces, from Christian Democrats and Liberals to Socialists and Communists, were Catalan nationalists as well. This meant, for instance, that all political parties in *Catalunya,* both during the anti-Franco resistance and since the establishment of Spanish democracy in 1977, were and are Catalan, not Spanish, although they are federated in most cases with similar parties in Spain, while keeping their autonomy as parties (for example, the Catalan Socialist Party is linked to the Spanish PSOE; the Unified Socialist Party of Catalunya to the Communists, and so on). In 1978, Article 2 of the new Spanish Constitution, declared Spain a "nation of nationalities," and, in 1979, the Statute of Autonomy of Catalunya provided the institutional basis for Catalan autonomy, within the framework of Spain, including the declaration of official bilingualism, with Catalan being enshrined as "Cataluña's own language." In the regional elections of *Catalunya,* the Catalan nationalist coalition *(Convergencia i Unio),* led by *Catalunya's* contemporary leader, an educated, cosmopolitan, medical doctor of modest background, Jordi Pujol, obtained a majority five consecutive times, still

[114]   Sole-Tura (1967).

being in power in 1996. The *Generalitat* (Catalan government) was strengthened, and became a dynamic institution, pursuing autonomous policies on all fronts, including the international arena. In the 1990s, Jordi Pujol is the president of the Association of European Regions. The city of Barcelona mobilized on its own, led by another charismatic figure, Catalan Socialist mayor Pasqual Maragall, a professor of urban economics, and the grandson of *Catalunya*'s national poet. Barcelona projected itself into the world, skillfully using the 1992 Summer Olympic Games to emerge internationally as a major metropolitan center, linking up historical identity and informational modernity. In the 1990s, the Catalan Nationalist party came to play a major role in Spanish politics. The inability of either the Socialist Party (in 1993) or the Conservative Partido Popular (in 1996) to win a majority of seats in the Spanish general elections made Jordi Pujol the indispensable partner of any parliamentary coalition to govern. He supported the Socialists first, the Conservatives later – at a price. *Catalunya* received the management of 30 percent of its income taxes, as well as exclusive competence in education (that is conducted in Catalan, at all levels), health, environment, communications, tourism, culture, social services, and most police functions. Slowly, but surely, *Catalunya*, together with the Basque Country, are forcing Spain to become, unwillingly, a highly decentralized federal state, as the other regions claim the same level of autonomy and resources that Catalans and Basques obtain. And yet, with the exception of a small, democratic, and peaceful pro-independence movement, mainly supported by young intellectuals, the Catalans, and the Catalan nationalist coalition, reject the idea of separatism, claiming they simply need institutions to exist as a nation, not to become a sovereign nation-state.[115]

What is, then, this Catalan nation, able to survive centuries of denial, and yet to refrain from entering the cycle of building a state against another nation, Spain, which became also part of *Catalunya*'s historical identity? For Prat de la Riba, probably the most lucid ideologist of conservative Catalan nationalism in its formative stage, "Catalunya is the long chain of generations, united by the Catalan language and tradition, that succeed to each other in the territory where we live."[116] Jordi Pujol also insists on the language as the foundation of Catalan identity, and so do most observers: "The identity of Catalunya is, to a very large extent, linguistic and cultural. Catalunya has never claimed ethnic or religious specificity, nor has insisted on geography, or being strictly political. There are many components of

---

[115]   Keating (1995).
[116]   Prat de la Riba (1894), cited by Sole-Tura (1967: 187); my translation.

our identity, but language and culture are its backbone."[117] Indeed, *Catalunya* was, for more than 2,000 years, a land of passage and migrations, between various European and Mediterranean peoples, thus forging its sovereign institutions in interaction with several cultures, from which it became clearly differentiated by the beginning of the twelfth century, when the name of *Catalunya* appears for the first time.[118] According to the leading French historian of *Catalunya*, Pierre Vilar, what made Catalans distinctive as a people, from an early age (as early as the thirteenth and fourteenth centuries), was the language, clearly distinct from Spanish or French, with a developed literature already in the thirteenth century, exemplified in the writings of Raimon Llull (1235–1315), using the *Catalanesc*, that evolved from Latin in parallel to Provençal and Spanish. Language as identity became particularly relevant in the last half of the twentieth century when a traditionally low birth rate of Catalans in modern times, coupled with the differential industrialization of *Catalunya*, led to massive migration from impoverished Southern Spain, thus submerging Catalan speakers, still fighting against the prohibition of their language, with wave after wave of Spanish-speaking workers, who set up their life and families in *Catalunya*, particularly in the Barcelona suburbs. Thus, after *Catalunya* recovered its autonomy under the 1978 Spanish Constitution, in 1983 the Catalan Parliament voted unanimously a "Law of Linguistic Normalization," introducing teaching in Catalan in all public schools and universities, as well as the Catalan language in the administration, in public places, streets and roads, and in public television.[119] The explicit policy was to reach, over time, full integration of the non-Catalan population into the Catalan culture, so as not to create cultural ghettos that would fracture the society probably along class lines. So, in this strategy, the state is used to reinforce/produce the nation, without claiming sovereignty from the Spanish state.

Why is language so important in the definition of Catalan identity? One answer is historical: it is, over hundreds of years, what has been the sign of identification of being Catalan, together with democratic political institutions of self-government when they were not suppressed. Although Catalan nationalists define as a Catalan whoever lives and works in *Catalunya*, they also add "and wants to be a Catalan." And the sign of "wanting to be" is speaking the language, or trying to (in fact, "trying to" is even better because it is a real sign of willingness to be). Another answer is political: it is the easiest way

[117]   Pujol (1995), quoted in Pi (1996: 176); my translation.
[118]   Salrach (1996).
[119]   Puiggene i Riera et al. (1991).

to expand, and reproduce, the Catalan population without resorting to criteria of territorial sovereignty that would then necessarily collide with the territoriality of the Spanish state. Yet, an additional, and more fundamental answer, may be linked to what language represents, as a system of codes, crystallizing historically a cultural configuration that allows for symbolic sharing without worshipping of icons other than those emerging in everyday life's communication. It may well be that nations without states are organized around linguistic communities – an idea on which I will elaborate below – although, obviously, a common language does not make a nation. Latin American nations would certainly object to this approach, as would the UK and the US. But, for the moment, let us stay in *Catalunya*.

I hope that, after this historical reminder, it can be conceded that it is not an invented identity. For at least over 1,000 years, a given human community, mainly organized around language, but with a great deal of territorial continuity as well, and with a tradition of indigenous political democracy and self-government, has identified itself as a nation, in different contexts, against different adversaries, being part of different states, having its own state, searching for autonomy without challenging the Spanish state, integrating immigrants, enduring humiliation (indeed, commemorating it every year), and yet existing as *Catalunya*. An effort has been made by some analysts to identify Catalanism with the historical aspirations of a frustrated industrial bourgeoisie asphyxiated by a pre-capitalist, bureaucratic Spanish monarchy.[120] This was certainly a major element present in the Catalanist movement of the late nineteenth century, and in the formation of the Lliga.[121] But class analysis cannot account for the continuity of explicit discourse of Catalan identity throughout history, in spite of all the efforts of Spanish centralism to eradicate it. Prat de la Riba denied that *Catalunya* was reducible to class interests, and he was right, although his Lliga was primarily a bourgeois party.[122] Catalanism has been often associated with nineteenth-century romanticism, but it was also connected to the modernist movement of the turn of the century, oriented toward Europe and the international movement of ideas, and away from traditional Spanish regenerationism searching for a new source of transcendent values after the loss of the remnants of the empire in 1898. A cultural community, organized around language and a shared history, *Catalunya* is not an imagined entity, but a constantly renewed historical product, even if nationalist movements construct/reconstruct

[120] Jutglar (1966).
[121] Sole-Tura (1967).
[122] Prat de le Riba (1906).

their icons of self-identification with codes specific to each historical context, and relative to their political projects.

A decisive characterization of Catalan nationalism concerns its relationship to the nation-state.[123] Declaring *Catalunya* at the same time European, Mediterranean, and Hispanic, Catalan nationalists, while rejecting separatism from Spain, search for a new kind of state. It would be a state of variable geometry, bringing together respect for the historically inherited Spanish state with the growing autonomy of Catalan institutions in conducting public affairs, and the integration of both Spain and *Catalunya* in a broader entity, Europe, that translates not only into the European Union, but into various networks of regional and municipal governments, as well as of civic associations, that multiply horizontal relationships throughout Europe under the tenuous shell of modern nation-states. This is not simply clever tactics in the 1990s. It comes from the centuries-old, pro-European standing of Catalan elites, in contrast with the splendid cultural isolationism practiced by most Castilian elites in most historical periods. It is explicit also in the thinking of some of the most universal Catalan writers or philosophers, such as Josep Ferrater Mora, who could write in 1960: "The catalanization of Catalunya may be the last historical opportunity to make Catalans 'good Spaniards', and to make Spaniards 'good Europeans.'"[124] This is because only a Spain that could accept its plural identity – *Catalunya* being one of its most distinctive – could be fully open to a democratic, tolerant Europe. And, for this to happen, Catalans have first to feel at home within the territorial sovereignty of the Spanish state, being able to think, and speak, in Catalan, thus creating their commune within a broader network. This differentiation between cultural identity and the power of the state, between the undisputed sovereignty of apparatuses and the networking of power-sharing institutions, is a historical innovation in relation to most processes of construction of nation-states, solidly planted in historically shaky soil. It seems to relate better than traditional notions of sovereignty to a society based on flexibility and adaptability, to a global economy, to networking of media, to the variation and interpenetration of cultures. By not searching for a new state but fighting to preserve their nation, Catalans may have come full circle to their origins as people of borderless trade, cultural/linguistic identity, and flexible government institutions, all features that seem to characterize the information age.

---

123 Keating (1995); Pi (1996); Trias (1996).
124 Ferrater Mora (1960: 120).

Nations of the information age

Our excursus at the two opposite extremes of Europe yields some knowledge of the new significance of nations and nationalism as a source of meaning in the information age. For the sake of clarity, I shall define nations, in line with the arguments and elaborations presented above, as *cultural communes constructed in people's minds and collective memory by the sharing of history and political projects.* How much history must be shared for a collectivity to become a nation varies with contexts and periods, as are also variable the ingredients that pre-dispose the formation of such communes. Thus, Catalan nationality was distilled over a thousand years of sharing, while the United States of America forged a very strong national identity, in spite of, or because of, its multi-ethnicity, in a mere two centuries. What is essential is the historical distinction between nations and states, which only came to merge, and not for all nations, in the modern age. Thus, from the vantage point of our end of millennium perspective, we know of nations without states (for example, Catalonia, the Basque Country, Scotland, or Quebec), of states without nations (Singapore, Taiwan, or South Africa), of pluri-national states (the former Soviet Union, Belgium, Spain, or the United Kingdom), of uni-national states (Japan), of shared-nation states (South Korea and North Korea), and of nations sharing states (Swedes in Sweden and Finland, Irish in Ireland and the United Kingdom, maybe Serbs, Croats, and Bosnian Muslims in a future Bosnia-Herzegovina). What is clear is that citizenship does not equate nationality, at least exclusive nationality, as Catalans feel Catalan first of all, yet, at the same time, most declare themselves Spanish, and even "European," as well. So, the assimilation of nations and states to the composite nation-state, beyond a given historical context, is simply contradicted by observation when the record is constructed over the long haul and in a global perspective. It seems that the rationalist reaction (Marxist or otherwise) against German idealism (Herder, Fichte), and against French nationalistic hagiography (Michelet, Renan), obscured the understanding of the "national question," thus inducing bewilderment when confronted with the power and influence of nationalism at the end of this century.

Two phenomena, as illustrated in this section, appear to be characteristic of the current historical period: first, the disintegration of pluri-national states that try to remain fully sovereign or to deny the plurality of their national constituents. This was the case of the former Soviet Union, of the former Yugoslavia, of the former Ethiopia, of Czechoslovakia, and maybe it could be the case, in the future, of Sri Lanka, India, Indonesia, Nigeria, and other countries. The result of this disintegration is the formation of *quasi-nation-states.* They are nation-states because they receive the attributes of sovereignty on the basis of a historically constituted national identity (for example, Ukraine). But they are "quasi" because the entangled set of relationships with their historical matrix forces them to share sovereignty with either their former state or a broader configuration (for example, the CIS; Eastern European republics associated with the European Union). Secondly, we observe the development of nations that stop at the threshold of statehood, but force their parent state to adapt, and cede sovereignty, as in the case of *Catalunya*, the Basque Country, Flanders, Wallonie, Scotland, Quebec, and, potentially, Kurdistan, Kashmir, Punjab, or East Timor. I label these entities *national quasi-states*, because they are not fully fledged states, but win a share of political autonomy on the basis of their national identity.

The attributes that reinforce national identity in this historical period vary, although, in all cases, they presuppose the sharing of history over time. However, *I would make the hypothesis that language, and particularly a fully developed language, is a fundamental attribute of self-recognition, and of the establishment of an invisible national boundary less arbitrary than territoriality, and less exclusive than ethnicity.* This is, in a historical perspective, because language provides the linkage between the private and the public sphere, and between the past and the present, regardless of the actual acknowledgment of a cultural community by the institutions of the state. And it is not because Fichte used this argument to build pan-German nationalism that the historical record should be discarded. But there is also a powerful reason for the emergence of language-based nationalism in our societies. If nationalism is, most often, a reaction against a threatened autonomous identity, then, in a world submitted to cultural homogenization by the ideology of modernization and the power of global media, language, as the direct expression of culture, becomes the trench of cultural resistance, the last bastion of self-control, the refuge of identifiable meaning. Thus, after all, nations do not seem to be "imagined communities" constructed at the service of power apparatuses. Rather, they are produced through the labors of shared history, and then spoken in the images of communal languages whose first word is *we*, the second is *us*, and, unfortunately, the third is *them*.

Ethnic Unbonding: Race, Class, and Identity in the Network Society

See you 100 Black Men. . . . See you jailed. See you caged. See you tamed. See you pain. See you fronting. See you lamping. See you want. See you need. See you dissed. See you Blood. See you Crip. See you Brother.

See you sober. See you loved. See you peace. See you home. See you listen.
See you love. See you on it. See you faithful. See you chumped. See you
challenged. See you change. See you. See you. See you . . . I definitely
wanna be you.

Peter J. Harris, "Praisesong for the Anonymous Brothers"[125]

Do *you* want, as well? Really? Ethnicity has been a fundamental source
of meaning and recognition throughout human history. It is a
founding structure of social differentiation, and social recognition, as
well as of discrimination, in many contemporary societies, from the
United States to Sub-Saharan Africa. It has been, and it is, the basis
for uprisings in search of social justice, as for Mexican Indians in
Chiapas in 1994, as well as the irrational rationale for ethnic cleansing,
as practiced by Bosnian Serbs in 1994. And it is, to a large extent, the
cultural basis that induces networking and trust-based transactions in
the new business world, from Chinese business networks (volume I,
chapter 3) to the ethnic "tribes" that determine success in the new
global economy. Indeed, as Cornel West writes: "In this age of globalization, with its impressive scientific and technological innovations in
information, communication, and applied biology, a focus on the
lingering effects of racism seems outdated and antiquated . . . Yet
race – in the coded language of welfare reform, immigration policy,
criminal punishment, affirmative action, and suburban privatization –
remains a central signifier in the political debate."[126] However, if
race and ethnicity are central – to America, as to other societies'
dynamics – their manifestations seem to be deeply altered by current
societal trends.[127] I contend that while race matters, probably more
than ever as a source of oppression and discrimination,[128] ethnicity is
being specified as a source of meaning and identity, to be melted not
with other ethnicities, but under broader principles of cultural self-
definition, such as religion, nation, or gender. To convey the
arguments in support of this hypothesis I shall discuss, briefly,
the evolution of African-American identity in the United States.

The contemporary condition of African-Americans has been transformed in the past three decades by a fundamental phenomenon:
their profound division along class lines, as shown in the pioneering
work of William Julius Wilson,[129] the implications of which shattered
for ever the way America sees African-Americans, and, even more

[125]   From Wideman and Preston (1995: xxi).
[126]   West (1996: 107–8).
[127]   Appiah and Gates (1995).
[128]   Wieviorka (1993); West (1995).
[129]   Wilson (1987).

importantly, the way African-Americans see themselves. Supported by
a stream of research in the past decade, Wilson's thesis, and its
development, points at a dramatic polarization among African-
Americans. On the one hand, spurred by the civil rights movement of
the 1960s, particularly thanks to affirmative action programs, a large,
well-educated, and relatively comfortable African-American middle
class has emerged, making significant inroads into the political power
structure, from mayoral offices to chairmanship of the Joint Chiefs of
Staff, and, to some extent, in the corporate world. Thus, about a third
of African-Americans are now part of the American middle class,
although men, unlike women, still make much less money than their
white counterparts. On the other hand, about a third of African-
Americans, comprising 45 percent of African-American children at or
below the poverty level, are much worse off in the 1990s than they
were in the 1960s. Wilson, joined by other researchers, such as Blakely
and Goldsmith, or Gans, attributes the formation of this "underclass"
to the combined effect of an unbalanced information economy, of
spatial segregation, and of misled public policy. The growth of an
information economy emphasizes education, and reduces the
availability of stable manual jobs, disadvantaging blacks at the entry
level of the job market. Middle-class blacks escape the inner city,
leaving behind, entrapped, the masses of the urban poor. To close the
circle, the new black political elite finds support among the urban
poor voters, but only as long as they can deliver social programs, which
is a function of how worrisome, morally or politically, urban poor are
for the white majority. Thus, new black political leadership is based
on its ability to be the intermediary between the corporate world, the
political establishment, and the ghettoized, unpredictable poor.
Between these two groups, the final third of African-Americans strives
not to fall into the poverty hell, hanging onto service jobs, disproportionately in the public sector, and to educational and
vocational training programs that provide some skills to survive in a
deindustrializing economy.[130] The punishment for those who do not
succeed is increasingly atrocious. Among poorly educated, central-city
black male residents in 1992, barely one-third held full-time jobs. And
even among those who do work, 15 percent are below the poverty line.
The average net worth of assets of the poorest fifth of blacks in 1995
was exactly zero. One-third of poor black households lives in sub-
standard housing, meaning, among other criteria, "to show evidence
of rats." The ratio of urban crime rate over suburban crime rate has
grown from 1.2 to 1.6 between 1973 and 1992. And, of course, inner-

---

[130]   Wilson (1987); Blakely and Goldsmith (1993); Carnoy (1994); Wacquant
(1994); Gans (1995); Hochschild (1995); Gates (1996).

city residents are those who suffer most from these crimes. Furthermore, the poor male black population is subjected to massive incarceration, or lives under the control of the penal system (awaiting trial, probation). While blacks are about 12 percent of the American population, in the 1990s they account for more than 50 percent of prison inmates.[131] The overall incarceration rate for black Americans in 1990 was 1,860 per 100,000, that is 6.4 times higher than for whites. And, yes, African-Americans are better educated, but in 1993 23,000 black men received a college diploma, while 2.3 million were incarcerated.[132] If we add all persons under supervision of the penal system in America in the 1996, we reach 5.4 million people. Blacks represented 53 percent of inmates in 1991.[133] The ratios of incarceration and surveillance are much higher among poor blacks, and staggering among black young males. In cities such as Washington DC, for age groups 18–30, the majority of black males are in prison or on probation. Women, and families, have to adjust to this situation. The notorious argument of the absent male in the poor African-American family has to account for the fact that many poor men spend considerable periods of their life in prison, so that women have to be prepared to raise children by themselves, or to give birth on their own responsibility.

These are well-known facts, whose social roots in the new techno-logical and economic context I shall try to analyze in volume III. But I am concerned, at this point in my analysis, with the consequences of such a deep class divide on the transformation of African-American identity.

To comprehend this transformation since the 1960s, we must go back to the historical roots of this identity: as Cornel West argues, blacks in America are precisely African and American. Their identity was constituted as kidnapped, enslaved people under the freest society of the time. Thus, to conciliate the obvious contradiction between the ideals of freedom, and the highly productive, slavery-based economy, America had to deny the humanity of blacks because only non-humans could be denied freedom in a society constituted on the principle that "all men are born equal." As Cornel West writes: "This unrelenting assault on black humanity produced the funda-mental condition of black culture – that of *black invisibility* and *namelessness*."[134] Thus, black culture, following Cornel's analysis, had to learn to cope with its negation without falling into self-annihilation.

---

[131]   Tonry (1995: 59).
[132]   Gates (1996: 25).
[133]   See volume III, chapter 2.
[134]   West (1996: 80).

It did. From songs to art, from communal churches to brotherhood, black society emerged with a deep sense of collective meaning, not lost during the massive rural exodus to the Northern ghettos, translated into extraordinary creativity in art, music, and literature, and into a powerful, multifaceted political movement, whose dreams and potential were personified by Martin Luther King Jr in the 1960s.

Yet, the fundamental divide introduced among blacks by the partial success of the civil rights movement has transformed this cultural landscape. But, how exactly? At first sight, it would seem that the black middle class, building on its relative economic affluence and political influence, could be assimilated into the mainstream, constituting itself under a new identity, as African-Americans, moving toward a position similar to that of Italian-Americans, or Chinese-Americans. After all, Chinese-Americans were highly discriminated against for most of California's history, yet they have reached in recent years a rather respected social status. Thus, in this perspective, African-Americans could become another, distinctive segment in the multi-ethnic quilt of American society. While, on the other hand, the "underclass" would become more poor than black.

Yet, this thesis of a dual cultural evolution does not seem to hold when checked against available data. Jennifer Hochschild's powerful study of the cultural transformation of blacks and whites in their relationship to the "American Dream" of equal opportunity and individual mobility shows exactly the contrary.[135] Middle-class blacks are precisely those who feel bitter about the frustrated illusion of the American Dream, and feel most discriminated against by the permanence of racism, while a majority of whites feel that blacks are being unduly favored by affirmative action policies, and complain about reverse discrimination. On the other hand, poor blacks, while fully conscious of racism, seem to believe in the American Dream to a greater extent than middle-class blacks, and, in any case, are more fatalistic and/or individualistic about their fate (it always was like this), although a temporal perspective in the evolution of opinion polls seems to indicate that poor blacks, too, are losing whatever faith in the system they had. Still, the major fact that clearly stands out from Hochschild's effort to bring to the analysis a wealth of empirical data is that, by and large, affluent African-Americans do not feel welcome in mainstream society. Indeed, they are not. Not only racial hostility among whites continues to be pervasive, but gains by middle-class black males still leave them way behind whites in education, occupation, and income, as shown by Martin Carnoy.[136]

[135]   Hochschild (1995).
[136]   Carnoy (1994).

So, race matters a lot.[137] But, at the same time, the class divide among blacks has created such fundamentally different living conditions that there is growing hostility among the poor against those former brothers that left them out.[138] Most middle-class blacks strive to get ahead not only from the reality of the ghetto, but from the stigma that the echoes from the dying ghetto project on them through their skin. They do so, particularly, by insulating their children from the poor black communities (moving to suburbs, integrating them into white-dominated private schools), while, at the same time, reinventing an African-American identity that revives the themes of the past, African or American, while keeping silent on the plight of the present.

In a parallel move, end-of-millennium ghettos develop a new culture, made out of affliction, rage, and individual reaction against collective exclusion, where blackness matters less than the situations of exclusion that create new sources of bonding, for instance, territorial gangs, started in the streets, and consolidated in and from the prisons.[139] Rap, not jazz, emerges from this culture. This new culture expresses identity, as well, and it is also rooted in black history, and in the venerable American tradition of racism and racial oppression, but it incorporates new elements: the police and penal system as central institutions, the criminal economy as a shop floor, the schools as contested terrain, churches as islands of conciliation, mother-centered families, rundown environments, gang-based social organization, violence as a way of life. These are the themes of new black art and literature emerging from the new ghetto experience.[140] But it is not the same identity, by any means, as the identity emerging in middle-class African-America through the careful reconstruction of the humanity of the race.

Yet, even accepting their cultural split, both sets of identities face what appear to be insuperable difficulties in their constitution. This is, for affluent African-Americans, because of the following contradiction:[141] they feel the rejection of institutional racism, so that they can only integrate into the American mainstream as leaders of their kin, as the "Talented Tenth" that Du Bois, the leading black intellectual at the turn of the century, considered to be the necessary saviors of "the negro race," as for all races.[142] But the social, economic, and

---

[137] West (1996).
[138] Hochschild (1995); Gates (1996).
[139] Sanchez Jankowski (1991, 1996).
[140] Wideman and Preston (1995); Giroux (1996).
[141] Hochschild (1995).
[142] Gates and West (1996: 133).

cultural divide between the "Talented Tenth" and a significant, growing proportion of black America is such that they would have to deny themselves, and their children, accomplishing such a role, to become part of a pluri-class, multiracial coalition of progressive social change. In their superb little book debating this question, Henry Louis Gates Jr and Cornel West seem to think, on the one hand, that there is no other alternative, and yet, they do have reasonable doubts of the feasibility of such an option. Gates: "The real crisis of black leadership is that the very idea of black leadership is in crisis."[143] West:

> Since a multi-racial alliance of progressive middlers, liberal slices of the corporate elite, and subversive energy from below is the only vehicle by which some form of radical democratic account-ability can redistribute resources and wealth and restructure the economy and government so that all benefit, the significant secondary efforts of the black Talented Tenth alone in the twenty-first century will be woefully inadequate and thoroughly frustrating.[144]

Indeed, Du Bois himself left America for Ghana in 1961 because, he said, "I just cannot take any more of this country's treatment . . . Chin up, and fight on, but realize that American Negroes can't win."[145]

Will this failure of full integration efforts lead to a revival of black separatism in America? Could this be the new basis for identity, in direct line with the radical 1960s movements, as exemplified by the Black Panthers? It would seem so, at least among the militant youth, if we were to pay attention to the renewed cult of Malcolm X, the growing influence of Farrakhan's Nation of Islam, or, even more so, the extraordinary impact of the 1995 "Million Men March" in Washington DC, built around atonement, morality, and black male pride. Yet, these new manifestations of cultural–political identity reveal further cleavages among African-Americans, and they are actu-ally organized around principles of self-identification that are not ethnic but religious (Islam, black churches), and strongly gendered (male pride, male responsibility, subordination of females). The impact of the "Million Men March," and its foreseeable development in the future, cuts across class lines, but shrinks the gender basis of African-American identity, and blurs the lines between religious, racial, and class self-identification. In other words, it was not based on identity but on the reflection of a disappearing identity. How can it be that, while society is reminding blacks every minute that they are

[143]   Gates (1996: 38).
[144]   West (1996: 110).
[145]   Gates and West (1996: 111).

black (thus, a different, stigmatized human kind, coming in a long journey from non-humanity), blacks themselves are living so many different lives, so as not to be able to share, and, instead, being increasingly violent against each other? It is this yearning for the lost community that is emerging in black America in the 1990s – because perhaps the deepest wound inflicted on African-Americans in the past decade has been the gradual loss of collective identity, leading to individual drifting while still bearing a collective stigma.

This is not a necessary process. Socio-political movements such as Jessie Jackson's "Rainbow Coalition," among others, continue to try hard to bring together black churches, minorities, communities, unions, and women, under a common banner to fight politically for social justice and racial equality. Yet, this is a process of building a political identity that only if fully successful in the long term could create a collective, cultural identity that would be necessarily new for both whites and blacks, if it is to overcome racism while maintaining historical, cultural differences. Cornel West, while acknowledging a "hope not hopeless but unhopeful," calls for "radical democracy" to transcend both racial divisions and black nationalism.[146] But in the ghetto trenches, and in the corporate boardrooms, historical African-American identity is being fragmented, and individualized, without yet being integrated into a multiracial, open society.

Thus, I formulate the hypothesis that ethnicity does not provide the basis for communal heavens in the network society, because it is based on primary bonds that lose significance, when cut from their historical context, as a basis for reconstruction of meaning in a world of flows and networks, of recombination of images, and reassignment of meaning. Ethnic materials are integrated into cultural communes that are more powerful, and more broadly defined than ethnicity, such as religion or nationalism, as statements of cultural autonomy in a world of symbols. Or else, ethnicity becomes the foundation for defensive trenches, then territorialized in local communities, or even gangs, defending their turf. Between cultural communes and self-defense territorial units, ethnic roots are twisted, divided, reprocessed, mixed, differentially stigmatized or rewarded, according to a new logic of informationalization/globalization of cultures and economies that makes symbolic composites out of blurred identities. Race matters, but it hardly constructs meaning any longer.

[146]   West (1996: 112).

Territorial Identities: the Local Community

One of the oldest debates in urban sociology refers to the loss of community as a result of urbanization first, and of suburbanization later. Empirical research some time ago, most notably by Claude Fischer and by Barry Wellman,[147] seems to have put to rest the simplistic notion of a systematic co-variation between space and culture. People socialize and interact in their local environment, be it in the village, in the city, or in the suburb, and they build social networks among their neighbors. On the other hand, locally based identities intersect with other sources of meaning and social recognition, in a highly diversified pattern that allows for alternative interpretations. So, where, in recent years, Etzioni sees the revival of community to a large extent on a local basis, Putnam watches the disintegration of the Tocquevillian vision of an intense civil society in America, with membership and activity in voluntary associations dropping substantially in the 1980s.[148] Reports from other areas of the world are equally conflicting in their estimates. However, I do not think it would be inaccurate to say that local environments, *per se*, do not induce a specific pattern of behavior, or, for that matter, a distinctive identity. Yet, what communalist authors would argue, and what is consistent with my own cross-cultural observation, is that people resist the process of individualization and social atomization, and tend to cluster in community organizations that, over time, generate a feeling of belonging, and ultimately, in many cases, a communal, cultural identity. I introduce the hypothesis that for this to happen, a process of social mobilization is necessary. That is, people must engage in urban movements (not quite revolutionary), through which common interests are discovered, and defended, life is shared somehow, and new meaning may be produced.

I know something about this subject, having spent a decade of my life studying urban social movements around the world.[149] Summarizing my findings, as well as the relevant literature, I proposed that urban movements (processes of purposive social mobilization, organized in a given territory, oriented toward urban-related goals) were focused on three main sets of goals: urban demands on living conditions and collective consumption; the affirmation of local cultural identity; and the conquest of local political autonomy and citizen participation. Different movements combined these three sets of goals in various proportions, and the outcomes of their efforts were

[147]   Wellman (1979); Fischer (1982).
[148]   Etzioni (1993); Putnam (1995).
[149]   Castells (1983).

equally diversified. Yet, in many instances, regardless of the explicit achievements of the movement, its very existence produced meaning, not only for the movement's participants, but for the community at large. And not only during the lifespan of the movement (usually brief), but in the collective memory of the locality. Indeed, I argued, and I argue, that this production of meaning is an essential component of cities, throughout history, as the built environment, and its meaning, is constructed through a conflictive process between the interests and values of opposing social actors.

I added something else, referring to the historical moment of my observation (the late 1970s, early 1980s), but projecting my view toward the future: urban movements were becoming critical sources of resistance to the one-sided logic of capitalism, statism, and informationalism. This was, essentially, because the failure of proactive movements and politics (for example, the labor movement, political parties) to counter economic exploitation, cultural domination, and political oppression had left people with no other choice than either to surrender or to react on the basis of the most immediate source of self-recognition and autonomous organization: their locality. Thus, so emerged the paradox of increasingly local politics in a world structured by increasingly global processes. There was production of meaning and identity: my neighborhood, my community, my city, my school, my tree, my river, my beach, my chapel, my peace, my environment. But it was a defensive identity, an identity of retrenchment of the known against the unpredictability of the unknown and uncontrollable. Suddenly defenseless against a global whirlwind, people stuck to themselves: whatever they had, and whatever they were, became their identity. I wrote in 1983:

> Urban movements do address the real issues of our time, although neither on the scale nor terms that are adequate to the task. And yet they do not have any choice since they are the last reaction to the domination and renewed exploitation that submerges our world. But they are more than a last symbolic stand and a desperate cry: they are symptoms of our own contradictions, and therefore potentially capable of superseding these contradictions . . . They do produce new historical meaning – in the twilight zone of pretending to build within the walls of a local community a new society they know unattainable. And they do so by nurturing the embryos of tomorrow's social movements within the local utopias that urban movements have constructed in order never to surrender to barbarism."[150]

[150]   Castells (1983: 331).

What has happened since then? The empirical answer is, of course, extraordinarily diverse, particularly if we look across cultures and areas of the world.[151] I would, however, venture, for the sake of the analysis, to synthetize urban movements' main trajectories in the 1980s and 1990s under four headings.

First, in many cases, urban movements, and their discourses, actors, and organizations, have been integrated in the structure and practice of local government, either directly or indirectly, through a diversified system of citizen participation, and community development. This trend, while liquidating urban movements as sources of alternative social change, has considerably reinforced local government, and introduced the possibility of the local state as a significant instance of reconstruction of political control and social meaning. I will return to this fundamental development in chapter 5, when analyzing the overall transformation of the state.

Secondly, local communities, and their organizations, have indeed nurtured the grassroots of a widespread, and influential, environmental movement, particularly in middle-class neighborhoods, and in the suburbs, exurbia, and urbanized countryside (see chapter 3). However, these movements are often defensive and reactive, focusing on the strictest conservation of their space and immediate environment, as exemplified, in the United States, by the "not in my backyard" attitude, mixing in the same rejection toxic waste, nuclear plants, public housing projects, prisons, and mobile home settlements. I will make a major distinction, which I will develop in chapter 3 when analyzing the environmental movement, between the search for controlling space (a defensive reaction), and the search for controlling time; that is, for the preservation of nature, and of the planet, for future generations, in a very long term, thus adopting cosmological time, and rejecting the instant time approach of instrumentalist development. Identities emerging from these two perspectives are quite different, as defensive spaces lead to collective individualism, and offensive timing opens up the reconciliation between culture and nature, thus introducing a new, holistic philosophy of life.

Thirdly, a vast number of poor communities around the world have engaged in collective survival, as with the communal kitchens that flourished in Santiago de Chile or Lima during the 1980s. Be it in squatter settlements in Latin America, in American inner cities, or in working-class neighborhoods in Asian cities, communities have built their own "welfare states" (in the absence of responsible public policies) on the basis of networks of solidarity and reciprocity, often

---

[151]   Massolo (1992); Fisher and Kling (1993); Calderon (1995); Judge et al. (1995); Tanaka (1995); Borja and Castells (1996); Hsia (1996); Yazawa (forthcoming).

around churches, or supported by internationally funded non-governmental organizations (NGOs); sometimes with the help of leftist intellectuals. These organized, local communities have played, and continue to play, a major role in the daily survival of a significant proportion of the world's urban population, at the threshold of famine and epidemic. This trend was illustrated, for instance, by the experience of community associations organized by the Catholic Church in São Paulo in the 1980s,[152] or by internationally sponsored NGOs in Bogota in the 1990s.[153] In most of these cases, a communal identity does emerge, although very often it is absorbed into a religious faith, to the point that I would risk the hypothesis that this kind of communalism is, essentially, a religious commune, linked to the consciousness of being the exploited and/or the excluded. Thus, people organizing in poor local communities may feel revitalized, and acknowledged as human beings, by and through religious deliverance.

Fourthly, there is a darker side of the story, concerning the evolution of urban movements, particularly in segregated urban areas, a trend that I foresaw some time ago:

> If urban movements' appeals are not heard, if the new political avenues remain closed, if the new central social movements (feminism, new labor, self-management, alternative communication) do not develop fully, then the urban movements – reactive utopias that tried to illuminate the path they could not walk – will return, but this time as urban shadows eager to destroy the closed walls of their captive city.[154]

Fortunately, the failure was not total, and the diversified expression of organized local communities did provide avenues of reform, survival, and self-identification, in spite of the lack of major social movements able to articulate change in the new society emerging in the past two decades. Yet, harsh policies of economic adjustment in the 1980s, a widespread crisis of political legitimacy, and the exclusionary impact of the space of flows over the space of places (see volume I), took their toll on social life and organization in poor local communities. In American cities, gangs emerged as a major form of association, work, and identity for hundreds of thousands of youths. Indeed, as Sanchez Jankowski has showed in his first-hand, comprehensive study of gangs,[155] they play a structuring role in many areas,

---

[152]   Cardoso de Leite (1983); Gohn (1991).
[153]   Espinosa and Useche (1992).
[154]   Castells (1983: 327).
[155]   Sanchez Jankowski (1991).

which explains the ambiguous feeling of local residents toward them, partly fearful, yet partly feeling able to relate to the gang society better than to mainstream institutions, which are usually present only in their repressive manifestation. Gangs, or their functional equivalent, are not, by any means, an American graffiti. The *pandillas* in most Latin American cities are a key element of sociability in poor neighborhoods, and so are they in Jakarta, in Bangkok, in Manila, in Mantes-la-Jolie (Paris), or in Meseta de Orcasitas (Madrid). Gangs are, however, an old story in many societies, particularly in America (remember William White's *Street Corner Society*). Yet there is something new in the gangs of the 1990s, characterizing the construction of identity as the twisted mirror of informational culture. It is what Magaly Sanchez and Yves Pedrazzini, on the basis of their study of the *malandros* (bad boys) of Caracas, call the *culture of urgency*.[156] It is a culture of the immediate end of life, not of its negation, but of its celebration. Thus, everything has to be tried, felt, experimented, accomplished, before it is too late, since there is no tomorrow. Is this really so different from the culture of consumerist narcissism *à la* Lasch? Have the bad boys of Caracas, or elsewhere, understood faster than the rest of us what our new society is all about? Is the new gang identity the culture of communal hyper-individualism? Individualism because, in the immediate gratification pattern, only the individual can be a proper accounting unit. Communalism because, for this hyper-individualism to be an identity – that is, to be socialized as value not just as senseless consumption – it needs a milieu of appreciation and reciprocal support: a commune, as in White's times. But, unlike White's, this commune is ready to explode at any time, it is a commune of the end of time, it is a commune of timeless time, characterizing the network society. And it exists, and explodes, territorially. Local cultures of urgency are the reverse expression of global timelessness.

Thus, local communities, constructed through collective action and preserved through collective memory, are specific sources of identities. But these identities, in most cases, are defensive reactions against the impositions of global disorder and uncontrollable, fast-paced change. They do build havens, but not heavens.

---

[156]   Sanchez and Pedrazzini (1996).

Conclusion: the Cultural Communes of the Information Age

The transformation of our culture and our society would have to happen at a number of levels. If it occurred only in the minds of individuals (as to some degree it already has), it would be powerless. If it came only from the initiative of the state, it would be tyrannical. Personal transformation among large numbers is essential, and it must not only be a transformation of consciousness but must also involve individual action. But individuals need the nurture of groups that carry a moral tradition reinforcing their own aspirations.

Robert Bellah et al., *Habits of the Heart*[157]

Our intellectual journey through communal landscapes provides some preliminary answers to the questions raised at the beginning of this chapter on the construction of identity in the network society.

For those social actors excluded from or resisting the individualization of identity attached to life in the global networks of power and wealth, cultural communes of religious, national, or territorial foundation seem to provide the main alternative for the construction of meaning in our society. These cultural communes are characterized by three main features. They appear as reactions to prevailing social trends, which are resisted on behalf of autonomous sources of meaning. They are, at their onset, defensive identities that function as refuge and solidarity, to protect against a hostile, outside world. They are culturally constituted; that is, organized around a specific set of values whose meaning and sharing are marked by specific codes of self-identification: the community of believers, the icons of nationalism, the geography of locality.

Ethnicity, while being a fundamental feature of our societies, especially as a source of discrimination and stigma, may not induce communes on its own. Rather, it is likely to be processed by religion, nation, and locality, whose specificity it tends to reinforce.

The constitution of these cultural communes is not arbitrary. It works on raw materials from history, geography, language, and environment. So, they are constructed, but materially constructed, around reactions and projects historically/geographically determined.

Religious fundamentalism, cultural nationalism, territorial communes are, by and large, defensive reactions. Reactions against three fundamental threats, perceived in all societies, by the majority of humankind, in this end of millennium. Reaction against

---

[157]   Bellah et al. (1985: 286).

globalization, which dissolves the autonomy of institutions, organizations, and communication systems where people live. Reaction against networking and flexibility, which blur the boundaries of membership and involvement, individualize social relationships of production, and induce the structural instability of work, space, and time. And reaction against the crisis of the patriarchal family, at the roots of the transformation of mechanisms of security-building, socialization, sexuality, and, therefore, of personality systems. When the world becomes too large to be controlled, social actors aim at shrinking it back to their size and reach. When networks dissolve time and space, people anchor themselves in places, and recall their historic memory. When the patriarchal sustainment of personality breaks down, people affirm the transcendent value of family and community, as God's will.

These defensive reactions become sources of meaning and identity by constructing new cultural codes out of historical materials. Because the new processes of domination to which people react are embedded in information flows, the building of autonomy has to rely on reverse information flows. God, nation, family, and community will provide unbreakable, eternal codes, around which a counter-offensive will be mounted against the culture of real virtuality. Eternal truth cannot be virtualized. It is embodied in us. Thus, against the informationalization of culture, bodies are informationalized. That is, individuals bear their gods in their heart. They do not reason, they believe. They are the bodily manifestation of God's eternal values, and as such, they cannot be dissolved, lost in the whirlwind of information flows and cross-organizational networks. This is why language, and communal images, are so essential to restore communication between the autonomized bodies, escaping the domination of a-historical flows, yet trying to restore new patterns of meaningful communication among the believers.

This form of identity-building revolves essentially around the principle of *resistance identity*, as defined at the beginning of this chapter. *Legitimizing identity* seems to have entered a fundamental crisis because of the fast disintegration of civil society inherited from the industrial era, and because of the fading away of the nation-state, the main source of legitimacy (see chapter 5). Indeed, cultural communes organizing the new resistance emerge as sources of identity by breaking away from civil societies and state institutions from which they originate, as is the case with Islamic fundamentalism breaking away from economic modernization (Iran), and/or from Arab states' nationalism; or with nationalist movements, challenging the nation-state and the state institutions of societies where they come into existence. This negation of civil societies and political institutions where cultural communes emerge leads to the closing of the boundaries of the commune. In contrast to pluralistic, differentiated civil societies, cultural communes display little internal differentiation. Indeed, their strength, and their ability to provide refuge, solace, certainty, and protection, comes precisely from their communal character, from their collective responsibility, cancelling individual projects. Thus, in the first stage of reaction, the (re)construction of meaning by defensive identities breaks away from the institutions of society, and promises to rebuild from the bottom up, while retrenching themselves in a communal heaven.

It is possible that from such communes, new subjects – that is collective agents of social transformation – may emerge, thus constructing new meaning around *project identity*. Indeed, I would argue that, given the structural crisis of civil society and the nation-state, this may be the main potential source of social change in the network society. As for how and why these new proactive subjects could be formed from these reactive, cultural communes, this will be the core of my analysis of social movements in the network society to be elaborated throughout this volume.

But we can already say something on the basis of the observations and discussions presented in this chapter. The emergence of project identities of different kinds is not a historical necessity. It may well be that cultural resistance will remain enclosed in the boundaries of communes. If this is the case, and where and when this is the case, communalism will close the circle of its latent fundamentalism on its own components, inducing a process that might transform communal heavens into heavenly hells.

— 2 —

The Other Face of the Earth: Social Movements against the New Global Order

Your problem is the same as many people have. It relates to the social and economic doctrine known as "neo-liberalism". This is a meta-theoretical problem. I am telling you. You start from the assumption that "neo-liberalism" is a doctrine. And by you I refer to all those with schemes as rigid and square as their head. You think that "neo-liberalism" is a capitalist doctrine to confront economic crises that capitalism charges are caused by "populism". Well, in fact "neo-classicism" is not a theory to explain crises or to confront them. It is the crisis itself, made theory and economic doctrine! This is to say that "neo-liberalism" does not have the slightest coherence, neither has plans or historical perspective. I mean, it's pure theoretical shit.

Durito, talking to Subcomandante Marcos in the Lacandon Forest, 1994[1]

Globalization, Informationalization, and Social Movements[2]

Globalization and informationalization, enacted by networks of wealth, technology, and power, are transforming our world. They are enhancing our productive capacity, cultural creativity, and communication potential. At the same time, they are disfranchising

---

[1] *Durito* is a usual character in the writings of Subcomandante Marcos, the *Zapatista* spokesperson. He is a beetle, but a very clever one: indeed, he is Marcos' intellectual adviser. The problem is he always fears being crushed by the too numerous guerrillas around him, so he begs Marcos to keep the movement small. This text by *Durito* is cited from *Ejercito Zapatista de Liberacion Nacional*/Subcomandante Marcos (1995: 58–9); my translation, with *Durito*'s benevolence.

[2] This chapter has benefited from valuable intellectual exchanges at the

societies. As institutions of state and organizations of civil society are based on culture, history, and geography, the sudden acceleration of the historical tempo, and the abstraction of power in a web of computers, are disintegrating existing mechanisms of social control and political representation. With the exception of a small elite of *globapolitans* (half beings, half flows), people all over the world resent loss of control over their lives, over their environment, over their jobs, over their economies, over their governments, over their countries, and, ultimately, over the fate of the Earth. Thus, following an old law of social evolution, resistance confronts domination, empowerment reacts against powerlessness, and alternative projects challenge the logic embedded in the new global order, increasingly sensed as disorder by people around the planet. However, these reactions and mobilizations, as is often the case in history, come in unusual formats and proceed through unexpected ways. This chapter, and the next one, explore these ways.

To broaden the empirical scope of my inquiry, while keeping its analytical focus, I will compare three movements that explicitly oppose the new global order of the 1990s, coming from extremely different cultural, economic, and institutional contexts, through sharply contrasting ideologies: the Zapatistas in Chiapas, Mexico; the American militia; and *Aum Shinrikyo*, a Japanese cult.

In the next chapter I will analyze the environmental movement, arguably the most comprehensive, influential movement of our time. In its own way, and through the creative cacophony of its multiple voices, environmentalism also challenges global ecological disorder, indeed the risk of eco-suicide, brought about by uncontrolled global development, and by the unleashing of unprecedented technological forces without checking their social and environmental sustainability. But its cultural and political specificity, and its character as a pro-active, rather than reactive, social movement, advise a separate analytical treatment of the environmental movement, as distinct from defensive movements built around the trenches of specific identities.

Before proceeding into the heart of the matter, let me introduce three brief methodological remarks that are necessary for understanding the analyses to be presented in the following pages.[3]

First, *social movements* must be understood in their own terms:

International Seminar on Globalization and Social Movements organized by the International Sociological Association's Research Committee on Social Movements, held at Santa Cruz, California, April 16–19, 1996. I thank the organizers of the seminar, Barbara Epstein and Louis Maheu, for their kind invitation.

[3] For a theoretical discussion of social movements directly relevant to the inquiry presented here, see Castells (1983); Dalton and Kuechler (1990); Epstein (1991); Riechmann and Fernandez Buey (1994); Calderon (1995); Dubet and

namely, *they are what they say they are.* Their practices (and foremost their discursive practices) are their self-definition. This approach takes us away from the hazardous task of interpreting the "true" consciousness of movements, as if they could only exist by revealing the "real" structural contradictions. As if, in order to come to life, they would necessarily have to bear these contradictions, as they bear their weapons and brandish their flags. A different, and necessary, research operation is to establish the relationship between the movements, as defined by their practice, their values, and their discourse, and the social processes to which they seem to be associated: for example, globalization, informationalization, the crisis of representative democracy, and the dominance of symbolic politics in the space of media. In my analysis I will try to conduct both operations: the characterization of each movement, in terms of its own specific dynamics; and its interaction with the broader processes that induce its existence, and become modified by this very existence. The importance I give to the movement's discourse will be reflected in my writing. When presenting and analyzing the movements, I will follow very closely their own *words*, not just ideas, as recorded in documents on which I have worked. However, in order to spare the reader from the minute details of reference citation, I have opted for giving generic references to the materials from which the discourses have been obtained, leaving the interested reader to find in these materials the precise words reported in my writing.

Secondly, social movements may be socially conservative, socially revolutionary, or both, or none. After all, we now have concluded (I hope for ever) that there is no predetermined directionality in social evolution, that the only sense of history is the history we sense. Therefore, from an analytical perspective, there are no "bad" and "good" social movements. They are all symptoms of our societies, and all impact social structures, with variable intensities and outcomes that must be established by research. Thus, I like the *Zapatistas*, I dislike the American militia, and I am horrified by *Aum Shinrikyo*. Yet, they are all, as I will argue, meaningful signs of new social conflicts, and embryos of social resistance and, in some cases, social change. Only by scanning with an open mind the new historical landscape will we be able to find shining paths, dark abysses, and muddled breakthroughs into the new society emerging from current crises.

Thirdly, to put some order into a mass of disparate material on the social movements to be examined in this and following chapters, I

Wieviorka (1995); Maheu (1995); Melucci (1995); Touraine (1995); Touraine et al. (1996); Yazawa (forthcoming).

find it useful to categorize them in terms of Alain Touraine's classic typology that defines a social movement by three principles: the movement's *identity*, the movement's *adversary*, and the movement's vision or social model, which I call *societal goal*.[4] In my personal adaptation (which I believe to be consistent with Touraine's theory), *identity* refers to the self-definition of the movement of what it is, on behalf of whom it speaks. *Adversary* refers to the movement's principal enemy, as explicitly identified by the movement. *Societal goal* refers to the movement's vision of the kind of social order, or social organization, it would wish to attain in the historical horizon of its collective action.

Having clarified the point of departure, let's depart for this voyage to the other face of the Earth, the one refusing globalization for the sake of capital and informationalization for the sake of technology. And where dreams of the past, and nightmares of the future, inhabit a chaotic world of passion, generosity, prejudice, fear, fantasy, violence, flawed strategies, and lucky strikes. Humanity, after all.

The three movements I have selected to understand insurgency against globalization are extremely different in their identity, in their goals, in their ideology, and in their relationship to society.[5] This is precisely the interest of the comparison because they are similar, however, in their explicit opposition to the new global order, identified as the enemy in their discourse and in their practice. And all of them are likely to have significant impacts on their societies, directly or indirectly. The *Zapatistas* have already transformed Mexico, inducing a crisis in the corrupt politics and unjust economy prevailing in Mexico, while putting forward proposals for democratic reconstruction that are being widely debated in Mexico, and throughout the world. The American militia, the most militant component of a broader socio-political movement self-identified as *The Patriots* (or *False Patriots*, as their critics call them), has much deeper roots in American society than is usually acknowledged, and may induce unpredictable, significant outcomes in America's tense political scene, as I will argue below. *Aum Shinrikyo*, while remaining a marginal cult in Japanese society, has dominated media attention and public debate for more than a year (in 1995–96), and it has acted as a

[4]   Touraine (1965, 1966). Touraine's formulation in fact uses a slightly different terminology, in French: *principe d'identité, principe d'opposition; principe de totalité*. I decided that it would be clearer for an international audience to use more plain words to say the same thing, at the risk of losing the authentic French flavor.

[5]   This comparative analysis is based on a joint study with Shujiro Yazawa and Emma Kiselyova, conducted in 1995. For a first elaboration of this study, see Castells et al. (1996).

symptom of unseen injuries, and unfolding dramas, behind the curtains of Japanese serenity. The point I am trying to make by bringing together these different, powerful insurgencies, is precisely the diversity of sources of resistance to the new global order. Together with the reminder that the neo-liberal illusion of the end of history is over, as historically specific societies take their revenge against their domination by global flows.

Mexico's *Zapatistas*: the First Informational Guerrilla Movement[6]

The Movimiento Civil Zapatista *is a movement that opposes social solidarity to organized crime from the power of money and government.*
Manifesto of *Movimiento Civil Zapatista*, August 1995

The novelty in Mexico's political history was the inversion of the control process against the powers that be, on the basis of alternative communication . . . The newness in Chiapas' political war was the emergence of various senders of information that interpreted events in very different ways.

The flow of public information reaching society, through the media, and through new technological means, was much greater than what conventional communication strategies could control. Marcos gave his opinion, the Church gave its opinion, and independent journalists, NGOs, and intellectuals, from the forest, from Ciudad de Mexico, from

[6]   The analysis of the *Zapatista* movement presented here is greatly indebted, as is often the case in this book, to contributions by two women. Professor Alejandra Moreno Toscano, a distinguished urban historian at the Universidad Nacional Autonoma de Mexico, and a former Secretary of Social Welfare of Mexico DF, was deputy to Manuel Camacho, the President's representative, during the critical period of negotiations between the Mexican government and the *Zapatistas* in the first months of 1994. She provided me with documents, opinion, and insights, and decisively helped my understanding of the overall process of Mexican politics in 1994–96. For her analysis (the most intelligent approach that I have read), see Moreno Toscano (1996). Secondly, Maria Elena Martinez Torres, one of my doctoral students at Berkeley, was a thorough observer of Chiapas peasantry. During our intellectual interaction, she provided me with her own analyses (Martinez Torres, 1994, 1996). Naturally, I bear exclusive responsibility for the interpretation, and possible mistakes, in the conclusions presented in this book. Additional sources used on the *Zapatista* movement are: Garcia de Leon (1985); Arquilla and Rondfeldt (1993); Collier and Lowery Quaratiello (1994); *Ejercito Zapatista de Liberacion Nacional* (1994, 1995); Trejo Delarbre (1994a, b); Collier (1995); Hernandez Navarro (1995); Nash et al. (1995); Rojas (1995); Rondfeldt (1995); Tello Diaz (1995); Woldenberg (1995).

the world's financial and political capitals, all gave their own opinion. These alternative opinions, made possible by open media, or by closed media that felt the pinch from open media, called into question forms of construction of "the truth", and induced, within the political regime as well, a variety of opinions. The view from power became fragmented.

Moreno Toscano, Turbulencia politica, p. 82

Mexico, the nation that generated the prototype of social revolution of the 20th century, is now the scene of a prototype transnational social netwar of the 21st century.

Rondfeldt, Rand Corporation, 1995

On January 1, 1994, the first day of the North American Free Trade Agreement (NAFTA), about 3,000 men and women, organized in the *Ejercito Zapatista de Liberacion Nacional*, lightly armed, took control of the main municipalities adjacent to the Lacandon Forest, in the Southern Mexican state of Chiapas: San Cristobal de las Casas, Altamirano, Ocosingo and Las Margaritas. Most of them were Indians from various ethnic groups, although there were also *mestizos*, and some of their leaders, and particularly their spokesperson, Subcomandante Marcos, were urban intellectuals. The leaders had their faces hidden behind ski masks. When the Mexican Army dispatched reinforcements, the guerrillas withdrew to the rainforest in good order. However, several dozen of them as well as civilians, and a number of soldiers and policemen, died in the confrontation or were summarily executed by soldiers in the aftermath. The impact of the uprising in Mexico, and the widespread sympathy that the *Zapatistas'* cause immediately inspired in the country, and in the world, convinced the Mexican president, Carlos Salinas de Gortari, to negotiate. On January 12, Salinas announced a unilateral ceasefire, and appointed as his "peace representative," Manuel Camacho, a respected Mexican politician, once considered his likely successor, who had just resigned from government after his presidential hopes were frustrated by Salinas (see my analysis of the Mexican political crisis in chapter 5). Manuel Camacho, and his trusted intellectual adviser, Alejandra Moreno Toscano, traveled to Chiapas, met with the influential Catholic Bishop Samuel Ruiz, and were able to engage in serious peace talks with the *Zapatistas* who quickly acknowledged the sincerity of the dialogue, although they remained justifiably wary of potential repression and/or manipulation. Camacho read to the insurgents a text in *tzotzil*, also broadcast in *tzeltal* and *chol*: the first time ever a leading Mexican official had acknowledged Indian languages. On January 27, an agreement was signed, setting a ceasefire, freeing prisoners on both sides, and engaging a process of negotiation on a broad agenda of political reform, Indian rights, and social demands.

Who are the *Zapatistas*?

Who were these insurgents, unknown until then to the rest of the world, in spite of two decades of widespread peasant mobilizations in the communities of Chiapas and Oaxaca? They were peasants, most of them Indians, *tzeltales, tzotziles,* and *choles,* generally from the communities established since the 1940s in the Lacandon rainforest, on the Guatemalan border. These communities were created with government support in order to find a way out of the social crisis created by the expulsion of *acasillados* (landless peasants working for landowners) from the *fincas* (farms), and ranches, owned by middle and large landowners, generally *mestizos.* For centuries, Indians and peasants have been abused by colonizers, bureaucrats, and settlers. And for decades they have been kept in constant insecurity, as the status of their settlements constantly changed, in accordance with the interests of government and landowners. In 1972, President Echeverria decided to create the "bioreserve" of Montes Azul, and to return most of the forest to 66 families of the original Lacandon tribe, thus ordering the relocation of 4,000 families that had resettled in this area, after their expulsion from their original communities. Behind the Lacandon tribes and the sudden love of nature, there were the interests of the forestry company Cofolasa, supported by the government development corporation, NAFINSA, which received logging rights. Most settlers refused to relocate, and started a 20-year struggle for their right to land, which was still lingering on when Salinas assumed the Presidency in 1988. Salinas finally accepted the rights of some colonists, but restricted his generosity to those few supporting the PRI (*Partido Revolucionario Institucional*), the government party. In 1992, a new decree abolished the legal rights of the Indian communities that had resettled for the second time. This time the pretext was the Rio Conference on the Environment, and the need to protect the rainforest. Cattle feeding in the area was also curtailed in order to help Chiapas ranchers, competing with cattle smuggling from Guatemala. The final blow to the fragile economy of peasant communities came when Mexican liberalization policies in the 1990s, in preparation for NAFTA, ended restrictions of imports of corn, and eliminated protection on the price of coffee. The local economy, based on forestry, cattle, coffee, and corn, was dismantled. Furthermore, the status of communal land became uncertain after Salinas' reform of the historic article 27 of the Mexican Constitution, which ended communal possession of agricultural property by the villagers (*ejidos*), in favor of full commercialization of individual property, another measure directly related to Mexico's alignment with privatization in accordance with NAFTA. In 1992 and 1993, peasants mobilized peacefully against these policies. But, after their powerful march of Xi' Nich, which brought thousands of peasants from Palenque to Ciudad de Mexico, was left without answer, they changed tactics. By the middle of 1993, in most communities of Lacandon, corn was not planted, coffee was left in the bushes, children withdrew from schools, and cattle were sold to buy weapons. The headline of the insurgents' Manifesto on January 1, 1994 read: "*Hoy decimos BASTA!*" (Today, we say ENOUGH!)

These peasant communities, mostly Indian, joined by other settlements from the Los Altos area, were not alone in the social struggles they had undertaken since the early 1970s. They were supported, and to some extent organized, by the Catholic Church, under the initiative of San Cristobal de las Casas' Bishop Samuel Ruiz, somewhat associated with liberation theology. Not only did the priests support and legitimize Indian claims, but they helped to form hundreds of cadres of peasants' unions. These cadres shared membership of the Church and of the unions. There were over one hundred *tuhuneles* (aides of priests), and over one thousand catechists, who provided the backbone of the movement, which developed in the form of peasant unions, each one of them based in a community (*ejido*). Strong religious feeling among Indian peasants was reinforced by education, information, and support from the Church, leading to frequent conflicts between the local Church, on the one hand, and Chiapas ranchers and Chiapas PRI apparatus, on the other hand. Yet, while the Church was decisive in educating, organizing, and mobilizing Indian peasant communities for many years, Samuel Ruiz and his aides strongly opposed armed struggle and were not among the insurgents, contrary to accusations by Chiapas ranchers. The cadres who organized the armed insurrection came, in their majority, from the Indian communities themselves, particularly from the ranks of young men and women who had grown up in the new climate of economic distress and social struggle. Other cadres came from Maoist groups formed in urban Mexico (particularly in Ciudad de Mexico, and in Monterrey) in the 1970s, in the aftermath of the student movement of 1968 crushed in the Tlatelolco massacre. The *Fuerzas de Liberacion Nacional* seem to have been active in the area for a long time, although accounts diverge on this point. In any case, whatever the origin, it seems that, after a series of setbacks in urban areas, a few revolutionaries, men and women, undertook the long march of establishing their credibility among the most oppressed sectors of the country, through patient work and daily sharing of their hardship and struggles. Marcos seems to have been one of these militants, coming to the region in the early 1980s, according to government sources, after completing studies in sociology and communication in Mexico and Paris, and teaching social sciences in one of the best universities in Mexico DF.[7] He is clearly a very learned intellectual, who speaks several languages, writes well, is extraordinarily imaginative, has a wonderful sense of humor, and is at ease in his relationship with the media. These revolutionary intellectuals, because of their honesty and dedication, were welcomed by the priests and, for a long time, in spite of ideological differences, they worked together in organizing peasant communities, and in supporting their struggles. It was only after 1992, when promises of reforms continued to go unfulfilled, and when the situation in the Lacandon communities become more dire because of the overall process of economic modernization in Mexico, that *Zapatista* militants set up their own structure and initiated preparations for guerrilla warfare. In May 1993 a first skirmish with the army took place, but the Mexican government downplayed the incident to avoid problems in the ratification of NAFTA by the US Congress. It should, however, be emphasized that the leadership of the *Zapatistas* is genuinely peasant, and mainly Indian. Marcos, and other urban militants, could not act on their own.[8] The process of deliberation, as well as negotiation with the government, consisted of lengthy procedures with the full participation of the communities. This was critical since, once a decision had been made, the whole community had to follow the common decision, to the extent that, in a few instances, villagers were expelled because of their refusal to participate in the uprising. Yet, during the two and a half years of the open insurgency process, the overwhelming majority of Lacandon communities, and a majority of Indians in Chiapas, showed their support for the insurgents, following them to the forest when the army took over their villages in February 1995.

The value structure of the *Zapatistas*: identity, adversaries, and goals

The deep causes of the rebellion are obvious. *But what are the insurgents' demands, goals, and values? How do they see themselves and how do*

---

[7]   The Mexican government claims to have identified Subcomandante Marcos and the main leaders of the *Zapatistas*, and its claim appears to be plausible. It has been widely reported in the media. However, since the *Zapatistas* are still insurgents at the time of writing, I do not feel it is proper to accept these claims as a matter of fact.

[8]   Moreno Toscano (1996).

they identify their enemy? On the one hand, they place themselves in historical continuity with five hundred years of struggle against colonization and oppression. Indeed, the turning point of the peasant movement was the massive demonstration in San Cristobal de las Casas on October 12, 1992, protesting the fifth centenary of the Spanish conquest of America by destroying the statue of Chiapas' conqueror, Diego de Mazariegos. On the other hand, they see the reincarnation of this oppression in the current form of the new global order: NAFTA, and the liberalizing reforms undertaken by President Salinas, which fail to include peasants and Indians in the modern- ization process. The changes in the historic article 27 of the Mexican Constitution, which had given formal satisfaction to the demands of agrarian revolutionaries championed by Emiliano Zapata, became the symbol of the exclusion of peasant communities by the new order of free traders. To this critique, shared by the whole movement, Marcos and others added their own challenge to the new global order: the projection of the socialist revolutionary dream beyond the end of communism and the demise of guerrilla movements in Central America. As Marcos wrote with irony:

> There is nothing to fight for any longer. Socialism is dead. Long life to conformism, to reform, to modernity, to capitalism and to all kind of cruel etceteras. Let's be reasonable. That nothing happens in the city, or in the countryside, that everything continues the same. Socialism is dead. Long life to capital. Radio, press, and television repeat it. Some socialists, now reasonably repentant, also repeat the same.[9]

Thus, the *Zapatistas*' opposition to the new global order is twofold: they fight against the exclusionary consequences of economic modernization; but they also challenge the inevitability of a new geopolitical order under which capitalism becomes universally accepted.

The insurgents affirmed their Indian pride, and fought for the recognition of Indian rights in the Mexican Constitution. However, it does not seem that the defense of ethnic identity was a dominant element in the movement. Indeed, the Lacandon communities have been created by forced resettlement which broke up original identi- ties from different communities and brought them together as peasants. Furthermore, it seems that, as Collier writes,

> Ethnic identity once *divided* indigenous communities from one another in the Chiapas central highlands. Recent events

---

[9]   EZLN (1994: 61); my translation.

underscore a transformation: now, in the wake of the Zapatista rebellion, peoples of diverse indigenous background are emphasizing what they share with one another in revindication of economic, social, and political exploitation.[10]

Thus, this new Indian identity was constructed through their struggle, and came to include various ethnic groups: "What is common to us is the land that gave us life and struggle."[11]

The *Zapatistas* are not subversives, but legitimate rebels. They are *Mexican patriots*, up in arms against new forms of foreign domination by American imperialism. And they are *democrats*, appealing to article 39 of the Mexican Constitution which proclaims "the right of the people to alter or modify its form of government." Thus, they call upon Mexicans to support democracy, ending *de facto* rule of one-party government based on electoral fraud. This call, coming from Chiapas, the Mexican state with the largest vote for PRI candidates, traditionally imposed by local *caciques*, elicited a strong echo in the urban middle-class sectors of a Mexican society craving freedom, and tired of systemic corruption. That the uprising took place precisely in the year of the presidential election, and in an election that was supposed to liberalize the PRI's hold on the state, is a sign of the tactical ability of the *Zapatistas*, and it was a major factor in protecting them from outright repression. President Salinas wanted to establish his legacy as both economic modernizer and political liberalizer, not only for his place in history, but for his next job: his candidacy to become the first secretary general of the newly constituted World Trade Organization, precisely the institution articulating the new world economic order. Under these circumstances, a Harvard-educated economist could hardly launch all-out military repression against a genuine peasant, Indian movement fighting against social exclusion.

---

[10]   Collier (1995: 1); a similar argument is put forward by Martinez Torres (1994). In the Manifesto issued by the *Zapatistas* over the Internet in November 1995, to commemorate the twelfth anniversary of the founding of their organization, they strongly emphasized their character as a Mexican movement for justice and democracy, beyond the defense of Indian identity: "The country we want, we want it for all the Mexicans, and not only for the Indians. The Democracy, Liberty, and Justice we want, we want for all Mexicans, and not only for the Indians. We do not want to separate from the Mexican Nation, we want to be part of it, we want to be accepted as equal, as persons with dignity, as human beings ... Here we are brothers, the dead of always. Dying again, but now to live" (EZLN, *Comunicado* on Internet, 17 November 1995; my translation).
[11]   *Zapatista* declaration, January 25, 1994; cited by Moreno Toscano (1996: 92).

The communication strategy of the *Zapatistas*: the Internet and the media

The success of the *Zapatistas* was largely due to their communication strategy, to the point that they can be called the *first informational guerrilla movement*. They created a media event in order to diffuse their message, while desperately trying not to be brought into a bloody war. There were, of course, real deaths, and real weapons, and Marcos, and his comrades, were ready to die. Yet, actual warfare was not their strategy. The *Zapatistas* used arms to make a statement, then parlayed the possibility of their sacrifice in front of the world media to force a negotiation and advance a number of reasonable demands which, as opinion polls seem to indicate, found widespread support in Mexican society at large.[12] Autonomous communication was a paramount objective for the *Zapatistas*:

> When the bombs were falling over the mountains south of San Cristobal, when our combatants were resisting attacks from federal troops, when the air smelled with powder and blood, the "Comite Clandestino Revolucionario Indigena del EZLN" called and told me, more or less: We must say our word and be heard. If we do not do it now, others will take our voice and lies will come out from our mouth without us wanting it. Look for a way to speak our word to those who would like to listen.[13]

The *Zapatistas'* ability to communicate with the world, and with Mexican society, and to capture the imagination of people and of intellectuals, propelled a local, weak insurgent group to the forefront of world politics. In this sense Marcos was essential. He did not have organizational control of a movement that was rooted in the Indian communities, and he did not show any signs of being a great military strategist, although he was wise in ordering retreat every time the army was to engage them. But he was extraordinarily able in establishing a communication bridge with the media, through his well-constructed writings, and by his *mise-en-scène* (the mask, the pipe, the setting of the interviews), somehow serendipitously found, as in the case of the mask that played such an important role in popularizing the revolutionaries' image: all over the world, everybody could become *Zapatista* by wearing a mask. Furthermore (although this may be an

[12] According to a poll conducted on December 8 and 9, 1994, 59 percent of Mexico City residents had a "good opinion" of the *Zapatistas*, and 78 percent thought that their demands were justified (published in the newspaper *Reforma*, December 11, 1994).

[13] Marcos, February 11, 1994; cited by Moreno Toscano (1996: 90).

over-theorization), masks are a recurrent ritual in pre-Colombian Mexican Indian cultures, so that rebellion, equalization of faces, and historical flashback played into each other in a most innovative theatrics of revolution. Essential in this strategy was the *Zapatistas'* use of telecommunications, videos, and of computer-mediated communication, both to diffuse their messages from Chiapas to the world (although probably not transmitted from the forest), and to organize a worldwide network of solidarity groups that literally encircled the repressive intentions of the Mexican government; for instance, during the army invasion of insurgent areas on February 9, 1995. It is interesting to underline that at the origins of the *Zapatistas'* use of the Internet are two developments of the 1990s: the creation of *La Neta*, an alternative computer communication network in Mexico and Chiapas; and its use by women's groups (particularly by *"De mujer a mujer"*) to link up Chiapas' NGOs with other Mexican women, as well as with women's networks in the US. *La Neta*.[14] originated in the linkup in 1989–93 between Mexican NGOs, supported by the Catholic Church, and the Institute for Global Communication in San Francisco, supported by skilled computer experts donating their time and expertise to good causes. In 1994, with the help of a grant from the Ford Foundation, *La Neta* was able to establish a node in Mexico with a private Internet provider. In 1993 *La Neta* had been established in Chiapas, with the purpose of getting local NGOs on line, including the Center for Human Rights "Bartolome de las Casas," and a dozen other organizations, which came to play a major role in informing the world during the *Zapatista* uprising. Extensive use of the Internet allowed the *Zapatistas* to diffuse information and their call throughout the world instantly, and to create a network of support groups which helped to produce an international public opinion movement that made it literally impossible for the Mexican government to use repression on a large scale. Images and information from and around the *Zapatistas* acted powerfully on the Mexican economy and politics. As Martinez Torres writes:

> Ex-President Salinas created a "bubble economy" which for several years permitted the illusion of prosperity based on a massive inflow of speculative investments in high-interest government bonds, that via a spiraling trade deficit and debt allowed the middle and working classes to enjoy for a while a multitude of imported consumer goods. Yet, as easy as it was to lure investors

[14] It seems necessary to clarify the multiple meaning of *La Neta* for non-Mexican readers. Besides being the figurative Spanish feminine of The Net, *la neta* is Mexican slang for "the real story."

in, any loss of investor confidence could potentially spiral into panic and run on Mexican bonds, with the possibility of causing a collapse of the system. In effect, the Mexican economy [in 1994] was an enormous confidence game. Since confidence is basically created by manipulation of information it can be destroyed in exactly the same way. In the new world order where information is the most valuable commodity, that same information can be much more powerful than bullets.[15]

This was the key to the *Zapatistas'* success. Not that they deliberately sabotaged the economy. But they were protected by their relentless media connection, and by their Internet-based worldwide alliances, from outright repression, forcing negotiation, and raising the issue of social exclusion and political corruption to the eyes and ears of world public opinion.

Indeed, experts of the Rand Corporation concur with this analysis,[16] having forecasted the eventuality of *Zapatista*-type "netwars" since 1993: "The revolutionary forces of the future may consist increasingly of widespread multi-organizational networks that have no particular national identity, claim to arise from civil society, and include aggressive groups and individuals who are keenly adept at using advanced technology for communications, as well as munitions."[17] The *Zapatistas* seem to have realized the worst nightmares of experts of the new global order.

The contradictory relationship between social movement and political institution

However, while the impact of the *Zapatistas'* demands shook up the Mexican political system, and even the Mexican economy, they became entangled in their own contradictory relationship to the political system. On the one hand, the *Zapatistas* called for the democratization of the political system, reinforcing similar demands being made within Mexican society. But they were never able to make precise the meaning of their political project, besides the obvious condemnation of electoral fraud. In the meantime, the PRI had been irreversibly shaken, divided into groups that were literally killing each other (see chapter 5). The presidential elections of August 1994 were reasonably clean, giving Zedillo, an obscure PRI candidate brought into the limelight by accidental circumstances, a triumph fueled by

---

[15]   Martinez Torres (1996: 5).
[16]   Rondfeldt (1995).
[17]   Arquilla and Rondfeldt (1993).

fear of the unknown. Ironically, political reforms in the election process, partly as a result of *Zapatista* pressure, contributed to the legitimacy of the election, after the agreement on January 27, 1994 between all presidential candidates. The leftist opposition party, whose leader had been rebuffed by the *Zapatistas*, suffered electorally for having sought Marcos' support. In August 1994, the *Zapatistas* called a National Democratic Convention in a site of the Lacandon Forest that they named Aguascalientes, the name of the historic site where, in 1915, revolutionary leaders (Villa, Zapata, Orozco) met to establish the Revolutionary Convention. In spite of massive partici- pation from grassroots organizations, leftist parties, intellectuals, and media, Aguascalientes exhausted itself in the symbolism of the event, this ephemeral gathering being unable to translate the new *Zapatista* language into conventional, leftist politics. Thus, in May 1995, in the midst of protracted negotiations with the government in San Andres Larrainzar, the *Zapatistas* organized a popular consultation on the possibility of becoming a civilian political force. In spite of the obvious difficulties (they were still an insurgent organization), almost 2 million people participated in the consultation throughout Mexico, supporting the proposal in their vast majority. Thus, in January 1996, to commemorate two years of their uprising, the *Zapatistas* decided to transform themselves into a political party, seeking full participation in the political process. They also decided, however, to keep their weapons until an agreement could be reached with the government on all points of contention. In January 1996 an important agreement on a future constitutional acknowledgment of Indian rights was reached, but negotiations were in process at the time of writing (in October 1996) concerning political reform, and economic matters. A difficult issue seemed to be the claim by the Indian communities to keep ownership of their land, including of their underground resources, a demand adamantly rejected by the Mexican government since it is widely believed that Chiapas is rich in hydrocarbons under- ground. As for political reform, the unwillingness of the PRI to release its hold on power made agreement very difficult.

The future potential of a *Zapatista* political party is uncertain. On the one hand, Marcos remains, by the end of 1996, one of the most popular leaders in Mexico. On the other hand, much of his popularity is linked to his status as a revolutionary myth. Marcos as a com- promising *politico* might lose much of his appeal, something that he seems to be aware of. Thus, he and his *companeros*, were, at the time of writing, hesitant to proceed with full institutionalization of their political standing, although this is a likely outcome of their in- surgency, albeit in the context of a still uncertain transformation of the Mexican political system.

Yet, regardless of the *Zapatistas'* fate, their insurgency did change Mexico, challenging the one-sided logic of modernization, characteristic of the new global order. Acting on the powerful contradictions existing inside the PRI between modernizers and the interests of a corrupt party apparatus, the debate triggered by the *Zapatistas* helped considerably to break PRI's hold on Mexico. The Mexican economy, buoyant and euphoric in 1993, was exposed in all its weakness, prompting US critics of NAFTA to claim vindication. An absent actor in the current Latin American modernization processes, the Indian peasantry (about 10 percent of the Mexican population) suddenly came to life. A constitutional reform, in the process of approval in November 1996, acknowledged the pluri-cultural character of Mexico, and gave new rights to the Indians, including the publication of textbooks in 30 Indian languages, to be used in public schools. Health and education services improved in many Indian communities, and limited self-government was in the process of implementation.

The affirmation of Indian cultural identity, albeit in a reconstructed manner, was connected to their revolt against outrageous abuse. But their fight for dignity was decisively helped by religious affiliation expressed in the deep current of populist Catholicism in Latin America, as well as by the last stand for the Marxist left in Mexico. That this left, built on the idea of the proletariat fighting for socialism with its guns, was transformed into an Indian, peasant movement of the excluded fighting for democracy, on behalf of constitutional rights, via the Internet and the mass media, shows the depth of the transformation of liberation avenues in Latin America. It also shows that the new global order induces multiple local disorder, caused by historically rooted sources of resistance to the logic of global capital flows. Chiapas Indians fighting against NAFTA by means of their alliance with ex-Maoist militants and liberation theologists are a distinctive expression of the old search for social justice under new historical conditions.

Up in Arms against the New World Order: the American Militia and the Patriot Movement in the 1990s[18]

In brief, the New World Order is a utopian system in which the US economy (along with the economy of every other nation) will be "global-ized"; the wage levels of all US and European workers will be brought down to those of workers in the Third World; national boundaries will for all practical purposes cease to exist; an increased flow of Third World immigrants into the United States and Europe will have produced a non-White majority everywhere in the formerly White areas of the world; an elite consisting of international financiers, the masters of mass media, and managers of multinational corporations will call the shots; and the United Nations peacekeeping forces will be used to keep anyone from opting out of the system.

William Pierce, *National Vanguard*[19]

The Internet was one of the major reasons the militia movement expanded faster than any hate group in history. The militia's lack of an organized center was more than made up for by the instant communication and rumor potential of this new medium. Any militia member in remote Montana who had a computer and a modem could be part of an entire

---

[18]   The main source of information on the American militia and the "Patriots" is the Southern Poverty Law Center, headquartered in Montgomery, Alabama. This remarkable organization has displayed extraordinary courage and effec-tiveness in protecting citizens against hate groups in America since its foundation in 1979. As part of its program, it has established a Klanwatch/Militia Task Force which provides accurate information and analysis to understand and counteract new and old, anti-government and anti-people extremist groups. For most recent information, used in my analysis, see Klanwatch/Militia Task Force (1996, subse-quently cited as KMTF). A well-documented account of the American militia in the 1990s is Stern (1996). I have also used the excellent analysis provided by my doctoral student Matthew Zook on militia groups and the Internet in 1996 (Zook, 1996). Additional sources specifically used in the analysis presented in this chapter are J. Cooper (1995); Anti-Defamation League (1994, 1995); Armond (1995); Armstrong (1995); Bennett (1995); Berlet and Lyons (1995); *Broadcasting and Cable* (1995); *Business Week* (1995d); Coalition for Human Dignity (1995); Cooper (1995); Heard (1995); Helvarg (1995); Jordan (1995); Ivins (1995); Maxwell and Tapia (1995); Sheps (1995); *The Nation* (1995); Orr (1995); Pollith (1995); Ross (1995); *The Gallup Poll Monthly* (1995); *The New Republic* (1995); *The New York Times Sunday* (1995a, b); *The Progressive* (1995); *Time* (1995); WEPIN Store (1995); Dees and Corcoran (1996); Winerip (1996).

[19]   Quote from White supremacist William Pierce's article in the March 1994 issue of his journal *National Vanguard*, cited by KMTF (1996: 37). Pierce is head of the National Alliance and author of the best-selling novel *The Turner Diaries*.

worldwide network that shared his or her thoughts, aspirations, organizing strategies and fears – a global family.

Kenneth Stern, *A Force upon the Plain*, p. 228

The blast of a truck loaded with fertilizer-based explosives in Oklahoma City on April 19, 1995 not only blew up a federal government building, killing 169 people, but it also exposed a powerful undercurrent of American society, until then relegated to traditional hate groups and political marginality. Timothy McVeigh, the main suspect in the bombing, used to carry with him William Pierce's novel about an underground cell, *The Patriots*, that bombs a federal building: McVeigh reportedly called Pierce's private number hours before the actual Oklahoma bombing. McVeigh, and his army buddy, Terry Nichols (both awaiting trial at the time of writing) were found to be loosely related to the Michigan Militia. The bombing occurred on the second anniversary of the Waco assault, in which most members of the Davidian cult, and their children, were killed in a siege by federal agents, an event denounced, as a rallying cry, by militia groups all around the United States.[20]

The militia groups are not terrorist, but some of their members may well be, organized in a different, but ideologically related form of movement, the "underground patriots." These are constituted on the basis of autonomous, clandestine cells, which set up their own targets in accordance with views pervasive throughout the movement. In 1994–6 a number of bombings, bank robberies, railroad sabotage, and other violent acts are believed to have been committed by such groups, and the intensity and lethality of their actions are increasing. Tons of explosives have been stolen from commercial sites, and stocks of military weaponry, including Stinger portable missiles, have disappeared from military arsenals. Attempts to develop bacteriological weapons have been discovered. And tens of thousands of "Patriots" around the United States are armed with war weapons, and undergo regular training in guerrilla tactics.[21]

The militia are the most militant, and organized, wing of a much broader, self-proclaimed "Patriot movement,"[22] whose ideological galaxy encompasses established, extreme conservative organizations,

[20]   The Texas Militia issued the following appeal a few days before April 19, 1995, the second anniversary of the Waco incident: "All able-bodied citizens are to assemble with their arms to celebrate their right to keep and bear arms and to assemble as militias in defense of the Republic" (cited in the editorial of *The Nation*, 1995: 656).

[21]   KMTF (1996).

[22]   KMTF (1996); Stern (1996).

such as the John Birch Society; a whole array of traditional, white supremacist, neo-nazi, and anti-semitic groups, including the Ku-Klux-Klan, and the Posse Comitatus; fanatic religious groups such as Christian Identity, an anti-semitic sect emanating from Victorian England's British Israelism; anti-federal government groups, such as the Counties' Rights Movements, Wise Use anti-environmental coalition, the National Taxpayers' Union, and defenders of "Common Law" courts. The Patriots' galaxy also extends, in loose forms, to the powerful Christian Coalition, as well as to a number of militant "Right to Life" groups, and counts on the sympathy of many members of the National Rifle Association, and pro-gun advocates. The direct appeal of the Patriots may reach to as many as 5 million people in America, according to well-informed sources,[23] although the very character of the movement, with its blurred boundaries, and the lack of organized membership, makes impossible an accurate statistical estimate. Still, its influence can be counted in millions, not thousands, of supporters. What these disparate groups, formerly un-related, came to share in the 1990s, and what broadens their appeal, is their common, declared enemy: the US federal government, as representative of the "New World Order," being set up against the will of American citizens. According to views pervasive throughout the Patriot movement, this "New World Order," aimed at destroying American sovereignty, is enacted by a conspiracy of global financial interests and global bureaucrats that have captured the US federal government. At the core of this new system are the World Trade Organization, the Trilateral Commission, the International Monetary Fund, and, above all, the United Nations, whose "peacekeeping forces" are seen as an international, mercenary army, spearheaded by Hong Kong policemen and Gurkha units, ready to suppress people's sovereignty. Four events seemed to confirm this conspiracy for the Patriots: the passing of NAFTA in 1993; the approval by Clinton of the Brady Bill in 1994, establishing limited controls on the sale of some types of automatic weapons; the siege of white supremacist Randy Weaver in Idaho, resulting in the killing of his wife by the FBI, in 1992; and the tragic siege of Waco, leading to the death of David Koresh and his followers in 1993. A paranoid reading of these events led to the conviction that the government was proceeding to disarm citizens, to subdue them later, submitting Americans to surveillance from hidden cameras, and black helicopters, and implanting bio-chips in the newborn. To this global threat, on jobs, on privacy, on liberty, on the American way of life, they oppose the Bible and the original American Constitution, expunged of its Amendments. In

---

[23] Berlet and Lyons (1995); KMTF (1996); Winerip (1996).

accordance with these texts, both received from God, they affirm the sovereignty of citizens and its direct expression in county governments, not acknowledging the authority of federal government, its laws, its courts, as well as the validity of the Federal Reserve Bank. The choice is dramatic. In the words of the Militia of Montana, created in February 1994, and an organizational inspiration for the whole movement: "Join the Army and Serve the UN or Join America and Serve the Militia" (Motto of WWW home page of the Montana Militia). Federal agents, particularly those from the Bureau of Alcohol, Tobacco, and Firearms, are considered to be in the frontline of the repression against Americans on behalf of the emerging world government. This, in the view of the militia, justifies making federal agents potential targets of the movement. Thus, as popular broadcaster Gordon Liddy put it in one of his talk shows: "They've got a big target [on their chest]: ATF. Don't shoot at that because they've got a vest on underneath that. Head shots, head shots. Kill the sons of bitches!"[24] In some segments of this highly diverse Patriot movement there is also a powerful mythology rooted in eschatological views of the world and End of Times prophecies (see chapter 1). Following the Book of Revelations, chapter 13, preachers such as tele-evangelist Pat Robertson, the leader of the Christian Coalition, remind Christians that they may be asked to submit to the satanic "Mark of the Beast," variously identified as new codes on paper money, supermarket bar codes, or microchip technology.[25] Resisting the new global, ungodly order, coming at the End of Times, is seen as a Christian duty and an American citizen's right. Yet, the sinister colorfulness of the movement's mythology sometimes obscures its profile, and actually downplays its political and social significance. This is why it is important to pay attention to the diversity of the movement, while still emphasizing its underlying commonality.

The militias and the Patriots: a multi-thematic information network

Militias, self-organized citizens armed to defend their country, religion, and freedom, are institutions that played an important role during the first century of America's existence.[26] The state militias were replaced by state national guards in 1900. However, in the 1990s, starting with the Montana Militia, right-wing populist groups have formed "unorganized militias," using some legal ambiguity in federal

---

24 Stern (1996: 221).
25 Berlet and Lyons (1995).
26 Whisker (1992); J. Cooper (1995).

laws to circumvent the legal prohibition to form military units outside of government control. The most distinctive feature of militia groups is that they are armed, sometimes with war weapons, and are structured in a military-style chain of command. By the end of 1995, KMTF could count 441 active militias in all 50 states, with paramilitary training sites in at least 23 states (see figure 2.1). Numbers of militia members are difficult to estimate. Berlet and Lyons ventured to evaluate them, in 1995, at between 15,000 and 40,000.[27] By all accounts they are growing rapidly. There is no national organization. Each state's militia is independent, and there are sometimes several, unrelated militia groups in the same state: 33 in Ohio, with about 1,000 members, and hundreds of thousands of sympathizers, according to police sources.[28] The Militia of Montana is the founding example, but the largest is the Michigan Militia, with several thousand active members. Their ideology, beyond the common opposition to the new world order and to the federal government, is highly diversified. Their membership is overwhelmingly white, Christian, and predominantly male. They certainly include a significant number of racists, anti-semites, and sexists among their ranks. Yet, most militia groups do not define themselves as racist or sexist, and some of them (for instance the Michigan Militia) make an explicit anti-racist statement in their propaganda. In Zook's analysis of militia pages in the World Wide Web, focusing on 11 of the most popular militia, seven of the home pages made anti-racist statements, four made no mention of race, and none contained overt racism.[29] Two pages took anti-sexist stands, two welcomed women, and the others did not mention sex. Indeed, the Michigan Militia refused to support the "Montana freemen," during their 1996 siege in a ranch, because they were racist. And one of the Militia Home Pages "E Pluribus Unum," part of the Ohio Militia, is run by an African-American Christian fundamentalist couple. To be sure, these statements could be faked, but given the importance of Internet posting to contact new members, it would be inconsistent to misrepresent the ideology on which new recruits are attracted. It seems that the militia and the Patriots, while including traditional racist, anti-semitic, hate groups, have a much broader ideological constituency, and this is exactly one of the reasons for their new success. Namely, their ability to reach out across the ideological spectrum to unite all sources of disaffection against the federal government. As KMTF's report says:

[27]   Berlet and Lyons (1995).
[28]   Winerip (1996).
[29]   Zook (1996).

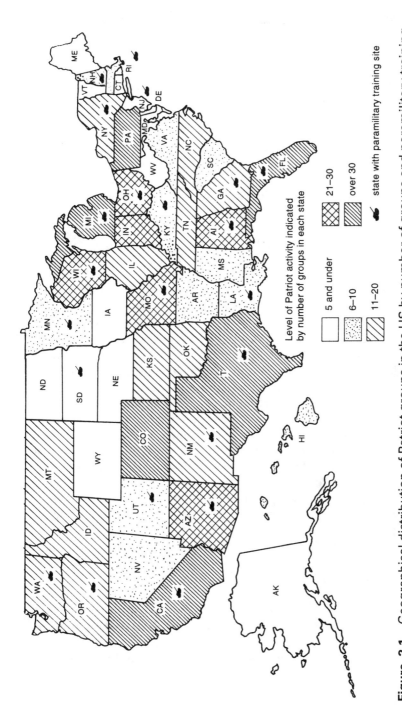

Figure. 2.1 Geographical distribution of Patriot groups in the US by number of groups and paramilitary training sites in each state, 1996

Source: Southern Poverty Law Center, Klanwatch/Militia Task Force, Montgomery, Alabama, 1996

Unlike their factious white supremacist predecessors, Patriots have been able to bridge minor ideological differences in favor of a broad unity on the anti-government agenda. As a result, they have created the most inviting insurgent force in recent history, home to a wide variety of anti-government groups whose organizational roles may differ dramatically.[30]

Two fast-expanding components of the Patriot movement are the Counties' Rights movement, and the "Common Law" courts. The first is a militant wing of the Wise Use coalition, which has growing influence in the Western states. The coalition opposes environmental regulation enforced by the federal government and appeals to the "customs and culture" of logging, mining, and grazing on public land. Land-use zoning is equated with socialism, and management of the ecosystem is considered to be a part of the new world order.[31] Consequently, the movement asserts the right of county sheriffs to arrest federal land managers, which prompted a number of violent incidents. People and communities are urged to acknowledge exclusively the authority of their elected officials at the municipal and county level, rejecting the federal government's right to legislate on their property. Seventy counties have passed Wise Use ordinances claiming local control over public land, and violent actions have intimidated environmentalists and federal land managers from New Mexico and Nevada to northern Idaho and Washington. Common Law courts have been established in 40 states, supported by an array of books and videos that claim to provide a legal basis for people to reject the judicial system, setting up their own "judges," "trials," and "juries." They have even established a national "Supreme Court of Common Law" with 23 justices, based on the Bible and on their own interpretation of law. Common Law followers declare themselves "sovereign," that is freemen, and refuse accordingly to pay taxes and social security, to comply with driving licensing, and to submit to all other government controls not contemplated in the original American legal body. To protect their sovereignty, and retaliate against public officials, they often file commercial liens against targeted public officials and judges, creating a nightmarish confusion in a number of county courts. As an extension of the Common Law movement, a rapidly expanding network of people, from Montana to California, refuse the authority of the Federal Reserve Bank to print money, and they issue their own bank documents, including cashier checks, with such good reproduction technology that they have often

---

[30]   KMTF (1996: 14).
[31]   Helvarg (1995).

been cashed, prompting a number of arrests for forgery and fraud. These practices are making the Common Law movement the most confrontational of all the Patriot groups, and were at the root of the three-month stand-off between "freemen" and the FBI in a ranch in Jordan, Montana, in 1996.

Such a diverse, almost chaotic, movement cannot have a stable organization, or even a coordinating instance. Yet, the homogeneity of its core world vision and, particularly, its identification of a common enemy are remarkable. This is because linkages between groups and individuals do exist, but they are carried out through the media (radio, mainly), through books, pamphlets, speaking tours, and alternative press, by Fax, and, mainly, through the Internet.[32] According to KMTF, "the computer is the most vital piece of equipment in the Patriot movement's arsenal."[33] On the Internet there are numerous militia bulletin board systems, home pages, and chat groups; for instance, the Usenet group MAM, established in 1995. Several reasons have been proposed for the widespread use of the Internet by militiamen. One is that, as Stern writes, "Internet was the perfect culture in which to grow the virus of conspiracy theory. Messages appeared on the screen with no easy way to separate junk from credible . . . For conspiracy enthusiasts like militia members, unverified statements from cyberspace reaffirmed their set conclusions by providing an endless stream of additional 'evidence.'"[34] Also, the frontier spirit characteristic of the Internet fits well with the freemen, expressing themselves, and making their statement without mediation or government control. More importantly, the network structure of the Internet reproduces exactly the autonomous, spontaneous networking of militia groups, and of the Patriots at large, without boundaries, and without definite plan, but sharing a purpose, a feeling, and, most of all, an enemy. It is mainly on the Internet (backed up by Fax and direct mailing) that the movement thrives and organizes itself. It was through the Associated Electronic Network News, organized by the Thompsons in Indianapolis, that a conspiracy theory was diffused according to which the Oklahoma bombing was a provocation by the federal government similar to Hitler's arson of the Reichstag in order to crack down on the militia. Other bulletin board systems, such as the "Paul Revere Net," link up groups around the country, exchange information, circulate rumors, and coordinate actions. For example, confidential reports inform browsers that Gorbachev, after giving a speech in California saying that "we are now

[32]   KMTF (1996); Stern (1996); Zook (1996).
[33]   KMTF (1996: 16).
[34]   Stern (1996: 228).

entering the new world order," went on to hide in a Southern California naval base to oversee the dismantling of America's armed forces in preparation for the arrival of the world order's army. Indeed, its arrival took place in May 1996, when a permanent base was established in New Mexico to train hundreds of German pilots in cooperation with the US Air Force. Or so thought the thousands of callers that submerged the Pentagon's switchboard after CNN reported the opening of such a base.

Radio talk shows are also important. Rush Limbaugh's audience of 20 million on 600 stations around the country is an instrument of political influence without parallel in 1990s America. While he is not a militia supporter, his themes ("femi-nazis," "eco-wacos") resonate in the movement. Other popular radio programs are more directly in tune with the Patriots: Gordon Liddy's call-in show, or *The Intelligence Report*, hosted by white supremacist Mark Koernke. Alternative cable channels, broadcasting similar topics to similar audiences, include National Empowerment Television, Jones Intercable, and Time–Warner-owned Paragon Cable in Florida, which features *Race&Reason*, an anti-semitic, racist show. A myriad of newspapers and bulletins, such as Washington DC's *Spotlight*, or the white supremacist tract *The Turner Diaries*, add to a highly decentralized, extensive network of alternative media. This network diffuses targeted information, airs people's resentment, publicizes right, extremist ideas, spreads rumors of conspiracies, and purveys the eschatological mythology that has become the cultural background for end-of-millennium right-wing populism. Thus, while the FBI looks in vain for proof of an organized conspiracy to overturn the government by force, the actual conspiracy, with no names (or multiple names), and with no organization (or hundreds of them), flows in the information networks, feeding paranoia, connecting anger, and maybe spilling blood.

The Patriots' banners

In spite of its diversity, the Patriot movement, with the militia at its forefront, does share some common goals, beliefs, and foes. It is this set of values and purposes that constructs a world vision and, ultimately, defines the movement itself.

There is an underlying, simple, but powerful view of the world and society which is expressed in different forms in the Patriot movement. According to this vision, America is divided into two kinds of people: producers and parasites. Producers, working people, are oppressed between two layers of parasites: corrupt government officials, wealthy corporate elites, and bankers, at the top; and stupid and lazy people, undeserving of the welfare they receive of society, at the bottom. The situation is being made worse by the current process of globalization, steered by the United Nations and international financial institutions, on behalf of corporate elites and government bureaucracies, which threatens to transform ordinary people into mere slaves of a world-wide plantation-like economy. God will prevail, but for this citizens must take up their guns to fight for "the future of America itself."[35] From this world vision emerges a specific set of targets for the movement, which organize its practice.

First of all, the militia, and the Patriots in general, are an extreme libertarian movement (and, in this sense, very different from traditional Nazis or fascists who call for a strong state). Their enemy is the federal government. In their view, the basic units of society are the individual, the family, and the local community. Beyond that immediate level of face-to-face acknowledgment, government is only tolerated as the direct expression of the citizens' will; for example, county governments, with elected officials who can be known and controlled on a personal basis. Higher levels of government are suspected, and the federal government is denounced outright as illegitimate, as having usurped citizens' rights and manipulated the Constitution to overstep the original mandate of the founding fathers of America. For militiamen, Thomas Jefferson and Patrick Henry are the heroes, and Alexander Hamilton the obvious villain. This rejection of the legitimacy of federal government expresses itself in very concrete, powerful attitudes and actions: rejection of federal taxes, refusal of environmental regulation and land-use planning, sovereignty of common law courts, jury nullification (namely deciding as jurors in court cases not in accordance with the law but according to their consciences), pre-eminence of county governments over higher authorities, and hatred of federal law-enforcement agencies. At the limit, the movement calls for civil disobedience against the government, backing it up, if and when necessary, with the guns of "natural law"-abiding citizens.

While the federal government and its enforcement agencies are the immediate enemies, and the immediate cause of the mobilization of the Patriots, a more ominous threat looms on the horizon: the new world order. The new world order, a notion popularized by tele-evangelist Pat Robertson, extrapolating from Bush's post-Cold War end-of-history ideology, implies that the federal government is actively working toward the goal of one world government in collaboration with Russia (particularly with Gorbachev, considered to be a key strategist in the plot). This project is supposedly being carried out by

[35]   M. Cooper (1995).

the intermediary of international organizations: the United Nations, the new World Trade Organization, and the International Monetary Fund. The placement of American military troops under the command of the United Nations, and the signing of NAFTA, are considered but the first steps toward such a new order, often explicitly associated with the coming of the Information Age. The actual impact on the American people is seen as their economic impoverishment for the benefit of multinational corporations and banks, and their political disfranchisement for the sake of global political bureaucracies.

Together with these localist, libertarian strands, a third major theme runs through the movement: a backlash against feminists (not against women as long as they remain in their traditional role), gays, and minorities (as beneficiaries of government protection). There is one clearly predominant characteristic in the Patriot movement: in a large majority, they are white, heterosexual males. The "Angry White Male" (actually the name of one Patriot organization) seem to have come together in this mixture of reactions to economic deprivation, reaffirmation of traditional values and privileges, and cultural backlash. Traditional national and family values (that is, patriarchalism) are affirmed against what are considered to be excessive privileges accorded by society to gender, cultural, and ethnic minorities, as exemplified by affirmative action and anti-discrimination legislation. While this theme does connect with a much older rejection of racial equality by white supremacist groups and anti-immigrant coalitions, it is new in its comprehensiveness, particularly because of the explicit rejection of women's rights, and in its hostile targeting of liberal values diffused by the mainstream media.

A fourth theme present in most of the movement is the intolerant affirmation of the superiority of Christian values, so linking up closely with the Christian fundamentalist movement, analyzed in chapter 1. Most Patriots seem to subscribe to the pretension that Christian values and rituals, as interpreted by their defenders, must be enforced through the institutions of society; for example, mandatory prayer in public schools and the screening of libraries and the media to censor what would be considered anti-Christian or anti-family values. The widespread anti-abortion movement, with fanatic assassins at its fringes, is its most notorious organizational instrument. Christian fundamentalism seems to be pervasive throughout the whole movement. It might seem paradoxical, this connection between an extreme libertarian movement, such as the militia, and Christian fundamentalism, a movement that aims at theocracy and therefore would seek government imposition of moral and religious values on its citizens. However, this is only a contradiction in the historical horizon, since in 1990s America both fundamentalists and libertarians converge on the destruction of a federal government that is perceived as being apart from both God and The People.

Guns and Bibles could well be the movement's motto.[36] Guns were the rallying point around which the militia came together in 1994 in response to the Brady Bill. A vast coalition was formed against this, and subsequent attempts at gun control. Around the powerful lobby of the National Rifle Association, controlling many votes in Congress, coalesced rural folks around the country, gun shop owners, extreme libertarians, and militia groups, to make the defense of the constitutional right to bear arms the last line of defense for America as it ought to be. Guns equal freedom. The Wild West rides again, on the streets of Los Angeles as on the Michigan farms. Two of the deepest features of American culture, its rugged individualism and its mistrust of despotic governments, from which many immigrants escape to come to America, provide the seal of authenticity to the resistance against threats generated by the informationalization of society, the globalization of economy, and the professionalization of politics.

Who are the Patriots?

A component of the movement is certainly made up of disaffected farmers in the Midwest and in the West, supported by a miscellaneous cast of small town societies, from coffeeshop owners to traditionalist pastors. But it would be inaccurate to consider that the appeal of the movement is limited to a rural world phased out by technological modernization. There are no demographic data on the movement's composition, but a simple look at the geographical distribution of the militia (figure 2.1) shows its territorial, thus social, diversity. The groups of states with the highest numbers of militia activity include such diverse areas as Pennsylvania, Michigan, Florida, Texas, Colorado, and California, more or less following the most populous states (minus New York, plus Colorado), but this is precisely the point: militia seem to be where people are, all over the country, not just in Montana. If we consider the Christian Coalition to be a part of the movement, then Patriots are present in the suburbs of most large metropolitan areas (there are about 1.5 million members of the Christian Coalition). Some militia groups, for instance in New Hampshire, and in California, seem to recruit among computer professionals. Thus, it does not seem that the Patriots are a class-based, or territorially specific movement. Rather, they are, fundamentally, a cultural and political movement, defenders of the

---

[36]   Maxwell and Tapia (1995).

traditions of the country against cosmopolitan values, and of self-rule of local people against the imposition of global order. However, if class is not relevant in the composition of the movement, it is relevant in the identification of its enemies. Corporate elites; bankers; the wealthy, powerful and arrogant big firms, and their lawyers; and scientists and researchers, are their enemies. Not as a class, but as representatives of an un-American world order. Indeed, the ideology is not anti-capitalist, but is, rather, an ideology in defense of free capitalism, opposed to a corporate manifestation of state capitalism that appears to be close to socialism. Thus, a class analysis of the Patriots does not seem to address the essence of the movement. It is a political insurgency that cuts across class lines and regional differentiation. And it relates to the social and political evolution of American society at large.

The militia, the Patriots, and American society in the 1990s

Right-wing populism is hardly a novelty in the United States; indeed, it is a phenomenon that has played an important role in American politics throughout the country's history.[37] Furthermore, angry popular reactions to economic distress have occurred in both America and Europe in different forms, from classic fascism and Nazism to the xenophobic and ultra-nationalist movements of recent years. One of the conditions that can help explain the fast spread of the militia, besides the Internet, is growing economic hardship and social inequality in America. Men's average income has deteriorated substantially in the past two decades, particularly during the 1980s. Families are barely maintaining the living standards of a quarter of a century ago by putting in the contribution of two wage earners instead of one. On the other hand, the top 1 percent of households increased its average income from $327,000 to about $567,000 between 1976 and 1993, while average family income remains at about $31,000. CEO's pay is 190 times higher than that of their average worker.[38] For the American worker and small entrepreneur, the age of globalization and informationalization has been the age of a relative, and often an absolute, decline in their standard of living, reversing the historical trend of the improvement of each generation's material well-being over that of previous generations. Occasionally, the culture of the new global rich adds insult to injury. For instance, Montana, the seedbed of the new militia, is also one of the favorite destinations of the new billionaires, fond of acquiring thousands of acres of pristine land to

---

37   Lipset and Raab (1978).
38   *The New York Times* (1995b).

build ranches from which to run their global networks. Ranchers in the area resented these moves.[39]

Furthermore, at the moment when the traditional family becomes indispensable as an instrument of both financial and psychological security, it has been falling apart, in the wake of the gender war ignited by the resistance of patriarchalism to women's rights (see chapter 4). Cultural challenges to sexism and to heterosexual orthodoxy confuse masculinity. In addition, a new wave of immigration, this time from Latin America and Asia, and the growing multi-ethnicity of America, although in continuity with the country's history, add to the feeling of loss of control. The shifts from agriculture and manufacturing to services, and from goods handling to information processing, undermine acquired skills and work subcultures. And the end of the Cold War, with the collapse of communism, eliminates the easy indentification of the external enemy, hampering the chances of bringing America together in a common cause. The age of information becomes the age of confusion, and thus the age of fundamental affirmation of traditional values and uncompromising rights. Bureaucratic, and sometimes violent, reactions by law-enforcement agencies to various forms of protest deepen the anger, sharpen the feelings, and seem to justify the call to arms, bringing the new American militia in direct confrontation with the emerging global order.

The Lamas of Apocalypse: Japan's *Aum Shinrikyo*[40]

The final goal of body techniques that Aum tries to develop by yoga and austerity is a mode of communication without any medium. Communication can be obtained by having resonance with others' bodies without relying on consciousness of identity as self, without using the medium of language.

Masachi Osawa, *Gendai*, October 1995[41]

---

[39] Stevens (1995).
[40] The analysis of *Aum Shinrikyo* presented here essentially reproduces the contribution to our joint study, and article, by Shujiro Yazawa, who conducted most of the research on *Aum*, although I also studied the movement, in cooperation with Yazawa, in Tokyo in 1995. Sources directly used in the analysis, besides reports in newspapers and magazines, are Aoyama (1991); Asahara (1994, 1995); *Vajrayana Sacca* (1994); Drew (1995); Fujita (1995); *Mainichi Shinbun* (1995); Miyadai (1995); Ohama (1995); Osawa (1995); Nakazawa et al. (1995); Shimazono (1995); Yazawa (forthcoming).
[41] Translated by Yazawa.

On March 20, 1995, an attack with sarin gas in three different trains on the Tokyo subway killed 12 people, injured over 5,000, and shook the foundations of the apparently stable Japanese society. The police, using information from a similar incident which had occurred in Matsumoto in June 1994, determined that the attack had been carried out by members of *Aum Shinrikyo*, a religious cult at the core of a network of business activities, political organizations, and paramilitary units. The ultimate goal of *Aum Shinrikyo*, according to its own discourse, was to survive the coming apocalypse, to save Japan, and eventually the world, from the war of extermination that would inevitably result from the competing efforts by Japanese corporations and American imperialism to establish a new world order and a united world government. To overcome Armageddon, *Aum* would prepare a new kind of human being, rooted in spirituality and self-improvement through meditation and exercise. Yet, to face the aggression of world powers that be, *Aum* had to defend itself by taking up the challenge of new weapons of extermination. The challenge came quickly indeed. The cult's founder and guru, Shoko Asahara, was arrested and put on trial (probably to be sentenced to death), along with the most prominent members of the cult. The cult itself continues to exist, albeit with a reduced constituency.

The debate over the origins, development, and goals of *Aum* went on for months in the Japanese media, and has not receded more than one and a half years later, at the time of writing. It prompted fundamental questions about the actual state of Japanese society. How could such acts be possible in one of the wealthiest, least unequal, safest, most ethnically homogeneous, and most culturally integrated societies in the world? Specially striking for the public was the fact that the cult had recruited particularly among scientists and engineers from some of the best Japanese universities. Coming in a period of political uncertainty, after the crisis of the LDP, Japan's governing party for almost five decades, the apparently senseless act was seen as a symptom. But a symptom of what? To understand a very complex development, with fundamental, but not so obvious, implications, we must reconstruct the evolution of the cult, starting with the biography of its founder, who played a crucial role in this development.

Asahara and the development of *Aum Shinrikyo*

Asahara was born blind in a poor family in Kumamoto Prefecture. He attended a special school for the blind, and, after completing his studies there, prepared for admission examinations into Tokyo University. His explicit project was to become Prime Minister. After failing the exam, he opened a pharmacy and specialized in the sale of traditional Chinese medicine. Some of these medicines were of questionable use, and his lack of a license eventually led to his arrest. After marrying and having a child, in 1977 he shifted his interest to religion. He educated himself in Sento, and tried to develop a spiritual health care method based on Taoism. The decisive change in his life came when he joined the Agon cult, a religious group preaching perfection through the practice of austerity.[42] Meditation, physical exercise, yoga, and esoteric Buddhism were essential practices of the group. Asahara combined Agon's teaching with his own ideas about creating a new religious world. In 1984, he opened a yoga school in Shibuya, Tokyo. At the same time, he established *Aum* as a corporation (*Aum* is a Sanskrit word meaning "deep wisdom"). He developed his yoga school's reputation by making claims in the media about his own supernatural powers, as shown by his ability to float in the air (a claim he backed up with photos showing himself in action, a first venture in special visual effects, which signaled *Aum*'s future emphasis on media technology). Stating that God had ordered him to build a utopia with a few elected ones, in 1985 the yoga master became a religious leader, and instructed his disciples at the school in search of perfection through the hard practice of austerity. In 1986 Asahara created the formal religious cult *Aum Shinsen*, with about 350 members. Most of them were inducted as priests, unlike other cults where only a small minority of members can devote themselves fully to the practice of austerity and meditation. This high ratio of priesthood was very important for the future of *Aum*, since it had to find substantial means of financial support for such a large number of priests. Thus, *Aum* requested donations of all assets from its recruits (sometimes by force), priced teachings and training seminars, and invested in various businesses. Among these business activities, it created a very profitable commercial chain of stores *(Mahaposha)*, selling personal computers at discount price, and specializing in distribution of pirate software. With the profits from these computer stores, *Aum* financed a number of eating and drinking outlets, and other miscellaneous businesses. In 1987, the name was changed to *Aum Shinrikyo* (the Japanese word for "truth"). A year later, as a step to utopia, *Aum* built its headquarters in a village in the foothills of Mount Fuji. In spite of some resistance from the authorities, it finally obtained recognition as a non-profit, tax-exempt, religious corporation. Having consolidated Aum's position, and with the support of about 10,000 members, Asahara decided to enter politics in order to transform society. In

---

[42] Austerity implies strenuous physical exercise and privation of food and bodily pleasure as a regular form of existence.

1990, he and 25 other *Aum* members ran for Congress but obtained almost no votes. They claimed their votes had been stolen. This political disappointment was a turning point for the ideology of *Aum*, which abandoned its attempts to participate in the political process. Future efforts would be directed toward confrontation with government. Shortly afterwards, an attempt to build a new hall for the cult in Naminomura was fiercely opposed by local residents, and, after a few incidents, *Aum* members were arrested. The media echoed rumors of kidnapping and extortions of former cult members. When a group of victims of *Aum* formed an association, their lawyer disappeared. The cult went into a paranoiac frenzy, feeling harassed by police, government, and the media.

In this context, Asahara started to emphasize the eschatological line of thinking that had been present in the cult's themes from its inception. Asahara, referring to the prophecies of Nostradamus, predicted that, around the year 2000, nuclear war between the US and the USSR would break out, and that, as a result, 90 percent of urban dwellers would die. Thus, the very best should prepare themselves to survive the disaster. To do so, hard physical exercise, austerity, and meditation, following the teachings of Asahara, would be needed in order to create a superhuman race. *Aum*'s meditation halls would be the birth places of a new civilization after Armageddon. Yet spiritual perfection would not be enough. The enemy would use all kinds of new weapons: nuclear, chemical, bacteriological. Therefore, *Aum*, as the last chance for humankind's survival, should be prepared for this terrible warfare at the End of Times. Consequently, *Aum* established several companies to buy and process materials for development of chemical and biological weapons. It imported one helicopter and several armored vehicles, bought on Russia's black market, and started to learn how to design and produce high-technology weapons, included laser-guided guns.[43]

In a logical development, in 1994, *Aum* decided to become a counter-state. It formed ministries and bureaux, mirroring the structure of the Japanese state, and appointed members to each ministry and agency, to constitute a shadow government, with Asahara at the top of this holy counter-state. The role of this organization would be to lead the cult and the few elected survivors in the final battle against the forces of evil, namely the united world government (dominated by multinational corporations) and its direct agents: American imperialists and Japanese police. In June 1994, a first experiment with nerve gas was carried out in Matsumoto, killing seven people. Police investigations of the cult, and reports in the media, prompted the

[43]   Drew (1995).

sense among cult members that confrontation was inevitable, and that the first episodes leading to the prophecy were taking place. The attack on Tokyo's subway, a few months later, propelled the cult, Japan, and maybe the world, into a new era of messianic critique potentially backed by weapons of mass extermination.

Aum's beliefs and methodology

The beliefs and teachings of *Aum Shinrikyo* are complex, and have been changing somewhat throughout the cult's evolution. Yet it is possible to reconstruct the essence of its vision and practice on the basis of available documents and reports. At the root of its purpose and method, *Aum* stresses the notion of deliverance (*gedatsu*), that is, according to Osawa, one of *Aum*'s best observers:

> Dissolving the integrity of the body as individual to overcome the locality of the body. Believers must transcend the boundary between the body and its external world by differentiating the body endlessly. By continual exercise, it is possible to reach the point where the body can be felt as fluid, gas, or wave of energy. The body tries to integrate itself as individual because we have self consciousness in the inner side of the integrated body. It is this inner side of the body that organizes the self. Therefore, to disintegrate our bodies to the extent that we feel our bodies as fluid or gas, means the disorganization of ourselves. This is deliverance.[44]

Deliverance means true freedom and happiness. Indeed, humans have lost their selves and become impure. The real world is in fact an illusion, and life as usually lived by people is full of burdens and pains. Realizing and accepting this harsh reality enables one to face death in truth. To reach this truth, through deliverance, *Aum* developed a technology of meditation and austerity (*Mahayana*), with precise indicators of the stage of perfection achieved by every believer at various stages.

However, for most followers, deliverance is uncertain at best. Thus, two additional elements provide coherence to *Aum*'s method and vision: on the one hand, faith in the guru's superpowers, guaranteeing salvation after a certain stage of perfection is achieved; on the other hand, a sense of urgency derived from the coming catastrophic crisis of civilization. In *Aum*'s view, there is a direct link between the end of the world and the salvation of believers, who are preparing for the apocalypse by acquiring supernatural powers. In this sense, *Aum*

---

[44]   Osawa (1995).

is at the same time a mystical cult and a practical corporation providing survival training for doomsday 2000 – at a price.

Aum and Japanese society

Most *Aum* priests were young university graduates. In 1995, 47.5 percent of its priests were in their twenties, and 28 percent in their thirties; 40 percent were women. Indeed, an explicit goal of *Aum* was "to solve gender differences" by changing "the inner world of gender." In the absence of a powerful feminist movement in Japan (as yet), *Aum* gained some influence among college-educated women frustrated by an extremely patriarchal society. A high proportion of the men were graduates in the natural sciences from distinguished universities.[45] *Aum*'s appeal to highly educated youth came as a shock to the Japanese public. According to Yazawa,[46] this appeal can be better understood by the alienation of Japanese youth, in the aftermath of the defeat of the powerful Japanese social movements of the 1960s. Instead of transformative social values, the "Information Society" was promised. But this promise fell short of cultural innovation and spiritual fulfillment. In a society with no mobilized social challengers, and without values of cultural transformation, a new generation has grown up since the 1970s in material affluence, but without spiritual meaning. It was seduced at the same time by technology and esotericism. Many *Aum* believers were people who could not find a place for their desires for change and meaningfulness in the bureaucratized structure of schools, administrations, and corporations, and were revolting against traditional, authoritarian family structures. They had no purpose in their lives, and not even enough physical space to express themselves in the congested conurbation of Japanese cities. The only thing left for them was their own bodies. For many of these youths, their desire was to live in a different world by using science and technology to help their bodies transcend natural and social limits. In Yazawa's concept, theirs was a desire based on the "informationalization of the body," meaning the transformation of human physical potential by the power of ideas, beliefs, and meditation. This is where *Aum*'s methodology of deliverance fitted particularly well. The promise of deliverance was that people could feel themselves and others at the same time. Community and belonging was restored, but as an expression of the self, through perfection and control of the body's own limits, not as a result of external imposition, enabling communication without a medium by directly connecting to other bodies. This new form of com-

---

[45]   *Mainichi Shinbun* (1995).
[46]   Castells et al. (1996); Yazawa (forthcoming).

munication was only considered to be possible among bodies that had already overcome their locality. Asahara's body, by having already escaped from his body's locality, would be the catalyst to induce the deliverance of others. As a result, a virtual community of communicating bodies was gradually formed, with Asahara as the sole center of this community.[47]

Some of these ideas and practices are not unusual in yoga and in Tibetan Buddhism. What was specific to *Aum*'s version of disembodied communication through yoga and meditation was, on the one hand, its technological implementation (for instance, through the extensive use of training videos, and of electronically stimulating devices), and, on the other hand, its political instrumentation. In some instances, experiments were carried out by means of electronic helmets attached to the followers' heads, to enable them to receive communication waves directly from the guru's brain (a little technological push to the theory of disembodied communication). Asahara's ideas developed finally into the identity of his self or "true self," in which the selves of all disciples were to be ultimately dissolved. Communication channels with the outside world were closed off, as it was declared the enemy, heading toward Armageddon. The inside network was structured in a hierarchical organization, in which communication came from the top, with no horizontal channels of communication among the believers. In this view, the outside world was unreal, and the virtual reality generated by a combination of technology and yoga techniques was the real world. The outside, unreal world was evolving toward its apocalypse. The inner, virtual reality, internally communicated world, was the fundamental reality, preparing itself for salvation.

In the latest stage of the discourse of *Aum*, a more precise social prediction took shape: future social change would be caused by a cycle of economic recession, then depression, followed by war and death. Natural disasters and economic depression would overtake Japan in the last years of the millennium. The reason: stepped up competition from other Asian countries using their comparative advantage of lower labor costs. To answer this challenge, Japan would develop its military industry and try to impose its will on Asia, in the interests of Japanese corporations striving to create a world government under the control of multinational corporations. In response, the United States would enter the war against Japan to protect its Asian vassals, and to advance its own project of world government. The war would linger on, and all kinds of high-technology weapons would be used. This would be a war of extermination, which could lead to the end of

[47]   Osawa (1995).

humankind. In this account, *Aum*'s vision reflected, in a distorted and schematic way, the fears of Japanese society about losing its competitive edge in the world economy, about a potential conflict with the United States, and about the catastrophic consequences of uncontrolled new technologies.

What distinguished *Aum* was its response to these threats. To be ready for such a war, and to survive it (as in some popular science fiction movies of the 1990s), would require both the rebirth of spirituality and the mastery of advanced weapons technology, particularly biological, chemical, and laser-guided weapons. As mentioned above, *Aum* did indeed try to acquire these weapons and hire scientists able to develop them in the United States, Israel, and Russia. While pursuing spiritual perfection, and uniting its members in a collective, spiritual body, *Aum* equipped itself to fight the survival war, and declared such a war in advance, against the supporters of the united world government looming on the horizon.

In a distorted way, *Aum*'s fears and ideas were similar to those found in many of the youth subcultures of Japan. According to Shinji Miyadai, two perceptions of the world could be found among them.[48] The first one was that of an "endless everyday life" without purpose, goals, or happiness. The second was that of possible commonality only in the case of a nuclear war that would force the survivors to unite. By building on both ideas – that is, by finding happiness in the inner self and preparing for the post-nuclear war commune – *Aum* directly connected with these expressions of cultural despair from youth alienated in an over-organized society. In this sense, *Aum* was not an act of collective madness, but the hyperbolic, amplified manifestation of educated rebels, manipulated by a messianic guru at the cross-roads between meditation and electronics, business and spirituality, informational politics and high-tech warfare. *Aum* appears to have been a horror caricature of Japanese Information Society, mirroring its government structure, its corporate behavior, and its worship of advanced technology mixed with traditional spiritualism. Perhaps the reason Japan became obsessed with *Aum* was because of the recognition of how truly Japanese this close-up vision of apocalypse was.

The Meaning of Insurgencies against the New Global Order

After analyzing three movements against globalization, in their practices, in their discourses, and in their contexts, I will venture their

---

[48]   Miyadai (1995).

comparison, seeking to draw conclusions for the broader analysis of social change in the network society. I will use my adaptation of Alain Touraine's typology as a way to read the movements in relation to the same analytical categories. Seen from this perspective, the three movements analyzed here coincide in the identification of their adversary: it is the new global order, designated by the *Zapatistas* as the conjunction of American imperialism and corrupt, illegitimate PRI government in NAFTA; incarnated by international institutions, most notably the United Nations, and the US federal government in the view of American militia; while for *Aum* the global threat comes from a unified world government representing the interests of multinational corporations, US imperialism and Japanese police. Thus, the three movements are primarily organized around their opposition to an adversary that is, by and large, the same: the agents of the new global order, seeking to establish a world government that will subdue the sovereignty of all countries and all people.

To such an enemy, each movement opposes a specific principle of identity, reflecting the sharp differences between the three societies where they come from: in the case of the *Zapatistas*, they see themselves as Indians and oppressed Mexicans fighting for their dignity, their rights, their land, and the Mexican nation; in the case of the militia, American citizens fighting for their sovereignty, and for their liberties, as expressed in the original, godly American Constitution. As for *Aum*, their identity principle is more complex: it is in fact their individual identity, expressed in their bodies, although such bodies

Chart 2.1   Structure of values and beliefs of insurgent movements against globalization

Movement	Identity	Adversary	Goal
Zapatistas	Oppressed, excluded Indians/Mexicans	Global capitalism (NAFTA), illegal PRI government	Dignity, democracy, land
American militia	Original American citizens	New world order, US federal government	Liberty and sovereignty of citizens and local communities
Aum Shinrikyo	Spiritual community of delivered bodies of believers	United world government, Japanese police	Survival of apocalypse

share each other in the guru's mind – it is the combination of physical individuality and reconstructed spiritual community. In each of the three cases, there is an appeal to authenticity in their identity principle, but with different manifestations: a historically rooted, broad community (the Indians of Mexico, as part of Mexicans); local/county communities of free citizens; and a spiritual community of individuals freed from dependence on their bodies. These identities are based on cultural specificity and on desire for control over their own destiny. And they are opposed to the global adversary on behalf of a higher societal goal, which in all three cases leads to integration between their specific identity and the well-being of society at large: Mexico, America, the surviving Humankind. Yet, this integration is sought through the fulfillment of different values for each movement: social justice and democracy for all Mexicans; individual freedom from government domination for all American citizens; and transcendence of materiality through spiritual liberation in the case of *Aum*. These societal goals, however, are the weakest element in each one of the three movements: they are primarily identity-based mobilizations in reaction to a clearly identified adversary. They are reactive, and defensive, rather than purveyors of a societal project, even if they do propose visions of an alternative society. Chart 2.1 lists the elements defining each movement.

The powerful impact of each of these movements has come, to a large extent, from their media presence and from their effective use of information technology. Media attention is sought, or found, by performing in the French anarchist tradition, briefly revived in May 1968, of *l'action exemplaire*: a spectacular action is undertaken which, by its powerful appeal, even through sacrifice, calls people's attention to the movement's claims, and is ultimately intended to wake up the masses, manipulated by propaganda and subdued by repression. Forcing a debate on their claims, and inducing people to participate, movements expect to put pressure on governments and institutions, reversing the course of submission to the new world order.

This is why weapons are essential in the three movements, not as a goal, but as a sign of freedom, and as an event-trigger device, calling media attention. This media-oriented strategy was particularly explicit, and skillfully executed, in the case of the *Zapatistas*, who tried carefully to minimize violence and to work via the media and the Internet to reach out to the world. But the paramilitary theatrics of the militia, and the deliberate exploitation of violent tactics, or the threat of it, to attract media attention are also a key component of American Patriots. Even *Aum*, distrustful of the media, did pay considerable attention to debates on television, and to press reports, dedicating some of its best members to such tasks. And its gas attacks seem to have had the double purpose of verifying the doomsday prophecy, and of diffusing in the world their warning, through the media. It would seem that the new protest movements cast their messages and project their claims in the form of symbolic politics characteristic of informational society (see chapter 6). Their media skills are fundamental fighting tools, while their manifestos and their weapons are means to create an event worth reporting.

New communication technologies are fundamental for these movements to exist: indeed, they are their organizational infrastructure. Without the Internet, Fax, and alternative media, the Patriots would not be an influential network, but a disconnected, powerless series of reactions. Without the communication capacity enabling the *Zapatistas* to reach urban Mexico, and the world, in real time, they may have remained an isolated, localized guerrilla force, as many of those still fighting in Latin America. *Aum* did not make much use of the Internet, simply because the Internet was hardly present in Japan in the early 1990s. But they did use extensively Fax, and video, and computers, as crucial tools in building a highly controlled, yet decentralized organizational network. Besides, they were trying a technological breakthrough (admittedly esoteric) by developing electronically stimulated, direct communication from brain to brain. The revolutionary cells of the information age are built on flows of electrons.

Alongside their similarity, the three movements also display profound differences, linked to their historical/cultural origins, and to the level of technological development of their societies. A sharp distinction must be drawn between the articulate political project of the *Zapatistas*, the confusion and paranoia of most militia groups, and the apocalyptic logic of *Aum*. This also relates to the difference between the eschatological component in both the militia and *Aum*, and the absence of such views of the End of Time in the *Zapatistas*. Thus, specific social contexts, cultures, historical processes, and levels of political consciousness do determine substantial differences in the processes of insurgency, even triggered by a similar cause.

The three movements have interacted closely with the political processes of the societies in which they take place. The *Zapatistas* deliberately launched their attack in the year of the Mexican presidential election, and they played a fundamental role in deepening the contradictions within the PRI, and in forcing the opening up of the Mexican political system (see chapter 5). *Aum* surged during a period when, in 1993, the formerly stable Japanese political system was crumbling down. By voicing, spectacularly, the alienation of a new generation of professionals and scientists, *Aum* amplified and accelerated the debate in Japan about the social model of the post-hypergrowth period, in which material affluence had been reached and threats of foreign domination had been superseded. After decades of accelerated modernization by waves of state intervention and national mobilization, Japan had to confront itself as a society, after the public realization that alienation, violence, and terrorism, could also be suffered and performed by Japanese against Japanese.

The American militia also grew in a context of widespread political disaffection and anti-government sentiment in the United States, a sentiment that was also expressed in electoral politics through the Republican Party's exploitation of the "neo-conservative revolution" (see chapter 5). A significant part of this new conservative vote has its origin in Christian fundamentalism, and other sectors of opinion related to the Patriot movement, as it manifested itself in the Republican congressional landslide victory in 1994, and in the relative impact of the Buchanan campaign during the Republican presidential primaries of 1996. There is indeed a loose connection between the deterioration of living conditions in America, the erosion of traditional party politics, the rise of right-wing libertarianism and populism within mainstream politics, the backlash of traditional values against processes of social change and family disintegration, and the emergence of the Patriot movement. These linkages are crucial to understanding the new relationship between American society and its political system.[49]

Thus, new social movements, in their diversity, react against globalization, and against its political agents, and act upon the continuing process of informationalization by changing the cultural codes at the root of new social institutions. In this sense, they surge from the depths of historically exhausted social forms, but decisively affect, in a complex pattern, the society in the making.

Conclusion: the Challenge to Globalization

The social movements I have analyzed in this chapter are very different. And yet, under different forms, reflecting their diverse social and cultural roots, they all challenge current processes of globalization, on behalf of their constructed identities, in some instances claiming to represent the interests of their country, or of humankind, as well.

The movements I have studied, in this and other chapters of this volume, are not the only ones opposing the social, economic, cultural,

[49]   Balz and Brownstein (1996).

and environmental consequences of globalization. In other areas of the world, for instance in Europe, similar challenges rise against capitalist restructuring, and against the imposition of new rules in the name of global competition, on the basis of the labor movement. For instance, the French strike of December 1995 was a powerful manifestation of such opposition, in the most classic French ritual of labor unions leading workers and students in the streets on behalf of the nation. Opinion polls showed strong support for the strike among the population at large, in spite of the daily inconvenience caused by the lack of public transportation. Yet, since there is an excellent sociological analysis available on this movement,[50] whose main lines of interpretation I share, I refer the reader to this analysis in order to diversify even further the cross-cultural picture of refusal of the process of globalization. These, and other movements spreading throughout the world, are ending the neo-liberal fantasy of creating a new global economy independent of society by using computer architecture. The grand exclusionary scheme (explicit or implicit) of concentrating information, production, and markets in a valuable segment of population, disposing of the rest in different forms, more or less humane according to each society's temper, is triggering, in Touraine's expression, a *"grand refus."* But the transformation of this rejection into the reconstruction of new forms of social control over new forms of capitalism, globalized and informationalized, requires the processing of social movements' demands by the political system and the institutions of the state. The ability, or inability, of the state to cope with the conflicting logics of global capitalism, identity-based social movements, and defensive movements from workers and consumers, will largely condition the future of society in the twenty-first century. Yet, before examining the dynamics of the state in the information age, we must analyze the recent development of different kinds of powerful social movements that are proactive rather than reactive: environmentalism and feminism.

[50] Touraine et al. (1996).

— 3 —

The Greening of the Self: the Environmental Movement

The Green approach to politics is a kind of celebration. We recognize that each of us is part of the world's problems, and we are also part of the solution. The dangers and potentials for healing are not just outside us. We begin to work exactly where we are. There is no need to wait until conditions become ideal. We can simplify our lives and live in ways that affirm ecological and human values. Better conditions will come because we have begun . . . It can therefore be said that the primary goal of Green politics is an inner revolution, "the greening of the self."

Petra Kelly, *Thinking Green*[1]

If we are to appraise social movements by their historical productivity, namely, by their impact on cultural values and society's institutions, the environmental movement of the last quarter of this century has earned a distinctive place in the landscape of human adventure. In the 1990s, 80 percent of Americans, and over two-thirds of Europeans consider themselves environmentalists; party and candidates can hardly be elected to office without "greening" their platform; governments and international institutions alike multiply programs, special agencies, and legislation to protect nature, improve the quality of life and, ultimately, save the Earth in the long term and ourselves in the short term. Corporations, including some notorious polluters, have included environmentalism in their public relations agenda, as well as among their most promising new markets. And throughout the globe, the old, simplistic opposition between development for the poor and conservation for the rich has been transformed into a multi-layered debate over the actual content of sustainable development for each country, city, and region. To be sure, most of our funda-

---

[1] *In Essays by Petra Kelly (1947–1992)* (Kelly, 1994: 39–40). In this quote, she refers to Joanna Macy's "the greening of the self" (Macy, 1991).

fundamental problems concerning the environment remain, since their treatment requires a transformation of modes of production and consumption, as well as of our social organization and personal lives. Global warming looms as a lethal threat, the rain forest still burns, toxic chemicals are deeply into the food chain, a sea of poverty denies life, and governments play games with people's health, as exemplified by Major's madness with British cows. Yet, the fact that all these issues, and many others, are in the public debate, and that a growing awareness has emerged of their interdependent, global character, creates the foundation for their treatment, and, maybe, for a reorientation of institutions and policies toward an environmentally responsible socioeconomic system. The multifaceted environmental movement that emerged from the late 1960s in most of the world, with its strong points in the United States and Northern Europe, is to a large extent at the root of a dramatic reversal in the ways in which we think about the relationship between economy, society, and nature, thus inducing a new culture.[2]

It is somewhat arbitrary, however, to speak of the environmental movement, since it is so diverse in its composition, and varies so much in its expressions from country to country, and between cultures. Thus, before assessing its transformative potential, I will attempt a typological differentiation of various components of environmentalism, and use examples for each type, to bring the argument down to earth. Then, I shall proceed to a broader elaboration on the relationship between environmentalists' themes, and fundamental dimensions on which structural transformation takes place in our society: the struggles over the role of science and technology, over the control of space and time, and over the construction of new identities. Having characterized the environmental movements in their social diversity and in their cultural sharing, I shall analyze their means and ways of acting on society at large, thus exploring the issue of their institutionalization, and their relationship to the state. Finally, consideration will be given to the growing linkage between environmental movements and social struggles, both locally and globally, along the increasingly popular perspective of environmental justice.

[2]   For an overview of the environmental movement, see (among other sources) Holliman (1990); Gottlieb (1993); Kaminiecki (1993); Shabecoff (1993); Dalton (1994); Alley et al. (1995); Diani (1995); Brulle (1996); Wapner (1996).

The Creative Cacophony of Environmentalism: a Typology

Collective action, politics, and discourses grouped under the name of environmentalism are so diverse as to challenge the idea of a movement. And, yet, I argue that it is precisely this cacophony of theory and practice that characterizes environmentalism as a new form of decentralized, multiform, network-oriented, pervasive social movement. Besides, as I will try to show, there are some fundamental themes that run across most, if not all, environmentally related collective action. However, for the sake of clarity, it seems helpful to proceed in the analysis of this movement on the basis of one distinction and one typology.

The distinction is between environmentalism and ecology. By *environmentalism* I refer to all forms of collective behavior that, in their discourse and in their practice, aim at correcting destructive forms of relationship between human action and its natural environment, in opposition to the prevailing structural and institutional logic. By *ecology*, in my sociological approach, I understand a set of beliefs,

Chart 3.1	Typology of Environmental Movements		
Type (Example)	*Identity*	*Adversary*	*Goal*
Conservation of nature (Group of Ten, USA)	Nature lovers	Uncontrolled development	Wilderness
Defense of own space (Not in my Back Yard)	Local community	Polluters	Quality of life/health
Counter-culture, deep ecology (Earth first!, ecofeminism)	The green self	Industrialism, technocracy, and patriarchalism	Ecotopia
Save the planet (Greenpeace)	Internationalist eco-warriors	Unfettered global development	Sustainability
Green politics (*Die Grünen*)	Concerned citizens	Political establishment	Counter-power

theories, and projects that consider humankind as a component of a broader ecosystem and wish to maintain the system's balance in a dynamic, evolutionary perspective. In my view, environmentalism is ecology in practice, and ecology is environmentalism in theory, but in the following pages I will restrict the use of the term "ecology" to explicit, conscious manifestations of this holistic, evolutionary perspective.

As for the typology, I shall again call upon Alain Touraine's useful characterization of social movements, as presented in chapter 2, to differentiate five major varieties of environmental movement, *as they have manifested themselves in observed practices* in the past two decades, at the international level. I suggest that this typology has general value, although most of the examples are drawn from North American and German experiences because they are the most developed environmental movements in the world, and because I had easier access to this information. Please accept the usual disclaimer about the inevitable reductionism of this, and all typologies, which I hope will be compensated for by examples that will bring the blood and flesh of actual movements into this somewhat abstract characterization.

To undertake our brief journey across the kaleidoscope of environmentalism by means of the proposed typology, you need a map. Chart 3.1 provides it, and requires some explanation. Each type is defined, analytically, by a specific combination of the three characteristics defining a social movement: *identity*, *adversary*, and *goal*. For each type, I identify the precise content of the three characteristics, resulting from observation, using several sources, to which I refer. Accordingly, I give a name to each type, and provide examples of movements that best fit each type. Naturally, in any given movement or organization there may be a mixture of characteristics, but I select, for analytical purposes, those movements that seem to be closer to the ideal type in their actual practice and discourse. After looking at Chart 3.1, you are invited to a brief description of each one of the examples that illustrate the five types, so that distinct voices of the movement can be heard through its cacophony.

The *conservation of nature*, under its different forms, was at the origin of the environmentalist movement in America, as enacted by organizations such as the Sierra Club (founded in San Francisco in 1891 by John Muir), the Audubon Society, or the Wilderness Society.[3] In the early 1980s, old and new mainstream environmental organizations came together in an alliance, known as the Group of Ten, that included, besides the above-cited organizations, the National Parks

[3]   Allen (1987); Scarce (1990); Gottlieb (1993); Shabecoff (1993).

and Conservation Association, the National Wildlife Federation, the Natural Resources Defense Council, Izaak Walton League, Defenders of Wildlife, Environmental Defense Fund, and the Environmental Policy Institute. In spite of differences in approach and in their specific field of intervention, what brings together these organizations, and many others created along similar lines, is their pragmatic defense of conservationist causes through the institutional system. In the words of Michael McCloskey, Sierra Club Chairman, their approach can be characterized as "muddling through": "We come out of a mountaineering tradition where you first decide that you're going to climb the mountain. You have a notion of a general route, but you find handholds and the footholds as you go along and you have to adapt and keep changing."[4] Their summit to be climbed is the preservation of wilderness, in its different forms, within reasonable parameters of what can be achieved in the present economic and institutional system. Their adversaries are uncontrolled development, and unresponsive bureaucracies such as the US Bureau of Reclamation, not caring to protect our natural preserve. They define themselves as nature lovers, and appeal to this feeling in all of us, regardless of social differences. They work through and by the institutions, using lobbying very often with great skill and political muscle. They rely on widespread popular support, as well as on donations from well-wishing, wealthy elites, and from corporations. Some organizations, such as the Sierra Club, are very large (about 600,000 members) and are organized in local chapters, whose actions and ideologies vary considerably, and do not always fit with the image of "mainstream environmentalism." Most others, such as the Environmental Defense Fund, focus on lobbying, analyzing, and diffusing information. They often practice coalition politics, but they are careful not to be carried away from their environmental focus, distrusting radical ideologies and spectacular action out of step with the majority of public opinion. However, it would be a mistake to oppose mainstream conservationists to the true, radical environmentalists. For instance, one of the historic leaders of the Sierra Club, David Brower, became a source of inspiration for radical environmentalists. Reciprocally, Dave Foreman, from Earth First!, was, in 1996, on the Board of Directors of the Sierra Club. There is a great deal of osmosis in the relationships between conservationists and radical ecologists, as ideologies tend to take second place to their shared concern about the relentless, multiform destruction of nature. This, in spite of sharp debates and conflicts within a large, diversified movement.

---

[4]   Quoted in Scarce (1990: 15).

The *mobilization of local communities in defense of their space*, against intrusion of undesirable uses, constitutes the fastest-growing form of environmental action, and the one that perhaps most directly links people's immediate concerns to broader issues of environmental deterioration.[5] Often labeled, somewhat maliciously, the *"Not in my Back Yard" movement*, it developed in the United States first of all under the form of the toxics movement, originated in 1978 during the infamous Love Canal incident of industrial toxic waste dumping in Niagara Falls, New York. Lois Gibbs, the homeowner who gained notoriety because of her fight to defend the health of her son, as well as the value of her home, went on to establish, in 1981, the Citizen's Clearinghouse for Hazardous Wastes. According to the Clearinghouse's counting, in 1984 there were 600 local groups fighting against toxic dumping in the United States, which increased to 4,687 in 1988. Over time, communities mobilized also against freeway construction, excessive development, and location of hazardous facilities in their proximity. While the movement is local, it is not necessarily localistic, since it often affirms residents' right to the quality of their life in opposition to business or bureaucratic interests. To be sure, life in society is made up of trade-offs among people themselves, as residents, workers, consumers, commuters, and travelers. But what is questioned by these movements is, on the one hand, the bias of location of undesirable materials or activities toward low-income communities and minority inhabited areas; on the other hand, the lack of transparency and participation in decision-making about the uses of space. Thus, citizens call for extended local democracy, for responsible city planning, and for fairness in sharing the burdens of urban/industrial development, while avoiding exposure to hazardous dumping or utilities. As Epstein concludes in her analysis of the movement:

> The demand of the toxics/environmental justice movement for a state that has more power to regulate corporations, a state that is accountable to the public rather than the corporations, seems entirely appropriate, and possibly a basis for a broader demand that state power over corporations be reasserted and expanded, and that state power be exercised on behalf of public welfare and especially the welfare of those who are most vulnerable.[6]

In other instances, in middle-class suburbs, residents' mobilizations were more focused on preserving their status quo against non-desired development. Yet, regardless of their class content, all forms of protest

---

[5] Gottlieb (1993); Szasz (1994); Epstein (1995).
[6] Epstein (1995: 20).

aimed at establishing control over the living environment on behalf of the local community, and in this sense, defensive local mobilizations are certainly a major component of broader environmental movement.

Environmentalism has also nurtured some of the counter-cultures that sprang from the 1960s and 1970s movements. By counter-culture, I understand the deliberate attempt to live according to norms different, and to some extent contradictory, from those institutionally enforced by society, and to oppose those institutions on the ground of alternative principles and beliefs. Some of the most powerful counter-cultural currents in our societies express themselves under the form of abiding only by the laws of nature, and thus affirming the priority of respect for nature over any other human institution. This is why I think it makes sense to include under the notion of *counter-cultural environmentalism* expressions as apparently distinct as radical environmentalists (such as *Earth First!* or the *Sea Shepherds*), the Animal Liberation movement, and ecofeminism.[7] In fact, in spite of their diversity and lack of coordination, most of these movements share the ideas of "deep ecology" thinkers, as represented, for instance, by Norwegian writer Arne Naess. According to Arne Naess and George Sessions, the basic principles of "deep ecology" are:

(1) The well-being and flourishing of human and non-human Life on Earth have value in themselves. These values are independent of the usefulness of the non-human world for human purposes. (2) Richness and diversity of life forms contribute to the realization of these values and are also values in themselves. (3) Humans have no right to reduce this richness and diversity except to satisfy vital needs. (4) The flourishing of human life and cultures is compatible with a substantial decrease of the human population. The flourishing of non-human life requires such a decrease. (5) Present human interference with the non-human world is excessive, and the situation is rapidly worsening. (6) Policies must therefore be changed. These policies affect basic economic, technological, and ideological structures. The resulting state of affairs will be deeply different from the present. (7) The ideological change is mainly that of appreciating life quality (dwelling in situations of inherent value) rather than adhering to an increasingly high standard of living. There will be profound awareness of the difference between big and great. (8) Those who subscribe to the foregoing points have an

---

[7]   For sources, see Adler (1979); Spretnak (1982); Manes (1990); Scarce (1990); Davis (1991); Dobson (1991); Epstein (1991); Moog (1995).

obligation directly or indirectly to try to implement the necessary changes.[8]

To respond to such an obligation, in the late 1970s a number of radical ecologists, led by David Foreman, an ex-Marine turned eco-warrior, created in New Mexico and Arizona *Earth First!*, an uncompromising movement that engaged in civil disobedience and even "ecotage" against dam construction, logging, and other aggressions to nature, thus facing prosecution and jail. The movement, and a number of other organizations that followed suit, were completely decentralized, formed by autonomous "tribes," that would meet periodically, according to the rites and dates of Native American Indians, and decide their own actions. Deep ecology was the ideological foundation of the movement, and it figures prominently in *The Earth First! Reader*, published with a foreword by David Foreman.[9] But equally, if not more, influential was Abbey's novel *The Monkey Wrench Gang*, about a counter-cultural group of eco-guerrillas, who became role models for many radical ecologists. Indeed, "monkeywrenching" became a synonym for eco-sabotage. In the 1990s, the animal liberation movement, focusing on outright opposition to experimentation with animals, seems to be the most militant wing of ecological fundamentalism.

Ecofeminism is clearly distant from the "macho-tactics" of some of these movements. And yet, ecofeminists share the principle of absolute respect for nature as the foundation of liberation from both patriarchalism and industrialism. They see women as victims of the same patriarchal violence that is inflicted upon nature. And so, the restoration of natural rights is inseparable from women's liberation. In the words of Judith Plant:

> Historically, women have had no real power in the outside world, no place in decision-making. Intellectual life, the work of the mind, has traditionally not been accessible to women. Women have been generally passive, as has been nature. Today, however, ecology speaks for the earth, for the "other" in human/environmental relations. And ecofeminism, by speaking for the original others, seeks to understand the interconnected roots of all domination, and ways to resist to change.[10]

Some ecofeminists were also inspired by Carolyn Merchant's controversial historical reconstruction, going back to prehistoric, natural

---

[8] Naess and Sessions (1984), reproduced in Davis (1991: 157–8).
[9] Davis (1991).
[10] Plant (1991:101).

societies, free of male domination, a matriarchal Golden Age, where there was harmony between nature and culture, and where both men and women worshipped nature in the form of the goddess.[11] There has also been, particularly during the 1970s, an interesting connection between environmentalism, spiritual feminism, and neo-paganism, sometimes expressed in ecofeminist and non-violent direct action militancy by witches belonging to the craft.[12]

Thus, through a variety of forms, from eco-guerrilla tactics, to spiritualism, going through deep ecology and ecofeminism, radical ecologists link up environmental action and cultural revolution, broadening the scope of an all-encompassing environmental movement, in their construction of *ecotopia*.

Greenpeace is the world's largest environmental organization, and probably the one that has most popularized global environmental issues, by its media-oriented, non-violent direct actions.[13] Founded in Vancouver in 1971, around an anti-nuclear protest off the coast of Alaska, and later headquartered in Amsterdam, it has grown into a transnational, networked organization that, as of 1994, had 6 million members worldwide and annual revenues in excess of $100 million. Its highly distinctive profile as an environmental movement derives from three major components. First, a sense of urgency regarding the imminent demise of life on the planet, inspired by a North American Indian legend: "When the earth is sick and the animals have disappeared, there will come a tribe of peoples from all creeds, colours and cultures who believe in deeds not words and who will restore the Earth to its former beauty. The tribe will be called 'Warriors of Rainbow.'"[14] Secondly, a Quaker-inspired attitude of bearing witness, both as a principle for action, and as a strategy of communication. Thirdly, a business-like, pragmatic attitude, largely influenced by Greenpeace's historic leader and chairman of the board, David McTaggart, "to get things done." No time for philosophical discussions: key issues must be identified by using knowledge and investigative techniques throughout the planet; specific campaigns must be organized on visible targets; spectacular actions geared toward media attention will follow, thus raising a given issue in the public eye, and forcing companies, governments, and international institutions to take action or face further unwarranted publicity. Greenpeace is at the same time a highly centralized organization, and

---

[11]   Merchant (1980); see also Spretnak (1982); Moog (1995).
[12]   Adler (1979); Epstein (1991).
[13]   Hunter (1979); Eyerman and Jamison (1989); DeMont (1991); Horton (1991); Ostertag (1991); Melchett (1995); Wapner (1995, 1996).
[14]   Greenpeace Environmental Fund, cited in Eyerman and Jamison (1989: 110).

a globally decentralized network. It is controlled by a council of country's representatives, a small executive board, and regional trustees for North America, Latin America, Europe, and the Pacific. Its resources are organized in campaigns, each one of them sub-divided by issues. In the mid-1990s, major campaigns were: toxic substances, energy and atmosphere, nuclear issues, and ocean/terrestrial ecology. Offices in 30 countries in the world serve to co-ordinate global campaigns, and raise funds and support, on a national/local basis, but most of the action aims at a global impact since main environmental problems are global. Greenpeace sees as its adversary a model of development characterized by a lack of concern with its consequences on life on the planet. Accordingly, it mobilizes to enforce the principle of environmental sustainability as the over-arching principle to which all other policies and activities must be subordinated. Because of the importance of their mission, the "rainbow warriors" are not inclined to engage in debates with other environmental groups, and do not indulge in counter-culture, regard-less of individual variation in the attitudes of their huge membership. They are resolutely internationalists, and see the nation-state as the major obstacle to accomplishing control over currently unfettered, destructive development. They are at war against an eco-suicidal model of development, and they aim to deliver immediate results on each front of action, from converting the German refrigeration industry to "green-freeze" technology, thus helping to protect the ozone layer, to influencing the restriction of whaling, and the creation of a whales sanctuary in Antarctica. The "rainbow warriors" are at the crossroads of science for life, global networking, communication technology, and intergenerational solidarity.

Green politics does not appear, at first sight, to be a type of movement by itself but, rather, a specific strategy, namely entering the realm of electoral politics on behalf of environmentalism. Yet, a close up of the most important example of green politics, *Die Grünen*, clearly shows that, originally, it was not politics as usual.[15] The German Green party, constituted on January 13, 1980, on the basis of a coalition of grass-roots movements, is not strictly speaking an environmental movement, even if it has probably been more effective in advancing the environmental cause in Germany than any other European move-ment in its country. The major force underlying its formation was the Citizen Initiatives of the late 1970s, mainly organized around the peace and anti-nuclear mobilizations. It uniquely brought

[15] See, among an ocean of sources on the German Green party, Langguth (1984); Hulsberg (1988); Wiesenthal (1993); Scharf (1994); and, particularly, Poguntke (1993) and Frankland (1995).

together veterans of the 1960s movements with feminists who discovered themselves as such by reflecting precisely on the sexism of 1960s revolutionaries, and with youth and educated middle classes concerned with peace, nuclear power, the environment (the forest disease, *waldsterben*), the state of the world, individual freedom, and grassroots democracy.

The creation and rapid success of the Greens (they entered the national parliament in 1983) stemmed from very exceptional circumstances. First of all, there were really no political expressions for social protest in Germany beyond the three main parties that had alternated in power, and even formed a coalition in the 1960s: in 1976, over 99 percent of the vote went to the three parties (Christian Democrats, Social Democrats, and Liberals). Thus, there was a potential disaffected vote, particularly among the youth, waiting for the possibility of expressing itself. Financial political scandals (the Flick affair) had rocked the reputation of all political parties and suggested their reliance on industry's contributions. Furthermore, what political scientists call the "political opportunity structure" supported the strategy of forming a party, and keeping unity among its constituents: among other elements, significant government funds were made available to the movement, and the German electoral law requiring at least 5 percent of the national vote to enter parliament disciplined the otherwise fractious Greens. Most Green voters were young, students, teachers, or members of other categories distant from industrial production, either unemployed (but supported by government), or working for the government. Their agenda included ecology, peace, defense of liberties, protection of minorities and immigrants, feminism, and participatory democracy. Two-thirds of Green party leaders were active participants in various social movements in the 1980s. Indeed, *Die Grünen* presented themselves, in Petra Kelly's words, as an "anti-party party," aimed at "politics based on a new understanding of power, a 'counter-power' that is natural and common to all, to be shared by all, and used by all for all."[16] Accordingly, they rotated representatives elected to office, and took most of the decisions in assemblies, following the anarchist tradition that inspired the Greens more than the Greens would accept. The acid test of real politics by and large dissolved these experiments after a few years, particularly after the 1990 electoral débâcle, mainly motivated by the Greens' total misunderstanding of the relevance of German unification, in an attitude coherent with their opposition to nationalism. The latent conflict between the *realos* (pragmatic leaders trying to advance the Green agenda through institutions) and the

---

[16]   Kelly (1994: 37).

fundis (loyal to the basic principles of grassroots democracy and ecologism) exploded into the open in 1991, leaving an alliance of centrists and pragmatics in control of the party. Reoriented, and reorganized, the German Green party recovered its strength in the 1990s, entered Parliament again, and won strong positions in regional and local governments, particularly in Berlin, Frankfurt, Bremen, and Hamburg, sometimes governing in alliance with the Social Democrats. Yet, it was not the same party. That is, it had indeed become a political party. Besides, this party had no longer the monopoly of environmental agenda since the Social Democrats, and even the Liberals, became much more open to new ideas put forward by the social movements. Furthermore, Germany in the 1990s was a very different country. There was no danger of war, but of economic decay. Widespread youth unemployment, and the retrenchment of the welfare state became more pressing issues for the "greying" green voters than cultural revolution. The murder of Petra Kelly in 1992, probably by her male companion, who then committed suicide, struck a dramatic chord, suggesting the limits of escaping society in everyday life while leaving untouched fundamental economic, political, and psychological structures. However, through green politics, the Green party became consolidated as the consistent left of *fin-de-siècle* Germany, and the 1970s rebellious generation still kept most of their values when ageing, and transmitted them to their children through the way they lived their lives. Thus, a very different Germany emerged from the green politics experiment, both culturally and politically. But the impossibility of integrating party and movement without inducing either totalitarianism (Leninism), or reformism at the expense of the movement (social democracy), received another historical confirmation as the iron law of social change.

The Meaning of Greening: Societal Issues and the Ecologists' Challenge

The conservation of nature, the search for environmental quality, and an ecological approach to life are nineteenth-century ideas that, in their distinct expression, remained for a long time confined to enlightened elites of dominant countries.[17] Often they were the preserve of a gentry overwhelmed by industrialization, as for the origins of the Audubon Society in the United States. In other instances, a communal, utopian component was the nest of early political ecologists, as in the case of Kropotkin, that linked for ever

[17]   Bramwell (1989, 1994).

anarchism and ecology, in a tradition best represented in our time by Murray Bookchin. But in all cases, and for almost one century, it remained a restricted intellectual trend, aimed primarily at influencing the consciousness of powerful individuals, who would foster conservationist legislation or donate their wealth to the good cause of nature. Even when social alliances were forged (for example, between Robert Marshall and Catherine Bauer in the United States in the 1930s), their policy outcome was packaged in a way in which economic and social welfare concerns were paramount.[18] Although there were influential, courageous pioneers, such as Alice Hamilton and Rachel Carson in the United States, it was only in the late 1960s that, in the United States, in Germany, in Western Europe, then rapidly diffusing to the entire world, North and South, West and East, a mass movement emerged, both at the grassroots and in public opinion. Why so? Why did ecological ideas suddenly catch fire in the planet's dried prairies of senselessness? I propose the hypothesis that there is a direct correspondence between the themes put forward by the environmental movement and the fundamental dimensions of the new social structure, the network society, emerging from the 1970s onwards: science and technology as the basic means and goals of economy and society; the transformation of space; the transformation of time; and the domination of cultural identity by abstract, global flows of wealth, power, and information constructing real virtuality through media networks. To be sure, in the chaotic universe of environmentalism we can find all these themes and, at the same time, none of them in specific cases. However, I contend that there is an implicit, coherent ecological discourse that cuts across various political orientations and social origins within the movement, and that provides the framework from which different themes are emphasized at different moments and for different purposes.[19] There are, naturally, sharp conflicts and strong disagreements in and between components of the environmental movement. Yet, these disagreements are more frequently about tactics, priorities, and language, than about the basic thrust in linking up the defense of specific environments to new human values. At the risk of oversimplification, I will synthesize the main lines of discourse present in the environmental movement in four major themes.

[18]   Gottlieb (1993).
[19]   For evidence of the presence, and relevance, of these themes in the environmental movements of several countries, see Dickens (1990); Dobson (1990); Scarce (1990); Epstein (1991); Zisk (1992); Coleman and Coleman (1993); Gottlieb (1993); Shabecoff (1993); Bramwell (1994); Porrit (1994); Riechmann and Fernandez Buey (1994); Moog (1995).

First, *an ambiguous, deep connection with science and technology.* As Bramwell writes: "the development of Green ideas was the revolt of science against science that occurred towards the end of the 19th century in Europe and North America."[20] This revolt intensified and diffused, in the 1970s, simultaneously with the information technology revolution, and with the extraordinary development of biological knowledge through computer modeling, that took place in the aftermath. Indeed, science and technology play a fundamental, albeit contradictory role in the environmental movement. On the one hand, there is a profound distrust of the goodness of advanced technology, leading in some extreme manifestations to neo-Luddite ideologies, as represented by Kirpatrick Sale. On the other hand, the movement largely relies on gathering, analyzing, interpreting, and diffusing scientific information about the interaction between man-made artifacts and the environment, sometimes with a high degree of sophistication. Major environmental organizations usually have scientists on their staff, and in most countries there is a tight connection between scientists and academics, and environmental activists.

Environmentalism is a science-based movement. Sometimes it is bad science, but it none the less pretends to know what happens to nature, and to humans, revealing the truth hidden by vested interests of industrialism, capitalism, technocracy, and bureaucracy. While criticizing the domination of life by science, ecologists use science to oppose science on behalf of life. The advocated principle is not the negation of knowledge, but superior knowledge: the wisdom of a holistic vision, able to reach beyond piecemeal approaches and short-sighted strategies geared toward the satisfaction of basic instincts. In this sense, environmentalism aims at retaking social control over the products of the human mind before science and technology take on a life of their own, with machines finally imposing their will on us, and on nature, a humankind's ancestral fear.

Struggles over structural transformation are tantamount to fighting for historical redefinition of the two fundamental, material expressions of society: space and time. And, indeed, *control over space, and the emphasis on locality* is another major, recurrent theme of various components of the environmental movement. I proposed, in volume I, chapter 6, the idea of a fundamental opposition emerging in the network society between two spatial logics, that of the space of flows and that of the space of places. The space of flows organizes the simultaneity of social practices at a distance, by means of telecommunications and information systems. The space of places privileges social interaction and institutional organization on the basis of physical contiguity.

---

[20]   Bramwell (1994: vii).

What is distinctive of new social structure, the network society, is that most dominant processes, concentrating power, wealth, and information, are organized in the space of flows. Most human experience, and meaning, are still locally based. The disjunction between the two spatial logics is a fundamental mechanism of domination in our societies, because it shifts the core economic, symbolic, and political processes away from the realm where social meaning can be constructed and political control can be exercised. Thus, the emphasis of ecologists on locality, and on the control by people of their living spaces, is a challenge to a basic lever of the new power system. Even in the most defensive expressions, such as in the struggles labeled "Not in my Back Yard," to assert the priority of local living over the uses of a given space by "outside interests," such as companies dumping toxics or airports extending their runways, bears the profound meaning of denying abstract priorities of technical or economic interests over actual experiences of actual uses by actual people. What is challenged by environmental localism is the loss of connection between these different functions or interests under the principle of mediated representation by abstract, technical rationality exercised by uncontrolled business interests and unaccountable technocracies. Thus, the logic of the argument develops into yearning for small-scale government, privileging the local community and citizen participation: *grassroots democracy is the political model implicit in most ecological movements*. In the most elaborated alternatives, the control over space, the assertion of place as source of meaning, and the emphasis on local government, is linked up to the self-management ideals of the anarchist tradition, including small-scale production, and emphasis on self-sufficiency, which leads to assumed austerity, the critique of conspicuous consumption, and the substitution of use value of life for exchange value of money. To be sure, people protesting against toxic dumping in their neighborhood are not anarchists, and few of them would actually be ready to transform the entire fabric of their lives as they are. But the internal logic of the argument, the connection between the defense of one's place against the imperatives of the space of flows, and the strengthening of economic and political bases of locality, allow for the sudden identification of some of these linkages in the public awareness when a symbolic event takes place (such as the building of a nuclear power plant). So are created the conditions for convergence between everyday life's problems and projects for alternative society: this is how social movements are made.

Alongside space, *the control over time is at stake in the network society, and the environmental movement is probably the most important actor in projecting a new, revolutionary temporality*. This matter is as important as complex, and requires slow-pace elaboration. In volume I, chapter 7, I proposed a distinction (on the basis of current debates in sociology and history, as well as of Leibniz's and Innis's philosophies of time and space) between three forms of temporality: clock time, timeless time, and glacial time. *Clock time*, characteristic of industrialism, for both capitalism and statism, was/is characterized by the chronological sequencing of events, and by the discipline of human behavior to a predetermined schedule creating scarcity of experience out of institutionalized measurement. *Timeless time*, characterizing dominant processes in our societies, occurs when the characteristics of a given context, namely, the informational paradigm and the network society, induce systemic perturbation in the sequential order of phenomena performed in that context. This perturbation may take the form of compressing the occurrence of phenomena, aiming at instantaneity (as in "instant wars" or split-second financial transactions), or else by introducing random discontinuity in the sequence (as in the hypertext of integrated, electronic media communication). Elimination of sequencing creates undifferentiated timing, thus annihilating time. In our societies, most dominant, core processes are structured in timeless time, yet most people are dominated by and through clock time.

There is still another form of time, as conceived and proposed in social practice: *glacial time*. In Lash and Urry's original formulation, the notion of glacial time implies that "the relation between humans and nature is very long-term and evolutionary. It moves back out of immediate human history and forwards into a wholly unspecifiable future."[21] Developing their elaboration, I propose the idea that the environmental movement is precisely characterized by the project of introducing a "glacial time" perspective in our temporality, in terms of both consciousness and policy. Ecological thinking considers interaction between all forms of matter in an evolutionary perspective. The idea of limiting the use of resources to renewable resources, central to environmentalism, is predicated precisely on the notion that alteration of basic balances in the planet, and in the universe, may, *over time*, undo a delicate ecological equilibrium, with catastrophic consequences. The holistic notion of integration between humans and nature, as presented in "deep ecology" writers, does not refer to a naive worshipping of pristine natural landscapes, but to the fundamental consideration that the relevant unit of experience is not each individual, or for that matter, historically existing human communities. To merge ourselves with our cosmological self we need first to change the notion of time, to feel "glacial time" running through our

[21] Lash and Urry (1994: 243).

lives, to sense the energy of stars flowing in our blood, and to assume
the rivers of our thoughts endlessly merging in the boundless oceans
of multiformed living matter. In very direct, personal terms, glacial
time means to measure our life by the life of our children, and of the
children of the children of our children. Thus, managing our lives
and institutions for them, as much as for us, is not a New Age cult, but
old-fashioned care-taking of our descendants, that is of our own flesh
and blood. To propose sustainable development as intergenerational
solidarity brings together healthy selfishness and systemic thinking in
an evolutionary perspective. The anti-nuclear movement, one of the
most potent sources of the environmental movement, based its radical
critique of nuclear power on the long-term effects of radioactive
waste, besides immediate safety problems, thus bridging to the safety
of generations thousands of years from us. To some extent, interest
in the preservation of and respect for indigenous cultures extends
backwards the concern for all forms of human existence coming from
different times, and affirming that we are them, and they are us. It is
this *unity of the species, then of matter as a whole, and of its spatiotemporal
evolution,* that is called upon implicitly by the environmental movement, and explicitly by deep ecologist and ecofeminist thinkers.[22] The
material expression unifying different claims and themes of environmentalism is their alternative temporality, demanding the assumption
by society's institutions of the slow-pace evolution of our species in its
environment, with no end to our cosmological being, as long as the
universe keeps expanding from the moment/place of its shared
beginning. Beyond the time-bounded shores of subdued clock time,
still experienced by most people in the world, the historical struggle
over new temporality takes place between the annihilation of time in
the recurrent flows of computer networks, and the realization of
glacial time in the conscious assumption of our cosmological self.

   Through these fundamental struggles over the appropriation of
science, space, and time, ecologists induce *the creation of a new identity,*
a biological identity, *a culture of the human species as a component of
nature.* This socio-biological identity does not imply denial of historical cultures. Ecologists bear respect for folk cultures, and indulge in
cultural authenticity from various traditions. Yet, their objective
enemy is state nationalism. This is because the nation-state, by definition, is bound to assert its power over a given territory. Thus, it breaks
the unity of humankind, as well as the interrelation between territories, undermining the sharing of our global ecosystem. In the words
of David McTaggart, the historic leader of Greenpeace International:
"The biggest threat we must address is nationalism. In the next

[22]   Diamond and Orenstein (1990); McLaughlin (1993).

century we are going to be faced with issues which simply cannot be addressed on a nation-by-nation basis. What we are trying to do is work together internationally, despite centuries of nationalist prejudice."[23] In what is only an apparent contradiction, ecologists are, at the same time, localists and globalists: globalists in the management of time, localists in the defense of space. Evolutionary thinking and policy require a global perspective. People's harmony with their environment starts in their local community.

This *new identity as a species*, that is a socio-biological identity, can be easily superimposed on multifaceted, historical traditions, languages, and cultural symbols, but it will hardly mix with state-nationalist identity. Thus, to some extent, environmentalism supersedes the opposition between the culture of real virtuality, underlying global flows of wealth and power, and the expression of fundamentalist cultural or religious identities. It is the only global identity put forward on behalf of all human beings, regardless of their specific social, historical, or gender attachments, or of their religious faith. However, since most people do not live their lives cosmologically, and the assumption of our shared nature with mosquitoes still poses some tactical problems, the critical matter for the influence of new ecological culture is its ability to weave threads of singular cultures into a human hypertext, made out of historical diversity and biological commonality. I call this culture *green culture* (why invent another term when millions of people already name it like this), and I define it in Petra Kelly's terms: "We must learn to think and act from our hearts, to recognize the interconnectedness of all living creatures, and to respect the value of each thread in the vast web of life. This is a spiritual perspective, and it is the foundation of all Green politics ... Green politics requires us to be both tender and subversive."[24] The tenderness of subversion, the subversion of tenderness: we are a long way from the instrumentalist perspective that has dominated the industrial era, in both its capitalist and statist versions. And we are in direct contradiction with the dissolution of meaning in the flows of faceless power that constitute the network society. Green culture, as proposed in and by a multifaceted environmental movement, is the antidote to the culture of real virtuality characterizing dominant processes in our societies.

Thus, the science of life versus life under science; local control over places versus an uncontrollable space of flows; realization of glacial time versus annihilation of time, and continued slavery to clock time; green culture versus real virtuality. These are the fundamental

---

[23] Interview in Ostertag (1991: 33).
[24] Kelly (1994: 37).

challenges of the environmental movement to dominant structures of the network society. And this is why it addresses the issues that people perceive vaguely as being the stuff of which their new lives are made. It remains that between this "fierce green fire" and people's hearths, the tenements of society stand tall, forcing environmentalism to a long march through the institutions from which, as with all social movements, it does not emerge unscathed.

Environmentalism in Action: Reaching Minds, Taming Capital, Courting the State, Tap-dancing with the Media

Much of the success of the environmental movement comes from the fact that, more than any other social force, it has been able to best adapt to the conditions of communication and mobilization in the new technological paradigm.[25] Although much of the movement relies on grassroots organizations, environmental action works on the basis of media events. By creating events that call media attention, environmentalists are able to reach a much broader audience than their direct constituency. Furthermore, the constant presence of environmental themes in the media has lent them a legitimacy higher than that of any other cause. Media orientation is obvious in the cases of global environmental activism such as Greenpeace, whose entire logic is geared toward creating events to mobilize public opinion on specific issues in order to put pressure on the powers that be. But it is also the daily staple of environmental struggles at the local level. Local TV news, radio, and newspapers are the voice of environmentalists, to the point that corporations and politicians often complain that it is the media rather than ecologists who are responsible for environmental mobilization. The symbiotic relationship between media and environmentalism stems from several sources. First of all, the non-violent direct action tactics, which permeated the movement from the early 1970s, provided good reporting material, particularly when news requires fresh images. Many environmental activists have imaginatively practiced the traditional French anarchist tactics of *l'action exemplaire*, a spectacular act that strikes minds, provokes debate, and induces mobilization. Self-sacrifice, such as enduring arrests and jail, risking their lives in the ocean, chaining themselves to trees, using their bodies as blocking devices against undesirable construction or evil convoys, disrupting official ceremonies, and so many other direct

---

[25]   See Epstein (1991); Horton (1991); Ostertag (1991); Costain and Costain (1992); Gottlieb (1993); Kanagy et al. (1994).

actions, coupled with self-restraint and manifest non-violence, introduce a witness-bearing attitude that restores trust and enhances
ethical values in an age of widespread cynicism. Secondly, the legitimacy of the issues raised by environmentalists, directly connecting to
the basic humanistic values cherished by most people, and often
distant from partisan politics, provided a good terrain for the media
to assume the role of the voice of the people, thus increasing their
own legitimacy, and making journalists feel good about it.
Furthermore, in local news, the reporting of health hazards or the
environmental disruption of people's lives brings home systemic
problems in a more powerful way than any traditional ideological
discourses. Often, environmentalists themselves feed the media with
precious images that say more than a thick report. Thus, American
environmental groups have distributed video cameras to grassroots
groups around the world, from Connecticut to Amazonia, for them
to film explicit violations of environmental laws, then using the technological infrastructure of the group to process, and diffuse,
accusatory images.

Environmentalists have also been at the cutting edge of new
communication technologies as organizing and mobilizing tools,
particularly in the use of the Internet.[26] For instance, a coalition of
environmental groups in the United States, Canada, and Chile,
formed around Friends of the Earth, the Sierra Club, Greenpeace,
Defenders of Wildlife, the Canadian Environmental Law Association,
and others, mobilized against approval of the North American Free
Trade Agreement (NAFTA) because of the lack of sufficient environmental protection provisions in it. They used the Internet to
coordinate actions and information, and they built a permanent
network that draws the battle lines of transnational environmental
action in the Americas in the 1990s. World Wide Web sites are
becoming rallying points for environmentalists around the world, as
with the sites established in 1996 by organizations such as *Conservation
International* and *Rainforest Action Network* to defend the cause of
indigenous people in tropical forests. *Food First*, a California-based
organization, has linked up with a network of environmental groups
in developing countries, connecting environmental and poverty
issues. Thus, through the Net, it was able to coordinate its action with
Global South, a Thailand-based organization that provides the environmental perspective from newly industrializing Asia. Through these
networks, grassroots groups around the world become suddenly able
to act globally, at the level where main problems are created. It seems
that a computer-literate elite is emerging as the global, coordinating

[26] Bartz (1996).

core of grassroots environmental action groups around the world, a phenomenon not entirely dissimilar to the role played by artisan printers and journalists at the beginning of the labor movement, orienting, through information to which they had access, the illiterate masses that formed the working class of early industrialization.

Environmentalism is not merely a consciousness-raising movement. Since its beginnings, it has focused on making a difference in legislation and governance. Indeed, the core of environmental organizations (such as the so-called Group of Ten in the United States) gears its efforts to lobby for legislation, and to support, or oppose, political candidates on the basis of their stand on certain issues. Even non-traditional, action-oriented organizations, such as Greenpeace, have increasingly shifted their focus to put pressure on governments, and on international institutions, to obtain laws, decisions, and implementation of decisions on specific issues. Similarly, at the local and regional level, environmentalists have campaigned for new forms of city and regional planning, for public health measures, for control of excessive development. It is this pragmatism, this issue-oriented attitude, that has given environmentalism an edge over traditional politics: people feel that they can make a difference right now and here, without mediation or delay. There is no distinction between means and goals.

In some countries, particularly in Europe, environmentalists have entered political competition, running candidates for office, with mixed success.[27] Evidence shows that green parties do much better in local elections, where there is still a direct linkage between the movement and its political representatives. They also perform relatively well in international elections, for example, the elections to the European Parliament, because, being an institution that holds only symbolic power, citizens feel comfortable about seeing their principles represented, with little cost in losing influence on decision-making. In national politics, political scientists have shown that chances for green parties are influenced less by people's environmental beliefs than by specific institutional structures framing the opportunities for political competition.[28] In a nutshell, the greater the accessibility of environmental themes and/or protest vote to mainstream parties, the lower the chances for the Greens; the greater the chances for a symbolic vote, without consequences for holding office, the better the performance by Green candidates. Indeed, it seems that Germany was the exception, not the rule, in the

[27]   Poguntke (1993); Dalton (1994); Diani (1995); Richardson and Rootes (1995).

[28]   Richardson and Rootes (1995).

development of green politics, as I argued above. Overall, it seems that there is a worldwide trend toward the greening of mainstream politics, albeit often in a very pale green, together with the sustained autonomy of the environmental movement. As for the movement itself, its relationship to politics increasingly mixes lobbying, targeted campaigning for or against candidates, and influencing voters through issue-oriented mobilizations. Through these diverse tactics, environmentalism has become a major public opinion force with which parties and candidates have to reckon in many countries. On the other hand, most environmental organizations have become largely institutionalized, that is, they have accepted the need to act in the framework of existing institutions, and within the rules of productivism and a global, market economy. Thus, cooperation with large corporations has become the rule rather than the exception. Corporations often fund a variety of environmental activities, and have become extremely aware of green self-presentation, to the point that environmental themes are now standard images in corporate advertising. But not all is manipulation. Corporations around the world have also been influenced by environmentalism, and have tried to adapt their processes and their products to new legislation, new tastes, and new values, naturally trying to make a profit out of it at the same time. However, because the actual production units in our economy are no longer individual corporations, but transnational networks made up of various components (see volume 1, chapter 3), environmental transgression has been decentralized to small business, and to newly industrializing countries, thus modifying the geography and topology of environmental action in the coming years.

Overall, with the extraordinary growth of environmental consciousness, influence, and organization, the movement has become increasingly diversified, socially and thematically, reaching from the corporate boardrooms to the fringe alleys of counter-cultures, passing through city halls and parliamentary houses. In the process, themes have been distorted, and in some cases manipulated. But this is the mark of any major social movement. Environmentalism is indeed a major social movement of our time, as it reaches out to a variety of social causes under the comprehensive banner of environmental justice.

Environmental Justice: Ecologists' New Frontier

Since the 1960s environmentalism has not been solely concerned with watching birds, saving forests, and cleaning the air. Campaigns against toxic waste dumping, consumers' rights, anti-nuclear protests, pacifism, feminism, and a number of other issues have merged with the defense of nature to root the movement in a wide landscape of rights and claims. Even counter-cultural trends, such as New Age meditation and neo-paganism, mingled with other components of the environmental movement in the 1970s and 1980s.

In the 1990s, while some major issues, such as peace and anti-nuclear protest, have receded into the background, partly because of the success of protests, partly because of the end of the Cold War, a variety of social issues have come to be a part of an increasingly diversified movement.[29] Poor communities and ethnic minorities have mobilized against being the target of environmental discrimination, submitted more often than the population at large to toxic substances, pollution, health hazards, and degradation of their living quarters. Workers have revolted against the source of occupational injuries, old and new, from chemical poisoning to computer-induced stress. Women's groups have shown that, being more often than not the managers of everyday family life, they are the ones that suffer most directly the consequences of pollution, of deteriorating public facilities, and of uncontrolled development. Homelessness is a major cause of declining quality of urban life. And, throughout the world, poverty has been shown, again and again, to be a cause of environmental degradation, from the burning of forests, to pollution of rivers, lakes, and oceans, to rampaging epidemics. Indeed, in many industrializing countries, particularly in Latin America, environmental groups have blossomed, and have linked up with human rights groups, women's groups, and non-governmental organizations, forming powerful coalitions that go beyond, but do not ignore, institutional politics.[30]

Thus, the concept of environmental justice, as an all-encompassing notion that affirms the use value of life, of all forms of life, against the interests of wealth, power, and technology, is gradually capturing minds and policies, as the environmental movement enters a new stage of development.

At first sight, it would seem to be opportunistic tactics. Given the success and legitimacy of the environmental label, less popular causes wrap themselves in new ideologies to win support and attract attention. And, indeed, some of the conservative, nature groupings of the environmental movement have grown wary of an excessively broad embrace that might take the movement away from its focus. After all, labor unions have fought for occupational health legislation since the onset of industrialization, and poverty is, and was, a major issue in its own right, without having to paint in green its sinister

[29] Gottlieb (1993: 207–320); Szasz (1994); Epstein (1995); Brulle (1996).
[30] Athanasiou (1996); Borja and Castells (1996).

darkness. Yet, what is happening in environmentalism goes beyond tactics. The ecological approach to life, to the economy, and to the institutions of society emphasizes the holistic character of all forms of matter, and of all information processing. Thus, the more we know, the more we sense the possibilities of our technology, and the more we realize the gigantic, dangerous gap between our enhanced productive capacities, and our primitive, unconscious, and ultimately destructive social organization. This is the objective thread that weaves the growing connectedness of social revolts, local and global, defensive and offensive, issue-oriented and value-oriented, emerging in and around the environmental movement. This is not to say that a new international of good-willing, generous citizens has emerged. Yet. As shown in this volume, old and new cleavages of class, gender, ethnicity, religion, and territoriality are at work in dividing and subdividing issues, conflicts, and projects. But this is to say that embryonic connections between grassroots movements and symbol-oriented mobilizations on behalf of environmental justice bear the mark of alternative projects. These projects hint at superseding the exhausted social movements of industrial society, to resume, under historically appropriate forms, the old dialectics between domination and resistance, between *realpolitik* and utopia, between cynicism and hope.

4

The End of Patriarchalism: Social Movements, Family, and Sexuality in the Information Age

> *If all who have begged help*
> *From me in this world,*
> *All the holy innocents,*
> *Broken wives, and cripples,*
> *The imprisoned, the suicidal –*
> *If they had sent me one kopeck*
> *I should have become "richer*
> *Than all Egypt"...*
> *But they did not send me kopecks,*
> *Instead they shared with me their strength,*
> *And so nothing in the world*
> *Is stronger than I,*
> *And I can bear anything, even this.*
>
> Anna Akhmatova, *Selected Poems* [1]

Patriarchalism is a founding structure of all contemporary societies. It is characterized by the institutionally enforced authority of males over females and their children in the family unit. For this authority to be exercised, patriarchalism must permeate the entire organization of society, from production and consumption to politics, law, and culture. Interpersonal relationships, and thus personality, are marked, as well, by domination and violence originating from the culture and institutions of patriarchalism. Yet, it is analytically, and politically, essential not to forget the rooting of patriarchalism in the family structure, and in the socio-biological reproduction of the species, as historically (culturally) framed. Without the patriarchal family, patriarchalism would be exposed as sheer domination, and

---

[1]   Akhmatova (1985: 84).

thus eventually overrun by the uprising of the "half of the heaven" historically kept under submission.

The patriarchal family, the cornerstone of patriarchalism, is being challenged in this end of millennium by the inseparably related processes of the transformation of women's work and the transformation of women's consciousness. Driving forces behind these processes are the rise of an informational, global economy, technological changes in the reproduction of the human species, and the powerful surge of women's struggles, and of a multifaceted feminist movement, three trends that have developed since the late 1960s. The massive incorporation of women into *paid* work increased women's bargaining power *vis à vis* men, and undermined the legitimacy of men's domination as providers of the family. Besides, it put an unbearable burden on women's lives by their daily, quadruple shift (paid work, homemaking, child rearing, and night shift for the husband). Contraception first, *in vitro* fertilization later, and genetic manipulation looming on the horizon, are giving women, and society, growing control over the timing and frequency of child bearing. As for women's struggles, they did not wait until this end of millennium to manifest themselves. They have characterized the entire span of human experience, albeit in a diversity of forms, most often absent from history books and from the written record altogether.[2] I have argued that many historical, and contemporary, urban struggles were, in fact, women's movements dealing with the demands and management of everyday life.[3] And feminism as such has an old history, as exemplified by the suffragists in the United States. Yet, I think it is fair to say that only in the last quarter of this century have we witnessed what amounts to a mass insurrection of women against their oppression throughout the world, albeit with different intensity depending on culture and country. The impact of such movements has been felt deeply in the institutions of society, and, more fundamentally, in the consciousness of women. In industrialized countries, a large majority of women consider themselves equal to men, entitled to their rights, and to women's control over their bodies and their lives. Such a consciousness is rapidly extending throughout the planet. This is the most important revolution because it goes to the roots of society and to the heart of who we are.[4] And it is irreversible. To say so does not mean that problems of discrimination, oppression, and abuse of women, and of their children, have disappeared, or even substantially diminished in their intensity. In fact,

[2] Rowbotham (1974).
[3] Castells (1983).
[4] Mitchell (1966).

while legal discrimination has been somewhat curtailed, and the labor market place shows equalizing trends as women's education soars, interpersonal violence and psychological abuse are widespread, precisely because of male anger, individual and collective, in losing power. This is not, and will not be, a velvet revolution. The human landscape of women's liberation and men's defense of their privileges is littered with corpses of broken lives, as is the case with all true revolutions. None the less, in spite of the sharpness of conflict, the transformation of women's consciousness, and of societal values in most societies, in less than three decades, is staggering, and it yields fundamental consequences for the entire human experience, from political power to the structure of personality.

I argue that the process that summarizes and concentrates this transformation is the undoing of the patriarchal family. If the patriarchal family crumbles, the whole system of patriarchalism, gradually but surely, and the whole of our lives, will be transformed. This is a scary perspective, and not only for men. This is why the challenge to patriarchalism is one of the most powerful factors presently inducing fundamentalist movements aimed at restoring the patriarchal order, as those studied in the previous chapters of this volume. Their backlash could indeed alter current processes of cultural change, since no history is pre-scripted. Yet, current indicators point to a substantial decline of traditional forms of patriarchal family. I will start my analysis by focusing on some of these indicators. Not that statistics, by themselves, can tell the story of the crisis of patriarchalism. But when changes are so widespread as to be reflected in national and comparative statistics, we can safely assume the depth and speed of these changes.

Then, we still have to account for the timing of this transformation. Why now? Feminist ideas have been present at least for a century, if not longer, albeit in their specific historical translation. Why did they catch fire in our time? I propose the hypothesis that the reason lies in a combination of four elements: first, the transformation of the economy, and of the labor market, in close association with the opening of educational opportunities to women.[5] Thus, I will try to present some of the data displaying such a transformation, linking them to the characteristics of the informational, global economy, and of the network enterprise, as presented in volume I. Secondly, there is the technological transformation in biology, pharmacology, and medicine that has allowed a growing control over child bearing, and over the reproduction of the human species, as argued in volume I, chapter 7. Thirdly, against this background of

[5]   Saltzman-Chafetz (1995).

economic and technological transformation, patriarchalism has been impacted by the development of the feminist movement, in the aftermath of the 1960s social movements. Not that feminism was a distinctive component of these movements. In fact, it started afterwards, in the late 1960s and/or early 1970s, among women who had been part of the movement, as a reaction to the sexism, and even abuse (see below) that they had had to suffer in the movement. But the context of social movement formation, with emphasis on the "personal as political," and with its multidimensional themes, freed the possibility of thinking away from the instrumental avenues of male-dominated movements (such as the labor movement, or revolutionary politics), and drifting toward a more experimental approach to the actual sources of oppression as felt, before they could be tamed by the discourse of rationality. The fourth element inducing the challenge to patriarchalism is the rapid diffusion of ideas in a globalized culture, and in an interrelated world, where people and experience travel and mingle, quickly weaving a hyperquilt of women's voices throughout most of the planet. Thus, after surveying the transformation of women's work, I will analyze the formation of a highly diversified feminist movement, and the debates emerging from the collective experience of constructing/reconstructing women's identity.

The impact of social movements, and particularly of feminism, on gender relations triggered a powerful shock wave: the calling into question of heterosexuality as the norm. For lesbians, separation from men as the subjects of their oppression was the logical, if not inevitable, consequence of their view of male domination as the source of women's plight. For gay men, the questioning of the traditional family, and the conflictive relationships between men and women, provided an opening to explore other forms of interpersonal relationships, including new forms of families, gay families. For all, sexual liberation, without institutional limits, became the new frontier of self-expression. Not in the homophobic image of endless cruising, but in the affirmation of the self, and in the experimentation with sexuality and love. The impact of gay and lesbian movements on patriarchalism is, of course, devastating. Not that forms of interpersonal domination cease to exist. Domination, as exploitation, always renews itself in history. But patriarchalism, as it has probably existed since the dawn of human times (Carolyn Merchant notwithstanding) is definitively shaken by undermining of the heterosexual norm. Thus, I will explore the origins and horizon of gay and lesbian movements, bridging from San Francisco to Taipei, to emphasize the growing cultural and geographical diversity of these movements.

Finally, I will address the issue of the transformation of personality in our society, as it results from the transformation of family structure and of sexual norms, since I think it can be argued that families constitute the basic socialization mechanism, and sexuality has something to do with personality. This is how the interaction between structural change and social movements – that is, between the network society and the power of identity – transforms us.

The Crisis of the Patriarchal Family

By the crisis of the patriarchal family I refer to the weakening of a model of family based on the stable exercise of authority/domination over the whole family by the adult male head of the family. It is possible, in the 1990s, to find indicators of such a crisis in most societies, particularly in the most developed countries. It is not obvious to use very rough statistical indicators as evidence of a feature, patriarchalism, that is political, cultural, and psychological. Yet, since a population's behavior and structure usually evolve at a very slow pace, the observation of sizeable trends affecting the structure and dynamics of the patriarchal family in comparative national statistics are, in my view, a powerful sign of change, and, I argue, of crisis of previously stable patriarchal patterns. I will summarize the argument before proceeding with a quick statistical scanning.

Dissolution of households of married couples, by divorce or separation, are a first indicator of disaffection with a model of family that relied on the long-term commitment of family members. To be sure, there can be (and this is the rule, in fact) successive patriarchalism: the reproduction of the same model with different partners. However, structures of domination (and mechanisms of trust) are undermined by the experience, both for women and for children, often caught in conflicting loyalties. Furthermore, with increasing frequency, dissolution of married households leads to the formation of single households and/or single-parent households, in this case ending patriarchal authority in the family, even if the structures of domination reproduce mentally in the new household.

Secondly, the increasing frequency of marital crises, and the growing difficulty of making marriage, work, and life compatible, seem to be associated with two other powerful trends: delaying coupling; and setting up partnerships without marriage. Here, again, the lack of legal sanction weakens patriarchal authority, both institutionally and psychologically.

Thirdly, as a result of these different tendencies, together with demographic factors, such as the aging of population, and the difference in mortality rates between sexes, an increasing variety of household structures emerges, thus diluting the prevalence of the classic nuclear family model (first time married couples and their children), and undermining its social reproduction. Single households, and single-parent households, proliferate.

Fourthly, under the conditions of family instability, and with the increasing autonomy of women in their reproductive behavior, the crisis of the patriarchal family extends into the crisis of social patterns of population replacement.[6] On the one hand, an increasing proportion of children are born out of wedlock, and are usually kept by their mothers (although unmarried couples jointly parenting a child are also part of the statistic). Thus, biological reproduction is assured, but outside traditional family structure. On the other hand, women, with heightened consciousness and facing hardship, limit the number of children they give birth to, and delay their first child. Ultimately, in some small circles, whose size seems to be increasing, women give birth to children for themselves, or adopt children alone.

Altogether, these trends, reinforcing each other, call into question the structure and values of the patriarchal family. It is not necessarily the end of the family, since other family arrangements are being experimented with, and may in the end reconstruct how we live with each other, and how we procreate and educate in different, maybe better, ways.[7] But the trends that I mention point to the end of the family as we have known it until now. Not just the nuclear family (a modern artifact), but the family based on patriarchal domination that has been the rule for millennia.

Let us have a look at some basic statistics. I will emphasize here a comparative approach, while reserving a more systematic overview of the crisis of patriarchal family in the United States, where the process seems to be more advanced, in a later section of this chapter.[8] While the trends indicated are most pronounced in developed countries, there is a general change in the same direction in much of the world. Thus, I will rely to a large extent on the report elaborated in 1995 by the Population Council on the transformation of families in the world,[9] which I will complement with various sources, as cited. I will

[6] In the European Union in 1995 the birth rate was the lowest in peacetime in the twentieth century: there were only 290,000 more births than deaths. In Germany and Italy, there were more deaths than births. Eastern Europe's population declined even further, particularly in Russia (*The Economist*, November 19, 1996).

[7] Stacey (1990).

[8] See United Nations (1970-95, 1995); Saboulin and Thave (1993); Valdes and Gomariz (1993); Cho and Yada (1994); OECD (1994b); Alberdi (1995); Bruce et al. (1995); De Vos (1995); Mason and Jensen (1995).

[9] Bruce et al. (1995).

focus on the 1970–95 period for reasons presented above in this chapter.

Table 4.1 shows, with one exception, a significant increase in the crude rate of divorce for selected countries: more than doubling in

Table 4.1 Rate of change in crude divorce rate in selected countries, 1971–90

Country	1971	1990	Rate of change 1971–90 Rate	%
Canada	1.38	2.94	1.56	113
France	0.93	1.86	0.93	100
Italy	0.32	0.48	0.16	50
Japan	0.99	1.27	0.28	28
UK	1.41	2.88	1.47	104
USA	3.72	4.70	0.98	26
USSR	2.63	3.39	0.76	29
Mexico	0.21	0.54	0.33	157
Egypt	2.09	1.42	–0.67	–32

Source: UN, *Demographic Yearbook* (1970–1995)

Table 4.2 Trends in divorce rates per 100 marriages in developed countries

Country	1970	1980	1990
Canada	18.6	32.8	38.3
Czechoslovakia	21.8	26.6	32.0[a]
Denmark	25.1	39.3	44.0
England and Wales	16.2	39.3	41.7[a]
France	12.0	22.2	31.5[a]
Greece	5.0	10.0	12.0
Hungary	25.0	29.4	31.0
Italy	5.0	3.2	8.0
Netherlands	11.0	25.7	28.1
Sweden	23.4	42.2	44.1
United States	42.3	58.9	54.8[b]
(former) West Germany	12.2	22.7	29.2

Note: Rates shown are a synthetic index calculated by summing duration-specific divorce rates in each year. (Original source incorrectly identifies rates as "per 1,000 marriages.")

[a] 1989
[b] 1985

Source: Monnier, Alain and de Guibert-Lantoine, Catherine (1993) "La conjoncture démographique: l'Europe et les pays développés d'outre-mer", *Population* 48(4):1043–67
Compiled and elaborated by Bruce et al. (1995)

the UK, France, Canada, and Mexico between 1971 and 1990. The less pronounced increases in the US (still +26 percent) and in the USSR (+29 percent) over the period are due to the fact that they had the highest rates in 1971. Interestingly enough, the one Muslim country that I selected for purposes of comparison displays a decrease in the divorce rate (probably reflecting trends toward Islamization of society), although it is still higher, in 1990, than that of Italy, Mexico, or Japan.

Table 4.2 shows the divorce rates per 100 marriages for selected, highly industrialized countries. There is a discrepancy between the levels of divorce for each country, but there is a general upward trend between 1970 and 1980, and between 1980 and 1990, with again the exception of the United States in 1990, partly because almost 55 percent of marriages ended up in divorce in this country in 1990.

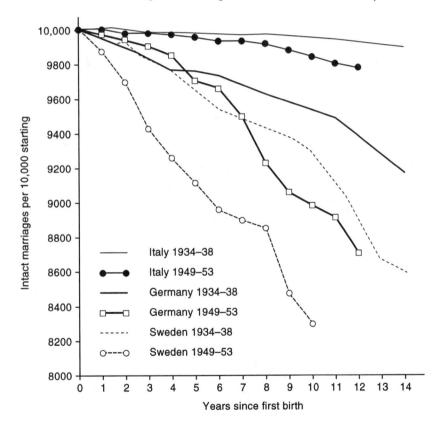

Figure 4.1   Marriage survival curves for Italy, West Germany, and Sweden: mothers born in 1934–38 and 1949–53
Source: Blossfeld et al. (1995)

Table 4.3 Percentage of first marriages dissolved through
separation, divorce, or death among women aged 40–49 in less-
developed countries

Region/country	Date	%
Asia		
Indonesia	1987	37.3
Sri Lanka	1987	25.6
Thailand	1987	24.8
Latin America/Caribbean		
Colombia	1986	32.5
Dominican Republic	1986	49.5
Ecuador	1987	28.9
Mexico	1987	25.5
Peru	1986	26.1
Middle East/North Africa		
Egypt	1989	22.8
Morocco	1987	31.2
Tunisia	1988	11.1
Sub-Saharan Africa		
Ghana	1988	60.8
Kenya	1989	24.2
Senegal	1986	42.3
Sudan	1989/90	28.2

Sources: United Nations (1987), table 47 in *Fertility Behaviour in the Context
of Development: Evidence from the World Fertility Survey* (New York: United
Nations), and tabulations from demographic and health surveys
Compiled and elaborated by Bruce et al. (1995)

De facto separations are not included in the statistics, nor are the rates
of the ending of cohabitation. However, we know, through survey
research, that cohabitation households are more likely to separate
than married couples,[10] and that separations correlate with the rate
of divorce, thus actually increasing the overall number, and proportion, of termination of households.[11] A global survey of divorce
patterns found that a growing proportion of divorces involve couples
with young children, thus increasing the likelihood that marital dissolution will lead to single parenthood.[12] Figure 4.1 shows the
decreasing rate of marriage survival between older and younger

[10] Bruce et al. (1995).
[11] Alberdi (1995).
[12] Goode (1993).

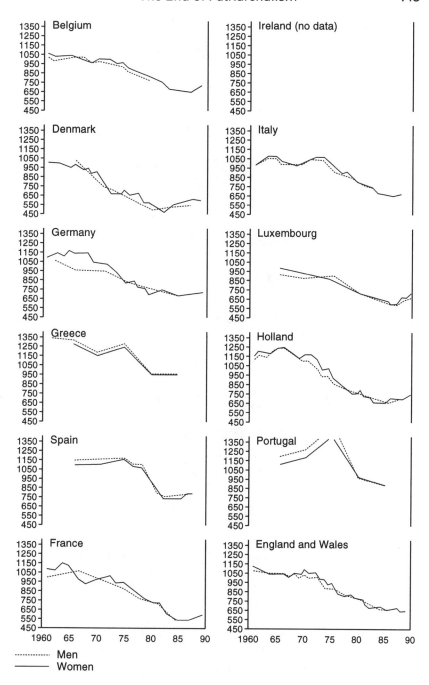

Figure 4.2   Evolution of first marriage in countries of the European
Union since 1960   *Source*: Alberdi (1995)

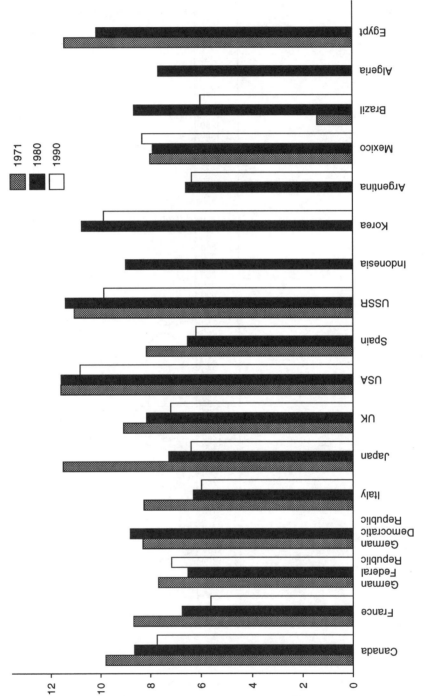

Figure 4.3 Crude marriage rates in selected countries   *Source:* United Nations, *Demographic Yearbook* (1970–95)

Table 4.4 Trends in percentage of women aged 20–24 who have
never been married

Region/country	Earlier date	%	Later date	%
Less-developed countries				
Asia				
Indonesia	1976	20	1987	36
Pakistan	1975	22	1990/91	39
Sri Lanka	1975	61	1987	58
Thailand	1975	42	1987	48
Latin America/Caribbean				
Colombia	1976	44	1986	39
Dominican Republic	1975	27	1986	39
Ecuador	1979	43	1987	41
Mexico	1976	34	1987	42
Peru	1978	49	1986	56
Middle East/North Africa				
Egypt	1980	36	1989	40
Morocco	1980	36	1987	56
Tunisia	1978	57	1988	64
Sub-Saharan Africa				
Ghana	1980	15	1988	23
Kenya	1978	21	1989	32
Senegal	1978	14	1986	23
Developed countries				
Czechoslovakia	1970	35	1980	33
Austria	1971	45	1980	57
France	1970	46	1980	52
Spain	1970	68	1981	59
United States	1970	36	1980	51

Sources: *Less-developed countries*: United Nations (1987), table 43 in *Fertility Behaviour in the Context of Development: Evidence from the World Fertility Survey* (New York: United Nations), and Westoff, Charles F., Blanc, Ann K. and Nyblade, Laura (1994) *Marriage and Entry into Parenthood* (Demographic and Health Surveys Comparative Studies no. 10. Calverton, Maryland: Macro International Inc.); *developed countries*: compiled by the United Nations Statistical Division for: United Nations (1995) *The World's Women 1970–1995: Trends and Statistics* (New York: United Nations)
Compiled and elaborated by Bruce et al. (1995)

cohorts of women for Italy, West Germany, and Sweden.[13]

This trend is by no means limited to industrialized countries. Table 4.3, for selected developing countries, displays rates of dissolution, for different causes, of first marriages for women aged 40–49: with the

[13]   Blossfeld (1995).

Table 4.5　Non-marital births as a percentage of all births by region (country averages)

Region/country (no. of countries)	1970	1980	1990
Developed countries			
Canada	n.a.	13.2	21.1[a]
Eastern Europe (6)	7.1	9.0	12.9
Northern Europe (6)	8.8	19.5	33.3
Southern Europe (5)	4.1	5.4	8.7
Western Europe (6)	5.6	8.3	16.3
Japan	1.0[b]	1.0[c]	1.0[d]
Oceania (2)	9.0[b]	13.4[c]	20.2[e]
United States	5.4[b]	14.2[c]	28.0
(former) USSR (14)	8.2	8.8	11.2
Less-developed countries			
Africa (12)	n.a.	4.8[f]	n.a.
Asia (13)	n.a.	0.9[f]	n.a.
Latin America/Caribbean (13)	n.a.	6.5[f]	n.a.

n.a. = not available.
[a] 1989　　　[c] 1975　　　[e] 1985
[b] 1965　　　[d] 1988　　　[f] 1975–1980 (average)

Sources: Eastern, Northern, Southern, and Western Europe, (former) USSR, and Canada: Council of Europe (1993) *Recent Demographic Developments in Europe and North America, 1992* (Strasbourg: Council of Europe Press); *USA, Oceania, and Japan:* United Nations (1992) *Patterns of Fertility in Low Fertility Settings* (New York: United Nations), and US Department of Health and Human Services (1993) *Monthly Vital Statistics Report* 42(3) supplement; *less-developed countries:* United Nations (1987) *Fertility Behaviour in the Context of Development* (New York: United Nations)
Compiled and elaborated by Bruce et al. (1995)

exception of Tunisia, it oscillates between 22.8 percent and 49.5 percent, with a peak of 60.8 percent in Ghana.

In the 1990s in Europe the number of divorces *vis à vis* marriages has stabilized, but this is mainly due to a reduction in the number of marriages since 1960, so that overall the number, and proportion, of dual-parent married households has decreased substantially.[14] Figure 4.2 displays the general trend toward the reduction of first marriages in countries of the European Union, and figure 4.3 presents the evolution of crude marriage rates for selected countries in different areas in the world. With the exception of Mexico and Germany, there is a decline over the 20-year period, with a significant drop in Japan.

The delay in the age of marriage is also a quasi-universal trend, and

[14]　Alberdi (1995).

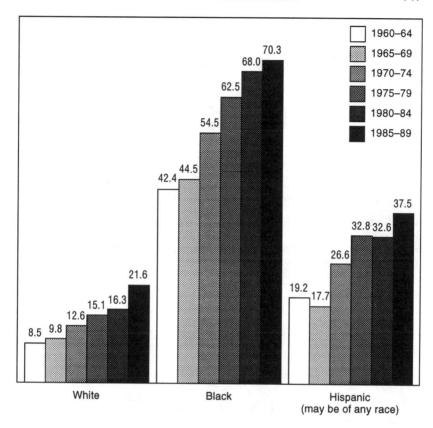

Figure 4.4   Percentage of women (15–34 years) with first birth
occurring before first marriage, by race and ethnic origin, in US,
1960–89
Source: US Bureau of the Census (1992a)

a particularly important one in the case of young women. Table 4.4
shows the percentage of women aged 20–24 who have never married.
The later dates are very diverse, so it is difficult to compare, but, with
the exception of Ghana and Senegal, between one-third and two-thirds
of young women are unmarried; with the exception of Spain and Sri
Lanka, the proportion of unmarried women 20–24 has increased since
1970. Worldwide, the proportion of married women aged 15 and older
declined from 61 percent in 1970 to 56 percent in 1985.[15]

An increasing proportion of children are born out of wedlock in
developed countries (table 4.5), and the most important observation
concerns the trend: in the United States, the proportion jumped from

[15]   United Nations (1991).

Table 4.6 Trends in single-parent households as a percentage of all households with dependent children and at least one resident parent in developed countries

Country	Early 1970s	Mid-1980s
Australia	9.2	14.9
France	9.5	10.2
Japan	3.6	4.1
Sweden	15.0	17.0
United Kingdom	8.0	14.3
United States	13.0	23.9
(former) USSR	10.0	20.0
(former) West Germany	8.0	11.4

Note: Single-parent households are households with dependent children and one resident parent.
Source: Burns, Ailsa (1992) "Mother-headed families: an international perspective and the case of Australia", *Social Policy Report* 6(1)
Compiled and elaborated by Bruce et al. (1995)

Table 4.7 Trends in percentage of households headed by women *de jure*

Region/country	Earlier date	%	Later date	%
Demographic survey data				
Asia				
Indonesia	1976	15.5	1987	13.6
Sri Lanka	1975	15.7	1987	17.8
Thailand	1975	12.5	1987	20.8
Latin America/Caribbean				
Colombia	1976	17.5	1986	18.4
Dominican Republic	1975	20.7	1986	25.7
Ecuador	1979	15.0	1987	14.6
Mexico	1976	13.5	1987	13.3
Peru[a]	1977/78	14.7	1986	19.5
Trinidad and Tobago	1977	22.6	1987	28.6
Middle East/North Africa				
Morocco	1979/80	11.5	1987	17.3
Sub-Saharan Africa				
Ghana	1960	22.0	1987	29.0
Sudan	1978/79	16.7	1989/90	12.6

Table 4.7 contd

Region/country	Earlier date	%	Later date	%
Census data				
Asia				
Hong Kong	1971	23.5	1991	25.7
Indonesia	1971	16.3	1980	14.2
Japan	1980	15.2	1990	17.0
Korea	1980	14.7	1990	15.7
Philippines	1970	10.8	1990	11.3
Latin America/Caribbean				
Brazil	1980	14.4	1989	20.1
Costa Rica	1984	17.5	1992	20.0
Panama	1980	21.5	1990	22.3
Peru	1981	22.1	1991	17.3
Uruguay	1975	21.0	1985	23.0
Venezuela	1981	21.8	1990	21.3
Sub-Saharan Africa				
Burkina Faso	1975	5.1	1985	9.7
Cameroon	1976	13.8	1987	18.5
Mali	1976	15.1	1987	14.0

Note: de jure = "usual" household headship.
[a] *de facto* = headship on day of interview.
Sources: *Demographic surveys*: Ghana: Lloyd, Cynthia B. and Gage-Brandon,
Anastasia J. (1993) "Women's role in maintaining households: family welfare
and sexual inequality in Ghana", *Population Studies* 47(1): 115–31. Ecuador:
Ono-Osaku, Keiko and Themme, A.R. (1993) "Cooperative analysis of recent
changes in households in Latin America", in IUSSP *Proceedings of
Conference on the Americas, Vera Cruz;* all other countries: Ayad, Mohamed
et al. (1994) *Demographic Characteristics of Households* (Demographic and
Health Surveys Comparative Studies no. 14. Calverton, Maryland: Macro
International Inc.); *censuses*: United Nations (1995) *The World's Women
1970–1995: Trends and Statistics* (New York: United Nations)
Compiled and elaborated by Bruce et al. (1995)

5.4 percent of all births in 1970 to 28 percent in 1990. The
phenomenon is ethnically differentiated: it reaches 70.3 percent for
African-American women in the age group 15–34 (figure 4.4). In
Scandinavian countries non-marital child bearing in the 1990s
accounts for about 50 percent of all child bearing.[16]

As a result of both separations and single motherhood, the proportion of single-parent households with dependent children (usually
female-headed) increased between the early 1970s and the mid-
1980s in developed countries (table 4.6), and the upward trend

[16]   Alberdi (1995); Bruce et al. (1995).

Table 4.8 Indicators of recent changes in family and household formation: selected Western countries, 1975–90

Region and country	Women 20–24 in cohabitation, c. 1985–90 (%)	Extramarital births, c. 1988 (%)	Rise in extramarital births, 1975–88 (%)	One-parent households with children c. 1985 (%)
Scandinavia				
Iceland	–	52	19	–
Sweden	44	52	19	32
Denmark	43	45	23	26
Norway	28	34	23	23
Finland	26	19	9	15
Northern Europe				
Netherlands	23	11	8	19
United Kingdom	24	25	16	14
France	24	26	18	10
West Germany	18	10	4	13
Austria	–	23	8	15
Switzerland	–	6	2	9
Luxembourg	–	12	8	18
Belgium	18	10	7	15
Ireland	4	13	8	7
Southern Europe				
Portugal	7	14	7	–
Spain	3	8	6	11
Italy	3	6	3	16
Greece	1	2	1	–
Malta	–	2	1	–
Cyprus	–	1	0	–
North America				
United States	8	26	12	28
Canada	15	21	14	26
Oceania				
Australia	6	19	7	15
New Zealand	12	25	9	–

Sources: Council of Europe (various issues); European Values Studies, 1990 Round; Moors and van Nimwegen (1990); United Nations (various years, 1990); personal communications from Larry Bumpass (United States), Peter McDonald, Lincoln Day (Australia), Thomas Burch (Canada), Ian Pool (New Zealand).
Compiled by Lesthaeghe (1995)

Table 4.9 Percentage of one-person households over total number
of households for selected countries, 1990–93

Country	Year	Total households (000s)	One-person households (000s)	%
Germany[a]	1993	36,230	12,379	34.2
Belgium	1992	3,969	1,050	26.5
Denmark[b]	1993	2,324	820	35.3
France	1992	22,230	6,230	28.0
Greece	1992	3,567	692	19.4
Great Britain	1992	23,097	6,219	26.9
Ireland	1991	1,029	208	20.2
Italy	1992	19,862	4,305	21.7
Luxembourg	1992	144	34	23.6
Netherlands	1992	6,206	1,867	30.1
Portugal	1992	3,186	399	12.5
Spain	1992	11,708	1,396	11.9
Estimates				
Finland	1993	2,120	716	33.8
Austria	1993	3,058	852	27.9
Sweden	1990	3,830	1,515	39.6
US	1993	96,391	23,642	24.5
Japan	1993	41,826	9,320	22.3

[a] Data from microcensus, April 1993.
[b] Data for Faeroe and Greenland not included.
Source: Statistiches Bundesamt (1995) *Statistisches Jahrbuch 1995 fuer das Ausland* (Wiesbaden: Metzer and Poeschel)

has continued in the 1990s in the US (see below). For developing countries, a similar trend can be detected on the basis of statistics on households headed by women *de jure*. Table 4.7 shows an overall upward trend in the proportion of female-headed households between the mid-1970s and the mid/late-1980s (with some exceptions, e.g. Indonesia), with Brazil showing over 20 percent of its households in this category in 1989, up from 14 percent in 1980.

Bringing together various indicators of household formation, Lesthaeghe constructed table 4.8 for OECD countries, whose data contrast northern Europe and North America with southern Europe, where traditional family structures resist better. Even so, excepting Ireland and Switzerland, the proportion of one-parent households with children in the mid-1980s represented between 11 percent and 32 percent of all households.

Table 4.9 shows the percentage of single households for selected countries in the early 1990s. It deserves a close look: with the exception of southern Europe, it oscillates between 20 percent and 39.6 percent of all households, with 26.9 percent for the UK, 24.5 percent for the US, 22.3 percent for Japan, 28.0 percent for France, and 34.2 percent for Germany. Obviously, most of these households are formed by single elderly, and thus the aging of the population accounts for a good part of the phenomenon. Still, the fact that between one-fifth and over one-third of households are single does call into question the pervasiveness of the patriarchal way of life. Incidentally, the resistance of traditional patriarchal families in Italy and Spain takes its toll: women counteract by not having children, so that both countries are the lowest in the world in fertility rate, way below the replacement rate for the population (1.2 for Italy, 1.3 for Spain).[17] In addition, in Spain the age of emancipation is also the highest in Europe: 27 years for women, 29 for men. Widespread youth unemployment and an acute housing crisis contribute to keep the traditional family together, at the cost of creating fewer families, and stopping the reproduction of Spaniards.[18]

This is, in fact, the most obvious consequence of the crisis of the patriarchal family: the precipitous decline of fertility rates in developed countries, below the rate of replacement of their population (see figure 4.5 for European countries). In Japan, the total fertility rate has been below replacement level since 1975, reaching 1.54 in 1990.[19] In the US, the total fertility rate has declined sharply in the past three decades, from its high historical point in the late 1950s, to reach a level below the replacement rate during the 1970s and 1980s, until stabilizing in the early 1990s at about the replacement level of 2.1. The number of births, however, increased because of the arrival of the baby boomer cohorts to procreation age (figure 4.6). Table 4.10 displays the total fertility rate by main regions of the world, with projections up to the mid-1990s. It has declined overall in the past two decades, and in the more developed regions has slipped below the replacement rate, and stays there. It should be noticed, however, that this is not an iron rule of population. Anna Cabre has shown the relationship between the recuperation of the fertility rate in Scandinavia in the 1980s and the generous social policy, and tolerance of society, in this privileged area of the world.[20] This is exactly why over 50 percent of children were conceived in an extra-marital relationship. Under conditions of psychological and material support, and not being penalized in their jobs, Scandinavian women

---

[17]   Alberdi (1995).
[18]   Leal et al. (1996).
[19]   Tsuya and Mason (1995).
[20]   Cabre (1990); Cabre and Domingo (1992).

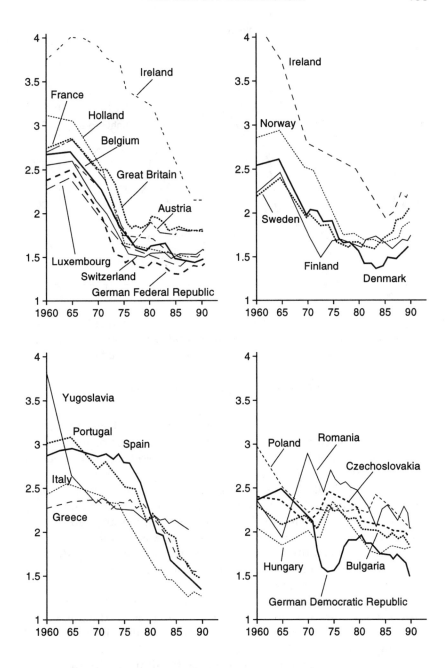

Figure 4.5   Synthetic index of fertility in European countries since 1960
Source: Alberdi (1995)

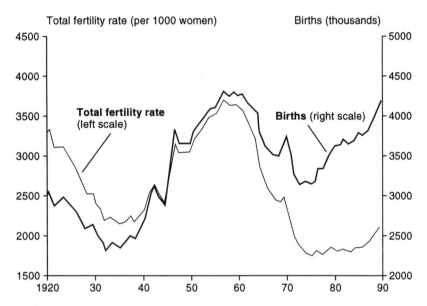

Figure 4.6 Total fertility rate and number of births in US, 1920–90
(total fertility rate = number of children that women would have by
the end of their child-bearing years based on age-specific birth rates
of a single year)
Source: US Bureau of the Census (1992a)

went back to having children, and their countries displayed in the
1980s the highest fertility rate in Europe. However, the recent picture
is not so rosy. Constraints on the Scandinavian welfare state reduced
the amount of support, and, accordingly, in the early 1990s
Scandinavian fertility rates stabilized, at replacement rate levels.[21]
Also, in a number of countries, particularly in the United States, the
total fertility rate is being pushed up by their immigrant population,
thus inducing multi-ethnicity and multiculturalism. One of the most
important socio-cultural differences might be the preservation of
patriarchalism among ethnic minority immigrant communities in
contrast to the disintegration of traditional families among native
ethnic groups (black and white) in industrialized societies. This trend
is, of course, self-reproducing, even accounting for a reduction in the
birth rate of immigrant minorities as soon as they improve their
economy and their education.

Overall, it seems that in most developed countries, with the major
exceptions of Japan and Spain, the patriarchal family is in the process

[21] Alberdi (1995).

Table 4.10   Total fertility rate by main regions of the world

	1970–75	1980–85	1990–95[a]
World	4.4	3.5	3.3
More-developed regions	2.2	2.0	1.9
Less-developed regions	5.4	4.1	3.6
Africa	6.5	6.3	6.0
Asia	5.1	3.5	3.2
Europe	2.2	1.9	1.7
Americas	3.6	3.1	–
Latin	–	–	3.1
Northern	–	–	2.0
Oceania	3.2	2.7	2.5
USSR	2.4	2.4	2.3

[a]   1990–95 as projections.
Sources: United Nations, *World Population Prospects*, estimates as assessed in 1984; United Nations, *World Population at the Turn of the Century* (1989), p. 9; United Nations Population Fund, *The State of World Population: Choices and Responsibilities* (1994)

of becoming a minority form in the way people live. In the United States, only about one-quarter of all households in the 1990s fits the ideal type of a married couple with children (see below). If we add the qualification "with the couple's children," the proportion drops. Certainly, not all is women's liberation. Demographic structure has something to do with it: another one-quarter of households in the US are one-person households, and the majority of them are elderly people, mainly women outliving their husbands. Yet, a statistical study conducted by Antonella Pinelli on the variables conditioning new demographic behavior in Europe concludes that:

> we see that marital instability, cohabitation, and extramarital births are taking place where there is a high-value on non-material aspects of the quality of life, and where women enjoy economic independence and relatively great political power. The conditions for women should be emphasized. Divorce, cohabitation, and extramarital fertility are the most widespread where women enjoy economic independence and are in a position to face the possibility of being a single mother without becoming, for this reason, a social subject at risk.[22]

Her conclusions must be corrected, however, by the observation that this is only part of the story. Children born out of wedlock in the United States result as much from poverty and lack of education as

[22]   Pinelli (1995: 88).

from women's self-affirmation. None the less, the general trend, as shown in a few statistical illustrations, is toward the weakening and potential dissolution of traditional family forms of unchallenged patriarchal domination, with wife and children clustering around the husband/father.

In developing countries similar trends are at work in the urban areas, but national statistics, overwhelmed by traditional rural societies (particularly in Africa and Asia), downplay the phenomenon, in spite of which we still have been able to detect some traces. The Spanish exception is fundamentally linked to youth unemployment, and to a serious housing shortage that precludes the formation of new households in the largest metropolitan areas.[23] As for Japan, cultural trends, such as the shame of non-marital births, help to consolidate patriarchalism, although recent trends seem to be eroding patriarchal ideology and women's relegation to the secondary labor market.[24] But my hypothesis about Japanese exceptionalism in preserving the patriarchal structure concerns mainly the absence of a significant feminist movement. Since such a movement is growing in the 1990s, I dare to forecast that in this matter, as in many others, Japanese uniqueness is to some extent a function of time. Without denying the cultural specificity of Japan, the forces at work, in the structure of society and in the minds of women, are such that Japan too will have to reckon with the challenge to patriarchalism from Japanese working women.[25]

If current trends continue to expand throughout the world, and I contend they will, families as we have known them will become, in a number of societies, a historical relic not too long in the historical horizon. And the fabric of our lives will have been transformed, as we already feel, sometimes painfully, the tremors of this transformation. Let us now turn to analyze the underlying trends at the root of this crisis and, it is to be hoped, at the source of new forms of togetherness between women, children, pets, and even men.

Women at Work

Work, family, and labor markets have been deeply transformed in the last quarter of this century by the massive incorporation of women to *paid labor*, in most cases outside their home.[26] Worldwide, 854 million

---

[23] Leal et al. (1996).
[24] Tsuya and Mason (1995).
[25] Gelb and Lief-Palley (1994).
[26] Kahne and Giele (1992); Mason and Jensen (1995).

Table 4.11 Labor force participation rates by sex (%)

	Men						Women					
	1973	1979	1983	1992	1993	1994[a]	1973	1979	1983	1992	1993	1994[a]
Australia	91.1	87.6	85.9	85.3	85.0	84.9	47.7	50.3	52.1	62.3	62.3	63.2
Austria	83.0	81.6	82.2	80.7	80.8	..	48.5	49.1	49.7	58.0	58.9	..
Belgium	83.2	79.3	76.8	72.6	..	..	41.3	46.3	48.7	54.1	..	..
Canada	86.1	86.3	84.7	78.9	78.3	..	47.2	55.5	60.0	65.1	65.3	..
Denmark	89.6	89.6	87.6	88.0	86.0	..	61.9	69.9	74.2	79.0	78.3	..
Finland	80.0	82.2	82.0	78.5	77.6	77.1	63.6	68.9	72.7	70.7	70.0	69.8
France	85.2	82.6	78.4	74.7	74.5	..	50.1	54.2	54.3	58.8	59.0	..
Germany	89.6	84.9	82.6	79.0	78.6	..	50.3	52.2	52.5	61.3	61.4	..
Greece	83.2	79.0	80.0	73.0	73.7	..	32.1	32.8	40.4	42.7	43.6	..
Ireland[b]	92.3	88.7	87.1	81.9	..	..	34.1	35.2	37.8	39.9	..	..
Italy	85.1	82.6	80.7	79.1	74.8	..	33.7	38.7	40.3	46.5	43.3	..
Japan	90.1	89.2	89.1	89.7	90.2	90.1	54.0	54.7	57.2	62.0	61.8	61.8
Luxembourg[b]	93.1	88.9	85.1	77.7	..	..	35.9	39.8	41.7	44.8	..	..
Netherlands	85.6	79.0	77.3	80.8	..	..	29.2	33.4	40.3	55.5	..	..
New Zealand	89.2	87.3	84.7	83.0	83.3	..	39.2	45.0	45.7	63.2	63.2	..
Norway	86.5	89.2	87.2	82.6	82.0	82.3	50.6	61.7	65.5	70.9	70.8	71.3
Portugal[c]	..	90.9	86.9	82.3	82.5	82.8	..	57.3	56.7	60.6	61.3	62.2
Spain	92.9	83.1	80.2	75.1	74.5	73.9	33.4	32.6	33.2	42.0	42.8	43.9
Sweden	88.1	87.9	85.9	81.8	79.3	78.1	62.6	72.8	76.6	77.7	75.7	74.6
Switzerland	100.0	94.6	93.5	93.7	92.5	91.0	54.1	53.0	55.2	58.5	57.9	56.9
United Kingdom	93.0	90.5	87.5	84.5	83.3	81.8	53.2	58.0	57.2	64.8	64.7	64.5
United States	86.2	85.7	84.6	85.3	84.9	85.4	51.1	58.9	61.8	69.0	69.0	70.5
North America	86.2	85.8	84.6	84.6	84.2	..	50.7	58.6	61.6	68.6	68.7	..
OECD Europe[d]	88.7	84.8	82.3	79.2	80.1	..	44.7	48.6	49.8	56.9	60.6	..
Total OECD[d]	88.2	85.9	84.3	82.9	81.3	..	48.3	53.1	55.1	61.9	61.6	..

[a] Secretariat estimates. [b] 1991 instead of 1992 for Ireland and Luxembourg.
[c] Labor force data include a significant number of persons aged less than 15 years.   [d] Above countries only.
Source: OECD *Employment Outlook* (1995)

Table 4.12 Total employment by sex (average annual growth rates in percentages)

	Men						Women					
	1973–75	1975–79	1979–83	1983–91	1992	1993	1973–75	1975–79	1979–83	1983–91	1992	1993
Australia	-0.3	0.6	-0.1	1.5[d]	-0.3	0.0	2.0	1.7	2.0	3.9[d]	0.6	0.8
Austria	-1.1	0.8	0.9	0.7	0.8	:	-1.2	1.0	0.8	2.1	3.3	:
Belgium	-0.4	-0.4	-1.8	0.0	-1.1	:	0.8	0.9	0.2	2.0	0.5	:
Canada	1.9	1.8	-0.6	1.1	-1.2	1.2	4.7	4.5	2.6	2.8	-0.4	1.1
Denmark	-1.8	0.7[b]	-1.7	0.9	:	:	-0.5	3.6[b]	0.9	1.4	:	:
Finland	0.7	-0.6[b]	0.9	-0.5	-7.6	-5.9	2.0	-0.0[b]	1.9	-0.1	-6.5	-6.3
France	-0.4	-0.2	-0.7	-0.1	-1.2	:	0.8	1.6	0.7	1.4	0.5	:
Germany	-2.5	0.3	-0.5	0.8[e]	-0.3	:	-1.0	0.9	-0.0	2.0[e]	1.7	:
Greece	-0.5	0.8	0.6	0.1	:	:	1.6	1.1	4.1	0.7	:	:
Ireland	-0.2	1.5	-1.4	-0.5	:	:	1.6	2.0	1.9	1.1	:	:
Italy	0.6	-0.1	0.0	0.1	-1.1	:[h]	2.4	2.7	1.3	1.6	0.3	:[h]
Japan	0.5	0.7	0.8	1.1	1.1	0.6	-1.7	2.0	1.7	1.7	1.0	-0.3
Luxembourg	1.0	-0.7	-0.7	2.3[f]	:	:	4.6	1.5	1.8	3.3[f]	:	:
Netherlands	-1.5	0.3	-0.8	2.1	1.3	:	2.9	2.7	4.0	5.3	3.2	:
New Zealand	2.1	0.2	-0.3	-1.0[d]	0.4	:	5.2	2.7	0.8	1.3[d]	0.6	:
Norway	0.9	1.1	-0.2	-0.4	-0.5	-0.5	2.9	4.4	1.8	1.40	-0.1	0.5
Portugal	-1.3[a]	0.3	0.4[c]	1.0	.[g]	-2.8	-1.5[a]	0.9	1.1[c]	3.0	.[g]	-1.2
Spain	-0.2	-1.7[b]	-1.8	0.8	-3.2	-5.4	-1.5	-1.3[b]	-1.7	3.0	0.3	-2.4
Sweden	1.0	-0.3	-0.6	0.1[c]	-5.1	-7.9	4.2	2.0	1.3	0.9[c]	-3.5	-6.2
Switzerland	-2.8	-0.5	0.8	0.8	-2.1	-2.5	-1.9	0.6	2.0	1.6	-2.4	-2.5
United Kingdom	-1.0	-0.2	-2.3	0.4	-3.3	-2.8	1.5	1.2	-1.0	2.3	-1.0	-1.3
United States	-0.6	2.5	-0.3	1.3	0.3	1.3	2.0	5.0	1.7	2.4	0.9	1.5
North America	-0.4	2.4	-0.4	1.2	0.2	1.3	2.2	4.9	1.8	2.4	0.8	1.5
OECD Europe[i]	-0.8	-0.2	-0.8	0.4	-2.0	:	1.2	1.4	0.5	2.0	-0.3	:
Total OECD[i]	-0.4	0.9	-0.3	0.9	-1.4	:	1.0	2.8	1.2	2.2	-0.1	:

[a] Break in series between 1973 and 1974.
[b] Break in series between 1975 and 1976.
[c] Break in series between 1982 and 1983.
[d] Break in series between 1985 and 1986.
[e] Break in series between 1986 and 1987.
[f] Data refer to 1983–90.
[g] Break in series between 1991 and 1992.
[h] Break in series between 1992 and 1993.
[i] Above countries only.

Source: OECD Employment Outlook (1995)

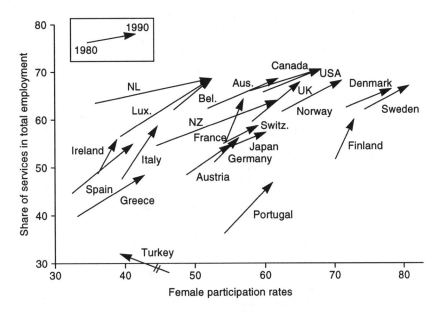

Figure 4.7 Growth in service sector employment and in female participation rates, 1980–90 (Aus., Australia; Bel., Belgium; Lux., Luxembourg; NL, Netherlands; NZ, New Zealand; Switz., Switzerland)
Source: OECD (1994b), Statistical Annex, tables A and D

women were economically active in 1990, accounting for 32.1 percent of the global labor force. Among women aged 15 years and over, 41 percent were economically active.[27] In OECD countries, the average labor force participation rate for women rose from 48.3 percent in 1973 to 61.6 percent in 1993, while for men it declined from 88.2 percent to 81.3 percent (see table 4.11). In the United States, women's labor participation rate went up from 51.1 percent in 1973 to 70.5 percent in 1994. Growth rates of employment for 1973–93 also indicate a general upward trend for women (reversed in some European countries in the 1990s), and a positive differential *vis à vis* men (table 4.12). Similar trends can be observed worldwide. Switching to the United Nations statistical categorization of "economic activity rate" (whose percentages are lower than those of labor force participation), tables 4.13 and 4.14 show a similar upward trend for women's economic activity rate, with the partial exception of Russia which already had a high level in 1970.

The massive entry of women into the paid labor force is due, on the one hand, to the informationalization, networking, and globalization

[27] United Nations (1995).

Table 4.13 Economic activity rates, 1970–90

			1970	*1975*	*1980*	*1985*	*1990*
OECD							
Canada	(15+)	Total	40.9(71)	44.6(76)			
		Men	53.3	55.6			
		Women	28.4	33.8			
France	(15+)	Total	42.0(71)	42.6	43.3	43.4(86)	44.8
		Men	55.2	55.1	54.4	52.6	51.6
		Women	29.4	30.5	32.7	34.6	38.2
Germany	(14+)	Total	43.9	43.4	44.9		49.6
		Men	59.2	57.1	58.4		60.8
		Women	30.0	30.9	32.6		39.2
Italy	(14+)	Total	36.6	35.4	40.2	41.1	42.0
		Men	54.7	52.2	55.2	54.6	54.3
		Women	19.3	19.4	26.0	28.2	30.3
Japan	(15+)	Total	51.0	48.6	48.4	51.5	51.7
		Men	63.4	62.3	60.2	63.6	62.4
		Women	39.1	35.2	36.8	39.8	41.3
UK	(16+)	Total	42.5		47.3(81)		50.3
		Men	51.7		59.4		58.4
		Women	33.0		35.8		42.6
USA	(16+)	Total	41.8	44.5	49.1		
		Men	53.9	55.6	56.8		
		Women	30.2	33.9	41.8		44.4(92)
Russian	(16+)	Total	48.4		51.7(79)		50.2
Federation		Men	52.1		55.7		55.0
		Women	45.3		48.1		45.8
Asia							
China	(15+)	Total			52.3(82)		
		Men			57.3		
		Women	44.25		47.0		
India	(15+)	Total	32.9(71)				37.5(91)
		Men	52.5				51.6
		Women	11.9				22.3
Indonesia	(15+)	Total	34.9(71)		35.5		
		Men	47.3		48.1		
		Women	22.8		23.5		
Korea	(15+)	Total	33.0	38.5	37.9		
		Men	42.8	46.9	46.3		
		Women	23.2	30.0	29.3		
Latin America							
Argentina	(14+)	Total	38.5		38.5	37.5	38.1
		Men	57.9		55.1	55.3	55.4
		Women	19.4		22.0	19.9	21.0
Mexico	(12+)	Total	26.9	27.6	33.0		29.6
		Men	43.6	42.9	48.2		46.2
		Women	10.2	12.0	18.2		13.6

Table 4.13 contd

			1970	1975	1980	1985	1990
Brazil	(10+)	Total	31.7		36.3		41.9
		Men	10.5		53.1		56.3
		Women	13.1		19.8		27.9
Africa							
Algeria	(6+)	Total	21.7(66)				23.6
		Men	42.2				42.4
		Women	1.8				4.4
Nigeria	(14+)	Total					30.3
		Men					40.7
		Women					19.7
Middle East							
Egypt	(6+)	Total	27.9(71)	30.2(76)			31.6
		Men	51.2	54.1			49.3
		Women	4.2	5.5			13.5

Note: Economic activity rate = economically active population/total population.
Source: ILO, Yearbook of Labour Statistics (1970–94)

Table 4.14 Growth rate of women's economic activity rate, 1970–90

	1970	1990	Growth rate (%)
France	29.4	38.2	29.9
Germany	30.0	39.2	30.7
Italy	19.3	30.3	57.0
Japan	39.1	41.3	5.6
UK	33.0	42.6	29.1
USA	30.2	44.4	47.0
Russia	45.3	45.8	1.1
India	11.9	22.3	87.4
Argentina	19.4	21.0	8.2
Mexico	10.2	13.6	33.3
Brazil	13.1	27.9	113.0
Algeria	1.8	4.4	144.4
Egypt	4.2	13.5	221.4

Note: Economic activity rate = economically active population/total
population.
Source: ILO, Yearbook of Labour Statistics (1970–94)

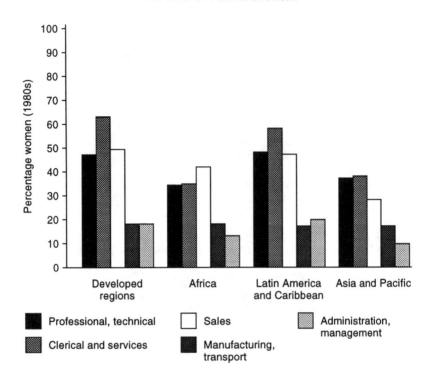

Figure 4.8a   Women as a percentage of the labor force by type of employment
Source: Prepared by the Statistical Office of the United Nations Secretariat (1991) from International Labour Office, *Yearbook of Labour Statistics* (various years)

of the economy; on the other hand, to the gendered segmentation of the labor market taking advantage of specific social conditions of women to enhance productivity, management control, and ultimately profits.[28] Let us look at some statistical indicators.[29]

When analyzing the transformation of employment structure in the informational economy (volume I, chapter 4), I showed the growth of service employment, and, within services, the strategic role played by two distinctive categories of services: business services, and social services, characteristic of the informational economy, as forecasted by early theorists of postindustrialism. Figure 4.7 displays the convergence between growth of services and of female employment in

[28]   Kahne and Giele (1992); Rubin and Riney (1994).
[29]   See Blumstein and Schwartz (1983); Cobble (1993); OECD (1993-95, 1994a, b, 1995); Mason and Jensen (1995); United Nations (1995).

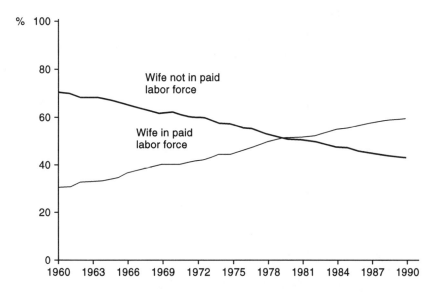

Figure 4.8b   Married couple families with wives in the labor force, in
US, 1960–90 (data for 1983 not available)
Source: US Bureau of the Census (1992a)

1980–90. Figure 4.8a shows the concentration of women in service
employment in different areas of the world. However, it should be
noticed that, in most of the world, the majority of labor is still agricultural (but not for long), and therefore, most women still work in
agriculture: 80 percent of economically active women in sub-Saharan
Africa, and 60 percent in southern Asia. Worldwide, about half of
economically active women are in services.[30] The proportion is much
higher in most developed countries, and has been increasing over
time, to reach about 85 percent of the female labor force in the US
and the UK. However, the most significant aspect is in which kind
of services women work. As shown in table 4.15, in most developed
countries, the bulk of female employment is in social services and
personal services. However, if we calculate the rate of increase of each
type of service in total female employment for the 1973–93 period
(table 4.16), we observe a spectacular increase in business services,
followed at some distance by social/personal services. Trade and
restaurant employment is the least dynamic segment in the evolution
of women's employment in advanced countries. Thus, there is a direct
correspondence between the type of services linked to informationalization of the economy and the expansion of women's employment

[30]   United Nations (1991).

Table 4.15 Female service employment by activities and rank of information intensity of total employment (%), 1973–93

		1 Financing, insurance, real estate, and business services	2 Community, social and personal services	2 Transport, storage and communications	3 Wholesale and retail trade, restaurants and hotels	(Rank of information intensity) Activities not adequately defined	Total
Canada	1975	11.2	40.2	4.0	25.8		81.2
	1983	12.1	40.9	4.2	25.4		82.6
	1993	13.6	43.9	3.7	24.8		86.0
USA	1973	9.1	41.5	3.5	23.9		78.0
	1983	11.9	41.9	3.3	24.5		81.6
	1993	12.6	46.6	3.5	22.7		85.3
Japan	1973	3.4	22.0	2.0	24.7	0.2	52.3
	1983	6.9	24.1	1.9	27.1	0.2	60.3
	1993	9.4	26.9	2.5	27.5	0.4	66.7
Germany	1973						
	1983	8.2	34.2	3.3	22.5		68.2
	1993	10.3	38.4	3.6	22.4		74.6
Italy	1977	1.7	31.0	1.8	18.8		53.3
	1983	3.1	34.6	2.0	21.0		60.6
	1993	8.1	36.4	2.7	22.6		69.8
UK	1973	7.4	36.0	2.8	24.7		70.7
	1983	9.8	42.2	2.8	25.0	0.1	79.9
	1993						84.9
Spain	1977	2.1	28.2	1.5	24.4		56.3
	1983	3.0	35.8	1.7	24.4		64.9
	1993	6.3	41.8	2.2	26.9		77.2

Source: OECD, *Labour Force Statistics* (1995)

Table 4.16 Rates of growth for each category of female service employment as a percentage of total female employment, 1973–1993[a]

Country	Business services (%)	Social and personal services (%)	Transportation, storage and communication (%)	Trade, hotels and restaurants (%)
USA	38.5	12.2	0	−5.0
Japan	176.5	22.2	25	1.3
Germany (1983–93)	25.6	12.3	9	−0.4
Italy (1977–93)	376.5	17.4	50	−3.9
UK	32.4	17.2	0	1.2
Spain (1977–93)	200.0	48.2	47	10.2

[a] Unless dates for calculations are otherwise indicated.
Source: Elaboration on data from table 4.15

in advanced countries. A similar conclusion results from observing the changing evolution of female employment by occupation between 1980 and 1989 in selected OECD countries (table 4.17). Overall, professional/technical and administrative/managerial categories have grown faster than others, although clerical workers still account, in general, for the largest group of women workers. Women are not being relegated to the lowest skilled service jobs: they are employed across the entire skills structure, and the growth of women's jobs is higher at the upper end of the occupational structure. This is exactly why there is discrimination: because they perform similarly qualified jobs at lower pay, with greater job insecurity, and with lower chances of careers to the top.

Globalization has also played a major part in involving women in the labor force around the world. The electronics industry, internationalized since the late 1960s, recruited mainly among young, unskilled women in Asia[31] The US *maquiladoras* in northern Mexico rely heavily on female labor. And the newly industrialized economies have brought into paid work underpaid women at almost all levels of the occupational structure[32] At the same time, a substantial share of urban employment for women in developing countries remains in the informal sector, particularly in providing food and services for metropolitan dwellers.[33]

[31] Salaff (1981, 1988).
[32] Standing (1990).
[33] Portes et al. (1989).

Table 4.17 Distribution of female employment by occupation,[a] 1980 and 1989 (%)

Country[b,c]	Professional, technical and related	Administrative and managerial	Clerical and related	Sales workers	Service workers	Agriculture and related	Production and related
Belgium							
1983	25.9	1.4	24.4	13.7	18.6	2.8	13.2
1988	28.2	1.4	27.3	14.6	14.4	2.1	11.6
Index (1983 = 100)	118.0	113.0	122.0	116.0	84.0	86.0	95.0
Canada							
1980	19.1	5.4	34.5	10.0	18.3	2.8	9.9
1989	20.9	10.7	30.5	9.9	17.0	2.2	8.9
Index (1980 = 100)	143.0	185.0	114.0	123.0	122.0	98.0	113.0
Finland							
1980	19.8	1.4	21.8	8.6	22.3	10.5	15.5
1989	31.2	1.9	22.7	11.5	16.2	6.5	10.0
Index (1980 = 100)	172.0	147.0	113.0	145.0	79.0	66.0	70.0
Germany							
1980	14.1	1.3	30.7	12.9	16.3	6.9	15.9
1986	16.2	1.5	29.8	12.8	16.1	5.5	13.3
Index (1980 = 100)	118.0	115.0	99.0	102.0	102.0	83.0	86.0
Greece							
1981	10.7	0.7	12.9	9.0	9.7	41.6	15.5
1989	14.4	0.8	14.6	10.8	11.5	34.0	13.9
Index (1981= 100)	156.0	130.0	131.0	138.0	137.0	95.0	104.0
Japan							
1980	9.6	0.5	23.1	14.3	12.7	13.1	26.5
1989	11.4	0.8	26.4	14.4	11.4	8.8	26.5
Index (1980 = 100)	173.0	132.0	116.0	104.0	77.0	116.0	250.0

Table 4.17 contd

Country [b,c]	Professional, technical and related	Administrative and managerial	Clerical and related	Sales workers	Service workers	Agriculture and related	Production and related
Norway							
1980	23.6	2.2	19.2	12.8	24.9	5.9	11.2
1989	28.3	3.5	19.8	12.4	22.3	3.9	9.4
Index (1980 = 100)	141.0	188.0	121.0	114.0	106.0	78.0	99.0
Spain							
1980	8.7	0.2	13.2	15.4	25.6	18.2	18.7
1989	15.2	0.4	18.2	15.4	25.2	11.1	14.4
Index (1980 = 100)	202.0	280.0	160.0	116.0	114.0	70.0	89.0
Sweden							
1980	30.6	0.8	21.6	8.7	22.8	3.0	12.4
1989	42.0	n.a.	21.9	9.3	13.2	1.8	11.7
Index (1980 = 100)	154.0	n.a.	114.0	120.0	65.0	66.0	106.0
United States							
1980	16.8	6.9	35.1	6.8	19.5	1.2	13.8
1989	18.1	11.1	27.8	13.1	17.7	1.1	11.1
Index (1980 = 100)	136.0	202.0	99.0	243.0	115.0	115.0	101.0

[a] Major groups of the International Standard Classification of Occupations (ISCO).
[b] Not all countries publish data according to ISCO. Countries in which occupational classification systems have changed during the relevant period are omitted.
[c] The index indicates the growth in total numbers employed in the occupation over the decade.
Source: ILO, Yearbook of Labour Statistics (various years)

Why women? First, because, in contrast with the misleading statements printed in the media, overall there has been a sustained job creation in the world in the past three decades, with the exception of Europe (see volume I, chapter 4). But, even in Europe, women's labor participation has increased while men's has declined. So, women's entry into the labor force is not just a response to labor demand. Also, women's unemployment is not always higher than for men: in 1994 it was lower than men's in the United States (6 percent v. 6.2 percent), and in Canada (9.8 percent v. 10.7 percent); and it was much lower than men's in 1993 in the United Kingdom (7.5 percent v. 12.4 percent). On the other hand, it was slightly higher in Japan and Spain, and significantly higher in France and Italy. Thus, the increase in women's labor participation rate goes on independently of their differential in unemployment *vis à vis* men, and of the growth of labor demand.

If labor demand, in purely quantitative terms, does not explain calling upon women, their appeal for employers must be explained by other characteristics. I think it is well established in the literature that it is the social gendering of women's work that makes them, as a whole, an attractive labor pool[34] This has certainly nothing to do with biological characteristics: women have proved that they can be firefighters and dockers around the world, and strenuous factory work by women marked industrialization from its beginning. Nor, for that matter, has young women's employment in electronics anything to do with the myth of their fingers' dexterity, but with the social acceptance of wasting their eyes in 10 years through microscopic assembly. Anthropologists have documented how, at the origins of women's employment in electronic factories in South-east Asia, there was the pattern of patriarchal authority extending from the family household into the factory, under agreement between factory managers and the paterfamilias.[35]

Neither, it seems, is the reason for hiring women to do with their lack of unionization. The causality seems to work the other way around: women are not unionized because they are often employed in sectors where there is little or no unionization, such as private business services or electronics manufacturing. Even so, women constitute 37 percent of union members in the United States, 39 percent in Canada, 51 percent in Sweden, and 30 percent in Africa, on average.[36] Garment workers in the United States and in Spain, women in the Mexican *maquiladoras*, and teachers and nurses

---

[34]   Spitz (1988); Kahne and Giele (1992); OECD (1994b).
[35]   Salaff (1981).
[36]   United Nations (1991).

throughout the world have mobilized in defense of their demands, with greater vehemence than male-dominated steel or chemical workers' unions in recent times. The supposed submissiveness of women workers is an enduring myth whose fallacy managers have come to realize, at their cost.[37] So, which are the main factors inducing the explosion of women's employment?

The first, and most obvious, factor concerns the possibility of paying less for similar work. With the expansion of universal education, including college education, particularly in most developed countries, women came to constitute a pool of skills that was immediately tapped by employers. Women's wage differential *vis à vis* men persists throughout the world, while, as we have seen, in most advanced countries differences in occupational profile are small. In the US, women earned 60–65 percent of men's earnings in the 1960s, and their share improved somewhat to 72 percent in 1991, but the main reason for this was the decline in men's real wages.[38] In the UK, women's earnings were 69.5 percent of men's in the mid-1980s. They were 73.6 percent in Germany in 1991, up from 72 percent in 1980. For France, the corresponding figures are 80.8 percent, up from 79 percent. Women's average wage is 43 percent of men's in Japan, 51 percent in Korea, 56 percent in Singapore, 70 percent in Hong Kong, and varies in a wide range between 44 percent and 77 percent in Latin America.[39]

I want to emphasize that in most cases women are not being deskilled, or reduced to menial jobs, but, quite the opposite. They are often promoted to multi-skilled jobs that require initiative, and education, as new technologies demand an autonomous labor force able to adapt, and reprogram its own tasks, as in the case studies of insurance and banking that I summarized in volume I, chapter 4. This is in fact the second major reason for hiring women, at a bargain price: their relational skills, increasingly necessary in an informational economy where the administration of things takes second place to the management of people. In this sense, there is an extension of the gendered division of labor between male's traditional production and female's traditional home-making, and social-making, under patriarchalism. It just happens that the new economy requires increasingly the skills that were confined to the private domain of relational work to be brought to the forefront of management and processing of information and people.

But there is something else that I believe is probably the most

[37]   Cobble (1993).
[38]   Kim (1993).
[39]   United Nations (1995).

Table 4.18 Size and composition of part-time employment, 1973–94 (%)

Part-time employment as a proportion of employment

	Men						Women					
	1973	1979	1983	1992	1993	1994	1973	1979	1983	1992	1993	1994
Australia	3.7	5.2	6.2	10.6	10.3	10.9	28.2	35.2	36.4	43.3	42.3	42.6
Austria	1.4	1.5	1.5	1.6	1.7	..	15.6	18.0	20.0	20.5	22.8	..
Belgium	1.0	1.0	2.0	2.1	2.3	2.5	10.2	16.5	19.7	28.1	28.5	28.3
Canada	4.7	5.7	7.6	9.3	9.8	9.5	19.4	23.2	26.1	25.8	26.2	26.1
Denmark	..	5.2	6.6	10.1	11.0	..	..	46.3	44.7	36.7	37.3	..
Finland	..	3.2	4.5	5.5	6.2	6.0	..	10.6	12.5	10.4	11.1	11.2
France	1.7	2.4	2.5	3.6	4.1	4.6	12.9	17.0	20.1	24.5	26.3	27.8
Germany[a]	1.8	1.5	1.7	2.6	2.9	..	24.4	27.6	30.0	30.7	32.0	..
Greece	..	..	3.7	2.8	2.6	3.1	..	..	12.1	8.4	7.6	8.0
Iceland	..	..	..	9.2	9.9	..	..	..	..	49.8	47.5	..
Ireland	..	2.1	2.7	3.9	4.8	..	..	13.1	15.5	18.6	21.3	..
Italy	3.7	3.0	2.4	2.8	2.5	2.8	14.0	10.6	9.4	11.5	11.0	12.4
Japan	6.8	7.5	7.3	10.6	11.4	11.7	25.1	27.8	29.8	34.8	35.2	35.7
Luxembourg	1.0	1.0	1.0	1.2	1.0	..	18.4	17.1	17.0	16.5	18.3	..
Mexico[b]	..	..	..	18.7	19.6	..	..	..	..	36.1	36.6	..
Netherlands[c]	..	5.5	7.2	13.3	13.6	14.7	..	44.0	50.1	62.1	63.0	64.8
New Zealand	4.6	4.9	5.0	10.3	9.7	9.7	24.6	29.1	31.4	35.9	35.7	36.6
Norway[d]	8.6	10.6	11.5	9.8	9.8	9.5	47.8	51.7	54.9	47.1	47.6	46.5
Portugal	..	2.5	..	4.1	4.5	4.7	..	16.5	..	11.3	11.1	12.1
Spain	..	..	..	2.0	2.4	2.6	..	..	..	13.7	14.8	15.2
Sweden[e]	..	5.4	6.3	8.4	9.1	9.7	..	46.0	45.9	41.3	41.4	41.0
Switzerland	..	..	..	8.3	8.6	8.8	..	..	..	53.7	54.1	55.4
Turkey	..	..	..	11.3	17.9	..	..	..	..	37.0	40.4	..
United Kingdom	2.3	1.9	3.3	6.2	6.6	7.1	39.1	39.0	42.4	43.5	43.8	44.3
United States[f]	8.6	9.0	10.8	10.8	10.9	11.5	26.8	26.7	28.1	25.4	25.3	27.7

Table 4.18 contd

	Part-time employment as a proportion of total employment						Women's share in part-time employment					
	1973	1979	1983	1992	1993	1994	1973	1979	1983	1992	1993	1994
Australia	11.9	15.9	17.5	24.5	23.9	24.4	79.4	78.7	78.0	75.0	75.3	74.2
Austria	6.4	7.6	8.4	9.0	10.1	..	85.8	87.8	88.4	89.6	89.7	..
Belgium	3.8	6.0	8.1	12.4	12.8	12.8	82.4	88.9	84.0	89.7	89.3	88.1
Canada	9.7	12.5	15.4	16.7	17.2	17.0	68.4	72.1	71.3	69.7	68.9	69.4
Denmark	..	22.7	23.8	22.5	23.3	..	..	86.9	84.7	75.8	74.9	..
Finland	..	6.7	8.3	7.9	8.6	8.5	..	74.7	71.7	64.3	63.1	63.6
France	5.9	8.1	9.6	12.5	13.7	14.9	82.3	82.1	84.3	83.7	83.3	82.7
Germany[a]	10.1	11.4	12.6	14.4	15.1	..	89.0	91.6	91.9	89.3	88.6	..
Greece	..	..	6.5	4.8	4.3	4.8	..	..	61.2	61.3	61.6	58.9
Iceland	..	..	..	27.8	27.3	..	..	..	..	82.1	80.4	..
Ireland	..	5.1	6.6	9.1	10.8	..	..	71.2	71.6	72.5	71.7	..
Italy	6.4	5.3	4.6	5.8	5.4	6.2	58.3	61.4	64.8	68.8	70.5	71.1
Japan	13.9	15.4	16.2	20.5	21.1	21.4	70.0	70.1	72.9	69.3	67.7	67.5
Luxembourg	5.8	5.8	6.3	6.9	7.3	..	87.5	87.5	88.9	88.9	91.2	..
Mexico[b]	..	..	..	24.0	24.9	..	..	..	..	46.3	46.1	..
Netherlands[c]	..	16.6	21.4	32.5	33.4	35.0	..	76.4	77.3	75.2	75.7	75.1
New Zealand	11.2	13.9	15.3	21.6	21.2	21.6	72.3	77.7	79.8	73.3	74.2	74.9
Norway[d]	23.0	27.3	29.6	26.9	27.1	26.5	76.4	77.0	77.3	80.1	80.5	80.6
Portugal	..	7.8	..	7.3	7.4	8.0	..	80.4	..	68.2	66.3	67.1
Spain	..	..	..	5.8	6.6	6.9	..	..	..	77.0	75.6	74.9
Sweden[e]	..	23.6	24.8	24.3	24.9	24.9	..	87.5	86.6	82.3	81.3	80.1
Switzerland	..	..	..	27.8	28.1	28.9	..	..	..	83.1	82.5	82.7
Turkey	..	..	..	19.3	24.8	..	..	..	..	59.3	50.2	..
United Kingdom	16.0	16.4	19.4	22.8	23.3	23.8	90.9	92.8	89.8	84.9	84.5	83.6
United States[f]	15.6	16.4	18.4	17.5	17.5	18.9	66.0	68.0	66.8	66.4	66.2	67.3

[a] Up to 1990 data refer to Western Germany; thereafter, they refer to the whole of Germany.   [b] 1991 instead of 1992.   [c] Break in series after 1985.
[d] Break in series after 1987.   [e] Break in series after 1986 and after 1992.   [f] Break in series after 1993.
Source: OECD, Employment Outlook (1995)

Table 4.19 Share of self-employment in total employment, by sex and activity (%)

| | All non-agricultural activities | | | | Service activities (1990) both sexes | | | |
| | Share of female employment | | Share of male employment | | Wholesale and retail trade, restaurants and hotels (ISIC 6) | Transport, storage and communications (ISIC 7) | Financing, insurance, real estate and business services (ISIC 8) | Community, social and personal services (ISIC 9) |
	1979	1990	1979	1990				
Australia	10.0	9.6	13.9	14.4	15.5	14.5	14.0	6.6
Austria	:	:	:	:	13.7	3.6	10.0	5.0
Belgium	8.8	10.3	12.6	16.7	36.0	5.5	21.7	8.2
Canada	6.0	6.4	7.2	8.3	7.2	6.4	10.4	8.5
Denmark	:	2.8	:	10.4	13.3	6.9	9.6	3.2
Finland	4.2	5.6	7.9	11.5	16.0	11.2	10.5	4.0
France	:	5.5	:	11.9	19.2	4.8	9.2	5.3
Germany	4.8	5.4	9.4	9.7	15.7	6.6	17.1	5.5
Greece	25.7	15.4	34.0	32.7	48.0	25.5	35.9	9.4
Ireland	:	6.1	:	16.8	24.4	13.7	13.6	6.8
Italy	12.8	15.1	21.7	25.8	45.8	14.1	8.9	15.5
Japan	12.9	9.3	14.6	12.1	15.0	4.8	8.1	12.0
Luxembourg	:	5.8	:	7.9	17.5	3.8	7.0	3.7
Netherlands	:	7.3	:	9.6	13.4	3.3	11.9	7.8
New Zealand	:	11.8	:	24.0	18.2	11.1	19.2	9.6
Norway	3.4	3.6	8.9	8.8	7.5	9.3	6.7	4.4
Portugal	:	12.3	:	18.3	38.3	8.6	13.7	4.6
Spain	12.5	13.9	17.1	19.2	34.0	26.8	13.7	6.0
Sweden	6.2	3.9	2.5	10.1	13.6	8.8	11.6	3.7
United Kingdom	3.2	7.0	9.0	16.6	15.9	10.5	14.2	7.8
United States	4.9	5.9	8.7	8.7	8.5	4.6	11.4	7.3

Source: OECD, *Employment Outlook* (1991), table 2.12; (1992) tables 4.A.2 and 4.A.8

important factor inducing the expansion of women's employment in the 1990s: their flexibility as workers.[40] Indeed, women account for the bulk of part-time employment and temporary employment, and for a still small but growing share of self-employment (tables 4.18 and 4.19). Relating this observation to the analyses presented in volume I, chapters 3 and 4, concerning the networking of economic activity, and the flexibilization of work as major features of the informational economy, it seems reasonable to argue that there is a fit between women's working flexibility, in schedules, time, and entry and exit to and from the labor market, and the needs of the new economy.[41] This fit is also a gendered condition. Since women's work has traditionally been considered as complementary to men's earnings in the family, and since women are still responsible for their household and, above all, for the rearing of their children, work flexibility fits, as well, survival strategies of coping with both worlds on the edge of a nervous breakdown.[42] Indeed, in the European Union (as everywhere else), marriage and children are the most important factors in inducing women's part-time employment (figure 4.9). Thus, the type of worker required by the informational, networked economy fits the survival interests of women who, under the conditions of patriarchalism, seek to make compatible work and family, with little help from their husbands.

This process of full incorporation of women into the labor market, and into paid work, has important consequences for the family. The first is that more often than not a woman's financial contribution becomes decisive for the household budget. Thus, female bargaining power in the household increases significantly. Under strict patriarchalism, women's domination by men was, to start with, a living matter: home-making was their job. Thus, rebellion against patriarchal authority could be only extreme, often leading to marginality. With women bringing pay home, and with men in many countries (for instance in the United States) seeing their real pay-checks decline, matters of disagreement could be discussed without necessarily escalating to all-out patriarchal repression. Furthermore, the ideology of patriarchalism legitimizing domination on the basis of the family provider's privilege was decisively undermined. Why could husbands not help at home if both members of the couple were equally absent for long hours, and if both were equally contributing to the family budget? The questions became more pressing with the increasing difficulty for women of assuming paid work, home work, child

[40] Susser (forthcoming).
[41] Thurman and Trah (1990); Duffy and Pupo (1992).
[42] Michelson (1985).

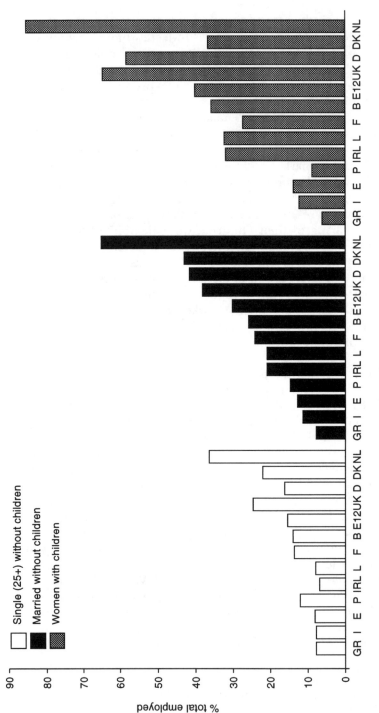

Figure 4.9 Women in part-time employment by family status in European Community member states, 1991 (GR, Greece; I, Italy; E, Spain; P, Portugal; IRL, Ireland; L, Luxembourg; F, France; B, Belgium; E12, average of member states; UK, United Kingdom; D, Germany; DK, Denmark; NL, Netherlands)

Source: European Commission, *Employment in Europe* (1993)

rearing, and management of husbands, while society was still organized on the assumption of the vanishing full-time housewife. With no proper child care, no planning of the spatial connection between residence, jobs, and services, and deteriorating social services,[43] women were confronted with their reality: their beloved husbands/fathers were taking advantage of them. And since their work outside the home opened their world, and broadened their social networks and their experience, often marked by sisterhood against daily harshness, they started to ask questions of themselves, and to give their answers to their daughters. The soil was ready for the seeding of feminist ideas that were *simultaneously* germinating in the fields of cultural social movements.

Sisterhood is Powerful: the Feminist Movement

The feminist movement, as manifested in its practice and discourses, is extraordinarily diverse. Its richness and depth increase as we analyze its contours in a global, comparative perspective, and as feminist historians and theoreticians unearth the hidden record of women's resistance and feminist thinking.[44] I will limit the analysis presented here to the contemporary feminist movement that surged in the late 1960s, first in the United States, then in Europe in the early 1970s, and diffused throughout the world in the next two decades. I will also focus on those features that are common to the movement, and that make it a transformative social movement challenging patriarchalism, while accounting for the diversity of women's struggles and the multiculturalism of their expression. As a preliminary, working definition of feminism, as understood here, I will follow Jane Mansbridge in broadly defining feminism as "the commitment to ending male domination."[45] I also concur with her view of feminism as a "discursively created movement." This does not imply that feminism is just discourse, or that the feminist debate, as expressed in the writings of various women, theorists and academics, is the primordial manifestation of feminism. What I contend, in line with Mansbridge and others,[46] is that the essence of feminism, as practiced and as narrated, is the (re)definition of woman's identity: sometimes by affirming equality between men and women, thus de-gendering biological/cultural differences; in other instances, on the contrary, as affirming

[43]   Servon and Castells (1996).
[44]   Rowbotham (1974, 1992); Kolodny (1984); Spivak (1990); Massolo (1992).
[45]   Mansbridge (1995: 29).
[46]   Butler (1990); Chodorow (1994); Whittier (1995).

the essential specificity of women, often in association with stating the superiority of women's ways as sources of human fulfillment; or else, claiming the necessity to depart from men's world, and recreate life, and sexuality, in sisterhood. *In all cases, through equality, difference, or separation, what is negated is woman's identity as defined by men, and as enshrined in the patriarchal family.* As Mansbridge writes:

> This discursively created movement is the entity that inspires movement activists and is the entity to which they feel accountable . . . This kind of accountability is an accountability through identity . . . It requires thinking of the collective as a worthy identity and oneself as part of that identity. Feminist identities are usually achieved, not given . . . Today, feminist identities are created and reinforced when feminists get together, act together, and read what other feminists have written. Talking and acting creates street theory and gives it meaning. Reading keeps one in touch and continues to make one think. Both experiences, of personal transformation and continuing interaction, make feminists "internally accountable" to the feminist movement.[47]

Thus, a fundamental commonality underlies the diversity of feminism: the historical effort, individual as well as collective, formal and informal, to redefine womanhood in direct opposition to patriarchalism.

To assess such an effort, and to propose a grounded typology of feminist movements, I will recall, succinctly, the trajectory of feminist movements in the past three decades. To simplify the argument, I will focus mainly on its place of rebirth, the United States, and I will try to correct the potential ethnocentrism of this approach with brief observations on other areas of the world, followed by a commentary on feminism in a comparative perspective.

American feminism: a discontinuous continuity[48]

American feminism has a long history in a country with a short history. From the official birth of organized feminism in 1848 at a village

[47]   Mansbridge (1995: 29).
[48]   For an excellent analysis of the evolution and transformation of the American feminist *movement* in the past three decades, see Whittier (1995); for an overview of feminist *organizations* in America, see Ferree and Martin (1995); for a well-organized and usefully commented collection of American feminist *discourses* since the 1960s, see Schneir (1994). Other sources used in my analysis are specifically cited in the text.

chapel in Seneca Falls, New York, American feminists undertook a protracted struggle in defense of women's rights to education, work, and political power, culminating in the conquest of their right to vote in 1920. Then, afterwards, for almost half a century, feminism was kept in the backstage of the American scene. Not that women ceased to fight.[49] In one of the most noted expressions of women's struggles, the 1955 bus boycott in Montgomery, Alabama, that arguably ushered in the civil rights movement in the South, and changed American history for ever, was enacted predominantly by African-American women organizing their communities.[50] Yet, an explicitly feminist mass movement surged only in and from the 1960s social movements, both from their human rights component, and from their counter-cultural, revolutionary tendencies.[51] On the one hand, in the wake of the work of John F. Kennedy's Presidential Commission on the Status of Women, in 1963, and of the approval of Title VII of the 1964 Civil Rights Act concerning women's rights, a group of influential women, headed by writer Betty Friedan, created the National Organization of Women (NOW) on October 29, 1966. NOW would become the most comprehensive national organization in defense of women's rights, and over the following three decades it demonstrated extraordinary political skill and perdurability, in spite of recurrent ideological and organizational crises. It came to epitomize the so-called liberal feminism, focusing on equal rights for women in all spheres of social, economic, and institutional life.

Around the same time, women participating in various radical social movements, and particularly in SDS (Students for a Democratic Society), started to organize separately as a reaction against pervasive sexism and male domination in revolutionary organizations that led not only to the personal abuse of women, but to the ridiculing of feminist positions as bourgeois and counter-revolutionary. What started in December 1965 as a workshop on "Women in the Movement" in the SDS Convention, and became articulated as Women Liberation in a 1967 convention at Ann Arbor, Michigan, generated a flurry of autonomous women's groups, most of which split from male-dominated revolutionary politics, giving birth to radical feminism. In these founding moments it is fair to say that the feminist movement was ideologically split between its liberal and radical components. Whereas NOW's first statement of purpose started by saying "We, MEN AND WOMEN [capitals in the original] who hereby constitute ourselves as the National Organization for Women, believe that the

[49]   Rupp and Taylor (1987).
[50]   Barnett (1995).
[51]   Evans (1979).

time has come for a new movement toward a fully equal partnership
of the sexes, as part of the world-wide revolution of human rights now
taking place within and beyond our national borders,"[52] the 1969
Redstockings Manifesto, that propelled radical feminism in New York,
asserted: "We identify the agents of our oppression as men. Male
supremacy is the oldest, most basic form of domination. All other
forms of exploitation and oppression (racism, capitalism, imperialism
etc.) are extensions of male supremacy; men dominate women, a few
men dominate the rest."[53]

Liberal feminism centered its goals on obtaining equal rights for
women, including the adoption of a constitutional amendment, that,
after being approved by Congress, failed to obtain the required
ratification by two-thirds of the states, being finally defeated in 1982.
Yet, the significance of this amendment was more symbolic than
anything else, since the real battles for equality were won in federal
and state legislation, and in the courts, from the right to equal pay for
equal work to reproductive rights, including the right of access to all
occupations and institutions. These impressive achievements, in less
than two decades, were obtained by skillful political lobbying, media
campaigns, and support for women candidates or pro-women candidates in their bids for public office. Particularly important was the
presence in the media of women journalists who were either feminists
or supportive of feminist causes. A number of somewhat feminist
commercial publications, most notably *Ms Magazine* founded in 1972,
were also instrumental in reaching out to American women beyond
organized feminist circles.

Radical feminists, while participating actively in equal rights
campaigns, and particularly in the mobilizations to obtain and defend
reproductive rights, focused on *consciousness raising* (CR), through the
organization of women-only CR groups, and the building of institutions of a women's autonomous culture. Defense of women against
male violence (anti-rape campaigns, self-defense training, shelters for
battered women, psychological counseling for abused women)
provided a direct link between women's immediate concerns and the
ideological critique of patriarchalism in action. Within the radical
stream, lesbian feminists (one of whose first public political
demonstrations, the "Lavender Menace," appeared in the Second
Congress to Unite Women, in May 1970 in New York) quickly became
a source of dedicated activism, cultural creativity, and theoretical
innovation. The relentless growth and widespread influence of
lesbian feminism in the feminist movement was to become both a

[52]   Reproduced in Schneir (1994: 96).
[53]   Reproduced in Schneir (1994: 127).

major force and a major challenge for the women's movement, which had to face its own internal prejudice about forms of sexuality, and to confront the dilemma of where (or whether) to draw the line for women's liberation.

For a while, socialist feminists tried to associate the radical feminist challenge to broader issues of anti-capitalist movements, linking up when necessary with the political left, and engaging in an enriching debate with Marxist theory. Some of them worked in the labor unions. For instance, in 1972 a Coalition of Labor Union Women was formed. However, in the 1990s the fading away of socialist organizations, and of socialism as a historical point of reference, as well as the declining influence of Marxist theory, lessened the impact of socialist feminism, which remained by and large confined to academia.[54]

However, the distinction between liberal and radical feminism was blurred in the practice of the movement, and in the ideology of individual feminists from the mid-1970s onwards. Several factors contributed to the overcoming of ideological cleavages in a feminist movement that kept its diversity, and featured vibrant debates as well as internecine fights, but established bridges and coalitions among its components.[55] On the one hand, as Zillah Eisenstein pointed out,[56] the issues to be tackled by liberal feminism, namely equal rights and de-gendering of social categories, involved such a level of institutional transformation that patriarchalism would be ultimately called into question, even within the most restrained strategy of being practical about achieving gender equality. Secondly, the anti-feminist backlash of the 1980s, supported by the Republican administration that governed America in 1980–92, prompted an alliance between different strings of the movement, that, regardless of their lifestyles and political beliefs, found each other together in the mobilizations to defend women's reproductive rights or in the building of women's institutions to provide services and assert cultural autonomy. Thirdly, most radical feminist organizations had faded away by the late 1970s, with their founders personally exhausted, and their local utopias confronting daily battles with "really existing patriarchalism." Yet, since most radical feminists never gave up on their basic values, they found refuge in the established organizations of liberal feminism, and in the enclaves that feminism managed to build within mainstream institutions, particularly in academia (women's studies programs), in

[54]   For an analysis of the rise and fall of one of the most dynamic and influential socialist feminist organizations, the Chicago Women's Liberation Union (CWLU), see Strobel (1995).
[55]   Ferree and Hess (1994); Ferree and Martin (1995); Mansbridge (1995); Spalter-Roth and Schreiber (1995); Whittier (1995).
[56]   Eisenstein (1981/1993).

non-profit foundations, and in women's caucuses of professional associations. These organizations and institutions were in need of militant support in their increasingly difficult task, when they began to move beyond the most obvious abuses of human rights into more controversial spheres, such as reproductive choice, sexual liberation, and advancement of women in men's various citadels. Indeed, it can be argued that the presence of liberal organizations helped radical feminism to survive as a movement, whereas most of men-based counter-cultural movements originated in the 1960s, with the major exception of ecologists, all but faded away, or were ideologically subdued during the 1980s. As a result of this multilayered process, liberalism and radicalism, in their different brands, became interwoven in their practice, and in the minds of most women supporting feminist causes and values. Even lesbianism became an accepted component of the movement, although still attached to some kind of tactical rejection within mainstream feminism (Betty Friedan opposed it), as exemplified by the tensions within NOW in the late 1980s after the "confession" of bisexuality by NOW's president Patricia Ireland.

Other distinctions became more relevant for the feminist movement, as it developed, diversified, and reached out, at least in their minds, to the majority of American women, between the mid-1970s and the mid-1990s. On the one hand, there were important distinctions in the kind of feminist *organizations*. On the other hand, there were substantial differences between what Nancy Whittier calls "political generations" within the feminist *movement*.[57]

In terms of organizations, Spalter-Roth and Schreiber[58] propose an empirically grounded, useful typology that differentiates between:

1 National membership organizations demanding equal rights, such as NOW or the Coalition of Labor Union Women, founded in 1972. They tried deliberately to avoid feminist language while advancing the cause of women in all domains of society, thus sacrificing principles for effectiveness in increasing women's participation in male-dominated institutions. Spalter-Roth and Schreiber conclude that "despite the hopes of organizations' leaders who wished to appeal to both liberals and radicals, the use of politically palatable language obscured relations of domination and subordination. Their efforts may have failed to raise the consciousness of the very women these organizations hoped to represent and empower."[59]

[57] Whittier (1995).
[58] Spalter-Roth and Schreiber (1995: 106–8).
[59] Spalter-Roth and Schreiber (1995: 119).

2 Direct service providers, such as the Displaced Homemakers
   Network, and the National Coalition against Domestic Violence.
   These are predominantly networks of local groups receiving
   support from government and corporations for their programs.
   Their main problem is the contradiction between assisting women
   and empowering them: usually, the urgency of the problem takes
   precedence over the long-term goals of consciousness raising and
   political self-organizing.
3 Staff-run and expert-based pro-women organizations, such as the
   Women's Legal Defense Fund, the Institute for Women Policy
   Research, the Center for Women Policy Studies, the Fund for
   Feminist Majority (supporting women in political institutions), the
   National Institute for Women of Color, or the National Committee
   for Pay Equity. The challenge for this type of organization is to
   broaden the range of their issues as more women are brought into
   the movement's sphere of influence, and as feminist themes
   become increasingly diversified, ethnically, socially, and culturally.

Beyond mainstream organizations, there are a myriad of local
organizations of the women's community, many of them originally
linked to radical feminism, then evolving along a great variety of
trajectories. Alternative women's health clinics, credit unions,
training centers, bookstores, restaurants, day-care centers, centers to
prevent violence against women and to cope with its injuries, theater
groups, music groups, writers' clubs, artists' studios, and a whole
range of cultural expressions, went through ups and downs and,
usually, when they survived they did so by downplaying their ideological character and becoming more integrated in society at large.
They are, in the broader sense, feminist organizations that, in their
diversity and with their flexibility, have provided the networks of
support, the experience, and the discursive materials for a women's
culture to emerge, thus undermining patriarchalism in its most
powerful site: women's minds.

The other major distinction to be introduced in understanding the
evolution of American feminism is Whittier's concept of political
generations and micro-cohorts. In her insightful sociological study of
the evolution of American radical feminism over three decades, she
shows both the continuity of feminism, and the discontinuity of feminist styles between the early 1970s, the 1980s, and the 1990s:

Political generations are important to social movement continuity in three ways. First, the collective identity of a political
generation remains consistent over time, as it has for women who
participated in the feminist movement of the 1970s. Second, even
when protest declines a social movement continues to have an

impact if a generation of movement veterans carry its key elements into societal institutions and other social movements. Institutions and innovations established by activists within these other settings serve not only as agents of change themselves but also as resources for the resurgence of a future wave of mobilization. Third, a social movement changes as new participants enter the movement and redefine its collective identity. The continual entry of micro-cohorts at regular intervals produces gradual changes. Each micro-cohort constructs a collective identity that is shaped by its context, and therefore activists who enter during movement resurgence, growth, peak and decline differ from each other. Despite the gradual shifts that occur continually within social movements, there are clearly sharper changes at certain points. At these times, a series of micro-cohorts converge into one political generation, as their similarities to each other outweigh their differences from a distinct set of incoming micro-cohorts that make up a second political generation . . . The passing of social movements from one political generation to another thus becomes key to movement survival over the long haul.[60]

Whittier shows, on the basis of her case study of Columbus, Ohio, as well as by reviewing evidence from secondary sources, the persistence and renewal of feminist movement, including radical feminism, over three decades, from the 1960s to the 1990s. She is supported in her argument by a number of other sources.[61] It seems that the "post-feminist age" was an interested manipulation of some short-term trends, excessively highlighted in the media.[62] But Whittier also emphasizes, convincingly, the profound transformation of radical feminism, leading sometimes to considerable difficulty in the understanding between generations: "Newcomers to the women's movement are mobilizing for feminist goals in different ways from longtime activists, who sometimes see their successors' efforts as apolitical or misdirected . . . Newcomers constructed a different model of themselves as feminists."[63] As a result of these sharp differences,

> it is painful for longtime feminists to see newer entrants to the movement dismissing their dearly held beliefs or changing

[60] Whittier (1995: 254–6).
[61] Buechler (1990); Staggenborg (1991); Ferree and Hess (1994); Ferree and Martin (1995).
[62] Faludi (1991); Schneir (1994).
[63] Whittier (1995: 243).

organizations they struggled to form. Recent debates within the feminist community exacerbate many women's feelings that they and their beliefs are vulnerable to attack. In the "sex wars" in particular, lesbian practitioners of sadomasochism, along with heterosexual women and others, argued that women should have the right to act freely on any sexual desires, and accused those who taught otherwise of being anti-sex, "vanilla", or puritanical.[64]

The main differences between feminist political generations do not seem to be related to the old divide between liberals and radicals, since Whittier concurs in her observation with the blurring of such an ideological definition in the collective action of the movement when confronted with a powerful patriarchal backlash. It seems that three different issues, somewhat interrelated, interfere with communication between veterans and newcomers in the radical feminist movement. The first concerns the growing importance of lesbianism in the feminist movement. Not that it was absent from radical feminism in earlier times, or that it is opposed by radical feminists. But the lifestyles of lesbians, and their emphasis on breaking the mold of heterosexual families, as well as the tactical problems in reaching out to mainstream women from the trenches of a movement with a lesbian heart, made the non-lesbian component of radical feminism increasingly uneasy about lesbian visibility. The second, and much sharper split, concerns the importance given to sexual expression in all its forms by the new generations of feminists. This includes, for instance, the breaking of the "classic" feminist dress code that used to avoid the traps of femininity, to emphasize sexiness and self-expression in women's self-presentation. It also extends to the acceptance of all manifestations of women's sexuality, including bisexuality, and experimentation. The third split is in fact the consequence of the two others. More assured of themselves, and more sharply separatist in their cultural and political values, younger radical feminists, and particularly lesbians, are more open than radical feminists were previously to cooperate with men's social movements, and to relate to men's organizations precisely because they feel less threatened by such alliances since they have already constructed their autonomy, often through separatism. The main point of alliance is between lesbians and gay men (for instance in Queer Nation), who share their oppression from homophobia, and meet in their defense of sexual liberation, and in their critique of the heterosexual/patriarchal family. However, Whittier also reports that old and new radical feminists share fundamental values and meet each other in the same struggles.

Other internal tensions in the feminist movement originate

---

[64] Whittier (1995: 239).

precisely from its expansion into the whole range of classes and ethnic groups in America.[65] While the 1960s pioneers who rediscovered feminism were overwhelmingly white, middle class, and highly educated, in the next three decades feminist themes linked up with the struggles that African-American women, Latinas, and other ethnic minorities have traditionally carried out in their communities. Women workers, both through labor unions and through autonomous women workers' organizations, mobilized in defense of their demands, using to their advantage the new context of legitimacy for women's struggles. It followed an increasing diversification of the women's movement, and a certain vagueness in their feminist self-definition. Yet, according to opinion polls, from the mid-1980s most women related positively to feminist themes and causes, precisely because feminism did not become associated with any particular ideological stand.[66] Feminism became the common word (and banner) for the whole range of sources of women's oppression as women, to which each woman, or category of women, would attach her personal or collective claim, and label.

Thus, through a variety of practices and self-identifications, women from different origins and with different goals, but sharing a common source of oppression that defined women from outside themselves, constructed a new, collective identity: this is in fact what made possible the transition from women's struggles to a feminist movement. As Whittier writes: "I propose to define the women's movement in terms of the collective identity associated with it rather than in terms of its formal organizations . . . What makes these organizations, networks, and individuals part of a social movement is their shared allegiance to a set of beliefs, practices, and ways of identifying oneself that constitute feminist collective identity."[67]

Are these questions and answers, inspired by the American experience, relevant to feminism in other cultures and countries? Can women's issues, and women's struggles, be generally related to feminism? How collective is this collective identity when women are seen in a global perspective?

Is feminism global?

To advance a tentative answer to such a fundamental question, even superficially, we must distinguish various areas of the world. In the

---

[65]   Morgen (1988); Matthews (1989); Blum (1991); Barnett (1995); Pardo (1995).

[66]   Stacey (1990); Whittier (1995).

[67]   Whittier (1995: 23–4).

case of Western Europe, Canada, and Australia, it seems apparent that a widespread, diverse, multifaceted feminist movement is active, and growing in the 1990s, albeit with different intensities and characteristics. In Britain, for instance, after a decline in the early 1980s, largely motivated by the neo-conservative assault prompted by Thatcherism, feminist ideas, and the cause of women, permeated throughout the society.[68] As in the United States, on the one hand, women fought for equality, and engaged in self-empowerment in work, social services, legislation, and politics. On the other hand, cultural feminism and lesbianism emphasized women's specificity, and built alternative women organizations. The emphasis on singular identities gives the impression of fragmentation in the movement. Yet, as Gabriele Griffin writes:

> It is the case that many women's groups give themselves titles which specify certain identities . . . This identification provides the impetus for their activism. On one level, feminist activism based on identity politics leads to the fragmentation which many feminists regard as typical for the current political climate, and which is supposed to be in direct contrast to the homogeneity, common purpose and mass mobilization of the Women's (Liberation) Movement, all with capital letters. The latter seems to me to be a myth, a nostalgic retrospective view of some golden age feminism that probably never was. Single issue or single identity feminist organizations such as are common in the 1990s may have the drawback of overly localized politics but their very specificity can also be a guarantee for expertise and impact, for maximum, clearly defined effort within a specific arena.[69]

Thus, single-issue organizations may work on a multiplicity of women's issues, and women may participate in different organizations. It is this intertwining and networking of individuals, organizations, and campaigns that characterizes a vital, flexible, and diverse feminist movement.

Throughout Europe, in every single country, there is a pervasive presence of feminism, both in the institutions of society, and in a constellation of feminist groups, organizations, and initiatives, that feed each other, debate each other (sometimes sharply), and keep inducing a relentless flow of demands, pressures, and ideas on women's condition, women's issues, and women's culture. By and large, feminism, as in the United States, and in Britain, has fragmented, and no single organization or institution can pretend to

[68]   Brown (1992); Campbell (1992); Griffin (1995); Hester et al. (1995).
[69]   Griffin (1995: 4).

speak on women's behalf. Instead, there is a transversal line cutting across the entire society that emphasizes women's interests, and women's values, from professional caucuses to cultural expressions, and political parties, many of which have established a minimum percentage of women among their leadership (usually the norm, rarely fulfilled, is set at 25 percent of leaders and deputies, so that women are "only" 50 percent under-represented).

Ex-statist societies present a peculiar situation.[70] On the one hand, statist countries helped/forced the full incorporation of women into paid work, opened up educational opportunities, and set up a wide-spread network of social services and child care, although abortion was banned for a long time, and contraception was not available. Women's organizations were present in all spheres of society, albeit under the total control of the Communist party. On the other hand, sexism was pervasive, and patriarchalism paramount in society, institutions, and politics. As a result, a generation of very strong women grew up, feeling their potential, yet having to fight their way every day to accomplish some of this potential. After the disintegration of Soviet-style communism, feminism as an organized movement is weak, and, until now, limited to a few circles of Westernized intellectuals, while the old-style, patronizing organizations are fading away. Yet, women's presence in the public sphere is increasing dramatically in the 1990s. In Russia, for instance, the Women's Party, although rather conservative in its position and membership, received about 8 percent of the vote in the 1995 parliamentary elections, while a number of women were in the way of becoming key political figures. There is a wide-spread feeling in Russian society that women could play a decisive role in rejuvenating leadership in Russian politics. In 1996, for the first time in Russian history, a woman was elected Governor of Koryakiya Territory. Furthermore, the new generation of women, educated in the values of equality, and with room to express themselves personally and politically, seem to be ready to crystallize their individual auton-omy in collective identity and collective action. It is easy to predict a major development of the women's movement in Eastern Europe, *under their own cultural and political forms of expression.*

In industrialized Asia, patriarchalism still reigns, barely challenged. This is particularly stunning in Japan, a society with a high rate of women's participation in the labor force, a highly educated female population, and a powerful string of social movements in the 1960s. Still, pressures from women groups, and from the Socialist party, led to legislation to limit work discrimination for women in 1986.[71] But,

---

[70] Funk and Mueller (1993).
[71] Gelb and Lief-Palley (1994).

overall, feminism is limited to academic circles, and professional women still suffer blatant discrimination. Structural features are fully present in Japan to unleash a powerful feminist critique, but the absence of such a critique on a scale large enough to impact society until now, clearly demonstrates that social specificity (in this case the strength of the Japanese patriarchal family, and men's fulfillment of their duties as patriarchs, in general) determines the actual develop-ment of a movement, regardless of structural sources of discontent. Korean women are even more subdued than Japanese women, although embryos of a feminist movement have appeared recently.[72] China is still on the edge of the contradictory statist model of supporting the rights of the "half of heaven," while keeping them under the control of the "half of hell." However, the development of a powerful feminist movement in Taiwan since the late 1980s belies the notion of the necessity of women's submission under the patriar-chal tradition of Confucianism (see below).[73]

Throughout the so-called developing world, the situation is complex, indeed contradictory.[74] Feminism as an autonomous ideo-logical or political expression is clearly the preserve of a small minority of intellectual and professional women, although their presence in the media amplifies their impact well beyond their numbers. Additionally, in a number of countries, particularly in Asia, women leaders have become towering figures in the politics of their countries (in India, Pakistan, Bangladesh, Philippines, Burma, maybe in Indonesia in a not too distant future), and they have come to repre-sent the rallying symbols for democracy and development. While femaleness does not guarantee womanhood, and most women politicians operate within the framework of patriarchal politics, their impact as role models, particularly for young women, and for the breaking of society's taboos, cannot be neglected.

The most important development, however, from the 1980s onwards, is the extraordinary rise of grassroots organizations, over-whelmingly enacted and led by women, in the metropolitan areas of the developing world. They were spurred by the simultaneous processes of urban explosion, economic crisis, and austerity policies, that left people, and particularly women, with the simple dilemma of fight or perish. Together with the growing employment of women, both in the new industries and in the urban informal economy, it has indeed transformed the condition, organization, and consciousness

[72]   Po (1996).
[73]   Po (1996).
[74]   Kahne and Giele (1992); Massolo (1992); Caipora Women's Group (1993); Jaquette (1994); Kuppers (1994); Blumberg et al. (1995).

of women, as it has been shown, for instance, by the studies conducted by Ruth Cardoso de Leite, or Maria da Gloria Gohn in Brazil, Alejandra Massolo in Mexico, or Helena Useche in Colombia.[75] From these collective efforts not only grassroots organizations have developed, and have impacted on policies and institutions, but a new collective identity, as empowered women, has emerged. Thus, Alejandra Massolo, concluding her analysis of women-based urban social movements in Ciudad de Mexico, wrote:

> The women's subjectivity of experiences of struggle is a revealing dimension of the process of social construction of new collective identities through urban conflicts. Urban movements of the 1970s and 1980s made visible, and distinguishable, the unusual collective identity of segments of popular classes. Women were part of the social production of this new collective identity – from their daily territorial bases, transformed into bases for their collective action. They gave to the process of constructing collective identity the mark of plural motivations, meanings, and expectations from the feminine gender, a complex set of meanings found in the urban movements, even when gender issues are not explicit, and when their membership is mixed and men are in their leadership.[76]

It is this massive presence of women in the collective action of grassroots movements around the world, and their explicit self-identification as collective actors, that is transforming women's consciousness and social roles, even in the absence of an articulate feminist ideology.

However, while feminism is present in many countries, and women's struggles/organizations are exploding all over the world, *the feminist movement displays very different shapes and orientations, depending upon the cultural, institutional, and political contexts where it arises.* For instance, feminism in *Britain* was marked, from its inception in the late 1960s, by a close relationship with the trade unions, the Labour party, the socialist left, and, moreover, the welfare state.[77] It was more explicitly political – that is, geared toward the state – than American feminism, and more directly connected to the daily problems of working women. Yet, because of its proximity to left politics and to the labor movement, it suffered, during the 1970s, from debilitating internal fights with and between different brands of socialist and

[75]   Cardoso de Leite (1983); Gohn (1991); Espinosa and Useche (1992); Massolo (1992).
[76]   Massolo (1992: 338); my translation.
[77]   Rowbotham (1989).

radical feminists. For instance, the popular "Wages for Housework" campaign of 1973 was criticized by some feminists because of its implicit acceptance of women's subordinate status at home, potentially inducing them to stay in their domestic enclosures. This contradictory linkage to labor and to socialist politics affected the movement itself. As Rowbotham wrote:

> There is probably some truth in the argument that the emphasis on trade-union support – much stronger in Britain than in many other women's liberation movements – influenced the terms in which the call for abortion was presented. Fusty trades council rooms are not the most commodious sites for learned perorations on the multiplicity of female desire. But . . . I think it is more likely to be partly because of an evasion within the women's liberation movement itself. The movement sought to avoid counterposing heterosexuality and lesbianism, but in the process the scope of sexual self-definition narrowed and any discussion of heterosexual pleasure went into defensive retreat.[78]

Partly as a result of this reluctance to face its diversity, and to drift away from the strategic rationality of traditional politics, British feminism was weakened by the 1980s' Thatcherite juggernaut. Yet, as soon as a new generation of feminists felt free of the old attachments of party politics and labor allegiance, feminism resurged in the 1990s, not only as cultural feminism, and lesbianism, but in a multiplicity of expressions that include, but not in an hegemonic position, socialist feminism, and institutionalized feminism.

Spanish feminism was even more obviously marked by the political context where it was born, the democratic movement against Franco's dictatorship in the mid-1970s.[79] Most women's organizations were linked to anti-Franquist, semi-clandestine opposition, such as the Communist party influenced *Asociacion de Mujeres Democratas* (a political association) and the *Asociaciones de Amas de Casa* (Housewives Associations, territorially organized). Every political tendency, particularly from the revolutionary left, had "its" women's "mass organization." In *Catalunya* and in the Basque Country, women's organizations, and feminists, also had their own organizations,

---

[78] Rowbotham (1989: 81).

[79] My understanding of Spanish feminism comes from direct, personal experience and observation, as well as from conversations with a number of women who played a significant role in the movement. I want to thank the women from whom I learned most, particularly Marina Subirats, Françoise Sabbah, Marisa Goñi, Matilde Fernandez, Carlota Bustelo, Carmen Martinez-Ten, Cristina Alberdi, and Carmen Romero. Naturally, responsibility for the analysis and information presented here is exclusively mine.

reflecting the national cleavages in Spanish politics. Toward the end of Franquism, in 1974–77, autonomous feminist collectives started to appear in the climate of cultural and political liberation that characterized Spain in the 1970s. One of the most innovative and influential was the Madrid-based *Frente de Liberacion de la Mujer*. Its membership was limited (less than one hundred women), but it focused its activity on impacting the media, using its network of women journalists, thus winning popularity for women's demands and discourses. It focused on abortion rights, divorce (both unlawful in Spain at that point), and free expression of women's sexuality, including lesbianism. It was mainly influenced by cultural feminism, and by the French/Italian ideas of *feminisme de la difference*, but it also participated in the political struggles pro-democracy, alongside communist and socialist women's organizations. However, with the establishment of democracy in Spain in 1977, and with the coming to power of the Socialist party in 1982, autonomous feminist movements all but disappeared, precisely because of their success at the institutional and political level. Divorce was legalized in 1981, and abortion, with restrictions, in 1984. The Socialist party promoted an *Instituto de la Mujer*, within the government, which acted as a lobby of feminists *vis à vis* the government itself. Many feminist activists, and particularly those from the *Frente de Liberacion de la Mujer*, joined the Socialist party, and occupied leadership positions in parliament, in the administration, and, to a lesser extent, in the cabinet. A leading socialist feminist, from the labor union movement, Matilde Fernandez, was appointed Minister of Social Affairs, and exercised her influence and strong will in strengthening women's causes in the second half of the Socialist regime. She was replaced as minister in 1993 by Cristina Alberdi, another veteran of the feminist movement, and a prestigious jurist. Carmen Romero, the country's first lady, and a socialist militant of long date, alongside her husband Felipe Gonzalez, was elected to parliament, and played a major role in modifying the party's traditional sexism. For instance, a rule was approved in the party's statutes reserving 25 percent of leadership positions to women (a promise that remained unfulfilled, although women's numbers did increase in the leadership of both party and government). Thus, on the one hand, feminism did have a major impact on improving Spanish women's legal, social, and economic condition, as well as in facilitating the entry of Spanish women to prominent positions in politics, business, and society at large. Attitudes of traditional machismo were dramatically eroded in the new generations.[80] On the other hand, the feminist movement practically disappeared as an

---

[80]   Alonso Zaldivar and Castells (1992).

autonomous movement, emptied from its cadres and entirely focused on institutional reform. There was little room left for lesbian feminism, and for an emphasis on difference and sexuality. Yet, the new tolerance won in Spanish society helped the growth of a new, more culturally oriented feminism in the 1990s, closer to current feminist trends in Britain or France, and distant from traditional politics, except in the Basque Country where it kept self-damaging links with the radical Basque separatist movement. Thus, Spanish feminism exemplifies the potential of using politics and institutions to improve women's status, as well as the difficulty of remaining an autonomous social movement under conditions of successful institutionalization.

Our last exploration of variations of feminism, according to the broader social context in which the movement develops, takes us to *Italy*, the site of what was, arguably, the most potent and innovative mass feminist movement in the whole of Europe during the 1970s.[81] As Bianca Beccalli writes: "From the historical survey of Italian feminism, two themes emerge clearly: the close association between feminism and the Left, and the particular significance of the intertwining of equality and difference."[82] Indeed, contemporary Italian feminism emerged, like most other feminist movements in the West, from the powerful social movements that shook Italy in the late 1960s and early 1970s. But, unlike its counterparts, the Italian feminist movement included an influential current within the Italian trade unions, and was welcome in, and supported by, the Italian Communist party, the largest Communist party outside the Communist world, and Italy's largest membership party. Thus, Italian feminists succeeded in popularizing their themes, as feminists, among large sectors of women, including working-class women, during the 1970s. Economic demands and demands for equality were interwoven with women's liberation, the critique of patriarchalism, and the subversion of authority in the family as in society. However, relationships between feminists and the left, and particularly with the revolutionary left were not easy. Indeed, in December 1975, *the servizio d'ordine* (self-appointed marshals) of *Lotta Continua*, the largest and most radical extreme-left organization, insisted on protecting the demonstration of *Lotta Continua*'s women in Rome, and when women refused their protection, they beat them up, prompting the secession of women

---

[81] My understanding of the Italian feminist movement comes, to a large extent, from my friendship and conversations with Laura Balbo, as well as from personal observation of social movements in Milan, Turin, Venice, Rome, and Naples throughout the 1970s. For a more recent analysis, see the excellent overview of the movement by Bianca Beccalli (1994). On the formative stage of the movement, and its development during the 1970s, see Ergas (1985) and Birnbaum (1986).
[82] Beccalli (1994: 109).

from the organization, and the dissolution of *Lotta Continua* itself a few months later. The increasing autonomy of the Communist-inspired organization *Unione delle Donne Italiane* (UDI) *vis à vis* the party led ultimately to the self-dissolution of UDI in 1978. Yet, overall, there were many linkages between women organizing, labor unions, and left political parties (except socialists), and a great deal of receptivity among party and union leaders to women's issues, and even to feminist discourses. This close cooperation resulted in some of the most advanced legislation on working women in the whole of Europe, as well as in the legalization of divorce (by a 1974 Referendum), and of abortion. For a long period, in the 1970s, this political collaboration went hand in hand with the proliferation of women's collectives which raised issues of women's autonomy, women's cultural difference, sexuality, and lesbianism, as separate trends, yet interacting with the world of politics and class struggle. And yet

> by the end of the decade [1970s] feminism was in decline; and the beginning of the 1980s saw it virtually disappear as a movement. It lost its visibility in political struggles and grew ever more fragmented and out of touch, as feminist activists increasingly committed their energies to private projects and experiences, whether of an individual or communal nature. Thus it was that the "new" feminist movement, following the example of other "new social movements" of the 1970s, evolved into just another form of lifestyle politics.[83]

Why so? Here, I will not put Beccalli's words into my own interpretation, although I do not think I contradict her account. On the one hand, Italian women conquered substantial legal and economic reforms, entered massively the labor force and educational institutions, undermining sexism and, more importantly, the traditional power exercised by the Catholic Church over their lives. Thus, the open, clear battles in which the left, the unions, and women could easily converge, were won, although the victory was not always exploited to its utmost, as in the Law on Equality that, as Beccalli argues, stopped way short of its British model. At the same time, the close connection between the women's movement and the left prompted the crisis of political feminism together with the crisis of the left itself. The revolutionary left, living in a Marxist/Maoist fantasy (elaborated with remarkable intelligence and imagination, thus making artificial paradises even more artificial), disintegrated in the second half of the 1970s. The labor movement, while not having to confront a neo-conservative backlash as in Britain or the United

---

[83]   Beccalli (1994: 86).

States, was faced in the 1980s with the new realities of globalization and technological change, and had to accept the constraints of Italian capitalism's international interdependence. The networking economy, which actually took Emilia Romagna as its model, made Italian small firms dynamic and competitive, yet at the price of decisively undermining union bargaining power concentrated in large factories and the public sector. The Communist party was brushed aside from its power bid by an anti-Communist front led by the Socialist party. And the Socialist party used the levers of power to illegally finance itself to buy its dream of *sorpasso* (that is, overtaking the Communists in the popular vote): the justice system caught up with the Socialists before they could reach the Communists who, in the meantime, had ceased to be Communists, and had joined the Socialist International. It is hardly surprising that Italian feminists, as political as they were, went home. That is, not to their husbands'/fathers' homes, but to the House of Women, to a diverse and vital women's culture which, by the late 1980s, had reinvented feminism, emphasizing *differenzia* without forgetting *egalita*. Luce Irigaray and Adrienne Rich replaced Marx, Mao, and Alexandra Kollontai, as the intellectual points of reference. Yet, new feminist collectives continued in the 1990s to link up feminist discourse and women's demands, particularly in the local governments controlled by the left. One of the most innovative and active campaigns concerned the reorganization of time, from working time to the opening hours of stores and public services, to make flexible schedules adapted to women's multiple lives. In the 1990s, in spite of the political threat from Berlusconi and the neo-fascists, calling for the restoration of traditional family values, the coming to power of a center-left coalition, including the now Socialist, ex-Communist *Partito Democratico di Sinistra* in 1996, opened the way for a renewal of institutional innovation. This time, on the basis of a decentralized, autonomous feminist movement that had learned the lessons of "dancing with the wolves."

Thus, feminism, and women's struggles, go up and down throughout the whole landscape of human experience in this end of millennium, always resurfacing, under new forms, and increasingly linking up with other sources of resistance to domination, while maintaining the tension between political institutionalization and cultural autonomy. The contexts in which feminism develops shape the movement in an array of forms and discourses. And, yet, I contend that an essential (yes, I said essential) nucleus of values and goals constituting identitie(s) permeates across the cultural poliphony of feminism.

Feminism: an inducive polyphony[84]

The strength and vitality of the feminist movement lies in its diversity, in its adaptability to cultures and ages. Thus, trying to find the nucleus of fundamental opposition and essential transformation that is shared across movements, we must first acknowledge this diversity. To read meaningfully through this diversity, I propose a typology of feminist movements based, on the one hand, on observation, as referred to in the cited sources; and, on the other hand, on Touraine's categorization of social movements, as presented in chapter 2. The use of this typology is analytical, not descriptive. It cannot render the multifaceted profile of feminism across countries and cultures in the 1990s. As all typologies, it is reductionist, a particularly unhappy circumstance concerning women's practices, since women have reacted, rightfully, against their constant cataloguing and labeling in their history as objects, rather than subjects. Furthermore, specific feminist movements, and individual women in the movements, often cut across these and other categories, mixing identities, adversaries, and goals in the self-definition of their experience and struggle. Besides, some of the categories may represent a very small segment of the feminist movement, although I consider them analytically relevant. Yet, overall, I believe it may be useful to consider the distinctions presented in Chart 4.1 as a way to begin with the diversity of feminist movements in a necessary step to investigate their commonality.

Under these types I have included, at the same time, collective actions and individual discourses which are debated in and around feminism. This is because, as stated above, feminism does not exhaust itself in militant struggles. It is also, and sometimes fundamentally, a discourse: a discourse subverting women's place in man's history, thus transforming the historically dominant relationship between space and time, as suggested by Irigaray:

> The gods, God, first create space . . . God would be time itself, exteriorizing itself in its action in space, in places . . . Which would be inverted in sexual difference? Where the feminine is experienced as space, but often with connotations of the abyss and

[84] In assessing the main themes of the feminist movement I do not pretend to give justice to the richness of the feminist debate, nor can I survey, even if I knew it, the full range of theories and positions that are now available for an in-depth understanding of women's sources of oppression and avenues of liberation. My analytical synthesis here is geared toward the theoretical purpose of this book: to interpret the interaction between social movements claiming the primacy of identity, and the network society, as the new structure of domination in the information age. If this disclaimer sounds defensive, it is.

Chart 4.1   Analytical typology of feminist movements

Type	Identity	Adversary	Goal
Women's rights (liberal, socialist)	Women as human beings	Patriarchal state and/or patriarchal capitalism	Equal rights (includes reproductive rights)
Cultural feminism	Women's commune	Patriarchal institutions and values	Cultural autonomy
Essentialist feminism (spiritualism, ecofeminism)	Female way of being	Male way of being	Matriarchal freedom
Lesbian feminism	Sexual/cultural sisterhood	Patriarchal heterosexuality	Abolition of gender through separatism
Women' specific identities (ethnic, national, self-defined: e.g. black lesbian feminist)	Self-constructed identity	Cultural domination	Degendered multi-culturalism
Practical feminism (workers, community self-defense, motherhood etc.)	Exploited/ abused women/ homemakers	Patriarchal capitalism	Survival/ dignity

night . . . while the masculine is experienced as time. The transition to a new age requires a change in our perception and conception of space-time, the inhabiting of places, and of containers, or envelopes of identity.[85]

This transition, and this change, are being operated through an array of women's insurgencies, some of which are presented in Chart 4.1, the content of which I will try to clarify by my commentary.

The *defense of women's rights* is the bottom line of feminism. Indeed, all other forms include this basic affirmation of women as human

---

[85]   Irigaray (1984/1993: 7).

beings, not as dolls, objects, things, or animals, in the terms of classic feminist critique. In this sense, feminism is indeed an extension of the human rights movement. This movement comes in two versions, liberal and socialist, although this inclusion as variants of one type may be surprising given their sharp ideological opposition. Indeed, they are different, but in terms of identity they both assert women's rights as equal to men. They differ in their analysis of the roots of patriarchalism, and in their belief, or disbelief, in the possibility of reforming capitalism and operating within the rules of liberal democracy while fulfilling the ultimate goals of equality. Both include economic rights and reproductive rights in women's rights. And both consider the winning of these rights as the movement's goals, although they may diverge sharply in tactical emphases and language. Socialist feminists see the struggle against patriarchalism as necessarily linked to the supersession of capitalism, while liberal feminism approaches socio-economic transformation with a more skeptical view, focusing on advancing the cause of women independently from other goals.

Cultural feminism is based on the attempt to build alternative women's institutions, spaces of freedom, in the midst of patriarchal society, whose institutions and values are seen as the adversary. It is sometimes associated with the "feminism of difference," although it does not imply essentialism. It starts with the double affirmation that women are different, mainly because of their differential history, and that in any case they can only rebuild their identity, and find their own ways, by constructing their own commune. In many cases this implies the will of separation from men, or at least from men-dominated institutions. But it does not lead necessarily to lesbianism or to separatism from males. It aims at building cultural autonomy as a basis of resistance, thus inspiring women's demands on the basis of alternative values, such as non-competitiveness, non-violence, cooperation, and multidimensionality of the human experience, leading to a new women's identity, and women's culture, which could induce cultural transformation in society at large.

The "consciousness-raising" movement, at the origins of radical feminism, was linked to cultural feminism, and induced a whole network of women's organizations and institutions that became spaces of freedom, protection, support, and unfettered communication among women: women's bookstores, health clinics, women's cooperatives. While these organizations were providing services to women, and became organizing tools for a variety of women's rights mobilizations, they also generated and diffused an alternative culture, which established the specificity of women's values.

Essentialist feminism goes a step further, and proclaims, simultaneously, women's essential difference from men, rooted in biology and/or history, and the moral/cultural superiority of womanhood as a way of life. In Fuss's formulation, "essentialism can be located in appeals to a pure or original femininity, a female essence, outside the boundaries of the social and thereby untainted (though perhaps repressed) by a patriarchal order."[86] For instance, for Luce Irigaray, an articulate and influential voice of essentialist feminism, "by our lips we are women."[87]

> How can I say it? That we are women from the start. That we don't have to be turned into women by them, labeled by them, made holy and profaned by them. That that has always happened, without their efforts. And that their history, their stories, constitute the locus of our displacement . . . Their properties are our exile. Their enclosures, the death of our love. Their words, the gag upon our lips . . . Let's hurry and invent our own phrases. So that everywhere and always we can continue to embrace . . . Our strength lies in the very weakness of our resistance. For a long time now they have appreciated what our suppleness is worth for their own embraces and impressions. Why not enjoy ourselves? Rather than letting ourselves be subjected to their branding. Rather than being fixed, stabilized, immobilized. Separated . . . We can do without models, standards, or examples. Let's never give ourselves orders, commands or prohibitions. Let our imperatives be only appeals to move, to be moved, together. Let's never lay down the law to each other, or moralize, or make war.[88]

Liberation is "making each woman 'conscious' of the fact that what she has felt in her personal experience is a condition shared by all women, thus allowing that experience to be politicized."[89] By accepting the specificity of their bodies women are not captured in biology, but, on the contrary, escape from their definition by men that has ignored their true nature. In a masculine order, women will be permanently annihilated because they are characterized from outside their primordial, bodily experience: their bodies have been reinterpreted, and their experience reformulated by men,[90] Only by reconstructing their identity on the basis of their biological and cultural specificity can women become themselves.

[86]   Fuss (1989: 2).
[87]   Irigaray (1977/1985: 210).
[88]   Irigaray (1977/1985: 215–17).
[89]   Irigaray (1977/1985: 164).
[90]   Fuss (1989).

For instance, the revival of Italian feminism in the early 1980s was somewhat marked by the affirmation of women's difference, and the primacy given to the reconstruction of women's identity on the basis of their biological/cultural specificity, as expressed in the highly popular *"Piu donne che uomini"* pamphlet published by the Women's Bookstore in Milan. It tried to address the inability of women to act in the public sphere by emphasizing the necessity of women working on their own personality, largely determined by their biological specificity. It found a wide echo among Italian women.[91]

Another stream of essentialism links womanhood to history and culture, and claims the myth of a matriarchal golden age when women's values, and the worshipping of the goddess, assured social harmony.[92] Spiritualism and ecofeminism are also among the most powerful manifestations of essentialism, bringing together biology and history, nature and culture, in the affirmation of a new age constructed around women's values and their merger with nature.[93]

Essentialism has come under spirited attack in the feminist movement, both on political grounds, and from opposing intellectual perspectives. Politically, it is argued,[94] that essentializing differences between men and women plays into the hands of traditional values of patriarchalism, and justifies keeping women in their private domain, necessarily in an inferior position. Intellectually, materialist feminists, such as Christine Delphy and Monique Wittig, consider anatomical sex as socially constructed.[95] For them, gender does not create oppression; rather, oppression creates gender. Womanhood is a man's category, and the only liberation consists in degendering society, cancelling the dichotomy man/woman.

Yet, the affirmation of women's irreducible specificity, and the proposal to rebuild society around women's values, does have an undeniable appeal among women, and feminists, while it provides the linkage to the powerful trends of spiritualism and radical ecologism characteristic of the information age.

Lesbian feminism has been the fastest growing, and most militant, component of the feminist movements in developed countries (and not only in the United States) in the past decade, organized in a number of collectives, as well as in caucuses and tendencies within broader feminist movements. It can certainly not be assimilated to a particular sexual orientation. Adrienne Rich proposes the notion of

---

[91]   Beccalli (1994).
[92]   Merchant (1980).
[93]   Spretnak (1982); Epstein (1991).
[94]   Beccalli (1994).
[95]   Delphy (1984); Wittig (1992).

a "lesbian continuum," to include a broad spectrum of women's experiences, marked by their oppression from, and resistance to, the inseparable institutions of patriarchy and compulsory heterosexuality.[96] Indeed, the 1970 Manifesto of American Radicalesbians, started with the following statement: "What is a lesbian? A lesbian is the rage of all women condensed to the point of explosion."[97] From this perspective, lesbianism, as women's radical, self-conscious separation from males as sources of their oppression, is the discourse/ practice of liberation. This explains the success of elective lesbianism for many women, as the way to express their autonomy *vis à vis* men's world in an uncompromising form. In Monique Wittig's words:

> The refusal to become (or to remain) heterosexual always meant to refuse to become a man or a woman, consciously or not. For a lesbian this goes further than the refusal of the role "woman". It is the refusal of the economic, ideological, and political power of a man . . . We are escapees of our class in the same way as the American runaway slaves were escaping slavery and becoming free. For us this is an absolute necessity; our survival demands that we contribute all our strength to the destruction of the class of women within which men appropriate women. *This can be accomplished only by the destruction of heterosexuality* as a social system which is based on the oppression of women by men and which produces the doctrine of the difference between sexes to justify this oppression.[98]

Because heterosexuality is the paramount adversary, lesbian feminism finds in the gay men's movement a potential, if ambivalent, ally (see below).

Increasingly, the feminist movement is being fragmented in a *multiplicity of feminist identities* that constitute the primary definition for many feminists. As I argued above, this is not a source of weakness but of strength in a society characterized by flexible networks and variable alliances in the dynamics of social conflicts and power struggles. These identities are self-constructed, even if they often use ethnicity, and sometimes nationality, as boundary making. Black feminism, Mexican American feminism, Japanese feminism, black lesbian feminism, but also sadomasochist lesbian feminism, or territorial/ethnic self-definitions, such as the Southall Black Sisters in England,[99] are but examples of endless possibilities of self-defined identities through

---

[96]   Rich (1980/1993).
[97]   Reproduced in Schneir (1994: 162).
[98]   Wittig (1992: 13–20); my italics.
[99]   Griffin (1995: 79).

which women see themselves in movement.[100] So doing, they oppose
the standardization of feminism, which they see as a new form of cultural domination, not alien to the patriarchal logic of overimposing
officialdom to actual diversity of women's experiences. In some
instance, self-identity starts with a pseudonym, as in the case of black
feminist writer bell hooks: "I chose the name bell hooks because it was
a family name, because it had a strong sound. Throughout childhood,
this name was used to speak to the memory of a strong woman, a
woman who spoke her mind . . . Claiming this name was a way to link
my voice to an ancestral legacy of women speaking – of woman power."
[101] Thus, the self-construction of identity is not the expression of an
essence, but a power stake through which women as they are mobilize
for women as they want to be. Claiming identity is power-making.

I have deliberately chosen a controversial term, *practical feminists*, to
refer to the widest and deepest stream of women's struggles in today's
world, particularly in the developing world, but also among working-
class women and community organizations in industrialized
countries. Of course, all feminists are practical, in the sense that they
all undermine everyday, in many different ways, the foundations of
patriarchalism, be it by fighting for women's rights or by demystifying
patriarchal discourses. But, it may also be that many women are feminist in practice, while not acknowledging the label or even having a
clear consciousness of opposing patriarchalism. Thus, the question
arises: *can feminism exist without feminist consciousness?* Aren't the struggles and organizations of women throughout the world, for their
families (meaning, mainly, their children), their lives, their work,
their shelter, their health, *their dignity*, feminism in practice? Frankly,
I am hesitant on this point, and my work on Latin American grassroots, and readings on other areas of the world, only deepens my
ambivalence, so that the best I can do is to convey it.[102]

On the one hand, I stand by the classic norm of "no class without
class consciousness," and by the fundamental methodological principle of defining social movements by the values and goals they
express themselves. From this perspective, the overwhelming majority
of women's struggles and organizations, in the developing world and
beyond, do not express a feminist consciousness, and, more importantly, do not oppose explicitly patriarchalism and male
domination, either in their discourse or in the goals of their move-

[100]   Whittier (1995); Jarrett-Macauley (1996).
[101]   hooks (1989: 161).
[102]   This issue has been discussed by some feminist historians. My category of
"practical feminism" is close to what they call "social feminism"; see Offen (1988);
Cott (1989).

ments. Issues of cultural feminism, of lesbian feminism, or of sexual liberation, are rarely present among common women's movements, although not absent, as the revealing experience of the Taiwanese lesbian movement shows (see below). Yet, overall, developing countries' explicit feminism is still, by and large, elitist. This would leave us with a rather fundamental split between feminism and women's struggles that would also have a North/South connotation. Indeed, the 1995 United Nations Women's Forum in Beijing showed some evidence of this split, amplified and highlighted by some interested parties, namely the "Crusade of the Half Moon" formed by the Vatican and Islamists, fighting hand in hand against feminism and women's reproductive rights.

On the other hand, through their collective action, women around the world are linking their struggle, and their oppression, to their everyday lives. They see the transformation of their condition in the family as connected to their intervention in the public sphere. Let us listen to the words of a woman in a Bogota shanty, as recorded by Helena Useche, in her women's stories reported from the trenches of activist social research:

> In recent years, women have made themselves noticed, and now men respect us. Just because of the fact that the compañero does not see the woman just at home, cooking, washing, ironing, but he also sees her as a compañera, contributing financially also. Because now it is very rare to see the husband telling the wife: I work and you stay home. Then, here there are the solutions we provide to our problems, such as building gardens, helping other women, making them aware of people's condition. Before, women were uninterested in all this. Now, we are concerned not only with being mothers, but with knowing how to be properly so.[103]

Is this feminism? Maybe the issue is one of cultural translation. Not between languages or continents, but between experiences. Maybe the parallel development of women's struggles and organizations, and feminist discourses and debates, is simply a stage in the historical development of a movement, whose fully fledged, global existence may result from the interaction and *reciprocal transformation* of both components.

If feminism is so diverse as to possibly include even women in movements who do not call themselves feminists, or even would object to the term, does it make sense to keep the word (after all invented by a man, Charles Fourier), or even to claim the existence of a feminist movement? I believe so, none the less, because of a major theoretical

---

[103] Espinosa and Useche (1992: 48); my translation.

reason: in all types of feminism, as presented in Chart 4.1, *the fundamental task of the movement, through struggles and discourses, is to
de/re/construct woman's identity by degendering the institutions of society.*
Women's rights are claimed on behalf of women as subjects
autonomous from men, and from the roles they are assigned under
patriarchalism. Cultural feminism builds the women's community to
raise consciousness, and reconstruct personality. Essentialist feminism affirms woman's irreducible specificity, and proclaims her
autonomous, superior values. Lesbian feminism, by rejecting heterosexuality, voids of meaning the sexual division of existence,
underlying both manhood and womanhood. Women's multiple identities redefine ways of being on the basis of their actual experience,
either lived or fantasized. And women's struggles for survival and
dignity empower women, thus subverting the patriarchalized woman,
precisely defined by her submission. Under different forms, and
through different paths, feminism dilutes the patriarchal dichotomy
man/woman as it manifests itself in social institutions and in social
practice. So doing, feminism constructs not one but many identities,
each one of which, by their autonomous existence, seizes micro-
powers in the world wide web of life experiences.

The Power of Love: Lesbian and Gay Liberation Movements[104]

*Any theory of cultural/political creation that treats lesbian existence as a
marginal or less "natural" phenomenon, as mere "sexual preference" or
as the mirror image of either heterosexual or male homosexual relations is
profoundly weakened thereby . . . A feminist critique of compulsory heterosexual orientation for women is long overdue.*
Adrienne Rich, "Compulsory heterosexuality
and lesbian existence", p. 229

*Our movement may have begun as the struggle of a minority but what we
should now be trying to "liberate" is an aspect of the personal lives of all
people – sexual expression.*
John D'Emilio, "Capitalism and gay identity", p. 474

[104] The analysis presented here does not include the study of gay and lesbian
issues and *values*, nor their relationship to social institutions. It is focused on
lesbian and gay *movements*, and on their impact on patriarchalism through sexual
liberation. In order to be specific, I will use two case studies, one for each movement. On the one hand, I will discuss the emergence of a powerful lesbian
movement in Taipei, in the 1990s, in interaction with the feminist movement, and

Patriarchalism requires compulsory heterosexuality. Civilization, as historically known, is based on taboos and sexual repression. Sexuality, as Foucault argued, is socially constructed.[105] The regulation of desire underlies social institutions, thus channeling transgression and organizing domination. There is an endless spiral between desire, repression, sublimation, transgression, and punishment, accounting for much of human passion, accomplishment, and failure, when the epics of history are observed from the hidden side of experience. This coherent system of domination, which links the hallways of the state to the pulse of the libido through mothering, fathering, and the family, does have a weak link: the heterosexual assumption. If this assumption is challenged, the whole system crumbles down: the linkage between controlled sex and reproduction of the species is called into question; sisterhood, and then women's revolt, become possible, by undoing the gendered division of sexual labor that splits women; and male bonding threatens manhood, thus undermining the cultural coherence of men-dominated institutions. While historical accounts show permissiveness for male homosexuality in some cultures, particularly in classical Greece,[106] lesbianism was severely repressed throughout most of human experience, not in spite but because of resistance to heterosexuality. As Adrienne Rich writes:

> The fact is that women in every culture and throughout history have undertaken the task of independent, non-heterosexual, woman-connected existence, to the extent made possible by their context, often in the belief that they were the "only ones" ever to

---

with the gay movement. This is a deliberate effort to move away from North American and Western European scenes of lesbian liberation, and to emphasize the increasing influence of lesbianism on cultures as patriarchal as the Chinese culture. On the other hand, I will succinctly analyze the formation and development of the gay community in San Francisco, arguably one of the most powerful and visible gay communities/movements in the world. My presentation of the lesbian movement in Taipei primarily relies on an excellent study by my Berkeley doctoral student Lan-chih Po, who is also an active militant in the feminist movement in Taipei (Po, 1996). I have also used for my understanding of Taipei's scene, besides my personal knowledge, my Taiwan connection. For this, I am grateful to You-tien Hsing, and to Chu-joe Hsia. As for San Francisco, I have relied on the fieldwork study I conducted in the early 1980s, with the cooperation of Karen Murphy (Castells and Murphy, 1982; Castells, 1983: 138–72), adding some observations on recent developments. There is really no place here for a review of the abundant, relevant literature on gay and lesbian issues. For a scholarly overview of this bibliography in the English language, see the excellent *Lesbian and Gay Studies Reader*, edited by Abelove et al. (1993).

[105]   Foucault (1976, 1984a, b).
[106]   Halperin et al. (1990).

have done so. They have undertaken it even though few women have been in an economic position to resist marriage altogether, and even though the attacks against unmarried women have ranged from aspersion and mockery to deliberate gynocide, including the burning and torturing of millions of widows and spinsters during the witch persecutions of the fifteenth, sixteenth, and seventeenth centuries in Europe.[107]

Male homosexuality was generally confined in time and space by "knowingly ignoring" adolescent impulses or hidden expressions in specific contexts (for example, in the religious orders of the Catholic Church). Because men kept their gender, class, and race privileges, repression of homosexuality was/is highly socially selective. Yet, the norm, the fundamental norm of patriarchalism was, and is, life organized around the heterosexual family, occasionally allowing the private expression of same-sex desire for men, as long as it would be kept in the back alleys of society.

While resistance to compulsory heterosexuality has existed in all times and cultures, it is only in the past three decades that social movements in defense of lesbian and gay rights, and affirming sexual freedom, have spurred throughout the world, starting in the United States in 1969–70, then in Europe and, thereafter, over much of the planet. Why in this period? There seem to be some common factors, and some specific elements for each one of these two distinct movements, explaining the timing and circumstances of their development.

Lesbianism is, in fact, a component of the feminist movement, as I proposed above, albeit lesbians often seek alliances with gay men in fighting cultural domination from heterosexual women. Once the feminist critique of gendered institutions eroded patriarchal orthodoxy, the calling into question of sexual norms was the logical line of development for those sectors in the feminist movement who wanted to express their identity in all dimensions. Furthermore, the identification of men as the source of oppression of women made increasingly difficult for women their emotional and sexual partnership with their "class enemies," thus favoring the expression of the latent lesbianism existing in many women.

As for gay men, their coming into a movement seems to have been induced by three concurrent factors: the insurgent climate of the 1960s movements in which self-expression and the questioning of authority made it possible to think and act the unthinkable, thus "coming out of the closet"; the impact of feminism on patriarchalism,

---

[107]   Rich (1980/1993: 230).

calling into question the category of woman, and therefore, of man, since they can only exist in their dichotomy; and the ferocity of repression by a homophobic society that radicalized even those gay men who simply wanted an accommodation.[108]

In my view, there were three additional factors in inducing the extraordinary development of both gay and lesbian liberation movements in America and elsewhere. One is structural: the formation of an advanced informational economy in the largest metropolitan areas led to a diversified, innovative labor market and flexible business networks, and created new kinds of jobs, at all levels of skills, independent of the large-scale organizations where individual behavior could be more easily regulated. The second factor refers to the popularity of sexual liberation as a theme of the 1960s movements. For instance, having been a close witness of the 1968 May movement in Paris (I was assistant professor of sociology in the Nanterre campus where the movement started), I can say that sexual liberation and self-expression were *the* paramount goals of the radical student movement: in fact, the movement started as a joint protest by males and females to obtain free access to their university's dormitories. Around the banner of sexual liberation, which also sustained the daily morale of the movement, both in France and in the United States, the utopian wish of freeing desire was the driving force of the 1960s, the rallying cry around which a whole generation felt the possibility of a different life. But sexual liberation, if it is to be liberation, has no limits. Thus, the liberation of sexuality led to rejecting the diktat of heterosexuality and, in many cases, to the abolition of all limits to desire, opening up the exploration of transgression, for instance in the fast-growing, and ideologically articulate, sadomasochist movement.

The third factor that, in my view, induced, in parallel, lesbian and gay movements, is more controversial. It refers to the separation, physical and psychological, created among both men and women by the feminist challenge to patriarchalism. By this I do not mean that women became lesbians and men became gay because they were quarreling with their heterosexual partners. Indeed, homosexuality has its own existence and pattern of development independently from heterosexuality. Yet, the profound cleavage introduced by the joint effect of the feminist challenge and the inability of most men to cope with the ending of their privileges, reinforced the likelihood of same-sex support networks and friendships, creating a milieu where all kinds of desires could be more easily expressed.

Finally, while sexual liberation is at the heart of gay and lesbian

[108]   D'Emilio (1983).

movements, *gayness and lesbianism cannot be defined as sexual preferences.*
They are, fundamentally, identities, and in fact two distinct identities:
lesbian, and gay men. As such identities, they are not given; they do
not originate from some form of biological determination. While
biological predispositions do exist, most homosexual desire is mixed
with other impulses and feelings (see figure 4.10), so that actual
behavior, the boundaries of social interaction, and self-identity, are
culturally, socially, and politically constructed. As for the specifics of
this political process of constructing identity, I now turn to the case
studies of the lesbian movement in Taipei, and of the gay community
in San Francisco.

Feminism, lesbianism, and sexual liberation movements in Taipei[109]

In Taipei, as in most of the world, the lesbian movement emerged as
a component of the feminist movement, and remained so, albeit in
the 1990s it acted in close alliance with an equally powerful gay men's
liberation movement. The fact that such a movement, with widespread influence among young women in Taipei, took place in a
quasi-authoritarian political context, and amidst a deeply patriarchal
culture, shows the breaking of traditional molds by global trends of
identity politics.

Taiwan's feminist movement started in 1972, under the initiative of
a pioneer intellectual woman, Hsiu-lien Lu who, returning to Taipei
after completing her master's degree in the United States, created a
women's group, set up "protection hot-lines," and founded the
Pioneer Publishing Company to print women-related books. Lu's
"new feminism" echoed closely the classic themes of liberal feminism,
combined with the idea of modernization in the labor market, challenging sex discrimination, and the confinement of women in certain
roles: "Women should first be human, and then women"; "women
should walk out of the kitchen"; "sex discrimination against women
should be removed and women's potential developed." At the same
time, she emphasized the genuine Chinese character of her movement, and opposed some of the values of Western feminism, such as
eliminating gender differences, or rejecting feminine dressing. For

---

[109] My analysis of Taipei's lesbian movement follows closely the study by Lan-
chih Po (1996). In addition to her observations, she also relies partially on the
papers (in Chinese) of a Conference on "New Maps of Desire: Literature, Culture,
and Sexual Orientation" organized on April 20, 1996 at National Taiwan
University, Taipei, and on the special issue of *Awakening* magazine (1995:
no. 158–61) on relationships between feminism and lesbianism.

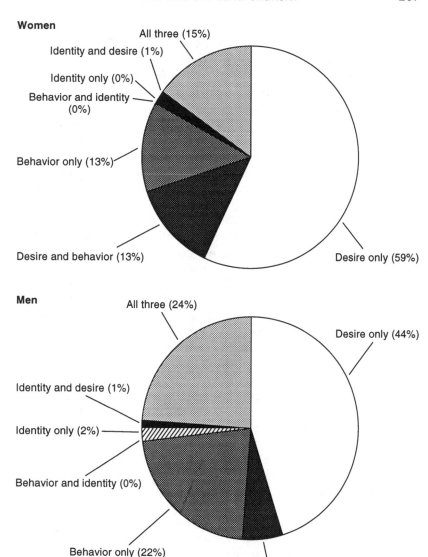

Figure 4.10   Interrelation of different aspects of same-gender
sexuality: for 150 women (8.6% of the total 1,749) who report any
adult same-gender sexuality; for 143 men (10.1% of the total 1,410)
who report any adult same-gender sexuality
Source: Laumann et al. (1994)

Lu, "women should be like they are." In the late 1970s, feminists joined the political opposition movement, and after the 1979 Kaoshiung riot, they were repressed, and Lu was imprisoned. The organized movement could not survive repression, but women's networks did, so that a second wave of feminism developed in the early 1980s. In 1982, a small group of women created Awakening Magazine, a monthly, to voice women's opinions, and to press for women's rights. In January 1987 hundreds of women took to the streets of Taipei to protest against the sex industry in the city. In 1987, after the lifting of the martial law that had subdued Taiwan's opposition for decades, the Awakening Foundation was formally established: it went on to become the coordinating instance of Taiwan's women's struggles, mixing liberal themes, radical causes, and support for a whole array of women's initiatives. In a largely spontaneous movement, in the late 1980s, numerous women's groups were formed, such as associations of divorced women, housewives, groups to rescue youth from prostitution, and the like. The media started to report the activities of these groups, increasing their visibility, and attracting a growing number of women, particularly among the educated and professional groups in Taipei.

With the beginning of democratic political life in the 1990s (indeed, the democratic opposition conquered the municipality of Taipei in the local elections), a diversified culturally oriented social movement emerged in Taipei. The women's movement both grew in numbers and influence, and became internally differentiated between its struggle for women's rights, its defense of women workers, and the expression of new women's identities, including lesbianism. University campuses were literally taken by feminism. In May 1995, the chairwoman of the "women's studies group" in National Taiwan University (Taiwan's premier university) was elected as chairperson of the student body, displacing both the government's party candidate, and the political opposition students. The support found by the feminist movement, outside the University, among women, particularly married women, of the new Taiwanese society prompted a series of debates, particularly around the notion of family, on the occasion of the revision of the "family law" in the Taiwanese parliament.

It is in this context of cultural effervescence and rise of feminist ideas that a number of young radical feminists started to introduce the lesbian debate in Taipei. The "Axis Collective" diffused ideas from radical feminists and lesbian theorists, such as Audre Lorde, Adrienne Rich, Gayle Rubin, and Christine Delphy, and translated some of their texts into Chinese. Following Lorde's notion of the "erotic as power," a new field of identity politics, centered on women's body and sexuality, was created. Alongside the rise of women's groups on campuses, the first explicitly lesbian group was formed in Taiwan in 1990: "Between Us (*wo-men-chih-chien*)."

On May 22, 1994, an "anti-sexual harassment parade" was organized by feminists in the streets of Taipei, with about 800 women, mainly students, marching from their campuses to the center of the city. During the march, Ho, a feminist scholar who had advanced the discourse of sexual liberation, improvised a slogan: "I want sexual orgasm, I don't want sexual harassment!" which was enthusiastically repeated by participants in the march, and sounded loudly in the streets of a shocked patriarchal Taipei. It made the headlines of most newspapers. The publicity of this incident raised a fundamental debate within the feminist movement. When the movement was winning legitimacy and acceptance, improving women's condition and asserting gender equality, many feminists felt that it was embarrassing, and potentially destructive, to identify feminism with sexual liberation in public opinion. Moreover, some feminists also argued that sexual liberation in the West was a trap for women, and in fact worked to the advantage of men. They suggested, instead, to fight for the "right to autonomy of the body." Ho and other feminists, related to the lesbian movement, argued for the need for a feminist approach to sexual liberation, seeking at the same time the emancipation of women and that of women's sexuality. In their view, sexual liberation is the radical way of challenging patriarchal culture, manifested in the control over a woman's body. The sexual liberation women's movement, including, but not exclusively, a strong lesbian component, went into action. In 1995, the women's studies groups in Taiwan University, mobilizing to elect their candidate to the student government, began showing pornographic movies in the women's dormitories. Simultaneously, a "women's erotic pioneering festival" was organized in different campuses. The activities of these women, most of them very young, were highly publicized in the media, shocked Taipei's society, and created considerable concern among feminist leaders, inducing a sharp, sometimes acrimonious, debate within feminism.

It is in this context of both feminist awakening and sexual liberation that lesbian and gay men's groups proliferated, breaking a deep-seated taboo in Chinese culture. Furthermore, in the 1990s, the traditional marginality of homosexuals in Taiwan had been reinforced, and rationalized, by the stigma of AIDS. And yet, after the creation of the lesbian group "Between Us," there followed an explosion of both lesbian and gay collectives, most of them on university campuses: lesbian groups such as "Between Us," ALN, "Lambda" (Taiwan University), and "I Bao"; gay men's groups such as "Gay Chat"

(Taiwan University), "NCA," and "Speak Out." Other groups joined forces between lesbians and gays: "Queer Workshop," "We Can" (Chin-hua University), DV8 (She-shin College), "Quist" (Chong-yung University), and so on. These groups created a homosexual community. They "collectively came out," and linked sexuality, enjoyment, and politics, rediscovering that "the personal is political." Bars were critical for information, networking, education, and, ultimately, for the production of gay and lesbian culture. As Po writes: "Just like pubs for the making of British working class, gay bars play important roles for the formation of urban gay/lesbian communities in Taipei."[110]

Yet, in the Information Age, in which Taiwan is fully immersed, gays and lesbians are not limited to bars in their networking. They use extensively the Internet, and BBSs, as forms of contact, communication, and interaction. They have also created "alternative media," particularly through a number of gay/lesbian underground radio stations. In addition, in 1996 two gay/lesbian programs were broadcast on mainstream radio stations in Taipei.

Beyond communication, networking, and self-expression, the lesbian movement, in close political alliance with the gay movement, has been active in a number of campaigns, social protests, and political demands. Particularly significant was the mobilization around AIDS policy. On the one hand, feminists, lesbians and gay men took to the streets to protest the incrimination of gay men by government policies as responsible for the epidemic. On the other hand, since heterosexual women are the fastest growing group of HIV infected in Asia, the feminist group "Awakening" took up the issue as a woman's survival matter. Indeed, in Taiwan, the largest group of HIV-infected women are housewives, defenseless victims of their husbands' prostitution habits. Women's groups in Taiwan acted on the contradiction of policies to prevent the spread of AIDS: how could women escape infection from their husbands if they could not have control over their sexual lives? By bringing down to earth the issues of sexual liberation, and showing women that they were facing deadly sexual oppression, the anti-AIDS movement built by feminists, lesbians, and gay men together introduced a fundamental challenge to the patriarchal structure of sexual domination.

A second major line of action by lesbian and gay movements in an extremely patriarchal society was the fight against traditional stigma and invisibility in the public image. Gay men had to fight the stigma of abnormality. Lesbians had to fight invisibility. For both, coming out in the public sphere became a paramount goal to achieve social

[110]   Po (1996: 20).

existence. Cultural activities were essential to that end. A 1992 film festival of "queer cinema" was the starting point of public, collective self-affirmation. Lesbian and gay audiences packed several movie theaters, and the films were introduced with debates on "queer theory." Incidentally, Taiwanese and Hong Kong activists have creatively translated into Chinese the term "queer" by "*tong-chii*," meaning "comrade," so that "comrade" does not refer any longer to communist fraternity but to "queer" identity. Starting with the film festival, a number of cultural activities, always communal and festive, substantially modified the perception of lesbian and gay culture in Taiwan to the point that in 1996, the movement felt strong enough to mark Valentine's Day by voting for the top ten "gay/lesbian idols" among prominent figures of entertainment, society, and politics (to be sure, not all of the chosen were enchanted with their popularity among gays and lesbians).

Thirdly, and not surprisingly, the lesbian and gay movements have been seeking control over public space, symbolized by their struggle around Taipei's New Park, which they vowed to "take back." The park, nearby the Presidential Hall, had become a "queer space," a major site for gathering and cruising for the gay community. In 1996, the new democratic municipal administration was planning the renewal of Taipei, including its parks. Fearful of being deprived of their "liberated space," lesbians and gays requested participation in the design project, as heavy users of the park, and organized themselves in the "Comrade Space Front Line" network, demanding free use of the park for their activities during daytime to escape their status as "the community in the darkness."

With the growing influence and militancy of lesbians, a series of conflicts emerged between them and the feminist movement at large. The major one concerned the revision of family law in the parliament. Lesbians criticized the proposal by women's groups because it assumed the norm of the heterosexual family, ignoring the rights of homosexuals. Thus, lesbians and gay men *mobilized actively for the legal sanction of same-sex marriage*, a fundamental issue, present in most lesbian/gay movements around the world, and on which I will elaborate below. The conflict stimulated thinking and debate in the feminist movement, particularly in the mainstream Awakening Foundation. Lesbians criticized the hypocrisy of feminist slogans, such as "women love women," as expressions of solidarity, while ignoring the sexual dimension of this love. Lesbians in 1996 were in the open within the feminist movement, and argued vehemently for their specific rights to be acknowledged, and defended, as a legitimate part of the women's movement.

Several elements deserve emphasis in this narrative of the lesbian movement in Taipei. It shattered the preconception of the solidity of patriarchalism, and heterosexuality, in cultures inspired by Confucianism. It was an extension of the feminist movement, while linking up at the same time with the gay liberation movement in a united front for the defense of rights to sexuality under all its forms. It joined the mobilization against AIDS, relating it to the consequences of housewives' sexual submission. It bridged the cutting-edge theoretical debates on feminism and lesbianism in the world with specific adaptations to Chinese culture and to Taiwan's social institutions in the 1990s. It used a whole range of cultural expressions to "come out collectively" in the midst of public attention. It made extensive use of the Internet, and of alternative means of communication, such as pirate broadcasting. It linked up with urban social movements and political struggles at the local level. And it deepened the critique of the patriarchal family, engaging in a legal and cultural battle to advance the notion of same-sex marriages, and non-heterosexual families. I will elaborate on these matters when summing up the relationship between lesbian and gay movements and their challenge to patriarchalism.

Spaces of freedom: the gay community in San Francisco[111]

The American gay liberation movement is generally considered to have as its starting point the Stonewall Revolt in New York's Greenwich Village on June 27, 1969, when hundreds of gays fought the police for three days in reaction to yet another brutal raid on The Stonewall, a gay bar. Thereafter, the movement grew with extraordinary speed, particularly in the major metropolitan areas, as gays came out of the closet, individually and collectively. In 1969 there were about 50 organizations nationwide; in 1973 the number had jumped to over 800. While New York and Los Angeles, because of their size, became home to the largest gay populations, San Francisco was the site of the formation of a visible, organized, and politicized gay community, which went on in the next two decades to transform the city in its space, its culture, and its politics. By my calculations (necessarily tentative, since, fortunately, there is no statistical recording of sexual preference), around 1980, the gay and lesbian population could account for about 17 percent of the city's adult residents (two-thirds of them gay men), and in important local elections, because of their high turn-out rate, they may have represented around 30

[111] For sources and methods for my study of San Francisco's gay community, see Castells (1983), particularly the Methodological Appendix, pp. 355–62.

percent of voters. My guess is that in the 1990s, in spite of decimation by the AIDS epidemics in the mid-1980s, the gay and lesbian population in San Francisco has increased, mainly because of an increase in lesbians, continuing gay immigration, and the consolidation of stable same-sex partnerships. More significantly, gays settled predominantly in certain areas of the city, forming authentic communes, in which residences, businesses, real estate, bars, restaurants, movie theaters, cultural centers, community-based associations, street gatherings and celebrations weaved a fabric of social life and cultural autonomy: a space of freedom. On the basis of this space, gays and lesbians organized politically, and came to exercise considerable influence in the San Francisco local government, including the mandatory recruitment of gays and lesbians by the police department, to make up at least 10 percent of the force. This spatial concentration of gay populations is indeed a mark of the gay culture in most cities, albeit in the 1990s, with greater social tolerance and many more openly gay people, they have diffused into most of American metropolitan geography, to the great fear of homophobic conservatives. The reason for this geographic concentration in the formative stage of gay culture is twofold: visibility and protection. As Harry Britt, a political leader of San Francisco's gays, told me in an interview years ago: "When gays are spatially scattered, they are not gay, because they are invisible." The fundamental liberating act for gays was/is "to come out," to publicly express their identity and their sexuality, then to resocialize themselves. But how is it possible to be openly gay in the middle of a hostile and violent society increasingly insecure about its fundamental values of virility and patriarchalism? And how can one learn a new behavior, a new code, and a new culture, in a world where sexuality is implicit in everybody's presentation of self and where the general assumption is heterosexuality? In order to express themselves, gays have always met together – in modern times in night bars and coded places. When they became conscious enough and strong enough to "come out" collectively, they earmarked places where they could be safe together and could invent new lives. The territorial boundaries of their selected places became the basis for the building of autonomous institutions, and the creation of cultural autonomy. Levine has shown the systematic patterning of spatial concentrations of gays in American cities during the 1970s.[112] While he and others used the term "ghetto," gay militants speak of "liberated zones": and there is indeed a major difference between ghettos and gay areas since the latter are usually deliberately constructed by gay people to create their own city, in the framework of the broader urban society.

[112] Levine (1979).

Why San Francisco? An instant city, a settlement for adventurers attracted by gold and freedom, San Francisco was always a place of tolerant moral standards. The Barbary Coast was a meeting point for sailors, travelers, transients, dreamers, crooks, entrepreneurs, rebels, and deviants – a milieu of casual encounters and few social rules where the borderline between the normal and the abnormal was blurred. Yet, in the 1920s, the city decided to become respectable, emerging as the cultural capital of the American West, and growing up grace-fully under the authoritative shadow of the Catholic Church, relying on the support of its Irish and Italian working-class legions. With the reform movement reaching City Hall and the police in the 1930s, "deviants" were repressed and forced into hiding. Thus, the pioneer origins of San Francisco as a free city are not enough to explain its destiny as the setting for gay liberation. The major turning point was World War II. San Francisco was the main port for the Pacific front. About 1.6 million young men and women passed through the city: alone, uprooted, living on the edge of death and suffering, and sharing it most of the time with people from their own sex, many of them discovered, or elected, their homosexuality. And many were dishonorably discharged from the Navy, and disembarked in San Francisco. Rather than going home to Iowa bearing the stigma, they stayed in the city, joined by thousands of other gay people at the end of the war. They met in bars, and they built networks of support and sharing. A gay culture started to emerge from the late 1940s. The tran-sition from the bars to the streets had to wait, however, for more than a decade, when alternative lifestyles flourished in San Francisco, with the beatnik generation, and around literary circles networked in the City Lights bookstore, with Ginsberg, Kerouac, and the Black Mountain poets, among others. This culture concentrated spatially in the old Italian North Beach area, near the red-light tourist zone of Broadway. Gays were fully accepted in this tolerant, experimental ambiance. When the media focused on the beatnik culture, they emphasized the widespread presence of homosexuality as a proof of its deviance. So doing, they publicized San Francisco as a gay Mecca, attracting thousands of gays from around America. City Hall responded with repression, leading to the formation, in 1964, of the Society of Individual Rights, that defended gays, in connection with the Tavern Guild, a business association of gay and bohemian bar owners fighting against police harassment. Then, in the late 1960s, the hippy culture, the social movements that took place in the San Francisco Bay Area, particularly in Berkeley/Oakland, and the emer-gence of the gay liberation movement throughout America, induced a qualitative change in the development of San Francisco's gay community, building on the strength of historically established networks. In 1971, for the first time, the California gay movement was strong enough to organize a march on the capital, Sacramento, in support of gay rights. In the 1970s, in San Francisco a gay community flourished in certain neighborhoods, particularly in the Castro area, buying or renting homes in a rundown, traditional working-class district, which came to be rehabilitated by gay households, gay realtors, and gay renovation companies. Gay-owned businesses also settled in the area. From scattered locations, following bars and counter-cultural areas, gays were able, by the 1970s, to concentrate on a neighborhood that they could call theirs. Figure 4.11 shows the expansion of gay residential areas in San Francisco between 1950 and 1980 on the basis of my fieldwork research.

Yet, the building of the gay community was not purely spontaneous. It was also the result of deliberate political action, particularly under the impulse of the historic leader of San Francisco's gay community, Harvey Milk. A graduate of the State University of New York at Albany,

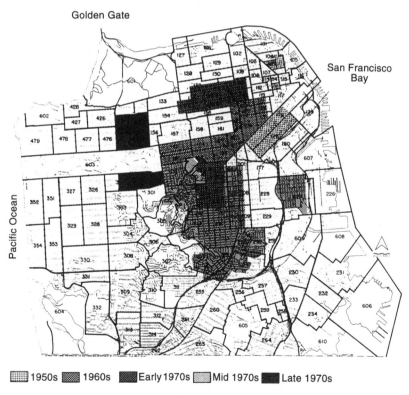

▦ 1950s ▨ 1960s ▩ Early 1970s ▧ Mid 1970s ■ Late 1970s

Figure 4.11   Gay residential areas in San Francisco
Source: Castells (1983)

he was not able to teach after being discharged from the Navy because of homosexuality. Like thousands of gays, he migrated to San Francisco in 1969. After leaving a job as a financial analyst, he opened a photography business, Castro Camera, on Castro Street. He conceived a plan for gays to evolve from community, to business, to power. He called for "gays to buy gay," so that Castro would be more than a cruising place, but a space owned by gays, lived by gays, and enjoyed by gays. Then, if gays could buy gay, and live as gays, they could also vote gay. In 1973, he ran for supervisor (council member) of the city of San Francisco, explicitly as a gay candidate. He did well, but was not elected. He went back to work on building a political basis, strengthening gays' political clubs, linking up with the Democratic party, and broadening his program to address issues of local urban policies, such as the control of real estate speculation. A political event changed his destiny. In 1975, a liberal California Senator, George Moscone, was elected mayor of San Francisco by a narrow margin. To secure the support of the by then strong gay community, Moscone appointed Harvey Milk to an important post in the local administration. For the first time an openly gay leader became a city official. Around the same time, the powerful neighborhood movement in San Francisco obtained a reform of the electoral law, establishing elections to the city council (Board of Supervisors) by local districts, instead of voting in the city at large. Then, on the basis of the territory that the gay community had conquered in the Castro area, which became an electoral district, Harvey Milk was elected supervisor in 1977. From his new platform, he mobilized gay power around the city, and around the state. In 1978 a conservative proposition was put in the ballot to California voters to ban homosexuals from teaching in public schools. The voters rejected it by 58 percent of the vote in California, 75 percent in San Francisco. Harvey Milk, with skillful media performance, was the leader of the campaign. In April 1978, the Board of Supervisors approved a very liberal Gay Rights Ordinance. At the same time, two lesbian leaders, Del Martin and Phyllis Lyon, holding City Hall Posts, received from the city of San Francisco a certificate of honor for their civic services – including support for lesbians – and for their 25 years of living together. These, and other gay breakthroughs, were more than the homophobic culture could take. On November 27, 1978, a conservative city supervisor, Dan White, an ex-policeman who had campaigned against tolerance toward "sexual deviants," shot and killed mayor George Moscone and supervisor Harvey Milk in their offices at City Hall. He later surrendered to his former colleagues in the police department. The mourning of Moscone and Milk was one of the most impressive political demonstrations ever seen in San Francisco: 20,000 people marched with candles, in silence, after listening to speakers who called on the movement to pursue the struggle in the way shown by Harvey Milk. It did. The new mayor, Dianne Feinstein, appointed another gay leader, Harry Britt, a socialist, to replace Harvey Milk in his post, and he was subsequently elected supervisor. Over the next decade, gay and lesbian leaders increased their representation in the 11-member city Board of Supervisors, and although they lost one election, in 1992, to a conservative mayor, they became again a major component of the coalition that helped to elect Willie Brown, a veteran Black Democratic leader, mayor of San Francisco in 1996. An anecdote of the 1996 campaign reveals the state of mental confusion of the homophobic culture in San Francisco, lost in the uncertainty of long cherished values. The incumbent mayor, an ex-police chief, may have lost his re-election bid after a major political blunder. Trailing in the polls, and trying to find a way to ingratiate himself with the gay audience, he let himself be photographed naked, while giving an interview in his shower with radio journalists in the same attire. The backlash from both gay and straight offended voters doomed his chances. The new mayor renewed the by then two decades old commitment from the city to respect and enhance gay rights, and gay culture, celebrated in parades and festivities several times in the year.

However, the gay community of the 1990s is not the same as the one formed in the 1970s because in the early 1980s AIDS struck.[113] In the next 15 years, about 15,000 people died from AIDS in San Francisco, and several other thousands were diagnosed infected with the HIV virus. The reaction of the gay community was remarkable, as San Francisco became a model for the entire world in self-organization, prevention, and political action geared toward controlling the AIDS epidemics, a danger for humankind. I believe it is accurate to say that the most important gay movement of the 1980s/1990s is the gay component of the anti-AIDS movement, in its different manifestations, from health clinics to militant groups such as ACT UP! In San Francisco, the first effort was directed toward helping the ill, and preventing the spread of the disease. A large-scale effort for the education of the community was undertaken, with safe-sex procedures taught and diffused. After a few years, the results were spectacular. In the 1990s, in San Francisco, and in California, the incidence of new cases of AIDS is much greater in the heterosexual population, as a result of drug use, prostitution, and infection of women by careless

[113] For a discussion of the relationship between the gay movement, the fight against AIDS, and society's reactions, see Coates et al. (1988); Mass (1990); Heller (1992); Price and Hsu (1992); Herek and Greene (1995); Lloyd and Kuselewickz (1995).

men, while the gay population, more educated and better organized, has seen a significant decline in new infections. The care of the ill was organized at all levels, with San Francisco General Hospital becoming the first hospital to establish a permanent AIDS section, and a whole network of volunteers providing help and comfort to people in the hospital and at home. Militant pressures to step up research efforts, and to obtain accelerated approval of experimental drugs as they became available, yielded significant results. The University of California at San Francisco Hospital became one of the leading centers in AIDS-related research. In a broader perspective, the 1996 worldwide AIDS Conference in Vancouver announced potential breakthroughs in controlling the disease and, maybe, in diminishing its lethality in the future.

But perhaps the most important effort by the gay community, in San Francisco and elsewhere, was the cultural battle to demystify AIDS, to remove the stigma, and to convince the world that it was not produced by homosexuality or, for that matter, by sexuality. Contact networks, including sexual contact, but comprising many other forms, were the lethal messengers, not homosexuality.[114] And the disconnection of these networks, thus controlling the epidemics, was not a matter of confinement but of education, organization, and responsibility, supported both by public health institutions and civic consciousness. That the gay community, starting in San Francisco, could win this uphill battle was a decisive contribution to humankind. Not only because a new crime against humanity was avoided, when the movement successfully fought back the calls for detection and confinement of HIV carriers. What was fundamentally at stake was the ability of the world to look AIDS directly into its horrifying eyes, and to face the epidemics in the terms of the virus(es) as it (they) is (are), not in terms of our prejudices and nightmares. We came very close, in the world at large, to considering AIDS as a deserved divine punishment against New Sodom, thus not taking the necessary measures to prevent an even greater spread of the disease until it may have been too late to control it at all. That we did not, that societies learned in time that AIDS was not a homosexual disease, and that the sources and vehicles of its spread had to be fought in society at large was, to a large extent, the work of the gay-community based, anti-AIDS movement, with its pioneers (many of them on their way to death) in the liberated city of San Francisco.

Not unrelated to the AIDS epidemic, another major trend took place in the 1990s in the San Francisco gay community. Patterns of sexual interaction became more stable, partly a sign of the aging and

---

[114]   Castells (1992c).

maturation of some segments of the community, partly as a way of channeling sexuality into safer patterns of love. The yearning for same-sex families became one of the most powerful cultural trends among gays and, even more so, among lesbians. The comfort of a durable, monogamous relationship became a predominant model among middle-aged gays and lesbians. Consequently, a new movement sprouted out from the gay community to obtain the institutional recognition of such stable relationships as families. Thus, certificates of partnership were sought from local and state governments, with this recognition carrying the entitlement to spousal benefits. Furthermore, the legalization of same-sex marriages became a major demand of the movement, taking conservatives at their word in promoting family values, and extending the value of the family to non-traditional, non-heterosexual forms of love, sharing, and child rearing. What started as a movement of sexual liberation came full circle to haunt the patriarchal family by attacking its heterosexual roots, and subverting its exclusive appropriation of family values.

Since any action brings a reaction, the relative taming of sexuality in new gay and lesbian families induced, in parallel, the development of sexual minority cultures (both heterosexual and homosexual), such as the sadomasochist movement, and voluntary sex-slave networks, a significant phenomenon in the San Francisco scene, particularly in the South of Market area, in the 1990s, although I identified the importance of this cultural/personal revolt in my fieldwork 15 years ago. Sadomasochists, whose culture includes some very articulate intellectuals, criticize mainstream gays for trying to define new norms of the "socially acceptable," thus reproducing the logic of domination that oppressed gays and lesbians throughout history. For sadomasochists the journey has no end. Thus, controlled violence, accepted humiliation, slave auctions, painful pleasure, leather dress, Nazi emblems, chains and whips, are more than sexual stimuli. They are cultural expressions of the need to destroy whatever moral values straight society has left them with since these values have traditionally been used to stigmatize and repress homosexuality, and sexuality. The considerable embarrassment that this cultural minority causes to most gays and lesbians is the symptom that they do address an important, if difficult, issue.

Left to itself, in its cultural ghetto, the gay community is unlikely to accomplish the sexual revolution and the subversion of patriarchalism that are, implicitly, the goals of the movement, even if they are not supported by the growing segment of male elites that consume rather than produce the gay movement. Strategic alliances with lesbians, and with the feminist movement at large seem to be a necessary condition for the fulfillment of gay liberation. Yet, gays are men, and their socialization as men, and the privileges they enjoy, particularly if they are white and middle class, limit their fully fledged incorporation into an anti-patriarchal alliance. This is why in San Francisco, in the 1990s, there is a growing split between a radically oriented gay and lesbian alliance, and a respectable gay elite that has established itself as an interest group to defend gay rights as a tolerated minority within the institutions of patriarchalism. Yet, if this diversity can be expressed within a broader movement that allows people freedom to chose whom they love, in contradiction with the heterosexual norm, it is because Harvey Milk, and other pioneers, built a free commune once upon a time in the West.

Summing up: sexual identity and the patriarchal family

Lesbian and gay movements are not simply movements in defense of basic human rights to choose whom and how to love. They are also powerful expressions of sexual identity, and therefore of sexual liberation. This is why they challenge some of the millennial foundations on which societies were built historically: sexual repression and compulsory heterosexuality.

When lesbians, in an institutional environment as repressive and patriarchal as the Chinese culture in Taipei, are able to openly express their sexuality, and to claim the inclusion of same-sex marriages in the family code, a fundamental breach has been opened in the institutional scaffolding constructed to control desire. If the gay community is able to overcome ignorant stigmatization, and to help prevent the plague of AIDS, it means that societies have become able to extract themselves from their darkness, and to look into the whole diversity of human experience, without prejudice and without violence. And if presidential electoral campaigns, in America for the moment, have unwillingly to reckon with the debate on gay rights, it means that the social movements' challenge to heterosexuality cannot be ignored or purely repressed any longer. Yet, the forces of transformation unleashed by sexual identity movements can hardly be confined within the limits of simple tolerance and respect for human rights. They bring into motion a corrosive critique of sexual normalization and of the patriarchal family. Their challenge is particularly frightening for patriarchalism because it comes at a historical time when biological research and medical technology allow the disassociation between heterosexuality, patriarchalism, and the reproduction of the species. Same-sex families, which will not give up rearing children, are the most open expression of this possibility.

On the other hand, the blurring of sexual boundaries, decoupling family, sexuality, love, gender, and power, introduces a fundamental cultural critique to the world as we have known it. This is why the future development of sexual liberation movements will not be easy. By shifting from the defense of human rights to the reconstruction of sexuality, family, and personality, they touch the nerve centers of repression and civilization, and they will be responded to in kind. There is a stormy horizon ahead for the gay and lesbian movements, and AIDS will not be the only hideous face of anti-sexual backlash. Yet, if the experience of the last quarter of the century has any indicative value, the power of identity seems to become magic when touched by the power of love.

Family, Sexuality, and Personality in the Crisis of Patriarchalism[115]

In the separating and divorcing society, the nuclear family generates a diversity of new kin ties associated, for example, with the so-called recombinant families. However, the nature of these ties changes as they are subject to greater negotiation than before. Kinship relations often used to be taken for granted on the basis of trust; now trust has to be negotiated and bargained for, and commitment is as much an issue as in sexual relationships.

Anthony Giddens, *The Transformation of Intimacy*, p. 96.

The incredibly shrinking family

The crisis of patriarchalism, induced by the interaction between informational capitalism and feminist and sexual identity social movements, manifests itself in the increasing diversity of partnership arrangements among people to share life and raise children. I will illustrate this point by using American data to simplify the argument. I do not imply, however, that all countries and cultures will follow this path. Yet, if the social, economic, and technological trends underlying the crisis of patriarchalism are present around the world, it is plausible that most societies will have to reconstruct, or replace, their patriarchal institutions under the specific conditions of their culture and history. The following discussion, empirically based on American trends, aims at identifying social mechanisms connecting the crisis of

---

[115] Data reported in this section are from the US Bureau of the Census and from *The World Almanac and Book of Facts* (1996), unless referred to otherwise. US Bureau of the Census publications used to retrieve these data are: US Department of Commerce, Economics and Statistics Administration, Bureau of the Census (1989, 1991, 1992a–d).

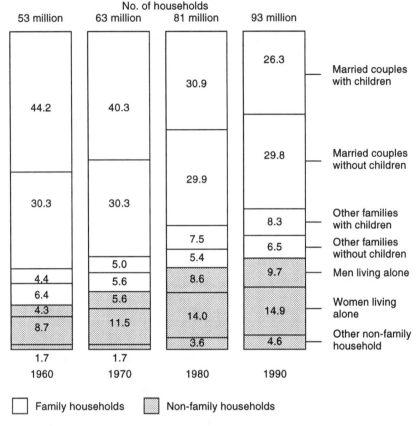

Figure 4.12a   Household composition in US, 1960–90 (%)
(children = own children under 18)
Source: US Bureau of the Census (1992a)

the patriarchal family, and the transformation of sexual identity, to the social redefinition of family life, thus of personality systems.

What is at issue is not the disappearance of the family but its profound diversification, and the change in its power system. Indeed, most people continue to marry: 90 percent of Americans do over their lifetime. When they divorce, 60 percent of women and 75 percent of men remarry, on average within three years. And gays and lesbians are fighting for their right to legal marriage. Yet, later marriages, frequence of cohabitation, and high rates of divorce (stabilized at about half of all marriages), and of separation, combine to produce an increasingly diverse profile of family and non-family life (figures 4.12a and 4.12b summarize its broad trends for 1960–90 and for 1970–95). The so-called "non-family households" doubled between

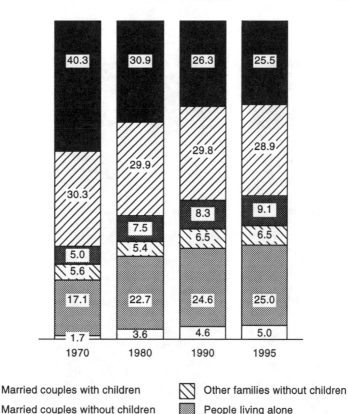

Legend:
- Married couples with children
- Married couples without children
- Other families with children
- Other families without children
- People living alone
- Other (non-related persons)

Figure 4.12b   Household composition in US, 1970–95 (%)
Source: US Bureau of the Census (1996)

1960 and 1995, increasing from 15 percent of all households to 29 percent of households, naturally including single elderly, and thus reflecting a demographic trend, as well as a cultural change. Women account for two-thirds of single-households. More significantly, the archetypical category "married couples with children" dropped from 44.2 percent of households in 1960 to 25.5 percent in 1995. Thus, the "model" of the patriarchal nuclear family is the reality for just over one-quarter of American households. Stacey quotes sources indicating that if we consider the most traditional version of patriarchalism, meaning the married couple with children in which the only breadwinner is the male, and the wife is a fulltime homemaker, the proportion drops to 7 percent of all households.[116]

---

[116]   Stacey (1990: 28).

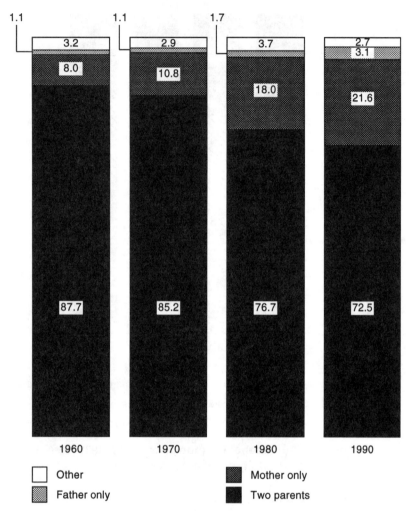

1.1   1.1   1.7

3.2	2.9	3.7	2.7
8.0	10.8	18.0	3.1
			21.6
87.7	85.2	76.7	72.5

1960   1970   1980   1990

☐ Other   ▓ Mother only

▒ Father only   ■ Two parents

Figure 4.13   Living arrangements of children under the age of 18, by
presence of parent, in US, 1960–90 (% distribution)
Source: US Bureau of the Census (1992a)

The life of children has been transformed. As figure 4.13 shows,
over one-quarter of children did not live with two parents in 1990, in
contrast to less than 13 percent in 1960. Furthermore, according to a
US Bureau of the Census study, in 1991 the proportion of children
living with their two biological parents was only 50.8 percent[117]. Other

[117]   US Bureau of the Census (1994).

sources also estimate that "nearly 50 percent of all children do not live with both of their genetic parents."[118] Adoptions have substantially increased over the past two decades, and 20,000 babies have been born from *in vitro* fertilization.[119] The *trends*, all pointing in the same direction of the fading away of the patriarchal nuclear family, are what really matters: the proportion of children living with a lone parent doubled between 1970 and 1990, reaching 25 percent of all children. Among these children, the proportion who lived with a never-married mother increased from 7 percent in 1970 to 31 percent in 1990. One-parent female-headed households with children increased by 90.5 percent in the 1970s, and by an additional 21.2 percent in the 1980s. One-parent male-headed households with children, while accounting only for 3.1 percent of all households in 1990, are growing even faster: by 80.6 percent in 1970s, and by 87.2 percent in the 1980s. Female-headed families without a husband present grew from 11 percent of all families in 1970 to 18 percent in 1994. The percentage of children living only with their mother doubled between 1970 and 1994, from 11 to 22 percent, while the proportion of children living only with their father trebled in the same period, going from 1 to 3 percent.

New profiles of living arrangements multiply.[120] In 1980, there were 4 million recombinant families (including children from a previous marriage); in 1990, 5 million. In 1992, one-quarter of single women over 18 had children; in 1993, there were 3.5 million unmarried couples, of which 35 percent had children in the household; the number of unmarried fathers with children doubled from 1980 to 1992; 1 million children were living with their grandparents in 1990 (10 percent up from 1960), out of a total of 3.5 million children sharing their household with a grandparent. Marriages preceded by cohabitation increased from 8 percent in the late 1960s to 49 percent in the mid-1980s, and half of cohabitating couples have children.[121] Furthermore, with the massive entry of women into the paid labor force, and their indispensable role in providing for the family, few children can enjoy their mother's or father's full-time care. In 1990, both husband and wife worked outside the home in about 70 percent of married couple families, and 58 percent of mothers with young children worked outside the home. Child care is a major problem for families, and was performed in their home by relatives or neighbors for two-thirds of children,[122] to which we should add unregistered

[118]	Buss (1994: 168).
[119]	Reigot and Spina (1996: 238).
[120]	Reigot and Spina (1996).
[121]	Coleman and Ganong (1993: 113).
[122]	Farnsworth Riche (1996).

home helpers. Poor women, unable to pay for child care, are faced with the choice of separating from their children or giving up work, then falling into the welfare trap that may lead eventually to their children being taken away from them.[123]

There are few reliable estimates on same-sex households and families. One of the few is by Gonsioreck and Weinrich, according to whom an estimated 10 percent of the American male population is gay, and between 6 and 7 percent of the female population lesbian.[124] They estimate that about 20 percent of the gay male population were married once, and that between 20 and 50 percent of them had children. Lesbians are often mothers, many of them from previous heterosexual marriages. A very wide range evaluation puts the figure of children living with their lesbian mothers at between 1.5 and 3.3 million. The number of children living with either gay or lesbian parents is estimated at between 4 and 6 million.[125] Among non-family households, the fastest growth is in the category "other non-family households," which increased from 1.7 percent of total households in 1970 to 5 percent in 1995. In this group are, according to the US census, room-mates, friends, and unrelated individuals. In fact, this category would include both heterosexual and homosexual couples in cohabitation without children.

As for projections toward the near future, using Harvard University's estimates of household formation to the year 2000, as a percentage of total households, married couples with children are expected to decline further, from 31.5 percent in 1980 to 23.4 percent in 2000, while single-person households may increase from 22.6 percent to 26.6 percent in 2000, statistically overtaking the household type of married couples with children.[126] Lone parents would increase slightly from 7.7 to 8.7 percent. Married couples without children would become the most numerous, but not predominant, household type, remaining at about 29.5 percent of all households, an effect of the longer survival of both spouses, together with the replacement of these formerly married couples with children by a more diversified

[123] Susser (1991).
[124] Gonsioreck and Weinrich (1991).The 10 percent threshold of homosexuality for the population at large is a demographic myth inspired by a superficial reading of the half-century old Kinsey Report (in fact reporting on American white males). As Laumann et al. (1994) suggest, with a strong empirical basis, there is no clear boundary of homosexuality that can be traced back to some distinctive biological impulse. The extent of homosexual behavior, in its different manifestations, evolves according to cultural norms and social contexts. For a discussion of the matter, see Laumann et al. (1994: 283–320).
[125] Reigot and Spina (1996: 116).
[126] Masnick and Ardle (1994); Masnick and Kim (1995).

array of household forms. Indeed, what they call "other households," comprising miscellaneous living arrangements are projected to increase their share from 8.8 percent in 1980 to 11.8 percent in 2000. Overall, in the Harvard University estimates and projections, while in 1960 three-quarters of all US households were formed by married couples, and non-family households accounted for only 15 percent of households, in the year 2000, married couples will account for about 53 percent, and non-family households will increase their share to 38 percent. What emerges from this statistical overview is a picture of diversification, of moving boundaries in people's partnerships, with a large and increasing proportion of children being socialized under family forms that were marginal, or even unthinkable, only three decades ago, an instant by the standards of historical time.[127]

So, what are these new arrangements? How do people live now, in and outside the family, on the borderlines of patriarchalism? We know something about it, after pioneer research by Stacey, Reigot and Spina, Susser, and others.[128] As Stacey writes:

> women and men have been creatively remaking American family life during the past three decades of post-industrial upheaval. Out of the ashes and residue of the modern family they have drawn on a diverse, often incongruous array of cultural, political, economic, and ideological resources, fashioning these resources into new gender and kinship strategies to cope with post-industrial challenges, burdens and opportunities.[129]

Similar conclusions are reached in the qualitative study by Reigot and Spina on new forms of families.[130] There is no new prevailing type of family emerging, diversity is the rule. But some elements seem to be critical in the new arrangements: *networks of support, increasing female-centeredness, succession of partners and patterns throughout the life-cycle.* Networks of support, often between members of families of divorced couples are a new, important form of sociability and burden-sharing, particularly when children have to be shared and supported between the two parents after they both form new households. Thus, a study

---

[127]   According to data cited by Ehrenreich (1983: 20), in 1957, 53 percent of Americans believed that unmarried people were "sick," "immoral," or "neurotic," and only 37 percent viewed them "neutrally." By 1976, only 33 percent had negative attitudes toward the unmarried, and 15 percent looked favorably upon people who remained single.
[128]   Stacey (1990); Susser (1991, 1996); Reigot and Spina (1996); see also Bartholet (1990); Gonsioreck and Weinrich (1991); Brubaker (1993); Rubin and Riney (1994); Fitzpatrick and Vangelisti (1995).
[129]   Stacey (1990: 16).
[130]   Reigot and Spina (1996).

of middle-class divorced couples in the San Francisco suburbs found one-third of them sustaining kinship ties with former spouses and their relatives.[131] Women's support networks are critical for single mothers, as well as for full-time working mothers, according to the case studies reported by Reigot and Spina, and by Susser, as well as by Coleman and Ganong.[132] Indeed, as Stacey writes "if there is a family crisis, it is a male family crisis."[133] Furthermore, since most people keep trying to form families in spite of disappointments or misfits, step-parent families and a succession of partnerships become the norm. Because of both life experience and complexity of the households, arrangements within the family, with distribution of roles and responsibilities do not adjust to tradition any longer: they must be negotiated. Thus Coleman and Ganong, after observing widespread family disruption, conclude: "Does this mean the end of the family? No. It does mean, however, that many of us will be living in new, more complex families. In these new families, roles, rules and responsibilities may have to be negotiated rather than taken for granted as is typical in more traditional families."[134]

So, patriarchalism in the family is altogether eliminated in the case of the growing proportion of female-headed households, and seriously challenged in most other families, because of the negotiations and conditions requested by women and children in the household. Additionally, another growing proportion of households, maybe soon reaching almost 40 percent, relates to non-family households, thus voiding the meaning of the patriarchal family as an institution in much of the practice of society, in spite of its towering presence as a powerful myth.

Under such conditions, what happens to the socialization of children, underlying the reproduction of gender division in society, and thus the reproduction of patriarchalism itself?

The reproduction of mothering under the non-reproduction of patriarchalism

There is no place within the limits of this chapter to enter the detail of a complex, diversified, and controversial empirical record, most of which is hidden in the clinical files of child psychologists, on the transformation of family socialization in the new family environment. But, I think a number of hypotheses can be advanced, on the basis of the

---

[131]　Cited in Stacey (1990: 254).
[132]　Coleman and Ganong (1993); Reigot and Spina (1996); Susser (1996).
[133]　Stacey (1990: 269).
[134]　Coleman and Ganong (1993: 127).

classic work by feminist psychoanalyst Nancy Chodorow. In her *Reproduction of Mothering*, Chodorow proposed a simple, elegant, and powerful psychoanalytical model of the production/reproduction of gender, a model that she refined and complemented in her later writings.[135] Although her theory is controversial, and psychoanalysis is certainly not the only possible approach to understanding personality changes in the crisis of patriarchalism, it provides, in my view, a useful starting point to theorize these changes. Let me first summarize Chodorow's analytical model in her own words, then elaborate on the implications of this model for personality and gender under the conditions of the crisis of patriarchalism. Following Chodorow, the reproduction of mothering is central to the reproduction of gender. It happens through a social-structurally induced psychological process, which is not the product of either biology or institutional role-training. In her words:

> Women, as mothers, produce daughters with mothering capacities and the desire to mother. These capacities and needs are built into and grow out of the mother–daughter relationship itself. By contrast, women as mothers (and men as not-mothers) produce sons whose nurturant capacities and needs have been systematically curtailed and repressed. This prepares men for their affective later family role and for their primary participation in the impersonal, extra-familial world of work and public life. The sexual and familial division of labor in which women mother and are more involved in interpersonal, affective relationships than men, produces in daughters and sons a division of psychological capacities which leads them to reproduce this sexual and familial division of labor . . . Women have primary responsibility for child care in families and outside them; women by and large want to mother, and get gratification for their mothering; and with all the conflicts and contradictions, women have succeeded at mothering.[136]

This model of reproduction has an extraordinary impact on sexuality, and therefore on personality and family life: "Because women mother, the development of heterosexual object-choice differ for men and women."[137] Boys retain their mother as their primary love object in their boyhood, and, because of the fundamental taboo, they have to go through the classic process of separation, and resolution of their oedipus complex, by repressing their attachment to the

---

[135] Chodorow (1989, 1994).
[136] Chodorow (1978: 7).
[137] Chodorow (1978: 191).

mother. When becoming adults, men are ready to find a primary relationship with someone *like* their mother (Chodorow's italics). Things are different for girls:

> Because her first love object is a woman, a girl, in order to attain her *proper heterosexual orientation*,[138] must transfer her primary object-choice to her father and men . . . For girls, as for boys, mothers are primary love objects. As a result, the structural inner object setting of female heterosexuality differs from that of males. When a girl's father does become an important primary person, it is in the context of a bisexual relational triangle . . . For girls, then, there is no absolute change of object, nor exclusive attachment to their fathers . . . The implications of this are two-fold. First, the nature of the heterosexual relationship differs for boys and girls. Most women emerge from their oedipus complex oriented to their father and men as primary *erotic* objects, but it is clear that men tend to remain *emotionally* secondary, or at most emotionally equal, compared to the primacy and exclusivity of an oedipal boy's tie to his mother and women. Second . . . women, according to Deutsch, experience heterosexual relationships in a triangular context, in which men are not exclusive objects for them. The implication of her statement is confirmed by cross-cultural examination of family structure and relations between the sexes, which suggests that conjugal closeness is the exception and not the rule.[139]

Indeed, men tend to fall in love romantically, while women, because of their economic dependence and their women-oriented affective system, engage *vis à vis* men in a more complex calculation, in which access to resources is paramount,[140] according to the cross-cultural

---

[138]   Adrienne Rich (1980) criticized Chodorow for not emphasizing the potential lesbian inclination of many women, in line with her theory. In my view, this criticism is unfair because Rich's "lesbian continuum" takes place within the context of institutionalized heterosexuality. What Chodorow explains is how the uninterrupted mother/daughter link is channeled toward the institutions of heterosexual marriage, from where it is also originates. It is essential for the psychoanalyst, and for the sociologist, to keep a distance between analysis and advocacy.

[139]   Chodorow (1978: 192–3).

[140]   Of course, the world's literature, as our personal experience, is full of examples of women abandoning everything in pursuit of romance. I would argue, however, that this is a manifestation of the ideological domination of the patriarchal model, and rarely resists the actual experience of the relationship. This is why it makes good material for novels!

study by Buss on strategies of human mating.[141] But let us pursue
Chodorow's logic:

> [Women] while they are likely to become and remain erotically
> heterosexual [Castells: albeit with more and more exceptions to
> the rule], they are encouraged both by men's difficulties with
> love and by their own relational history with their mothers to look
> elsewhere for love and emotional gratification. One way that
> women fulfill these needs is through the creation and mainte-
> nance of important personal relations with other
> women . . . However, deep affective relationships to women are
> hard to come by on a routine, daily, ongoing basis for many
> women. Lesbian relationships do tend to recreate mother-
> daughters, but most women are heterosexual . . . There is a
> second alternative . . . Given the triangular situation and
> emotional asymmetry of her own parenting, a woman's relation
> to a man *requires* on the level of psychic structure a third person,
> since it was originally established in a triangle . . . Then, a child
> completes the relational triangle for a woman [142]

Indeed, "women come to want and need primary relationships to children."[143] For men, again, it is different, because of their primordial
attachment to their mother, and, later on, to their mother-like figure:
"For men, by contrast, the heterosexual relationship alone recreates
the early bond to their mother; *a child interrupts it* [my italics]. Men,
moreover do not define themselves in relationships, and have come
to suppress relational capacities and repress relational needs. This
prepares them to participate in the affect-denying world of alienated
work, but not to fulfill women's needs for intimacy and primary
relationships."[144] Thus, "men's lack of emotional availability and
women's less exclusive heterosexual commitment help ensure
women's mothering." Ultimately,

> institutionalized features of family structure and the social
> relations of reproduction reproduce themselves. A psychoana-
> lytical investigation shows that women's mothering capacities
> and commitments, and the general psychological capacities and
> wants which are the basis of women's emotions work, are built
> developmentally into feminine personality. Because women are
> themselves mothered by women, they grow up with the relational

[141]   Buss (1994).
[142]   Chodorow (1978: 201).
[143]   Chodorow (1978: 203).
[144]   Chodorow (1978: 207).

capacities and needs, and psychological definition of self-in relationships, which commits them to mothering. Men, because they are mothered by women, do not. Women mother daughters who, when they become women, mother.[145]

Chodorow's model has been assailed, notably by lesbian theorists and materialist feminists, and unfairly accused of downplaying homosexuality, of fixing patriarchalism, and of predetermining individual behavior. In fact, it is not so. Chodorow herself has made clear her views: "I claim – against generalization – that men and women love in as many ways as there are men and women."[146] And she has refined her analysis by emphasizing that "differentiation is not distinctness and separateness, but a particular way of being connected to others."[147] The problem for women, she argues, and I concur, is not to claim their female identity, but their identification with an identity that has been socially devalued under patriarchalism. What Chodorow analyzes is not an eternal, biological process of male/female specificity, but a fundamental mechanism of reproduction of gender, and hence of identity, sexuality, and personality, *under the conditions of patriarchalism and heterosexuality*, as she has made clear repeatedly.

My question, then, is whether this institutional/psychoanalytical model can help us in understanding what happens when the patriarchal family disintegrates. Let me try to link up my observations on new forms of families and living arrangements with Chodorow's theory.[148] Under the classic, now fading, patriarchal/heterosexual condition, heterosexual women relate primarily to four kinds of objects: children as the object of their mothering; women's networks as their primary emotional support; men as erotic objects; and men as providers of the family. Under current conditions, for most families and women, the fourth object has been canceled as the exclusive provider. Women do pay a dear price, in working time, and in poverty, for their economic independence or for their indispensable role as family providers, but, by and large, the economic basis of family patriarchalism has been eroded, since most men also need women's income to reach decent living standards. As men were already secondary as assets of emotional

[145] Chodorow (1978: 209).
[146] Chodorow (1994: 71).
[147] Chodorow (1989: 107).
[148] I should remind the reader that Chodorow is primarily a psychoanalyst, focused on developing theory *on the basis of clinical evidence.* Therefore, this use of her cautious, psychoanalytical approach to construct my sweeping sociological generalizations goes far beyond her usual boundaries, and is undertaken, naturally, under my exclusive responsibility.

support, this leaves them, primarily, with their role as erotic objects, a dwindling source of interest for women in a time of widespread development of women's support networks (including expressions of affection in a "lesbian continuum"), and given women's focus on combining their mothering with their working lives.

Thus, the first living arrangement resulting from the crisis of patriarchalism, corresponding to the logic of Chodorow's model, is the formation of mother/children families, relying on the support of women's networks. These "women/children's communes" experience, from time to time, the visit of men, for heterosexual women, in a pattern of successive partnerships that leave behind additional children and further reasons for separatism. When mothers age, daughters mother, reproducing the system. Then, mothers become grandmothers, reinforcing the support networks, both *vis à vis* their daughters and grandchildren, and *vis à vis* the daughters and children of their networked households. This is not a separatist model, but a rather self-sufficient women-centered model, where men come and go. The main problem for the woman-centered model, as Barbara Ehrenreich pointed out years ago,[149] is its weak economic basis. Childcare, social services, and women's education and job opportunities are the missing links for this model to become a largely self-sufficient women's commune on a societal scale.

The situation for men, while being more socially privileged, is more complicated personally.[150] With the decline of their economic bargaining power, they usually cannot enforce discipline in the family any longer by withholding resources. Unless they engage in egalitarian parenting, they cannot alter the basic mechanisms by which their daughters are produced as mothers and they are produced as desirers of women/mothers *for themselves*. Thus, they continue to seek after *the* woman, as their object of love, not only erotic but emotional, as well as their safety blanket, and, not forgetting, their useful domestic worker. With fewer children, women working, men earning less and in less secure jobs, and with feminist ideas floating around, men face a number of options, none of which is the reproduction of the patriarchal family, if this analysis is correct.

The first is *separation*, "the flight from commitment,"[151] and, indeed, we observe such a trend in the statistics. Consumerist narcissism may help, particularly in the younger years. Yet, men do not do well in networking, solidarity, and relational skills, a feature that is also explained by Chodorow's theory. Male bonding is indeed a usual

[149] Ehrenreich (1983).
[150] Ehrenreich (1983); Astrachan (1986); Keen (1991).
[151] Ehrenreich (1983).

practice in traditional patriarchal societies. But, as I remember from my Spanish experience (old and recent), "men only" social gatherings are based on the assumption of family/female support waiting at home. It is only on a stable structure of domination satisfying basic affective needs that men can then play together, generally talking about, boasting about, and parading for women. The men's *peñas* [152] become silent and depressing when women disappear, suddenly transformed into drinking mortuaries of male power. Indeed, in most societies, single men have poorer health, lower longevity, and higher suicide and depression rates than married men. The contrary is true for women who divorce or separate, in spite of frequent, but short post-divorce depressions.

A second alternative is *gayness*. Indeed, it seems that gayness is expanding among men whose biological predispositions allow both forms of sexual expression, but that, under circumstances of privileged patriarchalism, may have chosen to abstain from the homosexual stigma. Gayness increases the chances of support networks, of which men are usually deprived. It also makes easier egalitarian, or negotiated, partnerships, since social norms do not assign dominant roles in the couple. Thus, gay families may be the experimental milieux of everyday life's egalitarianism.

Yet, for most men, the most acceptable, stable, long-term solution is to *renegotiate the heterosexual family contract*. This includes domestic work sharing, economic partnership, sexual partnership, and, above everything else, *full sharing of parenting*. This latter condition is critical for men because only under such circumstances can the "Chodorow effect" be altered, and women could be produced not only as mothers, but as men-desiring women, and men could be raised not just as women-lovers, but as children's fathers. Indeed, unless this mechanism is reversed, the simple reform of economic and power arrangements in the family cannot last as a satisfactory condition for men because, as they are still yearning for *the* woman as *their* exclusive love-object, and they are decreasingly needed by women, their conditional surrender in the reformed nuclear family is structurally filled with resentment. Thus, beyond individual bargaining in the reformed family, the future possibility for reconstructing viable heterosexual

---

[152]   The *peña* is a medieval Spanish institution, originally for men only, and still male dominated, which brought/brings together the youth of the village or neighborhood around the preparation of the annual religious/folk festivity of the village. It serves as a socializing network for drinking and enjoying together the annual round, as in the most famous *peñas*, those of Pamplona's San Fermines. The word *peña* means solid rock. The *peñas* are the rocks of male bonding.

families lies in the subversion of gender through the revolution of parenting, as Chodorow suggested in the first place. Without going into another round of statistical detail, let me just say that, while considerable progress has been made in this direction,[153] egalitarian parenting has still a long way to go, and its growth is slower than the rise of separatism for both men and women.

The main victims of this cultural transition are children, as they have become increasingly neglected under current conditions of family crisis. Their situation may even worsen, either because women stay with their children under difficult material conditions, or because women, looking for autonomy and personal survival, begin to neglect their children the way men do. Since support from the welfare state is dwindling, men and women are left to themselves in handling their children's problems, while losing control over their lives. The dramatic increase in child abuse in many societies, particularly in the United States, could well be an expression of people's bewilderment concerning their family life. By saying so, I am certainly not espousing the neo-conservative argument that blames feminism, or sexual liber-ation, for the plight of children. I am pinpointing a fundamental issue in our society that must be addressed without ideological prejudice: children are being massively neglected, as documented by social scientists and journalists.[154] The solution is not an impossible return to an obsolete, and oppressive, patriarchal family. The reconstruction of the family under egalitarian relations, and the responsibility of public institutions in securing material and psychological support for children, are possible ways to alter the course toward mass destruction of the human psyche that is implicit in the currently unsettling life of millions of children.

Body identity: the (re)construction of sexuality

There is a sexual revolution in the making, but not the one announced, and sought, by the 1960s/1970s social movements, although they have been important factors in inducing the really existing sexual revolution. *It is characterized by the de-linking of marriage, family, heterosexuality, and sexual expression* (or desire, as I call it). These four factors, linked under modern patriarchalism for the past two centuries, are now in the process of autonomization, as a number of observations reported in this chapter seem to show. As Giddens writes:

---

[153]   Shapiro et al. (1995).
[154]   Susser (1996).

Heterosexual marriage superficially appears to retain its central position in the social order. In reality, it has been largely undermined by the rise of the pure relationship and plastic sexuality. If orthodox marriage is not yet widely seen as just one life-style among others, as in fact it has become, this is partly the result of the complicated mixture of attraction and repulsion which the psychic development of each sex creates with regard to the other . . . Some marriages may still be contracted, or sustained, mainly for the sake of producing, or bringing up, children. Yet . . . most heterosexual marriages (and many homosexual liaisons) which do not approximate to the pure relationship are likely to evolve in two directions if they do not lapse into co-dependence. One is a version of a companionate marriage. The level of sexual involvement of the spouses with each other is low, but some degree of equality and mutual sympathy is built into the relationship. . . . The other form is where marriage is used as a home base for both partners who have only a slight emotional investment in one another.[155]

In both cases, sexuality is de-linked from marriage. This was indeed the case for most women throughout history,[156] but the affirmation of women's sexuality, of homosexuality for both men and women, and of elective sexuality, are inducing an increasing distance between people's desire and their families. However, this does not translate into sexual liberation, but, for the majority of the population, scared by the consequences of infidelity (for which men now also have to pay), and, in the 1980s and 1990s, by the AIDS epidemic, the consequence is sexual poverty, if not misery. This is at least what can be inferred from the most comprehensive, recent empirical survey of sexual behavior in America, conducted in 1992 on a representative national sample.[157] Some 35.5 percent of men reported having sex a few times a month, and another 27.4 percent a few times a year or not at all. For women, respective percentages were 37.2 percent and 29.7 percent. Only 7.7 percent of men and 6.7 percent of women reported having sex four or more times per week, and even in the 18–24 age group (the most sexually active), the percentage of high frequency was 12.4 percent both for men and women. High activity rates (over four times a week) are slightly lower for married couples than for the population at large (7.3 percent for men, 6.6 percent for women). These data also confirm the gender gap in reported orgasms: 75 percent of sexual encounters for men, only 29 percent

---

[155]   Giddens (1992: 154–5).
[156]   Buss (1994).
[157]   Laumann et al. (1994).

for women, although the gap is narrower in reporting "pleasure."[158] The number of sex partners in the last 12 months shows a limited range of sexual partnerships for the overwhelming majority of the population: 66.7 percent of men and 74.7 percent of women had only one partner; and 9.9 percent and 13.6 percent respectively, had none. So, no widespread sexual revolution in America in the early 1990s.

Yet, beneath the surface of sexual tranquility, the rich database of this University of Chicago study reveals trends toward an increasing autonomy of sexual expression, particularly among the younger age groups. For instance, there has been a steady decrease over the past four decades in the age of first intercourse: in spite of AIDS, teenagers are more sexually active than ever. Secondly, cohabitation before marriage has become the norm rather than the exception. Adults increasingly tend to form sexual partnerships outside marriage. About half of these cohabitations end within a year, 40 percent of them being transformed into marriages, 50 percent of which will end up in divorce, two-thirds of which will end up in remarriage, whose likelihood of divorce is even greater than the average for all marriages. It is this drying up of desire by successive efforts to link it up to living arrangements that seems to characterize 1990s' America.

On the other hand, "consumerist sexuality" appears on the rise, although the indications here are rather indirect. Laumann et al. analyze their sample in terms of sexual normative orientations following the classic distinction between traditional sexuality (pro-creational), relational (companionship), and recreational (oriented toward sexual enjoyment). They also isolate a "libertarian-recreational" type that seems closer to the images of pop-sexual liberation or, in Giddens' terms, "plastic sexuality." When analyzing their sample by major regions in America, they found that 25.5 percent of their sample in New England, and 22.2 percent in the Pacific region, could be included under such a "libertarian-recreational" category: this is about one-quarter of the population in some of the most culturally trend-setting areas of America.

A meaningful indicator of increasing sexual autonomy, as a pleasure-oriented activity, is the practice of oral sex which, I remind you, is catalogued as sodomy, and explicitly prohibited by law in 24 American states, albeit under conditions of doubtful enforcement. Figure 4.14 displays the occurrence of oral sex by cohort, by which is meant the percentages of women and men who have experienced either cunnilingus or fellatio in their lifetime by birth cohort. Laumann et al., commenting on these findings, assert that:

[158] Laumann et al. (1994: 116).

Men

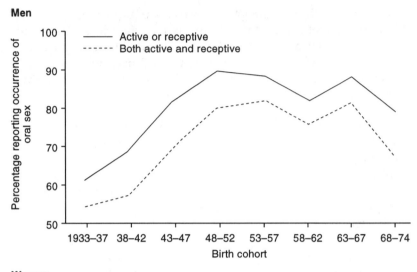

Women

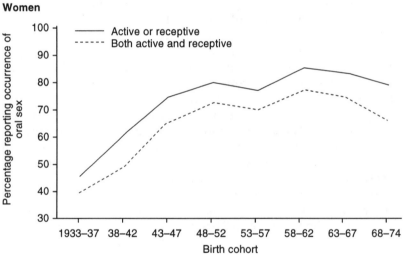

Figure 4.14   Lifetime occurrence of oral sex, by cohort: men and
women
Source: Laumann et al. (1994)

The overall trend reveals what we might call a rapid change in
sexual techniques if not a revolution. The difference in lifetime
experience of oral sex between respondents born between 1933
and 1942 and those born after 1943 is dramatic. The proportion
of men experiencing oral sex in their lifetime increases from 62

percent of those born between 1933–37 to 90 percent of those born between 1948–52 . . . The timing of sexual techniques appears to have been responsive to cultural changes in the late 1950s, changes that peaked in the mid to late 1960s, *when they approached saturation level of the population. The lower rates among the youngest groups in our survey are not necessarily evidence of decline in oral sex; these groups simply have not yet engaged in sexual relationships in which oral sex has become likely if not normative.*[159]

Incidentally, between 75 and 80 percent of women in the latest cohorts also experienced oral sex, and in the younger groups their occurrence is higher than for men. Laumann et al. also report widespread incidence of auto-eroticism (associated with high levels of partnered sexual activity), and of masturbation, hardly a novel technique, but that seems to involve two-thirds of men, and over 40 percent of women.

Thus, if instead of reading sexual behavior under the norm of heterosexual, repetitive partnership, we take a more "perverse" approach to it, the data reveal a different story, a story of consumerism, experimentation, and eroticism in the process of deserting conjugal bedrooms, and still searching for new modes of expression, while watching out for AIDS. Since these new patterns of behavior are more visible among younger groups, and in trend-setting cities, I feel safe to predict that, if, when, and where the AIDS epidemic comes under control, there will be one, two, three, many Sodoms, emerging from fantasies freed by the crisis of patriarchalism, and excited by the culture of narcissism. Under such conditions, as Giddens proposes, sexuality becomes the property of the individual.[160] Where Foucault saw the extension of apparatuses of power into the sexually constructed/construed subject, Giddens sees, and I concur, the fight between power and identity in the battleground of the body.[161] It is not necessarily a liberating struggle, because desire often emerges from transgression, so that a "sexually liberated society" becomes simply a supermarket of personal fantasies, in which individuals will consume each other rather than produce themselves. However, by assuming the body as identity principle, away from the institutions of patriarchalism, the multiplicity of sexual expressions empowers the individual in the arduous (re)construction of her/his personality.[162]

[159] Laumann et al. (1994: 103–4); my italics.
[160] Giddens (1992: 175).
[161] Giddens (1992: 31).
[162] Grosz (1995).

Flexible personalities in a post-patriarchal world

New generations are being socialized out of the traditional pattern of the patriarchal family, and are being exposed from an early age to the need to cope with different settings, and different adult roles. In sociological terms, the new process of socialization downplays to some extent the institutional norms of the patriarchal family and diversifies the roles within the family. In their insightful exploration of this matter, Hage and Powers propose that, as an outcome of such processes, new personalities emerge, more complex, less secure, yet more capable of adapting to changing roles in social contexts, as adaptive mechanisms are triggered by new experiences at an early age.[163] The increasing individualization of relationships within the family tends to emphasize the importance of personal demands beyond the rules of institutions. Thus, sexuality becomes, at the level of social values, a personal need that does not necessarily have to be channeled and institutionalized within the family. With the majority of the adult population, and one-third of children, living outside the boundaries of the traditional nuclear family, and with both proportions growing, the construction of desire increasingly operates on interpersonal relationships outside the lineage of traditional family context: it becomes an expression of the self. The socialization of teenagers under these new cultural patterns leads to a higher degree of sexual freedom than that of previous generations, including those in the liberated sixties, in spite of the menace of the AIDS epidemic.

Thus, the revolt of women against their condition, induced and allowed by their massive entry into the informational labor force, and the social movements of sexual identity have called into question the patriarchal nuclear family. This crisis has taken the form of a growing separation between the different dimensions that were previously held together in the same institution: interpersonal relationships between the two members of the couple; the working life of each member of the household; the economic association between members of the household; the performance of domestic work; the raising of children; sexuality; emotional support. The difficulty of coping with all these roles at the same time, once they are not fixed any longer in a formal, institutionalized structure, such as the patriarchal family, explains the difficulty of maintaining stable social relationships within the family-based household. For families to survive, new institutionalized forms of social relationships, in accordance with transformed relationships between genders, will have to emerge.

[163]   Hage and Powers (1992).

At the same time, technological change in biological reproduction has allowed the possibility of disassociating the reproduction of the species from the social and personal functions of the family. The possibilities of *in vitro* fertilization, of sperm banks, of surrogate mothers, of genetically engineered babies, open up a whole area of social experimentation that society will try to control and repress as much as possible because of its potential threat to our moral and legal foundations. Yet, the fact that women can have children on their own without having to even know the father, or that men, even after their death, can use surrogate mothers to have their children, severs the fundamental relationship between biology and society in the reproduction of human species, thus separating socialization from parenting. Under these historical conditions, families, and people's living arrangements, are being redefined in terms still unclear.

Because family and sexuality are fundamental determinants of personality systems, the calling into question of known family structures, and the coming into the open of personally projected sexuality, bring about the possibility of new types of personality that we are just beginning to perceive. Hage and Powers consider that the key ability to respond to current changes in society at the individual level is the ability to engage in "role redefinition," what they consider to be the "pivotal micro-process of postindustrial society."[164] While I concur with this most insightful analysis, I will add a complementary hypothesis to understand emerging personality systems. Daring to remain loyal to my psychoanalytical inclination, I would advance the idea that the open recognition of individual desire, as insinuated in the emerging culture of our society, would lead to such an aberration as the institutionalization of desire. Because desire is often associated with transgression, the recognition of sexuality outside the family would lead to extreme social strain. This is because as long as transgression consisted merely in expressing sexuality outside the family boundaries, society could easily cope with it, by channeling it through coded situations and organized contexts, such as prostitution, earmarked homosexuality, or condoned sexual harassment: this was Foucault's world of sexuality as normalization. Things are different now. If the patriarchal family is not there to be betrayed any longer, the transgression will have to be an individual act against society. The bumper function of the family is lost. This opens the way to the expression of desire in the form of non-instrumental violence. As welcome as it can be as a liberating development, the breakdown of the patriarchal family (the only one existing historically) is indeed giving way simultaneously to the normalization of sexuality (porno movies in

---

[164]   Hage and Powers (1992).

prime-time television), and to the spread of senseless violence in society through the back alleys of wild desire, that is, perversion.

Liberation from the family confronts the self with its own inflicted oppression. The escape to freedom in the open, networked society will lead to individual anxiety and social violence, until new forms of coexistence and shared responsibility are found that bring together women, men, and children in a reconstructed, egalitarian family better suited to free women, informed children, and uncertain men.

The End of Patriarchalism?

The continuing struggles in and around patriarchalism do not allow a clear forecasting of the historical horizon. Let me again repeat that there is no predetermined directionality in history. We are not marching through the triumphant avenues of our liberation, and, when we feel so, we had better watch out to see where these shining paths ultimately lead. Life muddles through life and, as we know, is full of surprises. A fundamentalist restoration, bringing patriarchalism back under the protection of divine law, may well reverse the process of the undermining of the patriarchal family, unwillingly induced by informational capitalism, and willingly pursued by cultural social movements. The homophobic backlash may undo the recognition of homosexual rights, as shown by the overwhelming vote by the US Congress in July 1996 to declare heterosexuality a requisite for legal marriage. And, around the world, patriarchalism is still alive and well, in spite of the symptoms of crisis that I have tried to emphasize in this chapter. However, the very vehemence of the reactions in defense of patriarchalism, as in the religious fundamentalist movements thriving in many countries, is a sign of the intensity of the anti-patriarchal challenges. Values that were supposed to be eternal, natural, indeed divine, must now be asserted by force, thus retrenching in their last defensive bastion, and losing legitimacy in people's minds.

The ability or inability of feminist and sexual identity social movements to institutionalize their values will essentially depend on their relationship to the state, the last resort apparatus of patriarchalism throughout history. However, the extraordinary demands placed upon the state by social movements, attacking institutions of domination at their root, emerge at the very moment when the state seems to be itself in the midst of a structural crisis, brought about by the contradiction between the globalization of its future and the identification of its past.

5

A Powerless State?

"What is specific to the capitalist state," wrote Nicos Poulantzas in 1978, "is that it absorbs social time and space, sets up the matrices of time and space, and monopolizes the organization of time and space that become, by the action of the state, networks of domination and power. This is how the modern nation is the product of the state."[1] Not any longer. State control over space and time is increasingly bypassed by global flows of capital, goods, services, technology, communication, and information. The state's capture of historical time through its appropriation of tradition and the (re)construction of national identity is challenged by plural identities as defined by autonomous subjects. The state's attempt to reassert its power in the global arena by developing supranational institutions further undermines its sovereignty. And the state's effort to restore legitimacy by decentralizing administrative power to regional and local levels reinforces centrifugal tendencies by bringing citizens closer to government but increasing their aloofness toward the nation-state. Thus, while global capitalism thrives, and nationalist ideologies explode all over the world, the nation-state, as historically created in the Modern Age, seems to be losing its power, although, and this is essential, *not its influence.*[2] In this chapter I shall explain why, and elaborate on the potential consequences of this fundamental development. I shall use illustrations of nation-states in various countries to emphasize that we are observing a systemic, global phenomenon, albeit with a great variety of manifestations. Indeed, the growing challenge to states' sovereignty around the world seems to originate from the inability of the modern nation-state to navigate

[1] Poulantzas (1978: 109); my translation.
[2] Tilly (1975); Giddens (1985); Held (1991, 1993); Sklair (1991); Camilleri and Falk (1992); Guehenno (1993); Horsman and Marshall (1994);Touraine (1994); Calderon et al. (1996).

uncharted, stormy waters between the power of global networks and the challenge of singular identities.[3]

Globalization and the State

The instrumental capacity of the nation-state is decisively under-mined by globalization of core economic activities, by globalization of media and electronic communication, and by globalization of crime.[4]

---

[3] The analysis of the crisis of the nation-state presupposes a definition, and a theory, of the nation-state. But since my work in this matter builds on already developed sociological theories, from various sources, I will refer the reader to the definition of Anthony Giddens in *The Nation-state and Violence* (1985: 121): "The nation-state, which exists in a complex of other nation-states, is a set of institutional forms of governance, maintaining an administrative monopoly over a territory with demarcated boundaries (borders), its rule being sanctioned by law, and direct control of the means of internal and external violence." Yet, as Giddens writes, "only in modern nation-states can the state apparatus generally lay successful claim to the monopoly of the means of violence, and only in such states does the administrative scope of the state apparatus correspond directly with territorial boundaries about which that claim is made" (p. 18). Indeed, as he argues, "a nation-state is a bordered power-container, the pre-eminent power-container of the modern era" (p. 120). So, what happens, and how should we conceptualize that state, when borders break down, and when containers are becoming contained themselves? My investigation starts, in theoretical continuity, from where the nation-state, as conceptualized by Giddens, appears to be superseded by historical transformation.

[4] For a definition and an analysis of globalization, as I understand it, see volume I, chapter 2. For a salutary critique of simplistic views on globalization, see Hirst and Thompson (1996). It has been often argued that globalization is not a new phenomenon, and has occurred in different historical periods, particularly with the expansion of capitalism at the end of the nineteenth century. It may be so, although I am not convinced that the new infrastructure based on information technology does not introduce a qualitative social and economic change, by enabling global processes to operate in real time. But I have really no quarrel with this argument: it does not concern my inquiry. I am trying to analyze, and explain, our society at the end of the twentieth century, in its variety of cultural, economic, and political contexts. So, my intellectual contribution should be discussed on its own ground, concerning contemporary processes as observed and theorized in the three volumes of this book. Undoubtedly, scholarly thinking would greatly benefit from comparative historical work contrasting current processes of inter-action between technology, globalization of economy and communications, politics, and political institutions with past experience of a similar transformation. I am hopeful that such an effort will be undertaken by colleagues, primarily by historians, and I will be more than happy to rectify my general theoretical state-ments on the basis of implications from such research. For the time being, the few attempts I have seen in this direction pay insufficient attention, in my opinion,

The transnational core of national economies

The interdependence of financial markets and currency markets around the world, operating as a unit in real time, links up national currencies. The constant exchange between dollars, yens, and the European Union's currencies (euros in the future) forces systemic coordination between these currencies, as the only measure able to keep some degree of stability in the currency market, and thus in global investment and trade. All other currencies in the world have become linked, for all practical purposes, to this triangle of wealth. If the exchange rate is systemically interdependent, so are, or will be, monetary policies. And if monetary policies are somehow harmonized at a supranational level, so are, or will be, prime interest rates, and, ultimately, budgetary policies. It follows that individual nation-states are losing and will lose control over fundamental elements of their economic policies.[5] In fact, this was already the experience of developing countries in the 1980s, and of European countries during the early 1990s. Barbara Stallings has shown how economic policies in developing countries were shaped during the 1980s by international pressures, as international financial institutions and private banks moved to stabilize developing economies as a prerequisite to international investment and trade.[6] In the European Union, the Bundesbank is already the *de facto* European Central Bank. For instance, when, in order to control German inflation after the government's irresponsible decision to set the exchange rate of one Western mark per one Eastern mark to unify Germany, the Bundesbank tightened up interest rates, it forced a deflation throughout Europe, regardless of the performance of national economies. In 1992 the Bundesbank went so far as to leak to the media its criticism of British monetary policy in order to force the devaluation of the pound, as eventually happened.

Japanese economic policy is essentially determined by the relationship between trade balance and exchange rate with the United States. As for the United States, the most self-sufficient economy, it could only remain so in spite of a substantial trade deficit during the 1980s by financing increased government spending

---

to the radically new processes in technology, finance, production, communications, and politics, so that while they may be right on the historical record, it is unclear why the present is just a repetition of past experience, beyond the rather pedestrian view that there is nothing new under the sun.

[5] Moreau Deffarges (1993); *Business Week* (1995a); Orstrom Moller (1995); Cohen (1996).

[6] Stallings (1992).

through borrowing, to a large extent from foreign capital. So doing, the main issue in American economic policy in the 1990s became the reduction of a gigantic budget deficit which threatened to become the black hole of the economy. America's economic independence was an illusion, likely to dissipate in the future when living standards will reflect competitiveness in the global economy, once the cushion of massive government borrowing, which became out of control under the Reagan Administration, is lifted.[7] It can be argued that the degree of freedom of governments' economic policy has been drastically reduced in the 1990s, with their budget policy caught between automatic entitlements inherited from the past, and high capital mobility experienced in the present, and probably increasing in the future.[8]

This increasing difficulty of government control over the economy (that some economists eagerly welcome) is accentuated by the growing transnationalization of production, not just under the impact of multinational corporations, but mainly through the production and trade networks in which these corporations are integrated.[9] It follows a declining capacity of governments to ensure, in their territories, the productive basis for generating revenue. As companies and wealthy individuals alike find fiscal havens around the world, and as accounting of value added in an international production system becomes increasingly cumbersome, a new fiscal crisis of the state arises, as the expression of an increasing contradiction between the internationalization of investment, production, and consumption, on the one hand, and the national basis of taxation systems, on the other.[10] Is it an accident that the two wealthiest countries in the world, in *per capita* terms, are Luxembourg and Switzerland? It may well be that one of the last stands of the nation-state is being fought in cyber-accounting space, between dutiful tax inspectors and sophisticated transnational lawyers.

A statistical appraisal of the new fiscal crisis of the state in the global economy

At this point in the analysis, it may be helpful to look at the evolution of government finances in the period of stepped-up globalization of national economies between 1980 and the early 1990s. To limit the complexity of the analysis, I have selected six countries: the three

[7]   Thurow (1992); Cohen (1993).
[8]   Chesnais (1994); Nunnenkamp et al. (1994).
[9]   Buckley (1994).
[10]   Guehenno (1993).

largest market economies (US, Japan, Germany); the most open of the large European economies (the UK); another European country, Spain, which, while being the eighth largest market economy in the world, is at a lower level of economic/technological development than G-7 countries; and one major economy of the newly industrialized world, India. On the basis of statistics compiled and elaborated by Sandra Moog, tables 5.1 and 5.2 have been constructed to provide an overview of some indicators of government finance and economic activity, related to the process of internationalization of economies. I will not comment in detail. Rather, I will use these tables to expand and specify the argument on globalization and the state as presented in the preceding pages.

Let us first examine the group of four countries (US, UK, Germany, and Spain) that seem to behave, in very broad terms, along similar lines, albeit with differences that I shall emphasize. Government expenditures have increased, and now represent between one-quarter and over 40 percent of GDP. Government jobs have decreased everywhere. The share of government consumption has decreased in the three major countries, while increasing in Spain. The share of government capital formation has increased in the US and declined in Germany. Central government's tax revenue has decreased in the US, while increasing in the other countries, substantially in Spain. Government deficit has increased, and substantially so in the US and Germany. Government debt has decreased in the UK, although it still represents about 34 percent of GDP, and has dramatically increased in Spain, Germany, and in the US, where in 1992 it represented 52.2 percent of GDP. The financing of government deficits has led the four countries to increase, in some cases substantially, dependency on foreign debt and foreign net lending. The ratios of government foreign debt and government net borrowing on GDP, central banks' currency reserves, government expenditures, and countries' exports show, in general terms, *an increasing dependence of governments on global capital markets*. Thus, for the United States, between 1980 and 1993, government foreign debt as a percentage of GDP more than doubled; as a percentage of currency reserves, it increased by 20 percent and, in 1993, represented almost ten times the level of total currency reserves; as a percentage of exports, it increased by 133 percent; and as a percentage of government expenditures, it almost doubled, to reach a level of 41.7 percent of total expenditures. As for the US government's net foreign borrowing, it increased in these 14 years by a staggering 456 percent, increasing by 203 percent its ratio to government expenditure, to reach a level equivalent to 6 percent of government expenditure. Since US direct foreign investment abroad, as a proportion of domestic investment, increased by 52.8 percent,

Table 5.1 Internationalization of the economy and public finance: rates of change, 1980–93 (and 1993 ratios, unless otherwise indicated)

	United States	United Kingdom	Germany	Japan	Spain	India
Gov. foreign debt/GDP %	104.2 (9.8)	31.8 (5.8/1992)	538.5 (p) (16.6) (p)	0.0 (0.3/1990)	1,066.7 (10.5)	−25.3 (5.9)
Gov. foreign debt/currency reserves %	20.1 (998.6)	44.7 (168.1/1992)	325.3 (p) (368.4) (p)	9.9 (12.2/1990)	674.5 (121.6)	−16.5 (149.4)
Gov. foreign debt/exports %	133.0 (134.0)	50.5 (32.2/1992)	590.8 (p) (75.3) (p)	9.5 (2.3/1990)	795.5 (79.7)	−55.6 (70.7)
Gov. foreign debt/gov. expenditures %	92.2 (41.7)	17.5 (13.5/1992)	423.5 (p) (44.5) (p)	—	586.8 (36.4)	−40.7 (35.4)
Gov. net foreign borrowing/gov. expenditures %	203.0 (6.12)	787.5 (14.2/1992)	223.4 (p) (15.2) (p)	—	—	10.3 (4.3)
Direct foreign investment abroad/domestic investment %	52.8 (5.5)	44.4 (17.9)	52.2 (3.5)	57.1 (1.1)	183.3 (2.8)	—
Inflow of direct foreign investment/domestic investment %	−35.5 (2.0)	−8.9 (10.2)	−50.0 (0.1)	—	236.7 (8.6)	—

(p) indicates preliminary data.

Note: For figures and details about sources and methods of calculation, please see the Methodological Appendix.

Sources: Compiled and elaborated by Sandra Moog from the following sources: *Government Finance Statistics Yearbook*, vol. 18 (Washington DC: IMF, 1994); *International Financial Statistics Yearbook*, vol. 48 (Washington DC: IMF, 1995); *The Europa World Yearbook* (London: Europa Publications, 1982, 1985, 1995); *National Accounts: Detailed Tables, 1980–1992*, vol. 2 (Paris: OECD, 1994); *OECD Economic Outlook*, vol. 58 (Paris: OECD, 1995); *World Tables, 1994* (The World Bank, Baltimore: The Johns Hopkins University Press, 1994)

Table 5.2 Government role in the economy and public finance: rates of change, 1980–92 (and 1992 ratios, unless otherwise indicated)

	United States	United Kingdom	Germany	Japan	Spain	India
Gov. expenditures/ GDP %	9.1 (24.0)	13.1 (43.2)	19.7 (34.6)	—	49.4 (25.1)	29.3 (p) (17.2) (p)
Budgetary central gov. tax revenue/GDP %	−15.6 (10.8)	8.0 (27.0)	11.6 (p) (13.5) (p)	18.2 (13.0/1990)	64.2 (17.4/1991)	17.3 (p) (11.2) (p)
Gov. budget deficit/GDP %	42.9 (4.8)	8.7 (5.0)	44.4 (2.6)	−78.6 (1.5/1990)	16.2 (4.3)	20.0 (p) (5.2) (p)
Gov. debt/GDP %	91.9 (52.2)	−26.0 (34.1)	78.1 (28.5)	30.1 (53.2/1990)	160.8 (39.9)	28.2 (p) (52.8) (p)
Gov. employment/ total employment %	−4.7 (16.2)	−3.1 (22.2)	−0.6 (16.4)	−20.9 (7.2)	—	—
Gov. capital formation/gross fixed capital formation %	21.2 (16.0)	—	−7.0 (27.9)	—	—	—
Gov. consumption/ private consumption %	−6.9 (27.2)	−2.7 (34.5)	−8.1 (32.7)	66.3 (16.3)	33.8 (26.9)	40.2 (p) (19.0) (p)

(p) indicates preliminary data.

Note: For figures and details about sources and methods of calculation, please see the Methodological Appendix.

Sources: Compiled and elaborated by Sandra Moog from the following sources: *Government Finance Statistics Yearbook,* vol. 18 (Washington DC: IMF, 1994); *International Financial Statistics Yearbook,* vol. 48 (Washington DC: IMF, 1995); *The Europa World Yearbook* (London: Europa Publications, 1982, 1985, 1995); *National Accounts: Detailed Tables, 1980–1992,* vol. 2 (Paris: OECD, 1994); *OECD Economic Outlook,* vol. 58 (Paris: OECD, 1995); *World Tables, 1994* (The World Bank, Baltimore: The Johns Hopkins University Press, 1994)

while inflow of direct foreign investment, also as a proportion of US domestic investment, decreased by 35.5 percent, it can be argued that the US federal government has become largely dependent on global capital markets and foreign lending.

The story is somewhat different for the UK, Germany, and Spain, but trends are similar. It is important to notice that, while the UK seems to be less dependent, Germany is increasing its dependency on foreign capital much faster than the US, as shown by several indicators: government foreign debt over GDP (538.5 percent increase), over currency reserves (325.3 percent increase), and over exports (590.8 percent increase). The German government's net foreign borrowing in 1993 reached a level representing over 15 percent of government expenditure, and its foreign debt is the equivalent of 44.5 percent of government expenditure, in both cases a higher percentage than those for the US. Thus, in spite of a strong export performance in the 1980s, Germany, unlike Japan, has substantially increased the international dependence of its national state.

Interestingly enough, India, while increasing government expenditure, consumption, and indebtedness, seems to be much less dependent on foreign debt: indeed, all its indicators of financial dependency show negative growth for the period, with the exception of the ratio of government foreign borrowing on government expenditure, still kept at a modest level. A sizeable increase in the share of tax revenue in GDP is only part of the explanation, the main one being the substantial acceleration of economic growth in India in the past decade. I should emphasize, however, that while the rate of change of indicators of the government's financial dependency in India has been negative over the period, the level of dependency remains very high (government foreign debt represents over 70 percent of exports, and almost 150 percent of currency reserves).

As is often the case, Japan is different. The Japanese government was not affected by foreign borrowing during the 1980s. Its budget deficit over GDP is by far the lowest, and it substantially declined during the period 1980–93. On the other hand, government consumption increased, government debt also increased, and Japan is as high as America in the ratio of government debt to GDP (over 50 percent). These observations indicate that the Japanese government's finances rely, rather, on domestic borrowing. This also reflects the greater competitiveness of the Japanese economy, and the considerable trade and balance of payments surplus accumulated by the country. So, the Japanese state is much more autonomous than other states *vis à vis* the rest of the world but the Japanese economy is much more dependent on trade performance, since Japanese capital finances its government with the proceeds from its competitiveness.

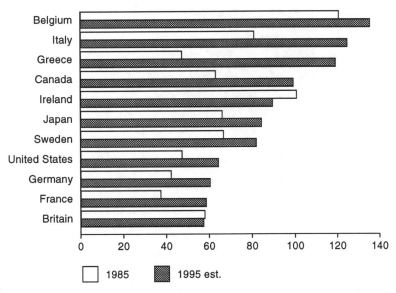

Figure 5.1 General government gross financial liabilities (% of GDP)
Source: OECD, elaborated by *The Economist* (January 20, 1996)

So, what appears to be an exception to the rule of government dependency, and increasing government deficit, is not. Japanese corporations take on the world economy, and their competitiveness finances the state, whose consumption has grown much faster than in any other of the countries studied. The Japanese state displays a second-order financial dependency on the movements of the international economy, via its borrowing from Japanese banks flourishing along with their *keiretsu*.

Three major trends can be underlined with regard to the arguments presented in this chapter:

1 In spite of a certain state's disengagement in the economy, particularly in terms of direct employment, and regulation, there is still a substantial economic role for the state that requires additional financing besides taxation, thus increasing the financial liability of the state, with the exception of the UK (see figure 5.1).

2 Governments' borrowing, with the major exception of Japan, is increasingly dependent on foreign lending, to an extent that already overwhelms central banks' currency reserves, and overshadows export performance. This reflects the broader phenomenon of an increasing gap between the faster growth of global financial markets in relation to the growth of global trade.

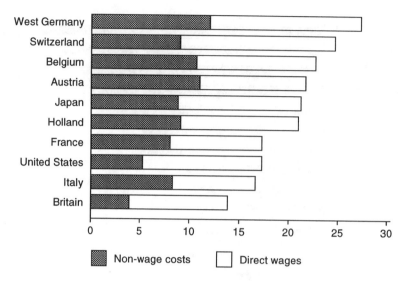

Figure 5.2   Labor costs in manufacturing, 1994 ($ per hour)
Source: Swedish Employers' Federation, elaborated by *The Economist*
(January 27, 1996)

3   The Japanese state has succeeded in establishing a measure of
fiscal autonomy *vis à vis* foreign capital. However, it has done so
on the basis of domestic borrowing, financed with Japanese corporations' earnings from protectionism and export performance; so
that the Japanese economy, and the Japanese state, have become
addicted to trade surpluses and recycling of profits in Japanese soil.
This state of affairs led to the Japanese "bubble economy" of the
late 1980s, and, subsequently, when the bubble burst, to the recession of the early 1990s.

Overall, the intertwining of national economies, and the dependency of government finance on global markets and foreign lending,
have created the conditions for an international fiscal crisis of the
nation-state, including the wealthiest and most powerful nation-states.

Globalization and the welfare state

The globalization of production and investment also threatens the
welfare state, a key element in the policies of the nation-state in the past
half-century, and probably the main building block of its legitimacy

in industrialized countries.[11] This is because it becomes increasingly contradictory for firms to operate in globalized, integrated markets, while experiencing major cost differentials in social benefits, as well as distinct levels of regulation between countries. This happens not only between North and South, but between different OECD countries, as well: for example, social benefits-related labor costs are much lower in the US than in Germany (see figure 5.2). But what is a comparative advantage of US location *vis à vis* Germany becomes a disadvantage *vis à vis* Mexico, after the implementation of the NAFTA Treaty. Since firms, because of information technology, can locate in many different sites and still link up to global production networks and markets (see volume I, chapter 6), there follows a downward spiral of social costs competition. The limits to such "negative competitiveness" in the past have been twofold: on the one hand, the productivity and quality lag between countries protected workers from advanced economies *vis à vis* less-developed competitors; on the other hand, domestic pressure induced protectionism, so as to increase the price of imports, via tariffs, to a level where the comparative advantage of external sourcing would disappear. Both limits are withering away. The new World Trade Organization is setting up a watch dog system to detect and penalize barriers to free trade. While the politics of international trade condition the actual impact of such controls, it would seem that, unless there is a dramatic reversal in the process of global economic integration, blatant, large-scale protectionism will become increasingly subject to retaliation from other countries. As for the quality and productivity lag, Harley Shaiken's study of American automobile factories in Mexico has shown the rapid catch-up of Mexican workers' productivity which equalled that of American workers in about 18 months. Similar processes have been observed in Asia.[12] And (Europeans should be reminded) American labor productivity is still the highest in the world, so canceling a potential European competitiveness differential that could still allow for a generous welfare state. In an economy whose core markets for capital, goods, and services are increasingly integrated on a global scale, there is little room for vastly different welfare states, with relatively similar levels of labor productivity and production quality. Only a global social contract (reducing the gap, without necessarily equalizing social and working conditions), linked to international tariff agreements, could avoid the demise of the most generous welfare states. Yet, because in the new liberalized, networked, global economy such a far-reaching social contract is unlikely, welfare states are being

---

[11]   Wilensky (1975); Janowitz (1976); Navarro (1994, 1995); Castells (1996).
[12]   Shaiken (1990); Rodgers (1994).

downsized to the lowest common denominator that keeps spiraling downwards.[13] So doing, a fundamental component of the legitimacy and stability of the nation-state fades away, not only in Europe but throughout the world, from middle-class welfare states in Chile or Mexico to the remnants of statist welfare states in Russia, China, or India, or to the urban welfare state induced in the United States by the social struggles of the 1960s.

Therefore, the nation-state is increasingly powerless in controlling monetary policy, deciding its budget, organizing production and trade, collecting its corporate taxes, and fulfilling its commitments to provide social benefits. In sum, it has lost most of its economic power, albeit it still has some regulatory capacity and relative control over its subjects.

Global communication networks, local audiences, uncertain regulators

The prospects for national regulation and control are not much better in another decisive area of state power: media and communication. Control of information and entertainment, and, through them, of opinions and images has historically been the anchoring tool of state power, to be perfected in the age of mass media.[14] In this realm, the nation-state confronts three major, interrelated challenges: globalization and interlocking of ownership; flexibility and pervasiveness of technology; autonomy and diversity of the media (see volume I, chapter 5). In fact, it has already surrendered to them in most countries.[15] Until the early 1980s, with the major exception of the United States, most television in the world was government-controlled, and radios and newspapers were under the severe potential constraint of government good will, even in democratic countries. Even in the United States, the Federal Communications Commission exercised a close control of electronic media, not always exempt from special interest biases,[16] and the three major television networks monopolized 90 percent of the audience, framing, if not shaping, public opinion. Everything changed in a decade.[17] The change was technology-driven. The diversification of communication modes, the link-up of all media in a digital hypertext, opening the way

[13] Sengenberger and Campbell (1994); Navarro (1995); Castells (1996).
[14] Mattelart (1991).
[15] Blumenfield (1994); Brenner (1994); Chong (1994); Graf (1995).
[16] Cohen (1986).
[17] Doyle (1992); Irving et al. (1994); Negroponte (1995); Scott et al. (1995); Campo Vidal (1996).

for interactive multimedia, and the inability to control satellites beaming across borders or computer-mediated communication over the 'phone line, blew up the traditional lines of regulatory defense. The explosion of telecommunications, and the development of cable, provided the vehicles for unprecedented broadcasting power. Business saw the trend and seized the opportunity. Mega-mergers took place, and capital was mobilized around the world to take position in the media industry, an industry that could link up power in the economic, cultural, and political spheres.[18] Pressure was brought to bear on national governments during the 1980s under various forms:[19] public, or published, opinion, yearning for freedom and diversity in the media; buy-outs of national media in difficulty; syndication of columnists to write the apology of unfettered communication; promises of political complacency, if not support, to almost everyone in power or with the chance to be in the near future; and, not least, personal benefits for those officials who were consenting adults. Symbolic politics, assimilating liberalization of media to technological modernization, played a major role in tilting elite opinion in favor of the new media system.[20] There is hardly any country, outside China, Singapore, and the Islamic fundamentalist world, where the institutional and business structure of the media did not experience a dramatic turnaround between the mid-1980s and the mid-1990s.[21] Television and radio were privatized on a large scale, and those government networks that remained often became indistinguishable from private television since they were submitted to the discipline of audience ratings and/or advertising revenues.[22] Newspapers became concentrated in major consortiums, often with the backing of financial groups. And, most importantly, media business went global, with capital, talent, technology, and corporate ownership spinning all over the world, away from the reach of nation-states (see figure 5.3). It does not entirely follow that states have no stake in the media. Governments still control important media, own stock, and have means of influence in a vast array of the media world. And business is careful not to antagonize the gatekeepers of potential markets: when Murdoch's Star Channel was chastised by the Chinese government for its liberal views on Chinese politics, Star obliged with newly found restraint, canceling BBC's news service from the

[18]   MacDonald (1990).
[19]   Gerbner et al. (1993); Campo Vidal (1996).
[20]   Vedel and Dutton (1990).
[21]   MacDonald (1990); Doyle (1992); Perez-Tabernero et al. (1993); Dentsu Institute for Human Studies (1994); *The Economist* (1994, 1996).
[22]   Perez-Tabernero et al. (1993).

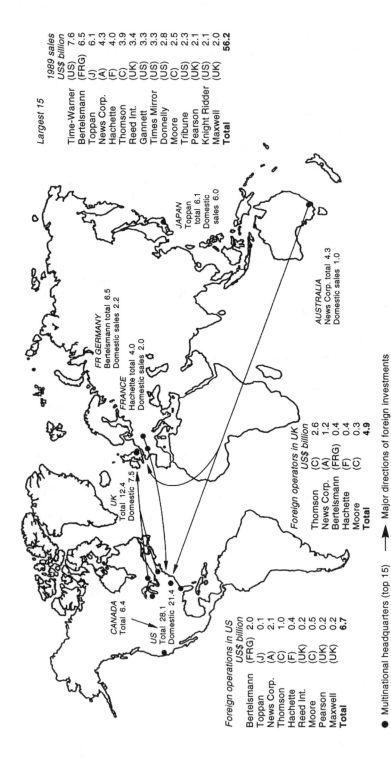

Largest 15		1989 sales US$ billion
Time-Warner	(US)	7.6
Bertelsmann	(FRG)	6.5
Toppan	(J)	6.1
News Corp.	(A)	4.3
Hachette	(F)	4.0
Thomson	(C)	3.9
Reed Int.	(UK)	3.4
Gannett	(US)	3.3
Times Mirror	(US)	3.3
Donnelly	(US)	2.8
Moore	(C)	2.5
Tribune	(US)	2.3
Pearson	(UK)	2.1
Knight Ridder	(US)	2.1
Maxwell	(UK)	2.0
Total		**56.2**

JAPAN
Toppan
total 6.1
Domestic
sales 6.0

FR GERMANY
Bertelsmann total 6.5
Domestic sales 2.2

FRANCE
Hachette total 4.0
Domestic sales 2.0

AUSTRALIA
News Corp. total 4.3
Domestic sales 1.0

UK
Total 12.4
Domestic 7.5

CANADA
Total 6.4

US
Total 28.1
Domestic 21.4

Foreign operations in US		US$ billion
Bertelsmann	(FRG)	2.0
Toppan	(J)	0.1
News Corp.	(A)	2.1
Thomson	(C)	1.0
Hachette	(F)	0.4
Reed Int.	(UK)	0.2
Moore	(C)	0.5
Pearson	(UK)	0.2
Maxwell	(UK)	0.2
Total		**6.7**

Foreign operators in UK		US$ billion
Thomson	(C)	2.6
News Corp.	(A)	1.2
Bertelsmann	(FRG)	0.4
Hachette	(F)	0.4
Moore	(C)	0.3
Total		**4.9**

● Multinational headquarters (top 15)   ⟶ Major directions of foreign investments

Figure 5.3 Size and location of activities of the 15 largest print and media multinationals (Germany, Canada, France, and Australia are major exporters; the US and UK are major importers)

Source: Fortune (April 23, 1990) and company annual reports, elaborated by MacDonald (1990)

channel's Chinese programming, and investing in an on-line edition of *People's Daily*. But, if governments still have influence over the media, they have lost much of their power, except for those media under the direct control of authoritarian states. Moreover, the media need to build their independence as a key ingredient of their credibility – not only *vis à vis* public opinion, but with regard to the plurality of power-holders and advertisers, since the advertising industry is the economic foundation of the media business. If a given medium becomes predominantly attached to an explicit political option or systematically represses certain kinds of information, it will restrict its audience to a relatively small segment, will hardly be able to make a profit in the marketplace, and will not appeal to the interests of a plurality of constituencies. On the other hand, the more a medium is independent, broad, and credible, the more it attracts information, sellers and buyers from a wide spectrum. Independence and professionalism are not only rewarding ideologies for the media: they translate into good business, including, sometimes, the possibility of selling this independence at a higher price when the occasion arises. Once media are acknowledged in their independence, once the nation-state acquiesces to this quality as an essential proof of its democratic character, the circle is closed: any attempt to curtail the media's liberty will become politically costly, since the citizenry, not necessarily picky concerning the accuracy of news, defends jealously the privilege of receiving information from sources that are not submitted to the state. This is why even authoritarian states are losing the battle over media in the Information Age. The ability of information, and images, to diffuse via satellite, video-cassette, or the Internet has dramatically expanded, so that news black-outs are increasingly ineffective in the main urban centers of authoritarian countries, precisely those places where the educated, alternative elites live. Furthermore, since governments all over the world want also to "go global," and global media are their accessing tool, governments often enter into negotiating two-way communication systems that, even when proceeding slowly and cautiously, ultimately undermine their hold on communication.

In a parallel movement to globalization of the media, there has also been, in many countries, thanks to new communication technologies, such as cost-sharing satellite transmission, an extraordinary growth of local media, particularly for radio and cable television. Most of these local media, which often share programming, have established a strong connection to specific, popular audiences, bypassing the standardized views of mass media. So doing, they escape the traditional channels of control (be it direct or indirect) that nation-states had set up *vis à vis* television networks and major newspapers. The growing political autonomy of local and regional media, using flexible communication technologies, is as important a trend as the globalization of media in shaping public attitudes. Furthermore, the two trends converge in many instances, with global media corporations buying into niche markets, on the condition of accepting the specificity of audiences built around local media.[23]

Computer-mediated communication is also escaping the control of the nation-state, ushering in a new era of extra-territorial communication.[24] Most governments seem to be terrified at the prospect. In January 1996, the French Minister of Information Technology announced the intention of his government to propose to the European Union a series of measures to ban free access to the Internet. The event that prompted this scheme of technological censorship from the country that spurred revolutionary ideals of liberty in Europe, as well as Minitel, was Mitterrand's last battle. After his death, a book was published by his doctor revealing that Mitterrand had had prostate cancer for all the 14 years of his presidency. The book was banned in France, at the request of Mitterrand's family, but everybody could read it on the Net. The fury of the French government went far beyond this particular issue. There was a clear understanding that government's or court's decisions over information could no longer be implemented. And the control of information has been, long before the Information Age, the foundation of state power.[25] Similar initiatives came, around the same time, from the Chinese, German, and American governments, on a variety of issues ranging from financial and political information in China to child pornography in the United States.[26] At the heart of the matter was the question of trans-border information flows that make it difficult to prosecute the source of information even if it were detected. It is still under debate what are the real technical possibilities of cutting access to the Internet without shutting off a whole country from the network. It would seem that *ex post facto* censorship and penalties, and self-operated screening devices, are easier than the jamming of communication. But even if external screening measures become effective, they will shrink the network, thus undermining access to much useful information and diminishing the extent and scope of interactivity. Furthermore, to be able to shrink the Net selectively, all countries connected to it will have to agree on

[23]   Levin (1987); Abramson et al. (1988); Scheer (1994); Spragen (1995); Fallows (1996).
[24]   Kahn (1994); *Financial Technology International Bulletin* (1995); Kuttner (1995); Ubois (1995).
[25]   Couch (1990).
[26]   Berman and Weitzner (1995); Faison (1996); Lewis (1996a).

the topics they want to see banned, and then set up a joint monitoring system that will certainly be challenged as unconstitutional in democratic countries. Indeed, in the United States, in June 1996, a federal judicial panel in Pennsylvania declared unconstitutional most of the new federal law intended to regulate pornographic material diffused over the Net. In a forceful decision, the three judges wrote: "Just as the strength of the Internet is chaos, so the strength of our liberty depends upon the chaos and cacophony of the unfettered speech the First Amendment protects."[27] Thus, for the years to come, nation-states will be struggling to control information circulating in globally interconnected telecommunication networks. I bet it is a lost battle. And with this eventual defeat will come the loss of a cornerstone of state power.

Altogether, the globalization/localization of media and electronic communication is tantamount to the de-nationalization and de-statization of information, the two trends being inseparable for the time being.

A lawless world?

The globalization of crime further subverts the nation-state, profoundly transforming processes of governance, and actually paralyzing the state in many instances. This is a crucial trend which is as easily acknowledged as promptly ignored in its consequences.[28] A whole chapter (in volume III, chapter 3) analyzes what is one of the most relevant trends of our world, and a distinctive one in respect of other periods, but it is necessary, at this point in the argument, to include such a critical trend in our understanding of the current crisis of the nation-state. What is new is not the pervasiveness of crime and its impact on politics. What is new is the global linkage of organized crime, its conditioning of international relations, both economic and political, because of the scale and dynamism of the criminal economy. What is new is the deep penetration, and eventual destabilization, of national states in a variety of contexts under the influence of transnational crime. While drug traffic is the most significant industrial sector in the new criminal economy, all kinds of illicit traffics come together in this shadow system that extends its reach and power over the world: weapons, technology, radioactive materials, art treasures, human beings, human organs, killers for hire, and smuggling of every

[27]   Cited by Lewis (1996b).
[28]   Arrieta et al. (1991); Roth and Frey (1992); Smith (1993); Lodato (1994); Sterling (1994); Golden (1995); Handelman (1995); Johnson (1995); WuDunn (1996).

profitable item from anywhere to anywhere are connected through the mother of all crimes – money laundering. Without it, the criminal economy would neither be global nor very profitable. And, through money laundering, the criminal economy is connected to the global financial markets, of which it is a sizeable component, and a relentless source of speculation. According to the United Nations Conference on the Global Criminal Economy held in Naples in October 1994,[29] a reasonable estimate would put the figure of capital from illegal sources being laundered in the global financial system at about US $ 750 billion a year. These capital flows need to be processed with greater mobility and flexibility than those originating from any other industry, since it is their constant swirling that makes them avoid tracking by law enforcement agencies.

The impact of these trends on national states occurs along three main lines:

1   In many instances, the entire structure of the state, often including the highest levels of power, is penetrated by criminal linkages, either through corruption, threats, or illegal political financing, thus creating havoc in the conduct of public affairs.
2   International relations between nation-states, in many countries, come to be dependent, in various degrees, on the handling or mishandling of cooperation in the fight against the criminal economy. The typical case until now has been that of relationships between the United States and some Latin American countries (Colombia, Bolivia, Mexico, Paraguay, Panama), but it is becoming a broader phenomenon, as the criminal economy diversifies (for instance, Germany's concern with Russian Mafia-originated traffic of radioactive materials; or the Russian government's worries about the increasing involvement of the Sicilian Mafia and of Colombian cartels with the Russian *Mafiya*).
3   The growing importance of financial flows from criminal origin are key elements in stimulating or destabilizing entire national economies, so that economic policy cannot be properly conducted in many countries and areas without including into the picture this highly unpredictable factor.

It used to be that national governments deeply affected by the wheelings and dealings of the criminal economy were a handful of usual suspects, such as Italy or Colombia. Not any more. The importance of the phenomenon, its global reach, the size of its wealth and influence, and its entrenched connection with international finance, make criminal linkages to political corruption a frequent feature in

[29]   United Nations, Economic and Social Council (1994).

major countries. For instance, the Japanese *Yakuza* has recently inter-nationalized its connections. And the open, and less open, linkages of the *Yakuza* with Japanese government leaders are well known, to the point that the Ministry of Construction was considered, over a long period, as the way to exchange government contracts in public works for generous contributions from *Yakuza*-sponsored businesses to the Liberal Democratic party – a system not too dissimilar to that of Italian Christian Democracy's *Mezzogiorno* development programs in relation to the Mafia. Or, when in 1996 a series of bank crises rocked Japan, resulting in unpaid loans for hundreds of billions of dollars, serious suspicions arose on the role of *Yakuza* in forcing bank managers to grant these loans, including the killing of two bankers.[30] In another context, the suspected penetration of internationally con-nected Russian criminal organizations in various spheres of government of one of the world's most powerful states, including the armed forces, is a worrisome development. And the chain of political scandals that have shaken governments all over the world in the 1990s (a topic that I shall analyze in chapter 6) is not unrelated, in many instances, to the continuing power struggle between the structures of global crime and the structures of nation-states. Furthermore, even major governments, which think they are rela-tively immune to penetration by crime in their higher levels, do suffer the aftershocks of criminal political maneuvering. For instance, when in 1994–95 the Mexican economy crumbled, in spite of massive US lending, because of a political crisis partly prompted, as I will argue below, by the penetration of drug traffickers in the highest levels of the Mexican ruling party, the dollar went sharply down, and the German mark skyrocketed in the currency markets, destabilizing the European monetary system, because of investors' fears that the US government deficit would balloon in the effort to lift Mexico out of its potential crash. In this entangled whirlwind of crime, capital, and power, there is no safe place. Or, for that matter, no safe national institutions.

Thus, globalization, in its different dimensions, undermines the autonomy and decision-making power of the nation-state. And this happens at the very moment when the exercise of state power in the international area is also subject to the constraints of multilateralism in defense, foreign policy, and global public policies, such as environ-mental policy.

[30] WuDunn (1996).

The Nation-state in the Age of Multilateralism

The post-Cold War period is characterized by increasing multilateral interdependence between nation-states.[31] This is due, primarily, to three factors: the dissolution or loosening of the military blocs built around the two superpowers; the dramatic impact of new technologies on warfare; and the social perception of the global character of major challenges to humankind because of increased knowledge and information, as in the case of environmental security.

With the disappearance of the Soviet Union, and regardless of possible future tensions between Russia, China, and NATO, the major mechanism for the stabilization of strategic links for most nation-states around the two superpowers disappeared as well.[32] While NATO continues to be organized around a US-led Western alliance, its functions are being redefined in the second half of the 1990s toward the fulfillment of security tasks on behalf of a broad consortium of nations, in association, whenever possible, with the United Nations. The new notion of global, collective security,[33] which emerged for the first time with the Gulf War to face the common threat to the oil supply from the Middle East, involves a symbiotic relationship between the most capable military forces (US and UK professional armies), the financiers of operations (Japan, Germany, the Arab princes, in the first place), and the rhetorical statements on behalf of the civilized world (often enacted by French leaders). The deliberate attempt by this NATO-based alliance to involve Russia in joint operations, as in Bosnia, is indicative of the transformation of military alliances from superpower domination to joint policing of a shaky world order, against potential unpredictable threats to the system. The new security system is being built, primarily, against outer barbarians without a name as yet.[34] So doing, nation-states, including the most powerful, are enmeshed in a web of interests and negotiations that reshapes itself into a different format for each issue to be tackled. Without the need for dramatic decisiveness in life and death situations, as was the case in the potential confrontation of superpowers and their allies in the Cold War nuclear age, the muddling through of a foreign policy with variable geometry translates into the growing inability of any state to act on its own in the international arena. Foreign policy is, by essence, multilateral in this end of millennium.[35]

[31] Baylis and Rengger (1992); McGrew et al. (1992); Falk (1995); Orstrom Moller (1995); Alonso Zaldivar (1996).
[32] Alonso Zaldivar (1996); McGrew (1992b).
[33] McGrew (1992a); Mokhtari (1994).
[34] Rosenau (1990); Berdal (1993); Guehenno (1993).
[35] Frankel (1988); McGrew et al. (1992).

Two major reservations concern the degree of integration into this system of collective security of Russia, still a nuclear superpower, and of China, superpower in the making.[36] Yet, since it is unlikely that any of them will organize a set of permanent allies around their interests (in spite of China's links to Pakistan), their relative isolation, and deep-seated distrust between them, does not contradict the multilateral character of the new security system, but simply adds complexity to it.

Fast changes in military technology are also undermining the capability of the nation-state to stand alone.[37] Warfare is now essentially dependent upon electronics and communications technology, as demonstrated by the Gulf War. The massive devastation that can be inflicted from a distance, through missile launchings and air strikes, can cripple in a few hours a sizeable army, particularly if its defenses are made blind by electronic counter-measures, and if targets have been identified by satellite and processed by computers thousands of kilometers away to direct actual fire in this invisible war. Conventional warfare is, as it always was, technologically dependent. The difference in the current period is, on the one hand, the speed of technological change, which makes weapons obsolete in a short time span.[38] This forces the continuous upgrading of weapons systems if armies are supposed to really fight other armies, instead of controlling their own people, as is still the case for much of humankind. Low-tech armies are not armies at all, but disguised police forces. On the other hand, the character of new military technology makes necessary a professional army in which personnel is equipped with advanced knowledge to manipulate semi-automated weaponry, and communication systems. This gives an advantage to countries with an advanced technological level, regardless of the size of their armed forces, as the cases of Israel and Singapore illustrate. Because of the essential role of technology, nation-states still wanting to assert their capacity to exercise violence become permanently dependent on technological suppliers, not just on hardware, but on human resources. This dependency, however, has to be placed in the context of a growing diversification of conventional war weapons, as countries industrialize and technology diffuses.[39] Thus, Brazil or Israel can be efficient suppliers of advanced warfare equipment. France, the UK, Germany, Italy, and China have increased their role, together with the United States and Russia, as suppliers of the world's armies. An increasingly

[36] Boardmann (1994); Alonso Zaldivar (1996).
[37] McInnes (1992).
[38] McInnes and Sheffield (1988); Grier (1995).
[39] McGrew (1992b).

complex pattern of cooperation and competition emerges, with China buying advanced fighters from Russia and communications technology from the United States, and France selling missiles to whoever wants to buy them, with after-sale services for training and maintenance included. Furthermore, illegal global markets for weapons, for any kind of weapons, have proliferated, making possible widespread diffusion of whichever technology becomes available, from "Stingers" to "Patriots," from nerve gas to electronic jamming devices. It follows that, unlike in other historical periods, no single state is self-sufficient in the production of warfare equipment, with the essential exception of the United States (since Russia is now technologically dependent on microelectronics and communications). But this does not imply that all nation-states are doomed to become an American colony. It is, rather, the opposite. The lack of a clear adversary has relaxed technology controls from the US Defense Department, so that most essential technologies and conventional weapons are widely available. Because nation-states cannot control sources for the supply of state-of-the-art equipment, they are permanently dependent, in the potential exercise of their war-making power, not on the US, but on diverse, global supplier networks. The fact that the United States is technologically self-sufficient (and only because of the Pentagon's effort to fight off dependency on Japanese semiconductor manufacturing equipment) gives to the United States the title of being the only true superpower. Yet, even this fact does not translate into full sovereignty in its foreign policy because of the weak financial and political position of the US toward committing its forces abroad.[40] Furthermore, as McInnes argues, "the character of modern warfare has led military thinkers to question whether a high intensity conflict could ever be worth the costs involved (regardless of whether nuclear weapons are used), and even if such a war did occur, whether it could be sustained by any length of time [given how expensive high-tech weapons are and how fast they can be destroyed]."[41]

Technological evolution adds a new twist to international relations toward multilateralism. Industrialization of new areas of the world, diffusion of scientific and technological knowledge, and illegal trade in everything have pushed, and are pushing, toward proliferation of nuclear, chemical, and biological warfare capabilities.[42] Thus, while nation-states are increasingly dependent on cutting-edge technology in conventional warfare, they may nevertheless have access to what I

[40]   Savigear (1992).
[41]   McInnes (1992: 156).
[42]   McGrew (1992b).

would call "veto technologies," that is, weapons of mass destruction
that by their existence can deter a more powerful state from winning.
The global "terror equilibrium" is in the process of being decentralized to many local "terror equilibria." This trend forces, on the one
hand, major powers to undertake concerted, multilateral action to
prevent the control of these weapons by new countries, political
forces, or terrorist groups. On the other hand, once some countries
come, anyway, into the possession of these weapons, the global security system is compelled to intervene and assist in balancing powers
of destruction in each area of the world to prevent dangerous local
confrontations.[43] It follows a complex, entangled web of different
levels of destructive power, controlling each other with *ad hoc*
agreements, and negotiated processes of disarmament and disengagement. In such a web no nation-state, not even the United States,
is free any longer, since a miscalculation, or an excess in exercising
superior power, could trigger a nuclear, or bacteriological, local
holocaust. Humankind will live for a long time with the monsters of
destruction we have created, either for mass, standardized annihilation, or miniaturized for customized carnage. Under such
circumstances, the most fundamental task of nation-states (and not
just for the superpowers as in the Cold War period) has become to
limit the actual exercise of their own military power, thus weakening
their original *raison d'être*.

Nation-states also confront the limits of their legitimacy, and thus
ultimately of their power, regarding the global management of the
planet's environment.[44] Science and technology are producing,
because of increased computing capacity, unprecedented new knowledge on the degradation of nature, and on its consequences for our
species. In a related development, as shown in chapter 3, the environmental movement has raised ecological consciousness in societies
around the world, putting increasing pressure on the responsibility of
governments to halt the path toward catastrophe. Yet, individual
nation-states are powerless, on their own, to act on issues such as
global warming, the ozone layer, the deforestation of the planet, the
pollution of water reserves, the depletion of life in the oceans, and the
like. Efforts for states to come together take, more often than not, the
form of international shows and solemn rhetoric, rather than actual
implementation of joint action programs. Lipschutz and Coca write,
in concluding their global survey on concerted environmental
policies:

[43] Daniel and Hayes (1995).
[44] Rowlands (1992); Vogler (1992); Morin and Kern (1993); Wapner (1995); Hempel (1996).

The possibility of an hegemonic direction or the emergence of a central coordinating authority seem remote with respect to environmental matters. And the likelihood of effective multilateral coordination seems small, as well, because of major uncertainties about the costs and benefits of environmental protection and management. To these barriers and conditions we would add a number of factors that stem from the nature of the state itself: the fundamental incapacity of governments to control the destructive processes involved, the scarcity of effective policy levers, and the importance of key resource-extraction (and hence environmental destruction) for key state-society alliances.[45]

This is not necessarily because of ignorance or ill-faith on the part of governments, but because each nation-state continues to act on behalf of its own interests, or of the interests of constituencies it values most.[46] So doing, multilateralism becomes a forum of debate and a negotiating arena, rather than a tool for exercising collective responsibility. Following a Habermasian logic of "crisis displacement," "the fundamental and global environmental-economic contradiction," as Hay puts it, "becomes displaced to the level of the nation-state."[47] This structurally induced stubbornness of nation-states paradoxically leads to their weakening as viable political institutions, as citizens around the world realize the incapacity of these rather expensive and cumbersome apparatuses in dealing with the major issues challenging humankind. Thus, to overcome their growing irrelevance, nation-states increasingly band together, shifting gears toward a new supranational order of governance.

Global Governance and the Super Nation-state

"If one wants a shorthand explanation for the renewed momentum of European integration in the mid-1980s," as Streeck and Schmitter wrote, "one would probably account for it as the result of an alignment between two broad interests – that of large European firms struggling to overcome perceived competitive advantages in relation to Japanese and US capital and that of state elites seeking to restore at least part of the political sovereignty they had gradually lost at the national level as a result of growing international interdependence."[48]

[45]   Lipschutz and Coca (1993: 332).
[46]   Castells (forthcoming).
[47]   Hay (1994: 87).
[48]   Streeck and Schmitter (1991: 148).

On both counts, for business interests and political interests, what was sought for was not supranationality, but the reconstruction of nation-based state power at a higher level, at a level where some degree of control of global flows of wealth, information, and power could be exercised. *The formation of the European Union (as I will argue in volume III) was not a process of building the European federal state of the future, but the construction of a political cartel, the Brussels cartel, in which European nation-states can still carve out, collectively, some level of sovereignty from the new global disorder, and then distribute the benefits among its members, under endlessly negotiated rules.* This is why, rather than ushering in the era of supranationality and global governance, we are witnessing the emergence of the super nation-state, that is of a state expressing, in a variable geometry, the aggregate interests of its constituent members.[49]

A similar argument can be extrapolated to the plurality of international institutions that share the management of the economy, of security, of development, of the environment, in this world *fin de millénium*.[50] The World Trade Organization has been set up to make compatible free trade with trade restrictions in a non-disruptive mechanism of control and negotiation. The United Nations is vying to establish its new, double role as a legitimate police force on behalf of peace and human rights, and as a world media center, staging global conferences every six months on the headlines of humankind: environment, population, social exclusion, women, cities, and the like. The G-7 countries club has appointed itself as the supervisor of the global economy, letting Russia watch through the window, just in case, and instructing the International Monetary Fund and the World Bank to keep financial markets and currencies under discipline, both globally and locally. Post-Cold War NATO has emerged as the nucleus of a credible military force to police the new world disorder. NAFTA is tightening up the economic integration of the Western hemisphere, with the potential incorporation of Chile belying its Northern label. MERCOSUR, on the other hand, is asserting South America's independence by increasingly trading with Europe rather than with the United States. Various Pacific cooperation international institutions are trying to build the commonality of economic interests, bridging over the historical mistrust between major players in the Asian Pacific (Japan, China, Korea, Russia). Countries around the world are using old institutions, such as ASEAN or the Organization

[49] Orstrom Moller (1995).
[50] Berdal (1993); Rochester (1993); Bachr and Gordenker (1994); Dunaher (1994); Falk (1995); Kraus and Knight (1995); Oversight of IMF/World Bank (1995).

of African Unity, or even post-colonial institutions, such as the British Commonwealth, or the French cooperation system, as platforms for joint ventures toward a diversity of goals that could hardly be reached by individual nation-states. Most assessments of this growing process of internationalization of state policies seem to doubt the feasibility of global governance as fully shared sovereignty, in spite of this notion's powerful rationale. Rather, global governance is usually considered as the negotiated convergence of national governments' interests and policies.[51] Nation-states, and their elites, are too jealous of their privileges to surrender sovereignty, except under the promise of tangible returns. In addition, according to opinion polls, it is highly unlikely, in the foreseeable future, that the majority of citizens in any country would accept full integration in a supranational, federal state.[52] The US experience of federal nation building is so historically specific that, in spite of its forceful appeal, it can hardly be a model for late millennium federalists in other areas of the world.

Furthermore, the growing incapacity of states to tackle the global problems that make an impact on public opinion (from the fate of whales to torture of dissidents around the world) leads civil societies to increasingly take into their own hands the responsibilities of global citizenship. Thus, Amnesty International, Greenpeace, *Medecins sans frontières*, Oxfam, and so many other humanitarian non-governmental organizations have become a major force in the international arena in the 1990s, often attracting more funding, performing more effectively, and receiving greater legitimacy than government-sponsored international efforts. The "privatization" of global humanitarianism is gradually undermining one of the last rationales for the necessity of the nation-state.[53]

In sum, what we are witnessing is, at the same time, the irreversible sharing of sovereignty in the management of major economic, environmental, and security issues, and, on the other hand, the entrenchment of nation-states as the basic components of this entangled web of political institutions. However, the outcome of such a process is not the reinforcement of nation-states, but the systemic erosion of their power in exchange for their durability. This is, first of all, because the processes of relentless conflict, alliance, and negotiation make international institutions rather ineffective, so that most of their political energy is spent in the process, rather than in the product. This seriously slows down the intervening capacity of states, unable to act by themselves, yet paralyzed when trying to act collec-

[51]   United Nations Commission on Global Governance (1995).
[52]   Orstrom Moller (1995).
[53]   Guehenno (1993); Rubert de Ventos (1994); Falk (1995).

tively. Moreover, international institutions, partly to escape from such a paralysis, partly because of the inherent logic of any large bureaucracy, tend to take on a life on their own. So doing, they define their mandate in ways that tend to supersede the power of their constituent states, instituting a *de facto* global bureaucracy. For instance, it is essentially wrong, as leftist critics often argue, that the International Monetary Fund is an agent of American imperalism or, for that matter, of any imperialism. It is an agent of itself, fundamentally moved by the ideology of neoclassical economic orthodoxy, and by the conviction of being the bulwark of measure and rationality in a dangerous world built on irrational expectations. The cold-bloodedness I have personally witnessed of IMF technocrats' behavior in helping to destroy Russian society in the critical moments of transition in 1992–95 had nothing to do with capitalist domination. It was, as in Africa, as in Latin America, a deep-seated, honest, ideological commitment to teach financial rationality to the people of the world, as the only serious ground to build a new society. Claiming victory in the Cold War for free-wheeling capitalism (a historical affront to the harsh combats of social democracy against Soviet communism), IMF experts do not act under the guidance of governments who appoint them, or of citizens who pay them, but as self-righteous surgeons skillfully removing the remnants of political controls over market forces. So doing, they may trigger a deep resentment among citizens all over the world, who feel the full impact of these global institutions on their lives, bypassing their obsolete nation-states.

Thus, the growing role played by international institutions and supranational consortia in world policies, cannot be equated to the demise of the nation-state. But the price paid by nation- states for their precarious survival as segments of states' networks, is that of their decreasing relevance, thus undermining their legitimacy, and ultimately furthering their powerlessness.

Identities, Local Governments, and the Deconstruction of the Nation-state

On December 25, 1632, the Count-Duke of Olivares wrote to his king, Philip IV:

> The most important business in your Monarchy is for Your Majesty to make yourself King of Spain; I mean, Sir, that Your Majesty should not be content with being King of Portugal, Aragon, Valencia, and Count of Barcelona, but should work and secretly scheme to reduce these kingdoms of which Spain is

composed to the style and laws of Castile, with no differentiation in the form of frontiers, custom posts, the power to convoke the Cortes of Castile, Aragon and Portugal wherever it seems desirable, and the unrestricted appointment of ministers of different nations both here and there . . . And if Your Majesty achieves this, you will be the most powerful prince in the world.[54]

The king acted on this advice, thus inducing a process that ultimately led to the Revolt of the Reapers in Catalonia, the revolt against the salt tax in the Basque Country, and the rebellion and eventual independence of Portugal. At the same time, he also built, in the process, the foundations of the modern, centralized, Spanish nation-state, albeit in such a precarious condition that prompted almost three centuries of uprisings, repressions, civil wars, terrorism, and institutional instability.[55] Although the Spanish state, until 1977, represented an extreme situation of imposed homogeneity, most modern nation-states, and particularly the French revolutionary state, have been built on the denial of the historical/cultural identities of its constituents to the benefit of that identity that better suited the interests of the dominant social groups at the origins of the state. As argued in chapter 1, the state, not the nation (defined either culturally or territorially, or both), created the nation-state *in the Modern Age*.[56] Once a nation became established, under the territorial control of a given state, the sharing of history did induce social and cultural bonds, as well as economic and political interests, among its members. Yet, the uneven representation of social interests, cultures, and territories in the nation-state skewed national institutions toward the interests of originating elites and their geometry of alliances, thus opening the way for institutional crises when subdued identities, historically rooted or ideologically revived, were able to mobilize for a renegotiation of the historical national contract.[57]

The structure of the nation-state is territorially differentiated, and this territorial differentiation, with its sharing, and not sharing, of powers, expresses alliances and oppositions between social interests, cultures, regions, and nationalities that compose the state. As I elaborated elsewhere,[58] the territorial differentiation of state institutions explains to a large extent the apparent mystery of why states are often ruled on behalf of the interests of a minority while not necessarily

---

[54]   Cited by Elliott and de la Pena (1978: 95); translation by Elliott.
[55]   Alonso Zaldivar and Castells (1992).
[56]   Norman (1940); Halperin Donghi (1969); Tilly (1975); Gellner (1983); Giddens (1985); Rubert de Ventos (1994).
[57]   Hobsbawm (1990): Blas Guerrero (1994).
[58]   Castells (1981).

relying on repression. Subordinate social groups, and cultural, national, regional minorities, do have access to power at lower levels of the state, in the territories where they live. Thus, a complex geometry emerges in the relationship between the state, social classes, social groups, and identities present in civil society. In each community and in each region, the social alliances and their political expression are specific, corresponding to the existing local/regional power relationships, the history of the territory, and its specific economic structure. This differentiation of power alliances according to various regions and communities is an essential mechanism for keeping in balance, overall, the interests of various elites which jointly benefit from the policies of the state, albeit in different proportions, in different dimensions, and in different territories.[59] Local and regional notables trade power in their territory for their allegiance to structures of dominance at the national level, where interests of national or global elites are more powerful. Local notables are intermediaries between local societies and the national state: they are, at the same time, political brokers and local bosses. Since agreements reached between social actors at the level of local government do not often correspond to the political alliances established between various social interests at the national level, the local system of power does not develop easily along strict party lines, even in the European situation of party-dominated democracies. Local and regional social alliances are frequently *ad hoc* arrangements, organized around local leadership. Thus, local and regional governments are, at the same time, the manifestation of decentralized state power, the closest point of contact between the state and civil society, and the expression of cultural identities which, while hegemonic in a given territory, are sparsely included in the ruling elites of the nation-state.[60]

I have argued, in chapter 1, that the increasing diversification and fragmentation of social interests in the network society result in their aggregation under the form of (re)constructed identities. Thus, a plurality of identities forwards to the nation-state the claims, demands, and challenges of the civil society. The growing inability of the nation-state to respond *simultaneously* to this vast array of demands induces what Habermas called a "legitimation crisis,"[61] or, in Richard Sennett's analysis, the "fall of public man,"[62] the figure that is the foundation of democratic citizenship. To overcome such a

---

[59] Dulong (1978); Tarrow (1978).
[60] Gremion (1976); Ferraresi and Kemeny (1977); Rokkan and Urwin (1982); Borja (1988); Ziccardi (1995); Borja and Castells (1996).
[61] Habermas (1973).
[62] Sennett (1978).

legitimation crisis, states decentralize some of their power to local and regional political institutions. This movement results from two convergent trends. On the one hand, because of the territorial differentiation of state institutions, regional and national minority identities find their easiest expression at local and regional levels. On the other hand, national governments tend to focus on managing the strategic challenges posed by the globalization of wealth, communication, and power, hence letting lower levels of governance take responsibility for linking up with society by managing everyday life's issues, so to rebuild legitimacy through decentralization. However, once this decentralization of power occurs, local and regional governments may seize the initiative on behalf of their populations, and may engage in developmental strategies *vis à vis* the global system, eventually coming into competition with their own parent states.

This trend is apparent all over the world in the 1990s. In the United States, the growing distrust of federal government goes hand in hand with a revival of local and state governments as sites of public attention. Indeed, according to opinion polls in the mid-1990s,[63] this re-localization of government offers the most immediate avenue for the re-legitimation of politics, be it in the form of ultra-conservative populism, as in the "county rights" movement or the born-again Republican party, building its hegemony on attacking the federal government.[64] In the European Union, while substantial areas of sovereignty have been transferred to Brussels, responsibility for many everyday life matters has been shifted to regional and local governments, including, in most countries, education, social policy, culture, housing, environment, and urban amenities.[65] Furthermore, cities and regions across Europe have gathered together in institutional networks that bypass national states, and constitute one of the most formidable lobbies, acting simultaneously on European institutions and on their respective national governments. In addition, cities and regions actively engage in direct negotiations with multinational corporations, and have become the most important agents of economic development policies, since national governments are limited in their actions by EU regulations.[66] In Latin America, the restructuring of public policy to overcome the crisis of the 1980s gave new impetus to municipal and state governments, whose role had been traditionally overshadowed by dependency on the national government, with the important exception of Brazil. Local, provin-

---

[63]   Roper Center of Public Opinion and Polling (1995).
[64]   Balz and Brownstein (1996).
[65]   Orstrom Moller (1995).
[66]   Borja et al. (1992); Goldsmith (1993); Graham (1995).

cial, and state governments in Mexico, in Brazil, in Bolivia, in Ecuador, in Argentina, in Chile, benefitted, in the 1980s and 1990s, from decentralization of power and resources, and undertook a number of social and economic reforms which are transforming Latin America's institutional geography. So doing, not only did they share power with the nation-state, but, most importantly, they created the basis for a new political legitimacy in favor of the local state.[67]

China is experiencing a similar fundamental transformation, with Shanghai and Guandong controlling the main avenues of access to the global economy, and many cities and provinces around the country organizing their own linkages to the new market system. While Beijing seems to be keeping political control with an iron hand, in fact the power of the Chinese Communist party relies on a delicate balance of power-sharing and wealth distribution between national, provincial, and local elites. This central/provincial/local arrangement of the Chinese state in the process of primitive accumulation may well be the key mechanism in ensuring an orderly transition from statism to capitalism.[68] A similar situation can be observed in post-Communist Russia. The balance of power between Moscow and local and regional elites has been critical for the relative stability of the Russian state in the midst of a chaotic economy, as in the sharing of power and profits between the federal government and the "oil generals" in Western Siberia; or between Moscow elites and local elites in both European Russia and in the Far East.[69] On the other hand, when demands of national identity were not duly acknowledged, and eventually mishandled, as in Chech'nya, the ensuing war was largely responsible for derailing the course of the Russian transition.[70] Thus, from the glory of Barcelona to the agony of Grozny, territorial identity and local/regional governments have become decisive forces in the fate of citizens, in the relationships between state and society, and in the reshaping of nation-states. A survey of comparative evidence on political decentralization seems to support the popular saying according to which national governments in the Information Age are too small to handle global forces, yet too big to manage people's lives.[71]

[67] Ziccardi (1991, 1995); Laserna (1992).
[68] Cheung (1994); Li (1995); Hsing (1996).
[69] Kiselyova and Castells (1997).
[70] Khazanov (1995).
[71] Borja and Castells (1996).

The Identification of the State

The selective institutionalization of identity in the state has a very important, indirect effect on the overall dynamics of state and society. Namely, not all identities are able to find refuge in the institutions of local and regional governments. In fact, one of the functions of territorial differentiation of the state is to keep the principle of universal equality, while organizing its application as segregated inequality. Separate and unequal from the norm that underlies, for instance, the strong local autonomy of American local government.[72] The concentration of poor people and ethnic minorities in America's central cities or in French *banlieues* tends to confine social problems spatially, while decreasing the level of available public resources precisely by keeping local autonomy. Local/regional autonomy reinforces territorially dominant elites and identities, while depriving those social groups who are either not represented in these autonomous government institutions or, else, are ghettoized and isolated.[73] Under such conditions, two different processes may take place. On the one hand, identities that tend to be inclusive use their control of regional institutions to broaden the social and demographic basis of their identity. On the other hand, local societies retrenched in a defensive position build their autonomous institutions as mechanisms of exclusion. An example of the first process is democratic Catalonia: it is run by Catalans and in Catalan, although in the 1990s the majority of the adult population was not born in Catalonia, since genuine Catalan women have been traditionally giving birth below the replacement rate. Yet, the process of cultural integration and social assimilation for immigrants from Southern Spain is relatively smooth, so that their children will be culturally Catalan (see above chapter 1). What is important in this example is to observe how a given cultural/national identity, to be Catalan, uses the control of the local/regional state to survive as an identity, both by reinforcing its bargaining position *vis à vis* the Spanish nation-state, and by using its hold on the regional/local institutions to integrate non-Catalans, thus producing them as Catalans, and reproducing Catalonia through surrogate families.

A totally different situation arises when identities and interests dominating in local institutions reject the notion of integration, as in ethnically divided communities. More often than not, the rejection of official culture is answered by the excluded building pride in their excluded identity, as in many Latino communities in American cities,

---

[72]   Blakely and Goldsmith (1993).
[73]   Smith (1991).

or with the young *beurs* of French North African ghettos.[74] These excluded ethnic minorities do not aim at the local state but call upon the national state in order to see their rights acknowledged, and their interests defended, above and against local/state governments, as in the case of American minorities requesting "affirmative action" programs to make up for centuries of institutional and social discrimination. However, the nation-state, in order to survive its legitimation crisis *vis à vis* the "majority," increasingly shifts power and resources to local and regional governments. So doing, it becomes less and less able to equalize the interests of various identities and social groups represented in the nation-state at large. Thus, mounting social pressures threaten the equilibrium of the whole nation. The nation-state's growing inability to respond to such pressures, because of the decentralization of its power, further de-legitimizes its protective and representative role *vis à vis* discriminated minorities. Subsequently, these minorities seek refuge in their local communities, in nongovernmental structures of self-reliance.[75] Thus, what started as a process of re-legitimizing the state by shifting power from national to local level, may end up deepening the legitimation crisis of the nation-state, and the tribalization of society in communities built around primary identities, as shown in chapter 1.

In the limit, when the nation-state does not represent a powerful identity, or does not provide room for a coalition of social interests that empower themselves under a (re)constructed identity, a social/political force defined by a particular identity (ethnic, territorial, religious) may take over the state, to make it the exclusive expression of such an identity. This is the process of formation of fundamentalist states, such as the Islamic Republic of Iran, or the institutions of American governance proposed by the Christian Coalition in the 1990s. At first glance, it would seem that fundamentalism gives a new, and powerful, breadth to the nation-state, in an updated historical version. Yet, it is in fact the deepest manifestation of the demise of the nation-state. As explained in chapter 1, the expression of Islam is not, and cannot be, the nation-state (a secular institution), but the *umma*, the community of believers. The *umma* is, by definition, transnational, and should reach out to the entire universe. This is also the case with the Catholic Church, a transnational, fundamentalist movement seeking to convert the entire planet to the only true God, using when possible the support of any state. Under this perspective, a fundamentalist state is not a nation-state, both in its relationship to the world and in its relationship to the

---

[74] Sanchez Jankowski (1991); Wieviorka (1993).
[75] Wacquant (1994); Trend (1996).

society living in the national territory. *Vis à vis* the world, the fundamentalist state has to maneuver, in alliance with other believers' apparatuses, states or not, toward the expansion of the faith, toward the molding of institutions, national, international, and local, around the principles of the faith: the fundamentalist project is a global theocracy, not a national, religious state. *Vis à vis* a territorially defined society, the fundamentalist state does not aim at representing the interests of all citizens, and of all identities present in the territory, but aims at helping those citizens, in their various identities, to find the truth of God, the only truth. Therefore, the fundamentalist state, while unleashing the last wave of states' absolute power, does so, in fact, by negating the legitimacy and durability of the nation-state.

Thus, the current death dance between identities, nations, and states, leaves, on the one hand, historically emptied nation-states, drifting on the high seas of global flows of power; on the other hand, fundamental identities, retrenched in their communities or mobilized toward the uncompromising capture of an embattled nation-state; in between, the local state strives to rebuild legitimacy and instrumentality by navigating transnational networks and integrating local civil societies.

Let me illustrate the full meaning of this proposition by focusing on contemporary developments in two major nation-states undergoing (as many others in the world) a structural crisis in the 1990s: Mexico and the United States.

Contemporary Crises of Nation-states: Mexico's PRI State and the US Federal Government in the 1990s

The analysis of the crisis of nation-states, as presented in this chapter, may be clarified by illustrating it with a summary account of specific crises. The reader should be aware, however, that observations and interpretation presented below are not intended to be fully fledged studies of state crises, given the limits of this chapter, even if they are grounded on empirical knowledge of the matter. From a wide range of possibilities around the world, I have selected, partly for reasons of personal acquaintance, two important cases. First, the Mexican PRI state because, *after having been one of the most stable political regimes in the world for about six decades, it disintegrated in a few years under the combined impact, I will argue, of globalization, identity, and a transformed civil society.* Secondly, I consider it meaningful to explore the actual effects of the processes described above on the US federal government, even if the US is an exceptional case because of the size of its economy, the flexibility of its politics, and the the high degree of decentralization in the structure of the state. Yet, it is precisely this exceptionalism[76] that makes the observation of the American nation-state analytically relevant. This is because *if even a state with a global reach, rooted in flexible federalism, becomes embattled by current trends as presented in this chapter, the proposed analysis might be considered to carry general value.*

NAFTA, Chiapas, Tijuana, and the agony of the PRI state[77]

After two decades of post-revolutionary instability, Mexico went on to build one of the most effective, if not most democratic, states in the world. It was organized around what came to be known as *Partido Revolucionario Institucional* (PRI), literally emphasizing the political project of institutionalizing the 1910–17 revolution in the diversity of its ideals and actors. The PRI state was able to subdue the competing power centers that haunted Latin American politics in most other countries of the region: the Army and the Catholic Church. It skillfully survived its unescapable, intimate connection with the United States, keeping alive Mexican nationalism and asserting political autonomy while enjoying generally good relations with its powerful neighbor. It managed to build a strong national, indigenous identity, bridging to the memories of pre-Colombian civilizations, while keeping in obscured marginality its 10 percent Indian population. It succeeded, also, in fostering substantial economic growth between 1940 and 1974, to create the world's twelfth largest economy by the 1990s. And, with the exception of targeted killings by landowners and local *caciques*, occasional political massacres (for example, Tlatelolco in 1968), and some limited action by leftist guerrillas, violence was rare in Mexican politics. Indeed, transmission of power from president to president was orderly, predictable, and unchallenged. Each president would designate his successor, and step out of the open political arena for ever. And each president would betray his predecessor, but never criticize him, and never investigate his actions. Systemic, widespread corruption was orderly, played by the rules, and,

---

[76] Lipset (1996).

[77] The analysis of Mexico presented here is based on three sets of sources: (a) newspapers and magazines from Mexico and other countries, as well as *Revista Mexicana de Sociologia*; (b) a number of published sources, including Mejia Barquera et al. (1985); Berins Collier (1992); Gil et al. (1993); Cook et al. (1994); *Partido Revolucionario Institucional* (1994); Trejo Delarbre (1994a,b); Aguirre et al. (1995); *Business Week* (1995c); Golden (1995); Marquez (1995); Perez Fernandez del Castillo et al. (1995); Summers (1995); *The Economist* (1995b, c); Tirado and Luna (1995); Woldenberg (1995); Ziccardi (1995); Moreno Toscano (1996); and (c) my personal knowledge of Mexico after 25 years of regularly studying that country.

in fact, was a major stabilizing factor in Mexican politics: each president renewed the distribution of political appointments in the entire structure of the state, leading to tens of thousands of new appointments every six years. During their tenure appointees would have the chance of benefitting personally from their position, under different forms. This collective rotation of political elites in a very rewarding system, ensured collective discipline, everybody waiting for his opportunity (it was usually *his*) which would likely come on the condition of respecting the rules of the game. The penalty for breaking the rules of discipline, silence, patience, and, above all, hierarchy was eternal exile from any relevant position of power and wealth in the country, including media presence and meaningful academic appointments. Inside the PRI, different political factions (*camarillas*) competed for power, but never breaking the collective discipline of the party, and never challenging the authority of the president, decider of last resort in any dispute. Yet, the key to social and political stability in the Mexican state was the elaborate system of connections between the PRI and the civil society. It relied on the organic incorporation of popular sectors, mainly through the trade unions (*Confederacion de Trabajadores Mexicanos*, CTM), which controlled the working class; the *Confederacion Nacional Campesina* (CNC), which controlled peasants and farmers, most of them in a system of communal use of the land on state property (*ejidos*), established by the agrarian revolution; and the *Confederacion Nacional de Organizaciones Populares* (CNOP), which tried to organize miscellaneous urban popular sectors, although with notably less success. This system of political clientelism was, for the most part, not based on manipulation and repression, but on actual delivery of jobs, wages, social benefits, goods (including land), and services (including urban amenities) in a comprehensive populist scheme. The Mexican bourgeoisie, and foreign capital, were essentially excluded from the power system, although their interests were frequently represented by the PRI, certainly a pro-capitalist party, albeit in a national populist version. Indeed, most business groups, with the exception of the autonomous Monterrey group, were outgrowths of the Mexican state. Last, and least, elections were systematically rigged by fraud and intimidation when necessary. But, in most cases, PRI would have won (although not in all cases, in all elections, as it came to be) because of the effectiveness of a populist system, socially engineered through networks, familism, and personal loyalties in a vertical chain of reciprocities covering the whole country. In this sense, the PRI system was not simply a political regime, but the very structure of the Mexican state, as it existed in the twentieth century.

Then, it all went down in less than a decade, between the mid-

1980s and the mid-1990s. Even in the unlikely event that the first Mexican president of the twenty-first century will again be a PRI candidate, he would preside over a very different state, since the political system above described has already collapsed. In 1994, the first year of the legal existence of NAFTA, the institutional expression of full-scale globalization of the Mexican economy, the following events took place: the *Zapatistas* insurged in Chiapas, on the first day of the year; the PRI presidential candidate, Luis Donaldo Colosio, was assassinated (the first time that such an event had occurred in half a century); the Mexican peso collapsed, and Mexico almost defaulted, in spite of unprecedented US and IMF support, sending shock waves throughout the world economy; the General Secretary of PRI, Jose Francisco Ruiz Massieu (whose first wife was President Salinas' sister) was assassinated, and his brother, Mexico's Deputy Attorney General was suspected of a cover-up in the assassination, and fled the country; Raul Salinas, brother of the then president Carlos Salinas, and a close business associate of the president, was accused of masterminding the assassination of Ruiz Massieu, and jailed; Raul Salinas' connections to the drug cartels, and to the laundering of hundreds of millions of dollars were exposed; President Carlos Salinas, a few days after stepping down in December 1994, rejected any wrong-doings, staged a 24-hour hunger strike, and, after receiving polite comfort from his successor, President Zedillo, left the country; his departure opened, for the first time ever, a flurry of public denunciations and reciprocal accusations by Mexican politicians from all factions, including former presidents, who decided that now it was all for all. Although the August 1994 presidential election was won by the PRI, in a relatively clean electoral process, widespread fear of instability and violence if the PRI were defeated was critical for such a victory. Electoral results in state, municipal, and congressional elections held afterwards indicated a clear upward trend of votes toward the conservative opposition, the *Partido de Accion Nacional* (PAN), and, to a lesser extent, toward the left-wing critics organized around the *Partido de la Revolucion Democratica* (PRD). President Zedillo relinquished considerable control over the electoral machine, appointed independents and members of PAN to high levels in his administration, and seemed to be prepared to be the president of the transition toward a different kind of regime, and, maybe, state. But the PRI seemed to think otherwise. In November 1996, it rejected the agreement with other parties on the law on political reform.

The political future of Mexico is unclear at the time of writing (1996) with political forces, and political leaders of various origins and ideologies, positioning themselves for the new political era. The only certainty is that the PRI state has ended its historical course.[78] And *the question is why, and how this major political event relates to the overall argument presented here on the crisis of the nation-state as a result of conflicts induced by the contradiction between globalization and identity.*

The current transformation of Mexico, and the demise of its nation-state, started in 1982, when Mexico became unable to pay interest on its foreign debt, in spite of the fact that Mexico's oil production picked up exactly at the time when the two oil supply crises of 1974 and 1979 substantially increased oil prices in the world. After Lopez Portillo's administration (1976–82) ended with the sudden nationalization of Mexico's banks, in a desperate attempt to reassert state control over a rapidly internationalizing economy, Mexico's political and business elites, the US, and international corporate interests decided somehow (I do not know exactly how) that Mexico was too important a country to be left to traditional populists to run it. A new generation of *tecnicos*, rather than *politicos*, came to power, substituting US-trained economists, financiers, and political scientists, for *licenciados* from the Universidad Nacional Autonoma de Mexico's Law School, as was the tradition. None the less, new elites still had to be *licenciados* of the UNAM as well, and they still had to be in the lineage of one of the traditional PRI political families. In the case of Carlos Salinas, it was the former president Miguel Aleman's network, via Salinas' father, Secretary of Commerce 1958–64, and Salinas' uncle, Ortiz Mena, Mexico's Treasury Secretary between 1958 and 1982. Miguel de la Madrid, a technocrat linked to Catholic integrist circles, was the transition president, in 1982–88, in charge of putting Mexico's finances in order, and grooming the new team of young, technically competent, politically daring leaders who would create a new country, and a new state, from within the PRI: Harvard's Carlos Salinas, Secretary of the Budget, and Princeton's Manuel Camacho, Secretary of Urban Development, were the leading figures. But the austerity program implemented by de la Madrid in the 1980s plunged Mexico into a recession, and for all practical purposes broke the social pact with labor and the urban popular sectors. Union leaders were careful not to jeopardize their privileges, but industrial workers, public sector employees, and popular neighborhoods felt the pain of restructuring. Then, in 1985, an earthquake struck Ciudad de Mexico, wrecking homes and businesses, and triggering social protests. An alternative political coalition, the FDN, organized by Cuauthemoc Cardenas (the

[78] In November 1996, local elections in the states of Mexico and Hidalgo were overwhelmingly won by opposition parties. The local elections sheduled for July 1997 in Mexico City and Monterrey are expected to inflict another major defeat on PRI.

son of General Cardenas, the 1930s' historic, populist leader of PRI) picked up steam, attracting the left of the PRI, from where Cuauthemoc Cardenas originated. The PRI barely survived the 1988 presidential election: Mexico City, Guadalajara, and Ciudad Juarez voted against the PRI. Carlos Salinas, the designated PRI candidate was elected because of fraud, this time the difference in votes being small enough that fraud became the decisive factor. Salinas, an intelligent, well-educated man, got the message. He appointed his old-time friend Manuel Camacho as *Regente* (Mayor) of Mexico City, and let him give free rein to his instincts: social programs, negotiation with civil society, democratization. The new president (with the influential help of the "Mexican Rasputin," French-born-of-Spanish-ancestry, international consultant Jose Cordoba) focused on ensuring the full integration of Mexico into the global economy. Salinas' views were straightforward: "We see an intense economic globalization of markets, and the revolution in knowledge and technology makes all of us live, more than ever, a single universal history."[79] Indeed, his career goal (and semi-official candidacy) for his after-presidency life, was to become the first Secretary General of the newly instituted World Trade Organization. Accordingly, he tightened Mexico's belt, sharply reduced public spending, modernized communications and telecommunications infrastructure, privatized most public enterprises, internationalized banking, liberalized trade, and set the country wide open for foreign investment. While standards of living plummeted for the majority of people, inflation was sharply reduced, the Mexican economy grew substantially, exports boomed, investment poured in, so that in 1993 Mexico became the country with the highest amount of foreign direct investment in the developing world. Currency reserves accumulated quickly. Foreign debt payments were under control. It was successful globalization at work. Salinas also launched an unprecedented attack on corrupt labor leaders (actually a warning to all organized labor), and vowed to fight corruption and drug traffic, although on these matters history, maybe soon, will judge his actual record. In the process, he dramatically reduced the real wages of Mexican workers and impoverished large sectors of the population. He did launch a charity program, *Pronasol,* led by one of his closest collaborators, Luis Donaldo Colosio, while charging Camacho with helping out restless Mexico City dwellers, and Ernesto Zedillo with modernizing the educational system. Against the background of much human suffering, the Mexican economy was indeed transformed in a few years, to the point that the US, and international investors, decided that it was time to graduate Mexico, welcoming this

---

[79] Cited by Berins Collier (1992: 134).

nation of over 90 million people into the First World Club (the OECD), even if over 50 percent of its citizens were living below the poverty line, and about 30 percent in absolute poverty. The signing of NAFTA, in 1993, was the high point of this strategy of integration of Mexico into the global economy. It was the moment of Salinas' triumph. It was also time to designate the next president-to-be. Instead of selecting Camacho, the strongest and most popular of his inner circle, he went for Colosio, another young *tecnico*, who, although not from the old guard of the PRI, was president of the party, and was considered more open to compromise by the party apparatus. Ironically, Camacho's best friend in the PRI, Ruiz Massieu, was the party's General Secretary. But, he was there precisely to fight off the "dinosaurs," the old guard. Camacho was disgruntled by his de- motion, both for personal and political reasons, and, for the first time in Mexican politics, he made clear his thoughts, to the president, and in public. But he had no option. By the end of 1993, everything seemed under control, and Salinas appeared to have succeeded in his *perestroyka* precisely by avoiding the mistake that, in his opinion, Gorbachev had committed: to reform politics before reforming the economy.

Then, on January 1, 1994, the first day of the NAFTA era, the *Zapatistas* attacked. I have already analyzed the causes, circumstances, and meaning of the *Zapatista* movement (chapter 2), so that I am simply considering here the movement's impact on the crisis of the Mexican state. It was devastating. Not because it really endangered state power from the military standpoint. But because it quickly became the rallying cry of a civil society that, in its large majority, was economically hurting and politically alienated. Furthermore, a genuinely Indian and peasant rebellion struck a major blow to PRI's mythology. The poor, the peasant, the Indian, were not the subdued, thankful, beneficiaries of the revolution, but the excluded, and they were fighting back. The veil of hypocrisy behind which Mexico had been living for decades was irreversibly torn. The king was naked, and so was the PRI.

Second act. Salinas, nervous with Camacho's reaction, decided to request his services again (with purposes and intentions unknown to me) to repair the damage in Chiapas. Camacho was appointed President's Commissioner for Peace. His skillful, conciliatory negoti- ation, and the popularity of the *Zapatistas*, triggered a new round of intrigue in the PRI in early 1994. With the Colosio campaign slow in taking off, the possibility of a reversal of the president's decision, nominating Camacho instead of Colosio, became the talk of the town. Colosio, the presidential candidate, a very capable and well- intentioned technocrat (a University of Pennsylvania-trained regional planner) was not a member of the old guard. The party apparatus was already tense about his appointment. But Camacho was too much: he was politically savvy, had his own party connections, grassroots support, good opinion polls, and an uncompromising attitude. Both Colosio and Camacho spelled future trouble for the party if they were to become presidents. But even worse than one or the other was the uncertainty about whom, and even the possibility of an alliance between them. As negotiations in Chiapas went on, and as Colosio's campaign seemed to be in a holding pattern, tensions in the party apparatus intensified, particularly in some sectors with very specific interests, and much to lose.

Having reached this point in the analysis, I have to introduce a new element that, in my informed opinion, is absolutely decisive, even if I have no hard evidence: *Mexico's new role in global organized crime.* Since the 1960s, Mexico cultivated, and exported, marihuana, but not more (actually less) than some areas in the US, such as northern California and Kentucky. Heroin production started on a limited scale in the 1970s. But the big change came in the 1980s when the formation of global drug networks, and stepped-up pressure on the Caribbean and Central American routes in the US, led the Colombian cartels to share part of the US-bound commerce with Mexican cartels, by giving them an amount of cocaine equivalent to what they were able to smuggle into the US at the service of the Colombians. Traffic skyrocketed, and powerful Mexican cartels were organized: in Tamaulipas and the Gulf around Garcia Abrego; in Ciudad Juarez around Amado Carrillo; in Tijuana around the Arellano Felix brothers, among others. They added profitable heroine cultivation, and traffic. Then, amphetamines. Then, everything. In the tens of billions of dollars. To work quietly, and professionally, they followed the Cali model, rather than Medellin's. Avoid unnecessary killing, be discreet. Just be cool, efficient, buy whomever you need: police, drug investigators, judges, prosecutors, local and state officials, and PRI bosses, as high as possible. Every dollar invested in corruption is profitable because it creates a network that, by extending itself, multiplies support, and ensures silence. Thus, while the new techno-political elite of Mexico was busy linking up with the global economy, important sectors of the traditional PRI apparatus, together with state and local officials of various political affiliations, established their own connection to the "other global economy." By 1994, the new "mafiocracy" was strong enough to defend its interests, but not established enough to cash out, and disappear into the financial avenues of money laundering. They needed more time, predictable time. And both Colosio and Camacho were unpredictable and dangerous to their interests. They decided to kill them both: Colosio, with a bullet; Camacho with a well-organized opinion campaign that blamed him, morally, for Colosio's fate. They succeeded. Not accidentally, Colosio was killed in Tijuana. Zedillo, Colosio's campaign manager, and one of the four of Salinas' inner circle (the other was Pedro Aspe, the Finance Minister), took his place. He is a competent, Yale-educated economist. Yet, his political connections were tenuous and his political skills untested. Not that the criminal connection had its way fully. But at least they changed the rules of the game. Whoever trespassed into their territory would do it at their peril.

Next in line was the Secretary General of the PRI, who appeared to go too far in investigating Colosio's death, still unsolved at the time of writing. This time, the assassin of Secretary General Jose Francisco Ruiz Massieu was traced back to a prominent PRI parliamentarian, to the Tamaulipas cartel, and, ultimately, to Raul Salinas, the brother, and close associate, of the president. Oddly enough, Ruiz Massieu's brother, who was the government's Special Prosecutor against Drug Traffic, has been formally accused of being on the cartels' payroll. It is too early to assert beyond doubt who was doing what, and certainly beyond my knowledge and competence. Yet, what is analytically relevant is that in the 1994 decisive political crisis, the drug traffickers–PRI connection played a major role in the assassinations, intimidations, and cover-ups that destroyed traditional rules of the political game, and opened the way for the demise of the PRI state. It must be emphasized that this was not a typical case of political infiltration by the mob. *It was the global reach of these criminal networks, their implication for US–Mexican relations, and the involvement of the higher levels of the state that make the crisis significant as an illustration of how the globalization of crime overwhelms powerful, stable nation-states.*

The political killings, the obvious infiltration of criminal elements in the state, the challenge from the *Zapatistas*, supported by a majority of public opinion, and the internal conflicts in the PRI, shook foreign investors' confidence in the stability of Mexico's emergent market. Capital outflow started in March 1994, after Colosio's assassination on March 23. In spite of this, Salinas, and his minister, Aspe, decided to keep the fixed exchange rate, using Mexico's abundant reserves to make up for loss of foreign capital. They were counting on reversing the trend. It did not happen. When Zedillo took control, on December 1, 1994, he panicked at the real situation, as reflected in secret book-keeping. He rushed a devaluation that made things worse. Ensuing capital flight left Mexico on the edge of defaulting, and shook up markets in Buenos Aires and Sao Paulo. The US president came to the rescue, NAFTA obliging, going as far as to bypass Congress, and to bring in $20 billion as collateral guarantee, pulled from the federal pockets. IMF also pitched in with an $8 billion loan (its largest ever), and arranged a few deals, so that by mid-1995 Mexico found itself somewhat cushioned by $50 billion, in exchange for which it lost its economic independence for ever.

Beyond economic restructuring, with its high social cost, and the new linkages with global crime, another essential element in the demise of the PRI state was the mobilization of Mexico's civil society, particularly in major urban centers. This mobilization was ambiguous because it was made up of very different social interests, cultures, and political projects. It brought together important sectors of the professional middle class, benefitting from the prospects of a dynamic economy, but yearning for democratization, clean government, and limits to bureaucracy. But it also threw into the battle against the PRI state, public sector employees threatened in their security; disaffected urban popular neighborhoods, fearful of the breakdown of mechanisms of redistribution of land and services; students, mobilizing around the renewed symbols of social change; and poor people, millions of them, in cities and the countryside, fighting to survive by any means. And although political skepticism is on the rise, and not many Mexicans truly believe that their fate depends on alternative political parties, there is consensus on the inability of the PRI state to deliver. The breakdown of populist legitimacy is tantamount to the end of populist, organic alliances at the heart of the system.

The democratizing effort during the Salinas administration took the form of devolution of power and resources to local and state governments, along with the tolerance of electoral victories for the opposition in a number of important states and cities, particularly in the North. The series of monographs on municipal governments in the 1990s, coordinated by Alicia Ziccardi,[80] show important improvements in local administration, particularly in Leon, Durango, Torreon, and in Mexico DF, among others. Yet, the political impact of these relative successes was to further undermine the PRI state, since in all these cases a stronger connection was established between the municipal administrations, in many instances in the hands of opposition parties, and local civil societies. Even in Mexico DF the municipal administration of presidential appointee, *Regente* Manuel Camacho, ended up establishing his own electoral basis among the population, bypassing the traditional PRI apparatus. Thus, overall, the effort at democratizing and decentralizing power to the lower levels of the state, while the president and his technocrats were riding the global economy, created greater distance between all segments of the population and the presidential quarters. Since the essence of the Mexican state was the godly status of the president while being

[80]   Ziccardi (1991, 1995).

president, the widespread lack of reverence, even in the moments of Salinas' triumph, rang the bell for one of the most durable political regimes in this century.

The Mexican nation-state will go on, in a new historical course, because the roots of nationalism are solidly planted in the hearts of Mexicans. However, it will not be the same nation-state created by the PRI, and, while still influential and resourceful, I dare to say, it will be increasingly powerless.

Economically, Mexico, and the world, have entered a new era, of which Mexico is probably a pioneer. Larry Summers, one of the most distinguished international finance experts, and a key player in the Mexican bail-out, wrote at the end of 1995, with the hindsight of time: "The form of Mexico's crisis [in 1994] was shaped by the financial innovations of recent years: and advances in information and communications technology caused it to be propagated in a way that is without precedent. It is little wonder, then, that the International Monetary Fund's Michel Camdessus, has labeled it as the first crisis of the 21st century."[81] This translated into the fact that Mexico's economic policy in the future, any kind of policy, will have to be closely coordinated with US economic policy, and with international financial markets.

Politically, Mexico has to reckon, from now on, with the penetration of its state apparatus, at any level, by global crime networks. It is doubtful that its own police and judicial system are immune from such penetration, so making extremely difficult the recovery of the state's full autonomy *vis à vis* crime. Indeed, it appears that most of the revelations about drug connections with the political system, including those referring to Raul Salinas, came from investigative work by US intelligence – which makes Mexican leaders dependent on American intelligence.

In domestic politics, a more educated and mobilized civil society is experimenting with new ways of expression and organization, all in direct contradiction to the PRI state, and often more developed at the local level. Increasing globalization and segmentation of the media are relaxing the grip that the Televisa group, a private multimedia empire traditionally allied with the PRI state, had on "infotainment."

And symbolically, the power of identity, as claimed by Marcos and the *Zapatistas*, has done more than to unveil Mexico's ideological self-complacency: it has built bridges between the real Indians, the real poor, and the educated urban sectors in search of new mobilizing utopias. In the process, the Mexican nation was reunited, this time against the PRI state.

[81] Summers (1995: 46).

The people versus the state: the fading legitimacy of US federal government [82]

The crisis of the American state in the 1990s is a crisis of legitimacy that, I contend, goes far beyond the traditional libertarian strain in US politics. It starts from the depths of civil society, expressing its griefs on several, distinct issues that converge into questioning the role, function, and power of the federal government, as asserted by the Supreme Court since its landmark decisions of 1810 and 1819. The immediate political impact of this renewed distrust of government is the growing ascendance of a rebuilt Republican party, clearly skewed to the right, as resoundingly expressed in the 1994 congressional and gubernatorial elections and to some extent confirmed in the 1996 congressional elections that kept the GOP in control of both the House and the Senate. Yet, the influence of anti-state feelings goes far beyond the Republican electorate to embrace independent voters, such as those represented by Ross Perot, who reject altogether the current party system. Anti-state standing also includes a growing number of democratic constituencies, so that President Clinton in his 1996 State of the Nation address went into announcing "the end of big government."

Indeed, Clinton's re-election in 1996 was largely due to his embracing of many of the Republican themes against the welfare state, and against government spending, together with a tough stand on law and order, and the promise to preserve entitlements for the middle class, thus skillfully occupying the center-right of the political spectrum. As Theda Skocpol stated, commenting on the 1996 presidential election results, "Regardless of the partisan balance, something about the shift in the debate that was registered in 1994 is going to stay with us. There is just a sense that you can't use the Federal Government for big initiatives even if the national problems are big."[83]

---

[82] One of the best accounts of political developments in the US in the first half of the 1990s is Balz and Brownstein (1996). I refer to this book for additional sources. To place American anti-government culture in a historical perspective, see Lipset (1996) and Kazin (1995). For additional, useful information and analyses underlying the matters covered in this section, see: Stanley and Niemi (1992); Davidson (1993); Bennett (1994); Black and Black (1994); Murray and Herrnstein (1994); Woodward (1994); Barone and Ujifusa (1995); Campbell and Rockman (1995); Greenberg (1995); Himmelfarb (1995); Pagano and Bowman (1995); Roper Center of Public Opinion and Polling (1995); Dionne (1996); Fallows (1996). For a rigorous, sociological critique of Murray's theses, see Fischer et al. (1995).

[83] Cited by Toner (1996).

Furthermore, the 1996 election registered increasing disaffection from the electorate toward all political candidates: only 49 percent of eligible voters bothered to vote, and Clinton obtained only 49 percent of this 49 percent. Keeping the executive and legislative powers in different political hands seemed to be the result of an implicit collective will to reinforce the system of checks and balances so to deny excessive power to any kind of government.

This powerful anti-state trend, for the time being, deeply affects politics but not the structure of the state. Yet, it seems to be on its way to transforming the institutional basis and political purpose of governance in America. If the proposals approved by the Republican Congress in 1995, or a modified version of these policies, become enacted, as is possible, the federal government would transfer to state governments by 2002 the responsibility and funds to manage dozens of major programs, including welfare, Medicaid, job training, and environmental protection, for a total estimated amount of $200 billion in annual spending.[84] Furthermore, funds would be provided as block grants, so that final decision for their use would be in the hands of the states, although with some provisions, whose content is the object of ferocious infighting in Congress. The Clinton administration was also planning to shift increasing responsibility to the states in several major areas, including transportation policy and welfare. In addition, efforts to cut the budget deficit in seven years, both by Republicans and by President Clinton, will lead to a substantial reduction in spending both at the federal and state levels. Medicaid spending may be reduced by 30 percent (that is, $270 billion) between 1995 and 2002. Federal agencies playing a major role in government regulation, such as the Environmental Protection Agency and the Federal Communications Commission, would most likely see their power and funding sharply curtailed. Indeed, reducing the budget deficit, while based on a strong economic rationale, has become the most powerful tool in shrinking the federal government, posting a $203 billion dollar annual deficit in 1995. The combined movement toward devolution of power to the states and counties, deregulation, disentitlement of welfare rights, drastic reduction of spending and borrowing, and tax cuts (including the possibility, in the future, of a true fiscal revolution, as illustrated by the recurrent debate on a flat income tax) are operating a fundamental redefinition of the power and aims of federal government, and thus of the American state.

The forces driving this transformation of the role of government in the United States emerge from a profound, explicit rejection of the federal government by a large majority of Americans in the 1990s (see

[84]   *Business Week* (1995e).

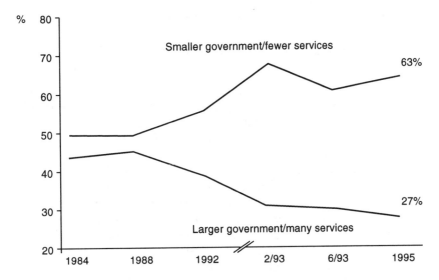

Figure 5.4 Public opinion attitudes toward size of government and service delivery, in US, 1984–95 (results of the survey question: "Would you say you favor smaller government with fewer services or larger government with many services?")
Source: Surveys by ABC News/*The Washington Post*, 1984, 1988, 1992, and February 1993; and *The Los Angeles Times*, June 1993 and January 1995

figure 5.4). Balz and Brownstein summarize data from opinion polls and political studies on the matter in the following way:

Discontent about government now runs down two powerful streams. On the one hand, the vast majority of Americans subscribe to a populist critique that assails Washington as wasteful, ineffective, in thrall to special interests, and crowded with duplicitous self-serving politicians who will say anything to be elected. (This populist alienation from government is strongest among working-class white voters – the same group that has faced the most economic pressure over the past two decades.) From a second front, a smaller, but still substantial number of Americans indict government on ideological grounds – as an overreaching behemoth that is eroding individual liberty and self-reliance, discouraging religion, and favoring minorities and the poor. The distrust of Washington has proven a huge hurdle for Democratic efforts to assemble support behind new government initiatives –

even those aimed at combating economic insecurity through expanded job training or guaranteed health care. Hostility toward Washington is now as much a part of American culture as reverence for the flag.[85]

It is precisely this divide between strengthened allegiance to the nation's symbol (the flag), and growing disobedience to the state's institutions (Washington) that characterizes a legitimacy crisis.

In chapter 2, while discussing social movements, I briefly analyzed the insurgency against the new global order in the United States, putting forward a number of ideas on the roots and characteristics of movements such as the American militia, the "county rights," "wise use" movement, and miscellaneous "patriot" anti-government mobilizations. In this chapter, my focus is on the impact of such movements, and of broader trends in public opinion on politics and the state. Anti-state feelings in 1990s' American society cannot be reduced to their most extreme manifestation, although the Patriot movement does epitomize the values and the anger expressed in large sectors of the society, as echoed in the diatribes of Rush Limbaugh's radio talk shows. Anti-federal government feelings and politics are the converging point of a vast array of ideological, economic, and social trends so deeply rooted in the relationship between globalization, construction of identity, and politics that it is safe to predict that whichever party wins in 2000, be it the GOP, or a renewed Democratic party, it may well be pushed into an overhaul of American political institutions in the twenty-first century. A review of the main components of this 1990s' conservative populism will help to understand the complexity of the process, and the extent of the crisis looming on the horizon, beyond variations of the political cycle.

A first, powerful, trend is a new brand of economic populism, reacting to the disfranchisement of a substantial proportion of American workers under the impact of global economic restructuring. Corporate profits and the stock market were at an all-time high in 1996, although the Dow Jones index was falling sharply each time substantial job creation was announced. Technology is, slowly but surely, inducing growth in productivity. Most women are now earning income. Jobs are being created in record numbers (10 million new jobs during the Clinton administration). Yet, deep-seated dissatisfaction and insecurity are a reflection of stagnant or declining living standards for the majority of the population, together with the structural instability introduced in the labor market by flexible work, networking of firms, and increasing dependence on transnational

---

[85]   Balz and Brownstein (1996: 13).

patterns of investment, production, and trade (see volume I). To be sure, this is an anti-corporate, rather than an anti-state feeling, and in fact implicitly calls for more active government intervention, as in the drive toward protectionism. Yet, it fuels anger against federal government because Washington is seen, correctly, as the manager of globalization, particularly after the signing of the NAFTA treaty, which came to symbolize increasing American economic interdependence. Policy issues involved in this movement lead, potentially, to economic protectionism, restriction of immigration, and discrimination against immigrants. Its implications lead to a frontal opposition to corporate interests, for whom free trade and free movement of capital, and of highly skilled labor, are essential, thus introducing an explosive contradiction within the Republican party, as demonstrated in the 1996 presidential primaries, with the alarm of GOP's leadership confronted with the initial success of Buchanan's populist candidacy. A similar contradiction exists also in the Democratic party, with most labor unions, and many minority groups, opposing NAFTA, and the full mobility of capital and jobs in an open, global economy, an agenda generally supported by Democratic leaders, and certainly fostered by Clinton.

Another current of public opinion, partly coincidental with economic protectionism, is the one proposing political isolationism, manifested by widespread popular opposition to committing American troops abroad in the absence of a clearly perceived threat to national security at home, a condition to which Somalia or Bosnia did not qualify. With the fading away of the Soviet Union, the rationale for national mobilization was lost in the minds and hearts of people, and the regular exercise of military superpower status, so appealing to economic, intellectual, and political elites, does not seem to justify cost or suffering. Rejection of American troops serving under the United Nations flag became the rallying point against multilateralism, and against the blurring of US sovereignty in the complex web of international institutions characterizing the post-Cold War era, such as the World Trade Organization.

A third current of opinion refers to a widespread rejection of what is considered to be government interference in private lives, family, and local communities. This is the case of the "home school movement," often associated with Christian fundamentalism, in which parents refuse to send their children to school, and reject the need for certification. Or of the "county rights" and "wise use" movements against environmental regulation, mixing defense of local autonomy, particularly in the West, with the interests of logging and mining companies. Or the growing, widespread concern about threats to privacy from the computerized state, fueling libertarianism of different brands, depending on levels of education and social context.

Family values, anti-abortion movements, anti-gay campaigns, and religious fundamentalism (most often from white evangelicals) form the basis of a wide, diversified social current, of which, as mentioned in chapters 1 and 2, the Christian Coalition is the most potent, and organized political expression, with 1.5 million members, and 1,200 chapters in 50 states. Indeed, the Christian Coalition has become, by the mid-1990s, the most important single bloc of voters in the Republican party, and a deciding force in many elections, at the local, state, and federal level, credited as being the functional equivalent of what organized labor used to be in the Democratic party. Christian fundamentalists are not, in principle, an anti-state movement. Indeed, their dream would be a theocracy, a God-abiding nation, with government enforcing the rules of God, as they have done in some school boards which they came to control in California, or in the vote of the Tennessee Senate in February 1996 to post the Ten Commandments in public offices and schools, requiring their observance. Yet, under the current constitutional regime of religious freedom, and separation between Church and state, the rebuilding of the Christian nation demands first of all the dismantlement of the secularized state, as it is today. The extraordinary development of Christian fundamentalism in the past decade in the United States, and its conversion into a well-organized political force, can be related to the reconstruction of identity, and to resistance to the disintegration of the traditional family. It is a rejection of feminism, gay liberation, and the end of patriarchalism. And of government efforts to implement laws supporting women's choice, gender equality, and cultural tolerance. But beyond this reaction, rooted in personal insecurity, there is an attempt at reconstructing identity and meaning on the basis of an idealized past, the past of family and community in a homogeneous society now being rebuilt in the new suburbia, and in the small towns of a vanishing rural life. This reaction is particularly dramatic against the background of the current collapse of the patriarchal family in America (see chapter 4). The insurgency against the crisis of patriarchalism is as powerful as the opposition to the new global economic order in challenging liberal values and the political establishment, thus delegitimizing their perceived enforcer, the federal government.

The critique of federal laws and institutions becomes even more vitriolic when it links up with class and racial hostility toward the poor and racial minorities. This is why the selective delegitimation of the welfare state, already embattled by economic trends, crystallizes popular sentiment, political votes, and anti-government hostility. I say selective because Social Security and Medicare (which account for

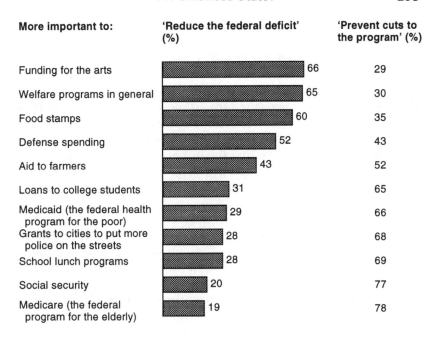

More important to:	'Reduce the federal deficit' (%)	'Prevent cuts to the program' (%)
Funding for the arts	66	29
Welfare programs in general	65	30
Food stamps	60	35
Defense spending	52	43
Aid to farmers	43	52
Loans to college students	31	65
Medicaid (the federal health program for the poor)	29	66
Grants to cities to put more police on the streets	28	68
School lunch programs	28	69
Social security	20	77
Medicare (the federal program for the elderly)	19	78

Figure 5.5 Attitudes toward federal government programs and reduction of federal budget deficit, in US, 1995 (results of the survey question: "For each of the following programs, do you think it is more important to reduce the federal budget or more important to prevent that program from being significantly cut?")
Source: Survey by the Gallup Organization for CNN/*USA Today*, February 24–26, 1995

about two-thirds of the budget of the US welfare state) continue to receive the support of a large majority of the population, so as to make the system very difficult to reform (see figure 5.5). On the other hand, welfare programs, social benefits for the poor, training programs, and affirmative action for minorities are under attack by a majority that refuses to pay taxes to sustain "the others," and stigmatizes the poor, blaming them for their behavior, for example attributing to welfare payments the exponential growth in the number of "babies born to babies." In the "theories" presented by the academic advisors of the anti-welfare movement, Victorian England and its rigorous morality becomes the model, and the poor and minorities are sentenced to a permanent lesser status by their biologically determined IQ.[86] A further manifestation of the break up of social solidarity is the special

[86]   Murray and Herrnstein (1994); Himmelfarb (1995).

rage developed by "angry white males," extending the rejection of affirmative action to women, thus inducing an additional potential split among disaffected citizens. The mobilization of a substantial proportion of civil society against the welfare state in America leads, at the same time, to segmentation of society and to the weakening of the state, increasingly pressured toward becoming, predominantly, a repressive apparatus against the rising "dangerous classes." The emphasis on community volunteerism and charity as substitutes for the welfare state, while stressing the importance of a concerned civil society, is essentially an ideological screen not to face the cynical abandonment of collective responsibility under the pretext of exercising individual responsibility.

All these dimensions of citizens' revolt are sometimes coincident with the unfettered interests of corporate capitalism (as in the critique of welfarism or environmentalism), sometimes sharply in opposition to them (as in the critique of globalization and work flexibility). But, while being very different, and stemming from different sources, they all converge into frontal opposition to the extensive role of federal government, characterizing the American nation-state as constituted in the past half-century.

But let me be clear on this point. As a whole, 1990s' conservative populism in America is not a libertarian movement, and does not echo the tradition of anti-government republicanism. Some of its most important components, as described above, demand, in fact, very statist policies, imposing values of some organized segments of society over individuals and families by the state. This is clearly the case of Christian fundamentalists, whose growing influence in local and state governments is seen as a means of imposing godly behavior over the whole society under their jurisdiction. This is also the case of protectionist economic policies, whose full implementation would require a decisive effort by federal government to control and gear the entire American economy. Therefore, *the crisis of the nation-state does not come, only, from the cultural hegemony of anti-state values, but from the convergence of challenges from various ideologies and interests into the calling into question of the US federal government, as it is historically constituted* – either to sharply reduce its role (traditional libertarianism), or to capture it on behalf of a new mission to rebuild the American nation under the guidance of God, and/or in isolation of the new global order. This is why this crisis of legitimacy, although underlying the "Republican revolution" of 1994, cannot be equated with it. It cuts across parties, and constituencies, and it affects industrial workers as much as farmers, angry males as much as angry tax-payers.

These very diverse, powerful currents often organize around two issues that become a shared banner for many of them: refuse taxes, bear arms. By depriving government, and particularly the federal government, of fiscal revenues, state action becomes gradually subdued. In a society and economy of rising demands *vis à vis* public policies, a dwindling tax base forces the state to concentrate on its core, strategic functions, essentially to keep law and order, and to provide the infrastructure for the new informational, global economy, while paying the interests of a debt inherited from Reagan's Cold War. Therefore, it becomes unable to perform other functions, and so is actually forced "off people's backs."

On the other hand, in the minds of a substantial proportion of the population, the right to bear arms is the ultimate foundation of citizens' freedom, under the invocation of the American constitution. Although many Americans do not agree with this state of affairs, the fact of the matter is that there are 300 million handguns in US households, and war weaponry is available on the open market.

Powerful organizations and lobbies, such as Americans for Tax Reform, the National Federation of Independent Business, and the legendary National Rifle Association, fight, with success, to undermine state control over money and guns. My God, my family, my community, my money, my gun, seem to be the set of values that shape the consciousness and behavior of an increasingly important proportion of American people, in direct opposition to the rules, programs, and personnel of the federal government, and with increasing hostility toward global corporatism and institutional multilateralism.

The diffusion of these themes and attitudes in American society has been helped by the increasing localization, segmentation, and differentiation of the media, and by the spread of interactive, electronic communication. The key development in this sense is the growing influence of local radio, broadcasting syndicated programs, and the explosion of talk shows and call-in talk radio. Between 1988 and 1995, the number of stations specializing in talk radio doubled, reaching 1,200. New satellite technology, and the loosening of regulations on distorted allegations, helped their development and influence. Rush Limbaugh, the star of talk shows, enjoyed a weekly audience of 20 million over 600 stations in the whole country, thus becoming a potent political force by himself. The new GOP, in 1994, paid homage, in a public dinner, to Limbaugh, the man who, more than anyone else, had popularized the cause of ultra-conservatism and anti-government stands throughout the country. Besides radio, the new populist, grassroots movement, as indicated in chapter 2, used all the potential of new communication technologies, including the Internet, but also Fax machines, to coordinate their action and ideas, and to diffuse them among targeted receivers and elected officials.

The de-massification of the media bypassed the traditional channels of indirect control between the political establishment and the audience, unleashing the diffusion of all kinds of information and ideas, including the most outrageous, distorted, and unfair, among millions of people. The borderline between publishing the fit and the unacceptable, carefully established over decades by a generally responsible freedom of the press, became irreversibly blurred.

However distorted are the expressions of anger, these social trends are not temporary moods of public opinion. Available opinion polls in the 1990s show their persistence, and their depth (see chapter 6). They are rooted in major structural transformations, as presented in this book, and processed under the specific culture and institutions of American society. As Balz and Brownstein write:

> Behind all these swirling, swelling movements on the Right is the fear of a world spinning out of control . . . As the economy restructures under the pressures of globalization and advancing technology, and society's cultural framework strains under the breakdown of the two-parent family, this is one of those times [when large numbers of Americans feel themselves uprooted by developments that they cannot understand or control]. "People feel they don't have control over their own lives," said Republican pollster Frank Luntz. "That they can no longer shape their future."[87]

And they blame for it the state they have built over the past half-century, yearning to retake control over their lives in their communities and with their families, and moving away from government. They are helped in this process by a Republican party that had been out of parliamentary power for three decades, and then saw the opportunity to assert its power for decades to come. But the GOP is doing so by riding the wave of anti-government, and anti-establishment feelings, thus playing with fire. As Balz and Brownstein conclude: "All the intellectual energy in the Republican party is now focused in finding new ways to reduce the scope and reach of the federal government."[88] However, since the GOP also represents powerful corporate interests, embedded in a global economy and in international institutions, by becoming the instrument of anti-state populism it builds an explosive internal contradiction between its anti-government and fundamentalist popular base, and its traditional role of representing corporate capitalism and the defense establishment. The coming into the open of such a contradiction, and the

---

[87]   Balz and Brownstein (1996: 173).
[88]   Balz and Brownstein (1996: 295).

ensuing probable disaffection of a powerful populist trend, that cuts across party lines, may induce a fundamental crisis in the American political system. It may well destabilize the careful balance that the founding fathers and the Supreme Court had historically established between the local and the federal, between government and society, thus potentially triggering the crisis of the American nation-state.

Structure and process in the crisis of the state

Let me emphasize the relevant analytical elements derived from these succinct case studies of state crisis. In both, Mexico and the United States, we observe the direct impact of globalization and capitalist restructuring on the legitimacy of the state, through the partial dismantlement of the welfare state, the disruption of traditional productive structures, increasing job instability, extreme social inequality, and the link up of valuable segments of economy and society in global networks, while large sectors of the population and territory are switched off from the dynamic, globalized system: all processes that I have analyzed in volume I, and which are shown to take their toll on the state's ability to respond to social demands, and, ultimately, on the state's legitimacy. Furthermore, the close connection of the Mexican economy with the US economy, institutionalized by NAFTA, and the electronic linkage of its financial markets with global markets in real time, made the collapse of the peso in 1994–95 very different from any previous economic crisis, actually exemplifying, as reported above, "the first financial crisis of the twenty-first century." Additionally, in the case of Mexico, the penetration of the state by the global criminal economy adds a powerful twist to the disorganization of political institutions and to their crisis of legitimacy.

In the case of the United States (not in Mexico, as yet), the crisis of patriarchalism, with its roots in the informational economy and in the challenge from social movements, deepened insecurity and fear among large sectors of people, prompting a withdrawal from the legal and political institutions that were receptive to women's rights, and from the secular state. For a significant segment of the population, it led to retrenchment in the affirmation of God, family, and community, as eternal values beyond contest from social challenges.

In both cases, the structural crises that undermined the state's legitimacy interacted with the development of social movements which, under forms specific to each society, affirmed alternative identities, and explicitly rejected the legitimacy of the federal government. Although these identity-based movements involved only a minority of activists, their demands and claims were indeed processed by the political system, and found an echo, admittedly distorted, in the population at large. There is an undeniable connection between the symbolic impact of the *Zapatistas* and the widespread rejection of the PRI state in Mexican society, ending what was one of the most perdurable political systems in the world. As for the United States, while the Patriots are more a symptom than a cause, the crisis of legitimacy manifests itself in the broad distrust of government, particularly of the federal government, and of politicians and parties, particularly of those linked to mainstream politics. The rise of popularity of conservative Republicans in the mid-1990s is, to a large extent, linked to their politically suicidal campaigning against the very government institutions which they want to control.

In both cases, Mexico and the United States, new electronic communication systems have been decisive in amplifying the impact of relatively small movements on public opinion at large by their feeding of the media and by their horizontal, unfettered networking.

Thus, there is an empirically observable, analytically meaningful connection between globalization, informationalization, capitalist restructuring, identity-based social movements, and the crisis of political legitimacy in both Mexican and American states, albeit with different forms, specific to each society. What is first in inducing causality is, methodologically, a wrong question because structure and process interact inseparably in the sequence leading to the crisis of the state. It would be difficult to imagine the impact of the *Zapatistas* on Mexico without the profound impact of globalization in economy and society. But the *Zapatistas* were not the result of economic crisis: they existed before, in the struggles of Indians and peasants supported by Catholic priests, and in the revolutionary will of refugees from the 1970s radical left movements. Libertarianism in America has a long tradition, and isolationism is a perennial temptation of a continental-sized, powerful country, as is the opposite temptation toward imperialism. That one or the other prevail in a particular historical period is not pre-scripted, since the precise outcome of interaction between the elements I have identified, constituting, at the same time, structure and process, is largely undetermined. So, in spite of the Republican revolution of 1994, Clinton still won the 1996 presidential election, to a large extent precisely because of the internal contradictions of the Republican electorate in being mobilized, at the same time, on behalf of corporate interests and by the themes of right-wing populism. Yet, Clinton himself, in order to win, had to depart sharply from the traditional Democratic platform, thus furthering the distance between the hopes of many Democrats and the realities of politics.

Why the social and political response to the new global disorder came from "the left" in Mexico and from "the right" in the United

States is due, partly, to specific political agencies, and, partly, to the characteristics of the crisis to be dealt with. Namely, since the state, in both cases, was unable to deliver its promised protection, and became, instead, the active manager of the globalization/restructuring process, the challenge against the state was mounted from outside the traditional basis of support for government-led reforms: the pro-federal government Democrats in the United States; the PRI populist system in Mexico. This does not preclude that a pro-welfare state, pro-government, left-wing movement could develop in the future in both countries, but it would have to grow away from the halls of the political establishment, precisely because of the crisis of its legitimacy.

This openness of political processes does not invalidate the interest of an in-depth, analytical understanding because the materials we have uncovered, and their linkages, are indeed the stuff of which political institutions and political processes are made in our time. As for analyzing the relationship between the sources of state crisis and the new forms of political struggle and competition, I need to consider, first, the specific dynamic of political actors in the new, informational paradigm – an exercise that I will attempt in chapter 6.

The State, Violence, and Surveillance: from Big Brother to Little Sisters

Is the state really powerless in the network society? Aren't we witnessing, instead, a surge of violence and repression throughout the world? Isn't privacy facing the greatest dangers in human history, because of the pervasiveness of new information technologies? Didn't Big Brother arrive, as Orwell predicted, around 1984? And how could the state be powerless when mastering a formidable technological capacity, and controlling an unprecedented stock of information?[89]

These essential, and usual, questions mix contradictory evidence with confused theory. Yet, their treatment is central in the understanding of the crisis of the state. First of all, the Big Brother imagery must be empirically dismissed, as it refers to the connection between our societies and the Orwellian prophecy. Indeed, George Orwell could well have been right, *vis à vis* the object of his prophecy, Stalinism, not the liberal, capitalist state, if political history and technology had followed a different trajectory in the past half-century, something that was certainly within the realm of possibility. But statism disintegrated in contact with new information technologies,

---

[89] Burnham (1983); Lyon (1994).

instead of being capable of mastering them (see volume III); and new information technologies unleashed the power of networking and decentralization, actually undermining the centralizing logic of one-way instructions and vertical, bureaucratic surveillance (see volume I). Our societies are not orderly prisons, but disorderly jungles.

However, new, powerful information technologies might indeed be put to the service of surveillance, control, and repression by state apparatuses (police, tax collection, censorship, suppression of political dissidence, and the like). But so might they be used for citizens to enhance their control over the state, by rightfully accessing information in public data banks, by interacting with their political representatives on-line, by watching live political sessions, and eventually commenting live on them.[90] Also, new technologies may enable citizens to videotape events, so providing visual evidence of abuses, as in the case of global environmental organizations that distribute video power to local groups around the world to report on environmental crimes, thus putting pressure on the ecological culprits. What the power of technology does is to extraordinarily amplify the trends rooted in social structure and institutions: oppressive societies may be more so with the new surveillance tools, while democratic, participatory societies may enhance their openness and representativeness by further distributing political power with the power of technology. Thus, the direct impact of new information technologies on power and the state is an empirical matter, on which the record is mixed. But, a deeper, more fundamental trend is at work, actually undermining the nation-state's power: the increasing diffusion of both surveillance capacity and the potential for violence outside the institutions of the state and beyond the borders of the nation.

Reports of the growing threat to privacy concern less the state as such than business organizations and private information networks, or public bureaucracies following their own logic as apparatuses, rather than acting on behalf of government. States, throughout history, have collected information on their subjects, very often by rudimentary but effective brutal means. Certainly, computers qualitatively changed the ability to cross-refer information, combining social security, health, ID cards, residence, and employment information. But with the limited exception of Anglo-Saxon countries, rooted in a libertarian tradition, people around the world, from democratic Switzerland to Communist China, have spent their lives dependent on files of information of residence, work, and on every domain of their relationship to government. On the other hand, if it is true that police work has been facilitated by new technologies, it has

[90]   Anthes (1993); Betts (1995); Gleason (1995).

also become extraordinarily complicated by the similar, and some-times superior, sophistication of organized crime in using new technologies (for instance, interfering with police communications, linking up electronically, accessing computing records and so on). *The real issue is somewhere else: it is in the gathering of information on indi-viduals by business firms, and organizations of all kinds, and in the creation of a market for this information.* The credit card, more than the ID card, is giving away privacy. This is the instrument through which peoples' lives can be profiled, analyzed, and targeted for marketing (or black-mailing) purposes. And the notion of the credit card as life in the public record must be extended to a variety of business offerings, from frequent flyer programs to consumer services of every possible item, and to membership of miscellaneous associations. *Rather than an oppressive "Big Brother," it is a myriad of well-wishing "little sisters," relating to each one of us on a personal basis because they know who we are, who have invaded all realms of life.* What computers do, indeed, is to make possible the gathering, processing, and using for specific purposes of a mass of individualized information, so that our name can be printed, and the offering personalized, or an offer mailed out, or beamed in, to millions of individuals. Or, in a telling illustration of new techno-logical logic, the V-chip, to be implanted in American TV sets in 1997, allows households to program censorship according to a system of codes that will also be implanted in the television signals emitted from the stations. So doing, it decentralizes surveillance rather than centralizing control.

David Lyon, in his insightful book on the matter, has insisted on the critical development of this extension of surveillance way beyond the boundaries of the state.[91] What he calls "the electronic eye" is indeed a surveillance "society," rather than a "surveillance state." This is, after all, the heart of Foucault's theory of micro-powers, although he confused many of his superficial readers by calling "state" what, in his own view, is in fact "the system;" that is, the network of sources of power in various domains of social life, including the power in the family. If, in the Weberian tradition, we restrict the concept of state to the set of institutions holding the legitimate monopoly of means of violence, and by nation-state the territorial delimitation of such a power,[92] it would seem that we are witnessing in fact the diffusion of the power of surveillance and of violence (symbolic or physical) into society at large.

This trend is even more apparent in the new relationship between state and media. Given the growing financial and legal independence

[91] Lyon (1994).
[92] Giddens (1985).

of the media, increased technological capacity puts into the hands of the media the ability to spy on the state, and to do so on behalf of society and/or of specific interest groups (see chapter 6). When, in 1991, a Spanish radio station recorded the conversation over cellular 'phones of two socialist officials, the broadcasting of their very critical remarks about the socialist Prime Minister triggered a political crisis. Or when Prince Charles and his friend indulged over the 'phone in postmodern elaborations on Tampax and related matters, the tabloid printing of these conversations shook the British Crown. To be sure, media revelations, or gossip, have always been a threat to the state, and a defense of citizens. But new technologies, and the new media system, have exponentially increased the vulnerability of the state to the media, thus to business, and to society at large. In historically relative terms, today's state is more surveilled than surveillant.

Furthermore, while the nation-state keeps the capacity for violence,[93] it is losing its monopoly because its main challengers are taking the form of, either, transnational networks of terrorism, or, communal groups resorting to suicidal violence. In the first case, the global character of terrorism (political, criminal, or both), and of their supplier networks in information, weapons, and finance, requires a systemic cooperation between nation-states' police, so that the operating unit is an increasingly transnational police force.[94] In the second case, when communal groups, or local gangs, renounce their membership of the nation-state, the state becomes increasingly vulnerable to violence rooted in the social structure of its society, as if states were to be permanently engaged in fighting a guerrilla war.[95] Thus the contradiction the state faces: if it does not use violence, it fades away as a state; if it uses it, on a quasi-permanent basis, there will go a substantial part of its resources and legitimacy, because it would imply an endless state of emergency. So, the state can only proceed with such a durable violence when and if the survival of the nation, or of the nation-state, is at stake. Because of the increasing reluctance of societies to support a lasting use of violence, except in extreme situations, the difficulty of the state to actually resort to violence on a scale large enough to be effective leads to its diminishing ability to do so frequently, and thus to the gradual loss of its privilege as holding the means of violence.

Thus, the capacity of surveillance is diffused in society, the monopoly of violence is challenged by transnational, non-state

---

[93]   Tilly (1995).
[94]   Fooner (1989).
[95]   Wieviorka (1988).

networks, and the ability to repress rebellion is eroded by endemic communalism and tribalism. While the nation-state still looks imposing in its shiny uniform, and people's bodies and souls still are routinely tortured around the world, information flows bypass, and sometimes overwhelm, the state; terrorist wars criss-cross national boundaries; and communal turfs exhaust the law and order patrol. The state still relies on violence and surveillance, but it does not hold their monopoly any longer, nor can it exercise them from its national enclosure.

The Crisis of the Nation-state and the Theory of the State

In his seminal article on democracy, the nation-state, and the global system, David Held summarizes his analysis by writing that

> the international order today is characterized by both the persistence of the sovereign state system and the development of plural authority structures. The objections to such a hybrid system are severe. It is open to question whether it offers any solutions to the fundamental problems of modern political thought which have been preoccupied by, among other things, the rationale and basis of order and toleration, of democracy and accountability, and of legitimate rule.[96]

Although he goes on to offer his own optimistic proposal for re-legitimizing the state in its postnational reincarnation, the powerful arguments against continuing state sovereignty that he puts forward in the preceding pages explain his hesitant concluding line: "There are good reasons for being optimistic about the results – and pessimistic."[97] In this context, I am not sure what "optimistic" and "pessimistic" mean. I have no particular sympathy for modern nation-states that have eagerly mobilized their people for reciprocal mass slaughter in the bloodiest century of human history – the twentieth century.[98] But this is a matter of opinion. *What really matters is that the new power system is characterized,* and I agree with David Held on this, *by the plurality of sources of authority (and, I would add, of power), the nation-state being just one of these sources.* This, in fact, seems to have been the historical rule, rather than the exception. As Spruyt argues, the modern nation-state had a number of "competitors" (city-states,

[96] Held (1991: 161).
[97] Held (1991: 167).
[98] Tilly (1995).

trading pacts, empires),[99] as well, I would add, as military and diplomatic alliances, which did not disappear, but coexisted with the nation-state throughout its development in the Modern Age. However, what seems to be emerging now, for the reasons presented in this chapter, is the de-centering of the nation-state within the realm of shared sovereignty that characterizes the current world's political scene. Hirst and Thompson, whose vigorous critique of simplistic views on globalization emphasizes the continuing relevance of nation-states, acknowledge, none the less, the state's new role:

> The emerging forms of governance of international markets and other economic processes involve the major national governments but in a new role: states come to function less as "sovereign" entities and more as components of an international "polity". The central functions of the nation-state will become those of providing legitimacy for and ensuring the accountability of supra-national and subnational governance mechanisms.[100]

Furthermore, in addition to its complex relationship to miscellaneous expressions of political power/representation, the nation-state is increasingly submitted to a more subtle, and more troubling, competition from sources of power that are undefined, and, sometimes, undefinable. These are networks of capital, production, communication, crime, international institutions, supranational military apparatuses, non-governmental organizations, transnational religions, and public opinion movements. And below the state, there are communities, tribes, localities, cults, and gangs. So, while nation-states do continue to exist, and they will continue to do so in the foreseeable future, they are, and they will increasingly be, *nodes of a broader network of power*. They will often be confronted by other flows of power in the network, which directly contradict the exercise of their authority, as it happens nowadays to central banks whenever they have the illusion of countering global markets' runs against a given currency. Or, for that matter, when nation-states, alone or together, decide to eradicate drug production, traffic, or consumption, a battle repeatedly lost over the past two decades everywhere – except in Singapore (with all the implications of this remark). Nation-states have lost their sovereignty because the very concept of sovereignty, since Bodin, implies that it is not possible to lose sovereignty "a little bit": this was precisely the traditional *casus belli*. Nation-states may retain decision-making capacity, but, having become part of a network

99   Spruyt (1994).
100   Hirst and Thompson (1996: 171).

of powers and counterpowers, they are powerless by themselves: they are dependent on a broader system of enacting authority and influence from multiple sources. This statement, which I believe to be consistent with the observations and elaborations presented in this chapter, has serious consequences for the theory and practice of the state.

The theory of the state has been dominated, for decades, by the debate between institutionalism, pluralism and instrumentalism in their different versions.[101] Institutionalists, in the Weberian tradition, have emphasized the autonomy of state institutions, following the inner logic of a historically given state once the winds of history planted its seeds in a territory that became its national basis. Pluralists explain the structure and evolution of the state, as the outcome of a variety of influences in the endless (re)formation of the state, according to the dynamics of a plural civil society, in a constant enacting of the constitutional process.

Instrumentalists, Marxists or historicists, see the state as the expression of social actors pursuing their interests and achieving domination, be it without challenge within the state ("the executive committee of the bourgeoisie"), or as the unstable result of struggles, alliances, and compromise. But, as Giddens, Guehenno, and Held argue, in all schools of thought, *the relationship between state and society, and thus the theory of the state, is considered in the context of the nation, and has the nation-state as its frame of reference.* What happens when, in Held's formulation, the "national community" is not any more the "relevant community" as such a frame of reference?[102] How can we think of non-national, diversified social interests represented in, or fighting for, the state? The whole world? But the unit relevant for capital flows is not the same as that for labor, for social movements, or for cultural identities. How to link up interests and values expressed, globally and locally, in a variable geometry, in the structure and policies of the nation-state? Thus, *from the point of view of theory* we must reconstruct the categories to understand power relationships without presupposing the necessary intersection between nation and the state, that is, separating identity from instrumentality. New power relationships, beyond the powerless nation-state, must be understood as the capacity to control global instrumental networks on the basis of specific identities, or, seen from the perspective of global networks, to subdue any identity in the fulfillment of transnational instrumental goals. The control of the nation-state, one way or the other, becomes just one means among others to assert power; that is the capacity to impose a

---

[101] Carnoy (1984).
[102] Held (1991: 142-3).

given will/interest/value, regardless of consensus. The theory of power, in this context, supersedes the theory of the state, as I shall elaborate in the Conclusion to this volume.

However, it does not follow that nation-states have become irrelevant, or that they will disappear. They will not, in most cases, at least for a long time. This is for paradoxical reasons that have to do more with communalism than with the state. Indeed, in a world of a-cultural, transnational global networks, societies tend, as proposed in the preceding chapters, to retrench themselves on the basis of identities, and to construct/reconstruct institutions as expressions of these identities. This is why we witness, at the same time, the crisis of the nation-state and the explosion of nationalisms.[103] The explicit goal of most, but not all, of these nationalisms is to build or rebuild a new nation-state, one based on identity, not just on historical heritage of territorial control. So doing, in many instances, nationalisms challenge, and ultimately bring into crisis, existing nation-states that were built on historic alliances, or on the total or partial negation of some of the identities that form their constituencies. Thus, contemporary nationalisms are, in fact, a major factor in prompting the crisis of nation-states as historically constituted, as illustrated by recent experiences in the Soviet Union, in Yugoslavia, and in Africa, and as may be the case in the future in Asia (India, Sri Lanka, Burma, Malaysia, Indonesia), and even (who knows?) in Europe (Spain, UK, Italy, Belgium). If and when these new, identity-based nationalisms reach the stage of statehood they will find the same limits of current nation-states *vis à vis* global flows of power. However, their construction will not be aimed at asserting sovereignty, but at resisting other states' sovereignty, while navigating the global system in an endless process of bargaining and adjustment. Some authors use the concept of "neo-medieval form of universal political order."[104] As with any "neo" characterization, I suspect it belies history. It is, however, an interesting image to convey the notion of autonomous, powerless states that remain none the less instruments of political initiative and sources of conditional authority.

Nation-states that remain strong in the middle of historical turbulence, such as Japan or South Korea, also do so on the basis of social homogeneity and cultural identity. Although even in such cases a growing contradiction is emerging between the interests of Japanese or Korean multinational corporations, now becoming truly global in order to survive cut-throat competition, and the territorial domain and political interests of Japanese or Korean states, thus undermining

---

[103] Cohen (1996).
[104] Bull (1977: 254), cited by Held (1991).

what constituted the historical basis of the successful, developmental state. [105]

Thus, communalism indeed constructs/maintains states in the newly globalized society, but, in the process, it weakens decisively the nation-state as constituted in the Modern Age, and maybe questions the very notion of the nation-state by capturing it into specific identities.[106]

Conclusion: the King of the Universe, Sun Tzu, and the Crisis of Democracy

So, whither the nation-state as far as historical practice is concerned? Answering this question, Martin Carnoy issues a resounding no.[107] He argues, and I concur with him, that national competitiveness is still a function of national policies, and the attractiveness of economies to foreign multinationals is a function of local economic conditions; that multinationals depend heavily on their home states for direct or indirect protection; and that national human–capital policies are essential for the productivity of economic units located in a national territory. Supporting this argument, Hirst and Thompson show that, if in addition to the relationship between multinational corporations and the state, we include the wide range of policies through which nation-states can use their regulatory powers to ease or block movements of capital, labor, information, and commodities, it is clear that, at this point in history, the fading away of the nation-state is a fallacy.[108]

However, in the 1990s, nation-states have been transformed from sovereign subjects into strategic actors, playing their interests, and the interests they are supposed to represent, in a global system of interaction, in a condition of systemically shared sovereignty. They marshall considerable influence, but they barely hold power by themselves, in isolation from supranational macro-forces and subnational micro-processes. Furthermore, when acting strategically in the international arena, they are submitted to tremendous internal stress. On the one hand, to foster productivity and competitiveness of their economies they must ally themselves closely with global economic interests, and abide by global rules favorable to capital flows, while their societies are being asked to wait patiently for the trickled down

[105] Johnson (1982); Castells (1992a).
[106] Guehenno (1993).
[107] Carnoy (1993: 88).
[108] Hirst and Thompson (1996).

benefits of corporate ingenuity. Also, to be good citizens of a multi-lateral world order, nation-states have to cooperate with each other, accept the pecking order of geopolitics, and contribute dutifully to subdue renegade nations and agents of potential disorder, regardless of the actual feelings of their usually parochial citizens. Yet, on the other hand, nation-states survive beyond historical inertia because of the defensive communalism of nations and people in their territories, hanging onto their last refuge not to be pulled away by the whirlwind of global flows. Thus, the more states emphasize communalism, the less effective they become as co-agents of a global system of shared power. The more they triumph in the planetary scene, in close part-nership with the agents of globalization, the less they represent their national constituencies. End of millennium politics, almost every-where in the world, is dominated by this fundamental contradiction.

Thus, it may well be that nation-states are reaching the status of Saint-Exupery's King of the Universe, fully in control of ordering the sun to rise every day. From the East. But, at the same time, while losing sovereignty, they emerge as major intervening players, in a purely strategic world, such as the one informing Sun Tzu's war treatise 2,500 years ago:

> It is the business of a general to be quiet and thus ensure secrecy; upright and just, and thus maintain order. He must be able to mystify his officers and men by false reports and appearances, and thus keep them in total ignorance. By altering his arrange-ments and changing his plans he keeps the enemy without definite knowledge. By shifting his camp and taking circuitous routes, he prevents the enemy from anticipating his purpose. At the critical moment the leader of an army acts like one who has climbed up a height and then kicks away the ladder behind him.[109]

This is how powerless states can still be victorious, and so increase their influence, on the condition of "kicking away" the ladder of their nations, thus ushering in the crisis of democracy.

---

[109] Sun Tzu (c.505–496 BC, 1988: 131–3).

— 6 —

Informational Politics and the Crisis of Democracy

Introduction: the Politics of Society

Power used to be in the hands of princes, oligarchies, and ruling elites; it was defined as the capacity to impose one's will on others, modifying their behavior. This image of power does not fit with our reality any longer. Power is everywhere and nowhere: it is in mass production, in financial flows, in lifestyles, in the hospital, in the school, in television, in images, in messages, in technologies . . . Since the world of objects escapes to our will, our identity is no longer defined by what we do but by what we are, thus making our societies somewhat closer to the experience of so-called traditional societies, searching for balance rather than for progress. Such is the central question to which political thought and action must respond: how to restore a link between the excessively open space of the economy, and the excessively closed, and fragmented world of cultures? . . . The fundamental matter is not seizing power, but to recreate society, to invent politics anew, to avoid the blind conflict between open markets and closed communities, to overcome the breaking down of societies where the distance increases between the included and the excluded, those in and those out.
Alain Touraine, Lettre à Lionel,
pp. 36–8, 42; my translation

The blurring of boundaries of the nation-state confuses the definition of citizenship. The absence of a clear situs of power dilutes social control and diffuses political challenges. The rise of communalism, in its different forms, weakens the principle of political sharing on which democratic politics is based. The growing inability of the state to control capital flows and ensure social security diminishes its relevance for the average citizen. The emphasis on local institutions of governance increases the distance between mechanisms of political control and management of global problems. The voiding of the social contract between capital, labor, and the state, sends everybody home to fight for their individual interests, counting exclusively on their own forces. As Guehenno writes:

> Liberal democracy was based on two postulates, currently called into question: the existence of a political sphere, site of social consensus and general interest; and the existence of actors provided with their own energy, who exercised their rights, and manifested their powers, even before society constituted them as autonomous subjects. Nowadays, instead of autonomous subjects, there are only ephemeral situations, which serve as support to provisional alliances supported by capacities mobilized for each occasion. Instead of a political space, site of collective solidarity, they are just dominant perceptions, as ephemeral as the interests that manipulate them. There is simultaneous atomization and homogenization. A society that is endlessly fragmented, without memory and without solidarity, a society that recovers its unity only in the succession of images that the media return to it every week. It is a society without citizens, and ultimately, a non-society. This crisis is not – as Europeans would like in the hope of escaping from it – the crisis of a particular model, the American model. The United States certainly pushes to the extreme the logic of confrontation of interests that dissolves the idea of a common interest; and the management of collective perceptions reaches in America a degree of sophistication without parallel in Europe. Yet, cases at the limit help us to understand average situations, and the American crisis reveals our future.[1]

The transformation of politics, and of democratic processes, in the network society is even deeper than presented in these analyses. Because, to the processes cited above, I shall add, as a major factor inducing this transformation, the direct consequences of new information technologies on the political debate and power-seeking strategies. This technological dimension interacts with the broader trends characteristic of the network society, and with the communal reactions to the dominant processes emerging from this social structure. But it adds a powerful twist to this transformation, inducing what I call *informational politics*. Thus, while Bobbio is correct in pinpointing the persistent differences between political right and political left throughout the world (basically because of their sharply divergent concern with social equality),[2] right, left, and center must process

---

[1] Guehenno (1993: 46); my translation.
[2] Bobbio (1994).

their projects and strategies through a similar technological medium if they wish to reach society, so securing the support of enough citizens to win access to the state. I contend that this technological sharing induces new rules of the game that, in the context of the social, cultural, and political transformations presented in this book, dramatically affect the substance of politics. The key point is that electronic media (including not only television and radio, but all forms of communication, such as newspapers and the Internet) have become the privileged space of politics. Not that all politics can be reduced to images, sounds, or symbolic manipulation. But, without it, there is no chance of winning or exercising power. Thus, everybody ends up playing the same game, although not in the same way or with the same purpose.

For the sake of clarity, let me warn the reader, from the outset of this analysis, against two simplistic, erroneous versions of the thesis according to which electronic media dominate politics. On the one hand, it is sometimes argued that the media impose their political choices on public opinion. This is not so, because, as I will elaborate below, the media are extremely diverse. Their linkages to politics and ideology are highly complex, and indirect, albeit with obvious exceptions, whose frequency depends on countries, periods, and specific media. In fact, in many cases, media campaigns may support the public against the political establishment, as was the case in America during the Watergate crisis, or in 1990s Italy, when most of the media supported the judicial anti-corruption drive against both traditional political parties, and against Berlusconi, in spite of Berlusconi's ownership of the three private national television channels. On the other hand, public opinion is often considered to be a passive recipient of messages, easily open to manipulation. Again, this is belied by the empirical record. As I argued in volume I, chapter 5, there is a two-way process of interaction between the media and their audience concerning the actual impact of messages, which are twisted, appropriated, and occasionally subverted by the audience. In the American context, the analysis by Page and Shapiro of citizens' attitudes toward policy issues in a long-term perspective shows the independence and commonsense of collective public opinion in most circumstances.[3] Overall, the media are rooted in society, and their interaction with the political process is highly undetermined, depending on context, strategies of political actors, and specific interaction between an array of social, cultural, and political features.

By pinpointing the critical role of electronic media in contemporary politics I am saying something different. I am saying that, because

---

[3]   Page and Shapiro (1992).

of the convergent effects of the crisis of traditional political systems and of the dramatically increased pervasiveness of the new media, political communication and information are essentially captured in the space of the media. Outside the media sphere there is only political marginality. What happens in this media-dominated political space is not determined by the media: it is an open social and political process. But the logic, and organization, of electronic media frame and structure politics. I shall argue, on the basis of some evidence, and with the help of a number of cross-cultural examples, that this framing of politics by their capture in the space of the media (a trend characteristic of the Information Age) impacts not only elections, but political organization, decision-making, and governance, ultimately modifying the nature of the relationship between state and society. And because current political systems are still based in organizational forms and political strategies of the industrial era, they have become politically obsolete, and their autonomy is being denied by the flows of information on which they depend. This is a fundamental source of the crisis of democracy in the Information Age.

To explore its contours, I will use data and examples from various countries. The United States is the democracy that first reached this technological stage, in a very open, unstructured political system, and thus it better manifests the broader trend. However, I certainly reject the idea that the "American model" will have to be followed by other countries in the world. Nothing is more specifically rooted in history than political institutions and political actors. Yet, in the same way that democratic habits and procedures, originated in England, America, and France, diffused around the world in the past two centuries, I would argue that informational politics, as it is practiced in the United States (for example, the dominance of television, computerized political marketing, instant polling as an instrument of political navigation, character assassination as political strategy and so on) is a good indicator of the times to come, with all due cultural/institutional translations. To broaden the scope of analysis, I will be discussing, as well, examples of recent political processes in the UK, Russia, Spain, Italy, Japan, and, in an effort to reach out to new democracies in less-developed countries, I shall focus on the case of Bolivia. On the basis of these observations, I shall try to link up processes of social, institutional and technological transformation at the roots of the crisis of democracy in the network society. In conclusion, I shall explore the potential for new forms of "informational democracy."

Media as the Space of Politics in the Information Age

Politics and the media: the citizens' connection

I shall state my argument before elaborating it empirically. In the context of democratic politics, access to state institutions depends on the ability to mobilize a majority of votes from citizens. In contemporary societies people receive their information, and form their political opinion, essentially through the media, and fundamentally from television (tables 6.1 and 6.2). Furthermore, at least in the United States, television is the most credible source of news, and its credibility has increased over time (figure 6.1). Thus, to act on people's minds, and wills, conflicting political options, embodied in parties and candidates, use the media as their fundamental vehicle of communication, influence, and persuasion. So doing, as long as the

Table 6.1 Sources of news in the US, 1959–92 (%)

Date	Tele-vision	News-papers	Radio	Magazines	People
December 1959	51	57	34	8	4
November 1961	52	57	34	9	5
November 1963	55	53	29	6	4
November 1964	58	56	26	8	5
January 1967	64	55	28	7	4
November 1968	59	49	25	7	5
January 1971	60	48	23	5	4
November 1972	64	50	21	6	4
November 1974	65	47	21	4	4
November 1976	64	49	19	7	5
December 1978	67	49	20	5	5
November 1980	64	44	18	5	4
December 1982	65	44	18	6	4
December 1984	64	40	14	4	4
December 1986	66	36	14	4	4
November 1988	65	42	14	4	5
December 1990	69	43	15	3	7
February 1991	81	35	14	4	6
November 1992	69	43	16	4	6

Note: The question asked was: "Where do you usually get most of your news about what's going on in the world today – from the newspapers, or radio, or television, or magazines, or talking to people or where?" (multiple responses permitted).
Source: Roper Organization Surveys for the Television Information Service (various years)

Table 6.2   Sources of political information of residents of
Cochabamba, Bolivia, 1996

Source of information	% declaring main source of information	% expressing preference for source
Newspapers	32.0	8.7
Radio	43.3	15.7
Television	51.7	46.0
Other	4.7	–

Source: Survey of Information Sources of Cochabamba Residents, Centro de
Estudios de la Realidad Economica y Social, Cochabamba, 1996

media are relatively autonomous from political power, political actors
have to abide by the rules, technology, and interests of the media. The
media frame politics. And because governance is dependent on re-
election, or election to a higher office, governance itself becomes
dependent on the daily assessment of the potential impact of government decisions on public opinion, as measured by opinion polls, focus
groups, and image analyses. Furthermore, in a world increasingly saturated by information, the most effective messages are the most simple,
and the most ambivalent, so that they leave room for people's own
projections. Images fit best into this characterization. Audiovisual
media are the primary feeders of people's minds, as they relate to
public affairs.

But who are the media? What is the source of their political
autonomy? And how do they frame politics? In democratic societies,
mainstream media are, essentially, business groups, increasingly
concentrated and globally interconnected, although they are, at the
same time, highly diversified and geared toward segmented markets
(see chapter 5, and volume I, chapter 5). Government-owned television and radio have come close to the behavior of private media
groups in the past decade, in order to be able to survive global competition, so becoming equally dependent on audience ratings.[4]
Audience ratings are essential because the main source of income in
the media business is advertising.[5] Performance in audience ratings
requires an appealing medium, and, in the case of news, credibility.
Without credibility, news is worthless, either in terms of money or
power. Credibility requires relative distance *vis à vis* specific political
options, within the parameters of mainstream political and moral

[4]   Perez-Tabernero et al. (1993).
[5]   MacDonald (1990).

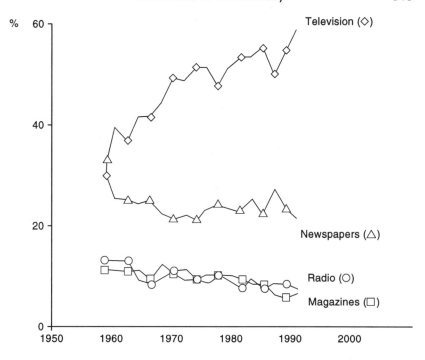

Figure 6.1 Credibility of news source in US, 1959–91
Source: Roper Organization, *America's Watching: Public Attitudes
toward Television* (New York, 1991)

values. Furthermore, only from a credible position of independence
can this independence be parlayed occasionally into an open, opportunistic political endorsement, or into a hidden financial deal in
exchange for support by diffusing or suppressing information. This
autonomy of the media, rooted in their business interests, also fits well
with the ideology of the profession, and with the legitimacy and self-
respect of journalists. They report, do not take sides. Information is
paramount, news analysis must be documented, opinion must be
regulated, and detachment is the rule. This double bind of independence, from corporations and from professionals, is reinforced by the
fact that the media world is submitted to relentless competition, even
if it is increasingly oligopolistic competition. Any breach in credibility
for a given TV network or newspaper, and the competition will take
audience (market) share away. Thus, on the one hand, the media
must be close to politics and government, close enough to access
information, to benefit from regulation, and, in many countries, to
receive considerable subsidies. On the other hand, they must be

neutral enough and distant enough to maintain their credibility, so being the intermediaries between citizens and parties in the production and consumption of information flows and images, at the roots of public opinion formation, voting, and political decision-making.

Once politics is captured in the space of the media, political actors themselves close the field of media politics by organizing political action primarily around the media: for instance, by leaking information to advance a given personal or political agenda. This leads, inevitably, to counter-leaks, so making the media the battleground in which political forces and personalities, as well as pressure groups, try to undermine each other, to collect the benefits in opinion polls, in the polling booths, in parliamentary votes, and in government decisions.

Naturally, media politics does not preclude other forms of political activity. Grassroots campaigns have proved their vitality in recent years, as shown by the Christian Coalition in the United States, the Green party in Germany, or the Communist party in Russia. Mass gatherings and street demonstrations are still essential rituals in Spanish, French, Italian, or Brazilian political campaigns. And candidates must still travel, appear, shake hands, go to meetings, kiss children (but carefully), address students, policemen, and every possible ethnic group (but not in France). Yet, with the exception of fundraising activities, the main target of these various forms of person-to-person politics is to stage the persona, or the message, in the media, be it prime-time TV news, a radio talk show, or a featured article in an influential newspaper. In Spanish political campaigns (and I suppose in other countries as well), leading candidates speaking at a public meeting are warned by a red light in their micro when there is live TV coverage (for one or two minutes), so that he/she switches automatically to a pre-programmed sound bite on a topic of choice, regardless of what he/she was saying to the live audience. In American elections, town meetings, school children's gatherings, stops along a candidate's bus, train, or plane route, are arranged in accordance with times and sites of potential media coverage. Cheerers and jeerers are on stage to provide the chance for interesting footage.

However, let me repeat again: to say that the media are the space of politics does not mean that television dictates what people decide, or that the ability to spend money in TV advertising or to manipulate images is, by itself, an overwhelming factor. All countries, and particularly the United States, are full of examples in which a television advertising barrage was not enough to elect a candidate, or a mediocre media performance did not preclude a candidate from winning (although examples also abound of the enhancing impact of TV presence in launching, and sustaining, a politician; for example, Ronald Reagan or Ross Perot in the United States, Felipe Gonzalez in Spain, Berlusconi in Italy, Jirinovsky in Russia in 1993, Aoshima in Tokyo in 1995). In 1990s' Brazil, Collor de Mello was elected president out of nowhere because of his masterful television performance, but people took to the streets to force his resignation once it became clear that he was a crook pillaging the state. Three years later, Fernando Henrique Cardoso, not unskillful on TV, but obviously disliking media gimmicks, was overwhelmingly elected president because, as Finance Minister, he was able to subdue hyperinflation for the first time in decades, although the support of *O Globo Televisao* for his candidacy did help. Neither television nor other media determine political outcomes by themselves, precisely because media politics is a contradictory realm, where different actors and strategies are played out, with diverse skills, and with various outcomes, sometimes resulting in unexpected consequences. *Mediacracy* is not contradictory to democracy because it is as plural and competitive as the political system is. That is, not much. Furthermore, if we consider the previous system, of a party-dominated democracy, where party organizations, largely insulated from the majority of citizens, entirely decided political programs and candidates, it is arguable which system provides for broader citizen input, at least once we passed the mythical times of communal town meetings.

Yet, *the critical matter is that, without an active presence in the media, political proposals or candidates do not stand a chance of gathering broad support.* Media politics is not all politics, but all politics must go through the media to affect decision-making. So doing, *politics is fundamentally framed, in its substance, organization, process, and leadership, by the inherent logic of the media system, particularly by the new electronic media.* As for how exactly this framing occurs it will help to refer to the actual evolution of media politics, starting with the American experience of the past three decades.

Show politics and political marketing: the American model

The transformation of American politics in the last decades of the twentieth century resulted from three interconnected processes: (a) the decline of political parties, and of their role in selecting candidates; (b) the emergence of a complex media system, anchored in television, but with an increasing diversity of flexible media, electronically interconnected; and (c) the development of political marketing, with constant opinion polling, feedback systems between polling and politicking, media spinning, computerized direct mailing and 'phone banks, and real time adjustments of candidates and issues to the format that can win.[6]

Although the transformation of the American political system has deep roots in social and cultural trends, the most direct manifestation of these transformations were the electoral reforms by the McGovern–Frazer Committee in response to the 1968 Democratic National Convention where the party apparatus chose Humphrey as a presidential candidate over the more popular Eugene McCarthy. Under the new system delegates to the convention were elected, in their vast majority, through direct primaries among presidential contenders.[7] Thus, while in the 1950s 40 percent of the delegates were chosen by this method, in the 1990s the proportion reached 80 percent.[8] In addition, a series of campaign finance reforms have forced candidates to rely more on their fundraising skills, and direct contacts with society, and much less on party support. Interest groups and citizens at large have pushed party organizations to the backstage of American politics.[9] Both trends have extraordinarily reinforced the role of the media: they have become the privileged intermediaries between candidates and the public, decisively influencing presidential primaries, as well as congressional and governatorial elections. And, because media advertising and media-oriented campaigning are very expensive, candidates have to rely on the support of private donors and political action committees external to the party system.[10]

The political role of the media has evolved considerably in the last three decades, both technologically and organizationally. Experts consider that the turning point in the relationship between media, polls, and politics was John Kennedy's campaign in 1960.[11] Not only did Kennedy base for the first time his campaign on polling and television strategy, but his victory was largely credited to his televised debate with Nixon (the first of the genre), which he dominated, while the radio audience of the same debate selected Nixon as the winner.[12] Subsequently, television became the agenda-setting device of American politics. While influential newspapers, such as *The New York Times* or *The Washington Post* are critical sources of investigative reporting, and of opinion trends, only events that are played out in

---

[6] Abramson et al. (1988); Patterson (1993); Roberts and McCombs (1994); Balz and Brownstein (1996).

[7] Patterson (1993: 30-3).

[8] Ansolabehere et al. (1993: 75).

[9] Magleby and Nelson (1990).

[10] Garber (1984, 1996); Gunlicks (1993).

[11] Jacobs and Shapiro (1995).

[12] Ansolabehere et al. (1993: 73).

television reach an audience large enough to set, or reverse, a trend in public opinion. Thus, television, newspapers, and radio work as a system, with newspapers often reporting an event, and elaborating on it, television digesting it and diffusing it to a broad audience, and radio talk shows providing the opportunity for citizen interaction, and for customized, partisan debate on the issues raised by television.[13] This increasingly central political role of television has induced two major features. On the one hand, political spending on television has skyrocketed: in the early 1960s, about 9 percent of the budgets of national political campaigns were spent on TV advertising, while in the 1990s, the proportion was about 25 percent of much larger budgets; in 1990, an estimated $203 million went on airtime political advertising;[14] and in 1994, $350 million were spent on television political advertising.[15] The figure for the 1996 elections may have been over $800 million. On the other hand, political spinning by advisors to political candidates has become an essential factor in political campaigning, as well as in obtaining support, or opposition, for government decisions. What really matters is not so much the event that is originally reported but the debate around it, how it is debated, by whom it is debated, and for how long it is debated. Victory, not explanation or clarification, becomes the critical matter. For instance, in 1993–94, after months of acrimonious debate on Clinton's health plan reform proposal, which occupied extensive media attention, polls indicated that the large majority of Americans were confused and unsure about the content of the proposal, and about the substance of criticisms aimed at the plan. Never mind. What the barrage of media controversy, fed by insurance companies, medical associations, and the pharmaceutical industry, succeeded in doing was to kill the proposal even before it came before Congress for a vote, let alone was discussed by the citizenry.[16] Media have become the main political arena.

Technology has transformed the political role of the media, not only by its effects on the media themselves, but by linking up the media system in real time with political marketing.[17] Starting in the late 1960s, the introduction of computers in the tabulation of polls led to the emergence of "strategic polling," testing different political strategies on targeted groups of potential voters, so as to modify the strategy, the form, and even the substance of the message

[13]   Friedland (1996).
[14]   Ansolabehere et al. (1993: 89).
[15]   Freeman (1994).
[16]   Fallows (1996).
[17]   D. West (1993).

as the campaign develops.[18] In the next two decades pollsters such as Patrick Caddell, Peter Hart, and Robert Teeter, decisively influenced campaign strategy, and became key intermediaries between candidates, citizens, and the media. Together with image makers and political advertisers, they built campaigns, platforms, issues and personas by feeding back opinion trends into media reports and vice versa.[19] As technology accelerated media reporting, and increased the speed and flexibility of information systems, feedback effects, and spins, became daily activities, so that in most high political offices, starting with the White House, communication strategists meet every day early in the morning to monitor the pulse of the nation, being ready to intervene in real time, even changing messages and schedules between morning and afternoon, depending on reporting in the main sources (CNN, TV networks, leading morning newspapers).[20] The fact that the media themselves are able to break the news any time, through uninterrupted reporting, means that communication warriors must be constantly on the alert, actually codifying and translating any political decision into the language of media politics, and measuring effects by polls and focus groups. Pollsters and image makers have become decisive political actors, able to make, and unmake, presidents, senators, congressmen, and governors, by blending information technology, mediology, political savvy, and cocky wizardry. And when they are mistaken, in their polls for instance, they still are influential, because their mistakes change political trends, as in the 1996 New Hampshire Republican primary, in which polls' errors undermined Forbes' performance by measuring his votes against mistaken upward predictions of polls in previous days.[21]

As the media diversified and decentralized their scope in the 1990s, their grasp on political attitudes and behavior became ever more comprehensive.[22] Local cable television and radio talk shows customized audiences and allowed politicians to better target their message, while interest groups and ideological constituencies were more able to forward their arguments without the cautious filter of mainstream media. VCRs became essential tools in distributing packaged video messages in town meetings and private homes through direct mailing. Around the clock coverage by C-Span and CNN allowed for instant delivery of politically packaged news and information. In one instance, Republican leader Newt Gingrich was able

[18]   Moore (1992: 128–9).
[19]   Mayer (1994).
[20]   Fallows (1996).
[21]   Mundy (1996).
[22]   Garber (1996); Hacker (1996).

to televise (by C-Span) a passionate, anti-liberal speech on the Congress floor, with no fear of stirring hostile reactions since, beyond the cameras' reach, the room was empty. Narrowcasting of messages to certain areas or social groups, through local stations, are fragmenting national politics, and undermining the influence of TV networks, yet embracing an even greater share of political expressions in the universe of electronic media. Additionally, the Internet has become in the mid-1990s the vehicle for campaign propaganda, controlled debate forums, and linking up with supporters.[23] Often, television programs, or ads, refer to an Internet address where information or development of arguments can be found, while computer-mediated communication picks up on media events, or on televised political advertising, to set up an electronic hook for concerned citizens.

By incorporating politics into their electronic space, the media decisively frame process, messages, and outcomes, regardless of the actual purpose or effectiveness of specific messages. Not that the medium is the message, because political options do differ, and the differences matter. But by entering the media space, political projects, and politicians, are shaped in particular ways.[24] In which ways?

To understand the framing of politics by the logic of the media, we must refer to *the overarching principles governing news media: the race for audience ratings, in competition with entertainment; the necessary detachment from politics, to induce credibility*. These translate into traditional assumptions in news coverage, as identified by Gitlin: "News concern the event, not the underlying condition; the person, not the group; conflict, not consensus; the fact that 'advances the story', not the one that explains it."[25] Only "bad news," relating to conflict, drama, unlawful deals, or objectionable behavior, is interesting news. Since news is increasingly framed to parallel (and compete with) entertainment shows, or sports events, so is its logic. It requires drama, suspense, conflict, rivalries, greed, deception, winners and losers, and, if possible, sex and violence. Following the pace, and language, of sports casting, "horse race politics" is reported as an endless game of ambitions, maneuvers, strategies and counter-strategies, with the help of insider confidences and constant opinion polling from the media themselves. The media provide decreasing attention to what politicians have to say: the average soundbite shrank from 42 seconds in 1968 to less than 10 in 1992.[26] The media's detached attitude turns

[23] Klinenberg and Perrin (1996).
[24] Patterson (1993); Balz and Brownstein (1996); Fallows (1996).
[25] Gitlin (1980: 28).
[26] Patterson (1993: 74).

into cynicism when literally everything is interpreted as a pure strategic game. News reporting provide the basis for these analyses, but they are considerably reinforced by pundit shows (such as CNN's *Crossfire*), which are built around sharply opposing, impolite, vociferous commentators, who of course, smile and shake hands at the end, thus underscoring that everything is a show. On the other hand, as James Fallows argues, the fast-paced, punchy, summary assessments of politics by increasingly popular television pundits directly impact the coverage of events in the TV news, and in newspapers.[27] In other words, media statements about politics become political events by themselves, with weekly announcements of winners and losers in the political race. As Sandra Moog writes:

> News stories are tending to devolve into mere discussions of public reactions to recent news coverage. Who are the winners and the losers, whose popularity ratings have crept up and whose have dropped, as a result of political events of the last month, last week, or last day. Frequent public opinion polling by news agencies makes this kind of hyper-reflexivity possible, by providing supposedly objective grounding for journalists' speculations about the impacts of political actions and the journalistic reactions to those actions, on the public's assessment of different politicians.[28]

An additional, and powerful, framing of political news reporting is the personalization of events.[29] Politicians, not politics, are the actors of the drama. And because they may change their programmatic proposals, while navigating the political waters, what remains in the minds of most people is personal motivation, and personal images, as the source of politics. Thus, questions of character come to the forefront of the political agenda, as the messenger becomes the message.

The framing of political news expands into the framing of politics itself, as strategists play in and with the media to influence voters. Thus, because only bad news is news, political advertising concentrates on negative messages, aimed at destroying the opponent's proposals, while advancing one's own program in very general terms. Indeed, experiments show that negative messages are much more likely to be retained, and to influence political opinion.[30] Furthermore, because politics is personalized in a world of image

[27]   Fallows (1996).
[28]   Moog (1996: 20).
[29]   Ansolabehere et al. (1993); Fallows (1996).
[30]   Ansolabehere and Iyengar (1995).

making and soap operas, character assassination becomes the most potent weapon.[31] Political projects, government proposals, and political careers can be undermined or even destroyed with the revelation of improper behavior (Nixon's Watergate inaugurated the new era); with the exposure of private life departing from strict moral standards, and of the cover-up of the information (Gary Hart); or with the accumulation of various accusations, rumors, insinuations, relayed one after another in the media, as soon as the impact of one allegation starts fading away (Bill and Hillary Clinton?). In some cases, unproven allegations lead to dramatic personal consequences, such as the suicide of the targeted politician (for example, French Socialist Minister of Finance Pierre Beregovoy in 1993). Therefore, the monitoring of personal attacks on a daily basis, and counter-attacking, or threatening to, with similar allegations, becomes a fundamental part of political life. Indeed, in the 1992 presidential campaign Clinton's advisers forced Republicans to downplay their focus on Clinton's extramarital affair by threatening to elaborate on Bush's alleged involvement with a former assistant at the White House: they had found another Jennifer.[32] Communication strategists and spokepersons are at the center of informational politics.

The increasing restriction of media exposure to the content of political proposals (except in segmented media away from a mass audience; for example, public television or newspapers' lengthy special reports) leads to an extreme simplification of political messages. Complex political platforms are scrutinized to select a few key issues that will be highlighted, for a broad audience, in dichotomous terms: pro-life or pro-choice; gay rights or gay-bashing; social security and budget deficit versus balanced budget and dismantling of Medicaid. Referendum politics mimics television game shows, with the electoral buzzer announcing winners and losers, and pre-electoral bells (polls) sounding warnings. Images, coded messages, and horse-race politics between heroes and villains (they switch roles periodically), in a world of faked passions, hidden ambitions, and back-stabbing: such is American politics as framed in and by the electronic media, thus transformed into political real virtuality, determining access to the state. Could this "American model" be the forebear of a broader political trend, characterizing the Information Age?

[31]   Garramone et al. (1990); Fallows (1996).
[32]   Swan (1992).

Is European politics being "Americanized"?

No and yes. No, because European political systems rely much more extensively on political parties, with a long, established tradition, and considerable roots in their specific history, culture, and society. No, because national cultures matter, and what is admissible in America would be inadmissible in most of Europe, and would actually backfire on the would-be aggressor: for instance, it was a known fact in French political circles that late President Mitterrand had a long-lasting, extramarital relationship, from which he had a daughter. It was never used against him, in spite of his many enemies, and, if it had been used, most citizens would have found it disgraceful to interfere with the privacy of the president. (UK media occupy an intermediate position between America and most of Europe concerning respect for political leaders' private lives.) Also, until the late 1980s, most of European television was controlled by government, so that political access to television was regulated, and paid advertising is still forbidden. Even with the liberalization and privatization of television, private networks (for example Britain's ITV, or Spain's Antena-3 TV) follow a self-regulating pattern of political balance to preserve their credibility. Thus, there are indeed substantial differences both in the media and in their relationship to political systems in America and in Europe.[33]

On the other hand, while candidates and programs are selected and decided by parties, the media have become as important in Europe as in America in deciding the outcome of political bids.[34] The media (and particularly television) are the fundamental source of political information and opinion for people, and the main attributes of informational politics, as identified in America, characterize European politics as well: simplification of messages, professional advertising and polling as political tools, personalization of options, negativism as a predominant strategy, leaking of damaging information as a political weapon, image-making and spin control as essential mechanisms in seizing power, and in keeping it. Let us briefly review some comparative evidence.

In the UK, television was the main source of political news for 58 percent of people in the 1980s: it increased to 80 percent in the 1990s,[35] with newspapers being the main source for the other 20 percent. However, paid TV advertising is illegal in Britain, and parties are given free broadcasts both during campaign times, and out of them. Yet, deregulation, privatization, and multiplication of sources

[33]   Siune and Truetzschler (1992); Kaid and Holtz-Bacha (1995).
[34]   Guehenno (1993); Kaid and Holz-Bacha (1995).
[35]   Moog (1996).

of televised information have driven audiences away from formal political advertising, and toward political reporting.[36] Commentary on parties' advertising in regular programs becomes more influential than advertising itself. For instance, in 1992, the Labour party broadcast a spot about Jennifer, a young girl who had to wait a year for an ear operation because of the crisis in the health system. When her identity (to be kept anonymous) was revealed, the real issue became the inability of Labour to keep confidential information, thus undermining its ability to be trusted in government.[37] Negative advertising, particularly from the Tories, became a focus of the 1992 campaign, and played a role in the Conservative victory.[38] Reliance on instant polling, targeted mailing, use of professional advertising and public relation firms, events and speeches oriented toward image-making and soundbites, slick professional advertisements using actors and photo montages, focus on image rather than on policy, are in the 1990s the staple of British politics, as much as they are in America.[39] Personalization of politics has a long tradition in Britain, with leaders as forceful as Winston Churchill, Harold Wilson, or Margaret Thatcher. However, the new wave of personalization does not relate to historic, charismatic leaders, but to anyone applying for the Prime Minister's job. Thus, in 1987, Labour focused its campaign on a "young and glamorous" couple, Neil and Glenys Kinnock, and ran as its main Party Election Broadcast (PEB), a televised biography titled *Kinnock*, produced by Hugh Hudson, the director of *Chariots of Fire*.[40] In 1992, two out of five Conservative PEBs focused on John Major (*Major – The Journey*, produced by Schlesinger, the director of *Midnight Cowboy*, depicting Major's rise from working-class Brixton).[41] Personalization leads to character assassination as political strategy, and such was the case as well in recent British politics: in the 1992 campaign, Kinnock was attacked in the Tory tabloid press (with the stories then being picked up by television news), with attacks ranging from alleged Mafia connections to his private life (the so-called "Boyo affair"). Paddy Ashdown, the Liberal Democrat leader, was publicly attacked with regard to his sex life. And while Axford et al. suggest that after the 1992 election, British media appeared ready to restrain themselves in the use of "dirty tricks," this new-found discipline does not seem to have spared the Royal Family.[42] Indeed, I feel safe in

[36]   Berry (1992).
[37]   Scammell and Semetko (1995).
[38]   Berry (1992); Scammel and Semetko (1995).
[39]   Axford et al. (1992); Philo (1993); Franklin (1994).
[40]   Philo (1993: 411).
[41]   Scammell and Semetko (1995: 35).
[42]   Axford et al. (1992).

forecasting, writing in 1996, that the next British general election, marked by the likelihood of a Labour victory, will be characterized by an explosion of "character assassination" attempts aimed at Tony Blair's emergent leadership.

The advent of Russian democracy meant also the introduction of American-style, television-oriented political campaigns since the parliamentary elections of December 1993.[43] In the decisive 1996 Russian presidential elections, Yeltsin was able to regain control of the electorate, in danger of turning to Zyuganov out of desperation, in the last weeks of the campaign, by launching a media barrage, and by using, for the first time in Russia, computerized direct mailing, targeted polling, and segmented propaganda. Yeltsin's campaign combined old and new strategies of media use, but, in both approaches, television was the focus. On the one hand, government and private television channels aligned themselves with Yeltsin, and used news and programming as vehicles of anti-Communist propa-ganda, including the broadcasting of several films on the horrors of Stalinism in the week before the vote. On the other hand, Yeltsin's political advertising was carefully designed. A political consulting company, "Niccolò M" (M for Machiavelli) played a major role in designing a media strategy in which Yeltsin would appear on regular television news while TV political advertising would focus on real people (I know one of them) who would explain their support for Yeltsin. The spots ended with the words "I believe, I love, I hope," followed by Yeltsin's signature, his only presence in the advertisement. Yekaterina Yegorova, director of "Niccolò M," understood that, in her own words: "The idea behind his absence is that Yeltsin, as president, appears so often on the screen [in the regular news] that if he were on commercials as well, people would get sick of him."[44] Thus, "absent personalization," by combining different forms of media messages, becomes a new, subtle strategy in a world saturated by audiovisual propaganda. Some California Republican consultants also played an advisory role on political technology in the Yeltsin campaign (albeit to a much lesser extent than they claimed), as well as a variety of media and political advisors, propelling Russia into informational politics even before it had time to become an information society. It worked: outfinanced, outpowered, and outsmarted, the Communists relied on large-scale grassroots organizing, too primitive a medium to counter the alliance of television, radio, and major newspapers that rallied around Yeltsin. Although other factors played a role in the Russian election (rejection of Communism, fear of disorder, electoral dema-

[43]   Hughes (1994).
[44]   *Moscow Times* (1996: 1).

goguery, skillful last-minute presidential decisions, particularly about Chech'nya, the incorporation of Lebed in the Yeltsin administration before the second round of the election), the old and new system of politics measured it up, and the result was a one-sided Yeltsin victory, after badly trailing in the polls four months earlier.

Spain's young democracy also learned quickly the new trades of informational politics.[45] In the 1982 general election, the skillful use of media and personalization, around the figure of an extraordinary leader, Felipe Gonzalez, led the socialists (PSOE) to an unprecedented electoral landslide. Subsequently, in 1986 and 1989, Gonzalez's Socialists were twice re-elected with an absolute majority, and even won in 1985 a national referendum to join NATO, in the most difficult conditions. In addition to Socialist policy's own merits, three major factors contributed to overwhelming political domination by the Socialist party in the 1980s: the charismatic personality of Felipe Gonzalez, and his powerful presence in the media, particularly in television, whether in face-to-face debates, journalists' interviews, or televised political events; the technological sophistication of Socialist political strategists, which, for the first time in Spain, used focused groups, constant polling, image analysis/design, and targeting of issues in time and space, in a coherent, sustained strategy of political propaganda that did not stop after election day; and the government monopoly on television, giving a clear edge to the government, until relentless criticism by the opposition on television coverage, as well as Gonzalez's democratic convictions, led to the liberalization and partial privatization of television in the 1990s. On the other hand, it was the losing of the battle in the media in the 1990s that first eroded the Socialist government in Spain in 1993, and later brought a center-right government into power in 1996. I will elaborate, in the following section, on scandal politics and the politics of corruption as an essential strategy of informational politics, again using, among other cases, this most revealing contemporary Spanish example. But it is important to underline, while discussing the possible extrapolation of American-style politics to Europe, that contemporary Spain had nothing to learn from America concerning techniques of media politicking, character assassination, and feedback loops between polling, broadcasting, and play acting.

Although in a less dramatic manner (after all, Spain is a high-drama country), politics in most European democracies has come to be dominated by similar processes. Thus, observers in France rebelled against "*telecratie*,"[46] while others emphasize the coming of "virtual

---

[45] Alonso Zaldivar and Castells (1992).

[46] *Esprit* (1994: 3–4).

democracy."[47] The sudden rise to power of Berlusconi in Italy was directly linked to the new role played by the media in Italian politics.[48] Comparative analysis of other European countries in the 1990s[49] describes a complex, transitional situation, of media dominating the diffusion of information, while parties are unequipped, under-financed, and strictly regulated, thus finding it hard to adapt to the new technological environment. The outcome seems to be that, on the one hand, political parties keep, by and large, their autonomy *vis à vis* the media, with the support of the state. On the other hand, because of restricted access of parties to the media, people increasingly form their political opinions from sources external to the political system, thus accentuating the distance between parties and citizens.[50] Thus, while institutions, culture, and history make European politics highly specific, technology, globalization, and the network society incite political actors and institutions to engage in technology driven, informational politics. I contend that this is a new, historical trend, affecting, by successive waves, the entire world, albeit under specific historical conditions that introduce substantial variations in political competition, and in the conduct of politics. Bolivia provides an exceptional opportunity to test this hypothesis.

Bolivia's electronic populism: *compadre* Palenque and the coming of *Jach'a Uru* [51]

If we had to select the most likely country in the world to resist globalization of culture, and to assert grassroots politics, Bolivia would be an obvious candidate. Its Indian identity is extremely present in the collective memory of its population (even if 67 percent consider themselves *mestizos*), and Aymara and Quechua are widely spoken. Nationalism is the paramount ideology of all political parties. Since the 1952 revolution, Bolivian miners and peasant unions have been among the most conscious, organized, and militant social actors in Latin America. The main nationalist-populist party, the *Movimiento*

[47] Scheer (1994).
[48] Di Marco (1994); Santoni Rugiu (1994); Walter (1994).
[49] Kaid and Holz-Bacha (1995).
[50] Di Marco (1993).
[51] I am indebted, for their help in the elaboration of this section on Bolivian media politics, to Fernando Calderon in La Paz, and to Roberto Laserna in Cochabamba. The analysis is based on the following studies by Bolivian researchers: Mesa (1986); Archondo (1991); Contreras Basnipeiro (1991); Saravia and Sandoval (1991); Laserna (1992); Albo (1993); Mayorga (1993); Perez Iribarne (1993a, b); Ardaya and Verdesoto (1994); Calderon and Laserna (1994); Bilbao La Vieja Diaz et al. (1996); Szmukler (1996).

Nacionalista Revolucionario, has been in and out of power for the past four decades, still holding the presidency in 1996, with the support of left nationalists of the *Movimiento Bolivia Libre*, and of the Katarist (indigenist) movement. Social tensions and political militancy in the country prompted frequent military coups, not always disliked by the US Embassy, until the open participation of the high ranks of the army in drug traffic in the late 1970s, and the change of policy under Carter, modified the US attitude, facilitating the restoration of stable democracy in 1982, with a left coalition coming to power. Since then, while social tensions did heighten, because of the structural adjustment policies introduced by the MNR in 1985 (later to be followed by other governments), democracy seems solidly established. A most lively political struggle developed, with parties being formed, split, and reformed, and the most unlikely political alliances being forged to reach state power. Thus, social mobilization and democratic politics were, and are, alive and well in Bolivia, apparently leaving little room for the transformation of the political scene by an Andean brand of informational politics. And yet, since 1989, the politics of La Paz–El Alto (the Bolivian capital and its periphery of popular settlements) has been dominated by a political movement built around Carlos Palenque, a former folk musician from humble origin, who became a radio and television show host, then the owner of a media network (RTP, *Radio Television Popular*), and finally leader of *Conciencia de Patria* (Condepa), founded on September 21, 1988, in Tihuanaco, the ancient capital of the Aymara world. Although the story may sound familiar to those aware of the old tradition of Latin American populism, it is in fact unusual, complex, and revealing.

Palenque's saga started in 1968 when, around his folk group, *Los Caminantes*, he created a radio program that gradually incorporated direct contact with the audience, using popular language, including a mixture of Spanish and Aymara, which made it easier for people from poor urban strata to communicate without being intimidated by the formalism of the medium. In 1978, he started a television show, where he offered a platform for people to voice their complaints. He introduced himself as the compadre of his audience, and he also referred to his interlocutors as *compadres* and *comadres*, thus leveling the field of communication, and introducing a reference to a fundamental communality, rooted in the Aymara and Catholic traditions.[52] In 1980, he succeeded in buying Radio Metropolitana,

[52] *Compadre* and *comadre* are terms signifying membership in the community. They bring together elements of Aymara tradition and of Catholic celebration (e.g godfathers and godmothers for christened children). As such, *compadres* and *comadres* are expected to understand, to contribute, to share, and to assume reciprocity.

and later on Canal 4, a television station in La Paz. They soon became the most listened-to media in the La Paz area, and they remain so: indeed, 25 percent of the radio audience declared that they listen exclusively to Metropolitana.

Five elements are critical in Palenque's communication strategy. The first is the personalization of the shows, with forceful *compadres* and *comadres* representing various constituencies, such as *comadre* Remedios Loza, a common woman (*mujer de pollera*), a human type never before seen on television, in spite of being the very image of La Paz's popular families; or *compadre* Paco, closer to the middle class; or his own wife, Monica Medina de Palenque, a former flamenco ballet dancer, assuming the role of the bottom-line, wise woman. The personalization of interaction with the audience does not stop with live shows, but extends to much of the programming. For instance, while Canal 4 broadcasts the same Latin American soap operas that capture attention throughout the entire Spanish-speaking world, *compadre* Palenque and his team personally comment on the events and drama of various episodes, and engage with their audience in relating the soap opera's story to the daily lives of *paceños*. Secondly, is the targeting of women, particularly of lower-class women, and the prominent presence of women in the programs. Thirdly, there is a direct connection to people's concerns, and joys, with programs such as *People's Saturdays* broadcast live with the participation of hundreds of people from urban locations; or *The People's Tribune*, in which people denounce live the abuses to which they are submitted by whoever. Fourthly, there is a willingness to listen to people's complaints, providing an ear open to the laments arising from the painful integration of rural and Indian life in the sprawling urban periphery of La Paz. And, fifthly, is the religious reference, legitimizing hope as God's will, with the promise of the coming of *Jach'a Uru*, the day when, according to the Aymara tradition, all suffering will come to an end.

However, Palenque's path to prominence was not a smooth one. Because of his criticism of authorities, under the pretext of a radio interview with a leading drug trafficker, RTP media network was twice closed by the government, in June and November 1988. But mass protests, and a decision by the Supreme Court, reopened it months later. Palenque answered by creating a party (Condepa), and running for president. In the first election in which it participated, in May 1989, Condepa became the fourth largest national party, and the first party in the capital. In the municipal elections, it won the Mayoralty of El Alto (fourth largest urban area of Bolivia), and entered in the municipal council of La Paz. In the next municipal election, Monica Medina de Palenque became the Mayor of La Paz, a post she kept until

1996. Condepa is also present in the National Congress: among other deputies, *comadre* Remedios played a leading role in pushing legislation for Bolivian women. In spite of its populism, Condepa did not develop a confrontational attitude toward various governments. In 1989 its votes helped to elect in the Congress President Jaime Paz Zamora, in spite of his third place in the popular vote. And when a new MNR President, Sanchez de Losada, was elected in 1993, Condepa, while not participating in the government, cooperated with the government in several legislative initiatives.

The success of *compadre* Palenque did not take place in a social vacuum. He had a pointed message, not just a medium, which seemed to fit well with the actual experience of the urban masses in La Paz. He appealed to the cultural identity of La Paz's recent immigrants, by the use of language, by the emphasis on Aymara traditions, by the reference to folk and religion. Against policies of economic adjustment, and integration in the global economy, he exposed the daily suffering of displaced workers and urban poor, the abuses imposed upon them under the pretext of economic rationality. *Compadre* Palenque became the voice of the voiceless. Using the media as platform, but linking up with local institutions where Condepa was present, Palenque ran a number of social programs, one of the most successful geared toward helping industrial workers displaced by economic restructuring and privatization. Refusing the categorical imperative of globalization, *compadre* Palenque proposed (albeit in rather vague terms) a model of "endogenous development," based on Bolivia's own resources, and counting on the communal spirit of its people. Thus, Condepa's influence is not just a media manipulation: its themes refer to the actual suffering of people in La Paz, and its language directly communicates to the cultural and local identity of popular strata in La Paz and El Alto (to the point that the movement remains by and large local, authorizing some analysts to speak of a "metropolitan ayllu").[53] However, without the power of the media, and without a perceptive communication strategy mixing entertainment radio and television with a space for public complaints, and with the building of charismatic trust between the leaders and the audience, Condepa would have been reduced to a minor role, as happened to other populist movements in Bolivia, such as Max Fernandez's *Unidad Cívica Solidaridad*. Indeed, in 1996, Bolivians trust the media more than they trust their political representatives (table 6.3).

So, media politics does not have to be the monopoly of influential

[53] *Ayllu* is the traditional form of a territorial/cultural community in the Aymara tradition.

Table 6.3   Opinion of Bolivian citizens on which institutions represent their interests

Institution	% of favorable opinion
Congress of Deputies	3.5
Any political party	3.4
President	3.3
Mayor	6.9
Neighborhood committee	11.3
Labor union	12.6
Mass media	23.4

Note: Answers to the question: "Do you feel that the following institutions represent your interests?" (percentage over total of polled citizens; national representative sample).
Source: Collective Author (1996)

interest groups, or of established political parties using the power of technology to perfect the technology of power. As *compadre* Palenque's ascendance seems to indicate, identity-based communalism, and poor people's movements, sometimes under the form of religious millennialism, can access the political mainstream by using the media. By so doing, they force other political actors to play a similar game (as is the case in Bolivia in the 1990s), thus contributing to the gradual enclosing of politics in the media space, albeit with specific characteristics fitting the Bolivian cultural tradition, economic condition, and political dynamics. Furthermore, in spite of the communal orientation of Condepa, we find in the experience of *compadre* Palenque a series of features not dissimilar to the broader trends of informational politics, as described above: the extreme personalization of leadership; the simplification of messages in dichotomous terms: good and evil; the pre-eminence of moral and religious judgments in framing public and personal life; the decisive importance of electronically broadcast language, images, and symbols in mobilizing consciousness and deciding politics; the volatility of public mood, lost in the feeling of a world spinning out of control; the difficulty of fitting these new political expressions into traditional political categories (to the point that some Bolivian analysts refer to the emergence of "informal politics," parallel to the "informal economy");[54] and, ultimately, we also find, among these *compadres* and *comadres*, a dependence on their financial ability to support media politics, thus creating a feedback loop (or a vicious circle) between power, media, and money. While the "resurrection of a metropolitan

[54]   Ardaya and Verdesoto (1994).

ayllu"[55] shows the limits to globalization, it is by inhabiting the space of media flows that traditional cultures and popular interests assert their power. So doing, they survive, but they transform themselves at the same time, entering a new world of sounds and images, of electronically modulated *charangos*, environmentally preserved condors, and television scripted *Jach'a Uru*.

Informational Politics in Action: the Politics of Scandal[56]

In the past decade, political systems have been shaken all over the world, and political leaders have been destroyed, in a relentless succession of scandals. In some cases, political parties solidly entrenched in power for about half a century have collapsed, taking along in their demise the political regime they had shaped in their interest. Among important examples of this evolution are: the Italian Christian Democrats, which literally disintegrated in the 1990s; Japan's Liberal Democratic Party which was split and lost the government, for the first time, in 1993, although the party as such survived, and still governs in coalition or in minority; or India's Congress Party, which, after governing the largest democracy in the world for 44 years of the more than 48 years since Independence, suffered a humiliating defeat, to the benefit of Hindu nationalists in the 1996 elections, after a major scandal involving Congress leader Narasimha Rao, seemingly putting an end to a political system built around uncontested domination of Nehru's successors. With the exception of Scandinavian

[55] Archondo (1991).
[56] This section is partly based on a reading of mainstream newspapers and magazines from different countries, as well as on personal knowledge of some events. I consider it unnecessary to provide detailed references for facts that are public knowledge. An international overview of political scandals is Longman (1990) *Political Scandals and Causes Célèbres since 1945*. A major scholarly, comparative volume on the topic is Heidenheimer et al. (1989). Historical accounts of American scandal politics can be found in Fackler and Lin (1995), and Ross (1988). A recent account of congressional scandals in America is in Balz and Brownstein (1996: 27ff). An annotated bibliography on American political corruption is Johansen (1990). Additional sources used in this section are: King (1984); Markovits and Silverstein (1988a); Bellers (1989); Ebbinghausen and Neckel (1989); Bouissou (1991); Morris (1991); Sabato (1991); Barker (1992); *CQ Researcher* (1992); Meny (1992); Phillips (1992); Swan (1992); Tranfaglia (1992); Barber (1993); Buckler (1993); DeLeon (1993); Grubbe (1993); Roman (1993); *Esprit* (1994); Gumbel (1994); Walter (1994); Arlachi (1995); Fackler and Lin (1995); Garcia Cotarelo (1995); Johnson (1995); Sechi (1995); Thompson (1995).

democracies, and a few other small countries, I cannot think of any
country in North America, Latin America, Western and Eastern
Europe, Asia, or Africa, where major political scandals, with significant, and sometimes dramatic, consequences, have not exploded in
recent years.[57]

In a few instances, scandals referred to the personal morality of a
leader (usually a man improperly driven by sexuality or drunkenness).
But, in most cases, the matter was political corruption, that is, in Carl
Friedrich's definition: "Whenever a powerholder who is charged with
doing certain things, i.e., who is a responsible functionary or office-
holder, is by monetary or other rewards not legally provided for,
induced to take actions which favor whoever provides the rewards and
thereby does damage to the public and its interests."[58] In some cases,
government officials simply took the money, without even needing to
run with it. Or so they believed. From South Korea's President Roh to
Brazil's President Collor de Mello, and from some members of
Russia's military, or of the United States' Congress, to some high-
ranking members of Spanish and French Socialist administrations,
wave after wave of corruption-related political scandals have become
the main staple of public life throughout the world in the 1990s. Why
so? Are our political systems the most corrupt in history? I doubt it.
Use and abuse of power for personal benefit is one of these features
that would qualify as "human nature," if such an entity were to exist.[59]
This is precisely one of the reasons why democracy was invented, and
became the most sought after, if not ideal, form of governance.
Behind the scenes, in situations of the control of information by the
state, political elites, in ancient times as in recent years, went happily
into establishing their personalized tax system on subjects and interest
groups, the main differences being in the degree of arbitrariness in
bribing, and in the variable disfunctionality of hidden contributions
for the conduct of public affairs. Thus, a first observation points to the
fact that denunciation of corruption could precisely be a good indicator of a democratic society, and of freedom of the press.[60] For
instance, Spain under the dictatorship of Franco suffered from direct
pillage of the country by the dictator's entourage, starting with Mrs
Franco's notorious visits to jewelry stores whose owners never dared
to send the bill to his excellency. No serious observer would assert that

[57]   Heidenheimer et al. (1989); Longman (1990); Garment (1991); *CQ Researcher*
(1992); Meny (1992); Grubbe (1993); Roman (1993); Gumbel (1994); Walter
(1994); Thompson (1995).
[58]   Friedrich (1966: 74).
[59]   Leys (1989).
[60]   Markovits and Silverstein (1988).

political corruption in Spain was more pervasive during the 1980s' Socialist governments than under Franco.[61] And yet, while, during the dictatorship, corruption was mainly a matter of gossip among reliable friends, political life in 1990s' Spanish democracy was entirely shaped by revelations, and allegations, of government corruption and unlawful behavior. Furthermore, in long-established democracies, with freedom of the press, such as the United States, the occurrence of political corruption, as reported in the press, goes up and down, with no clear long-term trend, as can be observed in figure 6.2, elaborated by Fackler and Lin for the past hundred years.[62] There is, however, a most spectacular surge of reporting on political corruption around the time of Nixon's Watergate, precisely the event that struck the imagination of both journalists and politicians with the possibility of bringing down the most powerful political office on earth, by obtaining and diffusing damaging information. The historical study by King on political corruption in nineteenth-century Britain[63] shows the pervasiveness of the phenomenon, prompting the 1867 Reform Act to curtail such practices, as democracy made progress. And Bouissou reports that in 1890 the Japanese press denounced widespread electoral fraud, with the newspaper *Asahi* writing that "whoever buys his election will be for sale once elected."[64] Moreover, in a most insightful analysis, Barker has shown that when unlawful actions by politicians do not provide enough ammunition to discredit them, other types of behavior (for example, improper sex) become the raw material for political scandal.[65] Thus, using the Longman international series of political scandals,[66] he calculated that the proportion of unlawful and not unlawful political scandals for all countries (73 : 27) was relatively close to the proportion in the US or France, but very different in the UK (41 : 59), so that sex and espionage became in Britain the functional equivalent of graft and bribery in other countries. Corruption *per se* seems to be less significant than scandals (that is, corruption or wrong doing revealed) and their political impact.[67]

So, why now? If it is unlikely that corruption is at a historical highpoint, why does it explode all over the media, and why does it so devastatingly affect political systems and political actors in the 1990s? There are a number of structural factors, and macro-political trends,

[61]   Alonso Zaldivar and Castells (1992).
[62]   Fackler and Lin (1995).
[63]   King (1989).
[64]   Bouissou (1991: 84).
[65]   Barker (1992).
[66]   Longman (1990).
[67]   Lowi (1988).

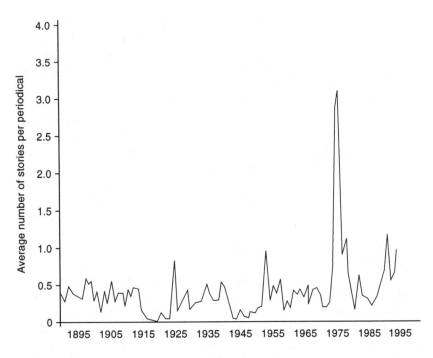

Figure 6.2   Average number of corruption stories per periodical in
US, 1890–1992
Source: Fackler and Lin (1995)

which have weakened political systems, making them more vulnerable
to turmoil created in public opinion. Political competition, and the
struggle to influence the center of the electorate's political spectrum,
have downplayed ideological contrasts, as parties/coalitions, having
secured their hard-core supporters, strive to steal adversaries' themes
and positions as much as possible. It follows a blurring of political
positions, and the tendency by citizens to be more sensitive to the
reliability of parties and candidates than to their professed positions
on issues. Personalization of politics also focuses attention on leaders,
and on their character, thus opening the way for attacks on precisely
those qualities as a form of winning votes. The rise of a potent global
criminal economy has penetrated state institutions in many countries,
often at the highest levels of government, thus providing ammunition
for scandal-making, and also using information to blackmail politicians into submission. Geopolitical factors also play a role: thus, the
Italian and Japanese political systems, organized around the Christian
Democratic and the Liberal Democratic parties respectively, were set
up in the aftermath of World War II, with considerable help and

influence from the US, to establish a bulwark against communism in two democracies that were critical in the Cold War context, and where communist and socialist parties were strong.[68] The long-standing, well-known connections of some leading Christian Democrats with the Mafia,[69] and of some Liberal Democrat leaders with the *Yakuza*,[70] were not an obstacle to the unrelenting support of international and domestic forces for these parties, as long as their replacement was an excessively risky operation. In the post-Cold War environment, each party is left to itself, to the movements of each country's political market; discipline inside the parties becomes less strict, because fierce competition can be better afforded in the absence of an external enemy. Guehenno has also suggested that, in a world of fading nation-states and uncertain ideological commitments, the rewards for being in office are no longer distinct from those offered in society at large, that is, ultimately, money, as the key to personal or organizational projects, from enjoying life to providing for the family, or helping humanitarian causes.[71]

All these factors seem to contribute to making political systems vulnerable to corruption. But there is something else, something that, in my view, changes the nature of political systems in contemporary societies. *I contend that scandal politics is the weapon of choice for struggle and competition in informational politics.* The argument goes like this. Politics has been, by and large, enclosed in the space of the media. The media have become more powerful than ever, technologically, financially, and politically. Their global reach, and networking, allow them to escape from strict political controls. Their capacity for investigative reporting, and their relative autonomy *vis à vis* political power, makes them the main source of information and opinion for society at large. Parties and candidates must act in and through the media to reach society. Not that the media are the Fourth Power: they are, instead, the ground for power struggles. Media politics is an increasingly expensive operation, made even more expensive by the whole paraphernalia of informational politics: polling, advertising, marketing, analyzing, image-making, and information processing. Current institutional systems of political financing are not up to the task. Political actors are chronically underfinanced, and the gap between necessary expenses and legal revenues has grown exponentially, and continues to grow.[72] Thus, after exhausting all legal sources,

---

[68] Johnson (1995).
[69] Tranfaglia (1992).
[70] Bouissou (1991); Johnson (1995).
[71] Guehenno (1993).
[72] Weinberg (1991); Freeman (1994); Pattie et al. (1995).

personal contributions, and business deals, parties and politicians
often resort to the only real source of money: under the table contributions from business and interest groups, obviously in exchange for
government decisions in favor of these interests.[73] *This is the matrix of
systemic political corruption, from which develops a shadow network of front
businesses and intermediaries.* Once corruption becomes widespread,
and after a few people add their personal take to the channels of political funding, everybody in politics, and in the media, knows (or thinks
he/she knows) that, if looking closely, and long enough, damaging
information can be found on almost anyone. Thus, the hunt starts, by
political advisors to prepare ammunition to attack or to defend; by
journalists to fulfill their job as investigative reporters, finding
material to boost their audience and their sales; by freelancers, and
crooks, to find information that can be used in potential blackmail,
or for sale to interested parties. In fact, most of the damaging material
published by the media is leaked by political actors themselves, or by
associated business interests. Finally, once the market of damaging
political information is created, if there is not enough clear-cut
material, then allegations, insinuations, and even fabrications, may
come in, depending, of course, on the individual ethics of politicians,
journalists, and the media. Indeed, the strategy in scandal politics
does not necessarily aim at an instant blow on the basis of one scandal.
It is the relentless flow of various scandals of different kinds, and with
different levels of likelihood, from solid information on a minor incident to shaky allegations on a major issue, that weave the thread where
political ambitions are finally strangled, and political dreams subdued
– unless a deal is made, thus feeding back into the system. What counts
is the final impact on public opinion, by the accumulation of many
different touches.[74] As in the old Russian saying: "I cannot remember
if she stole a coat, or if a coat was stolen from her."

The superior stage of scandal politics is the judicial or parliamentary investigation, leading to indictments, and, with increasing
frequency, to imprisonment of political leaders.[75] Judges, prosecutors, and investigative committee members enter into a symbiotic
relationship with the media. They protect the media (ensuring their
independence), and often feed them with calculated leaks. In
exchange, they are protected by the media, they become media
heroes, and, sometimes successful politicians with the support of the
media. Together, they fight for democracy and clean government,
they control the excesses of politicians, and, ultimately, they seize

[73]   Meny (1992).
[74]   Barker (1992); *CQ Researcher* (1992).
[75]   Garment (1991); Garcia Cotarelo (1995); Thompson (1995).

power away from the political process, diffusing it into the society. While doing so, they may also delegitimize parties, politicians, politics, and, ultimately, democracy in its current incarnation.[76]

The politics of scandal, as practiced in the 1990s against the governing Spanish Socialist party, offers an interesting illustration of this analysis. After the 1989 Socialist victory in the Spanish general election (the third in a row), a behind-the-scenes coalition of interest groups (*probably without the participation of the leaders of political opposition parties*) decided it was time to check the uncontested domination of the Socialists in Spain's political life, a domination that could be foreseen going into the twenty-first century.[77] Explosive political files were leaked, discovered, manipulated, or invented, and published in the press. Because of self-restraint by the main Spanish newspapers (*El Pais, El Periodico, La Vanguardia*) most of the potential anti-Socialist "scandals" were first published in *El Mundo*, a professionally sophisticated newspaper created in 1990. From there, weekly tabloids and radio talk show pundits (mainly from the Catholic Church-owned radio network) would hammer the audience until the rest of the media, including television, echoed the news. Scandals started to be revealed in January 1990 with information on the brother of the then vice-president of the government selling his assumed political influence to various businessmen. Although the wrongdoings of this little crook were not of great significance, and the courts cleared the vice-president of any impropriety, the "affair" occupied the political headlines of the Spanish media for almost two years, actually prompting the resignation of the vice-president, the influential number two of the Socialist party, who refused to condemn his brother publicly. As soon as this scandal started to fizzle out, a new media campaign started, focusing on illegal financing of the Socialist party, after a party accountant defected and gave information to the media, apparently out of a personal vendetta. A judicial investigation was opened, leading to the indictment of some Socialist leaders. When, in spite of all these accusations, the Socialist party still retained enough seats to form a government in the 1993 elections, scandal politics accelerated its tempo in the Spanish media and judicial scene: the Governor of the Bank of Spain was suspected of insider trading, and confessed to tax fraud; the first civilian director of the legendary Guardia Civil was caught requesting bribes, fled the country, was arrested in Bangkok, and returned to a Spanish prison, in a sequence that fell between the thriller and the burlesque; more seriously, a resentful officer of the Spanish military intelligence leaked papers

[76] Bellers (1989); Arlachi (1995); Garcia Cotarelo (1995); Fallows (1996).
[77] Cacho (1994); Garcia Cotarelo (1995); *Temas* (1995).

showing unlawful eavesdropping on Spanish leaders, including the king; and, to complete the disintegration of public morale, former special agents of the Spanish police, incarcerated for organizing assassinations in the "dirty war" carried on in the 1980s against Basque terrorists (emulating Thatcher's tactics against the IRA), turned their coats against the government, and involved the Minister of the Interior, and several high-ranking officials in the conspiracy. Of paramount importance in this political process was the attitude of the Spanish judges, who pursued earnestly the slightest possibility of embarrassing the Socialist party. Felipe Gonzalez executed what was considered a brilliant maneuver by recruiting the most famous of these zealous judges as an independent deputy in the Socialist ticket in the 1993 election, and appointing him to a high post in the Ministry of Justice. It was a disaster: whether because the post was not high enough (Socialist version), or that the judge was disappointed by what he saw (his version), he quit the government, and engaged in a most militant prosecution against any potential wrongdoing from the highest levels of the Socialist government. After parliamentary and judicial investigations were opened, some leading to indictments, others fizzling out because of lack of substance, political scandals became the daily headlines of the Spanish media for about five years, literally paralyzing the action of government, destroying a number of political and business figures, and shaking up the most potent political force in Spain. The Socialists were eventually defeated in 1996, although still surviving the onslaught thanks to the personal credibility of their charismatic leader.

Why and how this judicial/media anti-Socialist barrage happened in Spain is a complex matter that has not been brought to public light as yet. There was, in any case, a combination of several factors reinforcing each other: the illegal financing of the Socialist party, which involved several members of its leadership in setting up a network of shadow businesses; the actual corruption, and unlawful actions, of several high-ranking members of the Socialist administration, and of many local Socialist bosses; the exasperation of some groups against the government (some fringe businessmen, including a financial tycoon expropriated by the Socialists; some ultra-conservative forces; probably some elements of the integrist wing of the Catholic Church; some special interests; disaffected journalists who felt marginalized by Socialist power); the internal in-fighting in the Socialist party, with several leaders leaking information against each other to undermine the credibility of their rivals in the eyes of Felipe Gonzalez, the undisputed leader above the fray; the fight between two major financial groups, one of them representing traditional Spanish finance, close to the economic team of the Socialist government, the other organized around an outsider trying to make inroads into the system, and attempting alliances with some Socialist factions against others; a battle between media groups, jockeying for control of the new media system in Spain; personal vendettas, as the one by the editor of the most militantly anti-Socialist newspaper, convinced that he had lost his job as a result of government pressures; and a more complex, diffused opinion in the media world, and in other circles of Spanish life, according to which Socialist dominance was excessive, and the arrogance of some Socialist leaders intolerable, so that informed social elites should react and expose the true face of the Socialists to a seduced electorate which, in its majority, kept voting Socialist in four consecutive elections. Thus, ultimately, and regardless of personal motivation or specific business interests, the media asserted their power collectively, and, in alliance with the judiciary, made sure that the Spanish political class, including the conservatives (*Partido Popular*), learned the lesson for the future. While it is indisputable that there was unlawful behavior and a significant level of corruption in the Socialist administration and in the Socialist party, what really matters for our analytical purpose is the use of scandal politics in and by the media as the fundamental weapon utilized by political actors, business interests, and social groups to fight one another. So doing, they transformed for ever Spanish politics by making it dependent upon the media.

What is characteristic of scandal politics is that all political actors practicing it become entrapped by the system, often reversing roles: today's hunter is tomorrow's game. A case in point is the political adventure of Berlusconi in Italy. The facts are known: he parlayed his control of all three private TV networks into mounting a devastating campaign against the Italian corrupt political system.[78] Then, he created, in three months, an *ad hoc* "party" (*Forza Italia*, named after the fans' rallying cry for the Italian national football team), and, in alliance with the neo-Fascist party and the Northern League, won the 1994 general election and became Prime Minister. Control of government gave him, theoretically, authority over the three other, government-owned, TV networks. Yet, the autonomy of the media, and of journalists, was strongly asserted. In spite of his overwhelming presence in the media business (in newspapers and magazines, as well as in television), as soon as Berlusconi became Prime Minister, the judiciary and the media, again together, launched an all-out assault on Berlusconi's financial frauds and bribery schemes, undermining his business, bringing some of his associates to justice, indicting Berlusconi himself, and ultimately damaging his image in such a way

[78]   Walter (1994).

that parliament censored his government. Then, in 1996 the electorate rejected Berlusconi, electing instead *Il Ulivo*'s center-left
coalition, whose main component, the ex-Communist, now Socialist,
Partito Democratico di Sinistra, had not yet been in the national government, and thus had salvaged its reputation.

The extremely important lesson of this development in Italian politics is that overwhelming business influence in the media is not
tantamount to political control in informational politics. The media
system, with its symbiotic linkages to the judiciary and prosecutorial
institutions of democracy, sets its own pace, and receives signals from
the whole spectrum of the political system, to transform them into
sales and influence, regardless of the origin and destination of political impacts. The golden rule is that what is more valuable is what
makes the greater impact on any given situation. Once a politician, or
party, becomes irrelevant – they are no longer news matter. The political system becomes engulfed in the endless turbulence of media
reporting, leaking, counter-leaking, and scandal-making. To be sure,
some daring political strategists try to ride the tiger, by positioning
themselves in the media business, by making alliances, by targeting
and timing informational strikes. This is exactly what Berlusconi tried.
His fate ended up being similar to the fate of those financial speculators who pretended to know the course of navigation in
unpredictable, global financial markets. In scandal politics, as in
other domains of the network society, the power of flows overwhelms
the flows of power.

The Crisis of Democracy

Let us bring together the various threads we have identified
concerning the transformation of the nation-state, and of the political process in contemporary societies. When weaved into a historical
framework, they reveal the crisis of democracy as we have known it in
the past century [79]

The nation-state, defining the domain, procedures, and object of
citizenship, has lost much of its sovereignty, undermined by the
dynamics of global flows and trans-organizational networks of wealth,
information, and power. Particularly critical for its legitimacy crisis is
the state's inability to fulfill its commitments as a welfare state, because
of the integration of production and consumption in a globally interdependent system, and the related process of capitalist restructuring.

[79]   Minc (1993); Guehenno (1993); Patterson (1993); Ginsborg (1994);
Touraine (1995b); Katznelson (1996); Weisberg (1996).

Indeed, the welfare state, in its different manifestations, depending on the history of each society, was a critical source of political legitimacy in the reconstitution of government institutions after the Great Depression of 1930s, and World War II.[80] The rejection of Keynesianism, and the decline of the labor movement, may accentuate the demise of the sovereign nation-state because of the weakening of its legitimacy.

The (re)construction of political meaning on the basis of specific identities fundamentally challenges the very concept of citizenship. The state could only shift the source of its legitimacy from representing people's will and providing for their well-being, to asserting collective identity, by identifying itself with communalism to the exclusion of other values and of minorities' identities. This is indeed the source of fundamentalist nationalist, ethnic, territorial, or religious states, which seem to emerge from current political crises of legitimacy. I contend that they cannot, and will not, sustain democracy (that is, liberal democracy) because the very principles of representation between the two systems (national citizenship, singular identity) are contradictory.

To the crisis of legitimacy of the nation-state we must add the crisis of credibility of the political system, based on open competition between political parties. Captured into the media arena, reduced to personalized leadership, dependent on technologically sophisticated manipulation, pushed into unlawful financing, driven by and toward scandal politics, the party system has lost its appeal and trustworthiness, and, for all practical purposes, is a bureaucratic remainder deprived of public confidence.[81]

As a result of these three convergent and interacting processes, public opinion, and citizens' individual and collective expressions, display a growing and fundamental disaffection *vis à vis* parties, politicians, and professional politics. Thus, in the United States, according to a Times Mirror Center survey in September 1994: "Thousands of interviews with American voters this summer find no clear direction in the public's political thinking other than frustration with the current system and an eager responsiveness to alternative political solutions and appeals."[82] In 1994, 82 percent of respondents to a national Harris Poll did not think that the government represented their interests (against 72 percent in 1980), and 72 percent considered that in fact the government represented interest groups

---

[80]   Navarro (1995).
[81]   West (1993); Anderson and Comiller (1994). Mouffe (1995); Navarro (1995); Salvati (1995); Balz and Brownstein (1996).
[82]   Quoted by Balz and Brownstein (1996: 28).

Question: Do you approve or disapprove of the way Bill Clinton is handling his job as president?

United States

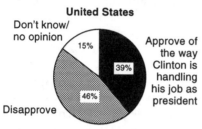

Don't know/no opinion 15%

Approve of the way Clinton is handling his job as president 39%

Disapprove 46%

Note: In a CBS News/*New York Times* survey conducted just before the November 1992 election, 37% of respondents said they approved of the way Bush was handling his job as president, 56% disapproved.
Source: Survey by CBS News/*New York Times*, June 21–24, 1993

Question: Are you satisfied or dissatisfied with Mr François Mitterrand as president of the Republic?

France

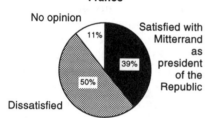

No opinion 11%

Satisfied with Mitterrand as president of the Republic 39%

Dissatisfied 50%

Source: Survey by the Institut Français d'Opinion Publique et d'Étude de Marchés (IFOP) for *Le Journal du Dimanche*, May 6–13, 1993

Question: Do you support the Miyazawa cabinet?

Japan

No answer/other 14%

Yes, support the Miyazawa cabinet 26%

Do not 59%

Source: Survey by the *Yomiuri Shimbun*, May 1993

Question: Are you satisfied or dissatisfied with Mr Major as prime minister?

Great Britain

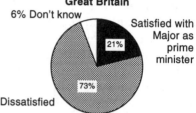

6% Don't know

Satisfied with Major as prime minister 21%

Dissatisfied 73%

Note: The percentage saying they are satisfied is the lowest ever for any British prime minister for which polling data is available.
Source: Survey by Social Surveys (Gallup Poll) Ltd, May 26–31, 1993

Question: Do you approve or disapprove of the way Brian Mulroney is handling his job as prime minister?

Canada

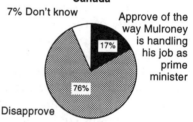

7% Don't know

Approve of the way Mulroney is handling his job as prime minister 17%

Disapprove 76%

Note: Brian Mulroney was succeeded as Prime Minister by Kim Campbell, June 25, 1993.
Source: Survey by Gallup Canada, January 13–18, 1993

Question: Are you happy or unhappy with the job done, in the last month, by Guiliano Amato as president of the cabinet?

Italy

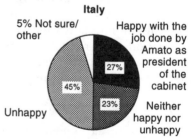

5% Not sure/other

Happy with the job done by Amato as president of the cabinet 27%

Neither happy nor unhappy 23%

Unhappy 45%

Source: Survey by DOXA, January 19, 1993

Figure 6.3 (opposite)   Approval ratings for various governments,
c. 1993
Source: Compiled and elaborated by Roper Center of Public Opinion
and Polling (1995)

(with 68 percent indentifying these groups as business interests);
along the same lines, a 1995 Roper Poll found that 68 percent of
respondents thought that there were not many differences between
Republicans and Democrats, and 82 percent wished that a new party
could be created.[83] Figure 6.3 displays widespread dissatisfaction with
governments of all political affiliations in six of seven countries,
members of the G-7 club, as reflected in public opinion polls.

However, this skepticism toward mainstream parties and politics
does not necessarily mean that people do not vote any longer, or that
they do not care about democracy. For that matter, in much of the
world, democracy has been attained only recently after a tremendous
effort, conquered with blood, sweat, and tears, so that people are not
easily ready to give up hope. Indeed, when people perceive the chance
of meaningful political action, they mobilize enthusiastically, as they
did around the election of Fernando Henrique Cardoso to the presidency of Brazil in 1994. Even in veteran democracies, where the rituals
of free elections have been practiced for two hundred years (except
for half of the people, that is women), political participation goes up
and down. People do not vote much in the United States (49 percent
in the 1996 presidential election, 54 percent in 1992, 51 percent in
1984, down from 68 percent in 1968), but participation rates are
consistently high (between 65 percent and 80 percent) in France,
Italy, Spain, Germany and most European countries (see table 6.4).
Yet, Europeans do not trust their politicians more than Americans
do.[84] It would seem than individualism, rather than political disaffection, accounts for American exceptionalism.[85]

There are, nevertheless, powerful expressions of growing political
alienation worldwide, as people observe the state's incapacity to solve
their problems, and experience cynical instrumentalism from professional politicians. One of these expressions is the increasing support
for a variety of "third party" forces, and for regional parties, since, in
most political systems, the final showdown to seize national executive
power takes place between two candidates, representing two broad
coalitions. Thus, voting for someone else becomes a protest vote

[83]   Cited by Navarro (1995: 55).
[84]   *Eurobarometer* (various years).
[85]   Lipset (1996).

Table 6.4 Turnout in elections to lower house of parliament: recent figures compared to rates for the 1970s and 1980s (%)

	1970s–1980s		
	Average turnout	*Turnout range*	*1990s (one election)*
France (1st ballot)	76.0	66.2–83.2	68.9 (1993)
Germany	88.6	84.3–91.1	79.1 (1994)
Italy	91.4	89.0–93.2	86.4 (1992)
Japan	71.2	67.9–74.6	67.3 (1993)
Spain	73.9	70.6–77.0	77.3 (1993)
United Kingdom	74.8	72.2–78.9	75.8 (1992)
United States	42.6	33.4–50.9	50.8 (1992)
			36.0 (1994)

Sources: 1970s and 1980s: *The International Almanac of Electoral History* (rev. 3rd edn, Thomas T. Mackie and Richard Rose, Washington, DC: Macmillan Press, 1991); recent elections: *The Statesman's Yearbook, 1994–1995 and 1995–1996* (Brian Hunter, ed., New York: St Martin's Press, 1994, 1995); United States: *Vital Statistics on American Politics*, 4th edn, Harold W. Stanley and Richard G. Niemi, Washington DC: CQ Press, 1994) Compiled by Sandra Moog

against the overall political system, and maybe the attempt to help build a different alternative, often on a local or regional basis. Sandra Moog and I have built an index of voting for mainstream parties for some major democracies in different continents, measuring its evolution at several points in time in the 1980s and 1990s.[86] As shown in figure 6.4, the overall trend seems to confirm the declining proportion of the vote for mainstream parties over time. There are, however, some inflexions of the tendency, when one party succeeds in mobilizing its electorate, as did the Conservative party in Spain in the 1996 election. Specific political rhythms introduce variations in the overall trend. Yet, at the macro-level, the predicted trend seems to appear distinctly. While the majority of voters are still geared toward instrumental voting – that is, supporting candidates with a real chance of being elected – the erosion of this support affects the very predictability of electoral chances, so reinforcing the crisis of credibility of major coalitions, and eventually precipitating their demise, as happened in Italian politics (Christian Democrats, Socialists), and in American politics (Democratic Congress) in 1994. However, Zaller and Hunt, in their excellent analysis of Ross Perot's 1992 presidential campaign, warn of the limits of "third party" politics: As they write:

[86] For sources, definitions and methods of calculation, see the Methodological Appendix.

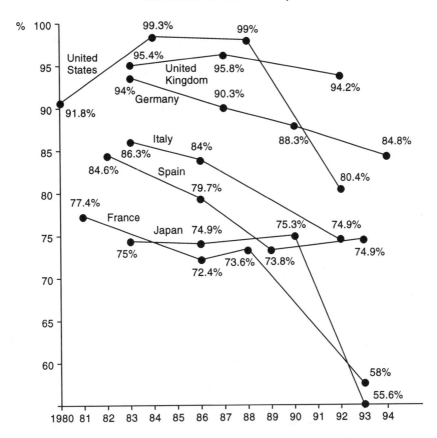

Figure 6.4   Level of support for mainstream parties in national elections, 1980–94 (US figures are for presidential elections; all others are returns for lower house of parliament)
Source: see Methodological Appendix for figures and sources; compiled and elaborated by Sandra Moog

Even in a mass democracy such as the United States, great skill as a communicator is insufficient to win the nation's highest office. One must still pass muster with the powers that be. The American system of choosing presidents, despite the inherent volatility of a nomination process that gives final authority to masses of volatile and often politically inattentive voters, remains a powerful institutional force capable of forcing candidates to run through it rather than around it.[87]

---

[87]   Zaller and Hunt (1994: 386).

The question is: until when? How much distance, and for how long, can be kept between the yearning of the electorate for alternative political options and their framing by the institutions of mainstream politics, in a situation where media politics can launch (and extinguish) new stars in a matter of hours?

Nevertheless, for the time being, most people in most countries are still constrained in their choices by the weight of institutions, political machines, and political traditions. Under these circumstances, an additional indicator of political disaffection with the traditional party system is the volatility of the electorate worldwide, bringing down governing parties, and accelerating the tempo of political alternation. In 1992–96, voters switched from Republicans to Democrats in the American presidency in 1992, from Democrats to Republicans in the congressional elections in 1994, and back to Clinton (after he emphasized his "new Democrat" look) in 1996 (but not back to Democrats in Congress); from Socialists to Gaullists in the French presidency; from center to right, then to center-left in Italy; from Socialists+ Nationalists to Conservatives+Nationalists in Spain; from Conservatives to a multiple coalition, then to Conservatives in minority government in Japan; from Socialists to Conservatives, then back to Socialists in Greece; from nowhere to Fernando H. Cardoso in Brazil; from democrats to Communists in the Russian parliamentary elections, then back to Yeltsin in the presidential elections; and, most likely, from Tories to Labour in the UK in 1997. Thus, people, discontented and disheartened, switch from one option to another at increasing speed, experiencing, in most cases, successive disappointments. With each new one, morale deteriorates, cynicism sets in, and hope fades away.

As a result of the trends presented above, another major feature is taking place: the growing fragmentation of the political system. Thus, if the 1996 Indian elections probably marked the end of an era of Congress Party dominance, Hindu nationalists, the winners of the election, could not hold onto government, having only one-third of the seats. A miscellaneous "united front" was constituted in May 1996 to bring into government an uncertain alliance of left parties, regional parties, and lower-caste parties, whose emergence in the election was the main reason for the crisis of the political regime. India, whose democratic political stability was the envy of the developing world, may have entered a condition of structural political fragmentation, and of regionalization of politics.

Among major democracies, only Germany seemed to keep political stability in the 1990s, but this was before Kohl undertook in 1996, under the pressures of global competition, the retrenchment of the German welfare state, and the reform of industrial co-determination, at the heart of the German political consensus.

As a consequence of these developments, we do not witness, in general terms, people's withdrawal from the political scene, but the penetration of the political system by symbolic politics, single-issue mobilizations, localism, referendum politics, and, above all, *ad hoc* support for personalized leadership. With political parties fading away, it is the time of saviors. This introduces systemic unpredictability. It could turn out to be the regeneration of politics, as with Fernando Henrique Cardoso, or maybe with Colin Powell (it would be ironic, but historically stimulating, to see a Republican African-American, the son of a Jamaican immigrant, re-legitimizing American politics). Or, else, it could end up in a demagogic flare up, disintegrating political institutions, jeopardizing world stability, or launching a new assault on reason.

Whatever the future, what the observation of the present seems to indicate is that, under different forms, and through the variety of processes I have outlined in this and previous chapters, we are witnessing the fragmentation of the state, the unpredictability of the political system, and the singularization of politics. Political freedom may still exist, as people will continue to fight for it. But political democracy, as conceived by the liberal revolutions of the eighteenth century, and as diffused throughout the world in the twentieth century, has become an empty shell. Not that it was just "formal democracy": democracy lives out of these very "forms," such as secret, universal suffrage, and respect of civil liberties.[88] But the new institutional, cultural, and technological conditions of democratic exercise have made obsolete the existing party system, and the current regime of competitive politics, as adequate mechanisms of political representation in the network society. People know it, and feel it, but they also know, in their collective memory, how important it is to prevent tyrants from occupying the vanishing space of democratic politics. Citizens are still citizens but they are uncertain of which city, and of whose city.

Conclusion: Reconstructing Democracy?

These are alarming words, indeed. It would be tempting at this point to seize the opportunity to lecture you on my personal model of informational democracy. Do not worry. For reasons that I will present in the general conclusion to this book (in volume III), I have forbidden myself normative prescriptions, and political admonition.

---

[88]   Katznelson (1996).

However, in strict fairness to political hope, I will conclude by commenting on potential paths of democratic reconstruction, *as they manifest themselves in the observed practice of societies in the mid-1990s*, regardless of my personal views on their goodness. Since, fortunately, embryos of new democratic politics are numerous, and diverse around the world, I will restrain my commentary to three trends that I consider particularly relevant for the future of informational politics.

The first one is the re-creation of the local state. In many societies around the world, local democracy, for reasons exposed in chapter 5, appears to be flourishing, at least in terms relative to national political democracy. This is particularly true when regional and local governments cooperate with each other, and when they extend their reach to neighborhood decentralization, and citizen participation. When electronic means (computer-mediated communication, or local radio and television stations) are added to expand participation and consultation by citizens (for example, in Amsterdam, or in Fukuoka Prefecture), new technologies contribute to enhanced participation in local government. Experiences of local self-management, such as the one developed by the municipality of Cuiaba, in the Brazilian Mato Grosso, show the possibility of reconstructing links of political representation to *share* (if not control) the challenges of economic globalization and political unpredictability. There are obvious limits to this localism since it accentuates the fragmentation of the nation-state. But, strictly in terms of observation, the most powerful trends legitimizing democracy in the mid-1990s are taking place, worldwide, at the local level.[89]

A second perspective often discussed in the literature,[90] and in the media,[91] is the opportunity offered by electronic communication to enhance political participation and horizontal communication among citizens. Indeed, on-line information access, and computer-mediated communication facilitate the diffusion and retrieval of information, and offer possibilities for interaction and debate in an autonomous, electronic forum, bypassing the control of the media. Indicative referendums on a variety of issues may provide a useful tool, when used carefully without yielding to the oversimplified frame of referendum politics. More importantly, citizens could form, and are forming, their own political and ideological constellations, circumventing established political structures, thus creating a flexible,

---

[89]   Cooke (1994); Graham (1995); Ziccardi (1995); Borja and Castells (1996).
[90]   Ganley (1991).
[91]   *The Economist* (1995a).

adaptable political field. However, serious criticism may be addressed, and has indeed been addressed to the prospects of electronic democracy.[92] On the one hand, should this form of democratic politics emerge as an important instrument of debate, representation, and decision, it would certainly institutionalize a form of "Athenian democracy," both nationally, and internationally. That is, while a relatively small, educated, and affluent elite in a few countries and cities would have access to an extraordinary tool of information and political participation, actually enhancing citizenship, the uneducated, switched off masses of the world, and of the country, would remain excluded from the new democratic core, as were slaves and barbarians at the onset of democracy in classical Greece. On the other hand, the volatility of the medium could induce an accentuation of "show politics," with the flaring up of fashions, and myths, once the rationalizing power of parties and institutions was bypassed by the flows of suddenly convergent and divergent political moods. In other words, on-line politics could push the individualization of politics, and of society, to a point where integration, consensus, and institution building would become dangerously difficult to reach.

To explore the matter, my students in the graduate seminar on Sociology of the Information Society at Berkeley proceeded with some on-line observation of the Internet in the spring of 1996. The results of their analysis reveal some interesting trends. Thus, Klinenberg and Perrin observed that, in the 1996 American presidential Republican primaries, Internet usage played an important role in diffusing information about the candidates (Dole), as well as in reaching out for support (Buchanan), and contributions (all candidates).[93] Yet, the channels of communication were monitored and tightly controlled, thus becoming, in fact, one-way communication systems, more powerful and flexible than television, but not more open to citizen participation. This could change in the future, but it seems that the logic of informational politics restrains openness of the system, since candidates must control the messages in their networks, not to be made responsible for positions or statements that are prejudicial, or out of touch with the electorate. Tight political control and electronic openness seem to be mutually exclusive in the present system. Thus, as long as political parties and organized campaigns control the political procedure, electronic citizen participation will take a back seat in informational politics, as it refers to formal elections and decision-making.

---

[92] High Level Experts Group (1996).
[93] Klinenberg and Perrin (1996).

Yet, on the other hand, Steve Bartz on the environmental movement, and Matthew Zook on the American militia movement, found a process of empowerment for grassroots groups using the Internet as an instrument of information, communication, and organization.[94] It appears that it is in the realm of symbolic politics, and in the development of issue-oriented mobilizations by groups and individuals outside the mainstream political system that new electronic communication may have the most dramatic effects. The impact of such developments on democracy is unclear. On the one hand, allowing issue mobilization to bypass formal politics may undermine even further the institutions of democracy. On the other hand, if political representation and decision-making could find a linkage with these new sources of inputs from concerned citizens, without yielding to a technologically savvy elite, a new kind of civil society could be reconstructed, thus allowing for electronic grassrooting of democracy.

The development of symbolic politics, and of political mobilization around "non-political" causes, electronically or otherwise, is the third trend that could be in the process of reconstructing democracy in the network society. Humanitarian causes, such as the ones supported by Amnesty International, *Medecins sans frontières*, Greenpeace, Oxfam, Food First, and thousands and thousands of both local and global, activist groups and non-governmental organizations around the world, are the most powerful proactive, mobilizing factor in informational politics.[95] These mobilizations develop around issues that receive a wide consensus, and that are not necessarily aligned with one or another political party. Indeed, in terms of official position, most political parties apparently support most of these causes. And most humanitarian organizations abstain from supporting a given political party, except on specific issues at specific times. Most of these mobilizations are in between social movements and political actions, since they address themselves to citizens, asking people to put pressure on public institutions or private firms that can make a difference on the particular matter targeted by the mobilization. In other instances, they do appeal to people's solidarity directly. Ultimately, their horizon is to act on the political process; that is, to influence the management of society by the representatives of society. But they do not necessarily, and in fact not frequently, use the channels of political representation and decision-making, for instance by electing their candidates to office. These forms of political mobilization, which could be defined as issue-oriented, non-

---

[94]   Bartz (1996); Zook (1996).
[95]   Guehenno (1993).

partisan politics, seem to win increasing legitimacy in all societies, and to condition the rules and outcomes of formal political competition. They re-legitimize the concern with public affairs in people's minds and lives. They do so by introducing new political processes, and new political issues, thus furthering the crisis of classic liberal democracy while fostering the emergence of the yet to be discovered, informational democracy.

Conclusion: Social Change in the Network Society

At the dawn of the Information Age, a crisis of legitimacy is voiding of meaning and function the institutions of the industrial era. Bypassed by global networks of wealth, power, and information, the modern nation-state has lost much of its sovereignty. By trying to intervene strategically in this global scene the state loses capacity to represent its territorially rooted constituencies. In a world where multilateralism is the rule, the separation between nations and states, between the politics of representation and the politics of intervention disorganizes the political accounting unit on which liberal democracy was built and came to be exercised in the past two centuries. The privatization of public agencies and the demise of the welfare state, while alleviating societies from some bureaucratic burden, worsen living conditions for the majority of citizens, break the historic social contract between capital, labor, and the state, and remove much of the social safety net, the nuts and bolts of legitimate government for common people. Torn by internationalization of finance and production, unable to adapt to networking of firms and individualization of work, and challenged by the degendering of employment, the labor movement fades away as a major source of social cohesion and workers' representation. It does not disappear, but it becomes, primarily, a political agent integrated into the realm of public institutions. Mainstream churches, practicing a form of secularized religion dependent either on the state or on the market, lose much of their capacity to enforce behavior in exchange for providing solace, and selling heavenly real estate. The challenge to patriarchalism, and the crisis of the patriarchal family, disturb the orderly sequence of transmitting cultural codes from generation to generation, and shake the foundations of personal security, thus forcing men, women, and children to find new ways of living. Political ideologies that emanate from industrial institutions and organizations, from nation-state-based democratic liberalism to labor-based socialism, find themselves deprived of actual meaning in the new social context. Therefore, they lose their appeal, and, trying to survive, they engage in a series of endless adaptations, running behind the new society, as dusty flags of forgotten wars.

As a result of these convergent processes, the *sources* of what I call in chapter 1 *legitimizing identities* are drained away. The institutions and organizations of civil society that were constructed around the democratic state, and around the social contract between capital and labor, have become, by and large, empty shells, decreasingly able to relate to people's lives and values in most societies. It is indeed a tragic irony that when most countries in the world finally fought their way to access the institutions of liberal democracy (in my view, the foundation of all political democracy), these institutions are so distant from the structure and processes that really matter that they appear to most people as a sarcastic grimace in the new face of history. In this end of millennium, the king and the queen, the state and the civil society, are both naked, and their children-citizens are wandering around a variety of foster homes.

The dissolution of shared identities, which is tantamount to the dissolution of society as a meaningful social system, may well be the state of affairs in our time. Nothing says that new identities have to emerge, new social movements have to re-create society, and new institutions will be rebuilt toward the *lendemains qui chantent*. At first sight, we are witnessing the emergence of a world exclusively made of markets, networks, individuals, and strategic organizations, apparently governed by patterns of "rational expectations" (the new, influential economic theory), except when these "rational individuals" suddenly shoot their neighbor, rape a little girl, or spread nerve gas in the subway. No need for identities in this new world: basic instincts, power drives, self-centered strategic calculations, and, at the macro-social level, "the clear features of a barbarian nomadic dynamic, of a Dionysian element threatening to inundate all borders and rendering international political-legal and civilizational norms problematic."[1] A world whose counterpoint could be, as we are seeing already in a number of countries, a nationalist reassertion by the remnants of state structures, abandoning any pretension to legitimacy, and clawing back from history to the principle of power for the sake of power, sometimes wrapping it in nationalist rhetoric. In the landscapes we have crossed in the first two volumes of this book, we have perceived the seeds of a society whose *Weltanschauung* would split between the old logic of *Macht* and a new logic of *Selbstanschauung*. [2]

[1] Panarin (1994: 37).
[2] *Macht* = strong power; *Weltanschauung* = culture-centered view of the world; *Selbstanschauung* (proposed neologism) = self-centered view of the world.

However, we have also observed the emergence of powerful resistance identities, which retrench in communal heavens, and refuse to
be flushed away by global flows and radical individualism. They build
their communes around the traditional values of God, nation, and the
family, and they secure the enclosures of their encampments with ethnic emblems and territorial defenses. Resistance identities are not
limited to traditional values. They can also be built by, and around,
proactive social movements, which choose to establish their autonomy
in their communal resistance as long as they are not powerful enough
to mount an assault on the oppressive institutions they oppose. This
is, by and large, the case of the women's movement, building women's
spaces where a new anti-patriarchal consciousness may rise; and it is
certainly the case of the sexual liberation movements, whose spaces of
freedom, from bars to neighborhoods, are essential devices of self-
recognition. Even the environmental movement, whose ultimate
horizon is cosmological, more often than not starts in the backyards
and communities around the world, protecting spaces before engaging in the conquest of time.

Thus, resistance identities are as pervasive in the network society as
are the individualistic projects resulting from the dissolution of former legitimizing identities that used to constitute the civil society of
the industrial era. However, these identities resist, they barely communicate. They do not communicate with the state, except to struggle
and negotiate on behalf of their specific interests/values. They rarely
communicate with each other because they are built around sharply
distinct principles, defining an "in" and an "out." And because the
communal logic is the key to their survival, individual self-definitions
are not welcome. Thus, on the one hand, the dominant, global elites
inhabiting the space of flows tend to consist of identity-less individuals ("citizens of the world"); while, on the other hand, people resisting
economic, cultural, and political disfranchisement tend to be
attracted to communal identity.

We should, then, add another layer to the social dynamics of the
network society. Together with state apparatuses, global networks, and
self-centered individuals, there are also communes formed around
resistance identity. However, all these elements do not glue together,
their logic excludes each other, and their coexistence is unlikely to be
peaceful.

The key issue becomes then the emergence of *project identities* (see
chapter 1), potentially able to reconstruct a new civil society of sorts,
and, eventually, a new state. On this matter, I will not be prescriptive
or prophetic, but, rather, I will elaborate on the provisional results of
my observation of social movements and political processes. My analysis does not preclude the possibility that social movements quite

different from those considered here may have a major role in constituting future society. But, as of 1996, I have not detected their signals.

New *project identities* do not seem to emerge from former identities of the industrial era's civil society, but from a development of current *resistance identities*. There are, I believe, theoretical reasons, as well as empirical arguments, for such a trajectory in the formation of new historical subjects. But, before proposing some ideas on the matter, let me clarify how project identities may emerge from the resistance identities we have observed.

The fact that a commune is built around a resistance identity does not mean that it will likely evolve toward building a project identity. It may well remain as a defensive commune. Or else, it may become an interest group, and join the logic of generalized bargaining, the dominant logic of the network society. Yet, in other cases, resistance identities may generate project identities, aiming at the transformation of society as a whole, in continuity with the values of communal resistance to dominant interests enacted by global flows of capital, power, and information.

Religious communes may develop into religious fundamentalist movements aimed at re-moralizing society, re-establishing godly, eternal values, and embracing the whole world, or at least the nearby neighborhood, in a community of believers, thus founding a new society.

The trajectory of nationalism in the Information Age is more undetermined, according to observation of recent experience. On the one hand, it can lead to retrenchment into a reconstructed nation-state, re-legitimizing it on behalf of the nation, rather than of the state. On the other hand, it may supersede the modern nation-state, by affirming nations beyond the state, and building multilateral networks of political institutions in a variable geometry of shared sovereignty.

Ethnicity, while being an essential ingredient of both oppression and liberation, seems to be usually framed in support of other communal identities (religious, national, territorial), rather than inducing either resistance or new projects by itself.

Territorial identity is at the root of the worldwide surge of local and regional governments as significant actors in both representation and intervention, better suited to adapt to the endless variation of global flows. The reinvention of the city-state is a salient characteristic of this new age of globalization, as it was related to the rise of a trading, international economy at the origin of the Modern Age.

Women's communes, and the spaces of sexual identity's freedom, project themselves into society at large by undermining patriarchalism, and by reconstructing the family on a new, egalitarian basis that

implies the degendering of social institutions, in opposition to patriarchal capitalism and to the patriarchal state.

Environmentalism shifts from the defense of one's environment,
health, and well-being, to the ecological project of integrating
humankind and nature, on the basis of the socio-biological identity of
the species, assuming humankind's cosmological meaning.

These identity projects emerge from communal resistance rather
than from the reconstruction of institutions of civil society, because
the crisis of these institutions, and the emergence of resistance identities, originate precisely from the new characteristics of the network
society that undermine the former and induce the latter. Namely,
globalization, capitalist restructuring, organizational networking, the
culture of real virtuality, and the primacy of technology for the sake
of technology, the key features of social structure in the Information
Age, are the very sources of crisis of state and civil society as constituted in the industrial era. They are also the forces against which
communal resistance is organized, with new identity projects potentially emerging around these resistances. Resistance and projects
contradict the dominant logic of the network society by engaging
defensive and offensive struggles around three foundational realms of
this new social structure: space, time, and technology.

The communes of resistance defend their space, their places,
against the placeless logic of the space of flows characterizing social
domination in the Information Age (volume I, chapter 6). They claim
their historic memory, and/or affirm the permanence of their values,
against the dissolution of history in timeless time, and the celebration
of the ephemeral in the culture of real virtuality (volume I, chapter 7).
They use information technology for people's horizontal communication, and communal prayer, while rejecting the new idolatry of
technology, and preserving transcendent values against the deconstructing logic of self-regulating computer networks.

Ecologists affirm the control of uses of space on behalf of both
people and nature against the a-natural, abstract logic of the space of
flows. They advance the cosmological vision of glacial time, integrating the human species into its evolving environment, and reject the
annihilation of time by de-sequencing, a logic embedded in timeless
time (volume I, chapter 7). And they support the use of science and
technology for life, while opposing the domination of life by science
and technology.

Feminists and sexual identity movements affirm the control of their
most immediate spaces, their bodies, over their disembodiment in the
space of flows, influenced by patriarchalism, where reconstructed
images of the woman, and fetishes of sexuality, dissolve their humanity and deny their identity. They also fight for the control of their time,

as the timeless logic of the network society piles up roles and functions over women without adapting their new lives to new timing; so that alienated timing becomes the most concrete expression of the chores of being a liberated woman in a non-liberated social organization. Women and sexual identity movements also aim at using technology to enhance their rights (for instance, their reproductive rights, and the right to control their bodies), against the patriarchal uses of science and technology, as expressed in the submission of women to arbitrary medical rituals and prejudices; or in the temporary lack of will of some scientific institutions in fighting AIDS so long as it was considered to be a homosexual disease. At the moment when humankind reaches the technological frontier of the social control over the biological reproduction of the species, a fundamental battle is being fought between bodies as autonomous identities, and bodies as social artifacts. This is why identity politics start with our bodies.

Thus, the dominant logic of the network society triggers its own challenges, in the form of communal resistance identities, and of project identities potentially emerging from these spaces, *under conditions and through processes that are specific to each institutional and cultural context*. The resulting contradictory dynamics is at the heart of the historical process through which a new social structure, and the flesh and blood of our societies, are being constituted. Where is power in this social structure? And what is power under these historical conditions?

Power, as argued, and to some extent shown, in this and in volume I of this book, is no longer concentrated in institutions (the state), organizations (capitalist firms), or symbolic controllers (corporate media, churches). It is diffused in global networks of wealth, power, information, and images, which circulate and transmute in a system of variable geometry and dematerialized geography. Yet, it does not disappear. *Power still rules society; it still shapes, and dominates, us.* Not only because apparatuses of different kinds can still discipline bodies and silence minds. This form of power is, at the same time, eternal, and fading away. It is eternal because humans are, and will be, predators. But, in its current form of existence, it is fading away: the exercise of this kind of power is increasingly ineffective for the interests that it is supposed to serve. States can shoot, but because the profile of their enemies, and the whereabouts of their challengers, are increasingly unclear, they tend to shoot randomly, with the probability that they may shoot themselves in the process.

The new power lies in the codes of information and in the images of representation around which societies organize their institutions, and people build their lives, and decide their behavior. The sites of this power are people's minds. This is why power in the Information Age is at the same time identifiable and diffused. We know what it is, yet we cannot seize it because power is a function of an endless battle around the cultural codes of society. Whoever, or whatever, wins the battle of people's minds will rule, because mighty, rigid apparatuses will not be a match, in any reasonable timespan, for the minds mobilized around the power of flexible, alternative networks. But victories may be ephemeral, since the turbulence of information flows will keep codes in a constant swirl. This is why identities are so important, and ultimately, so powerful in this ever-changing power structure – because they build interests, values, and projects, around experience, and refuse to dissolve by establishing a specific connection between nature, history, geography, and culture. Identities anchor power in some areas of the social structure, and build from there their resistance or their offensives in the informational struggle about the cultural codes constructing behavior and, thus, new institutions.

Under these conditions, who are the subjects of the Information Age? We already know, or at least I suggest we know, the sources from which they are likely to emerge. I would also add that I think we know from where they are not likely to develop. For instance, the labor movement seems to be historically superseded. Not that it will entirely disappear (although it is dwindling down in much of the world), or that it has lost all relevance. In fact, labor unions are influential political actors in many countries. And in many instances they are the main, or the only, tools for workers to defend themselves against abuses from capital and from the state. Yet, because of the structural features and historical processes that I have tried to convey in the first two volumes of this book, the labor movement does not seem fit to generate by itself and from itself a project identity able to reconstruct social control and to rebuild social institutions in the Information Age. Labor militants will undoubtedly be a part of new, transformative social dynamics. I am less sure that labor unions will.

Political parties have also exhausted their potential as autonomous agents of social change, caught into the logic of informational politics, and with their main platform, the institutions of the nation-state, having lost much of its relevance. They are still, however, essential instruments in processing the demands of society, spearheaded by social movements, into the realms of national, international, and supranational polities. Indeed, while social movements will have to provide the new codes under which societies may be re-thought, and re-established, political parties of some kind (maybe under new, informational incarnations) are still crucial agencies in institutionalizing social transformation. They are influential brokers rather than powerful innovators.

Thus, social movements emerging from communal resistance to

globalization, capitalist restructuring, organizational networking, uncontrolled informationalism, and patriarchalism – that is, for the time being, ecologists, feminists, religious fundamentalists, nationalists, and localists – are the potential subjects of the Information Age. In what forms will they express themselves? My analysis here is necessarily more speculative, although I feel obliged to suggest some hypotheses, as grounded as possible on the observations reported in this volume.

The agencies voicing identity projects aimed at changing cultural codes must be symbol mobilizers. They ought to act on the culture of real virtuality that frames communication in the network society, subverting it on behalf of alternative values, and introducing codes emerging from autonomous identity projects. I have observed two main sorts of such potential agencies. The first I will call *the Prophets*. They are symbolic personalities whose role is not that of charismatic leaders, or of shrewd strategists, but to give a face (or a mask) to a symbolic insurgency, so that they speak on behalf of the insurgents. Thus, voiceless insurgents have a voice, and their identity may enter the realm of symbolic struggles, and stand a chance of seizing power – in people's minds. This is, of course, the case of Subcomandante Marcos, Mexico's *Zapatistas* leader. But also of *compadre* Palenque in La Paz–El Alto. Or of Asahara, the guru of the murderous Japanese cult. Or, to emphasize the diversity of expression of such potential oracles, the case of the Catalan nationalist leader, Jordi Pujol, whose moderation, rationality, and strategic wit often hide his patient determination to insert *Catalunya* as a nation among other European nations, speaking on its behalf, and reconstructing a Carolingian identity for *Catalunya*. He may be the voice of a new, original, state-less brand of nationalism in informational Europe. In another, different example, ecological consciousness is often represented by popular rock singers, such as Sting in his campaign to save Amazonia; or by movie stars, such as Brigitte Bardot, engaging in a crusade on behalf of animal rights. A different kind of prophet could be the neo-luddite Unabomber in America, linking up the anarchist tradition to violent defense of essential nature against the evils of technology. In the Islamic or Christian fundamentalist movements, a number of religious leaders (I will not name names) assume a similar leading role by interpreting the holy texts, thus restating God's truth in the hope it will reach, and touch, the minds and souls of would-be believers. Human rights movements are also often dependent on the agency of symbolic, uncompromising personalities, as is the case in the tradition of Russian dissidents, historically represented by Sakharov, and exemplified in the 1990s by Sergei Kovalov. I deliberately chose to mix the genres in my examples to indicate that there are "good" and "bad" prophets, depending on individual preferences, including my own. But they are all prophets in the sense that they declare the path, affirm the values, and act as symbol senders, becoming a symbol in themselves, so that the message is inseparable from the messenger. Historical transitions, often operated in the midst of crumbling institutions and exhausted political forms, have always been a time for prophets. And it should be even more so in the transition to the Information Age, that is, a social structure organized around information flows and symbol manipulation.

However, the second and *main agency* detected in our journey across the lands inhabited by social movements, is a *networking, decentered form of organization and intervention, characteristic of the new social movements*, mirroring, and counteracting, the networking logic of domination in the informational society. This is clearly the case in the environmentalist movement, built around national and international networks of decentralized activity. But I have also shown this to be the case among women's movements, insurgents against the global order, and religious fundamentalist movements. These networks do more than organizing activity and sharing information. *They are the actual producers, and distributors, of cultural codes.* Not only over the Net, but in their multiple forms of exchange and interaction. Their impact on society rarely stems from a concerted strategy, masterminded by a center. Their most successful campaigns, their most striking initiatives, often result from "turbulences" in the interactive network of multilayered communication – as in the production of a "green culture" by a universal forum of putting together experiences of preserving nature and surviving capitalism at the same time. Or in the demise of patriarchalism resulting from the exchange of women's experiences in women's groups, women's magazines, women's bookstores, women's films, women's clinics, and women's networks of support in raising children. It is this decentered, subtle character of *networks of social change* that makes it so difficult to perceive, and identify, new identity projects coming into being. Because our historical vision has become so used to orderly battalions, colorful banners, and scripted proclamations of social change, we are at a loss when confronted with the subtle pervasiveness of incremental changes of symbols processed through multiform networks, away from the halls of power. It is in these back alleys of society, whether in alternative electronic networks or in grassrooted networks of communal resistance, that I have sensed the embryos of a new society, labored in the fields of history by the power of identity.

To be continued.

Methodological Appendix

Appendix for Tables 5.1 and 5.2

The ratios and rates of change in tables 5.1 and 5.2 were calculated using data from a number of different statistical sources. The tables below have been organized in order to show the actual figures used in the calculations, as well as the ratios and rates of change that were calculated using these data. In those rows in which the original data are presented, sources have been indicated in the far right-hand column, using the following abbreviations:

GFSY	=	*Government Finance Statistics Yearbook,* vol. 18 (Washington DC: IMF, 1994)
IFSY	=	*International Financial Statistics Yearbook,* vol. 48 (Washington, DC: IMF, 1995)
EWY	=	*The Europa World Yearbook* (London: Europa Publications, 1982, 1985, 1995)
OECDNA	=	*National Accounts: Detailed Tables, 1980–1992,* vol. 2 (Paris: OECD, 1994)
WT	=	*World Tables, 1994* (The World Bank, Baltimore: The Johns Hopkins University Press, 1994)

The tables are arranged alphabetically by country. For each country, table 5.1A provides data, calculations and sources for table 5.1, and table 5.2A provides information for table 5.2.

Listed below are a few definitions and explanations of our calculations. Full definitions of all categories included in these tables, and descriptions of the original sources of data and methods of calculation, can be found in the appendices of the source materials.

Exchange rates	=	period averages of market exchange rates and official exchange rates.
Currency reserves	=	reserves, other than gold, at national valuation.
Exports	=	merchandise exports, f.o.b.
Foreign debt	=	distinguished from domestic debt according to the residence of the lender, where possible, and otherwise, according to the currency in which the debt instruments are denominated.
Domestic investment	=	calculated by multiplying each country's figures in the IFSY's "Investment as Percent of GDP" world table by that country's GDP. Investment comprises Gross Fixed Capital Formation and Increase in Stocks.

A (p) following a figure indicates that it is a preliminary figure.

An (f) indicates a final figure.

An * indicates that there is a change in methods of calculation in relation to previous years' figures.

Tables 5.1 and 5.2 and these appendices have been compiled and elaborated by Sandra Moog.

Germany: Table 5.1A Internationalization of the economy and public finance
(in billions of deutschmarks, unless otherwise indicated)

	1980	1991	1992	1993	1994	Rate of change 1980–93%	Source
Average exchange rate (DM per US $)	1.8177	1.6595	1.5617	1.6533	1.6228		IFSY'95
GDP (DM) (1990 DM)	1,470.0 (1,942.4)	2,647.6 (2,548.6)	2,813.0 (2,593.5)	2,853.7 (2,549.5)	2,977.7 (2,608.3)		IFSY'95 IFSY'95
Gov. foreign debt	38.05	243.21	311.73*	472.87(p)		538.5	IFSY'95
Gov. foreign debt/GDP (%)	2.6	9.2	28.5	16.6			
Gov. net foreign borrowing	20.84	45.05	68.52*	161.14(p)			IFSY'95
Total currency reserves minus gold (in millions of US $)	48,592	63,001	90,967	77,640	77,363		
Total currency reserves minus gold (in billions of DM)	88.33	104.55	121.25	128.36	125.54		
Gov. foreign debt/currency reserves (%)	43.1	232.6	257.1	368.4		325.3(p)	
Exports	350.33	665.81	658.47	628.39	677.81		IFSY'95
Gov. foreign debt/exports (%)	10.9	36.5	47.3	75.3		590.8	
Gov. expenditures	447.54	860.74	1,022.95*	1,062.38(p)			IFSY'95

Gov. foreign debt/ gov. expenditures (%)	8.5	28.3	30.5	44.5		423.5(p)	
Gov. net foreign borrowing/ expenditures (%)	4.7	5.2	6.7	15.2		223.4	
Domestic investment (gr. fixed cap. form. + increases in stocks)	367.73	680.43	706.06	684.89	738.47		IFSY'95
Direct foreign investment abroad (in billions of US $)	4.7	23.72	19.67	14.48	14.65		IFSY'95
Direct foreign investment abroad (in billions of DM)	8.54	39.36	30.72	23.94	23.77		
Direct foreign investment abroad/ domestic investment (%)	2.3	5.8	4.4	3.5	3.2	52.2	
Inflow foreign direct investment (in billions of US $)	0.33	4.07	2.44	0.32	-3.02		IFSY'95
Inflow foreign direct investment (in billions of DM)	0.60	6.75	3.81	0.53	-4.90		
Inflow foreign direct investment/ domestic investment (%)	0.2	1.0	0.5	0.1	-0.7	-50.0	

Germany: Table 5.2A Government role in the economy and public finance
(in billions of deutschmarks, unless otherwise indicated)

	1980	1991	1992	1993	1994	Rate of change 1980–92(%)	Source
GDP	1,470.9	2,647.6	2,813.0	2,853.7	2,977.7		IFSY'95
Gov. expenditures	447.54	860.74	1,022.95*	1,062.38(p)			IFSY'95
Gov. expenditure/GDP (%)	30.4	32.5	36.4	37.2(p)		19.7	
Tax revenue (budgetary central gov.)	177.54	351.74	378.82(p)*				GFSY'90,'94
Tax revenue/GDP (%)	12.1	13.3	13.5(p)			11.6(p)	
Gov. budget deficit	−26.91	−62.29	−73.10*	−75.56(p)			IFSY'95
Gov. budget deficit/GDP (%)	1.8	2.3	2.6	2.6		44.4	
Gov. debt	235.77	680.81	801.57	902.52(p)			IFSY'95
Gov. debt/GDP (%)	16.0	25.7	28.5	31.6		78.1	
Gov. employment (employees in thousands)	3,929	4,307	4,340				OECDNA'92

Total employment	23,818	26,183	26,432				OECDNA'92
Gov. employment/ total employment (%)	16.5	16.5	16.4			−0.6	
Gov. consump.	298.0	466.5	502.9	508.5	520.2		IFSY'95
Private consump.	837.0	1,448.8	1,536.3	1,588.9	1,644.5		IFSY'95
Gov. consump./ private consump. (%)	35.6	32.2	32.7	32.0	31.6	−8.1	
Gov. capital expenditures	101.52	175.92	197.72	199.51			EWY'84,'95
Gross fixed capital formation	337.98	652.07	709.22	705.71			EWY'85,'95
Gov. capital expenditures/ gross fixed capital formation (%)	30.0	27.0	27.9	28.3		−7.0	

India: Table 5.1A Internationalization of the economy and public finance (in billions of rupees, unless otherwise indicated)

	1980	1991	1992	1993	1994	Rate of change 1980–93(%)	Source
Average exchange rate (rupees per US $)	8.659	22.724	25.918	30.493	31.374		IFSY'95
GDP (rupees) (1990 rupees)	1,360.1 (3,031.6)	6,160.6 (5,381.3)	7,028.3 (5,629.1)	7,863.6 (5,824.6)			IFSY'95
Gov. foreign debt	107.6	369.5	412.2(p)	464.5(f)			IFSY'95
Gov. foreign debt/GDP (%)	7.9	6.0	5.3(p)	5.9(f)		−25.3	
Gov. net foreign borrowing	7.0	54.2	46.8	55.8			
Total currency reserves minus gold (in millions of US $)	6,944	3,627	5,757	10,199	19,698		IFSY'95
Total currency reserves minus gold (in billions of rupees)	60.13	82.42	149.21	311.00	618.01		

Gov. foreign debt/currency reserves (%)	178.9	448.3	276.3(p)	149.4(f)		−16.5	IFSY'95
Exports	67.52	401.23	508.71	656.89	785.94		IFSY'95
Gov. foreign debt/exports (%)	159.4	92.1	81.0(p)	70.7(f)		−55.6	IFSY'95
Gov. expenditures	180.3	1,050.5	1,209.6(p)	1,310.7(f)			
Gov. foreign debt/gov. expenditures (%)	59.7	35.2	34.1(p)	35.4(f)		−40.7	
Gov. net foreign borrowing/ expenditures (%)	3.9	5.2	3.9	4.3		10.3	
Domestic Investment (gr. fixed cap. form. + increases in stocks)	284.26	1,410.78	1,637.59	1,674.95			IFSY'95

India: Table 5.2A Government role in the economy and public finance
(in billions of rupees, unless otherwise indicated)

	1980	1991	1992	1993	1994	Rate of change 1980–92(%)	Source
GDP	1,360.1	6,160.6	7,028.3	7,863.6			IFSY'95
Gov. expenditures	180.3	1,050.5	1,209.6(p)	1,310.7(f)			IFSY'95
Gov. expenditures/ GDP (%)	13.3	17.1	17.2(p)	16.7(f)		29.3(p)	
Tax revenue (consolidated central gov.)	132.7	673.6	787.8(p)	848.7(f)			GFSY'90,'94
Tax revenue/ GDP (%)	9.8	10.9	11.2	10.8(f)		17.3(p)	
Gov. budget deficit	–88.6	–358.2	–366.5(p)	–372.0			IFSY'95
Gov. budget deficit/GDP (%)	6.5	5.8	5.2	4.7		–20.0(p)	
Gov. debt	561.0	3,312.0	3,714.0(p)	4,136.6(f)			IFSY'95
Gov. debt/GDP (%)	41.2	53.8	52.8(p)	52.6		28.2	
Gov. consump.	130.8	694.6	785.9	910.5			IFSY'95
Private consump.	992.9	3,848.0	4,245.6	4,795.9			IFSY'95

					EWY'85,'95
Gov. consump./ private consump. (%)	13.2	18.1	18.5	19.0	40.2
Gross fixed capital formation	262.8	1,367.8	1,511.8	1,643.8	

Japan: Table 5.1A Internationalization of the economy and public finance (in billions of yen, unless otherwise indicated)

	1980	1991	1992	1993	1994	Rate of change 1980–93(%)	Source
Average exchange rate (yen per US $)	226.74	134.71	126.65	111.20	102.21		IFSY'95
GDP (yen) (1990 yen)	240,176 (271,500)	451,297 (422,720)	463,145 (428,210)	465,972	469,240		IFSY'95 (WT'94)
Gov. foreign debt	621	1,186 ('90)					IFSY'95
Gov. foreign debt/ GDP (%)	0.3	0.3				0.0('90)	
Total currency reserves minus gold (in millions of US $)	24,636	72,059	71,623	98,524	125,860		IFSY'95
Total currency reserves minus gold (in billions of yen)	5,586	9,707.1	9,071.1	10,956	12,864		
Gov. foreign debt/ currency reserves (%)	11.1	12.2				9.9('90)	
Exports	29,382	42,359	43,011	40,200	40,470		IFSY'95
Gov. foreign debt/ exports (%)	2.1	2.3('90)				9.5('90)	

Gov. expenditures	44,137						IFSY'95
Gov. foreign debt/ gov. expenditures	1.4						
Domestic investment (gr. fixed cap. form. + increases in stocks)	77,337	146,672	144,038	139,326	135,610		IFSY'95
Direct foreign investment abroad (in billions of US $)	2.39	30.74	17.24	13.74	17.97		IFSY'95
Direct foreign investment abroad (in billions of yen)	541.91	4,140.99	2,183.45	1,527.89	1,836.71		
Direct foreign investment abroad/ domestic investment (%)	0.7	2.8	1.5	1.1	1.4	57.1	
Inflow foreign direct investment (in billions of US $)	0.28	1.37	2.72	0.10	0.89		IFSY'95
Inflow foreign direct investment (in billions of yen)	63.49	184.55	344.49	11.12	90.97		
Inflow foreign direct investment/domestic investment (%)	0.08	0.13	0.23	0.01	0.07	(erratic)	

Japan: Table 5.2A: Government role in the economy and public finance
(in billions of yen, unless otherwise indicated)

	1980	1991	1992	1993	1994	Rate of change 1980–92(%)	Source
GDP	240,176	451,297	463,145	465,972	469,240		IFSY'95
Gov. expenditures	44,137						IFSY'95
Gov. expenditures/ GDP (%)	0.18						
Tax revenue (budgetary central gov.)	26,392	58,730('90)					GFSY'90,'94
Tax revenue/GDP (%)	11.0	13.0('90)				18.2('90)	
Gov. budget deficit	16,872	6,781('90)					IFSY'95
Gov. budget deficit/GDP (%)	7.0	1.5				−78.6('90)	
Gov. debt	98,149	239,932('90)					IFSY'95
Gov. debt/GDP (%)	40.9	53.2('90)				30.1('90)	
Gov. employment (employees in thousands)	43,070	54,185	55,381				OECDNA'92
Total employment	3,911	3,960	3,975				OECDNA'92

Gov. employment/ total employment (%)	9.1	7.3	7.2			−20.9	
Gov. consump.	23,568	41,232	43,258	44,666	46,108		IFSY'95
Private consump.	240,176	255,084	264,824	270,919	277,677		IFSY'95
Gov. consump./ private consump. (%)	9.8	16.2	16.3	16.5	16.6	66.3	
Gross fixed capital formation	75,420	143,429	142,999	141,322			EWY'85,'95

Spain: Table 5.1A Internationalization of the economy and public finance
(in billions of pesetas, unless otherwise indicated)

	1980	1991	1992	1993	1994	Rate of change 1980–93(%)	Source
Average exchange rate (pesetas per US $)	71.70	103.91	102.38	127.26	133.96		IFSY'95
GDP (psts) (1990 psts)	15,168 (37,305)	54,901 (51,269)	59,002 (51,625)	60,904 (51,054)	64,673 (52,064)		IFSY'95
Gov. foreign debt	133.6	2,968.8	3,259.9	6,364.6	5,893.0		IFSY'95
Gov. foreign debt/ GDP (%)	0.9	5.4	5.5	10.5	9.1	1,066.7	
Gov. net foreign borrowing		1,775.0	124.2	2,712.9	462.4		
Total currency reserves minus gold (in millions of US $)	11,863	65,822	45,504	41,045	41,569		IFSY'95
Total currency reserves minus gold (in billions of pesetas)	850.60	6,839.56	4,658.70	5,233.39	5,568.58		
Gov. foreign debt/ currency reserves (%)	15.7	43.4	70.0	121.6	105.8	674.5	
Exports	1,493.2	6,225.7	6,605.7	7,982.3	9,795.2		IFSY'95
Gov. foreign debt/ exports (%)	8.9	47.7	49.3	79.7	60.2	795.5	
Gov. expenditures	2,522.7	13,102.1	14,835.5	17,503.0	17,034.0		IFSY'95

Gov. foreign debt/ gov. expenditures (%)	5.3	22.7	22.0	36.4	34.6	586.8	
Gov. net foreign borrowing/ gov. expenditures (%)		13.5	0.9	15.5	2.7		
Domestic investment (gr. fixed cap. form. + increases in stocks)	3,518.98	13,505.65	13,393.45	12,119.90	12,740.85		IFSY'95
Direct foreign investment abroad (in millions of US $)	311	4,442	2,192	2,652	4,170		IFSY'95
Direct foreign investment abroad (in billions of pesetas)	22.30	461.57	224.42	337.49	558.61		
Direct foreign investment abroad/ domestic investment (%)	0.6	3.4	1.7	2.8	4.4	183.3	
Inflow foreign direct investment (in millions of US $)	1,493	12,493	13,276	8,144	9,700		IFSY'95
Inflow foreign direct investment (in billions of pesetas)	107.05	1,298.15	1,359.20	1,306.41	1,299.41		
Inflow foreign direct investment/ domestic investment (%)	3.0	9.6	10.1	8.6	10.2	236.7	

Spain: Table 5.2A Government role in the economy and public finance
(in billions of pesetas, unless otherwise indicated)

	1980	1991	1992	1993	1994	Rate of change 1980–92(%)	Source
GDP	15,168	54,901	59,002	60,904	64,673		IFSY'95
Gov. expenditures	2,552.7	13,102.1	14,835.5	17,503.0	17,034.0		IFSY'95
Gov. expenditures/ GDP (%)	16.8	23.9	25.1	28.7	26.3	49.4	
Tax revenue (budgetary central gov.)	1,602.4	9,530.6					GFSY'90,'94
Tax revenue/ GDP (%)	10.6	17.4				64.2('91)	
Gov. budget deficit	−555.8	−1,758.0	−2,523.5	−4,221.4	−4,943.9		IFSY'95
Gov. budget deficit/GDP (%)	3.7	3.2	4.3	6.9	7.6	16.2	
Gov. debt	2,316.7	20,837.3	23,552.7	28,708.9	34,448.0		IFSY'95
Gov. debt/GDP (%)	15.3	38.0	39.9	47.1	53.3	160.8	
Gov. employment (employees, in thousands)		2,041	2,084				OECDNA'92

						Source
Total employment	9,992	9,789	9,616				OECDNA'92
Gov. employment/ total employment (%)	20.1	20.8	21.7				
Private consump.		34,244	37,220	38,511	40,854		IFSY'95
Gov. consump.	2,008	8,882	10,027	10,669	10,992		IFSY'95
Gov. consump./ private consump. (%)		25.9	26.9	27.7	26.9	33.8	
Gross fixed capital formation	3,368	13,041	12,859	12,040	12,709		IFSY'95

United Kingdom: Table 5.1A Internationalization of the economy and public finance
(in billions of pounds sterling, unless otherwise indicated)

	1980	1991	1992	1993	1994	Rate of change 1980–93(%)	Source
Average exchange rate (pounds per US $)	0.4299	0.5652	0.5664	0.6658	0.6529		IFSY'95
GDP (pounds) (1990 pounds)	231.7 (423.49)	575.32 (540.31)	597.24 (537.45)	630.71 (549.59)	668.87 (570.72)		IFSY'95
Gov. foreign debt	10.14	28.45	34.89				IFSY'95
Gov. foreign debt/ GDP (%)	4.4	4.9	5.8			31.8('92)	
Gov. net foreign borrowing	1.43	5.50	4.71				
Total currency reserves minus gold (in billions of US $)	20.65	41.89	36.64	36.78	41.01		IFSY'95
Total currency reserves minus gold (in billions of pounds)	8.73	23.68	20.75	24.49	26.78		
Gov. foreign debt/ currency reserves (%)	116.2	120.1	168.1			44.7('92)	
Exports	47.36	104.88	108.51	120.94	133.03		IFSY'95
Gov. foreign debt/ exports (%)	21.4	27.1	32.2			50.5('92)	
Gov. expenditures	88.48	229.15	257.89				GSFY'90,'94

Gov. foreign debt/ gov. expenditures (%)	11.5	12.4	13.5			17.4('92)	
Gov. net foreign borrowing/ expenditures (%)	1.6	18.3	14.2			787.5('92)	
Domestic investment (gr. fixed cap. form. + increases in stocks)	38.94	92.63	91.97	95.24	103.67		IFSY'95
Direct foreign investment abroad (in millions of US $)	11.23	16.40	19.35	25.64	29.95		IFSY'95
Direct foreign investment abroad (in millions of pounds)	4.83	9.27	10.96	17.07	19.55		
Direct foreign investment abroad/ domestic investment (%)	12.4	10.0	11.9	17.9	18.9	44.4	
Inflow foreign direct investment (in millions of US $)	10.12	16.06	16.49	14.56	10.94		IFSY'95
Inflow foreign direct investment (in millions of pounds)	4.35	9.08	9.34	9.69	7.14		
Inflow foreign direct investment/domestic investment (%)	11.2	9.8	10.2	10.2	6.9	−8.9	

United Kingdom: Table 5.2A Government role in the economy and public finance
(in billions of pounds sterling, unless otherwise indicated)

	1980	1991	1992	1993	1994	Rate of change 1980–92(%)	Source
GDP (pounds) (1990 pounds)	231.7 (423.49)	575.32 (540.31)	597.24 (537.45)	630.71 (549.59)	668.87 (570.72)		IFSY'95
Gov. expenditures	88.48	229.15	257.89			13.1	GSFY'90,'94
Gov. expenditures/ GDP (%)	38.2	39.8	43.2				
Tax revenue (budgetary central gov.)	58.04	159.87	161.21			8.0	GSFY'90,'94
Tax revenue/ GDP (%)	25.0	27.8	27.0				
Gov. budget deficit	–10.73	–5.69	–30.0				IFSY'95
Gov. budget deficit/ GDP (%)	4.6	1.0	5.0			8.7	
Gov. debt	106.75	189.65	203.51				IFSY'95
Gov. debt/GDP (%)	46.1	33.0	34.1			–26.0	
Gov. employment (employees in thousands)	5,349	5,129	4,915				OECDNA'92

							OECDNA'92
Total employment	23,314	22,559	22,138				
Gov. employment/ total employment (%)	22.9	22.7	22.2			−3.1	
Gov. consump.	49.98	124.11	131.88	137.97	144.08		IFSY'95
Private consump.	138.56	364.97	381.72	405.46	428.08		IFSY'95
Gov. consump./ private consump. (%)	36.1	34.0	34.5	34.0		−2.7	
Gov. capital expenditures		20.23	20.08	19.64			EWY'95
Gov. fixed capital formation		41.79	45.99	49.56			EWY'95
Gov. capital expenditures/ gross fixed capital formation (%)	48.4	43.7	39.6				

United States: Table 5.1A Internationalization of the economy and public finance
(in billions of dollars, unless otherwise indicated)

	1980	1991	1992	1993	1994	Rate of change 1980–93(%)	Source
GDP ($) (1990 $)	2,708.1 (4,275.6)	5,722.9 (5,458.3)	6,020.2 (5,673.5)	6,343.3 (5,813.2)	6,738.4 (6,050.4)		IFSY'95
Gov. foreign debt	129.7	491.7	549.7	622.6			IFSY'95
Gov. foreign debt/ GDP (%)	4.8	8.6	9.1	9.8		104.2	
Gov. net foreign borrowing	0.2	68.8	57.6	91.4			IFSY'95
Total currency reserves minus gold	15.60	66.66	60.27	62.35	63.28		IFSY'95
Gov. foreign debt/ currency reserves (%)	831.4	737.6	912.1	998.6		20.1	
Exports	225.57	421.73	448.16	464.77	512.52		IFSY'95
Gov. foreign debt/ exports (%)	57.5	116.6	122.7	134.0		133.0	
Gov. expenditures	596.6	1,429.1	1,445.1	1,492.4			IFSY'95
Gov. foreign debt/ gov. expenditures (%)	21.7	34.4	38.0	41.7		92.2	

Gov. net foreign borrowing/gov. expenditures	0.03	4.8	4.0	6.12		203.0	
Domestic investment (gr. fixed cap. form. + increases in stocks)	541.62	875.60	939.15	1,052.99	1,246.60		IFSY'95
Direct foreign investment abroad	19.23	31.30	41.01	57.87	58.44		IFSY'95
Direct foreign investment abroad/domestic investment (%)	3.6	3.6	4.4	5.5	4.7	52.8	
Inflow foreign direct investment	16.93	26.09	9.89	21.37	60.07		IFSY'95
Inflow foreign direct investment/domestic investment (%)	3.1	3.0	1.1	2.0	4.8	−35.5	

United States: Table 5.2A Government role in the economy and public finance
(in billions of dollars, unless otherwise indicated)

	1980	1991	1992	1993	1994	Rate of change 1980–92(%)	Source
GDP	2,708.1	5,722.9	6,020.2	6,343.3	6,738.4		IFSY'95
Gov. expenditures	596.6	1,429.1	1,445.1	1,492.4			IFSY'95
Gov. expenditures/ GDP (%)	22.0	25.0	24.0	23.5		9.1	
Tax revenue (budgetary central gov.)	346.83	635.54	651.00	706.79			GFSY'88,'94
Tax revenue / GDP (%)	12.8	11.1	10.8	11.1		−15.6	
Gov. budget deficit	−76.2	−272.5	−289.3	−254.1			IFSY'95
Gov. budget deficit/GDP (%)	2.8	4.8	4.0			42.9	
Gov. debt	737.7	2,845.0	3,142.4	3,391.9			IFSY'95
Gov. debt/GDP (%)	27.2	49.7	52.2	53.5		91.9	
Gov. employment (employees in thousands)	14,890	16,893	16,799				OECDNA'95

							OECDNA'92
Total employment	87,401	103,499	103,637				
Gov. employment/total employment (%)	17.0	16.3	16.2			-4.7	
Gov. consump. & investment	507.1	1,099.3	1,125.3	1,148.4	1,175.3		IFSY'95
Private consump.	1,748.1	3,906.4	4,136.9	4,378.2	4,628.4		IFSY'95
Gov. consump./private consump. (%)	29.0	28.1	27.2	26.2	25.4	-6.9	
Gov. capital formation	72.7	139.6	150.6	155.1	160.8		IFSY'95
Gross fixed capital formation	549.8	876.5	938.9	1,037.1	1,193.7		IFSY'95
Gov. capital formation/gross fixed capital formation (%)	13.2	15.9	16.0	15.0	13.5	21.2	

Appendix for Figure 6.4: Level of Support for Mainstream Parties in National Elections, 1980–1994

The percentages in figure 6.4 have been calculated using the electoral returns for elections to the lower house of parliament, except in the case of the United States, in which returns for presidential elections were used. Parties were considered to be mainstream if they had served in government, with the exceptions of the French Communist Party and the Italian Communist Party.

For sources, see the last row of the table for each country below. All data come from one of the following sources:

EWY =   *Europa World Yearbook* (London: Europa Publications, 1982–1995)

SY   =   *Statesman's Yearbook* (ed. Brian Hunter, New York: St Martin's Press, 1994–1995, 1995–1996)

MDI =   *Ministerio del Interior* (cited in *Espana, fin del siglo*, by Carlos Alonso Zaldivar and Manuel Castells, Madrid: Alianza Editorial, 1992)

Valles =   "The Spanish general election of 1993," by Joseph M. Valles, *Electoral Studies*, 1994, 13 (1): 89

All figures in tables are percentages.

France   First round votes for National Assembly

	1981 (1st ballot)	1986 (1st ballot)	1988 (1st ballot)	1993 (1st ballot)
Mainstream parties				
RPR	20.8	11.2	19.2	20.4
UDF	19.2	8.3	18.5	19.1
RPR + UDF		21.5		
Socialists (PS)		31.0	34.8	17.6
MR de G		0.4	1.1	0.9
PS + MR de G	37.4			
Other parties				
Communists (PCF)	16.1	9.8	11.3	9.2
Other left wing	0.8	1.0	1.7	3.6
Extreme gauche	1.4	1.5		3.6
Other right wing	2.8	3.9	2.9	5.0
Extreme droit	0.4	0.2		
Front National		9.7	9.7	12.4
Ecologists		1.2		0.1
Les Vert				4.0
Regionalists		0.1		
Others			0.9	4.2
Total vote for mainstream parties	**77.4**	**72.4**	**73.6**	**58**
Source	EWY-82	EWY-88	EWY-90	EWY-95

Germany: Votes for Bundestag

	1983	1987	1990	1994
Mainstream parties				
CDU/CSU	48.8	44.2	43.8	41.5
Social Democratic Party (SPD)	38.2	37.0	33.5	36.4
Free Democrats (FDP)	7.0	9.1	11.0	6.9
Other parties				
Communists (DKP)	0.2			
Dem. Socialists (former Com.)				
Party of Dem. Soc. (PDS) (former Com. Party of GDR)			2.4	4.4
Republican Party			1.2	1.9
Nat. Dem. Party (NDP)	0.2	0.6		
Greens (+ Alliance '90 in 1990 & 1994)	5.6	8.3	5.0	7.3
Ecological Dem. Party (ODP)		0.3		
Women's Party		0.2		
Others		0.3	2.1	1.7
Total vote for mainstream parties	**94.0**	**90.3**	**88.3**	**84.8**
Source	EWY-84	EWY-88	EWY-92	EWY-95

Italy Votes for Chamber of Deputies

	1983	1987	1992
Mainstream parties			
Republicans (PRI)	5.1	3.7	4.4
Liberals (PLI)	2.9	2.1	2.8
Christian Democrats (DC)	32.9	34.3	29.7
Social Democrats (PSDI)	4.1	3.0	2.7
Socialists (PSI)	11.4	14.3	13.6
Communist Party (PCI)	29.9	26.6	
Dem. Party of the Left (formerly communists)			16.1
Refounded communists (formerly communists)			5.6
Other parties			
Italian Social Movement (MSI)	6.8	5.9	5.4
New United Left (Proletarian Democrats + Lotta Continua)			
Proletarian Dem.	1.5	1.7	
Radicals (PR)	2.2	2.6	
Regional parties			
Northern League			8.7
Sudtiroler Volkpartei	0.5		
La Rete			1.9
Greens		2.5	2.8
Others	2.7	3.3	6.3
Total vote for			
mainstream parties	**86.3**	**84.0**	**79.9**
Source	EWY-84	EWY-88	SY-94-5

Japan   Votes for House of Representatives

	1983	1986	1990	1993
Mainstream parties				
Liberal Dem. (LDP)	45.8	49.4	46.1	36.62
New Lib. Club (NLC)	2.4	1.8		
(rejoins LDP in '86)				
Dem. Soc. Party (DSP)	7.3	6.5	4.8	3.51
Socialists (JSP)	19.5	17.2	24.4	15.43
(becomes Soc. Dem. Party				
of Japan in 1992)				
Other parties				
Progressive Party			0.4	
Komeito	10.1	9.4	8.0	8.14
Japan New Party (JNP)				8.05
Japan Renewal Party				10.10
Soc. Dem. Fed. (SDF)	0.7	0.8	0.9	0.73
(+Un. Soc. Dem. P. in '93)				
Communists (JCP)	9.3	8.8	8.0	7.70
Independent	4.9	5.8	7.3	6.85
Sakigake				2.00
Others	0.1	0.2	0.1	0.23
Total vote for				
mainstream parties	**75.0**	**74.9**	**75.3**	**55.56**
Source	EWY-86	EWY-88	EWY-90	EWY-95

Spain   Votes for Congress of Deputies

	1982	1986	1989	1993
Mainstream parties				
ADP + PDP (+ PL in '88 = CP)	26.4	26.1		
Popular Party (AP -->PP in 1989)			26.0	34.6
Union de Centro Dem. (UCD)	9.8			
Social and Democratic		9.2	8.0	1.8
Center (CDS)				
Spanish Workers' Socialist	48.4	44.4	39.8	38.5
Party (PSOE)				
Other parties				
Span. Communist Party (PCE)	3.9			
United Left (IU)		4.7	9.1	9.5
Basque Nationalist Party (PNV)	1.9	1.5	1.2	1.2
Convergence and Union (CiU)	3.7	5.1	5.1	4.9
Others	5.9	9.1	10.8	9.4
Total vote for				
mainstream parties	**84.6**	**79.7**	**73.8**	**74.9**
Source	MDI	MDI	MDI	Valles

United Kingdom   Votes for House of Commons

	1983	1987	1992
Mainstream parties			
Conservatives	42.4	42.3	41.9
Liberals (+ Soc. Dem.)	25.4	22.6	17.9
Labour Party	27.6	30.9	34.4
Other parties			
Soc. and Dem. Lab. Party	0.4	0.5	0.5
Plaid Cymru	0.4	0.4	0.5
Scottish National Party	1.1	1.3	1.9
Sinn Fein	0.3	0.3	
Ulster Popular Unionist Party	0.1		
Ulster Unionists	0.8		
Dem. Unionist Party	0.5		
(All 3)		1.2	1.2
Others	1.0	0.5	1.8
Total vote for mainstream parties	**95.4**	**95.8**	**94.2**
Source	EWY-86	EWY-90	EWY-95

United States   Popular vote for President

	1980	1984	1988	1992
Mainstream parties				
Democrats	41.0	40.5	45.6	42.9
Republicans	50.8	58.8	53.4	37.5
Others				
John Anderson	6.6			
Ross Perot				18.9
Others	1.6	0.7	1.0	0.8
Total vote for mainstream parties	**91.8**	**99.3**	**99.0**	**80.4**
Source	EWY-81	EWY-88	EWY-90	EWY-94

Summary of Contents of Volumes I and III

Throughout this volume, reference has been made to the themes presented in volume I (published by Blackwell Publishers in 1996) and volume III (to be published in 1997). An outline of their contents is given below:

Volume I: *The Rise of the Network Society*

Prologue: The Net and the Self
1   The Information Technology Revolution
2   The Informational Economy and the Process of Globalization
3   The Network Enterprise: the Culture, Institutions, and Organizations of the Informational Economy
4   The Transformation of Work and Employment: Networkers, Jobless, and Flexitimers
5   The Culture of Real Virtuality: the Integration of Electronic Communication, the End of the Mass Audience, and the Rise of Interactive Networks
6   The Space of Flows
7   The Edge of Forever: Timeless Time
Conclusion: The Network Society

Volume III: *End of Millennium*

A Time of Change
1   The Crisis of Industrial Statism and the Collapse of the Soviet Union
2   The Rise of the Fourth World: Informational Captalism, Poverty, and Social Exclusion
3   The Perverse Connection: the Global Criminal Economy

References

Abelove, Henry, Barale, Michele Aina and Halperin, David M. (eds) (1993) *The Lesbian and Gay Studies Reader*, New York: Routledge.

Abramson, Jeffrey B., Artertone, F. Christopher and Orren, Cary R. (1988) *The Electronic Commonwealth: The Impact of New Media Technologies in Democratic Politics*, New York: Basic Books.

Adler, Margot (1979) *Drawing Down the Moon: Witches, Druids, Goddess-worshippers, and Other Pagans in America Today*, Boston: Beacon.

Aguirre, Pedro et al. (1995) *Una reforma electoral para la democracia. Argumentos para el consenso*, Mexico: Instituto de Estudios para la transicion democratica.

Akhmatova, Anna (1985) *Selected Poems*, trans. D. M. Thomas, London: Penguin.

Al-Azmeh, Aziz (1993) *Islams and Modernities*, London: Verso.

Alberdi, Ines (ed.) (1995) *Informe sobre la situacion de la familia en Espana*, Madrid: Ministerio de Asuntos Sociales.

Albo, Xavier (1993) *Y de Kataristas a MNRistas? La soprendente y audaz alianza entre Aymaras y neoliberales en Bolivia*, La Paz: CEDOIN-UNITAS.

Alexander, Herbert E. (1992) *Financing Politics. Money, Elections, and Political Reform*, Washington, DC: CQ Press.

Allen, Thomas B. (1987) *Guardian of the Wild. The Story of the National Wildlife Federation, 1936-1986*, Bloomington, Ind.: Indiana.

Alley, Kelly D. et al. (1995) "The historical transformation of a grassroots environmental group", *Human Organization*, 54 (4): 410–16.

Alonso Zaldivar, Carlos (1996) *Variaciones sobre un mundo en cambio*. Madrid: Alianza Editorial.

— and Castells, Manuel (1992) *Espana fin de siglo*, Madrid: Alianza Editorial.

Ammerman, Nancy (1987) *Bible Believers: Fundamentalists in the Modern World*, New Brunswick, NJ: Rutgers University Press.

Anderson, Benedict (1983) *Imagined Communities: Reflections on the Origin and Spread of Nationalism*, London: Verso (read in the 2nd edn, 1991).

Anderson, P. and Comiller, P. (eds) (1994) *Mapping the West European Left*, London: Verso.

Ansolabehere, Stephen and Iyengar, Shanto (1994) "Riding the wave and claiming ownership over issues: the joint effects of advertising and news coverage in campaigns", *Public Opinion Quarterly*, 58: 335–57.

— et al. (1993) *The Media Game: American Politics in the Television Age*, New York: Macmillan.

Anthes, Gary H. (1993) "Government ties to Internet expand citizens' access to data", *Computerworld*, 27, (34): 77.

Anti-Defamation League (1994) *Armed and Dangerous*, New York: Anti-Defamation League of B'nai B'rith.

Anti-Defamation League (1995) *Special Report: Paranoia as Patriotism: Far-Right Influence on the Militia Movement*, New York: Anti-Defamation League of B'nai B'rith.

Aoyama, Yoshinobu (1991) *Riso Shakai: kyosanto sengen kara shinri'e (The Ideal Society: from Communist Manifesto to Truth)*, Tokyo: AUM Press.

Appiah, Kwame Anthony and Gates, Henry Louis, Jr (eds) (1995) *Identities*, Chicago: The University of Chicago Press.

Archondo, Rafael (1991) *Compadres al microfono: la resurreccion metropolitana del ayllu*, La Paz: Hisbol.

Ardaya, Gloria and Verdesoto, Luis (1994) *Racionalidades democraticas en construccion*, La Paz: ILDIS.

Arlachi, Pino (1995) "The Mafia, Cosa Nostra, and Italian institutions", in Sechi (ed.): 153–63.

Armond, Paul (1995) "Militia of Montana meeting at the Maltby Community Center", *World Wide Web*, MOM site, February 11.

Armstrong, David (1995) "Cyberhoax!", *Columbia Journalism Review*, September/October.

Arquilla, John and Rondfeldt, David (1993) "Cyberwar is coming!", *Comparative Strategy*, 12 (2): 141–65.

Arrieta, Carlos G. et al. (1991) *Narcotrafico en Colombia. Dimensiones politicas, economicas, juridicas e internacionales*, Bogota: Tercer Mundo Editores.

Asahara, Shoko (1994) *Metsubo no Hi (The Doomsday)*, Tokyo: AUM Press.

— (1995) *Hi Izuru Kuni Wazawai Chikashi (Disasters Come Close to the Nation as the Rising Sun)*, Tokyo: AUM Press.

Astrachan, Anthony (1986) *How Men Feel: Their Response to Women's*

Demands for Equality and Power, Garden City, NY: Anchor Press/Doubleday.

Athanasiou, Tom (1996) *Divided Planet: The Ecology of Rich and Poor*, Boston: Little, Brown.

Awakening (1995) Special issue, no. 158–1961, Taipei (Chinese language).

Axford, Barrie et al. (1992) "Image management, stunts, and dirty tricks: the marketing of political brands in television campaigns", *Media, Culture, and Society*, 14 (4): 637–51.

Azevedo, Milton (ed.) (1991) *Contemporary Catalonia in Spain and Europe*, Berkeley: University of California, Gaspar de Portola Catalonian Studies Program.

Bachr, Peter R. and Gordenker, Leon (1994) *The UN in the 1990s*, New York: St Martin's Press.

Badie, Bertrand (1992) *L'etat importe: essai sur l'occidentalisation de l'ordre politique*, Paris: Fayard.

Bakhash, Shaul (1990) "The Islamic Republic of Iran, 1979-1989", *Middle East Focus*, 12 (3): 8–12, 27.

Balta, Paul (ed.) (1991) *Islam: Civilisations et sociétés*, Paris: Editions du Rocher.

Balz, Dan and Brownstein, Ronald (1996) *Storming the Gates: Protest Politics and the Republican Revival*, Boston: Little, Brown.

Barber, Benjamin R. (1993) "Letter from America, September 1993: the rise of Clinton, the fall of democrats, the scandal of the media", *Government and Opposition*, 28 (4): 433–43.

Barker, Anthony (1992) *The Upturned Stone: Political Scandals in Twenty Democracies and their Investigation Process*", Colchester: University of Essex, Essex Papers in Politics and Government.

Barnett, Bernice McNair (1995) "Black women's collectivist move- ment organizations: their struggles during the 'doldrums'", in Ferree and Martin (eds), pp. 199–222.

Barone, Michael and Ujifusa, Grant (1995) *The Almanac of American Politics 1996*, Washington: National Journal.

Barron, Bruce and Shupe, Anson (1992) "Reasons for growing popu- larity of Christian reconstructionism: the determination to attain dominion", in Misztal and Shupe (eds), pp. 83-96.

Bartholet, E. (1990) *Family Bonds, Adoption and the Politics of Parenting*, New York: Houghton Mifflin.

Bartz, Steve (1996) "Environmental organizations and evolving infor- mation technologies", Berkeley: University of California, Department of Sociology, unpublished seminar paper for SOC 290.2, May.

Baylis, John and Rengger, N.J. (eds) (1992) *Dilemmas of World Politics. International Issues in a Changing World*, Oxford: Clarendon Press.

Beccalli, Bianca (1994) "The modern women's movement in Italy", *New Left Review*, 204, March/April: 86-112.

Bellah, Robert N., Sullivan, William M., Swidler, Ann and Tipton, Steven M. (1985) *Habits of the Heart. Individualism and Commitment in American Life*, Berkeley: University of California Press (cited in the Perennial Library edition from Harper and Row, New York, 1986).

Bellers, Jurgen (ed.) (1989) *Politische Korruption*, Munster: Lit.

Bennett, David H. (1995) *The Party of Fear: the American Far Right from Nativism to the Militia Movement*, New York: Vintage Books.

Bennett, William J. (1994) *The Index of Leading Cultural Indicators: Facts and Figures on the State of American Society*, New York: Touchstone.

Berdal, Mats R. (1993) *Whither UN Peacekeeping?: An Analysis of the Changing Military Requirements of UN Peacekeeping with Proposals for its Enhancement*, London: Brassey's for International Institute of Strategic Studies.

Berins Collier, Ruth (1992) *The Contradictory Alliance. State-Labor Relationships and Regime Changes in Mexico*, Berkeley: University of California, International and Area Studies.

Berlet, Chips and Lyons, Matthew N. (1995) "Militia nation", *The Progressive*, June.

Berman, Jerry and Weitzner, Daniel J. (1995) "Abundance and user control: renewing the democratic heart of the First Amendment in the age of interactive media", *Yale Law Journal*, 104, (7) 1619-37.

Bernard, Jessie (1987) *The Female World from a Global Perspective*, Bloomington, Ind.: Indiana University Press.

Berry, Sebastian (1992) "Party strategy and the media: the failure of Labour's 1991 election campaign", *Parliamentary Affairs*, 45, (4): 565-81.

Betts, Mitch (1995) "The politicizing of cyberspace", *Computerworld*, 29 (3): 20.

Bilbao La Vieja Diaz, Antonio, Perez de Rada, Ernesto and Asturizaga, Ramiro (1996) "CONDEPA movimiento patriotico", La Paz: Naciones Unidas/CIDES, unpublished research monograph.

Birnbaum, Lucia Chiavola (1986) *Liberazione della donna: Feminism in Italy*, Middletown, Conn.: Wesleyan University Press.

Black, Gordon S. and Black, Benjamin D. (1994) *The Politics of American Discontent: How a New Party Can Make Democracy Work Again*, New York: John Wiley and Sons.

Blakely, Edward and Goldsmith, William (1993) *Separate Societies: Poverty and Inequality in American Cities*, Philadelphia: Temple University Press.

Blas Guerrero, Andres (1994) *Nacionalismos y naciones en Europa*, Madrid: Alianza Editorial.

Blossfeld, Hans-Peter (ed.) (1995) *The New Role of Women: Family Formation in Modern Societies*, Boulder, Colo.: Westview Press.

Blum, Linda (1991) *Between Feminism and Labor: The Politics of the Comparable Worth Movement*, Berkeley: University of California Press.

Blumberg, Rae Lesser, Rakowski, Cathy A. Tinker, Irene and Monteon, Michael (eds) (1995) *EnGENDERing Wealth and Well-being*, Boulder, Colo.: Westview Press.

Blumenfield, Seth D. (1994) "Developing the global information infrastructure", *Federal Communications Law Journal*, 47(2): 193–6.

Blumstein, Philip and Schwartz, Pepper (1983) *American Couples: Money, Work, Sex*, New York: William Morrow.

Boardmann, Robert (1994) *Post-socialist World Orders: Russia, China, and the UN system*, New York: St Martin's Press.

Bobbio, Norberto (1994) *Destra e sinistra: ragioni e significati di una distinzione politica*, Roma: Donzelli editore.

Borja, Jordi (1988) *Estado y ciudad*, Barcelona: Promociones y Publicaciones Universitarias.

— and Castells, Manuel (1996) *Local and Global: The Management of Cities in the Information Age*, London: Earthscan.

— et al. (1992) *Estrategias de desarrollo e internacionalizacion de las ciudades europeas: las redes de ciudades*, Barcelona: Consultores Europeos Asociados, Research Report.

Bouissou, Jean-Marie (1991) "Corruption à la Japonaise", *L'Histoire*, 142, March: 84–7.

Bramwell, Anna (1989) *Ecology in the 20th Century: A History*, New Haven: Yale University Press.

— (1994) *The Fading of the Greens: The Decline of Environmental Politics in the West*, New Haven: Yale University Press.

Brenner, Daniel (1994) "In search of the multimedia grail", *Federal Communications Law Journal*, 47 (2), pp: 197–203.

Broadcasting & Cable (1995) "Top of the week", May.

Brown, Helen (1992) *Women Organising*, London: Routledge.

Brown, Michael (1993) "Earth worship or black magic?", *The Amicus Journal*, 14 (4): 32–4.

Brubaker, Timothy H. (ed.) (1993) *Family Relations: Challenges for the Future*, Newbury Park, Calif.: Sage.

Bruce, Judith, Lloyd, Cynthia B. and Leonard, Ann (1995) *Families in Focus: New Perspectives of Mothers, Fathers, and Children*, New York: Population Council

Brulle, Robert J. (1996) "Environmental discourse and social movement organizations: a historical and rhetorical perspective on the development of US environmental organizations", *Sociological Inquiry*, 66 (1): 58–83.

Buci-Glucksman, Christine (1978) *Gramsci et l'état*, Paris: Grasset.

Buckler, Steve (1993) *Dirty Hands: the Problem of Political Morality*, Brookfield: Averbury.

Buckley, Peter (ed.) (1994) *Cooperative Forms of Transnational Corporation Activity*, London and New York: Routledge.

Buechler, Steven M. (1990) *Women's Movement in the United States*, Brunswick, NJ: Rutgers University Press.

Bull, Hedley (1977) *The Anarchical Society*, London: Macmillan.

Burgat, Francois and Dowell, William (1993) *The Islamic Movement in North Africa*, Austin, Texas: University of Texas Center for Middle Eastern Studies.

Burnham, David (1983) *The Rise of the Computer State*, New York: Vintage.

Business Week (1995a) "The future of money", June 12.

Business Week (1995b) "Hot money", March 20.

Business Week (1995c), "Mexico: Salinas is fast becoming a dirty word", December 25: 54–5.

Business Week (1995d) "The new populism", March.

Business Week (1995e) "Power to the states", August: 49–56.

Buss, David M. (1994) *The Evolution of Desire: Strategies of Human Mating*, New York: Basic Books.

Butler, Judith (1990) *Gender Trouble: Feminism and the Subversion of Identity*, New York: Routledge.

Cabre, Anna (1990) "Es compatible la proteccion de la familia con la liberacion de la mujer?", in Instituto de la Mujer (ed.), *Mujer y Demografia*, Madrid: Ministerio de Asuntos Sociales.

— and Domingo, Antonio (1992) "La Europa despues de Maastrich: reflexiones desde la demografia", *Revista de Economia*, 13: 63–9.

Cacho, Jesus (1994) *MC: un intruso en el laberinto de los elegidos*, Madrid: Temas de hoy.

Caipora Women's Group (1993) *Women in Brazil*, London: Latin American Bureau.

Calabrese, Andrew and Borchert, Mark (1996) "Prospects for electronic democracy in the United States: rethinking communication and social policy", *Media, Culture, and Society*, 18: 249–68.

Calderon, Fernando (1995) *Movimientos sociales y politica*, Mexico: Siglo XXI.

— and Laserna, Roberto (1994) *Paradojas de la modernidad*, La Paz: Fundacion Milenio.

— et al. (1996) *Esa esquiva modernidad: desarrollo, ciudadania y cultura en America Latina y el Caribe*, Caracas: Nueva Sociedad/UNESCO.

Calhoun, Craig (ed.) (1994) *Social Theory and the Politics of Identity*, Oxford: Blackwell.

Camilleri, J.A. and Falk, K. (1992) *The End of Sovereignty*, Aldershot: Edward Elgar.

Campbell, B. (1992) "Feminist politics after Thatcher." In H. Hinds, et al. (eds) *Working Out: New Directions for Women's Studies*, London: Taylor and Francis: 13–17.

Campbell, Colin and Rockman, Bert A. (eds) (1995) *The Clinton Presidency: First Appraisals*, Chatham, NJ: Chatham House.

Campo Vidal, Manuel (1996) *La transicion audiovisual*, Barcelona: B Ediciones.

Cardoso de Leite, Ruth (1983) "Movimientos sociais urbanos: balanco critico." In *Sociedade e politica no Brasil pos-64*, Sao Paulo: Brasiliense.

Carnoy, Martin (1984) *The State and Political Theory*, Princeton, NJ: Princeton University Press.

— (1993) "Multinationals in a changing world economy: whither the nation-state?", in Carnoy et al. (eds), pp. 45–96.

— (1994) *Faded Dreams: The Politics and Economics of Race in America*, New York: Cambridge University Press.

—, Castells, Manuel, Cohen, Stephen S. and Cardoso, Fernando H. (1993) *The New Global Economy in the Information Age*, University Park, PA: Penn State University Press.

Carre, Olivier (1984) *Mystique et politique: Lecture revolutionnaire du Coran by Sayyed Qutb*, Paris: Editions du Cerf-Presses de la Fondation Nationale des Sciences Politiques.

Carrere d'Encausse, Helene (1987) *Le grand defi: Bolcheviks et nations, 1917–1930*, Paris: Flammarion.

— (1993) *The End of the Soviet Empire: The Triumph of Nations*, New York: Basic Books (original French edition 1991).

Castells, Manuel (1981) "Local government, urban crisis, and political change", in *Political Power and Social Theory: A Research Annual*, Greenwich, CT: JAI Press, 2, pp. 1–20.

— (1983) *The City and the Grassroots: A Cross-cultural Theory of Urban Social Movements*, Berkeley: University of California Press, and London: Edward Arnold.

— (1992a) "Four Asian tigers with a dragon head: a comparative analysis of the state, economy, and society in the Asian Pacific rim", in Appelbaum, Richard, and Henderson, Jeffrey (eds) *States and Development in the Asian Pacific Rim*, Newbury Park, CA: Sage, pp. 33–70.

— (1992b) *La nueva revolucion rusa*, Madrid: Sistema.

— (1992c) "Las redes sociales del SIDA." Keynote address delivered at the Social Sciences Symposium, World Congress on AIDS research, Madrid, May 1992.

— (1996) "El futuro del estado del bienestar en la sociedad informacional", *Sistema*, 131, March: 35–53.

— and Murphy, Karen (1982) "Cultural identity and urban structure: the spatial organization of San Francisco's gay community", in

Fainstein, Norman I., and Fainstein, Susan S. (eds) *Urban Policy Under Capitalism*, Urban Affairs Annual Reviews, vol. 22, Beverly Hills, Calif.: Sage: 237–60.

—, Yazawa, Shujiro and Kiselyova, Emma (1996) "Insurgents against the global order: a comparative analysis of the Zapatistas in Mexico, the American Militia and Japan's Aum Shinrikyo", *Berkeley Journal of Sociology*, 40: 21–60.

Castells, Nuria (forthcoming) "Environmental policies and international agreements in the European Union: a comparative analysis", Amsterdam: University of Amsterdam, Economics Department, unpublished doctoral dissertation.

Chatterjee, Partha (1993) *The Nation and its Fragments: Colonial and Postcolonial Histories*, Princeton, NJ: Princeton University Press.

Chesnais, François (1994) *La mondialisation du capital*, Paris: Syros.

Cheung, Peter T.Y. (1994) "Relations between the central government and Guandong", in Y.M. Yeung and David K.Y. Chu (eds), *Guandong: Survey of a Province Undergoing Rapid Change*, Hong Kong: The Chinese University Press, pp. 19–51.

Cho, Lee-Jay and Yada, Moto (eds) (1994) *Tradition and Change in the Asian Family*, Honolulu: University of Hawaii Press.

Chodorow, Nancy (1978) *The Reproduction of Mothering: Psychoanalysis and the Sociology of Gender*, Berkeley: University of California Press.

— (1989) *Feminism and Psychoanalytical Theory*, New Haven: Yale University Press.

— (1994) *Feminities, Masculinities, Sexualities: Freud and Beyond*, Lexington, Ky: University Press of Kentucky.

Chong, Rachelle (1994) "Trends in communication and other musings on our future", *Federal Communications Law Journal*, 47 (2): 213–19.

Choueri, Youssef M. (1993) *Il fondamentalismo islamico: Origine storiche e basi sociali*, Bologna: Il Mulino.

Coalition for Human Dignity (1995) *Against the New World Order: the American Militia Movement*, Portland, Oregon: Coalition for Human Dignity Publications.

Coates, Thomas J. et al. (1988) *Changes in Sex Behavior of Gay and Bisexual Men since the Beginning of the AIDS Epidemics*, San Francisco: University of California, Center for AIDS Prevention Studies.

Cobble, Dorothy S. (ed.) (1993) *Women and Unions: Forging a Partnership*, New York: International Labour Review Press.

Cohen, Roger (1996) "Global forces batter politics", *The New York Times*, Sunday November 17, s. 4: 1–4.

Cohen, Stephen (1993) "Geo-economics: lessons from America's mistakes", in Carnoy et al. (eds), pp. 97–148.

Cohen, Jeffrey E. (1986) "The dynamics of the 'revolving door' on the FCC", *American Journal of Political Science*, 30 (4).

Coleman, Marilyn and Ganong, Lawrence H. (1993) "Families and marital disruption", in Brubaker (ed.), pp. 112–28.

Coleman, William E. Jr and Coleman, William E., Sr (1993) *A Rhetoric of the People: the German Greens and the New Politics*, Westport, Conn.: Praeger.

Collective Author (1996) *La seguridad humana en Bolivia: percepciones politicas, sociales y economicas de los bolivianos de hoy*, La Paz: PRON-AGOB-PNUD-ULDIS.

Collier, George A. (1995) *Restructuring Ethnicity in Chiapas and the World*, Stanford University, Department of Anthropology, Research Paper (published in Spanish in Nash et al. (eds), pp. 7–20).

— and Lowery Quaratiello, Elizabeth (1994) *Basta! Land and the Zapatista Rebellion in Chiapas*, Oakland, California: Food First Books.

Conquest, Robert (ed.) (1967) *Soviet Nationalities Policy in Practice*, New York: Praeger.

Contreras Basnipeiro, Adalid (1991) "Medios multiples, pocas voces: inventario de los medios de comunicacion de masas en Bolivia", *Revista UNITAS*, pp. 61–105.

Cook, Maria Elena et al. (eds) (1994) *The Politics of Economic Restructuring: State-society Relations and Regime Change in Mexico*, La Jolla: University of California at San Diego, Center of US–Mexican Studies.

Cooke, Philip (1994) *The Cooperative Advantage of Regions*, Cardiff: University of Wales, Centre for Advanced Studies.

Cooper, Jerry (1995) *The Militia and the National Guard in America since Colonial Times: a Research Guide*, Westport, Conn.: Greenwood Press.

Cooper, Marc (1995) "Montana's mother of all militias", *The Nation*, May 22.

Corn, David (1995) "Playing with fire", *The Nation*, May 15.

Costain, W. Douglas and Costain, Anne N. (1992) "The political strategies of social movements: a comparison of the women's and environmental movements", in *Congress and the Presidency*, 19 (1): 1–27.

Cott, Nancy (1989) "What's in a name? The limits of 'social feminism'; or, expanding the vocabulary of women's history", *Journal of American History*, 76: 809–29.

Couch, Carl J. (1990) "Mass communications and state structures", *The Social Science Journal*, 27, (2): 111–28.

CQ Researcher (1992) Special Issue: "Politicians and privacy", 2 (15), April 17.

Dalton, Russell J. (1994) *The Green Rainbow: Environmental Groups in Western Europe*, New Haven: Yale University Press.

— and Kuechler, Manfred (1990) *Challenging the Political Order: New Social and Political Movements in Western Democracies*, Cambridge: Polity Press.

Daniel, Donald and Hayes, Bradd (eds) (1995) *Beyond Traditional Peacekeeping*, New York: St Martin's Press.

Davidson, Osha Grey (1993) *Under Fire: the NRA and the Battle for Gun Control*, New York: Henry Holt.

Davis, John (ed.) (1991) *The Earth First! Reader*, Salt Lake City: Peregrine Smith Books.

Dees, Morris, and Corcoran, James (1996) *Gathering Storm: America's Militia Network*, New York: Harper-Collins.

Dekmejian, R. Hrair (1995) *Islam in Revolution: Fundamentalism in the Arab World*, Syracuse, NY: Syracuse University Press.

Delcroix, Catherine (1995) "Algeriennes et Egyptiennes: enjeux et sujets de societes en crise", in Dubet and Wieviorka (eds), pp. 257–72.

DeLeon, Peter (1993) *Thinking about Political Corruption*, Armonk, NY: M.E. Sharpe.

Delphy, Christine (ed.) (1984) *Particularisme et universalisme*, Paris: Nouvelles Questions Feministes, n. 17/17/18.

D'Emilio, John (1980/1993) "Capitalism and gay identity", in Abelove et al. (eds), pp. 467–76.

— (1983) *Sexual Politics, Sexual Communities: the Making of a Homosexual Minority in the United States, 1940–1970*, Chicago: University of Chicago Press.

DeMont, John (1991) "Frontline fighters", *Mclean's*, 104 (50): 46–7.

Dentsu Institute for Human Studies (1994) *Media in Japan*, Tokyo: DataFlow International.

Deutsch, Karl (1953) *Nationalism and Social Communication: an Inquiry into the Foundations of Nationality* (consulted in the 1966 edition, Cambridge, Mass.: MIT Press).

De Vos, Susan (1995) *Household Composition in Latin America*, New York: Plenum Press.

Diamond, Irene and Orenstein, Gloria (1990) *Reweaving the World: the Emergence of Ecofeminism*, San Francisco: Sierra Club Books.

Diani, Mario (1995) *Green Networks: a Structural Analysis of the Italian Environmental Movement*, Edinburgh: Edinburgh University Press.

Dickens, Peter (1990) "Science, social science and environmental issues: Ecological movements as the recovery of human nature", paper prepared for the meeting of the British Association for the Advancement of Science, University of Swansea, August.

Dietz, Thomas and Kalof, Linda (1992) "Environmentalism among nation-states", *Social Indicators Research*, 26: 353–66.

Di Marco, Sabina (1993) "Se la televisione guarda a sinistra", *Ponte*, 49 (7): 869–78.

— (1994) "La televisione, la politica e il cavaliere", *Ponte*, 50 (2): 9–11.

Dionne, E.J. (1996) *They Only Look Dead: Why Progressives Will Dominate the Next Political Era*, New York: Simon and Schuster.

Dobson, Andrew (1990) *Green Political Thought: an Introduction*, London: Unwin Hyman.

— (ed.) (1991) *The Green Reader: Essays toward a Sustainable Society*, San Francisco: Mercury House.

Doyle, Marc (1992) *The Future of Television: a Global Overview of Programming, Advertising, Technology and Growth*, Lincolnwood, Ill.: NTC Business Books.

Drew, Christopher (1995) "Japanese sect tried to buy US arms, technology, Senator says", *New York Times*, October 31: A5.

Dubet, François, and Wieviorka, Michel (eds) (1995) *Penser le sujet*, Paris: Fayard.

Duffy, Ann and Pupo, Norene (eds) (1992) *Part-time Paradox: Connecting Gender, Work and Family*, Toronto: The Canadian Publishers.

Dulong, Rene (1978) *Les regions, l'état et la société locale*, Paris: Presses Universitaires de France.

Dunaher, Kevin (ed.) (1994) *50 Years is Enough: the Case against the World Bank and the IMF*, Boston: South End Press.

Ebbinghausen, Rolf and Neckel, Sighard (eds) (1989) *Anatomie des politischen Skandals*, Frankfurt: Suhrkamp.

Ehrenreich, Barbara (1983) *The Hearts of Men: American Dreams and the Flight from Commitment*, Garden City, NY: Anchor Press/Doubleday.

Eisenstein, Zillah R. (1981/1993) *The Radical Future of Liberal Feminism*, Boston: Northeastern University Press.

Ejercito Zapatista de Liberacion Nacional (1994) *Documentos y comunicados*, Mexico: Ediciones Era (with preface by Antonio Garcia de Leon, and chronicles by Elena Poniatowska and Carlos Monsivais).

—/Subcomandante Marcos (1995) *Chiapas: del dolor a la esperanza*, Madrid: Los libros de la catarata.

Eley, Geoff, and Suny, Ronald Grigor (eds) (1996) *Becoming National: a Reader*, New York: Oxford University Press.

Elliott, J.H. and de la Pena, J.F. (1978) *Memoriales y cartas del Conde-Duque de Olivares*, Madrid: Alfaguara.

Epstein, Barbara (1991) *Political Protest and Cultural Revolution: Nonviolent Direct Action in the 1970s and 1980s*, Berkeley: University of California Press.

— (1995) "Grassroots environmentalism and strategies for social change", *New Political Science*, 32: 1–24.

Ergas, Yasmine (1985) *Nelle maglie della politica: femminismo, instituzione e politiche sociale nell'Italia degli anni settanta*, Milan: Feltrinelli.

Espinosa, Maria and Useche, Helena (1992) *Abriendo camino: historias de mujeres*, Bogota: FUNDAC.

Esposito, John L. (1990) *The Iranian Revolution: its Global Impact*, Miami: Florida International University Press.

Esprit (1994) "Editorial: face à la telecratie", 5: 3–4.

Etzioni, Amitai (1993) *The Spirit of Community: Rights, Responsibilities, and the Communitarian Agenda*, New York: Crown.

Evans, Sara (1979) *Personal Politics: the Roots of Women's Liberation in Civil Rights Movement and the New Left*, New York: Knopf.

Eyerman, Ron and Jamison, Andrew (1989) "Environmental knowledge as an organizational weapon: the case of Greenpeace", *Social Science Information*, 28 (1): 99–119.

Fackler, Tim and Lin, Tse-Min (1995) "Political corruption and presidential elections, 1929–1992", *The Journal of Politics*, 57 (4): 971–93.

Faison, Seth (1996) "Chinese cruise Internet, wary of watchdogs", *New York Times*, February 5, p. A1.

Falk, Richard (1995) *On Humane Governance: Towards a New Global Politics*, University Park, PA: Pennsylvania State University Press.

Fallows, James (1996) *Breaking the News: How the Media Undermine American Democracy*, New York: Pantheon.

Faludi, Susan (1991) *Backlash: the Undeclared War on American Women*, New York: Crown.

Farnsworth Riche, Martha (1996) "How America is changing – the view from the Census Bureau, 1995", in *The World Almanac and Book of Facts*, 1996: 382–83.

Fassin, Didier (1996) "Exclusions, underclass, marginalidad: figures contemporaines de la pauvreté urbaine en France, aux Etats-Unis et en Amerique Latine", *Revue Française de Sociologie*, 37: 37–75.

Ferraresi, Franco and Kemeny, Pietro (1977) *Classi sociali e politica urbana*, Rome: Officina Edizioni.

Ferrater Mora, Josep (1960) *Les formes de la vida catalana*, Barcelona: Editorial Selecta.

Ferree, Myra Marx and Hess, Beth B. (1994) *Controversy and Coalition: the New Feminist Movement across Three Decades of Change*, New York: Maxwell Macmillan.

— and Martin, Patricia Yancey (eds) (1995) *Feminist Organizations: Harvest of the Women's Movement*, Philadelphia: Temple University Press.

Ferrer i Girones, F. (1985) *La persecucio politica de la llengua catalana*, Barcelona: Edicions 62.

Financial Technology International Bulletin (1995) "A lawless frontier", 12 (12): 10.

Fischer, Claude S. (1982) *To Dwell among Friends: Personal Networks in Town and City*, Chicago: University of Chicago Press.

— et al. (1995) *Inequality by Design*, Princeton, NJ, Princeton University Press.

Fisher, Robert and Kling, Joseph (eds) (1993) *Mobilizing the Community: Local Politics in the Era of the Global City*, Thousand Oaks, CA: Sage.

Fitzpatrick, Mary Anne and Vangelisti, Anita L. (eds) (1995) *Explaining Family Interactions*, Thousand Oaks, CA: Sage.

Fooner, Michael (1989) *Interpol: Issues in World Crime and International Criminal Justice*, New York: Plenum Press.

Foucault, Michel (1976) *La volonté de savoir: histoire de la sexualité*, vol. I, Paris: Gallimard.

— (1984a) *L'usage des plaisirs: histoire de la sexualité*, vol. II, Paris: NRF.

— (1984b) *Le souci de soi: histoire de la sexualité*, vol. III, Paris: NRF.

Frankel, J. (1988) *International Relations in a Changing World*, Oxford: Oxford University Press.

Frankland, E. Gene (1995) "The rise, fall, and recovery of Die Grunen", in Richardson and Rootes (eds), pp. 23–44.

Franklin, Bob (1994) *Packaging Politics: Political Communications in Britain's Media Democracy*, London: Edward Arnold.

Freeman, Michael (1994) "Polls set spending record", *Mediaweek*, 4(44): 6.

Friedland, Lewis A. (1996) "Electronic democracy and the new citizenship", *Media, Culture, and Society*, 18: 185–211.

Friedrich, Carl J. (1966) "Political pathology", *Political Quarterly*, 37: 74.

Fujita, Shoichi (1995) *AUM Shinrikyo Jiken [The Incidents of AUM Shinrikyo]*, Tokyo: Asahi-Shinbunsha.

Funk, Nanette and Mueller, Magda (eds) (1993) *Gender Politics and Post-Communism: Reflections from Eastern Europe and the Former Soviet Union*, New York: Routledge.

Fuss, Diana (1989) *Essentially Speaking: Feminism, Nature, and Difference*, London: Routledge.

Ganley, Gladys G. (1991) "Power to the people via personal electronic media", *The Washington Quarterly*, Spring: 5–22.

Gans, Herbert J. (1995) *The War against the Poor: the Underclass and Anti-poverty Policy*, New York: Basic Books.

Garaudy, Roger (1990) *Integrismes*, Paris: Belfont.

Garber, Doris A. (1984) *Mass Media in American Politics*, 2nd edn, Washington DC: CQ Press.

— (1996) "The new media and politics – what does the future hold?", *Political Science and Politics*, 29 (1): 33–6.

Garcia Cotarelo, Ramon (1995) *La conspiracion*, Barcelona: Ediciones B.

Garcia de Leon, Antonio (1985) *Resistencia y utopia: memorial de agravios y cronica de revueltas y profecias acaecidas en la provincia de Chiapas durante los ultimos quinientos anos de su historia*, vol 2, Mexico: Ediciones Era.

Garcia-Ramon, Maria Dolors and Nogue-Font, Joan (1994) "Nationalism and geography in Catalonia", in Hooson (ed.), pp. 197–211.

Garment, Suzanne (1991) *Scandal: the Culture of Mistrust in American Politics*, New York: New York Times Books.

Garramone, Gina M. et al. (1990) "Effects of negative political advertising on the political process", *Journal of Broadcasting and Electronic Media*, 34 (3): 299–311.

Gates, Henry Louis, Jr (1996) "Parable of the talents", in Gates and West (eds), pp. 1–52.

— and West, Cornel (eds) (1996) *The Future of the Race*, New York: Alfred Knopf.

Gelb, Joyce and Lief-Palley, Marian (eds) (1994) *Women of Japan and Korea: Continuity and Change*, Philadelphia: Temple University Press.

Gellner, Ernest (1983) *Nations and Nationalism*, Ithaca, NY: Cornell University Press (originally published by Blackwell, Oxford).

Gerami, Shahin (1996) *Women and Fundamentalism: Islam and Christianity*, New York: Garland.

Gerbner, George, Mowlana, Hamid and Nordenstreng, Kaarle (eds) (1993) *The Global Media Debate: its Rise, Fall, and Renewal*, Norwood, NJ: Ablex.

Giddens, Anthony (1985) *A Contemporary Critique of Historical Materialism*, vol. II: *The Nation-state and Violence*, Berkeley: University of California Press.

— (1991) *Modernity and Self-identity: Self and Society in the Late Modern Age*, Cambridge: Polity Press.

— (1992) *The Transformation of Intimacy: Sexuality, Love and Eroticism in Modern Societies*, Stanford: Stanford University Press.

Gil, Jorge et al. (1993) "La red de poder mexicana: el caso de Miguel Aleman", *Revista Mexicana de Sociologia*, 3/95: 103–20.

Ginsborg, Paul (ed.) (1994) *Stato dell'Italia*, Milano: Il Saggiatore.

Giroux, Henry A. (1996) *Fugitive Cultures: Race, Violence and Youth*, New York: Routledge.

Gitlin, Todd (1980) *The Whole World is Watching: Mass Media in the Making and Unmaking of the New Left*, Berkeley: University of California Press.

Gleason, Nancy (1995) "Freenets: cities open the electronic door", *Government Finance Review*, 11 (4): 54–5.

Godard, Francis (ed.) (1996) *Villes*, Special issue of *Le Courrier du CNRS*, Paris: Centre National de la Recherche Scientique.

Gohn, Maria da Gloria (1991) *Movimientos sociais e luta pela moradia*, Sao Paulo: Edicoes Loyola.

Golden, Tim (1995) "A cocaine trail in Mexico points to official corruption", *New York Times*, April 19, pp. 1, 8.

Goldsmith, M. (1993) "The Europeanisation of local government", *Urban Studies*, 30: 683–99.

Gole, Nilufer (1995) "L'emergence du sujet islamique", in Dubet and Wieviorka (eds), pp. 221–34.

Gonsioreck, J.C. and Weinrich, J.D. (1991) *Homosexuality: Research Implications for Public Policy*, Newbury Park, CA: Sage.

Goode, William J. (1993) *World Changes in Divorce Patterns*, New Haven: Yale University Press.

Gottlieb, Robert (1993) *Forcing the Spring: the Transformation of the American Environmental Movement*, Washington DC: Island Press.

Graf, James E. (1995) "Global information infrastructure first principles", *Telecommunications*, 29 (1): 72–3.

Graham, Stephen (1995) "From urban competition to urban collaboration? The development of interurban telematic networks", *Environment and Planning C: Government and Policy*, 13: 503–24.

Granberg, A. (1993) "The national and regional commodity markets in the USSR: trends and contradictions in the transition period", *Papers in Regional Science*, 72: 1.

— and Spehl, H. (1989) *Regionale Wirstchaftspolitik in der UdSSR und der BRD*, Report to the Fourth Soviet–West German Seminar on Regional Development, Kiev, 1–10 October 1989.

Greenberg, Stanley B. (1995) *Middle Class Dreams: The Politics of Power of the New American Majority*, New York: Times Books.

Gremion, Pierre (1976) *Le pouvoir peripherique*, Paris: Seuil.

Grier, Peter (1995) "Preparing for the 21st century information war", *Government Executive*, 28 (8): 130–2.

Griffin, Gabriele (ed.) (1995) *Feminist Activism in the 1990s*, London: Francis and Taylor.

— et al. (eds) (1994) *Stirring It: Challenges for Feminism*, London: Francis and Taylor.

Grosz, Elizabeth (1995) *Space, Time, and Perversion*, London: Routledge.

Grubbe, Peter (1993) *Selbstbedienungsladen: vom Verfall der Demokratischen Moral*, Wuppertal: Hammer.

Guehenno, Jean Marie (1993) *La fin de la democratie*, Paris:

Flammarion. Read in the Spanish translation, Barcelona: Paidos, 1995 (quotations are my own translation into English).

Gumbel, Andrew (1994) "French deception", *New Statesman and Society*, 7, 328: 24.

Gunlicks Arthur B. (ed.) (1993) *Campaign and Party Finance in North America and Western Europe*, Boulder, Colo.: Westview Press.

Habermas, Jurgen (1973) *Legitimation Crisis*, Boston: Beacon Press.

Hacker, Kenneth L. (1996) "Missing links and the evolution of electronic democratization", *Media, Culture, and Society*, 18: 213–323.

Hadden, Jeffrey and Shupe, Hanson (1989) *Fundamentalism and Secularization Reconsidered*, New York: Paragon House.

Hage, Jerald, and Powers, Charles (1992) *Postindustrial Lives: Roles and Relationships in the 21st Century*, London: Sage.

Halperin, David M., Winkler, John J. and Zeitlin, Froma I.(eds) (1990) *Before Sexuality: the Construction of Erotic Experience in the Ancient Greek World*, Princeton, NJ: Princeton University Press.

Halperin Donghi, Tulio (1969) *Historia contemporanea de America Latina*, Madrid: Alianza Editorial.

Handelman, Stephen (1995) *Comrade Criminal: Russia's New Mafiya*, New Haven: Yale University Press.

Hay, Colin (1994) "Environmental security and state legitimacy", *Capitalism, Nature, Socialism*, 1: 83–98.

Heard, Alex (1995) "The road to Oklahoma City", *The New Republic*, May 15.

Heidenheimer, Arnold J., Johnston, Michael and LeVine, Victor T. (eds) (1989) *Political Corruption: a Handbook*, New Brunswick, NJ: Transaction.

Held, David (1991) "Democracy, the nation-state and the global system", *Economy and Society*, 20 (2): 138–72.

— (ed.) (1993) *Prospects for Democracy*, Cambridge: Polity Press.

Heller, Karen S. (1992) "Silence equals death: discourses on AIDS and identity in the gay press, 1981–1986", unpublished PhD dissertation, San Francisco: University of California.

Helvarg, David (1995) "The anti-enviro connection", *The Nation*, May 22.

Hempel, Lamont C. (1996) *Environmental Governance: the Global Challenge*, Washington DC: Island Press.

Herek, Gregory M. and Greene, Beverly (eds) (1995) *HIV, Identity and Community: the HIV Epidemics*, Thousand Oaks, CA: Sage.

Hernandez Navarro, Luis (1995) *Chiapas: la guerra y la paz*, Mexico: ADN Editores.

Hester, Marianne, Kelly, Liz and Radford, Jill (1995) *Women, Violence, and Male Power: Feminist Activism, Research and Practice*, Philadelphia: Open University Press.

Hicks, L. Edward (1994) *Sometimes in the Wrong, but Never in Doubt: George S. Benson and the Education of the New Religious Right*, Knoxville: University of Tennessee Press.

High Level Experts Group (1996) *The Information Society in Europe*, Report to the European Commission, Brussels: Commission of the European Union.

Himmelfarb, Gertrude (1995) *The De-moralization of Society: from Victorian Virtues to Modern Values*, New York: Alfred Knopf.

Hirkett, Mervyn (1992) *Some to Mecca Turn to Pray. Islamic Values in the Modern World*, St Albans: Claridge Press.

Hiro, Dilip (1989) *Holy Wars: The Rise of Islamic Fundamentalism*, New York: Routledge.

Hirst, Paul and Thompson, Grahame (1996) *Globalization in Question: the International Economy and the Possibilities of Governance*, Cambridge: Polity Press.

Hobsbawm, Eric J. (1990) *Nations and Nationalism since 1780*, Cambridge: Cambridge University Press.

— (1992) *Naciones y nacionalismo desde 1780*, Barcelona: Critica (expanded and updated version of original 1990 English publication).

— (1994) *The Age of Extremes: a History of the World, 1914–1991*, New York: Pantheon Books.

Hochschild, Jennifer L. (1995) *Facing up to the American Dream: Race, Class, and the Soul of the Nation*, Princeton, NJ: Princeton University Press.

Holliman, Jonathan (1990) "Environmentalism with a global scope", *Japan Quarterly*, July–September: 284–90.

hooks, bell (1989) *Talking Back: Thinking Feminist, Thinking Black*, Boston: South End Press.

— (1990) *Yearning: Race, Gender, and Cultural Politics*, Boston: South End Press.

— (1993) *Sisters of the Yaw: Black Women and Self-Recovery*, Boston: South End Press.

Hooson, David (1994a) "Ex-Soviet identities and the return of geography", in Hooson (ed.), pp. 134–40.

— (ed.) (1994b) *Geography and National Identity*, Oxford: Blackwell.

Horsman, M. and Marshall, A. (1994) *After the Nation State*, New York: Harper-Collins.

Horton, Tom (1991) "The green giant", *Rolling Stone*, September 5: 43–112.

Hsia, Chu-joe (1996) Personal communication.

Hsing, You-tien (1996) *Making Capitalism in China: the Taiwan Connection*, New York: Oxford University Press.

Hughes, James (1994) "The 'Americanization' of Russian politics:

Russia's first television election, December 1993", *The Journal of Communist Studies and Transition Politics*, 10 (2): 125–50.

Hulsberg, Werner (1988) *The German Greens: a Social and Political Profile*, London: Verso.

Hunter, Robert (1979) *Warriors of the Rainbow: a Chronicle of the Greenpeace Movement*, New York: Holt, Rinehart and Winston.

— "Issues, candidate image and priming: the use of private polls in Kennedy's 1960 presidential campaign", *American Political Science Review*, 88 (3): 527–40.

Inoguchi, Takashi (1993) "Japanese politics in transition: a theoretical review", *Government and Opposition*, 28 (4): 443–55.

Irigaray, Luce (1977/1985) *Ce sexe qui n'en est pas un*, read in the English translation (1985), Ithaca, NY: Cornell University Press.

— (1984/1993) *Ethique de la difference sexuelle*, read in the English translation (1993), Ithaca, NY: Cornell University Press.

Irving, Larry et al. (1994) "Steps towards a global information infrastructure", *Federal Communications Law Journal*, 47 (2): 271–9.

Ivins, Molly (1995) "Fertilizer of hate", *The Progressive*, June.

Jacobs, Lawrence R. and Shapiro, Robert Y. (1995) "The rise of presidential polling: the Nixon White House in historical perspective", *Public Opinion Quarterly*, 59: 163–95.

Janowitz, Morris (1976) *Social Control of the Welfare State*, Chicago: University of Chicago Press.

Jaquette, Jane S. (ed.) (1994) *The Women's Movement in Latin America. Participation and Democracy*, Boulder, Colo.: Westview Press.

Jarrett-Macauley, Delia (ed.), (1996) *Reconstructing Womanhood, Reconstructing Feminism: Writings on Black Women*, London: Routledge.

Jelen, Ted (ed.) (1989) *Religion and Political Behavior in America*, New York: Praeger.

— (1991) *The Political Mobilization of Religious Belief*, New York: Praeger.

Johansen, Elaine R. (1990) *Political Corruption: Scope and Resources: an Annotated Bibliography*, New York: Garland.

Johnson, Chalmers (1982) *MITI and the Japanese Miracle*, Stanford, Stanford University Press.

— (1995) *Japan: Who Governs? The Rise of the Developmental State*, New York: W.W. Norton.

Johnston, R.J, Knight, David and Kofman, Eleanore (eds) (1988) *Nationalism, Self-determination, and Political Geography*, London: Croom Helm.

Jordan, June (1995) "In the land of white supremacy", *The Progressive*, June.

Judge, David, Stokes, Gerry and Wolman, Hall (1995) *Theories of Urban Politics*, Thousand Oaks, CA: Sage.

Juergensmayer, Mark (1993) *The New Cold War? Religious Fundamentalism Confronts the Secular State*, Berkeley: University of California Press.

Jutglar, Antoni (1966) *Els burgesos catalans*, Barcelona: Fontanella.

Kahn, Robert E. (1994) "The role of government in the evolution of the Internet", *Communications of the ACM*, 37 (8): 15–19.

Kahne, Hilda and Giele, Janet Z. (eds). (1992) *Women's Work and Women's Lives: The Continuing Struggle Worldwide*, Boulder, Colo.: Westview Press.

Kaid, Lynda Lee and Holtz-Bacha, Christina (eds). (1995) *Political Advertising in Western Democracies*, Thousand Oaks, CA: Sage.

Kaminiecki, Sheldon (ed.) (1993) *Environmental Politics in the International Arena: Movements, Parties, Organizations, Policy*, Albany: State University of New York Press.

Kanagy, Conrad L. et al. (1994) "Surging environmentalisms: changing public opinion or changing publics", *Social Science Quarterly*, 75 (4): 804–19.

Katznelson, Ira (1996) *Liberalism's Crooked Circle: Letters to Adam Michnik*, Princeton, NJ: Princeton University Press.

Kazin, Michael (1995) *The Populist Persuasion: an American History*, New York: Basic Books.

Keating, Michael (1995) *Nations against the State: the New Politics of Nationalism in Quebec, Catalonia, and Scotland*, New York: St Martin's Press.

Keen, Sam (1991) *Fire in the Belly: on Being a Man*, New York: Bantam Books.

Kelly, Petra (1994) *Thinking Green: Essays on Environmentalism, Feminism, and Nonviolence*, Berkeley: Parallax Press.

Kepel, Gilles (1995) "Entre société et communauté: les musulmans au Royaume-Uni et au France aujourd'hui", in Dubet and Wieviorka (eds), pp. 273–88.

Khazanov, Anatoly M.(1995) *After the USSR: Ethnicity, Nationalism, and Politics in the Commonwealth of Independent States*, Madison: University of Wisconsin Press.

Khosrokhavar, Farhad (1995) "Le quasi-individu: de la neo-communauté à la necro-communauté", in Dubet and Wieviorka (eds), pp. 235–56.

Khoury, Philip and Kostiner, Joseph (eds) (1990) *Tribes and State Formation in the Middle East*, Berkeley: University of California Press.

Kim, Marlene (1993) "Comments", in Cobble (ed.), pp. 85–92.

King, Anthony (1984) "Sex, money and power: political scandals in Britain and the United States", Colchester, University of Essex, Essex Papers in Politics and Government.

King, Joseph P. (1989) "Socioeconomic development and corrupt campaign practices in England", in Heidenheimer et al. (eds), pp. 233–50.

Kiselyova, Emma and Castells, Manuel (1997) *The New Russian Federalism in Siberia and the Far East*, Berkeley: University of California, Center for Eastern European and Slavic Studies/Center for German and European Studies, Research Paper.

Klanwatch/Militia Task Force (KMTF) (1996) *False Patriots. The Threat from Antigovernment Extremists*, Montgomery, Alabama: Southern Poverty Law Center.

Klinenberg, Eric and Perrin, Andrew (1996) "Symbolic politics in the Information Age: the 1996 presidential campaign in cyberspace", Berkeley: University of California, Department of Sociology, Research Paper for Soc 290.2, unpublished.

Kolodny, Annette (1984) *The Land before Her: Fantasy and Experience of the American Frontiers, 1630–1860*, Chapel Hill: University of North Carolina Press.

Kozlov, Viktor (1988) *The Peoples of the Soviet Union*, Bloomington, Ind.: Indiana University Press.

Kraus, K. and Knight, A. (1995) *State, Society, and the UN System: Changing Perspectives on Multilateralism*, New York: United Nations University Press.

Kuppers, Gary (ed.) (1994) *Companeras: Voices from the Latin American Women's Movement*, London: Latin American Bureau.

Kuttner, Robert (1995) "The net as free-market utopia? Think again", *Business Week*, September 4, p. 24.

Lamberts-Bendroth, Margaret (1993) *Fundamentalism and Gender: 1875 to Present*, New Haven, CT: Yale University Press.

Langguth, Gerd (1984) *The Green Factor in German Politics: from Protest Movement to Political Party*, Boulder, Colo.: Westview Press.

Lasch, Christopher (1980) *The Culture of Narcissism*, London: Abacus, 1980.

Laserna, Roberto (1992) *Productores de democracia: actores sociales y procesos politicos*, Cochabamba: Centro de Estudios de la Realidad Economica y Social.

Lash, Scott and Urry, John (1994) *Economies of Signs and Space*, London: Sage.

Laumann, Edward O. et al. (1994) *The Social Organization of Sexuality: Sexual Practices in the United States*, Chicago: University of Chicago Press.

L'Avenc: Revista d'Historia (1996) Special issue: "Catalunya- Espanya", no. 200, February.

Lavrakas, Paul J. et al. (eds) (1995) *Presidential Polls and the New Media*, Boulder, Colo.: Westview Press.

Lawton, Kim A. (1989) "Whatever happened to the Religious Right?", *Christianity Today*, December 15: 44.

Leal, Jesus et al. (1996) *Familia y vivienda en Espana*, Madrid: Universidad Autonoma de Madrid, Instituto de Sociologia, Research Report.

Lechner, Frank J. (1991) "Religion, law, and global order", in Robertson and Garrett (eds), pp. 263–80.

Lesthaeghe, R. (1995) "The second demographic transition in Western countries: an interpretation", in Mason and Jensen (eds), pp. 17–62.

Levin, Murray B. (1987) *Talk Radio and the American Dream*, Lexington, MA: Heath.

Levine, Martin (1979) "Gay ghetto", in Martin Levine (ed.), *Gay Men*, New York: Harper and Row.

Lewis, Bernard (1988) *The Political Language of Islam*, Chicago: University of Chicago Press.

Lewis, Peter H. (1996a) "Judge temporarily blocks law that bars indecency on Internet", *New York Times*, February 16, pp. C1–C16.

— (1996b) "Judges turn back law to regulate Internet decency", *New York Times*, June 13, p. A1.

Leys, Colin (1989) "What is the problem about corruption?", in Heidenheimer et al. (eds), pp. 51–66.

L'Histoire (1993) Special dossier "Argent, politique et corruption: 1789-1993", May, 166: 48 ff.

Li, Zhilan (1995) "Shanghai, Guandong ruheyu zhongyang zhouxuan (How did Shanghai and Guandong negotiate with the central government?)", *The Nineties Monthly*, December, 311: 36–9.

Lienesch, Michael (1993) *Redeeming America: Piety and Politics in the New Christian Right*, Chapel Hill: University of North Carolina Press.

Lipschutz, Ronnie D. and Coca, Ken (1993) "The implications of global ecological interdependence", in Ronnie D. Lipschutz and Ken Coca (eds), *The State and Social Power in Global Environmental Politics*, New York: Columbia University Press.

Lipset, Seymour M. (1996) *American Exceptionalism: a Double-edged Sword*, New York: Norton.

— and Raab, Earl (1978) *The Politics of Unreason: Right-wing Extremism in America, 1790–1970*, New York: Harper and Row.

Lloyd, Gary A. and Kuselewickz J. (eds) (1995) *HIV Disease: Lesbians, Gays, and the Social Services*, New York: Haworth Press.

Lodato, Saverio (1994) *Quindici anni di Mafia*, Milan: Biblioteca Universale Rizzoli.

Longman (1990) *Political Scandals and Causes Célèbres since 1945*, London: Longman's International Reference Compendium.

Lowi, Theodore J. (1988) "Foreword", in Markovits and Silverstein (eds), pp. vii–xii.

Luecke, Hanna (1993) *Islamischer Fundamentalismus – Rueckfall ins Mittelalter oder Wegbereiter der Moderne?*, Berlin: Klaus Schwarz Verlag.

Lyday, Corbin (ed.) (1994) *Ethnicity, Federalism and Democratic Transition in Russia: A Conference Report*, Report of a Conference sponsored by the Berkeley-Stanford Program in Soviet and Post-Soviet Studies held at Berkeley on November 11–17, 1993.

Lyon, David (1994) *The Electronic Eye: the Rise of Surveillance Society*, Cambridge: Polity Press.

MacDonald, Greg (1990) *The Emergence of Multimedia Conglomerates*, Geneva: ILO, Multinational Enterprises Program, Working Paper 70.

McDonogh, Gary W. (ed.) (1986) *Conflict in Catalonia*, Gainsville: University of Florida Press.

McGrew, Anthony G. (1992a) "Global politics in a transitional era", in McGrew et al. (eds) pp. 312–30.

— (1992b) "Military technology and the dynamics of global militarization", in McGrew et al. (eds), pp. 83–117.

— Lewis, Paul G., et al. (1992) *Global Politics: Globalization and the Nation State*, Cambridge: Polity Press.

McInnes, Colin (1992) "Technology and modern warfare", in Baylis and Rengger (eds), pp. 130–58.

— and Sheffield, G.D. (eds) (1988) *Warfare in the 20th Century: Theory and Practice*, London: Unwin Hyman.

McLaughlin, Andrew (1993) *Regarding Nature: Industrialism and Deep Ecology*, Albany: State University of New York Press.

Macy, Joanna (1991) *World as Lover, World as Self*, Berkeley: Parallax Press.

Magleby, David B. and Nelson, Candice J. (1990) *The Money Chase: Congressional Campaign Finance Reform*, Washington DC: Brookings Institution.

Maheu, Louis (1995) "Les mouvements sociaux: plaidoyer pour une sociologie de l'ambivalence", in Dubet and Wieviorka (eds), pp. 313–34.

Mainichi Shinbun (1995), May 1.

Manes, Christopher (1990) *Green Rage: Radical Environmentalism and the Unmaking of Civilization*, Boston: Little, Brown.

Mansbridge, Jane (1995) "What is the feminist movement?", in Ferree and Martin (eds), pp. 27–34.

Markovits, Andrei S. and Silverstein, Mark (eds) (1988a) *The Politics of Scandal: Power and Process in Liberal Democracies*, New York: Holmes and Meier.

— and — (1988b) "Power and process in liberal democracies", in Markovits and Silverstein (eds), pp. 15–37.

Marquez, Enrique (1995) *Por que perdio Camacho*, Mexico: Oceano.

Marsden, George M. (1980) *Fundamentalism and American Culture: the Shaping of the 20th Century Evangelicalism, 1870–1925*, New York: Oxford University Press.

Martinez Torres, Maria Elena (1994) "The Zapatista rebellion and identity", Berkeley: University of California, Program of Latin American Studies, research paper (unpublished).

— (1996) "Networking global civil society: the Zapatista movement. The first informational guerrilla", Berkeley: University of California, seminar paper for CP 229 (unpublished).

Marty, Martin E. (1988) "Fundamentalism as a social phenomenon", *Bulletin of the American Academy of Arts and Sciences*, 42: 15–29.

— and Appleby, Scott (eds) (1991) *Fundamentalisms Observed*, Chicago: University of Chicago Press.

Masnick, George, S. and Ardle, Nancy M. (1994) *Revised US Households Projections: New Methods and New Assumptions*, Cambridge, Mass.: Harvard University, Graduate School of Design/ John F. Kennedy School of Government, Joint Center for Housing Studies, Working Papers Series.

— and Kim, Joshua M. (1995) *The Decline of Demand: Housing's Next Generation*, Cambridge, Mass.: Harvard University, Joint Center for Housing Studies, Working Papers Series.

Mason, Karen O. and Jensen, An-Magritt (1995) *Gender and Family Change in Industrialized Countries*, New York: Oxford University Press.

Mass, Lawrence (1990) *Dialogues of the Sexual Revolution*, New York: Haworth Press.

Massolo, Alejandra (1992) *Por amor y coraje: Mujeres en movimientos urbanos de la Ciudad de Mexico*, Mexico: El Colegio de Mexico.

Mattelart, Armand (1991) *La communication-monde: histoire des ideés et des strategies*, Paris: La Decouverte.

Matthews, Nancy A. (1989) "Surmounting a legacy: the expansion of racial diversity in a local anti-rape movement", *Gender and Society*, 3: 519–33.

Maxwell, Joe and Tapia, Andres (1995) "Guns and Bibles", *Christianity Today*, 39 (7): 34.

Mayer, William G. (1994) "The polls – poll trends: the rise of the new media", *Public Opinion Quarterly*, 58: 124–46.

Mayorga, Fernando (1993) *Discurso y politica en Bolivia*, La Paz, ILDIS-CERES.

Mejia Barquera, Fernando et al. (1985) *Televisa: el quinto poder*, Mexico: Claves Latinoamericanas.

Melchett, Peter (1995) "The fruits of passion", *New Statesman and Society*, April 28: 37–8.

Melucci, Alberto (1995) "Individualisation et globalisation: au-delà de la modernité?", in Dubet and Wieviorka (eds), pp. 433–48.

Meny, Yves (1992) *La corruption de la Republique*, Paris: Fayard.

Merchant, Carolyn (1980) *The Death of Nature: Women, Ecology, and the Scientific Revolution*, New York: Harper and Row.

Mesa, Carlos D. (1986) "Como se fabrica un presidente", in *Cuarto Intermedio*, pp. 4–23.

Michelson, William (1985) *From Sun to Sun: Daily Obligations and Community Structure in the Lives of Employed Women and their Families*, Totowa, NJ: Rowman and Allanheld.

Mikulsky, D.V. (1992) *Ideologicheskaya kontseptsiya Islamskoi partii vozrozhdeniya (Ideological Concept of Islamic Revival Party)*, Moscow: Gorbachev-Fund.

Minc, Alain (1993) *Le nouveau Moyen Age*, Paris: Gallimard.

Misztal, Bronislaw and Shupe, Anson (1992a) "Making sense of the global revival of fundamentalism", in Bronislaw and Shupe (eds), pp. 3–9.

— and — (eds) (1992b) *Religion and Politics in Comparative Perspective: Revival of Religious Fundamentalism in East and West*, Westport, Conn.: Praeger.

Mitchell, Juliet (1966) "Women: the longest revolution", *New Left Review*, 40, November/December.

Miyadai, Shinji (1995) *Owarinaki Nichijo of Ikiro (Live in Endless Everyday Life)*, Tokyo: Chikuma-Shobo.

Moen, Matthew C. (1992) *The Transformation of the Christian Right*, Tuscaloosa: University of Alabama Press.

— and Gustafson, Lowell S. (eds) (1992) *The Religious Challenge to the State*, Philadelphia: Temple University Press.

Mokhtari, Fariborz (ed.) (1994) *Peacemaking, Peacekeeping and Coalition Warfare: the Future of the UN*, Washington DC: National Defense University.

Monnier, Alain and de Guibert-Lantoine, Catherine (1993) "La conjoncture démographique: l'Europe et les pays développés d'outre-mer", *Population*, 48 (4): 1043–67.

Moog, Sandra (1995) "To the root: the mobilization of the culture concept in the development of radical environmental thought", Berkeley: University of California, Department of Anthropology, Seminar Paper for Anthro. 250X (unpublished).

— (1996) "Electronic media and informational politics in America", Berkeley: University of California, Department of Sociology, Research Paper for Soc 290.2 (unpublished).

Moore, David W. (1992) *The Superpollsters: How They Measure and*

Manipulate Public Opinion in America, New York: Four Walls Eight Windows.

Moreau Deffarges, Philippe (1993) *La mondialisation: vers la fin des frontieres?*, Paris: Dunod.

Moreno Toscano, Alejandra (1996) *Turbulencia politica: causas y razones del 94,* Mexico: Oceano.

Morgen, Sandra (1988) "The dream of diversity, the dilemmas of difference: race and class contradictions in a feminist health clinic" in J. Sole (ed.), *Anthropology for the Nineties,* New York: Free Press.

Morin, Edgar and Kern, Anne B. (1993) *Terre-Patrie,* Paris: Seuil.

Morris, Stephen D. (1991) *Corruption and Politics in Contemporary Mexico,* Tuscaloosa: The University of Alabama Press.

Moscow Times (1996), "Style beats substance in ad campaigns", May 30, p. 1.

Moser, Leo (1985) *The Chinese Mosaic: the Peoples and Provinces of China,* London: Westview Press.

Mouffe, Chantal (1995) "The end of politics and the rise of the radical right", *Dissent,* Fall: 488.

Mundy, Alicia (1996) "Taking a poll on polls", *Media Week,* 6 (8): 17–20.

Murray, Charles and Herrnstein, Richard (1994) *The Bell Curve: Intelligence and Class Structure in American Life,* New York: Free Press.

Nair, Sami (1996) "La crisis argelina", in *Claves,* April: 14–17.

Nakazawa, Shinichi et al. (1995) "AUM Jiken to wa Nandatta no ka (Was AUM an incident?)", in *Kokoku Hihyo,* June.

Nash, June et al. (1995) *La explosion de comunidades en Chiapas,* Copenhagen: International Working Group on Indian Affairs, Document IWGIA n. 16.

Navarro, Vicente (1994) *The Politics of Health Policy: The US Reforms, 1980–1994,* Oxford: Blackwell.

— (1995) "Gobernabilidad, desigualdad y estado del bienestar. La situacion en Estados Unidos y su relevancia para Europa", Barcelona: Paper delivered at the International Symposium on Governability, Inequality, and Social Policies, organized by the Institut d'Estudis Socials Avancats, 23–25 November (unpublished).

Negroponte, Nicholas (1995) *Being Digital,* New York: Alfred Knopf.

Norman, E. Herbert (1940) *Japan's Emergence as a Modern State: Political and Economic Problems of the Meiji Period,* New York: Institute of Pacific Relations.

Nunnenkamp, Peter et al. (1994) *Globalisation of Production and Markets,* Tubingen: Kieler Studien, J.C.B. Mohr.

OECD (1993–95) *Employment Outlook,* Paris: OECD.

OECD (1994a) *The OECD Jobs Study,* Paris: OECD.

OECD (1994b) *Women and Structural Change: New Perspectives*, Paris: OECD.

OECD (1995) *Labour Force Statistics*, Paris: OECD.

Offen, Karen (1988) "Defining feminism: a comparative historical approach", *Signs*, 14 (11): 119–57.

Ohama, Itsuro (1995) "AUM toiu Danso (AUM as an attempt to disconnect themselves from history)", in *Seiron*, July.

Orr, Robert M. (1995) "Home-grown terrorism plagues both the US and Japan", *Tokyo Business*, July.

Orstrom Moller, J. (1995) *The Future European Model: Economic Internationalization and Cultural Decentralization*, Westport, Conn.: Praeger.

Osawa, Masachi (1995) "AUM wa Naze Sarin ni Hashitakka (Why did AUM use sarin)?", in *Gendai*, October.

Ostertag, Bob (1991) "Greenpeace takes over the world", *Mother Jones*, March-April: 32–87.

Oumlil, Ali (1992) *Islam et etat national*, Casablanca: Editions Le Fennec.

Oversight of the IMF and the World Bank (1995) *A Meeting of a Multinational Group of Parliamentarians Involved in Oversight of the IMF and the World Bank*, Washington, DC: US Government Printing Office.

Page, Benjamin I. and Shapiro, Robert Y. (1992) *The Rational Public: Fifty Years of Trends in American's Policy Preferences*, Chicago: University of Chicago Press.

Pagano, Michael A. and Bowman, Ann O'M. (1995) "The state of American federalism, 1994-95", *Publius: The Journal of Federalism*, 25 (3): 1–21.

Panarin, Alexander S. (1994) "Rossia v evrazii: geopolitisichie vyzovy i tsivilizatsionnye otvety", Voprosy filosofii, 12: 19–31 (read from *Russian Social Science Review: A Journal of Translations*, May–June 1996: 35-53).

Pardo, Mary (1995) "Doing it for the kids: Mexican American community activists, border feminists?", in Ferree and Martin (eds), pp. 356–71.

Partido Revolucionario Institucional (1994) *La reforma del PRI y el cambio democratico en Mexico*, Mexico: Editorial Limusa.

Patterson, T. E. (1993) *Out of Order: How the Decline of the Political Parties and the Growing Power of the News Media Undermine the American Way of Electing Presidents*, New York: Alfred Knopf.

Pattie, Charles et al. (1995) "Winning the local vote: the effectiveness of constituency campaign spending in Great Britain, 1983–1992", *American Political Science Review*, 89 (4): 969–85.

Perez-Argote, Alfonso (ed.) (1989) *Sociologia del nacionalismo,* Vitoria: Argitarapen Zerbitzua Euskal Herriko Unibertsitatea.

Perez Fernandez del Castillo, German, et al. (1995) *La voz de los votos: un analisis critico de las elecciones de 1994,* Mexico: Miguel Angel Porrua Grupo Editorial.

Perez Iribarne, Eduardo (1993a) *La opinion publica al poder,* La Paz: Empresa Encuestas y Estudios.

— (1993b) "La television imposible", *Fe y Pueblo,* 3: 67–84.

Perez-Tabernero, Alfonso et al. (1993) *Concentracion de la comunicacion en Europa: empresa comercial e interes publico,* Barcelona: Generalitat de Catalunya, Centre d'Investigacio de la Comunicacio.

Phillips, Andrew (1992) "Pocketbook politics: Britain's Tories face a tough fight against Labour Party rivals in an April election", *Maclean's,* 105 (12): 22–25.

Philo, Greg (1993) "Political advertising, popular belief and the 1992 British general election", *Media, Culture, and Society,* 15 (3): 407–18.

Pi, Ramon (ed.) (1996) *Jordi Pujol: Cataluna, Espana,* Madrid: Espasa Hoy.

Pinelli, Antonella (1995) "Women's condition, low fertility, and emerging union patterns in Europe", in Mason and Jensen (eds), pp. 82–104.

Pipes, Richard (1954) *The Formation of the Soviet Union: Communism and Nationalism, 1917–23,* Cambridge, Mass.: Harvard University Press.

Piscatori, James (1986) *Islam in a World of Nation-states,* Cambridge: Cambridge University Press.

Pi-Sunyer, Oriol (1991) "Catalan politics and Spanish democracy: the matter of cultural sovereignty", in Azevedo (ed.), pp. 1–20.

Plant, Judith (1991) "Ecofeminism", in Dobson (ed.), pp. 100–4.

Po, Lan-chih (1996) "Feminism, identity, and women's movements: theoretical debates and a case study in Taiwan", Berkeley: University of California, Department of City and Regional Planning, research paper (unpublished).

Poguntke, Thomas (1993) *Alternative Politics: the German Green Party,* Edinburgh: Edinburgh University Press.

Pollith, Katha (1995) "Subject to debate", *The Nation,* 260 (22): 784.

Porrit, Jonathan (1994) *Seeing Green: the Politics of Ecology Explained,* Oxford: Blackwell.

Portes, Alejandro et al. (eds.) (1989) *The Informal Economy,* Baltimore: Johns Hopkins University Press.

Poulantzas, Nicos (1978) *L'etat, le pouvoir, le socialisme,* Paris: Presses Universitaires de France – Politiques.

Prat de la Riba, Enric (1906) *La nacionalitat catalana,* Barcelona: Edicions 62, republished in 1978.

Price, Vincent and Hsu, Mei-Ling (1992) "Public opinion about AIDS

policies: the role of misinformation and attitudes towards homosexuals", *Public Opinion Quarterly*, 56 (1).

Puiggene i Riera, Ariadna et al. (1991) "Official language policies in
contemporary Catalonia", in Azevedo (ed.), pp. 30–49.

Putnam, Robert (1995) "Bowling alone: America's declining social
capital", *Journal of Democracy*, 6 (1): 65–78.

Reigot, Betty Polisar and Spina, Rita K. (1996) *Beyond the Traditional
Family. Voices of Diversity*, New York: Springer Verlag.

Rich, Adrienne (1980/1993) "Compulsory heterosexuality and
lesbian existence", in Abelove et al. (eds), pp. 227–54.

Richardson, Dick and Rootes, Chris (eds) (1995) *The Green Challenge:
The Development of Green Parties in Europe*, London: Routledge.

Riechmann, Jorge and Fernandez Buey, Francisco (1994) *Redes que
dan libertad: introduccion a los nuevos movimientos sociales*, Barcelona:
Paidos.

Riesebrodt, Martin (1993) *Pious Passion: the Emergence of Modern
Fundamentalism in the United States and Iran*, Berkeley: University of
California Press.

Roberts, Marilyn and McCombs, Maxwell (1994) "Agenda setting and
political advertising: origins of the news agenda", *Political
Communication*, 11: 249–62.

Robertson, Roland and Garrett, William R. (eds) (1991) *Religion and
Global Order*, New York: Paragon House.

Rochester, J. Martin (1993) *Waiting for the Millennium: the UN and the
Future of World Order*, Columbia, SC: University of South Carolina
Press.

Rodgers, Gerry (ed.) (1994) *Workers, Institutions and Economic Growth
in Asia*, Geneva: International Institute of Labour Studies.

Rojas, Rosa (1995) *Chiapas: la paz violenta*, Mexico: Ediciones La
Jornada.

Rokkan, Stein and Urwin, Derek W. (eds) (1982) *The Politics of
Territorial Identity*, London: Sage.

Roman, Joel (1993) "La gauche, le pouvoir, les medias: à-propos du
suicide de Pierre Beregovoy", *Esprit*, 6: 143–6.

Rondfeldt, David (1995) "The battle for the mind of Mexico",
electronically published in June 1995 at RAND Corporation home
page. Available at: http://www.eco.utexas.edu/homepages/
faculty/cleaver/chiapas95/netawars.

Roper Center of Public Opinion and Polling (1995) "How much
government, at what level?: change and persistence in American
ideas", *The Public Perspective*, 6 (3).

Rosenau, J. (1990) *Turbulence in World Politics*, London: Harvester
Wheatsheaf.

Ross, Loretta J. (1995) "Saying it with a gun", *The Progressive*, June.

Ross, Shelley (1988) *Fall from Grace: Sex, Scandal, and Corruption in American Politics from 1702 to present*, New York: Ballantine.

Roth, Jurgen and Frey, Marc (1992) *Die Verbrecher Holding: das vereinte Europa im Griff der Mafia*, Piper and Co. (read in the Spanish translation, Madrid: Anaya/Mario Muchnik, 1995).

Rovira i Virgili, A. (1988) *Catalunya: Espanya*, Barcelona: Edicions de la Magrana (originally published in 1912).

Rowbotham, Sheila (1974) *Hidden from History: Rediscovering Women in History from the 17th Century to the Present*, New York: Pantheon Books.

— (1989) *The Past is Before Us: Feminism and Action since the 1960s*, London: Pandora.

— (1992) *Women in Movement: Feminism and Social Action*, New York: Routledge.

Rowlands, Ian H. (1992) "Environmental issues and world politics", in Baylis and Rengger (eds), pp. 287–309.

Rubert de Ventos, Xavier (1994) *Nacionalismos: el laberinto de la identidad*, Madrid: Espasa-Calpe.

Rubin, Rose M. and Riney, Rose (1994) *Working Wives and Dual-earner Families*, Westport, Conn.: Praeger.

Ruiz-Cabanas, Miguel (1993) "La campana permanente de Mexico: costos, beneficios y consecuencia", in Smith (ed.), pp. 207–20.

Rupp, Leila J. and Taylor, Verta (1987) *Survival in the Doldrums: the American Women's Rights Movement, 1945 to the 1960s*, New York: Oxford University Press.

Sabato, Larry J. (1991) *Feeding Frenzy: How Attack Journalism has Transformed American Politics*, New York: Free Press.

Saboulin, Michel and Thave, Suzanne (1993) "La vie en couple marie: un modele qui s'affaiblit", in INSEE, *La société française: données sociales*, Paris: INSEE.

Salaff, Janet (1981) *Working Daughters of Hong Kong*, Cambridge: Cambridge University Press.

— (1988) *State and Family in Singapore: Restructuring a Developing Society*, Ithaca: Cornell University Press.

— (1992) "Women, family and the state in Hong Kong, Taiwan and Singapore", in Richard Appelbaum and Jeffrey Henderson (eds), *States and Development in the Asian Pacific Rim*, Newbury Park, CA: Sage Publications.

Salmin, A. M. (1992) *SNG: Sostoyanie i perspektivy razvitiya*, Moscow: Gorbachev Fund.

Salrach, Josep M. (1996) "Catalunya, Castella i Espanya vistes per si mateixes a l'edad mitjana", *L'Avenc*, 200: 30–7.

Saltzman-Chafetz, Janet (1995) "Chicken or egg? A theory of relationship between feminist movements and family change", in Mason and Jensen (eds), pp. 63–81.

Salvati, Michele (1995) "Italy's fateful choices", *New Left Review*, 213: 79–96.

Sanchez, Magaly and Pedrazzini, Yves (1996) *Los malandros: la culture de l'urgence chez les jeunes des quartiers populaires de Caracas*, Paris: Fondation Humanisme et Developpement.

Sanchez Jankowski, Martin (1991) *Islands in the Street: Gangs and American Urban Society*, Berkeley: University of California Press.

Santoni Rugiu, Antonio (1994) "La bisciopedagogia", *Ponte*, 50 (2): 20–5.

Saravia, Joaquin and Sandoval, Godofredo (1991) *Jach'a Uru: la esperanza de un pueblo?*, La Paz: CEP-ILDIS.

Savigear, Peter (1992) "The United States: superpower in decline?", in Baylis and Rengger (eds), pp. 334–53.

Scammell, Margaret and Semetko, Holli A. (1995) "Political advertising on television: the British experience", in Kaid and Holtz-Bacha (eds), pp. 19–43.

Scanlan, J. (ed.) (1990) *Surviving the Blues: Growing up in the Thatcher Decade*, London: Virago.

Scarce, Rik (1990) *Eco-warriors: Understanding the Radical Environmental Movement*, Chicago: Noble Press.

Schaeffer, Francis (1982) *Time for Anger: the Myth of Neutrality*, Westchester, Ill.: Crossway Books.

Scharf, Thomas (1994) *The German Greens: Challenging the Consensus*, Oxford: Berg.

Scheer, Leo (1994) *La democratie virtuelle*, Paris: Flammarion.

Scheff, Thomas (1994) "Emotions and identity: a theory of ethnic nationalism", in Calhoun (ed.), pp. 277–303.

Schlesinger, Philip (1991) "Media, the political order and national identity", *Media, Culture, and Society*, 13: 297–308.

Schneir, Miriam (ed.), (1994) *Feminism in our Time: The Essential Writings, World War II to the Present*, New York: Vintage Books.

Scott, Allen (1995) *From Silicon Valley to Hollywood: Growth and Development of the Multimedia Industry in California*, Los Angeles, UCLA's Lewis Center for Regional Policy Studies, Working Paper no. 13, November 1995.

Scott, Beardsley et al. (1995) "The great European multimedia gamble", *McKinsey Quarterly*, 3: 142–61.

Sechi, Salvatore (ed.) (1995) *Deconstructing Italy: Italy in the Nineties*, Berkeley: University of California, International and Area Studies, Research Series.

Sengenberger, Werner and Campbell, Duncan (eds) (1994) *Creating Economic Opportunities: The Role of Labour Standards in Industrial*

Restructuring, Geneva: ILO, International Institute of Labour Studies.

Sennett, Richard (1978) *The Fall of Public Man*, New York: Vintage Books.

— (1980) *Authority*, New York: Alfred Knopf.

Servon, Lisa and Castells, Manuel (1996) *The Feminist City: a Plural Blueprint*, Berkeley: University of California, Institute of Urban and Regional Development, Working Paper.

Shabecoff, Philip (1993) *A Fierce Green Fire: The American Environmental Movement*, New York: Hill and Wang.

Shaiken, Harley (1990) *Mexico in the Global Economy: High Technology and Work Organization in Export Industries*, La Jolla, CA: University of California at San Diego, Center for US–Mexican Studies.

Shapiro, Jerrold L. et al, (eds) (1995) *Becoming a Father: Contemporary Social, Developmental, and Clinical Perspectives*, New York: Springer Verlag.

Sheps, Sheldon (1995) "Militia – History and Law FAQ", World Wide Web, September.

Shimazono, Susumu (1995) *AUM Shinrikyo no Kiseki (Trajectory of AUM Shinrikyo)*, Tokyo: Iwanami-Shoten.

Simpson, John H. (1992) "Fundamentalism in America revisited: the fading of modernity as a source of symbolic capital", in Misztal and Shupe (eds), pp. 10–27.

Singh, Tejpal (1982) *The Soviet Federal State: Theory, Formation, and Development*, New Delhi: Sterling.

Sisk, Timothy D. (1992) *Islam and Democracy: Religion, Politics, and Power in the Middle East*, Washington DC: United States Institute of Peace Press.

Siune, Karen and Truetzschler, Wolfgang (eds). (1992) *Dynamics of Media Politics. Broadcast and Electronic Media in Western Europe*, London: Sage.

Sklair, Leslie (1991) *The Sociology of the Global System*, London: Harvester/Wheatsheaf.

Slezkine, Yuri (1994) "The USSR as a communal apartment, or how a Socialist state promoted ethnic particularism", *Slavic Review*, 53 (2): 414–52.

Smith, Anthony D. (1986) *The Ethnic Origins of Nations*, Oxford: Blackwell.

— (1989) "The origins of nations", *Ethnic and Racial Studies*, 12 (3): 340–67 (quoted from Eley and Suny (eds) (1996), p. 125).

Smith, Michael P. (1991) *City, State and Market: The Political Economy of Urban Society*, Oxford: Blackwell.

Smith, Peter H.(ed.) (1993) *El combate a las drogas en America*, Mexico: Fondo de Cultura Economica.

Sole-Tura, Jordi (1967) *Catalanisme i revolucio burgesa: la sintesi de Prat de la Riba*, Barcelona: Edicions 62.

Spalter-Roth, Roberta and Schreiber, Ronnee (1995) "Outsider issues and insider tactics: strategic tensions in the women's policy network during the 1980s", in Ferree and Martin (eds), pp. 105–27.

Spence, Jonathan D. (1996) *God's Chinese Son: the Taiping Heavenly Kingdom of Hong Xiuquan*, New York: Norton.

Spitz, Glenna (1988) "Women's employment and family relations: a review", *Journal of Marriage and the Family*, 50: 595–618.

Spivak, Gayatri Chakravorty (1990) *The Postcolonial Critique: Interviews, Strategies, Dialogues* (ed. Sarah Harasym), New York: Routledge.

Spragen, William C. (1995) *Electronic Magazines: Soft News Programs on Network Television*, Westport, Conn.: Praeger.

Spretnak, Charlene (ed.) (1982) *The Politics of Women's Spirituality: Essays on the Rise of Spiritual Power within the Women's Movement*, New York: Anchor.

Spruyt, Hendrik (1994) *The Sovereign State and its Competitors*, Princeton, NJ: Princeton University Press.

Stacey, Judith (1990) *Brave New Families: Stories of Domestic Upheaval in Late Twentieth Century America*, New York: Basic Books.

Staggenborg, Susan (1991) *The Pro-choice Movement*, New York: Oxford University Press.

Stallings, Barbara (1992) "International influence on economic policy: debt, stabilization, and structural reform", in Stephan Haggard and Robert Kaufman (eds), *The Politics of Economic Adjustment*, Princeton, NJ: Princeton University Press, pp. 41–88.

Standing, Guy (1990) "Global feminization through flexible labor", *World Development*, 17 (7): 1077–96.

Stanley, Harold W. and Niemi, Richard G. (1992) *Vital Statistics on American Politics*, 3rd edn, Washington DC: CQ Press.

Starovoytova, Galina (1994) "Lecture at the Center for Slavic and East European Studies", University of California at Berkeley, 23 February.

Stebelsky, Igor (1994) "National identity of Ukraine", in Hooson (ed.), pp. 233–48.

Sterling, Claire (1994) *Thieves' World: the Threat of the New Global Network of Organized Crime*, New York: Simon and Schuster.

Stern, Kenneth S. (1996) *A Force upon the Plain: the American Militia Movement and the Politics of Hate*, New York: Simon and Schuster.

Stevens, Mark (1995) "Big boys will be cow boys", *The New York Times Sunday Magazine*, November 19: 72–9.

Streeck, Wolfgang and Schmitter, Philippe C. (1991) "From national corporatism to transnational pluralism: organized interests in the single European market", *Politics and Society*, 19 (2), pp. 133–63.

Strobel, Margaret (1995) "Organizational learning in the Chicago Women's Liberation Union", in Ferree and Martin (eds), pp. 145–64.

Summers, Lawrence (1995) "Ten lessons to learn", *The Economist*, December 23, pp. 46–8.

Sun Tzu (c.505-496 BC) *On the Art of War*, trans. with critical notes by Lionel Giles, Singapore: Graham Brash, 1988 (first published in English in 1910).

Suny, Ronald Grigor (1993) *The Revenge of the Past: Nationalism, Revolution, and the Collapse of the Soviet Union*, Stanford: Stanford University Press.

Susser, Ida (1982) *Norman Street: Poverty and Politics in an Urban Neighborhood*, New York: Oxford University Press.

— (1991) "The separation of mothers and children", in John Mollenkopf and Manuel Castells (eds), *Dual City: Restructuring New York*, New York: Russell Sage, pp. 207–24.

— (1996) "The construction of poverty and homelessness in US cities", *Annual Reviews of Anthropology*, 25: 411–35.

— (forthcoming) "The flexible woman: re-gendering labor in the informational society", *Critique of Anthropology*.

Swan, Jon (1992) "Jennifer", *Columbia Journalism Review* 31 (4): 36.

Szasz, Andrew (1994) *EcoPopulism: Toxic Waste and the Movement for Environmental Justice*, Minneapolis: University of Minnesota Press.

Szmukler, Monica (1996) *Politicas urbanas y democracia: la ciudad de La Paz entre 1985 y 1995*, Santiago de Chile: ILADES.

Tanaka, Martin (1995) "La participacion politica de los sectores populares en America Latina", *Revista Mexicana de Sociologia*, 3: 41–65.

Tarrow, Sydney (1978) *Between Center and Periphery*, New Haven, Conn.: Yale University Press.

Tello Diaz, Carlos (1995) *La rebelion de las canadas*, Mexico: Cal y Arena.

Temas (1995) Special issue "Prensa y poder", 5: 18–50.

The Economist (1994), "Feeling for the future: special survey of television", February 12.

The Economist (1995a) "The future of democracy", June 17: 13–14.

The Economist (1995b), "The Mexican connection", December 26: pp. 39–40.

The Economist (1995c) "Mexico: the long haul", August 26: pp. 17–19.

The Economist (1996) "Satellite TV in Asia: a little local interference", February 3.

The Gallup Poll Monthly (1995) April, 355: 2.

The Nation (1995) Editorial, May 15.

The New Republic (1995a) "An American darkness", May 15.

The New Republic (1995b) "TRB from Washington", May 15.

The New York Times (1995) "Where cotton's king, trouble reigns", October 9: A6.

The New York Times Sunday (1995a) "The rich: a special issue", November 19.

The New York Times Sunday (1995b) "The unending search for demons in the American imagination", July 23: 7.

The Progressive (1995) "The far right is upon us", June.

The World Almanac of Books and Facts, 1996 (1996) New York: Funk and Wagnalls Corporation, World Almanac Books.

Thompson, Dennis F. (1995) *Ethics in Congress: from Individual to Institutional Corruption*, Washington DC: The Brookings Institution.

Thurman, Joseph E. and Trah, Gabriele (1990) "Part-time work in international perspective", *International Labour Review*, 129 (1): 23–40.

Thurow, Lester (1992) *Head to Head: the Coming Economic Battle between Japan, Europe, and the United States*, New York: Morrow.

Tibi, Bassam (1988) *The Crisis of Modern Islam: a Pre-industrial Culture in the Scientific-technological Age*, Salt Lake City: Utah University Press.

— (1992a) *Die fundamentalische Herausforderung: der Islam und die Weltpolitik*, Munich: Beck Press.

— (1992b) *Religious Fundamentalism and Ethnicity in the Crisis of the Nation-state in the Middle-East: Superordinate Islamic and Pan-Arabic Identities and Subordinate Ethnic and Sectarian Identities*, Berkeley: University of California, Center for German and European Studies, Working Paper.

Tilly, Charles (ed.) (1975) *The Formation of Nation States in Western Europe*, Ann Arbor: University of Michigan Press.

— (1995) "State-incited violence, 1900–1999", *Political Power and Social Theory*, 9: 161–79.

Time (1995) "Hell raiser: a Huey Long for the 90s: Pat Buchanan wields the most lethal weapon in Campaign 96: scapegoat politics", November 6.

Tirado, Ricardo and Luna, Matilde (1995) "El Consejo Coordinador Empresarial de Mexico: de la unidad contra el reformismo a la unidad para el Tratado de Libre Comercio (1975–1993)", *Revista Mexicana de Sociologia*, 4: 27–60.

Toner, Robin (1996) "Coming home from the revolution", *The New York Times*, Sunday November 10, s. 4: 1.

Tonry, Michael (1995) *Malign Neglect: Race, Crime, and Punishment in America*, New York: Oxford University Press.

Touraine, Alain (1965) *Sociologie de l'action*, Paris: Seuil.

— (1966) *La conscience ouvrière*, Paris: Seuil.

— (1988) *La parole et le sang: politique et société en Amerique Latine*, Paris: Odile Jacob.

— (1992) *Critique de la modernité*, Paris: Fayard.

— (1994) *Qu'est-ce que la democratie?* Paris: Fayard.

— (1995a) "La formation du sujet", in Dubet and Wieviorka (eds), pp. 21–46.

— (1995b) *Lettre à Lionel, Michel, Jacques, Martine, Bernard, Dominique . . . et vous*, Paris: Fayard.

— et al. (1996) *Le grand refus: reflexions sur la grève de decembre 1995*, Paris: Fayard.

Tranfaglia, Nicola (1992) *Mafia, Politica e Affari, 1943-91*, Roma: Laterza.

Trejo Delarbre, Raul (1994a) *Chiapas: la comunicacion enmascarada. Los medios y el pasamontanas*, Mexico: Diana.

— (ed.) (1994b) *Chiapas: La guerra de las ideas*, Mexico: Diana.

Trend, David (ed.) (1996) *Radical Democracy: Identity, Citizenship, and the State*, New York and London: Routledge.

Trias, Eugenio (1996) "Entrevista: el modelo catalan puede ser muy util para Europa", *El Mundo*, June 30: 32.

Tsuya, Noriko O. and Mason, Karen O. (1995) "Changing gender roles and below-replacement fertility in Japan", in Mason and Jensen (eds), pp. 139–67.

Twinning, David T. (1993) *The New Eurasia: a Guide to the Republics of the Former Soviet Union*, Westport, Conn.: Praeger.

Ubois, Jeff (1995) "Legitimate government has its limits", *Midrange Systems*, 8 (22): 28.

United Nations (1970–1995) *Demographic Yearbook*, various years, New York: United Nations.

— (1995) *Women in a Changing Global Economy: 1994 World Survey on the Role of Women in Development*, New York: United Nations.

United Nations Commission on Global Governance (1995) *Report of the Commission*, New York: United Nations.

United Nations, Economic and Social Council (1994) "Problems and Dangers Posed by Organized Transnational Crime in the Various Regions of the World", Background Document for World Ministerial Conference on Organized Transnational Crime, Naples, 21–23 November (unpublished).

US Bureau of the Census (1994) *Diverse Living Arrangements of Children*, Washington DC: US Bureau of the Census.

US Bureau of the Census (1996) *Composition of American Households*, Washington DC: Department of Commerce, Bureau of the Census.

US Department of Commerce, Economics and Statistics Administration, Bureau of the Census, Current Population Reports Washington DC: Bureau of the Census:

— (1989) *Singleness in America: Single Parents and their Children. Married-couple Families with their Children.*

— (1991) *Population Profile of the United States, 1991*, Series P23, no. 173.

— (1992a) *Households, Families, and Children: a 30-year Perspective*, P23–181.

— (1992b) *When Households Continue, Discontinue, and Form* by Donald J. Hernandez, P23, no. 179.

— (1992c) *Marriage, Divorce, and Remarriage in the 1990s*, by Arthur J. Norton and Louisa F. Miller, P23-180.

— (1992d) *Population Trends in the 1980s*, P-23, no. 175.

Vajrayana Sacca (1994), August, no. 1. Tokyo: Aum Press.

Valdes, Teresa and Gomariz, Enrique (1993) *Mujeres latinoamericanas en cifras*, Madrid: Ministerio de Asuntos Sociales, Instituto de la Mujer.

Vedel, Thierry and Dutton, William H. (1990) "New media politics: shaping cable television policy in France", *Media, Culture, and Society*, 12 (4): 491–524.

Vicens Vives, Jaume (1959) *Historia social y economica de Espana y America*, Barcelona: Ariel.

— and Llorens, Montserrat (1958) *Industrials i Politics del Segle XIX*, Barcelona: Editorial Teide.

Vilar, Pierre (1964) *Catalunya dins l'Espanya Moderna*, Barcelona: Edicions 62.

— ed. (1987–90) *Historia de Catalunya*, Barcelona: edicions 62, 8 vols.

Vogler, John (1992) "Regimes and the global commons: space, atmosphere and oceans", in McGrew et al. (eds), pp. 118–37.

Wacquant, Loic J.D. (1994) "The new urban color line: the state and fate of the ghetto in postfordist America", in Calhoun (ed.), pp. 231-76.

Walter, David (1994) "Winner takes all: the incredible rise – and could it be fall – of Silvio Berlusconi", *Contents*, 23, (4/5): 18–24.

Wapner, Paul (1995) "Politics beyond the state: environmental activism and world civic politics", *World Politics*, April: 311-40.

— (1996) *Environmental Activism and World Civic Politics*, Albany, NY: State University of New York Press.

Weinberg, Steve (1991) "Following the money", *Columbia Journalism Review*, 30 (2): 49–51.

Weisberg, Jacob (1996) *In Defense of Government: the Fall and Rise of Public Trust*, New York: Scribner.

Wellman, Barry (1979) "The community question", *American Journal of Sociology*, 84: 1201–31.

WEPIN Store (1995), "Michigan Militia T-shirt", World Wide Web, West El Paso Information Network.

West, Cornel (1993) *Race Matters*, Boston: Beacon Press.

— (1996) "Black strivings in a twilight civilization", in Gates and West (eds), pp. 53–112.

West, Darrell M. (1993) *Air Wars: Television Advertising in Election Campaigns, 1952–1992*, Washington DC: CQ Press.

Whisker, James B. (1992) *The Militia*, Lewiston, NY: E. Mellen Press.

Whittier, Nancy (1995) *Feminist Generations: the Persistence of the Radical Women's Movement*, Philadelphia: Temple University Press.

Wideman, Daniel J. and Preston, Rohan B. (eds) (1995) *Soulfires: Young Black Men on Love and Violence*, New York: Penguin.

Wiesenthal, Helmut (1993) *Realism in Green Politics: Social Movements and Ecological Reform in Germany*, ed. John Ferris, Manchester: Manchester University Press.

Wieviorka, Michel (1988) *Sociétés et terrorisme*, Paris: Fayard.

— (1993) *La democratie à l'épreuve: nationalisme, populisme, ethnicité*, Paris: La Decouverte.

Wilcox, Clyde (1992) *God's Warriors: the Christian Right in 20th century America*, Baltimore: Johns Hopkins University Press.

Wilensky, Harold (1975) *The Welfare State and Equality: Structural and Ideological Roots of Public Expenditures*, Berkeley: University of California Press.

Williams, Lance and Winokour, Scott (1995) "Militia extremists defend their views", San Francisco Examiner, April 23.

Wilson, William Julius (1987) *The Truly Disadvantaged: the Inner City, the Underclass, and Public Policy*, Chicago: University of Chicago Press.

Winerip, Michael (1996) "An American place: the paramilitary movement. Ohio case typifies the tensions between Militia groups and law", *The New York Times*, June 23, p. A1.

Wittig, Monique (1992) *The Straight Mind*, Boston: Beacon Press.

Woldenberg, Jose (1995) *Violencia y politica*, Mexico: Cal y Arena.

Woodward, Bob (1994) *The Agenda: Inside the Clinton White House*, New York: Simon and Schuster.

WuDunn, Sheryl (1996) "Uproar over a debt crisis: does Japan's mob bear part of the blame?", *The New York Times*, February 14, p. C1.

Yazawa, Shujiro (forthcoming) *Japanese Social Movements since World War II*, Boston: Beacon Press.

Yoshino, Kosaku (1992) *Cultural Nationalism in Contemporary Japan*, London: Routledge.

Zaller, John and Hunt, Mark (1994) "The rise and fall of candidate Perot: unmediated versus mediated politics, part I", *Political Communication*, 11: 357–90.

Zaretsky, Eli (1994) "Identity theory, identity politics: psychoanalysis, marxism, post-structuralism", in Calhoun (ed.), pp. 198–215.

Zeskind, Leonard (1986) *The Christian Identity Movement: Analyzing its*

Theological Rationalization for Racist and Anti-semitic Violence, Atlanta, GA: National Council of the Churches of the Christ in the USA, Center for Democratic Renewal.

Ziccardi, Alicia (ed.) (1991) *Ciudades y gobiernos locales en la America Latina de los noventa*, Mexico: Miguel Angel Porrua Grupo Editorial.

— (ed.) (1995) *La tarea de gobernar: gobiernos locales y demandas ciudadanas*, Mexico: Miguel Angel Porrua Grupo Editorial.

Zisk, Betty H. (1992) *The Politics of Transformation: Local Activism in the Peace and Environmental Movements*, Westport, Conn.: Praeger.

Zook, Matthew (1996) "The unorganized militia network: conspiracies, computers, and community", Berkeley: University of California, Department of Sociology, Seminar paper for SOC 290.2 (unpublished).

Index

Page numbers in italics denote information in figures or tables.

The Information Age

Economy, Society and Culture

Volume III

End of Millennium

Para mi hija, Nuria Castells, alegría de mi vida, con la esperanza de que su milenio sea mejor que el mío

End of Millennium

Manuel Castells

First published 1998
Reprinted 1998 (three times)
Revised and updated edition published 1999

Blackwell Publishers Inc
350 Main Street
Malden, Massachusetts 02148, USA

Blackwell Publishers Ltd
108 Cowley Road
Oxford OX4 1JF, UK

Library of Congress Cataloging in Publication Data
Castells, Manuel
End of millennium / Manuel Castells
p.   cm. — (Information age : economy, society, and culture; v. 3)
Includes bibliographical references and index.
ISBN 1–55786–871–9 (alk. paper) — ISBN 1–55786–872–7 (pbk: alk. paper)
1. Social history—1970– . 2. Economic history— 1990– . 3. Technology
and civilization. 4. Information society. 5. Information technology—
Social aspects. 6. Information technology—Political aspects. I. Title.
II. Series: Castells, Manuel. Information age; v. 3.
HN17.5C354   1998   97–20968
306'.09 dc21   CIP

British Library Cataloguing in Publication Data
A CIP catalogue record for this book is available from the British Library

Printed and bound in Great Britain
by T. J. International Limited, Padstow, Cornwall

This book is printed on acid-free paper

Contents

Figures

Tables

Charts

Acknowledgments

This volume closes 12 years of research effort to elaborate an empirically grounded, cross-cultural, sociological theory of the Information Age. At the end of this journey, which has marked, and to some extent exhausted, my life, I want to publicly express my gratitude to a number of persons and institutions whose contribution has been decisive for the completion of this three-volume work.

My deepest gratitude goes to my wife, Emma Kiselyova, whose love and support gave me the life and energy I needed to write this book, and whose effective research work has been essential in several chapters, particularly chapter 1 on the collapse of the Soviet Union, which was researched by us both, in Russia and in California. It could not have been written without her personal knowledge of the Soviet experience, her analysis of Russian-language sources, and her correction of the many mistakes I made in successive drafts. She was also the primary researcher for chapter 3 on the global criminal economy.

Chapter 4 on the Asian Pacific relied on the input and comments of three colleagues who, over the years, have been constant sources for my ideas and information on Asian societies: Professor You-tien Hsing of the University of British Columbia; Professor Shujiro Yazawa of Tokyo's Hitotsubashi University; and Professor Chu-joe Hsia of Taiwan National University. Chapter 2 on social exclusion relied on the outstanding research assistance of my collaborator Chris Benner, a doctoral student at Berkeley during 1995–7.

Several people, besides those named above, provided their generous contribution, in information and ideas, to the research presented in this volume. For this, I particularly thank Ida Susser, Tatyana Zaslavskaya, Ovsey Shkaratan, Svetlana Natalushko, Valery Kuleshov, Alexander Granberg, Joo-Chul Kim, Carlos Alonso Zaldivar, Stephen Cohen, Martin Carnoy, Roberto Laserna, Jordi Borja, Vicente Navarro, and Alain Touraine.

I would also like to thank those colleagues who commented on drafts of this volume, and helped to rectify some of my mistakes: Ida Susser, Tatyana Zaslavskaya, Gregory Grossman, George Breslauer, Shujiro Yazawa, You-tien Hsing, Chu-joe Hsia, Roberto Laserna, Carlos Alonso Zaldivar, Stephen Cohen, and Jeffrey Henderson.

Throughout the years, a number of research institutions have provided essential support for the work presented here. I thank their directors and the colleagues in these institutions who taught me much of what I have learned about societies around the world. Foremost among these institutions is my intellectual home since 1979: the University of California at Berkeley, and particularly the academic units in which I work: the Department of City and Regional Planning, Department of Sociology, Center for Western European Studies, Institute of Urban and Regional Development, and the Berkeley Roundtable on the International Economy. Other institutions that have supported my work on the themes covered in this volume in the past decade are: Instituto de Sociologia de Nuevas Tecnologias, and Programa de Estudios Rusos, Universidad Autonoma de Madrid; Russian Sociological Association; Center for Advanced Sociological Study, Institute of Youth, Moscow; Institute of Economics and Industrial Engineering, Soviet (then Russian) Academy of Sciences, Novosibirsk; University of California, Pacific Rim Research Program; Faculty of Social Sciences, Hitotsubashi University, Tokyo; National University of Singapore; University of Hong Kong, Center for Urban Studies; Taiwan National University; Korean Institute for Human Settlements; Institute of Technology and International Economy, The State Council, Beijing; Centro de Estudios de la Realidad Economica y Social, Cochabamba, Bolivia; International Institute of Labour Studies of the International Labour Office, Geneva.

I reserve a special mention for John Davey, former editorial director at Blackwell Publishers. For over 20 years he has guided my writing and communicating skills, and has thoroughly advised me on publishing. His personal contribution in commenting on the conclusion to this volume has been decisive. My written work can never be separated from my intellectual interaction with John Davey.

I also wish to name a few people who have been essential in my overall intellectual development throughout the past 30 years. Their work and thinking is, in many ways, but under my exclusive responsibility, present in the pages of this book. They are: Alain Touraine, Nicos Poulantzas, Fernando Henrique Cardoso, Emilio de Ipola, Jordi Borja, Martin Carnoy, Stephen Cohen, Peter Hall, Vicente Navarro, Anne Marie Guillemard, Shujiro Yazawa, and Anthony Giddens. I have been fortunate to evolve together, in a global network, with an exceptional generation of intellectuals committed to both understanding and changing the world, while keeping the necessary distance between theory and practice.

Finally, I would like to thank my surgeons, Dr Peter Carroll and Dr James Wolton, and my physician, Dr James Davis, all of the University of California San Francisco Medical Center, whose care and professionalism gave me the time and energy to finish this book.

May 1997   Berkeley, California

The author and publishers gratefully acknowledge permission from the following to reproduce copyright material:

Carmen Balcells Literary Agency and Farrar Straus & Giroux Inc.: for extract from 'Too Many Names' from *Extravagaria* by Pablo Neruda, translated by Alastair Reid (Farrar Straus & Giroux, 1974), translation copyright © 1974 by Alastair Reid;

Blackwell Publishers: for table 1.4, Padma Desai (1987);

Carfax Publishing Company, PO Box 25, Abingdon, Oxon OX14 3UE: for tables 1.1, 1.2, and 1.3 and figures 1.1 and 1.2, Mark Harrison: *Europe–Asia Studies* 45 (1993);

The Economist: for figures 2.3 and 4.1, copyright © *The Economist*, London 1996, 1997;

Random House UK Ltd: for lines from a poem by Pablo Neruda from *Collected Poems* (Cape, 1970);

M.E. Sharpe Inc., Armonk, NY 10504: for figures 2.5, 2.6a, 2.6b, 2.7, and 2.8, Lawrence Mishel, Jared Bernstein and John Schmitt (1996);

V.H. Winston & Son Inc.: for table 1.6, D.J.B. Shaw: *Post-Soviet Geography* (1993), © V.H. Winston & Son Inc., 360 South Ocean Boulevard, Palm Beach, FL 33480. All rights reserved.

A Time of Change

The turn of a millennium is thought to be a time of change. But it is not necessarily so: the end of the first millennium was, by and large, uneventful. As for the second, those awaiting some kind of fateful lightning will have to make sure that they set their clocks correctly, since, in strictly chronological terms, the second millennium ends at midnight of December 31st, 2000, and not 1999 as most people will (have) celebrate(d). Furthermore, we are changing millennium only according to the Gregorian calendar of Christianity, a minority religion that is bound to lose its pre-eminence in the multiculturalism that will characterize the next century.

And, yet, this is indeed a time of change, regardless of how we time it. In the last quarter of this fading century, a technological revolution, centered around information, has transformed the way we think, we produce, we consume, we trade, we manage, we communicate, we live, we die, we make war, and we make love. A dynamic, global economy has been constituted around the planet, linking up valuable people and activities from all over the world, while switching off from the networks of power and wealth, people and territories dubbed as irrelevant from the perspective of dominant interests. A culture of real virtuality, constructed around an increasingly interactive audiovisual universe, has permeated mental representation and communication everywhere, integrating the diversity of cultures in an electronic hypertext. Space and time, the material foundations of human experience, have been transformed, as the space of flows dominates the space of places, and timeless time supersedes clock time of the industrial era. Expressions of social resistance to the logic of informationalization and globalization build around primary identities, creating defensive communities in the name of God, locality, ethnicity, or family. At the same time, founding social institutions as important as patriarchalism and the nation-state are called into question under the combined pressure of globalization of wealth and information, and localization of identity and legitimacy.

These processes of structural change, which I have analyzed in the two previous volumes of this book, induce a fundamental transformation of the macropolitical and macrosocial contexts that shape and condition social action and human experience around the world. This volume explores some of these macro transformations, while attempting to explain them as a result of the interaction between processes characterizing the Information Age: informationalization, globalization, networking, identity-building, the crisis of patriarchalism, and of the nation-state. While I do not claim that all important dimensions of historical change are represented in this volume, I believe that the trends documented and analyzed in the following chapters do constitute a new historical landscape, whose dynamics is likely to have lasting effects on our lives, and on our children's lives.

It is no accident that the volume opens with an analysis of the collapse of Soviet communism. The 1917 Russian Revolution, and the international communist movement that it sparked, has been the dominant political and ideological phenomenon of the twentieth century. Communism, and the Soviet Union, and the opposite reactions they have triggered throughout the world, have marked decisively societies and people for the span of the century. And yet, this mighty empire, and its powerful mythology, disintegrated in just a few years, in one of the most extraordinary instances of unexpected historical change. I argue that at the roots of this process, marking the end of a historical epoch, lies the inability of statism to manage the transition to the Information Age. Chapter 1 will try to provide empirical grounding for this statement.

The end of Soviet communism, and the hurried adaptation of Chinese communism to global capitalism, has left a new brand of leaner, meaner capitalism alone at last in its planetary reach. The restructuring of capitalism in the 1970s and 1980s showed the versatility of its operating rules, and its capacity to use efficiently the networking logic of the Information Age to induce a dramatic leap forward in productive forces and economic growth. Yet, it also displayed its exclusionary logic, as millions of people and large areas of the planet are being excluded from the benefits of informationalism, both in the developed and developing worlds. Chapter 2 documents these trends, relating them to the uncontrolled nature of global capitalist networks. Furthermore, on the fringes of global capitalism, a new collective actor has appeared, possibly changing the rules of economic and political institutions in the years to come: global crime. Indeed, taking advantage of the world disorder that

followed the disintegration of the Soviet empire, manipulating populations and territories excluded from the formal economy, and using
the instruments of global networking, criminal activities proliferate
throughout the planet, and link up with each other, constituting an
emergent, global criminal economy, that penetrates financial
markets, trade, business, and political systems in all societies. This
perverse connection is a significant feature of informational, global
capitalism. A feature whose importance is usually acknowledged in
the media, but not integrated in social analysis, a theoretical flaw that
I will try to correct in chapter 3 of this volume.

At the same time, there has been an extraordinary expansion of
capitalist growth, which includes hundreds of millions in the development process, particularly in the Asian Pacific (chapter 4). The
process of incorporation of dynamic areas of China, India, and of East
and South-East Asia, in the wake of Japanese development, into an
interdependent global economy, changes history, establishing a
multicultural foundation of economic interdependence: this signals
the end of Western domination, which characterized the industrial
era from its outset. It also signals the interdependence of economic
crises, arising in different continents.

Faced with the whirlwind of globalization, and with the shake up of
the cultural and geopolitical foundations of the world as it used to be,
European countries came together, not without problems, in the
process of European unification, which aims symbolically to unify
their currencies, and thus their economies, around the turn of the
millennium (chapter 5). However, the cultural and political dimensions, essential to the process of European unification, are still
unsettled, so that the fate of Europe will ultimately depend, as for
other areas of the world, on solving the historical puzzles posed by the
transition to informationalism, and by the shift from the nation-state
to a new interaction between nations and the state, under the form of
the network state.

After surveying these macrosocial/political transformations, which
define some of the major debates of our time, I shall conclude in a
more analytical vein. Not just about the themes presented in this
volume, but about the connections between these themes and the
social processes analyzed in the preceding two volumes. With the
reader's benevolence, the conclusion of this volume will propose
some materials to construct an open-ended, social theory of the
Information Age. That is to say that, after exploring our world, I shall
try to make sense of it.

— 1 —

The Crisis of Industrial Statism and the Collapse of the Soviet Union

When the Soviet Union will produce 50 million tons of pig iron, 60 million tons of steel, 500 million tons of coal, and 60 million tons of oil we will be guaranteed against any misfortune.

Stalin, Speech in February 1946[1]

The contradiction which became apparent in the 1950s, between the development of the production forces and the growing needs of society on the one hand, and the increasingly obsolete productive relations of the old system of economic management on the other hand, became sharper with every year. The conservative structure of the economy and the tendencies

This chapter was researched, elaborated, and written jointly with Emma Kiselyova. It relies mainly on two sets of information. The first is the fieldwork research I conducted between 1989 and 1996 in Moscow, Zelenograd, Leningrad, Novosibirsk, Tyumen, Khabarovsk, and Sakhalin in the framework of research programs of the Programa de Estudios Rusos, Universidad Autonoma de Madrid, and of the University of California's Pacific Rim Program, in cooperation with: the Russian Sociological Association; the Institute of Economics and Industrial Engineering, Russian Academy of Sciences, Siberian Branch; and the Center for Advanced Sociological Study, Institute of Youth, Moscow. Four major research projects were co-directed by myself with O.I. Shkaratan, V.I. Kuleshov, S.Natalushko, and with E. Kiselyova and A. Granberg, respectively. Specific references to each research project are given in the footnotes corresponding to each subject. I thank all my Russian colleagues for their essential contribution to my understanding of the Soviet Union, but I certainly exonerate them from any responsibility for my mistakes and personal interpretation of our findings. The second set of information on which this chapter is based refers to documentary, bibliographical, and statistical sources, primarily collected and analyzed by Emma Kiselyova. I also wish to acknowledge the thorough and detailed comments provided on the draft of this chapter by Tatyana Zaslavskaya, Gregory Grossman, and George Breslauer.

[1] Cited by Menshikov (1990: 72).

for extensive investment, together with the backward system of economic management gradually turned into a brake and an obstacle to the economic and social development of the country.

Abel Aganbegyan, *The Economic Challenge of Perestroika*, p. 49

The world economy is a single organism, and no state, whatever its social system or economic status, can normally develop outside it. This places on the agenda the need to devise a fundamentally new machinery for the functioning of the world economy, a new structure of the international division of labor. At the same time, the growth of the world economy reveals the contradictions and limits inherent in the traditional type of industrialization.

Mikhail Gorbachev, Address to the United Nations, 1988[2]

We will realize one day that we are in fact the only country on Earth that tries to enter the twenty-first century with the obsolete ideology of the nineteenth century.

Boris Yeltsin, *Memoirs*, 1990, p. 245[3]

The sudden collapse of the Soviet Union, and with it the demise of the international communist movement, raises a historical enigma: why, in the 1980s, did Soviet leaders feel the urgency to engage in a process of restructuring so radical that it ultimately led to the disintegration of the Soviet state? After all, the Soviet Union was not only a military superpower, but also the third largest industrial economy in the world, the world's largest producer of oil, gas, and rare metals, and the only country that was self-reliant in energy resources and raw materials. True, symptoms of serious economic flaws had been acknowledged since the 1960s, and the rate of growth had been decreasing since 1971 to reach a standstill by 1980. But Western economies have experienced a slowdown trend in productivity growth, as well as negative economic growth at some points in the past two decades, without suffering catastrophic consequences. Soviet technology seems to have lagged behind in some critical areas, but overall, Soviet science maintained its level of excellence in fundamental fields: mathematics, physics, chemistry, with only biology having some difficulty in recovering from Lysenko's follies. The diffusion of this scientific capacity in technological upgrading did not seem out of reach, as the advance of the Soviet space program over NASA's dismal performance of the 1980s seems to indicate.

[2] Reprinted in a special supplement of *Soviet Life*, February 1989, and Tarasulo (1989: 331).
[3] Our translation into English.

Agriculture continued to be in permacrisis, and shortages of consumer goods were customary, but exports of energy and materials, at least until 1986, were providing a hard currency cushion for remedial imports, so that the living conditions of Soviet citizens were better, not worse, in the mid-1980s than a decade earlier.

Furthermore, Soviet power was not seriously challenged either internationally or domestically. The world had entered an era of relative stability in the acknowledged spheres of influence between the superpowers. The war in Afghanistan was taking its toll in human suffering, in political image, and in military pride, but not to a greater level than that of the damage inflicted by the Algerian War on France or the Vietnam War on the United States. Political dissidence was limited to small intellectual circles, as respected as isolated; to Jewish people wanting to emigrate; and to kitchen gossip, a deeply rooted Russian tradition. Although there were a few instances of riots and strikes, generally associated with food shortages and price increases, there were no real social movements to speak of. Oppression of nationalities and ethnic minorities was met with resentment, and in the Baltic republics with open anti-Russian hostility, but such feelings were rarely articulated in collective action or in para-political opinion movements.

People were dissatisfied with the system, and expressed their withdrawal in different forms: cynicism, minor larceny at the workplace, absenteeism, suicide, and widespread alcoholism. But with Stalinist terror long superseded, political repression was limited and highly selective, and ideological indoctrination had become more of a bureaucratic ritual than an ardent inquisition. By the time the long Brezhnevian rule had succeeded in establishing normalcy and boredom in the Soviet Union, people had learned to cope with the system, going on with their lives, making the best of it, as far away as possible from the hallways of the state. Although the structural crisis of Soviet statism was brewing in the cauldrons of history, few of its actors seem to have realized it. The second Russian revolution, which dismantled the Soviet empire, so ending one of the most daring and costly human experiments, may be the only major historical change brought about without the intervention of social movements and/or without a major war. The state created by Stalin seems to have intimidated its enemies, and succeeded in cutting off the rebellious potential of society for a long period.

The veil of historical mystery is even thicker when we consider the process of reform under Gorbachev. How and why did this process go out of control? After all, against the simplistic image conveyed in the Western press, the Soviet Union, and before it Russia, had gone "from one *perestroika* to another," as Van Regemorter entitles his insightful historical analysis of reform processes in Russia.[4] From the New Economic Policy of the 1920s to Kosygin's reforms of economic management in the late 1960s, passing through Stalin's dramatic restructuring of the 1930s, and the revisionism of Khrushchev in the 1950s, the Soviet Union had progressed/regressed by leaps and bounds, making a systemic feature of alternating between continuity and reform. Indeed, this was the specific way in which the Soviet system responded to the issue of social change, a necessary matter for all durable political systems. Yet, with the major exception of Stalin's ruthless ability to constantly rewrite the rules of the game in his favor, the party apparatus was always able to control the reforms within the limits of the system, proceeding when necessary to political purges and changes of leadership. How, in the late 1980s, could such a veteran, shrewd party, hardened in endless battles of managed reform, lose political control to the point of having to resort to a desperate, hurried coup that ultimately precipitated its demise?

My hypothesis is that the crisis that prompted Gorbachev's reforms was different in its historical nature from the preceding crises, thus impinging this difference on the reform process itself, making it riskier, and eventually uncontrollable. I contend that the rampant crisis that shook the foundations of the Soviet economy and society from the mid-1970s onwards was the expression of the structural inability of statism and of the Soviet variant of industrialism to ensure the transition towards the information society.

By statism, I understand a social system organized around the appropriation of the economic surplus produced in society by the holders of power in the state apparatus, in contrast to capitalism, in which surplus is appropriated by the holders of control in economic organizations (see volume I, prologue). While capitalism is oriented toward profit-maximizing, statism is oriented toward power-maximizing; that is, toward increasing the military and ideological capacity of the state apparatus to impose its goals on a greater number of subjects and at deeper levels of their consciousness. By industrialism, I mean a mode of development in which the main sources of productivity are the quantitative increase of factors of production (labor, capital, and natural resources), together with the use of new sources of energy. By informationalism, I mean a mode of development in which the main source of productivity is the qualitative capacity to optimize the combination and use of factors of production on the basis of knowledge and information. The rise of informationalism is inseparable from a new social structure, the

---

[4]   Van Regemorter (1990).

network society (see volume I, chapter 1). The last quarter of the -
twentieth century has been marked by the transition from
industrialism to informationalism, and from the industrial society to
the network society, both for capitalism and statism, in a process that
is concomitant with the information technology revolution. In the
Soviet Union, this transition required measures that undermined
the vested interests of the state's bureaucracy and party's *nomenklatura*. Realizing how critical it was to ensure the transition of the
system to a higher level of productive forces and technological
capacity, the reformers, led by Gorbachev, took the gamble of
appealing to society to overcome the *nomenklatura*'s resistance to
change. *Glasnost* (openness) displaced *uskorenie* ([economic]acceler-
ation) at the forefront of *perestroika* (restructuring). And history has
shown that once Russian society comes into open political ground,
because it has so long been repressed, it refuses to mold to pre-pack-
aged state policies, takes a political life of its own, and becomes
unpredictable and uncontrollable. This is what Gorbachev, in the
tradition of Stolypin, learned again at his expense.

Furthermore, opening up political expression for Soviet society at
large unleashed the contained pressure of national identities –
distorted, repressed, and manipulated under Stalinism. The search
for sources of identity different from the fading communist ideology
led to the fracturing of the still fragile Soviet identity, decisively undermining the Soviet state. Nationalism, including Russian nationalism,
became the most acute expression of conflicts between society and the
state. It was the immediate political factor leading to the disintegration of the Soviet Union.

At the roots of the crisis that induced *perestroika* and triggered
nationalism was the incapacity of Soviet statism to ensure the transition to the new informational paradigm, in parallel to the process
that was taking place in the rest of the world. This is hardly an original hypothesis. Indeed, it is the application of an old Marxian idea,
according to which specific social systems may stall the development
of productive forces, admittedly presented here with an ironic historical twist. I hope that the added value of the analysis submitted to the
reader's attention in the following pages will be in its specificity. Why
was statism structurally incapable of proceeding with the necessary
restructuring to adapt to informationalism? It is certainly not the fault
of the state *per se*. The Japanese state, and, beyond the shores of the
Sea of Japan, the developmental state, whose origins and feats are
analyzed elsewhere (see chapter 4), have been decisive instruments
in fostering technological innovation and global competitiveness, as
well as in transforming fairly traditional countries into advanced information societies. To be sure, statism is not equivalent to state

interventionism. Statism is a specific social system oriented toward the maximization of state power, while capital accumulation and social legitimacy are subordinated to such an over-arching goal. Soviet communism (like all communist systems) was built to ensure total control by the party over the state, and by the state over society via the twin levers of a centrally planned economy and of Marxist–Leninist ideology enforced by a tightly controlled cultural apparatus. It was this specific system, not the state in general, that proved incapable of navigating the stormy waters of historical transition between industrialism and informationalism. The whys, hows, and ifs of this statement make the stuff of this chapter.

The Extensive Model of Economic Growth and the Limits of Hyperindustrialism

We have become so used to demeaning accounts of the Soviet economy in recent years that it is often overlooked that, for a long period of time, particularly in the 1950s and until the late 1960s, Soviet GNP grew generally faster than most of the world, albeit at the price of staggering human and environmental costs.[5] To be sure, Soviet official statistics grossly overestimated the growth rate, particularly during the 1930s. The important statistical work of G.I. Khanin,[6] fully recognized only during the 1990s, seems to indicate that Soviet national income between 1928 and 1987 did not grow 89.5 times, as Soviet statistics would make us believe, but 6.9 times. Still, by Khanin's own account (that we should consider the lower limit in the range of estimation: see tables 1.1–1.3 and figures 1.1 and 1.2), average annual growth of Soviet national income was 3.2 percent in the 1928–40 period, 7.2 percent in 1950–60, 4.4 percent in 1960–65, 4.1 percent in 1965–70, and 3.2 percent in 1970–75. After 1975 quasi-stagnation settled in, and growth became negative in 1980–82, and after 1987.

---

[5]   See, among other works, Nove (1969/1982); Bergson (1978); Goldman (1983); Thalheim (1986); Palazuelos (1990). For the debate on statistical accuracy in analyzing the Soviet economy, see Central Intelligence Agency (1990b).

[6]   Khanin (1991a). Khanin has been, for many years, a researcher at the Institute of Economics and Industrial Engineering, Russian Academy of Sciences, Siberian Branch. In addition to the reference cited, which corresponds broadly with his doctoral dissertation, much of his work has been published in the economic journal of the above-mentioned Institute, *EKO*; for example, see issues 1989(4); 1989(10); 1990(1); 1991(2). For a systematic review, in English, of Khanin's decisive contribution to the economic statistics of the Soviet Union, see Harrison (1993: 141–67).

Table 1.1 Soviet national income growth, 1928–87: alternative estimates (change over period, percentage per year)

Period	TsSu[a]	CIA	Khanin
1928–40	13.9	6.1	3.2[b]
1940–50	4.8	2.0	1.6[c]
1928–50	10.1	4.2	2.5
1950–60	10.2	5.2	7.2
1960–65	6.5	4.8	4.4
1965–70	7.7	4.9	4.1
1970–75	5.7	3.0	3.2
1975–80	4.2	1.9	1.0
1980–85	3.5	1.8	0.6
1985–87	3.0	2.7	2.0
1950–87	6.6	3.8	3.8
1928–87	7.9	3.9	3.3

[a] TsSU: Central Statistical Administration (of the USSR).
[b] 1928–41.
[c] 1941–50
Sources: compiled by Harrison (1993: 146) from the following sources –
TsSU; Khanin: net material product, calculated from Khanin (1991b: 85); CIA: GNP, calculated from CIA (1990a: table A-1).

Yet, overall, and for most of the existence of the Soviet Union, its economic growth was faster than that of the West, and its pace of industrialization one of the fastest in world history.

Furthermore, a system's performance must be evaluated according to its own goals. From such a perspective, the Soviet Union was for half a century an extraordinary success story. If we put aside (can we really?) the tens of millions of people (60 million?) who died as a result of revolution, war, famine, forced labor, deportation, and executions; the destruction of national cultures, history, and traditions (in Russia and the other republics alike); the systematic violation of human rights and political freedom; the massive degradation of a rather pristine natural environment; the militarization of the economy and the indoctrination of society; if, for one analytical moment, we can view the historical process with Bolshevik eyes, it can only be amazement at the heroic proportions of the communist saga. In 1917, the Bolsheviks were a handful of professional revolutionaries, representing a minority fraction of the socialist movement, itself only a part of the broader democratic movement that enacted the February 1917 Revolution almost exclusively in the main cities of a country

Table 1.2 Soviet output and inflation, 1928–90 (change over period, percentage per year)

	Real product growth			Wholesale price inflation	
	Industry	Construction	National income	True	Hidden
TsSU[a]					
1928–40	17.0	–	13.9	8.8	–
1940–50	–	–	4.8	2.6	–
1950–60	11.7	12.3[b]	10.2	–0.5	–
1960–65	8.6	7.7	6.5	0.6	–
1965–70	8.5	7.0	7.7	1.9	–
1970–75	7.4	7.0	5.7	0.0	–
1975–80	4.4	–	4.2	–0.2	–
1980–85	–	–	3.5	–	–
1985–87	–	–	3.0	–	–
1928–87	–	–	7.9	–	–
Khanin					
1928–41	10.9	–	3.2	18.5	8.9
1941–50	–	–	1.6	5.9	3.2
1950–60	8.5	8.4[b]	7.2	1.2	1.8
1960–65	7.0	5.1	4.4	2.2	1.6
1965–70	4.5	3.2	4.1	4.6	2.6
1970–75	4.5	3.7	3.2	2.3	2.3
1975–80	3.0	–	1.0	2.7	2.9
1980–85	–	–	0.6	–	–
1985–87	–	–	2.0	–	–
1928–87	–	–	3.3	–	–
1980–82	–	–	–2.0	–	–
1982–88	–	–	1.8	–	–
1988–90[c]	–	–	–4.6	–	–

[a] TsSU: Central Statistical Administration (of the USSR).
[b] 1955–60.
[c] Preliminary.
Sources: compiled by Harrison (1993: 147) from the following sources –
TsSU; 1928–87: 'National income' calculated from Khanin (1991b: 85); 'other columns' calculated from Khanin (1991a: 146 (industry); 167 (construction); 206, 212 (wholesale prices); 1980–90: calculated from Khanin (1991b: 29)

Collapse of the Soviet Union

Table 1.3 Soviet inputs and productivity, 1928–90 (change over period, percentage per year)

	Stock of fixed assets	Capital productivity	Output per worker	Materials intensity
TsSU[a]				
1928–40	8.7	4.8	11.9	–0.3
1940–50	1.0	3.1	4.1	–0.2
1950–60	9.4	0.8	8.0	–0.5
1960–65	9.7	–3.0	6.0	–0.2
1965–70	8.2	–0.4	6.8	–0.4
1970–75	8.7	–2.7	4.6	0.6
1975–80	7.4	–2.7	3.4	0.0
1980–85	6.5	–3.0	3.0	0.0
1985–87	4.9	–2.0	3.0	0.4
1928–87	7.2	0.5	6.7	–0.2
Khanin				
1928–41	5.3	–2.0	1.3	1.7[b]
1941–50	2.4	–0.8	1.3	1.1
1950–60	5.4	1.6	5.0	–0.5
1960–65	5.9	–1.4	4.1	0.4
1965–70	5.1	–1.0	3.0	0.4
1970–75	3.9	–0.6	1.9	1.0
1975–80	1.9	–1.0	0.2	1.0
1980–85	0.6	0.0	0.0	1.0
1985–87	0.0	2.0	2.0	–0.5
1928–87	3.9	–0.6	2.2	0.8
1980–82	1.5	–3.6	–2.5	2.5
1982–88	1.9	–0.2	1.4	0.7
1988–90[c]	–0.5	–4.1	–4.1	3.4

[a] TsSU: Central Statistical Administration (of the USSR).
[b] 1.7–2%.
[c] Preliminary.
Sources: compiled by Harrison (1993: 151) from the following sources – TsSU; 1928–87: calculated from Khanin (1991b: 85); 1980–90: calculated from Khanin (1991b: 29)

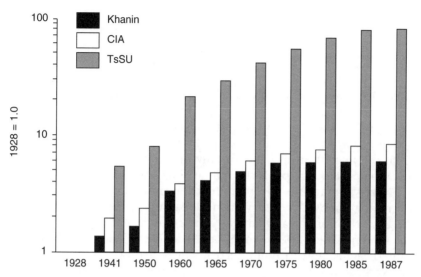

Figure 1.1   Soviet national income, 1928–87: alternative estimates
Source: compiled from figures in table 1.1 by Harrison (1993: 145)

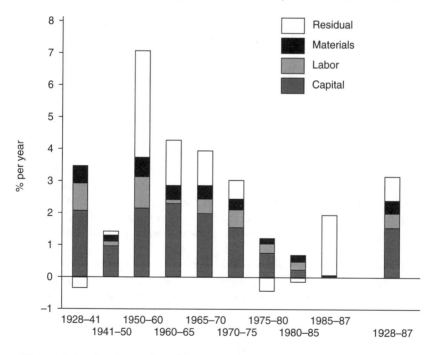

Figure 1.2   Soviet national income: role of inputs in output growth
Source: compiled from figures of Khanin (1991a, b)
by Harrison (1993: 149)

whose population was 84 percent rural.[7] Yet, they were able not only
to seize power in the October coup, eliminating competition from all
political forces, but still to win an atrocious revolutionary war against
the remnants of the Tsarist army, the White Guards, and foreign expe-
ditionary forces. They also liquidated in the process the anarchist
Makhno's peasant army and Kronstadt's revolutionary sailors.
Moreover, in spite of a narrow social base in a meager urban industrial proletariat, barely joined by scores of intelligentsia, the
Bolsheviks went on to build in record time, and despite international
isolation, an industrialized economy that was developed enough in
just two decades to provide the military hardware capable of crushing
the Nazi war machine. In a relentless determination to overtake capitalism, together with a somewhat understandable defensive paranoia,
the Soviet Union, by and large a poor country, managed to become
quickly a nuclear power, to maintain strategic military parity with the
United States, and to pull ahead in the space race by 1957, to the
shocked astonishment of Western governments which had believed
their own mythology about communism's inability to build an
advanced industrial economy.

Such undeniable feats were accomplished at the price of deform-
ing the economy forever.[8] At the root of Soviet economic logic was a
set of cascading priorities.[9] Agriculture had to be squeezed of its
products to subsidize industry and feed cities, and emptied of its
labor to provide industrial workers.[10] Consumer goods, housing, and
services had to concede priority to capital goods, and to the extraction of raw materials, so that socialism could rapidly be made
self-sufficient in all indispensable production lines. Heavy industry
itself was put at the service of military industrial production, since
military might was the ultimate purpose of the regime and the
cornerstone of statism. The Leninist–Stalinist logic, which considered sheer force as the *raison d'être* of the state – of all states in the
final analysis – permeated down through the entire institutional
organization of the Soviet economy, and reverberated throughout
the whole history of the Soviet Union under various ideological
forms.

To enforce such priorities under the strictest conditions, to "bring
politics to the command posts of the economy," as the communist slogan runs, a centrally planned economy was established, the first of its

[7]   See, among other works, Trotsky (1965); Conquest (1968, 1986); Cohen
(1974); Antonov-Ovseyenko (1981); Pipes (1991).
[8]   Aganbegyan (1988).
[9]   Menshikov (1990).
[10]   Johnson and McConnell Brooks (1983).

genre in world history, if we except some centrally controlled pre-industrial economies. Obviously, in such an economy, prices are simply an accounting device, and they cannot signal any relationship between supply and demand.[11] The entire economy is thus moved by vertical administrative decisions, between the planning institutions and the ministries of execution, and between the ministries and the production units.[12] Links between production units are not really horizontal since their exchanges have been pre-established by their respective parent administrations. At the core of such central planning, two institutions shaped the Soviet economy. The first was Gosplan, or State Board for Planning, which established the goals for the whole economy in five-year periods, then proceeded to calculate implementation measures for each product, for each production unit, and for the whole country, year by year, in order to assign output targets and supply quotas to each unit in industry, construction, agriculture, and even services. Among other details, "prices" for about 200,000 products were centrally set each year. No wonder that Soviet linear programming was among the most sophisticated in the world.[13]

The other major economic institution, less notorious but more significant in my opinion, was Gossnab (State Board for Materials and Equipment Supply), which was in charge of controlling all supplies for every transaction in the whole country, from a pin to an elephant. While Gosplan was preoccupied with the coherence of its mathematical models, Gossnab, with its ubiquitous antennae, was in the real world of authorizing supplies, actually controlling flows of goods and materials, and therefore presiding over shortages, a fundamental feature of the Soviet system. The Gosbank, or central bank, never played a substantial economic role, since credit and money circulation were the automatic consequence of Gosplan decisions, as interpreted and implemented by the state in accordance with the party's central committee instructions.[14]

To accomplish fast industrialization, and to fulfill the targets of plans, the Soviet state resorted to full mobilization of human and natural assets of an immense, resource-rich country, accounting for one-sixth of the earth's surface.[15] This extensive model of economic growth was characteristic of the Soviet Union not only during the

---

[11]   For a theoretical understanding of the logic of the centrally planned economy, see the classic work of Janos Kornai (1986, 1990).
[12]   Nove (1977); Thalheim (1986); Desai (1989).
[13]   Cave (1980).
[14]   Menshikov (1990).
[15]   Jasny (1961); Nove (1977); Ellman and Kontorovich (1992).

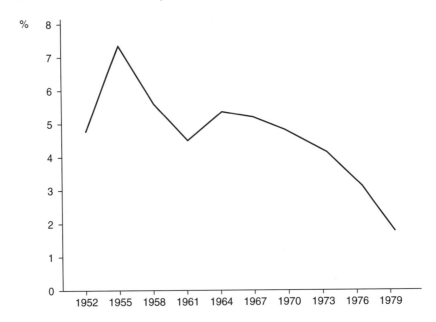

Figure 1.3   Soviet GNP growth rates, 1951–80. The annual growth rates are averaged over three years and plotted at the mid-year of each period

Source: elaborated from table 1.4, col. 2

phase of primitive accumulation in the 1930s,[16] but in the post-Stalin period.[17] Thus, according to Aganbegyan,

> in a typical post-war five-year period, usually in these five years the basic application of funds and capital investment increased one and a half times, the extraction of fuel and raw materials by 25–30 percent, and a further 10 to 11 million workers were recruited in the national economy, a large proportion of whom moved into new branches of production. This was characteristic of the whole period from 1956 to 1975. The last five-year period which involved a large growth in the use of resources was 1971–75. In that period a composite index for the increase of all resources used in production showed a growth of 21 percent.[18]

[16]   Wheatcroft et al. (1986).
[17]   Palazuelos (1990).
[18]   Aganbegyan (1988: 7).

Table 1.4   Growth rates of Soviet GNP, workforce, and capital stock, with investment–GNP and output–capital ratios

Year	Growth rate of			Gross investment– GNP ratio (%)	Ouput–capital ratio (average)
	GNP (%)	Workforce in man hours (%)	Capital stock (%)		
1951	3.1	−0.1	7.7		0.82
1952	5.9	0.5	7.5		0.81
1953	5.2	2.1	8.6		0.78
1954	4.8	5.1	10.5		0.74
1955	8.6	1.6	10.6		0.73
1956	8.4	1.9	10.3		0.72
1957	3.8	0.6	9.9		0.68
1958	7.6	2.0	10.0		0.66
1959	5.8	−1.0	9.7		0.64
1960	4.0	−0.3	9.2	17.8	0.61
1961	5.6	−0.7	8.9	18.1	0.59
1962	3.8	1.4	8.8	17.9	0.56
1963	−1.1	0.7	8.8	19.3	0.51
1964	11.0	2.9	8.6	19.1	0.52
1965	6.2	3.5	8.2	18.9	0.51
1966	5.1	2.5	7.7	19.2	0.50
1967	4.6	2.0	7.2	19.9	0.49
1968	6.0	1.9	7.1	20.2	0.48
1969	2.9	1.7	7.2	20.3	0.46
1970	7.7	2.0	7.8	21.0	0.46
1971	3.9	2.1	8.1	21.7	0.45
1972	1.9	1.8	8.2	22.9	0.42
1973	7.3	1.5	8.0	22.3	0.42
1974	3.9	2.0	7.8	23.0	0.40
1975	1.7	1.2	7.6	24.6	0.38
1976	4.8	0.8	7.2	24.5	0.37
1977	3.2	1.5	7.0	24.6	0.36
1978	3.4	1.5	6.9	25.2	0.35
1979	0.8	1.1	6.7	25.2	0.33
1980	1.4	1.1	6.5	25.4	0.31

GNP and investment (information for which is available from 1960) are in terms of 1970 rubles, whereas capital stock data are in terms of 1973 rubles. The output–capital ratios are average ratios, derived by dividing the absolute values of output and capital during a given year. The latter is the average of the capital stock at the beginning of two consecutive years.
Source: compiled and elaborated by Desai (1987: 17)

Thus, the Soviet model of economic growth was typical of an early industrial economy. Its rate of growth was a function of the size of capital investment and labor inputs, with technical change playing a minor role, thus potentially inducing diminishing returns as the supply of resources wears down (see table 1.4 and figure 1.3). In econometric terms, it was a model of growth characterized by a constant elasticity production function with constant returns to scale.[19] Its fate was dependent upon its capacity either to keep absorbing additional resources or else to increase its productivity through technological advance and/or the use of comparative advantages in international trade.

Yet, the Soviet economy developed in autarky, and for a long time in a hostile world environment that generated a siege mentality.[20] Trade was reduced to essential items, and always conditioned, both in imports and exports, by security considerations. Predatory acquisition of additional resources was never really an option for the Soviet Union, even after the Yalta Treaty acknowledged its occupation of Eastern Europe. Its vassal states, from East Germany to Cuba and Vietnam, were considered political pawns rather than economic colonies, some of them (for example, Cuba) being, in fact, very costly for the Soviet budget.[21] Interestingly enough, this priority of political over economic criteria was extended to the relationships between Russia and the non-Russian Soviet republics. The Soviet Union is a unique case of national domination in which there was reverse discrimination in the regional share of investment and resources, with Russia distributing to the other republics far more resources than it obtained from them.[22] Given the traditional Soviet distrust of foreign immigration, and with the belief in the unlimited potential of resources in the Asian and northern areas of the country, the *economic* emphasis was not on extending geographically the imperial reach but in mobilizing Soviet resources more fully, both natural and human (putting women to work outside the home; trying to make people work harder).

The shortcomings of this extensive model of economic growth followed directly from those features that assured its historical success in its politically assigned goals. The sacrifice of agriculture, and the brutal policy of enforced collectivization, hampered forever the

[19]   Weitzman (1970: 63), cited by Desai (1987: 63)

[20]   Holzman (1976); Desai (1987: 163–72; 251–73); Aganbegyan (1988: 141–56); Menshikov (1990: 222–64).

[21]   Marrese and Vanous (1983). For a critique (which I find questionable) of this analysis, see Desai (1987: 153–62).

[22]   See, among other sources, Korowkin (1994).

productivity of the countryside, not only in cultivation, but in harvesting, in storing, in distributing.[23] Very often, crops were left to rot in the fields, or were spoiled in warehouses, or on the long journey to distant silos, located as far as possible from peasant villages to prevent pillage by a distrusted, resentful rural population. Tiny private plots of land systematically contributed much higher yields, but they were too small, and too often submitted to controls and abuses, to make up for the difference in an otherwise ruinous agriculture. As the Soviet Union moved from a state of emergency to a society trying to feed its citizens, agricultural deficits became an onerous burden on the state budget and on Soviet imports, gradually taking away resources from industrial investment.[24]

The centrally planned economy, extremely wasteful, yet effective in mobilizing resources on priority targets, was also the source of endless rigidities and imbalances that decreased productivity as the economy became more complex, technologically advanced, and organizationally diversified. When the population was allowed to express consumption preferences above the level of survival, when technological change forced the transformation of established work procedures, and when the sheer size of the economy, functionally interdependent on a vast geographical scale, eluded the programming skills of Gosplanners, the command economy started to be plagued by systemic dysfunctions in the practice of implementing the plan. Vertical, heavy-handed bureaucracies, stranded in an age of flexibility, became increasingly aloof, wandering along the paths of their own interpretation of the plan's assignments.

This system also discouraged innovation at a time of fundamental technological change, in spite of the vast resources that the Soviet Union dedicated to science and research and development (R&D), and in spite of having a higher proportion of scientists and engineers in the working population than any other major country in the world.[25] Because innovation always entails risk and unpredictability, production units at every level were systematically discouraged from engaging in such risky ventures. Furthermore, the accounting system of the planned economy represented a fundamental obstacle to productivity-enhancing innovation, both in technology and in management. Let us explain. The performance of each unit was measured in the gross value of production measured in rubles. This value of output (or *valovaya produktsiya, val*) included the value of all

[23] Volin (1970); Johnson and McConnell Brooks (1983); Scherer and Jakobson (1993).
[24] Goldman (1983, 1987).
[25] Aganbegyan (1988).

inputs. The comparison of *val* between years determined the level of fulfillment of plan and, eventually, the premium for managers and workers. Thus, there was no interest in reducing the value of inputs in a given product, for instance by using better technology or better management, if the *val* system could not translate such improvements into higher value added.[26] Furthermore, the vertical organization of production, including scientific production, made it extremely difficult to establish synergistic linkages between production and research. The Academy of Sciences remained by and large isolated from industry, and each ministry had its own research support system, often separate from that of other ministries, and rarely working in cooperation. Piecemeal, *ad hoc* technological solutions were the rule in the Soviet economy at the very moment when uncharted technological innovation was breaking ground in advanced capitalist economies at the dawn of the Information Age.[27]

Similarly, the priorities politically assigned to each branch and sector of the economy allowed for the realization of the Communist party's goals, not the least being the achievement of superpower status in about three decades. But systemic priorities led to systemic imbalances between sectors, and chronic lack of adjustment between supply and demand in most products and processes. Since prices could not reflect such imbalances because they were set by administrative decision, the gap resulted in shortages. Shortages of everything became a structural feature of the Soviet economy.[28] And with shortages also came the development of methods to deal with shortages, from the consumer to the store, from the manufacturer to the supplier, and from one manager to another. What started as a pragmatic way of circumventing shortages, in a network of reciprocal favors, ended up as a vast system of informal economic exchange, increasingly organized on the basis of illegal payments, either in money or in goods. Since allegiance to and protection from supervising bureaucrats was a prerequisite for the system to work outside the rules on such a large scale, the party and the state became immersed in a gigantic shadow economy, a fundamental dimension of the Soviet system, which has been thoroughly investigated by Gregory Grossman, one of the leading scholars on the Soviet economy.[29] It has been sometimes claimed that such a shadow economy smoothed the rigidities of the system, creating a quasi-

[26]　Goldman (1987).
[27]　Golland (1991).
[28]　On the analysis of systemic generation of shortages in the command economy, see Kornai (1980).
[29]　Grossman (1977).

market mechanism that permitted the real economy to operate. In fact, as soon as managers and bureaucrats discovered the benefit of the shortage-ridden economy, shortages were constantly induced by strictly applying the rigid rules of the plan, thus creating the need for the softening of the system – at a price. The shadow economy, which grew considerably during the 1970s with the compliance of the party's *nomenklatura*, deeply transformed Soviet social structure, disorganizing and making more costly a planned economy that, by definition, was no longer allowed to plan, since the dominant interest of "gatekeepers" throughout the administrative apparatus was to collect their shadow rents rather than to receive their bonuses from the fulfillment of planned targets.[30]

The international isolation of the Soviet economy was functional to the system because it made possible the operation of the plan (not feasible practically in an open economy) and because it insulated production from external competitive pressures. But precisely for the same reason, Soviet industry and agriculture became unable to compete in the world economy, just at the historical moment of formation of an interdependent, global system. When the Soviet Union was forced to import goods, whether advanced machinery, consumer goods, or grain to feed cattle, it discovered the damaging limits of its scarce capacity to export manufactured goods in exchange. It resorted to massive exports of oil, gas, materials, and precious metals, which by the 1980s represented 90 percent of Soviet exports to the capitalist world, with oil and gas alone accounting for two-thirds of such exports.[31] This external trade structure, typical of underdeveloped economies, is susceptible to the secular deterioration of commodity prices *vis à vis* the prices of manufactured goods, and is excessively vulnerable to fluctuations in the price of oil in world markets.[32] This dependence on exports of natural resources diverted energy resources and raw materials from investment in the Soviet economy, further undermining the extensive model of growth. On the other hand, when the price of oil fell, in 1986, the import capacity of the economy was severely damaged, increasing shortages of consumer goods and agricultural inputs.[33]

Yet, perhaps the most devastating weakness of the Soviet economy was precisely what was the strength of the Soviet state: an overextended military–industrial complex and an unsustainable defense budget. In the 1980s, Soviet defense expenditure could be evaluated

[30] Grossman (1989).
[31] Menshikov (1990).
[32] Veen (1984).
[33] Aganbegyan (1988).

at about 15 percent of Soviet GNP, more than twice the equivalent proportion in the US at the peak of Reagan's defense build up. Some estimates put it at an even higher level, at about 20–25 percent of GNP.[34] About 40 percent of industrial production was defense related, and the production of enterprises that were engaged in the military–industrial complex reached about 70 percent of all industrial production. But the damage of such a gigantic military industry to the civilian economy went deeper.[35] Its enterprises concentrated the best talent in scientists, engineers, and skilled workers, and were also provided with the best machinery, and access to technological resources. They had their own research centers, the most technologically advanced in the country, and they had priority in the allocation of import quotas. Thus, they absorbed the best of Soviet industrial, human, and technological potential. And once these resources were allocated to the military sector, they were hardly returned to civilian production or applications. Technological spin-offs were a rarity, and the proportion of civilian goods to the total production of military enterprises was usually lower than 10 percent. Even so, most television sets and other electronic consumer goods were produced by military enterprises, as a by-product of their activity. Needless to say, attention to consumer satisfaction was minimal, given the organic dependence of such enterprises on the Ministry of Defense. The military–industrial sector operated as a black hole in the Soviet economy, absorbing most of the creative energy of society and making it disappear in an abyss of invisible inertia. After all, the militarization of the economy is a logical attribute of a system that assigns absolute priority to the power of the state for the sake of the power of the state. That an impoverished, massively rural, and barely developed country like the Soviet Union at the beginning of the century could become one of the greatest military powers in history in just three decades had necessarily to take its toll on the Soviet civilian economy and on its citizens' everyday life.

The Soviet leadership was not unaware of the contradictions and bottlenecks that were developing in the planned economy. Indeed, as mentioned above, Soviet history has been dominated by periodic efforts of reform and restructuring.[36] Khrushchev tried to bring the achievements of socialism closer to people's homes by improving agricultural production, and giving more attention to consumer goods, housing, and social benefits, especially pensions.[37] Furthermore, he

[34]   Steinberg (1991).
[35]   Rowen and Wolf (1990); Cooper (1991).
[36]   Van Regemorter (1990).
[37]   Gustafson (1981); Gerner and Hedlund (1989).

envisaged a new kind of economy, able to unleash the full development of productive forces. Science and technology would be put to the service of economic development, and the natural resources of Siberia, the far east and the central Asian republics would be brought to fruition. In the wake of the enthusiasm generated by the successful launching of the first sputniks, the 21st Party Congress, extrapolating on the basis of growth indicators, predicted that the USSR would reach economic parity with the United States in 20 years. Accordingly, the overall strategy to vanquish capitalism shifted from the inevitability of military confrontation to the stated policy of peaceful coexistence and peaceful competition. Khrushchev actually believed that the demonstration effect of the achievements of socialism would ultimately bring communist parties and their allies to power in the rest of the world.[38] Yet, before engaging the international communist movement in such a grandiose perspective (contested by Chinese communists), he knew that changes had to be made in the bureaucracy of the Soviet state. With the party hardliners put on the defensive by the revelation of Stalin's atrocities in the 20th Congress, Khrushchev eliminated the economic ministries, limited Gosplan's power, and transferred responsibility to regional economic councils (*sovnarkhozy*). The bureaucracy responded, predictably, by reconstructing informal networks of top-down control and management of scarce resources. The ensuing disorganization of the planning system led to falls in production, and to a substantial slowdown in the growth of agriculture, the core of Khrushchevian reforms. Before Khrushchev could react to the sabotage of his policies, admittedly flawed with excessive voluntarism, the party apparatus staged an internal coup that ended Khrushchev's tenure in 1964. Immediately afterwards, Gosplan's powers were reinstated, and new branch ministries were created, through which planning authorities could enforce their directives.

Economic reform was not completely stalled, but reoriented from the level of state administration to the level of the enterprise. The 1965 Kosygin reforms,[39] inspired by economists Liberman and Nemchinov, gave greater freedom of decision to enterprise managers, and experimented with a price system to pay for resources in production. More attention was also paid to consumer goods (whose production, for the first time, grew faster than that of capital goods in 1966–70). Incentives were provided to agriculture, resulting in a substantial increase in output in the 1966–71 period. Yet, when confronted with the logic of the planned economy, these reforms

[38] Taibo (1993b).
[39] Kontorovich (1988).

could not last. Enterprises that improved their productivity by using their newly obtained freedom found themselves assigned higher production quotas the following year. Entrepreneurial managers and workers (as in the enterprise that became the role model of the reforms in 1967, the chemical complex of Shchekino in Tula) felt trapped into being, in fact, punished with an intensification of their work pace while firms that had kept a steady, customary level of production were left alone in their bureaucratic routine. By the early 1970s, Kosygin had lost power, and the innovative potential of the half-hearted reforms faded away.

Yet, the first ten years of the Brezhnev period (1964–75)[40] witnessed moderate economic growth (above 4 percent per year, on average), coupled with political stability, and a steady improvement in the living conditions of the population. The term "stagnation" (*zastoi*), usually applied to the Brezhnev years, does not do justice to the first part of the period.[41] Relative stagnation did not settle in until 1975 onwards, and a zero growth level was reached in 1980. The sources of such stagnation seem to have been structural, and they were the immediate factors prompting Gorbachev's *perestroika*.

Padma Desai has provided empirical evidence, as well as an econometric interpretation, of the retardation in the growth of the Soviet economy (see figure 1.3), whose main reasons seem to be the declining rate of technical change, and the diminishing returns of the extensive model of accumulation.[42] Abel Aganbegyan also attributes the slowdown in economic growth to the exhaustion of the model of industrialization based on extensive use of capital, labor, and natural resources.[43] Technological backwardness led to decreasing returns in the oil and gas fields, in the coal mines, in the extraction of iron, and rare metals. The cost of exploring new resources dramatically increased with distance and with the geographical barriers created by the inhospitable conditions in the Northern and eastern areas of the Soviet territory. Labor supply dwindled in the Soviet economy as birth rates declined over time, as a result of education and economic development, and as women's incorporation into the labor force was almost complete. Thus, one of the pillars of the extensive model of accumulation, steady quantitative increases in labor, disappeared. Capital inputs were also limited by decreasing returns of investment under the same production function, characteristic of an earlier stage of industrialization. To produce the same quantity, under the new

---

[40] Goldman (1983); Veen (1984); Mitchell (1990).
[41] Van Regemorter (1990).
[42] Desai (1987).
[43] Aganbegyan (1988).

economic conditions, more capital had to be used, as the dramatic decline in output–capital ratio indicates (see table 1.4).

Retardation was also linked to the inherent dynamics and bureaucratic logic of the model of accumulation. Stanislav Menshikov, together with a team of young economists at the Institute of Economics of the Academy of Sciences in Novosibirsk in the 1970s, developed an intersectoral model of the Soviet economy. In his words:

> Economic analysis showed that our investment, production, and distribution decision-making was not, in fact, aimed at increasing the well-being of the population, promoting technological progress and keeping growth rates sufficiently high to maintain economic equilibrium. Rather, decisions were made with a view to maximizing the power of ministries in their struggle to divide up the excessively centralized material, financial, labour, natural, and intellectual resources. Our economic–mathematical analysis showed that the system had an inexorable inertia of its own and was bound to grow more and more inefficient.[44]

This inefficiency became particularly blatant when consumption demands from an increasingly educated, by now self-assured, population, started to put pressure on government, not in the form of social movements challenging the system, but as the loyal expression of the citizens' request for the gradual delivery of promised well-being.[45]

Yet, two major structural problems seemed to impede the ability of the system to reform itself by the 1980s. On the one hand, the exhaustion of the extensive model of economic growth implied the need to shift to a new production equation in which technological change could play a greater role, using the benefits of the unfolding technological revolution to increase substantially the productivity of the whole economy. This required that a share of the surplus could be set aside for social consumption without jeopardizing the updating of the military machine. On the other hand, the excessive bureaucratization of economic management, and the chaotic consequences of its corollary, the growth of the shadow economy, had to be corrected by shaking up the planning institutions, and by bringing under control the parallel circuits of appropriation and distribution of goods and services. On both counts – technological modernization and administrative regeneration – the obstacles to reckon with were formidable.

---

[44] Menshikov (1990: 8).
[45] Lewin (1988).

The Technology Question

In spite of the shortcomings of centralized planning, the Soviet Union did build a mighty industrial economy. When, in 1961, Khrushchev launched to the world the challenge that by the 1980s the USSR would produce more industrial goods than the United States, most Western observers ridiculed the statement, even in the wake of the sputnik shock. Yet, the irony is that, at least according to official statistics, in spite of economic retardation and social disarray, in the 1980s the Soviet Union produced substantially more than the US in a number of heavy industrial sectors: it produced 80 percent more steel, 78 percent more cement, 42 percent more oil, 55 percent more fertiliser, twice as much pig iron, and five times as many tractors.[46] The problem was that, in the meantime, the world's production system had shifted heavily toward electronics and specialty chemicals, and was tilting toward the biotechnology revolution, all areas in which the Soviet economy and technology were lagging substantially.[47] By all accounts and indicators, the Soviet Union missed the revolution in information technologies that took shape in the world in the mid-1970s. In a study I conducted in 1991–3, with Svetlana Natalushko, on the leading firms in microelectronics and telecommunications in Zelenograd (the Soviet Silicon Valley, 25 km from Moscow),[48] the immense technological gap between Soviet and Western electronic technologies became apparent, in spite of the generally high technical quality of the scientific and engineering personnel we interviewed. For instance, even at such a late date, Russian enterprises did not have the capability to design sub-micron chips, and their "clean rooms" were so "dirty" that they could not even produce the most advanced chips they could design. Indeed, the main reason we were given for their technological underdevelopment was the lack of appropriate equipment for semiconductor production. A similar story can be told about the computer industry, which, according to the observations of another study I conducted in the research institutes of the Siberian Branch of the Academy of Sciences in Novosibirsk, in 1990, seemed to be about 20 years behind the American or Japanese computer industry.[49] The PC revolution completely bypassed Soviet technology, as it did in fact with IBM. But, unlike IBM, the Soviet Union took more than a decade to start designing and producing its own clone, sus-

---

[46]   Walker (1986: 53).
[47]   Amman and Cooper (1986).
[48]   Castells and Natalushko (1993).
[49]   Castells (1991); for an abridged version of this analysis, see Castells and Hall (1994: ch. 4).

piciously looking like an Apple One.[50] At the other end of the spectrum, in high-performance computers, which should have been the
strong point of a statist technological system, the aggregate peak
performance of Soviet machines in 1991 – the highest year of such
production in the USSR – was over two orders of magnitude less than
that of Cray Research alone.[51] As for the most critical technological
infrastructure, the evaluation by Diane Doucette of the Soviet
telecommunications system in 1992 also showed its backwardness in
relationship to any major industrialized nation.[52] Even in key technologies with military applications, by the late 1980s the Soviet Union
was well behind the US. In a comparison of military technology
between the US, NATO, Japan, and the USSR, conducted by the US
Defense Department in 1989, the Soviet Union was the least advanced
country in 15 out of 25 technologies evaluated, and was not in parity
with the US in any technological field.[53] Malleret and Delaporte's evaluation of military technology also seems to confirm this fact.[54]

Here again, there is no obvious, direct reason for such backwardness. Not only had the Soviet Union a strong scientific basis, and a
technology advanced enough to have overtaken the US in the race to
space in the late 1950s,[55] but the official doctrine under Brezhnev
brought the "scientific and technical revolution" (STR) to the core of
Soviet strategy to overtake the West and build communism on a technological foundation spurred by socialist relations of production.[56]
Nor was this stated priority a purely ideological discourse. The importance given to the STR was backed by massive investment in science,
R&D, and the training of technical personnel, with the result that, by
the 1980s, the USSR had more scientists and engineers, relative to the
total population, than any other major country in the world.[57]

Thus, we are left anew with the idea that "the system", not the
people, and not the lack of material resources devoted to scientific
and technical development, undermined its foundations, provoking
technological retardation precisely at the critical moment of a major
paradigm shift in the rest of the world. Indeed, until the early 1960s

[50]   Agamirzian (1991).
[51]   Wolcott and Goodman (1993); see also Wolcott (1993).
[52]   Doucette (1995).
[53]   US Department of Defense (1989), compiled and cited by Alvarez Gonzalez
(1993).
[54]   Malleret and Delaporte (1991).
[55]   *US News and World Report* (1988).
[56]   Afanasiev (1972); Dryakhlov et al. (1972). For an English summary of these
themes, see Blyakhman and Shkaratan (1977).
[57]   See Fortescue (1986); Smith (1992: 283–309).

there is no evidence of substantial Soviet lagging behind in the main technological fields, with the major exception of biological sciences, devastated by Lysenkoism.[58] But, as soon as discontinuity took place in technological evolution, as it did in the West from the early 1970s, scientific research could not help technological progress, and efforts at learning through reverse engineering engaged the Soviet Union in a doomed race against the acceleration of technological innovation in America and Japan.[59] "Something" happened during the 1970s that induced technological retardation in the USSR. But this "something" happened not in the Soviet Union, but in the advanced capitalist countries. The characteristics of the new technological revolution, based on information technologies and on the rapid diffusion of such technologies in a wide range of applications, made it extremely difficult for the Soviet system to assimilate and to adapt them for its own purposes. It was not the crisis of the Brezhnevian stagnation period that hampered technological development. Rather, it was the incapacity of the Soviet system actually to integrate the much-vaunted "scientific technical revolution" that contributed to its economic stagnation. Let us be specific about the reasons for this incapacity.

The first reason was the absorption of economic resources, science and technology, advanced machinery, and brainpower into the industrial–military complex. This vast universe, which accounted in the early 1980s for about two-thirds of industrial production, and received, together with the armed forces, between 15 and 20 percent of Soviet GNP,[60] was a wasteful repository for science and technology: it received the best talent and best equipment available, returning to the civilian economy only mediocre electrical appliances and consumer electronics goods.[61] Few of the advanced technologies that were discovered, used, or applied in the military–industrial complex were diffused into society, mainly for security reasons, but also for the sake of controlling information which made the military enterprises virtual oligopolies of advanced industrial know-how. Furthermore, the logic of military enterprises, in the East as in the West, was and is, overall, to please their only client: the Defense Ministry.[62] Thus, technologies were developed, or adapted, to fit the

[58]   Thomas and Kruse-Vaucienne (1977); Fortescue (1986).
[59]   Goldman (1987).
[60]   Sapir (1987); Audigier (1989); Alexander (1990: 7620); Steinberg (1991).
[61]   Alvarez Gonzalez (1993).
[62]   Fieldwork by Manuel Castells, Svetlana Natalushko, and collaborators in electronics firms in Zelenograd (1991–3). See Castells and Natalushko (1993). On the problems of technological spin-offs from the defense industry in Western economies, see Kaldor (1981).

extremely specific requirements of military hardware, which explains the considerable difficulties of any conversion project both in Russia and in the US. Who needs, in the industrial or consumer market, a chip designed to withstand a nuclear blast? What saved American electronics defense industries from rapid obsolescence was their relative openness to competition from other American companies, as well as from Japanese electronics producers.[63] But Soviet enterprises, living in a closed economy, without incentive to export, and with no other purpose than to follow the specifications of a not necessarily up-to-date Ministry of Defense, were engaged in a technological trajectory increasingly removed from the needs of society and from the processes of innovation of the rest of the world.[64]

The logic imposed by military requirements on technological performance was largely responsible for the demise of Soviet computers, which were not far behind their Western equivalents between the mid-1940s and mid-1960s, and were a key element in the progress made by the early Soviet space program.[65] Computer design began at the Academy of Sciences in Kiev in the 1940s, under the direction of Professor S.A. Lebedev.[66] The first protoype, the MESM, was built in 1950, only four years after the first American computer, the UNIAC. From such prototypes developed, in the late 1950s and 1960s, a whole family of mainframes: the M-20, BASM-3M, BASM-4, M-220, and M-222. This line of development, reached its peak in 1968 with the production of a powerful machine, the BESM-6, capable of 800,000 operations per second, which became the workhorse of Soviet computing for the next two decades. Yet, this was the last major breakthrough of an endogenous Soviet computer industry. In 1965, under pressure from the military, the Soviet government decided to adopt the IBM model 360 as the core of the Unified Computer System of the Council of Mutual Economic Assistance (the Soviet-dominated Eastern European international organization). From then on, IBM and digital computers, and later some Japanese computers, became the norm in the Soviet Union. Instead of developing their own design and production line, Soviet electronic R&D centers and factories (all under the Ministry of Defense) engaged in the smuggling of computers from the West, proceeding to reverse engineering and to reproduce each model, adapting them to Soviet military specifications. The KGB was given, as a priority task, the acquisition of the

---

[63] Sandholtz et al. (1992).
[64] Cooper (1991).
[65] Fieldwork by Manuel Castells in Novosibirsk (1990) and in Zelenograd (1992–3); see also Hutching(1976); Amman and Cooper (1986).
[66] Agamirzian (1991).

most advanced Western technological know-how and machines, particularly in electronics, by whatever means.[67] Open and covert technology transfer from the West, both in design and in equipment, became the main source for the information technology revolution in the Soviet Union. This necessarily led to retardation, since the time lag between the moment that a new computer hit the world market (or even became available to KGB agents) and the moment that Soviet factories were able to produce it became increasingly longer *vis à vis* the state of the art, especially given the acceleration of the technological race in the late 1970s. Since the same procedure was followed for all electronics components and software, retardation in each segment of the industry interacted with each other, thus multiplying the technological lag. What had been a situation close to parity in computer design in the early 1960s became, in the 1990s, a 20-year difference in design and manufacturing capability.[68]

A similar development took place in software. Soviet machines of the 1960s were working on the endogenously developed ALGOL language, which would have paved the way for systems integration, the current frontier of computing. Yet, in the 1970s, in order to operate American-like computers, Soviet scientists developed their version of FORTRAN, quickly made obsolete by software developments in the West. Finally, they resorted to copying, without legal permission, whatever software appeared in America, thus introducing the same retardation mechanism to a field in which Russian mathematicians could have pioneered the world's scientific frontier.

Why so? Why, paradoxically, did the Soviet military and the KGB choose to become technologically dependent on the US?! The researchers I interviewed in the Academy of Sciences' Institute of Informatics Systems in Novosibirsk gave a convincing argument, drawn from their own experience. The development of Soviet computer sciences in isolation from the rest of the world was too uncertain in a field largely unexplored to satisfy the worried military and political leadership. What would happen to Soviet power, based on computing capacities, if their researchers missed a crucial new development, if the technological trajectory in which they were locked diverged dangerously from the West in an untested course? Would it not be too late to change course if the US one day realized

---

[67]   Andrew and Gordievsky (1990: 521ff.).

[68]   Evaluation by the director of the Institute of Informatics Systems, Russian Academy of Sciences, Siberian Branch. This evaluation was confirmed by six engineers and managers in telecommunications and electronics institutes in Zelenograd during my fieldwork; see Castells and Natalushko (1993); Castells and Hall (1994: ch. 4).

that the Soviet Union did not have the real computing capacity to defend itself effectively? Thus, the Soviet leadership (probably a high-level decision informed by the KGB) opted for a conservative, safe approach: let us have the same machines as "they" have, even if we take some extra time to reproduce "their" computers. After all, to activate Armageddon a few years' technological gap in electronic circuitry would not really be relevant, as long as it worked. Thus, the superior military interests of the Soviet state led to the paradox of making the Soviet Union technologically dependent on the United States in the crucial field of information technology.

However, Japanese electronics companies also proceeded to copy American technology in the early stages, and succeeded in catching up in several key areas in one or two decades, while the Soviet Union experienced the opposite result. Why so? The main reason seems to be that Japanese (and later other Asian countries) had to compete with the firms from whom they were borrowing the technology, so they had to keep apace, while the rhythm of technological development in Soviet enterprises was dictated by military procurement procedures and by a command economy that emphasized quantity over quality. The absence of international or domestic competition removed any pressure on Soviet firms to innovate faster than was needed in the view of the planners of the Ministry of Defense.[69] When the military-oriented technological acceleration of the "Star Wars" program made evident the much-feared technological gap between the Soviet Union and the US, the alarm of the Soviet high command, as expressed most openly by the chief of staff Marshal Ogarkov, was one of the factors that prompted *perestroika*, in spite of the political fall of Ogarkov himself.[70]

However, the Soviet Union had sufficient scientific, industrial, and technological resources outside the military sector to have been able to improve its technological performance even in the absence of military spin-offs. But another layer of statist logic precluded such development. The functioning of the command economy, as mentioned above, was based on the fulfillment of the plan, not on the improvement of either products or processes. Efforts at innovation always entail a risk, both in the outcome and in the ability to obtain the necessary supplies to engage in new areas of production. There was no incentive built into the system of industrial production toward such a goal. Indeed, there was the possibility of failure inscribed in any risk-taking initiative. Technological innovation had no rewards

[69]   Goldman (1987).
[70]   Walker (1986).

but could result in sanctions.[71] A simplistic, bureaucratic logic presided over technological decision-making, as in all other areas of economic management. A revealing anecdote may help to illustrate the argument.[72] Most US chip leads are spaced ¹⁄₁₀ inch apart. The Soviet Ministry of Electronics, in charge of copying American chips, mandated metric spacing, but ¹⁄₁₀ inch is equivalent to an odd metric measure: about 0.254 mm. To simplify things, as is often the case with the Soviet bureaucracy, rounding was decided upon, creating a "metric inch": 0.25 mm spacing. Thus, Soviet chip clones look like their American equivalents, but they do not fit in a Western socket. The mistake was discovered too late, with the net result that, even in 1991, Soviet semiconductor assembly equipment could not be used to produce Western-sized chips, thus excluding potential exports for Soviet microelectronics production.

Furthermore, scientific research and industrial production were institutionally separated. The powerful and well-provided Academy of Sciences was a strictly research-oriented institution with its own programs and criteria, disconnected from the needs and problems of industrial enterprises.[73] Unable to rely on the contributions of the Academy, enterprises used the research centers of their own ministries. Because any exchange between these centers would have required formal contacts between ministries in the context of the plan, applied research centers also lacked communication between each other. This strictly vertical separation, imposed by the institutional logic of the command economy, forbade the process of "learning by doing" that was critical in fostering technological innovation in the West. The lack of interaction between basic science, applied research, and industrial production led to extreme rigidity in the production system, to the absence of experimentation in scientific discoveries, and to a narrow application of specific technologies for limited uses, precisely at the moment when advancement in information technologies was predicated on constant interaction between different technological fields on the basis of their communication via computer networks.

Soviet leaders became increasingly concerned about the lack of productive interaction between science and industry, at least from 1955, when a conference convened by Bulganin met to discuss the problem. During the 1960s, Khrushchev, and then Brezhnev, were betting on science and technology to overtake capitalism. In the late

---

[71]   Berliner (1986); Aganbegyan (1989).
[72]   Reported by Fred Langa, chief editor of the journal *BYTE*; see the April 1991 issue, p. 128.
[73]   Kassel and Campbell (1980).

1960s, in the context of cautious economic reforms, "science–production associations" were introduced, establishing horizontal links between enterprises and research centers.[74] The results, again, were paradoxical. On the one hand, the associations won some autonomy and increased the interaction between their industrial and scientific components. On the other hand, because they were rewarded by their differential increase in production *vis à vis* other associations, they developed a tendency to be self-sufficient, and to cut off ties with other production associations, as well as with the rest of the science and technology system, since they were only accountable to their own parent ministries. Additionally, ministries were not keen to cooperate outside their controlled turfs, and the Academy of Sciences resisted any attempt at curtailing its bureaucratic independence, skillfully using the fears of regressing to the excessive submission of the Stalinist era. Although Gorbachev tried later to revive the experience, horizontal linkages between scientific research and industrial enterprises never really worked in the planned economy, thus precluding effective application of technological discoveries using different channels from vertically transmitted ministerial instructions.

A case in point, which illustrates the fundamental inability of the centrally planned economy to accommodate processes of rapid technological innovation, is the experiment of the science city of Akademgorodok, near Novosibirsk.[75] In 1957, Khrushchev, upon his return from the United States, aimed at emulating the American university campus model, convinced that, given the right conditions, Soviet science could surpass its Western equivalent. On the advice of a leading mathematician, Lavrentiev, he launched the construction of a science city in the Siberian birch forest, on the shores of the artificial Ob lake, adjacent to, but deliberately separated from, the main Siberian industrial and political center, Novosibirsk. Some of the best, young, dynamic scientific talent in the Soviet Union were given incentives to settle there, away from the academic bureaucracy of Moscow and Leningrad, and somewhat freer from direct ideological control. In the 1960s, Akademgorodok flourished as a major scientific center in physics, mathematics, informatics, advanced materials, and economics, among other disciplines. At its peak in the 1980s, Akademgorodok was home to 20 Institutes of the Academy of Sciences, as well as to a small, elite university, Novosibirsk State University. Altogether there were almost 10,000 researchers and

---

[74]   Kazantsev (1991).
[75]   Castells and Hall (1994: 41–56).

professors, 4,500 students, and thousands of auxiliary workers and technicians. These scientific institutions operated on the cutting edge of their disciplines. Indeed, in economics and sociology, Akademgorodok provided some of the first intellectual leaders of *perestroika*, including Abel Aganbegyan and Tatyana Zaslavskaya. Yet, regardless of the scientific excellence achieved by the Siberian science city, its link up with industry never took place. And this was in spite of its proximity to the Siberian industrial center, where were located major defense plants, including electronics and aircraft factories. The separation between the two systems was such that the Academy of Sciences established its own industrial workshops in Akademgorodok to produce the machines needed for scientific experimentation, while Novosibirsk electronics enterprises continued to rely on their Moscow-based research centers. The reason, according to the researchers I interviewed in 1990–2, was that industrial firms were not interested in state-of-the-art technology: their production plans were adjusted to the machinery they already had installed, and any change in the production system would mean failure to meet production quotas assigned to them. Therefore, technological change could happen only through the impetus of the corresponding Gosplan unit, which would have to order the introduction of new machines at the same time as it determined a new production quota. But Gosplan's calculations could not rely on potential machinery resulting from cutting-edge research in the academic institutes. Instead, Gosplan relied on off-the-shelf technology available in the international market, since the more advanced Western technology procured secretly by the KGB was reserved to the military sector. Thus, one of the boldest experiments of the Khrushchev era, designed to link up science and industry to form the core of a new development process in one of the world's richest regions in natural resources, ultimately failed under the inescapable burden of Soviet statism.

Thus, when technological innovation accelerated in the West, during the 1970s and early 1980s, the Soviet Union increasingly relied on imports of machinery and technology transfer for its leading industrial sectors, taking advantage of the cash bonanza resulting from Siberian oil and gas exports. There was considerable waste. Marshall Goldman interviewed a number of Western business executives engaging in technology exports to the Soviet Union in the early 1980s.[76] According to their accounts, imported equipment was poorly utilized (at about two-thirds of Western efficiency for the same machines); the Ministry of Foreign Trade attempted to save its scarce

---

[76]   Goldman (1987: 118 ff.).

hard currency resources, while major enterprises had a vested interest in stockpiling the most recent equipment and large amounts of spare parts whenever they were authorized to proceed with imports; distrust between ministries made it impossible to harmonize their import policies, resulting in incompatibility between equipment; and long periods of amortization for each type of equipment imported in a given factory led to technological obsolescence, and to the painful coexistence of machinery and procedures of highly diverse technological ages. Moreover, it soon became evident that it was impossible to modernize the technology of one segment of the economy without revamping the entire system. Precisely because the planned economy made its units highly interdependent, it was impossible to remedy technological lag in some critical sectors (for example, electronics) without enabling each element of the system to interface with the others. To close the circle, the logic of using scarce foreign technology resources for a shrunk, indispensable segment of the system, reinforced the priority given to the military–industrial sector, and firmly established a sharp separation between two increasingly incompatible technological systems, the war machine and the survival economy.

Last, but not least, ideological repression and the politics of information control were decisive obstacles for innovation and diffusion of new technologies precisely focused on information processing.[77] True, in the 1960s the excesses of Stalinism were left behind, to be replaced by the grand perspectives of "scientific and technical revolution" as the material basis of socialism. Lysenko was dismissed shortly after Khrushchev's fall, although only after exercising intellectual terror for 20 years; "cybernetics" ceased to be considered a bourgeois science; mathematical models were introduced in economics; system analysis was favorably commented upon in the Marxist–Leninist circles; and, most significantly, the Academy of Sciences received strong material support and considerable bureaucratic autonomy to take care of its own affairs, including exercising its own ideological controls. Yet, Soviet science and technology continued to suffer from bureaucracy, ideological control, and political repression.[78] Access to the international scientific community remained very limited, and available only to a select group of scientists, closely surveilled, with the ensuing handicap for scientific cross-fertilization. Research information was filtered, and the diffusion of findings was controlled and limited. Science bureaucrats

---

[77] Smaryl (1984).
[78] Fortescue (1986).

often imposed their views on challengers and innovators, finding support in the political hierarchy. KGB presence in major scientific centers continued to be pervasive until the end of the Soviet regime. Reproduction of information, and free communication among researchers, and between researchers and the outside world, remained difficult for a long time, constituting a formidable obstacle to scientific ingenuity and technological diffusion. Following Lenin's genial instinct to control paper supply as the basic device for controlling information in the aftermath of revolution, Soviet printing, copying, information processing, and communication machines remained under tight control. Typewriters were rare, carefully monitored devices. Access to a photocopying machine always required security clearance: two authorized signatures for a Russian text, and three authorized signatures for a non-Russian text. Use of long-distance telephone lines and telex was controlled by special procedures within each organization. And the very notion of a "*personal* computer" was objectively subversive to the Soviet bureaucracy, including science bureaucracy. Diffusion of information technology, both of machines and of the know-how, could hardly take place in a society where the control of information was critical to the legitimacy of the state, and to the control of the population. The more communication technologies made the outside world accessible to the imaginary representation of Soviet citizens, the more it became objectively disruptive to make such technologies available to a population which, by and large, had shifted from submissive terror into passive routine on the basis of a lack of information and of alternative views of the world. Thus, as its very essence, Soviet statism denied itself the diffusion of information technologies in the social system. And, without this diffusion, information technologies could not develop beyond the specific, functional assignments received from the state, thus making impossible the process of spontaneous innovation by use and networked interaction which characterizes the information technology paradigm.

Thus, at the core of the technological crisis of the Soviet Union lies the fundamental logic of the statist system: overwhelming priority given to military power; political-ideological control of information by the state; the bureaucratic principles of the centrally planned economy; isolation from the rest of the world; and an inability to modernize some segments of the economy and society technologically without modifying the whole system in which such elements interact with each other.

The consequences of this technological backwardness at the very moment when advanced capitalist countries were involved in a fundamental technological transformation, were full of meaning for the

Soviet Union, and ultimately became a major contributing factor in its demise. The economy could not shift from an extensive to an intensive model of development, thus accelerating its decline. The increasing technological gap disabled the Soviet Union in world economic competition, closing the door to the benefits of international trade beyond its role as supplier of energy and materials. The highly educated population of the country found itself trapped in a technological system that was increasingly distant from comparable industrial societies. The application of computers to a bureaucratic system and to a command economy increased the rigidity of controls,[79] verifying the hypothesis according to which technological rationalization of social irrationality increases disorder. Ultimately, the military machine itself came to suffer from a growing technological gap *vis à vis* its competing warriors,[80] thus deepening the crisis of the Soviet state.

The Abduction of Identity and the Crisis of Soviet Federalism

Many of our national problems are caused by the contradictory nature of the two principles which were laid as the cornerstones of the Russian Federation: the national-territorial principle and the administrative-territorial principle.

Boris Yeltsin, *Rossiyskaya gazeta*, February 25, 1994

Gorbachev's reforms were explicitly aimed, at their inception, at economic restructuring and technological modernization. Yet, these were not the only faults of the Soviet system. The foundations of the multinational, multi-ethnic, multilayered, Soviet federal state were built on the shaky sand of reconstructed history, and barely sustained by ruthless repression.[81] After massive deportations of entire ethnic groups to Siberia and central Asia under Stalin,[82] an iron-clad prohibition was imposed on the autonomous expression of nationalism among the more than a hundred nationalities and ethnic groups that populated the Soviet Union.[83] Although there were isolated nationalist demonstrations (for example, Armenia, April 1965;

---

[79]   Cave (1980).
[80]   Walker (1986); Praaning and Perry (1989); Rowen and Wolf (1990); Taibo (1993a).
[81]   Carrere d'Encausse (1978).
[82]   Nekrich (1978).
[83]   Motyl (1987); Lane (1990).

Georgia, April 1978), sometimes crushed by force (for example, Tbilisi, March 1956), most nationalist expressions were subdued for a long period, and only taken up by dissident intellectuals in rare moments of relative tolerance under Khrushchev or in the late 1970s.[84] Yet, it was the pressure of nationalism, utilized in their personal interest by the political elites of the republics, that ultimately doomed Gorbachev's reformist experiment, and led to the disintegration of the Soviet Union. Nationalism, including Russian nationalism, provided the ideological basis for social mobilization in a society where strictly political ideologies, not relying on historical-cultural identity, suffered the backlash of cynicism and disbelief generated by seven decades of indoctrination in the themes of communist utopia.[85] While the inability of Soviet statism to adapt to the technological and economic conditions of an information society was the most powerful underlying cause of the crisis of the Soviet system, it was the resurgence of national identity, either historically rooted or politically reinvented, that first challenged and ultimately destroyed the Soviet state. If economic and technological problems prompted the Andropov–Gorbachev reforms of the 1980s, the explosive issue of insurgent nationalism and federal relationships within the Soviet Union was the main political factor accounting for the loss of control of the reform process by the Soviet leadership.

The reasons for this irrepressible resurgence of nationalism in the Soviet Union during the *perestroika* years are to be found in the history of Soviet communism. It is, in fact, a complex story that goes beyond the simplistic image of sheer repression of national/ethnic cultures by the Soviet state. Indeed, it is argued by one of the leading historians of non-Russian nationalities in the Soviet Union, professor of Armenian history Ronald Grigor Suny, that:

> Lost in the powerful nationalist rhetoric is any sense of the degree to which the long and difficult years of Communist party rule actually continued the "making of nations" of the pre-revolutionary period. As the present generation watches the self-destruction of the Soviet Union, the irony is lost that the USSR was the victim not only of its negative effects on the non-Russian peoples but of its own "progressive" contribution to the process of nation building. . . . The Soviet state's deeply contradictory policy nourished the cultural uniqueness of distinct peoples. It thereby increased ethnic solidarity and national consciousness in the non-Russian republics, even as it

---

[84] Simon (1991).
[85] Carrere d'Encausse (1991); Khazanov (1995).

frustrated full articulation of a national agenda by requiring conformity to an imposed political order.[86]

Let us try to reconstruct the logic of this powerful political paradox.[87]

The Soviet Union was founded in December 1922 and its multinational, federal state was enshrined in the 1924 Constitution.[88] Originally it included: the Russian Soviet Federated Socialist Republic (RSFSR), itself incorporating, besides Russia, a number of non-Russian autonomous republics; the Ukrainian Soviet Socialist Republic; the Byelorussian Soviet Socialist Republic; and the Transcaucasian Federated Socialist Republic, a potentially explosive, artificial entity that brought together centuries-old inimical peoples, such as Georgians, Azeris, Armenians, and a number of smaller ethnic groups, among whom were Ingushis, Osetians, Abkhazians, and Metsketyans. Membership of the Union was open to all existing and future Soviet and Socialist Republics in the world. In the Fall of 1924, two additional republics were incorporated: Uzbekistan (formed by the forced territorial integration of the Uzbek population in Turkestan, Bukhara, and Khoresm), and Turkmenia. In 1936, three new Union Republics were created under the names of Tajikistan, Kirghizia, and Kazakhstan. Also in 1936, Transcaucasia was divided into three republics, Georgia, Armenia, and Azerbaijan, leaving inside each one of the three republics substantial ethnic enclaves that acted eventually as nationalist time bombs. In 1940, the forced absorption into the USSR of Estonia, Latvia, Lithuania, and Moldova (taken from Romania) completed the republican structure of the Soviet Union. Its territorial expansion also included the annexation of Karelia and Tuva, as autonomous republics within the RSFSR, and the incorporation of new territories in Western Ukraine and Western Byelorussia, extracted from Poland, in the 1939–44 period, and Kaliningrad, taken from Germany in 1945.[89]

The formation of the federal state of the Soviet Union was the result of a compromise following intense political and ideological debates during the revolutionary period.[90] Originally, the Bolshevik position denied the relevance of nationality as a significant criterion for the building of the new state, since class-based proletarian internationalism intended to supersede national differences between the

---

[86]   Suny (1993: 101, 130).
[87]   For a theoretical analysis of the relationship between nationalism and mobilization by Leninist elites, see Jowitt (1971, esp. part I), which sets his analytical foundation in a comparative perspective.
[88]   Pipes (1954).
[89]   Singh (1982); Hill (1985); Kozlov (1988).
[90]   Carrere d'Encausse (1987).

working and exploited masses, manipulated into inter-ethnic confrontations by bourgeois imperialism, as demonstrated by World War I. But in January 1918 the urgency of finding military alliances in the civil war that followed the Bolshevik October coup convinced Lenin of the importance of support from nationalist forces outside Russia, particularly in Ukraine. The Third All-Russian Congress of Soviets in January 1918 adopted the "Declaration of the Rights of Working and Exploited People," outlining the conversion of the former Russian Empire into the "fraternal union of Soviet Republics of Russia freely meeting on a federal basis."[91] To this "internal federalization" of Russia, the Bolsheviks added the project for the "external federalization" of other nations in April 1918, explicitly calling to the Union the people of Poland, Ukraine, Crimea, Transcaucasia, Turkestan, Kirghiz, "and others." But the critical debate concerned the principle under which ethnic and national identity would be recognized in the new Soviet state. Lenin and Stalin opposed the views of the Bundists and other socialists who wanted national cultures recognized throughout the whole structure of the state, making the Soviet Union truly multicultural in its institutions. *They opposed to such a view the principle of territoriality as the basis for nationhood.*[92] Furthermore, ethnic/national rights were to be institutionalized under the form of Union Republics, Autonomous Republics, and Autonomous Regions. The result was a complete encapsulation of the national question into the multilayered structure of the Soviet state: identities were recognized only as far as they could be marshalled within the institutions of governance. This was considered to be the expression of the principle of democratic centralism in reconciling the unitary project of the Soviet state with the recognition of the diversity of its territorial subjects.[93] Thus, the Soviet Union was constructed around the principle of a double identity: ethnic/national identities (including Russian) and Soviet identity as the foundation of the new culture of a new society.

Beyond ideology, the territorial principle of Soviet federalism was the application of a daring geopolitical strategy aimed at spreading communism throughout the world. A.M. Salmin has proposed an interesting model for interpreting the Leninist–Stalinist strategy underlying Soviet federalism.[94] The Soviet Union, in this view, was a centralized but flexible institutional system whose structure should remain open and adaptive to receive new members that would add to

[91]   Quoted by Singh (1982: 61).
[92]   Suny (1993: 110ff).
[93]   Rezun (1992).
[94]   Salmin (1992).

the system as the cause of socialism inexorably advanced in the world. This is why the Soviet Constitution of 1924 established the right of republics not only to enter the Union, but also to secede from it, making such decisions sovereign and reversible. History showed how difficult the application of such a right to secede became in the practice of the Soviet state. Yet, it was this principle, inherited from the early revolutionary debates and reproduced in the 1936 and 1977 Constitutions, that provided the legal/institutional basis for the separatist movements during the Gorbachev era, thus taking revolutionary ideology at its word and reversing, and ultimately dismantling, the odd construction of Soviet federalism.[95]

In the geopolitical model proposed by Salmin, which seems to fit with the historical evidence on the origins of the Soviet state,[96] five concentric circles were designed as both security areas and waves of expansion of the Soviet state as the standard-bearer of world communism. The first was Russia and its satellite autonomous republics, organized in the RSFSR. This was considered to be the core of Soviet power, to the point that, paradoxically, it was the only republic of the USSR not to have specific Communist party organizations, the only one without a president of the Republican Supreme Soviet, and the one with the least developed republican state institutions. In other words, the RSFSR was the reserved domain of the CPSU. Significantly, the RSFSR did not have land boundaries with the potentially aggressive capitalist world. Around this core of Soviet power, a protective second circle was formed by the Union republics, formally equal in rights to the RSFSR. Since several RSFSR autonomous republics (for example, Chechnya) were as non-Russian as some of the Union republics, it would seem that the actual criterion for their inclusion in one or other formation was precisely the fact that the Union republics had boundaries in direct contact with the outside world, thus acting as a territorial glacis for security purposes. The third circle was formed by the "people's democracies," outside the Soviet Union but under direct Soviet control, both militarily and territorially. Originally, this was the case for Khoresm and Bukhara (later dispatched between Uzbekistan and Turkmenia), Mongolia, and Tannu-Tura. In the 1940s, the People's Democracies of Eastern Europe also played such a role. The fourth circle was represented by the vassal states of pro-Soviet orientation (eventually, this category was formed by countries such as Cuba, Vietnam, and North Korea); China

[95] On the relationship between the national-territorial principle of Soviet federalism and the process of disintegration of the Soviet Union, see the insightful analysis of Granberg (1993b). For a recollection of the events, see Smith (1992).
[96] Suny (1993: 110ff).

was never really considered to be in such a category in spite of the triumph of communism: indeed, it was soon to be seen as a geopolitical threat. Finally, a fifth circle was formed by the international communist movement and its allies around the world, as embryos of the expansion of the Soviet state to the entire planet when historical conditions would precipitate the inexorable demise of capitalism.[97]

This constant tension between the a-historical, class-based universalism of communist utopia and the geopolitical interest of supporting ethnic/national identities as potential territorial allies determined the schizophrenia of Soviet policy toward the national question.

On the one hand, national cultures and languages were spurred, and in some cases reconstructed, in the union republics, autonomous republics, and ethnically based territories (*krai*). Nativization (*korenizatsiya*) policies were supported by Lenin and Stalin until the 1930s, encouraging the use of native languages and customs, implementing "affirmative action", pro-minority recruitment and promotion policies in the state and party apparatuses in the republics, and fostering the development of endogenous political and cultural elites in the republican institutions.[98] Although these policies suffered the backlash of anti-nationalist repression during the collectivization years, under Khrushchev and Brezhnev they were revived and led to the consolidation of powerful national/ethnic elites in the republics. Khrushchev, himself a Ukrainian, went so far in the non-Russian bias of Soviet federalism as to decide suddenly in 1954 on the transfer of the Crimea, a historically Russian territory, to Ukraine, reportedly after a night of heavy drinking on the eve of the Ukrainian national day. Furthermore, in the central Asian and Caucasian republics, during the Brezhnev period, traditional ethnic networks of patronage combined with party affiliation to establish a tight system that linked *nomenklatura*, clientelism, and the shadow economy in a hierarchical chain of personal loyalties that extended all the way up to the Central Committee in Moscow, a system that Helene Carrere d'Encausse calls "Mafiocracy."[99] Thus, when in December 1986 Gorbachev tried to clean up the corrupt party apparatus in Kazakhstan, the removal of a long-time Brezhnev protégé (Brezhnev himself started his career as party chief in Kazakhstan), the Kazakh Dinmukhammed Kunaev, and his replacement by a Russian as secretary of the party, provoked massive riots in Alma Ata in defense of ethnic, Kazakh rights.[100]

---

[97]   Conquest (1967); Singh (1982); Mace (1983); Carrere d'Encausse (1987); Suny (1993).

[98]   Suny (1993: ch. 3).

[99]   Carrere d'Encausse (1991: ch. 2).

The greatest paradox of this policy toward nationalities was that Russian culture and national traditions were oppressed by the Soviet state.[101] Russian traditions, religious symbols, and Russian folk were persecuted or ignored, depending upon the needs of communist politics at each point in time. Redistribution of economic resources took place in a reverse sense to what a "Russian imperialism" would have dictated: Russia was the net loser in inter-republican exchanges,[102] a situation that has continued into the post-communist era (see table 1.5). If we refer to Salmin's geopolitical theory of the Soviet state, the system operated as if the preservation of communist power in Russia was dependent on the ability of the party to lure into the system other nations, not only subduing them through repression, but also coopting their allegiance by providing resources and rights in excess of what Russian citizens were given. This does not exclude, of course, ethnic discrimination in major institutions of the state, for instance in the army and in the KGB, whose commanders were overwhelmingly Russian; or the policy of russification in the language, in the media, in culture, and science.[103] Yet, overall, Russian nationalism was generally repressed (except during the war when the assault of Nazi troops provoked Stalin into resurrecting Alexander Nevsky) as much as the cultural identity of the non-Russian subjected nations. As a consequence of this, when the relaxation of controls in Gorbachev's *glasnost* allowed nationalism to emerge, Russian nationalism was not only one of the most popularly supported but was actually the one that was decisive in dismantling the Soviet Union, in alliance with democratic nationalist movements in the Baltic republics. In contrast, in spite of their strong ethnic/national specificity, the Muslim republics of central Asia were the last bastion of Soviet communism, and only converted to independentism toward the end of the process. This was because the political elites of these republics were under direct patronage from Moscow, and their resources were highly dependent upon the politically motivated redistribution process within the Soviet state.[104]

On the other hand, autonomous nationalist expressions were

[100]   Wright (1989: 40–5, 71–4); Carrere d'Encausse (1991).
[101]   Suny (1993); Galina Starovoitova, Lecture at the Center for Slavic and Eastern European Studies, University of California at Berkeley, February 23, 1994, Emma Kiselyova's notes.
[102]   See, among other works by Alexander Granberg, Granberg and Spehl (1989) and Granberg (1993a).
[103]   Rezun (1992).
[104]   Carrere d'Encausse (1991).

Table 1.5   Balance of inter-republican exchange of products and resources, 1987

| | Output balance (billions of rubles) | | Full balance | |
| | | | Fixed assets (billions of rubles) | Labor resources (million person-years) |
Republic	Direct	Full		
Russia	3.65	−4.53	15.70	−0.78
Ukraine and Moldova	2.19	10.30	8.61	0.87
Byelorussia	3.14	7.89	1.33	0.42
Kazakhstan	−5.43	−15.01	−17.50	−0.87
Central Asia	−5.80	−13.41	20.04	−0.89
Transcaucasia	3.20	7.78	2.48	0.57
Baltic republics	−0.96	−0.39	−3.22	−0.05
Total	0.00	−7.37	−12.63	−0.74

Source: Granberg (1993a)

harshly repressed, particularly during the 1930s, when Stalin decided to break the back of all potential opposition to his program of accelerated industrialization and building of military power at whatever cost. The leading Ukrainian national communist, Mykola Skypnyk committed suicide in 1933, after realizing that the dreams of national emancipation within the Soviet Union had been another illusion in the long list of the Bolshevik revolution's unfulfilled promises.[105] The Baltic republics and Moldova were cynically annexed in 1940 on the basis of the 1939 Ribbentrop–Molotov pact, and national expressions in these areas were severely curtailed until the 1980s.[106] Furthermore, ethnic and national groups that were not trusted in their loyalty were submitted to massive deportation away from their original territories, and their autonomous republics abolished: such was the case for Crimean Tatars, Volga Germans, for Metsketyans, Chechens, Ingushi, Balkars, Karachai, Kalmyks.[107] Also, millions of Ukrainians, Estonians, Latvians, and Lithuanians suspected of collaboration with the enemy during World War II

---

[105]   Mace (1983).
[106]   Simon (1991).
[107]   Nekrich (1978).

Table 1.6 Ethnic composition of Russia's autonomous republics, 1989

Republic	Area (thousands of km²)	Percentage population share	
		Titular group	Russians
Bashkir	144	21.9	39.3
Buryat	351	24.0	70.0
Chechen-Ingush	19	70.7	23.1
Chuvash	18	67.8	26.7
Dagestan	50	27.5 (Avars)	9.2
Kabardino-Balkar	13	57.6	31.9
Kalmyk	76	45.4	37.7
Karelian	172	10.0	73.6
Komi	416	23.3	57.7
Mari	23	43.3	47.5
Mordva	26	32.5	60.8
North Ossetian	8	53.0	29.9
Tatar	68	48.5	43.3
Tuva	171	64.3	32.0
Udmurt	42	30.9	58.9
Yakut	3103	33.4	50.3

Source: Shaw (1993: 532)

suffered a similar fate. Anti-Semitism was a permanent feature of the Soviet state and permeated down to every single mechanism of political and professional promotion.[108] In addition, the policy of industrialization and settlement in the eastern regions led to the emigration (induced by the Soviet state) of millions of Russians into other republics, in which they became a sizeable minority, or even the largest ethnic group (as in Kazakhstan) while still being represented in the state by the native elites of each republic (see table 1.6). At the end of the Soviet Union, about 60 million citizens were living outside their native land.[109] This largely artificial federal construction was more a system of cooptation of local/regional elites than a recognition of national rights. The real power was always in the hands of the CPSU, and the party was hierarchically organized throughout the Soviet territory, directly conveying orders from

[108] Pinkus (1988).
[109] Suny (1993).

Moscow to the party organization in each republic, autonomous republic or *oblast*.[110] Furthermore, by mixing different national populations on such a large scale, and over a long period of time, a new Soviet identity did emerge, made up not just of ideology, but of family ties, friendships, and work relationships.

Thus, the Soviet state recognized national identity, with the odd exception of Russian identity, but it simultaneously defined identity in institutions organized on the basis of territoriality, while national populations were mixed all over the Soviet Union. At the same time, it practiced ethnic discrimination and forbade autonomous nationalist expressions outside the sphere of Communist power. This contradictory policy created a highly unstable political construction that lasted only as long as systemic repression could be enforced with the help of national Communist political elites which had their vested interests in the Soviet federal state. But by channeling identity into national/ethnic self-definition as the only admissible alternative expression to the dominant socialist ideology, the dynamics of the Soviet state created the conditions for the challenge to its rule. The political mobilization of nationally-based republics, including Russia, against the superstructure of the a-national federal state was the lever that actually brought about the collapse of the Soviet Union.

The creation of a new, soviet people (*sovetskii narod*) as an entity culturally distinct from each historic nationality was still too fragile to stand the assault of civil societies against the Soviet state. Paradoxically, this fragility was due to a large extent to the Communist emphasis on the rights of national cultures and institutions, as defined within the framework of the Soviet state. And this emphasis was directly motivated by the geopolitical interests of the CPSU, as the vanguard of a communist movement aiming at world power. Because people were allowed self-definition on the basis of their primary, national/ethnic identity, the ideological void created by the failure of Marxism–Leninism simplified the terms of the cultural debate into the opposition between subdued cynicism and rediscovered nationalism. While the nationalist fault produced only minor tremors under the iron hand of unabashed Communist authority, as soon as the pressure was released by the political expediency of the restructuring process, its shock waves wrecked the foundations of the Soviet state.

[110]   Gerner and Hedlund (1989).

The Last *Perestroika*[111]

In April 1983, about six months after Brezhnev's death, a closed seminar, organized in Novosibirsk by the Sociology Department of the Institute of Economics and Industrial Engineering of the Soviet Academy of Sciences, brought together 120 participants from 17 cities to discuss a daring report that denounced "the substantial lagging of production relations in the Soviet society behind the development of its productive forces."[112] The "Novosibirsk Report," intended to be

---

[111]   This section, and the one following, are mainly based on fieldwork, interviews and personal observation by myself and my Russian collaborators in Russia, as mentioned above, during the period 1989–96. Among relevant personalities interviewed were: A. Aganbegyan, T. Zaslavskaya, N. Shatalin, G. Yazov, B. Orlov, N. Khandruyev, Y. Afanasiev, G. Burbulis, Y. Gaidar, A. Shokhin, A. Golovkov, and several high-ranking officials of the Soviet Council of Ministers (1990, 1991), and of the Government of the Russian Federation (1991, 1992). A preliminary synthesis of these observations can be found in Castells (1992). Information on the political structure of the Soviet Union and of the political process between 1990 and 1993, based on Russian sources and interviews with political actors, is given in Castells, Shkaratan and Kolomietz (1993). (There is a Russian language version of the same report: Russian Sociological Association, Moscow.) Specific bibliographical references are given only when applicable to an argument or event mentioned in the text. I have not considered it necessary to provide specific references for reports in the Russian press of events and facts that are by now public knowledge. There are, in English, a number of excellent journalists' accounts of the process of reform and political conflict during the last decade of the Soviet Union. Two of the best are Kaiser (1991); and Pulitzer Prize Winner David Remnick (1993).

[112]   *Survey* (1984). The real story of the Novosibirsk Report differs from what was reported in the media, and accepted by the scholarly community. The generally acknowledged author of the report, sociologist Tatyana I. Zaslavskaya, wrote to Emma Kiselyova and myself to convey her own account of the origins and uses of the Novosibirsk Report. It did not originate in a meeting of the economic section of the Central Committee of the CPSU, as has been reported. Nor did the Central Committee ever discuss the document as such. The report was prepared for discussion in an academic meeting at the Institute of Economics and Industrial Engineering in Novosibirsk. Its distribution was forbidden, and it was stamped as a "restricted use document," each copy numbered for the exclusive use of participants at the meeting. During the meeting in Novosibirsk two of the copies disappeared. The KGB immediately tried to recover the copies, searching for them over the whole Institute, and confiscating all copies from the participants at the meeting, as well as the original manuscript of the report. Tatyana Zaslavskaya could not keep a single copy of her own report, and only received it in 1989 as a personal gift from the BBC in London. According to Zaslavskaya, Gorbachev read the report only after its publication in the West in August 1983. It seems plausible that he used some of the ideas in the elaboration of his own reformist strategy, as early as October 1984, in a Central Committee meeting on

exclusively for confidential use, was mysteriously leaked to *The Washington Post* which published it in August 1983. The impact of such a report *abroad* prompted Gorbachev, still not in full power, to read it and discuss it informally in the higher circles of the party. The report had been prepared under the direction of sociologist Tatyana Zaslavskaya at the Novosibirsk Institute. The director of the Institute at the time was one of the leading Soviet economists, Abel Aganbegyan. Only two years later, Aganbegyan became the top economic adviser of the newly appointed Secretary General Mikhail Gorbachev. Tatyana Zaslavskaya, as director of the first serious public opinion research institute in Moscow, was often consulted by Gorbachev, until her data started to show the decline of Gorbachev's popularity in 1988.

It is generally considered that the theses presented in the Novosibirsk document directly inspired Gorbachev's report to the 27th Congress of the CPSU on February 23, 1986. In his report the Secretary General called into question the predominance of "administrative methods" in the management of a complex economy, ushering in what appeared to be the most ambitious *perestroika* in Russian history.

Gorbachev's *perestroika* was born of Andropov's efforts to steer the Communist party ship out of the stagnant waters of the last Brezhnev years.[113] As KGB chief from 1967, Andropov had enough information to know that the shadow economy had spread all over the system to the point of disorganizing the command economy, bringing corruption to the highest levels of the state, namely to Brezhnev's family. Work discipline had broken down, ideological indoctrination was met with massive cynicism, political dissidence was rising, and the war in Afghanistan was revealing how the technology of Soviet armed forces lagged behind in conventional, electronic-based warfare. Andropov succeeded in obtaining the support of a younger generation of Soviet leaders who had grown up in post-Stalinist society, and were ready to modernize the country, to open it up to the world, ending the siege mentality that still prevailed among the Politburo's old guard.

Thus, the systemic contradictions, outlined in the preceding sections of this study, built up toward a critical point of potential

---

the management of the economy. Several observers trace back some key elements of Gorbachev's crucial report to the 27th Party Congress in February 1986 to the themes developed by Zaslavskaya in the Novosibirsk document. However, Zaslavskaya herself is much more skeptical concerning her intellectual influence on Gorbachev and on the Soviet leadership.

[113] For a documented analysis of the transition in the Soviet leadership from Brezhnev to Gorbachev, see Breslauer (1990),

breakdown. But the cautious Soviet leadership was not willing to take risks. As is often the case in history, structural matters do not affect historical processes until they align with the personal interests of social and political actors. In fact, these new actors were able to organize themselves in the CPSU around Andropov only because Brezhnev's designated successor, Andrei Kirilenko, was disabled by arteriosclerosis. In spite of his brief tenure (15 months between his election as Secretary General and his death), and his ailing health during these months, Andropov played a critical role in paving the way for Gorbachev's reforms: by appointing him as his deputy, and by purging the party and creating a network of reformers on whom Gorbachev could later capitalize.[114] These reformers were hardly liberals. Leading members of the group were Yegor Ligachev, the ideologist who went on to lead the resistance to Gorbachev during *perestroika*, and Nikolai Ryzhkov, who later, as Gorbachev's Prime Minister, defended the command economy against the liberal proposals of Shatalin, Yavlinsky, and other pro-market economists. Andropov's original blueprints for reform focused on restoring order, honesty, and discipline, both in the party and at the workplace, by means of a strong, clean government. Indeed, when Gorbachev was finally elected in March 1985, after the last stand of the old guard in the short-lived appointment of Chernenko, his first version of *perestroika* closely echoed Andropov's themes. The two main stated objectives of his policies were: technological modernization, starting with the machine-tools industry, and the restoration of labor discipline by calling on the responsibility of workers and by launching a decisive anti-alcohol campaign.

It soon became evident that the correction of failures in the Soviet system, as described in the Novosibirsk Report, required a major overhaul of the institutions and of domestic and foreign policy.[115] It was the historic merit of Gorbachev to have fully realized this need and to dare to take up the challenge, convinced as he was that the solidity of the Communist party, in whose fundamental principles he never ceased to believe, could endure the pain of restructuring so that a new, healthy, Socialist Soviet Union could emerge from the process. In the 1986 27th Congress of the CPSU he articulated the series of policies that will remain in history as Gorbachev's *perestroika*.[116]

The last Communist *perestroika*, as its predecessors in Soviet and Russian history, was a top-down process, without any participation by

---

[114]   An excellent report on the power struggles in the CPSU's Politburo after Brezhnev's death can be found in Walker (1986: 24ff.); see also Mitchell (1990).
[115]   See Aslund (1989).
[116]   See the series edited by Aganbegyan (1988–90).

the civil society in its inception and early implementation. It was not a response to pressures from below or from outside the system. It was aimed at rectifying internal failures from within the system, while keeping unscathed its fundamental principles: the Communist party monopoly of power, the command economy, and the superpower status of a unitary Soviet state.

In its strictest sense, Gorbachev's *perestroika* included a number of policies personally decided by Gorbachev, aimed at restructuring Soviet communism, between February 1986 (27th Congress) and September–November 1990, when Gorbachev rejected the "500 days plan" of transition to the market economy, and ceded to the pressures of the CPSU's Central Committee by appointing a conservative government which all but stalled the reforms and eventually engineered the August 1991 coup against Gorbachev himself.

Perestroika had four main distinct, yet interrelated, dimensions: (a) disarmament, release of the Soviet Empire in Eastern Europe, and end to the Cold War; (b) economic reform; (c) gradual liberalization of public opinion, media, and cultural expressions (the so-called *glasnost*); and (d) controlled democratization and decentralization of the political system. Significantly enough, nationalist demands within the Soviet Union were not on the agenda, until the Nagorno-Karabagh conflict, mobilization in the Baltic republics, and the 1989 Tbilisi massacre forced Gorbachev to deal with the issues involved.

The end of the Cold War will remain in history as Gorbachev's fundamental contribution to humankind. Without his personal decision to take the West at its word, and to overcome the resistance of Soviet hawks in the security establishment, it is unlikely that the process of disarmament and the partial dismantling of Soviet and American nuclear arsenals would have gone as far as they have, in spite of limitations and delays in the process. Furthermore, Gorbachev's initiative was decisive in the crumbling of communist regimes in Eastern Europe, since he even threatened (behind the scenes) the use of Soviet troops to thwart the Stasi's intention of shooting at demonstrations in Leipzig. To relinquish control over Eastern Europe was Gorbachev's masterful move to make disarmament and truly peaceful coexistence with the West possible. Both processes were indispensable in order to attack the problems of the Soviet economy and to link it up with the world economy, as was Gorbachev's ultimate design. Only if the burden of the gigantic military effort could be removed from the Soviet state could human and economic resources be reoriented toward technological modernization, production of consumer goods, and improvement in the living standards of the population, thus finding new sources of legitimacy for the Soviet system.

Yet, economic reforms proved to be difficult, even taking into account the promise of future disarmament.[117] The conversion of military enterprises proved so cumbersome that it is still unfulfilled after several years of post-Communist regime in Russia. World oil prices fell in 1986, contributing to lagging productivity and falling production in the Siberian oil and gas fields, so that the hard currency cushion, which for about a decade had spared the Soviet Union from major economic shortages, started to dwindle, increasing the difficulty of the transition. The dramatic nuclear accident at Chernobyl in April 1986 showed that the technological failure of Soviet industrialism had reached a dangerous level, and, in fact, helped liberalization by providing Gorbachev with additional arguments to shake up state bureaucracy. Yet, the most serious obstacles to economic reform came from the Soviet state, and even from the ranks of Gorbachev's reformers themselves. While there was agreement on the gradual movement toward the introduction of semi-market mechanisms in some sectors (mainly in housing and in services), neither Gorbachev nor his economic advisers really envisaged accepting the private property of land and means of production, liberalizing prizes throughout the economy, freeing credit from direct Gosbank control, or dismantling the core of the planned economy. Had they tried these reforms, as in the "500 days plan" elaborated by Shatalin and Yavlinsky in the summer of 1990, they would have faced the staunch opposition of the Soviet state apparatus and of the Communist party leadership. Indeed, this is exactly what happened when they hinted at such a possibility in the summer of 1990. At the root of the difficulties inherent in *perestroika* lay Gorbachev's personal and political contradiction in trying to reform the system by using the Communist party, while moving in a direction that would ultimately undermine the power of the Communist party itself. The "stop-and-go" policies that derived from such half-hearted reform literally disorganized the Soviet economy, provoking massive shortages and inflation. Inflation fueled speculation and illegal stockpiling, providing the ground for an even greater sprawling of the shadow economy in all areas of activity. From its subsidiary role, as a profitable parasite of the command economy, the shadow economy took over entire sectors of trade and distribution of goods and services, so that for a long time, and even more after the end of Communism, the former shadow economy, with its cohort of criminal mafias and corrupt officials, became the predominant organizational form of profit-making economic activity in the Soviet

[117] See Aganbegyan (1989).

Union, and in its successor societies.[118] The takeover of the most
dynamic economic sectors by the shadow economy further disorganized the formerly planned economy, plunging the Soviet economy
into chaos and hyperinflation by 1990.

Gorbachev was not a visionary idealist, but a pragmatic leader, a
veteran, skillful party politician, who had confronted the endemic
problems of Soviet agriculture in his native Stavropol province. He
was self-assured about his capacity to maneuver, convince, coopt, buy
off, and, when necessary, repress his political adversaries, as circumstances fitted to his design. His *perestroika* became both radicalized and
paralyzed because he sincerely believed that he could perfect the
system without fundamentally antagonizing the social interests that
supported Soviet Communism. In this sense, he was at the same time
sociologically naïve and politically arrogant. If he had paid closer
attention to the sociological analysis implicit in Zaslavskaya's document, he would have had a clearer vision of the social groups on which
he could have relied, and of those that would ultimately oppose any
significant attempt to ground the system on a different logic, whether
political democracy or market economy. In the final analysis, the
structure of society largely determines the fate of political projects.
This is why it is relevant to remember at this point in the analysis what
was the basic social structure underlying the power system in the
Soviet statist society. Four major interest groups represented
the essence of Soviet social power:[119]

1 The Communist ideologists, linked to the defense of
Marxist–Leninist values and of their dominance on social habits
and institutions. These were the doctrinaire leaders of the
Communist party (headed by Ligachev during the *perestroika*
years), but also included power-holders in the cultural and media
apparatuses of the Soviet Union, from the press, television and
radio, to the Academy of Sciences and universities, including also
official artists and writers.
2 The power elite of the state apparatus, interested in the continuation of its monopoly of power in the Soviet state, a source of
extraordinary privileges to the point of representing a caste, rather
than a class. This power elite was itself subdivided into at least four
major categories that obviously do not exhaust the complex structure of the Soviet state:

[118] See, for instance, Handelman (1995).
[119] See Lane (1990); Castells et al. (1993). For an insightful theoretical analysis
in understanding the social structure of socialist societies, see Verdery (1991). We
have also relied on work by Ivan Szelenyi. See, for instance, Szelenyi (1982).

(a)   The core political apparatus of the CPSU, which constituted the source of the *nomenklatura*, the actual ruling class of the Soviet Union. As it is known, the term *nomenklatura* has a precise meaning: it was the list of positions in the state and in the party, for which it was necessary to have the explicit agreement of the relevant party committee on the name of each person to be appointed; in the strictest, and most relevant sense, the top of the *nomenklatura* (literally thousands of positions) required explicit agreement by the Central Committee of the CPSU. This was the fundamental mechanism through which the Communist party controlled the Soviet state for seven decades.

(b)   The second, distinct elite group of the state apparatus was formed by Gosplan officers, who single-handedly managed the entire Soviet economy and gave instructions to the relevant ministries and administrative units. Gossnab, and to some extent Gosbank, executives, should also be included in this category.

(c)   A third group was formed by the commanders of the armed forces. Although they were always submitted to the party authority (particularly after their decimation by Stalin in the 1930s), they represented an increasingly autonomous group as the army grew in complexity, and became more reliant on technology and intelligence. They increasingly exercised their power of veto, and could not be counted on without serious consultation in the last decade of the Soviet Union, as the 1991 plotters learned too late.[120]

(d)   Last, but not least, KGB and Interior Ministry special forces continued to play an important, and relatively autonomous, role in the Soviet state, trying to embody the interests of the state beyond the variations of political rivalry within the party. It should be remembered that the contemporary KGB was created after Stalin's death, in March 1954, after the alliance of the party leadership and the armed forces suppressed an attempted coup by Beria and the MVD (the former political police) with whom the army always kept quarrel because of the memories of 1930s' terror. Thus, in spite of obvious continuities, the KGB of the 1980s was not the direct historical heir of Dzerzhinsky and Beria, but a more professional force, still dependent on the CPSU but more focused on the power and stability of the Soviet state than on the ideological purity of its

---

[120]   On the Soviet armed forces, see Taibo (1993a).

Communist construction.[121] This explains the paradoxical support of the KGB for the last round of reforms, from Andropov to Gorbachev, and its resistance to the 1991 coup, in spite of the active participation of Kryuchkov, the KGB chief.

3   A third group at the roots of Soviet power was formed by the industrial managers of large state enterprises, particularly in two major sectors: the military–industrial complex,[122] and the oil and gas industry.[123] This group, while professionally competent, and interested in technological modernization, was fundamentally opposed to the move toward the market, to the demilitarization of the economy, and to releasing control over foreign trade. Because of their economic, social, and political power in the enterprises and in key cities and regions around the country, the mobilization of this power elite against the reforms was decisive in blocking Gorbachev's efforts in the Central Committee of the CPSU, which in 1990 had come under the control of this group.[124]

4   Finally, another extremely important interest group was organized throughout the structure of the Soviet state. This was the network formed between the *nomenklatura* and the "bosses" of the shadow economy. In fact, this group was not different from those named above in terms of the persons involved. Yet their structural position in the Soviet power system was different: their power source came from their connection to the shadow economy. This group was opposed to the dismantling of the planned economy as it could only prosper in the cracks of this economy. However, once the command economy became disorganized, the shadow economy, deeply connected to the communist *nomenklatura*, took advantage of the situation, transforming the whole economy into a gigantic

---

[121]   Andrew and Gordievsky (1990).
[122]   See Castells and Natalushko (1993).
[123]   See Kuleshov and Castells (1993). (The original research report is in Russian and can be consulted at the Institute of Economics and Industrial Engineering, Russian Academy of Sciences, Siberian Branch, Novosibirsk, 1993). See also Kiselyova et al. (1996).
[124]   The group that controlled the Central Committee of the CPSU in the fall of 1990, who blocked the reforms, and whose initiatives paved the way for the preparation of the coup, was led by Lukyanov, chair of the Supreme Soviet of the USSR; Guidaspov, Leningrad's Party Secretary; Masljukov, Velitchko, and Laverov, leaders of military–industrial enterprises; and Baklanov, Secretary of the Military Commission of the Central Committee. Baklanov was considered to have played a decisive role in the preparation of the coup and he was one of the members of the "State of Emergency Committee" that seized power on August 19, 1991 (information from interviews with Russian political observers).

speculative mechanism. Because a shadow economy thrives particularly well in times of economic chaos, the quasi-criminal leaders
of the shadow economy, later transformed into wild proto-capitalism, were and are a major destabilizing factor during *perestroika*
and its aftermath.[125]

This was, in a nutshell, the set of powerful interest groups that
Gorbachev was up against to reform Communism without abolishing
the privileges generated by the system. He scored an easy victory
against the ideologists. When systems reach crisis point, mechanisms
for legitimating the values of the system can go the same way they
came in, as long as new forms of cultural domination are generated
and then embedded in the material interests of the dominant elites.
Ligachev and the Nina Andreyevas of the Soviet Union became the
perfect target against whom to size up the progress of reform. The
army was a more potent force to reckon with, since it is never easy for
the military to accept a decline in power, particularly when it goes in
hand with the shock of realizing that entire units cannot be repatri-
ated to the motherland because they would lack housing and basic
facilities. Yet, Gorbachev won their acquiescence to disarmament by
building on their understanding of the need to regroup and re-equip
after losing the technological race in conventional weapons. Marshal
Ogarkov, Chief of the General Staff, was dismissed in September 1984
a year after he had publicly claimed the need for higher military
budgets to update the technology of Soviet military equipment, whose
inferiority had been exposed in the 1982 Bekaa Valley air massacre of
Syrian jets by the Israeli Air Force. Yet, his message was received, and
Gorbachev, in fact, increased the military budget, even in the middle
of the harshest economic times. Gorbachev's military plans were not
too different from those of the American administration: they aimed
at reducing costs over time, dismantling a useless plethora of redundant nuclear missiles, while elevating the professional and
technological quality of the Soviet armed forces to the level of a superpower not aiming at nuclear holocaust. This strategy was, in fact,
supported by both the armed forces and the KGB which, therefore,
were not in principle opposed to the reforms, provided that two limits
were not transgressed: the territorial integrity of the Soviet state; and
the control of the military–industrial complex by the Ministry of
Defense. Thus, while Gorbachev seemed convinced of the support
of the army and security forces, these two non-negotiable conditions
were decisively damaging for Gorbachev's reforms because, in practice, they meant that nationalism had to be repressed (regardless of

[125]   See Handelman (1995).

Gorbachev's personal views), and that the core of industry could not operate under market rules.

Between 1987 and 1990, the party *nomenklatura*, the top state bureaucracy, the military–industrial complex, the oil generals, and the bosses of the shadow economy effectively resisted Gorbachev's reforms, conceding ideological battles, but retrenching themselves in the structure of the party and of the state bureaucracy. Gorbachev's decrees gradually became paper tigers, as had been so often the case in the history of Russian *perestroikas*.

But Gorbachev was a fighter. He decided not to follow Khrushchev in his historic defeat, and counted on the support of the new generation of Communist leaders, up against the Soviet gerontocracy, on the sympathy of the West, on the disarray of the state bureaucracy, and on the neutrality of the army and security forces toward political in-fighting. Thus, to overcome the resistance of interest groups that had become a political obstacle to *perestroika*, while still believing in the future of socialism and in a reformed Communist party as its instrument, he appealed to civil society to mobilize in support of his reforms: *uskorenie* led to *perestroika* and *perestroika* became dependent on *glasnost*, opening the way for democratization.[126] So doing, he inadvertently triggered a process that ultimately doomed the Communist party, the Soviet state, and his own hold on power. Yet, while for the majority of the Soviet people Gorbachev was the last Communist chief of state, and for the Communist minority he was the traitor who ruined Lenin's heritage, for history Gorbachev will remain the hero who changed the world by destroying the Soviet empire, although he did it without knowing it and without wanting it.

Nationalism, Democracy, and the Disintegration of the Soviet State

The liberalization of politics and the mass media, decided upon by Gorbachev to involve civil society in support of his reforms, resulted in widespread social mobilization on a variety of themes. The recuperation of historical memory, stimulated by an increasingly assertive Soviet press and television, brought into the open, public opinion, ideologies, and values from a suddenly freed society, often in confused expression, but with a shared rejection of all sorts of official

---

[126] See the excellent journalist's report on the influence of the media in the disintegration of the Soviet Union in Shane (1994).

truths. Between 1987 and 1991, in a social whirlwind of increasing intensity, intellectuals denounced the system, workers went on strike for their demands and their rights, ecologists exposed environmental catastrophes, human rights groups staged their protests, the Memorial Movement reconstructed the horrors of Stalinism, and voters used every opportunity in parliamentary and local elections to reject official candidates from the Communist party, thus delegitimizing the established power structure.

Yet, the most powerful mobilizations, and the direct challenge to the Soviet state came from nationalist movements.[127] In February 1988, the massacre of Armenians by Azeris in Sumgait revived the latent conflict in the Armenian enclave of Nagorno-Karabagh in Azerbaijan, a conflict that degenerated into open warfare and forced the intervention of the Soviet army and the direct administration of the territory from Moscow. Inter-ethnic tensions in the Caucasus exploded into the open, after decades of forced suppression and artificial integration. In 1989, hundreds of people were killed in the Ferghana Valley, in Uzbekistan, in rioting between Uzbeks and Metsketyans. On April 9, 1989, a massive, peaceful demonstration of Georgian nationalists in Tbilisi was repressed with poison gas, killing 23 people, and prompting an investigation from Moscow. Also in early 1989, the Moldavian National Front began a campaign for the independence of the republic and its eventual reintegration into Romania.

However, the most powerful and uncompromising nationalist mobilization came from the Baltic republics. In August 1988, the publication of the 1939 secret treaty between Stalin and Hitler to annex the Baltic republics led to massive demonstrations in the three republics and to the formation of popular fronts in each of them. Thereafter, the Estonian Parliament voted to change its time zone, shifting it from Moscow time to Finland time. Lithuania started issuing its own passports. In August 1989, to protest against the fiftieth anniversary of the Ribbentrop–Molotov pact, two million people formed a human chain stretching over the territories of the three republics. In the spring of 1989, the Supreme Soviets of the three republics declared their sovereignty, and their right to overrule legislation from Moscow, triggering an open confrontation with the Soviet leadership which responded with an embargo of supplies to Lithuania.

Significantly, the Muslim republics of central Asia and the Caucasus did not rebel against the Soviet state, although Islamism was on the rise, particularly among intellectual elites. Conflicts in the

---

[127]   Carrere d'Encausse (1991).

Caucasus and central Asia predominantly took the form of inter-ethnic confrontation and political civil wars within the republics (as in Georgia) or between republics (for example, Azerbaijan versus Armenia).

Nationalism was not only the expression of collective ethnic identity. It was the predominant form of the democratic movement throughout the Soviet Union, and particularly in Russia. The "democratic movement" that led the process of political mobilization in the main urban centers of the Soviet Union was never an organized front, nor was "Democratic Russia", the popular movement founded by Yuri Afanasiev and other intellectuals, a party. There were dozens of proto-parties of all political tendencies, but by and large the movement was profoundly anti-party, given the historical experience of highly structured organizations. The distrust of formalized ideologies and party politics led socio-political movements, especially in Russia, but also in Ukraine, in Armenia, and in the Baltic republics, to structure themselves loosely around two signs of identity: on the one hand, the negation of Soviet Communism in whatever form, whether it restructured or not; on the other hand, the affirmation of a collective primary identity, whose broadest expression was national identity, the only historical memory to which people could refer after the vacuum created by Marxism–Leninism and its subsequent demise. In Russia, this renewed nationalism found a particularly strong echo among the people as a reaction to the anti-Russian nationalism of other republics. Thus, as has often been the case in history, various nationalisms fed each other. This is why Yeltsin, against all the odds, became the only Russian political leader with massive popular support and trust, in spite of (and probably because of) all the efforts of Gorbachev and the CPSU to destroy his image and his reputation. Gennadi Burbulis, Yeltsin's main political adviser in the 1988–92 period, tried to explain in one of our conversations in 1991, the deep-seated reasons for Yeltsin's appeal to the Russian people. It is worth while to quote him directly:

> What Western observers do not understand is that, after 70 years of Stalinist terror and of suppression of all independent thinking, Russian society is deeply irrational. And societies that have been reduced to irrationality mobilize primarily around myths. This myth in contemporary Russia is named Yeltsin. This is why he is the only true force of the democratic movement.[128]

Indeed, in the critical demonstration of March 28, 1991 in Moscow, when the democratic movement definitively opposed Gorbachev and

[128] Interview with Gennadi Burbulis, April 2, 1991.

occupied the streets in spite of his prohibition, defying the presence of army troops, the hundreds of thousands of demonstrators shouted just two rallying cries: "*Rossiya!*" and "Yeltsin!, Yeltsin!" The affirmation of the forgotten past, and the negation of the present symbolized by the man who could say "No!" and still survive, were the only clearly shared principles of a newly born civil society.

The connection between the democratic movement, the nationalist mobilization, and the process of dismantlement of Soviet power was paradoxically predetermined by the structure of the Soviet Federal State. Because all the power was concentrated in the Central Committee of the CPSU and in the central institutions of the Soviet state (Congress of People's Deputies, Supreme Soviet of the USSR, Council of Ministers, and Presidency of the USSR), the process of democratization under Gorbachev took the form of allowing competing candidacies (but not free political association) for the soviets of cities, regions, and republics, while keeping under tighter control the USSR Congress of People's Deputies, and the USSR Supreme Soviet. Between 1989 and 1991, a majority of the seats in the local soviets of the main cities, and in the republican parliaments, went to candidates opposed to the official Communist candidates.

The hierarchical structure of the Soviet state seemed to limit the damage inflicted on the mechanisms of political control. Yet, the strategy, deliberately designed by political strategists of the democratic movement, and particularly those working with Yeltsin, was to consolidate power in the representative republican institutions, and then to use these institutions as a lever of opposition against the Soviet central state, claiming as much power as feasible for the republics. Thus, what appeared to be an autonomist or separatist movement was also a movement to break away from the discipline of the Soviet state, and ultimately to be freed from the control of the Communist party. This strategy explains why the key political battle in 1990–91 in Russia focused on increasing the power and autonomy of the Russian Federation, the only one not to have a president of its republican parliament. Thus, while Gorbachev thought he could claim victory when he won the majority of the popular vote in the referendum on a new Union Treaty on March 15, 1991, in fact the results of this referendum were the beginning of the end of the Soviet Union. Yeltsin's supporters were able to introduce in the ballot a question demanding direct popular election for the presidency of the Russian Federation, with a precise election date, June 12. The approval of this question by the electorate, thus automatically calling for such an election, was far more important than the approval given to the vague proposals of Gorbachev for a new federal state. When Yeltsin became the first Russian chief of state to be democratically elected a fundamental cleavage was created between the representative political structures of Russia and of other republics, and the increasingly isolated superstructure of the Soviet federal state. At this point, only massive, decisive repression could have turned the process back under control.

But the Soviet Communist party was not in a condition to launch repression. It had become divided, disconcerted, disorganized by Gorbachev's maneuvers, and by penetration into its ranks of the values and projects of a revived society. Under the impact of criticism from all quarters, the political *nomenklatura* lost its self-confidence.[129] For instance, the election of Yeltsin as chair of the Russian Parliament in March 1991 was only possible because an important faction of the newly established Russian Communist party, led by Rutskoi, joined the democrats' camp against the nationalist-communist leadership of Polozkov, leader of the majority of the Russian Communist party, who was in open opposition to Gorbachev. In fact, the most influential group of the Central Committee of the CPSU, loosely articulated around Anatoly Lukyanov, chairman of the USSR Supreme Soviet (and a law school classmate of Gorbachev), had decided to draw the line against further reforms in the fall of 1990. The then appointed Pavlov government aimed at re-establishing the command economy. Police measures were taken to restore order in the cities and to curb nationalism, starting with the Baltic republics. But the brutal assault on the television station in Vilnius by Interior Ministry special forces in January 1991 prompted Gorbachev to ask for restraint and to halt the repression. By July 1991, Gorbachev was ready to establish a new Union Treaty without six of the 15 republics (the Baltic republics, Moldova, Georgia, and Armenia), and to grant extensive powers to the republics as the only way to save the Soviet Union. In his speech to the Central Committee on July 25, 1991, he also outlined an ideological program for abandoning Leninism and converting the party to democratic socialism. He won an easy victory. The real forces of the Central Committee, and the majority of the Soviet government, had already embarked on a preparation of a coup against their Secretary General and President, after failing to control the process through standard institutional procedures that were no longer working because most of the republics, and particularly Russia, had broken loose from the control of the Soviet central state.

The circumstances of the August 1991 coup, the event that precipi-

---

[129] The loss of self-confidence by the party *nomenklatura* as a major factor in preventing an early reaction against Gorbachev's reforms was called to my attention by George Breslauer.

tated the disintegration of the Soviet Union, have not been fully exposed, and it is doubtful whether they will be in a long time, given the maze of political interests woven around the plot. On a superficial level, it seems surprising that a coup organized from the Central Committee of the CPSU with the full participation of the chief of the KGB, the Minister of the Interior, the Minister of Defense, the Vicepresident of the USSR, and most of the Soviet government, could fail. And indeed, in spite of all the analysis presented here about the inevitability of the crisis of the Soviet Union, the 1991 coup could have succeeded if Yeltsin and a few thousand supporters had not stood up to it, openly risking their lives, counting on the presence of the media as their symbolic defense, and if, all over Russia and in some Soviet republics, people of all social sectors had not met in their workplaces and voted their support for Yeltsin by sending tens of thousands of telegrams to Moscow to make their position known. After seven decades of repression, people were still there, confused but ready to fight if necessary to defend their new-found freedom. The possible success of the coup in the short term would not necessarily have meant that the crisis of the Soviet Union could have been halted, given the process of decomposition of the whole system. Yet the crisis would have had another denouement, and history would have been different. What determined the coup's failure were two fundamental factors: the attitude of the KGB and the army; and a misunderstanding of the Communist leadership about their own country as a result of their growing isolation at the summit of the Soviet state. Key units of the security forces refused to cooperate: the elite KGB's Alpha unit refused to obey the order to attack the White House, and received support from key KGB commanders; the paratroopers under the command of General Pavel Grachev declared their loyalty to Gorbachev and Yeltsin; and, finally, the Air Force Commander, General Shaposhnikov, threatened the Minister of Defense that he would bomb the Kremlin. Surrender came within hours of this ultimatum. These decisions resulted from the fact that the army and the KGB had been transformed during the period of *perestroika*. It was not so much that they were active supporters of democracy, but that they had been in direct contact with the evolution of society at large, so that any decisive move against the established chain of command could divide the forces and open the way for civil war. No responsible commander would risk a civil war in an army equipped with a gigantic and diverse nuclear arsenal. In fact, the organizers of the *putsch* themselves were not ready to start a civil war. They were convinced that a show of force and the legal removal of Gorbachev, following the historical precedent of Khrushchev's successful ousting, would be enough to bring the country under control. They underestimated Yeltsin's determination, and they did not understand the new role of the media, and the extent to which the media were outside Communist control. They planned and executed a coup as if they were in the Soviet Union of the 1960s, probably the last time they had been in the street without bodyguards. When they discovered the new country that had grown up in the last quarter of the century, it was too late. Their fall became the fall of their party-state. Yet, the dismantling of the Communist state and, even more, the break up of the Soviet Union were not a historical necessity. It required deliberate political action in the following months, enacted by a small group of decisive revolutionaries, in the purest Leninist tradition. Yeltsin's strategists, led by Burbulis, the undisputed Machiavelli of the new democratic Russia, took to the limit the plan of separation between the socially rooted institutions of the republics and the by then isolated superstructure of the Soviet Federal State. While Gorbachev was desperately trying to survive the dissolution of the Communist party, and to reform Soviet institutions, Yeltsin convinced the Ukrainian and Byelorussian Communist leaders, quickly reconverted to nationalism and independentism, to secede jointly from the Soviet Union. Their agreement in Belovezhskaya Pushcha on December 9, 1991, to dissolve the Soviet state, and to create a loose Commonwealth of Independent States as a mechanism to distribute the legacy of the defunct Soviet Union among the newly sovereign republics, signaled the end of one of the boldest and most damaging social experiments in human history. But the ease with which Yeltsin and his aides undertook the dismantlement process in only four months revealed the absolute decomposition of an overgrown state apparatus that had become uprooted from its own society.

The Scars of History, the Lessons for Theory, the Legacy for Society

The Soviet experiment marked decisively a twentieth century that, by and large, revolved around its development and consequences for the whole world. It cast a giant shadow not only over the geopolitics of states, but also over the imaginary constructions of social transformation. In spite of the horrors of Stalinism, the political left and social movements around the world looked to Soviet Communism for a long time at least as a motive of hope, and very often as a source of inspiration and support, perceived through the distorting veil of capitalist propaganda. Few intellectuals of the generations born in the first half of the century escaped the fascination of the debate about Marxism, communism, and the construction of the Soviet Union. A large number of leading social scientists in the West have constructed their theories for, against, and in relation to the Soviet experience. Indeed, some of the most prominent intellectual critics of Soviet Communism were influenced in their student years by Trotskyism, an ultra-Bolshevik ideology. That all this effort, all this human suffering and passion, all these ideas, all these dreams, could have vanished in such a short period of time, revealing the emptiness of the debate, is a stunning expression of our collective capacity to build political fantasies so powerful that they end up changing history, though in the opposite direction of intended historical projects. This is perhaps the most painful failure of the Communist utopia: the abduction and distortion of the revolutionary dreams and hopes of so many people in Russia, and around the world, converting liberation into oppression, turning the project of a classless society into a caste-dominated state, and shifting from solidarity among exploited workers to complicity among *nomenklatura* apparatchiks on their way to becoming ringleaders of the world's shadow economy. On balance, and in spite of some positive elements in social policies in the post-Stalin era, the Soviet experiment brought considerable suffering to the peoples of the Soviet Union, and to the world at large. Russia could have industrialized and modernized otherwise, not without pain but without the human holocaust that took place during Stalin's period. Relative social equality, full employment, and a welfare state were accomplished by social-democratic regimes in neighboring, then poor, Scandinavia, without resorting to such extreme policies. The Nazi machine was defeated not by Stalin (who, in fact, had decimated and weakened the Red Army just before the war to impose his personal control) but by the secular Russian will against the foreign invader. The domination of the Comintern over a large segment of the world's revolutionary and socialist movement sterilized energies, stalled political projects, and led entire nations to dead ends. The division of Europe, and of the world, into military blocs enclosed a substantial part of the technological advances and economic growth of the post-World War II years in a senseless arms race. To be sure, the American (and to a lesser extent European) Cold War establishment bears equal responsibility for engaging in the confrontation, for developing and using nuclear weapons, and for building up a bi-polar symmetry for the purpose of world domination.[130] However, without the coherence, strength, and

---

[130] The history of the Cold War is full of events and anecdotes that reveal how the two military blocs kept feeding their own defensive paranoia beyond reason-

threatening façade of Soviet power, Western societies and public opinion would hardly have accepted the expansion of their warfare states and the continuation of blatant colonial enterprises, as has been shown after the end of the Cold War. Furthermore, the building of a superpower without relying on a productive economy and an open society has proved to be unsustainable in the long run, thus ruining Russia, and the other Soviet republics, without much apparent benefit to their people, if we except job security, and some improvement of living conditions in the 1960–80 period: a period that is now idealized in Russia by many because of the desperate situation in which large segments of the population now find themselves in the wild transition to wild capitalism.

Yet, the most damaging historic irony was the mockery that the Communist state made of the values of human solidarity in which three generations of Soviet citizens were educated. While most people sincerely believed in sharing difficulties, and in helping each other to build a better society, they gradually discovered, and finally realized, that their trust had been systematically abused by a caste of cynical bureaucrats. Once the truth was exposed, the moral injuries thus inflicted on the people of the Soviet Union are likely to unfold for a long time: the sense of life lost; human values at the roots of everyday efforts degraded. Cynicism and violence have become pervasive throughout society, after the hopes inspired by democracy, in the aftermath of the Soviet collapse, quickly faded away. The successive failures of the Soviet experiment, of *perestroika*, and of democratic politics in the 1990s, have brought ruin and despair to the lands of Russia and the former Soviet republics.

As for intellectuals, the most important political lesson to be learnt from the Communist experiment is the fundamental distance that should be kept between theoretical blueprints and the historical development of political projects. To put it bluntly, all Utopias lead to Terror if there is a serious attempt at implementing them.

---

able limits. An illustration of this mentality, too quickly forgotten, is the 1995 revelation of the mystery of Soviet submarines in Swedish waters. As some may remember, for more than two decades Swedish naval forces, supported by the Western Alliance, claimed that the country's maritime borders were repeatedly intruded upon by Soviet submarines, and they resorted to regular dropping of explosive depth-charges broadcast by television all over the world. Only in 1995 did Sweden confirm "an embarrassing fact: that its defense forces have been hunting minkes, not Russian submarines . . . New hydrophonic instruments introduced into the Swedish navy in 1992 showed that minkes could give off sound patterns similar to those of submarines" (*New York Times*, February 12, 1995, p. 8). As for the fate of the minkes, there is no reference in the report.

Theories, and their inseparable ideological narratives, can be (and have been) useful tools for understanding, and thus for guiding collective action. But only as tools, always to be rectified and adjusted according to experience. Never as schemata to be reproduced, in their elegant coherence, in the imperfect yet wonderful world of human flesh. Because such attempts are at best cynical rationalizations of personal or group interests. At worst, when they are truly believed and enacted by their believers, such theoretical constructions become the source of political fundamentalism, always an undercurrent of dictatorship and terror. I am not arguing for a bland political landscape free of values and passions. Dreams and projects are the stuff of which social change is made. A purely rational, selfish subject, of the "free rider" type, would always stay at home, and let the work of historical change be done by "the others." The only problem with such an attitude (the best "economic rational choice") is that it assumes collective action from others. In other words, it is a form of historical parasitism. Fortunately, few societies in history have been constructed by parasites, precisely because they are too selfish to be involved. Societies are, and will always be, shaped by social actors, mobilized around interests, ideas and values, in an open, conflictive process. Social and political change is what ultimately determines the fate and structure of societies. Thus, what the Soviet experience shows is not the need for a non-political, value-free process of social transformation, but the necessary distance and tension between theoretical analysis, systems of representation of society, and actual political practice. Relatively successful political practice always muddles through the limits of history, not trying to progress by leaps and bounds, but adapting to the contours of social evolution and accepting the slow-motion process of transformation of human behavior. This argument has nothing to do with the distinction between reform and revolution. When material conditions and subjective consciousness are transformed in the society at large to a point where institutions do not correspond with such conditions, a revolution (peaceful or not, or in between) is part of the normal process of historical evolution, as the case of South Africa shows. When vanguards, who are almost invariably intellectual vanguards, aim at accelerating the historical tempo beyond what societies can actually take, in order to satisfy both their desire for power and their theoretical doctrine, they may win and reshape society, but only on the condition of strangling souls and torturing bodies. Surviving intellectuals may then reflect, from the comfort of their libraries, upon the excesses of their distorted revolutionary dream. Yet, what it is crucial to learn as the main political lesson of the Soviet experience, is that revolutions (or reforms) are too important and too costly in human lives to be left to dreams, or for that matter, to theories. It is up to the people, using whatever tools they may have in their reach, including theoretical and organizational tools, to find and walk the collective path of their individual lives. The artificial paradise of theoretically inspired politics should be buried for ever with the Soviet state. Because the most important lesson from the collapse of communism is the realization that there is no sense of history beyond the history we sense.

There are also important lessons to be drawn for social theory in general and for the theory of the information society in particular. The process of social change is shaped by the historical matrix of the society in which it takes place. Thus, the sources of statism's dynamics became at the same time its structural limitations and the triggers of contradictory processes within the system. The capture of society and economy by the state allows for the full mobilization of human and material resources around the objectives of power and ideology. Yet, this effort is economically wasteful because it has no built-in constraints in the use and allocation of scarce resources. And it is socially sustainable only as long as civil society is either subdued by sheer coercion or reduced to a passive role of contributing to work and public service at the lowest possible level. Under statism, as soon as society becomes active, it also becomes unpredictable in its relationship to the state. The state itself is weakened by its inability to mobilize its subjects, who refuse their cooperation, either through resistance or withdrawal.

Soviet statism faced a particularly difficult task in managing its relationship to economy and society in the historical context of the transition to informationalism. To the inherent wasteful tendencies of the command economy, and to the limits imposed on society by the structural priority given to military power, were added the pressures of adapting to the specific demands of informationalism. Paradoxically, a system built under the banner of the development of productive forces could not master the most important technological revolution in human history. This is because the characteristics of informationalism, the symbiotic interaction between socially determined processing of information and material production, became incompatible with the monopoly of information by the state, and with the closing of technology within the boundaries of warfare. At the level of organizations, the structural logic of vertical bureaucracies was made obsolete by the informational trend toward flexible networks, much as happened in the West. But, unlike in the West, the vertical command chain was at the core of the system, making the transformation of large corporations into the new forms of networked business organizations much more difficult. Furthermore, Soviet managers and bureaucrats did discover flexibility and networking as an organizational form. But they applied it to the development of the shadow economy, thus undermining the control capacity of the command economy from the inside, increasing the distance between the institutional organization of the Soviet system and the functional demands of the real economy.

Moreover, the information society is not the superstructure of a new technological paradigm. It is based on the historical tension between the material power of abstract information processing and society's search for meaningful cultural identity. On both counts, statism seems to be unable to grasp the new history. Not only does it suffocate the capacity for technological innovation, but it appropriates and redefines historically rooted identities in order to dissolve them into the all-important process of power-making. Ultimately, statism becomes powerless in a world where society's capacity to constantly renew information and information-embodying technology are the fundamental sources of economic and military power. And statism is also weakened, and ultimately destroyed, by its incapacity to generate legitimacy on the basis of identity. The abstraction of state power on behalf of a rapidly fading ideological construction cannot endure the test of time against the double challenge of historical traditions and individual desires.

Yet, in spite of these fundamental structural contradictions, Soviet statism did not collapse under the assault of social movements born of these contradictions. An important contribution of the Soviet experience to a general theory of social change is that, under certain conditions, social systems can disappear as a result of their own pitfalls without being decisively battered by consciously mobilized social actors. Such conditions seem to be the historical work of the state in destroying the foundations of civil society. This is not to say that the mosaic of societies that formed the Soviet Union was not capable of political insurgency, social revolt, or even revolutionary mobilization. Indeed, the nationalist mobilization of the Baltic republics, or the massive democratic demonstrations in Moscow and Leningrad in the spring of 1991, showed the existence of an active, politically conscious segment of the urban population lurching to overcome the Soviet state. Yet, not only was there little political organization, but, more importantly, there was no consistent, positive social movement projecting alternative views of politics and society. In its best expression, the Russian democratic movement toward the end of the Soviet Union was a free-speech movement, mainly characterized by the recovery of society's ability to declare and speak out. In its mainstream manifestation, the Russian democratic movement was a collective denial of the experience that society had lived through, without further affirmation of values other than the confused reconstruction of a historical, national identity. When the obvious enemy (Soviet Communism) disintegrated, when the material difficulties of the transition led to the deterioration of daily life, and when the gray reality of the meager heritage gained after seven decades of daily struggle settled in the minds of the ex-Soviet people, the absence of a collective project, beyond the fact of being "ex," spread political confusion, and fostered wild competition in a race for individual survival throughout society.

The consequences of a major social change resulting from the disintegration of a system, rather than from the construction of an alternative project, can be felt in the painful legacy that Russia and the ex-Soviet societies have received from Soviet statism, and from the pitfalls of *perestroika* policies. The economy was wrecked, to the unbearable pain of the people, by speculative maneuvers for the benefit of the *nomenklatura*; by irresponsible advice on abstract free-market policies by the International Monetary Fund, some Western advisers, and politically inexperienced Russian economists, who suddenly found themselves in the posts of high command; and by the paralysis of the democratic state as a result of byzantine quarrels between political factions dominated by personal ambitions. The criminal economy grew to proportions never witnessed in a major industrial country, linking up with the world's criminal economy, and becoming a fundamental factor to be reckoned with, both in Russia and in the international scene. Short-sighted policies from the United States, in fact aimed at finishing off the Russian Bear in world politics, triggered nationalist reactions, threatening to fuel again the arms race and international tension. Nationalist pressures within the army, political maneuvers in Yeltsin's Kremlin, and criminal interests in power positions, led to the catastrophic adventure of war in Chechn'ya. The democrats in power became lost between their novice faith in the power of the market and their Machiavellian strategies tailored for the backrooms of Moscow's political establishment but rather ignorant of the basic condition of a traumatized population, spread around the huge territory of an increasingly disarticulated country.

The most enduring legacy of Soviet statism will be the destruction of civil society after decades of systematic negation of its existence. Reduced to networks of primary identity and individual survival, Russian people, and the people of the ex-Soviet societies, will have to muddle through the reconstruction of their collective identity, in the midst of a world where the flows of power and money are trying to render piecemeal the emerging economic and social institutions before they come into being, in order to swallow them in their global networks. Nowhere is the ongoing struggle between global economic flows and cultural identity more important than in the wasteland created by the collapse of Soviet statism on the historical edge of the information society.

━ 2 ━

The Rise of the Fourth World:
Informational Capitalism, Poverty,
and Social Exclusion

The rise of informationalism in this end of millennium is intertwined with rising inequality and social exclusion throughout the world. In this chapter I shall try to explain why and how this is so, while displaying some snapshots of the new faces of human suffering. The process of capitalist restructuring, with its hardened logic of economic competitiveness, has much to do with it. But new technological and organizational conditions of the Information Age, as analyzed in this book, provide a new, powerful twist to the old pattern of profit-seeking taking over soul-searching.

However, there is contradictory evidence, fueling an ideologically charged debate, on the actual plight of people around the world. After all, the last quarter of the century has seen access to development, industrialization, and consumption for tens of millions of Chinese, Koreans, Indians, Malaysians, Thais, Indonesians, Chileans, Brazilians, Argentinians, and smaller numbers in a variety of countries. The bulk of the population in Western Europe still enjoys the highest living standards in the world, and in the world's history. And in the United States, while average real wages for male workers have stagnated or declined, with the exception of the top of the scale of college graduates, the massive incorporation of women into paid labor, relatively closing their wage gap with men, has maintained decent standards of living, overall, on the condition of being stable enough to keep a two-wage household. Health, education, and income statistics around the world show, on average, considerable improvement over historical standards.[1] In fact, for the population as a whole, only the former Soviet Union, after the collapse of statism, and Sub-Saharan Africa, after its marginalization from capitalism, have experienced a decline in living conditions, and for

[1] UNDP (1996).

some countries in vital statistics, in the past ten years (although most of Latin America regressed in the 1980s). Yet, as Stephen Gould entitled a wonderful article years ago, "the median isn't the message."[2] Even without entering into a full discussion of the meaning of the quality of life, including the environmental consequences of the latest round of industrialization, the apparently mixed record of development at the dawn of the Information Age conveys ideologically manipulated bewilderment in the absence of analytical clarity.

This is why it is necessary, in assessing the social dynamics of informationalism, to establish a distinction between several processes of social differentiation: on the one hand, *inequality, polarization, poverty,* and *misery* all pertain to the domain of relationships of distribution/consumption or differential appropriation of the wealth generated by collective effort. On the other hand, *individualization of work, over-exploitation of workers, social exclusion,* and *perverse integration* are characteristic of four specific processes *vis à vis* relationships of production.[3]

Inequality refers to the differential appropriation of wealth (income and assets) by different individuals and social groups, relative to each other. *Polarization* is a specific process of inequality that occurs when both the top and the bottom of the scale of income or wealth distribution grow faster than the middle, thus shrinking the middle, and sharpening social differences between two extreme segments of the population. *Poverty* is an institutionally defined norm concerning a level of resources below which it is not possible to reach the living standards considered to be the minimum norm in a given society at a given time (usually, a level of income per a given number of members of household, as defined by governments or authoritative institutions). *Misery,* a term I propose, refers to what social statisticians call "extreme poverty," that is the bottom of the distribution of income/assets, or what some experts conceptualize as "deprivation," introducing a wider range of social/economic disadvantages. In the United States, for instance, extreme poverty refers to those households whose income falls below 50 percent of the income that defines the poverty line. It is obvious that all these definitions (with powerful effects in categorizing populations, and defining social policies and resource allocation) are statistically relative and culturally defined, besides being politically manipulated. Yet, they at least allow us to be precise about what we say when describing/analyzing social differentiation under informational capitalism.

---

[2]   Gould (1985).
[3]   For an informed discussion on analyzing poverty and social exclusion in a comparative perspective, see Rodgers et al. (1995); Mingione (1996).

The second set of processes, and their categorization, pertains to the analysis of relations of production. Thus, when observers criticize "precarious" labor relations, they are usually referring to the process of individualization of work, and to its induced instability on employment patterns. Or else the discourse on social exclusion denotes the observed tendency to permanently exclude from formal labor markets certain categories of the population. These processes do have fundamental consequences for inequality, polarization, poverty, and misery. But the two planes must be analytically and empirically differentiated in order to establish their causal relationships, thus paving the way for understanding the dynamics of social differentiation, exploitation, and exclusion in the network society.

By *individualization of labor* I mean the process by which labor contribution to production is defined specifically for each worker, and for each of his/her contributions, either under the form of self-employment or under individually contracted, largely unregulated, salaried labor. I developed, empirically, the argument about the diffusion of this form of labor arrangement in volume I, chapter 4. I simply add here a reminder that individualization of labor is the overwhelming practice in the urban informal economy that has become the predominant form of employment in most developing countries, as well as in certain labor markets of advanced economies.[4]

I use the term *over-exploitation*[5] to indicate working arrangements that allow capital to systematically withhold payment/resource allocation, or impose harsher working conditions, on certain types of workers, below what is the norm/regulation in a given formal labor market in a given time and space. This refers to discrimination against immigrants, minorities, women, young people, children, or other categories of discriminated workers, as tolerated, or sanctioned, by regulatory agencies. A particularly meaningful trend in this context is the resurgence of child paid labor throughout the world, in conditions of extreme exploitation, defenselessness, and abuse, reversing the historical pattern of social protection of children existing under late industrial capitalism, as well as in industrial statism and traditional agricultural societies.[6]

---

[4] Portes et al. (1989).

[5] I use the term "over-exploitation" to distinguish it from the concept of exploitation in the Marxian tradition, that, in strict Marxist economics, would be applicable to all salaried labor. Since this categorization would imply accepting the labor theory of value, a matter of belief rather than of research, I prefer to bypass the debate altogether, but avoid creating further confusion by using "exploitation," as I would like to do for cases of systematic discrimination such as the ones I am referring to in my categorization.

[6] ILO (1996).

Social exclusion is a concept proposed by the social policy think-tanks of the European Union's Commission, and adopted by the United Nation's International Labour Office.[7] According to the European Commission's Observatory on National Policies to Combat Social Exclusion, it refers to "the social rights of citizens . . . to a certain basic standard of living and to participation in the major social and occupational opportunities of the society."[8] Trying to be more precise, I define *social exclusion as the process by which certain individuals and groups are systematically barred from access to positions that would enable them to an autonomous livelihood within the social standards framed by institutions and values in a given context.*[9] Under normal circumstances, in informational capitalism, *such a position is usually associated with the possibility of access to relatively regular, paid labor, for at least one member of a stable household.* Social exclusion is, in fact, the process that disfranchises a person as labor in the context of capitalism. In countries with a well-developed welfare state, inclusion may also encompass generous compensations in case of long-term unemployment or disability, although these conditions are increasingly exceptional. I would consider among the socially excluded the mass of people on long-term welfare assistance under institutionally punitive conditions, such as is the case in the United States. To be sure, among the English gentry, and among the oil sheiks, there are still a few independently wealthy individuals who could not care less about being demoted to non-labor: I do not consider them to be socially excluded.

Social exclusion is a process, not a condition. Thus, its boundaries shift, and who is excluded and included may vary over time, depending on education, demographic characteristics, social prejudices, business practices, and public policies. Furthermore, although the lack of regular work as a source of income is ultimately the key mechanism in social exclusion, how and why individuals and groups are placed under structural difficulty/impossibility

---

[7]   Rodgers et al. (1995).

[8]   Room (1992: 14).

[9]   By "autonomy," in this context, I mean the average margin of individual autonomy/social heteronomy as constructed by society. It is obvious that a worker, or even a self-employed person, is not autonomous *vis à vis* his/her employer, or network of clients. I refer to social conditions that represent the social norm, in contrast with people's inability to organize their own lives even under the constraints of social structure, because of their lack of access to resources that social structure mandates as necessary to construct their limited autonomy. This discussion of socially constrained autonomy is what underlies the conceptualization of inclusion/exclusion as the differential expression of people's social rights.

to provide for themselves follows a wide array of avenues of destitution. It is not only a matter of lacking skills or not being able to find a job. It may be that illness strikes in a society without health coverage for a substantial proportion of its members (for example, the United States). Or else drug addiction or alcoholism destroys humanity in a person. Or the culture of prisons and the stigma of being an ex-convict closes ways out of crime on return to freedom. Or the injuries of mental illness, or of a nervous breakdown, placing a person between the alternatives of psychiatric repression and irresponsible de-institutionalization, paralyze the soul and cancel the will. Or, more simply, functional illiteracy, illegal status, inability to pay the rent, thus inducing homelessness, or sheer bad luck with a boss or a cop, trigger a chain of events that sends a person (and his/her family, very often) drifting toward the outer regions of society, inhabited by the wreckage of failed humanity.

Moreover, the process of social exclusion in the network society concerns both people and territories. So that, under certain conditions, entire countries, regions, cities, and neighborhoods become excluded, embracing in this exclusion most, or all, of their populations. This is different from the traditional process of spatial segregation, as I shall try to show when examining the new features of American inner-city ghettos. Under the new, dominant logic of the space of flows (volume I, chapter 6), areas that are non-valuable from the perspective of informational capitalism, and that do not have significant political interest for the powers that be, are bypassed by flows of wealth and information, and ultimately deprived of the basic technological infrastructure that allows us to communicate, innovate, produce, consume, and even live, in today's world. This process induces an extremely uneven geography of social/territorial exclusion and inclusion, which disables large segments of people while linking up trans-territorially, through information technology, whatever and whoever may offer value in the global networks accumulating wealth, information, and power.

The process of social exclusion, and the insufficiency of remedial policies of social integration, lead to a fourth, key process characterizing some specific forms of relations of production in informational capitalism: I call it *perverse integration*. It refers to the labor process in the criminal economy. By criminal economy, I mean income-generating activities that are normatively declared to be crime, and accordingly prosecuted, in a given institutional context. There is no value judgment in the labeling, not because I condone drug trafficking, but because I do not condone either a number of institutionally respectable activities that inflict tremendous damage on people's lives. Yet, what a given society considers to be criminal is so, and it has substantial consequences for whoever engages in such activities. As I will argue in chapter 3, informational capitalism is characterized by the formation of a global criminal economy, and by its growing interdependence with the formal economy and political institutions. Segments of the socially excluded population, along with individuals who choose far more profitable, if risky, ways to make a living, constitute an increasingly populated underworld which is becoming an essential feature of social dynamics in most of the planet.

There are systemic relationships between informational capitalism, capitalist restructuring, trends in the relationships of production, and new trends in the relationships of distribution. Or, in a nutshell, between the dynamics of the network society, inequality, and social exclusion. I shall try to advance some hypotheses on the nature and shape of these relationships. But rather than proposing a formal, theoretical matrix, I shall survey the interaction between these processes, and their social outcomes, by focusing on three empirical matters, from which I will try to distill some analytical conclusions. I shall focus on the process of social exclusion of almost an entire continent, Sub-Saharan Africa, and of most of its 500 million people. I shall report on the spread and deepening of urban poverty in the country that boasts the leading economy, and the most advanced technology in the world, the United States. And I shall consider a different view of the process of global development and underdevelopment: the view of children. Beforehand, let me briefly overview the state of the world concerning inequality, poverty, and social exclusion.

Toward a Polarized World? A Global Overview

"Divergence in output per person across countries is perhaps *the* dominant feature of modern economic history. The ratio of per capita income in the richest versus the poorest country [between 1870 and 1989] has increased by a factor of 6 and the standard deviation of GDP per capita has increased between 60 and 100 percent" writes Pritchett, summarizing the findings of his econometric study for the World Bank.[10] In much of the world, this geographical disparity in the creation/appropriation of wealth has increased in the past two decades, while the differential between OECD countries and the rest of the

[10]   Pritchett (1995: 2–3).

Table 2.1 GDP per capita in a 55-country sample

Country	GDP/capita (in 1990 US$)			Index of GDP/capita (USA = 100)			Change in GDP/capita index (Numerical change)		Change in GDP/capita index (% change)	
	1950	1973	1992	1950	1973	1992	1950–73	1973–92	1950–73	1973–92
USA	9,573	16,607	21,558	100	100	100	0	0	0	0
Japan	1,873	11,017	19,425	20	66	90	47	24	239	36
16 Western European countries										
Austria	3,731	11,308	17,160	39	68	80	29	12	75	17
Belgium	5,346	11,905	17,165	56	72	80	16	8	28	11
Denmark	6,683	13,416	18,293	70	81	85	11	4	16	5
Finland	4,131	10,768	14,646	43	65	68	22	3	50	5
France	5,221	12,940	17,959	55	78	83	23	5	43	7
Germany	4,281	13,152	19,351	45	79	90	34	11	77	13
Greece	1,951	7,779	10,314	20	47	48	26	1	130	2
Ireland	3,518	7,023	11,711	37	42	54	6	12	15	28
Italy	3,425	10,409	16,229	36	63	75	27	13	75	20
Netherlands	5,850	12,763	16,898	61	77	78	16	2	26	2
Norway	4,969	10,229	17,543	52	62	81	10	20	19	32
Portugal	2,132	7,568	11,130	22	46	52	23	6	105	13
Spain	2,397	8,739	12,498	25	53	58	28	5	110	10
Sweden	6,738	13,494	16,927	70	81	79	11	–3	15	–3
Switzerland	8,939	17,953	21,036	93	108	98	15	–11	16	–10
UK	6,847	11,992	15,738	72	72	73	1	1	1	1
Average	4,760	11,340	15,912	50	68	74	19	6	37	8

3 Western offshoots										
Australia	7,218	12,485	16,237	75	75	75	0	0	0	0
Canada	7,047	13,644	18,159	74	82	84	9	2	12	3
New Zealand	8,495	12,575	13,947	89	76	65	-13	-11	-15	-15
Average	7,587	12,901	16,114	79	78	75	-2	-3	-2	-4
7 East European countries										
Bulgaria	1,651	5,284	4,054	17	32	19	15	-13	84	-41
Czechoslovakia	3,501	7,036	6,845	37	42	32	6	-11	16	-25
Hungary	2,480	5,596	5,638	26	34	26	8	-8	30	-22
Poland	2,447	5,334	4,726	26	32	22	7	-10	26	-32
Romania	1,182	3,477	2,565	12	21	12	9	-9	70	-43
USSR	2,834	6,058	4,671	30	36	22	7	-15	23	-41
Yugoslavia	1,546	4,237	3,887	16	26	18	9	-7	58	-29
Average	2,234	5,289	4,627	23	32	21	9	-10	36	-33
7 Latin American countries										
Argentina	4,987	7,970	7,616	52	48	35	-4	-13	-8	-26
Brazil	1,673	3,913	4,637	17	24	22	6	-2	35	-9
Chile	3,827	5,028	7,238	40	30	34	-10	3	-24	11
Colombia	2,089	3,539	5,025	22	21	23	-1	2	-2	9
Mexico	2,085	4,189	5,112	22	25	24	3	-2	16	-6
Peru	2,263	3,953	2,854	24	24	13	0	-11	1	-44
Venezuela	7,424	10,717	9,163	78	65	43	-13	-22	-17	-34
Average	3,478	5,616	5,949	36	34	28	-3	-6	-7	-18

Table 2.1 (contd)

Country	GDP/capita (in 1990 US$)			Index of GDP/capita (USA = 100)			Change in GDP/capita index (Numerical change)		Change in GDP/capita index (% change)	
	1950	1973	1992	1950	1973	1992	1950–73	1973–92	1950–73	1973–92
10 Asian countries										
Bangladesh	551	478	720	6	3	3	−3	0	−50	16
Burma	393	589	748	4	4	3	−1	0	−14	−2
China	614	1,186	3,098	6	7	14	1	7	11	101
India	597	853	1,348	6	5	6	−1	1	−18	22
Indonesia	874	1,538	2,749	9	9	13	0	3	1	38
Pakistan	650	981	1,642	7	6	8	−1	2	−13	29
Philippines	1,293	1,956	2,213	14	12	10	−2	−2	−13	−13
South Korea	876	2,840	10,010	9	17	46	8	29	87	172
Taiwan	922	3,669	11,590	10	22	54	12	32	129	143
Thailand	848	1,750	4,694	9	11	22	2	11	19	107
Average	762	1,584	3,881	8	10	18	2	8	20	89
10 African countries										
Côte d' Ivoire	859	1,727	1,134	9	10	5	1	−5	16	−49
Egypt	517	947	1,927	5	6	9	0	3	6	57
Ethiopia	277	412	300	3	2	1	0	−1	−14	−44
Ghana	1,193	1,260	1,007	12	8	5	−5	−3	−39	−38
Kenya	609	947	1,055	6	6	5	−1	−1	−10	−14
Morocco	1,611	1,651	2,327	17	10	11	−7	1	−41	9
Nigeria	547	1,120	1,152	6	7	5	1	−1	18	−21
South Africa	2,251	3,844	3,451	24	23	16	0	−7	−2	−31
Tanzania	427	655	601	4	4	3	−1	−1	−12	−29
Zaïre	636	757	353	7	5	2	−2	−3	−31	−64
Average	893	1,332	1,331	9	8	6	−1	−2	−14	−23

Source: Maddison (1995), calculated from table 1–3

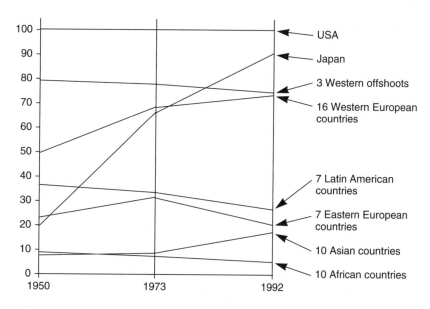

Figure 2.1   GDP per capita index in a 55-country sample (USA = 100)
Source: elaborated from table 2.1

planet, representing the overwhelming proportion of the population, is still abysmal. Thus, using the historical economic statistics elaborated by Maddison,[11] Benner and I have elaborated table 2.1, represented graphically in figure 2.1, displaying the evolution of GDP per capita index for a group of selected countries, ranked by the relative value of their index *vis à vis* the United States, between 1950, 1973, and 1992. Japan has succeeded in almost catching up in the past four decades, while Western Europe has improved its relative position, but still trails the US by a considerable margin. During the 1973–92 period, the sample of Latin American, African, and Eastern European countries studied by Maddison have fallen behind even further. As for ten Asian countries, including the economic miracles of South Korea, China, and Taiwan, they have substantially improved their relative position, but in absolute levels, in 1992, they were still poorer than any other region of the world except Africa, representing, as a whole, only 18 percent of the US level of wealth, although this is mainly due to China's population.

However, if the distribution of wealth between countries continues to diverge, overall the average living conditions of world's population,

[11]   Maddison (1995).

as measured by the United Nations Human Development Index, have improved steadily over the past three decades. This is due, primarily, to better educational opportunities, and improved health standards, which translate into a dramatic increase in life expectancy, which in developing countries went up from 46 years in the 1960s to 62 years in 1993, particularly for women.[12]

The evolution of income inequality presents a different profile if we take a global view, or if we look at its evolution within specific countries in a comparative perspective. In a global approach, there has been, over the past three decades, increasing inequality and polarization in the distribution of wealth. According to UNDP's 1996 Human Development Report, in 1993 only US$ 5 trillion of the US$ 23 trillion global GDP were from the developing countries even if they accounted for nearly 80 percent of total population. The poorest 20 percent of the world's people have seen their share of global income decline from 2.3 percent to 1.4 percent in the past 30 years. Meanwhile, the share of the richest 20 percent has risen from 70 percent to 85 percent. This doubled the ratio of the share of the richest over the poorest – from 30 : 1 to 61 : 1. The assets of the world's 358 billionaires (in US dollars) exceed the combined annual incomes of countries with 45 percent of the world's population. The gap in per capita income between the industrial and the developing worlds tripled, from $5,700 in 1960 to $15,000 in 1993.[13] "Between 1960 and 1991, all but the richest quintile [of the world's people] saw their income share fall, so that by 1991 more than 85 percent of the world's population received only 15 percent of its income – yet another indication of an even more polarized world."[14]

On the other hand, there is considerable disparity in the evolution of *intra-country inequality* in different areas of the world. In the past two decades, income inequality has increased in the United States,[15] United Kingdom,[16] Brazil, Argentina, Venezuela, Bolivia, Peru, Thailand, and Russia;[17] and, in the 1980s, in Japan,[18] Canada, Sweden, Australia, Germany,[19] and in Mexico,[20] just to cite a few relevant countries. But income inequality *decreased* in the 1960–90 period in India, Malaysia, Hong Kong, Singapore, Taiwan and South

---

[12] UNDP (1996: 18–19).
[13] UNDP (1996: 2–3).
[14] UNDP (1996: 13).
[15] Fischer et al. (1996).
[16] Townsend (1993).
[17] UNDP (1996).
[18] Bauer and Mason (1992).

Korea.[21] Also, according to data elaborated by Deininger and Squire, if we compare the level of income inequality, measured by Gini co-efficient, by major regions of the world, between the 1990s and the 1970s, in 1990 it was much higher in Eastern Europe, somewhat higher in Latin America, but lower in all other regions, when analyzed at a highly aggregate level.[22] This disparity in the evolution of inequality between the world's regions is probably associated with two main factors. For developing countries, this is the rate of rural–urban migration, since the main factor in the disparity of income distribution is the abysmal difference in income levels between rural areas and urban agglomerations, even accounting for widespread urban poverty.[23] For industrialized countries, the key issue is the differential development in welfare states, and in the level of wages and social benefits, directly related to the bargaining power of labor unions.[24]

But if the evolution of intra-country inequality varies, *what appears to be a global phenomenon is the growth of poverty, and particularly of extreme poverty.* Indeed, the acceleration of uneven development, and the simultaneous inclusion and exclusion of people in the growth process, which I consider to be a feature of informational capitalism, translates into polarization, and the spread of misery among a growing number of people. Thus, according to UNDP:

> Since 1980, there has been a dramatic surge in economic growth in some 15 countries, bringing rapidly rising incomes to many of their 1.5 billion people, more than a quarter of the world's population. Over much of this period, however, economic decline or stagnation has affected 100 countries, reducing the incomes of 1.6 billion people, again more than a quarter of the world's population. In 70 of these countries average incomes are less than they were in 1980 – and in 43 countries less than they were in 1970. [Furthermore], during 1970–85 global GNP increased by 40 percent, yet the number of poor increased by 17 percent. While 200 million people saw their per capita incomes fall during 1965–80, more than one billion people did in 1980–93.[25]

[19]   Green et al. (1992).
[20]   Skezely (1995).
[21]   UNDP (1996).
[22]   Deininger and Squire (1996: 584).
[23]   Jazairy et al. (1992).
[24]   Townsend (1993); Navarro (1997).
[25]   UNDP (1996: 1–2)

In the mid-1990s, taking as the extreme poverty line a consumption equivalent to one US dollar a day, 1.3 billion people, accounting for 33 percent of the developing world's population were in misery. Of these poor people, 550 million lived in South Asia, 215 million in Sub-Saharan Africa, and 150 million in Latin America .[26] In a similar estimate, using the one dollar a day dividing line for extreme poverty, ILO estimated that the percentage of the population below this line increased from 53.5 percent in 1985 to 54.4 percent in 1990 in Sub-Saharan Africa; from 23 percent to 27.8 percent in Latin America; and decreased from 61.1 percent to 59 percent in South Asia, and from 15.7 percent to 14.7 percent in East/South East Asia (without China).[27] The largest concentration of poverty was, by far, in the rural areas: in 1990, the proportion of poor among the rural population was 66 percent in Brazil, 72 percent in Peru, 43 percent in Mexico, 49 percent in India, and 54 percent in the Philippines.[28]

Thus, overall, *the ascent of informational, global capitalism is indeed characterized by simultaneous economic development and underdevelopment, social inclusion and social exclusion,* in a process very roughly reflected in comparative statistics. There is polarization in the distribution of wealth at the global level, differential evolution of intra-country income inequality, and substantial growth of poverty and misery in the world at large, and in most countries, both developed and developing. However, the patterns of social exclusion, and the factors accounting for them, require a qualitative analysis of the processes by which they are induced.

The De-humanization of Africa[29]

The rise of informational/global capitalism in the last quarter of the twentieth century has coincided with the collapse of Africa's

---

[26]   UNDP (1996: 27).

[27]   ILO (1995: table 13).

[28]   ILO (1994).

[29]   The analysis presented here is exclusively concerned with Sub-Saharan Africa, excepting South Africa and Botswana, as they are both special cases. Throughout this chapter, when writing on Africa, I shall be referring to this socio-economic unit, as defined by international institutions, minus Botswana and South Africa. I will deal with South Africa in the concluding pages of this section by analyzing its potential role in the overall development of the region. I will not deal with Botswana because its heavy specialization in diamond mining and exports (second largest producer in the world after Russia), and its interpenetration with South Africa's economy, invalidate comparison with the conditions in the rest of the region. However, I would like to point out that, after growing at a stunning

economies, the disintegration of many of its states, and the break-down of most of its societies. As a result, famines, epidemics, violence, civil wars, massacres, mass exodus, and social and political chaos are, in this end of millennium, salient features of the land that nurtured the birth of Lucy, perhaps the shared grandmother of humankind. I argue that structural, social causality underlies this historical coincidence. And I shall try, in the following pages, to show the complex interplay between economy, technology, society, and politics in the making of a process that denies humanity to African people, as well as to all of us in our inner selves.

Marginalization and selective integration of Sub-Saharan Africa in the informational/global economy

In the past two decades, while a dynamic, global economy has been constituted in much of the world, Sub-Saharan Africa has experienced a substantial deterioration in its relative position in trade, investment, production, and consumption *vis à vis* all other areas of the world, while its per capita GDP declined during the period 1980–95 (table 2.2). In the early 1990s, the combined export earnings of its 45 countries, with about 500 million people, amounted to just US$ 36 billion in current dollars, down from 50 billion in 1980. This figure represents less than half of Hong Kong's exports in the same period. In a historical perspective, from 1870 to 1970, during Africa's incorporation into the capitalist economy, under colonial domination, African exports grew rapidly, and their share of developing countries' exports increased. In 1950, Africa accounted for over 3 percent of world exports; in 1990, for about 1.1 percent.[30] In 1980, Africa was the destination of 3.1 percent of world exports; in 1995, of just 1.5 percent. World imports from Africa declined from 3.7 percent in 1980 to 1.4 percent in 1995.[31]

Furthermore, African exports have remained confined to primary commodities (92 percent of all exports), and particularly to agricultural exports (about 76 percent of export earnings in 1989–90). There is also an increased concentration of these agricultural exports in a few crops, such as coffee and cocoa, which accounted for 40 percent of export earnings in 1989–90. The ratio of manufactured goods exports to total exports fell from 7.8 percent in 1965 to 5.9 percent in

---

annual average of 13 percent in real GDP since its independence (1966), Botswana is also facing serious problems of unemployment and poverty in the 1990s. Interested readers should see Hope (1996).

[30] Svedberg (1993).

[31] UN (1996: 318–19).

Table 2.2 Per capita GDP of developing economies, 1980–96

	Annual rate of growth of per capita GDP (%)				Per capita GDP (1988 dollars)				
	1981–90	1991–95	1995[a]	1996[b]	1980	1990	1995[a]	1996[b]
Developing economies	1.0	2.9	3.3	4.0	770	858	988	1,028
Latin America	-0.9	0.8	-0.9	0.75	2,148	2,008	2,092	2,106
Africa	-0.9	-1.3	0.0	1.5	721	700	657	667
West Asia	-5.3	-0.6	0.4	0.25	5,736	3,423	3,328	3,335
South-East Asia	3.9	4.0	5.0	6.0	460	674	817	865
China	7.5	10.2	9.1	8.0	202	411	664	716
Least developed countries	-0.5	-0.9	0.4	1.75	261	249	238	243

[a] Preliminary estimate.
[b] Forecast.
Source: UN/DESIPA

Table 2.3   Value of exports from world, less-developed countries, and Sub-Saharan Africa, 1950–90

Region	1950	1960	1970	1980	1990
	Billions of current dollars				
World	60.7	129.1	315.1	2,002.0	3,415.3
LDCs	18.9	28.3	57.9	573.3	738.0
SSA	2.0	3.8	8.0	49.4	36.8
	Share of LDCs (%)				
World exports	31.1	21.9	18.4	28.6	21.6
	Share of SSA (%)				
World exports	3.3	2.9	2.5	2.5	1.1
LDC exports	10.6	13.4	13.8	8.6	5.0

LDCs, less-developed countries; SSA, Sub-Saharan Africa.
Source: UNCTAD 1979, 1989 and 1991, table 1.1; elaborated by Simon et al. (1995)

1985, while it rose from 3 percent to 8.2 percent in West Asia, from 28.3 percent to 58.5 percent in South/South-East Asia, and from 5.2 percent to 18.6 percent in Latin America.[32] Since the prices of primary commodities have been depressed since the mid-1970s, the deterioration in the terms of trade, as a result of the structure of exports, makes it extremely difficult for Africa to grow on the basis of an outward orientation of its economies. Indeed, according to Simon et al., adjustment policies, inspired by the IMF/World Bank to improve export performance, have actually increased dependence on primary commodities such as cotton and copper, thus undermining the efforts of some countries to diversify their economies to make them less vulnerable to the long-term deterioration of prices of primary commodities *vis à vis* higher value added goods and services.[33] Overall, the terms of trade deteriorated substantially for most African countries between 1985 and 1994 (see tables 2.3–2.6).

On the other hand, weak domestic markets have been unable to sustain import-substitution industrialization, and even agricultural production for domestic markets. Between 1965 and 1989, the ratio of total manufacturing value added to GDP did not rise above 11 percent, compared with an increase from 20 to 30 percent for all developing countries.[34] Agricultural production has lagged behind the 3 percent annual population growth rate. Thus, since the early 1980s, food imports have risen by about 10 percent per annum.[35]

---

[32]   Riddell (1993: 222–3).
[33]   Simon et al. (1995).
[34]   Riddell (1993: 22–3).
[35]   Simon et al. (1995: 22).

Table 2.4 Structure of exports (percentage share), 1990

Region	Fuels, minerals and metals	Other primary commodities	Machinery and transport equipment	Other manufacturing	Textiles and clothing
Sub-Saharan Africa	63	29	1	7	1
East Asia and Pacific	13	18	22	47	19
South Asia	6	24	5	65	33
Europe	9	16	27	47	16
Middle East and North Africa	75	12	1	15	4
Latin America and Caribbean	38	29	11	21	3
Low and middle-income countries	31	20	15	35	12
Low-income countries	27	20	9	45	21

Percentages are of respective regions' exports; data weighted by size of flows; all SSA classified as low income except: (a) lower-middle-income: Zimbabwe, Senegal, Côte d'Ivoire, Cameroon, Congo, Botswana, Angola, Namibia; (b) upper-middle-income: South Africa, Gabon; low-income includes India and China.
Source: World Bank (1992) *World Development Report 1992;* elaborated by Simon et al. (1995)

Table 2.5 Percentage share of Sub-Saharan Africa in world exports of major product categories

Product category	Share of product category in world exports		Sub-Saharan Africa's share of world exports		Share of product category in SSA exports	
	1970	1988	1970	1988	1970	1988
Crude oil (SITC 331)	5.3	6.0	6.5	6.9	14.0	34.5
Non-oil products (SITC 0–9 less 331)	94.7	94.0	2.2	0.8	86.0	65.5
Primary commodities[a] (non oil)	25.9	16.3	7.0	3.7	73.8	50.4
Agricultural commodities	7.0	2.8	6.3	3.6	12.3	8.2
Minerals and ores	7.5	3.8	9.7	4.2	30.0	14.6
18 IPC commodities[b]	9.1	4.3	16.1	10.0	59.1	35.6

[a] Standard International Trade Classification (SITC) 0, 1, 2–(233, 244, 266, 267), 4, 68 and item 522.56.
[b] What UNCTAD labels the Integrated Programme Commodities (IPC) (which supposedly are of greatest importance to developing countries): bananas, cocoa, coffee, cotton, and cotton yarn, hard fibers and products, jute and jute manufactures, bovine meat, rubber, sugar, tea, tropical timber, vegetable oils and oilseeds, bauxite, copper, iron ore, manganese, phosphates and tin.
SSA, Sub-Saharan Africa.
Sources: Derived on the basis of data from UNCTAD 1984, 1986, 1988, and 1989: various tables; UNCTAD 1980: tables 1.1 and 1.2; elaborated by Simon et al. (1995)

Table 2.7 shows that Africa's economy has consistently grown at a lower rate than any other area in the world in agriculture, industry, and services since 1973. Particularly noticeable is the collapse of industry in the 1980s, after a hefty growth in the 1960s, and a moderate increase in the 1970s. It appears that Africa's industrialization went into crisis at exactly the time when technological renewal and export-oriented industrialization characterized most of the world, including other developing countries.

Under these conditions, the survival of most African economies has come to depend on international aid and foreign borrowing. Aid, mainly from governments, but also from humanitarian donors, has become an essential feature of Africa's political economy. In 1990,

Table 2.6   Terms of trade of selected African countries, 1985–94

Country	Terms of trade (1987=100)	
	1985	1994
Burkina Faso	103	103
Burundi	133	52
Cameroon	113	79
Chad	99	103
Congo	150	93
Côte d'Ivoire	109	81
Ethiopia	119	74
Gambia (The)	137	111
Kenya	124	80
Madagascar	124	82
Malawi	99	87
Mali	100	103
Mozambique	113	124
Niger	91	101
Nigeria	167	86
Rwanda	136	75
Senegal	107	107
Sierra Leone	109	89
Tanzania	126	83
Togo	139	90
Uganda	149	58
Zimbabwe	100	84

Source: IBRD (1996), table 3, p.192

Africa received 30 percent of all aid funding in the world. In 1994, international aid represented 12.4 percent of GNP in Africa, compared with 1.1 percent for low and middle-income countries as a whole.[36] In a number of countries, it actually accounts for a substantial share of GNP (for example, 65.7 percent in Mozambique, 45.9 percent in Somalia).[37]

In the 1980s there was a massive influx of foreign loans (most of it from governments and international institutions, or endorsed by such institutions) to rescue the collapsing African economies. As a result, Africa has become the most indebted area in the world. As a percentage of GNP, total external debt has risen from 30.6 percent in 1980 to 78.7 percent in 1994;[38] and as a percentage of the value of

[36]   IBRD (1996).
[37]   Simon et al. (1995).
[38]   IBRD (1996).

Table 2.7 Sectoral growth rates (average annual percentage change of value added), 1965–89

Country group	Agriculture			Industry			Services		
	1965–73	1973–80	1980–89	1965–73	1973–80	1980–89	1965–73	1973–80	1980–89
Low-income economies	2.9	1.8	4.3	10.7	7.0	8.7	6.3	5.3	6.1
Middle-income economies	3.2	3.0	2.7	8.0	4.0	3.2	7.6	6.3	3.1
Severely indebted middle-income economies	3.1	3.6	2.7	6.8	5.4	1.0	7.2	5.4	1.7
Sub-Saharan Africa	2.2	–0.3	1.8	13.9	4.2	–0.2	4.1	3.1	1.5
East Asia	3.2	2.5	5.3	12.7	9.2	10.3	10.5	7.3	7.9
South Asia	3.1	2.2	2.7	3.9	5.6	7.2	4.0	5.3	6.1
Latin America and the Caribbean	3.0	3.7	2.5	6.8	5.1	1.1	7.3	5.4	1.7

Figures in italics in the 1980–89 columns are not for the full decade.
Source: World Bank (1990) *World Development Report 1990*, p.162; eleborated by Simon et al. (1995)

exports, it went up from 97 percent in 1980 to 324 percent in 1990.[39]

Since it is generally acknowledged that such a debt cannot be repaid, government creditors, and international institutions, have used this financial dependence to impose adjustment policies on African countries, exchanging their subservience against partial condonement of the debt, or renegotiation of payments servicing the debt. I shall discuss later the actual impact of these adjustment policies in the specific context of Africa's political economy.

Foreign direct investment is bypassing Africa at a time when it is growing substantially all over the world. According to Collier,

> while direct private investment into developing countries has increased enormously over the past decade, to around US$ 200 billion per annum, the share going to Africa has shrunk to negligible proportions: current estimates are that less than 1 percent of this flow is going to Sub-Saharan Africa. Even this level is falling: the absolute amount in 1992 was less in real terms than the inflow in 1985, the nadir of the economic crisis for much of the continent.[40]

Simon et al. also report that foreign direct investment in Africa declined consistently in both absolute and relative terms in the 1980s and early 1990s, representing in 1992 just about 6 percent of total foreign direct investment (FDI) in developing countries. While Africa represented 4 percent of UK worldwide net industrial FDI in the mid-1970s, its share went down to 0.5 percent in 1986.[41]

The reasons for this marginalization of Africa in the global economy are the subject of heated debate among experts, as well as among political leaders. Paul Collier has suggested a multi-causal interpretation, supported by the results of his survey of 150 foreign business executives in Eastern Africa.[42] It can be summarized under three headings: an unreliable institutional environment; lack of production and communications infrastructure, as well as of human capital; and erroneous economic policies which penalize exports and investment for the sake of local businesses favored by their association with state bureaucracy. Altogether, investing in Africa is a highly risky venture, which discourages even the most daring capitalists. Being unable to compete in the new global economy, most African countries represent small domestic markets that do not provide the basis for endogenous capital accumulation.

[39]   Simon et al. (1995: 25).
[40]   Collier (1995: 542).
[41]   Simon et al. (1995: 28).
[42]   Collier (1995).

However, not all of Africa is marginalized from the global networks. Valuable resources, such as oil, gold, diamonds, and metals, continue to be exported, inducing substantial economic growth in Botswana, and providing considerable earnings to other countries, such as Nigeria. The problem is the use of earnings from these resources, as well as of international aid funds received by governments.[43] The small, but affluent, bureaucratic class in many countries displays a high level of consumption of expensive imported goods, including Western food products and international fashion wear.[44] Capital flows from African countries to personal accounts and profitable international investment throughout the world, for the exclusive benefit of a few wealthy individuals, provide evidence of substantial private accumulation that is not reinvested in the country where the wealth is generated.[45] So, there is a selective integration of small segments of African capital, affluent markets, and profitable exports into the global networks of capital, goods, and services, while most of the economy, and the overwhelming majority of the population, are left to their own fate, between bare subsistence and violent pillage.[46]

Furthermore, while African businesses can hardly compete in the global economy, the existing linkages to this economy have deeply penetrated Africa's traditional sectors. Thus, subsistence agriculture, and food production for local markets, have plunged into a crisis, in most countries, as a result of the conversion to export-oriented agriculture, and specialized cash crops, in a desperate attempt to sell into international markets.[47] Thus, what is marginal globally, is still central in Africa, and actually contributes to disorganizing traditional economic forms.[48] In this sense, Africa is not external to the global economy. Instead, it is disarticulated by its fragmented incorporation to the global economy through linkages such as a limited amount of commodity exports, speculative appropriation of valuable resources, financial transfers abroad, and parasitic consumption of imported goods.

The consequence of this process of disinvestment throughout Africa, at the precise historical moment when the information technology revolution has transformed the infrastructure of production, management, and communications elsewhere, has been the de-linking of African firms and labor from the workings of the new

[43] Yansane (1996).
[44] Ekholm-Friedman (1993).
[45] Jackson and Rosberg (1994); Collier (1995).
[46] Blomstrom and Lundhal (1993); Simon et al. (1995).
[47] Jamal (1995).
[48] Callaghy and Ravenhill (1993).

economy characterizing most of the world, while linking up African elites to the global networks of wealth, power, information, and communication.

Africa's technological apartheid at the dawn of the Information Age

Information technology, and the ability to use it and adapt it, is the critical factor in generating and accessing wealth, power, and knowledge in our time (see volume I, chapters 2 and 3). Africa is, for the time being, excluded from the information technology revolution, if we except a few nodes of finance and international management directly connected to global networks while bypassing African economies and societies.

Not only is Africa, by far, the least computerized region of the world, but it does not have the minimum infrastructure required to make use of computers, thus making nonsense of many of the efforts to provide electronic equipment to countries and organizations.[49] Indeed, before moving into electronics, Africa first needs a reliable electricity supply: between 1971 and 1993 the commercial use of energy in Africa rose from only 251 kilowatts per capita to 288 kilowatts per capita, while in developing countries as a whole, consumption more than doubled, from 255 kW to 536 kW per capita. This compares with a consumption of 4,589 kW per capita in 1991 for industrial countries.[50] Furthermore, the critical aspect of computer use in the Information Age is its networking capability, which relies on telecommunications infrastructure and network connectivity. Africa's telecommunications are meagre, compared with current world standards. There are more telephone lines in Manhattan or in Tokyo than in the whole of Sub-Saharan Africa. In 1991, there was one telephone line per 100 people in Africa, compared to 2.3 for all developing countries, and 37.2 for industrial countries. In 1994, Africa accounted for only about 2 percent of world telephone lines.[51] Some of the obstacles to developing telecommunications come from government bureaucracies, and stem from their policy of keeping a monopoly for their national companies, thus slowing down their modernization. Permission is required from national telephone operators to install any telephone device. Import of telecommunications equipment is expensive, and uncertain, as it is often "lost" in

---

[49]   Odedra et al. (1993); Jensen (1995); Heeks (1996).
[50]   UNDP (1996: 183).
[51]   Hall (1995); Jensen (1995); UNDP (1996:167).

customs.[52] The Organization of African Unity established the Pan African Telecommunications Union to coordinate telecommunications policy in Africa, but the decision to locate the office in Zaïre, at Mobutu's insistence, limited its effectiveness, since Zaïre has one of the poorest telecommunications networks. Connection to the Internet is very limited because of insufficient international bandwidth, and lack of connectivity between African countries. Half of the African countries had no connection to the Internet in 1995, and Africa remains, by and large, the switched-off region of the world (see figure 2.2). However, what is significant is that, in 1996, 22 African capitals had full Internet connectivity, but in only one country (Senegal) was Internet access possible outside the capital city.[53] Thus, while some directional centers are being connected to the Internet, their countries remain switched off.

If the physical infrastructure is lagging behind, the human skills to operate information technology remain totally inadequate. An acute observer of Africa's information technology, Mayuri Odedra, writes that

> Sub-Saharan Africa lacks computer skills in all areas, including systems analysis, programming, maintenance and consulting, and at all operational levels, from basic use to management. Most countries lack the educational and training facilities needed to help people acquire the proper skills. The few training centers that do exist have not been able to keep up with demand. Only a handful of countries, such as Nigeria, Malawi, and Zimbabwe have universities that offer computer science degrees. The programs available in the other countries are mainly diplomas and certificates. As a result of unskilled and untrained personnel, user organizations are forced to hire expatriate staff, who in turn lack knowledge about local organizations and thus design poor systems.[54]

Most computing work is aimed at routine data processing, with little computed-aided decision-making. The public sector, the overwhelming force in African economies, proceeds with "blind computerization," induced by the ideology of modernization and/or by financial enticements by foreign computer companies, without actually using installed computer power to process relevant information. Regulations often impose centralized acquisition of computer equipment by the public sector, and tax private firms to discourage

[52] Adam (1996).
[53] Jensen (1995).
[54] Odedra et al. (1993: 1–2).

Figure 2.2 International connectivity
Source: copyright © 1995 Larry Landweber and the Internet Society

independent imports. The limited computerization of Africa has become another source of money-making for bureaucrats, without linkage to the needs of the economy or of public service.[55] In the 1980s, half of the computers introduced in Africa were aid-donated, most of them technologically obsolete, so that experts consider that Africa has become the dumping ground for a mass of equipment made obsolete by a fast-moving technological revolution. As for the private computer market, it is dominated by multinationals which generally ensure that they carry out the maintenance. Most of the systems are bought off the shelf, leading to some local knowledge of how to operate, but not of how to program or repair, the systems. The few indigenous software houses are only capable of undertaking small programming jobs.[56]

Technological dependency and technological underdevelopment, in a period of accelerated technological change in the rest of the world, make it literally impossible for Africa to compete internationally either in manufacturing or in advanced services. Other activities that also rely on efficient information processing, such as the promising tourist industry, come under the control of international tour operators and travel agencies, which take the lion's share of the tourists' share of lions, by controlling market information. Even agricultural and mineral exports, constituting the bulk of Africa's exports, are increasingly dependent on the management of information on international operations, as well as on electronic equipment and chemical/biotechnological inputs for advanced agricultural production. Because of the inability of African countries to produce/use advanced technological equipment and know-how, their balance of trade becomes unsustainable, as the added value of technology-intensive goods and services continues to increase *vis à vis* the value of raw materials and agricultural products, limiting their capacity to import inputs necessary to keep their commodity production systems in operation. It follows a downward spiral of competitiveness, as Africa becomes increasingly marginalized in the informational/global economy by each leap forward in technological change. The disinformation of Africa at the dawn of the Information Age may be the most lasting wound inflicted on this continent by new patterns of dependency, aggravated by the policies of the predatory state.

[55]   Bates (1988: 352).
[56]   Woherem (1994); Heeks (1996).

The predatory state

There seems to be a convergence in the views of a growing number of Africanists on the destructive role of African nation-states on their economies and societies. Frimpong-Ansah, a former governor of Ghana's central bank, considers that capital constraint is not the obstacle to development. What is critical is the institutional capacity to mobilize savings, and this was eroded in Africa from the mid-1970s because of the misuse of capital by the "vampire state," that is, a state entirely patrimonialized by political elites for their own personal profit.[57] From a different perspective, one of the most respected Africanists, Basil Davidson, thinks that "Africa's crisis of society derives from many upsets and conflicts, but the root of the problem is different from these . . . Primarily, this is a crisis of institutions. Which institutions? We have to be concerned here with the nationalism that produced the nation-states of newly independent Africa after the colonial period: with the nationalism that became nation-statism."[58] Fatton argues that the "predatory rule" characterizing most African states results from a process of individualization of ruling classes: "Their members tend to be mercenaries, as their hold on positions of privilege and power is at the mercy of the capricious decisions of an ultimate leader."[59] This seems to apply to bloody dictatorial rules, such as that of Mobutu in Zaïre or of "Emperor" Bokassa in the Central African Republic, as well as to benevolent pseudo-democracies, such as Houphouet-Boigny's regime in the Ivory Coast. As Colin Leys writes: "Few theorists of any of these persuasions [Marxists, dependency theorists] expected the post-colonial states of all ideological stripes to be corrupt, rapacious, insufficient, and unstable, as they have almost all been."[60]

Jean-François Bayart interprets Africa's plight as the result of a long-term historical trajectory dominated by "the politics of the belly" practiced by elites with no other strategy than reaping the riches of their countries, and of their countries' international linkages.[61] He proposes a typology of mechanisms of private appropriation of resources using positions of power in the state:

- Access to resources of "extraversion" (international connections), including diplomatic and military resources, as well as cultural resources, and Western know-how.

[57]   Frimpong-Ansah (1991).
[58]   Davidson (1992: 10).
[59]   Fatton (1992: 20).
[60]   Leys (1994: 41).
[61]   Bayart (1989).

- Jobs in the public sector, which provide a regular salary, a fundamental asset, regardless of its amount.
- Positions of predation, using power to extract goods, cash or labor: "In the countryside at least, most of the administrative and political cadres act this way."[62]
- Prebends obtained without violence or the threat of it, by being receptive to a variety of bribes and donations from various interests, constituting a widespread "state informal economy." Most technical or administrative decisions involving potential beneficiaries carry a price tag for the interested parties. Bayart cites the case of a regional commissar of the rich province of Shaba in Zaïre, in 1974, who received a monthly salary of US$ 2,000, complemented by about US$ 100,000 a month from prebends.[63]
- Links to foreign trade and investment are crucial sources of private accumulation, as custom duties and protectionist regulations offer the opportunity to circumvent them in exchange for a contribution to the chain of bureaucrats in charge of enforcing them.
- International development aid, including food aid, is channeled through private interests, and only reaches the needy, or the targeted development program, if ever, after substantial discount by government agencies, and their personnel, in charge of its distribution and implementation.
- State officials, and political elites at large, use some of this wealth to buy property, and invest in agriculture and transport businesses in their countries, constantly scanning opportunities for profitable, short-term investments, and helping each other to collectively control whatever source of profit appears in the country. However, a substantial amount of this private wealth is deposited in foreign bank accounts, representing a significant proportion of capital accumulated in each country. As Houphouet-Boigny, the (god)father of the Ivory Coast, put it "Who in the world would not deposit part of his goods in Switzerland?"[64] Mobutu's personal fortune in 1984, also deposited in foreign banks and invested abroad, was estimated at US$ 4 billion, roughly equivalent to Zaïre's total foreign debt.[65] By 1993, while Zaïre was in the process of disintegration, Mobutu's fortune outside the country was estimated to have increased to about US$ 10 billion.[66]

[62]   Bayart (1989: 76).
[63]   Bayart (1989: 78).
[64]   Cited by Bayart (1989: 101).
[65]   Sandbrook (1985: 91).
[66]   Kempster (1993).

Lewis, on the basis of his analysis of Nigeria, introduces an interesting distinction between *prebendalism* and *predation*.[67] "Prebendalism" is not essentially different from political patronage and systematic government corruption as practiced in most countries of the world. He argues, convincingly, that it was only in the late 1980s and early 1990s in Nigeria, under the Babangida regime, that the politics of predation became dominant, diffusing a model of "Zaïreanization" of the military-dominated state oligarchy. Although Lewis does not extend his analysis beyond Nigeria, it seems plausible, on the basis of information on other countries,[68] that this transition to predatory rule took place only in a later stage of Africa's crisis, with a different time of onset depending on each country. This is in contrast to Bayart's historical reconstruction that affirms the continuity of Africa's pillage by its own political elites from the pre-colonial period. In contrast to prebendalism, predatory rule is characterized by the concentration of power at the top, and the personalization of networks of delegation of this power. It is enforced by ruthless repression. Economic inducements to government personnel, and generalized corruption and bribery, become the way of life in government. This pattern of behavior leads to the erosion of political institutions as stable systems, being replaced by close-knit circles of personal and ethnic loyalties: the entire state is informalized, while power, and power networks, are personalized. While it is arguable whether predation was already the rule in pre-colonial times, or in the early period of African nationalism after independence (Bayart thinks the fomer, but he is challenged by Davidson, Leys, Lewis, and Fatton, among others), what matters, to understand current processes of social exclusion, is that the predatory model, and not just prebendalism, seems to characterize most African states in the 1990s, with the exception of South Africa, and a few other possible cases.

Three major consequences follow from this exercise of predatory rule, characteristic of most African states. First, whatever resources, from international or domestic sources, arrive into these state-dominated economies, are processed according to a logic of personalized accumulation, largely disconnected from the country's economy. What does not make sense from the point of view of the country's economic development and political stability makes a lot of sense from the point of view of its rulers. Secondly, access to state power is equivalent to accessing wealth, and the sources of future wealth. It

[67]   Lewis (1996).
[68]   Fatton (1992); Nzongola-Ntalaja (1993); Leys (1994); Kaiser (1996); *The Economist* (1996a).

follows a pattern of violent confrontation, and unstable alliances between different political factions competing for the opportunity to practice pillage, ultimately resulting in the instability of state institutions, and in the decisive role played by the military in most African states. Thirdly, political support is built around clientelistic networks which link the power-holders with segments of the population. Because the overwhelming share of wealth existing in the country is in the hands of the political/military elite and state bureaucrats, people must pay allegiance to the chain of patronage to be included in the distribution of jobs, services, and petty favors at all levels of the state, from internationally oriented agencies to local government benevolence. Under such a patronage system, various elites, at different levels of government, ultimately connected to the top of state power, engage in complex calculations and strategies: how to maximize support, and consolidate clienteles, while minimizing the amount of resources necessary to obtain this support. A mixture of criteria, encompassing ethnicity, territoriality, and economics, contribute to form networks of variable geometry that constitute the real-life politics in most of Africa.

While detailed empirical analyses are beyond the scope of this chapter, I shall illustrate the dynamics of African predatory states with a brief reference to the two largest countries, Zaïre (in 1997, Congo) and Nigeria.

Zaïre: the personal appropriation of the state

Zaïre became, at least before 1997, the epitome of predatory politics, as well as a warning of the consequences of social and political disintegration, as well as of human catastrophes (epidemics, pillage, massacres, civil wars), resulting from these politics.[69] The Zaïrean state was organized around the personal dictatorship of Sergeant Mobutu, supported by France, Belgium and the United States in the context of Cold War politics. Norman Kempster, a *Los Angeles Times* staff writer, summarized, in 1993, Mobutu's trajectory as follows:

> Mobutu is a former sergeant in Belgium's colonial army who seized power with US and Western backing in 1965, ending a chaotic rivalry between pro-Communist and anti-Communist factions. For three decades, he put his vast country, the second largest in Sub-Saharan Africa at the disposal of the CIA and other Western agencies, which used it as a staging base for activities

[69] Sandbrook (1985); Bayart (1989); Davidson (1992); Noble (1992); Kempster (1993); Press (1993); Leys (1994); French (1995); Weiss (1995); McKinley (1996).

throughout the continent. In exchange, he enjoyed a free hand
at home, diverting for his use billions of dollars from Zaïre's
mineral wealth while leaving most Zaïreans in poverty.[70]

Mobutu relied on a very simple system of power. He controlled the
only operational unit of the army, the presidential guard, and divided
politics, government, and army positions among different ethnic
groups. He patronized all of them, but also encouraged their violent
confrontation.[71] He concentrated on controlling mining business,
particularly cobalt, industrial diamonds, and copper, using government companies, in association with foreign investors, for his own
benefit. The "Zaïreanization" of foreign companies also put all valuable assets in the country into the hands of the bureaucracy and the
military. He disinvested in social services and infrastructure, focusing
on operating a few profitable ventures, and exporting earnings
abroad. He encouraged the entire army staff, and government agencies, to proceed in the same way. Thus, Bayart reports how the Zaïrean
Air Force engaged in pirate air transportation, then in smuggling, and
ultimately in the selling of spare parts of the aircraft, until all planes
became useless.[72] This made it possible for Mobutu to request additional aircraft equipment from his Western allies. Lack of control
over local and provincial governments led to the practical disintegration of the Zaïrean state, with most localities, including Kinshasa,
becoming out of control of central government. Army mutinies,
followed by indiscriminate pillage, as in September 1991, led to the
exodus of foreign residents, and ultimately to the retrenchment of
Mobutu in his native town of Gbadolite, in Equateur Province, kept
off limits by his private army, although the dictator spent much of his
time in his various mansions in Switzerland, France, Spain, and
Portugal. Provincial governments, left to themselves, followed the
leader's example in many instances, using their power to abuse and
steal from their own subjects, starting with the least powerful ethnic
groups. Ultimately, the rapacity of some provincial governments was
fatal for the whole enterprise, when, in 1996, the government of
Kivu, in Eastern Zaïre, moved to expropriate the lands of the
Banyamulenge, a Tutsi minority that had been settled in this area
for centuries, ordering them to leave the region. The subsequent
rebellion of the Banyamulenge and other ethnic groups, led by a
veteran revolutionary, Laurent Kabila, routed in a few months the
gangs of thugs posing as the Zaïrean army, and exposed the fiction of

---

[70]   Kempster (1993: 7).
[71]   Press (1993).
[72]   Bayart (1989: 235–7).
[73]   McKinley (1996); *The Economist* (1996c); French (1997).

the Zaïrean state leading to the end of Mobutu's regime in 1997.[73] The consequences of this three-decade long pillage of one of the richest countries in Africa by its own ruler and his associates, with the open complicity of Western powers, are dramatic and long lasting, for Zaïre, for Africa, and for the world. For Zaïre: because its entire communications, transportation, and production infrastructure has collapsed, deteriorating considerably below its level at the time of independence, while Zaïre's people have suffered massive mal-nutrition, and have been kept in illiteracy, and misery, losing in the process much of their subsistence agriculture. For Africa: because the disarticulation of one of its largest economies, at the very core of the continent, has blocked effective regional integration. Besides, the "Zaïrean model" acted as a magnetic example for other elites in the continent. It was personally promoted by Mobutu, who, as a privileged partner of the West, played an important role in the Organization of African Unity, and in Africa's political scene. For the world: because Zaïre has become a pre-eminent source of deadly "epidemics of dereliction," including the Ebola virus, whose potential for calamity may well impact upon the twenty-first century's livelihood. Furthermore, the indirect contribution of the West, and particularly of France, to the private appropriation of Zaïre by a military/bureaucratic clique removed much of the credibility for future policies of international cooperation in the minds of some of the best Africans. The probable disintegration of the Zaïrean state in the form inherited from Mobutu will mark the limits of predatory rule, underscoring its historical association with the politics of the Cold War and post-colonial domination patterns. Can we now think that this model has already had its historical time? Can it fade away with the last echoes of the superpowers' confrontation in Africa? Unfortunately, the experience of Nigeria seems to indicate that the predatory state has deeper structural and historical roots, linked both to Africa's colonial past and to its evolving pattern of selective link-ages with the global economy.

Nigeria: oil, ethnicity, and military predation

The fate of Nigeria, accounting for about one-fifth of the total popu-lation of Sub-Saharan Africa, is likely to condition the future of Africa. If so, prospects are bleak. The economy of Nigeria revolves around the state, and state control over oil revenues, which account for 95 percent of Nigerian exports, and 80 percent of government revenues. The politics and structure of the state are organized by and around the military, which have controlled the government for 26 of the 35 years of independence, canceling elections and imposing its will when necessary, as in the 1993 coup led by General Sani

Abacha.[74] The appropriation of oil wealth, exploited in consortium between the Nigerian National Petroleum Corporation and multi-national oil companies, is at the source of ethnic, territorial and factional struggles which have destabilized the Nigerian state since the 1966–70 civil war. Political struggles oppose factions organized around three axes: North (controlling the army) against the South (producing the oil); rivalries between the three major ethnic groups: the Hausa-Fulani (usually in control of armed forces' general staff), the Yoruba, and the Igbo; and opposition between these main ethnic groups and the 374 minority ethnic groups that, together, constitute the majority of the population but are excluded from power. Out of 30 states of Nigeria's federation, only four states in the Niger delta (Rivers, Delta, Edo, and Akwa-Ibom) produce virtually all the oil. They are home to ethnic minority groups, particularly the Ogoni, by and large excluded from the riches of their land. The Ogoni's opposition, and the ensuing ferocious repression by the military regime, were dramatically underscored in 1995 when Sane-Wiwa, and several other Ogoni leaders, were executed by the Abacha regime to put down social unrest in the oil-producing areas, and to suppress environmental denouncements by the Ogoni against the destruction of their land by the methods used in oil exploration and production, thus prompting international outcry.

The Nigerian state, an arbitrary colonial construction, was, at its origin, alien to the large majority of its constituencies. Thus, its leaders used control of resources to build enough support to maintain their power. As Herbst writes:

> Clientelism as it is practiced in Nigeria should not be seen merely as theft by individuals seeking to raid the coffers of the state . . . Rather, the distribution of state offices is legitimated by a set of political norms according to which the appropriation of such offices is not just an act of individual greed or ambition but concurrently the satisfaction of the short-term objectives of a subset of the population.[75]

Who is included in this subset, and how large it is, determine the dynamics of Nigerian politics, and access to resources that are, indirectly or directly, in the hands of the state. These patronage relationships expanded substantially with oil revenues, particularly in the 1970s, and with the "oil boomlet" of 1990–91. To reduce the threat of ethnic opposition from excluded groups, the federal government,

---

[74] *The Economist* (1993); Forrest (1993); Agbese (1996); Herbst (1996); Ikporukpo (1996); Lewis (1996).
[75] Herbst (1996: 157).

under military control, increased the number of states from 12 to 19, then to 30, to enhance cross-ethnic state clientelism, and to multiply the extent of government bureaucracies, and consequently of jobs, sinecures, and channels to government resources and rent-generating positions. Under pressure from international financial institutions and foreign companies and governments, there were, however, some attempts at stabilizing the Nigerian economy, bringing into line its productive sectors with global trade and investment. The most notable effort was in the first half of General Babangida's regime (1985–93), which partially deregulated the economy, dismantled the monopoly of marketing boards for agricultural exports, and restrained monetary supply and government debt for a short period. These efforts were undertaken without curtailing the privileges of the dominant, Northern military elite, at the expense of Southern states and ethnic minorities. When, in 1990, an attempt at a military coup by young officers, claiming support from Southern regions, almost succeeded, the regime, after a bloody repression, decided to stabilize its power by sharing wealth among a broader spectrum of Nigeria's ruling classes. Yet, to share the pie without diminishing its enjoyment, the pie had to be bigger, that is, more wealth had to be extracted from the public revenues. The result was, in the late 1980s and early 1990s, the shift from "prebendalism" to "predatory rule," following Lewis's analysis, and the extension of the realm of income-generating activities, by using the control of the state, to a whole array of illicit deals, including international drug trafficking, money laundering, and smuggling networks.[76] The use of the adjustment program, supported and financed by international institutions, for the private use of Nigeria's power-holders is summarized by Lewis in the following terms:

> In sum, the government managed the adjustment programme through a mixture of domestic political orchestration, compensatory measures, and coercion. For elites, the state provided special access to nascent markets and illegal activities, and manipulated key policies to provide the opportune rents . . . Faced with growing political contention, looming personal insecurity, and a fortuitous appearance of new revenues, the President [Babangida] engaged in increasingly reckless economic management. This involved a massive diversion of public resources, abdication of basic fiscal and monetary controls, and expansion of the illicit economy.[77]

[76] Lewis (1996: 97–9).
[77] Lewis (1996: 91).

With personal insecurity rampaging and economic and legal institutions breaking down, legal foreign investment and trade stalled. The regime tried to find a political issue through electoral mobilization around the competition between various members of the business elite in the 1993 election. Then, Babangida annulled the election, social protest mounted, including a general strike that affected oil transport, and regional factionalism threatened a new round of disintegration of the state. At that point, the army intervened again, establishing a new authoritarian rule, under General Abacha. The new dictator de-linked Nigeria's monetary flows from the international economy by re-evaluating the naira, decreeing negative interest rates, and reinforcing protectionism. This created anew the basis for personal accumulation of those in positions of control, while inducing capital flight, undermining legal exports, and favoring smuggling. The country was left with

> a legacy of weak central government, fractious ethnic competition, and centralised revenues that have sharply politicised economic management . . . Nigeria's political economy increasingly embodied the characteristics of such autocratic regimes as Mobutu Sese Seko's Zaïre, Haiti under Jean-Claude Duvalier, or the Somoza dynasty's Nicaragua. A transition was soon apparent from decentralised clientelist rule, or prebendalism, to purely avaricious dictatorship or predation.[78]

As for the Nigerian people, not despite but because of the oil boom and its political consequences, they were poorer in 1995 than at independence, their per capita income having declined by 22 percent between 1973 (date of increase in world oil prices) and 1987 (date of economic adjustment programme).[79]

Thus, nation-states in most of Africa have become, to a large extent, predators of their own societies, constituting a formidable obstacle not only to development but to survival and civility. Indeed, because of the extraordinary benefits resulting from control of states, various factions, closer to cliques and gangs than to parties and social groupings, have engaged in atrocious civil wars, sometimes on the basis of ethnic, territorial, and religious cleavages. It has followed the displacement of millions of people around the continent, the disruption of subsistence agricultural production, the uprooting of human settlements, the breaking down of social order, and, in a number of cases (Zaïre, Liberia, Sierra Leone, Somalia, among others), the disappearance of the nation-state for all practical purposes.

[78]   Lewis (1996: 102–3).
[79]   Herbst (1996: 159).

Why so? Why have nation-states in Africa come to be predatory? Is there a historical continuity, specific to the social structure of much of the continent, before, during, and after colonization, as Bayart suggests? Or, on the contrary, is it the result of the lasting wounds of colonialism and the perverse legacy of the political institutions invented and imposed by the Berlin Treaty, as Davidson proposes? Is the state's exteriority to African societies the result of an ethnic puzzle, reproducing ancestral inter-ethnic struggles, as the media often interpret? Why did the nation-state become predatory in Africa, while it emerged as a developmental agency in the Asian Pacific? Are the processes of state formation truly independent of the forms of Africa's incorporation (or lack of incorporation) into the new global economy, as argued by many critics of the dependency theory school? These are fundamental questions that require a careful, if tentative, answer.

Ethnic identity, economic globalization, and state formation in Africa

The plight of Africa is often attributed, particularly in the media, to inter-ethnic hostility. Indeed, in the 1990s, ethnic strife has exploded all over the continent, leading in some cases to massacres and attempted genocides. Ethnicity matters a lot, in Africa, as everywhere else. Yet, the relationships between ethnicity, society, the state, and the economy are too complex to be reducible to "tribal" conflicts. It is precisely this complex web of relationships, and its transformation in the past two decades, that lies at the root of the predatory state.

If ethnicity matters, the ethnic differences that are at the forefront of Africa's political scene today are politically constructed, rather than culturally rooted. From contrasting theoretical perspectives, Africanists as different as Bayart, Davidson, Lemarchand, and Adekanye, among others, converge toward a similar conclusion.[80] As Bayart writes:

> Most situations where the structuring of the political arena seems to be enunciated in terms of ethnicity relate to identities which did not exist a century ago or, at least, were then not as clearly defined . . . The colonisers conceptualised indistinct human land-scapes which they had occupied as specific identities, constructed in their imagination on the model of a bargain basement nation-state. With its Jacobin and prefectoral origins, the French

[80]   Bayart (1989); Davidson (1992, 1994); Lemarchand (1994a, b); Adekanye (1995).

Administration had an avowedly territorial concept of the state, British indirect rule, by contrast, being much more culturalist. Aside from such nuances, it was along these lines that the colonial regime was organised and that it aimed to order reality. To achieve this it used coercion, by an authoritarian policy of forced settlement, by controlling migratory movements, by more or less artificially fixing ethnic details through birth certificates and identity cards. *But the contemporary force of ethnic consciousness comes much more from its appropriation by local people, circumscribing the allocation of the state's resources.*[81]

Davidson anchors this ethnic classification of subjugated territories in the ideologically prejudiced, political-bureaucratic logic of colonial administrations:

Europeans had supposed that Africans lived in "tribes" – a word of no certain meaning – and that "tribal loyalties" were the only, and primitive, stuff of African politics. Colonial rule had worked on the assumption, dividing Africans into tribes even when these "tribes" had to be invented. But appearances were misleading. What rapidly developed was not the politics of tribalism, but something different and more divisive. This was the politics of clientelism. What tribalism had supposed was that each tribe recognized a common interest represented by common spokespersons, and there was thus the possibility of a "tribal unity" produced by agreement between "tribal representatives". But clientelism – the "Tammany Hall" approach – almost at once led to a dogfight for the spoils of political power.[82]

This redefinition of ethnic identity by colonial powers mirrored the structure of the colonial state, in a way that would reverberate in the long term for independent nation-states. First of all, states were made up arbitrarily, following the boundaries of conquest, uncertain maps of colonial geographers, and diplomatic maneuvers in the 1884–5 conference that led to the Berlin Treaty.[83] Furthermore, the functioning of the colonial state, largely reproduced in the post-independence period, followed the distinction in levels of a "bifurcated state," as conceptualized by Mahmood Mamdani in his brilliant analysis of state formation.[84] On the one hand there was the legal state, as a racialized entity, under the control of Europeans; on

[81] Bayart (1989: 51, my italic).
[82] Davidson (1992: 206–7).
[83] Davidson (1992); Lindqvist (1996).
[84] Mamdani (1996).

the other hand was the customary power of native power structures, as an ethnic/tribal identity. The unity of the former and the fragmentation of the latter were essential mechanisms of control under colonial administrations which usually dedicated scarce resources in personnel and equipment to maximize net gains in their ventures (Germany, for instance, had only five civil officers, and 24 military officers in Rwanda in 1914). Who was a member of which unit was decided administratively, in an effort of simplification that translated into assigning identities in ID cards, sometimes based on criteria of physical appearance according to summary classifications by physical anthropologists. Yet, once the structure of tribal chiefs was established, the customary state became a fundamental source of control over land and labor, so that belonging to a certain tribe was the only acknowledged channel to access resources, and the only recognized avenue of intermediation *vis à vis* the legal, modern state, that was the connection with the vast resources of the outside world, the international system of wealth and power. After independence, Africa's nationalist elites simply occupied the same structures of the legal/modern state which, therefore, were de-racialized. Yet, they kept in place the fragmented, ethnicized customary state. If and when the distribution of resources became difficult because of both growing scarcity in the country and the growing rapacity of the elites, a choice was made in favor of the ethnicized constituencies that were best represented in the legal state, and/or those who, on the basis of their larger numbers or their control of the military, came to power. Ethnicity became the main avenue to access the state's control over resources. But it was the state, and its elites, that shaped and reshaped ethnic identity and allegiance, not the other way around. According to Bayart:

> In Africa, ethnicity is almost never absent from politics, yet at the same time it does not provide its basic fabric . . . In the context of the contemporary state, ethnicity exists mainly as an agent of accumulation, both of wealth and political power. Tribalism is thus perceived as a political force in itself, as a channel through which competition for the acquisition of wealth, power, and status is expressed.[85]

Indeed, in many areas, and particularly in the Great Lakes region, this process of ethnic definition by the power structure, as a way of channeling/limiting access to resources, seems to have pre-dated colonial rule.[86] At this point in the analysis, its complexity could be

---

[85]   Bayart (1989: 55).
[86]   Mamdani (1996); Lemarchand (1970).

made somewhat clearer by a brief empirical illustration. For obvious reasons of actuality in this end of millennium, I have selected the violent confrontation between Tutsis and Hutus in Rwanda, Burundi, and beyond (eastern Zaïre, southern Uganda). As this is a well-known subject, on which exists a vast literature,[87] I will exclusively focus on a few matters that are relevant to the broader analysis of Africa's contemporary crises.

To start with, the "objective" distinction between Tutsis and Hutus is much less clear than is usually thought. As the leading Western expert on the matter, René Lemarchand, writes:

> As has repeatedly been emphasized, Hutu and Tutsi speak the same language – Kirundi in Burundi, Kinyarwanda in Rwanda – share the same customs, and lived in relative harmony side by side with each other for centuries before the advent of colonial rule. Contrary to the image projected by the media, the patterns of exclusion brought to light during and after independence cannot be reduced to "deep-seated, ancestral enmities". Although pre-colonial Rwanda was unquestionably more rigidly stratified than Burundi, and hence more vulnerable to Hutu-led revolutions, the key to an understanding of their contrasting political fortunes lies in the uneven rhythms at which processes of ethnic mobilization were set in motion in the years immediately preceding independence . . . In both instances it is the interplay between ethnic realities and their subjective reconstruction (or manipulation) by political entrepreneurs that lies at the root of the Hutu–Tutsi conflict.[88]

Even physical differences (the tall, lighter-skinned Tutsis, the stocky, darker-skinned Hutus) have been over-emphasized, among other things because of frequent inter-ethnic marriages and family formation. Thus, Mamdani reports that, during the 1994 massacres of Tutsis by the murderous Intrahamwe Hutu militia, identity was often checked through ID cards, and Tutsi wives were denounced and sent to their deaths by their Hutu husbands, fearful of appearing as traitors.[89] Besides, it is often forgotten that thousands of moderate Hutus were murdered along with the hundreds of thousands of Tutsis, underscoring the social and political cleavages behind a calculated strategy of extermination. Let me remind you of the overall story in a nutshell, trying then to sort out the analytical lessons.

In pre-colonial times, the state built in the lands that would become Rwanda and Burundi was under the control of a pastoralist/warrior

---

[87] Lemarchand (1970; 1993, 1994a, b); Newbury (1988); Adekanye (1995); Mamdani (1996).
[88] Lemarchand (1994a: 588).
[89] Mamdani (1996).

aristocracy, defining itself as Tutsis. Peasants (Hutu) (as well as bushmen, Batwa) were, by and large, excluded from the state and from power positions, almost entirely in Rwanda, less so in Burundi. However, accumulation of wealth (mainly cattle) would allow a Hutu family to move into the upper echelons of society (a process named Kwihutura), thus becoming Tutsi: so much for biological/cultural determination of ethnicity! As Mamdani writes:

> It is clear that we are talking of a political distinction, one that divided the subject from the non-subject population, and not a socio-economic distinction, between exploiters and exploited or rich and poor ... The Batutsi developed a political identity – they formed a distinct social category, marked by marriage and ethnic taboos, says Mafeje – a self-consciousness of being distinguished from the subject population. Thus the mere fact of some physical difference – often the nose, less often the height – could become symbolic of a great political difference.[90]

The colonial state – German first, Belgian afterwards – considerably sharpened and mobilized this political/ethnic cleavage, by giving the Tutsis full control over the customary state (even in areas that were before in the hands of the Hutu majority), and by providing them with access to education, resources, and administrative jobs, thus creating a Tutsi native state as a subordinate appendix to the colonial, Belgian state: a process not so different from the one that took place in Zanzibar, when British rulers established an Arab Sultanate to administer the native population. Under Belgian rule even the Kwihutura was abolished, and the system became a caste-like society. As could be expected, the process of independence, and its ensuing political mobilization, freed the explosive energy accumulated by the exclusion from all spheres of power of the Hutu majority (about 84 percent of the population). However, the political outcomes were different in Rwanda and Burundi. In Rwanda, the 1959 Hutu revolution led to Hutu majority rule, to pogroms and mass killings of Tutsis, and to the exile of a significant number of Tutsis, both to Burundi and to Uganda. In Burundi, a constitutional monarchy, around the prestigious figure of Prince Rwagasore, seemed to be able to organize ethnic coexistence around a national state. However, the assassination of the prince in 1961, and the failed Hutu coup attempt of 1965, allowed the Tutsi-dominated military to seize control of the country, making it a republic, and institutionalizing political marginalization of the Hutu, whose insurgency was repressed in a bloodbath:

[90]   Mamdani (1996: 10).

in 1972, the Tutsi army massacred over 100,000 Hutus in Burundi. Again, in 1988, massacres of thousands of Tutsis by Hutu peasants around Ntega/Marangara were responded to by the massacre of tens of thousands of Hutu civilians by the Tutsi army. In 1990, the invasion of Rwanda by Rwandan Tutsi exiles from Uganda (where they had participated in the victorious guerrilla war against Milton Obote) led to a civil war that, as is general knowledge, triggered the 1994 massacres when Hutu militia and the presidential guard went on the rampage, supposedly in retaliation for the killing of President Habyarimana when a missile hit his plane, in circumstances still obscure. The attempted genocide of Tutsis involved not only the Rwandan army and militia, but large segments of the Hutu civilian population, in every neighborhood and every village: it was a de-centralized, mass-participated holocaust. Thus, the military victory of the Tutsi-dominated Rwandan Patriotic Front, triggered an exile of millions, whose exodus to Zaïre, and its subsequent partial return to Rwanda by the end of 1996, may well have contributed to the full political destabilization of Central Africa. Meanwhile, in Burundi, the 1993 elections permitted for the first time a democratically elected Hutu president, Melchior Ndadye, to come to power. But only three months later he was assassinated by Tutsi military officers, triggering a new round of reciprocal massacres, the exodus of hundreds of thousands of Hutus, and a civil war, which was aggravated by a Tutsi military coup in July 1996, prompting a trade embargo to Burundi from its neighboring states.

After decades of mutual political exclusion, and repeated massacres, mainly organized around ethnic lines, it would be foolish to deny that there are Tutsi and Hutu identities, to the point that a majority rule, in a democratic polity, seems to be out of the question.[91] This situation seems to open the way for the establishment of Tutsi or Hutu ruthless domination, a protracted civil war, or the redrawing of political boundaries. Yet, what this dramatic experience seems to show is that the sharpening of ethnic differences, and the crystallization of ethnicity in social status and political power, came from the historical dynamics of the social basis of the state, colonial first, independent nation-state later. It also shows the incapacity of ethnically constituted political elites to transcend the definition inherited from the past, since they used their ethnicity as the rallying flag to seize state power or to resist it. In so doing, they made a plural, democratic state non-viable, as citizenship and ethnicity are contradictory principles of democratic political legitimacy. Furthermore, the memory of

---

[91] Mamdani (1996).

extermination, made fresh by atrocious repetition of the worst night-mares on both sides, marked in blood the ethnic boundaries of power as violence. From then on, ethnicity overtook politics, after having been shaped, and hardened, by the politics of the state. It is this complex interaction between ethnicity and the state, under the dominance of state logic, that we must have in mind to understand African politics, and beyond it, Africa's tragedy.

However, if the state is ethnicized, it is scarcely nationalized. Indeed, one of the key features explaining why a developmental state emerged in the Asian Pacific, as well as, with lesser fortune, in Latin America, and not in Africa, is the weakness of the nation in the African nation-state. Not that nationalism was absent from Africa's scene: after all, nationalist movements were the driving force to achieve inde-pendence, and, in the late 1950s and early 1960s, a fierce brand of nationalist leader (Sekou Ture, N'krumah, Kenyatta, Lumumba) shook the world, inspiring the promise of African renaissance. But they received a meager national heritage from colonialism, as the cultural/ethnic/historical/geographical/economic puzzle of Africa's political map confined, by and large, African nationalism to the educated elite of the legal/modern state, and to the small urban business class. As Davidson, in line with many other Africanists, writes: "An analysis of Africa's trouble has also to be an inquiry into the process – the process largely of nationalism – that has crystallized the division of Africa's many hundreds of peoples and cultures into a few dozen nation-states, each claiming sovereignty against the others, and then all of them sorely in trouble."[92] The lack of a national basis for these new African nation-states, a basis that in other latitudes was usually made up of shared geography, history, and culture (see volume II, chapter 1), is a fundamental difference between Africa and the Asian Pacific, with the exception of Indonesia, in the differential fate of their developmental processes (see chapter 4). It is true that two other elements (widespread literacy and a relatively high level of education in East Asia; and geopolitical support from the US and the openness of its market to Asian Pacific countries) were equally im-portant in facilitating a successful outward-looking development strategy in the Pacific. But Africa provided primary education on a large scale quite rapidly, at least in the urban centers, and France and Britain continued to "help" their former colonies, allowing access to markets in the former metropolises. The crucial difference was the ability of Asian Pacific countries to mobilize their nations, under authoritarian rule, around a developmental goal, on the basis of

[92]   Davidson (1992: 13).

strong national/cultural identity, and the politics of survival (see chapter 4). The weak social basis of the nationalist project considerably debilitated African states, both *vis à vis* their diverse ethnic constituencies and *vis à vis* foreign states competing for influence over Africa in the framework of the Cold War.

Africa, in the first three decades of its independence, has been the object of repeated interventions by foreign troops, and military advisers, from Western powers (particularly France, Belgium, Portugal, and white South Africa, but also the US, UK, Israel, and Spain), as well as from the Soviet Union, Cuba, and Lybia, thus making much of Africa a hot war battleground. The splitting of political factions, states, and regions in different geopolitical alignments contributed to the destabilization and militarization of African states, to the unbearable burden of gigantic defense budgets, and left the heritage of a formidable arsenal of military hardware, most of it in unreliable hands.[93] The short history of African nation-states, built on historically shaky ground, undermined nations and nationalism as a basis for legitimacy, and as a relevant unit for development.

There is another, fundamental element to be added to the equation explaining Africa's contemporary crisis. *This is the linkage between the ethnic politics of the [weak nation]-state, on the one hand, and the political economy of Africa in the past three decades, on the other hand.* Without reference to this connection, it is easy to descend to quasi-racist statements about the innately perverse nature of African politics. Colin Leys argues, and I concur, that Africa's crisis cannot be understood, including the role played by the state, without reference to economic history. For a number of reasons, which he hypothesizes, including the low development of productive forces, and the predominance of the household production system until the end of colonialism, "the timing of Africa's original incorporation in the world capitalist system, combined with the extreme backwardness of its precolonial economies and the limitations of subsequent colonial policy, prevented most of the continent from starting at all on the key transition to self-sustaining capital accumulation after independence."[94] I will briefly elaborate on this insight in my own terms.[95]

In historical sequence, in the 1960s Africa "got off to a bad start."[96] In the 1970s, in the context of world capitalism's crisis and restructuring, its development model collapsed, needing, by the end of

---

[93]   De Waal (1996).
[94]   Leys (1994: 45).
[95]   For relevant data, see Sarkar and Singer (1991) Blomstrom and Lundhal (1993); Riddell (1995); Yansane (1996); *The Economist* (1996a).
[96]   Dumont (1964).

the decade, a bail out from foreign lenders and international institutions. In the 1980s, the burden of the debt and the structural
adjustment programs, imposed as a condition for international
lending, disarticulated economies, impoverished societies, and destabilized states. It triggered, in the 1990s, the incorporation of some
minuscule sectors of some countries into global capitalism, as well as
the chaotic de-linking of most people and most territories from the
global economy. What were the reasons for these successive developments? In the 1960s, policies oriented toward agricultural exports and
autarkic industrialization contributed to destroying the local peasant
economy, and much of the subsistence basis of the population.
Domestic markets were too narrow to sustain large-scale industrialization. International economic exchanges were still dominated by
neo-colonial interests. In the 1970s, technological backwardness,
managerial inefficiency, and the persistence of post-colonial
constraints (for example, the Franc zone in ex-French Africa) made
it impossible to compete in international markets, while the deterioration of terms of trade made imports increasingly difficult precisely
when the modern sector needed new technology and the population
needed to import food. Indebtedness without criteria or control
(much of it was used in stepped-up defense spending, industrial
"white elephants," and conspicuous consumption; for example, the
construction of Yamassoukro, Houphouet-Boigny's dream capital in
his native village) led to bankruptcy in most of Africa. Structural
adjustment programs, advised/imposed by the International
Monetary Fund and the World Bank, aggravated social conditions
while failing by and large to make the economies dynamic. They
focused on downsizing the state and stimulating primary commodity
exports. This latter goal, in general terms, is a losing bet in today's
technological and economic environment; and in specific terms an
unrealistic proposition when confronted with persistent agricultural
protectionism in OECD markets.[97] While islands of economic efficiency have indeed emerged in some countries, including some large,
competitive African companies (for example, Ghana's Ashanti
Goldfields), material and human resources have been wasted and, as
documented above, the African economy as a whole is in substantially
worse shape in the 1990s than it was in the 1960s, both in production
and in consumption.

The massive shrinkage of resources, resulting from the economic
crisis and adjustment policies of the 1980s, dramatically affected the
political dynamics of nation-states, built on the capacity of the state

[97]   Adepoju (1993); Adekanye (1995); Simon et al. (1995).

elites to distribute to different clienteles, usually ethnically or territorially defined, and still keep enough for themselves. Three consequences followed from this shrinkage:

1   As international aid and foreign lending became a fundamental source of income, states engaged in the *political economy of begging*, thus developing a vested interest in human catastrophes that would gain international attention and generate charitable resources. This strategy was particularly important when the end of the Cold War dried up financial and military transfers from foreign powers to their African vassal states.

2   As resources from the formal, modern sector of the economy became scarcer, political leaders, military officers, bureaucrats and local businessmen alike engaged in *large-scale illicit trade*, including joint ventures with various partners in the global criminal economy (see chapter 3).

3   As resources decreased and the population's needs increased, *choices had to be made between different clienteles, usually in favor of the most reliable ethnic or regional groups* (that is, those closer to the dominant factions of the elite). Some factions, losing out in state power, resorted to political intrigue or military force, either to obtain their share or simply to appropriate the whole system of political control over resources. In their struggle for power they sought the support of those ethnic or regional groups that had been excluded by the state from a share of resources.

As factionalism increased, and national armies split, the distinction between banditry and violent political opposition became increasingly blurred. Since ethnic and regional affiliations became the only identifiable sources of membership and loyalty, violence trickled down to the population at large, so that neighbors, coworkers, and compatriots suddenly became, first, competitors for survival, then enemies, and, in the last resort, potential killers or victims. Institutional disintegration, widespread violence, and civil war further disorganized the economy, and triggered massive movements of population, escaping to uncertain safety.

Furthermore, people also learned the downgraded version of the political economy of begging, as their condition as refugees might, just might, entitle them to survival under the various flags of the United Nations, governments, and NGOs. In the end, by the mid-1990s, not only was Africa increasingly marginalized from the global/informational economy, but in much of the continent nation-states were disintegrating, and people, uprooted and harassed, were regrouping in communes of survival, under a variety of labels, depending on the anthropologist's taste.

Africa's plight

The deliberate attempt by international financial institutions to take Africa out of the 1980s debt crisis by homogenizing the conditions of trade and investment in Africa with the rules of the new global economy ended in a considerable fiasco, according to the evaluation of a number of observers and international agencies.[98] A study of the impact of structural adjustments in Africa, elaborated by the United Nations Population Fund, summarizes its findings in the following manner:

> There is consensus among the authors of this volume that, in the countries surveyed, one does not find a strong association between adjustment policies and economic performance. There are strong indications that adjustment policies may not be able to guarantee that African countries will overcome the effects of external shocks even in the long run, unless there is a more favourable external environment. In many African countries pursuing structural adjustment, what progress there is has been confined to nominal growth in GDP without any transformation of the structure of the economy. Ghana [the show case of the World Bank's evaluation], for example, achieved an average annual growth rate of 5 percent over 1984–88. But manufacturing capacity utilization has remained low, at 35 percent in 1988. In Nigeria it was just 38 percent in 1986–87. In most countries covered in this study, small and medium enterprises have been marginalized by the exchange rate and trade liberalization measures. High domestic interest rates, resulting from restrictive monetary and credit policies, created disruptive business climates. Industrial closures were rampant, four out of ten banks were shut down in Cameroon, whilst in many countries marketing boards for major commodities were scrapped. Although agriculture grew modestly in these countries, production of food stuffs declined. In Ghana, production of cereal fell by 7 percent and starchy staples by 39 percent between 1984 and 1988. Other countries had similar experiences. Although exports earnings generally increased, imports also rose, intensifying the balance of payments crisis . . . A United Nations-organized conference concluded that "adjustment measures have been implemented at high human costs and sacrifices and are rending the fabric of African society.[99]

---

[98]   Adepoju (1993); Ravenhill (1993); Hutchful (1995); Loxley (1995); Riddell (1995).

[99]   Adepoju (1993: 3–4).

The social, economic, and political cost of this failed attempt at glob-alizing African economies, without informationalizing its societies, can be shown along three main lines of argument, and one over-arching consequence: the growing dereliction of a majority of Africa's people.

First, formal urban labor markets stopped absorbing labor, gener-ating a substantial increase in unemployment and underemployment, which translated into a higher incidence of poverty levels. An ILO study on the evolution of labor markets in Africa, focusing on six French-speaking countries,[100] found a statistical relationship between employment status and incidence of poverty. In Sub-Saharan Africa as a whole, the urban unemployment rate doubled between 1975 and 1990, rising from 10 to 20 percent. Employment in the modern sector, and especially in the public sector, stagnated or declined. In 14 countries, salaried employment grew by an annual average of 3 percent in 1975–80, but only by 1 percent in the first half of the 1980s, way below what was needed to absorb labor increases from population growth and rural–urban migration. The informal sector of em-ployment, growing at 6.7 percent per year, became the refuge for surplus labor. Most labor in African cities is now in the categories of "irregular," "marginal self-employment," and "non-protected salaried worker", all leading to lower incomes, lack of protection, and a high incidence of poverty. For the population as a whole, in 1985, 47 percent of Africans lived below the poverty level, as compared to 33 percent for developing countries as a whole. The number of destitute persons in Africa increased by two-thirds between 1975 and 1985, and Africa is, according to projections, the only region of the world where poverty levels will increase in the 1990s.[101]

Secondly, African agricultural production per capita, and particu-larly food production, has declined substantially in the past decade (see figure 2.3), making many countries vulnerable to famine and epidemics when droughts, war, or other catastrophes strike. Agricultural crisis seems to be the result of a combination of excessive focus on export-oriented production and of ill-advised transition to technologies or product lines inappropriate to a country's ecological and economic conditions.[102] For instance, in West Africa, foreign forestry companies pushed for replacing acacias with non-indigenous trees, only to reverse the process a few years later when it became clear that acacias needed less water and less attention, besides helping to feed goats and sheep during the dry season. Or, in another illustra-tion of inappropriate technological change, at Lake Turkana, in East

[100]   Lachaud (1994).
[101]   Adepoju (1993) .
[102]   Jamal (1995).

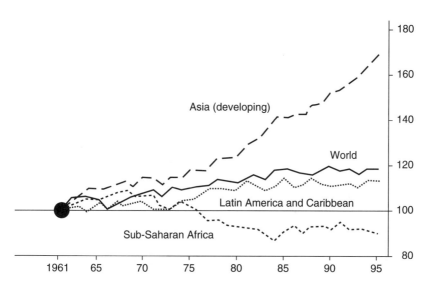

Figure 2.3   Food production per person (1961 = 100) (Sub-Saharan Africa excludes South Africa)
Source: compiled by *The Economist* (September 7, 1996) from figures from the Food and Agriculture Organization

Africa, Norwegian experts organized a program of conversion of Turkana cattlemen into producers of more marketable fish products, such as tilapia and perch. However, the cost of the equipment for chilling the fish was so high that production/distribution costs were higher than the fish price in accessible markets. Not being able to turn back to cattle-raising, 20,000 nomadic Turkana became dependent on food aid from donor agencies.[103] The difficulty of penetrating international markets for a small range of African agricultural products, and the transformation of government policies toward agriculture during the 1980s, made farming highly unpredictable. Thus, many farmers turned to short-term, survival strategies of cultivation, instead of investing in a long-term conversion to export-oriented, commercial agriculture, thus undermining their future chance of being internationally competitive.[104]

The third major trend in the social and economic evolution of Africa is the disorganization of production and livelihood induced by the disintegration of the state. The pattern of violence, pillage, civil

---

[103]   *The Economist* (1996a).
[104]   Berry (1993: 270–71).

wars, banditry, and massacres, which struck the large majority of African countries in the 1980s and 1990s, has thrown out of their towns and villages millions of people, ruined the economy of regions and countries, and reduced to shambles much of the institutional capacity to manage crises and reconstruct the material bases of life.[105]

Urban poverty, the crisis of agriculture, particularly of subsistence agriculture, institutional collapse, widespread violence, and massive population movements have combined to significantly deteriorate the living conditions of the majority of the African population in the past decade, as documented by the United Nations 1996 Human Development Report. Poverty, migration, and social disorganization have also contributed to creating the conditions for devastating epidemics that threaten the extermination of a substantial proportion of Africans, as well as the potential spread of diseases to the rest of the world. It should be emphasized that it is not only the conditions of hygiene and nutrition under which most Africans live that are the source of diseases and epidemics, but the lack of adequate health care and education greatly contribute to the diffusion of disease.

A dramatic case in point is the AIDS epidemic.[106] While the first HIV infections were reported in Africa in the early 1980s, by the mid-1990s, Sub-Saharan Africa accounted for about 60 percent of the estimated 17 million HIV-positive people in the world (see figure 2.4).[107] In countries such as Uganda, Rwanda, and Zambia, between 17 and 24 percent of the urban population were infected by about 1987 (see table 2.8). In general, this proportion has certainly increased in recent years in most countries, with some exceptions (Gabon). AIDS is now considered to the leading cause of death in Uganda, and a major cause in other countries. Because AIDS in Africa is transmitted through heterosexual contact in 80 percent of cases, women are particularly at risk, given their sexual subservience to men, and men's increased promiscuity at a time of migration and uprooting. About 4.5 million women are estimated to be HIV-positive. Their patriarchal submission limits their access to information and resources for prevention, and decreases their access to treatment for AIDS-related infections. Studies have shown that women are less likely to visit a hospital, die of HIV/AIDS at a younger age, and are more likely to stay with their spouses when the latter are diagnosed as HIV-positive than the other way round.[108] Thus, a large number of

[105]   Leys (1994); Adekanye (1995); Kaiser (1996).
[106]   Barnett and Blaikie (1992); Hope (1995); Philipson and Posner (1995); Boahene (1996); Kamali et al. (1996).
[107]   Boahene (1996).
[108]   Boahene (1996).

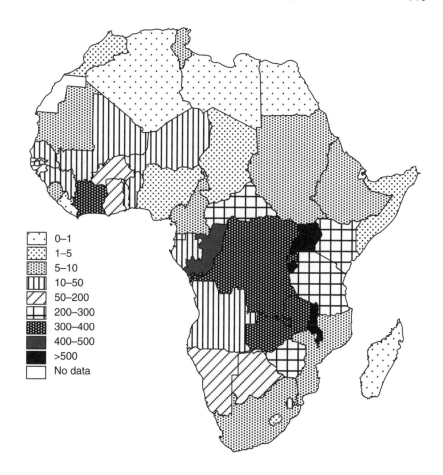

Figure 2.4   AIDS cases per million in Africa, 1990
Sources: WHO Epidemiological Record; WorldAIDS, 1990 and 1991,
elaborated by Barnett and Blaikie (1992)

women of reproductive age are HIV-positive. Over the next 10–25
years, the impact of AIDS on child survival is projected to be more
severe than the impact of the disease on the overall population. AIDS
is expected to cause more deaths in children in Sub-Saharan Africa
than either malaria or measles. Child and infant mortality rates
which were projected to decrease by 35–40 percent in the next
decade, are now expected to remain the same, or even increase,
because of AIDS. Child orphans are becoming a massive problem.
The prediction is that an estimated 10 million uninfected children

Table 2.8   Estimated seroprevalence for adults (15–49 years) for cities and rural areas in selected African countries, c.1987

Country	HIV seroprevalence (%)		Population infected with HIV (000s)
	Cities	Rural	
Uganda	24.1	12.3	894.3
Rwanda	20.1	2.2	81.5
Zambia	17.2	—	205.2
Congo	10.2	—	46.5
Côte d'Ivoire	10.0	1.3	183.0
Malawi	9.5	4.2	142.5
Central African Republic	7.8	3.7	54.3
Zaïre	7.1	0.5	281.8
Ghana	4.7	—	98.7
Burundi	4.3	—	15.0
Tanzania	3.6	0.7	96.6
Zimbabwe	3.2	0.0	30.9
Kenya	2.7	0.2	44.5
Cameroon	1.1	0.6	33.2
Mozambique	1.0	0.6	43.5
Sudan	0.3	—	6.8
Nigeria	0.1	0.0	8.1
Swaziland	0.0	—	0.0
Total infected persons, all African countries (incl. others not listed)			2,497.6
Total African population infected, 1987(%)			0.9

Source: Over (1990, reported by Barnett and Blakie (1992))

will lose one or two parents to the AIDS epidemic by the year 2000. Extended family systems are breaking down under the pressure of this wave of orphans.

The size and speed of diffusion of the AIDS epidemic in Africa are induced by social and economic conditions. As a leading expert on the matter, Kempe Ronald Hope writes: "Without a doubt, poverty and economic distress in the African countries have contributed greatly to the rapid spread of HIV and AIDS."[109] Lack of adequate health care, low levels of education, insanitary living conditions, lim-

[109]   Hope (1995: 82).

ited access to basic services, rapid urbanization, unemployment, and poverty are related phenomena, and they are all factors associated with HIV infection. Access to health care in Africa is extremely limited. Data for 1988–91 indicate that the population per doctor in Sub-Saharan Africa was 18,488, compared with 5,767 for all developing countries, and 344 for industrial countries.[110] Poverty limits access to information about prevention, as well as access to preventive methods. Agricultural crisis, famine, and wars have forced migration and disorganized families, communities, and social networks. Men who have migrated to urban areas, and periodically return to their communities of origin, are major carriers of HIV, spreading the virus through prostitutes, and diffusing it throughout trucking routes. Poor people who contract HIV tend to develop AIDS much faster than those of higher socio-economic status.

The potential spread of AIDS epidemic from Africa to other regions of the world represents a more serious risk than is usually acknowledged. South Africa provides striking evidence in this regard. While it is a country that borders areas where the epidemics began in the 1980s, and its black population was left for a long time in poor social and health conditions, South Africa's level of economic and institutional development is much higher than that of the rest of Africa. Yet, in the 1990s, the AIDS epidemic became rampant in South Africa, reproducing the patterns and the speed of diffusion experienced in neighboring countries a decade earlier. Certain groups, such as prostitutes and migrant laborers, are estimated to be infected in a 10–30 percent range. Among women of child-bearing age, estimates of HIV infection for the whole country are as high as 4.7 percent, with a higher incidence in some areas, such as Kwa/Zulu Natal. At current rates of diffusion, models of the future spread of HIV/AIDS estimate that, by the year 2010, 27 percent of the South African population will have been infected. More optimistic models, assuming a 40 percent reduction in the number of sexual partners, and a 20 percent increase in effective condom use, still project, for the same date, that 8 percent of the total population will have been infected.[111]

If Africa's plight is ignored or played down , it is unlikely to remain confined within its geographical boundaries. Both humankind and our sense of humanity will be threatened. Global apartheid is a cynic's illusion in the Information Age.

[110]   UNDP (1996).
[111]   Campbell and Williams (1996).

Africa's hope? The South African connection

Is Sub-Saharan Africa condemned to social exclusion in the new global economy, at least in the foreseeable future? This is a fundamental issue, but one that exceeds the limits of this chapter, and the purpose of this book, which is concerned with analysis rather than with policy or forecasting. However, on strictly empirical grounds, the end of apartheid in South Africa, and the potential linkage between a democratic, black-majority ruled South Africa and African countries, at least those in eastern/southern Africa, allows us to examine the hypothesis of the incorporation of Africa into global capitalism under new, more favorable conditions via the South African connection. Because of the implications for an overall analysis of the conditions reproducing or modifying social exclusion in the global economy, I will briefly examine this matter before moving out of Africa.

South Africa is clearly different from the rest of Sub-Saharan Africa. It has a much higher level of industrialization, a more diversified economy, and it plays a more significant role in the global economy than the rest of the continent. It is neither a low-wage dependent economy, nor a higher-skilled, competitive emerging economy. In fact, it combines aspects of both, and in some ways the processes of simultaneous inclusion and exclusion are more obvious and glaring in South Africa than in many other countries. The political environment is changing rapidly in the post-election, democratic period, and the economy is being helped by rapid reincorporation into the global economy after several decades of relative isolation, due both to sanctions and to high tariff barriers from South Africa's policies of import substitution industrialization.

South Africa accounts for 44 percent of the total GDP of all Sub-Saharan Africa, and 52 percent of its industrial output. It consumes 64 percent of the electricity consumed in Sub-Saharan Africa. In 1993, real GDP per capita for Sub-Saharan Africa (including South Africa) was US\$ 1,288, while for South Africa alone it was 3,127. There are nine times more telephone lines per capita in South Africa than in Sub-Saharan Africa.

The Johannesburg Stock Exchange is the tenth largest (by market capitalization) in the world. Yet the banking and financial system is dominated by four large commercial banks and has primarily serviced the major industrial sectors. Few funds have been available for small-scale entrepreneurs. At least since the discovery of diamonds in the nineteenth century, South Africa has played a role in the global economy. Mining was crucial in the overall development of the country over the past century, providing a growth engine for capital accumulation. Despite recent decline, gold mining is still the core of

South Africa's mining complex, constituting about 70 percent of mining exports and employment, and 80 percent of revenue.[112] Yet most of South Africa's gold reserves have been exhausted. Over the past century, over 45 thousand tonnes of gold have been removed, constituting over two-thirds of the original resource base, and the 20 thousand tonnes remaining tend to be deep and low grade. Other strategic mining and mineral-processing industries include iron, steel, zinc, tin, ferroalloys, manganese, copper, silver, aluminum and platinum. Mining still accounts for 71 percent of total foreign exchange earnings, though just over half of GDP comes from services and nearly a quarter from manufacturing.[113] The mining industry, more than any other industry, was dependent on the apartheid system because of its reliance on migrant and compound labor.

Manufacturing industry grew substantially in the 1960s, but began to slow in the 1970s and stagnated entirely in the 1980s. Manufacturing output growth in the 1970s averaged 5.3 percent per year.[114] But between 1980 and 1985, manufacturing output actually declined by 1.2 percent, and growth between 1985 and 1991 was only 0.7 percent, while employment in manufacturing actually declined by 1.4 percent.[115] South Africa's manufacturing sector is characterized by the classic problems of import substitution industrialization, with a strong capacity in consumer goods production, and a certain amount of heavy industry linked to the mining and mineral processing industries, but an absence of capital goods and many intermediate goods. However, South Africa is linked to the informational/global economy. It has the highest number of Internet hosts, for instance, of any non-OECD country.[116] Yet growth in technological capability is limited by a fragmented institutional environment and lack of effective government support. Business expenditure in R&D declined some 27 percent from 1983–4 to 1989–90 and there is a strong reliance on acquisition of technology from abroad, primarily through license agreements. R&D is significantly less than in other rapidly growing countries.[117] In 1993, at least, "there was little evidence that such technology transfer is accompanied by programmes of training to ensure effective assimilation."[118]

Overall employment has been on a downward trend since the mid-1970s, with falls in employment in agriculture, transport, mining, and

[112] MERG (1993).
[113] *The Economist* (1995).
[114] ISP (1995: 6).
[115] MERG (1993: 239).
[116] Network Wizards (1996).
[117] Industrial Strategy Project (1995: 239).
[118] MERG (1993: 232).

manufacturing. If there had not been substantial growth in public sector employment in the period 1986–90, total employment growth would have been negative in that period. From 1989 to 1992, total employment in the non-agricultural sectors of the economy declined by 4.8 percent, equivalent to the loss of about 286,000 jobs, with positive growth only in the public sector. Total private sector employment declined by 7.8 percent during this period. The proportion of the labor force employed in the formal economy in 1989 ranged from 61 percent in the Johannesburg/Pretoria area to only 22 percent in the poorest regions. While no reliable figures for unemployment exist, it is clear that a large and rapidly increasing gap exists between the number of people requiring employment and the capacity of the formal economy to provide employment. Real wage growth for African workers was negative in the period 1986–90. For African workers in the lowest educational and occupational categories, real wages between 1975 and 1985 declined at a rate of 3 percent per year.[119] The official unemployment rate was estimated at 32.6 percent by the Central Statistical Service in 1994, but the absence – relative to other African countries – of opportunities for earnings and subsistence from the land, and hence of a rural safety net, underlines the problem of mass unemployment. Unemployment is especially serious among the young, with 64 percent of the economically active population between the ages of 16 and 24 (about one million young people) being jobless in 1995.

Thus, many South Africans depend for survival on the informal economy, although estimates of their number vary. The Central Statistical Service estimated in 1990 that 2.7 million people, or 24 percent of the labor force, were active in the informal economy. This may be a significant understatement of informal economic activity, however. For instance, in a 1990 survey of residents of Alexandra township, a major township in the Johannesburg area, 48 percent of residents reported that they were self-employed, worked at home, or worked elsewhere in the township.[120] South Africa's informal economy is primarily an economy of bare survival. Approximately 70 percent of all informal enterprises involve street selling, primarily of food, clothing, and curios.[121] Only an estimated 15–20 percent involve some form of manufacturing enterprise, and sub-contracting seems to be much less common in the informal sector in South Africa than elsewhere. The reason for the low incidence of manufacturing in informal enterprises is explained not only by the apartheid policies

[119] MERG (1993: 149–50).
[120] Greater Alexandra/Sandton UDP Report (1990), cited by Benner (1994).
[121] Riley (1993).

that hindered black urbanization and prohibited blacks from becoming entrepreneurs, but also by the fact that blacks were systematically deprived of access to education, skills and the experience essential for the emergence of dynamic entrepreneurship, and especially informational skills. The South African economy also has high levels of concentration of capital and oligopolistic control.[122]

South Africa has an extremely unequal income distribution, by some measures the most unequal distribution in the world. It has a Gini coefficient of 0.65, compared with 0.61 for Brazil, 0.50 for Mexico, and 0.48 for Malaysia, and coefficients of 0.41 or less for the advanced industrialized countries. The bottom 20 percent of income-earners capture a mere 1.5 percent of national income, while the wealthiest 10 percent of households receive fully 50 percent of national income. Between 36 and 53 percent of South Africans are estimated to live below the poverty line. Poverty is overwhelmingly concentrated in the African and coloured population: 95 percent of the poor are African, and 65 percent of Africans are poor, compared with 33 percent of the coloured population, 2.5 percent for Asians and 0.7 percent for whites.[123]

Racial differences are still a major factor in inequality, despite an increase in the black middle class. For example, the October 1994 household survey of the Central Statistical Service found that only 2 percent of black men were employed in top management, compared with 11 percent of white men. Of this top management, 51 percent of black men earned over R2,000 (roughly US$ 500) a month, compared with 89 percent of white men who earned over R2,000 a month. Some 51 percent of black men were employed as "elementary workers" or "operators and assemblers," compared with 36 percent of white men.[124]

Thus, South Africa's economy and society are less buoyant than they look in comparison with its continental environment, constituted by the poorest countries in the world. Yet we must also consider South Africa's economic relations with its neighbors. The frontline states around Africa suffered a great deal during the anti-apartheid struggle, as South Africa waged a total war for control of the region and punished neighboring countries for their support of the African National Congress. Despite efforts at developing alternative transport routes and diversifying their trade relations, most southern African states remained heavily dependent on their relationship with South Africa throughout the 1980s. Starting in the early 1990s, the focus

---

[122]   Rogerson (1993); Manning (1993); Manning and Mashigo (1994).
[123]   South African Government (1996a).
[124]   South African Government (1996b).

shifted towards an evaluation of the extent to which South Africa could become a "growth engine" for the whole region. The entire southern Africa region is integrated, via South Africa, with most transport routes running through South Africa, and with many of the surrounding countries part of an extended migrant labor force for South African industries. For example, a total of 45 percent of the mining workforce in 1994 of 368,463 workers were foreign workers. This represents a decline from a peak in 1974 when 77 percent of all mine workers were foreign. Estimates of the number of undocumented people in South Africa from neighboring countries range widely. The South African Police Services estimate the number to be between 5.5 million and 8 million people. The Human Sciences Research Council calculated a similar figure of between 5 and 8 million.[125]

The unevenness of the relationship between South Africa and its neighbors is clear. The 11 countries of southern Africa have a combined population of 130 million people, but over 40 million of these live in South Africa. South Africa alone accounts for 80 percent of the entire area's GDP. South Africans are, on average, 36 times richer than Mozambicans. South African exports to the region are eight times bigger than the traffic in the other direction. There are, however, talks of regional integration as a free trade bloc. Efforts are underway to rebuild railways devastated by the war in Mozambique and to rebuild Mozambique's ports to handle exports from Zimbabwe, Botswana, and Zambia. However, looking at the differential economic structure between South Africa and its neighbors, two observations bear considerable significance: (a) all economies, including South Africa, are by and large commodity dependent in their export earnings; and (b) with the exception of South Africa's minuscule satellites, Botswana and Lesotho, there is little manufacturing capacity that could provide an export base for the large South African market. Indeed, trade data reveal that South African companies take over most of the limited import market capacity of neighboring countries.

Thus, in strictly economic terms, there is little complementarity between South Africa and its African environment. If anything, there will be competition in some key industries, such as global tourism. South Africa does not have the manufacturing and technological base to represent by itself a substantial center of accumulation on a scale large enough to propel development in its wake. Indeed, it has substantial social and economic problems that will require employment policies oriented toward its citizen population, with potentially

[125] South African Government (1996a).

disastrous consequences for migrants from other countries, whose remittances are a critical source of hard currency for the neighboring economies. The real problem for South Africa is how to avoid being pushed aside itself from the harsh competition in the new global economy, once its economy is open. Thus, regional cooperation programs may help the development of a transportation and technological infrastructure in the neighboring countries; and some spill-over from South Africa into southern Africa (for instance, investing in mining resources and in tourism) will certainly alleviate extreme conditions of poverty, as is already the case in Namibia, Botswana, and Mozambique. However, the vision of a new South Africa becoming the engine of development for much of the continent, through its multilayered incorporation into the global economy (in an African version of the "flying geese" pattern so much liked by Japanese strategists), seems, at close examination, utterly unrealistic. If the political fate of South Africa is indeed linked to its African identity, its developmental path continues to diverge from its ravaged neighbors – unless the end of the gold rush, a lagging technological capability, and increasing social and ethnic tensions push South Africa toward the abyss of social exclusion from which the African National Congress fought so bravely to escape.

Out of Africa or back to Africa? The politics and economics of self-reliance

Anthropologist Ida Susser, returning from her field trip in the Kalahari Desert, in Namibia, in 1996, reports that the lives of farmers and farm laborers go on, surviving in the interstices of the state. Their meager subsistence is covered on a day-to-day basis. There are no apparent signs of social disintegration and mass starvation: there is poverty, but not destitution.[126] They may not be representative of the diversity of subsistence economies that still allow survival for a sizeable proportion of Africans around the continent. Yet could these subsistence economies, and the traditional communities with which they are associated, constitute a refuge against the whirlwind of destruction and disintegration that blows across Africa? In fact, a growing number of voices in the intellectual and political world of Africa, or among those concerned with Africa, call for a reconstruction of African societies on the basis of self-reliance.[127] It would not imply remaining attached to primitive economies and to traditional societies, but to

[126] Susser, personal communication (1996).
[127] Davidson (1992, 1994); Aina (1993); Wa Mutharika (1995).

build from the bottom up, gaining access to modernity through a different path, fundamentally rejecting the values and goals predominant in today's global capitalism. Strong arguments for this position can be found in the current experiences of technological/economic marginalization of Africa, the rise of the predatory state, and the failure of IMF/World Bank-inspired adjustment policies, both in economic and in social terms. An alternative model of development, one that would in fact be more socially and environmentally sustainable, is not a utopia, and there is an abundance of realistic, technically sound proposals for self-reliant development models in a number of countries, as well as strategies for Africa-centered regional cooperation. In most cases, they assume the necessary partial de-linking of African economies from global networks of capital accumulation, given the consequences of current asymmetrical linkages, as presented in this chapter. However, there is a fundamental obstacle to the implementation of strategies of self-reliance: the interests and values of the majority of Africa's political elites and their networks of patronage. I have shown how and why what is a human tragedy for most Africans continues to represent a source of wealth and privilege for the elites. This perverted political system has been historically produced, and is structurally maintained by the European/American powers, and by the fragmented incorporation of Africa into global capitalist networks. It is precisely this selective articulation of elites and valuable assets, together with the social exclusion of most people and the economic devaluation of most natural resources, that is specific to the newest expression of Africa's tragedy.

Thus, the de-linking of Africa in its own terms would take a revolution, in the oldest, political meaning of this word – an unlikely event in the foreseeable future, considering the ethnic fragmentation of the population, and the people's devastating experience *vis à vis* most of their leaders and saviors. Yet the writing is on the wall if we refer to historical experience, according to which there is no oppression that is not met with resistance. As for the social and political outcomes of this resistance, uncertainty and experimentation are the only possible assessments, as the process of change muddles through the collective experience of rage, conflict, struggle, hope, failure, and compromise.

The New American Dilemma: Inequality, Urban Poverty, and Social Exclusion in the Information Age

The United States features the largest and most technologically advanced economy in the world. It is the society that first experienced the structural and organizational transformations characteristic of the network society, at the dawn of the Information Age. But it is also a society that has displayed, in the past two decades, a substantial increase in social inequality, polarization, poverty, and misery. To be sure, America is a highly specific society, with a historical pattern of racial discrimination, with a peculiar urban form – the inner city – and with a deep-seated, ideological and political reluctance to government regulation, and to the welfare state. None the less, its experience with social inequality and social exclusion, in the formative stage of the network society, may be a sign of the times to come in other areas of the world as well, and particularly in Europe, for two main reasons. First, the dominant ideology and politics of most capitalist countries emphasize deregulation of markets, and flexibility of management, in a sort of "recapitalization of capitalism" that closely echoes many of the strategies, policies, and management decisions experienced in America in the 1980s and 1990s.[128] Secondly, and perhaps more decisively, the growing integration of capital, markets, and firms, in a shared global economy, makes it extremely difficult for some countries to depart sharply from the institutional/macroeconomic environment of other areas – particularly if one of these "other areas" is as large and as central to the global economy as the United States. For European or Japanese firms, capital, and labor markets to operate under different rules, and with higher production costs, than firms based in the United States, one of two conditions has to be met. Their markets, including their capital and services markets, have to be protected. Or, else, productivity has to be higher than in America. But we know that the productivity of American labor, while lagging in productivity growth in the past two decades, is still the highest in the world in comparative terms. As for market protection, while it is still largely the case for Japan, new trade pacts, and increasing mobility of capital, are paving the way for a relative equalization of labor conditions across OECD countries. Thus, while each society will reckon with its own problems according to its social structure and political process, what happens in America regarding inequality, poverty, and social exclusion may be taken as a probable structural outcome of trends embedded in informational capitalism when market forces remain largely unchecked. Indeed, comparative studies show similar trends (but different levels) in the growth of poverty in Western Europe and the United States, particularly in the United Kingdom.[129] While sharp inequality between the upper and lower levels of society is a universal trend, it is particularly blatant in the United States.

[128]   Brown and Crompton (1994); Hutton (1996).
[129]   Funken and Cooper (1995); Hutton (1996).

To ground the discussion of the social implications of informational capitalism in advanced societies, I shall proceed with an empirical survey, as succinct as possible, of the evolution of inequality, poverty, and social exclusion in America during the past two decades, assessing these trends within the framework of categories proposed at the outset of this chapter.

Dual America

In the 1990s, American capitalism seems to have succeeded in becoming a most profitable system, under the conditions of restructuring, informationalism, and globalization.[130] After-tax profit rates at business-cycle peaks went up from 4.7 percent in 1973 to 5.1 percent in 1979, stabilized in the 1980s and then went up to 7 percent in 1995. Stock market values reached, in 1997, their highest historical level. Although they do go up and down, unless there is a catastrophic collapse of financial markets (always a possibility), the average plateau of the Dow Jones index seems to be established at an increasingly high level. Not only is capital rewarded, capitalist managers are also doing well. Counting in 1995 dollars, average total pay for chief executive officers (CEOs) in major US companies in the US went up from $1,269,000 a year in 1973 to $3,180,000 in 1989, and to $4,367,000 in 1995. The ratio of total CEO pay to total worker pay climbed from 44.8 times more in 1973 to 172.5 times more in 1995.

At the same time, median family income stagnated in the 1970s and 1980s, and declined in the first half of the 1990s (see figure 2.5). This is particularly the result of a decline in real average weekly earnings for production and non-supervisory workers that went from $479.44 in 1973 to $395.37 in 1995. Indeed, most families could cope only if and when two members were contributing to the household budget, as the median percentage contribution of working wives grew from around 26 percent of family income in 1979 to 32 percent in 1992, so that household structure becomes a major source of income difference between families. The decline of hourly wages for men was particularly concentrated among the lowest paid workers, while the highest paid (top percentile) were the only group that did not experience a decline (figure 2.6a). Yet even the most educated groups of male workers have, on average, experienced a decline in real wages: thus college-educated men with 1–5 years of experience saw their

---

[130]   The main source of data for this section on "Dual America" is the excellent annual study by Mishel et al. (1996), which provides their own insightful elaboration of reliable statistics. Unless otherwise indicated, data cited in the text are from this source.

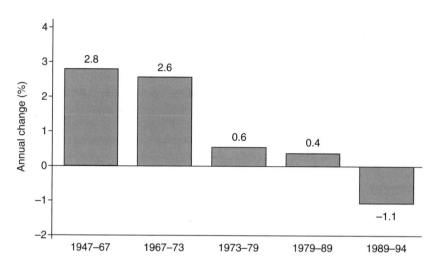

Figure 2.5 Annual growth of median family income, 1947–94
Source: US Bureau of the Census (1996), elaborated by Mishel et al.
(1996: 44)

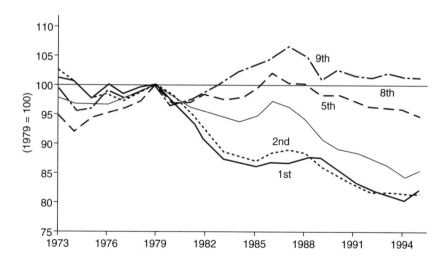

Figure 2.6a Hourly wages for men by wage percentile, 1973–95
Source: Mishel et al. (1996: 143)

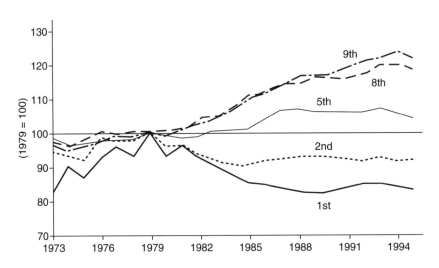

Figure 2.6b   Hourly wages for women by wage percentile, 1973–95
Source: Mishel et al. (1996: 145)

hourly wages decline by 10.7 percent in 1979–95. Only college-educated women have seen their wages increase, substantially for the experienced group, in this period, but they still, on average, lag behind the level of their male counterparts (figure 2.6b).

The average decline in income has affected differentially the upper, middle, and lower strata. Social inequality, as measured by the Gini coefficient, rose from 0.399 in 1967 to 0.450 in 1995. Furthermore, inequality has taken the shape of polarization: in 1973–95 the richer families increased their average annual income the fastest, while the poorer ones saw their income decline the most (see figure 2.7). According to Wolf's calculations,[131] a similar concentration and polarization exists in the distribution of wealth, and in its evolution in 1983–92. Thus, counting in 1992 dollars, while the median household's wealth in 1992 was $43,000, the average wealth for the top 1 percent of the distribution was $7,925,000. The richest 1 percent increased their wealth by 28.3 percent in 1983–92, while the bottom 40 percent of American families saw their assets *decline* by 49.7 percent during the same period. So, there is not only increasing inequality, but also increasing polarization. Poverty has also become widespread. The percentage of persons whose income is below the poverty line increased from 11.1 percent in 1973 to 14.5 percent in 1994: that is, over 38 million Americans, two-thirds of whom are white,

[131]   Wolf (1996).

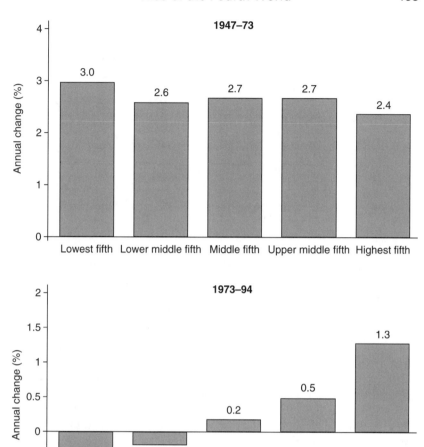

Figure 2.7   Average annual change in family income, 1947–94
Source: Mishel et al. (1996: 55)

including a substantial proportion in rural areas. Misery, or extreme poverty, has expanded even faster. Defining this category as those poor persons with incomes below 50 percent of the poverty level (in 1994: $7,571 annual income for a family of four), they accounted for almost 30 percent of all poor in 1975, and they reached 40.5 percent of all poor in 1994, which is about 15.5 million Americans.

The causes of increasing inequality, polarization, poverty, and misery in informational America are the object of raging debate, and I do not pretend to settle the question in a few paragraphs. I can, however, suggest some hypotheses relating to the main line of argument in this book. Traditional interpretations, from orthodox neoclassical or Marxist perspectives, do not seem to account for the size and pace of the phenomenon. The thesis of "skills mismatch," according to which inequality is a short-term phenomenon related to income premium for skills, which will even out over time as more are educated for current technology, has been empirically refuted by a number of experts, including the statistical work by Morris et al. that finds support, instead, for the hypothesis that relates polarization to the pattern of occupational growth characterizing the service/technology intensive economy.[132] As for the orthodox Marxist view of capitalist exploitation, it still has to explain why capitalism in the 1990s generates more inequality than in the 1950s or the 1960s, and why the lowest producers of value, the unskilled workers, are those that have experienced the steepest decline in their real wages.

To make a long story short, I think that empirical evidence supports an interpretation that links the growth of inequality and poverty in America to four interrelated processes: (a) deindustrialization, as a consequence of globalization of industrial production, labor, and markets; (b) individualization and networking of the labor process, induced by informationalization; (c) incorporation of women into paid labor in the informational economy, under conditions of patriarchal discrimination; and (d) the crisis of the patriarchal family. To these structural processes, I must add the socio-political factors that, by ensuring the domination of unrestricted market forces, accentuate the logic of inequality. However, the generalization of these pro-capitalist policies and ideologies, in very different institutional contexts and political cultures around the world, make me think that the above-mentioned structural trends exercise tremendous pressure in this direction, until and unless, checked by forces emerging for the new civil society still in the making.[133]

How do these mechanisms operate to induce increasing inequality and poverty? Deindustrialization, as a result of the geographical shift (not disappearance) of industrial production to other areas of the world, eliminates manufacturing jobs – the kind of semi-skilled, decently paid jobs that constituted the backbone of working America. The key issue here has been the dismantlement of the economic and organizational basis of organized labor, thus weakening labor unions and depriving workers of their instrument of collective defense. After

[132] Morris et al. (1994).
[133] Brown and Crompton (1994); Navarro (1997).

all, it was the existence of strong labor unions that explains why manufacturing jobs were better paid than service jobs at equivalent levels of skill.

The second mechanism, the individualization of work, and the concomitant transformation of firms under the form of the network enterprise, is the most important factor inducing inequality (see volume I, chapters 3 and 4). This is, on the one hand, because workers, as a group, are placed in highly specific working conditions for each one of them – and thus are left to their individual fates. On the other hand, the individualized bargaining process between employers and workers leads to an extraordinary diversity of labor arrangements and puts a decisive premium on workers who have unique skills, yet makes many other workers easily replaceable. Furthermore, by denying life-long career patterns, the successful worker today may become the discarded worker tomorrow, so that, overall, only those workers who are consistently at the top of the ladder, for a long enough period, can accumulate assets. This privileged minority has to do with a high level of education. But it does not follow that education will provide the solution, either for individuals or for social equality. It is a necessary, but not sufficient, condition to prosper in the informational economy. Data show that male college graduates have also seen their real wages stagnate in the past decade. The rewarded ones constitute a different group, hardly captured in traditional statistical categories. They are those workers/performers who, for whatever reason, provide an edge to business in their specific field of activity: sometimes it has more to do with image-making than with substance. This embodying of value-added induces an increasing disparity between a few, highly paid workers/collaborators/consultants, and a growing mass of individuals who, because they are individuals, must usually accept the lowest common denominator of what the market offers them. Such a disparity induces an increasingly skewed distribution of incomes and assets.

The massive incorporation of women into the informational economy has been critical in allowing the economy to operate efficiently at a much lower cost. While the wages of educated women have gone up substantially in America (particularly for white women), they are still, on average, about 66 percent of those of their equivalent male workers, so that the overall share of wages on total GDP has declined. It does not follow that women constitute the success story of workers in the informational economy. Indeed, the crisis of the patriarchal family (partly related to women's growing economic autonomy) has had punitive effects on most people, but particularly on women, and single mothers. Indeed, studies by Eggebeen and Lichter, Rodgers, and Lerman show the close connection between changing family structure and increasing poverty for women and their children.[134] Lerman estimates that the trend away from marriage toward single-parent households accounted for almost half the increase in child income inequality and for the entire rise in child poverty rates between 1971 and 1989.[135]

The poverty rate of persons not living in families grew by 2.2 percent in 1989–94 to reach 21.5 percent of this group, accounting for 14.5 percent of all persons. As for female-headed families, their poverty rate also increased by 2.2 percent in the same period, to reach, in 1994, 38.6 percent of all female-headed families. As a result, between 1973 and 1993, the number of white children living in poverty increased by 52.6 percent, for Hispanic children by 116 percent, and for black children by 26.9 percent.[136] Overall, 21.8 percent of American children were living in poverty in 1994, while the proportion for black children was 43.8 percent.

What characterizes the so-called "new poverty" is that it widely affects working people and families, who simply cannot maintain a livelihood on the basis of their earnings. As shown in figure 2.8, the share of workers earning poverty-level wages increased substantially for men, between 1973 and 1995, while decreasing for women, so that by 1995, almost 30 percent of American workers were earning poverty-level wages. One of the most striking faces of this new poverty is homelessness, which skyrocketed in the 1980s in American cities, and remains at a high level in the 1990s. Estimates of the homeless population vary widely. The 1994 Clinton Administration's "Priority: Home!" report estimated that the number of homeless in the second half of the 1980s was somewhere between 5 and 9 million people, and that about 7 percent of American adults have been homeless at some point during their lives. This estimate is probably exaggerated, but the most important matter is that a large proportion, and the fastest growing segment, of the homeless population comprises families with children. Indeed, they represent the majority in some cities, such as New York, where, in the early 1990s, families made up about three-quarters of the homeless.[137] The issue is that once poverty becomes shaped as misery and social exclusion – when life is on the street – stigma sits in, and the destruction of personality and social networks deepens the situation of distress.[138] This is how the set of relationships between dominant trends of informational capitalism, inequality, and

---

[134]   Eggebeen and Lichter (1991); Lerman (1996); Rodgers (1996).
[135]   Lerman (1996).
[136]   Cook and Brown (1994).
[137]   Da Costa Nunez (1996: 3–8).
[138]   Susser (1996).

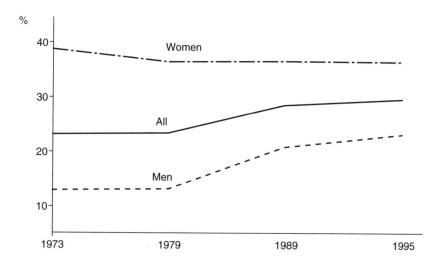

Figure 2.8   Share of workers earning poverty-level wages, 1973–95
Source: Mishel et al. (1996: 153)

poverty ultimately lead to the process of social exclusion, as epitomized in the dereliction of life in America's inner-city ghettos.

The inner-city ghetto as a system of social exclusion

The daily injuries of life in the ghetto constitute one of the oldest, and
most poignant, American social problems. For decades, the urban
social crisis, epitomized in inner-city areas segregated by race and
class, has been the focus of an array of public policies, as well as of
heated political debates, besides providing the ground for a distinguished research tradition in urban sociology.[139] And yet, in this end
of millennium, inner-city ghettos, particularly black ghettos, but also
some Latino ghettos, such as the one in East Los Angeles, concentrate
the worst expressions of inequality, discrimination, human misery,
and social crisis precisely at the time of the rise of informationalism
in America. Indeed, it can be argued that the social, economic, and
housing conditions in most inner-city ghettos have considerably
worsened over the past three decades, in spite (or because?) of a
sustained effort in urban social programs and welfare policies.[140] I

[139]   Drake and Cayton (1945).
[140]   Jones (1992); Massey and Denton (1993); Gans (1995); Van Kempen and
Marcuse (1996).

propose the hypothesis, along with William J. Wilson and other social scientists,[141] that there is a systemic relationship between the structural transformations I have analyzed as characteristic of the new, network society and the growing dereliction of the ghetto: the constitution of an informational/global economy, under the conditions of capitalist restructuring; the crisis of the nation-state, with one of its main manifestations in the crisis of the welfare state; the demise of the patriarchal family without being replaced by an alternative form of conviviality and socialization; the emergence of a global, yet decentralized, criminal economy, penetrating society and institutions at all levels, and taking over certain territories from which to operate; and the process of political alienation, and communal retrenchment, among the large segments of the population that are poor and feel disfranchised. Racial discrimination and spatial segregation are still major factors in the formation/reinforcement of ghettos as systems of social exclusion. But their effects take new meaning, and become increasingly devastating, under the conditions of informationalism – for reasons that I shall try to spell out in the following paragraphs.

To do so, I will rely on the powerful, empirically grounded analysis, proposed by William J. Wilson in his 1996 book *When Work Disappears*. However, while I find his interpretation convincing in its main thrust, I will recast it in my own terms, both to link up with the theory presented in this book, and to avoid making Wilson responsible for my own reading of his findings. I shall also use other sources when necessary.

The formation of large ghetto areas in the inner cities of metropolitan America is the result of a series of well-known processes.[142] Mechanization of Southern agriculture and the mobilization of an industrial labor force, during and after World War II, led to massive migration of black laborers who concentrated in the neighborhoods left vacant by the suburbanization process stimulated by federal housing and transportation policies. Massive displacement by the federal urban renewal program to preserve the business and cultural centers in the metropolitan cores further increased the concentration of blacks and other minorities in the most dilapidated neighborhoods. The location of public housing projects contributed to segregation. Slum landlordism and residential abandonment accelerated the process of escape from poor inner-city areas for whoever had the opportunity. The organization of schooling on the basis of residential location, in a decentralized system that split cities from

---

[141]   Wilson (1987, 1996); Wacquant (1993, 1996); Susser (1996).
[142]   Castells (1977: 379–427).

suburbs, concentrated disadvantaged children in an under-funded, under-staffed public school system in the inner city, which soon deteriorated. The perversion of the Jeffersonian tradition of local self-governance led to fiscal disparity between needs and resources, with suburbs enjoying higher resources and cities suffering greater needs. This is the pattern of formation of the classic American ghetto, whose social inequities triggered social revolts and political protests in the 1960s. The social policies that responded to grassroots pressure reduced institutional discrimination, somewhat empowered African-American political elites, and helped individual upward mobility for the most educated African-Americans, most of whom moved out of the inner city. Yet the residents of ghettos saw their condition dramatically deteriorate over the next quarter of the century. Why so?

Wilson anchors his interpretation, and I concur, in the transformation of work and employment under the conditions of informationalization and globalization of the economy. Not that new technologies induce unemployment: I showed in volume I, chapter 4 that both the empirical record and analytical insights reject the simplistic assumption of machines phasing out work and workers on a grand scale. Indeed, around the world, there is an unprecedented expansion of paid labor via the massive incorporation of women into the labor force, and the displacement of agricultural workers toward manufacturing, services, and the urban informal economy. It is precisely this globalization of manufacturing, and outsourcing of production in lower-cost areas, that greatly contributes to the elimination of those jobs that are costlier to perform in America, but not skilled enough to require location in a highly industrialized environment. Informationalization spurs job growth in the higher tier of skills in America, while globalization offshores low-skilled manufacturing jobs to newly industrializing countries.[143] Thus, in America, there is indeed a substantial reduction of manufacturing jobs, and particularly of low-skilled jobs, precisely the kind of jobs that brought black migrants into the urban areas and constituted the stable, hard core of their employment. Many of the new jobs of the informational economy require higher education and verbal/relational skills that inner-city public schools rarely provide. Besides, new manufacturing, and an increasing proportion of service jobs, have become suburbanized, decreasing accessibility for inner-city residents. Thus, there is a growing mismatch between the profile of many new jobs and the profile of poor blacks living in the inner city.[144]

Nevertheless, there are other sources of low-paid jobs, particularly

143   Carnoy et al. (1997).
144   Kasarda (1990, 1995).

in social services and in the public sector. Thanks to affirmative action policies, these are, indeed, the main employment opportunities for inner-city women, including black women.[145] Low-educated black men, however, are less likely to obtain these jobs. Furthermore, the shrinkage of public employment, following the retrenchment of social services in the past two decades, has reduced the availability of public jobs, and increased educational requirements for applicants.

There are also menial jobs in low-skill service activities (for example, janitorial services, food services, informal construction, repair and maintenance). Why black men do not easily get these jobs is less clear in Wilson's analysis. In my view, racial discrimination could be a reason. But Wilson does not find supportive evidence for it, emphasizing instead, for instance, that black employers are also reluctant to hire inner-city black men. Wilson hints at two possible factors. On the one hand, comparison with the much better performance of Mexican immigrants in the labor market for low-skill service activities seems to result from the willingness of Mexicans, and other immigrant groups, to accept low pay and hard work, under discriminatory conditions which are imposed upon them because of their vulnerability, often linked to their undocumented status. Thus, it would seem that the standards of work and pay that many poor blacks set for themselves, often resulting in complaints and dissatisfaction while performing a job, backfires in the perception of their prospective employers, inducing the notion of inner-city black males as being "difficult workers." Furthermore, new service jobs often require relational abilities that seem to be lacking among poor blacks, particularly among men, thus undermining their chances of employment. I would consider widespread racism among the population at large, particularly aimed at blacks, as an important factor, if not the only one, in the greater difficulty experienced in relating to a black employee outside a context of black-majority clientele.[146] Thus, although it may be true that deteriorating schools do not prepare the low-skilled labor force for relational and informational activities in the new service economy, this new handicap may interact with an older source of exclusion, namely the racial barriers that bias social interaction. I would also add that the crisis of family life, and the instability of living and working patterns in the ghetto, strongly interact with the difficulty for black men, particularly young black men, of fitting into the pattern of social acceptability and work ethic that still underlies hiring

[145]   Carnoy (1994).
[146]   West (1993).

decisions in many businesses. Finally, poverty and the family crisis in the black ghetto lead to an impoverishment of social networks, thus diminishing the chances of finding a job via personal connections. This, as Wilson argues, and as Alejandro Portes and his collaborators have demonstrated,[147] is in sharp contrast to the experience of Mexican and Latino immigrants/minorities, whose stronger family structure and broad social networks provide considerable support in job referrals and information.

As a result of these mutually reinforcing trends, formal work by and large disappears, particularly for men, and even more so for young men, in black ghetto areas. Wilson emphasizes that, in addition to high rates of unemployment in these areas, particularly among the youth, there is a considerable number of adults who have dropped out of the labor force, and are not even looking for a job. He cites findings of his studies on Woodlawn and Oakland (two poor neighborhoods on Chicago's South Side) where, in 1990, only 37 percent and 23 percent respectively of adults were working in a given week.[148] Furthermore, most poor men are also excluded from the programs of the urban welfare state.[149]

It does not follow that most adults are inactive or without access to sources of income. The informal economy, and particularly the criminal economy, become prevalent in many poor neighborhoods, which become the shopfloor of these activities, and increasingly influence the habits and culture of segments of their population. The explosion of crack cocaine's traffic and consumption in the black ghettos in the 1980s was a turning point for many communities.[150] Gangs became important forms of youth organization and patterns of behavior.[151] Guns are, at the same time, working tools, signs of self-esteem, and motives for peers' respect.[152] Widespread presence of guns calls for more guns, as everybody rushes to self-defense, after police gave up serious law enforcement in a number of poor neighborhoods.[153] Economic transactions in these inner-city areas often become marked by the criminal economy, as a source of work and income, as demand-generating activities, and as the operational unit for protection/taxation in the informal economy. Economic competition is often played out through violence, thus further destroying

[147]   Portes (1995); Wilson (1996).
[148]   Wilson (1996: 23).
[149]   Susser (1993).
[150]   Bourgois and Dunlap (1993); Bourgois (1995).
[151]   Sanchez Jankowski (1991).
[152]   Wilson (1996).
[153]   Susser (1995).

community life, and increasingly identifying gangs with surviving social networks, with the crucial exception of community-based churches.

The crisis of the ghetto goes beyond the issue of formal unemployment versus informal/criminal employment. It affects the patterns of family formation, in the context of the crisis of patriarchalism that I analyzed in volume II, chapter 4. Trends toward increasing single parenthood and births out of wedlock are, by no means, exclusively linked to poverty or to African-American culture. Indeed, in 1993, in America, 27 percent of all children under the age of 18 were living with a single parent, 21 percent of white children, 32 percent of Hispanic children, and 57 percent of black children. Between 1980 and 1992, the rate of births out of wedlock increased by 9 percent for blacks, but by a staggering 94 percent for whites.[154] This differential growth is due, partly, to the traditionally high rate of incidence of births out of marriage among African-Americans. Indeed, the crisis of the black family has been a critical argument of sociologists and social policy-makers for a long time. Yet, it could also be argued that, instead of seeing it as a symptom of social deviance, it could reflect a pioneering effort by black women to take control of their own lives, without begging men's lagging responsibility. Whatever the historical/cultural reasons for the weakness of the patriarchal family among urban African-Americans, this pattern, seen in historical perspective, seems to be a forerunner of the times to come for many Americans, as well as for many people in the world (see volume II, chapter 4).

A number of factors, identified by Wilson, seem to concur toward the single female-centeredness of a majority of families with children in poor black neighborhoods. First, there is the lack of employment opportunities for young black males, leading to uncertainty in their income, and thus undermining their ability to make commitments. I would also add that, given the high likelihood of imprisonment, injury, or even death among ghetto youth, in some cases it could actually be considered a responsible attitude not to set up a family, whose future care is at best uncertain. Secondly, Wilson documents, on the basis of his team's ethnographic studies, an extraordinary degree of distrust, and even hostility, between young women and men in the black neighborhoods that were studied. My only caveat on this most important observation is that similar studies among middle-class whites in large metropolitan areas may yield similar results. The difference, however, is in the coherent attitude of many young

[154] Wilson (1996: 87).

African-American women in deciding not to marry, and to have babies out of wedlock. This decision, Wilson hints, in line with Drake and Cayton's classic study of the black ghetto,[155] may be related to the lack of economic rewards and expectation of social mobility linked to marriage, in contrast with marriage patterns in the white middle class. With no apparent economic and social benefits from the marriage, and with a long-standing distrust of men's commitment, poor young black women have little incentive to marry, and to have to cope with men's problems in addition to their own. Thus, while in 1993, 9 percent of American children were living with a never-married parent, the proportion for black children was 31 percent, but it was even higher for poor blacks. According to Wilson's data, in Chicago's inner-city neighborhoods, almost 60 percent of black adults aged 18–44 years have never been married, and among black parents living in high-poverty areas, only 15.6 percent are married.[156] Why do black women, and particularly very young women, still choose to have children? It seems to be, primarily, a matter of self-esteem, of gaining respect, of becoming someone in their social environment, besides having someone of their own and a tangible goal in life. While most teenage pregnancies are the byproduct of love/sex without further thinking, the decision to keep the baby is usually associated with assuming womanhood, in contrast with the scarce chance of receiving education or a rewarding job under the conditions of ghetto life.[157] There seems to be little evidence to support the conservative argument according to which welfare provisions to help single mothers and their children offer an incentive to single motherhood.[158] However, once women have children on their own, fundamentally for personal reasons, it becomes increasingly difficult for them to leave the welfare trap.[159] This is because the kind of jobs they can access are so lowly paid that they cannot match the cost of child care, transportation, housing, and health care (usually not provided by most of their employers) with their wage. Thus, as difficult as it is to survive on welfare, it becomes a better option than working, particularly when health care for the children is taken into consideration. The deep cuts in welfare to single mothers with children mandated as of January 1997 are likely to have devastating effects on poor women and their children, thus assuring the further deterioration of social life in poor neighborhoods well into the twenty-first century.

[155]   Drake and Cayton (1945).
[156]   Wilson (1996: 89).
[157]   Plotnick (1990).
[158]   Wilson (1996: 94–5).
[159]   Susser and Kreniske (1987).

With many young men out of jobs and out of families, often reduced to the opportunities provided by the criminal economy, work ethics and job patterns hardly fit the expectations of prospective employers, thus providing a material basis to reinforce prejudicial attitudes toward employing inner-city black men, ultimately sentencing their fate. Thus, there is a link between joblessness and poverty for black men, but the link is specified by racial discrimination and by their rage against this discrimination.

Spatial structure interacts decisively with the economic, social, and cultural processes I have described. Urban segregation is reinforced by the increasing separation between the logic of the space of flows and the logic of the space of places I have identified as characteristic of the network society (volume I, chapter 6). The ghetto as a place has become increasingly confined in its poverty and marginality.[160] A decisive factor in this sense has been the upward mobility of a significant proportion of black urban families which, helped by politics, education, affirmative action programs, and their own effort, has earned them their place in mainstream society. In their vast majority, they left the inner city to save their children from a system that was reproducing social exclusion and stigma. Yet, by saving themselves individually, they left behind, trapped into the crumbling structures of the ghetto, most of the one-third of poor blacks (and over 40 percent of black children) that now form the most destitute segment of the American population. Furthermore, the emergence of the space of flows, using telecommunications and transportation to link up valuable places in a non-contiguous pattern, has allowed the reconfiguration of metropolitan areas around selective connections of strategically located activities, bypassing undesirable areas, left to themselves. Suburbanization first, ex-urban sprawl later, and the formation of "Edge City"'s peripheral nodes (see volume I, chapter 6) allowed the metropolitan world to exclude entirely inner-city ghettos from their function and meaning, disassociating space and society along the lines of urban dualism and social exclusion.[161] The spatial confinement of poor blacks replicated their growing exclusion from the formal labor market, diminished their educational opportunities, dilapidated their housing and urban environment, left their neighborhoods under the threat of criminal gangs, and, because of their symbolic association with crime, violence, and drugs, delegitimized their political options. American inner-city ghettos, and particularly the black ghetto, has become part of the earthly hell being built to punish the dangerous classes of the undeserving poor. And

[160]   Wacquant (1996).
[161]   Mollenkopf and Castells (1991).

because a large proportion of black children are growing up in these neighborhoods, America is systemically reproducing its deepest pattern of social exclusion, inter-racial hostility, and interpersonal violence.

When the underclass goes to hell

The ultimate expression of social exclusion is the physical and institutional confinement of a segment of society either in prison or under the supervision of the justice system, in probation and parole. America has the dubious distinction of being the country with the highest percentage of prison population in the world. The fastest growth of incarceration rates took place from 1980, a sharp increase *vis à vis* historical tendencies (see figure 2.9). On January 1, 1996, there were almost 1.6 million inmates in prisons and jails (local, state, and federal), and an additional 3.8 million people on probation and parole, giving a total of 5.4 million, representing 2.8 percent of all adults, under correctional supervision. This number has almost tripled since 1980, growing at an average annual rate of 7.4 percent (see figure 2.10). The proportion of inmates to general population in 1996 was 600 inmates per 100,000 US residents, a rate that has nearly doubled in ten years. Federal prisons in 1996 were operating at 26 percent over their capacity, and state prisons at between 14 and 25 percent over capacity.[162]

This prison population is socially and ethnically biased: in 1991, 53 percent of inmates were black, and 46 percent white, the proportion of blacks continuing to climb in the 1990s. Hispanics made up 13 percent of the prison population, and 14 percent of the jail population. Blacks also accounted for 40 percent of Death Row inmates, The ratio of incarceration rates of blacks *vis à vis* whites in 1990 was 6.44. Evidence shows that this is largely due to discrimination in sentencing, and preventive imprisonment, rather than because of the frequency or characteristics of the crimes committed.[163] As for adults on parole, in 1995, 49 percent were black, and 21 percent Hispanic.[164]

Let us look at the evolution of the incarceration system in a close up of California, the state that holds the distinction of having the largest prison population in the United States.[165] The number of prisoners in the state increased fourfold between 1980 and 1991. The total rate of

[162] Department of Justice (1996); Gilliard and Beck (1996).
[163] Tonry (1995).
[164] Department of Justice (1996).
[165] Hewitt et al. (1994); Koetting and Schiraldi (1994); Schiraldi (1994); Connolly et al. (1996).

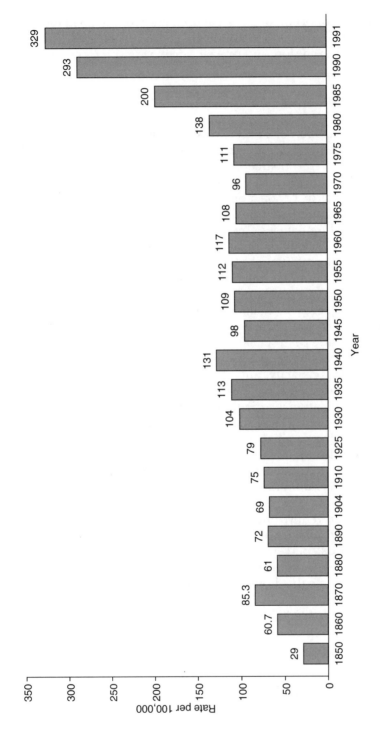

Figure 2.9 Incarceration rates in US, 1850–1991

Sources: Margaret Werner Cahalan, *Historical Corrections Statistics, 1850–1984* (Rockville, MD: Westat, 1986); Bureau of Justice Statistics, *Sourcebook of Criminal Justice Statistics, 1991* (Washington, DC: US Department of Justice 1992); Bureau of Justice Statistics, *Prisoners in 1991* (Washington, DC: US Department of Justice, 1992), elaborated by Gilliard and Beck (1996)

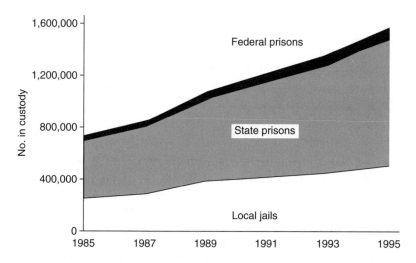

Figure 2.10 Number of inmates held in state or federal prisons or in local jails in US, 1985–95 (Figures include prisoners in custody, prisoners in local jails because of prison overcrowding, and prisoners supervised elsewhere, such as in treatment centers. Counts for 1994 and 1995 exclude persons who were supervised outside a jail. Total of people in custody of state, federal, or local jurisdictions per 100,000 US residents)
Source: Bulletin of the US Bureau of Justice Statistics, August 1996

incarceration in the mid-1990s was 626 per 100,000 people, which was nearly double that of South Africa or Russia. The incarceration rate for whites was 215 per 100,000, but for blacks it was 1,951 per 100,000. In 1990s California, about four in ten young African-American men were under some form of criminal justice control. These figures are particularly striking when compared with those for African-Americans in college education. In the early 1990s, 27,707 African-American students attended a four-year public university course in California, while 44,792 were in prison. The California Department of Corrections reported in 1996 that its prisons were operating at 194 percent capacity, and estimated that 24 new prisons would have to be built by 2005 to keep pace with the rate of incarceration. Projections were for the occupancy rate to reach 256 percent of capacity by 1996. The system was entirely geared toward punishment, and presumed deterrence. Rehabilitation as a goal of imprisonment was removed from the California Penal Code in 1977.[166]

[166] Connolly et al. (1996).

Irwin, Austin, Tonry, Welch, and Mergenhagen,[167] among others, have carefully established the profile of the prison population, the reasons for their incarceration, and the social consequences of their imprisonment. They found that the majority of offenders are non-violent. Indeed, in 1990, 28 percent of those sent to prison were admitted for parole violation, in two-thirds of the cases for technical violations of the parole, without committing a crime. For the 68 percent who received a court sentence, about 70 percent were sentenced for non-violent crimes (burglary, drugs possession or trafficking, robbery, public order offenses). In 1993, 26 percent of inmates were in prison for drug-related offenses, up from 8 percent in 1980, while the percentage of those imprisoned for violent offenses (including robbery) dropped from 57 to 45 percent.[168] In their survey, Irwin and Austin found that most crimes were "much pettier than the popular images promoted by those who sensationalize the crime issue . . . Our inner cities actually contain a growing number of young men, mostly non-white, who become involved in unskilled, petty crime because of no avenues to a viable, satisfying conventional life."[169] Indeed, 64 percent of inmates lack a formal high school education, and most of them are "uneducated, unskilled (at crime as well as other pursuits), and highly disorganized persons."[170] There has been a rapid increase in the number of juveniles dealt with in the criminal justice system: 600,000 in 1991, of which 100,000 were in prisons or juvenile detention facilities. Women are only 6 percent of prisoners, but their proportion is sharply up, from 4 percent in 1980; 6 percent of them come to prison pregnant. Most inmates are parents: 78 percent of women and 64 percent of men have children under 18. This, apparently, makes very good business for telephone companies, as inmates call collect to stay in touch with their children, so that, according to a report by *The Wall Street Journal*, a single prison telephone can gross as much as $15,000 a year. Furthermore, jails are dangerous places, plagued by drug consumption and violence, ruled by gangs, sometimes related to prison guards. Health is a major issue. One-third of state prison inmates participate in drug-treatment programs. And almost 3 percent of state prison inmates are HIV-positive, or sick with AIDS. The incidence of tuberculosis is four times higher than for the population at large, and about one-quarter of inmates have some type of clinical psychiatric problem.[171]

[167] Irwin (1985); Irwin and Austin (1994); Tonry (1995); Welch (1994, 1995); Mergenhagen (1996).
[168] Mergenhagen (1996).
[169] Irwin and Austin (1994; 59–60).
[170] Irwin and Austin (1994: 143).
[171] Mergenhagen (1996).

The prison society reproduces, and furthers, the culture of criminality, so that those who end up in prison see their chances of social integration substantially decreased, both because of social stigma and because of their inner injuries. In Irwin and Austin's words, "prisons have become true human warehouses – often highly crowded, violent, and cruel."[172] This, at a very high cost for taxpayers: about $39,000 a year per inmate. As in the old saying of criminologists: it costs more to send a young man to jail than to Yale. The state of California in the 1990s spends as much money on its prisons as its education system (about 9 percent of the state budget on each).

A number of studies has shown the small impact of punishment on the actual incidence of crime.[173] In the words of Robert Gangi, director of the Correctional Association of New York: "building more prisons to address crime is like building more graveyards to address a fatal disease."[174] Yet the mass punishment of social deviance does have a substantial effect, well beyond its instrumental value as a crime deterrent: it marks the boundaries of social exclusion in terms that blame the excluded for their plight, delegitimize their potential rebellion, and confine social problems into a customized hell. The making of a sizeable proportion of the underclass's young men into a dangerous class could well be the most striking expression of the new American dilemma in the Information Age.

Globalization, Over-exploitation, and Social Exclusion: the View from the Children

If any doubts were left about the fact that the main labor issue in the Information Age is not the end of work but the condition of workers, they are definitively settled by the explosion of low-paid, child labor in the past decade. According to the report released by the International Labour Office in November 1996,[175] about 250 million children between the ages of 5 and 14 were working for pay in developing countries, of which 120 million were working full time. These estimates, based on an improved methodology – and counting children of ages 5–10 years for the first time – doubled previous estimates. Some 153 million of these child workers were in Asia, 80 million in Africa, and 17.5 million in Latin America. However, Africa has the highest incidence of child labor, at around 40 percent of

---

[172]   Irwin and Austin (1994: 144).
[173]   Roberts (1994); Lynch and Paterson (1995).
[174]   Cited by Smolowe (1994: 55).
[175]   ILO (1996)

children aged 5–14. A 1995 ILO survey of child labor in Ghana, India, Indonesia, and Senegal found that 25 percent of all children between 5 and 14 years of age had engaged in economic activity, and that around 33 percent did not attend school. ILO also reports, without quantifying, a significant growth in child labor in Eastern European and Asian countries in transition to a market economy.[176] While the overwhelming majority of child workers are in the developing world, the phenomenon is also on the rise in advanced capitalist countries, particularly in the United States, where fast-food outlets prosper on the basis of teenage work, and other businesses – for example, commercial candy sales – are following apace. In 1992, the US Department of Labor registered 19,443 offenses against child labor laws, twice the level of 1980. Besides the main culprit, the fast-food industry, other cases reported concerned immigrant children working illegally in garment factories in Manhattan, in construction works in the Bronx, or on farms in Texas, California, and Florida. The National Safe Workplace Institute estimates that every year 300 children are killed and 70,000 injured on the job. Dumaine, citing experts, attributes the rise in child labor in America to the deterioration of working-class life conditions, and to increased undocumented immigration.[177] Lavalette found a similar expansion of child labor in Britain. He cites studies according to which, for school children aged 13–16, 80 percent of girls and 69 percent of boys had some form of employment; in Birmingham, a survey of 1,827 school students aged 10–16 found that 43.7 percent were working in some way, or had had a job in the recent past.[178] He states that "the existing studies of children's part-time jobs in advanced economies, though limited in number, all suggest that child employment is an extensive activity, carried out for little reward and performed in poor working conditions."[179] Out of reach of statistical observation, large numbers of children, both in developed and developing countries, are involved in income-generating activities linked to the criminal economy, particularly in drug traffic, petty thefts, and organized begging.[180] Much of the proliferation of street children is linked to these activities. Thus, studies in Brazil, whose cities, and particularly Rio de Janeiro, have been highlighted as the most striking example of thousands of children living in the street, show that, in fact, most of them return to their poor homes at the end of the day, bringing

[176] ILO (1996: 7–8).
[177] Dumaine (1993).
[178] Lavalette (1994: 29–31).
[179] Lavalette (1994: 1).
[180] Hallinan (1994); Pedrazzini and Sanchez (1996).

their meager gains to the family. A 1989 survey of street children in Rio found that those living by themselves on the streets, without their families, accounted for only 14.6 percent of street children, among whom 80 percent were drug addicts. Another 13.6 percent were homeless, but shared street life with their families; 21.4 percent were in the family home and worked in the streets under the control of their family. The majority (50.5 percent) have contact with their families, but worked in the streets independently, and occasionally slept there. Yet all categories shared a high risk of violence and death, often at the hands of "vigilantes" and policemen, engaging in "street clean-ups."[181] Pedrazzini and Sanchez report a similar situation among the "malandros" (bad boys) of Caracas.[182]

According to the ILO, child labor is present in a whole array of activities, many of them highly hazardous.[183] Besides the well-known case of rugs and carpet weaving, an export industry that in India and Pakistan utilizes child labor on a large scale, child workers are reported in the brassware industry of India; in the brick-making factories of Pakistan; in Muro-ami fishing (involving deep-sea diving) in South-East Asia; in the pesticide-poisoned plantations of Sri Lanka; in toxic fume-filled repair shops and woodwork shops in Egypt, the Philippines, and Turkey; in small-scale mines in Africa, Asia, and Latin America; and in millions of homes, as domestic workers, frequently exposed to abuse. Thus, around 5 million children are employed as domestic workers in Indonesia, and half a million in Sri Lanka. In Venezuela, 60 percent of the girls working between 10 and 14 years of age are in domestic work. A substantial proportion of child domestic workers are very young: 24 percent in Bangladesh, and 26 percent in Venezuela, were less than 10 years old. These domestic workers work as much as 10–15 hours a day, and studies report what ILO describes as "alarming evidence of physical, mental, and sexual abuse of adolescents and young women working as domestics."[184]

The rapid growth of global tourism, an industry currently employing about 7 percent of the total global workforce, is also a major source of child labor around the world.[185] Because it is a labor-intensive industry, seasonal and irregular in its activity, it is highly conducive to the employment of flexible, cheap labor, thus to child labor. Types of jobs include bell boys, waitresses, maids, collectors of fares in public taxis, masseuses, receptionists, "hospitality" workers,

[181]   Rizzini (1994).
[182]   Pedrazzini and Sanchez (1996).
[183]   ILO (1996).
[184]   ILO (1996: 15).
[185]   Black (1995).

ball boys, caddies, messengers, servers of tea and snacks, minders of deck-chairs and ponies on the beach and so on. Pay is extremely low: a study in Acapulco, Mexico, reported by Black, found that children of 7–12 years of age were employed as drink servers with no pay other than tips and a small commission per drink served.[186] This seems to be consistent with reports from other countries.

In some instances, child labor is involved in gruesome activities. Thus, in poverty-stricken, civil-war torn Kabul, in 1996, many children engaged, for the benefit of their families, in profitable robbing and smuggling of human bones. They obtained the bones from grave-yards, mixed them (to disguise their origin) with bones from dogs, cows, horses, and sold them to middlemen who ship them to Pakistan, where they are used for making cooking oil, soap, chicken feed, and buttons. A child in this trade made about 12 dollars a month, three times the salary of a civil servant in Taliban-dominated Afghanistan.[187]

A particularly exploitative type of child labor is bonded labor. As the 1996 ILO report writes: "Slavery is not dead. Societies are loath to admit to still harbouring it but, as can be surmised from cases reported to the ILO, numerous children are trapped in slavery in many parts of the world. Of all working children, surely these are the most imperiled."[188] Thus, according to a 1994 study of the US Department of Labor:

> in India, where conservative estimates of adult and child bonded laborers start at 3 million, debt bondage occurs when a person needing a loan and having no security to offer, pledges his/her labor, or that of someone under his/her control, as a security for the loan . . . There are increasing reports of child bonded laborers in both the service and manufacturing sectors in India . . . In some countries, recruiters comb the countryside paying for parents to recruit their children for work in factories. For example, in Thailand, many child workers come from poverty-stricken parts of the northeast regions, having been sold by their parents, or made part of a debt bondage arrangement. Unscrupulous "employment agencies" often negotiate the trans-action and deliver children to industries, like shrimp peeling, or prostitution. In the Philippines, two separate raids on a sardine canning factory found children, as young as 11, filling cans with sliced fish to repay the debt to the labor recruiter.[189]

[186]   Black (1995).
[187]   *The New York Times Magazine,* January 12, 1997: 30–2
[188]   ILO (1996: 15).
[189]   US Department of Labor (1994: 19).

This report is filled with case studies from a variety of countries documenting child bondage. Another US Department of Labor report provides ample evidence of child forced and bonded labor in commercial agriculture, as well as the damaging consequences of their early-age exposure to chemical fertilizers and pesticides.[190]

Why this surge in child labor? In the first place, it results from the simultaneous deepening of poverty and globalization of economic activity. The crisis of subsistence economies, and the impoverishment of large segments of the population, as documented above, force families, and their children, into all kinds of survival strategies: no time for schooling, the family needs as many income-earners as possible, and it needs them right now. Families, pushed by necessity, sometimes offer their children to bonded labor, or send them into the streets. Studies have shown the influence of large-size families on child labor: the higher the number of children, the more the likelihood of a family triage between those sent to school and into the streets. However, the same studies also show that the effect of family size on child labor is sharply reduced in countries or regions with more developed social welfare policies.[191]

On the other hand, the globalization of economic activities provides the opportunity for substantial gain by employing children, counting on the difference between the cost of a child laborer in developing countries and the price of goods and services in affluent markets. This is clearly the case in the international tourist industry. The luxurious services that middle-income tourists can afford in many "tropical paradises" rely to a large extent on the over-exploitation of local labor, including many children, as documented by Black.[192] Yet, the 1996 report by the ILO argues that labor costs are not necessarily the main determinants for hiring children. In India, for instance, savings from child labor seem to account for only 5 percent of the final price of bangles, and between 5 and 10 percent for carpets. Why then hire children? According to the report "the answer lies in *where* the gains from using child labor occur. In the carpet industry, for example, it is the loom owners who supervise the weaving who benefit directly. Many in number, they are usually poor, small contractors who work to a very slim profit margin and who can as much as double their meagre income by utilizing child workers."[193] Thus, *it is the networking between small producers, and larger firms, exporting to affluent*

[190]   US Department of Labor (1995).
[191]   Grootaert and Kanbur (1995)
[192]   Black (1995).
[193]   ILO (1996: 19).

markets, often through the intermediation of wholesale merchants and large department stores in these markets, that explains both the flexibility and the profitability of the industry. A 1994 US Labor Department study also found that, while most child workers were not directly working in export-oriented firms, the spread of sub-contracting networks, and of home-based production, in many countries were incorporating children into export industries. For instance, a study of a sample of seamstresses in the garment industry in Latin America, found that 80 percent of them were women working at home. Of those, 34 percent had their children help, and, for those working 50 hours a week, 40 percent had their children as helpers. In another example, the majority of workers in export-oriented Mexico's *maquiladoras* are young women, of 14–20 years of age; it is thought that among them there are also some who are younger than 14.[194]

However, the most important factor in employing children seems to be their *defenselessness*, leading to the relatively easy imposition of minimal pay and atrocious working conditions. As the ILO report states:

> Since the children do not have irreplaceable skills and are often not much less costly than adults, a major important explanation for hiring seems to be non-economic. There are many non-pecuniary reasons but the most important seems to be the fact that children are less aware of their rights, less troublesome and more willing to take orders and to do monotonous work without complaining, more trustworthy, less likely to steal, and less likely to be absent from work. Children's lower absentee rate is especially valuable for employers in informal sector industries where workers are employed on a daily, casual basis and a full contingent of workers must therefore be found each day.[195]

Children as ready-to-use, disposable labor are the last frontier of renewed over-exploitation under networked, global capitalism. Or is it?

The sexual exploitation of children

My question is indeed rhetorical. There is much worse in the current plight of many children: they have become sexual commodities in a large-scale industry, organized internationally through the use of advanced technology, and by taking advantage of the globalization

---

[194]   US Department of Labor (1994: 19).
[195]   ILO (1996: 20).

of tourism and images. The World Congress Against Commercial Sexual Exploitation of Children, which took place in Stockholm on August 27–31, 1996, put together an impressive set of documents providing evidence of the extent of this exploitation, of its rapid diffusion, and of the causes underlying the phenomenon.[196] Statistics cannot be precise on this matter, but reliable empirical estimates point toward the importance of the problem, and toward its fast growth, frequently associated with the globalization of tourism, and with the perverse search for sexual enjoyment beyond standardized sex consumption.[197] In Thailand, the hot spot of the global sex industry, the Center for Protection of Children's Rights, a well-established, non-governmental organization, estimates that as many as 800,000 children are in prostitution, with HIV infection being pervasive among them. Indeed, virginity is a well-paid merchandise, and sex without condoms is highly priced. A 1991 survey of *India Today* puts the number of child prostitutes in India somewhere between 400,000 and 500,000. In Sri Lanka, estimates range around 20,000. In the tiny Dominican Republic, over 25,000 minors were in prostitution. Another study counted 3,000 minors working as prostitutes in Bogota. Beyer estimates that Brazil has about 200,000 adolescent prostitutes, and Peru about half a million.[198] But the problem is not confined to developing countries by any means. The Council of Europe estimated that in Paris, in 1988, 5,000 boys and 3,000 girls were working as prostitutes on the streets; the Defence of the Child International evaluated at 1,000 the number of child prostitutes in The Netherlands in 1990; and a 1996 study presented to the World Congress indicated substantial growth of child prostitution among Russian, Polish, Romanian, Hungarian, and Czech children.[199] In Belgium, one of the largest political demonstrations ever took place in Brussels on October 20, 1996 to protest against the government cover-up of the implications of the murder of four little girls, apparently linked to a child prostitution ring in which leading politicians may have been involved.[200]

One of the fastest growing markets for child prostitution is in the United States and Canada, where, in 1996, estimates varied widely between 100,000 and 300,000 child prostitutes.[201] Some areas of the country are targeted. For instance, New York pimps like to recruit

[196] World Congress (1996).
[197] *Christian Science Monitor* (1996).
[198] Beyer (1996).
[199] World Congress (1996).
[200] *The Economist* (1996b); Trueheart (1996).
[201] Clayton (1996); Flores (1996).

their sex slaves in Kansas and Florida. Pimps move children from city to city, so as to keep them in unfamiliar surroundings; they keep them locked up, and give them no money. How do children end up in this situation? According to a report from the US Department of Labor, reasons may vary:

> Parents knowingly sell children to recruiters to augment family income, recruiters make false promises, children are kidnapped, or they run away and are lured into prostitution to survive on the streets . . . No matter what the cause, the outcome is the same. A large and profitable industry is willing to sexually exploit children to satisfy a demand for child prostitutes. The children are generally scarred for life – which may be short, since occupational hazards such as AIDS and other sexually transmitted diseases, or brutal physical abuse, often kill them.[202]

Related to prostitution, but as a distinct segment of the booming child sex industry, is child pornography. Technology is a major factor in spurring this industry. Camcorders, VCRs, home editing desks, computer graphics, have all moved the child porn industry into the home, making it difficult to police. The Internet has opened up new channels of information for those seeking access to children for sex. In some instances, computerized information systems have been operated from prison by incarcerated pedophiles. Thus, an impoverished, de-industrialized town in Northern Minnesota found their children specifically targeted in the records confiscated by police of a pedophile network operated from prison by inmates. Because pornographic images and video clips can be uploaded and downloaded almost anonymously, a global network of child pornography has developed, in a wholly decentralized manner, and with few possibilities for law enforcement.[203] Indeed, on-line child pornography is a major argument for establishing censorship of the Internet. It is easier to blame the messenger than to question the sources of the message; that is, to ask why our informational society engages in this activity on such a large scale. Major producers and distributors of child pornography (much of which concerns boys rather than girls) are legal firms located in permissive environments in high-technology societies, such as Japan, Denmark, Holland, and Sweden.[204]

Various analyses of the reasons for this staggering rise in a global industry of child sex (distinct from traditional sexual abuse of children

---

[202]   US Department of Labor (1995: 11).
[203]   World Congress (1996).
[204]   Healy (1996).

throughout history) converge toward a set of factors. First is the global-ization of markets for everything, and from everywhere to everywhere, whether it be organized sex tours or audiovisual distribution of porno-graphic material worldwide. Anonymity, guaranteed either by the electronic home or by exotic travel, helps break the barrier of fear for the masses of perverts who live among us. The escape into further transgression to find sexual excitement in a society of normalized sex-uality (see volume II, chapter 4), fuels the demand for new emotions, particularly among affluent segments of bored professionals.

On the supply side, poverty and the crisis of the family provide the raw material. The link up between supply and demand is often made by the global criminal networks that control much prostitution throughout the world, and are always striving to find new, more profit-able product lines and markets. Specifically, South-East Asian child prostitution networks buy children in the poorest rural areas of Thailand, Cambodia, the Philippines, and other countries, to feed their distribution networks in Asia, particularly targeting the interna-tional tourist hubs, and Japan, in cooperation with the Yakuza. Bangkok, Manila, and Osaka are internationally notorious places for child prostitution. Finally, as the 1996 World Congress document stated, media interest in child pornography and prostitution can unintentionally fuel demand, and the ease of access of information both opens up supply routes and increases demand.

Thus, the network society devours itself, as it consumes/destroys enough of its own children to lose the sense of continuity of life across generations, so denying the future of humans as a humane species.

The killing of children: war massacres and child soldiers

There is still more to report in this negation of ourselves. In this end of millennium in countries around the world, particularly (but not only, by any means) in the most devastated region, Africa, millions of children have been or are being killed by war. And tens of thousands of children have been or are being transformed into fighting/dying animals to feed the bloody, senseless, slow wars that haunt the planet. According to the 1996 UNICEF report on the *State of the World's Children*,[205] mainly devoted to the issue of the impact of war on chil-dren, during the past decade, as a direct effect of war, in this post-Cold War world, 2 million children were killed, between 4 and 5 million were disabled, over 1 million were orphaned or separated from their parents, 12 million were left homeless, and over 10 million were

---

[205]   Bellamy (1996).

psychologically traumatized. The increasing proportion of children among the victims of war is due to the character of these new, forgotten wars, once the affluent world decided to live in peace (see volume I, chapter 7). As the UNICEF report states:

> Rather than being set-piece battles between contending armies, these are much more complex affairs – struggles between the military and civilians, or between contending groups of armed civilians. They are likely to be fought in villages and suburban streets as anywhere else. In this case, the enemy camp is all around, and distinctions between combatant and non combatant melt away in the suspicions and confrontations of daily strife.[206]

But children are also brought into these wars as soldiers, in growing numbers. Cohn and Goodwin have researched this matter in depth.[207] They document the extent to which hundreds of thousands of children have been recruited into the regular armies of states (such as Iran or Bosnia), into rebel militia, and into gangs of bandits. In some instances, children were simply sent to die in the minefields. In other cases, as in Mozambique's RENAMO anti-government guerrillas, or in Cambodia's Khmer Rouge, they tortured children for a period to make them fierce warriors, albeit mentally damaged. In all cases, children join, or are forced to join, these courageous military leaders, out of lack of alternatives. Poverty, displacement, separation from their families, ideological or religious manipulation, all play a role.[208] In some cases, such as among the rebels of Eastern Zaïre in 1996, children are made to believe that they have magic powers and cannot die. In others, the feeling of power, of instilling fear, of "becoming a man," or a warrior, are powerful drives to entice a child. In all cases, children seem to be ferocious fighters, ready to kill, willing to die, with little awareness of the actual borderline between war and play, life and death. With new weapons technology providing extraordinary fire power in light, portable arms, these armies of kids are capable of inflicting tremendous casualties. To each other. For those who survive, in the words of Cohn and Goodwin Gill, "children who have participated in hostilities are often marked for life, mentally, morally, and physically."[209]

[206] Bellamy (1996: 14).
[207] Cohn and Goodwin (1994).
[208] Drogin (1995).
[209] Cohn and Goodwin (1994: 4).

Why children are wasted

So, what does informational capitalism have to do with this horror? Haven't children, after all, been abused, alas, throughout history? Yes and no. It is true that children have been historically victimized, often by their own families; that they have been submitted to physical, psychological, and sexual abuse by the powers that be in all historical periods; and that the rise of the industrial era also witnessed the massive use of child labor in mines and factories, often in conditions close to bondage. And, since children are people, the form in which societies have treated childhood inflicts lasting moral wounds on the human condition. But, I argue, there is something different in this beginning of the Information Age: there is a systemic link between the *current*, unchecked characteristics of informational capitalism, and the destruction of lives in a large segment of the world's children.

What is different is that we are witnessing a dramatic reversal of social conquests and children's rights obtained by social reform in mature industrial societies, in the wake of large-scale deregulation, and the bypassing of governments by global networks. What is different is the disintegration of traditional societies throughout the world, exposing children to the unprotected lands of mega-cities' slums. What is different is children in Pakistan weaving carpets for worldwide export via networks of suppliers to large department stores in affluent markets. What is new is mass, global tourism organized around pedophilia. What is new is electronic child pornography on the net, worldwide. What is new is the disintegration of patriarchalism, without being replaced by a system of protection of children provided either by new families or the state. And what is new is the weakening of institutions of support for children's rights, such as labor unions or the politics of social reform, to be replaced by moral admonitions to family values which often blame the victims for their plight.

Furthermore, informational capitalism is not an entity. It is a specific social structure, with its rules and its dynamics, which, through the processes documented in this chapter, are systemically related to children's over-exploitation and abuse, unless deliberate policies and strategies counter these trends.

At the roots of children's exploitation are the mechanisms generating poverty and social exclusion throughout the world, from Sub-Saharan Africa to the United States of America. With children in poverty, and with entire countries, regions, and neighborhoods excluded from relevant circuits of wealth, power, and information, the crumbling of family structures breaks the last barrier of defense for children. In some countries, like Zaïre, Cambodia, or Venezuela, misery overwhelms families, in rural areas as in shanty towns, so that children are sold for survival, are sent to the streets to help out, or end up running away from the hell of their homes into the hell of their non-existence. In other societies, the historical crisis of patriarchalism brings down the traditional nuclear family without replacing it, making women and children pay for it. This is why almost 22 percent of American children live in poverty, the worst child poverty rate in the industrialized world. This is also why, according to the documented analyses of Rodgers and of Lerman, there is a close relationship between changing family structure and the increase in women and child poverty in the United States.[210] Whoever challenges patriarchalism does it at her risk. And at her children's risk. A 1996 report from the US Department of Health and Human Services estimated that child abuse and neglect in the United States doubled between 1986 and 1993, growing from 1.4 million children affected to over 2.8 million in 1993. The number of children who were seriously injured quadrupled from 143,000 to 570,000. Children from the lowest income families were 18 times more likely to be sexually abused, almost 56 times more likely to be educationally neglected, and 22 times more likely to be seriously injured from maltreatment. Meanwhile, the percentage of cases investigated sharply declined.[211]

The supply of children provided by this weakened family structure, and by this impoverished childhood, is met, on the demand side, by the processes of globalization, business networking, criminalization of a segment of the economy, and advanced communication technologies, to which I have specifically referred in the analyses presented above. To both sets of supply and demand factors, we must add, as sources of children's over-exploitation, exclusion, and destruction, the disintegration of states and societies, and the massive uprooting of populations by war, famine, epidemics, and banditry.

There is something else, in the fragmented culture of our societies, that helps, and even rationalizes, the wasting of children's lives. Among the children themselves there is the diffusion of what Pedrazzini and Sanchez, on the basis of their fieldwork in the streets of Caracas, have labeled "the culture of urgency."[212] This is the idea that there is no future, and no roots, only the present. And the present is made up of instants, of each instant. So, life has to be lived as if each instant were the last one, with no other reference than the explosive fulfillment of individualized hyperconsumption. This

---

[210] Lerman (1996); Rodgers (1996).

[211] Sedlak and Broadhurst (1996).

[212] Pedrazzini and Sanchez (1996).

constant, fearless challenge to explore life beyond its present
dereliction keeps destitute children going: for a little while, until
facing utter destruction.

On the side of society at large, the crumbling of social institutions,
behind the façade of repetitive formulas on the virtues of a traditional
family that, by and large, has ceased to exist, leaves individuals, and
particularly men, alone with their desires of transgression, with their
power surges, with their endless search for consumption, characterized by an immediate gratification pattern. Why then not prey on the
most defenseless members of society?

And on the side of the economy, when global markets of everything
from everywhere to everywhere become possible, the ultimate
commodification drive, the one affecting our own kind, does not
seem to contradict the strictest rule of a sheer market logic as the only
guide for relationships among people, bypassing values and institutions of society. I am certainly not proposing the notion that
informational capitalism is made up of a mob of pimps and child
abusers. Conservative, capitalist elites are certainly fond of family
values, and major corporations fund and support child defense
causes. However, there is a structural link between unrestricted
market logic in a global, networked economy, empowered by
advanced information technologies, and the phenomena I have
described in this chapter. Indeed, it is frequent to find in the
economic development field, experts' views accepting, and
supporting, the spread of child labor, as a rational market response
which, under certain conditions, will yield benefits to countries and
families. The main reason why children are wasted is because, in the
Information Age, social trends are extraordinarily amplified by
society's new technological/organizational capacity, while institutions of social control are bypassed by global networks of
information and capital. And since we are all inhabited, at the same
time, by humanity's angels and devils, whenever and wherever our
dark side takes over it triggers the release of unprecedented, destructive power.

Conclusion: the Black Holes of Informational Capitalism

I have tried to show in this chapter the complex set of linkages
between the characteristics of informational capitalism and the rise
of inequality, social polarization, poverty, and misery in most of
the world. Informationalism does create a sharp divide between valuable and non-valuable people and locales. Globalization proceeds

selectively, including and excluding segments of economies and societies in and out of the networks of information, wealth, and power, that characterize the new, dominant system. Individualization of work leaves workers to each one of themselves, to bargain their fate *vis à vis* constantly changing market forces. The crisis of the nation-state, and of the institutions of civil society constructed around it during the industrial era, undermines institutional capacity to correct social imbalances derived from unrestricted market logic. At the limit, as in some African or Latin American states, the state, emptied of representativeness, becomes a predator of its own people. New information technologies tool this global whirlwind of accumulation of wealth and diffusion of poverty.

But there is more than inequality and poverty in this process of social restructuring. There is also exclusion of people and territories which, from the perspective of dominant interests in global, informational capitalism, shift to a position of structural irrelevance. This widespread, multiform process of social exclusion leads to the constitution of what I call, taking the liberty of a cosmic metaphor, the *black holes of informational capitalism*. These are regions of society from which, statistically speaking, there is no escape from the pain and destruction inflicted on the human condition for those who, in one way or another, enter these social landscapes. This is unless there is a change in the laws that govern the universe of informational capitalism, since, unlike cosmic forces, purposive human action *can* change the rules of social structure, including those inducing social exclusion.

These black holes concentrate in their density all the destructive energy that affects humanity from multiple sources. How people, and locales, enter these black holes is less important than what happens afterwards; that is, the reproduction of social exclusion, and the infliction of additional injuries to those who are already excluded. For instance, Timmer et al. have shown the diversity of paths toward homelessness in American cities.[213] The homeless population of the 1990s is composed of a mixture of "old homeless," classic skid-row types, or de-institutionalized mentally ill persons, and of newer characters, such as "welfare moms," young families left behind by de-industrialization and restructuring, tenants evicted by gentrification, runaway teenagers, migrants without a home, and battered women, escaping from men. Yet once they are in the street, the black hole of homelessness, as a stigma, and as a world of violence and abuse, acts upon the homeless indiscriminately, damning them to destitution if

---

[213] Timmer et al. (1994).

their life goes on in the street for some time. For instance, Ida Susser has shown the impact of shelters' regulations for the New York homeless on the separation of women from their children in a process that often triggers the wasting of children, in the sense made explicit in the preceding pages.[214]

In another instance, less often cited, functional illiteracy triggers mechanisms of unemployability, poverty, and, ultimately, social exclusion in a society that increasingly relies on some minimum capacity to decode language. This functional disability is much more widespread in advanced societies than is generally acknowledged. Thus, in 1988, a national literacy survey by the US Education Department found that 21–23 percent of a representative national sample – therefore, about 40–44 million adults in America – had blatantly insufficient levels of reading and writing in English, as well as of elementary arithmetic. Two-thirds of them had never completed secondary education. One-quarter of them comprised immigrants in the process of learning English, which still leaves over 30 million native Americans functionally illiterate. An additional 25–28 percent demonstrated abilities of what the study called level 2, a very narrow level of understanding that included an ability to receive written instructions, but did not extend to abilities such as writing a letter to explain an error in a credit card statement, or to plan meetings by using bus schedules or flight schedules. Functional illiteracy is a fundamental obstacle to integration in the formal labor market, at whatever level, and it is strongly correlated with low-wage employment and poverty: nearly half of the lowest level in the literacy scale were living in poverty. Likewise, the majority of the prison population in the US is functionally illiterate.[215]

Drug addiction, mental illness, delinquency, incarceration, and illegality are also avenues toward specific conditions of dereliction, increasing the likelihood of irreversibly stumbling away from the socially sanctioned right to live. They all have one attribute in common: poverty, from which they originate, or to where they lead.

These black holes often communicate with each other, while being *socially/culturally* out of communication with the universe of mainstream society. They are, however, economically connected to some specific markets (for example, through the criminal economy of drugs and prostitution), and bureaucratically related to the state (to the agencies set up for their containment, such as police and welfare). Drugs, illness (for example, AIDS), crime, prostitution, and violence are part of the same networks, each feature reinforcing the others (as

[214]   Susser (1991, 1993, 1996).
[215]   Kirsch et al. (1993); Newman et al. (1993).

in contracting HIV from sharing needles among drug addicts, and/or through prostituted sex).[216]

Social exclusion is often expressed in spatial terms. The territorial confinement of systemically worthless populations, disconnected from networks of valuable functions and people, is indeed a major characteristic of the spatial logic of the network society, as I argued in volume I, chapter 6. In this chapter, I have documented the spatial logic of social exclusion with an overview of the marginalization of Sub-Saharan Africa, and with reference to American inner-city ghettos. But there are many other instances of such a territorially shaped exclusion in the uneven geography of informational capitalism. Not the least striking is the fate of most Pacific islands, tropical paradises living in abject poverty and experiencing social disintegration induced by tourism, in the midst of a Pacific region transformed in the powerhouse of global capitalism.[217] Likewise, why people enter black holes, why and how territories become excluded or included, is dependent on specific events that "lock in" trajectories of marginality. It may be a rapacious dictator, as in Zaïre; or a police decision to abandon certain neighborhoods to drug traffickers; or "red lining" from housing lenders; or the exhaustion of mines or the devaluation of agricultural products on which a region was making a living. Whatever the reason, for these territories, and for the people trapped in them, a downward spiral of poverty, then dereliction, finally irrelevance, operates until or unless a countervailing force, including people's revolt against their condition, reverses the trend.

In this end of millennium, what used to be called the Second World (the statist universe) has disintegrated, incapable of mastering the forces of the Information Age. At the same time, the Third World has disappeared as a relevant entity, emptied of its geopolitical meaning, and extraordinarily diversified in its economic and social development. Yet, the First World has not become the all-embracing universe of neo-liberal mythology. Because a new world, the Fourth World, has emerged, made up of multiple black holes of social exclusion throughout the planet. The Fourth World comprises large areas of the globe, such as much of Sub-Saharan Africa, and impoverished rural areas of Latin America and Asia. But it is also present in literally every country, and every city, in this new geography of social exclusion. It is formed of American inner-city ghettos, Spanish enclaves of mass youth unemployment, French banlieues warehousing North Africans, Japanese Yoseba quarters, and Asian mega-cities' shanty

[216]   Susser (1996).
[217]   Wallace (1995).

towns. And it is populated by millions of homeless, incarcerated, prostituted, criminalized, brutalized, stigmatized, sick, and illiterate
persons. They are the majority in some areas, the minority in others,
and a tiny minority in a few privileged contexts. But, everywhere, they
are growing in number, and increasing in visibility, as the selective
triage of informational capitalism, and the political breakdown of the
welfare state, intensify social exclusion. In the current historical
context, the rise of the Fourth World is inseparable from the rise of
informational, global capitalism.

3

The Perverse Connection: the Global Criminal Economy

During the last few years, the international community has experienced an increasing number of political upheavals, geopolitical changes and technological restructuring. No doubt, organized transnational crime, a new dimension of more "traditional" forms of organized crime, has emerged as one of the most alarming of these challenges. Organized transnational crime, with the capacity to expand its activities and to target the security and the economies of countries, in particular developing ones and those in transition, represents one of the major threats that governments have to deal with in order to ensure their stability, the safety of their people, the preservation of the whole fabric of society, and the viability and further development of their economies.

United Nations, Economic and Social Council, 1994 p. 3

International criminal organizations have reached agreements and understanding to divide up geographical areas, develop new market strategies, work out forms of mutual assistance and the settlement of conflicts. . .and this on a planetary level. We are faced with a genuine criminal counter-power, capable of imposing its will on legitimate states, of undermining institutions and forces of law and order, of upsetting delicate economic and financial equilibrium and destroying democratic life.

Anti-Mafia Commission of the Italian Parliament [1]

Crime is as old as humankind. But global crime, the networking of powerful criminal organizations, and their associates, in shared activities throughout the planet, is a new phenomenon that profoundly affects international and national economies, politics, security, and, ultimately, societies at large. The Sicilian *Cosa Nostra* (and its associ-

[1] Report of the Anti-Mafia Commission of the Italian Parliament to the United Nations Assembly, March 20, 1990, cited by Sterling (1994: 66).

ates, *La Camorra, Ndrangheta,* and *Sacra Corona Unita*), the American
Mafia, the Colombian cartels, the Mexican cartels, the Nigerian criminal networks, the Japanese *Yakuza,* the Chinese Triads, the
constellation of Russian *Mafiyas,* the Turkish heroin traffickers, the
Jamaican Posses, and a myriad of regional and local criminal groupings in all countries, have come together in a global, diversified
network, that permeates boundaries and links up ventures of all sorts.
While drugs traffic is the most important segment of this worldwide
industry, arms deals also represent a high-value market. In addition,
is everything that receives added value precisely from its prohibition
in a given institutional environment: smuggling of everything from
everywhere to everywhere, including radioactive material, human
organs, and illegal immigrants; prostitution; gambling; loan-sharking;
kidnapping; racketeering and extortion; counterfeiting of goods,
bank notes, financial documents, credit cards, and identity cards;
killers for hire; traffic of sensitive information, technology, or art
objects; international sales of stolen goods; or even dumping garbage
illegally from one country into another (for example, US garbage
smuggled into China in 1996). Extortion is also practiced on an international scale; for instance, by the *Yakuza* on Japanese corporations
abroad. At the heart of the system, there is money laundering by the
hundreds of billions (maybe trillions) of dollars. Complex financial
schemes and international trade networks link up the criminal
economy to the formal economy, thus deeply penetrating financial
markets, and constituting a critical, volatile element in a fragile global
economy. The economies *and politics* of many countries (such as Italy,
Russia, the former Soviet Union republics, Colombia, Mexico, Bolivia,
Peru, Venezuela, Turkey, Afghanistan, Burma, Thailand, but also
Japan (see chapter 4), Taiwan, Hong Kong, and a multiplicity of small
countries which include Luxembourg and Austria) cannot be understood without considering the dynamics of criminal networks present
in their daily workings. The flexible connection of these criminal
activities in international networks constitutes an essential feature of
the new global economy, and of the social/political dynamics of the
Information Age. There is general acknowledgment of the importance and reality of this phenomenon, and a wealth of evidence,
mainly from well-documented journalists' reports, and the conferences of international organizations.[2] Yet, the phenomenon is largely

[2] The most authoritative, international source on global crime is the documentation assembled by the Economic and Social Council of the United Nations on
the occasion of the World Ministerial Conference on Organized Transnational
Crime held in Naples November 21–23, 1994. I have used these materials
extensively and wish to thank the people who provided them for me: Dr

ignored by social scientists, when it comes to understanding economies and societies, with the arguments that data are not truly reliable, and that sensationalism taints interpretation. I take exception to these views. If a phenomenon is acknowledged as a fundamental dimension of our societies, indeed of the new, globalized system, we must use whatever evidence is available to explore the connection between these criminal activities and societies and economies at large.

Organizational Globalization of Crime, Cultural Identification of Criminals[3]

In the past two decades, criminal organizations have increasingly set up their operations transnationally, taking advantage of economic globalization and new communication and transportation technologies. Their strategy is to base their management and production functions in low-risk areas, where they have relative control of the institutional environment, while targeting as preferential markets those areas with the most affluent demand, so that higher prices can be charged. This is clearly the case for the drug cartels, whether it is

---

Gopinath, Director of the International Institute for Labour Studies of the ILO, in Geneva, and Mr. Vetere, Chief of the Crime Prevention and Criminal Justice Branch of the United Nations, in Vienna. An excellent, documented overview of the expansion of global crime can be found in Sterling (1994). Although Sterling's work has been criticized for her sensationalism, I am not aware that the facts she reports, always backed by investigative reporting, and personal interviews, have been challenged. See also Martin and Romano (1992); and, although it is a bit old, Kelly (1986).

[3]   The source for data presented in this section, when not specifically cited, is the Background Report of the 1994 United Nations Conference on Organized Transnational Crime, given as United Nations, Economic and Social Council, (UN-ESC) (1994). On the impact of organized crime in Europe, besides Sterling's (1994) perceptive analysis, see Roth and Frey (1995). On the Italian Mafia, see Colombo (1990), Santino and La Fiura (1990), Catanzaro (1991), Calvi (1992), Savona (1993), Tranfaglia (1992) and Arlacchi (1995). On the recent transformation of American Mafia, see Potter (1994), and, again, Sterling (1994). On the impact of global crime on American crime, see Kleinknecht (1996). On the Chinese Triads, see Booth (1991); Murray (1994); Chu (1996). On heroin traffic in/from the Burmese/Thai Golden Triangle, see Renard (1996). On the Japanese *Yakuza*, see Kaplan and Dubro (1986), and Seymour (1996). On Africa, see Fottorino (1991). On Russia and Latin America, see below. In addition, I have used a number of sources from press reports, published in America, Europe, and Russia, collected and analyzed by Emma Kiselyova. Sources for specific information used in this section are cited in the footnotes.

cocaine in Colombia and the Andean region, or opium/heroin from the South-East Asian Golden Triangle, or from Afghanistan and Central Asia. But it is also the essential mechanism in weapons trade or traffic in radioactive material. Using their relative impunity in Russia and the former Soviet Union republics during the transition period, criminal networks, both Russian/ex-Soviet and from all around the world, took control of a significant amount of military and nuclear supplies to be offered to the highest bidder in the chaotic post-Cold War international scene. This internationalization of criminal activities induces organized crime from different countries to establish strategic alliances to cooperate, rather than fight, on each other's turf, through subcontracting arrangements, and joint ventures, whose business practice closely follows the organizational logic of what I identified as "the network enterprise," characteristic of the Information Age (volume I, chapter 3). Furthermore, the bulk of the proceeds of these activities are by definition globalized, through their laundering via global financial markets.

Estimates of profits and financial flows originating in the criminal economy vary wildly and are not fully reliable. Yet they are indicative of the staggering size of the phenomenon we are describing. The 1994 United Nations Conference on Global Organized Crime estimated that global trade in drugs amounted to about US$ 500 billion a year; that is, it was larger than the global trade in oil.[4] Overall profits from all kinds of activities were put as high as US$ 750 billion a year.[5] Other estimates mention the figure of US$ 1 trillion a year in 1993, which was about the same size as the US federal budget at that time.[6] In a very conservative estimate, the G-7 Financial Task Force declared in April 1990 that at least US$ 120 billion a year in drug money were laundered in the world's financial system. The OECD reported in 1993 the laundering of at least US$ 85 billion a year from drug traffic profits.[7] Sterling considers plausible the figure of US$ 500 billion as the likely global turnover of "narcodollars."[8] A substantial proportion of profits is laundered (with a commission for the launderers of between 15 and 25 percent of nominal dollars price), and about half of the laundered money, at least in the case of the Sicilian Mafia, is reinvested in legitimate activities.[9] This continuity between

[4]   UN-ESC (1994).
[5]   UN sources, reported by Cowell, (1994).
[6]   Washington-based National Strategy Information Center, reported by *Newsweek*, December 13, 1993.
[7]   *Newsweek*, December 13, 1993.
[8]   Sterling (1994).
[9]   Sterling (1994: 30).

profits from criminal activities and their investment in legitimate activities makes it impossible to limit the economic impact of global crime to the former, since the latter play a major role in ensuring, and covering up, the overall dynamics of the system. Furthermore, enforcement of deals also combines the skillful manipulation of legal procedures and financial systems in each country and internationally, with the selective use of violence, and widespread corruption of government officials, bankers, bureaucrats, and law-enforcement personnel.

At the sources of global crime, there are nationally, regionally, and ethnically rooted organizations, most of them with a long history, linked to the culture of specific countries and regions, with their ideology, their codes of honor, and their bonding mechanisms. These culturally based criminal organizations do not disappear in the new, global networks. On the contrary, their global networking allows traditional criminal organizations to survive, and prosper, by escaping the controls of a given state at a difficult time. Thus, the American Mafia, after considerably suffering from devastating strikes from the FBI in the 1980s, is being revived in the 1990s by an influx of Sicilian Mafia, and by alliances with the Chinese Triads, the Russian *Mafiyas*, and a variety of ethnic mobs.[10]

The Sicilian Mafia is still one of the most powerful criminal organizations in the world, using its historical control over the South of Italy, and its deep penetration of the Italian state. Its links with the Italian Christian Democratic Party (including, allegedly, to Andreotti, the towering figure of the party for almost half a century) allowed the Mafia to extend its presence to the entire country, to link up with the banking system, and, through it, with the entire political and business elite of the country, even coming very close to the Vatican through the Banco Ambrosiano which appears to have been under Mafia influence. In 1987, an agreement between the Sicilian Mafia and the Medellin cartel opened the way to swap heroin from Asia/Europe for cocaine from Colombia. Thus, the Colombians could enter the heroin market in the United States, shared until then between the Sicilian and American Mafias and the Chinese Triads. While using the Sicilian infrastructure, Colombian cartels could distribute their cocaine in Europe, paying a share to the Sicilians.[11] This was only the best documented of a series of international moves by the Sicilian Mafia, which included a deep penetration of Germany's criminal markets, and major speculative takeovers of Soviet property and currency during the transition period (see below).

[10]   Kleinknecht (1996).
[11]   Sterling (1994).

When the Italian state tried to regain its autonomy by confronting the Mafia, once the grip of the Christian Democrats and other traditional parties over the country was shaken in the early 1990s, the Mafia's reaction reached unprecedented brutality, including the killing of some leading figures in the anti-crime operations in Italy, most notably Judges Falcone and Borsalino. Popular reaction, exposure in the media, and the partial crumbling of corrupt Italian politics, weakened considerably the power of the Mafia in Italy itself, with the capture and imprisonment of its bloody *capo di tutti capi* Toto Riina. Yet the increased internationalization of Mafia activities in the 1990s allowed a new round of prosperity for its members, even if they had to relinquish some (but not most) of their control over local societies and government institutions in Italy.

In this internationalization process, the Italian Mafia coincides with the Chinese Triads, currently one of the largest and best articulated networks of criminal organizations in the world, counting, only in Hong Kong, some 160,000 members, divided between the 14k, the Sun Yee On, and the Wo Group. Another powerful network, the United Bamboo, is based in Taiwan. Like the Italian and American Mafias, the Triads are also rooted in history and ethnicity. They originated in southern China in the sixteenth century as a resistance movement against the Manchu invaders of the Qing dynasty. They fled China after the Communist revolution, and expanded throughout the world, particularly in the United States. The loss of their Hong Kong base in 1997 was anticipated ten years earlier, with a large-scale movement toward internationalization, and diversification, using primarily Chinese illegal immigrants to the United States, Europe, and Canada, often smuggled into the country by the Triads, and in some cases kept under their control. The Place d'Italie in Paris, and San Francisco's old (around Grant Street) and new (around Clemen Street) Chinatowns, witness the proliferation of Chinese businesses some of which may serve as support, and money-laundering devices, to a wide array of criminal activities, the most prominent of which continues to be the traffic of heroin from the Golden Triangle, historically controlled by drug lords' armies, originally members of Chiang Kai-shek's military, and supported by the CIA during the Cold War.[12]

The Japanese *Yakuza* (the *Boryokudan*, that is "the violent ones") has a quasi-legal existence in Japan, and is openly present in a wide array of businesses and political activities (usually ultra-nationalistic political associations). The most important gangs are *Yamagachi-gumi*, with 26,000 members in 944 networked gangs; *Inagawa-kai*, with 8,600

[12]   Renard (1996).

members; and *Sumiyoshi-kai*, with over 7,000 members. They also originated in the protection networks created by disaffected *samurai* among the poor population of cities in the early stages of Japanese urbanization in the nineteenth century. As with the other organizations, protection turned into preying on their own members. For a long time, the Japanese *Yakuza* felt so secure at home that its international activities were limited to smuggling weapons from the US into Japan, and to providing women sex slaves from other Asian countries to Japanese brothels and night clubs. Yet, they followed the globalization of Japanese corporations, and went into exporting to the United States their customary practice of blackmail and extortion of corporations, intimidating Japanese executives abroad by sending in their *Sokaiya* (violent *provocateurs*). They also imitated Japanese firms by investing heavily in real estate, particularly in America, and by manipulating stocks in financial markets. To operate in the United States and Europe, they made a number of deals with the Sicilian and American Mafias, as well as with various Russian criminal groups.

The dramatic expansion of several Russian criminal networks has made headline news in the whole world in the 1990s. Although some leaders of this underworld relate to the old Russian tradition of *vorovskoi mir* ("thieves' community" or "thieves' world"), organized crime in contemporary Russia and the ex-Soviet republics is the result of the chaotic, uncontrolled transition from statism to wild capitalism. Members of the Soviet *nomenklatura*, exceedingly entrepreneurial "capitalists" aspiring to become "end of millennium robber barons," and a myriad of ethnic mobs (with the Chechens as the most brutal and villified), constituted criminal networks in the wasteland created by the collapse of the Soviet Union. From there, they expanded throughout the world, linking up with organized crime everywhere, converging or competing, sharing profits with or killing each other, depending upon circumstances.[13]

[13] In one of the most striking cases of linkages between internationalized Russian crime and Latin American drug traffickers, in March 1997 the US Drug Enforcement Administration in Miami arrested Ludwig Fainberg, a Russian immigrant, and Juan Almeida and Nelson Yester, two Cubans considered to be middlemen for Colombian drug cartels. According to the DEA, Fainberg, owner of a strip bar near Miami Airport, was negotiating the sale of a Soviet submarine, complete with its crew, headed by a former admiral of the Soviet navy, to smuggle cocaine into ports along the West Coast of the United States. In fact, these partners had already done business together in 1992, when two Russian helicopters were sold to the cartels. Fainberg, a former dentist in the Soviet Union, was also organizing shipments of cocaine into Russia, and designing new methods of drug transportation to be operated jointly by Russian and Colombian criminal organizations (see Adams, 1997; Navarro, 1997).

Emerging from drug traffic in Latin America, the Medellin and Cali cartels in Colombia, the Tamaulipas and Tijuana cartels in Mexico, and similar groups almost in every Latin American country, organized a network of production, management, and distribution activities that linked up agricultural production areas, chemical laboratories, storage facilities, and transportation systems for export to affluent markets. These cartels focused almost exclusively on drug traffic, originally cocaine, but later they added marijuana, heroin, and chemical drugs. They set up their enforcement units, and their autonomous money-laundering schemes. They also favored penetration of police, judicial systems, and politicians, in a vast network of influence and corruption that changed Latin American politics, and will exercise its lasting influence for years to come. By their very essence, these cartels (actually made up of a coordinated network of smaller producers, under the control of cartel leaders through violence, finance, and distribution capability) were internationalized from the outset. They aimed essentially at exports to the United States, later to Europe, then to the whole world. Their strategies were, in fact, a peculiar adaptation of IMF-inspired export-oriented, growth policies toward the actual ability of some Latin American regions to compete in the high-technology environment of the new global economy. They linked up with national/local crime organizations in America and Europe to distribute their merchandise. And they set up a vast financial and commercial empire of money-laundering operations that, more than any other criminal organization, deeply penetrated the global financial system. Colombian and Latin American drug traffickers, as their Sicilian, Chinese, Japanese, or Russian counterparts, are also deeply rooted in their national, cultural identity. Pablo Escobar, the leader of the Medellin cartel made famous his slogan: "I prefer a tomb in Colombia than a prison in the United States." He succeeded in fulfilling his wish. His attitude, and similar attitudes among Latin America's drug kingpins reflect an obvious opportunism, since they are confident of their relative control over judges, police, and the penal system in their own countries. But there is undoubtedly something else, a more specific cultural component in their stand against the United States, and in their attachment to their regions and nations, a theme on which I will elaborate below.

The nationally and ethnically based criminal organizations that I have cited are the most notorious, but they are not, by any means, the only ones in the global scene. Turkish organized crime (enjoying significant influence in Turkey's politics and law-enforcement agencies) is a major player in the traditional Balkan route that brings heroin into Europe, a route now used for all kinds of additional traffic.

Diversified Nigerian criminal networks have become a force to reckon with, not only in Nigeria and in Africa (where they subcontract their knowledge of the field to international cartels), but in the world arena, where they excel, for instance, in credit-card fraud. In every country, and in every region, gangs, and networks of gangs, are now aware of their chances of linking up with broader chains of activities in this underworld that has a dominant presence in many neighborhoods, cities, and regions and that has even been able to buy most of the assets of some small countries, such as the island nation of Aruba, off the Venezuelan coast.

From these local, national, and ethnic bases, rooted in identity, and relying on interpersonal relationships of trust/distrust (naturally enforced with machine guns), criminal organizations engage in a wide range of activities. Drug traffic is the paramount business, to the point that the legalization of drugs is probably the greatest threat that organized crime would have to confront. But they can rely on the political blindness, and misplaced morality, of societies that do not come to terms with the bottom line of the problem: demand drives supply. The source of drug addiction, and therefore of most crimes in the world, lies in the psychological injuries inflicted on people by everyday life in our societies. Therefore, there will be mass consumption of drugs, for the foreseeable future, regardless of repression. And global organized crime will find ways to supply this demand, making it a most profitable business, and the mother of most other crimes.

Yet, besides drug trafficking, the criminal economy has expanded its realm to an extraordinary diversity of operations, making it an increasingly diversified, and interconnected, global industry. The 1994 United Nations Conference on Transnational Crime listed the main activities in which this kind of organized crime is engaged, *in addition to drug traffic*:

(1) *Weapons trafficking*   This is, of course, a multi-billion dollar business whose boundaries with the legal export of arms are not easy to determine. The critical matter in the business is the identity of the end-user, barred by international agreements or geopolitical considerations from receiving certain types of weapons. In some cases, these are states under an international embargo (such as Iran, Iraq, Libya, Bosnia, or Serbia). In other instances, they are guerrilla groups, or parties involved in a civil war. Still others are terrorist groups, and criminal organizations. The United States and the Soviet Union created the main supply of war weaponry in the world by providing it generously to various warring parties to influence them in their geopolitical games. After the end of the Cold War, weapons were left in often unreliable hands, which

used their stocks to feed the market. Other deals originate in semi-legal exports from arms-producing countries, such as France, the UK, China, the Czech Republic, Spain, or Israel. For instance, in May 1996, 2,000 AK-47 assault rifles, illegally imported from China, were seized in San Francisco in a sting operation, with a representative of China's main government-owned arms company being involved in the transaction.[14] According to the UN report: "Whoever the end user may be, however, black market arms deals have three characteristics: they are a covert activity, a large part of the cost is related to the surreptitious nature of the transaction, and the return flow of money is laundered."[15]

(2) *Trafficking of nuclear material* This involves the smuggling of nuclear weapons grade material, for eventual use in building these weapons and/or blackmailing by threatening their use. The disintegration of the Soviet Union provided a major opportunity for supplying this kind of material. Germany has been, in the 1990s, at the forefront of this kind of traffic, as criminal networks from the former Warsaw Pact countries have been smuggling nuclear material on behalf of international agents, sometimes in reckless ways, including carrying extremely radioactive items in the pockets of the smuggler.[16] According to the public testimony by Hans-Ludwig Zachert, President of the German Federal Police, in 1992 there were 158 case of illicit trade in radioactive material; and, in 1993, 241 cases. In these two years there was a total of 39 seizures, and in 1993 545 suspects were identified, 53 percent of whom were Germans, with the others being predominantly Czech, Polish, and Russian.[17] But the trade, while being supplied mainly from Eastern Europe, is international: on August 10, 1994, German police seized 350 grams of enriched plutonium, and arrested one Colombian and two Spaniards, although, in this case, reportedly, the deal was a set-up by the German Intelligence Service.[18] Other seizures of nuclear material took place in Budapest and Prague. Experts believe that Chinese nuclear stocks are also leaking some material into criminal trade.[19] At the source of this traffic, however, lies the catastrophic situation in Russia's nuclear weapons industry. It employs about 100,000 workers, who, in 1994, were paid (when they were paid

---

[14] *Time,* June 3, 1996.
[15] UN-ESC (1994: 18).
[16] Sterling (1994)
[17] UN-ESC (1994: 18).
[18] *Der Spiegel,* April, 4, 1995.
[19] *Time,* August 1, 1994.

at all) salaries of US$ 113 a month, on average. They resorted to strikes several times to call attention to their plight. In 1996, the director of the leading nuclear research institute related to the military nuclear complex in Russia committed suicide, out of despair. Under these circumstances, the temptation is too great for at least a few of these tens of thousands of workers, given the fact that the potential black-market price of a bomb-size amount of plutonium ranges in the hundreds of millions of dollars. Furthermore, the security conditions under which the dismantlement of Soviet bases outside Russia was conducted were very lax: in 1995, the Estonian government admitted that there had been a theft of radioactive material at the Padilski nuclear base.[20] In the Russian far east ports, radioactive wastes from nuclear submarines are piling up without proper storage facilities, not only representing a serious hazard, but inviting easy smuggling across a loosely guarded Eastern border.[21] The UN-ESC 1994 report concludes on this matter:

> It is clear that this trade has considerable potential for extortion, as well as for significant environmental damage, if only as a result of improper handling of the materials . . . The fact that nuclear materials are often procured from government-controlled organizations in the Russian Federation suggests the involvement of criminal organizations seeking profit. If they cannot obtain these profits in one way [by selling to a client], then it is only a small step to attempting to obtain them through some kind of nuclear blackmail. As nuclear disarmament continues, the availability of material is likely to increase rather than decrease.[22]

(3) *Smuggling of illegal immigrants*   The combination of misery around the world, displacement of populations, and dynamism in the core economies pushes millions of people to emigrate. On the other hand, increased border controls, particularly in the affluent societies, try to stem the immigration flow. These contradictory trends provide an exceptional opportunity to criminal organizations to tap into an immense market: "coyote" traffic on a global scale.[23] The 1994 United Nations report cites reliable

[20]   *Baltic Observer*, March 30–April 5, 1995.
[21]   *San Francisco Chronicle*, December 18, 1996.
[22]   UN-ESC (1994: 19).
[23]   "Coyote" is the nickname for smugglers of immigrants between Mexico and the US.

estimates that put the volume of illegal immigrant traffic from poor to richer countries at about one million people per year, about 20 percent of them being Chinese. This hardly accounts for about 700,000 undocumented immigrants who arrive every year in the United States by different means. The actual number of illegal immigrants in the world must be higher than the UN estimates. Criminally controlled illegal immigration is not only a source of profit from the payments of the would-be immigrants (for instance, an estimated US$ 3.5 billion a year in Mexico and the Caribbean alone). It also keeps many of them in bondage for a long time to repay their debt with a high interest. It exposes them, as well, to fraud, abuse, violence, and death. Furthermore, by threatening to overwhelm channels of lawful immigration, it triggers a xenophobic backlash which, manipulated by demagogic politicians, is destroying cultural tolerance and feelings of solidarity in most countries.

(4) *Trafficking in women and children*   Global tourism has become closely linked with a global prostitution industry, particularly active in Asia, where it is often under the control of the Triads and the *Yakuza*. It increasingly affects children as well (see chapter 2). In addition to child abuse and exploitation, there is also a growing industry in child adoption, particularly in Latin America, with destination to the United States. In 1994, Central American babies were being sold for 20,000 dollars to adoption rings, in most cases (but not always) with their parents' consent. It is believed that this traffic has grown into a multi-million dollar business.

(5) *Trafficking in body parts*   According to the United Nations 1994 report, there have been confirmed reports of such trafficking in Argentina, Brazil, Honduras, Mexico, and Peru, largely with destination to German, Swiss, and Italian buyers. In Argentina, there have been examples of the removal of corneas of patients who were declared brain dead after fabricated brain scans. The problem seems to be serious in Russia, mainly because of thousands of unclaimed bodies in the morgues: it was reported in 1993 that one company in Moscow had extracted 700 major organs, kidneys, hearts and lungs, over 1,400 liver sections, 18,000 thymus organs, 2,000 eyes, and over 3,000 pairs of testicles, all destined for transplant to high-paying clients.[24] The international conference on Commerce in Organs: Culture, Politics, and Bioethics of the Global Market, held at the University of California, Berkeley, on April 26–28, 1996, with the participation

[24]   *Times* November 18, 1993.

of leading academics and professionals from around the world, confirmed the importance of this expanding market. It also emphasized the thin line between criminal traffic and government-inspired trade. For instance, according to reports presented at this conference, the Chinese government seems to have routinely authorized the sale of body parts from people who have been executed, several hundreds of them every year, with the proceedings going, legally, into state coffers. Traffic seems to be particularly important in India and in Egypt, with destination to wealthy Middle Eastern patients. Most of these organs are voluntarily sold by people, either alive (one kidney, one eye), or by their families once they are dead. Yet, because of national and international legislation, the traffic is indeed illegal, and handled by smuggling networks, whose ultimate clients are, naturally, leading hospitals around the world. This is one of the links between global poverty and high technology.

(6) *Money laundering* The whole criminal system only makes business sense if the profits generated can be used and reinvested in the legal economy. This has become increasingly complicated given the staggering volume of these profits. This is why money laundering is the matrix of global crime, and its most direct connecting point to global capitalism. Money laundering[25] involves three stages. The first, and most delicate, requires the placement of cash into the financial system through banks or other financial institutions. In some instances, banks are located in countries with little control. Panama, Aruba, the Cayman Islands, the Bahamas, St Maertens, Vanuatu, but also Luxembourg and Austria (although in these two countries things are changing lately) are often cited in police reports as key entry points for dirty money into the financial system. In the leading economies, however, cash transactions over a certain sum (10,000 dollars in the US) must be reported. Thus, deposits operate through a large number of $9,999 (or less) transactions, a process called "smurfing." The second stage is "layering"; that is, separating funds from their source to avoid detection by future audits. What is critical here is the globalization of financial markets, and the availability of electronic transfer funds in seconds. Together with currency swaps, investments in different stocks, and use of some of this "dirty money" as collateral for loans from legitimate

[25] The origin of the term "money laundering" comes from 1920s Chicago, when one financier from the local Mafia bought a few automatic laundries where services could be paid for only in cash. Every evening, prior to declaring his daily earnings for tax purposes, he would add some "dirty" money to his "laundered" money (reported by *Literaturnaya Gazeta*, July 12, 1994).

funds, the speed and diversity of transactions makes it extremely difficult to detect the origin of these funds. Evidence of this difficulty is the very small amount of funds seized in the main capitalist countries.[26] The third stage is "integration"; that is, the introduction of laundered capital into the legal economy, usually in real estate or stocks, and generally using the weakest entry points of the legal economy, in countries with no or little anti-money-laundering legislation. After this integration, criminally-generated profits join the whirlwind of global financial flows.[27]

The key to the success and expansion of global crime in the 1990s is the flexibility and versatility of their organization. *Networking is their form of operation*, both internally, in each criminal organization (for example, the Sicilian Mafia, the Cali cartel), and in relation to other criminal organizations. Distribution networks operate on the basis of autonomous local gangs, to which they supply goods and services, and from which they receive cash. Each major criminal organization has its own means of enforcing deals. Ruthless violence (including intimidation, torture, kidnapping of family members, killings) are, of course, part of the routine, often subcontracted to contract killers. But more important is the "security apparatus" of organized crime, the network of law-enforcement agents, judges, and politicians, who are on the payroll. Once they enter this system, they are captive for life. While judicial tactics of plea bargains and crime witness-protection schemes have helped the repression of organized crime, particularly in America and Italy, the increasing ability of criminal leaders to find safe havens, and the global reach of killers-for-hire, are considerably limiting the effectiveness of classic repression methods of 1950s America and 1980s Italy.

This need to escape police repression based on nation-states makes *strategic alliances between criminal networks* essential in their new mode of operation. No one organization can by itself link up throughout the globe. Moreover, it cannot extend its international reach without entering the traditional territory of another criminal power. This is why, in strictly business logic, criminal organizations respect each other, and find points of convergence across national boundaries and turfs. Most of the killings are intranational: Russians killing Russians, Sicilians killing Sicilians, the Medellin cartel and the Cali cartel members killing each other, precisely to control their local/national base from which they can operate comfortably. It is this combination

[26] Sterling (1994).
[27] De Feo and Savona (1994).

of flexible networking between local turfs, rooted in tradition and identity, in a favorable institutional environment, and the global reach provided by strategic alliances, that explains the organizational strength of global crime. It makes it a fundamental actor in the economy and society of the Information Age. Nowhere is this global strategic role more evident than in the pillage of Russia during, and in the aftermath, of the transition from Soviet statism to wild proto-capitalism.

The Pillage of Russia[28]

Where does the mafia take its source from? This is simple, it begins with the common interests of politicians, business people, and gangsters. All others are hostage of this unholy alliance – all others means us.
                    Pavel Voshchanov, *Komsomolskaya Pravda*, p. 13

The chaotic transition of the Soviet Union to the market economy created the conditions for widespread penetration of business activities in Russia and the other republics by organized crime. It also induced the proliferation of criminal activities originating in and from Russia, and the ex-Soviet Union, such as the illegal traffic of weapons, nuclear materials, rare metals, oil, natural resources, and currency. International criminal organizations linked up with hundreds of networks of post-Soviet *Mafiyas*, many of them organized around ethnic lines (Chechens, Azeris, Georgians and so on), to launder money, to acquire valuable property, and to take control of prosperous illegal and legal businesses. A 1994 report on organized crime by the Analytical Center for Social and Economic Politics of the Presidency of Russia estimated that virtually all small private businesses were paying tribute to criminal groups. As for larger private

---

[28] This section is based on various sources. First, an analysis of press reports, both from Russian and Western sources, carried out by Emma Kiselyova. I have not considered it necessary to cite all these reports, since they are public knowledge. Secondly, the fieldwork research I conducted in Russia in 1989–96, as referred to and presented in chapter 1 of this volume, and in chapter 2 of volume 1. Although my research was not directly concerned with organized crime, I constantly found its traces among the processes of economic and political change that I tried to investigate. Thirdly, I have used a few important books and articles on the subject. The best account in English of Russian organized crime is Handelman (1995). Sterling (1994) has some powerful sections on Russia in her book on global crime. Voshchanov (1995) and Goldman (1996) articulate compelling arguments on the interpretation of the sources of criminalization of the Russian economy.

firms and commercial banks, it was reported that between 70 and 80 percent of them were also paying protection dues to criminal groups. These payments represented between 10 and 20 percent of capital turnover for these firms, an amount that was equivalent to over half of their profits.[29]

The situation did not seem to have improved in 1997. According to another *Izvestiya* report, it was estimated that about 41,000 industrial companies, 50 percent of banks, and 80 percent of joint ventures have criminal connections.[30] The report stated that the shadow economy, in all its manifestations, may account for as much as 40 percent of the Russian economy. Other observers, including Marshall Goldman, concur in estimating widespread penetration of business and government by organized crime.[31] The collapse of the taxation system is directly related to the payments of business to extortion organizations to solve their problems in the absence of a reliable state. Faced with the choice between an unresponsive administration and an effective, if ruthless, racketeering business, firms and people are growing accustomed to relying on the second, out of fear or convenience, or both.

In some cities (for example, Vladivostok), the local administration is highly conditioned in its functioning by its dubious connections. Furthermore, even if a given business is not related to organized crime, it operates in an environment in which the presence of criminal groups is pervasive, particularly in banking, import–export operations, trade in oil, and in rare and precious metals. The level of violence in the Russian business world in the mid-1990s was truly extraordinary: *Kommersant*, in 1996, was publishing a *daily* obituary section listing the businessmen killed in the line of duty. Contract killings became a way of life in the business world.[32] According to the Minister of the Interior, in 1995 about 450 contract killings were detected, and only 60 of them were solved by the police. Newly rich Russians were operating their Moscow businesses on line from their California mansions to escape the threats to them and their families, while still being daily involved in the wheelings and dealings that offered opportunities of making a fortune almost without parallel in the world. Enforcement of business deals, in an uncertain legal environment, was often carried on by intimidation, sometimes by killing. Organized crime was not usually satisfied with subcontracting violence or illegal operations for a price. They wanted, and usually obtained, a share of business, either in stocks or, more frequently, in

---

[29] Reported by *Izvestiya,* January 26, 1994.
[30] *Izvestiya,* February 18, 1997.
[31] Goldman (1996).
[32] Shargorodsky (1995).

cash, or else special favors, such as preferential loans or smuggling possibilities. In the private sector, businesses were paying "taxes" to criminal organizations instead of paying them to government. Indeed, the threat of denouncing a business's fiscal fraud to the government's tax inspectors was one of the extortion methods used by organized crime.

The widespread presence of international criminal cartels in Russia and the ex-Soviet republics was duly reciprocated by a dramatic expansion of post-Soviet criminal networks abroad, particularly in the United States and Germany. These criminal networks in America operated at a high level of financial and technological sophistication, usually organized by highly educated, young professionals, who did not hesitate in backing up their operations with extreme, but calculated, violence, often performed by ex-KGB officers, who found themselves a post-Cold War professional career.[33] Because of the strategic, economic, and political importance of Russia, and because of its large military and nuclear arsenal, its new, deep connection to global organized crime has become one of the most worrisome issues in this end of millennium, and a hot topic in geopolitical meetings around the world.[34]

How has this state of affairs come about? First of all, it must be said that this is *not* in historical continuity with past Russian experience, or with the underground economy of the Soviet Union, even though people involved in criminal or illegal activities in the former system are certainly very active in the new criminal economy. But they have been joined by many other actors in the criminal scene, and the mechanisms of formation and growth of the new criminal economy are entirely different. Criminal organizations have existed in Russia for centuries.[35] The *vorovskoi mir* ("thieves' world"), usually run from the prisons by an elite of *vory v zakonye* ("thieves-in-law"), survived repression, and kept their distance *vis à vis* the Czarist and Soviet states. They were, however, severely punished under Stalin, and subse-

---

[33] Kleinknecht (1996); Kuznetsova (1996); Wallace (1996).

[34] On the significance of Russian participation in global crime, see Ovchinsky (1993). On the persistence of criminal activity in Russia, a report by Interior Minister A. Kulikov of January 17, 1997, provided the following estimates: about 7 million crimes were committed in 1996, and about 2.62 million were reported. 29,700 murders and attempted murders were committed. More than 200 gangs were broken up by the police. Mr Kulikov acknowledged widespread corruption in his Ministry. The head of the Ministry's Technical and Military Supplies Administration, and 30 other officers were fired for embezzlement. About 10,000 Interior Ministry employees were brought to book in 1996, including 3,500 for criminal offenses.

[35] Handelman (1995).

quently weakened by their internal divisions and killings, particularly during the so-called "Scab Wars" of the 1950s. They reappeared during *perestroika*, but they had to share and compete for the control of the streets and criminal trafficking with a proliferation of ethnic *Mafiyas*, and a legion of newcomers to the business. In the 1990s they are just a component of a much broader picture, whose centers of power and wealth originated during the transition years. Nor are contemporary Russian *Mafiyas* a continuation of the networks that used to control the underground economy that grew up during the Brezhnev period. The underground economy was not in the hands of criminals, but of the Communist *nomenklatura*. It added flexibility to an increasingly rigid command economy, while providing rewards (rents) for the gatekeepers of each bureaucratic hurdle. As I described in chapter 1, this underground economy included barter between enterprises, as well as illegal sales of goods and services at all levels of the economic system, under the supervision, and for the personal benefit, of a gigantic network of bureaucrats, usually associated with the Communist power structure. The existence of this underground economy was entirely linked to the command economy, and thus its networks could not survive the collapse of the Soviet state. While many of these *nomenklatura* profiteers used their accumulated wealth and influence to take position in the new criminal economy of post-Soviet Russia, the structure of this criminal economy, and its mechanisms of connection to business and government, were entirely new.

The new criminal networks were formed in the 1987–93 period for the sake of proceeding with the pillage of Russia, and they consolidated their intertwining with the business world and the political system throughout the 1990s.[36] In trying to analyze this extraordinary development, I will propose a three-step explanation that I believe to

[36] The designation of 1987-93 as the period of formation of contemporary Russian *Mafiyas* is not arbitrary. In 1987 Gorbachev authorized the creation of private businesses (mainly under the form of cooperatives) in the most confusing terms, and without a proper legal environment, thus inducing an embryonic proto-capitalism that often had to operate under unlawful protection schemes. In October 1993, Yeltsin used tanks to crush the rebellion of the last Russian Parliament established during the Soviet era, actually ending the political transition. It was during this uncertain period, when nobody really knew who was in charge, except for the President himself, that organized crime set up its business networks, while many politicians positioned themselves in the generalized graft of Russian wealth. By the end of 1993, with a new Constitution, and a new, democratically elected Parliament, Russia entered into some kind of institutional normality. However, by this time, the intertwining of business, government, and crime, had already been consolidated, and became a feature of the new system.

be plausible in the light of available evidence.[37] I combine a structural interpretation, the identification of the actors involved in the uncontrolled appropriation of Soviet assets, and a description of the mechanisms used by these actors to accumulate wealth and power in a very short time.

The structural perspective

The economic chaos that resulted in the partial criminalization of business came, first of all, from a process of transition from a command economy to a market economy operated without institutions that could organize and regulate markets, and hampered by the collapse of state agencies, which became unable to control or repress developments. As Marshall Goldman writes:

> The break up of the Soviet Union was accompanied by the collapse of the economic infrastructure; Gosplan, the ministries, the wholesale operations – all simply disappeared. Eventually there was an institutional vacuum. On top of everything else, there was no accepted code of business behavior. Suddenly Russia found itself with the makings of a market but with no commercial code, no civil code, no effective bank system, no effective accounting system, no procedures for declaring bankruptcy. What was left over was not very helpful, especially the prevailing notion that it was perfectly appropriate to cheat the state.[38]

Under such conditions of institutional chaos, the accelerated transition to market mechanisms, including the liberalization of price controls, opened the way for a wild competition to grab state property by whatever means, often in association with criminal elements. As Goldman writes, "An argument can be made that to some extent the Russian reformers made the Mafia movement worse than it needed to have been."[39]

[37] See the sources cited in note 28 above. See, in addition, Bohlen (1993, 1994); Bonet (1993, 1994); Ovchinskyi(1993); Commission on Security and Co-operation in Europe (1994); Erlanger (1994a,b); Gamayunov (1994); *Izvestiya* (1994b,c); Kuznetsova(1996); Podlesskikh and Tereshonok (1994); Savvateyeva (1994); *The Current Digest of the Post-Soviet Press* (1994); Bennet (1997).
[38] Goldman (1996: 42).
[39] Goldman (1996: 40).The first government of democratic Russia, in 1992, was duly warned of the potential consequences of an accelerated transition to a market economy without previously setting up the institutions that would allow markets to operate properly. The international advisory committee to the Russian government that I chaired in 1992 (see explanation in chapter 1 of this volume,

This institutional chaos was made worse by the break up of the Soviet Union into 15 independent republics. Security agencies, and the armed forces, were disorganized; bureaucratic lines of command were blurred; legislation proliferated in disorder, while border controls were non-existent. Proto-capitalists and criminals moved around the different republics, picking up the most favorable environments, and still operating in the whole expanse of the ex-Soviet Union. Technological underdevelopment made it difficult to keep track of movements of capital, goods, and services in a huge territory. Local *Mafiyas* took control of local states, and established their own connection networks. The *Mafiyas*, and their business associates, jumped into the Information Age much faster than state bureaucracies. Controlling both the local nodes and the communication links, semi-criminal businesses bypassed most centralized controls still in place. They run the country through their own networks.

Identifying the actors

Who are the actors involved in the making of this wild process of accumulation, partly shaped by criminal interests? For one of the most respected observers of the Russian political scene, Pavel Voshchanov, the answer is unambiguous:

---

and in chapter 2 of volume I), delivered several notes and reports (which I still have), besides repeated verbal warnings, that indicated that markets required institutions and regulations, as demonstrated by the history of capitalist development in other countries. Burbulis told me in July 1992 that he agreed with our arguments but that "forces in the Kremlin" were in favor of a more pragmatic, less regulatory approach, that would provide greater freedom of maneuver. Gaidar, supported by the IMF, believed firmly in the intrinsic capacity of market forces to remove obstacles by themselves, once prices were liberalized, and people could use their vouchers to acquire shares. In 1996, acknowledging *ex post facto* some of the problems of uncontrolled privatization, which our committee had foreseen from March 1992, he blamed "the Communists and their allies". I personally do not think that Gaidar, Burbulis, and other leaders of the first Yeltsin cabinet were corrupt in 1992. I believe the key point is that they had really no legal, political, or bureaucratic power to control the results of their decisions. Thus, they liberalized, unleashing economic forces, and they were bypassed and overwhelmed by all kinds of pressure groups located inside and outside the state. When the process of liberalization and privatization became a free-for-all fight, and state institutions could offer no guarantee, various *Mafiyas* stepped in, and took partial control of the process. This is an important lesson for history. When and where there is no regulation and control by the legitimate forces of the state, there will be ruthless control by the illegitimate forces of violent, private groups. Unfettered markets are tantamount to wild societies.

How was the criminal Russian state born? In a way it emerged after the August 1991 coup. At that time the new political elite was pondering perhaps the most important question – how to make the post-coup economic and political changes irreversible. Those officials were unanimous that they must have their own social basis – a class of owners. It had to be rather large and be capable of supporting their patrons. The problem was to create this class starting from the point where all were roughly equal in terms of income and property . . . What was the major obstacle for the new nomenklatura at the Kremlin? It was the law. Any law was an obstacle as it, according to presidential aides in 1991, "hampered the progress of democracy."[40]

The strategic, political interests of reformers in power in 1991–2, induced a rapid process of liberalization and privatization that could create a large owners' class, with vested interests in the development of capitalism in Russia. Some of these reformers may, as well, have had it in mind to obtain personal benefit from their positions of power, as some eventually did in the following years. However, the most important point is that, inadvertently or not, they created opportunity for those with the money and power to seize state property – that is, the whole of Russia. These would-be capitalists were, first of all, leading members of the Communist *nomenklatura* that had accumulated wealth, particularly during the *perestroika* years, by diverting state funds into personal bank accounts abroad. I was told by high-ranking members of the Yeltsin cabinet in 1992 that, when they came to power, the gold and hard currency reserves of the Soviet state were almost entirely gone, a report that was later confirmed by various sources, and publicly stated, among others, by Yegor Gaidar in 1996. This was in addition to the secret foreign accounts of the Communist party of the Soviet Union that simply vanished in the global financial flows. Altogether this may represent, in all likelihood, tens of billions of dollars. A fraction of this capital was quite enough to buy a considerable amount of property, enterprises, banks, goods and services, in Russia, particularly if the political influence still in the hands of the *nomenklatura*'s friends facilitated the purchase of state property. Only a few months after the end of the Soviet Union, gigantic financial empires, with a highly diversified range of investments, emerged in the Russian economy. Soon, these conglomerates found connections in the new political system, since the institutional vacuum required some form of *ad hoc* government support to prosper in an uncertain environment, periodically shaken by a flurry of decrees.

[40]   Voshchanov (1995: 13).

There were other actors actively participating in the wild development of new Russian capitalism. Global organized crime, particularly the Sicilian Mafia and the Colombian cartels, seized the chance of Russian chaos to launder considerable sums of money, as well as mixing "dirty money" with counterfeited dollars by the billions.[41] Gaidar himself acknowledged in 1994 the existence of sizeable amounts of "dirty" money, laundered capital, and capital in the process of being laundered in Russia.[42] Having positioned themselves in Russia in the late 1980s and early 1990s, global criminal networks were able to take advantage of the privatization process, linking up with Russian organized crime, as well as inducing the development of new criminal organizations. They also linked up with the smuggling networks that sprung up around weapons depots, nuclear installations, oil fields, and precious and rare metals mines.[43]

When the institutional system broke down in 1991, and a disorderly market economy flourished at the street level, criminals of all kind, old and new, from various ethnic backgrounds, proliferated as parasites of whatever business, small or large, that emerged in Russia. Many non-profit, tax-exempt organizations came under *Mafiya* influence, for instance, the National Sports Foundation, the Russian Fund for Invalids of the Afghanistan War, and the All-Russian Society for the Deaf. Even the Russian Orthodox Church went into tax-exempt business, probably under the protection of the *Mafiya*, importing cigarettes duty-free for humanitarian aid, and investing in oil-trading companies.[44] Because of the absence of effective state regulation and control, a symbiotic relationship was established between the growth of private business, and its protection/extortion from criminal networks. This crime-penetrated business linked up with politicians at the local, provincial, and national levels, so that, ultimately, the three spheres (politics, business, crime) became intertwined. It does not mean that crime controls politics, or that most businesses are criminal. It means, none the less, that business operates in an environment deeply penetrated by crime; that business needs the protection of political power; and that many politicians, in the 1990s, have amassed considerable fortunes through their business contacts.

[41] Sterling (1994).
[42] Interview with Gaidar, *Trud*, February 10, 1994.
[43] Beaty (1994); Handelman (1995); Gordon (1996).
[44] *Business Week*, December 9, 1996; Specter(1996).

Mechanisms of accumulation

The mechanisms through which this kind of primitive capitalist accumulation in Russia has been performed are diverse: indeed, daring, imaginative schemes are the daily staple of Russian capitalists and crooks. But the essential mechanism has been *the process of privatization*, conducted with no transparency, scarce control, and unreliable accounting. It was through uncontrolled privatization that all valuable assets in Russia were sold for ridiculous prices to whoever had the money and the power to control the transaction. This is how and why government officials, ex-*nomenklatura*, and organized crime, Russian and international, came together, willingly or unwillingly.

Just prior to the privatization process several mega-scams helped to destabilize economic institutions, and provided seed capital to engage in primitive accumulation of Russian assets. Claire Sterling has identified, and carefully documented, what is probably the largest of these scams in 1990–92, initiated by global criminal networks, particularly by the Sicilian Mafia, with the complicity of contacts in the Soviet government, and, probably, of Western intelligence agencies as well. I refer to her account which lists a number of credible sources, citing names, places, dates, and figures.[45] In a nutshell, through a number of intermediaries posing as "international business men," criminal organizations and their contacts depreciated the ruble by buying billions of rubles in Russia at a large discount, with "dirty" dollars, and offering these rubles in the world market at a low price. Furthermore, they diffused rumors of even larger transactions, contributing to higher depreciation. Elements of the *nomenklatura* were interested in converting these worthless rubles into hard currency, both for their benefit, and, in some cases, for increasing the currency reserves of the Soviet state. These transactions fueled capital flight from the Soviet Union during the last period of *perestroika*. It seems that state gold reserves were used as a guarantee of some of these transactions. The devaluation of the ruble made assets and commodities much cheaper in Russia. Criminal networks, speculative intermediaries, and *nomenklatura* bosses used the billions of rubles they had amassed, and a few millions of dollars, to buy and smuggle oil, weapons, raw materials, rare and precious metals. They also invested in real estate, hotels, and restaurants. And they bought large packages of privatization vouchers from private citizens who did not know what to do with them, or were forced into selling. Once this speculative/criminal capital positioned itself in the economy it sought, and obtained, the support of the

---

[45]   Sterling (1994: 169–243).

Soviet, then Russian, government for investment in the country, and for import/export activities. This investment, originally made out of laundered money and/or from funds embezzled from the state, therefore multiplied considerably. Since much legitimate foreign investment was soon scared off from investing in Russia's insecure environment, Soviet and Russian legislation favoring foreign capital and trade worked largely in favor of para-criminal networks. Some of these scam creators were fully identified (Sterling cites Americans Leo Wanta and Marc Rich), but were never caught, and continued to run their businesses from their havens in other countries (Rich was based in Zug, Switzerland, in 1994). Sterling has evaluated the illicit smuggling of capital in 1992 at about US$ 20 billion, and the illicit outflow of oil and materials at another US$ 17 billion. This is several times the total foreign direct investment in Russia during the 1991–6 period. While Sterling's story has all the features of a fiction thriller, her documentation is serious enough to make it plausible, and the main thrust of her argument coincides with reports from other sources.[46] Furthermore, while I do not have factual evidence of my own, the picture of illegal deals and economic destabilization that I gathered during my fieldwork research in Russia in 1989–96, including interviews at the highest levels of Soviet and Russian government, does not contradict what Sterling, Handelman, Voshchanov, and many other observers, report.

Yet speculative maneuvers by global crime during the chaotic times of the Soviet collapse could not have sufficed to estabish the intertwining of politics, business, and crime that characterizes the Russian scene in the 1990s. The dramatic errors made by Gorbachev first, in disorganizing the Soviet system without replacing it, and the Russian democrats later, in pushing for an accelerated transition to the market economy without social and institutional control, created the conditions for the takeover of one of the largest, and naturally wealthiest countries in the world. It is this wild appropriation of wealth, enacted or tolerated by the powers that be, that explains the overwhelming presence of crime, not the other way around. But, unlike American "robber barons" who used all the means at their disposal to accumulate capital for investment, besides enriching themselves, wild Russian capitalism is deeply entrenched in global crime and in global financial networks. As soon as profits are generated, they are sent into the anonymous whirlwind of global finance, from which only a portion is reinvested, once conveniently laundered, into the

---

[46] Sterling's (1994) argument coincides with other sources as cited in the notes to this chapter.

rewarding, but risky, Russian economy. Thus, the pillage of Russia goes on, as a source of easy profits, and as a platform for international criminal activities, whose proceedings are diffused in the global financial networks.

Russian society, in its vast majority, is excluded from the Information Age in this end of millennium. But its crime-infested capitalism is fully immersed in the global flows of wealth and power that it has been able to access by perverting the hopes of Russian democracy.

Narcotrafico, Development, and Dependency in Latin America[47]

The extraordinary growth of the drug traffic industry since the 1970s has transformed the economics and politics of Latin America. Classic paradigms of dependency and development have to be rethought to include, as a fundamental feature, the characteristics of the drugs industry, and its deep penetration of state institutions and social organization. The industry is mainly centered around the production, processing, and export of coca and cocaine. However, in the 1990s heroin is becoming an increasingly important component, and

---

[47]   One of the best political-economic analyses of drug traffic in Latin America, although centered on Colombia, is Thoumi (1994). On the international structure of the drug industry in Latin America see Arnedy (1990); Tokatlian and Bagley (1990); Del Olmo (1991); Simposio Internacional (1991); Laserna (1991); and Bastias (1993). On the effects of coca production and cocaine traffic on national and regional economies, see Laserna (1995, 1996). To understand the psychology, social context, and political implications of drug traffic, probably the most inspiring document is the extraordinary report by Gabriel Garcia Marquez *Noticia de un secuestro* (1996). On the cultural dimensions of the world of drug traffic see De Bernieres (1991); Prolongeau (1992); and Salazar and Jaramillo (1992). On the links between the drug industry and US–Latin American relations, see the classic book by Scott and Marshall (1991). On Bolivia, see Laserna (1995) and Pasquini and De Miguel (1995). On Ecuador, Bagley et al. (1991). On Venezuela, Azocar Alcala (1994). On Mexico, Mejia Prieto (1988); Garcia (1991); and chapter 5 of volume II. On Peru, Turbino (1992); and Pardo Segovia (1995). A major source of information and ideas on the political economy of drug traffic in Latin America has been Roberto Laserna, Professor of Economics at the Universidad Mayor de San Simon, in Cochabamba. Our intellectual interaction for more than ten years has decisively shaped my thinking on this matter, although he bears no responsibility for my possible mistakes. Also, my stay in La Paz and Cochabamba in 1985, including a most interesting visit to the Chapare, by then one of the centers of coca cultivation in Latin America, were essential in my understanding of the drug industry.

marijuana, particularly in Mexico, is recovering some of the significance it had in the late 1960s and early 1970s. Around powerful criminal networks built from drug traffic, other criminal activities (particularly money laundering, smuggling, arms traffic, immigrants traffic, international prostitution, and kidnapping) are being organized, thus constituting a complex, criminal world, whose highly decentralized structure permeates, and marks, all Latin American societies. Several major features characterize *narcotrafico*'s industry.

(1) It is *demand driven and export oriented.* Its original, and still most important, market is the United States. However, Western Europe and affluent Asia are fast becoming important markets as well. As an illustration of the bottom-line economics of the cocaine industry, in 1991 the cost of producing one kilogram of cocaine in Colombia (including the cost of production of coca paste received from other countries) was estimated at US$ 750; its price for export from Colombia was about US$ 2,000; wholesale price for the same kilogram in Miami was US$ 15,000; and in the streets of American cities, sold by the gram, once conveniently "cut" with other ingredients, its value could reach up toUS$ 135,000.[48] Transportation and distribution costs, and protection of these distribution systems, are obviously linked to its illegality, and to its sustained demand in the United States.

(2) *The industry is fully internationalized, with a very strict division of labor between different locations.* Again focusing on cocaine, coca leaves are, and have been, cultivated and safely consumed for thousands of years in the Andean region.[49] Peru produces about 55 percent of coca leaves in the world, Bolivia about 35 percent, with the rest shared mainly between Ecuador, Colombia, Venezuela, and, recently, Brazil and Mexico. Transformation of coca leaves into coca paste, and, lately, into a base of coca, usually takes place in the cultivating countries, although at some distance from the fields to avoid detection. For instance, when I visited the then main coca-producing center in Bolivia, the Chapare, in Cochabamba province, coca paste was produced at about 100 km from Chapare, in villages of the valleys surrounding the city of Cochabamba, from where coca paste was carried on the backs of porters to clandestine land strips in the forest. From there, as well as from Alto Huallaga, the main producing area in Peru, coca paste and coca base were/are flown into Colombia, where the main centers of the industry have consolidated their control since

---

[48]   Thoumi (1994: 295).
[49]   Laserna (1996).

the late 1970s. In spite of repression, Colombia remains the main center for refining and advanced processing of cocaine. It also harbors management and commercial centers, from which is organized the most delicate operation: transportation into the affluent markets, particularly in the United States.

After primitive smuggling by human carriers in the early stages of the industry, the main form of transportation to the US is now by small planes flown from the Caribbean. This method was first organized by leading trafficker Carlos Lehder who bought an islet, Norman's Cay, in the Bahamas, and lent its landing strip to other exporters, thus constituting bases for cooperation – a flexible cartel – between exporters. But many other ways were and are used, as seizures by customs officers increased: commercial airlines, cargo ships, personal couriers, cocaine hidden in legally exported merchandise (construction materials, glass panels, fruits, cans, clothing and so on), as well as, particularly in the 1990s, land transportation across the Mexico–US border. Thus, Mexican drug cartels have developed strongly in the 1990s, first as intermediaries for the Colombians, then on their own, adding heroin, amphetamines, and marijuana to the cocaine they carried as partners of the Colombians.

In many instances, the method of transportation is straightforward: bribing customs officers of one or several countries. Long routes, such as to Europe or Asia, depend mainly on cargo ships, unloaded by smaller boats near the coast: this is the case in Galicia, Spain, one of the main entry points into Europe, in historical continuity with cigarette smuggling networks in Galicia. Networks of distribution in the United States tend to be controlled by Colombians, or their associates, often Mexican, using networks of immigrants from their national (or even regional) origin: trust-bonded networks. In Europe and Asia, Colombian cartels provide the merchandise, and leave the criminal organizations in charge of each territory to control distribution. Guayaquil plays a major role for sea shipments to the US. Venezuela is a staging point for air shipments to Europe.

Other critical inputs for the industry are chemical precursors, mainly imported from Switzerland, Germany, and the United States, but increasingly supplied by the Latin American chemical industry, particularly in Argentina and Brazil. Brazil, where a limited amount of coca is cultivated, has also joined the processing industry, as Colombian laboratories came under increasing pressure from the US Drug Enforcement Administration. While the geographical pattern of *narcotrafico* is evolving and extending its reach, it has maintained remarkable stability in its internal hierarchy, as the Colombian "cartels" have been able to maintain their domination, for reasons and with mechanisms that I will present below.

The three most important *transformations of this international division of labor of the drug industry in the 1990s* are: (a) the emergence of Mexico as a quasi-autonomous export center, benefiting from its proximity to the United States; (b) the strategic alliances between Colombian cartels and criminal organizations around the world, particularly with the Sicilian Mafia, the American Mafia, and the Russian criminal networks; (c) the widespread use of new communication technology, particularly mobile phones and portable computers, to communicate, and keep track of transactions, thus increasing the flexibility and complexity of the industry.

(3) The *critical component of the entire drugs industry is the money-laundering system.* It is also under the control of the main traffickers from Colombia and Mexico, but it is performed by specialized agents whose main locations are in the banks and financial institutions of Colombia, Venezuela, Panama, and Florida. Financial institutions in various small Caribbean countries, such as the Cayman Islands, Turcos y Caicos, Aruba, and the Bahamas, played an essential role as entry points of money laundering in the 1980s, but their exposure, and the small size of their financial systems, have diminished their role in global money laundering, although they still provide safe savings accounts for traffickers' personal finances.

(4) The whole set of transactions relies on *enforcement by an extraordinary level of violence.* All major criminal organizations have established their own networks of killers (for example, the Colombian *sicarios*), some of them highly specialized and professional. Many others, by the thousands, are in charge of policing and terrorizing entire cities, either as members of the organization or as subcontractors. Besides their enforcement function, these networks of killers are also instruments for competition, and for protection, when organizations fight each other for the control of a given market, or dispute the terms of profit-sharing. Indeed, as Thoumi observes, this high level of violence acts as a decisive "entry barrier" for would-be competitors in the industry.[50] Unless they have the resources, and the drive, to take the risk, they will simply be eliminated before they can position themselves in the market.

[50] Thoumi (1994).

(5) *The industry needs the corruption and penetration of its institutional environment to operate, at all points in the system.* Drug traffickers have to corrupt and/or intimidate local and national authorities, police, customs, judges, politicians, bankers, chemists, transportation workers, journalists, media owners, and businessmen. For most of these people, the alternative between obtaining considerable amounts of money or seeing their families terrorized is too powerful to be resisted. In the absence of a decisive affirmation of state power, *narcotrafico*'s networks take control of as many people and organizations as they need in their environment. True, a frontal assault against the state, as the one launched by Pablo Escobar and the Medellin cartel in Colombia in 1984–93, usually brings doom on the criminals. However, the Medellin tactics were extreme, and very much linked to the personality of its leaders, Rodriguez Gacha "el Mexicano," killed in 1989, and Pablo Escobar, deeply resentful against a government that had declared him to be a political outcast. The Cali cartel, as ruthless and violent as Medellin's, developed a more subtle strategy of penetration of the state, buying instead of killing, while reserving the killings for its Medellin rivals, and for low-level personnel who could be easily brought into subservience. As a result of this strategy, when the leaders of the Cali cartel, Miguel and Gilberto Rodriguez Orejuela, were finally apprehended, and brought to justice, in January 1997 they were sentenced to what, most likely, would amount to about three or four years in prison. Systematic corruption of the state, and extreme violence as a way of life, are essential components of the *narcotrafico* industry.

What are the economic consequences of the drugs industry for Latin America?

There is no doubt that the criminal economy represents a sizeable, and most dynamic, segment of Latin American economies in this end of millennium. Moreover, unlike traditional patterns of internationalization of production and trade in Latin America, this is a Latin American controlled, export-oriented industry, with proven global competitiveness. Even if, in the future, chemical drugs substitute for the real thing, the Colombian-based networks have the system in place to continue their pre-eminence in the market, including the R&D activities they finance for new product design and transportation technology. It is the United States that is dependent on drug consumption, and suffers an extraordinary burden of crime, social disintegration and police/judiciary/penitentiary costs, whose main origin lies in the criminalization of drugs and drugs traffic. Heroin from Asia also plays a part, and American and Sicilian Mafias, as well as home-grown gangs in many American cities, are significant in the crime scene. Yet, Latin American-based drugs traffic is an essential component of American crime, to the point that US policy toward Latin America is dominated by the obsession to fight drugs traffic at the point of supply. This is an impossible task, but one that has entirely transformed US–Latin American relations from old-fashioned imperialism to hysterical pursuit of a vanishing enemy which, in its repeated escapes, blows up entire political systems.

If *narcotrafico* has reversed the pattern of dependency is it developmental? Debate rages on the matter. A leading Latin American economist on the political economy of drugs traffic, Francisco Thoumi, thinks it is not. Others, like Sarmiento, link Colombian growth to foreign remittances, and investment, generated by drugs traffic.[51] Still others, such as Laserna, take an intermediate position, evaluating coca/cocaine's economic impact depending on which kind of development we are assessing, from which segment of the industry, and where it takes place.[52] I tend to concur with him. Areas of cultivation – in Bolivia, Peru, Ecuador, Colombia – improve their income, but not their living conditions. This is because the precariousness of the production blocks permanent investment in these settlements. These are frontier towns, always on the run, ready to be dismantled in one location, to start again 100 km deeper in the rain forest. What I saw in Chapare, in 1985, at the peak of its production boom, were poor huts, with no sanitary conditions, no water, scarce electricity, no schools, no health care, few women, and even fewer children. But I also saw, in a place with just 3 km of paved road, a proliferation of Mercedes and BMWs, an abundance of Japanese consumer electronics, and an unplugged IBM PC whose owner proudly told me that it was going to be the key to the education of his children. Most of the money generated in Chapare (about US$ 20,000 a year for a family of coca cultivators, collecting four crops a year) was changed for pesos in the streets, to buy a truck and build a house back in the village. A share of the money was deposited in banks in Cochabamba, from which this capital would be laundered through La Paz, the Caribbean, and Miami. Even Cochabamba did not display much wealth, except for half a dozen freshly built mansions. La Paz, and the Bolivian economy as a whole, has benefited to a much larger extent. As Peru did, somewhat: a share of its stunning capital

[51]   Sarmiento (1990a, b).
[52]   Laserna (1995, 1996).

investment in 1992–6 may have originated in the criminal economy. But peasants in Alto Huallaga, a region largely under the control of Sendero Luminoso guerrillas – allied to narcotraffickers – did not seem to have gained much advantage from this boom. Colombians appropriated a much larger share of the profits, even if the largest proportion was certainly recycled in the global financial markets for the profit of a small, criminally based business elite. But there was, from the mid-1980s, a significant boom of construction, real estate development, and investment in Colombia. In spite of the devastation of narco-terrorism, and of political instability, in 1995, the Bogota metropolitan area experienced an annual GDP growth of about 12 percent. During my most surrealist dinner with the Mayor of Medellin, in Bogota in December 1994, he laid out his grandiose plans for new development of the city, bridging into the twenty-first century. To be sure, this wave of investment in the mid-1990s cannot be rigorously traced back to criminal origins. Yet, given the prudent distance of regular foreign capital from the Colombian scene, it is plausible that some of this investment, and even more, the proliferation of intermediaries which are managing investment in construction, agriculture, industry, and advanced services in Colombia, can be related to a recycling of drugs traffic profits into legitimate business. Thus, Bogota, and Colombia, seem to have benefited economically from their central position in profitable drugs traffic, although the benefits of this trade have been partially offset by the destruction wrought by terrorism, by the climate of violence, and by the political instability generated by contradictory pressures from drug traffickers and from the US government.

Why Colombia?[53]

The dominance in the global cocaine industry of the Colombian cartels/networks, occupying for the first time a hegemonic position

[53] A documented social history of drug traffic in Colombia is Betancourt and Garcia (1994). A good journalistic account is Castillo (1991). For analyses of economic impacts in Colombia, see Sarmiento (1990); L.F.Sarmiento (1991); Kalmanovitz (1993); and Thoumi (1994). For social analyses of Colombian criminal subcultures and their relationship to everyday life, see Prolongeau (1992) and Salazar and Jaramillo (1992). For reports and analyses of the Medellin cartel, the most documented of cocaine-related criminal organizations, and on its wars with the Cali cartel see Veloza (1988); De Bernieres (1991); Gomez and Giraldo (1992); and Strong (1995). On the links between *narcotrafico* and paramilitary organizations in Colombia, with emphasis on Boyaca, see Medina Gallego (1990). For additional information, see also Camacho Guizado (1988); Perez Gomez (1988); and Arrieta et al. (1990). Again, the reading of Garcia Marquez's *Noticia*

in a major sector of the global economy, besides coffee exports, is linked to *cultural and institutional characteristics.* A brief reminder of how an export-oriented drugs traffic industry developed in Colombia, under Colombian control, will allow me to introduce a major theme of my interpretation of global crime: *the importance of cultural identity in the constitution, functioning, and strategies of criminal networks.*

Export-oriented drugs traffic in Colombia started in the late 1960s and early 1970s in the Atlantic Coast area of La Guajira, trading in marijuana cultivated in the sierras near Santa Marta (the famous "Santa Marta Gold" variety of marijuana). Social historians in Colombia report that the discovery of the potential of marijuana came from the enthusiasm shown for Colombian marijuana by young Americans sent to Colombia in the 1960s by the US Peace Corps. The American Mafia, linked to Colombia from Panama, organized the traffic in cooperation with a loose set of networks in La Guajira, around Barranquilla, an area that for centuries was a land of pirates, end of the world's immigrants, and smugglers. They came to be known as the *Marimberos* in the new prosperous era of the 1970s. It did not last. Marijuana was too bulky to transport, and the low price–volume ratio made it uncompetitive when faced with tougher controls by US customs. The US marijuana market began to be supplied by the United States. Humboldt County, in northern California, soon surpassed Colombia as a marijuana producer. US-induced repression of marijuana culture and traffic in Mexico and Colombia accentuated the shift of most production sites to within the US (for example, the Appalachian region) until the 1990s, when the control of Mexican cartels over large sections of the Mexican state made it possible to return to marijuana production for export across the border.

The networks that had been created around Colombia's marijuana exports survived to some extent. Panama-based American mafiosi mixed up Colombia with Bolivia (sic), and asked their Colombian contacts about the chances of switching to cocaine. Some entrepreneurial Colombians, in the smuggling business, seized the opportunity. They could also cultivate coca, but, more importantly,

de un secuestro (1996) is the most illuminating source for understanding the inter-action between *narcotrafico* and Colombian society. I also formed my analysis, and gathered information, during visits to Bogota in 1992 and 1994. I had the privilege of conversations and meetings with a number of colleagues and friends, whose names I prefer not to mention in a display of caution that is probably excessive. I do want, however, to express to all of them, and particularly to E.H., my deepest, if silent, gratitude.

they could take over the incipient traffic being developed in Bolivia, Ecuador, Peru, and Chile. One of them was a former student leader from Medellin, Pablo Escobar, who was making a killing in trafficking stolen tombstones, and who had already learned how to escape judicial repression by bribery and murder. He benefited from a favorable business environment.

Medellin, the capital of Antioquia, had traditionally been the seedbed of Colombia's entrepreneurialism, the equivalent of Sao Paulo in Brazil. In the 1970s, its traditional textile industry was in a shambles as a result of international competition from synthetic fibers. So was the other major entrepreneurial center of Colombia, Cali, the capital of the Valle del Cauca, whose sugar industry was struck by the new sugar quotas established in international trade. A third region, Boyaca, in the center of the country, was also undergoing turmoil because of a crisis in emerald mining and smuggling, its basic staple. These three areas became the centers of drug-traffic networks around cocaine. Boyaca, led by a bloody, populist leader, Rodriguez Gacha, joined the Medellin group, led by Pablo Escobar and the Ochoa family. Cali constituted its own network, and more often than not engaged in a ferocious war against the Medellin group. The Cali group, led by the brothers Rodriguez Orejuela, came from the upper-middle class of Cali, and never challenged the power of the traditional Colombian oligarchy, which has always controlled business, prestige, wealth, land, government, and the two parties *Conservador* and *Liberal.* These oligarchs still found a way of pitching *Liberales* against *Conservadores* in the most murderous civil war in Latin America, *La Violencia* of the 1950s, suggesting a pattern of violence that would become the trademark of Colombian criminal networks.

In contrast, the Medellin group, coming from the lower-middle class, had to settle its class differences with the local elite, in a culture where only wealth provides respect. They were also highly politicized, to the point that Pablo Escobar and a close political ally were elected to the Colombian Congress in 1982, only to be expelled thereafter when the US Embassy intervened. Also, the relationship between the two cartels and the marginal sections of the population were sharply different. Escobar financed a low-income housing program and social services for the poor in Medellin, and built significant social support among shanty-town dwellers. He even tried to defend the "human rights" of his youth gangs against the obvious abuses of the national police. The Cali cartel, on the other hand, practiced "social cleaning"; that is, randomly killing hundreds, maybe thousands, of "*desechables*" (discardables), who, in the drug traffickers' view, included the homeless, prostitutes, street children, beggars, petty thieves, and homosexuals. This practice is unfortunately carried on at this very moment in Bogota by paramilitary units, and upper-class-inspired "hunting parties," which bring terror to the city at night.

Yet, all drug-trafficking groups built up their military skills in the same killers' network: the MAS (*Muerte a Secuestradores*), which was created in 1981 in response to the kidnapping of Martha Nieves de Ochoa (from Medellin's Ochoa family) by the leftist guerrillas of M-19. Ms Ochoa was freed, after negotiations, but killings, by the hundred, went on for years: drug traffickers continued to send the message that they were strong enough, and determined enough, not to let anyone impose anything on them.

Yet, regardless of their violent divergences, and their contrasting tactics, both the Medellin and Cali groups hoped for their full integration into Colombian society. Repeatedly, they proposed to various presidents to pay off the Colombian foreign debt in cash (for different amounts, always in billions of dollars, at different times), and reinvest their capital in Colombia, thus becoming legitimate businessmen. It was not an impossible dream. But it was, indeed, a dream because the US government decided to draw the line, and use all means available to prevent drug traffickers making Colombia into a safe house. Thus, the main issue was the extradition of drug traffickers to the United States, a measure that the US succeeded in obtaining during the 1980s. But this was also the reason why the Medellin cartel launched a frontal assault against the Colombian state, on behalf of the "*Extraditables*" to reverse the law. It lost the battle, but won the war. After years of the most violent urban terrorism ever witnessed in Latin America, the Medellin cartel's leadership was decimated, and Pablo Escobar was gunned down on a Medellin roof in December 1993. Yet, in 1992, the new Colombian Constitution prohibited extradition of nationals.

The attachment of drug traffickers to their country, and to their regions of origin, goes beyond strategic calculation. They were/are deeply rooted in their cultures, traditions, and regional societies. Not only have they shared their wealth with their cities, and invested a significant amount (but not most) of their fortune in their country, but they have also revived local cultures, rebuilt rural life, strongly affirmed their religious feelings, and their beliefs in local saints and miracles, supported musical folklore (and were rewarded with laudatory songs from Colombian bards), made Colombian football teams (traditionally poor) the pride of the nation, and revitalized the dormant economies and social scenes of Medellin and Cali – until bombs and machine guns disturbed their joy. The funeral of Pablo Escobar was a homage to him by the city, and particularly by the poor of the city: many considered him to have been their benefactor.

Thousands gathered, chanting slogans against the government, praying, singing, crying, and saluting.

Why Colombia? Because of the original combination of dormant networks of drug traffic linking up to the United States, an existing entrepreneurial class marginalized by the failed industrialization of Latin America, and the strong rooting of the relatively educated, upwardly mobile smugglers into their cultures and local societies. This serendipitous formula, however, built on a tradition, and took advantage of a very favorable institutional environment. The tradition was the violence that has characterized Colombia throughout its history, and particularly in the 1950s. The *sicarios* of the 1980s were a reincarnation of the *pajaros* ("birds" = killers) that worked for both liberals and conservatives all over rural Colombia during *La Violencia*. And the Colombian drug traffickers took advantage of the perennial crisis of legitimacy and control of the Colombian state. Colombia is the only state in South America where, even in this end of millennium, sizeable areas of the country escape government control. Communist guerrillas, such as the *Fuerzas Armadas Revolucionarias Colombianas*, and other smaller groups, such as *Ejercito de Liberacion Nacional*, have controlled areas of the Colombian countryside, forests, and mountains, for the past half a century. In the 1980s, Rodriguez Gacha and Carlos Lehder organized "anti-communist free territories" in central Colombia, freely exercising their terror, with the tolerance of the army. The Colombian state has been, even more than other Latin American states, both captured by a narrow oligarchy, and deeply penetrated by corruption. When courageous leaders, such as Luis Carlos Galan, tried to reverse this course, they were simply murdered (in his case by Pablo Escobar's *sicarios*). Paramilitary groups, linked to elements in the police and the armed forces, have imposed their ferocious diktat over moderates in government, often going on a rampage of killings of elected officials, union leaders, community activists, intellectuals, and left-wing militants. And organized crime had its say in government well before cocaine traffic became significant in Colombia. Thus, Thoumi's hypothesis that points to the weakness of the Colombian state as a critical factor in fostering Colombia's preeminence in global cocaine traffic seems plausible.[54] It also suggests a broader trend. If large but weak states (such as Colombia) facilitate the location of command and control centers of global criminal networks, the power of these criminal centers is likely to overwhelm these states even further. It follows a downward spiral where, ultimately, criminal organizations may control some states: not by following the violent confrontation of the Medellin type of tactics, but

[54]   Thoumi (1994).

by combining bribery, intimidation, the financing of politics, and the affirmation of cultural identity with skillful international business management. Colombia, then Mexico, then Russia, then Thailand, then . . .

Globalization and identity interact in the criminal economy of Latin America. They organize the perverse connection that redefines development and dependency in historically unforeseen ways.

The Impact of Global Crime on Economy, Politics, and Culture

Money laundering, and its derivatives, have become a significant and troubling component of global financial flows and stock markets. The size of these capitals, while unknown, is likely to be considerable. But more important is their mobility. To avoid tracking, capital originating in the criminal economy shifts constantly from financial institution to financial institution, from currency to currency, from stock to stock, from investment in real estate to investment in entertainment. Because of its volatility, and its willingness to take high risks, criminal capital follows, and amplifies, speculative turbulences in financial markets. Thus, it has become an important source of destabilization of international finance and capital markets.

Criminal activity has also a powerful direct effect on a number of national economies. In some cases, the size of its capital overwhelms the economy of small countries. In other cases, such as Colombia, Peru, Bolivia, or Nigeria, it represents an amount sizeable enough to condition macroeconomic processes, becoming decisive in specific regions or sectors. Still in other countries, such as Russia or Italy, its penetration of business and institutions transforms the economic environment, making it unpredictable, and favoring investment strategies focused on short-term returns. Even in economies as large and solid as Japan, financial crises can be triggered by criminal maneuvers, as was the case in 1995 of the savings and loans defaults, for hundreds of billions of dollars, as a result of bad loans forced on some bankers by the *Yakuza*. The distorting effects of the unseen criminal economy on monetary policies, and on economic policies at large, make it even more difficult to control nationally based economic processes in a globalized economy, one component of which has no official existence.

The impact of crime on state institutions and politics is even greater. State sovereignty, already battered by the processes of globalization and identification, is directly threatened by flexible networks of crime that bypass controls, and assume a level of risk that no other organizations are capable of absorbing (see volume II, chapter 5). The technological and organizational opportunity to set up global networks has transformed, and empowered, organized crime. For a long time, its fundamental strategy was to penetrate national and local state institutions in its home country, in order to protect its activities. The Sicilian Mafia, the Japanese *Yakuza*, the Hong Kong-based, or Taiwan-based, or Bangkok-based Triads, the Colombian cartels relied on their capacity to build over time a deep connection with segments of national and regional states, both with bureaucrats and with politicians. This is still an important element in the operational procedures of organized crime: it can only survive on the basis of corruption and intimidation of state personnel and, sometimes, of state institutions. However, in recent times, globalization has added a decisive twist to the institutional strategy of organized crime. Safe, or relatively safe, houses have been found around the planet: small (Aruba), medium (Colombia), large (Mexico) or extra-large (Russia), among many others. Besides, the high mobility and extreme flexibility of the networks makes it possible to evade national regulations and the rigid procedures of international police cooperation. Thus, the consolidation of the European Union has handed organized crime a wonderful opportunity to take advantage of contradictions between national legislations and of the reluctance of most police forces to relinquish their independence. Thus, Germany has become a major operational center for the Sicilian Mafia, Galicia is a major staging point for the Colombian cartels, and The Netherlands harbors important nodes of heroin traffic of the Chinese Triads.[55] When pressure from the state, and from international forces (usually US intelligence agencies), becomes excessive in a given country, even in a region that was "safe" for organized crime (for example, the significant repression of crime in Sicily in 1995–6, or in Medellin and Cali in 1994–6), the flexibility of the network allows it to shift its organizational geometry, moving supply bases, altering transportation routes, and finding new places of residence for their bosses, increasingly in respectable countries, such as Switzerland, Spain, and Austria. As for the real thing, that is the money, it circulates safely in the flows of computerized financial transactions, managed from offshore banking bases that direct its swirling in time and space.

Furthermore, escaping police control through networking and globalization allows organized crime to keep its grip on its national bases. For instance, in the mid-1990s, while the Colombian cartels (particularly Medellin) suffered serious blows, Colombian drug

---

[55] Sterling (1994); Roth and Frey (1995).

traffickers survived by modifying their organization and decentralizing their structure. In fact, they were never a hierarchical, consolidated cartel, but a loose association of exporters, including, in Cali, for instance, over 200 independent organizations. Thus, when some leaders become too inconvenient (as, for example, Rodriguez Gacha, or Escobar), or are eliminated, these networks find new arrangements, new power relationships, and new, albeit unstable, forms of cooperation. By emphasizing local flexibility and international complexity, the criminal economy adapts itself to the desperate control attempts by rigid, nationally bound state institutions, that, for the time being, know they are losing the battle. With it, they are also losing an essential component of state sovereignty *and legitimacy*: its ability to impose law and order.

In a desperate reaction to the growing power of organized crime, democratic states, in self-defense, resort to measures that curtail, and will curtail, democratic liberties. Furthermore, since immigrant networks are often used by organized crime to penetrate societies, the excessive, and unjust, association between immigration and crime triggers xenophobic feelings in public opinion, undermining the tolerance and capacity of coexistence that our increasingly multiethnic societies desperately need. With the nation-state under siege, and with national societies and economies already insecure from their intertwining with transnational networks of capital and people, the growing influence of global crime may induce a substantial retrenchment of democratic rights, values, and institutions.

The state is not only being bypassed from outside by organized crime. It is disintegrating from within. Besides the ability of criminals to bribe and/or intimidate police, judges, and government officials, there is a more insidious and devastating penetration: *the corruption of democratic politics*. The increasingly important financial needs of political candidates and parties create a golden opportunity for organized crime to offer support in critical moments of political campaigns. Any movement in this direction will haunt the politician for ever. Furthermore, the domination of the democratic process by scandal politics, character assassination, and image-making also offers organized crime a privileged terrain of political influence (see volume II, chapter 6). By luring politicians into sex, drugs, and money, or fabricating allegations as necessary, organized crime has created a wide network of intelligence and extortion, which traffics influence against silence. In the 1990s, the politics of many countries, not only in Latin America, have been dominated by scandals and crises induced by the direct or indirect connection between organized crime and politics. But in addition to these known, or suspected, cases of political corruption, the pervasiveness of scandal politics suggests the possibility that

organized crime has discretely positioned itself in the world of politics and media in a number of countries, for instance in Japan
(*Yakuza*),[56] or Italy (Sicilian Mafia).

The influence of global crime also reaches the *cultural realm* in more
subtle ways. On the one hand, cultural identity nurtures most of these
criminal networks, and provides the codes and bonding that build
trust and communication within each network. This complicity does
not preclude violence against their own kind. On the contrary, most
violence is within the network. Yet there is a broader level of sharing
and understanding in the criminal organization, that builds on
history, culture, and tradition, and generates its own legitimizing
ideology. This has been documented in numerous studies of the
Sicilian and American Mafias, since their resistance to French occupation in the eighteenth century, or among the Chinese Triads, which
originated in southern resistance to northern invaders, and then
developed as a brotherhood in foreign lands. In my brief description
of the Colombian cartels I have given a glimpse of their deep rooting
in regional culture, and in their rural past, which they tried to revive.
As for Russian crime, which is probably the most cosmopolitan in its
projection, it is also embedded in Russian culture and institutions. In
fact, the more organized crime becomes global, the more its most
important components emphasize their cultural identity, so as not to
disappear in the whirlwind of the space of flows. In so doing, they
preserve their ethnic, cultural, and, where possible, territorial bases.
This is their strength. Criminal networks are probably in advance of
multinational corporations in their decisive ability to combine
cultural identity and global business.

However, the main cultural impact of global crime networks on
societies at large, beyond the expression of their own cultural identity, is in *the new culture they induce*. In many contexts, daring, successful
criminals have become role models for a young generation that does
not see an easy way out of poverty, and certainly no chance of enjoying

---

[56]   To mention just one example of penetration of government by organized
crime in Japan, let me summarize a report from a reliable Japanese magazine. On
January 3, 1997, former Minister of Defense of the Japanese government, Keisuke
Nakanishi, still a leading politician of the Shinshinto party, was attacked and
slightly injured at Haneda Airport by two members of the *Yakuza*. The attack
seemed to have been motivated by a dispute between the *Yakuza* and the ex-
Minister about his behavior while securing a large loan from a bank to a developer
for the benefit of the *Yakuza*. During the transaction, about 200 million yen
disappeared, and the *Yakuza* was using intimidation to recover the money.
Mr Nakanishi was suspected of engaging in various joint business ventures with
Yakuza groups during his tenure as Minister of Defense (from *Shukan Shincho*,
January 16, 1997).

consumption and live adventure. From Russia to Colombia, observers emphasize the fascination of local youth for the mafiosi. In a world of exclusion, and in the midst of a crisis of political legitimacy, the boundary between protest, patterns of immediate gratification, adventure, and crime becomes increasingly blurred. Perhaps Garcia Marquez, better than anyone else, has captured the "culture of urgency" of young killers in the world of organized crime. In his non-fiction book *Noticia de un secuestro* (1996), he describes the fatalism and negativism of young killers. For them, there is no hope in society, and everything, particularly politics and politicians, is rotten. Life itself has no meaning, and their life has no future. They know they will die soon. So, only the moment counts, the immediate consumption, good clothing, good life, on the run, together with the satisfaction of inducing fear, of feeling powerful with their guns. Just one supreme value: their families, and in particular their mother, for whom they would do anything. And their religious beliefs, particularly for specific saints that would help in bad moments. In striking literary terms, Garcia Marquez recounts the phenomenon that many social scientists around the world have observed: young criminals are caught between their enthusiasm for life and the realization of their limits. Thus, they compress life into a few instants, to live it fully, and then disappear. For those brief moments of existence, the breaking of the rules, and the feeling of empowerment, compensates for the monotone display of a longer, but miserable life. Their values are, to a large extent, shared by many other youngsters, albeit in less extreme forms.

The diffusion of the culture of organized crime is reinforced by the pervasiveness of the everyday life of the criminal world in the media. People around the world are probably more acquainted with the media version of the working conditions and psyche of "hit men" and drug traffickers than with the dynamics of financial markets where people invest their money. The collective fascination of the entire planet with action movies where the protagonists are the players in organized crime cannot be explained just by the repressed urge for violence in our psychological make up. It may well indicate the cultural breakdown of traditional moral order, and the implicit recognition of a new society, made up of communal identity and unruly competition, of which global crime is a condensed expression.

━━ 4 ━━

Development and Crisis in the Asian Pacific: Globalization and the State[1]

The Changing Fortunes of the Asian Pacific[2]

Before July 2, 1997 the Asian Pacific was considered, rightly, to be the world's success story of economic development and technological modernization of the past half-century. Indeed, between 1965 and 1996, average annual growth of GNP in real terms for the world at large was 3.1 percent. In contrast, in the Asian Pacific, China grew at an annual average rate of 8.5 percent, Hong Kong at 7.5 percent, South Korea at 8.9 percent, Singapore at 8.3 percent, Thailand at 7.3 percent, Indonesia at 6.7 percent, Malaysia at 6.8 percent, the Philippines at 3.5 percent, and Japan at 4.5 percent. In 1950, Asia accounted for just 19 percent of the world's income; in 1996, its share reached 33 percent. In the span of about three decades the Asian Pacific had become a major center of capital accumulation in the planet, the largest manufacturing producer, the most competitive

---

[1] This chapter was substantially revised in the fall of 1998 to introduce new material and analyses, taking into account the 1997–8 Asian crisis and its implications for states and societies in the Asian Pacific, as well as for the global economy.

[2] The data on the Asian crisis, for all countries, for 1996–8 have been obtained from standard business publications, particularly from *Far Eastern Economic Review, Business Week, The Economist, The Wall Street Journal, The Financial Times,* and *The International Herald Tribune,* as well as from sources on the Internet. Given that all these sources are in the public domain, I do not consider it necessary to provide specific references for each figure cited here. Several colleagues provided valuable ideas and information, including press clippings from Asian countries. I would particularly like to thank Chu-Joe Hsia of the National Taiwan University; Jeffrey Henderson of the University of Manchester; You-tien Hsing of the University of British Columbia; and Jong-Cheol Kim of the University of California, Berkeley.

trading region, one of the two leading centers of information technology innovation and production (the other is the US), and the fastest growing market. And, in a development full of implications, the hottest destination for global capital investment in emerging markets: during the 1990s Asian developing countries received a capital inflow estimated at over 420 billion US dollars. Together with China's rise as a world power, and with Japan's technological and financial might, it looked as though a geo-economic tectonic shift was in the making, ushering in the Pacific Era. Then, in a few months, in 1997 and 1998, entire economies collapsed (Indonesia, South Korea), others went into a deep recession (Malaysia, Thailand, Hong Kong, the Philippines), and the leading economy, Japan, the second largest in the world, was shaken by financial bankruptcies, prompting the international downgrading of Japanese bonds and stocks. Ultimately, the Japanese economy went into a recession as well. Taiwan and Singapore suffered much less, although they experienced moderate currency devaluation. Taiwan's growth slowed down, and Singapore declined, for the first time, in 1998. China seemed to absorb the shock at the onset of the crisis, and was the only country which contributed to stabilizing the region. Even if, in the future, the deepening of the crisis catches up with all Pacific countries, the differential behavior of the economies of China, Taiwan, and Singapore in the midst of the global turmoil of 1997 and 1998 is a most significant observation that may provide some clues for the explanation of the crisis and its aftermath. I will interpret the meaning of this observation at the end of the chapter.

The 1997 crisis unfolded over the following months (and years), substantially altering the economic and social landscape of the Asian Pacific, and provoking a chain of repercussions in the global economy. Why so? Why this dramatic reversal in what seemed to be the firmly established path of development and modernization? To be sure, at the turn of the millennium, the Asian Pacific is still a potentially dynamic region, and together with crisis there are underlying conditions for economic growth that will yield renewed prosperity for some sections of the population in core areas. At the same time, work and life will become much harsher for most of the labor force. The fact that Asia is going through a structural crisis does not imply that capitalist development will be halted in the Pacific Rim. In all likelihood, there will be a new round of economic growth, characterized by an accentuation of its capitalist character, thus further integrating the Pacific in global, informational capitalism. On the other hand, the kind of policies that will prove effective in overcoming the Asian financial crisis may reflect upon economic policies in the rest of the world, perhaps inducing a modification of the capitalist model itself. Therefore, a consideration of the causes and characteristics of the 1997–8 Asian crisis may help us to understand the specific process of integration of Asia in global capitalism, and thus the new features of global capitalism itself. There is, of course, a raging debate between economists on this matter, a debate whose detailed presentation would take us too far away from the central, analytical focus of this chapter. Besides, because this Asian crisis was not a single event, but is an ongoing process, any empirical evaluation of its contours will be outdated by the time you read these lines. Thus, I will concentrate on what is of general analytical value in interpreting the Asian crisis in the framework of the long-term process of Asian development, focusing on what I believe to be the central factor in this process: the evolving relationship between globalization and the state.

The Asian crisis was, at its source, a financial crisis, prompted by a currency crisis. After the devaluation of the Thai baht on July 2, 1997, most currencies in the region, with the exception of the not fully convertible yuan, began tumbling (the Indonesian rupiah, for instance, lost 80 percent of its value against the dollar in one year – although the six-month mark was much worse: –250 percent). The devaluation of currencies made it impossible for local banks to repay their short-term debt to foreign lenders, since they were operating in currencies that were until then pegged to the dollar. When governments acted, in most cases under IMF pressure, to raise interest rates in order to defend the currency, they put added pressure upon insolvent banks, and firms, and they ultimately stalled their economies by drying up capital sources. Furthermore, it has been convincingly argued, by leading economists such as Jeffrey Sachs, that the intervention of the IMF considerably aggravated the crisis.[3] Indeed, when the major issue at stake was the lack of credibility of a given currency, it was crucial to restore confidence in it. Instead, the IMF's alarming statements concerning the economies in crisis, and the unreliability of their banks and financial institutions, amplified the financial panic, prompting both international and domestic investors to withdraw their money, and cut off new lending. Therefore, currencies slid further, and bankruptcies were suffered by thousands of firms. Instability in Asian financial markets prompted speculative movements that diffused throughout the region's currency markets. When, on October 23, 1997, the Hong Kong dollar, a symbol of stability, came under sustained attack, the territory's economy was seriously undermined, with property values plunging by 40 percent

[3]   Sachs (1998).

between mid-1997 and mid-1998, wiping out 140 billion US dollars of Hong Kong's wealth. While China's determination to defend Hong Kong's financial system stabilized the currency for some time, the Hong Kong crisis was the turning point which alerted global investors to the dangers of Asian emerging markets. The most indebted economy, South Korea, the eleventh largest economy of the world at the time, actually collapsed. By the end of 1997, South Korea had to declare itself bankrupt, and surrender its economic sovereignty to the IMF in exchange for a 58 billion US dollar bail-out, the largest ever in the IMF's history. The austerity measures introduced in South Korea, and in the region at large, sent most Asian Pacific economies into a recession in 1998, except for China, and Taiwan.

Thus, at the root of the Asian crisis was the loss of investor trust and the sudden lack of credibility of Asian currencies and securities in global financial markets. What triggered the crisis was the brutal reversal in capital flows: the five most damaged economies (South Korea, Thailand, Indonesia, Malaysia, and the Philippines) posted a capital inflow of $93 billion in 1996, which became a capital out-flow of $12 billion in 1997 – a swing of $105 billion. But what was the cause of this credibility crisis? Some economists, such as Krugman and the IMF's Fischer, point to the economic weaknesses of Asian economies: for example, current account deficits, secluded financial systems, overvalued currencies, excessive short-term indebtedness, and the use of inflated real estate as loan collateral. Other economists, such as Sachs and Stiglitz, point, on the contrary, to the fundamentally sound features of most Asian economies: for example, budget surpluses, low inflation, high saving rates, export-oriented economies – all the features that are the usual staple of good developing economics. Indeed, this is what global investors used to think. Furthermore, there were considerable differences between the macroeconomic data and industrial mix of the various economies that, ultimately, shared the crisis; while other economies, particularly Taiwan, China, and to some extent Singapore, did weather the storm, initially avoiding a recession. So, on the one hand, there was an external source to the crisis, linked to the dynamics of global financial markets. On the other hand, economic diversity and institutional specificity led to very different outcomes in the impact of the crisis and its aftermath.[4] Let us consider these two observations, in sequence.

First of all, the external dimension of the crisis: why and how the

[4]   Henderson (1998a).

globalization of finance affected the financial stability of a number of countries. Some elements of the Asian economies (such as politically regulated banking practices and lack of accounting transparency) were worrisome for prudent capitalist investment. But these had been well-known features for years, and they did not deter massive foreign investment, both direct and in securities. Why, suddenly, in 1997 did this confidence vanish in a few months? How, in the investors' perception, did government protection mutate into crony capitalism and financial flexibility into irresponsible lending? One major reason for the instability of Asian finance seems to have been the excessively large volume of foreign lending, much of it short term. It had reached such a dimension that, as Jeffrey Sachs suggested, investors understood that if every investor stopped lending, countries such as Thailand, Indonesia, and South Korea would default. Thus, as soon as concerns emerged on the overvaluation of certain currencies (the baht, the won, in particular), there was a race among investors to take out their money before others did. It became a self-fulfilling prophecy. When real-estate prices collapsed as a result of economic uncertainty, most of the assets guaranteeing outstanding loans vanished. And government support became nonviable when confronted with the scale of assistance needed by numerous banks and corporations, all at the same time. Then, global agencies deepened the crisis. Private rating agencies, such as Moody's and Standard & Poor, sounded the alarm by downgrading entire countries – South Korea, for instance – a downgrading that extends automatically to all financial firms and corporations operating from the downgraded country (the so-called "sovereign ceiling doctrine"). Thus, inflows of foreign investment came to a halt, except for bargain price acquisition of domestic fledgling firms, particularly in the financial industry. On the other hand, IMF-imposed policies saved much of the money of foreign investors at the price of worsening the credibility crisis, and stagnating the domestic economies by making it even more difficult for firms to repay the loans, thus extending bankruptcy. The weakest economies, such as Indonesia, literally collapsed, giving rise to widespread deindustrialization and reverse migration to the countryside. There followed substantial social unrest: sometimes chaotic, turning to ethnic/religious hatred; sometimes beneficial for social and political change (for example, the end of Suharto's dictatorship; the strengthening of South Korean working-class movements; political change in Thailand).

There is another factor which must be taken into consideration to account for the timing and characteristics of the Asian crisis. This is the crisis of Japan itself, which cannot be equated with the processes

I have described, and which was a major factor in the inability of the region to react to the disruption provoked by volatile capital flows. Had Japan been able to lend capital, absorb imports, and reorganize financial markets, the Asian crisis would have been limited to a temporary turmoil. But, in fact, Japan had been suffering a structural crisis of its development model since the early 1990s. Furthermore, the Japanese state indulged in self-denial, with the result that Japan, instead of being a rampart against the crisis in Asia, itself suffered seriously from the impact of financial collapse throughout the region. The shaky condition of Japanese banks and financial institutions became exposed, and the whole economy went into a recession, after years of stagnation. I will return later in the chapter to the specific crisis in Japan, and its relationship to the Asian crisis as a whole.

This interpretation of the Asian crisis must, however, be placed in the framework of a broader analysis, in line with the theory of informational, global capitalism proposed throughout this book. I argue that the main reason why global financial markets overwhelmed the stability of Asian national economies was because, by the mid-1990s, global financial flows had penetrated these economies so deeply that they had become addicted to massive short-term borrowing, a practice that made economies extremely vulnerable to any sudden reversal of investment flows. Speculative maneuvering was certainly a factor in the demise of a number of currencies. Yet we should not equate speculation with the supposed action of a few sinister characters conspiring in a corporate room. Rather, I understand by speculation profit-making strategies by investors of all kinds, including hedge fund firms, as well as institutional investors, linking up anonymously via computer networks to create financial advantage on a run-away currency or on a fledgling stock market – thus decisively amplifying market trends.

Yet, why did global financial flows acquire such an overwhelming role in Asian economies? It seems that two main factors were at work: first, the success of these economies, and their prospects for high economic growth; secondly, the weakness of their financial institutions, entirely dependent on the state. Foreign investors were obtaining returns substantially higher than in the US or European markets – with no questions asked. Since Asian governments had, for a long time, fully backed their banks and financial institutions (in the case of Hong Kong, the main backer was, paradoxically, the PRC government, as shown in the 1997 crisis), the expectation was that if anything went wrong, it would be covered by governments. So, what have become the general complaints of global investors (lack of legal regulation, government interference) were the very reasons that prompted unprecedented capital investment in Asia in the first place.

There is still another important question to be asked: why were Asian financial institutions, banks, and securities firms so shaky? Why did the mechanisms of financial steering that had allowed governments to create the most extraordinary process of economic growth in Asian history become ineffectual in managing global lending and investment? My view is that, throughout the process of fast development, between the early 1960s and late 1980s, Asian economies were protected by their states from the whirlwind of global financial markets – and even, to some extent, from global trade competition – while, on the other hand, Asian firms sheltered in their economies were becoming global players in trade and investment. When the scale of these economies, the size of these firms, and their interconnection with global capitalist networks led to a two-sided integration in the global economy, states could no longer protect or control movements of capital, goods, and services. Thus, they were bypassed by global economic flows, and were not in a position to regulate or command their economies under the pre-existing rules, made obsolete by their own success. With no protection from the state, Asian financial markets, and firms, were taken by global capital flows that made substantial profits, and then left these markets when their lack of transparency made them too risky. Calculated or not, it was, overall, and in most cases, a profitable operation for global investors (including globalized Asian capital), since the international bail-out of defaulted loans was mainly aimed to cover their losses. In addition, the busting of local firms became a welcome opportunity for foreign firms, particularly American and Western European, that could finally crack the financial industry in Asian countries, through acquisitions, and joint ventures, under very favorable conditions. In sum, the institutional system that was at the heart of the Asian miracle, the developmental state, became the obstacle for the new stage of global integration and capitalist development in the Asian economy. For Asian economies to fully join the global economy, not just as competitors and investors, but as markets and recipients of global investment, they had to come under the discipline of global financial markets. This implied their submission to standard market rules, enforced, when necessary, through bankruptcy, bad ratings, and subsequent IMF-style imposed policies. This was not the result of a capitalist plot, but the inexorable consequence of a shared, global, capitalist logic, enacted through the integration of financial and currency markets. The historic journey of the Asian developmental state succeeded in bringing poor, peripheral economies into the high seas of informational capitalism. Then, upon reaching the stormy ocean of global financial networks, without a center, and without institutions, in most countries the developmental state sunk – a useless vessel, a captive of its anchoring in national shores. Economies and societies became gradually de-statized, while suddenly realizing the new tyranny of capital flows revealed by flashes of instructions on computer screens.

However, as Henderson has observed,[5] the pattern of development and crisis in the Asian Pacific varied greatly according to specific social, economic, and institutional environments. What happened in Japan, Korea, China, Singapore, Taiwan, Indonesia, or in any other country, was dependent upon the specific set of relationships between the state, economy, and society. Thus, we need to explain, at the same time, why each economy developed, why it suffered the crisis (or did not), and why the crisis affected, in varying degrees, countries with very different conditions. It is in the interplay of internal, social dynamics and external, financial flows, both mediated by the institutions of the state, that the explanation for the contradictory process of Asian Pacific development and crisis lies.

Thus, to understand the new historical stage of the Asian Pacific, and its relationship to the Information Age, I must retrace the social and institutional roots of its developmental saga, focusing on specific societies and developmental processes. Only after proceeding through a series of country-based analyses will I be able to return to the causes and consequences of the Asian crisis of 1997–8 to evaluate its potential outcome for the Pacific and for the world at large. Because societies are not global, but historically and culturally rooted, to proceed with the analysis of the rise of the Asian Pacific, I will summarize the historical journey of several societies over the past three decades. Because of the limits of my research capacity, I will have to omit from this observation some countries that are important for the understanding of the crisis, particularly Indonesia, Thailand, and Malaysia. However, I will try to integrate the analysis of their economic crises, in the context of the restructuring of the Asian Pacific, in the final section of this chapter. I will first focus on the process of development of the six lands that, together, constituted the core of the new Asian Pacific economy, and changed for ever the historical meaning of development. I will start with the decisive economy of the region – Japan – and will continue with a study of the four Asian "tigers", ending with a summary view of the transformation of the Middle Kingdom, home to one-fifth of humankind.

[5]   Henderson (1998b).

Heisei's Japan: Developmental State versus Information Society[6]

Japan's defeat was inevitable. Japan lacked raw materials, was backward in science, and the character of the people have long been corrupted and blind. You should consider Japan's defeat as providential and as a divine judgment, and should work joyously to contribute to the reconstruction of our new fatherland. The Japanese people should be reborn. Having come to this conclusion, I am a happy man today [on the day of his execution].

Last letter from a medical officer of the Japanese Navy,
executed in Guam in 1949.[7]

The process of economic growth, technological transformation, and social development achieved by Japan in the past half-century, emerging from the ashes of its crushed imperialistic ambitions, is nothing short of extraordinary. It has indeed changed the world, and our perception of world development, as it was able to combine growth with redistribution, raise real wages substantially, and reduce income inequality to one of the lowest levels in the world.[8] Furthermore, while Japanese social and environmental landscapes were deeply transformed, Japanese cultural identity was by and large preserved, in a powerful display of the historical feasibility of modernizing without Westernizing.[9] To be sure, these achievements required a strenuous effort from the entire Japanese society, with workers working many more hours than their American and European counterparts, consuming much less, and saving/investing much more

---

[6]   My analysis of Japanese society was mainly elaborated during my tenure as a visiting professor of sociology at Hitotsubashi University in 1995. I am particularly grateful to Professor Shujiro Yazawa, Dean of the Faculty of Social Sciences, both for his invitation, and for the most enlightening discussions we had, and continued to have later on. I am also indebted to the faculty and graduate students from various Japanese universities for their active participation and insightful input to my seminars at Hitotsubashi, and to my research assistant, Keisuke Hasegawa, who helped me with the analysis of Japanese material, and built a database on Japan's information society. Professor Kokichi Shoji, Chair of the Sociology Department at Tokyo University, generously provided me with a wealth of sociological studies on Japan, and shared with me his ideas on Japanese social transformation. Both Yazawa and Shoji have been sources of inspiration in my interpretation, but, naturally, they bear no responsibility for any of my statements or possible misunderstandings.

[7]   Quoted by Tsurumi (1970: 172).

[8]   Allen (1981); Tsuru (1993).

[9]   Reischauer (1988); Shoji (1991).

over a long period of time.[10] Japan was also paradoxically helped by the reforms imposed by the American occupation. Particularly important among these reforms were land reform, labor legislation, including the recognition of rights for organized labor, the prohibition of economic monopolies, leading to the dismantling of the *zaibatsu*, and new electoral laws that accorded women the right to vote. In addition, the military umbrella that the United States set up for Japan, in the context of the Cold War, freed the Japanese economy from the burden of military expenditures, and the Japanese state from foreign policy headaches that could have distracted it from its obsessive focus on production, technology, and exports. Yet, even taking into account this favorable context, the awesome process of development and structural transformation undergone by Japan can only be explained by the internal dynamics of Japanese society.

At the root of this dynamics was a project of affirmation of national identity, in historical continuity with 1868 *Ishin Meiji*. Japan was, and is, one of the most culturally and socially homogeneous societies in the world, albeit not as much as most Japanese think themselves, forgetting the millions of its residents who are Korean, Okinawan, and Ainu, as well as the culturally assimilated but socially excluded Burakumins. Its insular isolation for centuries reinforced this identity, which came under threat from Western colonialism's imposed opening to Western trade by the "black ships" of Commodore Perry in 1853. The reaction to this threat led to the Meiji Restoration, and to the accelerated modernization of the country in the following decades, as the only way to enable Japan to stand up to the Western challenge.[11] This is still the essential factor in understanding the social consensus and political legitimacy that have been the basis of Japan's developmental effort for more than a century. After the failure of both the democratic path to modernization during the Taisho period (1912–26), and of the militaristic, ultra-nationalist project in the second decade of Showa (1935–45), Japanese nationalism re-emerged in the form of a state-guided project of economic development oriented toward peaceful competition in the international economy.[12] An impoverished, defenseless country, entirely dependent in energy and natural resources, and confronted with self-doubt and, in progressive intellectual circles, with guilt and shame, Japan mobilized collectively: first to survive, then to compete, finally to assert itself by means of industrial production, economic

[10]   Tsuru (1993).
[11]   Norman (1940).
[12]   Kato (1987); Beasley (1990).

management, and technological innovation. This must be the starting point of any analysis of *Japanese development: it was the pursuit of national independence, and national power, by peaceful (economic) means*, in accordance with the 1947 Constitution, which renounced for ever war and armed forces. I will try to show the direct link between this nationalist project and the Japanese model of development that characterized both the hyper-growth period of 1956–73, and the bold techno-economic restructuring that successfully answered the challenges of the 1974 oil shock. However, the argument I put forward, in the context of my analysis of the emergence of the Pacific as a pivotal area for the twenty-first century, goes beyond a reassessment of this well-known experience of development. I suggest that *there is a fundamental crisis of the Japanese model of development in the* Heisei *period* (started on January 7, 1989), manifested during the 1990s in the instability of the political system, in sharp contrast to the preceding five decades; in the long recession that followed the bursting of the "bubble economy", and in the psychological confusion pervasive among significant sections of the youth, as dramatically revealed by the insurgency of *Aum Shinrikyo* (see volume II, chapter 3). I propose the hypothesis that *this multidimensional crisis results precisely from the success of the Japanese model of development, which induced new economic, social, and cultural forces that came to challenge the priority of the nationalist project, and therefore, the developmental state.* The conditions and forms of resolution of this crisis will deeply affect Japanese society, Japan's relations with the Pacific, and, ultimately, the fate of the whole Pacific area.

A social model of the Japanese developmental process[13]

It should be evident, after decades of research in the sociology of development, that processes of economic growth and structural

---

[13] In my opinion, the best political economic analysis on the origins and characteristics of Japanese development, from a Western perspective, is a little-known book by a distinguished English scholar, G.C. Allen (1981). Of course, the classic study on the formation and workings of the developmental state, and the one that invented the concept, is Chalmers Johnson's *MITI and the Japanese Miracle* (1982). For further elaboration of this perspective see a selection of his writings on Japan's political system in Johnson (1995). The best historical analysis of the emergence of Japan's modern state, starting with the Meiji Restoration, remains the one by Norman (1940). For a Japanese view of the process of economic development since the 1950s, see Tsuru (1993). On the cultural and psychological conditions under which the new developmental state emerged, see Tsurumi (1970). For a sweeping socio-political analysis of Japan's evolution in the period 1960–90, with emphasis on neo-nationalism, see Shoji (1991). For an analysis of Japanese social movements, see Yazawa (forthcoming). For a study of

transformation are embedded in institutions, oriented by culture, supported by social consensus, shaped by social conflict, fought over by politics, and guided by policies and strategies.[14] At the heart of the Japanese process of development, since the 1950s, is the nationalist project of the developmental state, enacted by the state bureaucracy on behalf of the nation.[15] In a nutshell, state bureaucracy has guided and coordinated Japanese corporations, organized in business networks (*keiretsu* and *kigyo shudan*), helping them through trade policy, technology policy, and credit, to compete successfully in the world economy. Trade surplus was recycled as financial surplus and, together with a high rate of domestic savings, allowed for non-inflationary expansion, making possible at the same time high rates of investment, rapidly rising real wages, and improvement in living standards. High rates of investment in R&D, and a focus on advanced manufacturing, enabled Japan to take a leading position in information technology industries at a time when their products and processes were becoming essential in the global economy. This economic performance relied on social stability and high labor productivity through management–labor cooperation, made possible by stable employment, and by seniority-based promotion, for the core labor force. Labor market flexibility was assured by part-time and

---

cultural nationalism, see Yoshino (1992). If you want to indulge in Western criticisms of Japanese society and politics (biased, in my opinion), you will find them in Van Wolferen (1989), and Harvey (1994). For a sympathetic Western perspective, see Reischauer (1988). For a theoretical interpretation of the Japanese state, see Kato (1984, 1987), and Taguchi and Kato (1985). An interesting chronicle of the internal dynamics of the Japanese state is Ikuta (1995). An excellent, up-to-date study of *Kanryo* (the Japanese bureaucracy) is Inoguchi (1995). An empirical analysis of Japanese political life can be found in Kishima (1991). For a study of Japanese political machines, including political corruption, see Schlesinger (1997). On Japanese neo-nationalism, see Watanabe (1996). On the condition of women, and women's mobilization in Japan see Ueno (1987); Gelb and Lief-Palley (1994); Shinotsuka (1994); and Yazawa (1995). On the Japanese family, see Seki (1987) and Totani and Yatazawa (1990). For an empirical view on Japanese schools, see Tsuneyoshi (1994). For a guided sociological bibliography of Japanese sources, see Shoji (1994). For Japanese business structure, industrial relations, work organization, labor markets, and employment practices, see my analysis in volume I, chapters 3 and 4. I will not repeat here references to sources used in these analyses, which can be found in volume I. Other sources used in my analysis in this section are cited in the footnotes to the text. Naturally, the overwhelming mass of potential sources on bibliography and data for the subjects covered in this section is not even touched. *I am referring only to those sources that I have directly used in my elaboration.*

[14]   Evans, (1995).

[15]   Kato (1984); Taguchi and Kato (1985); Johnson (1995).

contingent employment, usually made up of women, whose rate of participation in the labor force sky-rocketed. Overall social stability relied on three major factors: (a) people's commitment to rebuilding the nation; (b) access to consumption, and substantial improvement in living standards; and (c) a strong, stable patriarchal family, which reproduced traditional values, induced work ethics, and provided personal security for its members, at the cost of keeping women under submission. Political stability was ensured by organizing a coalition of interests and patronage constituencies under the umbrella of the Liberal Democratic Party, which controlled the government until 1993, counting on the adamant support of the United States, regardless of widespread corruption practices. The developmental state, while building its specific legitimacy by delivering the promise of economic development, benefited, additionally, from a double source of legitimacy: from people's votes for the LDP, and from the "Symbolic Emperor system," which provided historical continuity with the roots of national identity. Chart 4.1 attempts a synthetic representation of the social/institutional logic underlying Japan's economic development. I will go into a brief elaboration to clarify this excessively condensed summary.

As in all processes of social mobilization, it is essential to identify the sources of legitimacy that allow the dominant actor in the process (in this case the Japanese state) to find support in society, and to bring business under its coordination. The origins of the state's legitimacy are to be found outside the bureaucracy, in the so-called "Symbolic Emperor system" (*Shocho Tenno-sei*), and, since the 1947 Constitution, to a lesser extent, in the democratically elected political system. I say to a lesser extent because the government, while constitutionally elected, was dependent for almost five decades on "*Nagatacho* politics"; that is, the coalition of interests, factions, and patronage networks organized around the Liberal Democratic Party, rigged by corruption, and hardly valued in the eyes of most people. The guidance of the development process came essentially from an efficient, usually clean, state bureaucracy, which ensured the stability of policy-making, bridging over the quarrels between different factions of the LDP, formed of a miscellaneous coalition of interests, ideologies, and personalities.[16] Although formally dependent on the government, the state bureaucracy built its legitimacy on the values of an updated Symbolic Emperor system. Masao Maruyama wrote in 1946 a classic of Japanese political science, which is still considered to be the most insightful analysis of the Symbolic Emperor system, and

---

[16]   Inoguchi (1995); Schlesinger (1997).

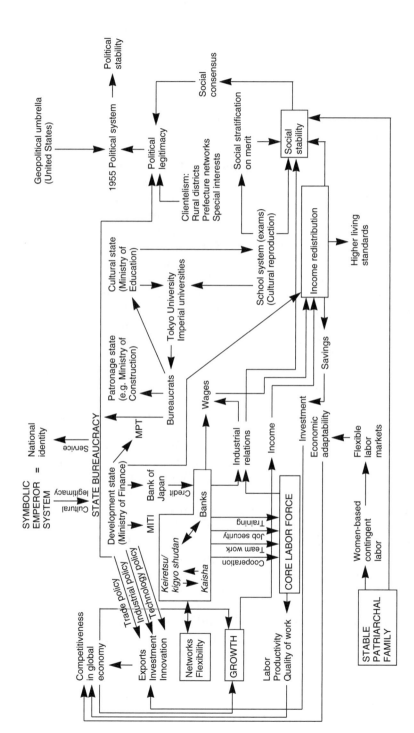

Chart 4.1 A social model of Japanese development, 1955–85

of its role in Japanese culture and politics. According to his analysis, "In Japan we are faced with a situation in which national sovereignty involves both spiritual authority and political power. The standard according to which the nation's actions are judged as right or wrong lies within itself (that is in the 'national polity')."[17] This is because

> whereas in the West national power after the Reformation was based on formal, external sovereignty, the Japanese state [after Meiji] never came to the point of drawing a distinction between the external and internal spheres and of recognizing that its authority was valid only for the former . . . Accordingly, until the day in 1946 when the divinity of the Emperor was formally denied in an Imperial Rescript, there was in principle no basis in Japan for freedom of belief. Since the nation includes in its "national polity" all the internal values of truth, morality, and beauty, neither scholarship nor art could exist apart from these national values . . . It was precisely when the success motive joined forces with nationalism that modern Japan was able to embark on its "rush towards progress". Yet, at the same time it was this very combination that led to Japan's decay. For the logic according to which private affairs cannot be morally justified within themselves but must always be identified with national affairs, has a converse implication: private interests endlessly infiltrate into national concerns.[18]

The social logic of what would become corporatist Japan, or Japan Inc. in the labeling of its critics, is implicit in Maruyama's analysis of political culture. After the humiliating defeat of the ultra-nationalist project, a revamped Symbolic Emperor system ensured historical continuity and political legitimacy for a bureaucracy that went on to reconstruct the country, and, in the process, discovered pragmatically how to create a strong, modern Japan by taking on the world economy. G.C. Allen and Chalmers Johnson have provided convincing empirical analyses of the rise of the Japanese developmental state, and its critical role in guiding strategically the nation's economic growth, at least between 1955 and 1985.[19] The dominating agency in this bureaucracy is the Ministry of Finance, which controls the purse, and thus has the material power of decision-making. Its two main instruments are the legendary MITI (Ministry of International Trade and Industry) and the Bank of Japan, since credit,

---

[17]   Maruyama (1963: 8).
[18]   Maruyama (1963: 6–7).
[19]   Allen (1981); Johnson (1982, 1995).

export/import allocations, and support for technological development are the essential tools through which state bureaucracy is able
to coordinate, help, organize competition, and, sometimes, subdue
Japanese business. Additionally, other infrastructure-oriented
ministries, particularly the Ministry of Posts and Telecommunications
(MPT), from the 1980s onwards, were also critical in providing the
material conditions of production, and in selectively organizing the
diffusion of technology. In parallel, and sometimes in conflict, other
ministries performed different functions, according to their specific
field of competence. Thus, the Ministry of Education had the care of
preserving cultural identity, and organizing an orderly system of stratification and social mobility by enforcing a hierarchical, rigid
examination system, which punctuated the entire lives of Japanese
children and young people, and thus encapsulated all families into
the ideology and rituals of meritocracy. Other ministries performed
more political functions. Thus, the Ministry of Construction, the
Ministry of Agriculture, and the Ministry of Transport seem to have
played a major role in channeling private funds into the political
campaigns of the LDP, and into securing local clienteles by distributing government funds to receptive local and provincial
governments.[20] The coherence of the state bureaucracy, including
that of the branches belonging to the developmental state, should not
be over-emphasized. As all states, the Japanese state is also torn by
internal conflicts, and contradictory interests, as various bureaucracies vie to establish their position in the power game. For instance,
the MPT's role was not limited to infrastructure and technology, since
its control of the largest source of savings, through the postal savings
system, gave it the power decisively to intervene in financial markets,
and into government funding of public and private investments.
Furthermore, while, in general terms, the state bureaucracy was
largely autonomous of the political elites, and less influenced by
interest groups, there was considerable cross-breeding between politicians and bureaucrats, as ministerial posts served as power bases for
various political factions, adding complexity to the system. However,
cultural homogeneity, and a shared belief in the superior interests of
the nation, still symbolically embodied in the Emperor system, were
assured through strict control of recruitment sources for the top
bureaucracy, from institutions carefully monitored by the Ministry of
Education. Key elements in this recruitment were (and still are) the
University of Tokyo, particularly its Faculty of Law, and the imperial
universities which, together with a few elite private universities,

[20]   Ikuta (1995); Johnson (1995).

supply practically all the members of the top bureaucracy. This social cohesion at the top permeates throughout society, since only about 1 percent of these recruits make it to the top of the state bureaucracy. The others, in the later stages of their career, "descend from heaven," taking positions as corporate executives, political leaders, or heads of para-public foundations in charge of structuring and guiding civil society. Thus, the cultural glue of the bureaucratic class diffuses by the circulation of elites between different spheres of social and economic life, ensuring the communication of ideas, the negotiation of interests, and the reproduction of ideology.

The mechanisms inducive to economic growth, designed and implemented by this nationalist bureaucracy, have been exposed in a flurry of monographs on the "Japanese miracle": an all-out export orientation, on the basis of outstanding competitiveness, made possible by substantial increases in labor productivity, by the quality of work, and by protection of domestic markets; abundance of capital, on the basis of a high savings rate, and short-term lending to the banks of *keiretsu* by the Bank of Japan, at a low interest rate; sustained effort in technological development with government-sponsored programs of technology acquisition, and technological innovation; emphasis on manufacturing; industrial policy, shifting from low-technology to medium-technology, then to high-technology industries, following the evolution of technology, of world demand, and of the productive capacity of Japanese industries. MITI, after clearing its programs with the Ministry of Finance, played a substantial role in strategic planning, and in helping, guiding, and supporting Japanese business networks, particularly in trade policy, in technology policy, and in industrial policy, deciding the sectors of priority for investment. Its decisions were not always successful, nor were they necessarily followed. For instance, the much-publicized Fifth Generation Computers Program in the 1980s was a fiasco. And most of the 26 Technopoles induced by MITI's Technopolis Program in prefectures around the country in the 1980s and 1990s, when and if successful, were agglomerations of branch plants rather than mini-Silicon Valleys, as MITI intended in its original vision. Yet, over time, more often than not, MITI's strategic planners were on target, and Japanese industries were able to move with remarkable speed from low value added to high value added products and processes, overtaking Europe first, and the United States later, in most key industries, from automobiles to semi-conductors, until the technological/managerial counter-offensive of American companies in the 1990s put them ahead of Japanese competitors in the higher tier of microcomputers, software, micro-electronics, telecommunications, and biotechnology. Yet, Japanese firms continue to dominate consumer electronics, memory chips, and semiconductors equipment manufacturing, and hold very strong competitive positions in a whole range of advanced manufacturing industries, with the important exceptions of pharmaceuticals and chemicals.

The effectiveness of administrative guidance was decisively helped by the networking structure of Japanese business, which I presented in some detail in volume I, chapter 3. By coordinating a few players, and by keeping competition between corporate networks at the top, the state bureaucrats were able to reach out to the entire economic structure without resorting to the self-destructive procedure of centralized planning. The Japanese model is a critical experience in showing how strategic, selective state intervention can make a market economy more productive, and more competitive, thus rejecting ideological claims about the inherent superior efficiency of *laissez-faire* economics.

But none of the above could have worked without full cooperation between management and labor, the source of productivity, stability, and long-range strategic investment, which were the ultimate determinants of Japanese competitiveness. Trade protectionism was widely practiced by Latin American economies, some of them very large, without ever being able to emerge as major players in high value added, global markets. It was labor's involvement at the shop-floor level, and the social peace enjoyed by Japanese business, that provided, early on, a decisive edge to the Japanese economy. This was particularly important in ensuring the Japanese transition to information-technology based manufacturing and services, requiring the full mobilization of labor's thinking capacity to make the best out of new technologies. But labor's involvement and cooperation with firms cannot be attributed to ethno-cultural idiosyncrasy. The strong cultural specificity of Japanese workers did not prevent them from mobilizing, striking, and organizing a militant labor movement when they had the freedom to do so, in the 1920s and early 1930s, and then again in the late 1940s and 1950s.[21] These struggles led to a series of labor and social policy reforms in the 1950s. On the basis of these reforms, around 1960 a new system of labor policy and industrial relations was set up by Japanese business and government. It was built around four major features. The first was a commitment by companies to long-term employment for the core labor force of large firms, either in the firm or in other firms of the *keiretsu*; in exchange, Japanese workers would also commit themselves to remain in the same firm for the duration of their working

---

[21] Yazawa (forthcoming).

lives. The second, was the seniority system for promotion, thus removing management's discretionary power to reward/punish workers, therefore dividing them through individual competition; this seniority system allowed for predictability in workers' life patterns. The third feature was the cooperative system of working practices, including a flat organizational hierarchy in supervisory work in factories and offices, the formation of work teams and quality control circles, and widespread use of workers' initiative in improving the efficiency and quality of the production process. The fourth factor was the company-based organization of labor unions, which identified the interests of union leaders and members with the interests of the firm. There were/are Japanese labor federations, and there is also collective bargaining of sorts at the national level for some sectors, preceded by symbolic mobilization (such as the ritual "spring offensives") in order to assert organized labor's potential. Yet, by and large, through firm-specific unionism, workers' participation at the shop-floor level, and joint commitment from management and labor to the well-being of the national economy, Japanese capitalism has enjoyed better industrial relations than any other market economy.

These labor practices were essential for the implementation of mechanisms that are usually associated with successful Japanese management practices, as I argued in my analysis of Japanese labor and working arrangements in volume I, chapters 3 and 4. Thus, the "just in time" system to eliminate inventories can only function in the absence of work stoppages, derived from a smooth system of industrial relations. The development and diffusion of "tacit knowledge" by workers which, according to Nonaka and Takeuchi's influential analysis is at the source of the "knowledge-generating company,"[22] is only possible if workers have incentives to invest their unique expertise, their insider knowledge of the company's production system, in the success of the firm to which they belong. In sum, labor productivity and quality of work, fundamental sources of Japanese competitiveness, were based on a system of working co-operation and industrial relations that was made possible by substantial gains for labor, including generous company benefits, and long-term commitment to keep jobs, even during downturns of the business cycle. It is also true, however, that some cultural elements, such as the search for *Wa* (harmony) in working relations, the communal spirit of teamwork, and the national mobilization to rebuild Japan, and to make it a strong, respected nation, also

[22] Nonaka and Takeuchi (1994).

contributed to the consolidation of the social pact achieved between business, labor, and government around 1960.

None the less, this cooperative dimension of labor relations is only part of the story of Japanese labor markets. Following the empirical analysis that I presented in volume I, chapter 4, flexibility of labor markets was assured by much more flexible labor practices, and fewer workers' rights, in small firms, in traditional sectors (such as retail trade), and for part-time workers in large firms. Much of this part-time and contingent employment was, and increasingly is, the lot of women, particularly of married women, who return to work after rearing children in their early years. The expanding women's labor market (currently reaching about 50 percent of adult women) is the key to flexibility and adaptability of labor markets, ensuring the stability of the core labor force, as the source of labor productivity, while still allowing firms to cushion themselves during recessions by firing contingent workers. In other industrialized countries there is a similar segmentation of labor markets, leading to an equally segmented social structure, thus to inequality and poverty. The true miracle of Japanese society is that this class segmentation is cancelled by the strength of the Japanese patriarchal family, which reunites within the family stable male workers and contingent female workers, so that social cleavages are dissolved in the unity of the family. This is particularly significant when we consider the high level of education of Japanese women, which means that this contingent labor is not less skilled, but simply less valued.

Patriarchalism is an essential ingredient of the Japanese developmental model. And not only for economic reasons. The patriarchal family has survived accelerated industrialization and modernization as a stable unit of personal stability and cultural reproduction. Rates of divorce, while increasing, are way below those in other advanced industrialized countries, except Italy and Spain (see volume II, chapter 3). Almost two-thirds of elderly Japanese were living with their adult children in 1980, and the majority still do, even if the proportion has declined rapidly in the past 30 years. Children are, by and large, kept under strict parental discipline, and the culture of shame is still a major determinant of their behavior. Women fulfill all their roles with little sign of widespread rebellion, to a large extent because most Japanese husbands, unlike in America, have honored their patriarchal commitments, usually not indulging in the pursuit of personal happiness outside family rules (see volume II, chapter 3). When necessary the state comes in to add a little institutional twist, rewarding patriarchalism. For instance, the Japanese tax code makes it nonsensical for women to add too much money beyond part-time wages, because the double-income household tax bracket becomes punitively high. The contribution of educated, hyper-active women to Japanese flexible labor markets, stable families and traditional culture is a critical component of the entire social and economic balance of Japan. And perhaps the weakest link in the Japanese model, if comparative experience is of any value.

Cultural reproduction is also assured by the state, particularly through the Ministry of Education, which closely supervises educational programs from pre-schools to leading universities. Emphasis is placed on traditional culture, and on a hierarchical, complex examination system which determines the occupational fate of each Japanese person, most often very early in his or her life. Strict discipline is the rule, as exemplified in a tragic incident in 1990 when a school girl was killed when trapped by the sliding gate installed by the school to keep out pupils arriving late for class. This stratified, cultural homogeneity is essential in ensuring cooperation, communication, and a sense of belonging in a communal/national culture, while acknowledging social differences and respecting everybody's relative place. The combined pressure of a strong patriarchal family from below, and of a strong Ministry of Education from above, smooths cultural reproduction, and exiles alternative values to radical challenges outside the system, thus marginalizing rebellion.

On the basis of rising standards of living, industrial cooperation, orderly reproduction of traditional values, and social mobilization on behalf of the nation, political stability was assured by a makeshift coalition of personalities, interest groups, and clienteles, hastily assembled under the name of the Liberal Democratic Party, in the wake of American occupation. The LDP was (much like the Italian Christian Democrats, built by the Vatican and the United States to resist communism and socialism) an unstable coalition of political factions, each one with its "capo" (the most powerful of whom was Kakuei Tanaka), around whom a web of interests, complicities, machinations, silences, and debts was weaved for five decades. Benefiting from American complacency (a fundamental matter for Japanese business, which needed a US-trusted interlocutor to assure critical access to American markets and supplies), the LDP's factions perfected the art of political intermediation. They exchanged votes for money, money for favors, favors for positions, positions for patronage, then patronage for votes, and so on. They constantly quarreled about control of resources in this patronage system, but always united around their common good. They were periodically rocked by scandals, particularly after the 1976 "Lockheed affair," which prompted the resignation of Prime Minister Tanaka, and showed the possibility of political revelations in the media, an event similar to the impact of Nixon's Watergate on US politics. As analyzed in volume II, chapter 6, political corruption was, in Japan as in most other countries, linked to the financing of political campaigns, and of political factions, adding also a little tip for the party's fundraisers. As mentioned above, the Ministries of Construction, Agriculture, and Transport seem to have been privileged mechanisms for channeling state funds to favored private companies, in exchange for which, companies funded the LDP's activities and leaders, and local bosses delivered votes.[23] But this was certainly not the only source of political funding. Furthermore, open links between the *Yakuza* and LDP leaders (including Prime Ministers) have been repeatedly exposed in the Japanese media.

Beyond political corruption, traditional patronage systems ensured widespread support for LDP candidates in rural districts and less-developed provinces. Electoral law over-represented these districts in Parliament, thus making it extremely difficult to challenge the LDP's repeated success. It worked. For almost five decades, for all its limitations, the LDP system ensured political stability in Japan, keeping conflicts within "the family," and letting the populace enjoy their hard-earned prosperity while becoming increasingly cynical about all politicians. However, this system was only able to survive, in spite of its limited legitimacy, because a higher authority, the Symbolic Emperor system, remained a moral guarantee for the Japanese people, and because a cast of enlightened despots took care of the affairs of the state, bringing business and workers together in the rebuilding of the nation.

This was the social model of development that stunned the world, scared America, and sent European governments running for the cover of the European Union. It was coherent, powerful, brilliant indeed. It was also short-lived by historical standards, as it reached its zenith in the mid-1980s, and entered into an open, structural crisis around the early years of the *Heisei* period.

Declining sun: the crisis of the Japanese model of development

Since the mid-1980s Japan has gradually gone into a structural crisis that manifests itself in different dimensions of the economic, social, and political landscape. The crisis unfolded in a series of apparently unrelated events, whose underlying relationships I hope to be able to show at the end of my analysis.

Let us focus first on the financial crisis that seems to be at the

---

[23]   Ikuta (1995); Johnson (1995); Schlesinger (1997).

forefront of Japan's structural crisis.[24] Boiling down the complexity of
the financial crisis to its essence, the main problem is the staggering
amount of bad loans accumulated by Japanese banks, estimated in
1998 at about 80 trillion yen, equivalent to 12 percent of Japan's GDP.
Foreign experts, assessing the situation of Japanese banks in 1998,
considered that only two of the top nineteen banks had an adequate
capitalization to cover their potential losses. The most blatant case was
that of one of the largest banks in the world, the Long Term Credit
Bank, which was intervened by the government in the fall of 1998,
after it became in default for over $US 7 billion. Other banks in a
desperate situation were Fuji Bank, with $17 billion in bad loans,
Sakura Bank, with another $11 billion in potential losses, and Nippon
Credit, $1.5 billion in debt, all probably merged, nationalized, or
liquidated by the time you read this. The near-default situation of
Japanese banks depreciated the value of their stocks and made it
prohibitively expensive for them to access international credit.
Accordingly, surviving banks drastically restricted their lending, thus
drying up credit for the economy. In 1998, for the first time since the
1970s oil crisis, Japan's economy shrunk, and the prospects to the end
of the century were for a prolonged recession. At the time of writing,
there is a chance that the combination of a bleak Asian environment,
domestic political instability, and economic policy blunders could
plunge Japan, and thus the world, into a depression.

   Therefore, the question remains, why were there so many bad
loans, and why was their potential default ignored for such a long
time? The answer lies in the contradictions built into the model
of Japanese development, aggravated by the growing exposure of
Japanese financial institutions to global financial markets. Let me
explain. Japan's high growth relied on a government-backed financial
system geared toward ensuring security for both savers and banks,
while providing low-interest, easy credit for firms. For a long time,
Japanese financial institutions operated in relative isolation from
international capital flows, and under regulations and policy guidelines set and interpreted by the Ministry of Finance. The stock market
was not a major source of finance, and did not provide an attractive
investment for savings. High saving rates were critical to fuel investment without inflation. But the intermediation between savings and
investments was channeled through deposits in the post office, in

---

[24]   The analysis of the Japanese financial crisis in the 1996–8 period is based on
reports in the business press, as cited in note 2. For useful overviews, see *The
Economist* (1997); Eisenstodt (1998); and the intriguing scenarios of Nakame
International Economic Research, Nikkei, and Global Business Network (1998).

banks, and in savings and loans. In 1997, the share of deposits over GDP was 92.5 percent in Japan, compared with 34 percent in the US. So, banks and savings institutions were loaded with cash, eager to lend it. Banks were linked to a *keiretsu*, and thus were obliged in their lending practices to preferred customers. In return, they were covered by the overall *keiretsu* structure. The government took care that no bank would go bankrupt. Loans were collateralized by property and shares. So, with low risk, and low interest rates, banks had a vested interest in high-volume lending, rather than in profit margins. As easy money propelled the economy, both internationally and domestically, high rates of growth seemed to assure the repayment of loans, providing more cash for future loans. Besides, real-estate prices sky-rocketed, particularly in Tokyo, and Osaka, providing more collateral value for an endless expansion of money-lending. The reasons for this overvaluation of land and real estate were twofold. On the one hand, rapid accumulation of capital in Japan, which was, mainly, the result of continuing trade surplus, made funds available for investment in real estate, pushing up land prices. On the other hand, the unplanned, chaotic nature of Japanese urbanization, in sharp contrast with the careful strategic planning of production and technology, induced a wild real-estate market.[25] Fast economic growth concentrated population and activities in dense urban areas, in a country already obsessed with the scarcity of usable land. Land prices increased dramatically because of mechanisms of political patronage which provided a special bonus to a large number of small landholders, many of them in the rural periphery of metropolitan areas. As an illustration, between 1983 and 1988 average prices of residential and commercial land rose, respectively, by 119 percent and 203 percent in the Tokyo area.[26] Real-estate speculation by petty landlords was helped by major financial firms, which benefited most from it. Local governments were assured of revenues, and of political support, precisely by not planning, and not providing housing alternatives, letting the market decide, making landowners, and banks, artificially rich in inflated real-estate values. At the same time, people aspiring to home ownership had to increase their savings, thus providing additional money to banks and financial institutions. In a related development, the stock market, also fueled by the proceeds of Japanese exports, multiplied its value, thus inducing additional lending, supposedly secured by inflated stock assets. As long as the system worked, based on competitiveness abroad, high earnings from

[25]   Machimura (1994).
[26]   Fukui (1992: 217).

exports, high saving rates, and inflated values at home, the financial system fueled its own expansion. Indeed, business consultants from around the world flocked to Tokyo to study, and praise, the miracle of a financial system able to self-generate value, while spurring industrial and trade competitiveness. By 1990, eight of the ten largest banks in the world, measured by the volume of their deposits, were Japanese.

There was also another, hidden, dimension to the practice of easy lending: the biased access to credit. Banks were obliged to lend to firms, individuals, or organizations that had a privileged access to the bank, regardless of the soundness of the investment or the risk of the loan. There were (are?) four main sources of this "preferred borrower" pattern. The first was the firms of the bank's *keiretsu*, so that lending policy was part of a broader corporate policy. Second was the advice, direct or indirect, of the Ministry of Finance concerning a particular loan deemed to be of interest to the Japanese economy. The third was the yielding of the bank (or savings and loans institution) to pressures from firms connected to the *Yakuza* (see above, chapter 3). The fourth was the financing of political parties, usually the government party, the LDP, or support for some of their personnel. After all, in return, banks were shielded from bad fortune precisely by the ultimate protection of the government, their *keiretsu*, and the banking industry at large. The circle was closed. With financial markets, individual investors, and consumers having little influence over the banking system, Japanese finance worked as a text-book case of state-capitalist corporatism. Banks had little autonomy: they were mainly an instrument for capturing savings and allocating them to targets decided by the entangled web of Japan Inc., to serve the national interest of Japan, and the personal interest of its representatives.

As long as it lasted, this system was highly dynamic, and reasonably efficient in fulfilling its own goals. But when it reversed itself, shifting from value creation to value destruction, it shattered the Japanese economy. Three sets of factors were critical in the demise of this financial system. First, the real-estate and stock-market bubble burst in 1991. Secondly the exposure of Japanese financial institutions to global financial markets made it increasingly difficult to follow Japanese customary financial practices. Thirdly, the government lost much of its capacity to cover bank debt and potential default. Let us examine these three developments in some detail.

First, the bubble burst because all bubbles do eventually. It is called the business cycle. But there were specific, aggravating circumstances in the Japanese case. An overheated economy pushed the yen's exchange rate upwards, undermining Japanese trade competitiveness. But a strong yen, and a buoyant stock market, induced

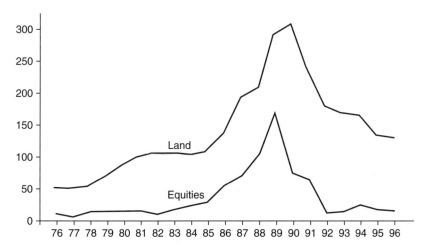

Figure 4.1   Japan's values in equities and land in billions of yen,
1976–96 (unrealized profits total value)
Source: *The Economist* (1997: 4)

corporations to enter financial investment and lent large sums, both internationally and domestically. Real-estate prices finally came down because of the structural incapacity of housing demand to absorb price increases and because of overcapacity in the office-building market. Stock markets followed the drop, destabilizing Japan's financial system, which was based on the risky assumption of a continuous, high-flying pattern. Fearful of inflation, the government put the brakes on the economy, inducing a recession in the early 1990s. The sharp decline of the stock market, together with the real-estate collapse, erased by 1996 most of the value artificially generated in the 1980s (see figure 4.1). For the first time in four decades, Japan's economy became stagnant, and only recovered in the mid-1990s, stimulated by government spending, albeit growing at a slow pace.[27] But this recovery was short-lived. Financial instability forced banks to tighten their lending practices. So, in spite of the government's effort to lower interest rates, which hit historic low levels in 1998 at around 1 percent, the economy was squeezed of money, halting growth. As in 1997, Japan slid into sharp downturn, which became a fully fledged recession in 1998.

Yet the most serious problem affecting Japanese finance came from its growing exposure to global financial markets. Three main issues

---

[27]   Asahi Shimbun (1995).

should be considered in this regard. First, faced with a stagnant
Japanese economy, and with a booming Asian Pacific market,
Japanese banks and financial institutions lent heavily in these
emerging markets. They reproduced the same lending practices that
they used at home: they lent short term, in large volume, to preferred
customers, regardless of their solvency, under the double guarantee
of major local corporations and governments. They took overvalued
real-estate property as collateral for many of their loans. In so doing,
they exposed their Asian lending to the same risks as their Japanese
loans. When the Asian real-estate bubble burst, many loans lost their
collateral, inducing their default. When the stock market collapsed in
Thailand, Indonesia, Malaysia, the Philippines, South Korea, and
Hong Kong, domestic firms which guaranteed the loans became
unable to repay them. When local currencies plunged, Japanese
banks were unable to recover their dollar, or yen, denominated loans.
And when they turned to Asian governments, including their expen-
sively acquired "friends" in government, asking them to honor their
commitments, governments simply could not do it. Governments
were faced with a mountain of financial debts which became due at
the same time. So, looking for salvation in the Asian markets, Japanese
financial institutions largely contributed to exporting their crisis,
which eventually came home to roost.

Secondly, when Japanese financial firms became global players, it
was more difficult for them to continue with insider trading and
borderline business practices that had been customary at home. This
is not because they went into a "cleaner environment." In fact, there
are numerous examples of questionable, risky, and even illegal practices in Western financial institutions. US and European governments
and banking industries have had their share of having to bail out
banks and financial institutions that would have collapsed, and
provoked financial panic, without decisive government action, often
using taxpayers' money. The bailing out of savings and loans associations in the US in the 1980s (at the staggering cost of $250 billion),
the closing of BCCI in Luxembourg, the salvaging of Crédit Lyonnais
in France (covering a financial hole of $US 100 billion), and the 1998
rescue of Long Term Capital Management in New York, are illustrations of a widespread pattern of risky financial practices in the global
economy. The problem for Japanese banks and securities firms was
that they did not have a precise grasp of the rules of the game abroad.
In other words, they did not have the same inside knowledge and
networks of contracts, globally, that they enjoyed in Japan. Moreover,
unlike in Japan, they could not count on the complicity of governments in the main financial markets around the world. By the time
they learned the global rules, the hard way, it was too late for many of

the banks and securities firms. Among others, Sanwa Bank was penalized in the United States; Nomura Securities was hit by scandal and huge losses in Japan and the US; and Yamaichi Securities, one of the largest firms in the world, was forced into bankruptcy in 1997.

Furthermore, by fully embracing global financial markets, Japanese banks and securities firms joined the growing legion of apparently mighty, yet powerless, financial groups. In other words, while accumulating, and investing, huge volumes of capital, they had little control on events that shape, and reshape, financial markets. So, Japanese firms were exposed to the same risks as others around the world. But there were two factors which became sources of higher risk for Japanese firms. First, they had built a financial pyramid, counting on repayment of risky loans, on the basis of high, sustained growth. Any downturn could cause a chain effect of financial losses, given the short-term horizon of a substantial part of their lending. Secondly, there is what I call the "weak giant paradox." Contrary to what common sense might dictate, the larger a financial institution in the current system of global finance, the more vulnerable it is to crisis. This is because size determines the extent of involvement around the world. The higher the volume of capital requiring return, the larger the scope and the scale of operation in which the financial institution has to be involved in order to ensure average profits. Global financial markets are interdependent, and turbulence in any node of these financial networks diffuses to other markets, for reasons largely independent of economic fundamentals. Thus, the larger the exposure of investments from a firm, the higher the probability of suffering a loss somewhere – or, simultaneously, multiple losses. Conversely, the probability of earning a profit, in successful markets, also increases with size. But since profits and losses are not predictable in time and space, volatility of returns on investment will increase with size and complexity of the financial firm. Thus, for a given level of risk, the larger the firm, and the larger the extent of its globalization, the higher will be the volatility of its financial yields. Hedge funds were supposed to be an answer to this paradox. Instead, they have become the most adventurous sources of investment patterns. Usually, hedge fund firms bet on alternative scenarios of a financial asset not to diminish risk, but to earn extra profits on the relative discrepancies in time and space between the two sides of the bet. Thus, ultimately, hedge funds increase financial volatility, rather than preventing it. In this context, when giant Japanese banks, loaded with cash from Japanese corporations' trade surpluses, went global, they became increasingly vulnerable to the instability of financial markets, accelerated by the speed of electronic transactions.

The third major development inducing the crisis of the Japanese financial system was the declining capacity of the Japanese government to cover the losses of financial institutions. This was due to several reasons. Losses grew in volume and size to such a level that public funds came up increasingly short of what was needed, particularly when losses took place at the same time, because of the ripple effect of financial pyramids. Trying to stimulate the economy out of stagnation, the Ministry of Finance lowered interest rates, depriving banks of additional revenue. Besides, available public funds were assigned to public works investment, reducing the financial margin of maneuver to bail out banks with taxpayers' money. Yet, the most important factor in accounting for the government's dwindling capacity to revamp the financial system was its political weakness. As I will discuss below, the end of the LDP's dominance of Japanese politics meant that decision-making had to be made accountable to opposition parties. When scandal after scandal wrecked public trust, the government lost the power to help financial friends in trouble behind the scene. Furthermore, the crisis of confidence affected, for the first time, the Japanese bureaucracy, particularly the formerly all-powerful Finance Ministry. In 1997–8, all calls for reform from the opposition began with the demand to set up an independent financial agency, separate from the Ministry of Finance, to oversee financial reform. Thus, the political weakness of both the LDP and the bureaucracy contributed to the crisis of the old financial system. And the deepening of the crisis contributed to weakening the government even further, thus making it increasingly difficult to refloat banks without political accountability.

Finally, the three factors I have analyzed – namely, the reversal of the business cycle, the contradictions inherent in the globalization of finance, and the crisis of political management – reinforced each other throughout the 1990s, spiraling the overall banking crisis out of control. While the government rushed to protect investors, irreversible damage was done to the credibility of Japanese financial institutions. The partial deregulation of financial transactions, allowing easier movement of capital flows, allowed for capital flight from Japan, bringing down the yen, and thus further increasing capital outflows. Since Japanese savers/investors will enjoy in the near future easier access to international mutual investment funds, and since interest rates are higher in foreign markets, the possibility of a hollowing out of Japan's finance looms on the horizon.

Faced with the collapse of stocks and real-estate prices at home, and unable to claim the large sums that they had lent in Japan and in Asia without sufficient guarantees, Japanese banks and financial firms called the government to their rescue. The government obliged, in 1997, with a package of more than $US 60 billion dollars, then with an additional infusion of cash in 1998. Banks were nationalized, merged, taken over. However, the pyramid that had been created in Japan by lending on fictitious value was so large, and so widespread were its effects among a vast number of firms, that government funds only delayed the day of reckoning. Furthermore, bailing out the financial system used up public funds, thus limiting public spending. The ensuing economic recession eliminated the basic mechanism that had been feeding Japan's easy money economy for decades: high economic growth. Instead of controlling inflation, the government had to face the threat of deflation, in a complete reversal of what had been the role and purpose of the developmental state.

Globalization also transformed the model of industrial development. In the mid-1980s, fears of protectionism from America and Europe, as well as the strong yen, and high costs of operating in Japan, finally pushed Japanese corporations toward global decentralization, relatively weakening Japan's manufacturing basis.[28] The first moves were to Asia, in search of lower production costs, and more favourable platforms to export to the advanced economies.[29] But by the late 1980s it accelerated, with the transfer of entire production units, comprising R&D centers together with factories and commercial establishments, to Japan's main markets, particularly in the United States, the United Kingdom, and Germany.[30] Asian countries also became a market and not just a production base. MITI tried to counter this migration of Japanese capital and technology by developing the Technopolis Program, in cooperation with the prefectures of less-developed provinces, to lure high-technology companies to a regional decentralization strategy as opposed to offshoring.[31] Kyushu greatly benefited from the Technopolis Program, partly because of the interest of foreign electronic companies in locating in the Japanese market. Japanese firms also decentralized some of their branch plants, while keeping their essential talent and high-level operations in the Tokyo–Yokohama milieu of innovation. Yet, the offshoring movement of manufacturing, commercial, and financial activities involved incomparably higher volumes of investment. Some of this offshoring aimed at producing at lower costs and shipping products back to Japan, so that a substantial part of Japan's trade with Asia is, in fact, back and forth shipping of Japanese production networks in Asia. But most of it, as empirically shown by Aoyama, in her Berkeley

[28] Aoyama (1996).
[29] Ozawa (1996).
[30] Aoyama (1996).
[31] Castells and Hall (1994)

doctoral dissertation on the international location strategies of Japanese consumer electronics firms,[32] amounts to a true globalization of Japanese companies beyond the shores of Japan. The trend is expanding in the late 1990s, pushed by fears of protectionism, and by the need to secure specific market knowledge, to access technology (in the case of the US), to tap labour markets (skilled, as well as unskilled), and to diversify export platforms. Overall, there has been a growing trend toward dissociation between Japanese multinationals and Japan's national economy. The most important consequence of this trend is that MITI, and the developmental state system, have lost much of their clout, and even influence, over Japanese corporations. This is not only because they are much bigger, and consider themselves strong enough to decide their own strategies, but also because they are global, and belong to global networks, so that their interests, as firms and groups of firms, are increasingly diversified, and require different strategies for different countries, different sectors, and different product lines.[33] To be sure, most of their assets are still in Japan (albeit in a decreasing proportion), and there is probably a higher cultural/geographical loyalty among Japanese companies toward their country than other companies of similar global reach. It is also still true that the Japanese state adopts policies favorable to its firms, as the US government does (for example, the support of the Department of Defense for the megamerger between Boeing and McDonnell Douglas in 1996 to counter competition from Airbus). But, in contrast to the 1960s or 1970s, MITI no longer has direct influence over Japanese corporations; nor do these corporations decide their strategies primarily within the framework of Japan's economic interest. The decoupling of systemic interaction between the developmental state and Japanese-based multinational networks introduces a new dynamic to Japan, and to the world at large.

Among the key elements of this new dynamic are the following. It is doubtful whether, exposed to conditions of global competition in a multilayered locational structure, Japanese companies can maintain the system of tenured employment for the entire core labor force. The gradual weakening of this system, and the expansion of contingent labor, are undermining Japanese institutions of stable industrial relations. It is also doubtful whether Fortress Japan can be kept for long under the new rules of the World Trade Organization, as the serious frictions in trade negotiations with the Clinton administration

---

[32]   Aoyama (1996).
[33]   Imai (1990).

seemed to indicate. Japanese attempts to multilateralize trade negotiations, to avoid direct confrontation with the US, may in fact heighten tensions, since the competitive position of Europe is even weaker. The over-exposure of Japanese financial investments throughout the world to the uncertainties of global flows makes it increasingly difficult for Japanese banks to fulfill their intra-*keiretsu* obligations. The constant swirl of financial flows in and out of the Japanese economy limits the impact of monetary controls by the Bank of Japan, so that the Finance Ministry is no longer able to determine interest rates, the cornerstone of Japanese industrial finance policy. Deregulation of telecommunications, media, and utilities is proceeding slowly but surely, opening up opportunities for investment from a variety of sources, including foreign sources.[34] Moreover, in 1998, the G7 group, the US government, and the International Monetary Fund felt Japan to be so weak that they were not afraid to prescribe to the Japanese government economic policies which they deemed necessary to overcome the crisis that threatened the global economy as a whole. While Japan adamantly refused to be advised by foreigners, these pressures were a factor in deciding several key measures in Japan, particularly those concerning financial reform and fiscal policy.

In sum, the system of administrative guidance that characterized Japan's miracle is in the process of disintegration, particularly because of the inability of the government to keep the financial system under control, and to cover financial losses, under the conditions of globalization of financial markets. There remains a series of cultural/institutional obstacles to the opening of Japanese markets, such as bureaucratic red-tape, the internal discipline of business networks, and the cultural nationalist habit of buying/consuming Japanese. The imposing state machinery set up over the past half-century is still there to guide/help/support Japanese business. It is a well-known rule of bureaucratic life that the instrument creates the function: MITI will always find something to do. There is, none the less, a fundamental transformation in the overall pattern of development, as companies try to identify Japan's interests with their interests (in plural), instead of serving the national interest, in line with Maruyama's prediction.

There is a more fundamental change in the making. As Sumiko Yazawa, Chizuko Ueno, and other researchers have argued,[35] on the basis of empirical studies, Japanese women are increasingly

[34]   Khan and Yoshihara (1994).
[35]   Ueno (1987); Yazawa (1995).

mobilizing, both at the grassroots level, and in the political system, particularly in local politics, in parallel with their massive entry into the labor force. While explicit feminism is still limited in its expression, women's struggles and women's rights have come to the fore in a growing number of local communities. The media focus on these activities is amplifying their impact, opening the way for a challenge to the current status of women as second-class workers and politically subdued subjects. When, and if, the women's movement expands, permeating into the private sphere of the patriarchal family, the entire Japanese social structure will come under stress, because of the interconnection of patriarchalism with the entire institutional system. And there are scattered, but significant, signs that these challenges are emerging in the 1990s.[36]

In the last resort, economic crisis and social change in Japan combined to induce a fundamental political crisis, potentially opening the way for a new model of relationship between the state and civil society.

The end of *"Nagatacho* politics"

The crisis of the Japanese model of development was compounded in the 1990s by the crisis of its political system. The crisis was ushered in by the loss of the 1993 election by the LDP, and the formation of a coalition government formed between new parties, splitting from the LDP, and the Socialists. Two years later, the game was changed, with the LDP returning to government in coalition with the Socialists. And in 1996 a new election brought a minority LDP government with parliamentary support from small parties, including a reduced Socialist party. The composition of parliament made clear, however, that new coalitions would form and dissolve, ushering in an era of instability in Japanese politics. Indeed, in July 1998, the LDP was crushed in the elections to the upper house of parliament, winning only 44 of the 126 seats being contested. The election saw the rise of Naoto Kan, leader of the opposition Democratic party, who became the most popular politician in Japan. In a significant development, the communist party, conducting an active, grassroots campaign, tripled the number of its seats. As a result of this electoral rebuke, the prime minister, and leader of the LDP, Hashimoto, resigned. He was replaced by an experienced, consensus-builder, party *apparatchik*, Keizo Obuchi, in a desperate attempt by the LDP to fight the centrifugal forces that were threatening to disintegrate the

---

[36]   Yazawa et al. (1992); Iwao (1993); Yazawa (1995).

party. Yet, at the time of writing, few observers were giving Obuchi much chance to put together a stable coalition, or the LDP to remain in control of government after the next election.

This political crisis is more important for what it reveals than because of its direct social consequences.[37] Indeed, it could be argued that no real change in the political personnel took place in 1993–8 since the Socialists lost considerable support, and the main reason that the LDP lost control of the government was that several of its factions left the LDP to create new parties. In some cases, the acrimonious intra-party fighting has made future coalitions between the LDP and ex-LDP groups difficult, notably in the case of Ichiro Ozawa's *Jiyu* party. Yet, the crisis is deeper than it looks. I will follow Shoji's suggestion that the "big change" came as a consequence of an accumulation of "small changes," foremost among which was a transformation in Japanese people's lifestyle.[38]

The gradual fragmentation of the LDP was facilitated by the end of the geopolitical state of emergency, under which the national unity of pro-American forces was paramount, both for Japanese business and social elites, and for American interests.[39] Furthermore, the open recognition of trade tensions with America showed that old-fashioned LDP politics were no longer instrumental in taming America's reluctance to acknowledge a new economic superpower. The diversification of Japan's national interests, in line with the globalization of its economy, and with the crisis in its finances, opened up the debate on policies and strategies, requiring the constitution of a truly competitive political system, beyond the coalition of caretakers that were rubber-stamping the policies of the bureaucrats of the developmental state. The full urbanization of Japan undermined traditional patronage networks. To acknowledge the new electoral map, a political reform redrew electoral districts in 1994–5, and combined single-constituency representation with a national vote in the election of the parliament. The public disgust with the systemic political corruption put politicians on the defensive, so that several of them tried a new departure, presenting themselves as regenerated political leaders. The opening up of political competition, and the relinquishing of loyalties in the LDP family, created opportunities for political jockeying, with personalities, political clubs, and special interests engaging in political marketing, and entering a new field of competitive politics. In the process, the LDP's dirty laundry was

---

[37]   Ikuta (1995); Johnson (1995); Schlesinger (1997).
[38]   Shoji (1995); Smith (1997).
[39]   Curtis (1993).

further exposed by increasingly daring, autonomous media, thus undermining the reconstruction of the coalition and spurring centrifugal forces. This is why most Japanese and foreign observers consider that the era of LDP domination is over.[40] What is next is a much more difficult prediction, since the Socialists are disintegrating even faster than the LDP, and local personalities, such as Tokyo's independent Governor Aoshima, elected in 1995 on an anti-corporate platform, quickly ran out of steam without stable popular support or a convincing program. It may well be that this era of "transitional politics" will not be transitional at all: that is, that the "party system" will be replaced by a "political market," dependent on media exposure and support from public opinion. Systemic political instability will follow, eliminating the convenient cushion of political parties between people's discontent and the heights of the state bureaucracy, acting on behalf of the Symbolic Emperor system. The loss of power of the Ministry of Finance during the 1997–8 financial crisis, and the distrust of business, opposition politicians, and people in general *vis à vis* the formerly untouchable bureaucracy, signaled the end of a cycle for the Japanese state. Not that the bureaucracy is out of power. In fact, it is probably the only coherent, stable power system left in Japan today. Yet its authority is challenged from so many quarters that it has become another node, if an essential one, in the entangled web of Japanese decision-making. From this direct confrontation between the aspirations of a new Japanese society and the old structures of historical legitimacy could result a more fundamental political crisis, affecting the heart of the Japanese national identity.

Some elements of this deeper social and political crisis surfaced in mid-1990s Japan. On the one hand, there has been a limited revival of social movements that have been dormant, by and large, since the political and cultural defeat of radical student movements in the 1960s. These incipient forms of social protest focus, primarily, on environmental and anti-nuclear issues, on women's causes, and on community and regional revitalization.[41] Often, they connect to local politics, for instance in successfully supporting populist candidates in municipal elections (as in Tokyo's and Osaka's 1995 municipal elections), or rejecting the building of nuclear power plants by popular referendum, as in the town of Maki, in August 1996. On the other hand, an increasingly confused society, particularly in its younger sections, having grown up in affluence, becomes deprived of

40   Curtis (1993); Johnson (1995); Schlesinger (1997).
41   Hasegawa (1994); Smith (1997); Yazawa (forthcoming).

meaningful values, as the traditional structures of familial patriarchalism and bureaucratic indoctrination lose their grip in a culture filled with information flows from diverse sources. A mixture of ritualistic Japanese traditions, American icons, and high-tech consumption fills the vacuum in social dynamics, cultural challenges, or personal dreams of a society that has finished its assigned task: to make Japan secure, rich, and respected within 50 years. Now, after their hard labor, the Japanese find the tunnel at the end of the light, as increasingly abstract, new technocratic challenges are proposed by a developmental state that has outlived the state of emergency. Or, even worse, financial crisis and the impact of globalization plunge Japan into a recession, and undermine stable employment, after decades of strenuous effort to be prosperous, secure, and independent. According to sociological studies, most people just want to enjoy the quiet consumption of the good life, meaning less *karoshi*, more vacation, better housing, better cities, and a life without exams;[42] while young people, bursting with the energy of their increasingly liberated passions, search for ways of experimentation. It is from these dark alleys, visited during such explorations, that symptoms of destructive revolt have surged, as epitomized by *Aum Shinrikyo* (see volume II, chapter 3). *Aum* was not, and will not remain, an isolated incident because the cracks in the mirror of Japanese society, revealed by Asahara and his followers, seem to originate in the fundamental contradiction emerging in *Heisei*'s Japan: the incompatibility between the developmental state – the actor of Japanese development and guarantor of Japanese identity – and the information society that this state decisively helped to bring to life.

Hatten Hokka and *Johoka Shakai*: a contradictory relationship[43]

The concept of "information society" (*Johoka Shakai*) is, in fact, a Japanese invention, exported to the West in 1978 by Simon Nora and

[42] Shoji (1994, 1995).

[43] This analysis of the Japanese information society is partly based on the database compiled and elaborated in 1995 by my assistant Keisuke Hasegawa, Department of Sociology, Hitotsubashi University. A prior overview of literature and data on Japan's information society was prepared by my assistant Yuko Aoyama, in 1990-94 in Berkeley, University of California, Department of City and Regional Planning. Additional information came from our study with Peter Hall on Japanese Technopoles (Castells and Hall, 1994), and from interviews I conducted in Japan in 1989 and in 1995. A major source of statistical data concerning the diffusion of information technologies in Japan is Ministry of Posts

Alain Minc in the title of their report to the French Prime Minister.[44] It was proposed for the first time in 1963 by Tadao Umesao in an article on an evolutionary theory of society based on the density of "information industries." The article was the object of debate in the January 1964 issue of the journal *Hoso Asahi*, whose editors, introducing the debate, used the term *Johoka Shakai* for the first time. It was popularized a few years later by Japanese futurologists, particularly Masuda and Hayashi. However, the reason that the information society became a major theme for prospective policy and strategic thinking was its adoption as the central issue of the Information Industry Section of MITI's Industrial Structure Council in 1967. Having reached the limits of the extensive model of development, based on traditional manufacturing, MITI was in search of new mobilizing goals for the nation, with the emphasis on finding industrial sectors that would be less polluting, and that could hold a competitive edge against the emerging Asian competitors producing at lower costs. Information technology industries were the obvious candidates, according to the document issued by the Council in 1969: "Tasks for Johoka – Report on the Development of Information Processing Industries."

This report was remarkable on two grounds: on the one hand, it foresaw the essential role of electronics in the new stage of global competition; on the other hand, it extended the concept of informationalism to the overall economy and society, calling for a profound transformation of Japan through the diffusion of information technology. Indeed, this new mode of development fitted very well with Japan's project of specializing in intelligence-intensive production and exports, and moving away from resource-consuming and energy-intensive industries, in which Japan was at a clear disadvantage because of its poor natural endowment. The oil crisis of 1973 underscored the accuracy of this diagnosis, propelling Japan in an all-out race to become the world leader in information technology. It almost succeeded: it came in second, after the United States, after an extra-

and Telecommunications (1995). See also Japan Information Processing Development Center (1994); Wakabayashi (1994); and InfoCom Research (1995). For a Western perspective on Japanese competitiveness in information technology industries, somewhat outdated by the mid-1990s in his statement of the "Japanese conquest," see the excellent overview by Forester (1993). For some glimpses of the discussion of analytical issues of social transformations linked to the informationalization of Japan, see Ito (1980, 1991, 1993, 1994a,b); Kazuhiro (1990); Watanuki (1990); and Sakaiya (1991).

[44]   Ito (1991).

ordinary competitive effort for over three decades.[45] In parallel with design, produce, and export information technology products, Japan also embarked on a rapid diffusion of new technologies in factories and offices of the corporate sector of the economy. Most of the world's factory robots are in Japan. Micro-electronics-based numerical control machines became a Japanese domain, and were widely used in Japanese factories earlier than in the rest of the world. VCRs, TV sets, video games, video cameras, and consumer electronics in general became a Japanese monopoly until the other Asian producers started to compete at the low-end of the industry. Karaoke machines dotted the vast majority of Japanese bars and entertainment centers. Government agencies, homes, and schools were much slower to access information technologies. None the less, Japan's technological modernization proceeded faster than the rest of the world, with the major exception of the United States. With the help of Keisuke Hasegawa, I have constructed some indicators of comparative levels and development of "informationalization" in Japan, the US, and the UK, in 1985 and 1992 (latest available statistics at the time of my study in 1995). According to our data (which I consider unnecessary to reprint here since they are widely available in Japanese statistical year-books), Japan still lagged behind the US, while being ahead of the UK, but its progression was very fast (although slower than the US in personal electronic equipment, such as home computers and mobile telephones).

Together with the production and diffusion of information tech-nology machines, Japan built a new mythology around a futurological view of the information society, which actually tried to replace social thinking and political projects with images of a computerized/ telecommunicated society, to which were added some humanistic, pseudo-philosophical platitudes. A flurry of foundations, publi-cations, seminars, and international conferences provided the apparatus of the new ideology, according to which the technological revolution would solve the future of Japan and, in passing, of the world as well. The developmental state (*Hatten Hokka* in Japanese) found a new gold mine of strategic initiatives: each ministry competed in creating technology-oriented programs which, in their respective areas of competence, aimed at transforming Japan by setting up the infrastructure of the information society.[46] Then, MITI launched the Technopolis Program, whose target was to mass-produce Silicon Valleys and, in the process, to patronize regional prefectures,

[45] Forester (1993).
[46] Castells and Hall (1994).

strengthening MITI's political position in the Information Age. The Ministry of Posts and Telecommunications asserted its privileged role in telecommunications and, among other initiatives, launched its Teletopia Program, to install interactive media in 63 model cities. The Ministry of Construction countered with its own Intelligent Cities Program, using its control of rights of way to install optical fiber networks, and its control of public works to construct smart buildings' office and residential complexes. The Japan Regional Development Corporation created the Science City of Tsukuba, and obtained from the national government the establishment of a new university, and the location in Tsukuba of 40 national research institutes, with emphasis on agricultural and biological research. Powerful prefectures developed programs of their own, so that most of Japan became involved in building the material basis of the new information society, as promised by an army of futurologists, led by retired top bureaucrats and executives heading a whole array of think-tank foundations. The problem was that, in the meantime, Japanese society evolved toward its culturally/historically specific model of the information society, and this came into contradiction not only with the technocratic blueprints of an abstract social model, but with the institutional and political interests of its procreators. Furthermore, after Japan bet its entire technological and economic development on the informational paradigm, the logic of the state came into contradiction with the full blossoming of this paradigm. Let me explain.

An information society is not a society that uses information technology. It is the specific social structure, associated with, but not determined by, the rise of the informational paradigm. The first volume of this book tried to present both the structural features and historic/cultural variations of this society which, in order to propose a more sociological characterization, I call the *network society*. Most of its features characterize 1990s Japan, albeit with Japanese characteristics. These features of the network society entered into contradiction with the institutions and logic of the Japanese state as historically constituted in the past half-century. I shall explain why and how.

First, the globalization of Japanese corporations, and financial markets, as mentioned above, undermined the influence of the developmental state, and exposed its bureaucratic, paralyzing dimension, which becomes a handicap in a world of variable geometry where freedom of maneuver and adaptability are critical for survival in a relentless, competitive race.

Secondly, the wave of deregulation and privatization, in the world and in Japan, forced the Japanese government gradually, but surely, to loosen its grip on telecommunications, the media, the utilities, construction work, and a number of other areas, thus losing many of its ways to control the economy, and to steer the country.

Thirdly, the weakness of Japanese science limited Japanese ability to improve existing technology, to make it better and cheaper, once Japanese companies reached the cutting edge of technological innovation. The success of American electronic companies to reverse the tide of Japanese competition in the 1990s, as well as the limited progress of Japanese firms in biotechnology and software, stem from this lagging behind in basic science and research training. The explanation for this gap between Japanese ability to adapt technology and to generate science-based technology lies in institutional, not cultural, factors, notwithstanding quasi-racist generalizations about Japanese innate capacities/incapacities. It lies, essentially, in the bureaucratic character of the Japanese university system, and in the examination-oriented, outdated pedagogic system, focused on assuring cultural reproduction rather than on stimulating intellectual innovation. As is known, universities are instructed not to work for corporations, professors are civil servants, usually forbidden to do business, graduate schools are weak, doctoral programs are geared toward in-house promotion, and endogamy is the rule in the recruitment of faculty, thus discouraging investment in time and resources studying abroad. Moreover, women are blatantly discriminated against in their academic careers, thus wasting an extraordinary potential for scientific innovation and quality teaching. Universities are degree-granting bureaucracies, primarily aimed at cultural reproduction and social selection, not centers of innovation and training for autonomous thinking. These facts are widely acknowledged by state institutions, but not easily remedied because their correction would contradict the fundamental mission embodied by the Ministry of Education: the preservation of Japanese identity, the transmission of traditional values, and the reproduction of meritocratic stratification. To open the system up to individual competition, autonomous thinking, variation of programs depending on market demands, and foreign influence would be tantamount to dismantling the bastion of *nihonjiron* (ideology of Japanese uniqueness). Let me be clear: I am not arguing that Japanese identity is contradictory to the information society, although, like any cultural identity, it will necessarily be modified by the course of history. My point is that the Japanese educational system, the source of production of the subjects of the information society, in its current structure and goals, is incapable of generating the critical mass of researchers and research programs on which business can rely to innovate in the new fields of industrial, technological, and cultural development, in spite of the astronomical number of engineering graduates. And because the imitation game at which Japanese firms excelled in the

1960s–1980s is now practiced by a plurality of competitors around the world, Japanese companies cannot rely any longer on Japanese institutions and Japanese-trained scientists and engineers to keep up with competition in the high tier of information-based industries. The Japanese government seemed to acknowledge this fact when, in August 1996, it approved a special plan to advance the effort in science and technology, investing US$ 155 billion over five years for programs to be conducted in 100 national universities and private schools.[47] Yet, unless there is a fundamental reform of educational institutions, additional funding would simply mean more, better-trained, bureaucratically minded graduates, in bureaucratically organized research centers, which would be decreasingly able to interact with the increasingly interactive universe of global research.

A fourth institutional limit to the flexibility requirements of the network society concerns the potential calling into question of the system of long-term employment tenure for the core labor force. This system was not just the result of bargaining between capital and labor. It came about in a situation of emergency and national mobilization for development called upon by the state. The growing interdependence of Japanese business with business practices around the world, and particularly in the Asian Pacific, characterized by labor flexibility, makes the preservation of the *choki koyo* system increasingly difficult (see volume I, chapter 4). This system is at the heart of social stability on three dimensions: the system of industrial relations; the legitimacy of the state, whose paternalism guarantees long-term security; and the patriarchal family, because only the assurance of stability of employment for the patriarch allows flexibility for women, as it makes it less risky for women to keep their double role as homemakers and temporary workers without building their own, independent future. Job insecurity, if it diffuses beyond the current trends of employment instability among young workers, will be particularly dramatic in Japan because most social benefits depend on the employing company.

Fifthly, the culture of real virtuality (see volume I, chapter 5) is diffusing fast in Japan. Multimedia, video games, karaoke, cable television, and, lately, computer-mediated communication are the new frontier of Japanese social life, particularly for the younger generations.[48] What characterizes the culture of real virtuality is the mixing of themes, messages, images, and identities in a potentially interac-

47 "Japan's blast-off in science," *Business Week*, September 2, 1996.
48 Dentsu Institute for Human Studies (1994).

tive hypertext. As a result of the simultaneous globalization and individualization of this culture, specific Japanese identities will merge and/or interact with this text, and be open to a variety of cultural expressions. What will be the outcome for Japanese identity? A superficial observer would notice the apparent Americanization of Japanese youth culture (from Rap to sports icons). Yet, a closer look reveals specific adaptations of these images into a twenty-first century Japanese way of being. Whatever it is, it is not traditional Japanese identity. Nor is it an updated version of Japanese culture. It is something else: a kaleidoscope of messages and icons from various cultural sources, including Japan's own, brewed and consumed in Japan and by Japanese, but never again in isolation from global alleys of the virtual hypertext. In this sense, the emphasis of traditional cultural apparatuses on enforcing loyalty to unique Japanese values enters into contradiction with the cultural environment in which the new generations are growing up. It follows cacophony rather than high fidelity.

Sixthly, the new avenues of identity-based social mobilization, around the defense of territorial community, gender, and the environment, directly contradict the myth of Japanese social homogeneity, and the image of a supreme national community represented by the state bureaucracy. True, the majority of Japanese are still cultural nationalists and express a clear feeling of cultural superiority *vis-à-vis* other cultures in the world, according to Shoji's surveys.[49] But the embryos of social movements, emerging in Japan in the 1990s, take exception to this image of national unity, and put forward their differential interests, not against the nation, but claiming diversity within the nation. This perspective directly contradicts the indissoluble unity of the national polity on which the Symbolic Emperor system is based.

Finally, the information society created in Japan over the past 20 years is an active, autonomous, assertive civil society, which has grown increasingly critical of a corrupt, inefficient political system, and rejects the routinization of the political debate.[50] This society requires a dynamic, open political system, able to process the fundamental debates emerging in Japan around what life should be after the end of the siege, and, consequently, beyond the siege mentality. Because the "1955 political system" was a control mechanism somewhat cosmetically added to the developmental state, it lacks the legitimacy and the capacity to transform itself into the citizens' *agora* of the

[49]   Shoji (1994).
[50]   Shoji (1995); Smith (1997); Yazawa (1997).

Information Age.[51] Thus, the demise of the political system's legitimacy directly exposes the developmental state to the claims and challenges of *Johoka Shakai*. This confrontation dominates, and will dominate, Japan as it enters the twenty-first century. For MITI's strategic planners the future is now. And, as is always the case in history, it looks messier than was forecast in their blueprints because it is filled with the actual needs, claims, fears, and dreams of the Japanese people.

Japan and the Pacific

The proof that the Symbolic Emperor system is alive and well in Japan is the, otherwise incomprehensible, stubborn refusal of Japanese political elites to apologize to their Asian neighbors for Japan's aggression and war crimes in the 1930s and 1940s. Had Germany adopted such an attitude, there would be no European Union today. And because Japan chose a different road, *rooted in its institutions of cultural nationalism*,[52] there will be no Pacific institutions of political integration, which are and will be consistently rejected by the Chinese, the Koreans, and the Russians.

On the other hand there is a growing economic interdependence in the Asian Pacific, and a set of interests largely built around Japanese companies' production networks in Asia. Furthermore, Japan's dependence for energy and raw materials and geographical proximity, and the explosive expansion of Asian markets, create powerful incentives for peaceful cooperation and exchange, in a process that could lead, eventually, to building institutions of Pacific cooperation. Nevertheless, the very institutions that propelled Japan, and the other Asian Pacific countries, toward the global economy and the information society are the main obstacles for further cooperation beyond the tense sharing of economic interests. This is because, both for Japan and the Asian Pacific countries, the engine of the development process has been the nationalist project at the heart of their respective developmental states. Therefore, only the superseding of the nationalist developmental state, in Japan and elsewhere, could create the conditions for new identities, new institutions, and new historical trajectories.

---

[51]   Inoguchi (1995).
[52]   Watanabe (1996).

Beheading the Dragon? Four Asian Tigers with a Dragon Head, and their Civil Societies[53]

The development of Japan, and its challenge to the West, came as only half a historical surprise. After all, Japan had industrialized since the late nineteenth century, and was able to build a formidable industrial and military machine in the 1930s. What really rang alarm bells around the orderly world of domination by cultures of European ancestry (naturally including Russia) was the rise of the four East Asian "tigers": South Korea, Taiwan, Singapore, and Hong Kong. That these barren territories, with their economies devastated by war and geopolitics, with no domestic markets or natural or energy resources, without industrial tradition or technological basis, were able to transform themselves in three decades into the most competitive producers and exporters in the world sent a clear signal that the new, global economy was paced and structured by new rules of the game – rules that these "tigers" seemed to have learned faster, and mastered better, than older industrialized countries. Among these rules was the ability to assimilate, use, and enhance new information technologies, both in products and in processes, and the strategic capacity to foresee the potential of new technologies, thus focusing on the technological overhaul of the countries' industries, management, and labor. Thus, analysis of the development process of the four "tigers" sheds light on the new relationships between technology, economy, state, and society, characterizing the transition to the informational, global economy. Furthermore, the Asian economic crisis that began in 1997

---

[53] This analysis largely relies on fieldwork, readings, and personal experience during my teaching, lecturing, and researching in Hong Kong (University of Hong Kong, 1983, 1987), Singapore (National University of Singapore, 1987, 1989), South Korea (Korean Research Institute of Human Settlements, and Seoul National University, 1988), and Taiwan (National Taiwan University, 1989). For my analysis of Hong Kong and Singapore, see Castells et al. (1990), which should be considered as a generic reference for sources on Hong Kong and Singapore, up to 1990 in order not to repeat here the bibliography contained in this monograph. I also wish to acknowledge the help and ideas of Professors Chu-Joe Hsia and You-tien Hsing about Taiwan, and from Professor Ju-Chool Kim about South Korea. Additional sources directly used in this section include: Lethbridge (1978); Amsdem (1979, 1985, 1989, 1992); Lau (1982); Lim (1982); Chua (1985); Gold (1986); Deyo (1987a); Krause et al. (1987); Kim (1987); White (1988); Winckler and Greenhalgh (1988); Robinson (1991); Sigur (1994); Evans (1995). I would also like to mention an interesting, prospective, little-known contribution by a young Korean researcher who died soon after finishing his book: Ahn (1994). Other materials consulted are specifically referred to in the footnotes of the text.

had very different impacts and manifestations in each one of the four "tigers." South Korea's economy, the largest of the four, collapsed, defaulting on its international debt payments on November 21, 1997. From October 1997 onwards, Hong Kong suffered a dramatic drop in the value of its stocks, and real estate, as mentioned above. Repercussions of the crisis in Singapore were in spite of a moderate depreciation of the Singapore dollar, and negative growth in 1998. And Taiwan seemed to withstand the crisis, overall, at least until the end of 1998. I believe, however, that if Japan goes deeper into its recession during the coming years, and if the economies of Indonesia, Thailand, Malaysia, and South Korea continue their deflationary trend, all Asian Pacific countries will eventually experience a substantial downturn, and perhaps a depression. Yet, for the analytical purpose of this book, the differential response to the crisis among the four "tigers" offers a great opportunity for an understanding of the nature of the crisis itself. Thus, after observing and interpreting the process of development of the four "tigers" in a comparative approach, I will extend this comparative analysis to the interpretation of their crisis.

I shall also attempt in this section to move beyond the analysis of processes of development, and crisis, to interpret the social and political contradictions triggered by these processes, inducing the transition to informational societies, and their integration in the global economy. Indeed, while the role of the developmental state (the "dragon" of my story) was critical in fostering, guiding, and ensuring economic growth and technological modernization for about three decades, in the 1990s civil society and corporate business grew increasingly uneasy about the suffocating presence of the state. And the globalization of the economy contradicted the nationalization of society. As a result, new social and political conditions were created in three of the four countries, with the fourth one, Singapore, transforming itself into an extraordinary experiment of a cybernetic, global node. It is in the evolving interaction between development, crisis, state, and society that we may find the explanation for the different forms of incorporation of these Asian societies in the global economy, and for their specific paths of social change.

Understanding Asian development

The understanding of social processes that, between 1960 and 1990, led to the spectacular economic growth and modernization of these four countries, albeit at the price of high social costs and political repression, remains obscured by the passion of ideological debate. This is because the performance of these economies challenges the conventional wisdom of both dogmatic dependency analysis and neo-classical economics in the field of development theory.[54] Against the prevailing left-wing view, according to which economic development cannot take place for dependent societies under capitalism, the four Asian "tigers" sustained the highest rate of GNP growth in the world for about three decades, and won substantial shares of world markets, transforming in the process their economic structure and their social fabric. Furthermore, while exploitation and oppression were integral parts of the development process (as they were in European industri-alization), economic growth was coupled with substantial improvement of living conditions (in wages, health, education, and housing). In addition, income inequality decreased in the 1960s, stabilized in the 1970s, and, although slightly increasing in the 1980s, was still lower in the mid-1980s than in the 1950s, and lower than in the US, the UK, France, and Spain. True, this economic and social transformation took place in a context of political and ideo-logical repression. But most developing societies in the world were under similar repressive conditions, while still being unable to over-come their obstacles to development, largely inherited from their colonial or semi-colonial past. Only the "tigers" could successfully break with that past, thus inspiring emulation in the rest of the Asian countries that, in the 1990s, seem to be following a similar path, albeit under different conditions, and with somewhat different policies, precisely because the development of the "tigers" changed the context in which they were operating, establishing the new Pacific connection to the global economy.

On the other hand, the economic success of the Asian "tigers" has been used to support the ideological discourse of some free-market economists and politicians who found, in their reconstructed version of Asian development, the lost paradise of neo-liberalism. And yet, any serious, unbiased observer of the Asian Pacific scene knows that systematic state intervention in the economy, as well as the state's strategic guidance of national firms and multinational corporations located in the country's territory, were fundamental factors in ensuring the transition of industrializing economies to each of the stages they were reaching in their developmental process.[55] As in Japan, the "developmental state" lies at the core of the experience of newly industrialized economies.[56] There is widespread acknowledg-ment of this fact concerning Singapore, South Korea, and Taiwan. On

[54]   Amsdem (1979); Evans (1995).
[55]   Deyo (1987a); Appelbaum and Henderson (1992).
[56]   Johnson (1987).

the basis of a stream of less well-known studies, including my own, I shall argue that this was also the case for Hong Kong.[57] But arguing that the state was the driving force in the economic development of these countries raises more questions than it answers for development theory. Because, given the widespread, and generally inefficient, state intervention in other developing economies, we must reconstruct the complex set of relationships between the state, society, and economy in the Asian Pacific to understand the specific social conditions explaining the successful outcome of the developmental process. I shall try to provide such an explanation, focusing first on the specific process of each country, then trying to raise analytical questions, and to answer them, in a comparative perspective. The sequence of presentation follows an order from the highest to the lowest level of state intervention: Singapore, South Korea, Taiwan, and Hong Kong.

Singapore: state nation-building via multinational corporations

In econometric terms, the analysis of Yuan Tsao, on sources of growth in Singapore for the 1965–84 period, shows the input of capital to be the main contributing factor, with labor input also having a positive effect, while total factor productivity had a negligible contribution.[58]

Concerning labor, in 1966 Singapore had an unemployment rate of 9 percent, with a labor participation rate of 42.3 percent. By 1983, the unemployment rate had gone down to 3 percent, with a labor force participation of 63 percent, mainly thanks to the massive incorporation of women into the labor force. Education of workers substantially improved, with mandatory English in schools, and the expansion of vocational training. Immigration was severely limited to avoid the location of low-wage activities, and to privilege Singapore citizens. Undocumented immigration was harshly repressed.

The critical factor, however, was the massive inflow of capital, from two main sources: (a) direct foreign investment which oscillated between 10 and 20 percent of GDP, during the 1970s; and (b) an exceptional rate of growth of gross national savings which reached 42 percent of GDP in the mid-1980s, the highest savings rate in the world. For the overall period 1966–85, gross national savings represented over 74 percent of total gross domestic capital formation. Much of it was generated by the public sector (46 percent), mainly

---

[57]   Castells et al. (1990).
[58]   Tsao (1986: 17–65).

through the Central Provident Fund, a government-controlled social security scheme designed to impose savings on the population. The government invested most, but not all, of these savings, much of it in social and physical infrastructure, some in public corporations (over 500 public companies in Singapore in the 1980s). Government also invested abroad, in stocks, and real estate, to decrease the vulnerability of government revenues *vis-à-vis* the cycles of Singapore's economy. Additionally, about one-quarter of total government revenue was kept in a government development fund to stabilize the economy, and allow for strategic government expenditures. This reserve provided the government with a substantial instrument to ensure monetary stability and to control inflation.

The government's fiscal prudence left the responsibility for investment and economic growth to foreign direct investment. The Singapore government decided from the moment of its independence, in 1965, that its impoverished, tiny territory could prosper only by offering itself as an export platform to multinational corporations.[59] Still, the central factor in Singapore's development process was the role of government to provide the necessary incentives to attract foreign capital, and to reach out to investors through the creation of an Economic Development Board (EDB), which did strategic planning on the future direction of the international economy. Among critical factors attracting investment to Singapore, mainly in manufacturing in the first stage, were: a favorable business environment, including low labor costs; social peace, after the repression and dismantlement of independent trade unions in the early 1960s; an educated labor force, largely English-speaking; business-friendly social and environmental legislation; excellent transportation and communications infrastructure; a supply of industrial land, fully equipped, including the possibility of "turn-key" factories built by the government; an advantageous inflation differential; stable fiscal policy; and political stability.[60]

The Singapore government was essential in making industrial diversification possible, as well as in upgrading the technical level of production operations performed in Singapore, enhancing the value of Singapore's products over time. Singapore shifted gradually from traditional services (regional trade) to manufacturing (mainly electronics assembly), then to advanced services (offshore finance, communications, business services). It moved from low-skill assembly manufacturing to advanced manufacturing products and processes,

[59]   Deyo (1981).
[60]   Chen (1983).

including R&D and wafer fabrication in micro-electronics; and from an economy dominated by maritime trade and petroleum refining to a highly diversified industrial structure, including machinery, electronics, transport equipment, producer services, and international finance. The government was largely responsible for this upgrading by creating the technological and educational infrastructure (including some of the best telecommunications and air transportation infrastructure in the world); by providing the real estate, the information systems, and the loosely regulated environment in which new, international business services could prosper; and by upgrading labor through a series of bold measures, including a deliberate, sharp increase of wages in 1979–82 to squeeze out companies looking for unskilled, cheap labor, after Singapore's economy had passed the survival stage. Efficient government management and political stability, ensured through ruthless domination and social integration mechanisms, gave the multinationals reason to believe Singapore was the safest haven in a troubled world. It was, except for intellectuals, independent journalists, political dissidents, unruly teenagers, undocumented immigrants, pregnant legal immigrants, smokers, drug addicts, and litter louts. Public housing of increasingly decent quality, most of it in planned, green, residential estates, fully equipped with amenities, was provided for 87 percent of the population, first as rented housing, then in ownership. In addition, heavily subsidized public health, public education, and mass transit, combined with rising real wages, and declining income inequality, dramatically improved the living conditions of the whole population: Singapore in the 1990s has a much higher per capita income than Britain. This material prosperity helped to pacify the social and inter-ethnic unrest that characterized Singapore in the 1950s and early 1960s. A sophisticated state security apparatus took discrete care of the few dissenters, and insulated Singapore from the influence of "non-Asian values." The restructuring process undertaken by Singapore in the early 1980s in order to upgrade its educational and technological basis led to a short economic recession in 1985–6. But the Lion City emerged from it leaner and meaner, as the government embarked on economic liberalization and internationalization, gradually transforming Singapore into the technological, financial, and business services center of South-East Asia, in close competition with Kuala Lumpur.

In the 1990s, when middle-skilled manufacturing product lines, such as computer disk drives, started to move out of Singapore, toward lower-cost production sites in South-East Asia, the government launched a major effort to anchor micro-electronics production in Singapore, to make sure that the manufacturing contribution to GDP would not fall below 25 percent, coherent with its strategic conviction that manufacturing matters to the wealth of the country. It aimed at high-value manufacturing – that is, R&D and wafer production of advanced chips. Since the Singapore government was now rich, it invested by itself in micro-electronics production. Government-owned Chartered Semiconductor Manufacturing built two plants in Singapore, for a total investment of US$ 1.1 billion, and was planning, in 1996, to build four more plants. The government also formed a joint venture with Texas Instruments, Canon and Hewlett Packard to build another two plants, with an investment of US$ 1.6 billion; and yet an additional joint venture with Hitachi and Nippon Steel to build another semiconductors plant for about US$ 1 billion. SGS–Thomson, counting on government support in training and tax subsidies, decided to expand its chip-making plant in Singapore with a new investment of US$ 710 million dollars by 1998. Altogether, Singapore's semiconductors industry is positioned to overtake, in quantity and quality, the micro-electronics production of any European country by the year 2000.

Furthermore, the fast growth of economies in the region, particularly of Thailand, Malaysia, and Indonesia, helped Singapore to climb up the ladder of informationalism, and to become one of the hubs of the global economy. It was not only growing fast, but transforming the quality of its growth, as companies around the world chose Singapore as their preferred base of operation for management and investment in the midst of the most dynamic economic region in the planet.

Thus, coming out of a devastated economy in the mid-1960s, forcibly cut off from its Malaysian hinterland in 1965, and abandoned as entrepôt and military base by a retreating British Empire in 1968, Singapore, against all the odds, established itself as the showcase of the new developmental process, building a national identity on the basis of multinational investment, attracted and protected by a developmental city-state.

South Korea: the state production of oligopolistic capitalism

American intervention in Korea was fundamental in creating the basis for a modern economy, in 1948–60, through land reform, military support for South Korea, and massive financial aid that allowed the reconstruction and survival of the country after one of the bloodiest wars in recent history. Yet, South Korea's fast developmental process started only under the Park Chung Hee regime, established by the military coup of May 1961, and institutionalized as the Third Republic by the rigged election of October 1963.

On the basis of military, financial, and political support from the

United States – a support determined by the meaning of the 38th parallel as the Berlin Wall of Asia – the South Korean military, and its political arm, the Democratic Republican Party, undertook the construction of a powerful economy as the foundation for its nationalist project. In the initial stages of development, the state assumed an entrepreneurial role via public corporations and government investments. Thus, in the period 1963–79, purchases by government and public corporations amounted to an annual average of almost 38 percent of gross domestic capital formation. The Park regime, however, heavily influenced by the Japanese model, aimed at creating an industrial structure based on large Korean companies, organized as conglomerates. To do so, it set up strong protectionist measures to preserve domestic markets. Yet, given the limited purchasing power of the domestic market, the government decided to sustain an all-out export strategy based on manufacturing. Using its control of the banking system, and of export–import licences, the state pushed Korean companies to merge, in the form of large, vertical networks (the *chaebol*), similar to the Japanese *keiretsu* but without financial independence (see volume I, chapter 3). By 1977, Korean firms employing over 500 workers, while representing only 2.2 percent of firms, accounted for 44 percent of the labor force. The government established an Economic Planning Board which designed and implemented a series of five-year economic plans. It guided Korean companies toward sectors considered strategic for the national economy, either in terms of building self-reliance or in fostering competitiveness in the world economy. Thus, South Korea methodically walked the path of industrial development, investing sequentially in textiles, petrochemicals, ship-building, steel, electrical machinery, consumer electronics, and (in the 1980s) in automobiles, personal computers, and micro-electronics (with some spectacular successes in this latter industry, including endogenous capacity to design and produce 256k chips earlier than Western Europe).[61] Often, some of the strategic decisions by state's agencies were grossly misguided, leading to economic setbacks.[62] But the government was there to absorb the losses, reconvert factories, and secure new loans.[63]

As in the case of Singapore, but on a much larger scale, the critical role of the state was to attract capital and to control and mobilize labor to make the formation and growth of *chaebol* possible during the 1960s

---

[61]   Lee (1988).
[62]   Johnson (1987).
[63]   Lim and Yang (1987).

and 1970s. A critical share of capital was of foreign origin, but with a crucial difference from the Singapore experience. The nationalism of the Korean government led to the rejection of the excessive presence of foreign multinational corporations, out of fear of their influence on society and politics. Thus, capital influx into South Korea mainly took the form of loans, guaranteed by the government under the sponsorship of the United States. Public loans, mainly from international institutions, such as the World Bank, were provided to the government to build a productive infrastructure. Private loans were channeled by the government to Korean companies, according to their compliance with the government's strategic plans. Foreign capital thus accounted for 30 percent of all gross domestic capital formation between 1962 and 1979. The ratio of foreign debt to GNP rose to over 26 percent in 1978, making South Korea one of the world's most indebted economies by the early 1980s. Yet, debt service as a proportion of exports was not excessive, and, in fact, declined from 19.4 percent in 1970 to 10.5 percent at the end of the decade. Indeed, the ratio of foreign trade (exports and imports) to GNP jumped from 22.7 percent in 1963 to 72.7 percent in 1979. The experience of South Korea indicates that indebtedness *per se* is not an obstacle to development: it is the proper use of the loans that determines the economic outcome. South Korea, in contrast to some Latin American military regimes (for example, Argentina), used the loans to build infrastructure and support exports. Its freedom of maneuver was guaranteed by the US footing the huge defense bill of the South Korean government, in compensation for being the Asian bulwark against communism.

Only in the 1970s, when the foundations of the South Korean economy were solidly established under tight control of the *chaebol*, guided by the state, did the government actively seek direct foreign investment. But even then, severe restrictions were imposed on foreign companies: foreign equity holding was limited to a maximum of 50 percent, forcing foreigners into joint ventures with Korean firms, except in Export Processing Zones insulated from the Korean market. The government was also very selective in allowing foreign investment, looking particularly for companies that could facilitate some technology transfer. Japanese companies invested in textiles, electrical machinery, and electronics. American companies established their presence mainly in petroleum and chemicals. Yet overall foreign investment remained limited, accounting in 1978 for only 19 percent of South Korean exports, and for 16 percent of total manufacturing output.

The state also organized the submissive incorporation of labor into the new industrial economy, under the principle of producing first, redistributing later. Korean labor, educated and hard working, was, as in the rest of East Asia, a critical factor in the developmental process. However, its mode of incorporation was much more repressive in Korea than in other societies.[64] The concentration of workers in large factories organized by quasi-military management favored the emergence of militant trade unionism. Yet independent workers' unions were forbidden, strikes were brutally repressed, and working and living conditions, in the factory and in the home, were kept to a minimum for a long period. Such a repressive attitude led to the formation of the most militant labor movement in Asia, as the frequency and violence of strikes in the 1980s and 1990s came to demonstrate. Keeping the growth of wages at a substantially lower level than productivity growth was a cornerstone of government economic policy.

Living conditions did improve, however, for the population at large as well as for industrial workers because of the impressive performance of the economy, under the impulse of export-led industrialization. For instance, during the critical developmental period 1972–9, government revenues increased at a stunning annual rate of 94.7 percent, the top 46 *chaebol* collected an annual increase in value added of 22.8 percent, and real wages grew at an annual rate of 9.8 percent. The proportion of the population below the poverty line declined from 41 percent in 1965 to 15 percent in 1975. And while income inequality worsened in the 1970s, overall, South Korea still displayed, in the 1980s, a more equitable income distribution than the United States.

Finally, an emphasis on science and technology, and the upgrading of products and process in Korean industry, have been the obsession of the South Korean state since the 1960s. It created and staffed a series of specialized R&D institutes, linking them to industry under the guidance of the Ministry of Science and Technology. South Korea is the industrializing country that has most rapidly climbed the technological ladder in the new international division of labor.[65] For instance, between 1970 and 1986, South Korean engineering exports grew at an average annual rate of 39 percent, far exceeding the performance of Japan, at 20 percent. In the 1990s, Korean microelectronics, consumer electronics, and computer industries have become serious competitors of Japanese and American companies, far outstripping European firms in winning world market share in electronics.

---

[64] Deyo (1987b).
[65] Ernst and O'Connor (1992).

South Korea was rightly dubbed by Alice Amsdem "Asia's next economic giant": it increased its share of world domestic production by 345 percent between 1965 and 1986.[66] The four leading South Korean *chaebol*, Samsung, Lucky Gold Star, Daewoo, and Hyundai, are, in the 1990s, among the world's 50 largest conglomerates. They are now investors with a global reach, penetrating markets in America, Europe, Asia, and Latin America, both with their exports and their direct investment. European and American regions fight each other to attract Korean investment. In 1996 the French government tried to sell for 1 franc its ailing "national champion," Thomson, to a consortium led by Daewoo, only to retreat from the deal after the announcement prompted nationalist outrage in France.

At the roots of such an extraordinary rise from the ashes of a destroyed and divided country, in about only three decades, lies the nationalist project of a developmental state that deliberately sought the creation of major Korean companies able to become global players in the world economy. It achieved its goal by using foreign loans, American military support, and the ruthless exploitation of Korean labor.

Taiwan: flexible capitalism under the guidance of an inflexible state

Even by the high standards of Asian Pacific development, Taiwan is probably *the* success story, in terms of the combination of a sustained high rate of growth (annual average of 8.7 percent in 1953–82, and of 6.9 percent in 1965–86), increase in world share of GDP (multiplied by a factor of 3.6 in 1965–86), increase in share of world exports (2 percent in 1986, above all other newly industrialized countries, including South Korea), increase in the share of world manufacturing output (multiplied by a factor of 6.8 in 1965–86, as compared to South Korea's 3.6). And this within the context of an income distribution less unequal than any other country, except for Scandinavia and Japan, with inequality declining rapidly during the growth process: Gini coefficient of 0.558 in 1953, and of 0.303 in 1980, well below that of the US or Western European average, although inequality increased somewhat during the 1980s.[67] There were also substantial improvements in the conditions of health, education, and general living standards.[68]

---

[66]   Amsdem (1989).
[67]   Kuo (1983).
[68]   Gold (1986).

Taiwanese growth was largely accomplished through productivity and competitiveness generated by a flexible production system,[69] put into practice in Taiwan before American academics discovered it in northern Italy. The flexibility concerns both the industrial structure itself, and its overall adaptability to changing conditions of the world economy, under the guidance of a strong state, supported and advised in the initial stages of development by the US Agency for International Development (AID). Throughout the process of development the model of economic growth changed quite dramatically, from an import-substitution emphasis in the 1950s, to export-oriented industrialization in the 1960s (the take-off period), to what Thomas Gold calls "export-oriented import substitution" during the 1970s and 1980s (that is, the deepening of the industrial base to feed exports of manufactured goods).[70] In the 1980s, as Taiwan became an economic power in its own right, Taiwanese companies took on the world market, internationalizing their production and investments both in Asia (particularly in China) and in the OECD countries (particularly in the United States).[71]

At each of these four stages in the process, we observe a different industrial structure that evolves and superimposes upon itself without major crises. But in all instances two features are critical for the understanding of the process: (a) the Kuomintang (KMT) state was at the center of the structure; and (b) the structure is a network, made up of relationships between firms; between firms and the state; between firms and the world market through trading companies (mainly Japanese), and worldwide commercial intermediaries (see volume I, chapter 3).

During the 1950s, the KMT state, with massive economic aid and military protection from the US, undertook the reform of the economy, after bringing society under its total control by means of the bloody repression of 1947–50 and the "white terror" of the 1950s. An American-inspired land reform destroyed the landowning class and created a large population of small farmers who, with state support, increased agricultural productivity substantially. Agricultural productivity was the first source of surplus accumulation. It generated capital for investment, and freed labor for work in the urban–industrial sector. The government forced farmers into unequal exchange with the industrial economy by controlling credit and fertilizers, and organizing a barter system that exchanged

[69]   Greenhalgh (1988).
[70]   Gold (1986).
[71]   Hsing (1997a).

agricultural inputs for rice. With the control of the banks (generally government-owned), and of import licenses, the state geared the Taiwanese economy toward import substitution industrialization, forming an incipient capitalist structure in an entirely protected market. It also provided, with the support of USAID, the necessary industrial and communications infrastructure, and emphasized the education of the labor force. To implement these strategies, several government agencies were established, and four-year plans were elaborated.

By the end of the 1950s, the domestic market had exhausted its demand potential to stimulate growth. Following, again, the advice of US experts, the KMT state embarked on an ambitious program of economic restructuring, this time following an outward orientation. In 1960, the 19-point "Program of Economic and Financial Reform" liberalized trade controls, stimulated exports, and designed a strategy to attract foreign investment. Taiwan was the first country to create an Export Processing Zone, in Kaoshiung. In 1964, General Instruments pioneered electronics assembly offshoring in Taiwan. Japanese medium-sized companies quickly moved to benefit from low wages, lack of environmental controls, educated labor, and government support. Yet the nucleus of Taiwanese industrial structure was home grown. It was made of a large number of small and medium firms, set up with family savings and cooperative savings networks (the famous *huis*), and supported when necessary with government bank credits. Most of these firms started in the rural fringes of metropolitan areas, where families shared work on the land and in industrial shops at the same time. For instance, in 1989, I visited a rural–industrial area of Chang-hua county, near Taichung, where networks of small firms were supplying about 50 percent of the world's umbrellas. The Taiwanese state attracted foreign investment as a way of obtaining capital and access to international markets. But foreign corporations were linked through subcontracting arrangements to a wide network of small firms that provided a substantial base for industrial production. In fact, with the exception of electronics, direct foreign investment did not, and does not, represent a major component of Taiwan's economy. For instance, in 1981, direct capital stock of foreign companies in Taiwan represented only 2 percent of GNP, employment in foreign firms was about 4.8 percent of total employment, their output about 13.9 percent of total output, and their exports only 25.6 percent of total exports.[72] Access to world markets was initially facilitated by Japanese trading companies and by

[72]   Purcell (1989: 81).

buyers of American department stores looking for direct supplies from Taiwanese firms.

Thus, the outward orientation of the economy did not imply control of it by multinationals (as in Singapore), nor the formation of large national conglomerates (as in Korea), although a number of industrial groups did grow up under the auspices of the state, and in the 1990s there are several very large, fully internationalized Taiwanese companies. But most of Taiwan's development was enacted by a flexible combination of decentralized networks of family-based Taiwanese firms, acting as subcontractors for foreign manufacturers located in Taiwan, and as suppliers of international commercial networks, usually linked through intermediaries. This is how "Made in Taiwan" merchandise penetrated the whole realm of our everyday life.

In spite of the importance of Taiwan's medium and small firms in winning competitiveness through flexibility, the role of the state in the development process cannot be overlooked, at least until the mid-1980s. It was the central actor in guiding and coordinating the process of industrialization, in setting up the necessary infra-structure, in attracting foreign capital, in deciding priorities for strategic investment, and imposing its conditions when necessary. For instance, the first attempt to start automobile production in Taiwan failed when the government rejected the conditions requested by Toyota.

As in the case of the other "tigers," a critical factor in enhancing economic productivity was the high yield of labor through a com-bination of low wages, decent education, hard work, and social peace. The social control of labor in Taiwan was achieved, first, by estab-lishing the precedent of unrestrained repression of any challenge to state authority. But, in addition to repression, a number of factors contributed decisively to diffuse conflict and to quell workers' demands. The state did provide a safety net in the form of subsidized health and education, but not housing. Housing cooperatives, helped by government banks, played a role in delaying the housing crisis that finally came into the open in the late 1980s, triggering active urban social movements. However, the most important factor in keeping social peace was the industrial structure itself, made up of thousands of small companies, many of which were based on family members and primary social networks, sometimes linked to part-time agricultural activity. In multinational corporations, the bulk of the unskilled labor force, as in other Asian societies, were young women who were subjected to the double patriarchalism of family and factory. While this is changing, with the growth of a powerful feminist move-ment in Taiwan in the 1990s (see volume II, chapter 3), the gendering of the labor force was an important factor in ensuring social peace during the critical period of industrial take-off.

From the mid-1970s onward, to fight the threat of protectionism in world markets, and to counter the threat of international isolation after the diplomatic recognition of China by the United States, the KMT state engaged in a process of upgrading and modernizing industry, particularly in high-technology manufacturing. This effort included the launching of Taiwan's micro-electronics, personal computer, and computer peripheral industries, and the building of one of the most successful technology parks in Asia: Hsinchu, near Taipei.[73] A number of Taiwanese companies became major suppliers to large electronics firms such as DEC and IBM, while others, linked up in networks, set up shop in Silicon Valley, and other US locations, and thrived on their own.[74] Other industrial sectors, such as garments and textiles, were advised by the government to raise the quality and value of their products to circumvent import restriction quotas in foreign markets, usually calculated by volume.

By the mid-1980s Taiwan had become a mature, diversified economy, with a solid footing in world markets, and the largest currency reserves in the world. Taiwanese firms felt strong enough to take on China, investing through Hong Kong, and becoming a key player in the Chinese economic miracle (see below). Because of rising wages and the increasing organization of workers in Taiwan, together with the tightening of quotas *vis-à-vis* Taiwanese-originated exports, the largest Taiwanese companies proceeded to offshore production in China and South-East Asia. For instance, Taiwan is currently the world's largest exporter of shoes, but a large proportion of Taiwanese firms' production actually takes place in China.[75] However, this consolidation of Taiwan's firms in international markets, combined with the growth of a civil society, led to an increasing rejection of KMT's grip, resulting in a transformation of the Taiwanese state when Teng Hui Lee, a native Taiwanese, assumed the presidency in January 1988. The process of development begun by KMT to regain new legitimacy in Taiwan, and, across the Taiwan strait, in China itself, created a complex industrial economy, and an affluent, educated society, which made the KMT state obsolete.

[73]   Castells and Hall (1994).
[74]   Ernst and O'Connor (1992).
[75]   Hsing (1997a).

Hong Kong model versus Hong Kong reality: small business in a world economy, and the colonial version of the welfare state

Hong Kong remains the historical reference for the advocates of unfettered capitalism. While the prominent role of the state in the hypergrowth economies of Japan, South Korea, Singapore, and Taiwan is too obvious to be denied, Hong Kong, with its early take-off in the 1950s, and its apparent *laissez-faire* brand of capitalism, embodies the dreams of stateless capitalism, supported by the Hong Kong government's explicit policy of "positive non-intervention." Thus, the Hong Kong model may well survive 1997. It was, as the saying goes, a society built in a borrowed place, on borrowed time.

And, yet, a careful analysis of Hong Kong's economic development since the mid-1950s reveals the decisive role of the state in creating conditions for growth and competitiveness, albeit in a more subtle, indirect, but no less important, mode of intervention than the ways followed by the other three "tigers."[76]

Let us first review certain facts. In the free-market paradise of Hong Kong, all land (with the exception of communal village land of the New Territories) was Crown land, which the government leased, not sold, over the years, in a land market entirely manipulated by government control in order to increase public revenue. This land policy also allowed the government to subsidize its public housing projects (land was provided at no cost), as well as government-developed industrial estates, and factories with flats, which played a substantial role in housing small manufacturing firms in the first stage of industrialization. Furthermore, during the critical years of economic take-off (1949–80), while GDP grew by an impressive factor of 13, real government expenditure grew by 26 times, and government social expenditures (including housing, education, health, and social welfare) grew by an astounding 72 times. Thus, government expenditure as a proportion of GDP reached 20.3 percent in 1980. Government share of total capital formation grew during the 1960s and 1970s, from 13.6 percent in 1966 to 23.4 percent in 1983, before declining to around 16 percent in the late 1980s.[77]

Government regulation was more important than is usually acknowledged. It was, for instance, significant in the banking industry, after a series of financial scandals in the early 1980s threatened to

---

[76] Leung et al. (1980); Youngson (1982); Schiffer (1983); Castells et al. (1990).

[77] Ho (1979); Youngson (1982); Castells et al. (1990).

wreck Hong Kong's markets.[78] But what was really crucial was the role played by government in creating the conditions for competitiveness of Hong Kong's economy in world markets. I shall summarize the argument.

The classic econometric study by Edward K.Y. Chen on the sources of economic growth in Hong Kong for the period 1955–74 showed that capital and labor inputs played in Hong Kong, as in Singapore, a much greater role than in advanced industrial economies.[79] He also identified exports and international trade as the leading causes of Hong Kong's growth. This interpretation was confirmed, and expanded, in the careful statistical analysis of Tsong-Biau Lin, Victor Mok, and Yin-Ping Ho on the close relationship between exports of manufacturing goods and economic growth.[80] This was hardly a surprising finding, but still constituted an observation full of meaning, particularly from the vantage point of the 1990s, when the rise of Hong Kong as a financial and advanced services center somehow obscures the original sources of the Territory's prosperity. Their study showed that exports were concentrated over time in the same few industries – textiles, garments, footwear, plastics, consumer electronics – in a different pattern from that observed in the other three "tigers." The expansion of exports was mainly due to what Lin et al. have called "changes due to differential commodity composition";[81] that is, changes of product line and in the value of the products within the same industry. In this sense, *what was fundamental was the flexibility of Hong Kong manufacturers to adapt quickly and effectively to the demand of world markets within the same industries.*

We still need to explain the competitiveness of these industries besides their ability to adapt to demand. Another econometric study by E.K.Y. Chen provided the clue: *the critical explanatory variable in Hong Kong's growth equation was the differential between Hong Kong's relative prices and the level of income in the United States, the main market for Hong Kong's exports.*[82] Since the level of prices for manufactures in Hong Kong was mainly determined by wage levels in labor-intensive industries, it was the ability of Hong Kong firms to keep wage increases well below the increase in US income, while still assuring an efficient, skilled, healthy, and motivated labor force, that provided the ground base for the expansion of manufactured exports, and thus for

[78]   Ghose (1987).
[79]   Chen (1979).
[80]   Lin et al. (1980).
[81]   Lin et al. (1980).
[82]   Chen (1980).

economic growth. Thus, *flexibility of manufacturing, and competitive prices on the basis of relatively low production costs, were the main factors explaining Hong Kong's growth*. But the "explanatory variables" are themselves the result of a specific industrial structure and of a given institutional environment that made the flexibility and competitiveness of the economy possible.

On one hand, *flexibility was the result of an industrial structure characterized by small business*: more than 90 percent of manufacturing firms in Hong Kong in 1981 employed fewer than 50 workers, and large firms (over 100 workers) accounted for only 22.5 percent of manufacturing contribution to GDP. Since 90 percent of manufactured goods were exported, we may assume that small businesses were equally significant in exports, although there are no available data to show it directly. We do know, however, that foreign manufacturers accounted for a small proportion of Hong Kong's manufacturing exports (10.9 percent in 1974, 13.6 percent in 1984). In fact, the average size of manufacturing establishments in Hong Kong decreased over time: from an average of 52.5 workers per establishment in 1951 to 20 in 1981. The mystery lies in how these small firms were able to link up with the world market. Unlike Taiwan, foreign trading companies were not important in Hong Kong. There were, indeed, the traditionally established British trading "Hongs" (such as the legendary Jardine Matheson or Swire groups, whose personas populated James Clavell's novels), but their role in manufacturing exports was rather small. According to a classic study by Victor Sit, about 75 percent of local exports were handled by local export/import firms.[83] The great majority of these small firms were small businesses themselves. There were more than 14,000 such firms in Hong Kong in 1977. It was only in the 1980s that large department stores from the United States, Japan, and Western Europe set up their own offices in Hong Kong to place orders with local firms. Thus, the basic industrial structure of Hong Kong consisted of networks of small firms, networking and subcontracting among themselves on an *ad hoc* basis, following the orders channeled by small firms specializing in export/import. Such a flexible structure, originating from the initial nucleus of 21 Shanghainese industrialists who relocated to Hong Kong after the Chinese revolution, with their know-how and small family savings, became an effective business tool for adapting to rapidly changing demand in an expanding world market.

But how were these small businesses able to obtain information about the world market, to upgrade their production, to improve

---

[83]   Sit (1982).

their machinery, to increase their productivity? The Hong Kong government played a significant, albeit not decisive, role in this matter. First, it organized the distribution of export quotas allowed under the MultiFiber Agreement among different firms in the textile industry, thus shaping the production networks under the guidance of the Industry Department. Secondly, it established (in the 1960s) several information and training centers, such as the Hong Kong Productivity Center, engaged in training programs and consulting and technology services; and the Hong Kong Trade Development Council, with offices around the world to promote exports, and to disseminate information among Hong Kong's firms. Other services, such as the Hong Kong Credit Insurance Corporation, served to cover some of the risks incurred by exporters. In the late 1970s, when the need for restructuring and upgrading of Hong Kong's economy became necessary to answer the challenge of protectionism in core markets, the government appointed a Committee on Industrial Diversification, which elaborated a strategic plan for Hong Kong's new stage of industrialization, a plan that was implemented by and large during the 1980s.

The fundamental contribution, however, of Hong Kong's government to the flexibility and competitiveness of small business was its widespread intervention in the realm of collective consumption. The key element in this intervention was a large public housing program, the second largest in the capitalist world, in terms of the proportion of the population housed in it: about 45 percent, in the 1980s. Although the first estates were of appalling quality, they improved over time, with the building of several large new towns, fully equipped with urban amenities. In the late 1980s, the government undertook the upgrading of the program, demolishing and rehabilitating old structures, and building new housing for displaced tenants. In addition, a comprehensive system of public education, public health, subsidized mass transport, social services, and subsidized foodstuffs was put into place over the years, amounting to a major subsidy of indirect wages for the labor force. Schiffer calculated the impact of non-market forces on household blue-collar expenditures in 1973–4: on average it amounted to a 50.2 percent subsidy of total expenditures for each household.[84] Yu and Li estimated a transfer-in-kind to the average public housing tenant equivalent to 70 percent of household income.[85] Thus, public housing and the special brand of welfare state that emerged in Hong Kong subsidized workers, and allowed them to

[84]   Schiffer (1983).
[85]   Yu and Li (1985).

work long hours without putting too much pressure on their employers, most of whom had little margin to afford salary increases. By shifting onto the government's shoulders much of the responsibility for workers' well-being, small business could concentrate on competitive pricing, shrinking and expanding their labor force according to the variations of demand.

Hong Kong's colonial welfare state did perform two other important functions directly related to the competitiveness of the economy. First, it made possible industrial peace for a long period, a matter of some consequence given the historical tradition of social struggle (often overlooked) among Hong Kong's working class, an underlying current that surfaced with rampaging violence in the urban riots of 1956, 1966, and 1967.[86] Secondly, it created a safety net for low-risk entrepreneurialism that characterized the small business scene in Hong Kong. In fact, small businesses in Hong Kong, as everywhere else, had a high failure rate: on average, an entrepreneur succeeded only after seven attempts.[87] But most businesses were started by workers who betted their small savings, and relied on family support, and on the safety net of public housing and subsidized public amenities to take their chance. If and when their entrepreneurial dreams were busted, they were able to land softly in this safety net, to regroup, and try again.

Thus, social stability and subsidized collective consumption were critical for moderating the pressure of direct wages on business, for stable industrial relations, and for the creation of a burgeoning nest of small- and medium-sized entrepreneurs who were, indeed, the driving force of Hong Kong's development, but under social and institutional conditions quite different from those imagined by Milton Friedman in his fiction writing about the Hong Kong economy. Chart 4.2 provides a synthetic view of the set of relationships that, according to my research and sources, characterized Hong Kong's development process between the early 1950s and the mid-1980s.

After the conclusion of the 1984 Sino–British agreement on the transfer of sovereignty at the historically established date of 1997, Hong Kong went into a new model of development, pushed at the same time by new competitive pressures from the world economy, and by the imminent transformation of its institutional environment. Its new economy relied on three major strategic moves. First, Hong Kong deepened its role in manufacturing exports by decentralizing most

---

[86]   Hong Kong Government (1967); Endacott and Birch (1978); Chesnaux (1982); Chan et al. (1986).
[87]   Sit (1982).

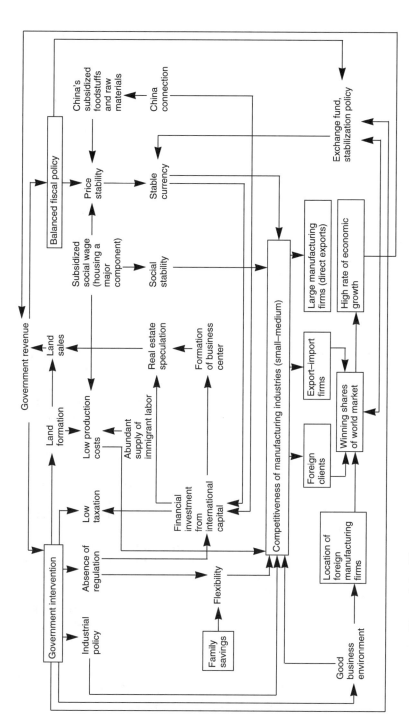

Chart 4.2 The structure and process of economic development in Hong Kong, 1950–85

of its production into the Pearl River delta across the border (see volume I, chapter 6). According to estimates, 10, or 6, or no fewer than 5 million workers were engaged in manufacturing for Hong Kong firms in and around the Pearl River delta, in Guandong province, in the mid-1990s. Secondly, Hong Kong expanded its role as international business center that had been established in the 1980s, taking advantage of its flexible financial regulations, its excellent communications and business infrastructure, and its networks of connections. Thirdly, Hong Kong became, as it had been in history, but this time on a much larger scale, the link with China, and with the Chinese miracle. Most investment in China circulates through Hong Kong. Thus, Hong Kong anticipated its destiny by becoming indispensable to China's incorporation into the global economy, and by betting on its ability to adapt to a new environment, and to thrive in a potentially Chinese-dominated Pacific century. Yet, for Hong Kong to be able to sell itself, to China and to the world, it relies on its economic growth performance of the past half-century – a process that belies the so-called Hong Kong model, but suggests a wealth of developmental lessons to be learned from the Hong Kong reality.

The breeding of the tigers: commonalities and dissimilarities in their process of economic development

In the preceding pages I have tried to summarize the underlying political/economic logic specific to the development process in each of the four lands under consideration. To make progress in the path of theorizing their experience, I will now attempt to think comparatively, by focusing on both the commonalities and the dissimilarities between the four processes, as clues to understanding the social and institutional conditions inducing development in the global economy.

Let us start with the *differential factors*, those that clearly differ in each case, and therefore cannot be considered to be critical elements in the development process. The most important dissimilarity is the industrial structure of each country. In particular, we should reject the "new international division of labor" thesis, according to which new industrialization "in the periphery" is mainly due to productive decentralization from multinational corporations from "the core." Multinationals are fundamental to Singapore, but they played a secondary role in Taiwan's industrialization, and they were, and still are, minor players in South Korea and Hong Kong (although in Hong Kong multinational *financial* corporations became an important factor from the mid-1980s). As mentioned above, the industrial structure of Singapore is characterized by the direct linkage between multinational corporations and the state, including a number of significant state-owned, or state-participated, corporations. The South Korean economy was/is centered around the Korean *chaebol*, nurtured, supported and guided by the state; indeed, in the mid-1990s, the four largest *chaebol* still accounted for 84 percent of Korea's output. Taiwan blends a flexible structure of small- and medium-sized, family business networks; a few large, national firms; and a significant, but minority, presence of foreign firms, either large (American), or medium (Japanese). Hong Kong's economic growth, until the mid-1980s was mainly engineered by local manufacturing firms, most of them small and medium, supported by a benevolent, colonial state, which provided the productive infrastructure, subsidized collective consumption, and ventured into a subtle form of industrial policy. Therefore, there is no relationship between a given industrial structure and economic growth.

Nor is the sectoral specialization of the economies a common feature. It was not the concentration of industrial effort on textiles or on electronics that explained competitiveness, since South Korea, and Taiwan to a lesser extent, gradually diversified their activities into a variety of sectors. Singapore began with petroleum and electronics (mainly semiconductors), and went on to deepen its electronics specialization (adding computer disk drives, of which it became the main world producer in the 1980s, and then advanced micro-electronics in the 1990s), but reaching out to a whole range of advanced services, finance, and trade activities. Hong Kong, on the other hand, deepened and upgraded its early specialization in five sectors: textiles, garments, plastics, footwear, and consumer electronics, adding, like Singapore, a buoyant advanced services industry. So, the only common feature of the four development processes is the adaptability and flexibility of firms and policies in dealing with world market demand. But this flexibility was performed either by a simultaneous presence in several sectors (Taiwan), or by a succession of priority sectors (as in South Korea), or by upgrading the traditional sectors (as in Hong Kong). Competitiveness does not seem to result from "picking the winners" but from learning how to win.

The existence of a welfare state of sorts, through subsidized collective consumption, was a decisive element in the development of city-states – Hong Kong and Singapore – but was clearly not so in South Korea, where the state did not take care of workers' needs and only the *chaebol* introduced some elements of "repressive paternalism," such as company housing. Nor was it the case in Taiwan, where the state aimed at reducing income inequality, and assured education, but let the market provide the basic goods for the population, trusting the trickle-down effect from economic growth.

Last but not least, the myth of social peace as a major component of the development process in East Asia does not stand up to observation. Singapore became stable only after massive state repression, and the outlawing of the independent, majority trade union movement in the early 1960s. Taiwan was tensely pacified only after the execution of an estimated 10,000 to 20,000 Taiwanese resisting KMT's occupation, and the widespread "white terror" of the 1950s. Besides, social conflicts in Taiwan started to develop again after the 1977 Chung Li riot, and social movements of all kinds proliferated in the late 1980s, without endangering economic dynamism. Hong Kong had, for a long time, a relatively high degree of unionization in its workforce, and the largest labor federation was controlled by PRC's Communists. Hong Kong's "social peace" was repeatedly shattered by the riots of 1956, 1966, and 1967, the last one followed by several months of protest, including bombings. Since the late 1970s, powerful community movements in Hong Kong have created the foundation of what is today an active "democracy movement," which raises serious concerns among the authorities, both in Hong Kong and in Beijing. South Korea went from the 1960 student uprising that toppled Syngman Rhee to an endless succession of student demonstrations, workers' struggles (most of them subdued and ignored), and citizens' and workers' insurrections, most notably the 1980 Kwangju uprising that was repressed by the dictatorship of Chun Doo Hwan, resulting in the killing of possibly 2,000 people. Korean social movements and political protest brought down the military regime in 1987, and opened the door for democracy. Political turmoil, and workers' daily resistance and powerful strikes, challenged the authoritarianism of the *chaebol*, but did not undermine South Korea's growth, which continued to proceed at a brisk pace in the 1990s, with annual rates of growth oscillating between 5 and 9 percent in 1991–6.

Thus, while the search for social stability, and the partial achievement of this goal, was a fundamental element in the development policy of the four countries, it was not a given of the society. Quite the opposite: all four societies began their development process with volatile social and political situations, so that important segments of society had to be repressed, tamed, and later integrated, in order to keep a minimum order under which the economy could grow. And when social movements appeared again on the surface, economic development adapted to social tensions, and the four countries were able to keep growth and redistribution, together with democratic liberalization, except in Singapore. Social stability was not a prerequisite for development, but an always uncertain result of it.

I also find commonalities in my observation of Asian development. Without them, we could not think about a recurrent pattern that would shed light on our understanding of new historical processes of development. The first common factor concerns the *existence of an emergency situation in the society*, as a result of major tensions and conflicts, both national and geopolitical. It is obvious in the cases of South Korea and Taiwan. It should also be recalled that Hong Kong dramatically changed in 1949 as a consequence of the Chinese revolution, losing most of its traditional role as an entrepôt for China trade, thus being forced into manufacturing exports as a way to survive without being a burden on the Crown's budget. Indeed, it was its role *vis à vis* China, together with its economic success, that prevented Hong Kong from joining the decolonization process, since neither the United Kingdom nor China could accept its independence. This was also the case for Singapore, first prevented by British troops from being annexed by Indonesia, then expelled from the Federation of Malaysia in 1965, and abandoned to its fate by Britain in 1965–8, then saved politically and economically because of its support for the American effort in the Vietnam War. The critical geopolitical element in East Asia, in contrast with Latin America, was that the US perceived much of Asia as being in danger of being taken over by communists and their allies, and in fact there were elements to support this perception. Strategic considerations overshadowed all other calculations for US policy in the region, giving considerable freedom of maneuver to Asian states in the running of their economies, on the condition that they would remain "vassal states" of the United States in terms of foreign policy and repression of domestic communism, a condition to which they gladly agreed. If there is a fundamental common thread to the policies of the four "tigers" (including Hong Kong) it is that, at the origin of their process of development, we find *policies dictated by the politics of survival.*

Another consequence of this context, dominated by the Asian Cold War, was the importance of American and British support for these governments and for their economies. American aid was the major element in the reconstruction and orientation of the economies of South Korea and Taiwan during the second-half of the 1950s. Although Hong Kong contributed more to Britain than Britain did to Hong Kong, some crucial functions, like defense, remained on British shoulders. And, most importantly, Hong Kong was allowed to export to the Commonwealth, and received strong support from the UK in securing export quotas that were decisive for its early penetration of world markets. While Singapore did not receive much foreign aid, the economy got its jump-start from profitable oil and ship repairing commerce with the American military in Vietnam during the 1960s. Geopolitics provided the ground for the politics of survival to become successful developmental policies.

A second major common factor is that all four development processes were based on an *outward orientation of the economy, and, more specifically, on their success in exporting manufactured goods*, particularly targeting the US market. It is true that for both South Korea and Taiwan import-substitution policies were essential to establish an industrial base at the outset of the development process. Yet, their high growth came only when, starting from their protected domestic markets, they succeeded in exporting. In this sense, the explosion of world trade in the 1960s, and the process of formation of a new, global economy seem to have been the indispensable habitat of the Asian "tigers."

A third common factor is the *absence of a rural, landowning class*, non-existent in Hong Kong and Singapore, and obliterated (or transformed into industrialists) in South Korea and Taiwan by the American-inspired land reforms of the 1950s. The existence of a powerful landowning class is an obstacle to development because of the usually speculative character of their investments, and because of their reluctance to embark on processes of modernization that would jeopardize their social and cultural domination. It seems that this was one of the obstacles to the Indonesian development process, until the internationalization of its economy in the 1980s, under the aegis of the state, bypassed the interests of traditional rural/financial oligarchies.[88]

A fourth common factor in the development of the four countries was the *availability of educated labor, able to reskill itself during the process of industrial upgrading, with high productivity and a level of wages that was low by international standards*. Labor was kept, by and large, under control, in terms of work discipline, and labor demands, with the exception of South Korean labor in large factories in the late 1980s. Disciplined, efficient, relatively cheap labor was a fundamental element in Asian development. But this discipline and effectiveness did not come from the supposedly submissive nature of Asian labor (plainly a racist statement) nor, in more sophisticated vein, from Confucianism. Confucianism does explain the high value placed on education, and therefore the high quality of labor once the state provides the conditions for access to education. But Confucianism does not explain subordination since, in Confucian philosophy, authority must be legitimate, and exercised in legitimate ways, or else it should be resisted. Indeed, the long history of popular uprisings in China, as well as the tradition of revolutionary working-class movements in Shanghai and Canton, contradicts such ill-informed, ideological

[88]   Yoshihara (1988).

statements.[89] As mentioned above, in all four countries labor discipline was imposed first by repression. But in all cases there were also, subsequently, powerful elements of social integration that explain why a historically rebellious population ultimately accommodated to the exploitative conditions that characterized working and living conditions for most people for most of the development period. Paramount among the integrative factors was the actual betterment of workers' living standards. What was a low wage for an American or a Japanese worker was a fortune for the industrial labor force of poor East Asian countries. Furthermore, data show a decrease in income inequality in the first stage of development, and a dramatic rise in real wages over three decades. Besides, in the case of Hong Kong and Singapore, a peculiar version of the welfare state, materially organized around public housing projects and new towns, was essential in both improving living conditions and establishing the state's social control and political legitimacy. In the case of Taiwan, the integration of rural and urban life in the same families, and the vitality of social networks, provided, at the same time, the safety net to resist the shocks of fast industrialization and the peer-group social-control mechanisms to discourage workers from challenging the system. Thus, through a combination of state repression, state integration, economic improvement, and social network protection and control, an increasingly educated labor force (much of which was made up of women) found it in its best interests to fulfill the expectations of a system that was as dynamic as it was ruthless. Only when the survival stage was passed did spontaneous social resistance start to take shape in a labor movement, and political alternatives, particularly in South Korea.

A fifth common factor in East Asian industrialization was the *ability of these economies to adapt to the informational paradigm and to the changing pattern of the global economy*, climbing the ladder of development through technological upgrading, market expansion, and economic diversification. What is particularly remarkable (as in the case of Japan, which provided the role model for development, except in Hong Kong) is their understanding of the critical role played by R&D and high-technology sectors of the new global economy. Their emphasis on science and technology (stronger in South Korea and Taiwan, but also present in the city-states) was decided and implemented by the state, but it was welcomed and internalized by industrial firms. The four countries, over three decades, made the transition into the advanced productive structures of the

---

[89]   Chesnaux (1982); Chan et al. (1986).

informational economy, albeit still keeping many low-tech activities, as was also the case in the US.

It was this ability to shift from one level of development to another, and from peripheral incorporation into the global economy into a more dynamic, competitive positioning, in higher-value generating activities, that led to sustained growth, in contrast with the short-lived bursts of growth that characterized most Latin American economies.[90]

Behind most of the critical factors common to the experiences of the four East Asian "tigers" is what seems to be the most significant of all commonalities: *the role of the state in the development process.* The production of high-quality labor and its subsequent control, the strategic guidance through the hazardous seas of the world economy, the ability to lead the economy in the transition to informationalism and globalization, the process of diversification, the creation of a science and technology base, and its diffusion in the industrial system – these are all critical policies whose success determined the feasibility of the development process.

Policies are, of course, the outcome of politics, enacted by the state. Behind the economic performance of Asian "tigers" breathes the dragon of the developmental state.

The developmental state in East Asian industrialization: on the concept of the developmental state

If the characterization of East Asian industrialization I have presented in the preceding pages is plausible, then understanding this development experience requires a sociological analysis of the formation and intervention of the developmental state in these countries.

But, first, I need to define the precise meaning of developmental state, which I have already used in my analysis of Japan. I take it from Chalmers Johnson's conceptualization, and I do not disagree with the meaning giving to it by Johnson, Peter Evans, Alice Amsdem, and other scholars in the field of development theory. I think, however, it would be useful to provide my own definition, as I understand it, on the basis of my analysis of East Asian "tigers," although it can be used in other contexts.

A state is developmental when it establishes as its principle of legitimacy its ability to promote and sustain development, understanding by development the combination of steady high rates of economic growth and structural change in the productive system, both domestically and in its relationship to the international economy. This definition needs, however, to specify the

---

[90]   Fajnzylber (1983).

meaning of "legitimacy" in a given historical context. Many political scientists remain prisoner to an ethnocentric conception of legitimacy, related to the democratic state. Under this conception, the state is legitimate when it establishes hegemony or consensus *vis-à-vis* the civil society. Yet, this particular form of legitimacy presupposes acceptance by the state itself of its submission to the principle of representation of society as it is. But we know that states that have tried over history to break away from the existing order did not recognize civil-society-as-it-was as the source of their legitimacy. And yet, they were not pure apparatuses of naked power, as has been the case with defensive military dictatorships in many instances. The clearest examples are revolutionary states, particularly those emerging from communist revolutions or national liberation movements. They have never pretended to be legitimate in terms of the acquiescence of their subjects, but in terms of the historical project they embodied, as *avant-gardes* of the classes and nations that were not yet fully aware of their destiny and interests. The obvious, and significant, political and ideological differences between communist and revolutionary states and the right-wing dictatorships of East Asia have, in my opinion, led to the overlooking of some fundamental similarities that go beyond formal resemblances to the heart of the logic of the state: the legitimacy principle holding together the apparatus, and structuring and organizing the codes and the principles for accessing power and for exercising it. In other words, the legitimacy principle may be exercised on behalf of society (the democratic state) or on behalf of a societal project. When the state substitutes itself for society in the definition of societal goals, when such a societal project involves a fundamental transformation of the social order (regardless of our value judgment on the matter), I refer to it as a revolutionary state. *When the societal project respects the broader parameters of social order (for example, global capitalism), but aims at fundamental transformations of the economic order (regardless of the interests or desires of the civil society), I propose the hypothesis that we are in the presence of the developmental state.* The historical expression of this societal project generally takes the form (and was the case in most East Asian experience) of the building, or rebuilding, of national identity, affirming the national presence of a given society, or a given culture, in the world. Sometimes this national affirmation does not even coincide with the territory under the political control of the developmental state: for example, the Kuomintang state speaking on behalf of the "Republic of China," behind the safe refuge provided by the US Seventh Fleet.

   Thus, ultimately, *for the developmental state, economic development is not a goal but a means.* To become competitive in the world economy, for all Asian "tigers," was first their way of surviving, both as a state and as a society. Secondly, it also became their only way of asserting their national interests in the world – that is, to break away from a situation of dependency, even at the price of becoming an unconditional front-line for the United States. I propose the idea that the developmental state effects the transition from a political subject "in itself" to a political apparatus "for itself" by affirming the only legitimacy principle that does not seem to be threatening for the international powers overseeing its destiny: economic development.

The rise of the developmental state: from the politics of survival to the process of nation-building

The East Asian developmental state was born of the need for survival, and then it grew on the basis of a nationalist project, affirming cultural/political identity in the world scene. *Survival came first.*

Singapore was a nonentity at the outset of its independence in 1965. An abandoned military outpost of the crumbled British Empire, a bankrupt entrepôt economy cut off from its ties with Indonesia, an integral part of Malaysia expelled from the Federation of Malaysia against its will, and a pluri-ethnic society subjected to the pressure of its Malay environment and torn by internal, violent ethnic and religious strife between the Chinese majority and the Muslim Malay and Hindu Tamil minorities, it could have easily become another Sri Lanka. The first concern of Lee Kwan Yew's People's Action Party (PAP), which led the anti-colonial struggle against the British, was to hold Singapore together and to make it viable, while fighting off what was perceived as the menace from guerrillas of the Malaysian Communist Party, led by Chinese, and supported by the PRC.

South Korea had just survived an all-out assault from communist North Korea, and barely escaped being caught in the middle of a nuclear war between MacArthur's imperial fantasies and the victorious Chinese People's Liberation Army. In 1953, the country was in a shambles, the nation divided, and Syngman Rhee's First Republic was but a superstructure for the United States to build a strong defensive line, based on a new, war-hardened, South Korean army, on the northern Asian frontier between communism and the Free World.

Taiwan was not yet Taiwan. It was an impoverished and terrorized island that had become the last bastion of the vanquished Kuomintang armies, kept in reserve by the United States as a potential threat, and as a political standpoint against the rising power of the PRC. In fact, it was the communist invasion of South Korea that brought the United States to the decision to draw the line in the

Taiwan Strait, a decision that saved the KMT and allowed it to live its ideological fantasy of reconstructing the Republic of China from Taiwan Province, a fantasy not shared by Chinese capitalists, most of whom emigrated elsewhere.

Hong Kong was rapidly becoming an anachronism after the Chinese revolution and the embargo on China imposed by the United Nations on the occasion of the Korean War. With its entrepôt commerce with China downgraded to smuggling, it was on its way to being the last colony of a fading empire. Fundamental doubts about China's willingness to let it live outside Chinese control, as well as political fears that either the Labour party or British public opinion would include the Territory in the next round of decolonization, kept Hong Kong wondering about its fate, while wave upon wave of Chinese immigrants/refugees were making the colony into their own trap, escaping either from revolution or misery.

The first reflex of state apparatuses that later became developmental (PAP state in Singapore, the Park Regime in South Korea, the KMT in Taiwan, and the colonial state in Hong Kong) was to ensure the physical, social, and institutional viability of the societies they came to be in charge of. In the process, they constructed and consolidated their own identity as political apparatuses. However, according to the hypothesis I am proposing, they shaped their states around the developmental principle of legitimacy on the basis of specific political projects that had, in each case, specific political actors, all of which were created in rupture with the societies they were about to control and lead.

In Singapore, the PAP did lead the anti-colonialist struggle, but it did so in the 1950s in close alliance with the left-wing movement (including the left-wing labor unions), and even with the communists, until the events of the early 1960s convinced Singapore's national leader, Lee Kwan Yew, that he had to repress the left (which he did ruthlessly) to affirm an autonomous political project aimed at transforming Singapore from a colonial outpost into a modern nation.[91] The PAP was, in fact, organized along Leninist lines, with tight mechanisms of social control and social mobilization, centralized forms of party power, and direct guidance of the economy through a well-trained, well-paid, usually clean, state technocracy. The social policies of the PAP, including public housing and community services, aimed at blending into one national culture the complex pluri-ethnic structure of Singapore, while the emphasis on Confucianism and on Mandarin literacy among the Chinese deliberately sought to break up

---

[91]   Chua (1985).

the subcultures organized around dialects spoken by Chinese networks of various regional origins. Economic development was the means to achieve both goals of making Singapore a viable country and of building it as a new nation.

In Taiwan, once the KMT had to accept the reality of having lost China, it tried to convert Taiwan into a showcase of what a reformed KMT could do for China and the Chinese people, after acknowledging the disastrous economic management and the damage that their unrestrained corruption had done to their political control over China.[92] A quasi-Leninist party, explicitly organized around the principles of democratic centralism, the KMT attempted to reform itself, made its adherence to Sun Yat-Sen's "three principles of the people" official ideology, and derived from it its policies of land reform, reduction of inequality, and emphasis on education. The critical matter for the consolidation of KMT power in Taiwan was its ability to assure the island's growing prosperity. The KMT considered the success of its developmental project to be critical in obtaining the support of Chinese all over the world for its future challenge to communist power on the mainland. In fact, the Chinese "open-door policy" of the 1980s was partly an answer to the impact of Taiwan's economic miracle, not only among the informed Chinese population, but among the Chinese leadership itself.

The origins of the Park Regime in South Korea can also be traced back to the emergence of a new political actor, breaking away both from the colonial order and from the corrupt, inefficient Rhee regime that had seen the remnants of the pro-Japanese commercial bourgeoisie prosper through the state redistribution of US aid, while the country continued to suffer from the devastation of war.[93] Although the 1961 coup toppled the short-lived civilian government of John Chang, issued from student-led rebellion against Syngman Rhee, the ideology and practice of military plotters went beyond a simple law-and-order reflex. The leaders of the coup were young, nationalist, military officers of low rank, with the exception of Major General Park, who was trained in Japan and had served in the Japanese Army in Manchuria. The South Korean military was an entirely new institution, whose organization and growth was obviously linked to the Korean War. It grew from 100,000 in 1950 to 600,000 in 1961, making it one of the most numerous, well-trained, and more professional armies in the world. Given the military interest of the US in Korea, most of the effort of modernization and support was focused

---

[92]   Gold (1986).
[93]   Cole and Lyman (1971); Lim (1982).

on the armed forces. Thus, the army's professional training and organizational capacity seems to have been above the rest of South Korean society in the 1960s, if we except a small group of students, and an even smaller intelligentsia. Thus, in the presence of the disintegration of the state, economy, and society, the military officers who seized power in 1961–3 appear to have been close to the "Nasserite" brand of nationalist military regimes. Lacking a social basis, and feeling uncertain of the support of the United States toward the national projection of Korea beyond its geopolitical function, the Park Regime conceived the developmental strategy as an instrument of rebuilding the Korean nation, and of winning degrees of political freedom.

But what about Hong Kong? How did the half-hearted, more subtle brand of Hong Kong's semi-developmental state come into being? How could a colonial government identify itself with the destiny of the colony? If the traditional Hongs and the new entrepreneurs cared only about their business, if the British old-timers mainly dreamed about their retirement in Surrey, and the Chinese industrialists about their green (residence) cards in California, how could a collective political actor emerge in Hong Kong to make it into a thriving city-state projecting itself in the world economy? Let us examine the question in historical close-up.

Institutional power in Hong Kong, during the entire development process, was concentrated in the hands of the colonial governor, appointed by Westminster. Once appointed, however, the Governor was almost entirely autonomous in deciding domestic Hong Kong policies.[94] From 1957, the Hong Kong budget did not require formal approval from London. Thus, the Colony was run as an autonomous state, centered on the Governor and a series of appointed Committees, headed by Secretaries, also appointed by the Governor. This executive branch of government relied on the support of a number of legislative and advisory bodies made up of official and unofficial members, most of them also appointed by the government until the political reforms of the 1980s. These institutions were served by a numerous, well-trained, and efficient government public service, numbering 166,000 civil servants in the 1980s. However, behind this formal structure of power, the empirical study by Miron Mushkat, the historical–anthropological monograph of Henry Lethbridge, and a number of other studies,[95] including my own fieldwork, reveal a different, fascinating story about the real power structure of Hong

[94]   Miners (1986).
[95]   Lethbridge (1970); Mushkat (1982); Kwan and Chan (1986).

Kong. The core of this power structure seems to have been in the hands of what Mushkat calls the "administrative class," a small, select group of civil servants who, until the 1970s, were recruited overwhelmingly in Britain by the Colonial Civil Service, out of the best British universities, and generally from Oxford and Cambridge. Between 1842 and 1941 there were only 85 "cadets" (as they were called until 1960) of the Hong Kong Colonial Civil Service. Even after the huge expansion of personnel in the 1970s, including the massive recruitment of Chinese, there were only 398 "general grade administrative officers."[96] It was this administrative class, with strong social and ideological cohesion, shared professional interests and cultural values, that seems to have controlled power within the Hong Kong state for most of the history of the Colony. They exercised power while keeping in mind the interests of the business elite, but only to the extent that business would assure the economic prosperity of Hong Kong, on which the power, income, prestige, and ideological self-legitimation of the administrative class depended. Their interest in relation to the future of Hong Kong was twofold: to maintain the Colony in the midst of the turmoil of decolonization and the threatening stands of the British Labour party; and to show the world that the Colonial Service, on behalf of what was left of the tradition of the British Empire, was more able than any other political institution (including the new independent national states) to ensure the prosperity of the new Asian world, including to a large extent the well-being of its people, in a paternalistic attitude that evokes the historical precedent of "enlightened despotism." Although my ethnographic material on the subject is too unsystematic to be conclusive, it did convince me that the dedication and effectiveness of the elite Colonial Civil Service of Hong Kong was tantamount to the last hurrah of the British Empire. The "Hong Kong cadets" aimed at building Hong Kong's prosperity as an ideological monument to the historic memory of the lost Empire, while also taking care of their retirement years, in England.

Thus, under different forms specific to each society, the developmental state in the newly industrialized Asian countries seems to have been the instrument of nation (or city) building (or rebuilding) processes enacted by political actors largely autonomous of their societies. However, it was only because these political actors were able both to mobilize and to control their civil societies that they could implement their developmental strategy.

---

[96]   Scott and Burns (1984).

The state and civil society in the restructuring of East Asia: how the developmental state succeeded in the development process

To identify the main actors of the development process in the Asian Pacific (the developmental states) does not solve the fundamental issue of why they were able to succeed, if by success we understand the achievement of their vision of economic development. To identify the factors explaining their success I must address three questions: (a) the relationship between Asian developmental states and other states in the international system; (b) the internal logic of developmental states; and (c) the relationship between developmental states and their societies.

First, it is important to remember that the first stages of East Asian industrialization were extraordinarily favored by the geopolitical context in which these economies took shape: the Asian Cold War and the full support of the United States to these regimes, and, in the case of Hong Kong, the support of Britain. However, we must reject the leftist oversimplification of seeing these states as "puppets of American imperialism": in fact, these states did show their autonomy by fostering their own nation-building projects. To understand their historical specificity, I propose the concept of "vassal state" for this particular political form. By *vassal state*, using the analogy with feudalism, *I understand a state that is largely autonomous in the conduct of its policies, once it has abided by the specific contribution it has to make to its "sovereign state."* Thus, the states of the Asian tigers were not "dependent states" in the sense in which dependent societies and dependent states are defined by the structural-historical theory of dependency. These are states with very limited autonomy *vis-à-vis* the overall geopolitical system to which they belong, in exchange for which they receive protection along with a significant degree of autonomy in the conduct of their domestic affairs. I propose the notion that Taiwan, at least until the early 1970s, and South Korea, at least until 1987, were vassal states of the United States, while Hong Kong was all along a vassal city-state (rather than a colony) of the UK. As for Singapore, it was a semi-vassal state of the United States, from the Vietnam War, including some curious linkages such as the organizing and training of its military by the Israelis. This "vassal" condition created a security umbrella, relieved much of the burden of the defense budget of these countries, and played a role in the critical initial stages in facilitating access to world markets.

The second element explaining the success of the developmental strategy was *the construction of an efficient, technocratic, state apparatus.* This has little to do with the traditional distinction between corrupt bureaucracies and clean bureaucracies. Corruption was widespread in South Korea, significant in Taiwan, present in Hong Kong, and more limited, but not absent, in Singapore. And, yet, the four states were able to operate with a high level of efficiency, served by well-trained civil servants, and organized on flexible lines that changed according to the needs of each stage of development. In functional terms, corruption is only an obstacle to efficiency when it prevents the bureaucracy from fulfilling its assigned task. And it is only an obstacle to legitimacy if there is a democratic state, accountable to a civil society that expects public service to prevail over private interests. In South Korea, for instance, corruption was the pay-off exacted by military officers and party officials from Korean industrialists in exchange for running the country toward developmental aims that created huge benefits for these state-sponsored industrialists. Overall, these states were more technocratic than bureaucratic, since their apparatuses were set up to implement a strategic, historical project, and not only (but also) to reap the benefits of dictatorship.

Yet, the fundamental element in the ability of developmental states to fulfill their project was *their political capacity to impose and internalize their logic on their societies*. The autonomy of developmental states, and their ability to implement their project with few concessions to society's demands, must be explained in empirical, historical terms, without calling upon the metaphysics of Confucianism.

The first explanation is a simple one: repression. The Kuomintang began to establish its hold on the island by the Kaoshiung massacre of May 9, 1947. It went on to set up a ruthless political control apparatus which, for the next three decades, arrested, tortured, and killed political dissenters, whether from right or left, all lumped under the communist label. The PAP in Singapore liquidated all serious political opposition in the period 1961–5, banning the main trade union, and arresting leaders of the opposition Barisan Socialists, which led to the expulsion of the PAP from membership of the Socialist International. Later, it often used the British Colonial Internal Security Act, allowing the government to detain without charge for an indefinite period anyone suspected of "subversion." Hong Kong used British troops to quell the riots of 1956, 1966, and 1967, and kept a very large and efficient police force of over 20,000, which did not hesitate to deport on the spot to China any dissident considered a threat to public order. South Korea, under the aegis of one of the most effective, and brutal, police forces in the world (the Korean CIA), arrested, tortured, imprisoned, and killed dissidents, while forbidding all independent union activity and most independent political activity until the demise of the authoritarian regime in the late 1980s.

Most Third World countries, however, practice similar repressive policies, without much success either in containing protest or, even less, in mobilizing their societies on the path to development. Thus, other factors must have accounted for the organizational capacity demonstrated by the East Asian developmental states *vis-à-vis* their societies.

An important element was that *the traditional, dominant social classes were either destroyed, disorganized, or made subordinate to the state*, with the partial exception of Hong Kong. Land reforms in Korea and Taiwan, and the absence of a non-colonial bourgeoisie in Singapore, destroyed the traditional oligarchy in these societies. What was left of the commercial–industrial bourgeoisie was made an appendage of the developmental strategy decided by the state. With no domestic base from which to accumulate, the role of the state as gatekeeper to the world economy made any local capitalist entirely dependent on import–export licenses and government-sponsored credit. In Singapore, the multinationals quickly understood that the Lion City could be a tropical paradise for them only on the condition of "not messing up" with the government. In Hong Kong, as usual, a more complex pattern developed. The bourgeoisie, both traditional (the British Hongs), and newcomers (the Shanghainese industrialists), were co-opted via a number of government committees. The Chinese bourgeoisie was left to run its own business on the condition of reporting to the government and abiding by its instructions. The Jockey Club socially "glued" the political and business elites together, but under the clear leadership of the "cadets." And a significant number of high-ranking government officials retired to become representatives of Hong Kong business associations, thus establishing an informal and effective channel of communication between government and business, in a harmonious division of labor, generally led by government's enlightened technocracy.[97]

As for the working class, the four states devised strategies of integration to complement repression and, if possible, to substitute for it in the long run. All four states counted on economic growth and the improvement of living standards, including access to education and health, to keep workers content. In fact, the strategy was effective for most of the period.

In addition to improving living conditions, there were policies explicitly designed for social integration. Taiwan emphasized reduction in income inequality. Both Hong Kong and Singapore created an Asian version of the British welfare state, centered around

---

[97]   Lethbridge (1978); King and Lee (1981); Scott (1987); Castells et al. (1990).

public housing and social services. Public housing estates played a fundamental role in social integration. In the case of Hong Kong, tenancy in public housing was the *de facto* citizenship accorded to a largely immigrant working class. In the case of Singapore, social engineering through the public housing/new towns program was essential in diffusing inter-ethnic tensions in everyday life.[98] South Korea practiced a much harsher policy toward the working class, and as a result had to confront what is today one of the most militant labor movements in Asia. Yet, the extraordinary improvement in living conditions, the emergence of an affluent middle class, and the particularly strong persistence of patriarchalism in the family allowed South Korea to keep labor conflicts under control until the 1980s.

Thus, the developmental states were fully aware of the need to integrate their societies to the extent that this integration remained compatible with economic conditions necessary to be competitive in the world economy. They were not just repressive dictatorships. Their project consisted of a double-edged plowshare that they did not hesitate to transform into a sword when required.

However, the process of development they succeeded in implementing not only transformed the economy but completely changed the society. A new, more assertive capitalist class, ready to take on the world, emerged in the 1980s, increasingly confident that it no longer needed a state of technocrats, racketeers, and political police. A new, consumer-oriented, educated, liberal middle class decided that life was all too good to be sacrificed for the historical project of an artificially invented nation. And new, more conscious, better organized social movements, workers, students, citizens, women, environmentalists, appeared to be ready to raise questions about the conditions, goals, and sharing of development. The success of developmental states in East Asia ultimately led to the demise of their apparatuses and to the fading of their messianic dreams. The societies they helped to engender through sweat and tears are indeed industrialized, modern societies. But, at the end of the millennium, their actual historical projects are being shaped by their citizens, now in the open ground of history making.

Divergent paths: Asian "tigers" in the economic crisis[99]

The economic crisis of the late 1990s was felt very differently in the four lands we are analyzing. South Korea's economy collapsed. Hong

---

[98]   Castells et al. (1990).
[99]   This section is intellectually indebted to the contributions of Jeffrey

Kong, between October 1997 and June 1998, lost about $US 300 billion in the value of stocks and property: roughly the equivalent of all deposits in local banks. In 1998 Hong Kong's economy suffered its first recession in three decades. Singapore experienced a moderate downturn, declining by about 1 percent in 1998. Taiwan continued to grow in 1998 at a good pace, at around 5 percent. Although both Singapore's and Taiwan's economies suffered the impact of the Asian crisis, to understand their greater resilience to the crisis may open the way to comprehending future paths of development in the twenty-first century.

There was a sharp difference in the origins of the crisis in Hong Kong and in South Korea. In Hong Kong, the collapse of the property market, and its impact on stocks, played a decisive role in the financial crisis. In South Korea, it was the crisis of profitability of the large *chaebol* that prompted their risky borrowing from foreign funds, inducing the default of their debt payments. In both cases, however, speculative attacks on their currencies by global capital sources, acting on the opportunity provided by a shaky financial system, amplified the crisis. To simplify the analysis, I will contrast Hong Kong with Singapore, then South Korea with Taiwan.

In Hong Kong, real-estate values in the private market sky-rocketed during the 1990s. Between 1990 and 1996, the price of housing multiplied fourfold. This was partly due to a clause in the 1984 agreement between the UK and the PRC, under which auctions of government land would be limited to 50 hectares per year, unless otherwise authorized by the PRC. Thus, land supply shrunk, while demand on land increased at a fast pace, as a result of the boom in financial and business services in Hong Kong. The Hong Kong government benefited from rising land prices. As I showed above, land revenues were a major source of income for the government – indeed, the substitute for tax revenue. Furthermore, in the 1990s Hong Kong transformed its economy from manufacturing to services. Instead of upgrading technologically, Hong Kong manufacturers opted for cutting costs by shifting production across the border, and investing in business services, financial markets, and real estate. They were joined by overseas Chinese investors, who made Hong Kong one of their main bases of operation, as well as their preferred stock market. There followed an extraordinary revaluation of stocks and property, which attracted

Henderson, Chu-Joe Hsia, You-tien Hsing, and Jong-Cheol Kim, though all responsibility for errors of interpretation is mine. For analytical developments and sources of information, see Dolven (1998); Dornbusch (1998); Henderson (1998a, b); Henderson et al. (1998); Kim (1998); Stiglitz (1998); Thompson (1998).

short-term, speculative capital from around the world. Hong Kong lacked proper financial regulation, and the currency board system, established to keep the exchange rate stable, limited the government's capacity to act on monetary policy. Thus, the October 1997 run on the Hong Kong dollar undermined investors' confidence. Only the determination of the PRC to defend the Hong Kong currency kept it pegged to the US dollar. But the cost was staggering. High interest rates, and loss of investor confidence, led to a plunge in both the property market and the stock market. In the summer of 1998, the Hong Kong government tried to play cat and mouse with speculative financial flows, buying and selling Hong Kong stocks without warning, just to inflict punitive losses on speculators and discourage their moves. It was a desperate strategy, tantamount to using a bucket to contain a financial *tsunami*. After losing over 10 billion dollars, the Hong Kong government stopped the fight, and let the PRC take full responsibility for its currency. Having transformed itself into a financial and services economy, and losing competitiveness *vis-à-vis* its neighbors because of its stubborn refusal to devalue, Hong Kong learnt the meaning of recession.

Meanwhile, Singapore, the other city-state, followed a very different path in the 1990s, a path that eventually allowed it to absorb much of the shock of the crisis. Property values were kept under control, by and large. The much larger proportion of the population in public housing (87 percent) limited the impact of speculation on real-estate prices, since land, as in Hong Kong, was in the public domain. But, unlike in Hong Kong, land revenues had a limited role in government finance, so the government had little interest in pursuing the risky adventure of becoming itself a speculative landholder. Instead, the government continued to rely on the flow of funding accumulated in the Central Provident Fund, as well as on the proceeds of the vast, and mostly profitable, public enterprise sector. Indeed, in 1998, the government and government-related business were generating about 60 percent of Singapore's GDP.

Furthermore, while Singapore became a major financial hub and an advanced service economy, it made a point of remaining a leading manufacturing center as well. Manufacturing was, essentially, a multinational operation, but, as shown above in this chapter, it received steady support from government policies. The Singapore government designed a strategy of technological upgrading for Singapore-based companies so that the 25 percent of total employment in manufacturing would translate into a higher share of manufacturing in GDP because of the high value-added of manufactured products. With stronger regulations than Hong Kong in the financial markets (particularly after the collapse of Barings Bank in Singapore), tighter control on property values, a strong, productive public sector, and opportunities for profitable investment in manufacturing and business services, Singapore did not suffer the same speculative attacks as Malaysia or Hong Kong. To be sure, the strong connection between Singapore and the surrounding South-East Asian economies induced a downturn in its economic growth and a mild recession in 1998. The continuation of the Asian crisis still could inflict considerable pain on its economy. Yet, the strength and decisiveness of the Singaporean state, and its strong links with multinational manufacturing companies, proved to be better assets to weather the crisis than Hong Kong's free-wheeling financial markets, and orthodox economic policies, under the conditions of the new global economy.

South Korea and Taiwan are very different from the city-states. They both depend, fundamentally, on the competitiveness of their manufacturing industries. But their industrial structures are very different: large, vertically integrated *chaebol* in the case of South Korea; flexible, entrepreneurial small and medium companies, some of which grew considerably in scale through their competitiveness, in the case of Taiwan. State control was also different: the South Korean state was deeply involved with the *chaebol*, and entirely controlled their finance during the period of high growth. The Taiwanese state, instead, provided decisive support in technology, infrastructure, and trade policy, as presented above, but let firms decide their own strategies for themselves. Besides, while the Taiwanese state owned, or participated in, the major banks of Taiwan, it rarely used bank lending as an instrument of industrial policy. Instead, entrepreneurial start-ups in 1990s Taiwan relied on the well-provided venture capital market which channeled domestic savings into productive investment. The differential trajectories of the two countries during the crisis highlight the importance of these differences.

The South Korean crisis started with the bankruptcy, in January 1997, of one of the large *chaebol*, Hanbo, which specialized in the steel and construction industries. In the following months, a number of other *chaebol*, all among the thirty largest, followed suit in declaring themselves bankrupt: Sammi, Jinnro, Daenong, Kia, Sangbangul, Haitai. By September 1997, defaulted loans and bankruptcies came to represent 32 trillion won; that is, about 7.5 percent of GDP. The subsequent decline in stock prices, and the downgrading of South Korean securities by international rating agencies, led to a stampede of foreign debtors, who called in their loans. Capital flight followed. After spending most of its reserves defending the currency, the South Korean government gave up, and the won collapsed. On November 21, 1997, the South Korean government declared insolvency in international payments, and asked for help from the IMF in exchange for surrendering its economic sovereignty. Thus, the financial crisis and the currency crisis were prompted by the bankruptcy of large South Korean corporations, which, not long before, had been among the fiercest competitors in the global economy.

Three factors seem to have been decisive in their demise. First, South Korean manufacturers had lost competitiveness substantially since the early 1990s, particularly in the US market. South Korean companies were producing at too high a cost to compete with the lower tier of new Asian producers, while not being able to match the technological level of Japanese, American, or even Taiwanese companies. This trend was particularly visible in semiconductors, where the relative dominance of Korean companies in memory chips (40 percent of the world market) was being eroded by more flexible and innovative Taiwanese firms (Acer, Powerchip, Windbond) which had taken about 9 percent of the world market by the end of 1998. The automobile company Kia suffered a major fiasco in its export strategy. The reaction of Korean *chaebol*, which had been accustomed to push through their own way, counting on the all-out support of the state, was to borrow, and invest, to increase their competitiveness. But the South Korean state, and the global economy, had changed by the early 1990s. Under Kim Young Sam's administration, the Economic Planning Board was moved to the Ministry of Finance and lost its strategic capacity to guide the economy. The financial system was deregulated, making direct access by the *chaebol* to foreign lending possible. Financial transactions were now mediated not by the state, but by loosely regulated South Korean banks. Japanese financial firms, unable to obtain high interest rates at home, were happy to lend to the *chaebol*, always counting on the customary protection of the South Korean state. Thus, the debt/equity ratio of South Korean firms sky-rocketed, sending the financial system on a risky path.

The third, and decisive, factor in triggering the crisis was the changing attitude of the South Korean state. This time, it did not bail out the *chaebol*, concentrating instead on protecting those *chaebol* in which the government had a personal or political interest. The resulting default of several *chaebol* precipitated the crisis of confidence among foreign debtors that prompted the overall financial crisis. But why did the state not prevent the bankruptcies by intervening earlier? First, the largest *chaebol* had become global players, quite independent of the state. The *chaebol* took advantage of financial deregulation to tap into a much larger, global source of credit than the one formerly provided by state-controlled banks. Secondly, the South Korean state, in the democratic context, had become accountable to society at large, so that its margin of maneuver was limited. The close links between the *chaebol* and the political class continued during the democratic regime, but it was a clientelistic relationship, rather than a systemic feature of the state. Various political factions had their own connections with specific *chaebol*, thus entering the game of supporting their cronies, rather than preserving the state/*chaebol* system as a whole. In other words, there was a change from corporatist state capitalism to corrupt government practices on behalf of specific business interests. Lack of regulation, and loose government control of the financial system, rather than excessive government intervention, were critical factors which allowed the financial crisis to ruin the economy.

Thus, the South Korean crisis may have been induced by the inability of the *chaebol* to continue to grow and compete in the global economy without the support of the developmental state. The South Korean developmental state could not deliver the same level of support as it had in the past. This was, on the one hand, because social mobilization and political democracy had imposed limits on the use of state resources for the exclusive benefit of *chaebol*; on the other hand, because the integration of the South Korean economy in the global economy, and the deregulation of financial markets and currency controls under pressure from the US, had removed essential policy tools from the hands of the state. The global whirlwind of speculative financial flows filled the gap thus created between the needs of the *chaebol* and the limited capacity of the state, providing easy money to South Korean firms. But short-term, high-risk lending is the kind of money that is recalled at the first sign of potential default.

To sum up, the South Korean crisis resulted from the cumulative effect of the following factors: a crisis in the profitability of large South Korean export manufacturers; the weakness of financial institutions in South Korea, exploited by speculative, high-risk foreign moneylenders, particularly Japanese; and the substantial limitation of the state's developmental capacity which resulted from new controls established by a democratic society and from international (namely, US) pressure pushing toward the liberalization of trade and finance.

In contrast, the Taiwanese state played a secondary role in the growing competitiveness of Taiwanese firms during the 1990s. Networks of these firms, in Taiwan, in Asia, and in the United States (particularly in Silicon Valley), found their own way out of the semiconductor slump. Indeed, they took on South Korean and Japanese competitors, winning market share in memory chips, in personal computers, in LCD screens, in software products. Taiwan's vast foreign currency reserves, the largest in the world, discouraged most speculative attacks. However, the currency was devalued by 6.5 percent, supposedly in a political ploy to bring down the yuan, thus taking the Chinese economy off track. But markets pushed the NT upward later on, in a clear indication of the basic soundness of the

Taiwanese economy. Indeed, while Taiwan did suffer from the crisis because of the loss of substantial export markets in Asia, it was spared most of the financial turmoil. Its property market played a minor role in capital accumulation. Its banking system was largely de-linked from export manufacturers, which had their own funding sources. And the value of stocks in the stock market was mainly determined by the profitability of the companies traded in it. Taiwan thus offers a good example to appreciate the difference between suffering the impact of an external crisis and a home-grown crisis resulting from domestic economic and institutional flaws. The Taiwanese developmental state became weaker in the 1990s, as in the case of South Korea, because it had to reckon with democratic politics and an active civil society. It considerably downplayed its *dirigisme.* But because of its entre-preneurial flexibility, Taiwanese business did not need the state any longer. Relying on the competitiveness of its manufacturers, and on their domestic capital market, Taiwan's economy was not taken over by uncontrollable financial flows of global origin. Thus, financial turmoil did not ruin the economy, although it did jeopardize Taiwan's projected "March to the South," aimed at expanding invest-ment and trade in South-East Asia.

Overall, no clear-cut pattern is emerging on the sources of the crisis in the four "tigers" since each case seems to be different. But we can say that the presence of the developmental state, and excessive inter-ventionism, did not induce the crisis since Singapore provides evidence of effective state intervention which limited the impact of the crisis, while Hong Kong's deregulated environment and currency board policy, following orthodox economic prescriptions, led to a devastating destruction of financial value. Indeed, it would seem that, in the case of South Korea, it was the disorderly withdrawal of the developmental state from economic management, and its loose regu-lation of the banking system, that precipitated the crisis. So, it was not state intervention that caused the crisis, but the inconsistency of this intervention. Both the "soft landing" of Taiwan's *dirigisme* and the continuation of state control in Singapore avoided the pitfalls produced by the chaotic withdrawal of the state in South Korea and erratic government intervention in Hong Kong.

A second observation is that manufacturing competitiveness, in Taiwan and Singapore, continued to be at the root of their relatively solid economic performance, while the deindustrialization of Hong Kong, and the loss of competitiveness of the South Korean *chaebol,* weakened their economies. An advanced service economy still needs a solid link to a dynamic manufacturing sector – postindustrialist myths notwithstanding. Lastly, the destabilizing role of short-term movements by global financial flows remains the most important source of the crisis. But economies are further exposed to their destructive influence when they bring down their domestic regulations and become addicted to easy money. Institutional weaknesses are critical factors in the differential resistance of national economies to the disruptive effects of global finance. These institutional weaknesses can be traced back, in the last resort, to the crisis of the state. And the crisis of the developmental state seems to be a function of the changing patterns of relationship between state and society.

Democracy, identity, and development in East Asia in the 1990s

On August 26, 1996, former South Korean dictator and president General Chun Do Hwan was sentenced to death in Seoul for his participation in the 1979 coup, and his responsibility for the 1980 Kwangju massacre of pro-democracy demonstrators. His successor, and former protégé, Roh Tae Woo, who presided over South Korea's transition to democracy, received a 22-year minimum jail term. By this highly symbolic gesture, Korean democracy, under President Kim Young Sam, was asserting itself against the authoritarian state. Not only was the military dictatorship on trial: the corrupt linkage between the authoritarian regime and South Korean business was condemned as well. The heads of eight *chaebol* received prison sentences for bribing former president Roh. The sentences were suspended, but the trial was a break with the past.

An even greater break took place when, in December 1997, Kim Dae Jung, the undisputed leader of the South Korean radical democratic opposition, was elected president. The fact that he came to preside over an economy in shambles was equally symbolic. The South Korean developmental state had failed, both in its economic performance and in its political control. Kim Dae Jung, in a highly symbolic gesture, pardoned the former dictator, Chun Do Hwan, the man who had sentenced him to death. Democracy was strong enough to make gestures of national reconciliation, paving the way for the eventual reunification with the North in a future democratic nationalist project. But the rebuilding of this political project – breaking with the authoritarian developmental state – required an attack on the corrupt roots of South Korean politics. In September 1998, the public prosecutor accused the former government's Grand National Party of using tax collectors to extract from the *chaebol* 6 million dollars for its electoral campaign. President Kim Dae Jung asked the party to apologize for its "tax theft," prompting a new political crisis. So, in a sequence of events in the 1990s, South Korean politics shifted its center of gravity from the remnants of military bureaucracy to a new democratic, political elite, rooted in the professional middle class. This transformation of politics, and of the state, could not have taken place without the transformation of civil society under the impulse of social movements.

On December 27, 1996, hundreds of thousands of Korean workers went on a general strike that, under various forms, lasted several weeks. They were protesting against a new law proposed by President Kim Young Sam, and approved by the government's parliamentary majority, which made it easier for Korean companies to dismiss workers, in an adaptation, according to proponents of the law, to the flexibility of labor markets required by new global competition. Workers were also protesting against the lack of legal recognition of the main confederation of trade unions. After weeks of strikes, demonstrations, and repeated clashes with police, the trade unions, with the support of public opinion and the political opposition, obtained the recognition of their union, as well as some concessions in labor legislation. Subsequently, labor unions grew in influence, in spite of the economic crisis. But, faced with the collapse of the South Korean economy, in 1998 they agreed to a social pact with business and government, so that President Kim Dae Jung could have a chance to manage the country toward recovery.

Four elements combined to transform the relationship between state, society, and the economy in South Korea, after 1987, when Chun ceded to pressures from democratic quarters to engage in a process of controlled liberalization. The first factor in bringing down the military regime was the increased assertiveness of civil society, in which powerful social movements were spreading. There was the traditionally militant student movement. But radical students had been isolated from society at large in their many years of struggle against the regime. By the late 1980s, they were joined by a revitalized labor movement, springing out of hundreds of wild-cat strikes that shook up South Korea's repressive control of its working class. The strikes and demonstrations of December 1996 and January 1997 were a display of strength by the trade unions that made it clear that workers had shattered the domination exercised by government and business over labor. Community movements, particularly for housing and against urban renewal, often supported by churches, mobilized large sections of a predominantly urban society in Korea. And an educated, prosperous middle class aspired to live a "normal life" in a "normal country." Altogether, they contributed to changing the political landscape.

A second factor was the increasing distance of the Korean *chaebol* from the state, as they became global companies, diversified their interests, and resented the imposition of government policies. A third factor was international pressure, particularly from the United States, to stabilize a democratic South Korea, whose defense against North Korea would be acceptable on political grounds, when the disappearance of tension with the USSR undermined the geopolitical rationale of the US military commitment. The 1988 Olympic Games symbolized the opening of the new Republic of Korea to the world.

The fourth factor is less known but, in my opinion, was, and is, fundamental to understanding South Korea's political dynamics: the regionalization of politics. Surprising as it may seem in such an ethnically homogeneous nation, and in a geographically small country, regional identity is a critical factor in Korean politics, and the failure of the military regime to meld these identities into the nationalist project doomed its efforts for political control. For instance, in the first democratic parliamentary elections of 1988, Kim Young Sam's party took 15 out of 16 seats in his native Pusan province, and performed strongly in nearby South Kyungsang. His rival in the democratic opposition, Kim Dae Jung, took 31 out of 32 seats in his own regional base, North and South Cholla provinces. And "the third Kim," Kim Jong Pil, dominated in South Chungchung. As for the military-sponsored party, the DJP, it won overwhelmingly in Roh's home province, North Kyungsang. Only Seoul/Inchon, with its metropolitan population formed by waves of migration, appeared to have a diversified political constituency. In the 1997 presidential election, Kim Dae Jung's victory was based, again, on his overwhelming dominance in Cholla. But, in this election, Kim Dae Jung was able to marshal broad support in Seoul/Inchon, particularly because of the middle-class sector's discontent with the persistence of corruption under Kim Young Sam. This fractioning of South Korean politics on the basis of regional identity favored the organization of opposition to the military regime, on the basis of trusted, popular regional leaders, thus undermining military control, as soon as plural political expression was tolerated. Yet, on the other hand, it was also a weakening factor for the democratic opposition because of the division that it implied, thus undermining the electoral chances of democrats to defeat the government party. In fact, the stalemate was only overcome in the 1990s, when Kim Young Sam, in a brilliant, but risky, political maneuver, joined forces with Roh Tae Woo, thus being able to succeed Roh as president, in exchange for providing democratic legitimacy to the remnants of pro-military politicians. Yet, the fragmentation of regional identity continues to be a major factor in both mobilization and instability in South Korea. In my personal conversations with Kim Young Sam, at his home in Seoul in 1988, when he still embodied the ideals of a section of the democratic opposition, he pointed out to me what seems to be the critical goal in reorienting Korea's divisive politics. In his view, it was essential to take the nationalist project away from the non-democratic military and put it into the hand of the democrats. Only then could Korean regional identity be subsumed into a strong Korean national identity. But such democratic nationalism had to fulfill an essential task: Korean reunification. Korean reunification has indeed been the motto of democratic movements in Korea for a long time, and Korean democracy in the 1990s is still dominated by the debates on how to proceed in this direction – not an easy project because North Korean communism is more deeply entrenched in the country than, say, East German communism was. Yet, Korean democratic leaders, Kim Dae Jung, as well as Kim Young Sam, were convinced that reunification was essential to build a strong Korea for the twenty-first century, a Korea strong enough to survive the formidable challenge presented by the parallel rise of Japan and China to the summits of world power and influence, and stable enough to continue to be the home base for newly globalized Korean corporations. Thus, the rebuilding of the project of nationalist identity on democratic grounds is essential in the dismantling of the former developmental state, once the legitimacy principle shifted from developmental nationalism to citizen-based nationalism.

Identity is also crucial in the orientations and debates of Taiwan's democratic politics in the 1990s. Taiwan society has always suffered a problem of blurred identity, of what Taiwanese scholar Chu-joe Hsia calls "the orphan syndrome." The KMT and the Chinese Communist party agreed on only one thing: that Taiwan was not Taiwan, but a province of China. But since this was not its reality, for the past half-century, after being a Japanese colony for most of the previous half-century, Taiwan's people did not belong to anything. Matters were made worse by the fundamental split, in Taiwan, between Mainlanders and Taiwanese, and by the further split, among Taiwanese, between native Taiwanese, Fujien, and Hakka. Thus, even if, from an ethnic point of view, they were all Han Chinese, there was a sharp social/cultural divide among Taiwan's population, a division that permeated all levels of the state, as KMT leadership was firmly in the hands of Mainlanders until Chiang Ching Kuo's death in 1988. With the lifting of martial law in 1987 (significantly, the same year that South Korean democratization started), an effort was made to establish Taiwan's political system on Taiwan's new historical reality. In 1990, Teng Hui Lee, a Taiwanese-born, highly educated, KMT leader, was elected president. He presided over the democratization of Taiwan, and aimed at asserting Taiwan's autonomous existence in the international arena, negotiating Taiwan's economic and industrial power into its right to existence. A significant section of the democratic opposition went further: the leading opposition party, the Democratic Progressive Party (DPP), created in 1986, made Taiwan's independence its overarching goal. China strongly opposed both moves and threatened military action if Taiwan went all the way toward becoming an independent country. The United States came, again, to the rescue of Taiwan, but within certain limits. That is, Taiwan had to behave, and remain in political limbo as long as China kept a cooperative attitude toward the United States. Thus, Taiwan in the 1990s went back to the beginning of its peculiar history: having been born out of the geopolitical strategy of the US *vis-à-vis* China, it remains, by and large, entirely dependent on US–China relations for the foreseeable future. The problem is that, in the meantime, there are 20 million people living in an island that has become an economic power house, fully networked into the global economy, and whose investments in China have played a significant role in the development of southern China's new capitalism. Taiwan's civil society has sprung powerfully in the 1990s, with very active community movements, an environmental movement, student movement, women, gay, and lesbian movements (see volume II, chapter 3), somewhat revitalized labor unions, and an informed and educated public opinion, served by independent, influential media. The convergence of these social movements, and the search for a national and *local identity*, led the independence party, the DPP, to victory in Taipei's municipal elections of 1995, providing a power base for the implementation of democratic reforms. The new elected mayor, Chen Shui-pien, found widespread people's support for his slogan: "A citizens' city." National politics, however, remained dominated by the KMT, as President Lee was re-elected until the twenty-first century, mainly from the people's concern that electing pro-independence leaders would provoke China, while Lee was assertive enough to be personally targeted as a foe by the Chinese government. But this is a very different KMT from the one that set up a bloody dictatorship in the island 50 years before. It is searching for a new legitimacy, both international and domestic, trying, for instance, to link up with community movements to set up mechanisms of participatory democracy. By contrast, the independence movement is increasingly split between its fundamentalist wing, striving for independence and national identity, and its social movement wing, aiming at democracy and social change, without entering the geopolitical debate. There is, however, convergence of opinions on the need to shrink, or even dismantle, the developmental state. Taiwan's business networks, both from large or small businesses, have now found their niches in the global or Asian economies. State economic guidance is generally considered a hindrance. Demands from Taiwan's civil society to the government concern consumption and the quality of life, rather than production and technology. And the search for identity increasingly shifts from the public to the private, from nation to family and the individual, from the impossible Taiwanese cultural identity to the daily personal identity of Chinese people who have struggled, survived, and lived in the barren island where they have ended up by the shifts of history.

Hong Kong's future is even more deeply woven in historical ambiguity. It is now part of China. But it will always be a very special part of China. This is, on the one hand, because it will continue to play the role that it has played for many years: the main link between China and the international economy, as well as China's capitalist business school and testing ground. But it is also, on the other hand, because, throughout the 1980s, Hong Kong became an active, civil society, where community movements, and a large, well-educated middle class, openly expressed their democratic values. Tens of thousands of professionals left Hong Kong for their havens in the United States, UK, Australia, and Canada. Additional tens of thousands hold resident cards or passports from foreign countries, and commute between their profitable jobs in Hong Kong and their families' new residences in Vancouver or Perth. But Hong Kong people are in Hong Kong. And businesses – local and multinational – are tied to Hong Kong because Hong Kong is still, and will continue to be, a major node of the global economy, even after its devastating real-estate and financial crisis. The future of Hong Kong people is less than certain, but their identity is sure. They are an essential component of the new China, a China made of transnational networks of business and regional societies, managed by, and interacted with, a complex web of national/provincial/local governments. And they will share, as well, China's uncertain future.

The last "tiger" of our story, Singapore, baffles me, as everybody else. Unlike the three other countries, no civil society has really developed in Singapore in the 1990s, and the state seems to be as powerful and active as ever, in spite of statements to the contrary. This applies to authoritarian politics, and the control of information, as much as to the steering and monitoring of Singapore's development. The state continues to work in close contact with multinational corporations, as was the case 30 years ago, but, having become rich, it also now uses its own resources to invest in companies, either by itself or in joint ventures. Per capita income in Singapore now exceeds the average of the European Union. The city-state works smoothly in a fully planned metropolitan system. The island is the first country to be entirely wired with optic fiber, and is poised to become the first smoking-free and drug-free country (drug traffickers are sentenced to death, and often executed). The city is clean: littering the streets is penalized with heavy fines, and with community work performed in green uniforms, with the culprits exposed in the media. Political and cultural dissent is kept to a minimum, without the need to resort to extreme repression. There is formal democracy, and token opposition. When an opposition leader denounces government abuses, he is sued in court by the corresponding government official, and the court takes care that the daring critic is heavily fined or jailed. There is effective management of inter-ethnic tensions. And there is relatively peaceful coexistence with its surrounding Muslim world, although the whole population continues to be organized in armed militia, and the Singaporean Air Force is on a constant state of alert to proceed with retaliatory bombing of large cities just minutes away in their flight plans. The towering figure of Lee Kwan Yew, while no longer Prime Minister, continues to permeate Singapore's political culture and institutions. He succeeded in inventing a society out of nowhere, and making it the historical proof of the superiority of "Asian values," a project probably dreamed in his Oxford years, as a nationalist without a nation.[100] In fact, he rediscovered Victorian England, with its cult of moral virtues, its obsession with cleanliness, its abhorrence of the undeserving poor, its belief in education, and in the natural superiority of the few highly educated. He added a high-tech twist, actually funding studies to establish a scientific basis for the biological superiority of certain groups. Not on a racial basis, but on a class basis. His beliefs directly shaped Singapore's policies. For instance, college-educated women in Singapore received, in the 1980s, special allowances from the state to give birth to as many children as possible, as well as family leaves to educate their children, while working-class women (Chinese or Malay) were taxed for having too many children. The aim was to improve the quality of the Singaporean population by increasing the proportion of children born to educated families. The whole of Singapore is based on the simple principle of survival of the fittest. The ultimate goal of state policies is to enable Singapore to survive, and win, against the implacable competition of the global economy, in an interdependent world, by means of technology, social engineering, cultural cohesiveness, self-selection of the human stock, and ruthless political determination. The PAP implemented this project, and continues to do so, in accordance with the principles of Leninism that Lee Kwan

[100]   Chua (1998).

Yew knew, and appreciated, in his resistance years as a labor lawyer in the anti-colonialist movement. And, indeed, it is probably the only true Leninist project that has survived, outlasting its original matrix. Singapore represents the merger of the revolutionary state with the developmental state in the building of legitimacy, in its control of society, and in its maneuvering in the economy. It may also prefigure a successful model for the twenty-first century: a model that is being sought, consciously, by the Chinese Communist state, pursuing the developmental goals of a nationalist project.

While most of the Asian "tigers," and their newly industrializing neighbors, with the exception of Singapore, seem to be in the process of beheading the dragon of the developmental state, a much larger dragon (remember dragons are beneficial creatures in Chinese mythology) has emerged from its millennial isolation to take on the world, and, for good or bad, surely change it for ever.

Chinese Developmental Nationalism with Socialist Characteristics[101]

The policy of taking economic construction as the key link must never be changed; the reform and open-door policy must never be altered. The party's basic line must not be shaken for 100 years. We must properly

---

[101] My analysis of China relies on two main sources of first-hand observation. First was my own visits and fieldwork in China during the 1980s. Particularly important for my understanding of Chinese reforms was the fieldwork I conducted in 1987, together with Martin Carnoy and Patrizio Bianchi, to study technology policy and economic modernization at the invitation of the State Council's Institute of Technology and International Economy. We interviewed Chinese government officials, managers of Chinese factories, managers of American and European companies, and local and provincial representatives, in Beijing, Shanghai, Guangzhou, and Shenzhen. For a summary of our study, see Bianchi et al. (1988). Things have changed in China since then. This is why I relied extensively on a second source of direct observation: the fieldwork conducted between 1992 and 1997, all over China, but particularly in Guandong, Fujian, Shanghai, and Beijing, by Professor You-tien Hsing, from the University of British Columbia, who graciously provided me with extensive notes and documentation from her fieldwork, and followed this up with extensive personal conversations and e-mail communications on the matter. I am truly indebted to her for this critical help. However, the responsibility for this analysis is exclusively mine, and she should not be held accountable for my errors and excesses. For a partial view of her own analysis, see Hsing (1997a, b). I have also consulted a number of sources on Chinese developments in the 1990s, just a minute sample

draw the lesson from the former Soviet Union and handle well the relationships between the party centre and localities. We must uphold the leadership of the CCP. The CCP's status as the ruling party must never be challenged.

Deng Xiaoping, 1994[102]

China's Socialist modernization drive, the practice of the reform and open-door policy, and new developments in the world situation [must be synthesized by the party] so as to develop Marxism while adhering to it.

Jiang Zemin, 1990 [103]

Who are the biggest beneficiaries of the current policy? Careerists and capitalist-style politicians. The people are hurting badly. Chairman Mao's country will be destroyed by this people. From Confucius to Sun Yat-sen there has been a great deal of historical continuity in the development of our nation. History will condemn those who deny this. Allowing only admiration, and forbidding any mention of actual problems and difficulties, indicates a big cover-up of shortcomings and errors.

Mao Yingxing, 1970[104]

---

of a vast literature. An excellent overview of events can be found in Lam (1995). Useful journalistic, economic appraisals can be found in *The Economist*, August 17, 1996, and in Overhalt (1993). A comprehensive historical account is Spence (1990). A classic work on Chinese social and political relations under communism is Walder (1986), followed up for the more recent period in Walder (1995). On overseas Chinese business networks, besides Hsing (1997a, b), see *Business Week*, November 29, 1993 (special report of "Asia's Wealth"); Clifford (1994); and Ong and Nonini (1997). On central local relations in China, see Hao and Zhimin (1994). On *guanxi* and informal networks, see Yang (1994). On Chinese fiscal policies and central–local relations, see Wong et al. (1995). On democracy movements, see Lin (1994); and Walder (1992). For specific, selected bibliography, both in Chinese and English, on the characteristics of the new Chinese capitalism, see Hsing (1997a). And for those intellectuals who fantasized 30 years ago about the Cultural Revolution, I advise reading the documents collected and translated by Walder and Gong (1993). Additional sources consulted in writing this section are: Granick (1990); Nathan (1990); White (1991); Mackie (1992); Bowles and White (1993); Cheung(1994); Naughton (1994); Yabuki (1995); and Li (1996).

[102]   Speech while touring Qingdao, probably his last public political instructions, quoted in Lam (1995: 386).

[103]   Quoted by Lam (1995: 12).

[104]   A woman teacher in Jingning County, Guasu Province, who was executed on April 14, 1970, accused of being an "active counter-revolutionary" by the Department of Public Security, quoted in Walder and Gong (1993: 77). These words were from her last letter.

The new Chinese revolution

The Middle Kingdom, breaking with a millennial pattern of absolute or relative isolation, and deliberately incorporating itself into the rest of the world, has changed the world's history. Less than two decades after the beginning of the "open-door policy," China's economic growth, the fastest in the planet, and its competitiveness in international trade, have stunned governments and firms alike, arousing contradictory feelings. On the one hand, the promise of adding a market of 1.2 billion people, even at a fraction of the level of the West's solvent demand, may well diffuse any crisis of overproduction for a long time, thus solidifying the rise of global capitalism into the twenty-first century. From a broader point of view, the growing interaction with humankind's oldest civilization, with its extraordinary cultural tradition, is certain to enhance spiritual enrichment and reciprocal learning. Yet, on the other hand, the emergence of China as a major economic and military power, the persistence of the Communist party's control over society, and the unyielding attitude of the Chinese government toward international and domestic objections on human rights and political democracy, have triggered, particularly in Asia, but also in other countries, such as the United States, serious concerns about a potential, new Cold War, which would loom dangerously into the twenty-first century. Alternatively, some observers (whose views, frankly, I do not share) also fear a period of chaos and civil confrontation in China if the Asian economic crisis finally brings down the Chinese economy, and if poverty and unemployment fuel social protests and link up with the political challenge of the pro-democracy movement. But, whatever the views and feelings on China's transformation in the 1990s, I believe that many of them reflect a profound misunderstanding of the social and political characteristics of Chinese development, thus giving rise to misleading inferences concerning the future of its economy, politics and international relations. Within the limits of this section, I shall try to suggest an alternative hypothesis that is based on a premise.

The premise: *China's modernization and international opening up is, and was, a deliberate state policy, designed and controlled so far, by the leadership of the Communist party.* This was the work of Deng Xiaoping, after emerging victorious from his struggles against Maoists in the late 1970s, and against liberal reformers in the late 1980s. Jiang Zemin continued Deng's centrist, cautious policy, asserting his leadership after Deng's death without any significant challenge, or internal conflict within the party. Consequently, the motivations, orientations, and developments of the open-door policy have to be understood from the perspective of a specific political project, elaborated and implemented on the basis of the interests of the Communist party, as self-declared representative of the interests of the people and of the nation. Furthermore, in order to understand these interests, it is essential to recall that the *Chinese revolution was, primarily, a nationalist revolution with socialist characteristics.* It was the Japanese invasion, and the inept resistance of a corrupt, unpopular Kuomintang regime, that paved the way for the influence and growth of the People's Liberation Army, the backbone of Chinese communist power, and the stronghold of Mao's charismatic leadership. And it was the decisive participation of Chinese communists in World War II against Japan, in the context of the Western–Soviet alliance in that effort, that created the political and military conditions for their final run against KMT armies, routed in 1945–9 in spite of American support. Mao's ideology, and the Communist party's practice, never considered the Chinese revolution to be a socialist one: it was a "democratic revolution," based on a strategy of class alliances against "imperialism and its lackeys." It relied on the mobilization of poor peasants against the corrupt urban world of the compradore bourgeoisie. The "proletarian vanguard" was almost absent from this revolution, among other reasons because there was a very small proportion of industrial proletarians in sparsely industrialized China. While the categorization of Marxist–Leninist terminology clearly fails to apprehend the complexities of class structure and political ideology of twentieth-century China, it is a good indicator, none the less, of the predominantly nationalist rationale of the Chinese revolution. It was the defense of a humiliated China against foreign powers, including the brotherly Soviet Union, that rallied significant support around Chinese communists, together with an agrarian reform that reinforced the village structure, and eliminated the hated landowners, rather than persecuting kulaks. Agrarianism and nationalism were the two "marching legs" of the Chinese revolution. But the brain, the engine, and the gun were embodied in the Communist party. And because it was (and is) communist, that is Leninist, it imprinted "socialist" characteristics on Chinese revolutionary nationalism throughout the whole process of construction of a new state, a new economy, and a new society. Paramount among them, as in the Soviet Union, was the control of the party over the economy by a central planning system, and over society by an extensive ideological apparatus that ensured the dominance of Marxist–Leninist ideology and kept tight control over information and communication. The political system as well was molded in the Leninist–Stalinist tradition, with the party controlling all levels and branches of government institutions, including the army through the network of political commissars. At the heart of power system was (and is) the Central Military Commission of the Central Committee of the party. The chairmanship of this Commission was the only position that Mao always held, the last one that Deng relinquished in 1989, and the one held by Jiang Zemin in 1997. For Chinese communists, then as now, "power lies in the barrel of the gun." But the party was also a powerful, decentralized political machine, present in every village, neighborhood, and production unit throughout the country, forming an immense, hierarchical net that, for the first time in history, actually controlled China to the smallest corner. And this is not just ancient history: in 1998, the 54-million member Chinese Communist party (CCP) was alive and well, and its local leaders and cadres were enjoying the highest level of power and influence, if not popularity, in their districts. This is a fundamental reality that conditions, and shapes, the evolution of China. At the top of the power system, as in all communist regimes – with no historical exceptions, except for brief interregnum periods – there is an extreme personalization of leadership, in fact a personality cult. After Mao Zedong's Thought, in the 1990s it was the time for Deng Xiaoping's Thought (even if Deng himself politely refused the term), as the People's Liberation Army was mandatorily engaged in reading and commenting on Deng's Selected Works. Discussions of the historical continuity of personalized leadership in China ("the new Emperors") do not seem especially significant, since this is a communist characteristic as much as a Chinese characteristic. The extreme personalization of leadership in Chinese communism lends political voluntarism a powerful hand. Whatever is decided by the leader becomes a material force by the chain of command that reverberates throughout society and the centers of power. This is the only way we can explain the extraordinary, destructive adventures of the Great Leap Forward, and of the Great Proletarian Cultural Revolution, decided and directed by Mao Zedong, against the will of the party's collective leadership, to the point that *his* "revolutionary guards," with the backing of the PLA, went on a rampage mainly aimed at Communist party cadres and organizations. That the CCP survived its own suicidal tendencies (that is Maoism) shows a political strength far greater than that of any other communist experience. But Maoism was not a folly (although many of its acts were). It actually expressed one answer to the fundamental problem of the Chinese revolution: how to make China strong, and independent, while preserving Communist power, in a world dominated by superpowers, and where technological and economic development were proceeding apace on the opposite shores of the China Sea. Deng's and Liu Shao-shi's answer, since the 1950s, was accelerated industrialization, economic growth, and technological modernization, along the lines of the Soviet model, the only model available to Chinese Communists at that time. Mao's own answer was self-reliance, emphasis on ideology, preservation of ruralism, and decentralized, guerrilla warfare ("people's war") to resist any invader, while relying on nuclear armament as a deterrent of last resort (although at one point, at the height of the Cultural Revolution, Mao talked seriously about constructing socialism on the nuclear ruins of capitalism). In the middle, Zhu En-Lai obtained an agreement from the warring factions to steer a centrist course, preserving China's technological–military complex, as the necessary guarantee of its national independence. As a result, this technological–military complex remained relatively undisturbed by the political turmoil of the 1960s and 1970s. When, after the defeat of the "Gang of Four," Deng Xiaoping, who had survived the Cultural Revolution sweeping the streets of his native Chungking, returned to power, he went back to his basic idea that economic prosperity, and technological modernization were the fundamental pillars of Chinese power and independence. Furthermore, after the disastrous impact of the Cultural Revolution on people's lives and minds, not only did the independence of China have to be preserved, but the legitimacy of the Communist party had to be restored. After such a murderous ideological orgy, only the immediate improvement of living conditions, the diffusion of property rights, and the prospects of a better life in their lifetime, could rally the Chinese again around a revamped Communist regime. As Deng would state to the 13th Central Committee years later, in 1990: "If the economy improves, other policies could succeed and the Chinese people's faith in socialism will be enhanced. If not, socialism not only in China but in the rest of the world will be endangered."[105] But, in 1978, the Soviet Union was China's enemy and the Soviet economic model was clearly ailing, while, all around China, the Asian Pacific and particularly the ethnically Chinese economies were growing and modernizing at the fastest pace in history. Thus, the dramatic turn-round taken by the Central Committee, at Deng's initiative, on a cold December day in Beijing in 1978, was aimed at ensuring China's entry into the capitalist global economy and into the informational paradigm (even if the proponents of the open-door policy and of the "four modernizations" policy would not recognize these words), using the lessons from the Asian "tigers" (called "dragons" in China). However, this new developmental path should proceed in a way that would preserve "socialism;" that is, the power, control, and influence of the Communist party, as the representative of the Chinese people. In this sense, it was not

[105] Quoted in Lam (1995: 5).

fundamentally different from what Gorbachev would try to do in the Soviet Union only seven years later. But, unlike Gorbachev, who was too arrogant to imagine he could fail, the Chinese leadership understood that to release the Communist grip over society in a period of rapid economic, and therefore social, change, could derail the process toward "capitalism with Chinese characteristics," thus putting them out of business. Deng, and his entourage, were rightly obsessed with this idea, and the fate of Gorbachev, and of the Soviet Union, fully confirmed their diagnosis, at least in their view. This is why the "Singapore model" was, and is, so popular among Chinese Communist leaders. The idea of a fully-fledged economic and technological development process without yielding to the pressures of civil society, and keeping the capacity to maneuver in the global arena firmly in the hands of the state, appeals strongly to a party whose ultimate *raison d'être* is the assertion of China as a world power, if possible coupled with the preservation of Communist mythology. Yet, the experience of tiny Singapore can hardly be extrapolated to a country that accounts for 20 percent of humankind. And the Soviet experience of communist-controlled transition to capitalism ended in disaster. This is why Chinese communists navigate, with extreme caution and pragmatism, in uncharted historical waters. And this is why the actual process of transformation in China does not follow Deng's tentative blueprint of the early 1980s, but results from *ad hoc* decisions from a plurality of actors, and from the interests, compromises, conflicts, and alliances triggered and revealed by economic reform policies.

To sum up, China's economic development and technological modernization, within the framework of the new global economy, were (are) pursued by the Chinese communist leadership both as an indispensable tool for national power, and as a new legitimacy principle for the Communist party. In this sense, Chinese communism in the 1990s represents the historical merger of the developmental state and the revolutionary state. But, in order to fulfill this strategic aim, the Communist party, led in the 1990s by Deng Xiaoping, Jiang Zemin and Zhu Rongji, had to reckon with a series of formidable problems: the form of integration in the global economy; the controlled decentralization of state power; the management of social contradictions triggered by rural exodus and social inequality; the repression of political democracy; the control of an emerging civil society; and the balancing of power and influence among the power elite, keeping ideologues at bay without risking excessive factionalism in the army and in the party. I shall briefly elaborate on these various issues, building my argument toward an over-arching hypothesis: *that this complex act of balance is being accom-*

plished, with reasonable, but not certain, chances of future success, by inter-
twining regional developmental states with a nationalist project of China as a
great power, able to liberate itself for ever from the foreign devils. Capitalism,
and the uncertain fate of democracy, are but means to that fundamental goal, even if, in the process, the power elite considerably
benefits from the new sources of wealth and prestige.

Guanxi capitalism? China in the global economy

China's integration into the global economy began on a false note
in the early 1980s: the Special Economic Zones policy, creating
four Export Processing Zones, facing Hong Kong, Macau, and Taiwan, and aimed at offering cheap labor and land, tax breaks, and
social discipline to foreign investors, particularly multinational corporations, to be used as export platforms. The zones were designed
to be physically, and legally, separated from the rest of Chinese territory, so that socialism would not be contaminated. Chinese workers
would be shipped to these zones, but other Chinese citizens would
be excluded from these areas. In this scheme, Special Economic
Zones would attract foreign capital and technology, generate revenue, and provide valuable expertise for China. The underlying
project was tantamount to creating four, then many, new Chinese
dragons, but this time under the control of the Chinese government,
and for the benefit of China as a whole. It did not work. In my conversations on these matters with middle-level Chinese officials in
1987 I understood their fundamental mistake: they had read, and
believed, the "new international division of labor theory," proposed
by some Western Marxists, and they were eager to offer multinational
corporations a fraction of Chinese labor to be exploited – at the
price, mainly, of technology transfer. Yet, as I explained to them at
the time, multinational corporations had no interest in going into
China, with all its political unknowns and poor infrastructure, in
search of cheap labor and tax breaks, when they could obtain similar
conditions in a wide range of developing countries, under much
more favorable political circumstances. What multinational corporations wanted was to penetrate the Chinese market, planting seeds of
investment toward its future expansion. But, for this, they needed
access to China at large, beyond the restrained Special Economic
Zones; they needed to import their own supplies, without or with few
excise duties; and they needed freedom to create their own network
of suppliers and distributors. In a word: they needed to enter China's
economy, not just to use Chinese labor and land for exporting purposes. But their obvious business requests spelled trouble for the
prudent Chinese leaders. On the one hand, they had to protect

the interests of the state-owned companies, which would be displaced by the competition of foreign firms in China. On the other hand, what China really needed was to export manufactured goods and import technology and know-how, not just simply let foreign producers take over China's industry, and foreign products overrun Chinese markets. Thus, while the Chinese government formally opened much of China's urban–industrial regions to foreign investment and trade, under the 14 Coastal Cities policy, restrictions and red-tape made sure that the process would be under government control. Multinational corporations reacted by restraining investment, withholding technology, and negotiating market shares directly with the government. In my interviews with American and European companies in Shanghai and Beijing in 1987, they described their operations as an industrial island in an ocean of technological and economic backwardness, some of them importing as much as 90 percent of the inputs they needed to manufacture their products. None was making a profit. All were trading capital investment and transfer of old technology for presence in China, in the hope of future opportunities. Things have changed since then, and the production of Japanese, American, and European companies has substantially increased, particularly through high-technology markets for government orders, and through regional markets protected by provincial governments (for example, Volkswagen in Shanghai, German beer in Shendang). Some symbolic agreements, such as the US\$ 1 billion investment by General Motors in 1994, reflect the government's determination to lure foreign investors. Yet, at least until the mid-1990s, multinational corporations, and Western and Japanese investments, were not the main linkage between China and the global economy. Indeed, as table 4.1 shows, between 1979 and 1992, of the US\$ 116.4 billion pledged for investment in China, 71.7 percent came from Hong Kong and Taiwan, 7 percent from the US, and 5.8 percent from Japan. Individual European countries' share of investment is even lower. Similarly, only a fraction of China's imports originate in OECD countries. On the other hand, not counting weapons sales, a substantial proportion of Chinese exports (either from Chinese firms or from joint-venture companies located in China) are exported to Western Europe and the United States. Indeed, the United States seems to be in danger of running a trade deficit with China larger than it has with any other country. But the new competitiveness of China did not come from its inefficient state enterprises, nor, for the most part, from its still infant private business sector. It was organized around investment, know-how, and world market expertise from overseas Chinese investors which, in cooperation with a special kind

Table 4.1 Contracted foreign investment in China by source,
1979–92 (US$ million, percentage shares in brackets)

	1979–90	1991	1992	1979–92
National total	45,244	12,422	58,736	116,402
	(100)	(100)	(100)	(100)
Hong Kong	26,480	7,531	40,502	74,513
	(58.5)	(60.6)	(69.0)	(64.0)
Taiwan	2,000	1,392	5,548	8,968
	(4.4)	(11.2)	(9.4)	(7.7)
US	4,476	555	3,142	8,163
	(9.9)	(4.5)	(5.3)	(7.0)
Japan	3,662	886	2,200	6,748
	(8.1)	(7.1)	(3.7)	(5.8)

Between 1979 and 1989, the total value of pledged (contracted) FDI in China
was US$ 32.37 billion, the actual (realized) was US$ 15.61 billion, 48% of the
total pledged FDI. If we use 48% as the percentage of the actual FDI in total
pledged FDI, the national total of realized FDI in China between 1979 and
1992 is about US$ 56 billion.
Source: Sung (1994: 50)

of institutional partner (see below), constituted the fundamental link
between China and the global economy in the 1980s and 1990s.

The ethnic connection of China's global integration is indeed an
extraordinary story, full of practical and theoretical implications. But
it must be told, as You-tien Hsing has done,[106] without the
romanticizing and anecdotal evidence that characterizes much
of the cottage-industry research generated on the "Chinese business networks" operating in the "China circle." These ethnic business
networks are essential to contemporary Chinese development, but
they came to life in China by taking advantage of the opportunity
provided by the open-door policy. Investment in China was risky, but
could yield very high profits in a largely untapped market, with negligible labor costs, on the condition of knowing how to operate in a
complex environment. Chinese investors from Hong Kong and
Taiwan used the opening to decentralize their production, particularly in the Pearl River Delta, and in other areas of southern China,
when higher production costs at home, and a reduction of their
export quotas threatened their competitive position. To minimize
risks, they used their *guanxi* (relationship) networks, particularly
looking for people who were from the same place of origin (*tong-
xiang*), their relatives or friends, or for dialect-group acquaintances.

[106] Hsing (1997a, b).

The building of the necessary infrastructure to support international connections (hotels, business services, airports, roads, property development) created an immediate market for large Hong Kong-based firms, which went into this kind of investment very early in the process of economic reform (I enjoyed an international hotel developed by Hong Kong's business in Guangzhou as early as 1983). As analyzed in volume I, chapter 6, the mega-region Hong Kong – Shenzhen – Guangzhou – Zhuhai – Macau – Pearl River Delta, comprising about 60 million people, had become an economic unit by the early 1990s, constituting one of the potential global nodes of the twenty-first century. To answer in kind, Shanghai, with the support of the Beijing political elite, largely dominated by the "Shanghai group," launched in the early 1990s the new enterprise zone of Pudong, poised to become the major financial and advanced services center of China.

Once the investment networks from Hong Kong and Taiwan were established, by the late 1980s, capital flowed from all over the globe, much of it from overseas Chinese, from Singapore, Bangkok, Penang, Kuala Lumpur, Jakarta, California, New York, Canada, and Australia. The statistical pre-eminence of Hong Kong is, in fact, a mirage. It reflects the management of plural sources of investment by Hong Kong-based Chinese firms. It should be interpreted as "global capital." But this "global capital," which can be, and is, from any source, from Japanese banks to money launderers, is administered, and to a large extent controlled, by Chinese business networks, more often than not based on family relationships, and inter-linked among themselves, in spite of fierce rivalry in specific markets and projects. Why does Chinese business have an advantage over other foreign investors, and why does it not risk as much as Western or Japanese investors in the uncertain conditions of proto-capitalist China? I have grown skeptical of cultural explanations about insider knowledge and personal connections. After all, reading Yang's excellent anthropological account of rural *renqing* and urban *guanxi* practices in contemporary China,[107] I do not see any substantial difference from my knowledge of similar practices in Latin America. And yet, US investors have dominated Latin American economies for decades, and Mexico, one of the most *guanxi*-oriented countries that I know, benefited in the 1990s from a flurry of direct international investment without much need of Mexican mediation, while Mexican business networks continued to export their savings abroad, instead of investing in Mexico. In the case of China, overseas Chinese business networks are indeed the main intermediaries between global capital,

[107] Yang (1994).

including overseas Chinese capital, and China's markets and producing/exporting sites. But the reason is not that they and their southern China partners both like steamed cod. It is because *China's multiple link to the global economy is local, that is, it is performed through the connection between overseas Chinese business and local and provincial governments in China,* the *sui generis* capitalist class that Hsing calls the "bureaucratic entrepreneurs."[108]

China's regional developmental states and the bureaucratic (capitalist) entrepreneurs

To overcome ideological resistances to economic reform from the CCP and PLA's high-ranking cadres, Deng sought the support of local and provincial governments from the outset of reform. To short-circuit the power of the conservatives, concentrated in the Beijing headquarters, and in the northern provinces, he proclaimed the principle of *yindizhiyi* ("to each locality according to its own characteristics"), proceeding during the 1980s to a considerable fiscal decentralization: the center's share of GDP declined from 37 percent in 1978 to 19 percent in 1992, and the center's share of total tax revenue amounted to only 35 percent in 1993.[109] He particularly courted Guandong and Shanghai, China's historical links to foreign trade and investment. In 1992, he went on his famous *nanxun* (imperial tour) of the south, encouraging Guandong, in particular, to overtake the Asian Pacific dragons, by accelerating its growth rate and its opening to the international economy. "Only development," he argued, "passes the test of reason."[110] Guandong, Shanghai, but also most other provinces, and localities, took Deng at his word, and asserted their economic autonomy, both in fiscal matters and in credit policy, to finance its own infrastructure, create new businesses, and attract foreign investors. The overheating of the economy, and consequent inflationary surges, in 1988, 1992, and 1993, led the central government to tighten controls, and to reverse fiscal decentralization by instituting, in 1993, a dual tax system, under which the central government would keep its own source of revenue. Provincial governments, with Guandong leading the charge, used their new political and economic muscle to resist new revenue-sharing schemes. But their drive for autonomy (at the source of their new wealth) was mainly implemented not by subtracting resources from the center but

---

108 Hsing (1997a, b).
109 Lam (1995: 88).
110 Quoted by Lam (1995: 132).

by creating new sources of revenue for themselves, using precisely their new freedom of maneuver. If Deng wanted to infuse collective entrepreneurialism (probably too much sophistication for the pragmatist he was) he succeeded. Provincial and local governments in China (which I include under a "regional" label, for the sake of simplicity) invested in new market-oriented businesses, often in joint ventures with foreign investors, and became the source of "private" capitalist accumulation, as collective entrepreneurs who shared the benefits of their enterprises. In 1993, state enterprises ("wholly people's owned firms") accounted for 48.4 percent of the total value of industrial production; private ownership (including foreign-participated business) for only 13.4 percent; while "collective enterprises" (that is, businesses with participation of specific government administrations, most of them regional and private investors) represented 38.2 percent of the total, and growing.[111] Furthermore, industrial production was not the main sector of investment for regional governments, and their foreign partners, most frequently overseas Chinese. Property development was the entry point for these foreign investors: it was less risky, offered immediate pay-offs in a country that became, in its coastal areas, an instant, gigantic construction site, and provided a solid footing into local networks. Besides, control over their own land was an undisputed resource for local/provincial governments. Finance was also a critical sector for the strengthening of provincial autonomy and the introduction of capitalist economic management. A bold financial experiment was initiated, again, by Guandong government as early as 1981. The Guandong Branch of the People's Bank gained the autonomy to use a specific amount of capital and to issue short- and medium-term loans.[112] The establishment of the province's own financial institution, the shareholding Guandong Development Bank, was approved and incorporated in 1988. Then, Guandong was also allowed to develop a stock and security market, set up foreign exchange adjustment centers, and handle foreign exchange account business. The province was also able to obtain foreign borrowing and to issue its own bonds abroad, subject to central approval. When the central government imposed fiscal austerity in 1994, Guangzhou's municipal government began to raise funds from international financial markets, either through foreign partners of joint ventures in Guangzhou, or through the municipal government-owned Guangzhou International Trust

[111]   Lam (1995: 94–5).
[112]   Cheung (1994: 26–39).

and Investment Corporation, and Yuexiu Enterprise in Hong Kong.[113] Between June and November 1994, in the midst of national austerity measures, six foreign banks in Guangzhou provided US$ 380 million in loans to local enterprises.[114] In addition to borrowing from abroad, Guandong also attracted capital from other provinces in China. Thus, while many regions were suffering from austerity measures, in the mid-1990s, cities and counties in the Pearl River Delta continued with their expansion plans, running a budget two to five times higher than allowed by government's central plans, and financing it with bonds and loans. In the midst of the controversy over the overheating of the economy, the mayor of Dongguan, a Pearl River Delta city, proclaimed: "How the Pearl River Delta could catch up with the four East Asian dragons if we take cautious steps?"[115] Guandong's local government attracted capital by offering exceptionally high interest rates (18–20 percent; that is, eight points higher than in Sichuan or Hunan provinces), under the principle of "water flows to low lands, people move to high places, and money goes to profits," in a display of the rapid assimilation of capitalist principles by Chinese slogan makers.[116] It is only thanks to this access to outside financial resources that Guandong, Shanghai, and other fast-growing areas in China have been able to short-circuit economic controls from the central planning system. This system is still in place, but its main role is to subsidize an unproductive state sector, and assure enough revenue collection to provide for the center's priorities. Among these priorities are technology and military investments, and the self-reproduction of the state and party apparatuses.

Through these, and similar processes, *a new capitalist class has emerged in China, mainly constituted of "bureaucratic entrepreneurs;" that is, by individuals (more often than not members of the Communist party) whose access to resources stems from their control of government institutions and finances.* Using these resources, they invest in business on behalf of the government institutions they represent, either by themselves, in association with other bureaucracies, or, increasingly, linking up with foreign investors. These mixed enterprises are the core of China's new capitalism. It is a highly decentralized capitalism because it follows the contours of provincial and local alliances, and of the business networks to which they connect: a capitalism that is oligopolistic in local markets, and competitive at the national and international

---

[113]   Lu (1994a).
[114]   Lu (1994b).
[115]   Quoted by Lu (1993).
[116]   Quoted by Hsing (1997a).

levels. And it is a capitalism that knows that it has to generate enough surplus to pay its share (formally or informally) to higher levels of government, not directly involved in business, and to indispensable participants in the local/provincial enterprises, such as high-ranking military officers and party cadres whose protection is necessary to shrug off the planned economy.

This process of "bureaucratic capitalist development" was, by the mid-1990s, under the supervision of the state. However, as the market economy spread, it became increasingly difficult to exercise political control, without creating chaos, for three main reasons: first, because the centers of capital accumulation were mainly in the hands of this constellation of provincial/local enterprises, directly linked to foreign markets and financial sources. The second reason refers to the rapid growth of thousands of *gumin* ("stocks-crazed specu-lators") who, using information technology to trade in the Bourses of Beijing, Shanghai, and Shenzhen, from anywhere in China, were channeling savings and bypassing government controls. And the third, and fundamental, reason is that the new power equilibrium in China has taken the form of a complex pattern of interdependence between the center and the regions, interconnected by the party and by the army. Any decisive attempt by the center to curtail the regions' economic autonomy, particularly *vis-à-vis* the rich provinces, could not only derail economic reforms (fundamentally based on provincial government capitalism), but call into question the fragile status quo reached in the reformed Communist state, under the twin banners of China's national power and of Deng's slogan: "It's glorious to be rich."

Weathering the storm? China in the Asian economic crisis

By the end of 1998, the only Asian economy holding to a steady path of high economic growth, at about 7 percent, was China. To be sure, its future was uncertain, as China's development is largely dependent upon the overall performance of the Asian Pacific. Moreover, in spite of its initial success in defending the yuan against speculative attack, by the time you read this it is possible that China will have devalued its currency. The still pending, and important, question is by how much. Yet, in 1997–8, China asserted its economic power and kept relative stability by resisting the destructive assault of financial flows, and by preventing a fall into recession. The Chinese government even felt strong enough to save the Hong Kong dollar from devaluation. The PRC's determination, backed by its $US 140 billion in hard currency reserves, allowed Hong Kong's currency board system to survive, at least for a while. China had very good reasons to support

Hong Kong's economy, in addition to the fact that the territory is now fully part of China. China's government, and banks, are the largest landholders, and among the largest stockholders, in Hong Kong, so they tried to limit their losses. But even more important is the fact that Hong Kong is the main source of foreign investment in China, most of it from overseas Chinese business, processed through Hong Kong firms. To stabilize Hong Kong it was essential to link up international investors with China's market at a time when China had to counter the trends of capital outflow. To preserve stable exchange rates for both the Hong Kong dollar and the yuan China was ready to sacrifice some of its trade competitiveness, as exports from its Asian competitors became substantially cheaper as a result of the devaluation of their currencies. China suffered on two grounds: export growth declined considerably, falling from a 22 percent growth rate in 1997 to about 5 percent in 1998. And capital outflows, as in other Asian countries, sky-rocketed: $US 20 billion moved out in 1997, and a much larger sum was expected to follow in 1998, as investors feared the devaluation of the yuan. And yet, the Chinese economy suffered, overall, much less impact from the crisis than the rest of the Pacific. To understand why this was so has extremely important analytical implications, even if a new wave of the Asian crisis ultimately hits China hard.

The main factor explaining China's relative capacity to absorb the shock of the crisis is its limited integration in the global economy, particularly in terms of its financial markets. The yuan, in 1998, was not fully convertible, so it was much better protected from speculative attack than currencies traded in the open market. The banking system in China was, in 1997–8, in as much trouble as the one in Japan. Banks were at least $US 240 billion in bad debt and most of them were insolvent. Other reports, from Standard&Poor, put bad bank loans at about 60 percent of China's GDP. However, the government was backing the banks, only forcing bankruptcy under controlled circumstances; and, because of tight controls on foreign lending, Chinese banks were not strangled by short-term foreign debt, the source of most of the financial crisis in the rest of Asia. In spite of the fact that some banks borrowed foreign money through Hong Kong-based banks, the Hong Kong "bumper" prevented in China the kind of financial panic that struck Indonesia and South Korea. Thus, government control of the links between the Chinese financial system and global markets provided a cushion to resist the wild movements of financial flows around the world.

A second factor which helped to keep China on the development path was government management of the pace of integration in international trade. In spite of China's push to become a member of the

World Trade Organization, with its implications for open trade policy, in 1998 China compensated for its declining exports by restrictions on imports, thus maintaining a healthy current balance. To stop the flow of cheap, low-end products from Asian competitors into its market, China resorted to red tape, and to currency controls on import companies, to favor local production. But in the critical sector of high technology, and high-value manufactured goods, China was able to control imports because of the good technological level of its advanced manufacturing industries. Indeed, while much has been written on the obsolescence of the state enterprise sector, some of these state-controlled companies, particularly in telecommunications, have been able to improve their productivity, and technological quality, winning market share from their foreign competitors in China, even on those product lines that are manufactured in China by foreign companies. Relying on state-controlled companies, such as Huawei, Datang, and Great Dragon, Chinese companies have increased their share of the Chinese telecommunications market from 10 percent in 1995 to about 55 percent in 1998. While government support in some contracts, particularly at the provincial level, has helped Chinese manufacturers, industry observers consider that the high quality and hard work of low-wage, innovative Chinese engineers, and the R&D effort of Chinese local manufacturers, have been the most important factors in gaining competitiveness over foreign firms.[117] A similar trend is perceived in the automobile industry, in which sales of the Alto, produced in China by an all-Chinese company, Norinco, have taken on imports of foreign cars. Thus, the ability to upgrade, protect, and expand its manufacturing industry, geared primarily toward the domestic market, has been a key factor in China's avoiding a dramatic slump, at least during the first phase of the crisis.

Yet, none of these circumstances would have pulled China out of a potential recession had it not been for government economic policies. Zhu Rongji, prime minister since March 1998, and the architect of the anti-inflation program of the 1990s, understood, well before the International Monetary Fund did, that the real problem faced by Asia was deflation, not government spending. Thus, instead of putting the brakes on the economy, and implementing austerity policies, as the IMF was forcing Indonesia, Thailand, and South Korea to do, the Chinese government embarked on an ambitious plan of government spending, most of it on infrastructure and housing. To pay for it, the government counted on mobilizing the estimated

---

[117]   *The Economist* (1998: 64–6).

$US 560 billion savings deposited in state-run commercial banks. To use the banks as intermediaries, the government first used $US 32 billion to refloat the banks, and allow them to go back into the lending business, so stimulating the economy. Thus, what seems to have been at the root of China's initial success in weathering the financial crisis was Keynesianism on a grand scale, shielded from disruptive financial flows and guided by government through currency controls and managed trade policy. Major problems remain unsolved, on which I will elaborate below, and it is not certain by any means that China can continue to be "a little bit global" and "a little bit capitalist," while preserving Communist leadership and strong government intervention in the economy. Yet, the first results of the Chinese experience in handling the crisis, in contrast with what has happened in other "emerging markets" in the world, seem to support the argument concerning the decisive role of the state in managing the impacts of globalization.

Democracy, development, and nationalism in the new China

Observers of the new China often start their forecasts from the implicit assumption of the necessary association between development and democracy. Thus, their prognosis is for either the gradual erosion or the sudden overrun of Communist power, as the new urban middle classes grow, and a stronger, influential civil society comes to life. At the time of writing (fall of 1998), available information does not support this view. The network of Communist party organizations is firmly in control of most voluntary associations and expressions of civic life. The party overwhelms *shimin shehui* (civil society). There is openness and diversity in the media, but within the margins of political correctness. There are new electronic media, but even foreign satellite broadcasting companies, such as Murdoch's Star TV, practice self-restraint as regards Chinese politics to avoid losing a giant market. The Internet is in China, but China is the only country in the world which is having some success in controlling web sites and hook ups, although at the cost of impoverishing its collective access to the worldwide net. As for the middle class, it is too busy making money and consuming it, thus vindicating Deng's vulgar economicist approach to the new stage of the revolution. Furthermore, since access to government institutions, and to party-controlled resources, is critical to be in business, and since opportunities are plenty, there is little interest in dismantling the system, or opening it up, while everybody is dedicated to their personal "primitive accumulation." This is why *guanxi* is so important, but so dependent on the existence of a formal system of planned economy, whose daily bypassing provides a major source of rent for its gatekeepers. The emerging market system in China develops by using competitive advantages obtained by positioning in the cracks of the still predominant command economy. Thus, with little incentive to undermine communist control, and considerable risk in trying to do so, the new urban middle class, while disliking the state, can shrug off its dislike as long as its families keep prospering.

To be sure, there are many democrats in China, particularly among the intelligentsia and students. And, in such a large country, it is easy to count them by the hundreds of thousands, mostly concentrated in the major metropolitan areas. But Tian An Men did teach some lessons. On the one hand, it showed the determination of the communist state not to lose control of the transition process. On the other hand, it also showed, although it is usually not acknowledged, that the student movement could go as far as it did because of the relative tolerance (if not encouragement) provided by Zhao Ziyang, fully engaged in his struggle against the left of the party. Who manipulated whom (for instance, were the students, instead, manipulated by the left to provoke a law and order reaction leading to the demise of Zhao Ziyang and to counter-reform?) we will probably never know. But what became clear was that the movement was limited, lacked widespread popular support, and was entirely dependent for its fate on internal struggles in the CCP.

Thus, the ability of autonomous civil society to expand, and for political democracy to develop, will depend, essentially, on how able the CCP is to keep its unity, and how well the Chinese state manages conflicts between different levels of government, and between different provinces vying for economic gains. A key element in the treatment of both issues is the strength, unity, and orientation of the People's Liberation Army. Probably, Deng's main political legacy will be his skillful maneuvering in the minefield of military command during his last years. In the early 1990s he essentially proceeded, successfully, with four key operations. First, he eliminated opposition from leftists, ideologues, and non-reliable officers at the top, particularly by dismissing General Yang Shangkung, vice-chairman of the Central Military Commission, together with his brother and 300 other officers, suspected of organizing a leftist network, in 1992. Secondly, he moved on to appointing pro-reform officers in the highest positions, while adopting a conciliatory attitude toward the traditional left in the army, as long as they would not plot against their new commanders. He also gave greater representation to the Army in the party's leading organs: in the 14th Congress of the CCP in 1992, the army's representation in the Central Committee went up from 18 to 22 percent, and a professional officer, General Liu Huaquing, was given a permanent seat in the Politburo. Thirdly, with the support of army commanders, Deng moved to put greater emphasis on professionalism and technology, to create what he labeled "an elite corps with Chinese characteristics." The PLA, like the Soviet army, had been greatly impressed by the performance of high-tech weapons and of the Western airforce in the Gulf War, undermining the position of those officers who were still emphasizing people's war tactics based on ideological motivation. As a result, the army decided to support economic and technological modernization which appeared to be indispensable to bring Chinese forces up to the level of twenty-first century warfare. Last but not least, Deng and Jiang made sure that the PLA fully participated in China's economic bonanza. Military factories were given the opportunity of targeting the civilian market, which they did with considerable success, counting on tariff protection against foreign imports. Individual officers were appointed to state companies, and to state supervising agencies, and were allowed to receive profits from their commercial activities. Provincial governments seconded this policy, so that thousands of military officers ended up on the boards of new "collective businesses," and became integrated into the new class of bureaucratic entrepreneurs. Furthermore, since officers on active duty could not dedicate themselves entirely to business, their sons and daughters were given the opportunity, both in China and in Hong Kong, so that a vast network of family interests linked up with overseas business networks, bureaucratic entrepreneurs, party leaders, PLA leaders, and their families, thus constituting China's dominant class in an inseparable web of political positions and business interests. In fact, the conversion of the PLA from the bastion of the left to a pro-business institution went too far for the political interests of the Chinese state. In 1998, Jiang Zemin issued several directives to limit the involvement of high-ranking officers in business because the army was losing discipline, and military readiness, given the excessive dedication of many officers to their business ventures. Yet, overall, the army continued to be a significant part of the new, profitable state capitalist economy in China. Thus, with party and army unity largely assured by their new economic bonds, and with society under control, the Chinese communist state seemed to be poised for a gradual transition to an economy and a polity that would respond to the interests of these elites in the context of China's integration into the global economy.

At the end of the millennium, however, China has to face a number of difficult problems, whose effective resolution would condition its future, as well as the fate of the Pacific in the twenty-first century. None of them relates to democracy, which is a Western concern, rather than a real issue for most of China. But a democratic movement could indeed spur from the social conflicts generated around some of these issues. I have been able to identify at least four such problems. Perhaps the most immediate is the massive rural exodus provoked by the modernization and privatization of agriculture, which is estimated to affect about 200 million peasants during the 1990s. A fraction of them are being absorbed into the small towns being developed by the Chinese government to stand the shock. Others are being employed in the new urban economy, and in the factories and shops scattered in semi-rural areas. Many of them (perhaps as many as 50 million) seem to be in the category of "floating urban population," wandering around Chinese cities looking for work and shelter. This mass of uprooted migrants can hardly be assimilated to the notion of a "civil society." They are unorganized, lack cultural and political resources to represent an articulate force of opposition. But they are an extraordinarily volatile element, whose potential rage could destabilize the whole process of transition to a market economy, should they come into contact with messianic leaders or with splintering factions of the Communist party.

A second major problem refers to the existence of bitter inter-provincial conflicts. For reasons mentioned above, the opposition between the center and provinces, particularly with the rich provinces of the south and of coastal China, seem to be intelligently cushioned by the co-optation of provincial leaders (most notably from Shanghai) to the Beijing government, and by the freedom given by the center to the provinces to prosper on their own in the inter-national economy. With the CCP and the PLA structuring their interests around central government and provincial institutions, the sharp conflicts that do exist between the center and the coastal provinces seem to have proper channels for their treatment. Besides, unlike in the former Soviet Union, the ethnic/national factor, in spite of Tibetan resistance and Muslim unrest, does not represent a major source of contradiction because Han Chinese constitute about 94 percent of the population. So, outside Tibet, Xinjiang, and Inner Mongolia, the ethnic basis for national or regional resistance to the center is very weak. However, what is being witnessed in the mid-1990s is intense rivalry and fierce competition between provinces, particularly pitching the poor regions of inland China against the rich coastal provinces that participate fully in the market economy and international exchange. In 1996, the Ministry of Civil Affairs revealed that over 1,000 disputes, and some "bloody fights," had taken place between provinces and regions concerning the definition of their territorial borders. Using their autonomy, some provinces ban the sale of products from other provinces within their borders, and follow tax, credit and industrial policies of their own. Since the political clout of provinces still largely depends on their influence in Beijing, their infighting is exported into the central apparatuses of party and government, with potential destabilizing tendencies. For instance, Shanghai's current dominance in the Beijing government is strongly resented in Guandong. The incorporation of Hong Kong may reinforce this tension, since the economic might of the mega-region Hong Kong/Guandong does not have commensurate political influence in Beijing. Furthermore, as regional disparities increase dramatically between the poor, subsidized regions and the self-sufficient market-oriented regions, the ideological conflicts about the extent and perdurability of the command economy and of the socialist safety net are taking, and will increasingly take, a regional connotation. The potential regional conflicts emerging in China will not look like the break up of the Soviet Union, but, rather, there will be regionalism with Chinese characteristics, perhaps threatening to degenerate into a new period of warring states, as the one that took place, among Han Chinese, for about 200 years, 24 centuries ago.

The third major problem confronting China is how to move toward a market economy while avoiding mass unemployment and the dismantling of the safety net. There are two main issues in this regard. The first is the privatization of housing. On the one hand, this is the government's secret weapon to stimulate the Chinese economy, by mobilizing the large, untapped mass of private savings, into a gigantic housing mortgage market. On the other hand, the largest section of the urban population does not have the means to access the new property market. Thus, displacement, urban segregation, and massive homelessness could be the consequence of fast-paced housing privatization. This is why the "big bang" of the privatization program announced for July 1998 was postponed to a later date, in order to proceed cautiously city by city.[118]

The second major issue which slows down Chinese economic reforms is the low productivity, and low profitability, of many (but not all, as I pointed out above) of the state enterprises, which survive on subsidies, and still employ the largest section of the industrial work-force. The problem is compounded by the fact that large state enterprises, as well as government administrations, are critical for all spheres of life for Chinese workers, from housing to health plans, from kindergartens to vacations. Privatization has proceeded apace, but most state enterprises find no buyers, and the government keeps financing them. For how long? All indications are that Chinese

[118] Po (forthcoming).

Communists are determined not to make the same mistakes as their European counterparts. While listening to Western economists on the handling of the international sector of the economy, they seem poised to ensure a long period of transition based on subsidizing the public sector and the welfare state, as the basis for their own power and legitimacy. For this, keeping the central planning system, as a system of accounting and management of the public sector, is crucial, thus justifying the function, and jobs, of millions of government employees who depend on them for their living. Therefore, the new Chinese economy is developing through the juxtaposition of three sectors: a public sector, insulated from market competition; an internationally oriented sector, geared toward foreign investment and trade; and a domestic market-oriented, capitalist sector, mainly built around bureaucratic entrepreneurs. The connections and passages between the three sectors is assured by the party's business networks, the so-called "red capitalists." Yet the complexity of the system, and the number of potential conflicts of interest, opens the door for acute power struggles.

The fourth problem is of a different character, but I consider it critical for the feasibility of the "Singapore model," which Chinese Communist leaders seem to be seeking to implement. Indeed, it was, as I tried to argue in chapter 1, a major factor in the disintegration of the Soviet Union. It refers to technology, and particularly to information technology. If China's economy is going to compete in the global area, and if China's state is going to project its military might, a strong technological base is essential. China does not yet possess it. It certainly did not when I had the opportunity to evaluate it, even superficially, in 1987.[119] However, recent information suggests that China has made substantial progress in the past decade, particularly in telecommunications and personal computers, as mentioned above. Yet, the speed of technological change is such that China will have to step up its technological upgrading *vis-à-vis* the United States, Japan, the Asian "tigers," and multinational corporations around the world. Yes, China can put satellites in orbit, and has remarkable scientific teams. It is also a nuclear power, with missile-launching capability, including, probably, a limited stock of ICBMs. Yet satellite-launching is mainly a business practiced by other medium-tech countries, such as India; most science seems to develop in isolation from industry; and the ability to blow up part of the planet is a military deterrent of last resort, but not an indication of the technological capacity to project conventional warfare power. The question is, as it was for the

[119]   Bianchi et al. (1988).

Soviet Union, whether the current technological revolution, based on information technology, can be developed in a closed society, in which endogenous technology is secluded in the national security system, where commercial applications are dependent on foreign licensing or imitation, and, most fundamentally, where individuals, private business, and society at large, cannot appropriate technology and develop its uses and its potential; for instance, by freely accessing the Internet. I think not, and the experience of the Soviet Union seems to prove it, albeit it must be conceded that other important factors played a role in the Soviet crisis, and that Chinese communists have the benefit of hindsight with the Soviet experience. Chinese leaders think they can manage the contradiction by acquiring technology from abroad, by buying machines, by obtaining licenses, by technology transfer from foreign companies, and by sending their own scientists and engineers for training abroad. In my exchanges with some of their experts on this matter in 1987, and in our study of their technology policy, I realized that Chinese officials had an outdated, industrialist notion of what technology is. They still thought that technology was machines, and that with the scientific and technical excellence of Chinese professionals, they could handle everything if they just had the proper machinery. Hence their emphasis on licensing, on importing machinery, and on seeking the location of technologically advanced multinationals which would have a demonstrable effect on China's industrial structure. This is simply wrong, although this is not the place to lecture you on what technology is today. In the informational paradigm, the uses of technology cannot be separated from technology itself. The machines can easily be bought everywhere, except for specific military hardware. What is essential is to know what to do with them, how to program, reprogram, and interact, in a largely serendipitous process that requires an open, uncensored network of interaction and feedback. The essential technology is in our brains and experience. China continues to send students and professionals abroad, as the most effective means of building its technological potential. But, as faculty members of major universities around the world know, most of these bright young Chinese scientists and engineers are not truly welcome back home, suffocated by a bureaucratic system of science, by low-level uses of technology, and a generally oppressive cultural atmosphere. Thus, after their training, they bureaucratize themselves, or go into more profitable business, or, in many cases, just stay in the West or get a good job in the thriving Pacific outside China. I will not go so far as to say that without democracy China cannot truly gain access to the information technology paradigm, so vital for its grand design: political processes cannot be reduced to simple statements.

But, without some form of open society, it probably cannot, for reasons argued in volume I, and in chapter 1 of this volume. Yet, there seems to be some evidence of technological improvement in Chinese high-technology industries, particularly in telecommunications equipment. This is to a large extent due to technology transfer from multinational corporations, and from overseas Chinese companies, cooperating with technologically advanced state enterprises, and counting on the excellence of Chinese technological universities. The question is whether this technological upgrading can be sustained without fully fledged modernization of the overall manufacturing industry, and without the much broader exposure of Chinese universities to international exchanges. To sum up, China is muddling through the contradiction of developing information technology in an information-controlled society. But this pragmatic policy will face a much greater challenge when Chinese companies need a higher level of technological innovation, one that cannot be satisfied by reverse engineering.

Thus, while democracy is not a dramatic issue in China, and while Deng's succession seems to be under control by an able Communist leadership led by Jiang Zemin and Zhu Rongji, the promise of party rule for the next century, and the viability of implementing the "Singapore model," are under question, given the widespread range of conflictive issues that have to be tackled in this end of millennium.

If conflicts flare up, if China feels the political pressure of the outside world, and if domestic politics grows restless, it is highly likely that the Chinese state will seek to perpetuate itself in the form of uncompromising nationalism. With revolutionary legitimacy exhausted among the people for all practical purposes, if consumerism does not reach a broad enough segment of the population to ensure social stability, the regime will emphasize its nationalist identity, as the defender of China, and of Chinese people around the world, finally being able to stand up to the East, West, and North, imposing respect simultaneously on Japan, the US, and Russia. In 1996, sabre rattling in the China Sea, confronting Taiwan, Vietnam, and Japan on the sovereignty of several islets, and open threats to Taiwan, seemed to indicate that this is a possible path of political evolution for the Chinese regime. It may rely on considerable popular support. Nationalism runs strong in China in this end of the century. Students spontaneously demonstrated against Japan's arrogance with such enthusiasm in August 1996 that the government had to step in to calm down the movement before it went out of control. Thus, after half a century of communism, China has come full circle to affirm itself as a nation and as a civilization rather than as an alternative social system, while sharing by and large the risks and riches of global capitalism. But this renewed Chinese nationalism displays marked socialist characteristics. And it projects itself in the Pacific and beyond, daring for the first time to take on the world as a major power.

Conclusion: Globalization and the State

Enough evidence has been presented in this chapter to support the argument that the developmental state has been the driving force in the extraordinary process of economic growth and technological modernization of the Asian Pacific in the past half-century. To the cases we have analyzed, others could be added. Malaysia was as developmental as Singapore, albeit weakened by its internal, potentially explosive, ethnic and religious contradictions. Indonesia, like Thailand, in the 1980s, was a quasi-developmental state. Certainly, Suharto's regime was based on the Suharto family's appropriation of a significant share of the country's wealth through their control of the military, the government, and the banking system. Suharto's personal dictatorship enabled him, and his cronies, to form an alliance with the multinational corporations (particularly the Japanese), and with the wealthy Chinese business community, to allow them to run the country's economy for a share of the profits. Yet, while the developmental strategy, in both Indonesia and Thailand, included, as an essential element, the personal enrichment of the rulers, the policies of the state focused on linking up the country with the global economy to industrialize and dynamize the national economy. These policies met with considerable success in terms of growth and modernization. After all, in the states of South Korea, Taiwan, and even Japan, systemic corruption was also present. And personal dictatorship was, for a long time, a central feature of the state in South Korea, Taiwan, and Singapore. Thus, with the exception of Marcos's Philippines (a predatory state), militaristic Myanmar, and war-torn Cambodia and Laos, the developmental state, in different degrees, and in various forms, was the main actor in the successful development process of the Asian Pacific.

Its own success led to its demise, with the exception of China. The developmental state was based on the premise of a double-edged, relative autonomy. Relative autonomy *vis-à-vis* the global economy, making the country's firms competitive in the international realm, but controlling trade and financial flows. Relative autonomy *vis-à-vis* society, repressing or limiting democracy, and building legitimacy on the improvement of living standards rather than on citizen participation. All this under the banner of serving the nation, or even creating it, while serving the rulers themselves. On both grounds, the autonomy of the state was challenged by the outcome of the developmental process. Full integration into the global economy made it increasingly difficult for the state to control financial flows, trade, and, therefore, industrial policy. Firms nurtured by the state became global corporations, or global networks of firms. Financial institutions tapped the international financial markets on their own. And global investors found their direct line into the booming Asian economies, the new Wild East of unfettered capitalism. The traditional mechanisms set up by the developmental state were made obsolete, but new rules and regulations, adapted to the globalization of financial markets, were not in place. We know that capitalism does not mean free markets. Unfettered markets without reliable institutions and regulations are tantamount to pillage, speculation, abusive, private appropriation, and ultimately chaos, if the lessons of history are of any value. The institutional void created by the confused transition from the developmental state to a new, regulatory capitalist framework was quickly filled by global financial lenders, speculators, and their local cronies.

The success of the developmental state in modernizing the economy led, in most cases, to the emergence of a civil society, asserting itself against the authoritarian state. When social change and democracy fought their way through the political institutions, the margin of maneuver for the developmental state was reduced, so that it became increasingly unable to ensure, at the same time, the management of global competition and the rulers' personal prosperity. No one seemed to understand better the connection between preserving this dual autonomy and the survival of the developmental state than Malaysia's national leader, Mahathir Mohamad. His response to the crisis was three-pronged. First, to partly de-link Malaysia from the global economy by making the ringgit non-convertible, and establishing strict controls on financial exchanges, while still supporting the direct, productive investment of multinationals in Malaysia. Secondly, to crack down on civil society and democracy, firing his liberal-minded deputy and finance minister, Anwar Ibrahim, jailing him under ridiculous pretexts, and beating up people demonstrating their support for Anwar. Thirdly, he rallied Malaysian nationalism, and called upon religious identity, by denouncing global financial strategies as a new form of colonialism and of Western domination, probably, it was said, inspired by Jews, and certainly orchestrated by George Soros. While most of these gestures had predominantly symbolic value, they signaled the refusal of at least one developmental state to be brought down by the process of globalization that the development states had helped to create.

There are, as presented in this chapter, three important exceptions that do not fit in this analysis: Taiwan, Singapore, and, above all, China. It may well be that, by the time you read this, the three countries will also have been engulfed by the crisis, thus making the following discussion academic. But remember this is an academic book. So, I think it is analytically useful to reflect on the specific crisis management in Taiwan, Singapore, and China in the framework of understanding the relationship between globalization and the state.

Taiwan offers no mystery. The Taiwanese economy, by the mid-1990s, had already made the transition to flexible, entrepreneurial networks linked up around, and across, the Pacific, with markets and manufacturing networks. The state was strong enough to partly shield the banking system, but not strong enough to impose crony capitalism or to suffocate the emerging civil society. Thus, overall, Taiwan's firms, and the country as a whole, were fully integrated in the rules and procedures of advanced global capitalism, with the benefits and risks of full integration. Taiwan was, by and large, globalized.

Singapore was, and remains, the ultimate developmental state, clearly perfecting its Japanese blueprint. And, yet, its economy was brought down eventually only as a consequence of the overall decline in South-East Asia. And its society, while affluent and modernized, cannot be characterized as a civil society, in the Gramscian sense. State control over economy, and society, is still unabated. I consider it an exception. Because it is fully integrated in the global economy, its currency is convertible, it is a leading financial center, it is fully open to multinational corporations, and still the state keeps considerable control over the economy and over wild fluctuations in the financial markets. And while the potential for state policing of individuals and organizations is ever present, it is the people's self-inflicted withdrawal and censorship, rather than brute force, which rule Singapore. I do not know of any state or society in the world that comes even close to Singapore's experience. It may prefigure a future model of human civilization, exactly what Lee Kwan Yew wanted. If so, an in-depth study of Singapore as a laboratory for one possible social future for the twenty-first century becomes an essential task. I propose to build a Futurology Center in Singapore, and concentrate there the best futurologists in the world, for them to try to make sense of the experience. I wish them eternal happiness in the Lion City – a city-state which still baffles (and fascinates) me.

China is a different matter, even if Chinese leaders would like to adapt the Singapore model. For the time being, China demonstrates the possibility of benefiting from globalization while partly shielding the country's economy from uncontrollable global market forces. By limiting the convertibility of the yuan, and keeping tight control over financial flows, with a banking system under full government control, the Chinese government was able to spur the competitiveness of Chinese firms in export markets and attract foreign investment, lured by market size. Thus, China was able to sustain high rates of economic growth, acting on inflation or on deflation depending on the business cycle. The obvious backdrop to a strategy of controlling financial flows is the reluctance of global investors to lend/invest in China. So, over time, foreign investment, which was one of the major sources of China's hypergrowth in the 1990s, could dwindle, threatening to stall growth. There is, however, a major alternative source of financing: a high rate of domestic savings. And, for a share of these savings to be in hard currency, what is needed is export competitiveness in world markets. After all, it was precisely this formula, engineered by the developmental state, which spurred growth in the Asian Pacific countries before China joined, and surpassed them. Thus, while the developmental state seems to be failing in most of the Asian Pacific, the Chinese developmental state, as a tool of nationalist affirmation and political legitimacy, could be on the rise. The size of China, its scientific potential, its deep connections with dynamic, overseas Chinese business networks, may provide breathing space for the largest of all dragons. It is possible to follow here a Gerschenkronian logic as I hypothesize that the comparative advantage of the Chinese developmental state comes partly from its late arrival to the global economy. Thus, over time, this advantage will fade away, forcing China to face the same contradictions as its more precocious neighbors. However, history is not a pre-scripted scenario. The very fact that China can still behave as a developmental state changes the context because China is not a small exception to the global rule, as Singapore could be. If China succeeds in managing globalization, and marshalling society, in its transition to the Information Age, it means that the developmental state is alive and well for at least one-fifth of humankind. And if nations and states around the world feel increasingly powerless *vis-à-vis* global financial markets, they may look for alternatives and find inspiration in the Chinese experience. But this, of course, is only one of several possible courses of action. It may well happen, instead, that China loses control of its economy, and a rapid sequence of alternative deflation and inflation wrecks the country, triggers social explosions, and induces political conflict. If so, the developmental state will have run its historic course, and global flows of capital and information may reign uncontested – unless a new form of state, the network state, potentially exemplified by the European Union, comes to the rescue of societies, enslaved by their economies. The relationship between globalization and the state, at the heart of development and crisis in the Asian Pacific, is the dominant political issue at the end of this millennium.

— 5 —

The Unification of Europe: Globalization, Identity, and the Network State

The unification of Europe around the turn of the second millennium, when and if completed, will be one of the most important trends defining our new world.[1] It is important, first of all, because it will probably (but not surely) bring to an end the millennial war-making between major European powers, a recurrent practice that brought destruction and suffering to Europe, and in recent times to the world, throughout the entire span of recorded history, peaking with extraordinary violence in the first half of the twentieth century. It is also important because a unified Europe, with its economic and technological might, and its cultural and political influence, together with the rise of the Pacific, will anchor the world power system in a poly-

[1]   This chapter is intellectually indebted to my interaction with a number of Europeanists, both faculty and graduate students, at the University of California, Berkeley, where I chair the Center for Western European Studies in 1994–99. I am also grateful to the many European scholars and speakers (including government officials from different countries) who have visited the Center during these years. My discussion of information technology in relation to European economies and societies has been partly informed by exchanges with my colleagues in the European Commission's High Level Expert Group on the Information Society, on which I served during 1995–7. I thank Luc Soete, chair of the group, for facilitating these exchanges. I have benefited, as well, from my participation in a research program organized at Berkeley by the Center for German and European Studies, and by the Center for Slavic and Eastern European Studies, in 1995–8, on "Europe East and West: Challenges to National Sovereignty from Above and from Below." I thank the directors of this research program, Victoria Bonnell, and Gerald Feldman, for their kind invitation to join the effort. Last, but not least, my conversations with Alain Touraine, Felipe Gonzalez, Javier Solana, Carlos Alonso Zaldivar, Jordi Borja, Roberto Dorado, Peter Schulze, Peter Hall, Stephen Cohen, Martin Carnoy, and John Zysman, on the topics covered in this chapter, have shaped my thought, and considerably enriched my information.

centric structure, precluding the existence of any hegemonic super-power, in spite of the continuing military (and technological) pre-eminence of the United States. And, I argue, it is also significant as a source of institutional innovation that may yield some answers to the crisis of the nation-state. This is because, around the process of formation of the European Union, new forms of governance, and new institutions of government, are being created, at the European, national, regional, and local levels, inducing a new form of state that I propose to call *the network state.*

However, the actual content of this unification, and the actors involved in it, are still unclear, and will be so for some time. It is precisely this ambiguity that makes unification possible, while charac-terizing its process as a debate rather than as a blueprint. Indeed, European unification grew in the past half-century from the conver-gence of alternative visions and conflicting interests between nation-states, and between economic and social actors. The very notion of Europe, as based on a common identity, is highly question-able. The noted historian Josep Fontana has documented how European identity, throughout history, was always constructed against "the other," the barbarians of different kinds and different origins.[2] The current process of unification is not different in this sense, as it was made from a succession of *defensive political projects* around some common interests among the participating nation-states. Yet, Europe at the turn of the millennium is something else, and more complex. It results from the internal dynamics of the unification process, building on these defensive projects, then recently twisted, supported, and challenged by the two macro-trends that characterize the Information Age: the globalization of economy, technology, and communication; and the parallel affirmation of identity as the source of meaning. Because of the failure of the classic nation-state in ar-ticulating the reponse to these symmetrical, opposing challenges, European institutions are trying, just trying, to cope with both trends by using new forms and new processes, thereby attempting the construction of a new institutional system, the network state. This is the story I shall recount in this chapter, without having the opportu-nity, or harboring the intention, of presenting the whole economic and political complexity that surrounds the construction of the European Union, thus referring the interested reader to an abun-dant, well-informed literature on these matters.[3] My focus here is in

[2] Fontana (1994).
[3] Much of the information on which my analysis relies can be found in general newspapers and magazines, such as *El País, Le Monde, New York Times, The Economist,* and *Business Week.* I find it unnecessary to provide specific references to widely known facts. Nor do I intend to provide the reader with a dense

showing how the trends I have identified as critical in configuring the
Information Age – globalization, identity, and the crisis of the nation-
state – are shaping European unification, and thus the world of the
twenty-first century.

European Unification as a Sequence of Defensive Reactions: a Half-century Perspective

The European Union resulted from three outbursts of political initiatives and institution-building aimed at defending the participating
countries against three perceived series of threats in three historical
moments: the 1950s, the 1980s, and the 1990s. In all three cases, the
*goal was primarily political, and the means to reach this goal were, mainly,
economic measures.*

In 1948, several hundreds of European leaders met in The Hague
to discuss the prospects of European integration. Beyond ideological
proclamations, and technocratic ambitions, the essential goal of
European integration was to avoid a new war. For this, a permanent
form of accommodation had to be found with Germany, in sharp
contrast to Germany's humiliating condition following World War I
which led to World War II. The accommodation had to be primarily
between Germany and the other European continental power,
France, and it had to be blessed by the United States, Europe's
protector in the aftermath of a most destructive war. Furthermore, the
Cold War, with its front line passing through Germany, called for an
economically strong, politically stable Western Europe. NATO
provided the necessary military umbrella, and the Marshall Plan
helped to rebuild European economies, while paving the way for

---

bibliography on a set of highly specialized matters concerning European integration. I shall simply mention a few sources that I have found useful in refreshing
my memory, and stimulating my thinking on a subject that I have followed very
closely for the past quarter of a century in France, and Spain. Probably one of the
most intelligent, informed analyses of the subject can be found in Alonso Zaldivar
(1996). For a perceptive overview, whose argument I largely share, see Orstrom
Moller (1995). A major source of ideas is Keohane and Hoffman (1991b). A
seminal article on the political dimensions of European integration is Waever
(1995). On multiculturalism and the crisis of democracy in Europe, see Touraine
(1997). Additional, useful readings are: Ruggie (1993); Sachwald (1994); Ansell
and Parsons (1995); Bernardez (1995); Estefanía (1996, 1997); Hill, ed. (1996);
Hirst and Thompson (1996); Parsons (1996); Pisani-Ferry (1996); Tragardh
(1996); Zysman et al. (1996); Zysman and Weber (1997). It is also refreshing to
go back to the classic texts by Ernst Haas (1958a,1958b, 1964), where many of the
current political debates are advanced in analytical terms.

investment by American multinationals. But political institutions were required to stabilize relationships among nation-states that had been historically constituted fighting each other, or seeking alliances for the next war. No wonder that the first move toward European integration was a common market in the coal and steel industries, which made autonomous national development impossible in the industries that, at that time, were strategically central to any future war effort. The European Coal and Steel Community (ECSC) was created in Paris, in April 1951, by West Germany, France, Italy, and the Benelux countries. The good results of this initiative led to the two Treaties of Rome of March 25, 1957, creating Euratom, to coordinate policy in nuclear energy, the new strategic industry, and the European Economic Community, oriented toward improving trade and investment among the six nations.

The rapid increase of economic integration on the continent brought to the forefront of the European debate competing visions of the integration process. The technocrats who originated the blueprint of a unified Europe, and particularly Jean Monnet, dreamed of a federal state. None of the nation-states truly believed in it or wanted it. However, the inertia of the European institutions led to the accumulation of considerable influence (if not power) in the hands of European bureaucracy, while Germany, constrained in its international role, saw the EEC as a convenient international platform. The accession of de Gaulle to the French presidency put the brakes on the process of the transfer of sovereignty, and emphasized the option that would come to be known as intergovernmental, that is, placing European-wide decisions in the hands of the council of heads of executive powers from each country. De Gaulle tried to add a new political objective to the EEC: to assert its independence *vis à vis* the United States. This is why France vetoed twice, in 1963 and in 1966, the British application to join the EEC, considering that Britain's close ties to the United States would jeopardize European autonomous initiatives. Indeed, Britain represented, and still represents, in the clearest possible terms, a third, different vision of European integration: the one focusing on the development of a free-trade area, without conceding any significant political sovereignty. When Britain finally joined the EEC (together with Ireland and Denmark), in 1973, after de Gaulle's departure, this economic vision of European integration became predominant for about a decade, downplaying the political dynamics, and in fact slowing down the pace of integration, since the negotiation of national economic interests consumed most of the energy, and budget, of the EEC. The 1973 and 1979 economic crises ushered in the era of euro-pessimism, when most European nations felt deprived of political power by the two superpowers, technologically outclassed by the development of the information technology revolution largely beyond European shores, and economically lagging behind not only the United States but also new Pacific competitors.

The inclusion of Greece, in 1981, and particularly that of Spain and Portugal in 1986, did add breathing space to the European economy (after all, Spain was at the time the eighth largest market economy in the world), and brought in some dynamic new players. But it also added depressed regions, and complicated negotiations in key areas, such as agriculture, fishing, labor legislation, and voting procedures. Yet it was the feeling that Europe could become an economic and technological colony of American and Japanese companies that led to the second major defensive reaction, represented by the Single European Act (SEA) of 1987, setting up steps toward the constitution of a truly unified market by 1992. Economic measures were combined with an emphasis on technology policy, in coordination with the European-wide Eureka program, created at the initiative of the French government, this time under Mitterrand, aimed at counteracting the American technological onslaught that came to be symbolized by the Star Wars program. Furthermore, with Mitterrand softening the French position against supranationality, and Spain (under Felipe Gonzalez) supporting Germany's emphasis on European institutions, broader powers were given to the European Commission; the European Council (representing heads of executives) obtained majority voting procedures in several key domains, and the European Parliament received some limited powers, beyond its previously symbolic role.

The reason why Spain is, probably, together with Germany, the most federalist country is also political: to be anchored in a strong, unified Europe would prevent the country, in the view of Spanish democrats, from returning to the demons of political authoritarianism and cultural isolationism, which have dominated Spanish history for most of the past 500 years. Under the double impulse of southern Europe becoming fully democratic, and France and Germany defending the techno-economic autonomy of Europe in the new global system, the EEC became the EC: the European Community. Once again, an economic measure, the establishment of a truly common market for capital, goods, services, and labor, was, essentially, a measure to further political integration, ceding parts of national sovereignty to ensure some degree of autonomy for the member states in the new global environment. When Thatcher tried to resist, retrenching Britain in outdated state-nationalism, it cost her her job. Most British political and economic elites had understood the opportunity represented by a unified Europe, and had decided to go along, while reserving the possibility of opting out of undesirable policies, such as (for the Conservatives), workers' social rights.

Just when Europe had decided on an accelerated pace of economic integration, and on a moderate pace of political supranationality, the overall geopolitical environment suddenly changed, on November 9, 1989, prompting another round of European construction, to respond to the new political issues arising on the continent. The unexpected unification of Germany had necessarily to affect deeply the unification of Europe, since the neutralization of geopolitical tensions between Germany and its European neighbors was the original goal of European integration. The new, unified Germany, with 80 million people, and 30 percent of the European Community's GNP, represented a decisive force in the European context. Furthermore, the end of the Cold War allowed Germany to be truly independent of the tutelage under which it had been kept for over four decades by the victors of World War II. Thus, it became imperative again, for the whole of Europe, to strengthen the economic and political ties between Germany and the rest of the continent, by reinforcing the European Community, and accommodating German interests within it. The essence of the negotiation amounted to fully integrating the German economy with the rest of Europe, by moving toward a single European currency, the euro, and an independent, European Central Bank. For Germany to sacrifice its hard-won solid deutschmark, and to overcome the resistance of the Bundesbank, three major compensations were necessary:

1   The European economies had to absorb the deflationary policies made necessary by the alignment of monetary policies on the needs and pace of the German economy, particularly after the political decision of setting up the exchange rate between Western and Eastern German currencies on the parity of one mark for one mark, a decision that triggered inflationary pressures in Germany.
2   The European institutions would be reinforced in their powers, moving toward a higher level of supranationality, thus overcoming traditional French resistance, and British rejection, to any project approaching federalism. Again, the push toward further European integration was the only way for Germany to start projecting its weight in the international scene without triggering fear and hostility from most European countries. What Japan has never been able to do – that is, to bury the specters of World War II – is being accomplished by Germany via its full participation in supranational, European institutions.
3   Germany requested an additional concession from the 12 EC members, supported by Britain for its own, different reasons: the

enlargement of the EC toward the north and east. In the case of Austria, Sweden, and Finland, the goal was to balance the European Community with richer countries, and more developed economies, to compensate for the inclusion of southern Europe, with its burden of poor regions. In the case of Eastern Europe, Germany was (and is) trying to share with the rest of Europe the need to stabilize, economically and politically, these unsettled countries, as a way of preventing future turmoil from spilling over into Germany, either through immigration, or through geopolitical conflicts. Thus, Germany could play its traditional role of a Central/Eastern European power, without being suspected of reconstructing Bismarck's imperial dream.

In this regard, it is interesting to observe the persistence of historical perceptions of what a geopolitical threat is. Eastern European countries put all kinds of pressures on Germany to join the European Union, and on the US to join NATO, fundamentally for security reasons: to escape, for ever, from Russian influence. Germany supported their case also with the goal of establishing a territorial glacis between its Eastern border and Russia. And, yet, the terms under which these strategic aims are being discussed seem to be utterly obsolete. First of all, the large-scale wars of the Information Age can be fought, and will be fought, essentially from the air, and through electronic communications and jamming of signals, making meaningless a few more minutes of flight for missiles or aircraft. Besides, Russia in the mid-1990s is no less democratic or less capitalist than the Visegrad countries (Poland, Hungary, Czech Republic, Slovakia), and its foreign policy does not show signs of hostility toward the West in the foreseeable future. Furthermore, except for its status as a nuclear superpower, the state of the Russian military, and the economic weakness of the country, do not allow Russian nationalism to project ambitions of geopolitical power for many years to come. And, yet, centuries of confrontation between Russian and German military power in Eastern Europe, with ferocious battles fought in these lands, have left a mark that goes beyond the transformation of the actual conditions of geopolitical confrontation in Europe today. Because of the fear of Russian power (real or potential), Russia, one of the oldest European cultures, will not become a member of the European Union. Eastern European countries have been taken under the "protection" of NATO, and will be associated with the European Union, under forms that will vary for each country. The enlargement of the European Union to the East, which will probably be delayed until the middle of the first decade of the twenty-first century, will in fact create greater difficulties for effective integration in the EU. This

is because of the vast disparity of economic and technological conditions between ex-statist countries and even the poorest of the EU
members. Furthermore, by pure game theory, the larger the number
of members, the more complex the decision-making process, threatening to paralyze European institutions, thus reducing the European
Union to a free-trade area, with a weak degree of political integration.
This is, in fact, the main reason why Britain supports the process of
enlargement: the larger and more diverse the membership, the lower
the threat to national sovereignty. Hence, the paradox of seeing
Germany (the most federalist country) and Britain (the most anti-
federalist country) supporting enlargement for entirely different
reasons.

The Maastricht Treaty, signed in December 1991, and revised in the
Intergovernmental Conference held in 1996–7, after the 1993 Danish
and French Referenda, and British parliamentary opposition, threatened to reject it, reflected the compromise between these different
interests, and the ambiguity of the institutional formulas aimed at
continuing with the process of integration without openly confronting the fundamental issue of supranationality. In essence, by
deciding the creation of the euro currency, of the European Monetary
Institute, and the harmonization of fiscal policies, Maastricht made
an irreversible commitment to a fully unified European economy,
which will come into existence, if not in 1999, early in the third millennium. By reinforcing the decision-making power of European
institutions, particularly by making it more difficult to form a blocking
minority vote in the European Council, European-wide policies began
to take precedence over national policies, in areas as varied as infrastructure, technology, research, education, environment, regional
development, immigration, justice and police, in a process of political
integration symbolized by the change of name from European
Community to European Union. It is true, however, that foreign
policy, security, and defense are not truly integrated, as they have
been, for a long time, areas of indecision and confusion in the
European Union in spite of rhetorical proclamations of convergence,
as the catastrophic management of the war in Bosnia shows. But, in
reality, NATO is the fundamental security instrument of the
European Union, in close alliance with the United States. The election of a Spanish Socialist leader, Javier Solana, to the post of General
Secretary of NATO, symbolized this transformation of a Cold War
alliance into the operative tool of political/military coordination of
European (and United States) initiatives in the new geopolitical
context. An evolution that seems to sentence to oblivion the Gaullian
dream of a Europe militarily and strategically autonomous as regards
the United States. Britain and Germany never wanted this autonomy,

and none of the European countries' electorates was/is ready to foot the bill, in taxes and military effort, to be a world power, thus making Europe irreversibly dependent on the United States in strategic terms.

Thus, for all its limits and contradictions, the Maastricht Treaty marked an irreversible process of economic and political integration in the European Union, a process by and large confirmed in December 1996 by the "stability (and growth) pact" reached in Dublin. On the other hand, British, Swedish and Danish reluctance to go along with conceding sovereignty through the euro currency, together with the diversity of situation among the countries negotiating their future membership, led to the "Europe *à la carte*"; that is, to different levels of integration depending upon countries and issues. This "variable geometry" of European construction,[4] for all its incoherence, is an essential instrument of the construction itself, as it prevents frontal conflicts among major partners, while allowing European institutions to muddle through the challenges presented by the two processes that, at the same time, further and oppose integration: economic globalization and cultural identity.

Globalization and European Integration

European integration is, at the same time, a reaction to the process of globalization and its most advanced expression. It is also the proof that the global economy is not an undifferentiated system made up of firms and capital flows, but a regionalized structure in which old national institutions and new supranational entities still play a major role in organizing economic competition, and in reaping, or spoiling, the benefits of it. However, it does not follow that globalization is just an ideology. As I argued in volume I, chapter 2, and in volume II, chapter 5, while most economic activity, and most jobs in the world are national, regional, or even local, the core, strategic economic activities are globally integrated in the Information Age through electronically enacted networks of exchange of capital, commodities, and information. It is this global integration that induces and shapes the current process of European unification, on the basis of European institutions historically constituted around predominantly political goals.

The foremost dimension in the globalization process concerns financial markets and currency markets. They are truly global, with the potential of working as a unit in real time, through electronic flows, and the ability to bypass, or overwhelm, government controls.

---

[4]   Pisani-Ferry (1995).

The central decision that anchors the unification of Europe is the creation of the euro in 1999–2002, and the phasing out of national currencies, with the possible exception of the British pound, which will be, in fact, either pegged to the euro or pegged to the US dollar. In the 1990s, it became imperative to keep a minimum degree of monetary and financial stability in the European economies, after two revealing experiences. One was the failed attempt, in the early 1980s, of the first Mitterrand administration in France to embark independently on an expansionary policy, only to be forced to three successive devaluations of the franc, and to impose for a decade, both by Socialist and Conservative administrations, the most stringent budgetary policy of the whole continent. The second experience took place in the two-stage crisis of the European monetary system in the fall of 1992, and in the summer of 1993, when the pound and the lira were forced out of the system, and the peseta and the escudo were forced to devalue, in spite of the large-scale commitment of several European central banks, including the Italian, the British, and the Spanish, whose interventions were swept away by the movement of about US$ 1 trillion in a week of October 1992 in the European currency markets. After such an experience it became clear that, within closely linked economies, the floating of exchange rates between their national currencies constituted a permanent temptation to induce capital market turbulences, since capital flows in the global financial markets were/are in relentless movement to maximize instant opportunities to enhance their return. In this context, the notion of speculation is simply misleading. What we are witnessing is not "speculation," but the domination of financial markets over all other investment opportunities in maximizing profits as a structural feature of the new global, informational economy. This does not mean that banks, or financial institutions, dominate industrial capital, an obsolete formulation that does not do justice to the intertwining of capital movements between different sectors in the networked economy, a theme that I will develop in the conclusion to this book.

The integration of capital markets, and the establishment of a single currency, require the homogenization of macro-economic conditions in the different European economies, including fiscal policies. Budgets may still vary according to national policies, but only by giving priority to some budget items over others within the constraints of similar fiscal prudence. Furthermore, the alignment of European economies on a given set of macro-economic parameters is but one step toward their alignment on international standards, at least vis à vis OECD countries. Indeed, the basic requirements established by the Maastricht Treaty, and made more precise by the Dublin "Stability and Growth Pact" of December 1996, closely mirror the standard criteria imposed by the International Monetary Fund around the world: low budget deficit (less than 3 percent of GDP); relatively low public debt (no more than 60 percent of GDP); low inflation; low long-term interest rates; and stable exchange rate. The harmonization of European economies is inseparable from the harmonization of global macro-economic parameters, to be watched over, and imposed if necessary, by the G-7 annual meetings of the rich countries, and by the International Monetary Fund for the rest of the world. It is in this sense that we can truly speak of globalization of capital, and of the conditions of circulation of capital, not a small matter in a capitalist economy. Down the line, an attempt at stabilizing the exchange rate between the euro, the US dollar, and the yen is to be expected. And since the speed and volume of electronic exchanges in the currency markets will make it impossible to control highly destabilizing movements (as was the case in euro-currency markets), the three dominant currencies will be likely to be pegged to each other in the future, thus eliminating economic national sovereignty for all practical purposes, although national pride will preclude the creation of a global currency, and technical obstacles will make a return to the gold standard unlikely.

There is a second, major dimension of globalization: information technology, at the heart of the productive capacity of economies, and the military might of states. As I mentioned above, in the mid-1980s, the intensification of European integration came partly as a response to a perceived technological deficit *vis à vis* the United States and Japan. In fact, most European technology policy initiatives failed, with the extremely important exception of Airbus and the aeronautics industry in general, predicated more on a successful commercial strategy than on technological excellence. Yet, Europe definitively lost step with US companies in the critical areas of micro-electronics and software, and with Japanese and Korean companies in micro-electronics and advanced consumer electronics (with the exception of Nokia). The policy of "national champions" deteriorated in a wasteful subsidy to oversized, inefficient companies, as the (failed) attempt by the French government to sell Thomson to a consortium led by Daewoo for 1 franc in 1996 dramatically underscored. The European Union's research programs (such as Esprit) were too removed from industrial R&D, and the universities that most benefited from them were not advanced enough to break through new technological paths. Eureka's efforts at stimulating innovative businesses were too limited, and too dependent on a series of bureaucratic rules in establishing multi-country partnership, actually to make a difference in the over-all picture. Telecommunications was the fundamental area in which European companies (particularly Alcatel, Siemens, and Ericsson) had cutting-edge know-how, a powerful industrial base, and well-established market connections. However, their dependence on electronic components and computers also made European technological autonomy unthinkable. So that, by the late 1990s, no serious policy-maker or industrial strategist in Europe thinks about European technological independence in the way that de Gaulle or Mitterrand would have suggested. But the terms of this debate have been made obsolete by the nature of information technology industries in the new, global economy. High technology firms are all dependent on global networks of technological and economic exchange. True, there are some oligopolies, such as Microsoft in PC software, or Intel in advanced micro-electronics. And consumer electronics, with its array of critical technologies, such as HDTV or liquid crystal display, are, by and large, a Japanese (and increasingly Korean) domain. Yet the acceleration of technological change, the need to link up to specific markets, and the strategy of hedging technological bets among different partners (see volume I, chapters 1 and 3) have induced a fully fledged networking of multinational corporations, and medium-level firms, in a model of interpenetration of technology, production, and markets that I have defined as "the network enterprise." Thus, instead of opposing American and Japanese companies to European companies, the globalization of information technology results in the complete entangling of research, R&D, production, and distribution between the advanced areas, firms, and institutions of the United States, the Pacific, and the European Union. Information technology is now asymmetrically globalized, and the relevance of European firms and markets assures that Europe is deeply integrated into the dominant technological networks. For instance, in the next technological wave, genetic engineering, Japan lags way behind, while European laboratories are on the cutting edge of cloning; and while R&D is most dynamic in the United States, some of the advanced American research, and researchers, have been acquired by giant pharmaceutical companies in Switzerland, Germany, and France. Thus, while it is true that American-based and Japanese-based information technology research and production continue to be far more advanced than in Europe, access to new sources of knowledge and application is guaranteed to European firms and institutions by the intertwining of information technology networks. In this sense, the fundamental productive base of Europe in the Information Age is truly globalized.

   The globalization of capital and information technology force us to consider the classic subject of the integration of trade and investment in a new perspective. A major theme of debate about Europe and globalization concerns the potential decline of European competitiveness in a truly global market, under the double squeeze of US and Japanese technology from above, and the lower production costs of newly industrialized countries from below. Yet, in the 1990s, the European Union's balance of trade *vis à vis* the United States and, recently, *vis à vis* Japan is rather equilibrated, year in, year out. There is a deficit in relation to newly industrialized countries, but European imports from these countries are not large enough to induce an overall imbalance. How is this possible? How does Europe, as a whole, keep its competitive position, in spite of higher labor costs, inferior entrepreneurialism, the financial conservatism of firms, and lower level of technological innovation? Part of the answer concerns timing. Markets for goods and services are not truly globalized *yet*. Some traditional sectors, such as textiles or garments, have been hurt by competition from Asia and Latin America. But most European trade is within the European Union, and the lowering of tariffs in strategic sectors, such as automobiles or farm products, still has a long way to go, and will have to operate on a reciprocity basis, in application of the Uruguay Round GATT agreements. But there is something more important: networking of trade and investment across national boundaries. Japanese, American, and Asian Pacific companies are investing and producing in Europe besides exporting from their various platforms. And European firms are producing in Asia and in the United States. As much as one-third of world trade seems to be intra-firm, or intra-network, movements of goods and services, thus largely invisible to trade statistics (see volume I, chapter 2). And European companies, when faced with decreasing competitiveness for exports from their European bases, tend to invest in America, the Asian Pacific, and Latin America, both to serve these markets and to export back to Europe from their offshore production sites, such as Singapore. Thus, in 1994–6, while German industrial companies sharply reduced their investments in Germany, they went on an investment spree around the world, particularly in Asia. For instance, in 1995, investment abroad by German companies almost doubled, reaching a record US$ 32 billion, while investment fell in Germany. Thus, it is the global movement of investment, and the constitution of trans-border production networks, both in manufacturing and services, that characterize the process of globalization, rather than the constitution of a single, global market.

While globalization does characterize the movement of capital, technology, and productive investment in the Europe of the 1990s, it does not seem to affect the movement of labor excessively. As I showed in volume I, chapter 4, the proportion of foreign population *legally recorded* in France or Britain has not substantially increased since the mid-1980s, and it remains below 5 percent across the European Union, with the exception of Germany, after its one-time absorption of Eastern European refugees during the crumbling of statism. The catastrophic predictions about 25 million Russians emigrating to Western Europe have translated into a few hundred thousands, not millions, who have emigrated in the past five years, in spite of an extreme deterioration in living conditions. Famine, war, and devastation of Africa have increased African immigration to Europe by hundreds of thousands, yet nothing comparable to the millions of foreign workers who arrived in France, Germany, Holland, Switzerland, Belgium, and England during the years of high growth in the 1960s. While Fourth World poverty is indeed increasing *illegal immigration* in desperate conditions, particularly in the entry-point countries, such as Italy and Spain, strict immigration controls, widespread xenophobia, lack of immigrant social networks, and, above all, lack of job opportunities, have considerably limited the much-feared waves of immigrations from south and east to the European Union. What has really happened is that some countries that did not have immigrants, such as Spain and Italy, now have several hundred thousands, and, most importantly, that the foreign-born population in Europe is having children at a much higher rate than the native population, thus making Europe irreversibly multi-ethnic. But ethnic diversity does not equate with globalization of the labor force.

However, if there is not a global labor force, there is a certain degree of globalization of working conditions. That is, with increased mobility of capital, and cross-border networking of trade and investment, European firms may choose to invest in other countries where labor costs are lower, unions are less resilient, and, more importantly, flexibility of labor is the rule. They increasingly tend to do so. The historical limit to this practice was the lower productivity level, and lower skills of the labor force, leading to reduced quality and reliability of production. Conditions have dramatically changed because, with new technologies and with the diffusion of industrialization and advanced services, a number of countries offer an equivalent or superior labor force at lower cost (not only the Asian Pacific, but the United States or the UK *vis à vis* other European countries). Thus, the process of industrialization throughout the world, the networking of firms, and the interpenetration of markets offer the opportunity for European firms to expand elsewhere to take on the global market, rather than digging themselves into their home turfs. It follows, tendentially, relative disinvestment in Europe *vis à vis* other areas of the world, particularly in manufacturing. This trend is at the root of growing unemployment rates in the European Union, in clear contrast with the substantial growth of employment in the United States, and in the Asian Pacific, in the 1990s.

There are two additional dimensions of globalization that directly affect the process of European unification, which I simply mention here for the sake of coherence of the argument, without repeating it, since their analysis can be found elsewhere in this book. On the one hand, the globalization and interdependence of communication media (see volume I, chapter 5, and volume II, chapter 5) create a European audiovisual space that fundamentally transforms European culture and information, in a process, by and large, independent of the nation-states. On the other hand, the rise of a global criminal economy (see chapter 3 of this volume) finds a wonderful opportunity to prosper in a half-integrated institutional system, such as the one currently characterizing the European Union. Indeed, national controls are easily bypassed by the new mobility of capital, people, and information, while European police controls are slow to develop, precisely because of the resistance of national bureaucracies to give up their monopoly of power, thus inducing a historical no man's land where crime, power, and money link with each other.

The shaping of European unification by this multidimensional globalization has profound and lasting consequences for European societies. Probably the most important one is the difficulty of preserving the European welfare state in its present form. This is because the mobility of capital, and the networking of production, create the conditions for investment to move around the world to areas of lower social costs. But it is also because the search for flexibility in the labor markets, and the process of disinvestment in Europe, reduces the employment basis on which the fiscal stability of the welfare state relies. Without job creation, and without a relative equalization of social costs in the internationally networked system, it is difficult to see how a comprehensive welfare state can be maintained in Europe, under the conditions of relatively similar, or lower, productivity *vis à vis* other areas of production (for example, the United States). Indeed, the UK, under Thatcher and Major, embarked on a major retrenchment of the welfare state from the 1980s, and, in the mid-1990s, Germany, France, Spain, and (to a lesser extent) Italy have at the top of their agenda the significant shrinkage of the welfare state. If the UK experience is of any value, not to speak of the United States, a dramatic increase in inequality, poverty, and social exclusion will follow. Ultimately, political legitimacy will be undermined, since the welfare state is one of its pillars.[5]

A similar process of relative equalization of working arrangements between European and American/Asian economies is taking place in the labor markets, as the push for flexibility and networking, characteristic of informational capitalism, is clearly on in most European

---

[5]   Castells (1996); Navarro (1996).

countries. According to a 1996 report from the German *Länder* of Bavaria and Saxony, it was projected that by 2015 about 50 percent of German workers would not hold a stable, full-time job.[6] If such were to be the case, the entire European social fabric would be transformed.

I do not imply, however, that these consequences of globalization on European integration, and on European societies, are inexorable. There is, as Alain Touraine argues, an ideology of globalization that considers it as a natural force, reducing societies to economies, economies to markets, and markets to financial flows.[7] This is simply a crude rationalization of strictly capitalist interests, often defended with more vehemence by neo-liberal ideologists than by capitalists themselves, since many firms have a worldview broad enough to understand their social responsibility, and the need to preserve social stability. But Alain Touraine also points out that, too often, the opposition to globalization in Europe, and particularly in France, is carried out by social actors who defend narrow, corporatist interests, linked to an obsolete public sector subsidized by the taxpayer, without gaining much benefit from it.[8] However, together with the corporatism of privileged sectors of workers, such as Air France pilots, there is a widespread popular reaction, in France, and elsewhere, against the shrinkage and potential dismantlement of the welfare state, and against flexibility in the labor markets at the expense of workers' stable lives, an opposition often expressed in terms of the people against the politicians, the nation against the European state.[9] While the sources of this opposition are, to a great extent, rooted in social and economic interests, they tend to express themselves in the language of nationalism, and in the defense of cultural identity against the impersonal forces of global markets and the diktats of Eurocrats. The political debate and the social conflicts around the ways to control, and guide, the transformation of European societies throughout their gradual integration into an increasingly globalized economy cannot be reduced to the elementary opposition between a-historical neo-liberalism and archaic public bureaucratism. In its reality, this debate is expressed in the language of the Information Age – that is in the opposition between the power of flows and the power of identity.

[6] Touraine (1996c).
[7] Touraine (1996b).
[8] Touraine (1996b, c).
[9] Touraine et al. (1996).

Cultural Identity and European Unification

The whirlwind of globalization is triggering defensive reactions around the world, often organized around the principles of national and territorial identity (volume II, chapters 1 and 2). In Europe, this perceived threat is materialized in the expanding powers of the European Union. Widespread citizen hostility to the process of unification is reinforced by the discourse of most political leaders presenting the European Union as the necessary adaptation to globalization, with the corollary of economic adjustment, flexibility of labor markets, and shrinkage of the welfare state, as the *sine qua non* conditions for the integration of each country in the European Union.[10] Thus, since the acceleration of the integration process has coincided with stagnation of living standards, rising unemployment, and greater social inequality in the 1990s, significant sections of the European population tend to affirm their nations against their states, seen as captives of European supranationality. It is revealing that, with the partial exception of Britain, the political establishment of all countries, both on the center-right and on the center-left, are unquestionably pro-European, while most public opinions are sharply divided, at best.[11]

> Debate over European integration is not a matter of *raison d'état* but rather a matter of *raison de nation*. Whether European integration is allowed to proceed will depend on the ability of nations to secure their own survival. A nation will only allow integration when it is secure that its national identity will not be threatened, that it may even be strengthened by its exposure to different identities. If a nation feels that it is only able to survive through a close correspondence with a state that is sovereign and independent, if it does not believe that the state can be integrated while its culture is reproduced, it will block further integration.[12]

This insecurity is enhanced by the growing multi-ethnicity and multiculturalism of European societies, which trigger racism and xenophobia as people affirm their identity both against a supranational state and against cultural diversification.[13] The utilization of this insecurity by political demagogues, such as Le Pen in France, amplifies the expression of cultural nationalism throughout the political system and the mass media. The linkage, in the public mind,

[10]   Touraine (1996b).
[11]   Alonso Zaldivar (1996).
[12]   Waever (1995: 16).
[13]   Wieviorka (1993).

between crime, violence, terrorism, and ethnic minorities/ foreigners/the other leads to a dramatic surge in European xeno- phobia, precisely at the high point of European universalism. This is, in fact, in historical continuity with the previous unification of medieval Europe around Christianity – that is, an intolerant, religious boundary, exclusive of infidels, pagans, and heretics.[14]

There is an additional, fundamental source of people's distrust *vis à vis* European institutions: what has come to be labeled "the demo- cratic deficit." While significant powers affecting the livelihood of citizens have been transferred to the European Union (mainly to the Council of Ministers, representing European nation-states), and some essential economic policy decisions have even been made "automatic," under the control, in the near future, of the European Central Bank, the capacity of citizens to influence these decisions has been considerably reduced. Between the act of choosing, every four years, from two usually unsatisfactory options of government, and the daily management of a complex, pan-European system, there is so much distance that citizens feel definitively left out. There are prac- tically no effective channels of citizen participation in the European institutions. And moreover, as Borja pointedly writes, there are no "European conflicts."[15] Indeed, the democratic process is not only based on representation and consensus building, but in democrati- cally enacted conflicts between different social actors vying for their specific interests. Other than farmers littering the streets of Brussels with their produce (still unhappy in spite of being entirely subsidized by all other Europeans, and, indirectly, by most of the developing world), the expressions of transnational collective mobilization aimed at European decision-making are negligible. The apprentice- ship of European citizenship is absent, to a large extent because European institutions are usually happy to live in their secluded world of technocratic agencies and deal-making councils of ministers. For instance, the possibilities of using networks of computer-medi- ated communication for dissemination of information and citizen participation have been all but ignored.[16] Thus, confronted with a decline in democracy and citizen participation, at a time of global- ization of the economy and Europeanization of politics, citizens retrench in their countries, and increasingly affirm their nations. Nationalism, not federalism, is the concomitant development of European integration. And only if the European Union is able to handle, and accommodate, nationalism will it survive as a political

[14] Fontana (1994).
[15] Borja (1996: 12).
[16] HLEGIS (1997).

construction. As Waever, based on Anthony Smith's insights, proposes, while European institutions may adopt the French version of national identity, built around political identity, European nations may be heading toward the adoption of the German version of national identity, based on a linguistically united *Volk*.[17] As paradoxical as it may sound, it is possible that only the institutional and social articulation of both identity principles can make possible the development of a European Union that is something else than a common market.

But if nations, independently from the state, become the sources of identity-based legitimacy for the European construction, the issue arises of which nations. It seems relatively clear in the case of France: after the successful extermination of plural national identities by the French Revolution on behalf of the universal principle of democratic citizenship, when French people react against Europe they do so in the name of "La France," in terms that would be equally understood by General de Gaulle and the French Communists. For different reasons, it is also clear in Germany, where the ethnic purity of the nation, even among Kazakhstan's Germans, remains untainted by the millions of immigrants, and sons of immigrants, that will never be German. The greatest fear of Eurocrats is that this Germanity may find an eternal expression in the deutschmark, and that in the event of a political crisis, the German constitutional court will rule against the European institutions, in application of the principle of *Superrevisionsinstanz*, that it affirmed in its landmark verdict of October 12, 1993.

But the appeal to national identity is more complicated in other countries, based on pluri-national states, as is the case in Spain, in the United Kingdom, and Belgium. Would *Catalunya* or Scotland affirm their identity against the European institutions, or, on the contrary, in favor of the European Union, bypassing, rather than opposing, the Spanish or British governments?[18] Furthermore, the affirmation of a "Padania" identity in northern Italy has been superficially ridiculed because of the extravagant character of Bossi, the leader of the *Lega Nord*. And yet, while it is true that the foundation of this identity is essentially economic, and even more narrowly fiscal, it also has historical roots in the artificial integration of Italy in the late nineteenth century, and its dynamics may go well beyond the political anecdote. Not that Padania exists, but in linguistic, cultural, social, and political terms, it is highly doubtful whether Italy existed until well into the twentieth century, with the Mezzogiorno, even today, having very little

[17]   Waever (1995: 23).
[18]   Keating (1995).

in common with Lombardy, Piedmont or Emilia-Romagna.[19] The retrenchment around the principle of national identity is strengthening the nation-states against the European Union in some countries, while reinforcing the European Union against the current nation-states in others.

The search for identity as an antidote to economic globalization and political disfranchisement also permeates below the level of the nation-state, adding new dynamism to regions and cities around Europe. As Orstrom Moller writes, the future European model may be made up of the articulation of economic internationalization and cultural decentralization.[20] Regional and local governments are playing a major role in revitalizing democracy in the 1990s, and opinion polls show a higher degree of citizen trust in these lower levels of government as compared with national and supranational levels. Cities have become critical actors in establishing strategies of economic development, in negotiated interaction with internationalized firms. And both cities and regions have established European networks that coordinate initiatives, and learn from each other, putting into action a novel principle of cooperation and competition, whose practice we have described elsewhere.[21] On the light side, an illustration of this double dynamic of local identity and European networking, which I consider to be extremely important, is the structuring of professional sports, such as football or basketball, in the past decade. As everybody knows, the local team is an essential rallying point for people's identity. While national competitions continue to be played, maximum attention is given to European competitions (of which there are three for football, for instance), so that the reward for teams in the national competition is to become "European," a goal that many teams can reach, in contrast with only a few three decades ago. At the same time, the opening of labor markets for European players, and the mass migration to Europe of players from other countries, means that a significant proportion of players in the local team are foreigners. The result is that people mobilize around the identity of their city, as represented by a group of largely foreign professional players competing in various European leagues. It is through this kind of basic life mechanisms that the real Europe is coming into existence – by sharing experience on the basis of meaningful, palpable identity. How, then, can unification proceed between the high winds of globalization and the warm hearth of locality?

[19] Ginsborg (1994).
[20] Orstrom Moller (1995).
[21] Borja and Castells (1997).

The Institutionalization of Europe: the Network State

When we reflect on the contradictory visions and interests sur-rounding the unification of Europe, and we consider the lack of enthusiasm among citizens of most countries, it seems miraculous that the process of integration is as advanced as it is at the turn of the millennium. Part of the explanation for this unlikely success can be found in the fact that the European Union does not supplant the existing nation-states but, on the contrary, is a fundamental instru-ment for their survival on the condition of conceding shares of sovereignty in exchange for a greater say in world, and domestic, affairs in the age of globalization. But this convergence of interests still had to find an institutional expression to be operational. It found it in a complex, and changing, geometry of European institutions that combines the control of decision-making by national governments (the Council of Ministers, the rotating presidency, the executive summits every six months), the management of common European business by a competent, if unpopular, euro-technocracy, directed by the politically appointed European Commission, and the symbolic expressions of legitimacy in the European Parliament, the Court of Justice, and the Court of Auditors.

The relentless negotiations within this set of institutions, and between the national actors pursuing their strategies in the frame-work of these institutions, may look cumbersome and inefficient. Yet it is precisely this indeterminacy and this complexity that make it possible to accommodate in the European Union various interests and changing policies, not only from different countries, but from the different political orientations of parties elected to government. The process becomes even more complicated with the introduction of a single currency, and with the process of enlargement. Some countries, like Britain and Denmark, may exercise their opt-out clause. Others will negotiate exceptions to the general rules. And because of increasing disparity between the conditions of countries within the Union, voting procedures will change, depending on issues. On the one hand, a majority vote in the Council of Ministers will make it possible for large countries to go ahead with strategic decisions without being paralyzed by the specific interests of one country, or of a minority coalition. On the other hand, the price to be paid for this reinforcement of majority powers will be flexibility in the application of Union decisions to some countries in some areas and for some time. As Alonso Zaldivar writes, under this system, the federal and confederal logics are not mutually exclusive:

For instance, in matters of defense, police, and public spending, the confederal or intergovernmental [logic] could take precedence, while in monetary policy, trade, residence, and circulation of capital, goods, and people, the functioning of the Union would be closer to federalism or supranationality. Other matters, such as foreign policy, environment, taxes, and immigration would occupy an intermediate position. The future, enlarged European Union must be less uniform and more flexible . . . It is possible that the organigram of such an institution will be closer to a network than to a tree, and political theory still does not have a simple term adequate to this kind of configuration, but this is not an obstacle to building it. However, it will not be enough that enlightened bureaucrats conceive this institution: it will also be necessary for the citizens to accept it.[22]

The key element in gradually establishing the European Union's legitimacy, without jeopardizing its policy-making capacity, is the ability of its institutions to link up with subnational levels of government – regional and local – by a deliberate extension of the subsidiarity principle, under which the Union institutions only take charge of decisions that lower levels of government, including nation-states, cannot assume effectively. The Committee of the Regions, an advisory body composed of 222 members representing regional and local governments from all the countries of the Union, is the most direct institutional expression of this concern. The real process of relegitimization of Europe appears to be taking place in the burgeoning of local and regional initiatives, in economic development, as well as in cultural expressions, and social rights, which link up horizontally with each other, while also linking up with European programs directly or through their respective national governments.[23]

Reflecting on the growing complexity and flexibility of European political process, Keohane and Hoffman propose the notion that the European Union "is essentially organized as a network that involves the pooling and sharing of sovereignty rather than the transfer of sovereignty to a higher level."[24] This analysis, developed and theorized by Waever,[25] brings European unification closer to the characterization of institutional neo-medievalism; that is, a plurality of overlapping powers, along the lines suggested years ago by Hedley

[22]   Alonso Zaldivar (1996: 352–3); my translation.
[23]   Borja (1992).
[24]   Keohane and Hoffman (1991b: 13).
[25]   Waever (1995).

Bull, and echoed by a number of European analysts, such as Alain Minc.[26] Although historians may object to such a parallel, the image illustrates powerfully the new form of state epitomized by European institutions: *the network state. It is a state characterized by the sharing of authority (that is, in the last resort, the capacity to impose legitimized violence) along a network.* A network, by definition, has nodes, not a center. Nodes may be of different sizes, and may be linked by asymmetrical relationships in the network, so that the network state does not preclude the existence of political inequalities among its members. Indeed, all governmental institutions are not equal in the European network. Not only national governments still concentrate much decision-making capacity, but there are important differences of power between nation-states, although the hierarchy of power varies in different dimensions: Germany is the hegemonic economic power, but Britain and France hold far greater military power, and at least equal technological capacity. However, regardless of these asymmetries, the various nodes of the European network state are interdependent on each other, so that no node, even the most powerful, can ignore the others, even the smallest, in the decision-making process. If some political nodes do so, the whole system is called into question. This is the difference between a political network and a centered political structure.

Available evidence, and recent debates in political theory, seem to suggest that the network state, with its geometrically variable sovereignty, is the response of political systems to the challenges of globalization. And the European Union may be the clearest manifestation to date of this emerging form of state, probably characteristic of the Information Age.

European Identity or European Project?

In the end, however, the unification of Europe will probably not be fulfilled only by skillful political engineering. In the context of democratic societies, Europe will only unify, at various degrees and under forms yet to emerge, if its citizens want it. On the basis of the exploration of social trends presented in the three volumes of this book, it is unlikely that this acceptance will take place exclusively on the basis of instrumental interests of managing globalization, particularly when this management will certainly hurt considerable sections of the population. If meaning is linked to identity, and if identity remains exclusively national, regional or local, European integration may not

[26]   Bull (1977); Minc (1993).

last beyond the limits of a common market, parallel to free-trade zones constituted in other areas of the world. European unification, in a long-term perspective, requires European identity.

However, the notion of European identity is problematic at best. Because of the separation of Church and state, and the tepid religiosity of most Europeans, it cannot be built around Christianity, as was the case historically, even if the widespread anti-Muslim reaction signals the historical persistence of the Crusader spirit. It cannot be built around democracy: first, because democratic ideals are shared around the world; secondly, precisely because democracy is in crisis in its current dependency on the nation-state (see Volume II, chapter 6). It will be difficult, and dramatic, to build it around ethnicity at a time when Europe is becoming increasingly diverse in ethnic terms. It is by definition impossible to build it on national identity, albeit if the preservation of national identity will be necessary for European unification to proceed. And it will not be easy to defend a European economic identity ("Fortress Europe") as core economic activities become globalized, and cross-border production networks articulate the European Union with the rest of the world, starting with Eastern Europe and South-East Asia. Do most people feel European – besides feeling French, Spanish, or Catalan – according to opinion polls in the 1990s? Yes. Do they know what it means? In their majority, not. Do *you* know? Even with the euro in circulation (2000?, 2005?), its extra-economic meaning will be lost unless there is a broader cultural transformation of European societies.

So, by and large, there is no European identity. But it could be built, not in contradiction, but complementary to national, regional, and local identities. It would take a process of social construction that I have identified, in volume II, as *project identity*; that is, a blueprint of social values and institutional goals that appeal to a majority of citizens without excluding anybody, in principle. That was what democracy, or the nation-state, historically represented at the dawn of the industrial era. What could be the content of such a European identity project in the Information Age? I have my preferences, as everybody else, but they should not interfere with our exploration of history in the making. What are the elements that *actually appear in the discourse, and practice, of social actors opposing globalization and disfranchisement without regressing to communalism?*[27] The defense of the welfare state, of social solidarity, of stable employment, and of workers' rights; the concern about universal human rights and the plight of the Fourth World; the reaffirmation of democracy, and its extension to citizen participation at the local and regional level; the

[27] Touraine (1997)

vitality of historically/territorially rooted cultures, often expressed in language, not surrendering to the culture of real virtuality. Most European citizens would probably support these values. Their affirmation, for instance in the defense of the welfare state and stable employment against the pressures of globalization, would take extraordinary changes in the economy and in institutions. But this is precisely what an identity project is: not a utopian proclamation of dreams, but a struggle to impose alternative ways of economic development, sociability, and governance. There are embryos of a European project identity. And, probably, only if these embryos find political expression will the process of European unification ultimately be accomplished.

Conclusion:
Making Sense of our World

This means to say that scarcely
have we landed into life
than we come as if new-born;
let us not fill our mouths
with so many faltering names,
with so many sad formalities,
with so many pompous letters,
with so much of yours and mine,
with so much signing of papers.

I have in mind to confuse things,
unite them, make them new-born,
mix them up, undress them,
until all light in the world
has the oneness of the ocean,
a generous, vast wholeness,
a crackling, living fragrance.

Pablo Neruda, fragment of "Too Many Names," *Estravagario*

This is the general conclusion of the three-volume book, *The Information Age: Economy, Society, and Culture.* I have tried to avoid repetition. For definition of theoretical concepts used in this conclusion (for example, informationalism, or relationships of production), please refer to the Prologue of the book in volume I. See also the conclusion of volume I for an elaboration of the concept of network society, and the conclusion of volume II for an analysis of the relationships between cultural identity, social movements, and politics.

Genesis of a New World[1]

A new world is taking shape in this end of millennium. It originated in the historical coincidence, around the late 1960s and mid-1970s, of three *independent* processes: the information technology revolution; the economic crisis of both capitalism and statism, and their subsequent restructuring; and the blooming of cultural social movements, such as libertarianism, human rights, feminism, and environmentalism. The interaction between these processes, and the reactions they triggered, brought into being a new dominant social structure, the network society; a new economy, the informational/global economy; and a new culture, the culture of real virtuality. The logic embedded in this economy, this society, and this culture underlies social action and institutions throughout an interdependent world.

A few, decisive features of this new world have been identified in the investigation presented in the three volumes of this book. The information technology revolution induced the emergence of informationalism, as the material foundation of a new society. Under informationalism, the generation of wealth, the exercise of power, and the creation of cultural codes came to depend on the technological capacity of societies and individuals, with information technology as the core of this capacity. Information technology became the indispensable tool for the effective implementation of

---

[1] In discussions in my seminars in recent years a recurrent question comes up so often that I think it would be useful to take it to the reader. It is the question of newness. What is new about all this? Why is this a new world? I do believe that there is a new world emerging in this end of millennium. In the three volumes of this book I have tried to provide information and ideas in support of this statement. Chips and computers are new; ubiquitous, mobile telecommunications are new; genetic engineering is new; electronically integrated, global financial markets working in real time are new; an inter-linked capitalist economy embracing the whole planet, and not only some of its segments, is new; a majority of the urban labor force in knowledge and information processing in advanced economies is new; a majority of urban population in the planet is new; the demise of the Soviet Empire, the fading away of communism, and the end of the Cold War are new; the rise of the Asian Pacific as an equal partner in the global economy is new; the widespread challenge to patriarchalism is new; the universal consciousness on ecological preservation is new; and the emergence of a network society, based on a space of flows, and on timeless time, is historically new. *Yet this is not the point I want to make.* My main statement is that it does not really matter if you believe that this world, or any of its features, is new or not. My analysis stands by itself. This is our world, the world of the Information Age. And this is my analysis of this world, which must be understood, used, judged, by itself, by its capacity, or incapacity, to identify and explain the phenomena that we observe and experience, regardless of its newness. After all, if nothing is new under the sun, why bother to try to investigate, think, write, and read about it?

processes of socio-economic restructuring. Particularly important was its role in allowing the development of networking as a dynamic, self-expanding form of organization of human activity. This prevailing, networking logic transforms all domains of social and economic life.

The crisis of models of economic development for both capitalism and statism prompted their parallel restructuring from the mid-1970s onwards. In capitalist economies, firms and governments proceeded with a number of measures and policies that, together, led to a new form of capitalism. It is characterized by globalization of core economic activities, organizational flexibility, and greater power for management in its relation to labor. Competitive pressures, flexibility of work, and weakening of organized labor led to the retrenchment of the welfare state, the cornerstone of the social contract in the industrial era. New information technologies played a decisive role in facilitating the emergence of this rejuvenated, flexible capitalism, by providing the tools for networking, distant communication, storing/processing of information, coordinated individualization of work, and simultaneous concentration and decentralization of decision-making.

In this global, interdependent economy, new competitors, firms and countries came to claim an increasing share of production, trade, capital, and labor. The emergence of a powerful, competitive Pacific economy, and the new processes of industrialization and market expansion in various areas of the world, broadened the scope and scale of the global economy, establishing a multicultural foundation of economic interdependence. Networks of capital, labor, information, and markets linked up, through technology, valuable functions, people, and localities around the world, while switching off from their networks those populations and territories deprived of value and interest for the dynamics of global capitalism. There followed the social exclusion and economic irrelevance of segments of societies, of areas of cities, of regions, and of entire countries, constituting what I call "the Fourth World." The desperate attempt by some of these social groups and territories to link up with the global economy, to escape marginality, led to what I call "the perverse connection," when organized crime around the world took advantage of their plight to foster the development of a global criminal economy. It aims at satisfying forbidden desire and supplying outlawed commodities to endless demand from affluent societies and individuals.

The restructuring of statism proved to be more difficult, particularly for the dominant statist society in the world, the Soviet Union, at the center of a broad network of statist countries and parties. Soviet statism proved incapable of assimilating informationalism, thus stalling economic growth and decisively weakening its military machine, the ultimate source of power in a statist regime. Their awareness of stagnation and decline led some Soviet leaders, from Andropov to Gorbachev, to attempt a restructuring of the system. In order to overcome inertia and resistance from the party/state, reformist leadership opened up information, and called upon civil society for support. The powerful expression of national/cultural identities, and the people's demands for democracy, could not be easily channeled into a pre-scripted reform program. The pressure of events, tactical errors, political incompetence, and the internal split of statist apparatuses led to the sudden collapse of Soviet Communism, in one of the most extraordinary events in political history. With it, the Soviet Empire crumbled also, while statist regimes in its global area of influence were decisively weakened. So ended, in what amounted to an instant by historical standards, the revolutionary experiment that dominated the twentieth century. This was also the end of the Cold War between capitalism and statism, which had divided the world, determined geopolitics, and haunted our lives for the past half-century.

In its communist incarnation, statism ended there, for all practical purposes, although China's brand of statism took a more complicated, subtle way toward its historical exit, as I tried to show in chapter 4 of this volume. For the sake of coherence of the argument presented here, let me remind the reader that the Chinese state in the 1990s, while fully controlled by the Communist party, is organized around China's incorporation into global capitalism, on the basis of a nationalist project represented by the state. This Chinese nationalism with socialist characteristics is quickly moving away from statism into global capitalism, while trying to find a way to adapt to informationalism, without an open society.

After the demise of statism as a system, in less than a decade capitalism thrives throughout the world, and it deepens its penetration of countries, cultures, and domains of life. In spite of a highly diversified social and cultural landscape, for the first time in history, the whole planet is organized around a largely common set of economic rules. It is, however, a different kind of capitalism than the one formed during the Industrial Revolution, or the one that emerged from the 1930s Depression and World War II, under the form of economic Keynesianism and social welfarism. It is a hardened form of capitalism in its goals, but is incomparably more flexible than any of its predecessors in its means. It is informational capitalism, relying on innovation-induced productivity, and globalization-oriented competitiveness to generate wealth, and to appropriate it selectively. It is, more than ever, embedded in culture and tooled by technology. But, this time, both culture and technology depend on the ability of knowledge and information to act upon knowledge and information, in a recurrent network of globally connected exchanges.

Societies, however, are not just the result of technological and economic transformation, nor can social change be limited to institutional crises and adaptations. At about the same time that these developments started to take place in the late 1960s, powerful social movements exploded almost simultaneously all over the industrialized world, first in the United States and France, then in Italy, Germany, Spain, Japan, Brazil, Mexico, Czechoslovakia, with echoes and reactions in numerous other countries. As a participant in these social movements (I was an assistant professor of sociology at the Nanterre campus of the University of Paris in 1968), I bear witness to their libertarianism. While they often adopted Marxist ideological expressions in their militant vanguards, they had little to do with Marxism or, for that matter, with the working class. They were essentially cultural movements, wanting to change life rather than seizing power. They intuitively knew that access to the institutions of state co-opts the movement, while the construction of a new, revolutionary state perverts the movement. Their ambitions encompassed a multi-dimensional reaction to arbitrary authority, a revolt against injustice, and a search for personal experimentation. While often enacted by students, they were not by any means student movements, since they permeated throughout society, particularly among the young people, and their values reverberated in all spheres of life. Of course, they were politically defeated, because, as most utopian movements in history, they never pretended to political victory. But they faded away with high historical productivity, with many of their ideas, and some of their dreams, germinating in societies and blossoming as cultural innovations, to which politicians and ideologues will have to relate for generations to come. From these movements sprang the ideas that would be the source of environmentalism, of feminism, of the endless defense of human rights, of sexual liberation, of ethnic equality, and of grassroots democracy. The cultural movements of the 1960s and early 1970s, in their affirmation of individual autonomy against both capital and the state, placed a renewed stress on the politics of identity. These ideas paved the way for the building of cultural communes in the 1990s, when the legitimacy crisis of institutions of the industrial era blurred the meaning of democratic politics.

The social movements were not reactions to the economic crisis. Indeed, they surged in the late 1960s, in the heyday of sustained growth and full employment, as a critique of the "consumption society." While they induced some workers' strikes, as in France, and helped the political left, as in Italy, they were not a part of the right/left politics of the industrial era that had been organized around the class cleavages of capitalism. And while they coexisted, broadly speaking, with the information technology revolution, technology was largely absent from either the values or critiques of most movements, if we except some calls against de-humanizing machinism, and their opposition to nuclear power (an old technology in the Information Age). But if these social movements were primarily cultural, and independent of economic and technological transformations, they did have an impact on economy, technology, and ensuing restructuring processes. Their libertarian spirit considerably influenced the movement toward individualized, decentralized uses of technology. Their sharp separation from traditional labor politics contributed to the weakening of organized labor, thus facilitating capitalist restructuring. Their cultural openness stimulated technological experimentation with symbol manipulation, constituting a new world of imaginary representations that would evolve toward the culture of real virtuality. Their cosmopolitanism, and internationalism, set up the intellectual bases for an interdependent world. And their abhorrence of the state undermined the legitimacy of democratic rituals, in spite of the fact that some leaders of the movement went on to renew political institutions. Moreover, by refusing the orderly transmission of eternal codes and established values, such as patriarchalism, religious traditionalism, and nationalism, the 1960s movements set the stage for a fundamental split in societies all over the world: on the one hand, active, culturally self-defined elites, constructing their own values on the basis of their experience; on the other hand, increasingly uncertain, insecure social groups, deprived of information, resources, and power, digging their trenches of resistance precisely around those eternal values that had been decried by the rebellious 1960s.

The revolution of technology, the restructuring of economy, and the critique of culture converged toward a historical redefinition of the relationships of production, power, and experience, on which societies are based.

A New Society

A new society emerges when and if a structural transformation can be observed in the relationships of production, in the relationships of power, and in the relationships of experience. These transformations lead to an equally substantial modification of social forms of space and time, and to the emergence of a new culture.

Information and analyses presented in the three volumes of this book provide a strong indication of such a multidimensional transformation in this end of millennium. I shall synthesize the main features of transformation for each dimension, referring the reader to the respective chapters covering each subject for empirical materials that lend some credibility to the conclusions presented here.

Relationships of production have been transformed, both socially and technically. To be sure, they are capitalist, but of a historically different brand of capitalism, which I call informational capitalism. For the sake of clarity, I shall consider, in sequence, the new characteristics of the production process, of labor, and of capital. Then, the transformation of class relationships can be made visible.

Productivity and competitiveness are the commanding processes of the informational/global economy. Productivity essentially stems from innovation, competitiveness from flexibility. Thus, firms, regions, countries, economic units of all kinds, gear their production relationships to maximize innovation and flexibility. Information technology, and the cultural capacity to use it, are essential in the performance of the new production function. In addition, a new kind of organization and management, aiming at simultaneous adaptability and coordination, becomes the basis for the most effective operating system, exemplified by what I label the network enterprise.

Under this new system of production, labor is redefined in its role as producer, and sharply differentiated according to workers' characteristics. A major difference refers to what I call generic labor versus self-programmable labor. The critical quality in differentiating these two kinds of labor is education, and the capacity of accessing higher levels of education; that is, embodied knowledge and information. The concept of education must be distinguished from skills. Skills can be quickly made obsolete by technological and organizational change. Education (as distinct from the warehousing of children and students) is the process by which people, that is labor, acquire the capability constantly to redefine the necessary skills for a given task, and to access the sources for learning these skills. Whoever is educated, in the proper organizational environment, can reprogram him/herself toward the endlessly changing tasks of the production process. On the other hand, generic labor is assigned a given task, with no reprogramming capability, and it does not presuppose the embodiment of information and knowledge beyond the ability to receive and execute signals. These "human terminals" can, of course, be replaced by machines, or by any other body around the city, the country, or the world, depending on business decisions. While they are collectively indispensable to the production process, they are individually expendable, as value added by each one of them is a small fraction of what is generated by and for the organization. Machines, and generic labor from various origins and locations, cohabit the same subservient circuits of the production system.

Flexibility, enacted organizationally by the network enterprise, requires networkers, and flextimers, as well as a wide array of working arrangements, including self-employment and reciprocal subcontracting. The variable geometry of these working arrangements leads to the coordinated decentralization of work and to the individualization of labor.

The informational/global economy is capitalist; in fact, more so than any other economy in history. But capital is as transformed as labor is in this new economy. The rule is still production for the sake of profit, and for the private appropriation of profit, on the basis of property rights – which is the essence of capitalism. But how does this appropriation of profit take place? Who are the capitalists? Three different levels must be considered in answering this fundamental question. Only the third level is specific to informational capitalism.

The first level concerns *the holders of property rights*. These are, basically, of three kinds: (a) shareholders of companies, a group in which institutional, anonymous shareholders are increasingly predominant and whose investment and disinvestment decisions are often governed solely by short-term financial considerations; (b) family owners, still a relevant form of capitalism, particularly in the Asian Pacific; and (c) individual entrepreneurs, owners of their own means of production (their brains being their main asset), risk-takers, and proprietors of their own profit-making. This last category, which was fundamental to the origins of industrial capitalism and then became largely phased out by corporate industrialism, has made a remarkable comeback under informational capitalism, using the pre-eminence of innovation and flexibility as the essential features of the new production system.

The second level of capitalist forms refers to *the managerial class*; that is, the controllers of capital assets on behalf of shareholders. These managers, whose pre-eminence Berle and Means had already shown in the 1930s, still constitute the heart of capitalism under informationalism, particularly in multinational corporations. I see no reason not to include among them managers of state-owned companies who, for all practical purposes, follow the same logic, and share the same culture, minus the risk for losses underwritten by the taxpayer.

The third level in the process of appropriation of profits by capital is both an old story and a fundamental feature of the new informational capitalism. The reason lies in the nature of *global financial markets*. It is in these markets that profits from all sources ultimately converge in search of higher profits. Indeed, the margins of gain in the stock market, in the bond market, in the currency market, in futures, options, and derivatives, in financial markets at large, are, on average, considerably greater than in most direct investments, excepting a few instances of speculation. This is so not because of the nature of financial capital, the oldest form of capital in history. But because of the technological conditions under which it operates in informationalism. Namely its annihilation of space and time by electronic means. Its technological and informational ability relentlessly to scan the entire planet for investment opportunities, and to move from one option to another in a matter of seconds, brings capital into constant movement, merging in this movement capital from all origins, as in mutual funds investments. The programming and forecasting capabilities of financial management models makes it possible to colonize the future, and the interstices of the future (that is, possible alternative scenarios), selling this "unreal estate" as property rights of the immaterial. Played by the rules, there is nothing evil about this global casino. After all, if cautious management and proper technology avoid dramatic crushes of the market, the losses of some fractions of capital are the wins of others, so that, over the long term, the market balances out and keeps a dynamic equilibrium. However, because of the differential between the amount of profits obtained from the production of goods and services, and the amount that can be obtained from financial investments, individual capitals of all kinds are, in fact, dependent on the fate of their investments in global financial markets, since capital can never remain idle. Thus, *global financial markets, and their networks of management, are the actual collective capitalist, the mother of all accumulations.* To say so is not to say that financial capital dominates industrial capital, an old dichotomy that simply does not fit the new economic reality. Indeed, in the past quarter of a century, firms around the world have, by an large, self-financed the majority of their investments with the proceeds of their trade. Banks do not control manufacturing firms, nor do they control themselves. Firms of all kinds, financial producers, manufacturing producers, agricultural producers, service producers, as well as governments and public institutions, use global financial networks as the depositories of their earnings and as their potential source of higher profits. It is in this specific form that *global financial networks are the nerve center of informational capitalism.* Their movements determine the value of stocks, bonds, and currencies, bringing doom or bonanza to savers, investors, firms, and countries. But these movements do not follow a market logic. The market is twisted, manipulated, and transformed, by a combination of computer-enacted strategic maneuvers, crowd psychology from multicultural sources, and unexpected turbulences, caused by greater and greater degrees of complexity in the interaction between capital flows on a global scale. While cutting-edge economists are trying to model this market behavior on the basis of game theory, their heroic efforts to find rational expectation patterns are immediately downloaded in the computers of financial wizards to obtain new competitive advantage from this knowledge by innovating on already known patterns of investment.

The consequences of these developments on *social class relationships* are as profound as they are complex. But before identifying them I need to distinguish between different meanings of class relationships. One approach focuses on social inequality in income and social status, along the lines of social stratification theory. From this perspective, the new system is characterized by *a tendency to increased social inequality and polarization*, namely the simultaneous growth of both the top and the bottom of the social scale. This results from three features: (a) a fundamental differentiation between self-programmable, highly productive labor, and generic, expendable labor; (b) the individual-ization of labor, which undermines its collective organization, thus abandoning the weakest sections of the workforce to their fate; and (c) under the impact of individualization of labor, globalization of economy, and delegitimation of the state, the gradual demise of the welfare state, so removing the safety net for people who cannot be individually well off. This tendency toward inequality and polarization is certainly not inexorable: it can be countered and prevented by deliberate public policies. But inequality and polarization are pre-scripted in the dynamics of informational capitalism, and will prevail unless conscious action is taken to countervail these tendencies.

A second meaning of class relationships refers to *social exclusion*. By this I mean the de-linking between people-as-people and people-as-workers/consumers in the dynamics of informational capitalism on a global scale. In chapter 2 of this volume, I tried to show the causes and consequences of this trend in a variety of situations. Under the new system of production, a considerable number of humans, probably in a growing proportion, are irrelevant, both as producers and consumers, from the perspective of the system's logic. I must empha-size, again, that this is not the same as saying that there is, or will be, mass unemployment. Comparative data show that, by and large, in all urban societies, most people and/or their families work for pay, even in poor neighborhoods and in poor countries. The question is: what kind of work for what kind of pay under what conditions? What is happening is that the mass of generic labor circulates in a variety of jobs, increasingly occasional jobs, with a great deal of discontinuity. So, millions of people are constantly in and out of paid work, often included in informal activities, and, in sizeable numbers, on the shop floor of the criminal economy. Furthermore, the loss of a stable relationship to employment, and the weak bargaining power of many workers, lead to a higher level of incidence of major crises in the life of their families: temporary job loss, personal crises, illness, drugs/alcohol addictions, loss of employability, loss of assets, loss of credit. Many of these crises connect with each other, inducing the downward spiral of social exclusion, toward what I have called "the black holes of informational capitalism," from which, statistically speaking, it is difficult to escape.

The borderline between social exclusion and daily survival is increasingly blurred for a growing number of people in all societies. Having lost much of the safety net, particularly for the new generations of the post-welfare state era, people who cannot follow the constant updating of skills, and fall behind in the competitive race, position themselves for the next round of "downsizing" of that shrinking middle that made the strength of advanced capitalist societies during the industrial era. Thus, processes of social exclusion do not only affect the "truly disadvantaged," but those individuals and social categories who build their lives on a constant struggle to escape falling down to a stigmatized underworld of downgraded labor and socially disabled people.

A third way of understanding new class relationships, this time in the Marxian tradition, is concerned with *who the producers are and who appropriates the products of their labor*. If innovation is the main source of productivity, knowledge and information are the essential materials of the new production process, and education is the key quality of labor, the new producers of informational capitalism are those knowledge generators and information processors whose contribution is most valuable to the firm, the region, and the national economy. But innovation does not happen in isolation. It is part of a system in which management of organizations, processing of knowledge and information, and production of goods and services are intertwined. So defined, this category of informational producers includes a very large group of managers, professionals, and technicians, who form a "collective worker"; that is, a producer unit made up of cooperation between a variety of inseparable individual workers. In OECD countries they may account for about one-third of the employed population. Most other workers may be in the category of generic labor, potentially replaceable by machines or by other members of the generic labor force. They need the producers to protect their bargaining power. But informational producers do not need them: this is a fundamental cleavage in informational capitalism, leading to the gradual dissolution of the remnants of class solidarity of the industrial society.

But who appropriates a share of informational producers' work? In one sense, nothing has changed *vis à vis* classic capitalism: their employers do, this is why they employ them in the first place. But, on the other hand, the mechanism of appropriation of surplus is far more complicated. First, employment relationships are tendentially individualized, meaning that each producer will receive a different deal. Secondly, an increasing proportion of producers control their own work process, and enter into specific, horizontal working relationships, so that, to a large extent, they become independent producers, submitted to market forces, but playing market strategies. Thirdly, their earnings often go into the whirlwind of global financial markets, fed precisely by the affluent section of the global population, so that they are also collective owners of collective capital, thus becoming dependent on the performance of capital markets. Under these conditions, we can hardly consider that there is a class contradiction between these networks of highly individualized producers and the collective capitalist of global financial networks. To be sure, there is frequent abuse and exploitation of individual producers, as well as of large masses of generic labor, by whoever is in charge of production processes. Yet, segmentation of labor, individualization of work, and diffusion of capital in the circuits of global finance have jointly induced the gradual fading away of the class structure of the industrial society. There are, and will be, powerful social conflicts, some of them enacted by workers and organized labor, from Korea to Spain. Yet, they are not the expression of class struggle but of interest groups' demands and/or of revolt against injustice.

The *truly fundamental social cleavages of the Information Age* are: first, the internal fragmentation of labor between informational producers and replaceable generic labor. Secondly, the social exclusion of a significant segment of society made up of discarded individuals whose value as workers/consumers is used up, and whose relevance as people is ignored. And, thirdly, the separation between the market logic of global networks of capital flows and the human experience of workers' lives.

Power relations are being transformed as well by the social processes that I have identified and analyzed in this book. The main transformation concerns the *crisis of the nation-state as a sovereign entity, and the related crisis of political democracy*, as constructed in the past two centuries. Since commands from the state cannot be fully enforced, and since some of its fundamental promises, embodied in the welfare state, cannot be kept, both its authority and its legitimacy are called into question. Because representative democracy is predicated on the notion of a sovereign body, the blurring of boundaries of sovereignty leads to uncertainty in the process of delegation of people's will. Globalization of capital, multilateralization of power institutions, and decentralization of authority to regional and local governments induce a new geometry of power, perhaps inducing a new form of state, the network state. Social actors, and citizens at large, maximize the chances of representation of their interests and values by playing out strategies in the networks of relationships between various institutions, at various levels of competence. Citizens of a given European region will have a better chance of defending their interests if they support their regional authorities against their national government, in alliance with the European Union. Or the other way around. Or else, none of the above; that is, by affirming local/regional autonomy against both the nation-state and supranational institutions. American malcontents may revile the federal government on behalf of the American nation. Or new Chinese business elites may push their interests by linking up with their provincial government, or with the still powerful national government, or with overseas Chinese networks. In other words, the new structure of power is dominated by a network geometry, in which power relationships are always specific to a given configuration of actors and institutions.

Under such conditions, informational politics, enacted primarily by symbol manipulation in the space of the media, fits well with this constantly changing world of power relationships. Strategic games, customized representation, and personalized leadership substitute for class constituencies, ideological mobilization, and party control, which were characteristic of politics in the industrial era.

As politics becomes a theater, and political institutions are bargaining agencies rather than sites of power, citizens around the world react defensively, voting to prevent harm from the state in place of entrusting it with their will. In a certain sense, *the political system is voided of power*, albeit not of influence.

Power, however, does not disappear. In an informational society, *it becomes inscribed, at a fundamental level, in the cultural codes through which people and institutions represent life and make decisions, including political decisions.* In a sense, power, while real, becomes immaterial. It is real because wherever and whenever it consolidates, it provides, for a time, individuals and organizations with the capacity to enforce their decisions regardless of consensus. But it is immaterial because such a capacity derives from the ability to frame life experience under categories that predispose to a given behavior and can then be presented as to favor a given leadership. For instance, if a population feels threatened by unidentifiable, multidimensional fear, the framing of such fears under the codes of immigration = race = poverty = welfare = crime = job loss = taxes = threat, provides an identifiable target, defines an us versus THEM, and favors those leaders who are most credible in supporting what is perceived to be a reasonable dose of racism and xenophobia. Or, in a very different example, if people equate quality of life with conservation of nature, and with their spiritual serenity, new political actors could emerge and new public policies could be implemented.

Cultural battles are the power battles of the Information Age. They are primarily fought in and by the media, but the media are not the power-holders. Power, as the capacity to impose behavior, lies in the networks of information exchange and symbol manipulation, which relate social actors, institutions, and cultural movements, through icons, spokespersons, and intellectual amplifiers. In the long run, it does not really matter who is in power because the distribution of political roles becomes widespread and rotating. There are no more stable power elites. There are however, *elites from power*, that is, elites formed during their usually brief power tenure, in which they take advantage of their privileged political position to gain a more permanent access to material resources and social connections. Culture as the source of power, and power as the source of capital, underlie the new social hierarchy of the Information Age.

The transformation of *relationships of experience* revolves primarily around *the crisis of patriarchalism*, at the root of a profound redefinition of family, gender relationships, sexuality, and, thus, personality. Both for structural reasons (linked to the informational economy), and because of the impact of social movements (feminism, women's struggles, and sexual liberation), patriarchal authority is challenged in most of the world, albeit under various forms and intensity depending upon cultural/institutional contexts. The future of the family is uncertain, but the future of patriarchalism is not: it can only survive under the protection of authoritarian states and religious fundamentalism. As the studies presented in volume II, chapter 4 show, in open societies the patriarchal family is in deep crisis, while new embryos of egalitarian families are still struggling against the old world of interests, prejudices, and fears. Networks of people (particularly for women) increasingly substitute for nuclear families as primary forms of emotional and material support. Individuals and their children follow a pattern of sequential family, and non-family, personal arrangements throughout their lives. And while there is a rapidly growing trend of fathers' involvement with their children, women – whether single or living with each other – and their children, are an increasingly prevalent form of reproduction of society, thus fundamentally modifying patterns of socialization. Admittedly, I am taking as my main point of reference the experience of the United States, and of most of Western Europe (with southern Europe being, to some extent, an exception in the European context). Yet, as I argued in volume II, it can be shown that women's struggles, whether or not avowedly feminist, are spreading throughout the world, thus undermining patriarchalism in the family, in the economy, and in the institutions of society. I consider it very likely that, with the spread of women's struggles, and with women's increasing awareness of their oppression, their collective challenge to the patriarchal order will generalize, inducing processes of crisis in traditional family structures. I do see signs of a recomposition of the family, as millions of men appear to be ready to give up their privileges and work together with women to find new forms of loving, sharing, and having children. Indeed, I believe that rebuilding families under egalitarian forms is the necessary foundation for rebuilding society from the bottom up. Families are more than ever the providers of psychological security and material well-being to people, in a world characterized by individualization of work, destructuring of civil society, and delegitimation of the state. Yet the transition to new forms of family implies a fundamental redefinition of gender relationships in society at large, and thus of sexuality. Because personality systems are shaped by family and sexuality, they are also in a state of flux. I characterized such a state as flexible personalities, able to engage endlessly in the reconstruction of the self, rather than to define the self through adaptation to what were once conventional social roles, which are no longer viable and which have thus ceased to make sense. *The most fundamental transformation of relationships of experience in the Information Age is their transition to a pattern of social interaction constructed, primarily, by the actual experience of the relationship.* Nowadays, people produce forms of sociability, rather than follow models of behavior.

Changes in relationships of production, power, and experience converge toward *the transformation of material foundations of social life, space, and time.* The space of flows of the Information Age dominates the space of places of people's cultures. Timeless time as the social tendency toward the annihilation of time by technology supersedes the clock time logic of the industrial era. Capital circulates, power rules, and electronic communication swirls through flows of exchanges between selected, distant locales, while fragmented experience remains confined to places. Technology compresses time to a few, random instants, thus de-sequencing society, and de-historicizing history. By secluding power in the space of flows, allowing capital to escape from time, and dissolving history in the culture of the ephemeral, the network society disembodies social relationships, introducing the culture of real virtuality. Let me explain.

Throughout history, cultures have been generated by people sharing space and time, under conditions determined by relationships of production, power, and experience, and modified by their projects, fighting each other to impose over society their values and goals. Thus, spatio-temporal configurations were critical for the meaning of each culture, and for their differential evolution. Under the informational paradigm, a new culture has emerged from the superseding of places and the annihilation of time by the space of flows and by timeless time: *the culture of real virtuality*. As presented in volume I, chapter 5, by real virtuality I mean a system in which reality itself (that is, people's material/symbolic existence) is fully immersed in a virtual image setting, in the world of make believe, in which symbols are not just metaphors, but comprise the actual experience. This is not the consequence of electronic media, although they are the indispensable instruments of expression in the new culture. The material basis that explains why real virtuality is able to take over people's imagination and systems of representation is their livelihood in the space of flows and in timeless time. On the one hand, dominant functions and values in society are organized in simultaneity without contiguity; that is, in flows of information that escape from the experience embodied in any locale. On the other hand, dominant values and interests are constructed without reference to either past or future, in the timeless landscape of computer networks and electronic media, where all expressions are either instantaneous, or without predictable sequencing. All expressions from all times and from all spaces are mixed in the same hypertext, constantly rearranged, and communicated at any time, anywhere, depending on the interests of senders and the moods of receivers. This virtuality is our reality because it is within the framework of these timeless, placeless, symbolic systems that we construct the categories, and evoke the images, that shape behavior, induce politics, nurture dreams, and trigger nightmares.

This is the new social structure of the Information Age, which I call *the network society* because it is made up of networks of production, power, and experience, which construct a culture of virtuality in the global flows that transcend time and space. Not all dimensions and institutions of society follow the logic of the network society, in the same way that industrial societies included for a long time many pre-industrial forms of human existence. But all societies in the Information Age are indeed penetrated, with different intensity, by the pervasive logic of the network society, whose dynamic expansion gradually absorbs and subdues pre-existing social forms.

The network society, as any other social structure, is not absent of contradictions, social conflicts, and challenges from alternative forms of social organization. But these challenges are induced by the characteristics of the network society, and thus, they are sharply distinct from those of the industrial era. Accordingly, they are incarnated by different subjects, even though these subjects often work with historical materials provided by the values and organizations inherited from industrial capitalism and statism.

The understanding of our world requires the simultaneous analysis of the network society, and of its conflictive challenges. The historical law that where there is domination there is resistance continues to apply. But it requires an analytical effort to identify who the challengers are of the processes of domination enacted by the immaterial, yet powerful, flows of the network society.

The New Avenues of Social Change

According to observation, and as recorded in volume II, social challenges against patterns of domination in the network society generally take the form of constructing autonomous identities. These identities are external to the organizing principles of the network society. Against the worshipping of technology, the power of flows, and the logic of markets, they oppose their being, their beliefs, and their bequest. What is characteristic of social movements and cultural projects built around identities in the Information Age is that they do not originate within the institutions of civil society. They introduce, from the outset, an alternative social logic, distinct from the principles of performance around which dominant institutions of society are built. In the industrial era, the labor movement fought fiercely against capital. Capital and labor had, however, shared the goals and values of industrialization – productivity and material progress – each seeking to control its development and for a larger share of its harvest. In the end they reached a social pact. In the Information Age, the prevailing logic of dominant, global networks is so pervasive and so penetrating that the only way out of their domination appears to be out of these networks, and to reconstruct meaning on the basis of an entirely distinct system of values and beliefs. This is the case for communes of resistance identity I have identified. Religious fundamentalism does not reject technology, but puts it at the service of God's Law, to which all institutions and purposes must submit, without possible bargaining. Nationalism, localism, ethnic separatism, and cultural communes break up with society at large, and rebuild its institutions not from the bottom up, but from the inside out, the "who we are" versus those who do not belong.

Even proactive movements, which aim at transforming the overall pattern of social relationships among people, such as feminism, or among people and nature, such as environmentalism, start from the rejection of basic principles on which our societies are constructed: patriarchalism, productivism. Naturally, there are all kind of nuances in the practice of social movements, as I tried to make clear in volume II, but, quite fundamentally, their principles of self-definition, at the source of their existence, represent a break with institutionalized social logic. Should institutions of society, economy, and culture truly accept feminism and environmentalism, they would be essentially transformed. Using an old word, it would be a revolution.

The strength of identity-based social movements is their autonomy *vis à vis* the institutions of the state, the logic of capital, and the seduction of technology. It is hard to co-opt them, although certainly some of their participants may be co-opted. Even in defeat, their resistance and projects impact and change society, as I have been able to show in a number of selected cases, presented in volume II. Societies of the Information Age cannot be reduced to the structure and dynamics of the network society. Following my scanning of our world, it appears that our societies are constituted by the interaction between the "net" and the "self," between the network society and the power of identity.

Yet, the fundamental problem raised by processes of social change that are primarily external to the institutions and values of society, as it is, is that they may fragment rather than reconstitute society. Instead of transformed institutions, we would have communes of all sorts. Instead of social classes, we would witness the rise of tribes. And instead of conflictive interaction between the functions of the space of flows and the meaning of the space of places, we may observe the retrenchment of dominant global elites in immaterial palaces made out of communication networks and information flows. Meanwhile people's experience would remain confined to multiple, segregated locales, subdued in their existence and fragmented in their consciousness. With no Winter Palace to be seized, outbursts of revolt may implode, transformed into everyday senseless violence.

The reconstruction of society's institutions by cultural social movements, bringing technology under the control of people's needs and desires, seems to require a long march from the communes built around resistance identity to the heights of new project identities, sprouting from the values nurtured in these communes.

Examples of such processes, as observed in contemporary social movements and politics, are the construction of new, egalitarian families; the widespread acceptance of the concept of sustainable development, building intergenerational solidarity into the new model of economic growth; and the universal mobilization in defense of human rights wherever the defense has to be taken up. For this transition to be undertaken, from resistance identity to project identity, a new politics will have to emerge. This will be a cultural politics that starts from the premise that informational politics is predominantly enacted in the space of media, and fights with symbols, yet connects to values and issues that spring from people's life experience in the Information Age.

Beyond this Millennium

Throughout the pages of this book I have adamantly refused to indulge in futurology, staying as close as possible to observation of what we know the Information Age brings to us, as constituted in the last lapse of the twentieth century. In concluding this book, however, with the reader's benevolence, I would like to elaborate, for the span of just a few paragraphs, on some trends that may configure society in the early twenty-first century. When you are reading this, we will be at most two years away from that century (or perhaps already in it) so that my writing hardly qualifies as futurology. It is, rather, an attempt to bring a dynamic, prospective dimension to this synthesis of findings and hypotheses.

The information technology revolution will accentuate its transformative potential. The twenty-first century will be marked by the completion of a global information superhighway, and by mobile telecommunication and computing power, thus decentralizing and diffusing the power of information, delivering the promise of multimedia, and enhancing the joy of interactive communication. In addition, it will be the century of the full flowering of the genetic revolution. For the first time, our species will penetrate the secrets of life, and will be able to perform substantial manipulations of living matter. While this will trigger a dramatic debate on the social and environmental consequences of this capacity, the possibilities open to us are truly extraordinary. Prudently used, the genetic revolution may heal, fight pollution, improve life, and save time and effort from survival, so as to give us the chance to explore the largely unknown frontier of spirituality. Yet, if we make the same mistakes as we made in the twentieth century, using technology and industrialization to massacre each other in atrocious wars, with our new technological power we may well end life on the planet. It turned out to be relatively easy to stop short of nuclear holocaust because of the centralized control of nuclear energy and weaponry. But new genetic technologies are pervasive, their mutating impacts not fully controllable, and their institutional control much more decentralized. To prevent the evil effects of biological revolution we need not only responsible governments, but a responsible, educated society. Which way we go will depend on society's institutions, on people's values, and on the consciousness and determination of new social actors to shape and control their own destiny. Let me briefly review these prospects by pinpointing some major developments in the economy, polity, and culture.

The maturing of the informational economy, and the diffusion and proper use of information technology as a system, will likely unleash the productivity potential of this technological revolution. This will be made visible by changes in statistical accounting, when twentieth-century categories and procedures, already manifestly inadequate, will be replaced by new concepts able to measure the new economy. There is no question that the twenty-first century will witness the rise of an extraordinarily productive system by historical standards. Human labor will produce more and better with considerably less effort. Mental work will replace physical effort in the most productive sectors of the economy. However, the sharing of this wealth will depend for individuals on their access to education and, for society as a whole, on social organization, politics, and policies.

The global economy will expand in the twenty-first century, using substantial increases in the power of telecommunications and information processing. It will penetrate all countries, all territories, all cultures, all communication flows, and all financial networks, relentlessly scanning the planet for new opportunities of profit-making. But it will do so selectively, linking valuable segments and discarding used up, or irrelevant, locales and people. The territorial unevenness of production will result in an extraordinary geography of differential value-making that will sharply contrast countries, regions, and metropolitan areas. Valuable locales and people will be found everywhere, even in Sub-Saharan Africa, as I have argued in this volume. But switched-off territories and people will also be found everywhere, albeit in different proportions. The planet is being segmented into clearly distinct spaces, defined by different time regimes.

From the excluded segments of humankind, two different reactions can be expected. On the one hand, there will be a sharp increase in the operation of what I call "the perverse connection," that is, playing the game of global capitalism with different rules. The global criminal economy, whose profile and dynamics I tried to identify in chapter 3 of this volume, will be a fundamental feature of the twenty-first century, and its economic, political, and cultural influence will penetrate all spheres of life. The question is not whether our societies will be able to eliminate the criminal networks, but, rather, whether criminal networks will not end up controlling a substantial share of our economy, of our institutions, and of our everyday life.

There is another reaction against social exclusion and economic irrelevance that I am convinced will play an essential role in the twenty-first century: the exclusion of the excluders by the excluded.

Because the whole world is, and will increasingly be, intertwined in the basic structures of life, under the logic of the network society, opting out by people and countries will not be a peaceful withdrawal. It takes, and it will take, the form of fundamentalist affirmation of an alternative set of values and principles of existence, under which no coexistence is possible with the evil system that so deeply damages people's lives. As I write, in the streets of Kabul women are beaten for improper dress by the courageous warriors of the Taliban. This is not in accordance with the humanistic teachings of Islam. There is however, as analyzed in volume II, an explosion of fundamentalist movements that take up the Qū'ran, the Bible, or any holy text, to interpret it and use it, as a banner of their despair and a weapon of their rage. Fundamentalisms of different kinds and from different sources will represent the most daring, uncompromising challenge to one-sided domination of informational, global capitalism. Their potential access to weapons of mass extermination casts a giant shadow on the optimistic prospects of the Information Age.

Nation-states will survive, but not so their sovereignty. They will band together in multilateral networks, with a variable geometry of commitments, responsibilities, alliances, and subordinations. The most notable multilateral construction will be the European Union, bringing together the technological and economic resources of most, but not all European countries: Russia is likely to be left out, out of the West's historical fears, and Switzerland needs to be off limits to keep its job as the world's banker. But the European Union, for the time being, does not embody a historical project of building a European society. It is, essentially, a defensive construction on behalf of European civilization to avoid becoming an economic colony of Asians and Americans. European nation-states will remain and will bargain endlessly for their individual interests within the framework of European institutions, which they will need but, in spite of their federalist rhetoric, neither Europeans nor their governments will cherish. Europe's unofficial anthem (Beethoven's "Hymn of Joy") is universal, but its German accent may become more marked.

The global economy will be governed by a set of multilateral institutions, networked among themselves. At the core of this network is the G-7 countries club, perhaps with a few additional members, and its executive arms, the International Monetary Fund, and the World Bank, charged with regulation and intervention on behalf of the ground rules of global capitalism. Technocrats and bureaucrats of these, and similar, international economic institutions, will add their own dose of neo-liberal ideology and professional expertise in the implementation of their broad mandate. Informal gatherings, such as the Davos meetings, or their equivalents, will help to create the cultural/personal glue of the global elite.

Global geopolitics will also be managed by multilateralism, with the United Nations, and regional international institutions ASEAN, OEA, or OAU, playing an increasing role in the management of international or even national conflicts. They will increasingly use security alliances, such as NATO, in the enforcement of their decisions. When necessary, *ad hoc* international police forces will be created to intervene in trouble spots. For instance, in the fall of 1996, the Clinton administration proposed to several African countries, and to the Organization of African Unity, the creation of an African rapid intervention force, attached to the UN, armed and trained by the US, and financed by the US, the European Union, and Japan. This proposal did not prosper, but it may be the characteristic model for future international armies, ready to preserve the peace of global networks and their constituencies and/or prevent genocides of the Rwandan kind: in this dual role of international intervention lies the ambiguity of multilateralism.

Global security matters will be likely to be dominated by three main issues, if the analyses contained in this book are proved correct. The first is the rising tension in the Pacific, as China asserts its global power, Japan goes into another round of national paranoia, and Korea, Indonesia, and India react to both.

The second is the resurgence of Russian power, not only as a nuclear superpower, but as a stronger nation, no longer tolerating humiliation. The conditions under which post-Communist Russia will be or will not be brought into the multilateral system of global co-management will determine the future geometry of security alignments. The third security issue is probably the most decisive of all, and will be likely to condition safety for the world at large for a long period of time. It refers to the new forms of warfare that will be used by individuals, organizations, and states, strong in their convictions, weak in their military means, but able to access new technologies of destruction, as well as find the vulnerable spots of our societies. Criminal gangs may also resort to high-intensity confrontation when they see no other option, as Colombia experienced in the 1990s. Global or local terrorism is already considered a major threat worldwide in this end of millennium. But, I believe this is only a modest beginning. Increasing technological sophistication leads to two trends converging toward outright terror: on the one hand, a small determined group, well financed, and well informed, can devastate entire cities, or strike at nerve centers of our livelihood; on the other hand, the infrastructure of our everyday life, from energy to transportation to water supply, has become so complex, and so intertwined, that its vulnerability has increased exponentially. While new technologies help security systems, they also make our daily life more exposed. The price for increased protection will be to live within a system of electronic locks, alarms systems, and on-line police patrols. It will also mean to grow up in fear. It is probably not different from the experience of most children in history. It is also a measure of the relativity of human progress.

Geopolitics will also be increasingly dominated by a fundamental contradiction between the multilateralism of decision-making and the unilateralism of military implementation of these decisions. This is because, after the demise of the Soviet Union, and the technological backwardness of the new Russia, the United States is, and will be for the foreseeable future, the only military superpower. Thus, most security decisions will have to be either implemented or supported by the United States to be truly effective or credible. The European Union, for all its arrogant talk, gave a clear demonstration of its operational inability in the mishandling of the absurd, atrocious Bosnian war, which had to be stopped, and provisionally settled, in Dayton, Ohio. Germany is barred by its Constitution from sending combat forces abroad, and I doubt that its citizens will tolerate otherwise for a long time. Japan has forbidden itself to build an army, and the pacifist feeling in the country runs deeper than the support for ultra-nationalist provocations. Outside the OECD, only China and India may have enough technological and military might to access global power in the foreseeable future, but certainly not to match the United States or even Russia. So, excepting the unlikely hypothesis of an extraordinary Chinese military build up, for which China simply does not yet have the technological capacity, the world is left with one superpower, the United States. Under such conditions, various security alliances will have to rely on American forces. But the US is confronted with such deep domestic social problems that it will certainly not have the means, nor the political support, to exercise such a power if the security of its citizens is not under direct threat, as American presidents discovered several times in the 1990s. With the Cold War forgotten, and no credible equivalent "new Cold War" looming on the horizon, the only way America may keep its military status is to lend its forces to the global security system. And have other countries pay for it. This is the ultimate twist of multilateralism, and the most striking illustration of the lost sovereignty of the nation-state.

The state does not disappear, though. It is simply downsized in the Information Age. It proliferates under the form of local and regional governments, which dot the world with their projects, build up constituencies, and negotiate with national governments, multinational corporations, and international agencies. The era of globalization of the economy is also the era of localization of polity. What local and regional governments lack in power and resources, they make up in flexibility and networking. They are the only match, if any, to the dynamism of global networks of wealth and information.

As for people, they are, and will be, increasingly distant from the halls of power, and disaffected from the crumbling institutions of civil society. They will be individualized in their work and lives, constructing their own meaning on the basis of their own experience, and, if they are lucky, reconstructing their family, their rock in this swirling ocean of unknown flows and uncontrolled networks. When subjected to collective threats, they will build communal havens, whence prophets may proclaim the coming of new gods.

The twenty-first century will not be a dark age. Neither will it deliver to most people the bounties promised by the most extraordinary technological revolution in history. Rather, it may well be characterized by informed bewilderment.

What is to be Done?

Each time an intellectual has tried to answer this question, and seriously implement the answer, catastrophe has ensued. This was particularly the case with a certain Ulianov in 1902. Thus, while certainly not pretending to qualify for this comparison, I shall abstain from suggesting any cure for the ills of our world. But since I do feel concerned by what I have seen on my journey across this early landscape of the Information Age, I would like to explain my abstention, writing in the first person, but thinking of my generation and of my political culture.

I come from a time and a tradition, the political left of the industrial era, obsessed by the inscription on Marx's tomb at Highgate, his (and Engel's) eleventh thesis on Feuerbach. Transformative political action was the ultimate goal of a truly meaningful intellectual endeavor. I still believe that there is considerable generosity in this attitude, certainly less selfish than the orderly pursuit of bureaucratic academic careers, undisturbed by the labors of people around the world. And, on the whole, I do not think that a classification between right-wing and left-wing intellectuals and social scientists would yield significant differences in scholarly quality between the two groups. After all, conservative intellectuals also went into political action, as much as the left did, often with little tolerance for their foes. So, the issue is not that political commitment prevents, or distorts, intellectual creativity. Many of us have learned, over the years, to live with the tension, and the contradiction, between what we find and what we would like to happen. I consider social action and political projects to be essential in the betterment of a society that clearly needs change and hope. And I do hope that this book, by raising some questions and providing empirical and theoretical elements to treat them, may contribute to informed social action in the pursuit of social change. In this sense, I am not, and I do not want to be, a neutral, detached observer of the human drama.

However, I have seen so much misled sacrifice, so many dead ends induced by ideology, and such horrors provoked by artificial paradises of dogmatic politics that I want to convey a salutary reaction against trying to frame political practice in accordance with social theory, or, for that matter, with ideology. Theory and research, in general as well as in this book, should be considered as a means for understanding our world, and should be judged exclusively on their accuracy, rigor, and relevance. How these tools are used, and for what purpose, should be the exclusive prerogative of social actors themselves, in specific social contexts, and on behalf of their values and interests. No more meta-politics, no more *"maîtres à penser,"* and no more intellectuals pretending to be so. The most fundamental political liberation is for people to free themselves from uncritical adherence to theoretical or ideological schemes, to construct their practice on the basis of their experience, while using whatever information or analysis is available to them, from a variety of sources. In the twentieth century, philosophers have been trying to change the world. In the twenty-first century, it is time for them to interpret it differently. Hence my circumspection, which is not indifference, about a world troubled by its own promise.

Finale

The promise of the Information Age is the unleashing of unprecedented productive capacity by the power of the mind. I think, therefore I produce. In so doing, we will have the leisure to experiment with spirituality, and the opportunity of reconciliation with nature, without sacrificing the material well-being of our children. The dream of the Enlightenment, that reason and science would solve the problems of humankind, is within reach. Yet there is an extraordinary gap between our technological overdevelopment and our social underdevelopment. Our economy, society, and culture are built on interests, values, institutions, and systems of representation that, by and large, limit collective creativity, confiscate the harvest of information technology, and deviate our energy into self-destructive confrontation. This state of affairs must not be. There is no eternal evil in human nature. There is nothing that cannot be changed by conscious, purposive social action, provided with information, and supported by legitimacy. If people are informed, active, and communicate throughout the world; if business assumes its social responsibility; if the media become the messengers, rather than the message; if political actors react against cynicism, and restore belief in democracy; if culture is reconstructed from experience; if humankind feels the solidarity of the species throughout the globe; if we assert intergenerational solidarity by living in harmony with nature; if we depart for the exploration of our inner self, having made peace among ourselves. If all this is made possible by our informed, conscious, shared decision, while there is still time, maybe then, we may, at last, be able to live and let live, love and be loved.

I have exhausted my words. Thus, I will borrow, for the last time, from Pablo Neruda:

*Por mi parte y tu parte, cumplimos,
      compartimos esperanzas e
      inviernos;*

*y fuimos heridos no solo por los
      enemigos mortales*

*sino por mortales amigos (y esto
      pareció más amargo),*

*pero no me parece más dulce
      mi pan o mi libro
      entretanto;*

*agregamos viviendo la cifra que
      falta al dolor,*

*y seguimos amando el amor y con
      nuestra directa conducta*

*enterramos a los mentirosos y
      vivimos con los verdaderos.*

*For my part and yours, we comply,
      we shared our hopes and
      winters;*

*and we have been wounded not only
      by mortal enemies*

*but by mortal friends (that seemed
      all the more bitter),*

*but bread does not seem to taste
      sweeter, nor my book, in the
      meantime;*

*living, we supply the statistics that
      pain still lacks,*

*we go on loving love and in our
      blunt way*

*we bury the liars and live among the
      truth-tellers.*

Summary of Contents of Volumes I and II

Throughout this volume, reference has been made to the themes presented in Volume I (published by Blackwell Publishers in 1996) and Volume II (published by Blackwell Publishers in 1997). An outline of their contents is given below. The conclusion to this volume stands as a conclusion to the three-volume book.

References

Adam, Lishan (1996) "Africa on the line?" *Ceres: the FAO Review*, 158, March–April.

Adams, David (1997) "Russian Mafia in Miami: 'Redfellas' linked to plan to smuggle coke in a submarine", *San Francisco Examiner*, March 9: 3.

Adekanye, J. Bayo (1995) "Structural adjustment, democratization and rising ethnic tensions in Africa", *Development and Change*, 26 (2): 355–74.

Adepoju, Aderanti (ed.) (1993) *The Impact of Structural Adjustment on the Population of Africa: the Implications for Education, Health and Employment*, Portsmouth, NH: United Nations Population Fund and Heinemann.

Afanasiev, V.G. (1972) *Nauchno-teknicheskaya revolyutsiya, upravleniye, obrazovaniye*, Moscow: Nauka.

Agamirzian, Igor (1991) "Computing in the USSR", *BYTE*, April, pp. 120–9.

Aganbegyan, Abel (1988) *The Economic Challenge of Perestroika*, Bloomington: Indiana University Press.

—— (1988–90) *Perestroika Annual*, vols 1–3. Washington, DC: Brassey.

—— (1989) *Inside Perestroika: The Future of the Soviet Economy*, New York: Harper and Row.

Agbese, Pita Ogaba (1996) "The military as an obstacle to the democratization enterprise: towards an agenda for permanent military disengagement from politics in Nigeria", *Journal of Asian and African Studies*, 31 (1–2): 82–98.

Ahn, Seung-Joon (1994) *From State to Community: Rethinking South Korean Modernization*, Littleton, CO.: Aigis

Aina, Tade Akin (1993) "Development theory and Africa's lost decade: critical reflections on Africa's crisis and current trends in development thinking and practice", in Margareta Von Troil (ed.), *Changing Paradigms in Development – South, East and West*, Uppsala: Nordiska Afrikainstitutet, pp. 11–26

Alexander, A.J. (1990) *The Conversion of the Soviet Defense Industry*, Santa Monica, CA: Rand Corporation.

Allen, G.C. (1981) *The Japanese Economy*, New York: St Martin's Press.

Alonso Zaldivar, Carlos (1996) "Variaciónes sobre un mundo en cambio", Madrid: Alianza

Alvarez Gonzalez, Maria Isabel (1993) "La reconversion del complejo industrial-militar sovietico", unpublished thesis, Madrid: Universidad Autonoma de Madrid, Departamento de Estructura Económica.

Amman, R. and Cooper, J. (1986) *Technical Progress and Soviet Economic Development*, Oxford: Blackwell.

Amsdem, Alice (1979) "Taiwan's economic history: a case of etatisme and a challenge to dependency theory", *Modern China*, 5 (3): 341–80.

—— (1985) "The state and Taiwan's economic development", in Peter Evans et al. (eds), *Bringing the State Back In*, Cambridge: Cambridge University Press.

—— (1989) *Asia's Next Giant: South Korea and Late Industrialization*, New York: Oxford University Press.

—— (1992) "A theory of government intervention in late industrialization", in Louis Putterman and Dietrich Rueschemeyer (eds), *State and Market in Development: Synergy or Rivalry?*, Boulder, CO.: Lynne Rienner.

Andrew, Christopher and Gordievsky, Oleg (1990) *KGB: the Inside Story of its Foreign Operation from Lenin to Gorbachev*, London: Hodder and Stoughton.

Anonymous (1984) "The Novosibirsk Report", April 1983, translated into English in *Survey*, 28 (1): 88–108.

Ansell, Christopher K. and Parsons, Craig (1995) *Organizational Trajectories of Administrative States: Britain, France, and the US Compared*, Berkeley: University of California, Center for Western European Studies, Working Paper.

Antonov-Ovseyenko, Anton (1981) *The Time of Stalin*, New York: Harper and Row.

Aoyama, Yuko (1996) "From Fortress Japan to global networks: the emergence of network multinationals among Japanese electronics industry in the 1990s", unpublished PhD thesis, Berkeley: University of California, Department of City and Regional Planning.

Appelbaum, Richard P. and Henderson, Jeffrey (eds) (1992) *States and Development in the Asian Pacific Rim*, London: Sage.

Arbex, Jorge (1993) *Narcotráfico: um jogo de poder nas Américas*, São Paulo: Editora Moderna.

Arlacchi, Pino (1995) "The Mafia, Cosa Nostra, and Italian institutions", in Salvatore Secchi (ed.), *Deconstructing Italy: Italy in the Nineties*, Berkeley: University of California, International and Area Studies Series.

Arnedy, B. Alejandro (1990) *El narcotráfico en America Latina: sus conexiones, hombres y rutas*, Cordoba: Marcos Lerner Editora.

Arrieta, Carlos G. et al. (eds) (1990) *Narcotráfico en Colombia: dimensiones políticas, económicas, juridicas e internacionales*, Bogotá: TM Editores.

Asahi Shimbun (1995) *Japan Almanac 1995*, Tokyo: Asahi Shimbun Publishing Company.

Aslund, Anders (1989) *Gorbachev's Struggle for Economic Reform*, Ithaca, NY: Cornell University Press.

Audigier, P. (1989) "Le poids des dépenses de défense sur l'économie sovietique", *Défense Nationale*, May.

Azocar Alcala, Gustavo (1994) *Los barones de la droga: la historia del narcotráfico en Venezuela*, Caracas: Alfadil Ediciones.

Bagley, Bruce, Bonilla, Adrian and Paez, Alexei (eds) (1991) *La economía política del narcotráfico: el caso ecuatoriano*, Quito: FLACSO.

Barnett, Tony and Blaikie, Piers (1992) *AIDS in Africa: its Present and Future Impact*, London: Belhaven Press.

Bastias, María Veronica (1993) "El salario del miedo: narcotráfico en América Latina", Buenos Aires: SERPAJ-AL

Bates, R. (1988) "Governments and agricultural markets in Africa", in R. Bates (ed.), *Toward a Political Economy of Development: a Rational Choice Perspective*, Berkeley: University of California Press.

Bates, Timothy and Dunham, Constance (1993) "Asian-American success in self-employment", *Economic Development Quarterly*, 7(2) 199–214.

Bauer, John and Mason, Andrew (1992) "The distribution of income and wealth in Japan", *Review of Income and Wealth*, 38(4): 403–28.

Bayart, Jean-François (1989) *L'état en Afrique: la politique du ventre*, Paris: Librairie Artheme Fayard. (English trans., London: Longman, 1993).

Baydar, Nazli, Brooks-Gunn, Jeanne and Furstenberg, Frank (1993) "Early warning signs of functional illiteracy: predictors in childhood and adolescence", *Child Development*, 63(3).

Beasley, W.G. (1990) *The Rise of Modern Japan*, London: Weidenfeld and Nicolson.

Beaty, Jonathan (1994) "Russia's yard sale", *Time*, April 18: 52–5.

Bellamy, Carol (director) (1996) *The State of the World's Children 1996*, New York: Oxford University Press for UNICEF.

Benner, Christopher (1994) "South Africa's informal economy: reflections on institutional change and socio-economic transformation", unpublished research seminar paper for geography 253, Berkeley: University of California.

Bennett, Vanora (1997) "Interchangeable cops and robbers: Russian police moonlighting for organized crime", *San Francisco Chronicle*, April 7: 12.

Bergson, Abram (1978) *Productivity and the Social System: the USSR and the West*, Cambridge, MA: Harvard University Press

Berliner, J.S. (1986) *The Innovation Decision in Soviet Industry*, Cambridge, MA: MIT Press.

Bernardez, Julio (1995) *Europa: entre el timo y el mito*, Madrid: Temas de Hoy.

Berry, Sara (1993) "Coping with confusion: African farmers' responses to economic instability in the 1970s and 1980s", in Callaghy and Ravenhill, (eds), pp. 248–78.

Berryman, Sue (1994) "The role of literacy in the wealth of individuals and nations", *NCAL Technical Report TR94-13*, Philadelphia: National Center for Adult Literacy.

Betancourt, Dario and Garcia, Martha L. (1994) *Contrabandistas, marimberos y mafiosos: historia social de la mafia colombiana (1965–1992)*, Bogotá; TM Editores.

Beyer, Dorianne (1996) "Child prostitution in Latin America", in US Department of Labor, Bureau of International Labor Affairs, *Forced Labor: the Prostitution of Children, Symposium Proceedings*, Washington DC: US Department of Labor.

Bianchi, Patrizio, Carnoy, Martin and Castells, Manuel (1988) "Economic modernization and technology transfer in the People's Republic of China", Stanford: Stanford University, Center for Educational Research at Stanford, Research Monograph.

Black, Maggie (1995) *In the Twilight Zone: Child Workers in the Hotel, Tourism, and Catering Industry*, Geneva: International Labour Office.

Blomstrom, Magnus and Lundhal, Mats (eds) (1993) *Economic Crisis in Africa: Perspectives and Policy Responses*, London: Routledge.

Blyakhman, L. and Shkaratan, O. (1977) *Man at Work: the Scientific and Technological Revolution, the Soviet Working Class and Intelligentsia*, Moscow: Progress.

Boahene, K. (1996) "The IXth International Conference on AIDS and STD in Africa", *AIDS Care*, 8(5): 609–16.

Bohlen, Celestine (1993) "The Kremlin's latest intrigue shows how real life imitates James Bond", *The New York Times*, November 23.

—— (1994) "Organized crime has Russia by the throat", *The New York Times*, October 13.

Bonet, Pilar (1993) "El laberinto ruso", *El País Semanal*, December 12.

—— (1994) "La mafia rusa desafia al gobierno de Yeltsin con el uso de coches-bomba", *El País*, June 9.

Booth, Martin (1991) *The Triads: the Growing Global Threat from the Chinese Criminal Societies*, New York: St Martin's Press.

Borja, Jordi (1992) *Estrategias de desarrollo e internacionalización de las ciudades europeas: las redes de ciudades*, Report to the European Community, Directorate General XVI, Barcelona: Consultores Europeos Asociados.

—— (1996) "Ciudadanos europeos?", *El País*, October 31: 12.

—— and Castells, Manuel (1997) *Local and Global: the Management of Cities in the Information Age*, London: Earthscan.

Bourgois, P. (1995) "The political economy of resistance and self-destruction in the crack economy: an ethnographic perspective", *Annals of the New York Academy of Sciences*, 749: 97–118.

—— and Dunlap, E. (1993) "Exorcising sex-for-crack: an ethnographic perspective from Harlem", in P. Bourgois and E. Dunlap (eds), *Crack Pipe as Pimp: an Ethnographic Investigation of Sex-for-Crack Exchange*, New York: Lexington.

Bowles, Paul and White, Gordon (1993) *The Political Economy of China's Financial Reforms*, Boulder, CO.: Westview Press.

Breslauer, George W. (1990) "Soviet economic reforms since Stalin: ideology, politics, and learning", *Soviet Economy*, 6(3): 252–80.

Brown, Phillip and Crompton, Rosemary (eds) (1994) *Economic Restructuring and Social Exclusion*, London: UCL Press.

Bull, Hedley (1977) *The Anarchical Society: a Study of Order in World Politics*, London: Macmillan.

Business Week (1996) "Helping the Russian Mafia help itself", December 9: 58.

Callaghy, Thomas (1993) "Political passions and economic interests: economic reform and political structure in Africa", in Thomas Callaghy and John Ravenhill (eds), pp. 463–519.

—— and Ravenhill, John (eds) (1993), *Hemmed In: Responses to Africa's Economic Decline*, New York: Columbia University Press.

Calvi, Maurizio (1992) *Figure di una battaglia: documenti e riflessioni sulla Mafia dopo l'assassinio di G. Falcone e P. Borsellino*, Bari: Edizioni Dedalo.

Camacho Guizado, Alvaro (1988) *Droga y sociedad en Colombia*, Bogotá: CEREC/CIDSE-Universidad del Valle.

Campbell, C.M. and Williams, B.G. (1996) "Academic research and HIV/AIDS in South Africa", *South African Medical Journal*, 86(1): 55–63.

Carnoy, Martin (1994) *Faded Dreams*, New York: Cambridge University Press.

——, Castells, Manuel and Benner, Chris (1997) "What is happening to the US labor market?" Research report of the Russell Sage Foundation, New York.

Carrere d'Encausse, Helene (1978) *L'empire éclate*, Paris: Flammarion.

—— (1987) *Le grand défi: Bolcheviks et nations, 1917–30*, Paris: Flammarion.

—— (1991) *La fin de l'empire soviétique: le triomphe des nations*, Paris: Fayard.

Castells, Manuel (1977) *The Urban Question*, Cambridge, MA: MIT Press.

—— (1989) *The Informational City: Information Technology, Economic Restructuring, and the Urban-regional Process*, Oxford: Blackwell.

—— (1991) *La ciudad científica de Akademogorodok y su relación con el desarrollo económico de Siberia*, Madrid: UAM/IUSNT, research report.

—— (1992) *La nueva revolución rusa*, Madrid: Sistema.

—— (1996) "El futuro del Estado del Bienestar en la sociedad informacional", *Sistema*, March: 35–53.

—— and Hall, Peter (1994) *Technopoles of the World: the Making of 21st Century Industrial Complexes*, London: Routledge.

—— and Nataluskho, Svetlana (1993) *La modernización tecnológica de las empresas de electrónica y de telecomunicaciónes en Rusia*, Madrid: UAM/IUSNT, research report.

——, Goh, Lee and Kwok, Reginald Y.W. (1990) *The Shek Kip Mei Syndrome: Economic Development and Public Housing in Hong Kong and Singapore*, London: Pion.

——, Shkaratan, Ovsei and Kolomietz, Viktor (1993) *El impacto del movimiento político sobre las estructuras del poder en la Rusia post-comunista*, Madrid: UAM/IUSNT, research report.

Castillo, Fabio (1991) *La coca nostra*, Bogotá: Editorial Documentos Periodisticos.

Catanzaro, Raimondo (1991) *Il delito come impresa: storia sociale della mafia*, Milan: Rizzoli.

Cave, Martin (1980) *Computers and Economic Planning: the Soviet Experience*, Cambridge: Cambridge University Press.

Chan, M.K. et al. (eds) (1986) *Dimensions of the Chinese and Hong Kong Labor Movement*, Hong Kong: Hong Kong Christian Industrial Committee.

Cheal, David (1996) *New Poverty: Families in Postmodern Society*, Westport, CT: Greenwood Press.

388 References

Chen, Edward K.Y. (1979) *Hypergrowth in Asian Economies: a Comparative Analysis of Hong Kong, Japan, Korea, Singapore, and Taiwan*, London: Macmillan.
—— (1980) "The economic setting", in David Lethbridge (ed.), *The Business Environment of Hong Kong*, Hong Kong: Oxford University Press.
Chen, Peter S.J. (1983) *Singapore: Development Policies and Trends*, Singapore: Oxford University Press.
Cheru, Fantu (1992) *The Not So Brave New World: Problems and Prospects of Regional Integration in Post-Apartheid Southern Africa*, Johannesburg: South African Institute of International Affairs.
Chesneaux, Jean (1982) *The Chinese Labor Movement: 1919–1927*, Stanford: Stanford University Press.
Cheung, Peter (1994) "The case of Guandong in central-provincial relations", in Hao and Zhimin (eds), pp. 207–35.
Christian Science Monitor (1996) "Safeguarding the children", series of reports, August 22–September 16.
Chu, Yiu-Kong (1996) "International Triad movements: the threat of Chinese organized crime", London: Research Institute for the Study of Conflict and Terrorism, Conflict Studies Series, July/August.
Chua, Beng-Huat (1985) "Pragmatism and the People's Action Party in Singapore", *Southeast Asian Journal of Social Sciences*, 13 (2).
—— (1998) "Unmaking Asia: revenge of the real against the discursive", paper presented to the Conference on Problematising Asia, National Taiwan University, Taipei, July, 13–16.
CIA, Directorate of Intelligence (1990a) *Measures of Soviet GNP in 1982 Prices*, Washington, DC: CIA.
—— (1990b) *Measuring Soviet GNP: Problems and Solutions. A Conference Report*, Washington, DC: CIA.
Clayton, Mark (1996) "In United States, Canada, new laws fail to curb demand for child sex", *Christian Science Monitor*, September 3: 11.
Clifford, Mark (1994) "Family ties: heir force", *Far Eastern Economic Review*, November 17: 78–86.
Cohen, Stepehn (1974) *Bukharin and the Bolshevik Revolution*, New York: Alfred Knopf.
Cohn, Ilene and Goodwin Gill, Guy (1994) *Child Soldiers: the Roles of Children in Armed Conflict*, Oxford: Clarendon Press.
Cole, D. C. and Lyman, J.A. (1971) *Korean Development: the Interplay of Politics and Economics*, Cambridge, MA: Harvard University Press.
Collier, Paul (1995) "The marginalization of Africa", *International Labour Review*, 134(4–5): 541–57.
Colombo, Gherardo (1990) *Il riciclaggio: gli istrumenti guidiziari di controllo dei flussi monetari illeciti con le modifiche introdotte dalla nuova legge antimafia*, Milan: Giuffre Editore.
Commission on Security and Cooperation in Europe (1994) *Crime and corruption in Russia*, Briefing of the Commission, Implementation of the Helsinki Accord, Washington, DC: June.

Connolly, Kathleen, McDermid, Lea, Schiraldi, Vincent and Macallair, Dan (1996) *From Classrooms to Cell Blocks: How Prison Building Affects Higher Education and African American Enrollment*, San Francisco: Center on Juvenile and Criminal Justice.

Conquest, Robert (ed.) (1967) *Soviet Nationalities Policy in Practice*, New York: Praeger.

—— (1968) *The Great Terror*, New York: Oxford University Press.

—— (1986) *The Harvest of Sorrow*, New York: Oxford University Press.

Cook, John T. and Brown, J. Larry (1994) "Two Americas: comparisons of US child poverty in rural, inner city and suburban areas: a linear trend analysis to the year 2010", Medford, MA: Tufts University School of Nutrition, Center on Hunger, Poverty and Nutrition Policy, Working Paper No. CPP-092394.

Cooper, J. (1991) *The Soviet Defence Industry: Conversion and Reform*, London: Pinter.

da Costa Nunez, Ralph (1996) *The New Poverty: Homeless Families in America*, New York: Insight Books.

Cowell, Alan (1994) "138 nations confer on rise in global crime", *The New York Times*, November 22.

Curtis, Gerald L. (1993) *Japan's Political Transfigurations: Interpretation and Implications*, Washington, DC: Woodrow Wilson International Center for Scholars.

Davidson, Basil (1992) *The Black Man's Burden: Africa and the Crisis of the Nation-State*, New York: Times Books.

—— (1994) *A Search for Africa: History, Culture, Politics*, New York: Times Books.

De Bernieres, Louis (1991) *Señor Vivo and the Coca Lord*, New York: Morrow.

De Feo, Michael and Savona, Ernesto (1994) "Money trails: international money laundering trends and prevention/control policies", Background Paper presented at the International Conference on Preventing and Controlling Money-Laundering and the Use of the Proceeds of Crime: a Global Approach, Courmayeur, Italy, June, 18–20.

Deininger, Klaus and Squire, Lyn (1996) "A new data set measuring income inequality", *The World Bank Economic Review*, 10,(3): 565–91.

Del Olmo, Rosa (1991) "La geopolítica del narcotráfico en América Latina", in *Simposio Internacional*: 29–68.

Del Vecchio, Rick (1994) "When children turn to violence", *San Francisco Chronicle*, May 11.

Dentsu Institute for Human Studies (1994) *Media in Japan*, Tokyo: DataFlow International.

Desai, Padma (1987) *The Soviet Economy: Problems and Prospects*, Oxford: Blackwell.

—— (1989) *Perestroika in Perspective: the Design and Dilemmas of Soviet Reforms*, Princeton, NJ: Princeton University Press.

Deyo, Frederic (1981) *Dependent Development and Industrial Order: An Asian Case Study*, New York: Praeger.

—— (ed.) (1987a) *The Political Economy of East Asian Industrialism*, Ithaca, NY: Cornell University Press.

—— (1987b) "State and labor: modes of political exclusion in East Asian development", in Deyo (ed.).

Dolven, Ben (1998) "Taiwan's trump", *Far Eastern Economic Review*, August, 6: 12–15.

Dornbusch, Robert (1998) "Asian crisis themes" (http://www.iie.com/news98–1.htm).

Doucette, Diane (1995) "The restructuring of the telecommunications industry in the former Soviet Union", unpublished PhD dissertation, Berkeley: University of California.

Drake, St Clair, and Cayton, Horace (1945) *Black Metropolis: a Study of Negro Life in a Northern City*, New York: Harcourt Brace Jovanovich, rev. edn 1962.

Drogin, Bob (1995) "Sending children to war", *Los Angeles Times*, March 26, A1-A14.

Dryakhlov, N.I. et al. (1972) *Nauchno-teknischeskaya revolyutsiya i obshchestvo*, Moscow: Nauka.

Dumaine, Brian (1993) "Illegal child labor comes back", *Fortune* 127(7), April 5.

Dumont, René (1964) *L'Afrique Noire est mal partie*, Paris: Éditions du Seuil.

Eggebeen, David and Lichter, Daniel (1991) "Race, family structure, and changing poverty among American children", *American Sociological Review*, 56.

Ehringhaus, Carolyn Chase (1990) "Functional literacy assessment: issues of interpretation", *Adult Education Quarterly*, 40(4).

Eisenstodt, Gail (1998) "Japan's crash and rebirth", *World Link*, September/October: 12–16.

Ekholm-Friedman, Kajsa (1993) "Afro-Marxism and its disastrous effects on the economy: the Congolese case", in Blomstrom and Lundhal (eds), pp. 219–45.

Ellman, M. and Kontorovich, V. (eds) (1992) *The Disintegration of the Soviet Economic System*, London: Routledge.

Endacott, G.B. and Birch, A. (1978) *Hong Kong Eclipse*, Hong Kong: Oxford University Press.

Erlanger, Steven (1994a) "Russia's new dictatorship of crime", *The New York Times*, May 15.

—— (1994b) "A slaying puts Russian underworld on parade", *The New York Times*, April 14.

Ernst, Dieter and O'Connor, David C., (1992) *Competing in the Electronics Industry: the Experience of Newly Industrializing Economies*, Paris: OECD, Development Centre Studies.

Estefanía, Joaquin (1996) *La nueva economía: la globalización*, Madrid: Temas para el Debate.

—— (1997) "La paradoja insoportable", *El País Internacional*, April 14: 8.

Evans, Peter (1995) *Embedded Autonomy: States and Industrial Transformation*, Princeton, NJ: Princeton University Press.

Fainstein, Norman (1993) "Race, class and segregation: discourses about African Americans", *International Journal of Urban and Regional Research*, 17(3): 384–403.

—— and Fainstein, Susan (1996) "Urban regimes and black citizens: the economic and social impacts of black political incorporation in US cities, *International Journal of Urban and Regional Research*, 20(1): March.

Fajnzylber, Fernando (1983) *La industrialización truncada de America Latina*, Mexico: Nueva Imagen.

Fatton Jr, Robert (1992) *Predatory Rule: State and Civil Society in Africa*, Boulder, CO.: Lynne Rienner.

Fischer, Claude et al. (1996) *Inequality by Design*, Princeton, NJ: Princeton University Press.

Flores, Robert (1996) "Child prostitution in the United States", in US Department of Labor, Bureau of International Labor Affairs, *Forced Labor: the Prostitution of Children, Symposium Proceedings*, Washington DC: US Department of Labor.

Fontana, Josep (1994) *Europa ante el espejo*, Barcelona: Critica.

Forester, Tom (1993) *Silicon Samurai: How Japan Conquered the World's IT Industry*, Oxford: Blackwell.

Forrest, Tom (1993) *Politics and Economic Development in Nigeria*, Cambridge: Cambridge University Press.

Fortescue, Stephen (1986) *The Communist Party and Soviet Science*, Baltimore: The Johns Hopkins University Press.

Fottorino, Eric (1991) *La piste blanche: l'Afrique sous l'emprise de la drogue*, Paris: Balland.

French, Howard (1995) "Mobutu, Zaïre's 'guide', leads nation into chaos", *The New York Times*, June 10: 1.

—— "Yielding power, Mabutu flees capital: rebels prepare full takeover of Zaïre", *The New York Times*, May 17: 1.

Frimpong-Ansah, Jonathan H. (1991) *The Vampire State in Africa: the Political Economy of Decline in Ghana*, London: James Curley.

Fukui, Harushiro (1992) "The Japanese state and economic development: a profile of a nationalist-paternalist capitalist state", in Richard Appelbaum and Jeffrey Henderson (eds), *States and Development in the Asian Pacific Rim*, Newbury Park, CA: Sage, pp. 190–226.

Funken, Claus and Cooper, Penny (eds) (1995) *Old and New Poverty: the Challenge for Reform*, London: Rivers Oram Press.

Gamayunov Igor (1994) "Oborotni", *Literaturnaya gazeta*, December 7: 13.

Gans, Herbert (1993) "From 'underclass' to 'undercaste': some observations about the future of the postindustrial economy and its major victims" *International Journal of Urban and Regional Research*, 17(3): 327–35.

—— (1995) *The War against the Poor: the Underclass and Antipoverty Policy*, New York: Basic Books.

Garcia, Miguel (1991) *Los barónes de la cocaína*, Mexico, DF: Planeta.

Garcia Marquez, Gabriel (1996) *Noticia de un secuestro*, New York: Penguin.

Gelb, Joyce and Lief-Palley, Marian (eds) (1994) *Women of Japan and Korea: Continuity and Change*, Philadelphia: Temple University Press.

Gerner, Kristian and Hedlund, Stefan (1989) *Ideology and Rationality in the Soviet Model: a Legacy for Gorbachev*, London: Routledge.

Ghose, T.K. (1987) *The Banking System of Hong Kong*, Singapore: Butterworth.

Gilliard, Darrell K. and Beck, Allen J. (1996) "Prison and jail inmates, 1995", *Bulletin of the Bureau of Justice Statistics*, Washington, DC: US Department of Justice, August.

Ginsborg, Paul (ed.) (1994) *Stato dell'Italia*, Milan: Il Saggiatore/Bruno Mondadori.

Gold, Thomas (1986) *State and Society in the Taiwan Miracle*, Armonk, NY: M.E. Sharpe.

Goldman, Marshall I. (1983) *USSR in Crisis: the Failure of an Economic System*, New York: W.W. Norton.

—— (1987) *Gorbachev's Challenge: Economic Reform in the Age of High Technology*, New York: W.W. Norton.

—— (1996) "Why is the Mafia so dominant in Russia?", *Challenge*, January–February: 39–47.

Golland, E.B. (1991) *Nauchno-teknicheskii progress kak osnova uskorenia razvitia narodnogo khoziaistva*, Novosibirsk: Nauka.

Gomez, Ignacio and Giraldo, Juan Carlos (1992) *El retorno de Pablo Escobar*, Bogotá: Editorial Oveja Negra.

Gordon, Michael R. (1996) "Russia struggles in a long race to prevent an atomic theft", *The New York Times*, April 20: 1–4.

Gould, Stephen Jay (1985) "The median isn't the message", *Discover*, June: 40–2.

Granberg, Alexander (1993a) "The national and regional commodity markets in the USSR: trends and contradictions in the transition period", *Papers in Regional Science*, 72(1): 3–23.

—— (1993b) "Politika i uchenyy, kotoryy zanimayetsya ey po dolgu sluzhby", *EKO*, 4: 24–8.

—— and Spchl, II. (1989) "Regionale Wirstchaftspolitik in der UdSSR und der BRD", report to the Fourth Soviet–West German Seminar on Regional Development, Kiev, October 1–10.

Granick, David (1990) *Chinese State Enterprises: a Regional Property Rights Analysis*, Chicago: University of Chicago Press.

Green, Gordon et al. (1992) "International comparisons of earnings inequality for men in the 1980s", *Review of Income and Wealth*, 38(1): 1–15.

Greenhalgh, Susan (1988) "Families and networks in Taiwan's economic development", in Winckler and Greenhalgh (eds).

Grindle, Merilee S. (1996) *Challenging the State: Crisis and Innovation in Latin America and Africa*. Cambridge: Cambridge University Press.

Grootaert, Christiaan and Kanbur, Ravi (1995) "Child labor: a review", Washington, DC: World Bank policy research working paper no. 1454.

Grossman, Gregory (1977) "The second economy of the USSR", *Problems of Communism*, 26: 25–40.

—— (1989) "Informal personal incomes and outlays of the Soviet urban population", in Portes et al. (eds), pp. 150–72.

Gugliotta, Guy, and Leen, Jeff (1989) *Kings of Cocaine: Inside the Medellin Cartel*, New York: Simon and Schuster.

Gustafson, Thane (1981) *Reform in Soviet Politics*, New York: Cambridge University Press.

Haas, Ernst B. (1958a) *The Uniting of Europe: Political, Social, and Economic Forces, 1950–57*, Stanford: Stanford University Press.

—— (1958b) "The challenge of regionalism", *International Organization*, 12(4): 440–58.

—— (1964) *Beyond the Nation-State: Functionalism and International Organization*, Stanford: Stanford University Press.

Hall, Tony (1995) "Let's get Africa's act together . . .", report on the UNESCO/ITU/UNECA African Regional Symposium on Telematics for Development, Addis Ababa, Ethiopia, May.

Hallinan, Joe (1994) "Angry children ready to explode", *San Francisco Examiner*, May 22.

Handelman, Stephen (1993) "The Russian *Mafiya*", *Foreign Affairs*, 73(2) 83–96.

—— (1995) *Comrade Criminal: Russia's New Mafiya*, New Haven, CT: Yale University Press.

Hao, Jia and Zhimin, Lin (eds) (1994) *Changing Central–Local Relations in China: Reform and State Capacity*, Boulder, CO.: Westview Press.

Harrison, Mark (1993) "Soviet economic growth since 1928: the alternative statistics of G.I. Khanin", *Europe–Asia Studies*, 45(1): 141–67.

Harvey, Robert (1994), *The Undefeated: the Rise, Fall and Rise of Greater Japan*, London: Macmillan.

Hasegawa, Koichi (1994) "A comparative study of social movements for a post-nuclear energy era in Japan and the United States", paper delivered at the 23rd World Congress of Sociology, Research Committee on Collective Behavior and Social Movements, Bielefeld, Germany, July 18–23.

Healy, Margaret (1996) "Child pornography: an international perspective", working document prepared for the World Congress against Commercial Sexual Exploitation of Children, Stockholm, Sweden, August 27–31.

Heeks, Richard (1996) *Building Software Industries in Africa*, downloaded from: http://www.sas.upenn.edu/African_Studies/Acad_Research/ softw_heeks.htaml.

Henderson, Jeffrey (1998a) "Danger and opportunity in the Asian Pacific", in G. Thompson (ed.), *Economic Dynamism in the Asian Pacific*, London: Routledge, pp. 356–84.

—— (1998b) "Uneven crises: institutional foundations of East Asian economic turmoil", paper delivered at the Annual Conference of the Society for the Advancement of Socio-economics, Vienna, July, 13–16.

——, Hama, Noriko, Eccleston, Bernie and Thompson, Grahame (1998) "Deciphering the East Asian crisis: a roundtable discussion", *Renewal*, 6(2).

Herbst, Jeffrey (1996) "Is Nigeria a viable state?", *The Washington Quarterly*, 19(2) : 151–72.

Hewitt, Chet, Shorter, Andrea and Godfrey, Michael (1994) *Race and Incarceration in San Francisco, Two Years Later*, San Francisco: Center on Juvenile and Criminal Justice.

High Level Expert Group on the Information Society (HLEGIS) (1997) "The European information society", report to the European Commission: Brussels, European Commission, Directorate General V.

Hill, Christopher (ed.) (1996) *The Actors in European Foreign Policy*, London: Routledge.

Hill, Ronald J. (1985) *The Soviet Union: Politics, Economics and Society. From Lenin to Gorbachev*, London: Pinter.

Hirst, Paul and Thompson, Grahame (1996) *Globalization in Question*, Oxford: Blackwell.

Ho, H.C.Y. (1979) *The Fiscal System of Hong Kong*, London: Croom Helm.

Holzman, Franklyn D. (1976) *International Trade under Communism*, New York: Basic Books.

Hondagneu-Sotelo, Pierrette (1994) "Regulating the unregulated?: domestic workers' social networks", *Social Problems*, 41:(1).

Hong Kong Government (1967) *Kowloon Disturbances, 1966: Report of the Commission of Inquiry*, Hong Kong: Hong Kong Government.

Hope, Kempe Ronald (1995) "The socio-economic context of AIDS in Africa", *Journal of Asian and African Studies*, 30: 1–2.

—— (1996) "Growth, unemployment and poverty in Botswana", *Journal of Contemporary African Studies*, 14: 1.

Hsing, You-tien (1997a) *Making Capitalism in China: the Taiwan Connection*, New York: Oxford University Press.

—— (1997b) "Transnational networks of Chinese capitalists and development in local China", paper presented at the Bamboo Networks and Economic Growth in the Asia Pacific Region Research Workshop on the Work of Chinese Entrepreneur Networks, Vancouver, University of British Columbia, Institute of Asian Research, April 11–12 (unpublished in 1997).

Hutchful, Eboe (1995) "Why regimes adjust: the World Bank ponders its 'star pupil'", *Canadian Journal of African Studies*, 29: 2.

Hutching, Raymond (1976) *Soviet Science, Technology, Design*, London: Oxford University Press.

Hutton, Will (1996) *The State We're In*, rev. edn, London: Vintage.

Ikporukpo, C.O. (1996) "Federalism, political power and the economic game: conflict over access to petroleum resources in Nigeria", *Environment and Planning C: Government and Policy*, 14: 159–77.

Ikuta, Tadahide (1995) *Kanryo: Japan's Hidden Government*, Tokyo: NHK.

Imai, Ken'ichi (1990) *Jouhon Network Shakai no Tenkai* [The development of the information network society], Tokyo: Tikuma Shobou.

Industrial Strategy Project (ISP) (1995) *Improving Manufacturing Performance in South Africa*, Cape Town/Ottawa: UCT Press and International Development Research Centre.

InfoCom Research (1995) *Information and Communications in Japan, 1995*, Tokyo: InfoCom Research.

Inoguchi, Takashi (1995) "Kanryo: the Japanese bureaucracy in history's eye", paper delivered at a conference on Crisis and Change in Japan Today, Seattle, October 20–21 (read in a revised version, supplied by the University of Tokyo, March 1996).

International Bank for Reconstruction and Development (IBRD) (1994) *Adjustment in Africa: Reforms, Results and the Road Ahead*, Oxford: Oxford University Press.

—— (1996) *World Development Report 1996: From Plan to Market*, Oxford: Oxford University Press.

International Labour Office (ILO) (1994) *World Labour Report 1994*, Geneva: ILO.

—— (1995) *World Employment Report 1995*, Geneva: ILO.

—— (1996) *Child Labour: Targeting the Intolerable*, Geneva: ILO.

Irusta Medrano, Gerardo (1992) *Narcotráfico: hablan los arrepentidos – personajes y hechos reales*, La Paz: CEDEC.

Irwin, John (1985) *The Jail: Managing the Underclass in American Society*, Berkeley: University of California Press.

—— and Austin, James (1994) *It's about Time: America's Imprisonment Binge*, Belmont, CA: Wadsworth.

Ito, Youichi (1980) "The *Johoka Shakai* approach to the study of communication in Japan", *Keio Communication Review*, 1: 13–40.

—— (1991) "Birth of *Johoka Shakai* and *Johoka* concepts in Japan and their diffusion outside Japan", *Keio Communication Review*, 13: 3–12.

—— (1993) "How Japan modernised earlier and faster than other non-Western countries: an information sociology approach", *The Journal of Development Communication*, 4(2).

—— (1994a) "Why information now?", in Georgette Wang (ed.), *Treading Different Paths: Informationization in Asian Nations*, Norwood, NJ: Ablex.

—— (1994b) "Japan", in Georgette Wang (ed.), *Treading Different Paths: Informationization in Asian Nations*, Norwood, NJ: Ablex.

Iwao, Sumiko (1993) *The Japanese Woman*, New York: Free Press.

Izvestiya, (1994a) "Krestnye ottsy i inoplanetyane", January 27.

—— (1994b) "Rossiiskaya mafia sobiraet dos'ye na krupnykh chinovnikov i politikov", January 26: 1–2.

—— "Ugolovnaya rossiya", October 18, 19: 1–2.

Jackson, Robert H. and Rosberg, Carl G. (1994) "The political economy of African personal rule", in David Apter, and Carl Rosberg (eds), *Political Development and the New Realism in Sub-Saharan Africa*, Charlottesville: University of Virginia Press.

Jamal, Vali (ed.) (1995) *Structural Adjustment and Rural Labour Markets in Africa*, New York: St Martin's Press for the ILO.

James, Jeffrey (1995) *The State, Technology and Industrialization in Africa*, New York: St Martin's Press.

Japan Information Processing Development Center (1994) *Informatization White Paper*, Tokyo: JIPDEC.

Jasny, N. (1961) *Soviet Industrialization, 1928–1952*, Chicago: University of Chicago Press.

Jazairy, Idriss et al. (1992) *The State of World Rural Poverty: an Inquiry into its Causes and Consequences*, New York: New York University Press.

Jensen, Leif (1991) "Secondary earner strategies and family poverty: immigrant–native differentials, 1960–1980", *International Migration Review*, 25: 1.

Jensen, Mike (1995) Draft discussion paper for UNESCO/ITU/UNECA African Regional Symposium on Telematics for Development in Addis Ababa, May, downloaded from http://www.idsc.gov.eg//aii/ddpf.htm#tele.

—— (1996) "Economic and technical issues in building Africa's information technologies", presentation to Conference on Africa and the New Information Technologies, Geneva, October 17–19.

Johnson, Chalmers (1982) *MITI and the Japanese Miracle*, Stanford: Stanford University Press.

—— (1987) "Political institutions and economic performance: the government–business relationship in Japan, South Korea, and Taiwan", in Deyo (ed.).

—— (1995) *Japan: Who Governs? The Rise of the Developmental State*, New York: W.W. Norton.

Johnson, D. Gale, and McConnell Brooks, Karen (1983) *Prospects for Soviet Agriculture in the 1980s*, Bloomington: Indiana University Press.

Jones, J. (1992) *The Dispossessed: America's Underclasses from the Civil War to the Present*, New York: Basic Books.

Jowitt, Kenneth (1971) *Revolutionary Breakthroughs and National Development: the Case of Romania, 1944–65*, Berkeley: University of California Press.

Kaiser, Paul (1996) "Structural adjustment and the fragile nation: the demise of social unity in Tanzania", *Journal of Modern African Studies*, 34: 2.

Kaiser, Robert G. (1991) *Why Gorbachev Happened: His Triumphs and his Failures*, New York: Simon and Schuster.

Kaldor, Mary (1981) *The Baroque Arsenal*, New York: Hill and Wang.

Kalmanovitz, Salomon (1993) *Análisis macro-económico del narcotráfico en la economía colombiana*, Bogotá: Universidad Nacional de Colombia, Facultad de Ciencias Económicas.

Kamali, A. et al. (1996) "The orphan problem: experience of a sub-Saharan African rural population in the AIDS epidemic", *AIDS Care*, 8(5): 509–15.

Kaplan, David E. and Dubro, Alec (1986) *Yakuza: the Explosive Account of Japan's Criminal Underworld*, Menlo Park, CA.: Addison-Wesley.

Kasarda, John D. (1990) "Urban industrial transition and the underclass", *Annals of the American Academy of Political and Social Science*, 501: 26–47.

—— (1995) "Industrial restructuring and the changing location of jobs", in Reynolds Farley (ed.), *State of the Union: America in the 1990s*, New York: Russell Sage Foundation.

Kassel, Simon and Campbell, Cathleen (1980) *The Soviet Academy of Sciences and Technological Development*, Santa Monica, CA: Rand Corporation.

Kato, Tetsuro (1984) "A preliminary note on the state in contemporary Japan", *Hitotsubashi Journal of Social Studies*, 16(1): 19–30.

—— (1987) "Der neoetatismus im heutigen Japan", *Prokla*, 66: 91–105.

Kazantsev, Sergei (1991) "Ozenka ekonomicheskogo effekta NTP v sisteme tsentralizovannogo upravleniya nauchno-tekhnicheskim progressom", in

E. Golland, and T. Rybakova (eds), *Tekhnologicheskiyi progress i ekonomicheskoye razvitiye*, Novosibirsk: Nauka, pp. 162–74.

Kazuhiro, Imamura (1990) "The computer, interpersonal communication, and education in Japan", in Adriana Boscaro, Franco Gatti, and Massimo Raveri (eds), *Rethinking Japan*, Folkestone, Kent: pp. 97–106.

Keating, Michael (1995) *Nations against the State: the New Politics of Nationalism in Quebec, Catalonia, and Scotland*, New York: St Martin's Press.

Kelly, R.J. (ed.) (1986) *Organized Crime: a Global Perspective*, Totowa, NJ: Rowman and Littlefield.

Kempster, Norman (1993) "US consider seizing vast wealth of Zaïre's Mobutu to force him out", *Los Angeles Times*, March 3.

Keohane, Robert O. and Hoffman, Stanley (1991a) "Institutional change in Europe in the 1980s", in Keohane and Hoffman (eds).

—— and —— (eds) (1991b) *The New European Community: Decision Making and Institutional Change*, Boulder, CO.: Westview Press.

Khan, Sikander and Yoshihara, Hideki (1994) *Strategy and Performance of Foreign Companies in Japan*, Westport, CT: Quorum Books.

Khanin, G.I. (1988) "Ekonomicheskii rost: al'ternativnaya otsenka", *Kommunist* 17.

—— (1991a) *Dinamika ekonomicheskogo razvitiya SSSR*, Novosibirsk: Nauka.

—— (1991b) "Ekonomicheskii rost v SSSR v 80-e gody", *EKO*, 5.

Khazanov, Anatoly M. (1995) *After the USSR: Ethnicity, Nationalism and Politics in the Commonwealth of Independent States*, Madison: University of Wisconsin Press.

Kibria, Nazli (1994) "Household structure and family ideologies: the dynamics of immigrant economic adaptation among Vietnamese refugees", *Social Problems*, 41:1.

Kim, Jong-Cheol (1998) "Asian financial crisis in 1997: institutional incompatibility of the development state in global capitalism", unpublished seminar paper for Sociology 280V, Berkeley: University of California, Department of Sociology, May.

Kim, Kyong-Dong, (ed.) (1987) *Dependency Issues in Korean Development*, Seoul: Seoul National University Press.

Kim, Seung-Kuk (1987), "Class formation and labor process in Korea", in Kim (ed.).

King, Ambrose Y.C. and Lee, Rance P. (eds.) (1981) *Social Life and Development in Hong Kong*, Hong Kong: Chinese University Press.

King, Roy (1994) "Russian prisons after perestroika: end of the gulag?" *British Journal of Criminology*, 34, special issue.

—— and Mike Maguire (1994) "Contexts of imprisonment: an international perspective", *British Journal of Criminology*, 34, special issue.

Kirsch, Irwin, Jungeblut, Ann, Jenkins, Lynn and Kolstad, Andrew (1993) *Adult Literacy in America: a First Look at the Results of the National Adult Literacy Survey*, Washington, DC: US Department of Education.

Kiselyova, Emma, Castells, Manuel and Granberg, Alexander (1996) *The Missing Link: Siberian Oil and Gas and the Pacific Economy*, Berkeley:

University of California, Institute of Urban and Regional Development, Research Monograph.

Kishima, Takako (1991) *Political Life in Japan: Democracy in a Reversible World*, Princeton, NJ: Princeton University Press.

Kleinknecht, William (1996) *The New Ethnic Mobs: the Changing Face of Organized Crime in America*, New York: The Free Press.

Koetting, Mark and Schiraldi, Vincent (1994) *Singapore West: the Incarceration of 200,000 Californians*, San Francisco: Center on Juvenile and Criminal Justice.

Kontorovich, V. (1988) "Lessons of the 1965 Soviet economic reform", *Soviet Studies*, 40, 2.

Kornai, Janos (1980) "Economics of shortage", Amsterdam: North-Holland

—— (1986) *Contradictions and Dilemmas: Studies on the Socialist Economy and Society*, Cambridge, MA: MIT Press.

—— (1990) *Vision and Reality, Market and State*, New York: Routledge.

Korowkin, Wladimir (1994) "Die wirtschaftsbeziehungen Russlands zu den Staaten der ehemaligen UdSSR", *Osteuropa*, 2 (February): 161–74.

Kozlov, Viktor (1988) *The Peoples of the Soviet Union*, Bloomington: Indiana University Press.

Kozol, Jonathan (1985) *Illiterate America*, New York: Anchor Press.

Krause, Lawrence, Koh Ai Tee and Lee (Tsao) Yuan (1987) *The Singapore Economy Reconsidered*, Singapore: Institute of South-East Asian Studies.

Kuleshov, Valery and Castells, Manuel (directors) (1993) "Problemas socio-económicos del complejo de gas y petroleo en Siberia Occidental en el contexto del la reforma económica", Madrid: UAM/IUSNT, research report.

Kuo, Shirley W.Y. (1983) *The Taiwan Economy in Transition*, Boulder, CO.: Westview Press.

Kuznetsova, N.F. (1996) "Konferenciya po problemam organizovannoi prestupnosti", *Gosudarstvo i Pravo*, 5: 130–37.

Kwan, Alex Y.H. and Chan, David K.K. (eds) (1986) *Hong Kong Society*, Hong Kong: Writers and Publishers Cooperative.

Lachaud, Jean-Pierre (1994) *The Labour Market in Africa*, Geneva: International Institute for Labour Studies.

Lam, Willy Wo-Lap (1995) *China after Deng Xiaoping: the Power Struggle in Beijing since Tiananmen*, Singapore: Wiley.

Lane, David (1990) *Soviet Society under Perestroika*, London: Unwin and Hyman.

Laserna, Roberto (ed.) (1991) *Economía política de las drogas: lecturas Latinoaméricanas*, Cochabamba: CERES/CLACSO.

—— (1995) "Coca cultivation, drug traffic and regional development in Cochabamba, Bolivia", unpublished PhD thesis, Berkeley: University of California.

—— (1996) *20 juicios y prejuicios sobre coca-cocaína*, La Paz: Clave Consultores.

Lau, Siu-kai (1982) *Society and Politics in Hong Kong*, Hong Kong: The Chinese University Press.

Lavalette, Michael (1994) *Child Employment in the Capitalist Labour Market*, Aldershot: Avebury.

Lee, Chong Ouk (1988) *Science and Technology Policy of Korea and Cooperation with the United States*, Seoul: Korea Advanced Institute of Science and Technology, Center for Science and Technology Policy.

Leitzel, Jim et al. (1995) "Mafiosi and Matrioshki: organized crime and Russian reform", *The Brooking Review*, winter: 26–9.

Lemarchand, René (1970) *Rwanda and Burundi*, London: Pall Mall.

—— (1993) "Burundi in comparative perspective: dimensions of ethnic strife", in John McGarry and Brendan O'Leary (eds), *The Politics of Ethnic Conflict Regulation: Case Studies of Protracted Ethnic Conflicts*, London and New York: Routledge.

—— (1994a) "Managing transition anarchies: Rwanda, Burundi, and South Africa in comparative perspective", *Journal of Modern African Studies*, 32(4): 581–604.

—— (1994b) *Burundi: Ethnocide as Discourse and Practice*, New York: Woodrow Wilson Center Press and Cambridge University Press.

Lerman, Robert (1996) "The impact of changing US family structure on child poverty and income inequality", *Economica*, 63: S119–39.

Lethbridge, H. (1970) "Hong Kong cadets, 1862–1941", *Journal of the Hong Kong Branch of the Royal Asiatic Society*, 10: 35–56.

—— (1978) *Hong Kong: Stability and Change: a Collection of Essays*, Hong Kong: Oxford University Press.

Leung, Chi-keung et al. (1980) *Hong Kong: Dilemmas of Growth*, Hong Kong: University of Hong Kong, Centre of Asian Studies.

Lewin, Moshe (1988) *The Gorbachev Phenomenon: a Historical Interpretation*, Berkeley: University of California Press.

Lewis, Peter (1996) "From prebendalism to predation: the political economy of decline in Nigeria", *Journal of Modern African Studies* 34(1): 79–103.

Leys, Colin (1994) "Confronting the African tragedy", *New Left Review*, 204: 33–47.

Li, Linda Ch. (1996) "Power as non-zero sum: central–provincial relations over investment implementation, Guandong and Shanghai, 1978–93", Hong Kong: City University of Hong Kong, Department of Public and Social Administration, working paper 1996/2.

Lim, Hyun-Chin (1982) *Dependent Development in Korea: 1963–79*, Seoul: Seoul National University Press.

—— and Yang, Jonghoe (1987) "The state, local capitalists and multinationals: the changing nature of a triple alliance in Korea", in Kyong-Dong Kim (ed.), *Dependency Issues in Korean Development*, Seoul: Seoul National University Press: pp. 347–59.

Lin, Jing (1994) *The Opening of the Chinese Mind: Democratic Changes in China since 1978*, Westport, CT: Praeger.

Lin, Tsong-Biau, Mok, Victor and Ho, Yin-Ping (1980) *Manufactured Exports and Employment in Hong Kong*, Hong Kong: Chinese University Press.

Lindqvist, Sven (1996) *Exterminate All the Brutes*, New York: The New Press.

Loxley, John (1995) "A review of *Adjustment in Africa: Reforms, Results and the Road Ahead*", *Canadian Journal of African Studies*, 29: 2.

Lu, Jia (1993) "*Jingji guore wnti geshuo gehua* (Disagreement between the central and the provincial government on the problems of overheated economy)", *China Times Weekly*, 61, February 28–March 6: 44–5.

—— (1994a) "*Zhonggong yabuzhu difang haiwai juzhaifeng* (The Chinese communists cannot control the trend of local government's foreign borrowing)", *China Times Weekly*, 150, November 13–19: 6–9.

—— (1994b) "*Laozi jiufen juyou zhongguo tese* (Labor disputes have Chinese characteristics)", *China Times Weekly*, 116, March 20–6; 11–13.

Lynch, Michael J. and Paterson, E. Britt (eds) (1995) *Race and Criminal Justice: a Further Examination*, New York: Harrow and Heston.

McDonald, Douglas (1994) "Public imprisonment by private means: the re-emergence of private prisons and jails in the United States, the United Kingdom, and Australia", *British Journal of Criminology*, 34, special issue.

Mace, James E. (1983) *Communism and the Dilemmas of National Liberation: National Communism in Soviet Ukraine, 1918–33*, Cambridge, MA: Harvard Ukrainian Research Institute.

Machimura, Takashi (1994) *Sekai Toshi Tokyo no Kozo* [The structural transformation of a global city: Tokyo], Tokyo: Tokyo University Press.

Mackie, J.A.C. (1992) "Overseas Chinese entrepreneurship", *Asian Pacific Economic Literature*, 6(1): 41–64.

McKinley, James C. (1996) "Old revolutionary is a new power to be reckoned with in Central Africa", *The New York Times*, November 27.

Maddison, Angus (1995) *Monitoring the World Economy, 1820–1992*, Paris: OECD Development Centre Studies.

Malleret, T. and Delaporte, Y. (1991) "La conversion des industries de défense de l'ex-URSS", *Le Courrier des Pays de l'Est*, November.

Mamdani, Mahmood (1996) "From conquest to consent as the basis of state formation: reflections on Rwanda", *New Left Review*, 216: 3–36.

Manning, Claudia (1993) "Subcontracting in the South African economy: a review of the evidence and an analysis of future prospects", paper prepared for the TASKGRO Workshop, May 21–3.

—— and Mashigo, Angela Pinky (1994) "Manufacturing in South African microenterprises", *IDS Bulletin*, 25(1).

Marrese, Michael and Vanous, Jan (1983) *Soviet Subsidization of Trade with Eastern Europe: a Soviet Perspective*, Berkeley: University of California, Institute of International Studies.

Martin, John M. and Romano, Anne T. (1992) *Multinational Crime*, London: Sage.

Maruyama, Masao (1963) *Thought and Behaviour in Modern Japanese Politics* (ed. Ivan Morris), London: Oxford University Press.

Massey, Douglas S. and Denton, Nancy A. (1993) *American Apartheid: Segregation and the Making of the Underclass*, Cambridge, MA: Harvard University Press.

——, Grow, Andrew and Shibuya, Kumiko (1994) "Migration, segregation and the geographic concentration of poverty", *American Sociological Review*, 59: 425–45.

Medina Gallego, Carlos (1990) *Autodefensas, paramilitares y narcotráfico en Colombia*, Bogotá: Editorial Documentos Periodisticos.

Mejia Priete, Jorge (1988) *Mexico y el narcotráfico*, Mexico, DF: Editorial Universo.

Menshikov, Stanislas (1990) *Catastrophe or Catharsis? The Soviet Economy Today*, Moscow and London: Inter-Verso.

MERG (Macro-Economic Working Group) (1993) *Making Democracy Work: a Framework for Macroeconomic Policy in South Africa*, Belleville, South Africa: Center for Development Studies.

Mergenhagen, Paula (1996) "The prison population bomb", *American Demographics*, 18(2): 36–40.

Minc, Alain (1993) *Le nouveau Moyen Âge*, Paris: Gallimard.

Miners, N.J. (1986) *The Government and Politics of Hong Kong*, Hong Kong: Oxford University Press.

Mingione, Enzo (1993) "The new urban poverty and the underclass: introduction", *International Journal of Urban and Regional Research*, 17(3).

—— (ed.) (1996) *Urban Poverty and the Underclass*, Oxford: Blackwell.

—— and Morlicchio, Enrica (1993) "New forms of urban poverty in Italy: risk path models in the north and south", *International Journal of Urban and Regional Research*, 17(3).

Mishel, Lawrence, Bernstein, Jared and Schmitt, John (1996) *The State of Working America, 1996–97*, Washington, DC: Economic Policy Institute.

Mita Barrientos, Fernando (1994) *El fenomeno del narcotráfico*, La Paz: AVF Producciones.

Mitchell, R. Judson (1990) *Getting to the Top in the USSR: Cyclical Patterns in the Leadership Succession Process*, Stanford, CA: Hoover Institution Press.

Mollenkopf, John and Castells, Manuel (eds) (1991) *Dual City: Restructuring New York*, New York: Russell Sage.

Morris, Martina, Bernhardt, Annette and Handcock, Mark (1994) "Economic inequality: new methods for new trends", *American Sociological Review*, 59: 205–19.

Motyl, Alexander M. (1987) *Will the Non-Russians Rebel? State, Ethnicity, and Stability in the USSR*, Ithaca, NY: Cornell University Press.

Muntarbhorn, Vitit (1996) "International perspectives and child prostitution in Asia", in US Department of Labor, Bureau of International Labor Affairs, *Forced Labor: the Prostitution of Children, Symposium Proceedings*, Washington, DC: US Department of Labor.

Murray, Diane H. (with Qin Baogi) (1994) *The Origins of the Truandihui: the Chinese Triads in Legend and History*, Stanford: Stanford University Press.

Mushkat, Miron (1982) *The Making of the Hong Kong Administrative Class*, Hong Kong: University of Hong Kong, Centre for Asia Studies.

Nakame International Economic Research, Nikon Keizai Shimbun Inc. (Nikkei), and Global Business Network (1998) *Scenarios for the Future of Japan*, Emeryville, CA, Global Business Network.

Nathan, Andrew J. (1990) *China's Crisis: Dilemmas of Reform and Prospects for Democracy*, New York: Columbia University Press.

National Center for Adult Literacy (NCAL) (1995) "Adult literacy: the next generation", *NCAL Technical Report TR95-01*, Philadelphia: NCAL.

Naughton, Barry (1995) *Growing Out of the Plan: Chinese Economic Reforms, 1978–1993*, New York: Cambridge University Press.

Navarro, Mireya (1997) "Russian submarine surfaces as player in drug world", *The New York Times*, March 5: 1–8.

Navarro, Vicente (1996) "La unidad monetaria, Maastricht y los Estados del Bienestar: notas comparativas de la UE con EEUU", paper presented at the Conference on New Social and Economic Policies for Europe, Fundación Sistema, Madrid, December 18–19.

—— (1997) *Neoliberalismo y estado del bienestar*, Madrid: Alianza Editorial.

Nekrich, Aleksandr M. (1978) *The Punished Peoples: the Deportation and Tragic Fate of Soviet Minorities at the End of the Second World War*, New York: W.W. Norton.

Network Wizards (1996) Internet Survey, July, downloaded from: http://www.nw.com.

Newbury, Catherine (1988) *The Cohesion of Oppression: Clientship and Ethnicity in Rwanda, 1860–1960*, New York: Columbia University Press.

Newman, Anabel, Lewis, Warren and Beverstock, Caroline (1993) "Prison literacy: implications for program and assessment policy", *NCAL Technical Report TR93-1*, Philadelphia: NCAL.

Noble, Kenneth (1992) "As the nation's economy collapses, Zaïreans squirm under Mobutu's heel", *The New York Times*, August 30: 14.

Nonaka, Ikujiro and Takeuchi, Hirotaka (1994) *The Knowledge-creating Company: How Japanese Companies Created the Dynamics of Innovation*, New York: Oxford University Press.

Norman, E. Herbert (1940) *Japan's Emergence as a Modern State: Political and Economic Problems of the Meiji Period*, New York: Institute of Pacific Relations.

Nove, Alec (1969/1982) *An Economic History of the USSR*, Harmondsworth: Penguin.

—— (1977) *The Soviet Economic System*, London: Allen and Unwin.

Nzongola-Ntalaja, Georges (1993) *Nation-building and State-building in Africa*, SAPES Trust Occasional Paper Series no. 3, Harare: Sapes Books.

Odedra, Mayuri et al. (1993) "Sub-Saharan Africa: a technological desert", *Communications of the ACM*, 36(2): 25–9.

OECD (1995) *Literacy, Economy and Society: Results of the First International Adult Literacy Survey*, Paris: OECD.

Ohmae, Kenichi (1990) *The Borderless World: Power and Strategy in the Interlinked Economy*, New York: Harper.

Orstrom Moller, J. (1995) *The Future European Model: Economic Internationalization and Cultural Decentralization*, Westport, CT: Praeger.

Ovchinsky, Vladimir (1993) *Mafia: Neob'yavlennyi vizit*, Moscow: INFRA-M.

Over, Mead (1990) "The economic impact of fatal adult illness from AIDS and other causes in Sub-Saharan Africa: a research proposal", Research Department of the World-Bank, Washington, unpublished.

Overhalt, William H. (1993) *The Rise of China*, New York: W.W. Norton.

Ozawa, Terutomo (1996) "Japan: the macro-IDP, meso-IDPs and the technology development path (TDP)", in John H. Dunning and Rajneesh Narula (eds), *Foreign Direct Investment and Governments: Catalysts for Economic Restructuring*, London: Routledge: pp. 142–73.

Palazuelos, Enrique (1990) *La economía sovietíca mas alla de la perestroika*, Madrid: Ediciones de Ciencias Sociales.

Panos Institute (1992) *The Hidden Costs of AIDS: the Challenge to Development*, London: Panos Institute.

Pardo Segovia, Fernando (ed.) (1995) *Narcotráfico: situación actual y perspectivas para la acción*, Lima: Centro Peruano de Relaciones Internacionales.

Parsons, Craig (1996) "Europe's identity crisis: European Union dilemmas in the 1990s", Berkeley: University of California, Center for Western European Studies, research paper.

Pasquini, Gabriel and De Miguel, Eduardo (1995) *Blanca y radiante: mafias, poder y narcotráfico en la Argentina*, Buenos Aires: Planeta.

Pease, Ken (1994) "Cross-national imprisonment rates: limitations of method and possible conclusions", *British Journal of Criminology*, 34, special issue.

Pedrazzini, Yves and Sanchez, Magaly (1996) *Malandros, bandes et enfants de la rue: la culture d'urgence dans la métropole latino-américaine*, Paris: Fondation Charles Léopold Mayer pour le Progrès de l'Homme.

Perez Gomez, V. (1988) *Historia de la drogadicción en Colombia*, Bogotá: TM Editores/Uniandes.

Peterson, G. and Harrell, Adele V. (eds) (1993) *Drugs, Crime, and Social Isolation*, Washington, DC: The Urban Institute Press.

Pfeffer, Max (1994) "Low-wage employment and ghetto poverty: a comparison of African-American and Cambodian day-haul farm workers in Philadelphia", *Social Problems*, 41(1).

Philipson, Thomas and Posner, Richard A. (1995) "The microeconomics of the AIDS epidemic in Africa", *Population and Development Review*, 21(4): 835–48.

Pinkus, Benjamin (1988) *The Jews of the Soviet Union: the History of a National Minority*, Cambridge: Cambridge University Press.

Pipes, Richard (1954) *The Formation of the Soviet Union: Communism and Nationalism, 1917–23*, Cambridge, MA: Harvard University Press.

—— (1991) *The Russian Revolution*, New York: Alfred Knopf.

Pisani-Ferry, Jean (1995) "Variable geometry in Europe", paper presented at the Conference on Reshaping the Transatlantic Partnership: an Agenda for the Next Ten Years, Bruges: The College of Europe, March 20-2.

Plotnick, Robert D. (1990) "Determinants of teenage out-of-wedlock childbearing", *Journal of Marriage and the Family*, 52: 735–46.

Po, Lan-chih (forthcoming) "Economic reform, housing privatization and changing life of women in China", unpublished PhD dissertation, Berkeley: University of California, Department of City and Regional Planning.

Podlesskikh, Georgyi and Tereshonok, Andrey (1994) *Vory V Zakone: Brosok k Vlasti*, Moscow: Khudozestvennaya Literatura.

Portes, Alejandro (ed.) (1995) "The economic sociology of immigration: essays on networks, ethnicity and entrepreneurship", New York: Russell Sage.

—— and Sensenbrenner, Julia (1993) "Embeddedness and immigration: notes on the social determinants of economic action", *American Journal of Sociology*, 98(6): 1320–50.

——, Castells, Manuel and Benton, Lauren (eds) (1989) *The Informal Economy: Studies on Advanced and Less Developed Countries*, Baltimore: The Johns Hopkins University Press.

Potter, Gary W. (1994) *Criminal Organizations: Vice, Racketeering and Politics in an American City*, Prospect Heights, IL: Waveland Press.

Praaning, R. and Perry, C. (eds) (1989) *East–West Relations in the 1990s: Politics and Technology*, Dordrecht/Boston: M. Nijhoff.

Press, Robert M. (1993) "Some allege Mobutu is stirring up deadly tribal warfare in Zaïre", *Christian Science Monitor*, August 17: 1.

Pritchett, Lant (1995) *Divergence, Big Time*, Washington, DC: The World Bank, Policy Research Working Paper, no. 1522.

Prolongeau, Hubert (1992) *La vie quotidienne en Colombie au temps du cartel de Medellin*, Paris: Hachette.

Psacharopoulos, George et al. (1995) "Poverty and inequality in Latin America during the 1980s", *Review of Income and Wealth*, 41(3): 245–63.

Purcell, Randall P. (ed.) (1989) *The Newly Industrializing Countries in a World Economy*, Boulder, CO: Lynne Rienner.

Ravenhill, John (1993) "A second decade of adjustment: greater complexity, greater uncertainty", in Callaghy and Ravenhill (eds).

Reischauer, Edwin O. (1988) *The Japanese Today: Change and Continuity*, Cambridge, MA: The Belknap Press of Harvard University Press.

Remnick, David (1993) *Lenin's Tomb: the Last Days of the Soviet Empire*, New York: Random House.

Renard, Ronald D. (1996) *The Burmese Connection: Illegal Drugs and the Making of the Golden Triangle*, Boulder, CO: Lynne Rienner.

Renaud, Bertrand (1997) "The 1985 to 1994 global real estate cycle: an overview", *Journal of Real Estate Literature*, 5: 13–44.

Rezun, Miron (ed.) (1992) *Nationalism and the Breakup of an Empire: Russia and its Periphery*, Westport, CT: Praeger.

Riddell, Barry (1995) "The World Bank speaks to Africa yet again", *Canadian Journal of African Studies*, 29:2.

Riddell, Roger (1993) "The future of the manufacturing sector in Sub-Saharan Africa", in Callaghy and Ravenhill (eds), pp. 215–47.

Riley, Thyra (1993) "Characteristics of and constraints facing black businesses in South Africa: survey results", paper prepared for the World Bank's presentation to the Seminar on Small and Medium Business Enterprises, Johannesburg, June 1-2.

Rizzini, Irene (ed.) (1994) *Children in Brazil Today: a Challenge for the Third Millennium*, Rio de Janeiro: Editora Universitaria Santa Ursula.

Roberts, Albert E. (1994) *Critical Issues in Crime and Justice*, Thousand Oaks, CA: Sage.

References

Robinson, Thomas W. (ed.) (1991) *Democracy and Development in East Asia*, Washington, DC: The American Enterprise Institute Press.

Rodgers, Gerry, Gore, Charles and Figueiredo, Jose B.(eds) (1995) *Social Exclusion: Rhetoric, Reality, Responses*, Geneva: International Institute of Labour Studies.

Rodgers, Harrell (1996) *Poor Women, Poor Children*, Armonk, NY: M.E. Sharpe.

Rogerson, Christian (1993) "Industrial subcontracting in South Africa: a research review", paper prepared for the PWV Economic Development Forum, June.

Rohwer, Jim (1995) *Asia Rising*, New York: Simon and Schuster.

Room, G. (1992) *Observatory on National Policies to Combat Social Exclusion: Second Annual Report*, Brussels: Commission of the European Community.

Roth, Jurgen and Frey, Marc (1995) *Europa en las garras de la mafia*, Barcelona: Anaya and Mario Muchnik (orig. pub. in German in 1992).

Rowen, H.S. and Wolf Jr, Charles, (eds) (1990) *The Impoverished Superpower*, San Francisco: Institute for Contemporary Studies.

Ruggie, John G. (1993) "Territoriality and beyond: problematizing modernity in international relations", *International Organization*, 47(1): 139–74.

Sachs, Jeffrey (1998) "The IMF and the Asian flu", *The American Prospect*, March/April: 16–21.

Sachwald, Fredrique (1994) *European Integration and Competitiveness: Acquisitions and Alliances in Industry*, Aldershot: Edward Elgar.

Sakaiya, Taichi (1991) *The Knowledge–Value Revolution: or a History of the Future*, Tokyo: Kodansha International.

Salazar, Alonso and Jaramillo, Ana Maria (1992) *Medellin: las subculturas del narcotráfico*, Bogotá: CINEP.

Salmin, A.M. (1992) *SNG: Sostoyanie i perspektivy razvitiya*, Moscow: Gorbachev Fund.

Sanchez Jankowski, Martin (1991) *Islands in the Street*, Berkeley: University of California Press.

Sandbrook, Richard (1985) *The Politics of Africa's Economic Stagnation*, Cambridge: Cambridge University Press.

Sandholtz, Wayne et al. (1992) *The Highest Stakes: Economic Foundations of National Security*, New York: BRIE/Oxford University Press.

Santino, Umberto and La Fiura, Giovanni (1990) *L'impresa mafiosa: dall'Italia agli Stati Uniti*, Milan: Franco Angeli.

Sapir, J. (1987) *Le système militaire soviétique*, Paris: La Découverte.

Sarkar, Prabirjit and Singer, H.W. (1991) "Manufactured exports of developing countries and their terms of trade since 1965", *World Development*, 19(4): 333–40.

Sarmiento, Eduardo (1990) "Economía del narcotráfico", *Desarrollo y Sociedad*, September 26: 11–40.

Sarmiento, Luis Fernando (1991) *Cocaina and Co.: un mercado ilegal por dentro*, Bogotá: Universidad Nacional de Colombia, Instituto de Estudios Políticos y Relaciones Internacionales.

Savona, Ernesto (ed.) (1993) *Mafia Issues*, Milan: International Scientific and Professional Advisory Council of the United Nations Crime Prevention and Criminal Justice Program.

Savvateyeva, Irina (1994) "Kontrrazvedka sobirayetsya proveryat' chinovnikov: dlya chego?", *Izvestiya*, April 28: 2.

Scherer, John L. and Jakobson, Michael (1993) "The collectivisation of agriculture and the Soviet prison camp system", *Europe–Asia Studies*, 45 (3): 533–46.

Schiffer, Jonathan (1983) *Anatomy of a Laissez-faire Government: the Hong Kong Growth Model Reconsidered*, Hong Kong: University of Hong Kong, Centre for Urban Studies.

Schiraldi, Vincent (1994) *The Undue Influence of California's Prison Guards' Union: California's Correctional-Industrial Complex*, San Francisco: Center on Juvenile and Criminal Justice, report, October.

Schlesinger, Jacob M. (1997) *Shadow Shoguns: the Rise and Fall of Japan's Postwar Political Machine*, New York: Simon and Schuster.

Scott, Ian (1987) "Policy making in a turbulent environment: the case of Hong Kong", Hong Kong: University of Hong Kong, Department of Political Science, research report.

—— and Burns, John P. (eds) (1984) *The Hong Kong Civil Service*, Hong Kong: Oxford University Press.

Scott, Peter D. and Marshall, Jonathan (1991) *Cocaine Politics: Drugs, Armies and the CIA in Central America*, Berkeley: University of California Press.

Sedlak, Andrea and Broadhurst, Diane (1996) *Executive Summary of the Third National Incidence Study of Child Abuse and Neglect*, Washington, DC: US Department of Health and Human Services.

Seki, Kiyohide (1987) "Population and family policy: measuring the level of living in the country of familism", Tokyo: Nihon University, Population Research Institute, Research Paper Series no. 25.

Seymour, Christopher (1996) *Yakuza Diary: Doing Time in the Japanese Underworld*, New York: Atlantic Monthly Press.

Shane, Scott (1994) *Dismantling Utopia: How Information Ended the Soviet Union*, Chicago: Ivan R. Dee.

Shargorodsky, Sergei (1995) "In troubled Russia, contract killings are a way of life", *San Francisco Chronicle*, November 17.

Shaw, Denis J. B. (1993) "Geographical and historical observations on the future of a federal Russia", *Post-Soviet Geography*, 34(8).

Shinotsuka, Eiko (1994) "Women workers in Japan: past, present and future", in Gelb and Lief-Palley (ed.) : 95–119.

Shoji, Kokichi (1991) "Rising neo-nationalism in contemporary Japan – changing social consciousness of the Japanese people and its implications for world society", Tokyo: University of Tokyo, Department of Sociology, research paper.

—— (1994), "Sociology", in *An Introductory Bibliography for Japanese Studies*, vol. 9, part 1, Tokyo: The Japan Foundation: pp. 150–216.

—— (1995) "Small changes make big change: changing Japanese life-style and political change", Tokyo: University of Tokyo, Department of Sociology, research paper.

Sigur, Christopher J. (1994) Continuity and Change in Contemporary Korea, New York: Carnegie Council on Ethics and International Affairs.

Silver, Hilary (1993) "National conceptions of the new urban poverty: social structural change in Britain, France and the United States", International Journal of Urban and Regional Research, 17(3): September.

Simon, David (1995) "Debt, democracy and development: sub-Saharan Africa in the 1990s", in Simon et al. (eds).

——, van Spengen, Wim, Dixon, Chris and Naarman, Anders (eds) (1995) Structurally Adjusted Africa: Poverty, Debt and Basic Needs, London: Pluto Press.

Simon, Gerhard (1991) Nationalism and Policy toward the Nationalities in the Soviet Union: from Totalitarian Dictatorship toward Post-Stalinist Society, Boulder, CO.: Westview Press.

Simposio Internacional (1991) El impacto del capital financiero del narcotráfico en América Latina, La Paz: Centro para el estudio de las relaciones internacionales y el desarrollo.

Singh, Tejpal (1982) The Soviet Federal State: Theory, Formation and Development, Delhi: Sterling.

Sit, Victor (1982) "Dynamism in small industries: the case of Hong Kong", Asian Survey, 22: 399–409.

Skezely, Miguel (1995) "Poverty in Mexico during adjustment", Review of Income and Wealth, 41(3): 331–48.

Smaryl, O.I. (1984) "New technology and the Soviet predicament", Survey, 28(1): 109–11.

Smith, Gordon B. (1992) Soviet Politics: Struggling with Change, New York: St Martin's Press.

Smith, Patrick (1997) Japan: a Reinterpretation, New York: Pantheon.

Smolowe, Jil (1994) "Lock 'em up and throw away the key", Time, February 7: 55–9.

South African Government (1996a) "Restructuring the South African labour market", report of the Presidential Commission to Investigate Labour Market Policy.

—— (1996b) "Employment and occupational equity: policy proposals", Department of Labour Green Paper.

Specter, Michael (1996) "Cemetery bomb in Moscow kills 13 at ceremony", The New York Times, November 11: A1–A4.

Spence, Jonathan D. (1990) The Search for Modern China, New York: Norton.

Staebler, Martin (1996) "Tourism and children in prostitution", paper prepared for the World Congress against Commercial Sexual Exploitation of Children, Stockholm, August 27–31.

Steinberg, Dimitri (1991) Soviet Defense Burden: Estimating Hidden Defense Costs, Washington, DC: Intelligence Decision Systems, research report.

Sterling, Claire (1994) Thieves' World: the Threat of the New Global Network of Organized Crime, New York: Simon and Schuster.

Stiglitz, Joseph (1998) "Sound finance and sustainable development in Asia" (http://www.worldbank.org/html/extdr/extme/jsso031298.html).

Strong, Simon (1995) *Whitewash: Pablo Escobar and the Cocaine Wars*, London: Macmillan.

Sung, Yun-wing (1994) "Hong Kong and economic integration of the China circle", paper presented at the China Circle Conference organized by the Institute of Global Cooperation and Conflict, University of California, Hong Kong: December 8–11.

Suny, Ronald Grigor (1993) *The Revenge of the Past: Nationalism, Revolution, and the Collapse of the Soviet Union*, Stanford: Stanford University Press.

Survey (1984) "The Novosibirsk Report", *Survey* 28(1): 88–108 (English trans.).

Susser, Ida (1991) "The separation of mothers and children", in John Mollenkopf and Manuel Castells (eds), *Dual City: Restructuring New York*, New York: Russell Sage: pp. 207–24.

—— (1993) "Creating family forms: the exclusion of men and teenage boys from families in the New York City shelter system, 1987–1991", *Critique of Anthropology*, 13(3): 267–85.

—— (1995) "Fear and violence in dislocated communities", paper presented to the 94th Annual Meeting of the American Anthropological Association, Washington, DC.

—— (1996) "The construction of poverty and homelessness in US cities", *Annual Reviews of Anthropology*, 25: 411–35.

—— and Kreniske, John (1987) "The welfare trap: a public policy for deprivation", in Leith Mullings (ed.), *Cities of the United States*, New York: Columbia University Press, pp. 51–68.

Svedberg, Peter (1993) "Trade compression and economic decline in Sub-Saharan Africa", in Magnus Blomstrom and Mats Lundahl (eds), *Economic Crisis in Africa: Perspectives on Policy Responses*, Routledge: London and New York, pp. 21–40.

Szelenyi, Ivan (1982) "The intelligentsia in the class structure of state-socialist societies", in Michael Burawoy and Theda Skocpol (eds), *Marxist Inquiries*, special issue of the *American Journal of Sociology*, 88: 287–327.

Taguchi, Fukuji and Kato, Tetsuro (1985) "Marxist debates on the state in post-war Japan", *Hosei Ronsyu* (Journal of Law and Political Science), 105: 1–25.

Taibo, Carlos (1993a) "Las fuerzas armadas en la URSS", unpublished PhD dissertation, Madrid: Universidad Autonoma de Madrid.

—— (1993b) *La Unión Soviética (1917–1991)*, Madrid: Editorial Sintesis.

Tarasulo, Isaav T. (ed.) (1989) *Gorbachev and Glasnost: Viewpoints from the Soviet Press*, Wilmington, DE: Scholarly Resources Books.

Tevera, Dan (1995) "The medicine that might kill the patient: structural adjustment and urban poverty in Zimbabwe", in David Simon, Wim van Spengen, Chris Dixon and Anders Naarman (eds), *Structurally Adjusted Africa: Poverty, Debt and Basic Needs*, London: Pluto Press.

Thalheim, Karl (1986) *Stagnation or Change in the Communist Economies?* (with a note by Gregory Grossman), London: Center for Research in Communist Economies.

The Current Digest [of Post-Soviet press] (1994) "Crime, corruption pose political, economic threat", *Current Digest*, 45(4): 14–16.

The Economist (1993) "Let down again: a survey of Nigeria", special supplement, August 21.

—— (1995) "Coming of age: a survey of South Africa", special supplement, May 20.

—— (1996a) "Africa for the Africans: a survey of Sub-Saharan Africa", special supplement, September 7.

—— (1996b) "Belgium: crony state", October 26: 61–2.

—— (1996c) "Death shadows Africa's Great Lakes", October 19: 45–7.

—— (1997) "A survey of Japanese finance: a whopping explosion", special report, June 27: 1–18.

—— (1998) "Silicon Valley, PRC", June 27: 64–6.

Thomas, John and Kruse-Vaucienne, Ursula (eds) (1977) *Soviet Science and Technology*, Washington, DC National Science Foundation.

Thompson, Grahame (1998) *Economic Dynamism in the Asian Pacific*, London: Routledge.

Thoumi, Francisco (1994) *Economía política y narcotráfico*, Bogotá: TM Editores.

Timmer, Doug A., Eitzen, D. Stanley, and Talley, Kathryn (1994) *Paths to Homelessness: Extreme Poverty and the Urban Housing Crisis*, Boulder, CO: Westview Press.

Tipton, Frank B. (1998) *The Rise of Asia: Economics, Society, and Politics in Contemporary Asia*, Honolulu: University of Hawaii Press.

Tokatlian, Juan G. and Bagley, Bruce (eds) (1990) *Economía política del narcotráfico*, Bogotá: CEREC/Uniandes.

Tonry, Michael (1994) "Racial disproportion in US prisons", *British Journal of Criminology*, 34, special issue.

—— (1995) *Malign Neglect: Race, Crime, and Punishment in America*, New York: Oxford University Press.

Totani, Osamu and Yatazawa, Noriko (eds) (1990) [*The Changing Family*: in Japanese], Tokyo: University of Tokyo Press.

Touraine, Alain (1995) "De la globalización al policentrismo", *El País*, July 24.

—— (1996a) "La deconstrucción europea", *El País*, April 4.

—— (1996b) "La globalización como ideología", *El País*, September 16.

—— (1996c) "Detras de la moneda: la economía", *El País*, December 22.

—— (1997) *Pourrons-nous vivre ensemble? Égaux et différents*, Paris: Fayard.

—— et al. (1996) *Le grand refus: réflexions sur la grève de décembre 1995*, Paris: Fayard.

Townsend, Peter (1993) *The International Analysis of Poverty*, London: Harvester/Wheatsheaf.

Tragardh, Lars (1996) "European integration and the question of national sovereignty: Germany and Sweden, 1945–1995", paper presented at the

Center for Slavic Studies/Center for German and European Studies Symposium, University of California, Berkeley, November 22.

Tranfaglia, Nicola (1992) *Mafia, politica e affari: 1943–91*, Roma: Editori Laterza.

Trotsky, Leon (1965) *La Révolution Russe* (trans. from Russian), Paris: Maspero.

Trueheart, Charles (1996) "String of crimes shocks Belgium: national pride damaged by pedophilia, murder, coverups", *Washington Post*, September 25.

Tsao, Yuan (1986) "Sources of growth accounting for the Singapore economy", in Lim Chong-Yah and Peter J. Lloyd (eds), *Singapore: Resources and Growth*, Singapore: Oxford University Press.

Tsuneyoshi, Ryoko (1994) "Small groups in Japanese elementary school classrooms: comparisons with the United States", *Comparative Education*, 30(2): 115–29.

Tsuru, Shigeto (1993) *Japan's Capitalism: Creative Defeat and Beyond*, Cambridge: Cambridge University Press.

Tsurumi, Kazuko (1970) *Social Change and the Individual: Japan Before and After Defeat in World War II*, Princeton, NJ: Princeton University Press.

Turbino, Fidel (1992) *Violencia y narcotráfico en Amazonia*, Lima: Centro Amazónico de antropologia y aplicación práctica.

Ueno, Chizuko (1987) "The position of Japanese women reconsidered", *Current Anthropology*, 28(4): S75-S82.

UNICEF (1996) *The State of the World's Children 1996*, Oxford: Oxford University Press.

United Nations, Department for Economic and Social Information and Policy Analysis (1996) *World Economic and Social Survey 1996: Trends and Policies in the World Economy*, New York: United Nations.

United Nations Development Programme (UNDP) (1996) *Human Development Report 1996*, New York: Oxford University Press.

United Nations Economic and Social Council (UN-ESC) (1994) "Problems and dangers posed by organized transnational crime in the various regions of the world", Background Document for the World Ministerial Conference on Organized Transnational Crime, Naples, November, 21–23, Document E/CONF.88.2.

US Department of Defense (1989) *Critical Technologies Plan*, Washington, DC: Department of Defense.

US Department of Justice (1996) "Probation and parole population reaches almost 3.8 million", Washington, DC: US Department of Justice press release, June 30.

US Department of Labor (1994) *By the Sweat and Toil of Children: Vol. I. The Use of Child Labor in US Manufactured and Mined Imports*, Washington, DC: US Department of Labour.

—— (1995) *By the Sweat and Toil of Children: Vol. II. The Use of Child Labor in Agricultural Imports and Forced and Bonded Child Labor*, Washington, DC: US Department of Labour.

US News & World Report (1988) "Red Star Rising", pp. 48–53.

Van Kempen, Ronald and Marcuse, Peter (1996) *The New Spatial Order of Cities*, New York: Columbia University Press.

Van Regemorter, Jean-Louis (1990) *D'une perestroika à l'autre: l'évolution économique de la Russie de 1860 à nos jours*, Paris: SEDES, Les Cours de la Sorbonne.

Van Wolferen, Karel (1989) *The Enigma of Japanese Power: People and Politics in a Stateless Nation*, New York: Alfred Knopf.

Veen, Hans-Joachim (ed.) (1984) *From Brezhnev to Gorbachev: Domestic Affairs and Soviet Foreign Policy*, Leamington Spa: Berg.

Velis, Jean-Pierre (1990) *Through a Glass Darkly: Functional Illiteracy in Industrialized Countries*, Paris: UNESCO.

Veloza, Gustavo (1988) *La guerra entre los carteles del narcotráfico*, Bogotá: G.S. Editores.

Venezky, Richard (1996) "Literacy assessment in the service of literacy policy", *NCAL Technical Report TR95-02*, Philadelphia: National Center for Adult Literacy.

Verdery, Katherine (1991) "Theorizing socialism: a prologue to the "transition"", *American Ethnologist*, August, pp. 419–39.

Volin, Lazar (1970) *A Century of Russian Agriculture: from Alexander II to Khrushchev*, Cambridge, MA: Harvard University Press.

Voshchanov, Pavel (1995) "Mafia godfathers become fathers of the nation", *Konsomolskaya Pravda* (read in the English version in *Business World of Russia Weekly*, 18/169, May: 13–14).

de Waal, Alex (1996) "Contemporary warfare in Africa: changing context, changing strategies", *IDS Bulletin*, 27(3): 6–16.

Wacquant, Loic (1993) "Urban outcasts: stigma and division in the black American ghetto and the French urban periphery", *International Journal of Urban and Regional Research*, 17(3): September.

—— (1996) "The rise of advanced marginality: notes on its nature and implications", *Acta Sociologica*, 12: 121–39.

Waever, Ole (1995) "Identity, integration, and security: solving the sovereignty puzzle in EU studies", *Journal of International Affairs*, 48(2): 1–43.

Wagner, Daniel (1992) "World literacy: research and policy in the EFA decade", *Annals of the American Academy of Political and Social Sciences*, 520, March 1992.

Wakabayashi, Hideki (1994) *Japan's Revolution in Wireless Communications*, Tokyo: Nomura Research Institute.

Walder, Andrew G. (1986) *Communist Neo-traditionalism: Work and Authority in Chinese Industry*, Berkeley: University of California Press.

—— (1992) *Popular Protest in 1989: Democracy Movement*, Hong Kong: Chinese University Press.

—— (1995) "Local governments and industrial firms: an organizational analysis of China's transitional economy", *American Journal of Sociology*, 101(2): 263–301.

—— and Gong, Xiaoxia (eds) (1993) "China's great terror: new documentation on the Cultural Revolution", *Chinese Sociology and Anthropology*, 26(1), special issue.

Walker, Martin (1986) *The Waking Giant: Gorbachev's Russia*, New York: Pantheon.

Wallace, Bill (1996) "Warning on Russian crime rings", *San Francisco Chronicle*, March 18.

Wallace, Charles P. (1995) "The Pacific paradox: islands of despair", *Los Angeles Times*, March 16: A1–A30.

Wa Mutharika, Bingu (1995) *One Africa, One Destiny: Towards Democracy, Good Governance and Development*, Harare: Sapes.

Watanabe, Osamu (1996) "Le néo-nationalisme japonais", *Perspectives Asiatiques*, 1: 19–39.

Watanuki, Joji (1990) "The development of information technology and its impact on Japanese society", Tokyo: Sophia University, Institute of International Relations, research paper.

Weiss, Herbert (1995) "Zaire: collapsed society, surviving states, future polity", in I. William Zartman (ed.), *Collapsed States: the Disintegration and Restoration of Legitimate Authority*, Boulder, CO.: Lynne Rienner.

Weitzman, Martin L. (1970) "Soviet postwar economic growth and capital-labor substitution", *American Economic Review*, 60(4): 676–92.

Welch, Michael (1994) "Jail overcrowding: social sanitation and the ware-housing of the urban underclass", in Roberts (ed.).

—— (1995) "Race and social class in the examination of punishment", in Lynch and Patterson (eds).

West, Cornel (1993) *Race Matters*, Boston: Beacon Press.

Wheatcroft, S.G., Davies, R.W. and Cooper, J.M. (eds) (1986) "Soviet indus-trialization reconsidered: some preliminary conclusions about economic development between 1926 and 1941", *Economic History Review*, 39, 2.

White, Gordon (ed.) (1988) *Developmental States in East Asia*, New York: St Martin's Press.

—— (ed.) (1991) *The Chinese State in the Era of Economic Reform*, Armonk, NY: M.E. Sharpe.

Wieviorka, Michel (1993) *La démocratie à l'épreuve: nationalisme, populisme, ethnicité*, Paris: La Découverte.

Wilson, William Julius (1987) *The Truly Disadvantaged: the Inner City, the Underclass, and Public Policy*, Chicago: University of Chicago Press.

—— (1996) *When Work Disappears: the World of the New Urban Poor*, New York: Alfred Knopf.

Winckler, Edwin A. and Greenhalgh, Susan (eds.) (1988) *Contending Approaches to the Political Economy of Taiwan*, Armonk, NY: M.E. Sharpe.

Woherem, Evans (1994) *Information Technology in Africa: Challenges and Opportunities*, Nairobi: African Centre for Technology Studies Press.

Wolcott, P. (1993) "Soviet advanced technology: the case of high-perfor-mance computing", unpublished PhD dissertation, Tucson: University of Arizona.

—— and Goodman, S.E. (1993) "Under the stress of reform: high-perfor-mance computing in the Soviet Union", *Communications of the ACM*, 36(10): 26.

Wong, Christine et al. (1995) *Fiscal Management and Economic Reform in the People's Republic of China*, Hong Kong: Oxford University Press.

World Congress (1996) "Documents of the World Congress against the Commercial Sexual Exploitation of Children", Stockholm, August 27–31, downloaded from http://www.childhub.ch/webpub/csechome/21ae.htm.

Wright, Martin (ed.) (1989) *Soviet Union: the Challenge of Change*, Harlow, Essex: Longman.

Yabuki, Susumu (1995) *China's New Political Economy: the Giant Awakes*, Boulder, CO.: Westview Press.

Yang, Mayfair Mei-lui (1994) *Gifts, Favors, and Banquets: the Art of Social Relationships in China*, Ithaca, NY: Cornell University Press.

Yansane, Aguibou Y. (ed.) (1996) *Development Strategies in Africa: Current Economic, Socio-political, and Institutional Trends and Issues*, Westport, CT: Greenwood Press.

Yazawa, Shujiro (1997) *Japanese Social Movements*, New York: Aldeen.

Yazawa, Sumiko (1995) "Political participation of Japanese women and local self-government – its trend and review", Tokyo: Tokyo Women's Christian University, research paper.

——— et al. (1992) *"Toshi josei to seiji sanka no new wave, kanagawa network undo no chosakara"* [New wave of political participation by urban women: research results of Kanagawa network movement], in *Yokohama Shiritsu daigaku keizai kenkyujo "keizai to boeki"*, no. 161 (as cited and summarized by Yazawa 1995).

Yeltsin, Boris (1990) *Memorias* (trans. from Russian), Madrid: Temas de Hoy.

——— (1994) "Ob ukrepleniyi Rossiyskogo gosudarstva", *Rossiyskaya gazeta*, February 25.

Yoshihara, Kunio (1988) *The Rise of Ersatz Capitalism in South East Asia*, Singapore: Oxford University Press.

Yoshino, K. (1992) *Cultural Nationalism*, London: Routledge.

Youngson, A.J. (1982) *Hong Kong: Economic Growth and Policy*, Hong Kong: Oxford University Press.

Yu, Fu-lai and Li, Si-Ming (1985) "The welfare cost of Hong Kong's public housing program", *Urban Studies*, 22: 133–40.

Zartman, I. William (ed.) (1995) *Collapsed States: the Disintegration and Restoration of Legitimate Authority*, Boulder, CO.: Lynne Rienner.

Zimring, Franklin and Hawkins, Gordon (1994) "The growth of imprisonment in California", *British Journal of Criminology*, 34, special issue.

Zysman, John and Weber, Stephen (1997) "Economy and security in the new European political architecture", Berkeley: University of California, Berkeley Roundtable on the International Economy, research paper.

———, Doherty, Eileen and Schwartz, Andrew (1996) "Tales from the 'global economy': cross-national production networks and the reorganization of the European economy", Berkeley: University of California, Berkeley Roundtable on the International Economy, working paper.

Index